Dictionary of Building Preservation

Dictionary of Building Preservation

Edited by
WARD BUCHER, A.I.A.

CHRISTINE MADRID
Illustration Editor

Preservation Press

John Wiley & Sons, Inc.
New York • *Chichester* • *Brisbane* • *Toronto* • *Singapore* • *Weinheim*

The publisher wishes to thank the Prints & Photograph Division and the Photoduplication Service, both of the Library of Congress, for their generous assistance in printing the measured drawings from the Historic American Buildings Survey collection.

This text is printed on acid-free paper.

Published by John Wiley & Sons, Inc.

Library of Congress Cataloging in Publication Data:

Dictionary of building preservation / William Ward Bucher III, editor ; Christine Madrid, illustration editor.

p. cm.

Includes bibliographical references and index.

ISBN 0-471-14413-4 (alk. paper)

1. Architecture—Dictionaries. 2. Building—Dictionaries. 3. Architecture—Conservation and restoration. I. Bucher, William Ward. II. Madrid, Christine.

NA31.D55 1996

720'.3—dc20 96-19947

Printed in the United States of America

10 9 8 7 6 5 4 3 2 1

To William Ward Bucher Jr.,
who taught me to love old things, and
William Ward Bucher IV,
who continues to learn new things.

Introduction

Back in twelfth-century Britain, *mullion* was a brand new word. It was invented to describe one of the technical and stylistic changes associated with Early English Gothic tracery. The word *tracery* would wait another 500 years for its first recorded use by the English architect Sir Christopher Wren.

Also in the twelfth century, Bernard of Chartres is reported to have said:

> We are as dwarfs standing on the shoulders of giants. Our vision is extended by all those who have gone before.

Several years of research on this project have given me a profound appreciation of both the evolution of words and Bernard's remark. Nearly all of the data contained in this volume is based on the work of fellow authors and preservationists, both previous and contemporary.

The lineage of Western dictionaries of architecture can be traced back to Vitruvius, the Roman compiler of Classic styles. As the modern day is approached the number and variety of dictionaries, and their authors, increase exponentially. This volume attempts to clarify the vision of those who have gone before and to occupy a particular niche in the contemporary lexicon as a guide for those interested in the world of preservation.

The *Dictionary of Building Preservation* is intended to serve two main purposes: first, to clarify the specialized terms used in the preservation field in the United States and Canada; and second, to allow a recorder to fully describe a historic resource.

Due to the constraints of time and the limits of my expertise, this dictionary is more focused on buildings than structures, sites, or objects. I have explained in the following some of the other limitations of definitions found herein:

Names of people are excluded unless they identify a style or movement. For example, *Richardsonian* is defined, but *A. J. Downing* is not.

Tools and methods of production are omitted unless the tool or process is synonymous with the product. For example, *wrought iron* is included, but *forging* is not. Manufacturing buildings or complexes, such as an *ironworks,* that may be of historic or cultural significance are also included.

Descriptions of parts of buildings are limited to nouns. Where the verb form and the noun form are similar, the noun form indicating the state of the material or element is used. For example, *rived,* rather than *rive,* is included in the dictionary. Also, building parts are limited to those known to have been used in North America, whatever the original source of the word may have been. While rooms of ancient Greek temples and

Roman houses are generally not included, many Latin and Greek terms are defined because they refer to the architecture of the various revival styles or are in current use in altered form.

The *types of building elements and materials* included are also generally limited to those in use before World War II. Although a few unique post-war properties have been determined to be historic, this book is intended to serve preservationists involved with the multitude of earlier ones.

Only a few *basic architectural styles* are included, as this volume is not intended as a substitute for the many excellent field guides currently available. Rather, the definitions and illustrations will help the reader find some of the associated physical characteristics of most of the common architectural styles.

Building materials found or manufactured in North America are included. Raw materials defined include metal, stone, and wood. Some imported materials known to have been used in North America are also defined. However, most rare materials, such as exotic wood veneers, are omitted.

Woods are defined under their respective tree. The most commonly lumbered trees are included, but the list is not inclusive. Where several varieties of a single family, such as *pine,* are defined, the varieties included are listed under the family name and defined under the variety name. Where information is available, the period of maximum use of the particular wood is part of the definition.

Only *current preservation usage* is defined. Many words have multiple meanings, only some of which are applicable to preservation. For example, in the nineteenth century, *dinette* was a little dinner or luncheon. The twentieth-century meaning is used—a dining alcove in a dwelling.

It was my original intent to exclude well known words such as *room* or *house.* However, during the compilation of this work I concluded that basic words of this type should be included as a reference for their many multiple variations and subtypes. I also discovered that many words I had thought to be constant in meaning have evolved over time. Therefore, the inclusion of words that are commonly understood today may assist current and future researchers.

The spelling of the words defined herein is generally English as used in the United States. Words with multiple spellings have the preferred spelling listed first. Words used only in Canada have the British or Canadian spelling. Words of other languages, such as Spanish or French, have the spelling and accent marks of their native language, unless they have been adapted into English. Generally the singular, rather than plural, form of nouns is used. Irregular pluralization is noted in parentheses after the word being defined, such as *anta (pl. antae).*

A parenthetically enclosed date or period preceding a definition, such as (18c) or (pre-20c), indicates when a word was in common use or the only period from which a written reference was found. Similarly, a locational notation, such as (western U.S.) signifies the geographical area where a term is most often used. A bracketed language preceding a definition, such as [Spanish], means that the word is primarily used by speakers of that language. These notations are not meant to imply that the word is never used outside of this context, but are intended to provide the reader with a more complete understanding of the word and its meaning.

I expect that many specialists looking on the preservation pyramid from different vantage points will have additional data and words they believe should have been included. I hope that they will pass this information on to me for incorporation into future editions that will allow us all to see farther.

In conclusion, I would like to thank the many generous individuals who provided essential assistance with the research and editing of this volume. I have been astonished at the apparently universal willingness of preservationists to joyfully give large chunks of time to extend my view.

At the beginning there were those who provided essential encouragement and motivation, including Patricia Poore, Editor in Chief, *Old-House Journal;* James C. Cope, Director of Environmental Policy, Executive Office of Transportation and Construction, Massachusetts; and, especially, Rick Brown, National Project Director, Pacific Institute.

Several reviewers took on the significant task of reviewing every one of the thousands of definitions. Their comments and suggestions were invaluable in making the final product more focused, accurate, and useful. They include Richard Longstreth, Director, Historic Preservation Program, The George Washington University, Washington, D.C.; Hugh C. Miller, Director, Virginia Department of Historic Resources, Richmond, Virginia; and Ward Jandl, National Park Service, Washington, D.C. Hugh Miller in particular provided a tremendous amount of suggestions, information, and editing. Sara B. Chase, Preservation Consultant, Lexington, Massachusetts, deserves special mention for going beyond her agreed task of reviewing paints and coatings definitions to comment on the entire draft.

A number of reviewers provided extensive comments and information on specific portions of the dictionary. Elizabeth Merritt, Esq., Corporation Counsel's Office, National Trust for Historic Preservation, provided substantial advice and information for all the legal definitions. Susan Sherwood, World Monuments Fund, commented on items related to corrosion and scientific analysis and provided substantial information on stone and geology. Veronica Vaillancourt, Heritage Canada, reviewed Canadian-related terms and provided extensive updated information. Janet Rumbarger, American Institute of Architects, assisted with the final copyediting.

Buckley Jeppeson and Janet Walker, former editors of *Preservation Press,* helped define the scope of the dictionary. Jan Cigliano, Preservation Press/Wiley, was invaluable in speeding the manuscript on its way to the printing press.

Numerous other individuals helped with advice, information, and referrals to other specialists. These include Gordon Boch, Editor, *Old-House Journal;* John Burns, HABS; William Cissel, National Park Service, St. Croix, Virgin Islands; Ellen Delage, Program Officer, ICOMOS/US; Eric DeLony, HAER; Diana Godwin, Navarre, Florida; Elizabeth Hennings, SITES, Smithsonian Institution; Janis James, Jeltrups' Books, St. Croix, Virgin Islands; Susan Ford Johnson, Association for Preservation Technology International; Clem Labine, Publisher, *Traditional Building;* Diane Maddex, Archetype Press; Dr. Gregory P. Marchildon, Deputy Provincial Secretary, Saskatchewan; Jane Merritt, Early American Studies, University of Pennsylvania; Robert Mitchell, A.I.A., Historical Architect, State Historical Society of North Dakota; Joni Monnich, Finishing Consultant, Alameda, California; Terry Morton, former Executive Director, ICOMOS/US; Fran Rehwaldt, Weichert Realtors, Washington D.C.; Gary Scott, National Park Service, National Capital Region; Anne and David Sellin, Washington, D.C.; William Taylor, Architect, St. Croix, Virgin Islands; and Bill Wagner, F.A.I.A., Preservation Architect, Dallas Center, Iowa.

At the end was Chris Madrid, National Park Service, National Capital Region, who cheerfully haunted the Library of Congress and the HABS/HAER Library to gather the hundreds of illustrations herein. Marilyn Ibach of the Prints and Photographs Division, Library of Congress, provided crucial assistance.

My thanks to all those noted above and others who I may have omitted. Standing together we observe both the past and the future.

WARD BUCHER
Washington, D.C.

Abbreviations

1c	1st century
15c	15th century
16c	16th century
17c	17th century
18c	18th century
19c	19th century
20c	20th century
abbr.	abbreviation
ca.	circa
WWI	World War I (1914–1919)
WWII	World War II (1939–1946)
2×	two by

Dictionary of Building Preservation

A

Aaron's rod An ornament consisting of a straight molding with a circular cross section that ends in leafy carving or scrollwork.

AASLH American Association for State and Local History

abaciscus, abaculus (pre-19c) A paving tile, slab, or **tessera.**

abacus The uppermost member of a column capital; in classical style columns, typically square or a hollowed square in plan, with the hollowed plan having concave indentations on each of four faces and truncated corners. Also known as **tailloir.** See also **Classical orders.**

abamurus (pre-20c) A masonry support, especially a buttress.

Abandoned Shipwreck Act of 1987 U.S. federal legislation that transfers ownership of the remains of a historic wrecked ship located within three miles of the coast to the adjoining state; protects such sites from commercial salvage operations or looters.

abated A lowered stone or metal background, as in **bas relief** sculpture.

abatement The removal or reduction to an acceptable level of health risk from **hazardous materials,** such as those containing **asbestos** or **lead,** at a site; may include selective demolition and removal, or encapsulation, of the materials; the acceptable level of risk may be regulated by national or local governments.

abat-jour, abat jour A roof or wall opening through which daylight is cast downward; types include (1) a sloped sill or lintel in a thick wall; (2) a **skylight;** (3) a window covering that slopes out and upward; used to prevent prisoners from seeing below; (4) any window shade.

abattoir Same as **slaughterhouse.**

abat-vent, abat vent (pre-20c) From the French for **dampened wind,** describes any construction that breaks the force of the wind; types include (1) a **louver** with large boards; (2) a chimney **cowl;** (3) a **windbreak;** and (4) a sloping roof.

abrasive blasting See **blast cleaning.**

abraum A red ocher used to color mahogany.

abreuvoir, abbreuvoir, abrevoir A masonry joint between two stones.

ABS Abbr. for **acrylonitrile-butadiene-styrene,** a type of plastic.

absorbing well A shaft or hole sunk below impervious underground material to a permeable level that can be used for discharge of wastewater. Also known as **drain well, waste well.** See also **dry well.**

abstract of title A statement of the history of ownership, liens, and easements of a property; prepared by research at the local government office that records real estate titles.

abutment **1.** The portion of a wall that supports the weight and resists the thrust of an arch, vault, or truss. **2.** The end support of a bridge or arched colonnade, as opposed to the intermediate piers. **3.** The joining of two pieces of wood so that their grains are perpendicular.

abutment arch The first or last of a series of arches next to an **abutment.**

abutment joint (pre-WWI) **1.** The end joint between two axially aligned iron compression members, such as one column on top of another column. **2.** Same as **butt and butt** or **T-joint.**

abutting joint Same as **abutment joint.**

acanthine In the form of an **acanthus,** or decorated with stylized acanthus leaves.

acanthite A silver sulfide that forms shiny, faceted, black, orthorhombic crystals on silver, sometimes in a foliated shape resembling acanthus leaves.

acanthus A classical style design motif of vertical, symmetrical foliage with scalloped edges, named after the Mediterranean plant; common on Corinthian, Composite, and Gothic style column capitals.

access door A hinged panel providing access to equipment, ducts, and other hidden spaces.

accessibility Provision of access to and through a building or site for physically impaired individuals, including those who are in wheelchairs and sight or hearing impaired. Also known as **handicap accessibility.** See also **Americans with Disabilities Act, Fair Housing Act of 1988, Architectural Barriers Act of 1968, Uniform Federal Accessibility Standards.**

accessibility audit Evaluation of an existing building's barriers to accessibility by persons with disabilities; usually compares existing **accessibility** conditions to those required by legislation, such as the **Americans with Disabilities Act Accessibility Guidelines,** or by building codes.

accessory building A structure, such as an outhouse or stable, that is related but subordinate to the principal building on a site.

accidental fire An unintentional, destructive building fire; the most common types are caused by problems with the heating system; other sources include defective electrical wiring, lightning, cigarettes, and renovation activities, such as stripping paint with flaming torches and spontaneous combustion of chemicals. See also **arson.**

accolade A hood molding in the form of an ogee arch, tangent to the extrados of the arched opening below and rising to a finial peak.

accompanying documentation The U.S. Geological Survey map, photographs, and sketch maps that accompany a completed National Register registration form.

accordion door A folding door with more than two leaves; similar in appearance to the bellows of an accordion. See also **bifold door.**

accouplement Having pairs of closely spaced columns or pilasters; typically the abacuses of the capitals touch without being joined; common in neoclassical architecture.

accretion **1.** An accumulation of extraneous material, such as dirt or salts, on the surface of a monument or building. **2.** The addition of elements to a building after the initial construction due to expansion or other alterations.

achelor (pre-20c) Same as **ashlar.**

ACHP **Advisory Council on Historic Preservation**

acid deposition The delivery of acidic materials in rain to an exterior surface; may be atmospheric particles or soluble gases, especially sulfur and nitrogen oxides.

acid rain Rain that is more acidic than normal (pH 5.5), especially with a reading below pH 5.0. See also **acid deposition, dry deposition, wet deposition.**

ACM Abbr. for **asbestos-containing material.** See also **asbestos abatement.**

acorn A rounded tip attached to one of the ends of a **butt hinge** knuckle.

acorn ventilator A sheet-metal fabrication that approximates the shape of an acorn with the pointed end up; used for ventilating roofs and skylights.

Acoustalith Trade name for an early 20c plaster with acoustical deadening properties.

acoustical tile A interior finish tile made of compressed fibers with a surface texture that absorbs sound; range in size from 1 × 1 foot to 2 × 4 feet; may be dropped in a **ceiling grid,** stapled to furring, or glued in place; manufactured 1925–present. See also **suspended ceiling.**

acre A unit of measure of land area; equals 160 square rods, 4,840 square yards, 43,560 square feet, or 4,047 square meters; originally an English measure equal to the area plowed by a yoke of oxen in one day.

acreage Area of a property measured in acres.

acropodium A pedestal for a large statue. See also **acroterion.**

acroterion, acroterium, (pre-20c) **acroter** (pl. **acroteria, acroteres**) **1.** Pedestals to support statues at the apex and lower corners of a classical style pediment or other gable end. **2.** A statue or ornament on an acroterion. **3.** Any ornament at the apex of a building. **4.** (18c) "sharp pinnacles or spiry battlements, that stand in ranges about flat buildings, with rails and balusters" (*The Builder's Dictionary*).

acrylic A synthetic resin composed of **polymethyl acrylate,** developed late 20c; used in paints, especially as an emulsion in **acrylic latex paint,** and in glazing, such as **Lucite®, Plexiglas®.**

acrylic latex paint A 20c type of paint composed of a suspension of acrylic and polyvinyl resins in water, other resins, pigments, and extenders; typically used on plaster and drywall. Also known as **acrylic paint.** See also **latex.**

acrylic paint Same as **acrylic latex paint.**

actinic glass Glass that screens out **actinic light.**

actinic light The active green, blue, and ultraviolet wavelengths of sunlight or artificial light sources; highly photochemically interactive and therefore extremely damaging to fabric and finishes. See also **ultraviolet light.**

action hinge (19c) Same as **double-acting hinge.**

acuminated Terminating in a point, as in a church spire.

acute-pointed arch A **two-centered arch** with the centers on the spring line outside the intrados, creating a sharply pointed arch; common in Gothic Revival style. Also called **lancet arch.**

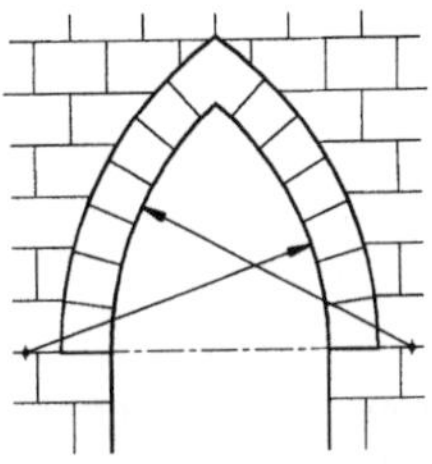

acute-pointed arch

ADA **Americans with Disabilities Act**

ADAAG **Americans with Disabilities Act Accessibility Guidelines**

Adam style Architectural style named for Robert Adam (1728–92) and his three brothers, English architects renowned for designing country estates and groups of London town houses in the latter half of the 18c characterized by imposing neoclassical style facades with delicately ornamented interiors, especially bas-relief plaster scrollwork ceilings and Neoclassical furnishings in coordinated pastel

Adam style
Congress Hall
Ceiling ornament, Senate Chamber
Philadelphia, Pennsylvania, ca. 1789

colors; strongly influenced the **Federal style** in the U.S.; the ceiling of George Washington's house at Mount Vernon, Virginia, is an early example (1775) in North America. Also known as **Adamesque style.**

adaptation A modern product, such as a lighting fixture, that has the general appearance of the original but is not an exact copy.

adaptive use Changing an existing, often historic, building to accommodate a new function; may include extensive **restoration** and/or **renovation** of both the interior and exterior of the building and removal of some existing building elements. Also known as **adaptive re-use.**

adaptive re-use Same as **adaptive use.**

addition Construction that increases the size of the original structure by building outside its existing walls and/or roof.

additive massing A building form created by joining simple volumes along their outer surfaces, as in a lean-to addition.

Adirondack Rustic style Architectural style of the mountain camps built in late 19c and early 20c in the Adirondack Mountains of eastern U.S.; characterized by buildings with peeled log walls and beams, fieldstone fireplaces, peeled branch railings and brackets, and steeply pitched roofs; ranged from small cabins to large buildings of the wealthy.

Adirondack sandstone Same as **Malone sandstone.**

adjusted basis The initial cost of a property (basis) plus capital improvements less depreciation; typically includes land value except when used in calculating an **investment tax credit.**

adjuster A hardware device for opening casement windows; typically has a sliding bar with one end pivoted on the bottom rail and the other held with a thumbscrew. See also **transom adjuster.**

adobe **1.** A large, sun-dried building block made from aluminous clay; straw was often added to the clay after 1540; typical sizes range from 10 × 14 × 4 inches to 12 × 18 × 5 inches. **2.** Buildings whose walls are constructed with adobes and mud mortar and covered with mud stucco; used in arid climates such as found in Mexico, Arizona, New Mexico, and southern California and often associated with Native American and Spanish colonial construction; typical coursing is running bond; elements may include **adobine, alacena, canale, cedro, laja, latia, portal, roof bearing, sala, viga, zaguan.** See also **Sante Fe style, Spanish Colonial style, Spanish Colonial Revival style, Territorial style.**

adobine An extra long **adobe** brick, ranging in length from two to six feet.

adverse effect An effect of a U.S. federally assisted undertaking on a historic property that may diminish the integrity of the property's location, design, setting, materials, workmanship, feeling, or association. See also **Section 106, National Environmental Policy Act of 1969.**

Advisory Board on National Parks, Historic Sites, Buildings and Monuments A panel that advises the U.S. secretary of the interior on the acquisition and management of national parks, designation of national landmarks (historic and natural), and general administrative policies pertaining to historically and archaeologically significant federal sites, buildings, and properties; created by the Historic Sites Act of 1935; members are appointed by the secretary of the interior.

Advisory Council on Historic Preservation An independent U.S. federal agency created by the National Historic Preservation Act of 1966 (NHPA) that advises the president and Congress and assists other federal agencies in reviewing the effects of their actions and decisions on properties of historical, architectural, archaeological, and cultural significance, including review of Environmental Impact Statements, and other activities, such as giving awards; has issued regulations (36 C.F.R. Part 800) defining a consultation process that all federal agencies must follow in order to comply with **Section 106** of the NHPA. See also **adverse effect, Environmental Impact Statement, Memorandum of Agreement, undertaking.**

AE, A/E, A & E Abbr. for **architecture and engineering.**

aerial photography The process and product of taking photographs from above ground, such as from an airplane, satellite, or balloon.

aerugo Same as **verdigris.**

Aesthetic movement The philosophical basis of the **Queen Anne style,** resulting from the reaction of the younger generation of the English upper middle class to the **Gothic Revival style** in the mid-19c; espoused modeling architecture, furnishings, and clothing on English domestic examples of the 17c and 18c.

aft gate Same as **tail gate.**

agate A translucent quartz stone with colored bands or irregular markings; found in many different colors, often is artificially stained; used as ornamental stone.

aggregate The solid material used with a cement or binder to form a mixture such as **asphalt**

concrete, concrete, or **plaster;** usually sand and crushed stone or gravel but may be any material, including broken brick, sawdust, or shells.

Ag-panels Premanufactured agricultural sheet-metal roofing panels with rolled ribs; commonly galvanized.

Agreements for Recreation and Conservation (ARC) A program that created partnerships between Parks Canada and provincial or territorial governments that developed Cooperative Heritage Areas, Heritage Canals, Heritage Trails, and Canadian Heritage Rivers throughout Canada; examples include the Canada-Ontario Rideau-Trent-Severn (CORTS) Agreement, the Red River Agreement, the Alexander Mackenzie Heritage Trail, and the Canadian Heritage Rivers System.

aha Same as **ha-ha.**

AIA **1. American Institute of Architects. 2. American Institute of Archaeology.**

AIC **American Institute of Conservation of Historic and Artistic Works**

Aich's metal A ductile **brass** alloy composed of copper, zinc, and iron; patented by J. Aich in 1860.

aileron One of a pair of half gable ends or wing walls abutting a taller middle portion of a building; in neoclassical architecture, the parapet is typically shaped as a large single scroll or curve to disguise the sloped roof behind.

air balancing The process of adjusting air flow in a **heating, ventilating and air conditioning system** to achieve the proper rate of flow to all spaces. Also known as **balancing.**

air brick **1.** A brick with openings to allow ventilating air into the interior of a building. **2.** A brick-sized metal louver built into a brick wall.

air conditioning (1906–present) The process of mechanically treating the air supply of a building to control the humidity and temperature and to remove airborne particles; beginning ca. 1900 mainly used for manufacturing mills; central systems installed for comfort became widespread in the 1920s for public, workplaces, and residences; the first air-conditioned office building was built in 1928; American engineer Stuart Cramer first used the phrase. See also **heating, ventilating, and air conditioning.**

air drain **1.** (19c) A masonry flue that supplies combustion air to a fireplace. **2.** (19c) "A channel around a foundation that promotes dryness by allowing free circulation of air" (*Funk & Wagnalls,* 1899). See also **areaway.**

air dried Any material, such as **seasoned wood,** that has had its moisture content reduced by natural evaporation. See also **kiln dried.**

air duct (19c–present) A pipe or boxlike construction that conveys air from one part of a building to another; in the 20c usually made of sheet metal but may also be other materials, such as asbestos cement, fiberglass, or plastic; pre-20c also wood or masonry; types include **trunk duct, ventiduct.**

air heading A passage in a mine that is smaller than and parallel to the main gangway; used for ventilation. See also **airway.**

air heating furnace See **furnace.**

air hole (pre-20c southern U.S.) One of several openings in a masonry foundation wall to permit ventilation of the crawl space.

air loop (pre-20c) A narrow window.

air pipe (19c) Same as **vent pipe.**

air rights The legal right to use the space above a facility to construct a building (for example, above a highway or subway station).

air space A continuous cavity between two building elements, such as the vertical space between inner and outer parts of a masonry wall. See also **cavity wall.**

air trap Same as **trap** (sense 1).

air trunk Same as **trunk duct.**

airway A passage used for ventilation, especially in a mine. See also **air heading.**

air wood (19c) Wood that is seasoned by being **air dried,** as opposed to **kiln dried.**

aisle, (pre-19c) **aile, ile, isle** **1.** (19c–present) A space created by dividing the interior of a building into parallel areas by rows of columns, especially the space between the nave of a church and the outside walls. **2.** (18c–present) The walkway between the ends of rows of seats or pews. See also **alley.**

à jour, ajouré **1.** A carving that is undercut and pierced so that light can pass through it. **2.** (19c) Having a transparent or translucent background.

Alabama marble Fine-grained, creamy white marble quarried in the state of Alabama.

alabaster A soft, smooth translucent stone composed of gypsum; commonly color is white but may also be red, yellow, or gray; often used for bas-relief carvings; varieties include **Fort Dodge alabaster.**

alabaster glass A translucent, yellowish white glass. Also known as **rice stone glass.** See also **milk glass.**

alacena A recessed cupboard built into the wall of an adobe house. See also **adobe.**

à la grecque (19c) Designed in classical Greek style, especially with fret, key, or meander decoration.

Alaska cedar A softwood tree with a hard, yellow wood; found in the Pacific Northwest, especially in Alaska; used for lumber and fine cabinetry; *Chamaecyparis nootkatensis.* Also known as **Alaska cypress, yellow cedar, yellow cypress.**

Alaska cypress Same as **Alaska cedar.**

albarium **1.** A thin, white stucco. **2.** A white lime produced by heating marble, commonly used in stucco work.

Alberene Trade name for a very dense, blue-gray **soapstone** quarried in Virginia.

albronze An alloy of aluminum and copper. See also **bronze.**

alcove **1.** (18c–19c) A deep recessed space in a bedroom designed to contain the bed, typically with curtains that conceal the bed when drawn across the opening. **2.** Any recess or niche, especially one having a lower ceiling than the main space. **3.** A recess in a wall or hedge of a pleasure garden. **4.** (late 18c–19c) Any secluded place, such as a bower or summerhouse in a garden.

alder Any of the hardwood trees or shrubs of the genus **alnus,** with reddish colored wood; used in cabinet or veneer work.

ale house (pre-18c) A building where ale and other spirits are sold. See also **ordinary, tavern.**

alette, allette **1.** The portion of a pier that is visible on either side of a pilaster centered on the face of the pier. **2.** A small wing of a building. **3.** (19c) A pilaster. **4.** (19c) A doorjamb.

Alhambraic (19c) Architecture in the style of the Alhambra, a richly decorated, red stone medieval Moorish palace in Granada, Spain; from the Arabic for “the red” (*al-hambra*). See also **arabesque.**

aligreek (19c) Same as **meander;** probably a corruption of **à la grecque.**

A list The properties with the highest significance listed on a Canadian heritage list.

alizarin red A brilliant red, **aniline color** paint pigment.

alkaline A compound, such as lye or lime, that is chemically basic, the opposite of an acid. See also **pH.**

alkathene Same as **polyethylene.**

alkyd A petroleum-based, gelatinous, synthetic resin used as a solvent base in oil-base paints and stains after 1940 as a substitute for linseed oil.

allée A narrow walkway or road, especially one in a garden bordered with tall hedges or rows of trees.

allège A part of an exterior wall that is thinner than the rest of the wall, especially under a window sill.

alley, (pre-18c) **ally** **1.** A walkway or roadway between adjacent buildings leading to their rear. **2.** A passageway in or under a house providing access to a rear yard or central court; common in Boston houses 1810–40. **3.** (pre-20c) an **aisle,** as in a church. **4.** A long, narrow building, such as a bowling alley. **5.** (pre-20c) Same as **allée.** Also known as **passageway, passway.**

alley dwelling A dwelling that fronts on a rear alley; often a secondary house located behind the main structure; until mid-20c usually the lowest-quality housing available in urban areas.

alligatoring A cracking pattern that approximates a rectangular grid; typically caused by shrinkage of a surface coating material, such as paint or plaster, at a rate different from that of the substrate.

alloy Two or more metals combined by fusion; types include **amalgam, bronze, brass, monel, pot metal, queen's metal, steel, solder, terne.**

alloy steel Any of various alloys of steel with another metal, such as **stainless steel.**

all-mine pig Pig iron smelted entirely of ore from a single source.

almshouse, alms house (pre-19c) Same as **poorhouse.**

aloes A resin made from the juices, thickened by evaporation, of the aloe plant; used to make varnish. See also **gilt varnish.**

alpha tracker A testing device that measures the number of alpha particles present; used to detect the presence of **radon.**

altar, (pre-19c) **alter** **1.** A table or other raised surface on which religious offerings are made. **2.** A raised area in a church where a communion service is conducted; sometimes enclosed with an **altar rail.** See also **high altar.**

altar cavity A niche or recess in an **altar** to hold religious relics.

altarpiece, altar piece, (pre-19c) **alter piece, aulter peace** A decorative painting, mosaic, or bas-relief on the wall above and behind an **altar;** required by colonial Anglican church law to be tablets inscribed with the Ten Commandments. See also **reredos.**

altar rail, altar railing A railing that separates an **altar** (sense 2) from the front of the chancel of a church.

alteration Any physical changes to an existing structure or building; generally excludes maintenance work such as painting and repairs.

alto-relievo, alto-rilievo Same as **high relief;** used in reference to sculpture.

aluminum, (Canada, pre-20c U.S.) **aluminium,** (pre-20c) **alumium** A lightweight, nearly colorless, ductile elemental metal; corrosion resistant; the Hall-Heroult process for reducing from bauxite ore invented in 1886; in commercial use by 1892; used for all types of metalwork, including windows, railings, roofing, siding, and ornamental castings. See also **anodized.**

aluminum bronze An **alloy** of aluminum and copper with a pale gold color. Also known as **aluminum gold.** See also **bronze.**

aluminum foil Sheets of aluminum that are less than 0.005 inch thick.

aluminum gold Same as **aluminum bronze.**

aluminum paint A silver colored **oil-base paint** with powdered or flaked aluminum pigment; in use by 1924 with heavy-bodied boiled linseed oil; typically used as a protective coating on exterior metal.

aluminum solder An alloy of gold, silver, and copper used to solder aluminum; may also contain a small amount of zinc.

alure A passageway, cloister, gallery, gangway, or walk, especially behind the battlement of a **fortification.** See also **banquette, chemin-de-ronde.**

alveated A vault or cupola having the concave shape of a beehive.

amalgam An alloy of mercury with another metal. See also **silvered, amalgam gilding, amalgam silvering.**

amalgam gilding Gold gilding applied to another metal, especially copper or silver, by mixing the gold with mercury and heating the metal to drive off the mercury; used for furniture hardware, light fixtures, and similar decorative metalwork.

amalgam silvering Silver applied to another metal, especially copper or brass, by mixing the silver with mercury and heating the metal to drive off the mercury; used for furniture hardware, light fixtures, and similar decorative metalwork. See also **fire silvering.**

amber varnish Any **varnish** made with amber resin dissolved in a solvent, such as **white varnish.**

ambry (19c) **1.** A food pantry. **2.** In a church, the wall cupboard in which the communion vessels are kept.

amenity A feature of a development that is pleasant, agreeable, or beautiful; in zoning or planning, indicates a contribution to the public good that is above and beyond the normal standard.

American basement A **basement house** with the main entrance through a ground-level basement containing a kitchen and an entrance vestibule at the foot of the main stair; found after 1880.

American beech A tall hardwood tree with light red colored, dense, straight, smooth-grained wood; found in eastern U.S. and Canadian maritime provinces; used for flooring; *Fagus grandifolia.*

American bond Same as **common bond.**

American chestnut A hardwood tree with light reddish brown, relatively weak, coarse-grained heartwood with light-colored sapwood; used for framing lumber and, because it is durable in contact with soil, palisades and fence posts and rails; popular from 19c to WWII for natural finished paneling and trim; now rare due to chestnut blight imported from Asia ca. 1904; *Castanea dentata.*

American cypress Common cedar tree found in eastern U.S.; not a true **cypress;** *Chamaecyparis sphaeroidea.* See also **white cedar.**

American elm A tall hardwood tree with light-colored, hard, tough, cross-grained wood; found in eastern half of the U.S. and southeastern Canada; lumbered in small quantities for flooring; peak lumbering production was in 1929; *Ulmus americana.*

American hemlock Same as **eastern hemlock.**

American holly An evergreen hardwood tree with light-colored, dense, weak, fine-grained wood; lumbered in small quantities for use in parquet and other inlay work; *Ilex opaca.*

American Institute of Architects (AIA) U.S. professional association whose principal members are registered architects; involved in various preservation activities and is a signatory to the Historic American Building Survey **tripartite agreement;** headquartered in Washington, D.C.

American National Standards Institute (ANSI) U.S. organization that promulgates testing and design standards. See also **American Society for Testing and Materials.**

American Society for Testing and Materials (ASTM) Professional organization that promulgates voluntary standards, guides, practices, and test procedures for various construction materials and methods; established in 1898 and headquartered in Philadelphia, Pennsylvania. See also **American National Standards Institute.**

American Society of Landscape Architects (ASLA) U.S. professional association for landscape architects.

American Standard beam Any of various sizes of rolled steel I-beams manufactured to a standardized shape and weight beginning in 1896; characteristics include narrow flanges and thin, deep webs. See also **wide flange beam.**

American Style (19c) Same as **Italianate.**

Americans with Disabilities Act (ADA) A 1990 U.S. civil rights law that includes requirements for accessibility of public accommodations, including historic sites, by removal of existing physical barriers as defined in the **Americans with Disabilities Act Accessibility Guidelines** (ADAAG); changes that would "threaten or destroy" the historic significance of a building or facility are not required. See also **accessibility.**

Americans with Disabilities Act Accessibility Guidelines (ADAAG) A written and illustrated description of a barrier-free environment as required by the **Americans with Disabilities Act** (ADA).

American system A truss construction system using pinned connections at joints so that strains are axial along the length of the members.

American turpentine Turpentine manufactured in the U.S. from the longleaf pine. Also known as **white turpentine.** See also **Canadian turpentine, Carolina turpentine.**

American vermilion A brilliant, nonfading red paint **pigment** composed of basic lead chromate ($PbCrO_4$). See also **chrome yellow, vermilion.**

Amherst sandstone Sandstone quarried in Lorain County, Ohio; buff, variegated, or gray.

amicus curiae Latin for "friend of the court"; a party (an individual or organization) with special expertise who is not directly involved in a legal suit and who submits a brief or argument on an issue before a court; for example, the National Trust for Historic Preservation may submit an amicus curiae brief in a local court case involving preservation issues.

ammonium sulfamate A chemical compound used as a fungicide; often used to kill moss on concrete.

amortizement, amortissement The sloped top of a buttress or projecting pier, designed to shed rainwater.

amphiprostyle A building with columns across the full width of the front and rear porticoes but with no columns on the sides. See also **columniation.**

amphitheater **1.** An elliptical-shaped building with tiers of seats surrounding a central open area; may be roofed or open to the sky; used for public entertainment. **2.** Tiers of seats on a bowl-shaped slope of ground facing a central stage; typically with a semicircular or semielliptical arrangement. **3.** A room with tiers of seats arranged in a manner similar to those described in 2. **4.** Any arena or place of public competition.

amygdaloid Volcanic rock with almond-shaped cavities filled with other minerals; for example, the Brighton amygdaloid found near Boston.

anaglyph Ornamentation carved in relief; has more depth than bas-relief. See also **coelanaglyph.**

Anaglypta Trade name for an embossed wall covering made of cotton pulp and decorated with various bas-relief patterns; often used on ceilings and as wainscoting; invented in 1887 by Thomas J. Palmer, a manager at the **Lincrusta-Walton** factory in England.

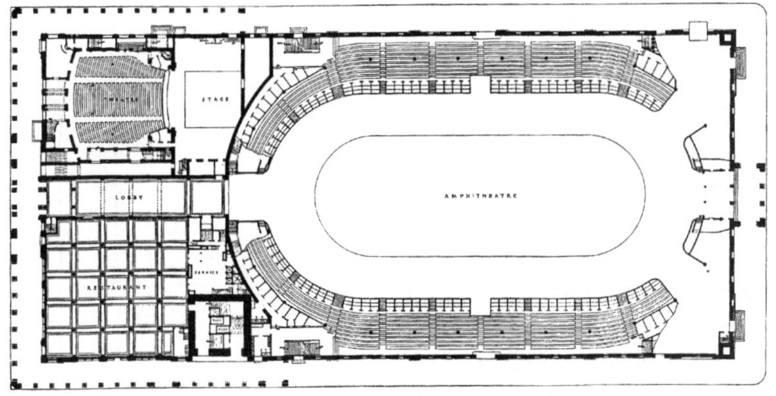

amphitheater (sense 1)
Madison Square Garden
New York City, ca. 1891

anastylosis Rebuilding fallen masonry elements in their assumed position in the original structure, including restacking fallen column drums.

anatase A paint **pigment** composed of a variety of **titanium dioxide;** owing to its chalking characteristics, has largely been replaced by **rutile** titanium dioxide. Also known as **octahedrite.**

anchor **1.** Metal fabrications used to fasten building elements together, especially a structural member to masonry or concrete; types include **anchor bolt, anchor plate, angle anchor, cramp, government anchor, side joist anchor.** **2.** A stylized pointed anchor with two flukes; used in decorative moldings. See also **egg and anchor, dart.** **3.** One of the principal retail businesses in a development that attracts patrons to the development; often a department or merchandise store or a supermarket. Also known as **anchor tenant, key tenant.** **4.** A **historic building** that establishes the identity or character of a site or historic district.

anchor and collar **1.** Part of a heavy **hinge** for a door, gate, or shutter; consists of a collar ring with an anchor bar inserted into a masonry jamb; receives the **pintle** attached to a **hanging stile** or **heel post.** **2.** A **hinge** composed of a **pintle** attached to a jamb that supports a collar ring.

anchor bolt A bolt with its head embedded in the structure; may be a machine bolt or various bent shapes with one threaded end; used to attach a structural member, such as a **sole** to a foundation wall; types include **J-bolt, swage bolt.**

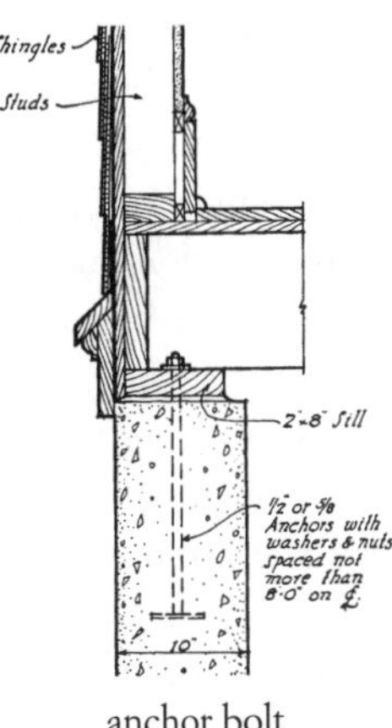

anchor bolt

anchor dart Same as **anchor** (sense 2).

anchor plate In masonry construction, a metal plate on a wall that holds the end of a tie rod; may be of a decorative form; shapes include **earthquake washer, fish plate, S-iron, star anchor, T-head, triangular washer.** Also known as **wall washer.** See also **skewback.**

anchor tenant An **anchor** (sense 3) business that leases the ground or building it occupies in a development. Also known as **key tenant.**

anchor tie **1.** A metal fabrication used to attach a masonry veneer to its backing. **2.** Same as **anchor** (sense 1).

ancillary (pre-19c) Same as **accessory building.**

ancon, (pre-20c) **ancone** (pl. **ancones**) **1.** A scroll-shaped **bracket** that supports the cornice or entablature over a door, window, or mantel. See also **console. 2.** Same as **crossette** (sense 1). **3.** (18c) A bracket at a corner of a wall or where crossbeams meet a rafter. **4.** (pre-20c) A console ornament on a **keystone. 5.** (pre-20c) The angle of a **knee timber. 6.** (19c) The corner or quoin of a wall.

androsphinx An Egyptian-style sphinx with the head of a man and the body of a lion.

angel light One of several small openings at the top of a window with Gothic style tracery; typically glazed with stained glass angels.

angle anchor An **anchor** formed by two short pieces of angle iron bolted together through a hole in the end of a steel beam.

angle bar **1.** An **angle iron. 2.** A mullion with an angled cross section, such as at the intersection of two faces of a bay window.

angle bead **1.** A projecting, vertical bead molding at an outside corner of a wall; typically circular in cross section; may be less than full height and turned at the top and bottom. Also known as **bowtell.** See also **angle staff, staff bead. 2.** Same as **corner bead** (sense 1).

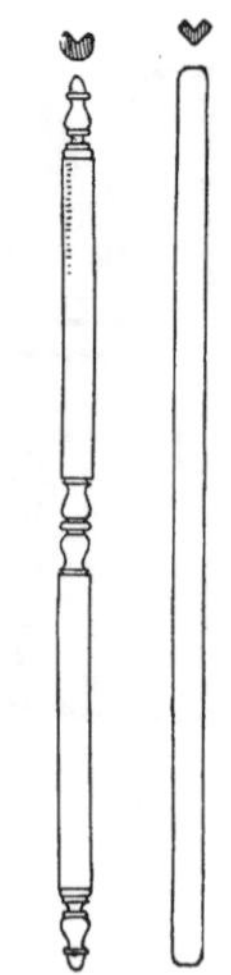

angle bead (sense 1)

angle beam **1.** A beam composed of two members intersecting at an angle; typically the angle is 90 degrees. **2.** Same as **angle iron. 3.** A beam composed of steel plates attached with angle iron.

angle block (19c) A block or shoe, often of cast iron, that ties together the ends of two or more truss members meeting at an angle.

angle brace **1.** A **brace** across the corner of a rectangular frame or structure. **2.** A diagonal tie terminating at an inside corner of a frame.

angle bracket A cornice bracket at an inside corner; usually has two perpendicular decorative sides.

angle brick A specially shaped brick for use at an outside corner of a building.

angle bulb An L-shaped angle iron with the end of one leg expanded into a circular cross section; typically used as a small beam.

angle buttress A pair of buttresses at right angles at the outside corner of a building, with each buttress parallel to a wall.

angle capital A column capital at the corner of a colonnade or other structure; in the Ionic

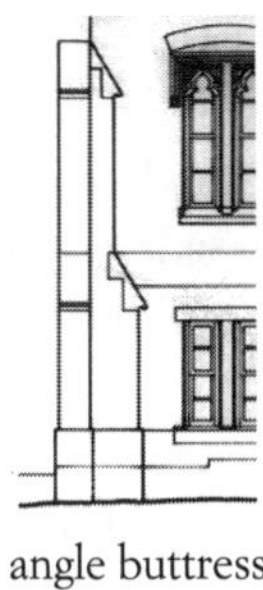
angle buttress

order, the angle capital is designed to have volutes perpendicular to each other on both of the outer faces.

angle chimney Same as **corner chimney.**

angle cleat Same as **angle iron.**

angle column (late 19c–early 20c) A column composed of steel plates attached with **angle iron;** typically H-shaped in cross section. See also **channel column.**

angle girder (late 19c–early 20c) A beam or girder with **angle iron** flanges attached to a web of plate steel or wrought iron to form an I-shaped cross section; the plate web is often reinforced with vertical angle iron; in use by 1859. See also **riveted beam girder.**

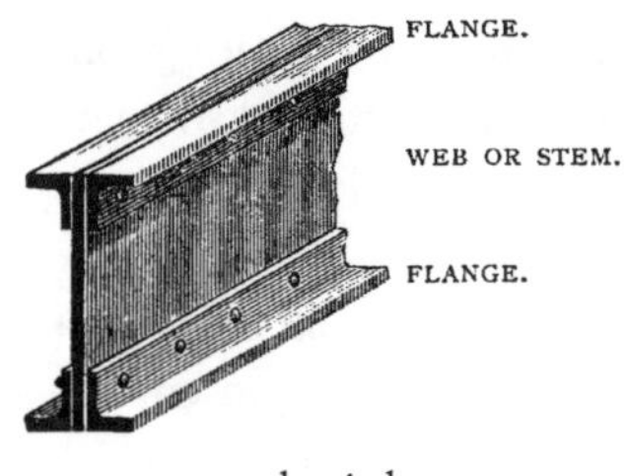

angle girder

angle iron A bar of iron or steel with an L-shaped or, less frequently, V-shaped cross section.

angle joint A joint between two members in the same plane that meet at an angle other than 90 or 180 degrees.

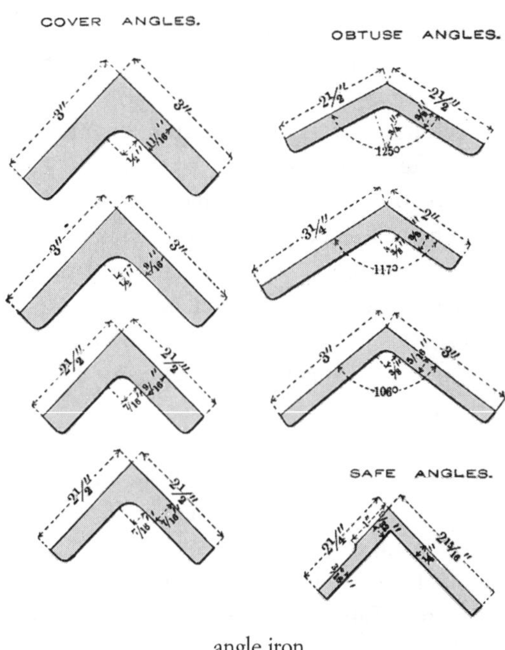

angle iron

angle joist A **joist** that runs diagonally from an interior support across an outside corner; used to support the foot of a hip rafter or other overhanging member.

angle leaf **1.** Same as **spur. 2.** (19c) A decorative structural bracket used to reinforce an inside corner; typically in the form of stylized foliage.

angle modillion A **modillion** at a corner of a cornice.

angle niche A niche formed in a corner of a building.

angle of repose **1.** The steepest angle of an earthen slope that will remain stable; refers to all types of materials including **sand** and **gravel. 2.** The steepest angle of an arch bed joint that will hold a **voussoir** stone without slipping.

angle of skew The angle between the axis of a **skew arch** or **skew vault** and its abutting walls.

angle of slide Same as **angle of repose.**

angle post A stair handrail post about which winders turn.

angle rafter **1.** Same as **hip rafter.** **2.** A principal rafter directly under a hip rafter.

angle rib **1.** Same as **diagonal rib.** **2.** A projecting molding along the intersection of two plane surfaces. **3.** A curved timber supporting a corner of an arched ceiling.

angle shaft **1.** A column within a 90-degree recess. See also **jamb shaft.** **2.** Same as **staff bead.**

angle staff **1.** Same as **angle iron.** **2.** An angular wood molding projecting from an outside corner of a wall, such as **square staff.** See also **staff bead, corner bead.**

angle steel **Angle iron** made of steel.

angle stone Same as **quoin.**

angle tie Same as **angle brace.**

angle volute One of the four corner volutes of a Corinthian capital, with an axis at 45 degrees to the face of the abacus.

anglet A V-shaped groove, typically with sides at 45 degrees.

angular capital (19c) Same as **angle capital.**

aniline color, aniline dye Any of several paint **pigments** or dye tints manufactured from coal tar derivatives; the first aniline colors, manufactured in 1865, were mauve and magenta; colors include **alizarin red, chinolin, coal tar indigo, nigrosene black, para red.** Also known as **coal tar color.**

animation Re-enactment or demonstration of the history of a place, often in period costumes.

annealed glass Same as **heat-strengthened glass.**

annual ring One of the circular lines found in wood end grain; formed by the different rates of growth of the tree during summer and winter; typically each ring represents one year of growth. See also **dendrochronology, grain.** Also known as **growth ring.**

annular lamp An **Argand lamp** with the fuel reservoir in the shape of a hollow ring around the burner; designed to reduce the shadow cast by the earlier side-reservoir models; common types in the early 19c included **astral lamp, sinumbra.**

annular vault A barrel vault in which the center axis, in plan, is the shape of a circle segment.

annulated Encircled by a ring or rings, especially a column or group of engaged columns.

annulet, annulus A small ridge or molding with a rectangular cross section forming a ring, especially one of the projecting rings at the base of a Doric capital under the quarter round molding. Also known as **annulus, bandelet, cincture, fillet, listel, square and rabbet, supercilium, tinea.**

annunciator **1.** (19c–WWI) A central monitoring device in a hotel or large house that indicates a remote bell handle was pulled or an electric bell button was pushed. Also known as **bell telegraph.** **2.** (late 19c–WWII) A telephone switchboard in a hotel. **3.** (late 20c) A panel with indicator lights to show firemen the portion of a building in which sprinklers have discharged and alarms or a smoke detectors signaled.

anodizing A protective coating on aluminum produced by an electrolytic oxidation process; typically clear or various shades of yellow and brown.

ANSI **American National Standards Institute**

anta (pl. **antae**) **1.** (19c–present) A square or rectangular pier at the end of a wall, especially one of a pair of antae at the parallel side walls of an opening with columns; classical Greek style antae have a capital and base but are typically of a different order than the columns between them. Also known as **parastas.** See also **in antis.** **2.** A smooth **pilaster** with a rectangular cross section and without a capital or base.

antebellum, (19c) **ante-bellum** (southern U.S., 19c–present) The period before the U.S. Civil War.

antechamber, (pre-20c) **ante-chamber, anti-chamber** A lobby or waiting area outside a main room. Also known as **anteroom.**

antechoir A screen-enclosed area in front of a church **choir.**

antefix (pl. **antefixae, antefixes**) In classical Greek style architecture, the ornamental vertical elements at the eaves that terminate each row of roof **imbrex** tiles; also used as decorative elements with other roofing materials; typically with an **anthemion** or mask design.

antepagment, antepagmentum (pl. **antepagmenta**), (18c) **antipagment** **1.** Sculpted stone or stucco relief ornamentation on the surface of a door architrave or jamb. **2.** Same as **architrave.**

antepagment (sense 1)
Philosophy Building
detail at main entrance
Columbia University, New York City

anteroom Same as **antechamber.**

anthemion A stylized **palmette** or **honeysuckle** decoration used in classical architecture. Also known as **bouquet.** See also **antefix, anthemion band.**

anthemion band, (19c) **anthemion moulding** A classical Greek style decorative molding with bas-relief or painted anthemion leaf clusters; two types of anthemion designs are often alternated along the band.

antiscrape The policy of a group of mid-19c English preservationists, led by John Ruskin, who opposed removal of finishes from and later alterations to Gothic cathedrals. See also **scrape.**

anticipatory demolition **Demolition** of a historic building or structure by an owner before governmental controls or reviews take effect, such as under **Section 106** of the **National Historic Preservation Act;** owner may be a potential applicant or in the early stages of applying for government assistance or permits.

antipagment (18c) Same as **antepagment.**

antiquarian One who collects and/or studies historic artifacts.

antiquary (pre-20c) **1.** A student or collector of historic artifacts, especially as curiosities. **2.** A **curator** of historic artifacts.

antique **1.** Object that has acquired additional cultural and/or monetary value because of its age; U.S. Treasury rulings in the late 19c defined antique articles as those made before 1700 A.D.; generally not an appropriate term for describing North American buildings. See also **Antiquities Act of 1906.** **2.** (18c) Architecture that dates from the classical Greek period to about 600 A.D. **3.** **Marble** recycled from an unknown source.

Antiquities Act of 1906 U.S. federal legislation authorizing the president to designate historic and natural resources of national significance located on federally owned or controlled lands as national monuments, and providing for protection of all historic and prehistoric ruins and objects of antiquity located on federal lands; the first U.S. preservation legislation. See also **Historic Sites Act.**

antlerite A green, basic copper sulfate that forms on outdoor bronze or copper sculpture.

Antwerp blue Same as **Prussian blue.**

APA **1.** American Planning Association **2.** American Plywood Association

apartment **1.** (pre-19c) A **suite** reserved for use by a particular individual or function, such as a government office. **2.** (pre-20c) A partitioned room within a building. **3.** (After ca. 1870) One of several dwellings within a single building; types include **duplex, flat, studio apartment, tenement, triplex.** See also **tenement.** **4.** (pre-20c) A compartment.

apartment building Same as **apartment house.**

apartment hotel A building with multiple dwelling units that do not have private kitchen facilities; typically rented on a short-term basis. See also **apartment house.**

apartment house (After ca. 1870) A building with multiple dwellings, each of which has complete kitchen facilities; originally the term was reserved for buildings occupied by the wealthy and/or those without kitchens. Also known as **apartment building, flat house.** See also **apartment hotel, tenement house.**

APE **Area of Potential Effects**

aperture Any opening in the exterior of a building, such as a door, window, or chimney.

apex stone The stone at the top of a gable end, vault, or dome. See also **saddle stone.**

apophyge **1.** The concave curve formed where the base or top of a classical style column curves inward to meet the shaft; tangent to the shaft and perpendicular to the adjoining fillet. Also known as **scape, scape molding, scapus.** **2.** (19c) A hollow molding immediately below the echinus of some Doric style capitals. See also **classical orders.**

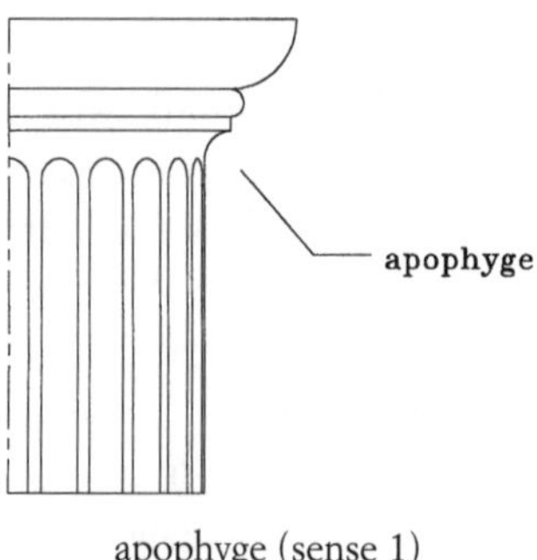

apophyge (sense 1)

apparatus floor (19c–early 20c) The ground floor of a firehouse where the horses and fire-extinguishing equipment are stored.

appentice (pre-20c) Same as **penthouse** (senses 1 and 2). Also known as **pent.**

Appleton Charter Abbreviated reference to the **Appleton Charter for the Protection and Enhancement of the Built Environment,** written in 1983 by the English-Speaking Committee of the International Council on Monuments and Sites (Canada); serves as a guideline for management and conservation of the built environment in Canada.

applied aggregate Same as **pebbledash.**

applied column Same as **engaged column.**

applied mold A molding that is produced separately and attached to a finish surface. See also **flush mold, solid mold.**

appliqué **1.** Applied to a surface for decorative effect. **2.** (19c) An accessory decorative element attached to the structure of a building.

appraised value The current **market value** of a property; may be determined by comparison to the sale price and condition of other similar properties, by analyzing the net income generated, or by estimating the replacement cost; typically estimated by a private or local government appraiser. See also **assessed value, highest and best use.**

appropriateness See **certificate of appropriateness.**

apron **1.** The casing molding below the projecting lip of a window stool, counter, or similar casework. **2.** Same as **counterflashing. 3.** The ornamental work below the cornice of a veranda. **4.** A paved area that serves as a transition element; for example, as between a garage entrance and a driveway or between a driveway and a road.

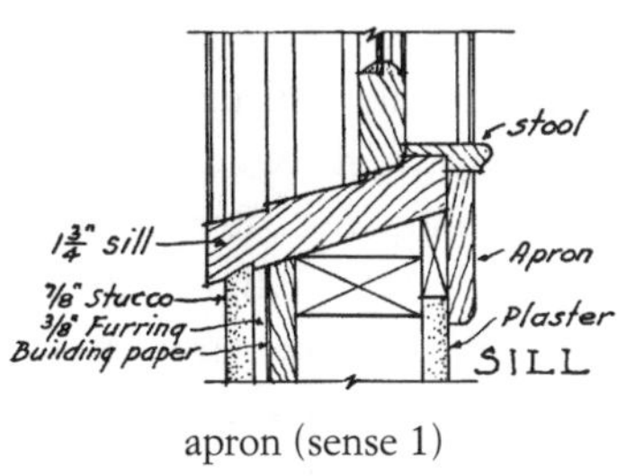

apron (sense 1)

apron piece A stair framing member that supports stringers and landing joists. Also known as **pitching piece.**

apse, apsid, apsis A large recessed space within a building, especially a church, that has a half dome concha and a semicircular (or similarly shaped) exterior wall.

apsidiole A small apse, especially one that opens off a larger apse.

APT **Association for Preservation Technology International.**

APT Bulletin The technical journal of the **Association for Preservation Technology International.**

apteral Descriptive of a classical building with columns across the width of the portico at one or both ends of the building but with no columns on the sides. See also **columniation.**

APTI **Association for Preservation Technology International**

aqueduct, (17c) **aquaduct** A **structure** that carries a water supply, especially to a community from a distant source such as a river or **reservoir;** portions of the conduit may be elevated, on grade, or underground; before 19c, sometimes used to refer to a building **gutter.**

aqueduct
High Bridge, Harlem River

Aquia Creek sandstone A Cretaceous sandstone quarried in Stafford County, Virginia; composed of quartz sand with inclusions of pebbles, thin clay beds, and pellets, all cemented with silica; used as building stone for the White House and the original facade of the U.S. Capitol; colors include tawny white, pink, and buff.

arabesque, (18c) **arabesk** **1.** Interlocking geometric decoration in the style of Moorish architecture. **2.** Ornate, decorative scrollwork or other ornament covering a flat surface, especially stylized vine patterns, in the style of Roman or Renaissance architecture; sometimes contains illustrations of classical vases, people, and animals.

Arabesque style A literal or loose imitation of the Moorish architectural style of Spain, characterized by masonry walls with multicolored Mooresque decoration in plaster; precious stones or glazed tiles on most surfaces; arches of horseshoe, pointed, ogive, or multifoil shape; interior courtyards surrounded by colonnades; flat or pointed-dome roofs; and, sometimes, wide horizontal stripes and stalactite ornament.

araeostyle, areostyle Columns that are spaced four or more diameters between centers. See also **intercolumniation.**

araeosystyle, areosystyle Columns that are spaced alternately **araeostyle** and **systyle.** See also **intercolumniation.**

ARB Abbr. for **architectural review board.**

arbor, arbour, (pre-19c) **arber, harbour** **1.** An open framework of wood or metal designed to be covered with vines, especially a freestanding structure in a park or garden. See also **pergola. 2.** A shaded walk or recess, especially within a garden. See also **bower. 3.** (pre-20c) A lawn, garden, or orchard. **4.** An open area used for religious revival meetings, as well as temporary or permanent shelter for the preacher and congregation. See also **tent.**

arc, (pre-19c) **arch** **1.** A segment of a curved geometric shape, such as between two cusps of a foiled arch or tracery. See also **segment,** and various compound words beginning with **compass. 2.** (pre-19c) Same as **arch.**

ARC See **Agreements for Recreation and Conservation.**

arcade **1.** A series of continuous arches, especially when an ornamental architectural feature. See also **arcading, arcature, surface arcade. 2.** A covered passageway with a series of open archways on one or both sides; not common in North America before the 18c. Also known as **piazza. 3.** A covered passageway with stores facing both sides, often multistoried and skylighted. Also known as a **galleria. 4.** A vaulted passageway or street.

arcading An arcade immediately in front of a solid wall so that there is insufficient space to walk between the arcade and the wall. See also **surface arcade.**

arcature **1.** A small arcade, as in a balustrade. **2.** Same as **arcade.**

arc-boutant An arch buttress, such as a **flying buttress.**

arc-doubleau (pl. **arcs-doubleaux**) **1.** An **arch band** in the shape of a rectangular pilaster that forms the soffit of an arch. See also **arch. 2.** Same as **transverse arch.**

arc en tiers point A two-centered **pointed arch.**

arc formeret Same as **wall rib.**

arch **1.** Multiple masonry units combined to structurally bridge over an opening in a wall by translating the vertical load into diagonal thrust at the sides of the arch, with the joints between the units radiating from a common center or centers; shapes can grouped according to the number of centers of the radii of the intrados and include **flat arch (jack arch, camber arch), one-centered arch (semicircular arch, segmental arch, pointed round arch), two-centered arch (blunt-pointed arch, equilateral pointed arch, acute-pointed arch, segmental pointed arch), three-centered arch (basket-handle arch, trefoil arch), four-centered arch (two-cusped arch, ogee arch, Tudor arch), five-centered arch (basket-handle, cinquefoil), elliptical arch, parabolic arch, catenarian arch,** and **multifoil arch;** other shape variations include **compound arch, drop arch, Gothic arch, horseshoe arch, interlaced arch, mixed arch, Moorish arch, pointed arch, Queen Anne arch, rampant arch, semiarch, skew arch, splayed arch, stepped arch, stilted arch, surbased arch, surmounted arch, Syrian arch, triangular arch,** and **Venetian arch;** types by use include **abutment arch, back arch, floor arch, inverted arch, relieving arch, safety arch, squinch,**

and **straining arch;** components of an arch include **architrave, archivolt, chord, crown, degree, depth, extrados, haunches, impost, intrados, keystone, rise, skewback, soffit, springer, spring line, voussoir.** Also known as **arc.** See also **abutment, arched, built arch, crossette, dome, extradosed, French arch, hand arch, haunched arch, inverted arch, joggled arch, miter arch, ogive, rowlock arch, shoot, spandrel, tile arch, vault, Welsh arch. 2.** A nonstructural opening in the shape of an arch. **3.** Part of a circle or other curved shape, such as an ellipse.

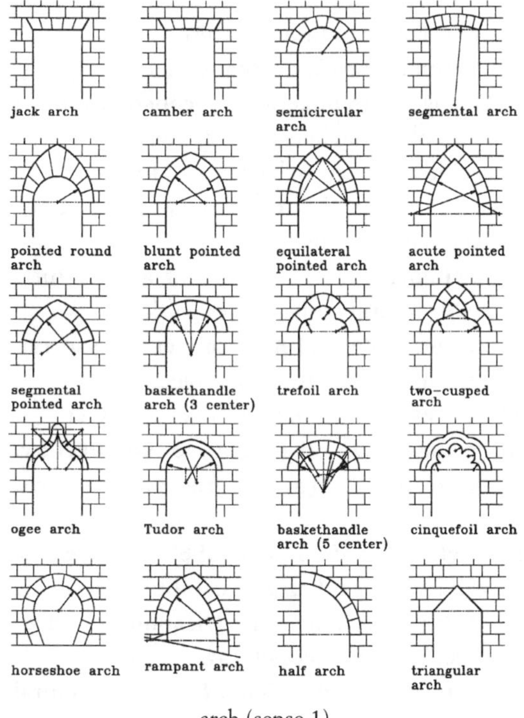

arch (sense 1)

archaeological artifact, archeological artifact An object made by people, or material altered by human activity, usually recovered from or found at an **archaeological site;** may be out of context in relation to other objects because of disturbance of or removal from a site.

Archaeological Resources Protection Act of 1979 (ARPA) U.S. federal legislation that prohibits the removal, excavation, or alteration of any archaeological resource from federally owned or controlled land or Indian reservations without a permit; permits are granted only for scientific research.

archaeological site, archeological site A place containing evidence of previous human activity that has been or can be investigated by an **archaeologist.** See also **archeological district, lumper, splitter.**

archaeologist, archeologist A professional with a graduate degree in archaeology, anthropology, or a closely related field, with specialized experience in research, field survey, and excavation work and analysis of archaeological sites and artifacts.

archaeology, archeology The scientific study of the physical remains of past human life, including prehistoric and historic societies; types include **conservation archaeology, crisis archaeology, historical archaeology, industrial archaeology, marine archaeology.** See also **archaeological artifact, archaeological site, archaeologist.**

arch band **1.** A horizontal wall band that continues around an arch as part of the archivolt or the intrados. **2.** The visible portion of a vault rib.

arch bar **1.** A curved top member of a window sash. **2.** An upward curved top member of a truss. **3.** A cambered iron bar.

arch barrel A wide **arch ring.**

arch brace One of a pair of curved braces at the bottom of a timber roof truss that create an arch shape.

arch brick **1.** A specially shaped brick used as a **voussoir** in a brick arch; can be shaped by rubbing, molding, or cutting. Also known as **com-**

pass brick, featheredge brick, radial brick, radiating brick, radius brick, voussoir brick. **2.** A hard, burned brick from the vault of a brick kiln, used for extra durability.

arch buttant Same as **arc-boutant.**

arch buttress, arch-buttress Same as **flying buttress.**

arch culvert A **culvert** with an arch-shaped top; may also have an arched floor; made of masonry and, beginning in the late 19c, concrete.

arched Having the curved shape of an **arch** or **vault,** such as a doorway or ceiling. See also compound words beginning with **compass.**

arched beam A beam formed with a substantial upward curve; has little or no outward thrust. See also **arch bar, camber beam.**

arched impost An impost block with moldings that continue around the archivolt.

arched truss Same as **bowstring truss.** See also **trussed arch.**

arched tympanum A **tympanum** with a top cornice in the shape of a circle segment.

Archeological and Historic Preservation Act of 1974 Directs preservation of historic and archaeological data that would otherwise be lost as a result of U.S. federal construction or other federally licensed or assisted activities; administered by the secretary of the interior.

archeological district (U.S.) A significant concentration, linkage, or continuity of sites important in history or prehistory.

archeology Same as **archaeology;** the spelling used by U.S. government agencies.

arch face Same as **archivolt** (sense 1).

arching **1.** The system of arch construction in a building. **2.** The process of constructing an arch or series of arches.

architect, (pre-20c) **architectus** One who designs buildings based on principles learned in formal education and communicates the design by means of drawings and specifications; a recognized profession in North America beginning in the late 18c; licensing required by individual states between 1897 (Illinois) and 1951 (Vermont and Wyoming) and in Canada by Provincial Architectural Associations under the Provincial Architects Acts (not directly by government); typically has overall responsibility for ensuring that the project meets legal requirements for health, safety, and the public welfare; formerly, a master **builder** who designed the building and also supervised its construction. Also known as **architector, architectress.** See also **American Institute of Architects, construction documents, contractor, engineer, landscape architect, restoration architect.**

architectonic, (pre-20c) **architectonick** **1.** Pertaining to **architecture** or **construction,** or resembling architecture. **2.** Relating to an **architect,** such as having the function of a designer and director of construction, especially a master builder.

architectonics **1.** The science of **architecture.** **2. Structural** design or design skill.

architector (pre-20c) An **architect** or a superintendent of a construction project.

architectress (pre-20c) A woman **architect.**

architectural Of or relating to **architecture,** including its design, construction, principles, and style.

Architectural Barriers Act of 1968 U.S. federal legislation regarding **accessibility;** superseded by the **Americans with Disabilities Act of 1990.** See also **accessibility.**

architectural classification The **architectural style** or other descriptive term by which a property can be identified on a National Register registration form.

architectural conservation The process of maintaining and/or repairing the materials of a building or structure to reduce or reverse physical deterioration; based on a philosophy of conserving rather than replacing existing architectural elements; sometimes uses scientific diagnostic techniques developed by museum conservators and other researchers; examples include cleaning wallpaper, reattaching loose plaster, repointing masonry joints, and consolidating decayed wood. See also **maintenance, restoration.**

architectural conservator A **conservator** who specializes in **architectural conservation.**

architectural design The process of analysis of a **program** that results in the creation or alteration of a building or similar structure; usually refers to **new construction,** sometimes within existing buildings; may result in the production of **construction documents.** See also **construction observation, engineering, restoration, renovation.**

architectural engineering (20c) The art and science of building construction, as opposed to the art of **architectural design.**

architectural element Any portion of the structure or decoration of a building; restoration and renovation projects may include new partitions, interior finishes, exterior walls, windows, and roofing. See also **structural, mechanical, electrical.**

architectural historian A specialist in the history of the built environment, with particular expertise in architecture.

architectural history The field of study of the history of **architectural style** including the theoretical basis of design and the evolution of design vocabularies and construction techniques.

architectural precast concrete (1920's–present) High quality **precast concrete;** typically composed of portland cement, sand, and colored aggregates, reinforced with steel; the aggregates are exposed on the surface by removing the cement skin by sandblasting or chemicals; used for large wall panels or structural elements. See also **cast stone.**

architectural review board (ARB) An appointed local body that reviews proposed alterations to existing buildings and new construction in a **historic district** or to buildings that are in a **register of historic places** for conformance to established **design guidelines** and/or good design practice. Also known as **board of architectural review (BAR).** See also **preservation commission, zoning.**

architectural significance The importance of a property based on physical aspects of its design, materials, form, style, or workmanship; used for a National Register nomination.

architectural style **1.** The overall appearance of the **architecture** of a **building** or **structure,** including its construction, form, and ornamentation; may be a unique individual expression or part of a broad cultural pattern. **2.** A category of architecture of similar buildings distinguished by common characteristics of structure, arrangement of elements, and ornament; may also be defined partly by the buildings' age, such as **period architecture** or a **revival style;** types include **Adam style, Adirondack Rustic style, Art Deco, Art Moderne, Art Nouveau, Barroco-mudéjar style, Chateauesque, chinoiserie, Churrigueresque, Classical Revival style, classical style, Colonial Revival style, Craftsman style, Eastlake style, Empire style, Exotic Revival style, Federal style, French Eclectic style, Georgian, Georgian Revival, Gothic Revival, Greek Revival style, International Style, Italianate, Jacobean Revival style, Jeffersonian, Mission style, Monterey style, neoantique, neoclassical, Oriental style, Palladian, Prairie Style, Pueblo Revival style, Quebec style, Queen Anne style,**

Regency Revival style, Renaissance Revival style, Richardsonian Romanesque style, Romanesque Revival style, Second Empire style, Shingle Style, Spanish Colonial Revival style, Stick Style, Territorial Style, Tudor Revival style, Vitruvian. See also **aesthetic movement, arch order, Arts and Crafts movement, beaux-arts, Chicago School, colonial architecture, folk architecture, functionalism, high style, modern architecture, period house, postmedieval architecture, pre-Columbian architecture, transitional style.**

architectural terra-cotta Terra-cotta clay that has been formed and fired for use as a nonstructural wall finish or ornamental element, typically with mortared joints and internal voids; often glazed, especially when used on the exterior; can be machine extruded or hand-molded; finishes include **combed, full glaze, mat glazed, oak bark, tooled,** and **smooth;** common on U.S. commercial buildings from 1880–1930. Also known as **hollow pottery.** See also **structural terra cotta.**

architecturalist (pre-20c) A student or connoisseur of architecture.

architecture **1.** The art and science of designing and constructing a **building, fortification,** or similar structure, especially with emphasis on beauty; may relate to **new construction** or an **alteration.** See also **folk architecture, landscape architecture, vernacular building. 2.** The collective buildings produced in a particular period, location, style, or similar grouping, such as colonial architecture, Ontario architecture, Gothic Revival architecture; types include **modern architecture, period architecture;** before the 19c the term usually referred to work of a **classical style.** See also **architectural style, modern architecture, pre-Columbian architecture. 3.** (pre-20c) The process of designing and constructing a building or a structural form.

architectus (pre-20c) Same as **architect.**

architrave, (18c) **archytrive,** (19c) **arcatrive** **1.** In classical architecture, the bottom band of an **entablature,** located immediately above the column capitals. Also known as **epistyle.** See also **jack architrave, classical orders. 2.** A molded trim band surrounding the sides and top of a rectangular wall opening; types include **banded architrave, circular architrave, double architrave, kneed architrave, shouldered architrave, single architrave.** Also known as **architrave door, architrave trim, facing.** See also **architrave-cornice. 3.** (18c) A large wood beam bearing directly on the column capitals. Also known as **master-beam, reason-piece, summer. 4.** The bottom band of an entablature over a door or window. Also known as **hyperthyron. 5.** The molding at the outside edge of the extrados of an **arch.**

architrave door An **architrave** (sense 2) surrounding a door opening.

architrave trim Same as **architrave** (sense 2).

architrave-cornice An entablature without a frieze.

archives, archive A repository for historic documents that can be accessed for research; often the repository of the official papers of a government, such as the National Archives.

archivolt **1.** The surface of an **arch** parallel to the wall and between the intrados and extrados, especially when formed with moldings or other raised decorations similar to an architrave. Also known as **circular architrave,** especially by builders. See also **returned archivolt, ring. 2.** The underside or soffit of an arch.

arch of discharge (19c) Same as **relieving arch.**

arch of the tierce Same as **equilateral arch.**

arch order A Roman architectural style characterized by a series of arched openings with an entablature above the head of the arch and an engaged column that appears to support the entablature between adjacent arches. Also known as **Roman order.** See also **Classical orders.**

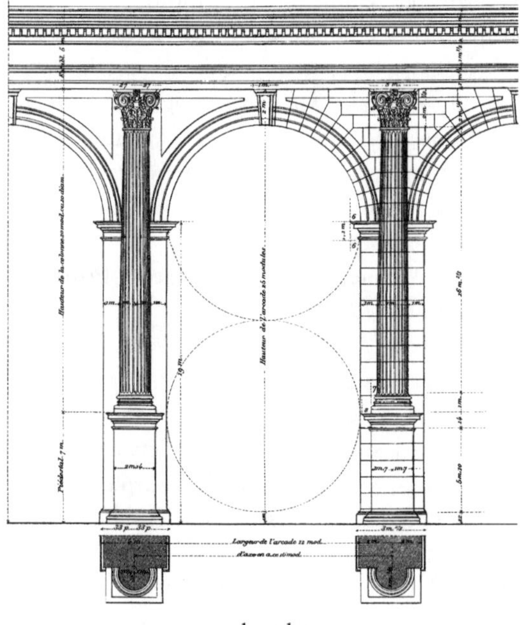

arch order

arch of the third point Same as **equilateral arch.**

arch rib An arched ceiling rib perpendicular to the main axis of a building; common in the Romanesque Revival style.

arch ring The primary curved structural member of an arched structure.

arch solid (19c) A **voussoir.**

arch surround Same as **archivolt** (sense 1).

arch truss Same as **bowstring truss.** Also known as **arched truss.** See also **trussed arch.**

archway **1.** An arched gateway, especially in a freestanding wall. **2.** An arched passageway, as under a barrel vault.

arc lamp An electric lighting fixture with an **arc light.**

arc lamp

arc light An artificial light produced by electrical current jumping across a space between two carbon or metal electrodes; typically the electrodes are surrounded by a glass globe; discovered by Humphrey Davies in 1808; type includes **electric candle.** Also known as **voltaic light.** See also **hanger board.**

arc ogive Same as **diagonal rib.**

arcuate, arcuated A building constructed with arches or archlike curves, as opposed to a **trabeated** building.

arcuated lintel Same as **Syrian arch.**

arcuation **1.** The use of arches. **2.** A series of arches.

arc welding The process of melting and fusing abutting pieces of metal by means of an electric current arcing between an electrode and the metal.

area **1.** Same as **areaway.** **2.** Any interior or exterior horizontal open space. **3.** The amount of surface enclosed within a defined boundary; may be expressed in **square measure** or other units such as an **acre.** **4.** The enclosed space around the outside of a building.

area drain A **drain** located in an **areaway.** See also **air drain** (sense 2).

Area of Potential Effects The geographic area within which a federal undertaking or federally licensed or assisted undertaking may cause changes in the character or use of historic properties; determined jointly by the federal agency with authority over the undertaking, the state historic preservation officer, and the President's Advisory Council on Historic Preservation, as part of the consultation process under **Section 106.** Also known as **APE.**

area of significance According to National Register criteria, the aspect of historic development in which a property made contributions, such as agriculture or politics/government.

area wall (19c) A retaining wall surrounding an **area.**

areaway An open sunken space adjacent to basement windows or doors to provide light and air and/or access to the lower level. See also **air drain** (sense 2), **dry area.**

Argand lamp, Argand burner An **oil lamp** constructed so that air passes both inside and outside of a hollow tubular wick that is fed whale oil from an elevated reservoir; the cylindrical flame is surrounded by a glass chimney; invented by the Frenchman Francois Pierre Auir Argand ca. 1783 and first imported to North America by Thomas Jefferson ca. 1794; common in wealthy homes from late 18c–mid-19c; types include **annular lamp, Bude light.** See also **solar lamp.**

argenite Black silver sulfide; the result of corrosion of silver. See also **acanthite.**

argillaceous slate Same as **argillite.**

argillite, argillyte A dense sedimentary rock composed mainly of clay and aluminum silicate; some varieties split into smooth slates; used for sinks, counters, and roofing slates.

arkose **1.** Same as **Arkosic sandstone.** **2.** A framented rock formed of crystals of disintegrated granite.

arkosic sandstone **1.** A type of **sandstone** containing feldspar. **2.** Same as **brownstone** (sense 1).

armature **1.** An iron bar reinforcing the structure of a building. **2.** A hidden structural support for a sculpture or other decorative element, such as plasterwork.

armored cable Insulated electric wires, with a separate ground wire, spiral-wrapped with galvanized steel; required by codes in place of **BX cable** beginning in the 1950s. See also **electric wiring, flexible metal conduit.**

armory, (pre-20c) **armoury** **1.** A place for storing weapons and ammunition. Also known as an **arsenal.** See also **magazine, powder house.** **2.** A building used by a militia for a training facility and for storage of weapons and equipment. **3.** (U.S.) A manufacturing plant for weapons.

ARPA **Archaeological Resources Protection Act of 1979**

arris, aris **1.** A sharply defined outside corner where straight or curved profiles meet, especially in reference to moldings, the corners of dressed stone blocks, and between column flutings. See also **flat arris, sharp arris.** **2.** A line on a block of stone for leveling it during construction.

arris fillet A wood shim with a triangular cross section used to raise slates or shingles where they abut a wall, such as at a dormer or skylight. See also **flat arris.**

arris gutter A hung, V-shaped wooden roof gutter that has an arris shape when viewed from below.

arris rail A triangular railing typically formed by cutting a square section diagonally; the longest side of the triangle forms the base of the rail.

arris tile A triangular-shaped tile.

arrowhead Same as **dart.**

arsenal Same as **armory** (senses 1 and 3); typically refers to a public facility.

arson The malicious, criminal act of setting a building on fire; the most common types are juvenile arson by teenagers and arson for profit, sometimes used to avoid restrictions on development of historic structures. See also **accidental fire.**

Art Deco A decorative design style intended to renounce all of the various revival styles practiced in the early 20c; characterized by vertical massing and surface ornamentation of angular geometric forms such as zigzags, chevrons, and stylized floral motifs, sometimes combined with polychromy; frequently combined with **Art Moderne** elements; featured at the Paris Exposition Internationale des Arts Decoratifs et Industrieles Modernes in 1925; applied to jewelry, clothing, furniture, and handicrafts; architectural expressions found primarily on skyscrapers and other commercial buildings, especially in New York City (e.g., Rockefeller Center); most North American examples were constructed in the 1920s and '30s. Also known as **Zigzag.** See also **International Style.**

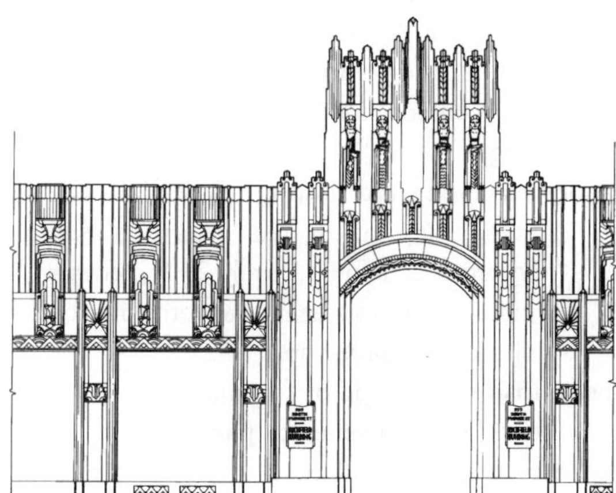

Art Deco
Richfield Oil Building
detail at east entrance
Los Angeles, California

art gallery A **museum** or **gallery** that displays works of art, such as paintings and sculpture; public art galleries were not common in North America before mid-19c.

Art Glass A type of decorative **leaded glass** window in which scenes or patterns are produced by using colored, rather than stained, glass; common in **Art Nouveau** work.

articles of agreement (pre-19c) A construction contract that included a general description of the size, type, and quality of the building; the specifics of materials, workmanship, and design were assumed to be common knowledge unless an ususual feature was requested.

artifact Any individual product of human manufacture, such as cutlery, glassware, pottery, textiles, tools, and weapons. See also **archaeology.**

artificial stone (ca. 1870–WWI) **Concrete** architectural elements, especially when finished to resemble stonework, such as concrete paving scored to look like flagstone or a facade finished with **cast stone.**

artificial wood Any of various mixtures that are molded to simulate wood; often with sawdust, paper, or other wood fiber as a major ingredient mixed with glue. See also **wood fiber ornament, composition.**

art metal Decorative metal elements, such as sheet-metal cornices or pressed tin ceilings.

Art Moderne A design style characterized by horizontal elements, rounded corners, flat roofs, glass block, smooth walls, and asymmetrical massing, all intended to look streamlined; windows often continue around corners without interruption by a column; most North American examples were constructed in the period 1925–WWII; frequently combined with **Art Deco** elements. Also known as **Streamline Moderne, Style Moderne.** See also **International Style.**

Art Nouveau An antihistorical, romantic, and individualistic design style of the late 19c–early 20c characterized by flowing lines and undulating forms drawn from nature; largely a European design movement, North

American architectural examples are rare; the foremost practitioner in the U.S. was Louis Comfort Tiffany (1848–1933), who designed and manufactured colored glass lamps and windows. Also known as **style 1900.** See also **Art Deco.**

Arts and Crafts Movement A late 19c design movement founded in England by William Morris and his associates; focused on handcrafted furniture and other household objects and such decorative furnishings as wallpapers, printed textiles, art tile, and art glass based on stylized natural forms; led to the establishment of C. R. Ashbee's Arts and Crafts Exhibition Society in London in 1888; strongly influenced the **Queen Anne style** and the **Craftsman style.**

art tile A glazed ceramic tile with bas-relief decorative patterns; typically with natural scenes or classical motifs; popular in the late 19c and early 20c, often with **faience** glazing.

asbestic **1.** Containing asbestos fibers. **2.** After 1895, having fireproofing qualities like asbestos.

asbestine Small, fluffy asbestos particles used in paint to help suspend the pigment.

Asbestone Trade name for a mid-20c composition flooring material.

asbestos Fibers of the mineral chrysotile, an excellent heat insulator; the separated fibers were in common use early 19c–late 20c for insulating pipes and boilers and for floor **deafening;** also used since ca. 1900 as reinforcement in concrete to create many fire-resistant materials, including **asbestine, Asbestone, asbestos board, asbestos corrugated roofing, asbestos felt, asbestos paper, asbestos shingle, asbestos slate, sprayed asbestos, asbestos tile;** now recognized as a potential health hazard and classified as a **hazardous material;** regulated in the U.S. by the Environmental Protection Agency under the Asbestos Hazard Emergency Response Act of 1986. Also known as **cork fossil.** See also **asbestic, asbestos abatement, friable asbestos, serpentine.**

asbestos abatement Removal or encapsulation of asbestos-containing material (ACM) that is considered a potential health hazard, especially **friable asbestos,** in a manner that minimizes risk to abatement workers and the public.

Asbestos Air Cell Board (20c) Trade name for a fire-resistant **asbestos board.**

asbestos board A type of **composition board** composed of cement reinforced with asbestos fibers, such as **Asbestos Air Cell Board** or **Transite;** used to protect flammable materials near stoves and for fire stopping; sometimes laminated with other materials. Also known as **cement asbestos board.**

asbestos cement pipe (20c) **Pipe** composed of **Portland cement** reinforced with **asbestos** fibers; typically 3–18 inches in diameter; most often used for **drainpipe** or **vent pipe.**

asbestos cement shingle Same as **asbestos shingle.**

asbestos corrugated roofing A mid-20c roofing system using corrugated sheets of asbestos reinforced cement; typically 27.5 inches wide and fastened to a steel framework with screws, nails, or aluminum wire.

asbestos felt A type of **felt** made with asbestos fibers. See also **asbestos paper.**

asbestos paper A thin, flexible sheet material made from asbestos fibers; used for fire stopping. See also **asbestos felt.**

asbestos rope A woven rope composed of asbestos fibers; used to caulk lead plumbing joints.

asbestos shingle A **shingle** composed of cement reinforced with asbestos fibers; manufactured early–late 20c in various sizes, shapes, and textures; typically of uniform thickness. Also known as **asbestos cement shingle.** See also **asbestos slate.**

asbestos slate An artificial roofing **slate** manufactured during mid-20c with asbestos reinforced cement. See also **asbestos shingle.**

asbestos sprayed fireproofing Same as **sprayed asbestos.**

asbestos tile Any type of flooring tile reinforced with asbestos fibers, such as **vinyl asbestos tile.**

as-built drawings Plans that incorporate the changes made during construction to record accurately the actual construction of the building, as opposed to the initial construction documents. See also **measured drawings.**

as-found drawings Same as **measured drawings.**

ASC Archaeological Survey of Canada

ASCE American Society of Civil Engineers

ash See **black ash, white ash.**

ash house An outbuilding used to store ashes for later use as fertilizer or in making soap; typically of small size.

ashlar, (pre-20c) **ashler, achelor 1.** A wall constructed of quarried stone building blocks that have been squared and finished with a smooth surface; beginning in the 19c the term indicates facing backed by rubble or brick walls; a single stone is referred to as a block of ashlar; types include **bastard ashlar, coursed ashlar, random ashlar, random coursed ashlar, random broken coursed ashlar.** Also known as **broad stone.** See also **blocked, hacking, rough ashlar, rustication. 2.** A stud used in **ashlaring.**

ashlar anchor A **cramp** or similar fastener.

ashlaring, (19c) **ashlering** Wall studs that frame a **knee wall** between sloped roof rafters and the attic floor.

ashlar pavement Paving composed of large, squared stone blocks.

ashpit A void built into the base of a masonry chimney for disposal of ashes from a fire.

ashpit door A cleanout door that accesses an **ashpit,** such as below a fireplace or in a coal furnace. Also known as **chimney-ash door, cleanout door.**

ASLA American Society of Landscape Architects

asphalt 1. A naturally occurring insoluble mineral pitch; used as a weather-resistant binder in building or paving materials. Also known as **asphaltum, pitch mineral. 2.** A distilled substitute for natural asphalt; manufactured from coal tar in the 19c and petroleum in the 20c; product types include **asphaltic concrete, asphalt mastic, asphalt shingles, asphalt tile, asphaltic felt, rolled roofing, roofing felt.** See also **macadam.**

asphalt block A 20c **paver** composed of asphaltic concrete; may be hexagonal or rectangular; sometimes laid on a concrete slab-on-grade.

asphalt felt See **asphaltic felt.**

asphaltic concrete A road-paving material composed of gravel aggregate mixed with an asphalt binder; typically applied hot and then compacted by heavy rollers; used in various paving systems, including **macadam, vulcanite pavement.**

asphaltic felt A flexible, waterproof material composed of asbestos or rag felt saturated with asphalt. See also **roofing felt.**

asphalt mastic A cement composed of a bituminous substance, such as asphalt, mixed with a filler such as sand or asbestos.

asphalt shingle (1903–present) A **shingle** composed of rag felt or, after 1970, fiberglass, saturated with asphalt; typically manufactured in large pieces divided on the bottom edge with slots to resemble the size of wood shingles.

asphalt tile A 20c resilient floor tile composed of asphaltic resins, asbestos fibers, inert fillers, and pigments; typical dimensions were ⅛ × 9 × 9 inches.

asphaltum Naturally occurring asphalt.

assemblage A **parquet floor** pattern with small strips forming two overlapping square grids at a 45-degree angle to one another.

assemblage of orders Same as **superposition.** See also **Classical orders.**

assembly room **1.** (18c–19c) A room or suite of rooms used for social gatherings; typically a ballroom plus smaller ancillary spaces; often part of a tavern or other commercial venture. **2.** (19c–present) A public or institutional space for dancing, lectures, and similar activities; typically without fixed seating. See also **auditorium.**

assessed value The **appraised value** of a particular piece of **real estate** as determined by a local government for the purpose of levying real estate taxes.

assize **1.** One of the individual blocks of stone forming a column. **2.** One course of ashlar.

associated historic contexts The historic contexts included in a **National Register** multiple property listing and common to the sites being nominated; may have been identified in a state comprehensive planning process or have been created for the purpose of documenting the multiple property group. See also **associated property types, nomination.**

associated property types The different types of properties included in a **National Register** multiple property listing; may include buildings, sites, structures, objects, districts, or any combination of these, and be associated by events, processes, institutions, design, construction, settlement, migration, ideals, beliefs, lifeways, and other facets of development or maintenance of cultural systems. See also **associated historic contexts, nomination, Thematic Group Format.**

association **1.** The link of a historic property with a historic event, activity, or person. **2.** The quality of integrity through which a historic property is linked to a particular past time and place.

Association for Preservation Technology International (APT, APTI) An international association that promotes the development and dissemination of technical preservation information; founded in 1968 as the Association for Preservation Technology, a joint Canadian and U.S. organization.

associative value For purposes of the **National Register,** the historic significance of a property owing to its **association** with or linkage to events or persons of local, state, or national importance. See also **nomination.**

ASTM **American Society for Testing and Materials**

astragal, (pre-19c) **astragalus** **1.** A projecting molding with a half round cross section; often carved into a series of slightly rounded parts such as **pearls and olives** or **bead and reel** when used in a **Classical Revival style.** Also known as **bead, fusarole.** **2.** A molding at the top of the shaft of a classical style column, composed of a bead, fillet, and congé. **3.** The molding on one of a pair of double doors that overlaps the joint between the doors when closed; shapes include **T-astragal, flat astragal.** **4.** (pre-20c) A rabbeted sash bar that holds window glass. **5.** (18c) A ring with a round cross section at the bottom of a column. See also **bead, chaplet.**

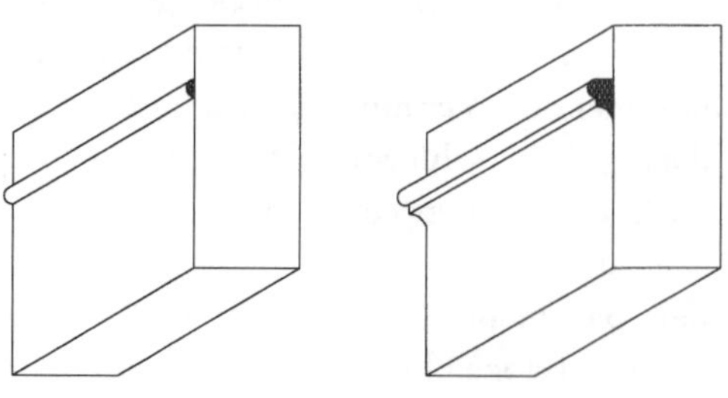

astragal (senses 1 and 2)

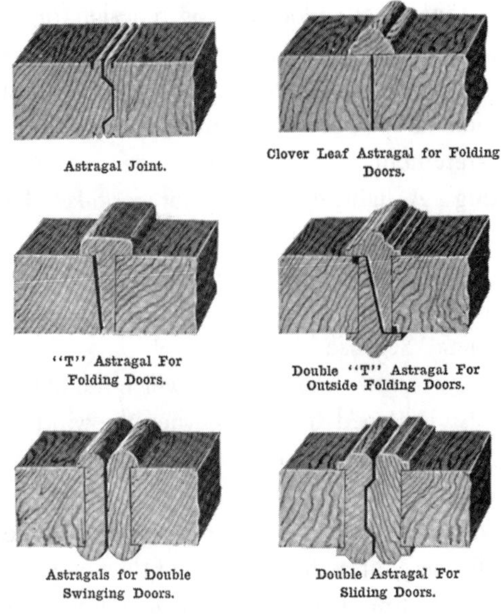

astragal (sense 3)

astragal joint A molding shape that projects on the meeting stile of one of a pair of sliding doors, and recedes on the other door, so that the opening is sealed when the doors are pulled together.

astragal tile (pre-19c) Same as **scallop tile.**

astral lamp A suspended **annular lamp** patented by Bordier-Marcet in 1809; named for the light coming from above like the stars.

astylar Without columns or pilasters, generally used to refer to building facades.

asylum An institution or facility for the care of ill or destitute persons, such as an orphan asylum; beginning in the 19c the term generally was used to describe an instituition for the mentally ill or insane. See also **hospital.**

atacamite Emerald or blackish-green copper chloride; the result of corrosion of copper or bronze.

Athens Charter An international charter expressing 111 principles concerning dwellings, recreation, work, transportation, and historic Buildings; enacted by CIAM (Congrès International d'Architecture Moderne) on a cruise from Athens to Marseilles in 1933; had a strong effect on city planning, especially the encouragement of restrictive use zones rigidly separated by greenbelts, and "high, widely spaced apartment blocks wherever the necessity of housing high densities of population exists"; its antihistorical and antiurban core bias had a negative effect on preservation. See also **Venice Charter.**

atlas (pl. **atlantes**) A column carved in the form of a male figure; often used to refer to the muscular, bearded, half-figures common in the 18c; in Greek mythology the god who supported heaven on his shoulders. Also known as **telamon.** See also **caryatid, herm, term.**

atrium **1.** A central courtyard or skylighted space, especially when surrounded by arcades or balconies; from the Latin for the central courtyard of a Roman house. **2.** (pre-20c) Same as **cemetery** or **churchyard;** from the courtyard in front of early churches.

attached column Same as **engaged column.**

attached house A house that shares one or more common walls with another house; types include **row house, semidetached house.**

attic, (pre-19c) **attick** (from Attica, the region of Greece where Athens is located; not commonly used before the 19c) **1.** In classical style buildings, a low story built behind the parapet above the main wall cornice. **2.** An ornamental wall construction above the entablature that is inscribed or decorated. **3.** The space immediately below a sloped roof, especially when built behind an attic (sense 2) above. See also **cockloft, garret, loft.**

attic base **1.** A circular Ionic column base with an upper and lower **torus** joined by a concave **scotia** molding bordered with a pair of **quadra** fillets. **2.** A pedestal that supports a classical style Greek column. See also **classical orders.**

attic order An **order,** typically with pilasters, used on the front of an **attic** wall; usually subordinate to the main order of the facade. See also **classical orders.**

automatic fire detection system A system of sensing devices that trigger an alarm when smoke or fire is present; the sensing devices may detect heat or smoke particles; the devices may sound a local alarm or be remotely monitored. See also **fire detector, fire suppression system.**

automatic sprinkler See **sprinkler.**

avant-corps The part of a building that projects out from the main structure and appears to be separate.

aventurine Glass or glazing containing reflective particles of metal or metallic oxides.

avenue **1.** A wide, public thoroughfare, especially when lined with trees; sometimes used in the U.S. as a street name without reference to its physical character. **2.** A wide axial approach to a building, lined with rows of trees or statues.

aviary A large enclosure or cage in which live birds are kept.

avoidance The relocation or redesign of proposed development to avoid negative impacts on a historic place; one of the alternative actions reviewed in an **environmental impact statement.**

awning A lightweight, exterior rooflike shade that projects over a window or door; before late 20c, usually made of canvas fabric on a metal framework, also may be wood, plastic or metal. See also **blind.**

awning window A window in which the opening sash is hinged at the top; when the window is open, the bottom of the sash projects out at an angle.

axis of Ionic capital A line that passes perpendicularly through the center of the volute.

azotea In **Spanish Colonial** style architecture, a flat roof or terrace.

azulejo A patterned, glazed, earthenware tile common in Mexico and the southwestern U.S.; the patterned glazing is slightly raised from the background and of bright colors, especially blue.

azurite Blue copper carbonate; the result of corrosion of copper or one of its alloys.

B

back **1.** The process of finishing or trimming the rear or top of a building element (e.g. **backing** the top of a hip rafter; to back off a block of stone). **2.** The top surface of the voussoirs at the extrados of an arch or vault. See also **backing.** **3.** (pre-20c) Same as **principal rafter,** especially as part of a timber frame truss. **4.** The upper face of a slate. See also **bed, head.**

back air Same as **back vent.**

back arch An **arch** that supports an inner wall where the outer wall is supported in a different manner (e.g., a brick back arch behind a horizontal stone lintel). See also **relieving arch.**

backband, back band **1.** One of various molding shapes designed to overlap another element, such as a **back molding.** **2.** The narrow band at the edge of a projecting architrave, jamb casing, or quoin where it returns to the wall. Also known as **back fillet.**

backbar, back bar Same as **randle bar.**

back building (pre-20c) Same as **backhouse.**

back catch A hardware device mounted on an exterior wall to engage a **blind fast** to lock an exterior shutter in the open position. See also **sill catch.**

backer rod A cylindrical, compressible filler inserted in an **expansion joint** as support for the caulking or sealant when it is initially applied.

backfill, back fill **1.** The earth placed in an excavation after the below-grade construction is complete or after an archaeological dig is complete; originally referred to the masonry or earth fill over vaulted construction such as tunnels and sewers. **2.** Rough masonry in between the finished faces of a wall. **3.** Rough brickwork used to fill the spaces between studs in a frame building. See also **nogging.**

back fillet Same as **backband.**

back flap The part of a bifold or multiple-fold shutter or door that folds against the wall or jamb when the shutter or door is open.

back flap hinge (19c) A hinge attached to the **back flap** of an interior folding shutter that folds inside a casing, as beside a window.

back gutter A gutter between a sloping roof and a chimney or other vertical wall. See also **cricket.**

back hearth The floor within the firebox of a fireplace.

backhouse (pre-WWI) An **outbuilding** at the rear of the main building, especially a latrine. Also known as **back building, outhouse.**

backing **1.** The masonry that rests on the extrados of an arch or vault. **2.** The inner portion of a masonry wall. **3.** Beveling at the top of a hip rafter that allows the sheathing to lie flat at the hip. See also **back.**

backing up (19c) A rough masonry retaining wall, or the process of constructing this type of wall.

backing-up brick Same as **salmon brick;** used for the **backing** of a masonry wall.

backing-up coat Any coat of material on the back side of an element (e.g. **backplastering** on the inside of stucco lath).

back-kerf A series of kerf cuts on the back of a wood molding or similar element that enables it to be bent to conform to a curved surface.

backjoint, (pre-20c) **back joint** A hidden rabbet in the face of a masonry wall to allow attachment of other construction, such as a mantelpiece or window frame.

back lining Casing or sheathing at the rear of a recess, such as: (1) the inside portion of a **shutter box** farthest from a window; (2) the part of a window **sash pocket** that abuts the masonry or framing; (3) the sheathing between the sill and floor below a recessed window.

back lintel A lintel supporting the interior wythes of a masonry wall.

back molding, (19c) **back moulding** An L-shaped molding that overlaps the side of casing trim and conceals the joint between the trim and the wall. Also known as **backband.** See also **back fillet.**

back nail, back-nail (18c) A flat shank **nail** designed for nailing without splitting the wood; used for arris gutters or similar plank construction. Also known as **bottom nail.**

backplastering, back plastering **1.** Plaster brown coats applied to lathing between the exterior studs of a wood frame building, leaving a small air space between the backplaster and the sheathing to keep out drafts and provide insulation. **2.** Plaster applied to the inside of lath, opposite the finish side of the wall. See also **backing-up coat.**

back prime To apply primer paint to the unexposed side of woodwork.

back shutter The **back flap** of a bifold shutter.

backstair, back stair A rear secondary stair or any similar stair in a house, typically used by servants.

back vent An air **vent pipe** connected to the sewer side of a plumbing drain to prevent water from being siphoned out of the trap. Also known as **back air, countervent.**

backup The material used to provide structural support to a masonry veneer, such as face brick with concrete block backup.

backyard (19c–present) An open area at the opposite side of a house from the main entrance. See also **yard.**

badigeon A patching compound composed of plaster and powdered stone, especially limestone; used as a **filler** for stone or wood.

bagnio, (pre-19c) **bannio** (pre-20c) **1.** Same as **bathhouse. 2.** Same as **bathroom. 3.** A brothel.

bag trap An S-shaped, lead plumbing **trap** in which the vertical inflow pipe at the top aligns with the outflow pipe at the bottom.

bague The ring of an annulated column.

baguette, baguet, bagnette **1.** A small diameter **bead** molding, especially at an outside corner of a wall. See also **astragal, chaplet. 2.** (18c) A roll molding at the outside corner of a hip roof, or the outside corner itself.

bahut **1.** A solid masonry parapet, especially when undecorated. **2.** A low wall behind a balustrade and gutter that supports the main roof; typically undecorated, as opposed to an **attic;** from the resemblance to a chest of the same name with a setback upper portion. **3.** (pre-20c) A convex top course of a wall or parapet.

baked enamel A hard, glossy metal finish composed of synthetic resins baked in an oven. See also **porcelain enamel.**

bakehouse, (pre-20c) **bake-house, bake house** (late 18c–present) A building containing an oven used for baking; typically refers to a urban, commercial establishment.

Bakelite A trademark for a synthetic resin composed of phenol and formaldehyde; used to form plastic parts and in electric wire insulation during the period ca. 1920–WWII.

balanced step One of a series of winders whose tread width near the inside of the turn approximately equals those treads in the straight run; the width is typically measured 18 inches from the handrail.

balancing Same as **air balancing.**

balcon corrido In Spanish Colonial style architecture, a continuous balcony that connects two or more doorways; typically constructed of wrought iron with scroll-shaped braces that extend above the top of the railing.

balconet A low railing outside a window that gives the appearance of a balcony. See also **vignette.**

balcony **1.** (18c–present) A railed or balustraded platform that projects from a wall; typically in front of a window or door. See also **balcon corrido, balconet.** **2.** A tier of upper-level seating in a theater. See also **parquet.**

baldachin Same as **ciborium.**

bald cypress **1.** A deciduous softwood tree with light brown to reddish-brown, soft, straight-grained wood with a high tannic acid content; grows in wetlands in coastal southeastern and southern U.S., especially Florida and the Mississippi valley; very decay resistant and therefore often used in contact with soil and for exposed elements such as **shingles;** also used for lumber, flooring, and trim; peak lumbering was in the period 1870–1915; *Taxodium distichum* or *Taxodium ascendens.* See also **cypress.**

bale house (pre-20c southern U.S.) Same as **warehouse.**

balk, baulk **1.** A squared timber at least 13 inches wide; may have one side with **wane;** often used as a rafter or pole in barns and other outbuildings. **2.** A **tie beam** in a roof. **3.** (18c) A small, trimmed fir tree.

balk tie A horizontal balk used to connect the exterior wall posts of a timber frame structure.

ball A spherical-shaped ornament, such as at the top of a post, flagpole, lantern, or cupola. See also **globe.**

ballast **1.** Rough masonry filling that adds stability to construction, as in the fill above the haunches of a vault. **2.** Gravel used as the bed of a **railroad track;** usually of a hard crushed stone such as basalt or granite.

ball and flower Same as **ball-flower.**

ball-bearing butt hinge A **butt hinge** with ball bearings between two or more of the knuckles; common on heavy doors by 1900.

ball cock An automatic plumbing water valve that is opened and closed by a lever arm attached to a floating ball; used in water tanks, especially for a **water closet.** See also **waste preventer.**

ball-flower A carved decoration in the form of three stylized petals enveloping a sphere; typically one of a series on a concave molding; used as a decorative element in Gothic style architecture, especially the **Decorated style.** Also known as **ball and flower.**

balloon, (18c) **ballon** **1.** A spherical ornament on top of a pier or pillar. **2.** Same as **ball.**

balloon frame A wood framing system composed entirely of 2× members, with corner posts and studs running continuously from the sill plate at the foundation to the roof plate and intermediate floors supported on ribbands attached to the studs; racking is prevented by diagonal board sheathing or braces; less expensive to construct than a **timber frame,** and often used for one- or two-story, detached, brick veneer buildings because of the small amount of vertical movement of the frame;

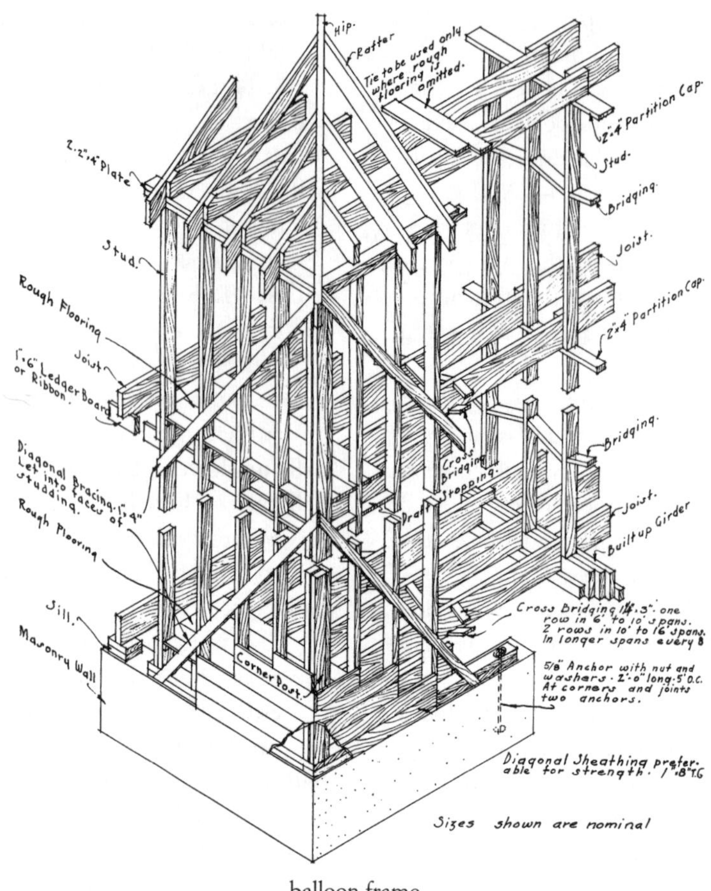

balloon frame

used in Chicago in the 1830s and common in the midwest beginning in the mid-19c; largely replaced by the **platform frame** by mid-20c. See also **braced frame.**

ballroom, (pre-19c) **ball room** A large room used for dancing or other social gatherings. See also **assembly room, reception room.**

ball valve A **ball cock.**

balm-of-Gilead fir Same as **balsam fir.**

balsam fir A softwood tree with yellowish brown, soft, brittle, coarse-grained wood; found in the Appalachian Mountains and New England, and in Canada from Labrador to the Yukon; used for interior trim; *Abies balsamea.* Also known as **balm-of-Gilead fir, fir balsam, pine fir.**

balsam poplar A large hardwood tree with greenish to tan, soft, straight-grained wood; found in northern U.S. and Canada; used primarily for painted millwork; *Populus balsamifera.* Also known as **Ontario poplar, poplar, tacamahac.**

Balsam Wool (20c) A trademarked insulating material composed of sheets of shredded wood fiber.

balteus The vertical bead between the two scrolls at the side of an Ionic capital. See also **bolster.**

Baltimore heater Same as **Latrobe.**

Baltimore truss A **Petit truss** with horizontal top and bottom chords. See **truss** for illustration.

baluster, (18c) **balister, ballester, balluster 1.** One of several small columns or rods that support a railing or balustrade; may be of any size or shape, including a square wrought-iron bar; a thin turned wood spindle; or a neoclassical stone column with base, shaft, and capital; often largest near the base, creating a bottle shape. See also **baluster order, balustrade, double baluster, banister, railing, uncut baluster. 2.** Same as a **bolster.**

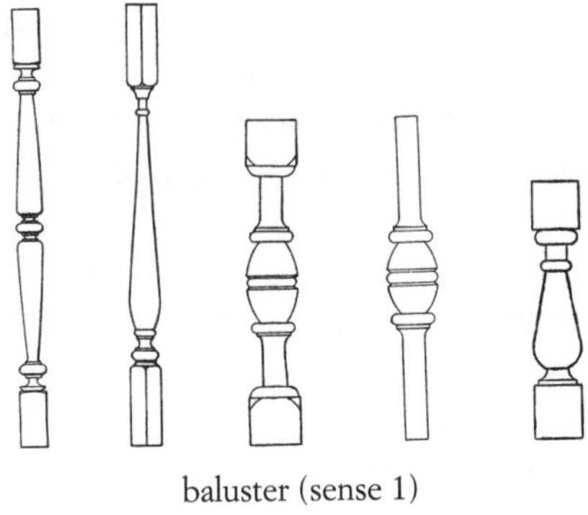

baluster (sense 1)

baluster column A short, thick column.

baluster side The rounded side of an Ionic capital.

balustrade 1. A railing with upper and lower rails, balusters, and pedestals; the rail moldings usually continue across the pedestals; typically refers to massive stone or similar appearing constructions of wood or sheet metal, with the lower rail resting on the same plane as the pedestals. See also **banister. 2.** A parapet with balusters, sometimes alternating between solid and pierced sections.

balustrade order One of the neoclassical orders of balusters and rails. See also **Classical orders.**

Banbury lock (18c) An inexpensive **stock lock** in which the mechanism is attached to a wood casing rather than an iron plate; originally manufactured only in Banbury, England.

band A wide, flat molding; typically refers to horizontal elements with a rectangular cross section. See also **fascia.**

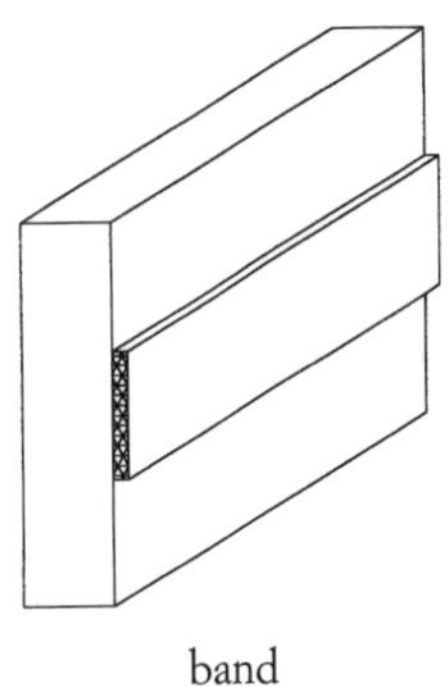

band

band and hook hinge Same as **hook and band hinge.**

band course A masonry **stringcourse** or band.

bandage A metal strap or chain encircling a tower, silo, or dome to resist the outward thrust of the structure.

banded architrave A door or window architrave with smooth rectangular blocks interrupting the moldings; found in neoclassical style architecture. See also **Gibbs surround.**

banded column A column with alternating larger and smaller drums along the shaft.

banded door A wood door with a thin band or strip applied to the outside edge of the face of each stile and the top and bottom rail; typically the band is molded. See also **friction strip.**

banded rustication Alternating courses of smooth ashlar and rusticated stone blocks; used in Renaissance style architecture.

bandelet, bandlet 1. A small, flat molding, larger than a **fillet** and smaller than a **fascia.**

2. A ring with a rectangular cross section encircling a column, an **annulet.**

banderol, banderole A carved ribbon or scroll bearing an inscription.

banister, bannister A slender **baluster** used in a balustrade or in a railing at the edge of a staircase or light well within a building, especially a turned wooden one; the plural form, "the banisters," refers to all of the balusters, rails, and newel posts within a single stairway and is more commonly used than the more formal **balustrade.**

bank **1.** A sloped ground surface; may be natural or earth piled against the side of a structure. See also **embankment.** **2.** A building or office that houses a banking establishment; beginning in the late 18c, typically has a banking hall, counting room, vault, and related offices. Also known as **bank-house, banking house.** **3.** A long **timber** that is 4 to 10 inches square; "usually of unslit fir wood." (*Funk & Wagnalls,* 1899).

bank barn (20c) A barn built into a slope, or with a **bank** of earth against one side, so that the main floor is at grade on one side and one story above grade on the other side; allowed hay or grain wagons to enter the barn for unloading on the upper banked side or to pull alongside at the lower level for loading; most common in the mid-Atlantic states, especially Pennsylvania and Delaware, beginning in the second quarter of the 19c. See also **driveway floor, Pennsylvania barn.**

banquet room A large room used for formal dining and other social gatherings. See also **assembly room, ballroom.**

banquette, banquet **1.** (southern U.S.) A sidewalk. **2.** A raised platform behind a fortification wall for firing weapons. **3.** A raised walkway next to a bridge railing or parapet. **4.** An upholstered, built-in bench, especially a narrow **window seat.**

baptistery A building, or a portion of a church, used exclusively for baptismal services.

bar, (17c) **barr** **1.** An architectural or structural element with a small cross section in relation to its length; types include (a) a horizontal timber connecting two parts of a framework; (b) a **muntin** or **mullion** dividing a window; (c) a piece of lumber used to bolt a door; (d) one of the divisions of a **grate;** (e) a **rail** of a fence that can be moved lengthwise to provide passage; (f) a flat iron strip fastening a door, hatch, or shutter; (g) a solid iron or steel wrought or **rolled section** 6 inches or less in width and 0.203 inch or more in thickness, or 6 to 8 inches in width and 0.230 inch or more in thickness; typically smooth surfaced and square, rectangular or round in section; types include **flat bar, reinforcing bar,** and various special shapes such as half round, hexagon, oval, round edge flat, and round cornered square. See also **bar iron.** **2.** Anything that blocks access, including (a) a railing in a public space, such as a courtroom, that separates the public from those involved in the proceedings; the origin of the phrase "before the bar"; (b) a grille that can be lowered over the serving counter in a tavern. See also **barroom.** **3.** a counter where liquor or other refreshments are served; from the bar of sense 2b. **4.** Same as **barroom.**

BAR **Board of Architectural Review**

barabara An Alaskan sod house with a whale-rib or log frame.

barandal A Spanish Colonial style railing; typically wrought iron; often supported on projecting stonework when part of an 18c balcony; from the Spanish **baranda,** or railing.

barb bolt A metal rod with a head and a barbed end that secures it when driven into a structural element.

bare The portion of a roof or wall slate, shingle, or tile that is exposed to the weather. See also **naked.**

barefoot A balloon frame post or stud that is not secured with a mortise-and-tenon joint at its base.

barff, barffing Same as **Bower-Barff.**

bargeboard, (pre-19c) **vargeboard, vergeboard** One of a pair of sloped boards at the edge of a projecting eave at a gable end; replaces or covers one of the rafters of a **barge couple;** often decoratively carved or scrolled, especially in **Gothic Revival style** houses. Also known as **gableboard.** See also **barge couple.**

bargeboard

barge couple, bargecouple One of a pair of rafters that supports the outer edge of a projecting eave at a gable end; often covered with a **bargeboard.**

barge cornice (18c) A **raked cornice** at the top of a gable end.

barge course, bargecourse **1.** Tiles or slates along the outer edge of a gable end, often projecting slightly over the bargeboards. See also **barge stone.** **2.** The portion of a gable roof that projects past the gable end. **3.** A projecting brick wall coping formed with rowlocks on a **gable end** (sense 1).

barge rafter, bargerafter **1.** Same as **barge couple.** **2.** (19c) A rafter in a barge course.

barge spike A large nail with a square cross section; used for timber framing.

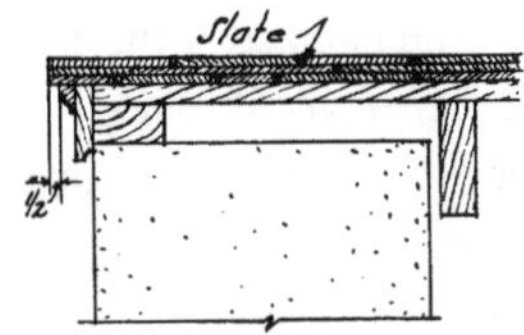

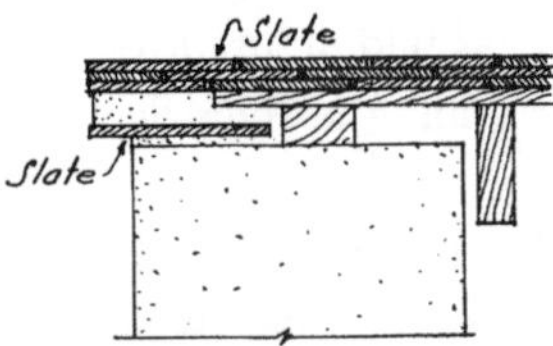

bargecourse (sense 1)

barge stone, bargestone One of the sloping coping stones of a masonry gable end wall. See also **barge course.**

bar iron **1.** (19c) A malleable type of iron with less carbon than **cast iron** and more carbon than **steel;** used for bars, angles, and similar shapes. **2.** Wrought iron fabricated into a **bar** (sense 1g).

barite A crystalline mineral composed of barium sulfate; used to make **barium white.** Also known as **barytes, heavy spar.**

barium sulfate, barium sulphate See **barium white.**

barium white An inert, nearly colorless, white **pigment** composed of barium sulfate ($BaSO_4$); used as a paint extender and pigment since ca. 1820. Also known as **blanc fixe.** See also **barite, lithopone.**

barium yellow An intense lemon yellow paint **pigment** composed of barium chromate.

bar joist An **open web joist** with diagonal struts made of round or square steel bars and top and bottom chords made of pairs of steel angles.

bark, (17c) **barke** **1.** The outer layer of a tree trunk or branch; used for roofing and siding on some colonial and frontier dwellings and as an interior finish material; type includes **cork.** **2.** The surface texture on the exposed face of a **brick** in the stylized form of rough, parallel tree bark. See also **oak bark.**

barked Wood that has been stripped of bark. See also **sapped.**

bark edge Same as **wane.**

bark house **1.** A house or hut covered with **bark.** **2.** A building used to store or process bark for tanning leather. See also **bark mill, tannery.**

bark mill The machinery used to grind bark for tanning or dyeing and its shelter; typically a separate structure from a **bark house.**

bark pit A **tan vat** used to soak leather in a tanning infusion made from bark.

barley twist Small parallel **bead** moldings that spiral around a turned element.

bar lift A horizontal metal bar attached to the inside of a heavy window sash to assist in raising the sash.

barn **1.** A farm building used for storing crops such as hay and grains; may also be used to house farm animals and store equipment or as a threshing area; types include **bank barn, Pennsylvania barn, tobacco barn.** Also known in southern U.S. as **house,** for example, **cotton house.** **2.** (U.S.) Same as **stable.**

barn framing **Timber framed** construction without wall studs between the posts. See also **pegged braced frame.**

barn raising The **raising** (sense 2) of a barn or similar structure.

barnyard A fenced open area for animals adjacent to a barn. See also **yard.**

baroque **1.** Ornately decorated, especially in the European Baroque style of mid-16c–mid-18c characterized by elaborate symmetrical ornamentation with scrolls, curves, and distorted classical forms, such as a **solomonic column;** from the French for the Italian term **barocco;** named for the founder of the style Frederigo **Barocci** (1528–1612). See also **Barroco-mudéjar style, rocaille.** **2.** Fantastic or irregularly shaped.

barracks, barrack **1.** A plain building for housing workmen or soldiers. See also **fortification.** **2.** (pre-20c) A number of temporary shelters within an enclosure; in the 18c sometimes referred to temporary pole structures used by an army. **3.** A hip roof covering for a haystack made of thatch or other rough material and supported on four poles; the barracks is lowered as the hay is consumed by adjusting pins in the poles supporting the frame.

barracoa A type of raised grain house used by Native Americans living along the northwestern coast of the U.S. and Canada.

barrel bolt A cylindrical metal rod and casing that locks a door or window by sliding into a hole in the jamb. See also **bolt drop.**

barrel drain A masonry **drain** with a circular cross section.

barrel roof A roof formed by a **barrel vault,** or with a cross section in the shape of a semicircle. Also known as **wagon roof.**

barrel vault, barrel roof An arched space in the form of a half cylinder or a similar space with various cross sections, such as a **semicircular vault,** a semiellipse, or a **pointed arch.** Also known as **cradle vault, fornix, tunnel vault, wagon vault.** See also **arch, cul de four, simple vault.**

Barroco-mudéjar style An architectural style of the Mexican colonial period that employs Italian Baroque features and Moorish decorative motifs; typically includes thick stuccoed adobe or stone walls, scrolled parapet copings, elaborately carved stone window and door surrounds, and **conchas.** Also known as **Mexican Baroque.** See also **baroque, Mudéjar-Gothic, Spanish Colonial.**

barroom, bar room, (18c) **barr room** **1.** (18c) A small area in a tavern where liquor was stored;

typically enclosed with a counter and a **bar** (sense 2b) that could be lowered when the server was absent. **2.** (19c–present) A room with a **bar** (sense 3), especially where liquor is served.

bar size angle A small **angle iron.**

bar tracery Gothic Revival style window tracery with slender, vertical, molded stone mullions that divide at their heads to form **tracery.** See also **interlaced tracery, net tracery.**

barytes Same as **barite.**

basalt A dense, dark gray to black volcanic rock formed of augite, plagioclase, and, usually, magnetite; often full of small cavities that may contain olivine and other minerals; used as a building stone.

bascule bridge A **drawbridge** with one or two balanced leaves that pivot vertically on a **trunnion** located at one end of the span. See also **counterweight.**

base **1.** The lowest of the three principal parts of a column. See also **attic base, order, subbase.** **2.** The lowest part of a wall or pier, especially when ornamented with projecting moldings. **3.** Same as **baseboard,** or a similar element. **4.** The bottom of a sculpture. See also **self-base.** **5.** The liquid that carries the **pigment** in paint, such as **oil-base paint.** See also **vehicle.** **6.** The elements that support a plaster finish. See also **furring, grounds, lathing.**

baseboard, (19c) **base board** (19c–present) A projecting band around the bottom of an interior wall; typically wood but may also be of stone, tile, or other material; may be a single piece, such as a **sanitary base,** or have a **base cap** and **shoe mold.** Also known as **base, mopboard, scrub board, skirting board, washboard.** See also **base molding, subbase, surbase.**

base block A solid, rectangular piece of material forming the bottom member of a door or window surround, such as the casing of a door jamb; stock wood base blocks are plain surfaced or milled with horizontal moldings; types include **plinth block.**

base cabinet A **kitchen cabinet** that rests on the floor and supports the counter. See also **wall cabinet.**

base cap Molding that rests on or overlaps the top of a **baseboard.**

base coat **1.** The first coat of a **plaster** finish, typically composed of lime, cement, and sand; before late 19c plaster often had hair or other binder in the mix. **2.** The first layer of any coating applied in a liquid or plastic state, such as paint.

base course The lowest course of a masonry wall or pier; may also be part of the footing.

base-court **1.** (19c) The inferior, outer court of a mansion. **2.** (19c) The rear yard of a farmhouse formed by the connecting outbuildings and used for domestic animals.

base isolation A late 20c system of making a building earthquake resistant by supporting all of the load-bearing elements on structural shock absorbers known as isolators; **seismic retrofit** of an existing building involves cutting a trench around the perimeter down to the lowest level and underpinning the foundation and columns with isolators; typically the isolators are composed of 12–24 inch square sandwiches of rubber and steel plates; most often used on simple, rectilinear, freestanding buildings.

base map A graphic representation of a defined area, such as a particular site or a neighborhood, town, region, or state or province, showing legal boundaries and physical features; additional data is displayed on the map as more information is gathered about the site or area. See also **land status map, survey, topographic map, USGS map.**

basement **1.** A story or stories of a building below the main level, at or partly below grade; typically used to refer to habitable space; before mid-19c a below-grade area was commonly known as a **cellar.** See also **basement house.** **2.** (19c) The lowest portion of the facade when differentiated from upper stories; may be more than one story high. **3.** Same as **base** (sense 1).

basement house (19c) A town house in which the main entrance is below the main floor level; variations include **American basement, English basement, French basement.**

base molding The molding immediately above a **baseboard** or column **plinth.** See also **base cap.**

base shoe Same as **shoe mold.**

basilica A church in the form of a rectangular hall divided into nave and side aisles by rows of columns and with an apse at the east end; from the Roman hall of justice adopted for worship by early Christians; originally a portico on the Athens agora where the archon-bacileus dispensed justice; the term was not commonly used to refer to North American buildings until early 19c.

basin, (pre-19c) **bason** **1.** (19c–present) A ceramic bowl with a drain set below a marble slab or other counter; typically located in a bathroom. Also known as **washbasin.** **2.** Any of various artificially constructed bays of navigable water, including: (a) the area between two canal locks; (b) a widened area of a canal or waterway for turning or passing boats; (c) a widened area of a river for anchoring boats at a wharf or pier. **3.** A **reservoir** where water is retained at high tide. **4.** (pre-19c) A decorative pond in a pleasure garden. **5.** A bowl used to hold baptismal water; typically wider than it is deep.

basket-handle arch An **arch** that approximates a semiellipse; may be a **three-centered arch** with two small-radius end segments with their centers on the spring line, and a large-radius center segment with its center below the spring line, or a similar **five-centered arch** composed of five circle segments.

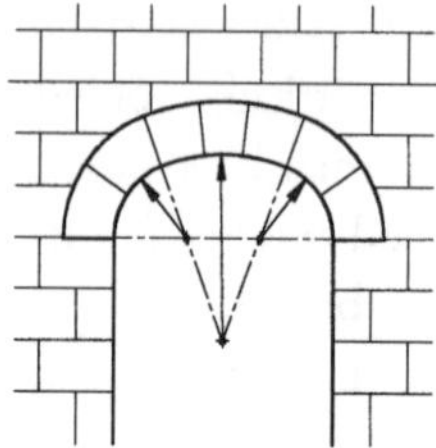
basket-handle arch (3-center)

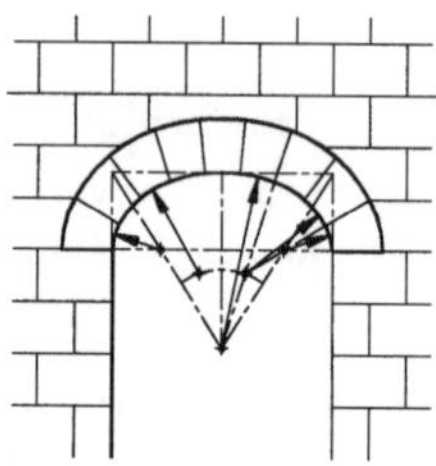
basket-handle arch (5-center)

basket weave bond A brick checkerboard pattern composed of squares of vertical bricks alternating with squares of horizontal bricks; typically has three **stretchers** alternating with three **soldiers** for walls, and two **sailors** alternating with two **shiners** for floors.

bason (pre-19c) Same as **basin.**

bas-relief, (19c) **bas relief,** (18c) **bass relief** A low **relief** carving in which no portion of the form is undercut; types include **stiacciato.** Also known as **basse-taille, basso-relievo.**

basse-taille (17c) Same as **bas-relief.**

basso-relievo Same as **bas-relief.**

bastard False, or not of the highest quality.

bastard ashlar A thin stone veneer cut to resemble solid blocks of stone; typically the bedding of the stone is vertical. See also **ashlar.**

bastard cedar Same as **redwood.**

bastard cut Same as **plain sawn.**

bastard grain The wood grain running from the center of the tree to the circumference. See also **silver grain.**

bastard granite A stone, such as gneiss, that is not a true granite.

bastard sawn Same as **plain sawn.**

bastard spruce Same as **Douglas fir.**

bastard stucco A coarse **stucco.**

bastard tuck pointing Same as **beaded joint.**

bastion A projecting portion of a **fortification** designed to defend the adjacent curtain wall with flanking fire; typically approximates a semihexagon, with two outer faces meeting at an acute angle and two flanks abutting a curtain wall on each side.

baston Any large molding with a rounded convex shape.

bat **1.** A broken or cut brick that has one complete end remaining and is less than half a full brick in length. Also known as **brickbat.** **2.** One of a series of shallow parallel grooves cut into the face of stone blocks; depth varies with the number of bats per inch and ranges 1/32–1/16 inch deep. See also **machine tooled, stonework.**

bath **1.** A plumbing fixture used to immerse or spray the body with water; variations include **bathtub, douche bath, needle bath, rain bath, Scotch bath, shower bath, sitz bath.** See also **swimming bath.** **2.** Same as **bathroom.** **3.** Same as **bathhouse** (sense 1).

bath-cock A combined hot and cold water faucet with two handles and a single outlet; may be mounted on the inside face of a cast iron bathtub, or on the outside with the handles and outlet pipe on the inside.

bathhouse, bath-house **1.** A building with bathing facilities; may be an outbuilding of a house or a commercial establishment with var-

bath-cock

ious kinds of baths, saunas, and steam rooms. Also known as **bagnio, bathing house.** **2.** (19c–present) A building adjoining a beach or swimming pool used for changing clothes; may include toilet facilities and/or showers.

bathing house (late 18c–early 19c) Same as **bathhouse.**

bathing room (pre-20c) A room with unplumbed bathing facilities, such as a washstand and freestanding tub. See also **bathroom.**

bathroom, (19c) **bath-room** (late 19c–present) A room with bathing facilities; typically contains a plumbed **bathtub, water closet,** and **lavatory.** See also **bathing room, half bath, lavatory, shower bath, toilet room.**

bathtub

bathtub, (19c) **bath tub, bathing tub** A large open vessel that holds water for bathing by immersion; typically of rectangular plan with rounded ends and, beginning in the 19c, fitted with overflow and drain pipes and water faucets; 19c tubs were manufactured of wood lined with zinc or copper, or of cast or sheet iron coated with paint, galvanizing, or porcelain enamel, or of stoneware or porcelain and glass; nearly all 20c pre–WWII bathtubs are cast iron coated with porcelain enamel. Also known as **tub.** See also **bath, shower.**

bath stove A cast iron **grate** with a solid decorative front and projecting flat hobs at the top.

bâtons rompus Parallel zigzag moldings; typically with a round cross section; common in **Romanesque Revival style** architecture. Also known as **zigzag moulding.**

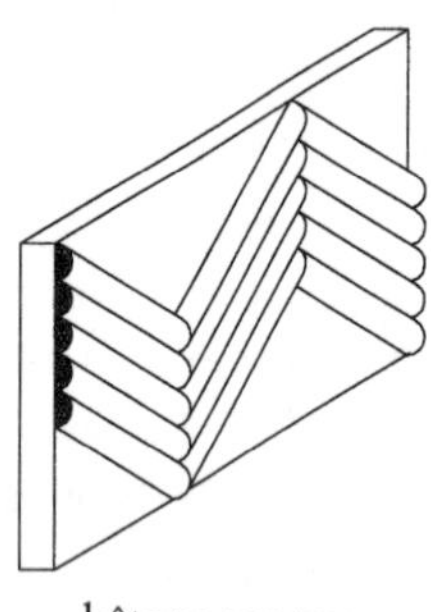

bâtons rompus

batswing burner A **gaslight burner** with a slotted domed tip; creates an efficient, flat flame approximately in the shape of an inverted flying bat; invented in England ca. 1816; often fitted with noncorroding tips in the 1850s. Also known as **batwing jet.**

batted work Same as **broad tooled.** See also **bat** (sense 2).

batten, (18c) **battain, batton** **1.** A **board** less than 4 inches wide. See also **slating batten.** **2.** A narrow board applied on a surface, especially when used to cover a joint between siding boards or to give the appearance of paneling. See also **batten door, board-and-batten, ledger.** **3.** A rib with a rectangular cross section between flat panels of a sheet-metal roof.

batten brad (18c) A finish nail used for softwood wainscoting.

batten door **1.** A door formed of full height boards glued edge to edge with horizontal and vertical battens applied to give the appearance of paneling; a single batten door has battens on one side, and a double batten door has them on both sides. **2.** A rough door formed of full height boards attached edge to edge by horizontal boards nailed to the verticals; typically used on barns and other outbuildings. See also **door band, doornail.** **3.** A door constructed of vertical tongue-and-groove boards lapped by board stiles and rails; typically used on stables, garages and similar buildings.

batten plate **1.** A short plate used to connect members of a structural frame, especially in steel construction. **2.** Same as **fish.**

batten roof A **sheet-metal roof** in which the vertical panels are divided by metal-covered wood battens.

batter The slight slope of a wall face inward toward the top; the slope may be a straight line or a concave curve.

batter

batter brace The inclined brace at the end of a truss, such as a **Pratt truss.**

battery A level platform supporting artillery and protected with an earthen berm or a parapet; not completely enclosed at the perimeter. See also **casemate, fortification.**

battery box A wooden box filled with sand; used to build a **battery** parapet.

batt insulation Loosely matted, fibrous **insulation** more than one inch thick; types of fibers include **fiberglass, wood.** See also **flexible insulation, felt insulation.**

battlement, (pre-20c) **battelment** **1.** A **fortification** wall with alternating higher and lower sections to provide protection for the defenders; components include **alure, crenel, merlon, parapet of the crenel.** **2.** A decorative parapet or crest with merlons and crenels located at the top of a wall or roof ridge.

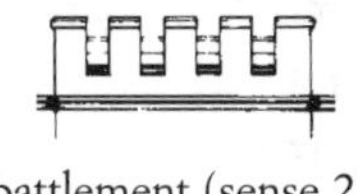

battlement (sense 2)

battleship linoleum An extra-thick type of linoleum.

batwing jet Same as **batswing burner.**

bay **1.** Each individual space defined by a structural grid; includes, for example, the spaces between the bents of a timber frame barn, the rectangular space enclosed by four columns of a steel skeleton frame, and the spaces between piers of a bridge. See also **vault bay.** **2.** A repetitive vertical subdivision of an exterior facade; may be defined by various means, including pilasters and wall openings. **3.** A door or window opening in a facade, especially when defined by repetitive columns or arches.

bayberry wax, bayberry tallow A slow-burning candle wax made from bayberries of the wax myrtle shrub *Myrica cerifira,* which is found in coastal regions of New England and eastern Canada.

bay leaf garland Molding in the form of bay leaves wrapped with ribbons; often used on a torus which is part of a column base.

bay stall A **window seat** constructed in a bay window.

bay window A projection from the main wall of a building with windows on all sides and its own foundation and roof; relatively small compared with the main portion of the building; a common feature of various **architectural styles,** including **Gothic Revival** and **Queen Anne style.** See also **bow window, oriel.**

bayonet base An **incandescent lamp** with two projecting prongs on its base that are inserted in an electrical socket.

BC, B.C. Abbr. for **bottom chord.**

beacon house (pre-19c) Same as **lighthouse.**

beacon tower A tower or other structure with a signaling device that guides boats or airplanes to a channel or runway or away from obstructions.

bead **1.** A small, linear molding with a round cross section that ranges from **quarter round** to **three-quarter round;** may be continuous or a series of beadlike bumps; typically at or below the adjoining surface and ⅛ to nearly ¾ inch in width; types include **angle bead, bead and reel, boultin, center bead, cock bead, double bead, flush bead, nosing bead, parting bead, pearls and olives, quirk bead, rabbet bead, return bead.** Also known as **astragal,** especially when projecting above the adjoining surface. See also **bead and butt, bead and cove, beaded board, casing bead, reed.** **2.** A continuous ridge of material deposited to form a metal joint by soldering, brazing, or welding. **3.** One of a series of carved, domed decorations on a molding, such as on a **bead and reel** molding. Also known as **olive, pearl. 4.** A raised ridge on sheet metal.

bead and butt Wood paneling in which the exposed face of the panels is flush with the face of the stiles and rails, and the long edges of the panels, in the direction of the grain, have a flush bead that abuts the stiles. Also known as **bead butt.** See also **bead butt and square, bead and flush.**

bead and cove A **solid sticking** mold in which the shapes are arranged as follows: fillet, quarter round bead, fillet, quarter round cove, and fillet; the cove is at the outer edge of the mold. See also **cove and bead.**

bead and flush Wood paneling with **bead and butt** on all edges of the panels and with the surface of the panels flush with that of the stiles and rails.

bead and quirk Same as **quirk bead.**

bead and reel An astragal molding that alternates a circular **bead** or **olive** with a **reel** or pair of reels. Also known as **reel and bead.**

bead butt, bead butt work Same as **bead and butt.**

bead butt and square Wood paneling with **bead and butt** on one face and square reveals on the other face; used on doors.

bead chamfer A beveled corner with a raised bead along the center.

beaded board A tongue-and-groove board decorated with bead patterns at one edge and the middle; often used in the 19c for wainscoting and porch ceilings.

beaded joint **1.** A recessed **mortar joint** in the form of a quirked bead. **2.** A single-color mortar joint with a raised bead in the center that projects past the surface of the brick or stone. See also **tuck pointing.**

bead flush work Same as **bead and flush.**

beading **Bead**-like ornamentation.

bead molding, bead mold **1.** Same as **bead** (sense 1). **2.** Same as **paternoster.**

beak **1.** A projecting molding that forms a drip at the bottom of a cornice or soffit, especially when convex on top and concave below. **2.** Any beaklike ornamental projection.

beaking joint (pre-20c) A row of several aligned head joints, especially the ends of floor boards or planks. See also **joint.**

beam, (pre-18c) **beame** **1.** A principal structural member that spans horizontally between supports and carries a vertical load; types by form include **American Standard beam, angle iron, arched beam, balk, box beam, bulb beam, built beam, channel beam, flitch beam, Hodgkinson beam, open web joist,** and steel sections noted by their resemblance to various letters, such as **H-beam, I-beam, L-iron;** types by use include **architrave, binding beam, collar beam, cross beam, girder, hammer beam, sister, straining beam, strut beam, summer, tie beam.** See also **girder, rolled beam, truss. 2.** Any building element that carries a vertical load over a span, such as **joist, lintel, purlin, rafter, solive, stringer;** these subsidiary or repetitive elements are more often referred to only by their specific names. See also **bearing, bridging, hanger, trabeated.**

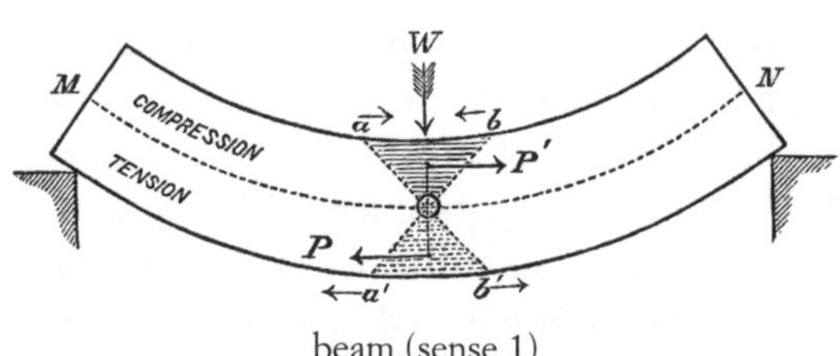

beam (sense 1)

beam anchor A metal strap that attaches a beam end to a masonry wall; types include **side joist anchor, spur anchor.** See also **beam hanger.**

beam box A cast-iron box that is set into a masonry wall to support a heavy timber beam;

beam truss bridge
Plainfield, New Jersey

used in **slow burning mill construction.** Also known as **girder box, wall box.** See also **beam hanger.**

beam box girder (late 19c–present) A **box girder** composed of a pair of parallel I-beams with continuous steel plates across their top and bottom flanges; used for supporting interior masonry walls in the late 19c.

beam ceiling A wood ceiling having the appearance of exposed beams projecting below the floor above.

beam clip A sheet-metal fabrication that attaches the bottom of a steel joist to the top flange of a structural steel girder.

beam filling Masonry in the space between adjoining joists or rafter ends above a masonry wall. Also known as **wind filling.**

beam hanger A projecting metal device that supports the sides and bottom of the end of a wood beam; may be a bent rectangular bar, formed sheet metal, or cast iron; types include **joist hanger, stirrup, strap hanger, wall hanger.** See also **beam anchor, beam box.**

beam house At a **tannery,** a building where hides are scraped; named for the board on which the hide is placed to be curried.

beam iron Same as **beam anchor.**

beam shoe Same as a column **bolster.**

beam truss bridge A **truss bridge** supported by a **truss** that acts as a beam spanning between supports.

bear a body (18c) The ability of a paint pigment to be ground to an oily smoothness so that it mixes easily with the oil base.

beard **1.** A sharp edge of a board. **2.** A spring on the back of a lock that prevents it from rattling.

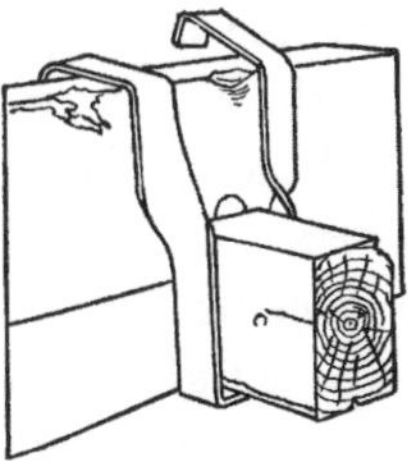

beam hanger

bearer, (pre-20c) **bareer** **1.** One of several small supports, such as framing carrying a stair winder or projecting beams supporting a gutter. **2.** (18c) A post or projecting brick wall that helps support the end of a beam. **3.** A piece of wood blocking installed crosswise between joists to provide structural support for another member. See also **cross bearing.** **4.** A **girt** let into a two story tall **timber frame** stud; may support the ends of the second-floor joists. See also **ribband.**

bearing **1.** The area that supports the weight at the end of a structural member, such as a beam or column. **2.** (19c) Incorrectly, the span of a beam between the end bearings.

bearing cleat A ledger that supports the bottom of **cross bearing** installed between floor joists below a partition.

bearing partition An interior **bearing wall** (sense 1).

bearing plate **1.** A metal plate at the end of a beam or bottom of a column to distribute the weight over a larger surface. **2.** A metal plate attached to the web of a structural member to provide a thicker web at a pinned connection.

bearing wall **1.** A wall with relatively small openings that transfers loads from above down to the foundation along its entire length. **2.** (19c) A wall that supports a beam.

beaufait Same as **buffet.**

beaufet Same as **buffet.**

beaux-arts An inexact adjective indicating architectural work of various classical styles designed according to the principles of the **École des Beaux-Arts,** especially by architects who studied at the school in Paris; style common for large public buildings and dwellings of the wealthy in the late 19c and early 20c; characterized by symmetrical plans and facades, often with exuberant exterior detail including monumental stairs, rusticated bases, balustrades, paired columns on plinths, carved floral swags, and quoins. See also **Second Empire, vista.**

bed **1.** A horizontal layer of mortar, cement, or soil in which a masonry unit or ceramic tile is placed. **2.** The face of a masonry unit, such as a brick or stone block, which is in contact with the horizontal joint; the top of the unit is known as the "upper bed" and the bottom as the "lower bed." **3.** The under surface of a roof shingle, tile, or slate, as opposed to the **back.** **4.** The face of a block of stone that is parallel to its primary cleavage plane, also known as the **bedding plane, natural bed, quarry bed.** **5.** (mid-18c–present) A plot of ground prepared for planting, especially in a garden; may be level with the adjoining surface or raised above grade; often combined with the the name of the plants grown within, such as **radish bed** or **flower bed.** Also known as **square.**

bedchamber, bed-chamber (late 17c–19c) Same as **bedroom;** through the early 19c, often a principal ground-floor room used for socializing as well as sleeping. See also **chamber.**

bedded Placed in a **bed** (sense 4); a block of stone is bedded vertically when the natural bedding plane is installed vertical.

bedding molding (pre-20c) Same as **bed molding.**

bedding plane See **bed** (sense 4).

Bedford limestone A buff, gray, or variegated calcite-cemented calcareous Mississippian **limestone** formed of shells and shell fragments, practically noncrystalline in character; quarried almost entirely in Lawrence, Monroe, and Owen counties in Indiana. Also known as **Bedford stone, Indiana limestone.**

Bedford stone Same as **Bedford limestone.**

bed joint The horizontal joint between courses of masonry.

bed molding **1.** A molding or group of moldings that support the corona of a classical style entablature; often composed of a bottom ogee, a band, a quarter round, and a top band. **2.** A similar molding used as the bottom of a cornice or as a rake molding.

bedplate, bed plate A piece of 2× framing lumber resting directly on top of a foundation wall to support and attach the wood frame wall above. See also **sill, sole.**

bedroom (ca. 1725–present) A **room** used for sleeping. See also **bedchamber, dormitory, sleeping porch.**

bed sill (pre-19c) Same as **mudsill.**

bed site (19c) A recess for a bed.

bed timber Same as **bolster beam.**

beech See **American beech.**

beehive oven A type of **blast furnace** shaped like a conical beehive.

bee house (18c) Same as **house apiary.**

bee shed (18c) Same as **house apiary.**

belection moulding (19c) Same as **bolection molding.**

belfry **1.** A bell tower; may be detached or be part of a larger building. **2.** The room in a bell tower where bells are hung. **3.** The room where bell ringers stand; beginning in early 18c, includes an open paved area under a bell tower. Also known as **belfry chamber, bell chamber.** **4.** Same as **bell cage.**

belfry chamber Same as **belfry** (sense 3).

belfry tower Same as **bell tower.**

Belgian block A paving stone roughly cut to the shape of a truncated pyramid with a 5–6 inch square base and 7–8 inch height; the top is not more than 1 inch smaller than the base dimension; typically a hard stone, such as granite.

Belgian pavement Paving composed of Belgian blocks.

Belgian truss Same as a **cambered Fink truss.**

Belgic tile (pre-20c) Same as **pantile.**

bell **1.** The shape of a Composite or Corinthian style capital without ornamentation; has a double curved profile that curves outward at the top. Also known as **campana, tambour, vase.** **2.** The echinus of a Corinthian capital. **3.** The enlarged end of a pipe that receives the end of an adjoining pipe. See also **bell and spigot joint.**

bell (sense 1)

bell and spigot joint A plumbing joint in which the narrow end of one pipe is inserted in the **bell** end of another pipe; typically sealed with **oakum** covered with molten **lead** until late 20c, when compression joints using neoprene or rubber gaskets were introduced. Also known as **spigot and faucet joint, spigot joint.**

bell-and-spigot pipe Same as **bell pipe.**

bell cage The structure that supports the bells in a **bell tower;** designed to absorb the shock of the bell ringing. Also known as **belfry.**

bell carriage **1.** Same as **bell cage.** **2.** The stock piece that directly supports a large bell. Also known as **bell hanging.**

bell cast roof A form of **mansard roof** in which the lower roof slopes downward in a straight line and then curves outward at the eave.

bell chamber (19c) Same as **belfry** (sense 3).

bell cot, bell cote A small structure projecting out from a wall or up from a roof to shelter one or more bells; often in the form of a turret with spire (e.g., Old Dutch Church, Sleepy Hollow, New York). See also **bell gable.**

bell crank An L-shaped or triangular lever used to change the direction of a bell wire 90 degrees at a corner of a room. See also **bell hanging.**

bell deck The level of the bell tower from which the bells are hung.

bell gable A gable end parapet with an opening that supports a bell. See also **bell cot.**

bellflower A stylized representation of one of the bell-shaped flowers of the genus *Campanula;* typically one of a series of flowers joined in a straight garland; commonly used in the late 18c and early 19c as bas-relief decoration on mantelpieces.

bell hanging **1.** (19c) The process or trade of installing a signaling system of wires and bells. **2.** A **bell carriage** (sense 2).

bell of the cap Same as **bell.**

bell pipe A pipe that has an expanded connecting hub at one end that receives the smaller end of an adjoining pipe; typically of large diameter and made of terra-cotta or cast iron. Also known as **bell-and-spigot pipe.** See also **socket sewer pipe.**

bell pull A knob or handle used to ring a mechanical annunciator system with bells. See also **bell hanging.**

bell roof A roof with a cross section in the approximate shape of a bell, especially when the roof has a circular or regular polygonal plan. See also **ogee roof.**

bell telegraph (19c) Same as **annunciator** (sense 1).

bell tower A tower that encloses the **bell carriage** of large bells, with wall openings to let out the sound; typically attached to a church. Also known as **belfry tower, campanile.**

bell trap (19c) A plumbing drain trap in the shape of an inverted bell pierced with a center pipe that is covered with a metal dome and located directly below the outlet of the sink or floor drain; a seal is formed by the water between the outside of the dome and the inside of the bell.

bell trap

bell wire **1.** A small-diameter steel wire used in **bell hanging.** **2.** A small-diameter copper wire used to connect electric door bells and similar devices to a power source.

belly **1.** The convex curve of the lower part of a baluster; from the resemblance to a fat human stomach. **2.** Any outward- or downward-curving architectural feature. See also **bombé, pulvinated.**

belowstairs (pre–WWII) Servant work areas below the main floor of a house.

belt course Same as **stringcourse.**

belt-driven elevator A 19c type of **elevator** with a platform supported by cables over a pulley and a counterweight; operated by a series of belts and pulleys driven by a constantly turning shaft powered by steam or electricity; the belt around the hoisting drum is engaged or released from the elevator platform.

belvedere, (pre-19c) **belvidere** **1.** A small structure with open sides used for enjoying the view; either a separate building or on the rooftop of a larger building. See also **cupola.** **2.** (19c) A circular or octagonal building used as a **camera obscura.** **3.** (19c) A summerhouse located on a hill.

bema The area surrounding the altar of a Greek Orthodox church. See also **chancel, prothesis.**

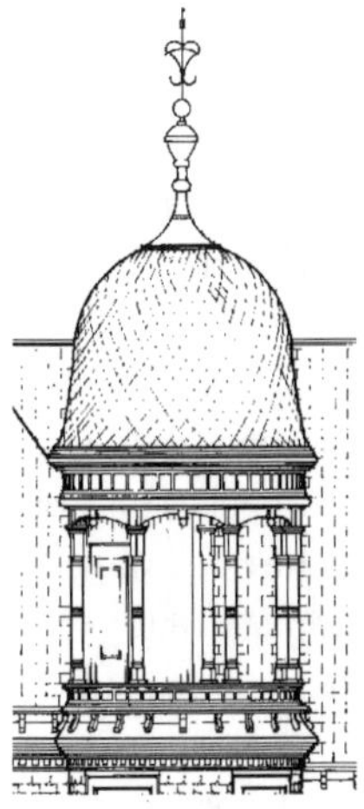
belvedere (sense 1)

bench **1.** A horizontal ledge constructed partway up the earth slope of a civil engineering work. Also known as **berm.** **2.** A courtroom podium or desk for the presiding judge. **3.** A long seat that can accommodate several people; may have a back or be backless, and be fixed or movable.

bench mark A surveying reference point, such as a stone block or wood stake, with a fixed location and height, often marked with a cross-shaped notch.

bench table A projecting lower part of the inside of a masonry wall that creates an exposed shelf and corresponds to the exterior **water table.**

bend A **pipe fitting** that is curved or bent to change the direction of the flow; types include **quarter bend, sanitary bend.**

bent One of a series of transverse structural frames of a building or structure, including (1) in **timber frame** construction, a pair of posts, one or more connecting beams, and often corner braces; see also **raising;** (2) a steel frame with a pair of large beams in the form of a shallow V-shape and assembled into a **three-hinged arch.**

bent principal (20c) Same as **knee rafter** (sense 2).

bent sash A window sash that is curved in plan.

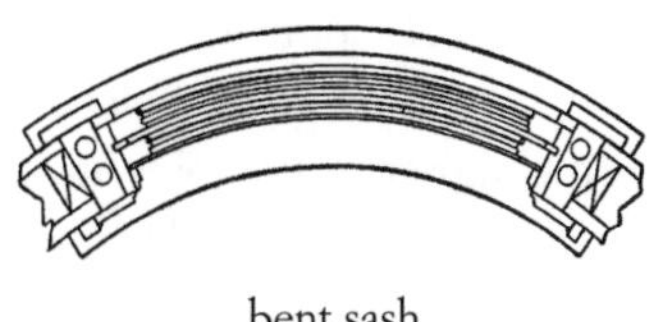
bent sash

bent window A window that is curved in plan; typically with a bent sash; jambs may be parallel or radial.

benzotriazole A chemical used to inhibit copper corrosion, especially on bronze. Also known as **BTA.**

Berea sandstone A dark, fine-grained sandstone containing brine and oil; quarried primarily in the vicinity of Berea, Ohio, and in Pennsylvania; used for building stone and grindstones.

Berlay metal lumber (mid-20c) A trade name for **metal lumber;** includes an I-beam joist built-up of two sheet-metal channels.

Berlin blue Same as **Prussian blue.**

Berlin iron A soft **iron** containing phosphorus; used for fine ornamental castings. See also **cast iron.**

berm **1.** The bank of a canal opposite a towpath. Also known as **berm-bank.** **2.** Same as **bench.** **3.** A narrow, level area between the foot of the outside of a fortification slope and the top of the scarp wall below; used to prevent eroded material from falling into the ditch. **4.** (20c) A linear mound of earth with sloped sides; may be flat on top; used to divert water flow and for landscaping. **5.** The sloped shoulder of a road. See also **bank.**

berm-bank Same as **berm** (sense 1).

best best iron (19c) A highly uniform, high quality rolled iron; used for bridges. See also **best iron.**

best iron (19c) The standard quality of iron used for rolled shapes. See also **best best iron.**

Bethlehem column (early 20c) A rolled steel **H-section** used as a column; popularized by Bethlehem Steel Company as a replacement for columns built-up of steel plate and angles.

béton, béton Coignet (19c–present) A concrete composed of lime, sand, and hydraulic cement mixed with gravel, invented in France.

bettering house (late 18c) Same as **workhouse.**

between glass The total difference in dimension between the glass width and the **outside opening** of a window.

between joints, (pre-19c) **betwixt joints** (New England) The height of a building between the sill and the wall plate. Also known as **pitch.**

betwixt joints Same as **between joints.**

bevel, (18c) **bevil** The inclined face or end of a member. See also **chamfer.**

beveled glass Glass panes in which the perimeter is continuously beveled; creates prismatic effects.

beveled molding A molding with an inclined plane surface.

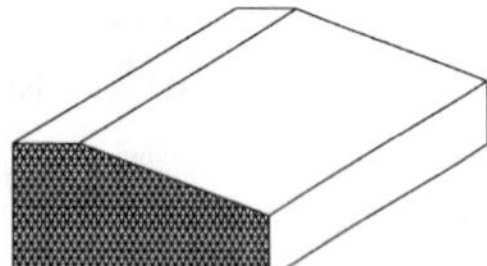

beveled molding

beveled tile A fiber tile with a beveled edge used as a ceiling finish between WWI and WWII; sizes range from 12 × 12 to 16 × 48 inches.

bevel joint Any **joint** in which the ends of the two abutting elements are cut at an angle, especially when not forming a right angle. See also **miter.**

bevel lap A **lap joint** in which a beveled tongue on the end of one wood member overlaps a beveled notch in the side of another member.

bevel siding, beveled siding Tapered **clapboards** installed with the thinner part of the boards at the top.

bevel washer Same as **triangular washer.**

Beverly jog A narrow addition on the end of a house with the back slope of its roof in the same plane as the back slope of the main roof; originally found on late 18c houses in the Boston, Massachusetts, area; now found in other areas.

bezant, byzant A decorative motif of abutting or overlapping flat disks, especially on the face of the archivolt of an arch; often used in **Romanesque Revival style** architecture; from the medieval Byzantine gold coin of the same name.

bibb A wall-mounted **faucet** with a turned-down end. Also known as **bibb cock, bibcock, sill cock.** See also **hose bibb.**

bibb cock, bibcock Same as **bibb.**

bice A paint pigment prepared by grinding naturally occurring carbonate of copper; azurite produces blue bice (light blue) and malachite produces green bice (yellow-green).

bidet **1.** (pre-20c) A basin on a stand on which one sits to bathe the posterior parts of the body. **2.** A plumbing fixture that sprays water upward to clean the posterior parts of the body. See also **douche bath, sitz bath.**

bidding The process of extending invitations to and receiving price proposals from contractors or subcontractors for a defined scope of work; in construction, typically based on the **construction documents.** See also **tender.**

bifold door A pair of two-leafed **folding doors.** See also **accordion door.**

big house (southern U.S.) Same as **great house.**

bilection Same as **bolection.**

bill brad (18c) A flooring nail with a protruding bill on one side of the head. Also known as **quarter head.**

billet **1.** One of a series of projecting shapes that form a **billet molding** by alternating with a concave space; types include **billet rod, square billet.** See also **roll billet molding.** **2.** A bar of partially finished metal; typically iron and steel are approximately 1.5–4 inches square.

billet banding Same as **billet molding.**

billet molding A molding characterized by three staggered rows of projections alternating with voids; the projections may be a **billet rod** or a **square billet;** common in Romanesque Revival style architecture. Also known as **segmental billet.**

billet rod A short, horizontal, cylindrical **billet** projection used in a **billet molding.**

bill of lumber Same as **bill of scantling.**

bill of scantling (18c–19c) A list of the quantity and dimensions of all the framing lumber required to construct a particular building. Also known as **bill of lumber.** See also **scantling.**

bimetallic wire Any wire composed of two separate metals, such as (1) wire with a steel core surrounded by copper; typically both metals are in equal proportion; used for **telegraph wire** and **telephone wire;** (2) wire with two metals fused side by side; used in thermostats.

binder **1.** A girder that supports multiple floor joists. **2.** A substance that holds other materials together (e.g., the asphalt that is mixed with crushed stone for road paving). **3.** Same as a brick **header** or a **bondstone.** **4.** A resinous **paint** component that attaches the pigment particles together and sticks to the surface below the paint film; types include **acrylic,** gelatin, hide glue, **linseed oil,** natural gums, salt, **vinyl.**

binder joist Same as **binding beam.**

binding beam **1.** A transverse timber girder that spans between posts or masonry walls and supports floor joists, or both floor and ceiling joists. **2.** One of a series of timber beams spanning between walls or girders and supporting **bridging joists.** Also known as **binder, binder joist, binding joist, summer.** See also **double floor.**

binding joist Same as **binding beam** (sense 2).

binding stone (19c) Same as **bondstone.**

birch One of several hardwood trees of the genus *Betula;* species include **black birch, paper birch, yellow birch.**

bird of paradise An **ornamental cast iron** pattern in the stylized form of intertwined foliated scrolls with a bird's head at the center of the bottom spiral.

bird's-eye A pattern of small dark circles in wood, especially maple, said to resemble birds' eyes.

bird's-eye pine Same as **lodgepole pine.**

bird's-mouth A **seat cut** notch at the bottom of a diagonal timber, such as a rafter, in the shape of an inverted L; fits around the wall plate or other base framing.

bird's-beak molding Same as **beak** (sense 1).

bisection (18c Philadelphia) Same as **bolection.**

Bishopric board A brand-name stucco lath composed of beveled creosoted boards attached to a fiberboard coated with asphalt mastic; the adjoining boards form dovetailed slots for the stucco keys.

bitter spar Same as **dolomite.**

bitumen A solid or semisolid hydrocarbon formed of asphalt, mineral tar, or similar substances. Also known as **pitch mineral.**

bituminous paint A thick, black, coating material composed of **bitumen;** used for patching roofs, **dampproofing,** and **waterproofing.**

bituminized fiber pipe **Pipe** composed of cellulose and asbestos fibers impregnated with coal tar pitch; typically 3–6 inches in diameter; joined with tapered ends that fit into a coupling sleeve; used for underground **drainpipe** and **sewer pipe.**

black and white work 1. Same as **graffito. 2.** Exposed timber framing with plaster infill (e.g., a painted **half-timbered** building in which the timbers are black and the plaster white).

black ash A hardwood tree with dark brown, tough, elastic wood; used for lumber and staves; *Fraxinus nigra.*

black birch A small **birch** tree with dark reddish brown, strong, hard, heavy, close-grained heartwood with wide, pale yellow sapwood; found in upland areas of the Appalachian Mountain region from northern Georgia to West Virginia, to southern Maine and scattered areas in Michigan and southern Ontario; used for millwork; *Betula lenta.*

black brick (19c) Bricks that have been waterproofed by dipping in hot coal tar.

black cherry A small hardwood tree with reddish brown, hard, relatively lightweight heartwood with thin, yellow sapwood; found in the eastern half of the U.S. and Canada; used for naturally finished interior trim and paneling; *Prunus serotina.* Also known as **wild black cherry.**

black hemlock Same as **mountain hemlock.**

black iron Untinned, malleable iron. See also **black japan, gray iron, white iron.**

black iron pipe Malleable iron or steel pipe, as opposed to **galvanized pipe** or **tin-plate pipe;** typically 2 inches or less in diameter and with male threads; made of wrought iron until the late 19c; used for gas and water pipes, and sometimes for railings. See also **wrought iron pipe.**

black japan (19c) A hard, jet-black lacquer coating for sheet metal composed of asphalt, linseed oil, and varnish. Also known as **Brunswick black, japan black.**

black lead Same as **graphite.**

black locust Same as **locust.**

black oak A moderately sized **oak** tree with reddish brown, heavy, hard, strong, coarse-grained heartwood with narrow, light-colored sapwood; found in the eastern U.S. and southern Ontario; used for flooring and lumber; *Quercus velutina.* Also incorrectly known as **red oak.**

black pipe Same as **black iron pipe.**

black shellac Shellac mixed with lampblack, used for **ebonizing** woodwork and furniture.

black spruce A tall **spruce** tree with pale buff yellow, soft, relatively weak, lightweight, stiff, straight-grained wood; found from West Virginia to Labrador and west to Alaska; used for lumber, masts, and pulpwood; *Picea mariana.* Also known as **blue spruce, bog spruce, eastern spruce, spruce pine, swamp spruce.** See also **red spruce.**

black walnut A tall hardwood tree with dark brown, strong, dense wood; durable in contact with soil; used mainly for natural finished paneling and trim; the most popular interior trim wood in the U.S. from 1855–1865; peak production was in 1929; *Juglans nigra.*

blade (pre-20c) **1.** Same as **principal rafter,** especially as part of a timber frame truss. **2.** A long, thin **tenon.**

bladed scarf joint A **scarf joint** connecting two **timber frame** members end to end with long, thin, interlocking mortise and tenons.

blanc fixe Same as **barium white.**

blank bolt An unthreaded metal **bolt** with a fixed head. See also **pin.**

blank door A false **door,** finished only on one side. See also **jib door.** Also known as **sham door.**

blanket insulation Same as **flexible insulation.**

blank hinge (19c) Same as **blind hinge** (sense 1), especially when used on a **blank door** or **jib door.**

blank wall A flat wall without openings. Also known as **blind wall, dead wall.**

blank window A recess in an exterior wall filled with masonry and having the same enframement as glazed windows in the building. Also known as **blind window.** See also **false window.**

blast cleaning Use of a pressurized stream of air and/or water, often mixed with small abrasive particles, to clean surfaces; types include **sandblasting, water blasting.**

blast furnace A tall, cylindrical smelting furnace with a fire intensified by a continuous air blast; most often used for producing **iron** from ore.

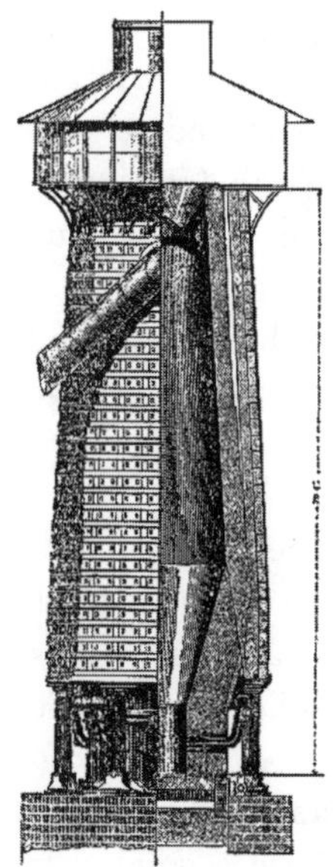

blast furnace

bleachers (19c–present) Uncovered, outdoor seating for spectators. Also known as **bleachery.** See also **bleaching boards.**

bleachery **1.** (19c) Same as **bleaching board.** **2.** A place where bleaching is done.

bleaching agent **1.** An acid applied to wood to lighten its color; used to make **pickled wood.** **2.** Light, weather, or chemicals (such as chlorine) that whiten material upon exposure.

bleaching boards (19c) **Bleachers** consisting of temporary boards for standing and sitting. Also known as **bleachery.**

blind **1.** A building or part of a building that has no windows, such as a blind story. **2.** Any of various devices that obscure the light or view at windows; types include **Persian blind, shutter, Venetian blind.** See also **shade.** **3.** A camouflaged structure used by hunters; typically used in a compound phrase with the type of quarry, such as **duck blind.**

blind adjuster **1.** A device for placing the slats of a window shutter or Venetian blind at a particular angle. See also **rolling slats.** **2.** A device for securing folding window shutters at a particular position.

blind arcade A **surface arcade.**

blind arch An arch whose opening is sealed with the same masonry as the wall; the masonry within may be recessed from the main face of the wall.

blind bond A brick wall bond with concealed headers behind continuous stretcher courses; types include **clip bond, split bond.** See also **blind header.**

blind dado A **dado** groove with an open end at the edge of the member covered with molding.

blind door **1.** A door with slats like a window shutter. **2.** Same as **blank door.**

blind door (sense 1)

blind fast A spring catch for securing an exterior blind or shutter in the open or closed position; clicks into a **sill catch** in the closed position and into a **back catch** in the open position. Also known as **holdback.** See also **shutter dog.**

blind flooring Same as **subfloor.**

blind header A brick header concealed behind the outer wythe of the wall.

blind hinge **1.** A hinge designed so that it is not visible when the door is closed. **2.** (19c) A hook-and-eye hinge with an inclined plane on the base of the pin that automatically shuts the blind or door after it is opened.

blind mortise Same as **closed mortise.**

blind nailing Nailing in a hidden joint so that there is no exposed nailhead, such as in tongue-and-groove flooring; often done with **skew nailing.** Also known as **nailed in the edge, secret nailing.**

blind stop The molding against which an outside door or window shutter or blind rests in the closed position; holds in the outer sash of a double hung window; typically a 1.25-inch thick rectangular molding that abuts the inside face of the masonry in veneer construction.

blind valley The portion of a **long valley** between the head of a dormer and the main roof ridge; concealed within the main roof.

blind wall (pre-20c) Same as **blank wall.**

blind window Same as **blank window.**

blister steel A highly crystalline steel manufactured in the 19c by placing wrought iron bars in layers of charcoal and heating them to high temperatures for two or three days. Also known as **cement steel.**

block **1.** Same as **concrete block.** **2.** An unfinished piece of stone as it comes from the quarry. **3.** A solid piece of wood used in **blocking.** **4.** A short post or log used to support a building above the ground. **5.** Same as **corner block.**

block and cross bond A brick wall bond with one face in Flemish bond and the other in cross bond.

block bond Same as **Flemish bond** or **English bond.**

block cornice A **modillion cornice** with a series of **block modillions;** usually the modillions are more closely spaced than in a typical modillion cornice.

blocked Carved integrally from a stone block (e.g., a **blocked** bracket).

blockhouse, (17c) **blockehowse** **1.** A small **fortification** structure that blocks access, such as through a pass or a river; typically with an overhanging second story and loopholes for firing weapons; may be freestanding or part of a walled compound; often built of logs or planks in North America, sometimes with a masonry base. **2.** A **log house** constructed of squared timbers.

block-in-course bond A bond in an arch of concentric rowlock courses formed by a voussoir or a block of soldier bricks placed at intervals.

blocking Lumber attached to framing and used as a **nailer** to which the finished trim or other material is attached; types include **show blocking, solid blocking.** See also **fire stopping.**

blocking course A plain masonry parapet exposed above a cornice; typically supports the rafters of an attic behind the parapet or balustrade. See also **bahut, stringcourse.**

block modillion A plain, rectangular, solid cornice modillion, as opposed to a carved scroll shape; typically as wide as it is deep. Also known as **uncut modillion.** See also **block cornice.**

block tin Solid tin, as opposed to **tin-plate.**

block-tin pipe (pre–WWI) A corrosion-resistant pipe composed of solid tin; used for water suction pipes from cisterns and wells.

block veneer (20c) Concrete block masonry used as a veneer on a balloon frame building. See also **brick veneer.**

blonde shellac A light-yellow, translucent **shellac** made from bleached lac dissolved in alcohol.

blown joint A joint formed when pipes of soft metal, especially lead, are melted together with a blowtorch. See also **wiped joint.**

Blue Amherst A light blue-gray, fine-grained **sandstone** quarried in the vicinity of Amherst, Ohio; fire resistant and even textured. See also **Gray Canyon sandstone.**

blue brick A dense, hard brick manufactured by heating clay in a low-oxygen reducing fire.

blue bronze **Bronze powder** that is blue.

blue glass See **cobalt glass.**

blue oak A large **oak** tree with light-colored, hard, coarse-grained, extremely strong wood; used for lumber, millwork, and flooring; found in California; *Quercus douglasii.* Also known as **mountain white oak.**

blueprint, blue print **1.** A paper copy of a drawing produced by the cyanotype process invented by Sir John Herschel in 1842; has a Prussian blue background and white lines. **2.** Incorrectly used to refer to copies created by the diazo process, which have blue lines on a white background or, in the plural, to any set of drawing copies.

blue spruce **1.** A large **spruce** tree with whitish colored, brittle, weak wood; found in the central Rocky Mountain area; used regionally for log cabins; *Picea pungens.* Also known as **prickly spruce.** **2.** Same as **black spruce.**

blue stain Same as **sap stain.**

blue steel See **tempered steel.**

bluestone Any of the blue-gray, fine-grained, argillaceous sandstones; used locally as flagstone, and for steps, sills, and lintels; easily split along its bedding plane; varieties include **Euclid bluestone, Hudson River bluestone, North River bluestone, Pennsylvania bluestone, Wyoming Valley stone.**

blue verdigris See **verdigris.**

bluing See **tempered steel.**

blunt-pointed arch A **two-centered arch** with the centers on the spring line inside the intrados. Also known as **drop arch.**

blushing An opaque or translucent film in a lacquer coating caused by improper drying.

board **1.** A long, thin piece of lumber cut from a log; typically with a rectangular cross section less than 2.5 inches thick and 4.5 inches or more in width; boards can be **rived, hand-hewn, hand-sawn,** or **mill-sawn.** See also **batten, deal, plank, weatherboard.** **2.** To cover the frame of a building with sheathing boards. **3.** (southern U.S.) A rived slab of wood used for roofing. Also known as **clapboard.**

board and batten Wood siding construction in which wide vertical boards are covered at the joints by narrow boards.

board and brace A partition system in which boards with kerfed edge grooves alternate with thinner boards inserted in the grooves.

boarded wall (pre-19c) A wall with board **siding.**

board fashion Long hand-split shingles installed with approximately one-half the length of the shingle exposed.

board foot A measurement of lumber equal to 1 square foot 1 inch thick before sawing or planing; used in **board measure.**

board frame Same as **vertical plank frame.**

boarding The boards covering any plane surface of a building; includes **flooring, sheathing, siding.**

boardinghouse, (pre-20c) **boarding house** A building where rooms are rented and meals provided to residents for a fixed term. See also **hotel, lodging house, tavern.**

boarding joist (pre-20c) The floor joists to which wood floor boards are directly nailed; one of the members of a **carcase floor.**

board measure A system of calculating the quantity of lumber by the **board foot;** lumber is typically sold in quantities of a thousand board feet (M).

Board of Architectural Review (BAR) Same as **Architectural Review Board.**

board-on-board Wood siding, fencing, or roofing characterized by overlapping vertical boards that alternate forward and back. See also **plank-on-plank.**

board shantie A board-frame house.

boardwalk (U.S.) A walkway whose surface is constructed of parallel planks, especially one along a beach.

board wall Same as **horizontal plank frame;** espoused by Orson Fowler in his 1853 book *The Octagon House.* See also **boarded wall.**

boast To roughly shape stone before final dressing, especially with a flat, 2-inch-wide boaster or a **drove** chisel.

boasted The rough, hand-cut surface texture of stone blocks shaped with a broad drove chisel. See also **stonework.**

boat nail Same as **clamp nail.** See also **nail.**

boat spike A large nail with a square cross section and a wedge-shaped point. Also known as **ship spike.**

bobeche A disk on top of a **candleholder** that catches dripping wax; may be metal or glass.

BOCA Code A U.S. national building code promulgated by the organization of Building Officials and Code Administrators; section 3406.0 waives strict compliance with the code for historic buildings or structures under certain conditions.

bodega **1.** A wine vault or cellar. **2.** A wineshop. **3.** A storeroom or warehouse.

body range, body vault The main vault with which other smaller, lower vaults intersect, as in a groin or ribbed vault.

boghouse (pre-20c) Same as **outhouse** (sense 2).

bog spruce Same as **black spruce.**

boiler A closed metal vessel used to heat water; types include **double boiler, steam boiler, water boiler, water heater.**

boiler felt Same as **boilermaker's felt.**

boiler iron (19c) Same as **boiler plate.**

boilermaker's felt (19c) A thick wool or hair **felt** used to insulate steam pipes and boilers. Also known as **boiler felt.**

boiler plate Rolled iron or steel sheets .25–.50 inch thick with a tensile strength of at least 40,000 pounds per square inch; used to construct steam boilers.

boiler tube Same as **water tube.**

boiserie Richly decorated wood paneling, especially when installed floor to ceiling.

bolection, (pre-20c) **balection, belection, bilection, bolexion,** (18c Philadelphia) **bisection** A molding that projects beyond the adjoining surfaces, such as at the joint between a panel and a stile or rail of a door. Also known as **raised molding.**

bollard (mid-19c–present) A short, large-diameter post used for tying up boats at a quay or for restricting vehicular traffic from certain areas; may be made of stone, metal, or wood.

Bollman truss A bridge **truss** with tension rods that radiate from the top of the two end posts to the bottom of the evenly spaced vertical chords; the roadbed is supported between the bottom of two Bollman trusses.

bolster **1.** A horizontal timber set across the top of a column to support the parallel ends of girders above it; used to increase the bearing area. Also known as **head tree.** See also **bolster beam.** **2.** Same as **cushion.** **3.** Same as **pulvinar.** **4.** A short length of timber used to support a bridge walkway.

bolster beam A timber or iron beam that supports the end of a bridge truss on an abutment or pier; set perpendicular to the trusses. Also known as **bed timber.**

bolster work Rusticated stonework in which each course bulges outward.

bolt **1.** A rod or **pin** that holds together parts of a building, structure, or object, especially with a permanent head on one end; in the 20c generally indicates a metal **machine screw** fastened with a **nut** unless further modified; types include **barb bolt, blank bolt, bridge bolt, carriage bolt, clevis bolt, collar bolt, coupling bolt, drift bolt, expansion anchor, eyebolt, fox bolt, lag bolt, Lewis bolt, socket bolt, stud bolt, stud pin, T-bolt, through bolt.** **2.** A sliding rod for locking a door, gate or window; types include **barrel bolt, dead bolt, drop bolt, slide bolt.**

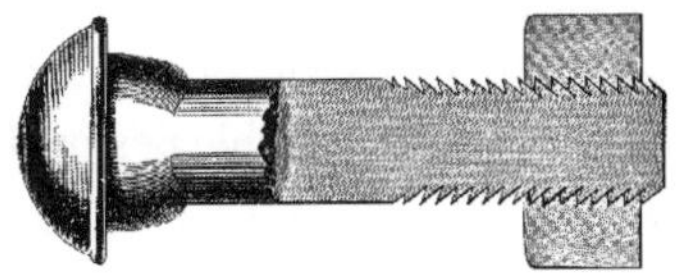

bolt (sense 1)

bolt drop The handle of a horizontal door bolt that hangs down when the bolt is not in use. See also **slide bolt.**

bolted connection A connection between structural members made with plates and bolts, as opposed to such other methods as **riveted construction** or **welding.**

boltel, bowtel A quarter circle or other similar convex shape, including (1) the coping of a parapeted gable end; (2) a torus or ovolo molding, especially the torus immediately below the abacus of a Doric or Tuscan column capital; (3) a **roll molding.** Also known as **boultin.**

bolting house, (pre-19c) **boulting house** A building in which flour is sifted through fine cloth or wire sieves. Also known as **bolting mill.**

bolting mill, (pre-19c) **boulting mill** Same as **bolting house.**

bombé A shape that swells outward. See also **belly, cushion, pulvinated.**

bond Anything that holds two or more objects together, including (1) the pattern of interlocking units and joints in a masonry structure; types include **basket weave bond, blind bond, block-and-cross bond, block-in-course bond, chain bond, clip bond, common bond, cross bond, dog's-tooth bond, English bond, Flemish bond, flying bond, garden wall bond, heading bond, heart bond, in-and-out bond, raking bond, running bond, stack bond, tapestry brick, timber bond;** see also **ashlar, brick, pattern bond, structural bond;** (2) the connection between masonry units or the unit and the mortar bed; (3) the connection of multiple timbers by another timber that crosses them at right angles, such as a **wall plate;** (4) (19c) the amount that one slate or shingle overlaps the second one beneath it; (5) same as **bondstone.**

bond course A horizontal row containing brick headers or bondstones in a masonry structure. Also known as **heading course.**

bonder Same as **bondstone.**

bond header A **bondstone** exposed on both faces of the wall.

bonding brick A specially shaped brick that connects both faces of a wall.

bond plaster A gypsum plaster manufactured so that it can be used as a scratch coat directly on concrete.

bondstone, (pre-20c) **bond stone** A block of stone that projects into a masonry wall and connects the face blocks to the backing; may be a **perpend** or be exposed on only one face. Also known as **bond, bonder.**

bond timber A wood framing member that connects other members, such as a **lintel** or a **plate.** See also **timber bond.**

bone black Same as **drop black.**

bone glass Same as **opal glass.**

bonnet **1.** Same as **vent-cap.** **2.** (pre-19c Virginia) Same as **pent.**

bonnet hip tile Same as a **cone tile.**

book matched Wood veneer or sliced marble installed so that the grain of pairs of the pieces is aligned at the center. See also **herringbone matched.**

book tile (19c) A lightweight roof-deck tile or ceiling tile formed in the shape of a closed book, with one concave edge and one convex edge; installed with the flat ends supported by T-bars and the rounded edges nested together.

booked chill A process of producing a **cast-on** with a hinged mold clamped over the pieces to be joined, such as **iron-wire fence** wires.

booster pump A **water pump** that increases the pressure in a building or system; may be used for domestic water or a sprinkler system to boost the pressure supplied by the **main** or other source.

boot The top of a drainpipe that receives the foot of a **downspout;** typically cast iron.

borate A salt of boric acid; used as a wood preservative to prevent growth of fungi; typically small rods inserted in holes drilled in the wood dissolve and diffuse the salt when water is present.

Borden system A system of coded identification for archaeological sites that designates each site by four letters for the geographic coordinates plus a number. See also **geocode, UTM.**

border **1.** A decorative edging, such as the wood trim between a fireplace hearth and the floorboards. **2.** A linear planting or raised bank forming a separation or edge in a garden.

border stone A curb stone.

borescope A fiber optic device for looking into hidden cavities, often through a hole drilled through the finish material; one bundle of fibers acts as a light source and a second bundle is used for viewing; may be used with a short, straight rod or a longer flexible rod; typically attached to a video camera or still camera for recordation.

boss **1.** A projecting mass of stone that terminates raised moldings, especially when decoratively carved; commonly refers to the carved keystones at the intersection of the ribs of Gothic style vaults. Also known as **knob.** **2.** A projecting piece on a stone block to aid handling and which is later cut away or decoratively carved. Also known as **bossage.**

bossage **1.** Projecting blocks in a stone wall, especially in a rusticated wall. **2.** An unfinished block of stone that is cut into a molding after being set.

Boston hip A hip, or wall corner, joint made by alternately overlapping shingles or slates from each side.

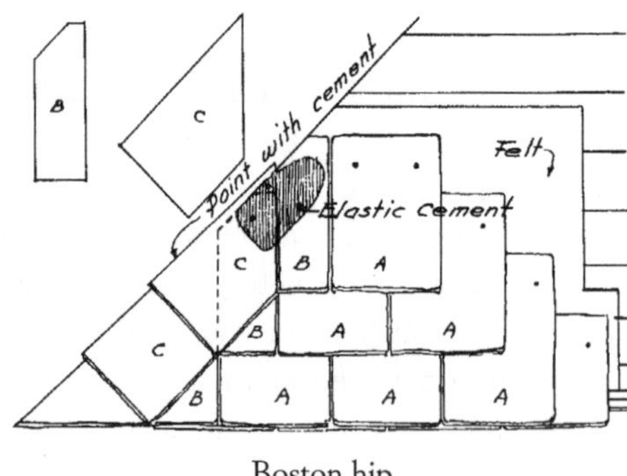

Boston hip

Bostwick lath A brand-name **expanded-metal lath** similar to **Truss-loop lath.**

botanical garden, (pre-19c) **botanick garden** (late 18c–present) A garden and/or greenhouse, or portion of one, in which many varieties of exotic plants are grown for scientific research and recreational viewing.

bottom chord A **chord** along the lower perimeter of a **truss;** one of a pair with the **top chord.**

bottom cripple A short section of stud framing between a header or the bottom of a window and the wall plate below. See also **cripple, top cripple.**

bottom cut Same as **seat cut.**

bottom nail (18c) Same as **back nail.** See also **nail.**

bottom stone Same as **footing stone.**

boulder A naturally occurring **stone** that is more than 12 inches in diameter and separated from its original bed; usually rounded, may also be angular.

boultin, boultine (pre-19c) Same as **boltel.**

boulting house (pre-19c) Same as **bolting house.**

boulting mill (pre-19c) Same as **bolting house.**

bound masonry Masonry in which the units are bonded together. See also **bond.**

boundary The outer edge of a defined area, especially a plot of land; may be unmarked, defined by a series of boundary markers, or coincident with a fence. See also **bounds, metes and bounds, verbal boundary description.**

boundary marker An object, such as a **monument** or **lead and tack,** located on the boundary of a property; often located where the perimeter changes direction. See also **metes and bounds.**

bounds **1.** Same as **boundary. 2.** A defined land area beyond which students, or pre-19c prisoners, may not pass.

bouquet **1.** The decorative ornament at the top of a finial or other projection in a floral or foliated form. **2.** Same as **anthemion.**

bousillage Chinking or nogging composed of clay reinforced with materials such as twigs, straw, Spanish moss, and/or animal hair, sometimes with gravel galleting; used in French colonial construction.

bow A bend in the large face of a piece of wood along its length. See also **warp.**

bower **1.** A rustic shelter in a garden; typically made from the branches of living plants twined together or vines on a framework. See also **arbor. 2.** (pre-19c) A rough dwelling made of branches and bark.

Bower-Barff A black, noncorrosive, magnetic iron oxide coating on iron or steel; common in the mid-19c. Also known as **barff.**

bowfat (Early English colonial) Same as **buffet.**

bow-fett Same as **buffet.**

bow knot A decorative element in the stylized shape of a ribbon tied in a bow; often in the form of repetitive open loops containing rosettes.

bowl A **basin,** or a similar plumbing fixture.

bowl

bowl capital An undecorated **capital** in the shape of a bowl.

bowling green A large, level lawn area used for playing the English game of bowls; common mid-17c–early 19c.

bowl light An electric light fixture with a translucent glass bowl suspended below a ceiling-mounted lamp; common in the period 1910–20.

bowstring girder A girder composed of a truss with an upward-curved beam with a horizontal chord connected to the beam with vertical tie rods.

bowstring roof A curved roof supported by bowstring trusses.

bowstring truss A **truss** with a curved top chord that meets the horizontal bottom chord at the bearing points; the top chord acts as an arch and the bottom chord acts as a horizontal tie; when used for bridges, the loads are suspended from the top chord by posts and diagonal ties. Also known as **arched truss, arch truss.**

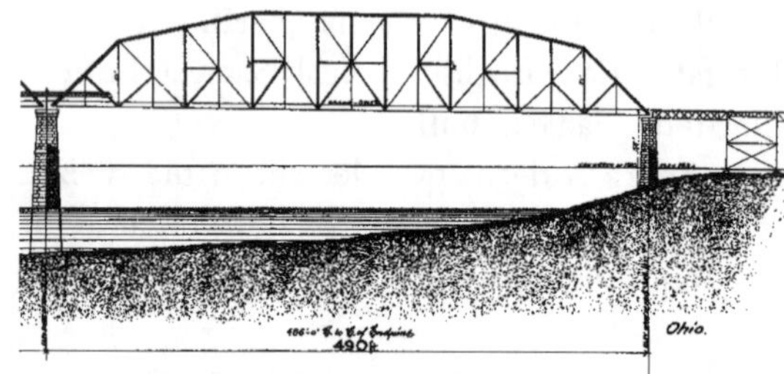

bowstring truss
Cincinnati Bridge, Ohio
by the Phoenix Bridge Co., Pennsylvania, ca. 1888

bowtell Same as **boltel.**

bow window **1.** A **bay window** in which the outer wall plan is in the shape of a segment of a circle. **2.** (18c) Any shape of **bay window.**

box **1.** The area within a rail or partition that encloses a group of seats, such as in a church, theater, stadium, or courtroom; types include **jury box, proscenium box.** See also **box seat.** **2.** A hole that receives the latch or bolt of a **lock;** may be behind a **strike plate. 3.** A small house or wood compartment used as a hunter's blind. **4.** Same as **loose stall. 5.** A small building for a sentry or watchman. **6.** (pre-19c) A small house in the country used as a retreat. **7.** (pre-20c) One of several sitting areas in a public garden enclosed with wood partitions on three sides and containing a table; sometimes with built-in benches and a curtain across the open side. See also **beam box, electric box.**

box beam **1.** A rectangular structural tube formed with pieces of wood or metal. Also known as **built beam.** See also **box girder. 2.** Wood casing that provides a finish around a structural beam or that creates a false beam.

box bed A bed enclosed with wood paneling that can be closed in cold weather.

box bridge An enclosed bridge. See also **covered bridge.**

box cornice, boxed cornice A wood cornice formed by enclosing the framing members below overhanging rafter tails; may be of various configurations with a horizontal or sloped soffit. See also **open cornice.**

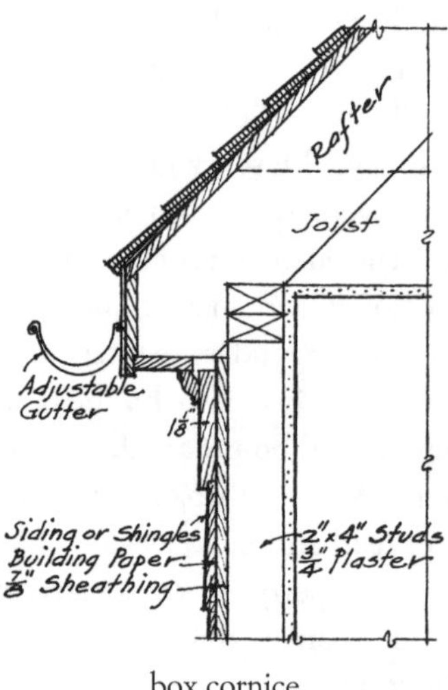

box cornice

box culvert A **culvert** with a rectangular cross section; made of wood, stone, or, beginning in the late 19c, reinforced concrete.

box drain A masonry **drain** with a rectangular cross section; typically covered with flat paving stones to allow maintenance access.

boxed **1.** Constructed with **boxing. 2.** Enclosed with boards in a box shape.

boxed heart rot Decay of the heartwood in a standing tree, leaving the sapwood intact. See also **decay tunnel.**

boxed out Box-shaped framing around an opening or penetration, such as in a floor around a vertical pipe.

boxed shutter, boxing shutter, box shutter An interior window shutter that folds into the **boxing** at the side of the jamb; typically with upper and lower sections that can be operated independently.

box frame **1.** Same as **vertical plank frame.** **2.** (19c) Same as **sash pocket.**

box girder (19c–present) A **box beam** used as a **girder;** typically built-up of steel angles and plate; types include **beam box girder.**

box-head window A double-hung window in which the sashes slide up into a recess at the top of the window.

boxing **1.** Wide vertical boards enclosing the corners of a **vertical plank frame** house or **log cabin.** **2.** A millwork enclosed recess at the side of a window that receives a **boxed shutter** when closed. **3.** Same as **sheathing.**

boxing shutter Same as **boxed shutter.**

box lobby A theater lobby that includes box office windows.

box lock A surface-mounted lock with the mechanism in a rectangular metal or wood casing, as opposed to a **mortise lock;** originally with a wood case and an iron mechanism.

box office The ticket sales booth of a theater, stadium, or similar facility.

box room An enclosed, dry, storage area.

box seat One of the seats in a **box,** as in a theater or stadium; usually in a preferred location.

box shutter Same as **boxed shutter.**

box sill A C-shaped support at the base of an exterior stud wall, composed of three 2× members with the top horizontal 2× projecting beyond the studs to support the edge of the flooring, and the bottom horizontal 2× resting on the foundation wall.

box stair **1.** A wood stair with two closed strings that form a boxlike shape with the treads and risers; typically preconstructed in a millwork shop. **2.** Same as **closed string stair.**

box stall Same as **loose stall.**

box staple Same as **box** (sense 2).

box stoop (1880–present) Entrance stairs with a raised quarter-turn landing; the flight of steps runs parallel to the face of the building. See also **stoop.**

box string Same as **closed string.**

box tenon A tenon with an L-shaped cross section.

box valve A pipe **valve** with a box-shaped casing and an access door.

Boyd Block (20c) A trade name for a type of concrete **granite block** manufactured by Boyd Brothers in the Ottawa Valley in the 20c.

BPP **Building Preservation Plan**

bracciale An ornamental wall bracket for holding a torch or flagpole; typically with a foliated arm with a claw holding a ring at its base; from the Italian term for those used on palazzos.

brace, (pre-18c) **brase** A structural element that holds something in place, including: (1) a diagonal member that prevents a **timber frame** or truss **panel** from changing shape, acting in either tension or compression, such as a **wind brace;** (2) same as **strut;** (3) a latent support acting in compression, such as a **truss brace.**

braced arch A truss in the shape of a reticulated arch.

braced frame **1.** A **wood frame** system with large corner posts and girts stiffened with diagonal corner braces and with the exterior and interior bearing walls composed of 2 × 4 studs; common before 1850 and used until ca. 1900. See also **balloon frame, pegged braced frame, timber frame.** **2.** (20c) A **skeleton**

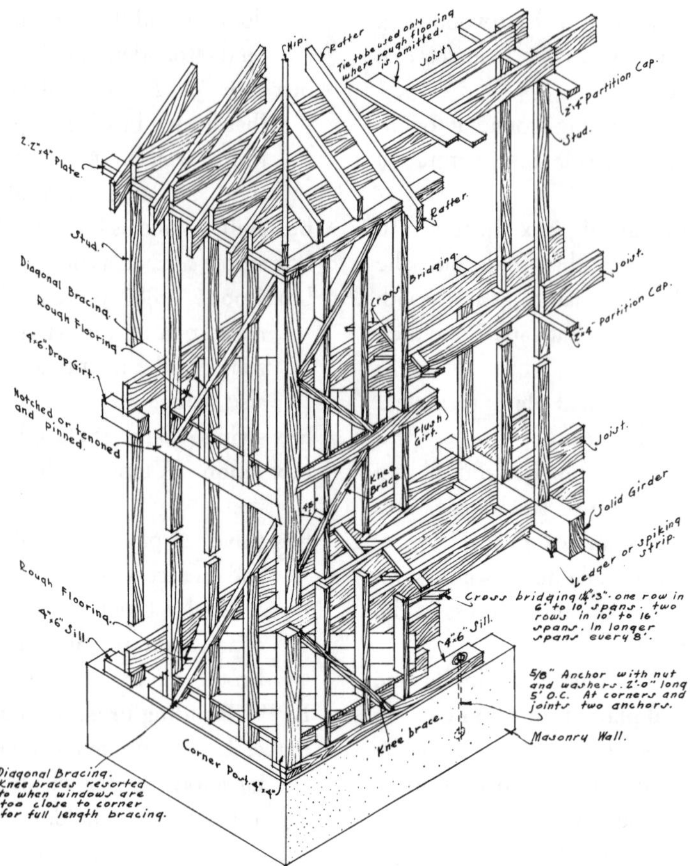

braced frame (sense 1)

construction frame braced with diagonal members between the columns and girders to resist wind forces.

braced header A wall **header** with a pair of 45-degree diagonal wood braces that slope from the top of the header toward the center of the partial wall above the opening.

braced partition (20c) A stud partition with diagonal 1×s or 2×s from the sole plate to the top plate.

brace molding An angled molding composed of two ogee moldings with the convex sides butting; in section, the molding resembles a printer's brace symbol.

bracket 1. An angled support that helps transfer the load of a horizontal structural member to a vertical one; similarly, various decorative elements in the corner of an opening or below a

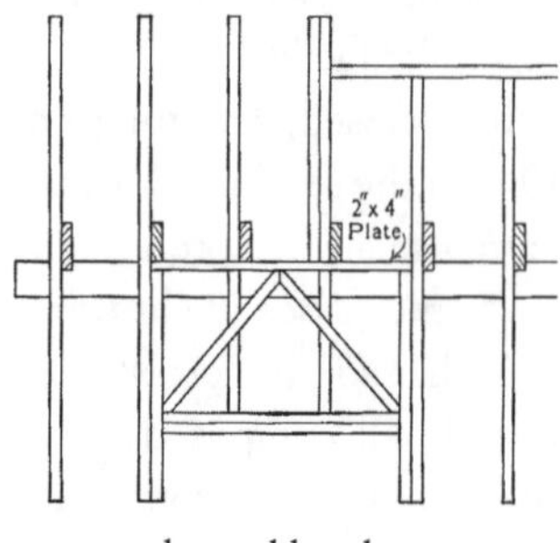

braced header

projection; types include **angle bracket, console, cut bracket.** See also **bracketed string, hanger, modillion, strut. 2.** A wall-mounted **gas fixture.** Also known as **wall bracket.**

bracketed cornice A deep cornice having large, widely spaced ornamental brackets supporting an overhanging eave; common in the **Italianate style.**

bracketed cornice

bracketed string, bracketed stringer An open string of a stair with triangular brackets on top of the string that support the treads.

bracketed style (19c) Same as **Italianate.**

bracket joint A **joint** stiffened by a bracket.

bracted red fir Same as **noble fir.**

brad 1. A short **finish nail** with a small cross section; may be a **wrought nail, cut nail,** or **wire nail. 2.** (before mid-19c) A **wrought nail** with a slightly flat, rectangular cross section and headless or with a slight projecting bill on one side, and of any size; types include **batten brad, bill brad.**

branch A nearly horizontal **drainpipe** or **vent pipe** that connects to another pipe, such as a **stack.**

branch line A subsidiary water pipe.

branch rib One of the ribs of a Gothic style cross vault. Also known as **lierne.**

brander To install furring strips across the bottom of ceiling joists in preparation for installing the lath for plaster.

brandy house (18c–19c Delaware) A building where liqueurs are distilled.

brass 1. (18c–present) A ductile alloy composed of copper and zinc; varieties, in order of increasing zinc content, include **violet brass (0.05 percent), orange brass (0.73 percent), red-yellow brass (9.6 percent), deep yellow brass (15.3 percent), pale yellow brass (16.69 percent), common brass (36 percent), Muntz metal (40 percent), white brass (66 percent);** used for hardware and decorative plating. See also **hard solder, similor, tombac. 2.** Any of various alloys of copper; varieties include **Aich's metal, cock metal, copper-red brass, bronze, English brass, green brass, ormolu, Pinchbeck, sterro metal, white tombac.**

brass pipe Pipe made of solid brass; typically .5–2 inch diameter, with brazed or screwed joints; used for drain and vent pipes, exposed gas piping, and water supply pipes.

bratticing, brattishing Carved ornamental work, especially at the top of a cornice or screen wall; forms include miniature battlements, Tudor flowers, and foliation.

brauna A tropical hardwood tree with brownish, intricately grained wood imported from South America; used for veneer wood; *Melanoxylon brauna.* Also known as **Brazil wood.**

brazil wood, brazil 1. One of several species of hardwood tree imported from South America and the West Indies as early as the 19c for veneer; varieties include *Caesalpinia echinata, Brauna* and *Garauna.* **2.** (ca. 12c–present) A reddish orange lake-color pigment made from wood of various trees of the genus *Caesalpinia;* used for paint and dyestuffs; the country Brazil was named for the wood exported to Europe beginning in the 17c.

brazing, (pre-20c) **braizing** Joining two pieces of metal by melting a thin piece of **hard solder** between them at temperatures above 800 degrees Fahrenheit. Also known as **hard soldering.** See also **welding.**

brazing solder Same as **hard solder.**

break **1.** A gap in an element. **2.** A change in direction of an element. See also **return.** **3.** A projection of a portion an element beyond the main plane. See also **offset.**

breaker Same as **circuit breaker.**

breakfast nook (20c) A three-sided, recessed space with parallel, built-in benches and table; often adjoins the kitchen.

breakfast nook

breakfast room (late 18c–present) A dining room in which breakfast and informal meals are eaten; typically smaller than the main dining room.

breaking in Cutting a recess in masonry to receive the end of a beam or other element.

breast **1.** The portion of a chimney that projects into a room; especially above the fireplace opening. **2.** The bottom of a handrail, beam, or similar element, as opposed to the **back.** **3.** The part of a wall that is between a windowsill and the floor. **4.** A closed railing in front of a gallery.

breast girt A breast-high horizontal member that spans between the end posts and the center post of a bent adjoining the center space of a **timber frame** barn; supported by breast studs; used to keep hay out of the interior driveway.

breast molding **1.** A windowsill molding. **2.** Paneling between a windowsill and the floor. See also **back lining.**

breast stud A stud that supports a **breast girt.** See also **timber frame.**

breastsummer, breast summer, bressumer, brestsomer, (pre-19c) **brest summer, brissumer** A wood **summer beam** lintel over a large opening such as a shop window or fireplace, supported by side walls or pillars; sometimes carved; originally a large timber at the top of a one-story wall of a house with a half-timber frame above supported by corbels or brackets, so that the base of the half-timber wall is outside the masonry wall. See also **dragon beam.**

breast wall A retaining wall.

breast wheel A vertical **waterwheel** in which the water flow arrives at the level of the horizontal shaft. Also known as **breastshot wheel.** See also **overshot wheel, undershot wheel.**

breastwork **1.** A low-height, temporary **fortification** wall quickly erected (typically breast high); may be the parapet of an entrenchment. **2.** (pre-20c) A building parapet.

breastshot wheel (pre-19c) Same as **breast wheel.**

breccia A stone conglomerate composed of angular fragments cemented together. See also **puddingstone.**

breccia marble **Marble** with chunky, angular inclusions in a fine-grained background.

breeder's stable A **stable** on a horse breeding farm; typically a large, barnlike structure with a central aisle opening to the stalls. Also known as **training stable.**

breeze block Concrete block manufactured from **breeze concrete.**

breeze concrete A nailable, lightweight concrete manufactured using **coke breeze** as an aggregate; used in the early 20c.

breezeway A covered, open-sided walkway between two buildings.

brest summer (pre-19c) Same as **breastsummer.**

brewery A building in which beer or similar beverages are manufactured by brewing grains in vats. Also known as **ale house, brewhouse.**

brewhouse Same as **brewery.**

brick A dense, fired-clay building component; typically with rectangular faces and uniform size, may also be formed into ornamental shapes; used primarily in walls, foundations, and exterior paving; early bricks were solid, while some 20c bricks have vertical holes in the interior; types by their orientation at the face of a wall include **header, rowlock, stretcher, soldier, sailor, or shiner;** types by use or shape include **air brick, angle brick, arch brick, compass brick, face brick, fire brick, ventilating brick, well brick;** types by manufacturing process include **chuff brick, pressed brick, sandstruck brick, water smoked, water-struck brick, wire-cut brick;** types by composition include **adobe, blue brick, clinker brick, common brick, Dutch brick, glazed brick, sand-lime brick, slag brick, salmon brick, stone brick;** types by size include **common brick, engineer brick, modular brick, Norman brick, Roman brick, utility brick;** types by color and texture include **barks, flare header, rugs, smooth, stippled.** See also **closer, black brick, bond, diaper, frog, Milwaukee brick, Philadelphia brick.**

brick and brick Brickwork in which the bricks touch one another without mortar between, except to fill small gaps.

brick-and-stud work Same as **brick nogging.**

brick ashlar An ashlar stone wall with brick backup.

brickbat Same as **bat** (sense 1).

brick bond See **bond.**

brick dust mortar A masonry mortar colored with brick dust.

brick fender (19c) A brick foundation wall that supports a hearth at the lowest level of a building.

bricking A false brick wall made by filling grooves cut in plaster with plaster mortar.

brick mold, brick mould One of various wood moldings used on the exterior to trim the edge of windows in a masonry opening and, by extension, the edge molding of a window used with any type of siding.

bricknog Same as **brick nogging.**

brick nogging Brick masonry **nogging** infilled between wall timbers. Also known as **brick-and-stud work, brick nog.**

bricks-and-mortar An expression used to describe the actual construction work of a project and, by inference, the hard construction costs; sometimes used to refer to grants or funding for historic preservation projects. See also **hard cost, soft cost.**

brick veneer A single wythe of face brick forming the exterior wall finish and supported horizontally by an independent building frame; developed in the mid-19c in conjunction with residential **balloon frame** construction, used with various types of **backup** and **wall tie** in any type of construction, including **plank frame.** See also **block veneer.**

brickwork Masonry construction composed of **bricks** and **mortar.** See also **brick and brick, bond.**

bridge A structure that spans over a depression or waterway; typically carries a transportation way, such as a footpath, road, or railway, or sometimes a utility line, such as a water main; types include **beam truss bridge, deck bridge, drawbridge, suspension bridge, tres-**

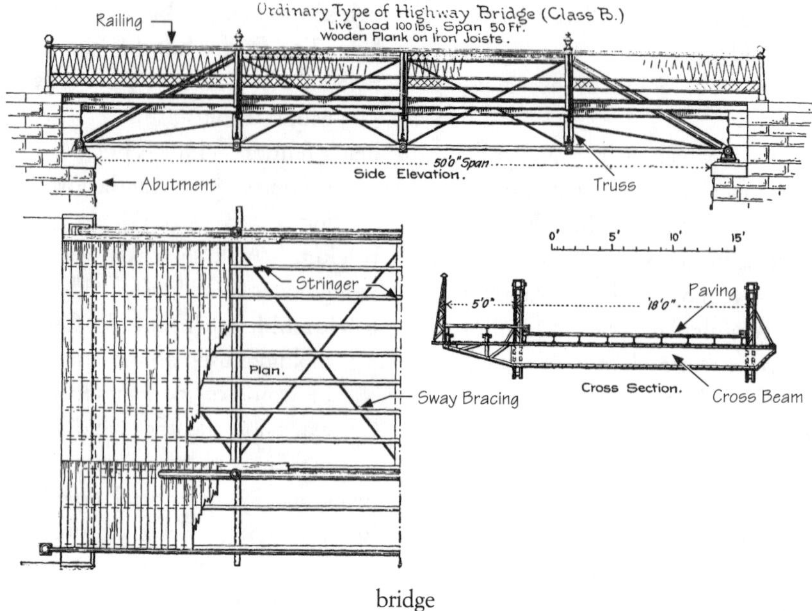

bridge

tle, through bridge, truss bridge, vertical-lift bridge; components may include **abutment, arch, counterweight, cross beam, girder, paving, pier, railing, stringer, sway bracing, trough plate, truss, trunnion, turntable, wing wall, zore.**

bridgeboard, bridge board A notched wood stair **stringer.**

bridge bolt (19c) Same as **rivet.**

bridge-letting (19c) A request for proposals to build a bridge; the proposals typically included both the design and construction.

bridging A continuous row of stiffeners between floor joists or other parallel structural members to prevent rotation about their vertical axes; types include **cross bracing, single bridging, solid bridging, strap bridging, wire tension bridging.**

bridging beam **1.** A floor beam supported at one or both ends by a girder, so that the beam does not span the entire distance between bearing walls. See also **binding beam. 2.** Same as **bridging joist.**

bridging floor A **double floor** with **bridging joists.**

bridging joist, (pre-19c) **bridging joice** One of a series of parallel beams supported on top of the **binding beams** and/or girders of a **double floor** system; the floorboards are laid on top and sometimes notched at each joist.

bridle iron (19c) Same as **stirrup** or **strap hanger.**

bridle joint, bridled joint A carpentry joint connecting a slotted end of one timber to the double-notched end of another timber; used for various connections, such as to connect a rafter to a tie beam or two rafters at a ridge.

bridled scarf joint A **scarf** connecting two timbers end to end with a **bridle joint.**

bright Having a shiny finish.

bright tin Pure **tin,** as opposed to an alloy. See also **block tin.**

brilliant-cut glass Plate glass with a refractive, decorative pattern cut into the surface by a glass-cutting lathe and then polished; common in **frosted glass** and **flash glass** in the 19c.

brimstone Same as **sulfur.**

bringing forward Painting existing surfaces so that chipped areas will be filled in flush with the main surface.

brise-soleil Fixed louvers or grillwork on the exterior of a building to screen out sunlight.

brissumer (pre-19c) Same as **breastsummer.**

Bristol stone A creamy white **limestone** quarried in the vicinity of Bristol, England; imported pre-19c to coastal Maryland, Virginia, and the Carolinas for use as pavers and, sometimes, building stone.

Britannia metal Same as **pewter.**

British thermal unit (abbr. **Btu**) A unit of heat measurement equal to the amount of heat required to raise the temperature of 1 pound of water by 1 degree Fahrenheit.

brixon plank A herringbone **parquet floor** pattern of interlocked, elongated rectangles.

broach **1.** A **spire** that rises from the top of a tower without a parapet or other transition at the base. See also **needle spire.** **2.** A hipped corner at the base of an octagonal broach spire on a rectangular tower. **3.** To roughly dress stone with a broach chisel, typically with parallel diagonal grooves.

broach post (pre-WWI) Same as **king post.**

broach stop Same as **chamfer.**

broad ax, broad axe See **rough hewn.**

broad gauge, broad gage A railroad track that is greater in width between the rails than **standard gauge;** typically more than 56.5 inches, measured perpendicularly at a point ⅝ inch below the top of the rail.

broad glass (19c) Same as **cylinder glass.**

broad stone **1.** (18c) Wide stones, 2–3 inches thick, used as pavers. **2.** Same as **ashlar.**

broad tooled Stone scored by a batting chisel with continuous, fine, parallel vertical or diagonal marks.

brob A wedge-shaped spike driven alongside the end of an abutting timber to keep it from moving laterally; usually one of a pair.

brochantite A bright-green copper sulfate **corrosion** that forms on copper and bronze.

broken arch A segmental arch whose architrave is interrupted by decorative work at the crown.

broken ashlar Same as **random ashlar.**

broken joint A pattern in which the elements are installed so that adjacent butt joints between pieces are not aligned, such as for flooring or brickwork.

broken joint floor Flooring of random-width boards in which some of the joints between the sides of boards are discontinuous.

broken pediment A pediment with a gap at its apex or base; common in **Renaissance Revival style** and **Beaux-Arts** architecture. Also known as **open pediment.**

broken rangework Same as **random broken coursed ashlar.**

bronze **1.** A reddish-brown metal alloy composed of 58–95 percent copper, with the remaining 5–42 percent of tin and, sometimes, other metals, such as lead or zinc; when the copper is alloyed with large quantities of other metals it is referred to in its compound form (e.g., **aluminum bronze** or **leaded phosphor bronze**); used for statuary, hardware, and decorative grilles; types include **phosphor bronze, statuary bronze, white bronze.** Also known as **brass** before the 19c. See also **albronze, bronzine, Fontainemoreau's bronze.** **2.** The process of covering the surface of a material with **bronze powder** or bronze paint to give the appearance of gold or other metals.

bronze disease Self-perpetuating **corrosion** in copper alloys caused by the interaction of oxygen, water, and chloride compounds that creates pitting.

bronze liquid, bronze paint **Bronze powder** mixed with varnish, lacquer, or tung oil; used to produce the appearance of gilding; most common base is amyl acetate from banana oil. See also **aluminum paint.**

bronze powder Fine particles of bronze, or another metal, used for ornamental finishes and for making **bronze liquid;** types by color include **blue bronze, gold bronze, silver bronze.** See also **bronzine, Dutch metal.**

bronzine A metal used to imitate bronze.

brotch A twig bent into a U-shape and used to secure thatch to a roof. Also known as **spar.**

brothel A building in which prostitutes entertain men. Also known as **house of rendezvous, whorehouse.**

brown coat The second layer of a **plaster** finish, applied over the **scratch coat** and floated smooth to receive the **finish coat;** composed of **coarse stuff** with more sand than the scratch coat, giving it a distinctive brown color. Also known as **browning, floated coat, straightening coat.**

browning Same as **brown coat.**

brown pine (19c) Same as **longleaf pine.**

brownstone **1.** Any one of several reddish brown to brown sandstones, especially the arkosic sandstones found in Connecticut, New Jersey, and Pennsylvania; varieties include **Connecticut brownstone, Hummelstown brownstone;** similar sandstones quarried in North Carolina, western Massachusetts, Colorado, and other locations. **2.** (Mid-Atlantic to New York region, 19c–present) An urban dwelling with a brownstone facade; constructed primarily in the late 19c.

brow piece (19c) A beam over a door.

brow post (19c) A cross beam.

B-shape lamp An **incandescent lamp** with a candle-flame shape and a straight tip. See also **C-shape lamp, flame shape lamp.**

Brunswick black Same as **black japan.**

BTA Abbr. for **Benzotriazole.**

Btu Abbr. for **British thermal unit.**

BtuH Abbr. for **British thermal units per hour.**

buck **1.** The rough frame around a door opening to which the finished jamb and head are attached. **2.** (20c) A preformed metal doorframe. Also known as **door buck.**

bucket and pulley A mechanism consisting of a bucket on a rope or chain that passes over a pulley mounted on a frame; used for drawing water from a well or lifting loose materials from an excavation or up to a scaffold.

bucket and windlass A mechanism for drawing water from a well; consists of a bucket on a rope that winds around a horizontal piece of wood turned by a crank arm and mounted on a frame over the top of the well.

buckle Same as **brotch.**

buckled sheet (19c) Same as **corrugated iron.**

buckled plate, buckle-plate A domed iron plate with flat edges; placed on iron or steel beams to support a concrete slab or asphalt or stone paving; used in the 19c for bridges and fireproof floors; typically ¼–⅜ inch thick, 3–4 feet square, with a 2–3 inch rise; plates with multi-

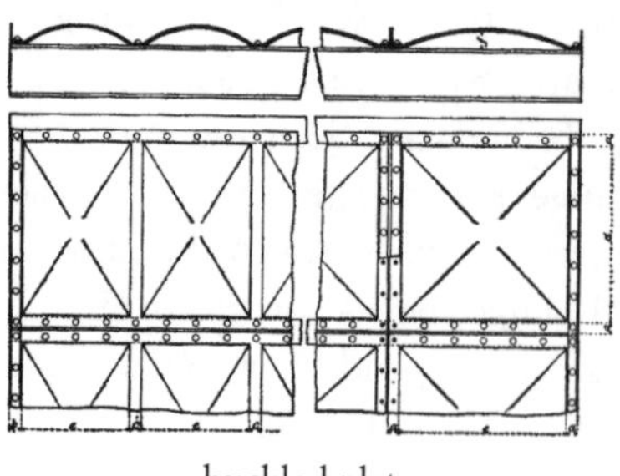

buckled plate

ple rectangular domes also manufactured in late 19c.

buckler A shield-shaped bas-relief ornament used in friezes; named after the round defensive shield used with swords.

buckstay (20c) A vertical rolled-steel section attached vertically to a **sheet pile** to provide rigidity; commonly used when the sheet piling is to be left in place after excavation.

bucranium, bucrane A sculpted ornament in the form of an ox skull, often decorated with garlands; common on **Doric** style friezes. Also known as **bull's head.**

bud **1.** An Egyptian style column capital in the form of a stylized lotus bud. **2.** A small, foliated portion of a Corinthian capital located between the base of two acanthus leaves above the caulicoles.

Bude light (19c) An **Argand lamp** with oxygen piped to the center of the gas flame.

buffet, (18c) **beaufait, beaufet, bowfat, bow-fett, buffat, bufet** **1.** (18c–present) A place used for storing and displaying china and glassware, especially in a public room; may be a recess separated from a main room by columns, a glass-doored cupboard, or a freestanding piece of furniture. See also **butler's pantry. 2.** (19c) A public place for lunch or light refreshments, as opposed to a more elaborate restaurant.

build **1.** A vertical masonry joint. **2.** The dimension of stone block perpendicular to the **quarry bed.**

builder (18c–present) The person who directs the construction of a house or other structure; may also be the **developer.** Also known as **undertaker.** See also **architect, contractor.**

builder's hardware All of the metal fittings and connectors used for framing a building and constructing millwork; includes both **finish hardware** and **rough hardware.**

builder's plastic Same as **carbon-filled polyethylene** in sheet form; the black film is typically 4 or 6 mm thick.

building, (pre-18c) **buylding** **1.** A **structure** enclosing a space and providing protection from the elements; typically includes walls, a roof, and other components; commercial types include **bank, bark mill, brewery, casino, exchange, factory, foundry, forge, garage, gunnery, hangar, laundry, mill, mortuary, office building, railroad station, shot tower, smith's shop, store, theater, trading post, warehouse, weave shed,** and various types listed under **house;** residential types include **apartment building, barracks, dormitory, hotel, house, outbuilding, quarters, shack, shanty, villa;** institutional types include **academy, amphitheater, armory, arsenal, asylum, aviary, Capitol, city hall, church, courthouse, fortification, herbarium, hospital, jail, lazaretto, library, lyceum, museum, natatorium, post office, rotunda, sanatorium, school;** agricultural and rural types include **barn, blind, cellar, dovecot, farrowing house, kennel, pole structure, potato hole, potato house, Quonset hut, shed, stable, smokehouse, storehouse.** See also **room, silo. 2.** For National Register purposes, may also be used to refer to a historically and functionally related unit, such as a courthouse and jail or a house and barn.

building block (19c) Same as **concrete block.**

building brick (late 20c) Same as **common brick.**

building code Government-adopted regulations governing the safe and healthy design and construction of individual structures, both for new construction and rehabilitation; usually refers to those codes that govern structural and architectural matters, as opposed to a **mechanical code, plumbing code,** or **electri-**

cal code; although typically developed locally beginning in the late 19c, most are developed nationally, regionally, or by states by the late 20c; usually administered by the local **building official;** many codes have specific waivers for historic structures; types include **BOCA Code, CABO Code, National Building Code, Uniform Building Code.** See also **Americans with Disabilities Act Accessibility Guidelines, egress requirements, separation of occupancies, zoning code.**

building envelope The outer bounds, both vertically and horizontally, of an enclosed structure; the maximum extent is often defined by **zoning.**

building inspector **1.** A **building official,** usually employed by a local government, who visits construction sites to observe work in progress and enforce **building codes.** **2.** A private sector firm or individual that conducts a prepurchase inspection of a property. See also **construction observation, testing.**

building line An imaginary line set at a fixed distance from a street or other right-of-way, beyond which no building facade may be constructed. See also **setback line.**

building material Any or all of the products and raw materials used to construct a building, including **bricks, cement, lime, lumber, pipe, sand;** generally does not include **builder's hardware** or mechanical and electrical fixtures and equipment. Also known as **tignum.**

building occupancy A general classification of the type of use of a structure, such as residential or business; used in **building codes** to determine the level of fire hazard and, consequently, the size and type of construction permitted, egress requirements, and other restrictions.

building official An employee of a government agency that administers a **building code;** may be an architect or engineer who reviews plans or a **building inspector** experienced in construction methods.

building paper **1.** A heavy, water-resistant paper used on sheathing below siding or roofing or below finish flooring. See also **roofing felt.** **2.** (19c) Any heavy paper used in a building, such as for acoustical or thermal insulation. See also **felt.**

building permit Written authorization from the appropriate government agency to proceed with construction work; typically a permit is required for (1) constructing, enlarging, altering, or demolishing a building or structure; (2) changing the use of a building; (3) installing or altering mechanical, plumbing, or electrical systems; common types include a basic **building permit,** and a **mechanical permit, plumbing permit, electrical permit** related to the individual trades.

Building Preservation Plan (BPP) A standardized, automated system used by the U.S. General Services Administration for the analysis, management, and treatments of its historic buildings; includes ratings of the historic significance of a building's elements. See also **historic structure report.**

building stone Any type of stone suitable for use in exterior construction; includes **dolomite, diorite, granite, limestone, quartzite, sandstone,** and some types of **marble.** See also **ornamental stone, stonework, wall stone.**

building survey A detailed investigation and recording of the present appearance and condition of a structure; in addition to visual inspection, diagnostic instruments may be used. See also **building inspector, historic structure report, measured drawing.**

built arch (19c) A nonmasonry structure having the shape of an **arch,** such as a laminated wood arch or an **arched truss.**

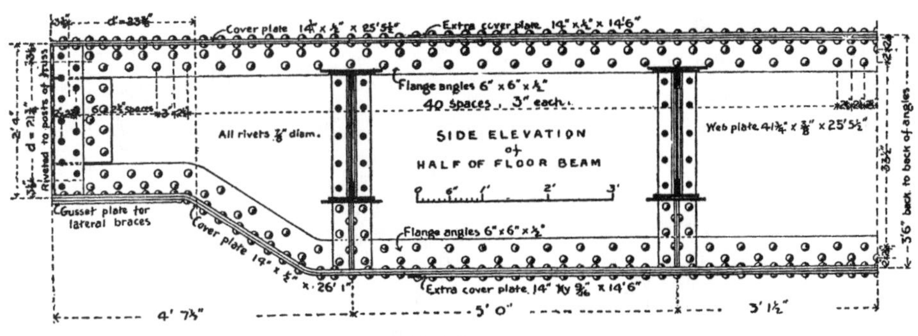

built beam

built beam, built-up beam A beam composed of multiple parts; types include **box beam, compound beam, flitch beam, lattice beam, plate beam.** See also **angle girder.**

built environment That portion of the physical surroundings created by humans, as opposed to the natural environment; includes **site, building, structure, object.** See also **cultural landscape, townscape.**

built terrace A terrace constructed by filling above the existing grade of a sloped hillside. Also known as **terrace of construction.**

built-up A wood framing member composed of two or more individual pieces, such as a built-up plate. See also **built arch, built beam.**

built-up roof A water-resistant coating on a low-slope roof composed of asphalt mopped on a flexible material; (18c–early 19c) asphalt- or tar-soaked canvas held down by wood battens or gravel; (19c–present) several overlapping layers of roofing felt sealed with a heated asphalt compound and usually protected by spread gravel on the top surface; types include **three ply, four ply, gravel roof, slag roof.** Also known as **ready roofing.**

bulb angle A **rolled section** in the form of an L-shaped angle with a thickened, rounded end on the longer leg.

bulb beam A bulb angle or bulb-tee used as a beam.

bulb-tee, bulb-T An iron or steel rolled section with a T-shaped cross section with a thickened, rounded bottom leg. Also known as **deck beam, T-bulb.** See also **angle bulb.**

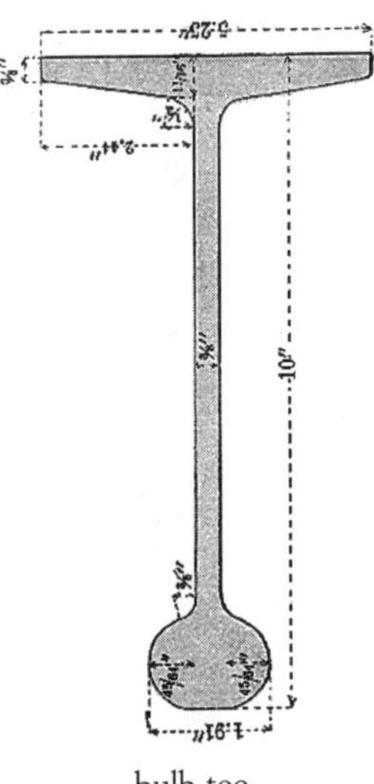

bulb-tee

bulkhead, (18c) **bolk head** **1.** A penthouse with a sloped roof covering the top of a stair or elevator, or a similar structure projecting above a floor. **2.** (mid-19c–present) A sloped hatchway that opens to a cellar stairway. Also known as **cellar cap. 3.** (20c) A lowered portion of the ceiling at the edge of a room. Also known as **soffit.** See also **draft stop. 4.** A protective vertical retaining wall along a shoreline or around a bridge pier; may be of timber or masonry. See also **seawall.**

bulkhead light A cellar window above an entrance door; enclosed on the interior by a bulkhead that projects above the floor above the cellar.

bull header Same as **rowlock.**

bullion, bullion point Same as **bull's-eye** (sense 2).

bullnose, bull nose, (19c) **bull's nose** A rounded corner, as in a bullnose brick, corner bead, or edge tile.

bullnosed step The bottom step or steps of a flight of stairs that project beyond and return to the stringer with a half round end.

bull pine An inexact name used for **ponderosa pine, yellow pine** (sense 1), and several other species.

bull stretcher Same as **shiner.**

bull's-eye **1.** A small circular window; also known as **oculus, oeil-de-boeuf.** **2.** The raised circular center of a piece of hand-blown glass; also known as **bullion, roundel.** See also **crown glass, rondelle.** **3.** An ornamental device with concentric circles similar to an archery target.

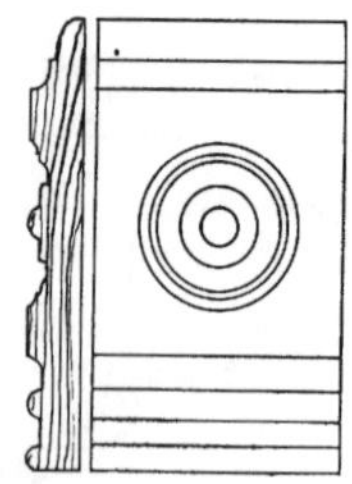

bull's-eye (sense 3)

bull's-eye light A single window opening glazed with a crown glass **bull's-eye;** refracts light into an interior space.

bull's head Same as **bucranium.**

bundle pier A pier with an undulating outline, used in Gothic style architecture; the separation of forms is less distinct than that in a **compound pier.**

bungalow An inexact term for a late 19c–mid-20c type of small house, borrowed from the 19c British term for a one-story house in India with an encircling veranda and tile or thatched roof; in North America, more a set of concepts than a building type; characterized by materials that express their natural state, interconnected interior spaces, low, broad form, and lack of applied ornamentation; often has a

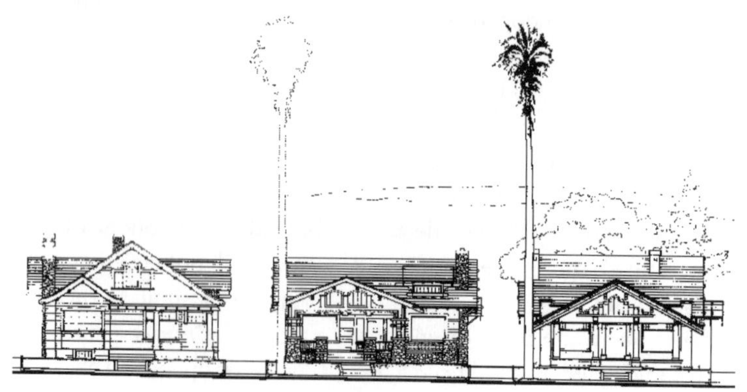

bungalow
Hanchett Residence Park
San Jose, California, ca. 1905

low-pitched gable or hip roof and a porch with massive columns; common details include wide, overhanging eaves with exposed rafter tails, projecting beam ends, and triangular knee braces at gable eaves, attached pergolas, and bungalow windows; although most often in the **Craftsman style,** may be any 20c style or combination of styles.

bungalow door (20c) Any of various front door designs featuring lights in the top portion of the door; usually with divided lights above two or three long, vertical, flat panels.

bungalow door

bungalow window (20c) A double-hung window with a single light in the bottom sash and rectangular, divided lights in the upper sash.

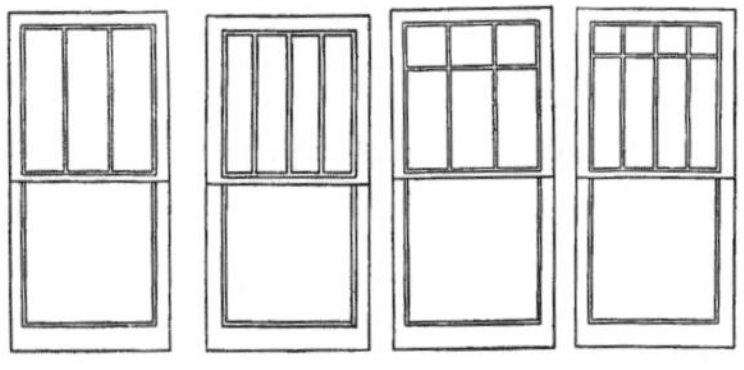

bungalow window

bunk A small compartment, shelf, or recess used as a sleeping place; typically one of several.

bunkhouse A simple dormitory building with a number of **bunks** and/or beds.

Burgundy pitch A yellowish, hard, brittle **pitch** made by boiling down Norway spruce sap.

burial ground Same as **graveyard.**

burl A knot in a tree that produces wood with large, swirling grain distortions.

burnetizing (19c) A trade name process for adding chemical preservatives to wood; used for bridge timbers.

burning fluid A volatile, potentially explosive mixture of alcohol and turpentine; used in a **burning fluid lamp.**

burning fluid lamp Any of various types of **oil lamp** fueled by **burning fluid,** ca. 1830–1860; displaced by the **kerosene lamp.** Also known as **camphene lamp.**

burnt Charred by fire; used on the tops and bottoms of fence posts to prevent rot.

burnt Sienna A rich, brownish red paint **pigment** made by roasting **raw Sienna.**

burnt umber A chocolate brown paint **pigment** made by roasting **raw umber.**

burying ground Same as **graveyard.**

bus bar A large, bare-metal bar used to distribute the main electric current within a building or main switchboard; typically copper or aluminum; also known as **bus-rod, bus-wire.**

bus duct A linear enclosure for a **bus bar.**

bushhammered, bush hammered The tooled surface texture of soft stone blocks produced by the serrated face of a bushhammer; may be hand or machine tooled. See also **hammer-dressed work, patent bush hammered, stone work.**

bus-rod (19c) A **bus bar** with a circular cross section.

busybody Same as **window mirror.**

bus-wire (19c) A **bus bar** with a circular cross section.

butler's pantry A small room between the kitchen and dining room fitted with a sink, counter, and cupboards. Also known as **butler's room.** See also **buffet, buttery, pantry.**

butler's room Same as **butler's pantry.**

butment (18c) Same as **abutment.**

buts Same as **butt hinge.**

butt **1.** The back or bottom end of a building element, such as the hinged edge of a door or the squared end of a stud. **2.** The thick, lower edge of a shingle. **3.** The wider end of a log. **4.** Same as **butt joint.**

butt and butt A **butt joint** formed where the butt ends of two building elements touch each other.

butt-and-strap hinge Same as **cross-garnet** or **T-hinge.**

butt block A wood block with one end cut at a right angle to the grain of the truss member it abuts. See also **normal cut.**

butt end Same as **butt** (senses 3 and 4).

butter joint A very narrow **mortar joint** made with mortar of butterlike consistency.

butterfly hinge (20c) Same as **dovetail hinge.**

butterfly roof Two shed roofs that meet in a valley.

butternut A hardwood tree with light brown, soft, coarse-grained wood that polishes to a satiny luster; used for interior millwork; found in the eastern half of the U.S. from the northern Gulf states to the Great Lakes and southern Maine; *Juglans cinerea.* Also known as **white walnut.**

buttery **1.** (pre-19c) A dairy room adjacent to the kitchen. **2.** (pre-19c) A storeroom for bulk food and/or kitchen implements. **3.** A **butler's pantry** where china and condiments are stored.

butt hinge, (18c) **but hinge, buts** A plate **hinge** mortised into both the edge of a door and the frame; composed of two rectangular **leafs** with **knuckles** that surround a **hinge pin;** only the knuckles are exposed when the door is closed; types include **loose joint hinge, parliament hinge, rising-butt hinge, spring-butt hinge.** See also **olive-knuckle hinge, paumelle hinge, pivot hinge.**

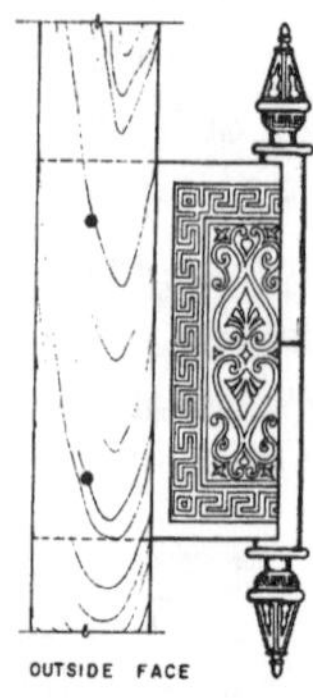

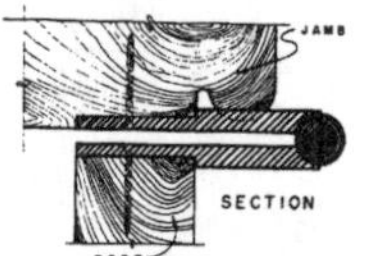

butt hinge

butt joint **1.** A **joint** formed by the squared end of one building element resting against another but not overlapping; types include **butt and butt, T-joint.** Also known as **abutment joint, butt.** See also **lap joint.** **2.** A stonework mortar joint in which the adjoining stone blocks have squared edges. See also **quirk joint.** **3.** A carpentry joint in which two pieces of wood touch with their grains at right angles to one another.

button **1.** An electrical push button. **2.** A piece of wood or metal mounted onto the casing next to a door, casement window, or shutter, and rotated to secure it. **3.** A small, carved decoration between a caulicole and a bud of a Corinthian capital. **4.** Any protruding fixed knob, such as a door pull or the end of a tracery cusp.

button head A domed head, such as used on rivets.

button lac A dark brown, translucent **shellac** made from unbleached lac dissolved in alcohol.

buttress A projecting pier used to stiffen a masonry wall, especially when on the exterior of the wall; forms include **angle buttress, clasping buttress, diagonal buttress, flying buttress, setback buttress, setoff buttress.**

buttress pier An exterior wall pier that both supports the weight of the masonry wall and receives the thrust from an interior vault.

butts and bounds (pre-20c) The short and long dimensions of a rectangular plot of land.

butt weld A welded joint connecting two pieces of metal that are butted together but not overlapping.

buyer's agent A **real estate agent** who represents the purchaser or lessee of a property, rather than the seller or lessor.

buylding (pre-18c) Same as **building.**

BX cable Insulated electric wires spiral wrapped with steel cut from galvanized sheets; first used in 1901 and common from 1910 to ca. 1950. See also **armored cable, electric wiring, flexible metal conduit.**

BXL cable BX cable with lead sheathing around the wires inside the spiral steel covering.

bypass, (pre-20c) **bye-pass** An alternate route for flow, including (1) a pipe or channel in or around a valve that allows fluid to flow even though the valve is in the closed position; (2) (20c) a road that diverts traffic around a congested area; (3) A channel that deflects floodwaters; (4) a passage in poorly designed plumbing that allows sewer gas into a building.

bypath (19c) A secondary, secluded, or indirect path.

Byrkit lath A brand-name of **sheathing lath.**

byzant Same as **bezant.**

Byzantine arch Same as **horseshoe arch.**

Byzantine Revival style An architectural **style** of the late 19c characterized by use of Byzantine forms and decoration, including domes supported on high drums, arcades with plain, shafted columns, structural polychromy, and bas-relief decorative work.

cabaña **1.** [Spanish] A rustic hut or cabin. **2.** (20c) A bathhouse at the beach.

cabildo In a Spanish colonial cathedral, a chapter house used for meetings of an ecclesiastical group such as monks or nuns.

cabin, (pre-19c) **caban, cabane, cabbin, cabine** **1.** A small, crudely constructed dwelling; may have a living room with a fireplace plus one or more small rooms; in the 17c also referred to Native American dwellings. **2.** A room aboard a vessel. See also **log cabin, slave cabin.**

cabin (sense 1)

cabinet **1.** (pre-19c) A closet or small room, especially the innermost of a series of rooms used as a study or a room aboard a vessel. **2.** (pre-20c) A room used for display of precious or scientific objects. **3.** The room in which a council or cabinet meets. **4.** A built-in or freestanding piece of furniture fitted with drawers and/or shelves, with the shelves typically behind one or a pair of doors.

cabinet finish (19c) A varnished, paneled hardwood room interior, as opposed to a painted, softwood board interior.

cabinet molding (19c) Same as **cable molding.**

cabinet window A projecting display window; common in stores in the early 19c.

cabinetwork Fine woodwork that includes such elements as built-in shelves, drawers, and cabinets. See also **casework, millwork.**

cabin roof, (pre-19c) **cabbin roof** A method of constructing the gable end and roof structure of a **log cabin** by stacking **gable logs** of decreasing length on the two end walls to create steps on which a series of log roof beams are placed lengthwise.

cable **1.** Twisted strands of copper or other metals for supplying electric power. **2.** A heavy wire rope used to support or apply tension to a structural element. **3.** The bead of a **cabled column** or **cabled flute.**

cabled column A column with a shaft in the stylized shape of twisted strands of a large fiber rope; the cross section of the surface has the form of parallel half rounds. See also **solomonic column, twisted column, spiral fluted column.**

cabled flute, cable fluted, cable fluting Having semicircular convex moldings in the center of column or pilaster flutes, usually starting at the base of the column and stopping at one-third to one-half of the shaft height; may be plain or **cable molding.** See also **cabled column, stopped flute.**

cabling **1.** Same as **cable molding.** **2.** Having **cabled flutes.**

cable molding A molding with parallel, diagonal half rounds in the stylized form of twisted strands of a fiber rope. Also known as **rope molding, rope torus, rudenture.**

CABO Code Abbr. for Council of American Building Officials One- and Two-Family Dwelling Code.

CAD (late-20c) Abbr. for Computer Assisted Drafting.

CADD (late-20c) Abbr. for Computer Assisted Design and Drafting.

caement (18c) Same as **cement.**

Caen stone cement A plaster material composed of crushed limestone from Caen, France, mixed with cements; used to imitate stone and typically scored and finished to resemble ashlar.

cage **1.** (pre-20c) A single room structure used to temporarily confine prisoners. See also **jail.** **2.** A timber frame lining a mining shaft.

cage construction **1.** (late 19c) **Skeleton construction** with self supporting exterior masonry walls. **2.** (20c) Same as **skeleton construction.**

cairn A pile of stones used as a marker or monument.

caisson **1.** Same as **coffer.** **2.** A watertight enclosure used for underwater construction.

calathus The bell of a Corinthian, or similar, capital.

calcareous cement Any of several varieties of **cement** composed of calcareous material (calcined limestone or chalk) mixed with argillaceous material (clay or slate) or siliceous material (sand, quartz, or slag); types include **hydraulic cement, Maya cement, natural cement, portland cement, Roman cement, slate cement.**

calcimine, kalsomine An interior **paint** composed of a mixture of clear glue, whiting or zinc white, and water; colored pigments may be added; typically used on plaster surfaces.

calcine **1.** The process of heating a substance so that water or other vapors are driven off and it becomes a powder. **2.** Naturally occurring calcium carbonate, such as limestone or chalk, that has been crushed and heated until it becomes a powder. See also **lime, plaster.**

calcined plaster Same as **plaster of Paris.**

calcium light Same as **Drummond light.**

calf's-tongue molding, calves'-tongue molding A molding with a series of pointed elements raised above their background; common in early medieval style archivolts.

calico marble A **breccia marble** with inclusions up to several inches in diameter; quarried at Point of Rocks, Maryland; used for columns in the Old Hall of Representatives in the U.S. Capitol. Also known as **Frederick County marble, Potomac breccia.**

caliduct (pre-20c) **1.** A hot air duct. **2.** (pre-19c) A hot water or steam pipe.

California balsam poplar A large hardwood tree with greenish to tan, soft, straight-grained wood found on the Pacific coast from San Diego to British Columbia; used primarily for painted millwork; *Populus trichocarpa.* See also **balsam poplar, poplar.**

California nut pine Same as **Sabine's pine.**

California valley (late 20c) Same as **swept valley.**

California white oak Same as **western oak.**

calotte **1.** A cap-shaped element, especially a cupola or half cupola. **2.** The lead covering of a spire. **3.** (18c) Same as **conch.**

Calway River marble A deep red, white-veined **marble** quarried in the vicinity of the Calway River, Quebec.

camber The slight upward curve of the bottom of an arch, beam, or truss, designed to counteract sagging from the weight of the structure.

camber arch A **flat arch** with an intrados that has a slight concave rise toward the center. See also **jack arch.**

camber beam A beam formed with a slight upward bend in the middle, so that after loading the beam does not sag below level.

cambered Fink truss A **Fink truss** with a cambered bottom chord. Also known as **Belgian truss, French truss.**

cambered Howe truss A triangular **Howe truss** with a pair of bottom chords that slope upward to the bottom of a center post; used as a roof truss. Also known as **English truss.**

came (pl. **came**) An H-shaped metal strip that holds the pieces of stained or cut glass in a window; typically composed of cast lead, **turned lead,** or other soft metals. Also known as **window lead.** See also **leaded window.**

camelback A house type in which the front part of the house is one-story tall and the rear is two stories; popular in New Orleans in the late 19c.

camelback
Kuntz "Shotgun" House
side elevation
Louisville, Kentucky, ca. 1889

camelback truss A **Pratt truss** with the overall shape of a **bowstring truss.**

cameo glass Flash glass cut with a decorative pattern so that the clear glass shows through the colored glass.

camera obscura **1.** (19c) A structure in which spectators view images of exterior views projected on a white table or mirror in the center of a darkened room. Also known as **belvedere, optick chamber. 2.** An optical device that projects the image of an exterior object on a plane surface.

camerated (18c) Vaulted or arched.

campana **1.** The **bell** of a Corinthian capital. **2.** Same as **gutta** (senses 1 and 2).

campanile A **bell tower,** especially when freestanding; from the Italian term.

camp ceiling Same as **tray ceiling.**

camphene (pre-20c) Same as **turpentine,** especially as an ingredient in **burning fluid.**

Canada Mortgage and Housing Corporation (CMHC) The Canadian federal agency that administers housing and urban development policies.

Canada pitch Same as **hemlock pitch.**

Canadian Association of Professional Conservators (CAPC) A Canadian association that accredits conservators of historic objects, artwork, and other artifacts.

Canadian Conference on Historical Resources (CCHR) A self-directed forum established in 1961 that meets annually for an informal and open exchange on heritage resource conservation and management issues within federal/provincial/territorial jurisdictions.

Canadian hemlock Same as **eastern hemlock.**

Canadian Heritage Information Network (CHIN) A special operating agency of the Cultural Development and Heritage Sector of the federal Department of Canadian Heritage (Canada), created in 1972 to establish a comprehensive inventory of Canadian museum collections and to provide collection management services to institutions in all regions of the country; mandate broadened by Canadian Museum Policy of 1990 to include the development of services that increase museum participation in the network, types of information available, analysis of technology and its use in museums, and better information standards;

has three national databases: humanities, natural sciences, and archaeological sites.

Canadian Heritage Rivers System (CHRS) Established in 1984 by the federal, provincial, and territorial governments to give national recognition to, and conserve and protect, the important rivers of Canada.

Canadian Institute of Quantity Surveyors (CIQS) A national membership organization for professional quantity surveyors in Canada.

Canadian Inventory of Historic Buildings (CIHB) A computer-based national archive of the architectural heritage of Canada established in 1970 by the National Historic Sites Directorate, **Parks Canada.**

Canadian Mortgage and Housing Corporation (CMHC) A federal Crown corporation established by the **National Housing Act** as Canada's national housing agency; mandate includes construction of new houses, repair and modernization of existing houses, and the improvement of housing and living conditions.

Canadian Parks Service The predecessor to **Parks Canada.**

Canadian Register of Heritage Properties (CRHP) A national list of properties in Canada recognized as being of notable heritage significance and worthy of preservation; created in 1992 and reported on annually by the Federal/Provincial/Territorial Conference of Ministers Responsible for Culture and Historic Resources. See also **Canadian Inventory of Historic Buildings, Register of Federal Heritage Buildings.**

Canadian turpentine Turpentine manufactured in Canada from balsam fir. See also **American turpentine, Carolina turpentine.**

canal **1.** An artificially constructed waterway; used for transportation, for moving water for mill power or irrigation, or for a decorative landscape feature; components may include **embankment, lift-lock, towpath.** See also **sluice.** **2.** A groove or channel in an architectural feature, such as a drip in a soffit, the recessed space between two decorative elements, or the groove between the fillets of an Ionic volute. Also known as **canalis, channel, flute, kennel.** See also **canale, cannelated.**

canale A **viga** with a large groove cut into the top surface at the end to drain water away from the roof; projects through the parapet of some flat-roofed **adobe** or stone buildings found in southwestern U.S. and Mexico. See also **Pueblo, Spanish Colonial.**

canalis Same as **canal** (sense 2).

canal lift **1.** An inclined railroad with a cradle that transports a canal boat between different levels of a canal. **2.** Same as **canal lock.**

canal lock A **lift-lock** used along a navigation canal.

canary glass A yellow glass manufactured with uranium oxide.

cancela In Spanish Colonial style architecture, a wood latticework gate; the grillwork is often formed by turned spindles, **cancelli,** or scrollwork. Also known as **porton.**

cancelli Thin bars or balusters of a lattice work railing or screen. See also **cancela.**

candle An open-flame lighting device composed of a fiber wick encased in a rod of fuel; fuel types include beeswax, **bayberry wax** (17c–present), tallow (pre-20c), **spermaceti** (mid-18c–early 19c), animal fat stearin (early–late 19c), paraffin (ca. 1860–present).

candle holder Any device that supports a lighted candle; may be portable or a fixture; candlelight was the primary source of night lighting until mid-19c. See also **light fixture.**

candlesnuffer A projecting, three-quarter round turret with a conical roof, with the base of the turret starting above the ground level; the shape of the turret approximates that of a traditional candlesnuffer with a conical top.

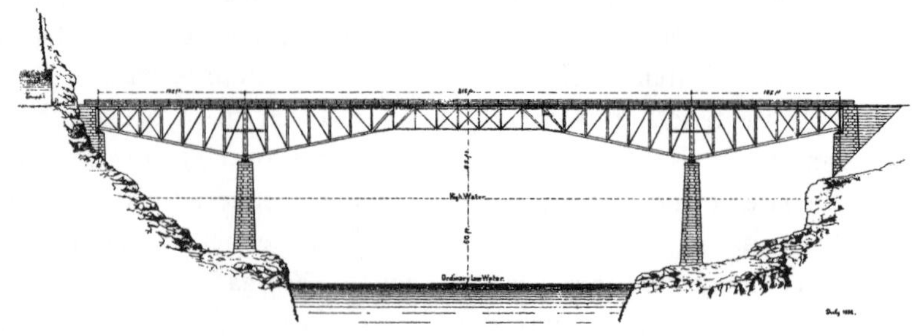

cantilever
Fraser River Bridge
Niagara Falls

candlewood pine A large **pine** tree with very pitchy wood; found in Mexico; used for lumber and turpentine; *Pinus teocote.* Also known as **okote pine.**

cane bolt A **drop bolt** in the form of a metal rod with a bent head.

canephora, canephore A **caryatid** with a basket-shaped capital on the woman's head.

cannelated Having a grooved or fluted surface. See also **canal, reeding.**

canoe birch Same as **white birch.**

canopy **1.** (20c) A projecting roof structure that shelters an entrance to a building. See also **appentice.** **2.** An ornamental covering over an altar, niche, statue, tomb, or similar feature; may project from a wall or be supported on columns. See also **sounding board, type.**

cant An inclined surface; of greater extent than a **bevel.** See also **cant board, cant moulding, cant strip.**

cantaliver **1.** (18c–19c) One of a series of cantilevered or bracketed supports of a cornice and eaves or balcony; similar in appearance to a **modillion.** **2.** (19c) Same as **cantilever.**

cant board A board with its face set at an angle to shed water, as on a coping.

cantilever, (pre-20c) **cantaliver** A beam or truss with an unsupported end projecting past the bearing; may support any kind of projecting element including a building overhang, part of a bridge, or a balcony.

cant moulding (19c) **1.** Any **molding** with a beveled back; used for placing in a corner. See also **spring molding.** **2.** Any molding with a beveled slope on the front face.

cantoned (18c) Having projecting decoration at an exterior corner, such as quoins or pilasters.

cant strip **1.** A filler piece cut at an angle (commonly 45 degrees) to make a transition from a horizontal roof to a vertical surface. **2.** A wood strip with a small rectangular cross section placed below the bottom edge of the lowest course of slate to make its slope the same as the upper courses.

caoutchouc (19c) Same as rubber cement or rubber. Also known as **gum elastic.** See also **gutta percha.**

CAP **Conservation Assessment Program**

cap **1.** An element, such as a molding or projection, that covers or forms the top of an architectural feature, including a door entablature or lintel and a mantelshelf. See also **cap flashing, cap of the triglyph, capped rail, capstone, cap trim.** **2.** Abbr. of **capital** (sense 1). **3.** The rotating top of a windmill. **4.** A cylindrical cover for the end of a plumbing pipe.

CAPC **Canadian Association of Professional Conservators**

Cape Cod house **1.** A simple, timber frame, one- or one-and-one-half-story side-gable house with a central chimney and steeply pitched wood shingle roof; built beginning ca. 1700 in eastern Massachusetts, by 1740 found in most of New England and Long Island, New York; typically with wood shingle or clapboard siding, multipaned windows, and flat wood trim at openings and corners; variations include **half house, three-quarter house, full cape;** 19c examples often have Greek Revival details. **2.** A Colonial Revival style house based on the original; popular in the U.S. in the 1920s and 1940–50s; common additions to the original style include brick veneer, dormers, and a Georgian style entry door.

cap flashing Same as **counterflashing.**

capital, (pre-20c) **capitel,** (pre-19c) **capitol** **1.** The topmost portion of a column or pier; types include **cushion capital, protomai capital, scalloped capital, water-leaf capital.** Also known as **cap.** See also **classical orders.** **2.** Funds invested in a development project. **3.** The head of a chimney or still.

capital improvement An improvement made to **real estate** that has an extended lifetime and increases the property's value, such as new construction, rehabilitation, or replacement of mechanical equipment, as opposed to maintenance work, such as painting.

capital value The market value of **real estate** minus debts owed against it, such as a mortgage.

capitol **1.** (18c–present) The building occupied by the legislative body of a national, state, or

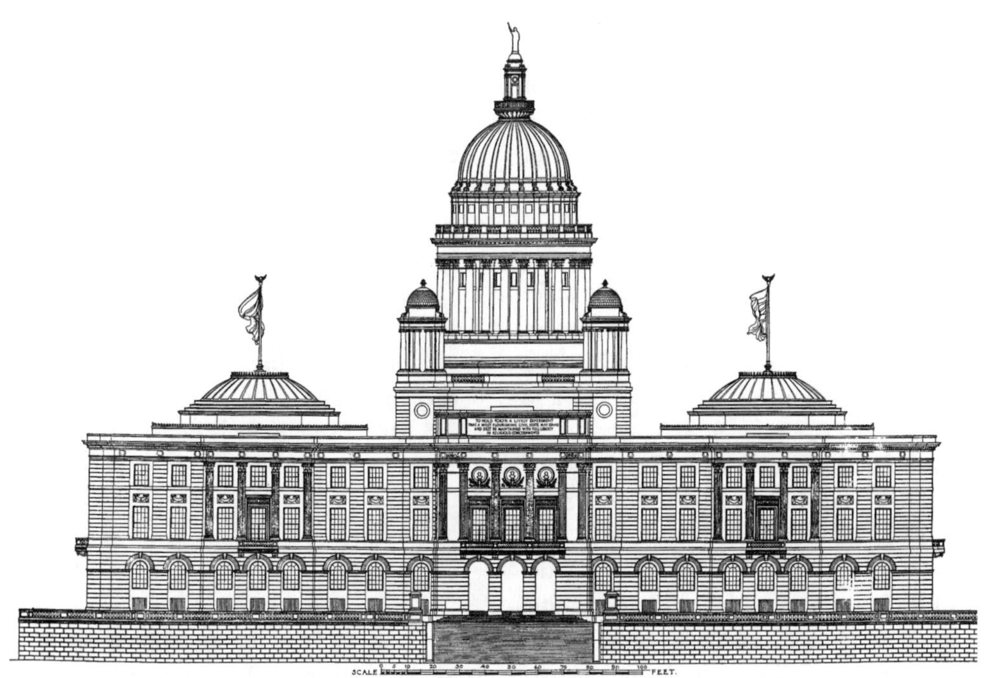

capitol (sense 1)
Rhode Island State Capitol
Providence, Rhode Island

provincial government. Also known as **statehouse.** **2.** (pre-19c) Same as **capital.**

cap of the triglyph A narrow molding with a rectangular cross section at the top of a Doric frieze; wraps around the top of the **triglyph.**

caponier, caponière Part of a **fortification** located in or across a ditch, especially a single or double row of stockade or a row of palisades; enables firing in both directions along the ditch. **2.** An unroofed passage with walls on both sides that connects various areas of a fortification.

capped rail A steel-topped iron railroad **rail.**

capstone **1.** Same as **coping stone.** **2.** The top row of stones on a retaining wall, or the top stone of a pier. **3.** The top stone of a corbeled vault.

cap screw A **machine screw** with a cylindrical slotted head.

cap trim **1.** Any wood molding that overlaps the top of elements such as wainscots or baseboards. See also **surbase.** **2.** (20c) A wood molding approximately in the shape of the top portion of a classical style cornice; typically with overall dimensions of 1⅜ × 3½ inches.

caracole, caracol (pre-19c) Same as **spiral stair.**

carbon black Any black pigment composed of relatively pure carbon; varieties include **drop black, ivory black,** and soot. See also **graphite.**

carbon-black-filled polyethylene **Polyethylene** containing **carbon black** pigment; resists deterioration by ultraviolet rays; often used as a vapor barrier. Also known as **builder's plastic.**

carbon dioxide system A **foam extinguishing system** that floods a space with carbon dioxide gas to put out a fire by displacing the oxygen normally present; used primarily in such areas as storage for museum collections or in electrical equipment that would be damaged by water from a **sprinkler system;** cannot be used in spaces that are normally occupied by people; may not extinguish smoldering fires.

carbon-filament bulb An incandescent electric lamp that uses a thin, glowing piece of carbon fiber; invented by Thomas A. Edison and used ca. 1880–ca. 1910. Also known as **hairpin filament bulb.**

carbon steel Same as **soft steel.**

carborundum finish A very smooth, machine-cut surface texture of stone blocks. See also **stonework.**

carcass, carcase **1.** (pre-20c) The wood framing of a structure, without sheathing or flooring. **2.** (pre-20c) The wood framing and sheathing of a structure, including the floors, roof, and partitions but excluding lathing and trim. See also **case, hull.** **3.** A building shell remaining after the interior finishes and trim have been removed. See also **gut rehab.** **4.** The shell of a building, such as a factory, without equipment, fixtures, or machinery.

carcass floor, carcase floor (pre-20c) The structural girders and joists that support a subfloor and finish floor.

Carolina turpentine **Turpentine** manufactured in North or South Carolina from the longleaf pine. See also **Canadian turpentine, American turpentine.**

carpenter ant Any of various ants that nest in galleries of tunnels bored in wood; in North America of the genus *Camponotus* such as *Formica pennsylvanica.* See also **carpenter bee, termite.**

carpenter bee A solitary bee that lays its eggs in holes bored in dead wood; North American species include the bumblebee-sized *Xylocopa viginica.* See also **carpenter ant, termite.**

Carpenter Gothic, Carpenter's Gothic Vernacular wood **Gothic Revival style** architecture

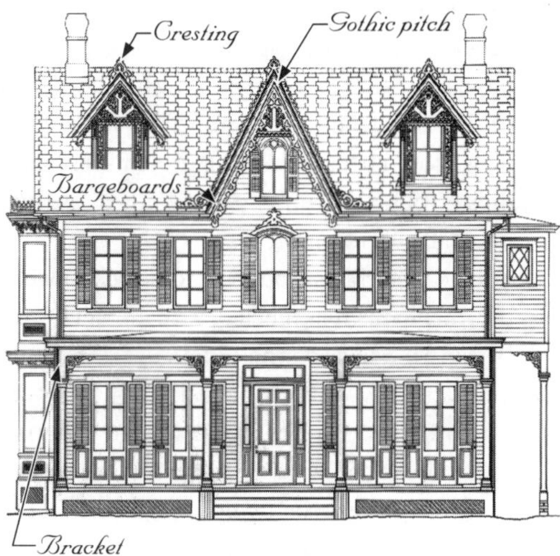

Carpenter Gothic
J. Stratton Ware House
Cape May, New Jersey

with ornate wood scrollwork tracery, especially bargeboards, cresting, and brackets. Also known as **steamboat Gothic.**

carport (20c) A roofed automobile shelter adjoining a house and open on two or more sides; term first used by Frank Lloyd Wright in connection with his Usonian houses. See also **garage.**

Carrara glass A trade name for thick, solid-color **structural glass** cast in panels and used as a wall veneer; common 1900–40, especially on **Art Deco** style buildings.

Carrara marble A fine, white marble quarried in the vicinity of Carrara, Italy.

carreau A small pane of glass or an encaustic tile; typically square or diamond shaped. Also known as **tessera.**

carrelage (19c) Paving of fired-clay units, such as encaustic tile, terra-cotta, or bricks.

carriage Same as **stringer.**

carriage bolt A cylindrical metal rod with a domed head and a threaded end; a square shank below the bottom of the head prevents the bolt from rotating.

carriage house (late 18c–present) An outbuilding for sheltering horse-drawn carriages, coaches, or automobiles; frequently combined with a **stable** or an upper level for storage or servants' quarters. Also known as **chair house, chaise house, coach house.** See also **cart house, garage.**

carriage porch (19c) A covered drive for sheltering passengers. See also **porte cochere.**

carrying capacity (20c) The number of visitors that can be accommodated at a facility, such as a park or historic site, at any particular time.

cart house An outbuilding which shelters a horse-drawn, two-wheeled cart. See also **carriage house.**

carton pierre A product composed of papier-mâché and formed to resemble stone carving; often composed of paper, glue, whiting, and chalk.

cartouche, (18c) **cartouse, cartouze** **1.** A bas-relief, scroll-shaped ornament. **2.** A raised circular or oval decoration, especially when in the center of other bas-relief elements.

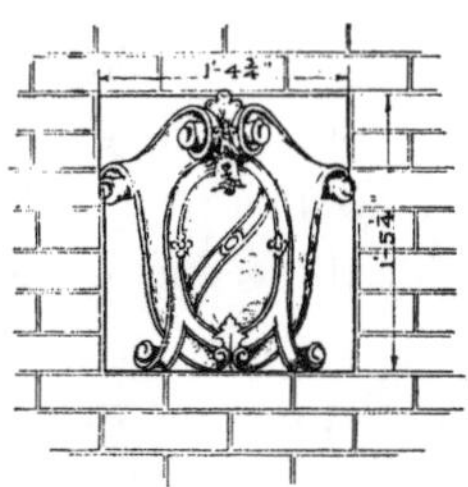

cartouche (sense 2)

cartridge (18c) Same as **cartouche.**

caryatic order A series of caryatids and the entablature they support. See also **Classical orders.**

caryatid A column or pilaster in the form of a robed female figure; typically used to represent virtues such as justice, prudence, and temperance; named by the ancient Greeks for the captive women of Caria. See also **atlas, herm, term.**

casa [Spanish] Same as **house.**

Casberg block A trade name for **concrete block** with small chips of colored glass exposed on the surface; manufactured in Wisconsin.

case **1.** The exterior covering of a building, including **ashlar, brick veneer, siding.** See also **casing** and terms beginning with **cased.** **2.** Same as **doorframe** or **window frame.** **3.** The metal box enclosing the workings of a lock. **4.** (West Indies) A complete, small, wood frame house from the sill up; may be movable or permanently attached to a pile foundation; originally a slave dwelling that was moved to different sugar cane fields at harvest time. **5.** The lining of a mine **gallery.** **6.** (pre-20c) A measure of **crown glass** equal to 225 square feet.

case bay (19c) An interior floor or roof **bay** (sense 2). See also **tail bay.**

cased Covered with another material, especially wood boards.

cased beam Same as **box beam.**

cased frame The wood **window frame** of a double-hung window, including the **sash pockets.**

cased glass Two or more layers of glass of different colors fused together; types include **flash glass.**

cased opening An interior window or doorway trimmed with casing but without a sash or door. Also known as **trimmed opening.**

case hardened Same as **tempered steel.**

casein A protein component of various types of animal milk; precipitated by bacteria in sour milk or rennet and used for **casein glue** and **casein paint.**

casein glue A wood glue composed of **casein** dissolved in a solution of borax, or casein mixed with hydrated lime. See also **casein paint.**

casein paint A water-based paint composed of **casein, quicklime,** pigments, and, sometimes, oil; used most frequently on fresh plaster; hard to dissolve when dry, it must be made fresh daily from cheese, milk, or proteins similar to those found in milk. Also known as **milk paint, farmers paint.**

case lock A surface-mounted door lock in which the mechanism is enclosed in a metal **case** (sense 3). See also **stock lock.**

casemate **1.** A vaulted, bombproof chamber with a wall opening for firing a large gun; used in fortifications ca. 1800–65; sometimes also used for storage or living quarters. **2.** (18c) Same as **casement** (sense 3).

casement **1.** A window sash hinged on one side so that it opens by swinging in or out; types include **French casement, lattice window.** **2.** (18c–19c) A **cavetto** molding, one-quarter or one-sixth of a circle. Also known as **scotia.**

casement window A **window** with one or more casement sashes; may also have fixed lights; the most common type of window in North America until the early 18c.

case steps (pre-20c) A millwork **stair.**

casework High-quality shelving and display cases, such as for a store; often used to mean **cabinetwork,** especially kitchen cabinets.

casing **1.** The wood trim on the surface of the wall surrounding a window or door, at a right angle to the jambs. **2.** (18c) Exterior stucco scored to resemble ashlar. **3.** Same as **well casing.** See also **well curb.**

casing bead A metal strip used to form the edge of a plaster surface at an opening, such as the edge of a door or window.

casino, (19c) **cassino** **1.** A building or room used for public recreation such as dancing, music, and social gatherings. **2.** (20c) A building, or a portion of a building, housing a gambling establishment; from the card game of the same name. **3.** (19c) A house that is, or appears to be, a one-story structure in a garden.

castellate Built like, or in the appearance of, a castle, especially with battlements or turrets.

cast glass Same as **plate glass** or **rolled glass.**

cast-in-place **Cast stone, concrete,** or a similar material that is formed in situ, as opposed to being **precast.**

cast iron A hard, brittle, high carbon content (2.5–4 percent) **iron** formed by casting in foundry molds; used for structural and decorative building components in North America beginning in the 1830s with a complete cast-iron building system patented in the U.S. by James Bogardus in 1849; typically used in the mid-19c for the front facade and interior columns in buildings up to six stories in height in combination with brick side walls and wood joists; varieties include **gray iron, malleable iron, ordnance iron, silicon iron, stove-plate, white iron;** individual products include **cast-iron pipe, cast-iron stove, cast-on, illuminated tile, skew-back lintel.** See also **Berlin iron, I-beam, steel, wrought iron.**

cast-iron pipe Pipes and fittings molded in various shapes from cast iron; typically with diameters larger than 2 inches; types include heavy (used for drains) and extra-heavy (used for sewers); commonly in the form of a **bell pipe.**

cast-iron stove **1.** A heating device for individual rooms, manufactured of cast iron starting in the 1830s; burns wood or coal; vented to the exterior through sheet-metal stovepipes or masonry flues. **2.** A cooking stove made of cast iron.

cast lead Sheet lead produced by pouring molten lead on an extremely smooth bed of sand. See also **milled lead.**

cast-on A cast-iron decoration cast-in-place on another element, such as over the intersections of iron-wire fence. See also **booked chill, iron-wire fence.**

cast pipe A lead pipe manufactured by casting lead in a mold. See also **blown joint, soldered pipe, wiped joint.**

cast stone (late 19c–present) Any of various manufactured products that resemble stone; in the late 20c most often refers to elements molded from dense **concrete** composed of white portland cement and aggregates of marble, quartz, or similar stones; used for counters, sinks, masonry units, sculpted ornamental elements, and fireplace mantels; types include **Coade stone, Permastone, Victoria stone.** Also known as **artificial stone.** See also **cast-in-place, precast.**

catalog house Same as **mail-order house.**

cataloging The process of systematically recording objects in a museum collection or from an **archaeological site;** includes a description of the physical nature and **provenance** of each item. See also **catalog number, registration.**

catalog number The number assigned to each artifact recovered from an **archaeological site** and to objects in a museum collection.

cat and clay chimney (18c) Same as **stick chimney.**

catch, (pre-19c) **ketch** **1.** A hardware device for fastening a movable element, such as a shutter or window sash, in a particular position; types include **back catch, sill catch.** See also **lock.** **2.** Same as **keeper.** See also **catch bolt.**

catch basin A masonry- or concrete-walled pit that collects surface stormwater and directs it into a storm sewer; typically has a pit below the sewer inlet to catch debris; the inflow may be a grate at the top or an aperture at the side. Also known as **catch reservoir.**

catch bolt The bolt of a **spring lock.**

catch drain **1.** A ditch along a canal that carries surplus water. **2.** A drain on a sloped grade that receives surface water runoff.

catch reservoir (19c) Same as **catch basin.**

catchwork An **earthwork** that collects surface water runoff and distributes it via a series of irrigation ditches.

catenary, (18c) **catenaria,** (19c) **catenarian-curve** A curve in the shape of the line of a chain hung between two points.

catenary arch, (18c–20c) **catenarian arch** An **arch** that has an intrados in the shape of an inverted catenary curve; extremely rare because of the difficulty of layout and construction.

catenated Having a decorative motif in the form of a linked chain.

catery (19c) Same as **catery closet.**

catery closet (pre-19c) A storeroom for household provisions.

Catherine wheel Same as **wheel window.**

cathetus **1.** An imaginary vertical line that passes through the axis of a cylinder, especially a column. **2.** An imaginary plumb line that connects the outside of the bottom of the cymatium of an Ionic capital with the center of the volute below.

catlinite A stone composed of indurated red clay of variable composition quarried in Minnesota and Wisconsin, especially in the vicinity of Pipestone City, Minnesota; named for George Catlin, American painter of western scenes. Also known as **Indian pipestone.**

CAT scan Abbr. for **computerized axial tomography scanning,** an electromagnetic medical device used to produce images of internal organs; occasionally used to produce an image of interior decay in wood artifacts.

Catskill sandstone A Devonian sandstone quarried in the Catskill Mountains, New York.

catslide (southern U.S.) A gable-roofed house with a lean-to addition. See also **saltbox.**

cat step Same as **crow step.**

cattail pine Same as **foxtail pine.**

caulicole **1.** (pre-20c) Same as **cauliculus.** **2.** (18c) Same as **helix** (sense 2).

cauliculus, (pre-20c) **caulicole,** (pre-19c) **caulicolus** One of the eight small ornaments that rise between the second row of acanthus leaves on a **Corinthian** capital to the base of the volutes; may be a carved cabbage stalk with a bud at the tip or a curly leaf.

caulis, caule One of the eight large leaves in the second row of acanthus leaves at the base of a **Corinthian** capital; supports the cauliculi. See also **cauliculus.**

caulking, cauking, calking Flexible sealant material used to close joints between materials; includes tar and oakum, lead, putty, and modern elastomerics such as silicone and polyurethane.

caulk tenant, caulk tennant (pre-20c) Same as **dovetail;** from variant spelling of **cock tenon.**

caustic stripper An alkaline **paint remover** with potassium hydroxide or sodium hydroxide as the active ingredient.

cavalier A raised, earthen platform in a fort for a gun emplacement or a lookout post.

cavasion (18c) Same as **excavation.**

cavate lodge, cavated lodge A dwelling excavated in a cliff or steep hillside; formerly used by Native Americans in southwestern U.S., especially along the Rio Grande, San Juan River, and the Rio Verde, and in the San Francisco Mountains.

cavernous Stone containing irregular cavities or of a porous texture, such as **travertine.**

cavetto A concave molding with a quarter round or similar curve bounded by two flat faces at right angles to one another. Also known as **mouth.** See also **casement, congé, scotia.**

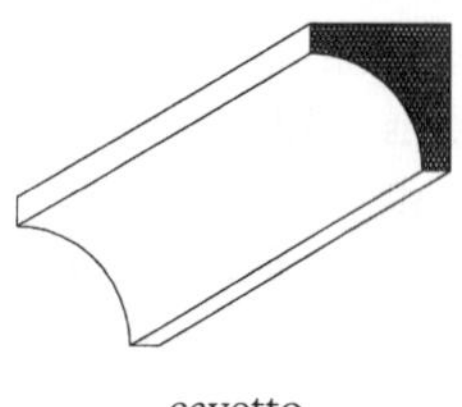

cavetto

cavity iron (pre-20c) A small, iron **wall tie** for a cavity wall.

cavity wall A masonry wall in which the outer and inner wythes are separated by a vertical **air space** and connected by bonding units or metal ties; intended to reduce water infiltration to the building interior.

cavo-relievo, cavo-rilievo Same as **sunk relief.**

CBD Central Business District

CCHR Canadian Conference on Historical Resources

cedar, (pre-19c) **seader** **1.** One of several trees of the genus *Juniperus,* including **eastern red cedar** and **western cedar.** **2.** One of several trees of the genus *Chamaecyparis,* especially **Alaska cedar, Port Orford cedar, white cedar.** **3.** One of the large softwood trees of the genus *Thuja,* especially **western red cedar** and **northern white cedar.** **4.** The Mexican tree *Cedrela mexicana.* See also **Washington cedar.**

cedar shingle See **shingle.**

cedro A hand-split cedar plank that spans between the **viga** beams of a flat-roofed adobe or stone building in southwestern U.S. or northern Mexico; forms the finished ceiling below and supports the earthen roof above.

ceil To install a finished ceiling, especially of planks or boards. See also **seal.**

ceiling, (pre-20c) **cieling, sealing, seeling, sieling,** (pre-18c) **ceilinge** **1.** A finished upper surface of an interior space; before the 20c the term was primarily limited to a covering that hides overhead joists or rafters, especially of planks or boards. See also **suspended ceiling.** **2.** (20c) Tongue-and-groove beaded boards; typically ⅝ or ⅞ inch thick.

ceiling beam Same as **ceiling joist.**

ceiling block Same as **rosette** (sense 3).

ceiling button Same as **plaster button.**

ceiling cutout An electrical **rosette** (sense 3) with an integral fuse.

ceiling fixture Same as **ceiling light.**

ceiling grid A rectangular grid of metal supports for a **suspended ceiling,** especially for **acoustical tile;** typically the members are inverted T-shapes.

ceiling joist One of a series of beams that support the finish ceiling and are separate from the floor joists or rafters above.

ceiling light Any type of **light fixture** attached to a ceiling. See also **chandelier.**

ceiling medallion A bas-relief ornament on a ceiling, especially a relatively large, circular one located in the center of a room. Also known as **rosace.** See also **rosette.**

ceinture Same as **cincture.**

celature Decorative chased, repoussé, or engraved metalwork.

cell One of the parts of a groin vault defined by the lines of intersection between two vaults. See also **vaulting cell.**

cellar, (pre-19c) **celler, sellar,** (pre-18c) **seller** **1.** The part of a building enclosed by the foundation walls and with more than one-half its height below grade. See also **basement.** **2.** A freestanding structure that is partly or wholly underground; types include **earth cellar, root cellar, storm cellar, wine cellar.** Also known as **cellar house.**

cellar cap (18c) Same as **bulkhead** (sense 2).

cellar door, cellar flap A door to a cellar on a sloping **bulkhead.**

cellar house (pre-20c) Same as **cellar** (sense 2).

celler (pre-19c) Same as **cellar.**

cement **1.** Any substance used to bind materials together by hardening as it dries or cures; types include **cold cement, hot cement, slate cement.** **2.** A calcium-based binder used for **mortar, plaster,** or **concrete;** types include **Caen stone cement, calcareous cement, hydraulic cement, Keene's cement, Maya cement, portland cement, Rosendale cement.** **3.** Same as **concrete;**

technically incorrect, but in common usage during the 20c.

cement asbestos board Same as **asbestos board.**

cement-base paint Same as **cement-water paint.**

cement block (early 20c) Same as **concrete block.**

cement mortar A masonry mortar with cement, especially portland cement, as an ingredient.

cement pipe A cast concrete pipe; typically of large diameter and in the form of a bell pipe; used for sewers.

cement siding (early 20c) Same as **stucco** made with portland cement.

cement steel Same as **blister steel;** from the manufacturing process.

cement stone Stone used to manufacture calcareous cement, especially limestone used for hydraulic cement.

cement-water paint A water-based **paint** that uses portland cement as the binder; used on masonry walls. Also known as **cement-base paint.**

cemetery (late 18c–present) A **graveyard;** beginning in the 19c, especially a relatively large area designed as a park. See also **gravestone, monument.**

cemetery beacon A lantern tower located in a cemetery; also known as **lantern of the dead.**

cenotaph A tomblike **monument** to a deceased person who is not buried there.

center bead, centre bead A **flush bead** located along the middle of a board.

centering The temporary frame used to support an arch while it is being constructed.

center mold, (19c) **centre mould** A pivoted thin board cut to a molding profile and used to cut circular molds in plaster.

center passage A building with a central passage or stair hall axially aligned on the front facade and extending from front to back; types include **I-house.**

centerpiece, center piece, centrepiece, (pre-20c) **centre piece** An elaborate decorative element at the center of a composition, especially on a ceiling.

center post The middle post of each bent of a **timber frame** building; runs from the cross-sill to the main beam.

center splice A wood frame butt joint commonly used for joists above the center of a hallway; each pair of joists is connected by lumber of the same size as the joists nailed across both sides of the joint.

center to center, (Canada and pre-20c U.S.) **centre to centre** Same as **on center.**

centimeter In the **metric system,** a measure of length that equals 0.01 **meter;** in the U.S. equals 0.3937 inches.

central business district (CBD) The main commercial area in an urban area, with concentrated office and retail uses.

central tower A tower that rises from the crossing of a church or similar structure.

centrum phonicampticum (18c) The place where the sound of an echo returns. See also **centrum phonicum, echo, whispering gallery.**

centrum phonicum (18c) The point of origin of sound in an echo. See also **centrum phonicampticum, echo, whispering gallery.**

CEQ **Council on Environmental Quality**

ceramic See **architectural terra-cotta, tile.**

ceramic veneer (20c) Architectural terra-cotta formed in large, thin slabs ranging in thickness from 1⅛–2½ inches; typically used as a glazed exterior wall finish on commercial structures.

cerro A Mexican pyramid.

Certificate of Appropriateness An authorization from a local **architectural review board** or preservation commission to alter or demolish a historic property, or to construct a new building, in a historic district; required by most local historic preservation ordinances; typically part of a defined application and public hearing process, often in conjunction with criteria for determining whether the proposed action is appropriately consistent with the character of the historic district or site.

certificate of occupancy (C of O) A permit from a local government agency granting permission to use a building or site, or a portion thereof, for a particular purpose; issued after the satisfactory completion of **construction** that requires a **building permit.** Also known as **occupancy permit, use and occupancy permit.**

certification **1.** The process by which a nominating authority, such as a state or federal historic preservation officer, signs a National Register form or continuation sheet to verify the accuracy of the documentation and to express his or her opinion on the eligibility of the property for National Register listing. **2.** The process and signature by which the Keeper of the Register acts on a request for listing, a determination of eligibility, or other action. See also **Certification of Significance.**

Certification of Significance The result of a process defined in Section 2124 of the U.S. Tax Reform Act of 1976 for **investment tax credit** projects; includes certification as a historic building due to being listed on the **National Register of Historic Places** (or eligible for listing), and certification of proposed rehabilitation work by the state historic preservation officer and the National Park Service as meeting the **Secretary of the Interior's Standards for Rehabilitation** and **Guidelines for Rehabilitating Historic Buildings;** 75 percent of exterior walls must remain in their original position after the rehabilitation. See also **certified historic structure.**

certified historic structure A structure the U.S. National Park Service has determined is eligible to obtain a **Certification of Significance.**

Certified Local Government (CLG) In the U.S., a local government certified by the state historic preservation officer and the National Park Service as having met the following criteria: (1) adopted and enforced a local ordinance providing for the designation and protection of historic properties; (2) established an adequate and qualified historic preservation review commission; (3) maintained a system for the survey and inventory of historic properties; and (4) provided for adequate public participation in the local historic preservation program, including the process of recommending properties for nomination to the National Register; CLGs are eligible for federal matching grants and can participate directly in the National Register nomination process.

Certified Rehabilitation Project A rehabilitation project that has obtained a **Certification of Significance.**

ceruse A pure form of **white lead.**

cesspool A masonry, concrete, or metal pit for receiving sewage from a building; typically covered; types include **leaching cesspool, tight cesspool.** Also known as **sink.** See also **hydrant cesspool, septic tank.**

CFC (chlorofluorocarbon) (20c) An **air conditioning** refrigerant composed of chlorofluorocarbon molecules; phased out of use beginning in the late 20c because of its negative effects on upper atmosphere ozone.

chaff house An outbuilding used to store cornhusks, finely cut hay, or similar fodder. See also **fodder house.**

chain Same as **chain molding.** See also **Gunter's chain.**

chain bolt A door bolt with an attached chain.

chain bond A masonry wall bond formed by horizontal metal bars or pieces of lumber built into the wall; types include **hoop iron bond, timber bond.**

chain course A course of stone bonded together by continuous metal cramps.

chain house An outbuilding used to store a surveying chain and related equipment. See also **Gunter's chain.**

chain-link fence A 20c fence system composed of steel wire woven in a diamond pattern, with steel-pipe posts and top rails; typically without any decorative elements. See also **wire fence.**

chain molding A carved decoration in the stylized form of a linked chain.

chain of title The sequence of ownership of a property; typically determined by a **title search.**

chain timber A piece of **timber** used for a **timber bond.**

chair Marble that is carnation pink or the color of caucasian flesh.

chair board Same as **chair rail.**

chair house (mid-18c–early 19c) A **carriage house** for sheltering a light, two-wheeled chaise for two passengers drawn by a single horse. See also **cart house, chaise house.**

chair rail One of various horizontal moldings installed on an interior wall to protect the wall finish from the backs of chairs and other furniture; may be a single beaded board or the top part of a dado or wainscot.

chaise house, shay house (to mid-19c) A **carriage house** for sheltering a light, two- or four-wheeled vehicle drawn by one, or sometimes two, horses. See also **cart house, chair house.**

chalcedony Hard, translucent minerals composed of cryptocrystalline silica; typically found in cavities of igneous rocks; forms include agate, carnelian, **chert, flint,** jasper, opal, and **onyx.**

chalet, châlet A wood house in the style of a Swiss mountain house, with exposed beams and columns, wide eaves, balconies, and ornately carved and scrolled woodwork.

chalk A soft white, gray, or buff colored limestone composed of microscopic skeletons of foraminifera and sometimes the larger shells of mollusks; used for marking, as an **extender** in oil paints, and as a pigment in distemper paints. See also **calcine, carton pierre.**

chalking A powdery deposit on the surface of paint (or a similar material) caused by degradation of the binder or pigment by ultraviolet light.

chamber **1.** (17c–19c) A **room** in a house, especially a bedroom; types include **bed chamber, chamber chamber, hall chamber, hall back chamber, inner chamber, outer chamber.** **2.** (pre-19c) Any full-height sleeping area above the ground floor, exclusive of attic areas. **3.** A room for meetings of a legislative body. **4.** (pre-19c) A principal ground-floor sleeping area; typically also used for informal socializing. Also known as **inner room, parlor.** **5.** Same as **lock chamber.** **6.** An enlarged space in a mine.

chamber chamber A room over a **chamber.**

chamber floor Same as **chamber story.**

chamber story (19c) A floor of a house occupied entirely by bedrooms; typically located above the ground floor.

chamber summer beam A large **tie beam** in a **timber frame** building.

chambranle (pre-20c) **1.** A structural enframement of a masonry wall opening, composed of one horizontal and two vertical elements. **2.** A decorative door or window surround in the form of sense 1.

chambrel (19c) Same as **gambrel.**

chamfer **1.** A 45-degree bevel cut at an outside corner of a building element; used with wood, stone, and concrete to reduce impact damage and for ornamentation. See also **bead chamfer, hollow chamfer, stop chamfer.** **2.** A groove, channel, or bevel in a wood element. Also known as **broach stop.**

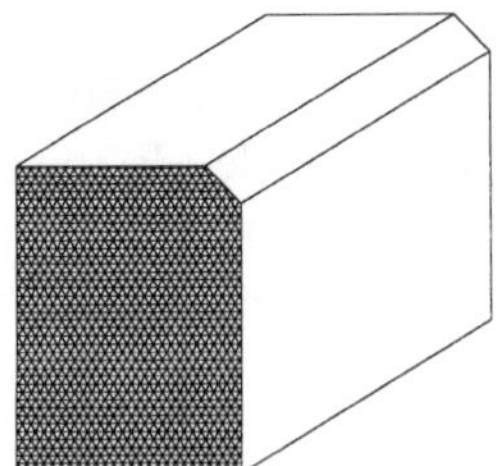

chamfer (sense 1)

chamfered door A wood door with the corners of the stiles and rails adjacent to the panels beveled at a 45-degree angle.

chamfered joint Same as **miter.**

chamfered rustication Rusticated stone blocks with 45-degree beveled edges aligned so that the joints form a right angle V-shaped groove. See also **rustication.**

chamfer stop Same as **stop chamfer.**

Champion Pink A light pink **marble** with waves of darker shades and occasional veins or crow's-feet quarried in the vicinity of Knoxville, Tennessee.

chancel, (pre-19c) **chancell, chancil** **1.** In a large church, the part located beyond the transept; typically contains the altar and choir. **2.** The space at the east end of an Episcopalian or Roman Catholic church containing the altar and sometimes pews or seats for the clergy; typically separated from the rest of the church by a raised floor and a screen or railing. **3.** An area in a Protestant church containing the pulpit and surrounded by a railing.

chandelier A fixture with multiple arms hung from the ceiling to support lights; originally for candles but later manufactured with gas and electric lights; typically imported before the 19c; may be made of brass, glass, wood with metal arms, or tinplate. See also **crystal chandelier, gasolier.**

change order A document that changes the scope and/or the cost of the work of a construction contract; typically executed by the **architect, contractor,** and **owner;** may be for changes requested by the owner, hidden conditions of the property, or delays caused by weather conditions.

channel **1.** Any decorative groove. **2.** One of several parallel grooves in a surface, especially semiellipses that abut in an arris; typical on Doric style column shafts. See also **flute.** **3.** The groove of a Doric triglyph. **4.** A rolled iron or steel or extruded aluminum shape with a vertical flange and horizontal top and bottom webs that project on the same side of the flange. **5.** (18c) The groove that forms the volute of an Ionic capital.

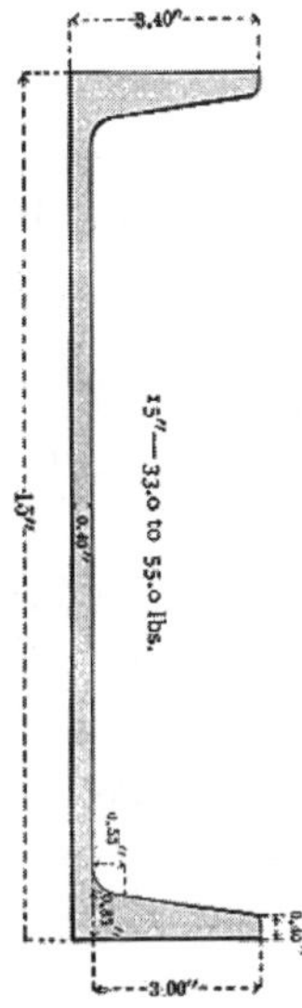

channel (sense 4)

channel bar (19c) Same as **channel iron.**

channel beam A channel (sense 4) used as a beam, typically with the web in the vertical position.

channel column A hollow steel column composed of a pair of channels attached with plates so that the flanges are facing outward.

channel iron A small channel (sense 4); also known as **channel bar.**

channel of the larmier (18c) The channel of a cornice soffit below the corona; forms a drip in the shape of a pendant mouchette.

chantlate A projection of the roof sheathing beyond the ends of the rafters to carry the roof tiles or slates and create a drip; used where the rafters do not form eaves.

chantry A **chapel** used for subsidiary services in a church; originally a chapel in a monastery or church endowed for daily chanting of services for the founder or a deceased loved one.

chapel, (pre-19c) **chaple, chappel, chappell, chappelle, chapple** **1.** A small church or place of worship; pre-19c generally referred to a Roman Catholic or Anglican church; types include **chapel of ease.** **2.** An area within a large church where services may be held separately from the main nave; types include **chantry.**

chapel of ease (pre-19c southern U.S.) A secondary Anglican church for the use of parishioners who live far away from the main parish church.

chaplet A small-diameter bead molding decorated with continuous carved ornamentation, such as pearls, ribbons, and foliage.

chaptrel **1.** (18c) A voussoir; see **arch.** **2.** (18c) Same as **impost.** **3.** A small capital. **4.** The capital of a pilaster, especially when supporting vaulting ribs.

charged An architectural element with raised surface decoration.

charter A nonbinding set of principles that guide an organization, nation or movement; examples include **Appleton Charter, Athens Charter, Venice Charter, New Orleans Charter.**

chase **1.** (19c) A vertical recess, especially in a wall, in which such elements as plumbing pipes or wires are inserted. **2.** A covered recess in a wall that forms a vertical shaft.

Châteauesque style A house style based on 16c French châteaux with a mixture of Gothic and Renaissance style details; popular for large houses and mansions in the late 19c and early 20c; typical exterior details include massive stone walls, steeply pitched mansard or hip roofs, dormers with pinnacles and parapeted gables, turrets, Gothic tracery or relief carving, corbeling, and hood molds with label stops.

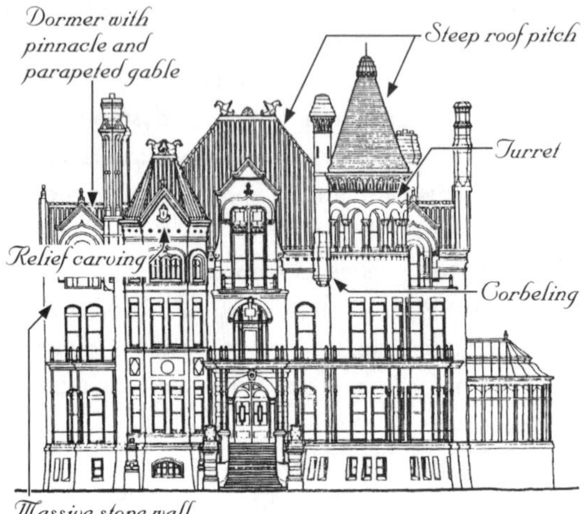

Châteauesque style
Walter Gresham House
Galveston, Texas

chat sawed A coarse, pebbled, surface texture of soft stone ashlar blocks produced by using a coarse sand abrasive during gang sawing; resembles sand-blasted stone and sometimes contains shallow saw marks or parallel scores. See also **shot sawed, stonework.**

check **1.** A rabbet cut at the edge of a stone block that permits the stones to overlap when installed; the face of the stone block may have a notch in the corner or a lug that projects up or down; common in uncoursed and random coursed masonry. See also **pien check.** **2.** A radial crack along the grain of sawn lumber or a pole that does not go entirely through the wood. See also **checking, shake, split.**

checker, chequer **1.** A square grid with differing treatment of alternate squares, such as bas-relief and alto-relief or black and white colors. **2.** A diaper pattern with decoration within the divisions of a square grid; common in the Romanesque Revival style.

checkered plate (19c–present) A nonslip steel plate with a bas-relief grid having diamond-shaped recesses; typically 3⁄16–3⁄4 inch thick.

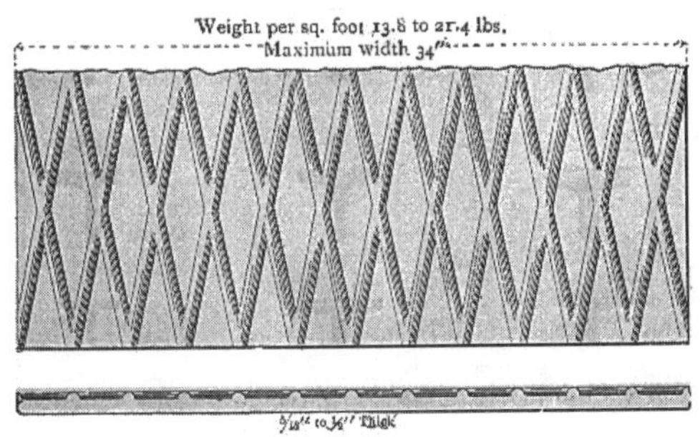

checkered plate

checkerwork, chequerwork, (19c) **checker-work** **1.** (19c) Same as **checker** (sense 1). **2.** Stonework with a **stackbond.**

checking Cracking of wood with the grain, caused by rapid drying after initial sawing. See also also **seasoning.**

checking hinge A spring hinge with a mechanism that allows a door to check in the open position.

check rail A window meeting rail that is thicker than the rest of the sash, so that it fills the gap between the upper and lower sash made by the **check strip;** typically beveled.

check strip A small molding on a window jamb that holds a vertically sliding sash in place.

cheek **1.** One of two facing parts of an architectural element, such as a recessed window opening, the inside facing of an **embrasure,** or one of the vertical sides of a door or window frame. See also **jamb.** **2.** One of the vertical side faces of the exterior of a **dormer window** or similar projecting element. **3.** One of the sides of a mortise, or one of the two pieces cut from the end of a timber to make a tenon.

cheek cut A beveled saw cut at the foot of a **hip rafter, valley rafter,** or **jack rafter.**

cheek wall Same as **wing wall.**

Chelmsford granite A light pinkish gray to gray, medium-grained muscovite-biotite granite quarried in the vicinity of West Chelmsford, Massachusetts.

chemin-de-ronde A continuous covered walkway behind a rampart. See also **alure, banquette.**

Cherokee A bluish white **marble** with clouds of darker shades, quarried in Pickins County, Georgia; polishes well.

cherry See **black cherry.**

chert An impure form of **chalcedony.**

cherub The winged head of an infant; common on 17c and 18c tombstones and in 19c painted interiors and ornament in revival architectural styles.

chestnut See **American chestnut.**

chevaux-de-frise, (18c–19c) **chevaux-de-frize** **1.** (17c–present) A series of horizontal poles with radiating iron points or spiked pickets used as a barricade to obstruct cavalry; from the French for Friesland horse (cheval-de-Frise) after the device's first use at the siege of Groningen in Friesland province, Netherlands, in 1658; later used to indicate any similar device, such as those placed in the Hudson River during the Revolutionary War. **2.** (19c–present) An assemblage of sharp points on top of a wall to prevent access; includes both radiating, pointed wood bars and broken glass set in mortar.

chevet The semicircular end of a church apse or nave; common in the **Gothic Revival style.**

chevron A decorative pattern in the form of a flattened, inverted V.

chevron molding A molding with chevrons or zigzags. See also **bâtons rompus.**

Chicago plan See **transfer of development rights.**

Chicago School A design movement begun by midwestern architects in the last quarter of the 19c and characterized by high-rise commercial buildings with a steel skeleton frame and curtain wall exterior that clearly expresses the structure behind; the buildings often have simple, nonhistorical exteriors; notable practitioners include the firms of Adler and Sullivan, Burnham and Root, and Holabird and Roche. See also **Prairie Style, skyscraper.**

chicken coop A **coop** for chickens.

chicken house (19c–present) Same as **henhouse.**

chicken wire **Wire cloth** composed of 20-gauge wire woven into a series of 1-inch-wide hexagons; used for lath and fencing, especially around poultry yards.

chimaera A sculpture or decoration in the form of an imaginary monster of any shape; after the legend of the Chimaera of Lycia.

chimney, (pre-18c) **chimnie, chimny** **1.** A vertical construction that leads the hot gases and smoke from an interior heating fire to the outside; usually made of masonry or metal with the top higher than the adjacent roof; may be connected to a **boiler, fireplace, furnace, stove, water heater,** or other source; types include **chimney stack, corner chimney, inside chimney, outside chimney, steam chimney, stick chimney, Welsh chimney;** components may include **chimney arch, chimney back, chimney bar, chimney breast, chimney cap, chimney cheeks, chimney pot, chimney throat, chimney shaft, cowl, damper, fireback, fire board, firebox, flue, lintel, manteltree, smoke shelf, throat.** See also **hearth, fireplace, mantel.** **2.** (pre-18c) Same as **fireplace.**

chimney arch The arch over a fireplace opening that supports the chimney breast above.

chimney-ash door Same as **ashpit door.**

chimney back **1.** The rear wall of the inside of a fireplace; may be constructed of **firebrick.** **2.** (pre-19c) A one-piece cast-iron **fireback.**

chimney bar A wood or iron beam spanning across a fireplace opening to support the masonry above.

chimney board, chimneyboard Same as **fireboard.**

chimney breast The projecting interior face of a chimney containing the fireplace opening and flues.

chimney brick Same as **salmon brick.** See also **firebrick.**

chimney cap The decorative masonry or metalwork that crowns a chimney; may include a cover to keep out rain; may be corbeled, an abacus, or a cornice. See also **cowl, chimney pot, hoveling.**

chimney cheeks The jambs of a mantelpiece or fireplace opening.

chimney corner (19c) Facing built-in benches with backs in front of a fireplace. Also known as **inglenook.**

chimney glass A mirror in an overmantel or on the wall above a mantel.

chimney gorge (18c) The portion of a mantelpiece between the chambranle and the crown below the mantelshelf, of various shapes.

chimney hook **1.** (19c) A device in a fireplace on which to suspend a pot; often on a swing arm and adjustable in height. **2.** (18c) A brass or steel hook placed in a chimney jamb to hold fire tongs and shovel.

chimney jack A chimney **cowl** with rotating metal vanes.

chimney jamb The interior sides of a fireplace; frequently splayed.

chimney lug An iron bar inside a fireplace from which pots are suspended. See also **randle bar.**

chimneypiece, chimney piece, chimney-piece **1.** (pre-20c) Same as **mantelpiece.** **2.** A picture or other decorative device on the wall above a fireplace.

chimney post A post at the end of **timber frame** bents on each side of a central chimney.

chimney pot An extension of the top of a chimney above the masonry; usually of decorative terra-cotta and in a cylindrical, octagonal, or spiral shape; common on Tudor Revival style buildings. See also **chimney cap, tall boy.**

chimney rock In Florida, a porous phosphate rock that hardens on exposure to air; commonly used in construction of chimneys.

chimney shaft The narrow portion of a chimney above its base or above the roof.

chimney stack **1.** The entire masonry construction containing several fireplaces and flues. **2.** A tall chimney shaft for a power plant or similar use, especially when nearly freestanding; may be masonry or, beginning in 1898, reinforced concrete. Also known as **stack.** **3.** A **chimney shaft** that contains several flues.

chimney throat The flue space immediately above a fireplace where the walls narrow toward the top; popularized by Count Rumford in the late 18c as a means of increasing the draft of a fireplace.

chimney tile A **Dutch tile** used as a fireplace surround or as a lining in a firebox.

chimney valve (19c–present) A damper that permits room air to flow into a chimney for ventilation but prevents backdrafts; invented by Benjamin Franklin.

chimney wing One of the angled side walls of a fireplace interior at the gathering-in of the throat.

CHIN **Canadian Heritage Information Network**

China-wood oil Same as **tung oil.**

chin-beak A projecting quarter round or other molding that is convex above and flat, or concave, below.

Chinese (late 18c–late 19c) Same as **chinoiserie.**

Chinese blue Same as **Prussian blue.**

Chinese railing (18c) Wood bars forming a geometric pattern within a rectangular frame in imitation of railings found in Chinese architecture.

Chinese wax (pre-WWI) A hard, white wax secreted by an insect on the twigs of a Chinese ash tree; used for candles and **wax paint.** Also known as **pela, white wax, vegetable insect wax.**

Chinese white Same as **zinc oxide.**

chink **1.** A long, narrow crack or gap, such as between two logs in a log house or the stones of a rubble wall. **2.** The end grain pattern of wood sawed across the grain.

chinking The material used to fill a **chink,** especially between logs of a log house; often consists of clay mixed with other materials including sand, lime, stones, and hair; (pre-20c) generally referred to the material between the logs that is then covered with daubing; types include stones, pieces of wood, moss, and newspapers. See also **nogging.**

chinoiserie (late 19c–present) In the style of Chinese style of art and architecture; some influence in the U.S. during 18c and early 19c (e.g., the **Chinese railings** at Monticello).

chinolin An **aniline color** paint pigment.

chipolin painting (19c) A faux marble imitation of cipollino marble with light gray or greenish veins.

chisel A pattern formed by rows of **shingles** with angled bottoms.

chisel-drafted corner A hand-chiseled **draft** at the edge of a stone block.

chiseled **1.** Cut, gouged, or shaped by a chisel. See also **tooled. 2.** Having a beveled end like a chisel.

chlorofluorocarbon (CFC) See **CFC.**

chocolate paint (pre-19c) A dark brown **oil-base paint** colored with **lampblack** and **Spanish brown** pigments.

choir The part of a large church where the singers sit, especially the chancel beyond the crossing in a cruciform plan; common in Gothic Revival style churches; term not generally used in U.S. until early 19c. See also **antechoir, chancel, church, retrochoir.**

choir aisle One of the aisles on both sides of a choir. See also **deambulatory.**

choir loft An elevated seating area for a church choir; may be in the front, rear, or side of the church.

choir screen A railing, gate, or partition that separates a choir from the rest of the church or from the choir aisles. See also **rood screen, screen.**

choir vestry A changing room for a church choir. See also **vestry.**

chord **1.** One of the principal members of a **truss,** typically one of a horizontal pair separated by diagonal or vertical **web** members; types include **bottom chord, top chord. 2.** The imaginary chord of one of the circle segments that form the intrados of an **arch. 3.** (18c) The **spring line** of an arch.

Christian door (colonial New England) A paneled door in which the center stile and rail are in the form of a cross. See also **cross and bible, colonial panel door.**

chroma The intensity of color, indicating the degree of departure from white; typically used in reference to pigment or paint, as in having **high chroma.**

chrome Same as **chromium.**

chrome green (early 19c–present) A green paint **pigment** composed of a mixture of **Prussian blue** and **chrome yellow;** a fairly permanent color. See also **chrome oxide green.**

chrome oxide green (early 19c–present) A compound used for green paint **pigment;** color ranges from dull olive to bluish green; very nonfading. See also **chrome green.**

chrome plated A thin layer of **chromium** electroplated onto another metal to provide corrosion resistance and/or a shiny finish; common in the 20c. See also **nickel plated.**

chrome yellow (early 19c–present) A bright, opaque paint **pigment** composed of lead chromate ($PbCrO_4$) compounds; colors range from canary through red-orange; commercial manufacture began ca. 1818; used for protective metal coatings and house paints; a fairly permanent color. See also **American vermilion.**

chromium A shiny, silver, corrosion-resistant **metal** element; used in alloys and plating, and as a component of paint pigments, including **chrome green, chrome oxide green, chrome yellow;** discovered in 1797. Also known as **chrome.** See also **chrome plated.**

chromochronology A sequential listing of colors, pigments, paint types, and relative dates, used for dating elements of a historic structure; typically established by **paint analysis.**

CHRS **Canadian Heritage Rivers System**

chuff brick, chuffy brick A **brick** puffed out by internal steam during firing. Also known as **salmon brick.** See also **sand-lime brick.**

church A building used for Christian worship; may be of any **architectural style;** forms include **basilica, cruciform, round church, triapsidal;** components may include **aisle, altar, altarpiece, altar rail, antechoir, apse, belfry, bell tower, bema, chancel, chapel, choir, crossing, cupola, exonarthex, lady chapel, narthex, nave, organ gallery, pew,**

presbytery, pulpit, reredos, retrochoir, royal door, sanctuary, screen, spire, steeple, stoup, tabernacle, tomb, transept, triforium, vestry; types include **chapel, meetinghouse.** Also known as **house of God, house of prayer.** See also **oratory, temple.**

churchyard The space immediately surrounding the exterior of a church, especially when fenced; may include a **graveyard.**

Churrigueresque, Churriguresco style Architecture in the Baroque style of Don José Churriguera (1650–1723) of Salamanca, Spain, and his sons in late 17c–early 18c Spain; characterized by elaborate decoration and picturesque assemblages including broken pediments, twisted columns, deformed scrolls, and extensive gilding; common in colonial buildings of Mexico and southwestern U.S. See also **Mudéjar-Gothic style.**

ciborium **1.** A permanent ornamental canopy over an altar; may be supported on columns, projected from a wall, or suspended from the ceiling. **2.** A tabernacle or recessed cupboard that houses the communion vessels near a church altar.

cieling (pre-20c) Same as **ceiling.**

ciferd (pre-19c) Same as **ciphered.**

CIHB **Canadian Inventory of Historic Buildings**

cilery, silery **1.** The sculpted foliage or drapery on a capital. **2.** Same as **volute.**

cima, cimatium Same as **cymatium.** See also **Classical orders.**

cimborio A lantern that provides natural light over the crossing of a church; common in colonial churches in Mexico and southwestern U.S.

cimellarc, cimeliarch A room in a church used for storage of vestments and valuables.

ciment (18c) Same as **cement.**

cincture A narrow fillet or other molding separating the top of the base or the bottom of the capital of a classical style column or pilaster from the shaft, especially a fillet next to an **apophyge.** Also known as **annulet, ring.**

cinderblock A lightweight **concrete block** with aggregate made of coal or slag cinders; patented in the U.S. by F. J. Straub in 1917; manufactured only in the early 20c due to poor strength and durability. See also **Straublox.**

cinder concrete A lightweight, low-strength, nailable concrete made of coal cinder aggregate with small amounts of lime or cement; used for short-span floors and fireproofing.

cinnabar A mineral composed of mercuric sulphide (HgS); used to make **American vermilion.**

cinnabar green Same as **chrome green.**

cinquefoil A circular opening with five cusps; used in Gothic and Gothic Revival architecture. Also known as **quintefoil.** See also **cinquefoil arch.**

cinquefoil arch A **three-centered arch** with the intrados in the form of five lobes with cusps; the overall form of the arch may be semicircular or pointed.

cinquefoil arch

ciphered, (pre-19c) **ciferd, cyphered, siphered** Paneling, sheathing, or wainscoting having overlapping beveled joints between adjoining boards.

cipollino American A slightly yellowish to dark green **marble** with green shading and veins of light green to brownish green, quarried in the vicinity of West Rutland, Vermont; polishes medium well.

CIQS **Canadian Institute of Quantity Surveyors**

circuit breaker An electric switch that automatically opens during a current overload on the circuit. Also known as **breaker.** See also **fuse.**

circular architrave A raised, curved molding surrounding a semicircular wall opening. Also known as **archivolt.**

circular loom Electric wire **fibrous wrapped insulation** made of a seamless woven tube of cotton impregnated with an insulating compound and rolled in mica dust; slid around the wire for installation. Also known as **duraduct, flexible tubing.**

circular stair Same as **spiral stair.**

circulation **1.** The movement of a fluid, such as air or water, through a closed system so that it eventually returns to the point of origin. **2.** The movement of people through a space.

circumvolution A flat spiral, especially that of an Ionic volute.

cissing A preparatory operation for graining wood that includes wetting the surface with beer and coating it with whiting.

cistern A watertight structure used to store water; may be located either inside or outside of a building; most commonly underground masonry parged on the interior and covered with a shallow dome or vault with an access hole or pump at the center, may also be a tank with wood staves.

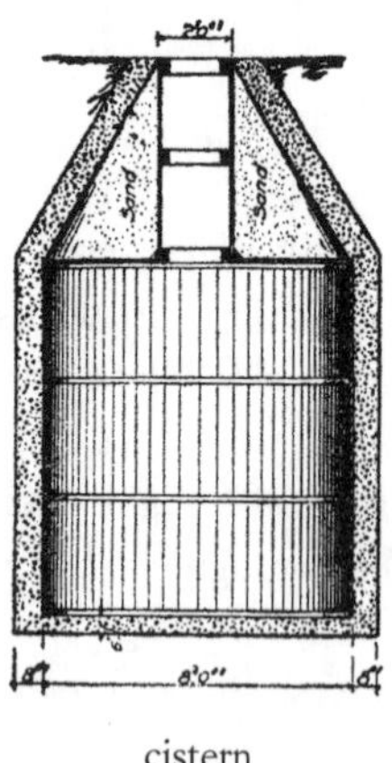

cistern

citadel A fortified stronghold in a city, often on a high point of land.

citarilla A masonry fence of balustrade with pierced openings created by brick or tile units in various shapes; common in Mexican Spanish Colonial style construction.

city **1.** An area with a relatively dense concentration of buildings, and related civil engineering works, and in which people live and work; typically larger in area and population than a **town;** may be incorporated as in sense 2. **2.** (U.S. and Canada) A local geographic and political jurisdiction incorporated by act of a state or provincial legislature.

City Beautiful Movement A city planning movement of the late 19c and early 20c inspired by the symmetrical, classical buildings and landscapes of the 1893 Columbian Exposition in Chicago; largely the work of citizens' organizations that pressed for progressive local government, urban park systems, and a monumental, classical city core as a means of improving the quality of life.

city hall The building housing the administrative offices of a city. See also **hall.**

city planning See **planning.**

cityscape See **townscape.**

cladding The exterior, nonstructural finish material of a building, such as **siding.**

clamp **1.** A wood or metal piece that holds other elements in position; most often iron, such as a **crampon.** See also **armature.** **2.** A temporary brick kiln made by stacking layers of bricks and fuel. **3.** A wood or iron piece mortised or fastened across the grain of one or more pieces of wood to prevent warping.

clamping Joining the ends of several parallel boards by fastening them to a perpendicular board (e.g., a batten door).

clamp nail A large, broad-headed **nail** used for framing; named for its use in fastening boat clamps. Also known as **boat nail.**

clamp rail A cleat or batten that holds the ends of several boards; typically grooved to receive the tongues on the end of the boards.

clamshell molding (20c) A smooth curved molding used for casings; typically 2.25 inches wide.

clapboard, (pre-19c) **clabboard** **1.** One of a series of boards used for siding, roofing, or, sometimes, flooring; most often has a tapered cross section; beginning mid-17c refers to a thin, rived board 4–5 feet in length used as **weatherboard;** by late 19c most commonly refers to **beveled siding;** a corruption of **clayboard,** from the clay chinking used with early colonial rived boards. Also known as **board.** See also **clapboarding, shingle.** **2.** (New England) Four-foot-long beveled siding boards radially cut from a log. **3.** (Appalachia) The outside strip of wood, with one rounded side, remaining after the larger boards have been split from a log. Also known as **slab.**

clapboard house A relatively lightweight **timber frame** building in which much of the structural rigidity is provided by rived **clapboarding;** has common rafters rather than principal rafters and purlins, and is typically supported on short piles or a ground sill; developed in the Chesapeake Bay region in the late 17c. Also known as **Virginia house.** See also **English frame.**

clapboarding **Weatherboard** siding or roofing composed of a series of **clapboards** with overlapping edges; when used for roofing, sometimes covered with shingles.

Clarendon A bluish white **marble,** with small rows or bands of gray spots, quarried in the vicinity of Clarendon, Vermont.

Clark's design A method of fastening two stacked halves of a **compound beam** by nailing continuous diagonal boards to the vertical faces; typically the boards are 6–8 inches wide by 1.25–2 inches thick.

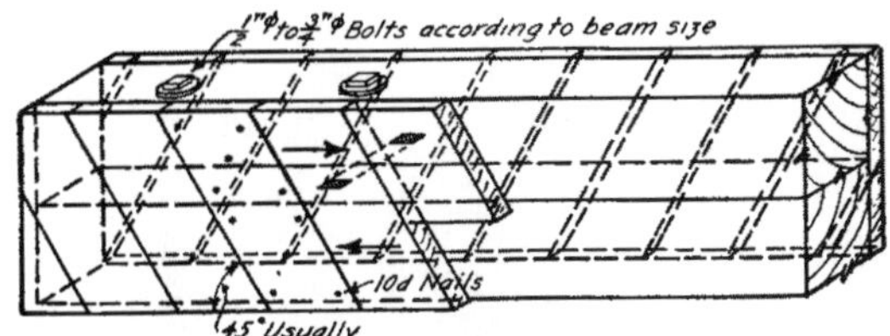

Clark's design

clasping buttress A buttress that wraps around a corner of a building.

clasp nail A **nail** having two spur points under its T-shaped head; used for trim with the head driven below the surface of the wood; originally a **wrought nail** formed by hammering down the head of a rose nail on opposite sides; typically a **cut nail** by the end of the 19c.

classic See **classical.**

classical, Classical (17c–present) Of the style or period of premedieval Greek and Roman art, architecture, or literature; originally referred to a member of the Roman tax-paying upper class, later "first class" or of the highest quality. See also **classicism, classical style, neoclassical.**

classical orders, (pre-19c) **classic orders** The combinations of column and entablature components used in a **classical style;** each order has a column with base, shaft, and capital, and an entablature with architrave, frieze, and cornice; some orders also have pedestals with base, die, and cap to support the columns; the most common orders are the **Composite order, Corinthian order, Doric order, Ionic order,** and **Tuscan order,** also referred to as the **Five Orders;** each order has its own rules of proportion of its various elements. See also **arch order, attic**

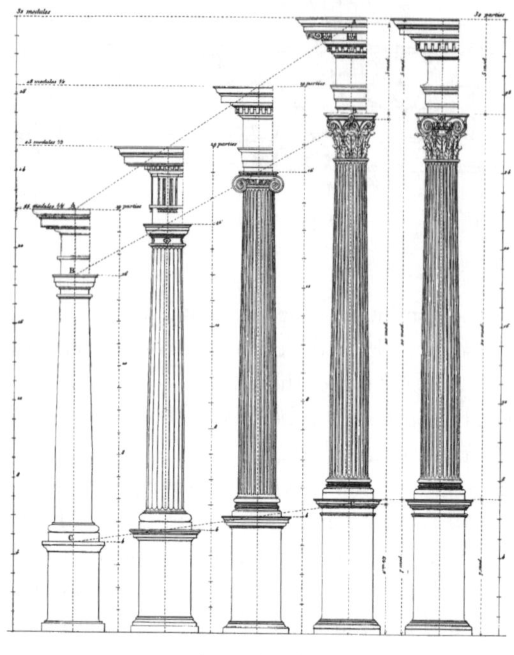

classical orders

order, balustrade order, columniation, intercolumniation, superposition.

Classical Revival style **1.** Late 18c–early 19c architecture that imitates the style of all or a part of an individual premedieval **classical** building and incorporates one of the **classical orders.** See also **Greek Revival style, Jeffersonian, neoclassical.** **2.** A late 19c–early 20c revival of the **classical** style with elements assembled using the beaux-arts tradition; especially popular for public buildings, such as those in the Federal Triangle in Washington, DC.

classical style, Classical style The system of design used by the Greeks and Romans from 700 B.C.–330 A.D.; See also **classical orders, classicism, Classical Revival style, Greek Revival style, Jeffersonian, neoantique, neoclassical.**

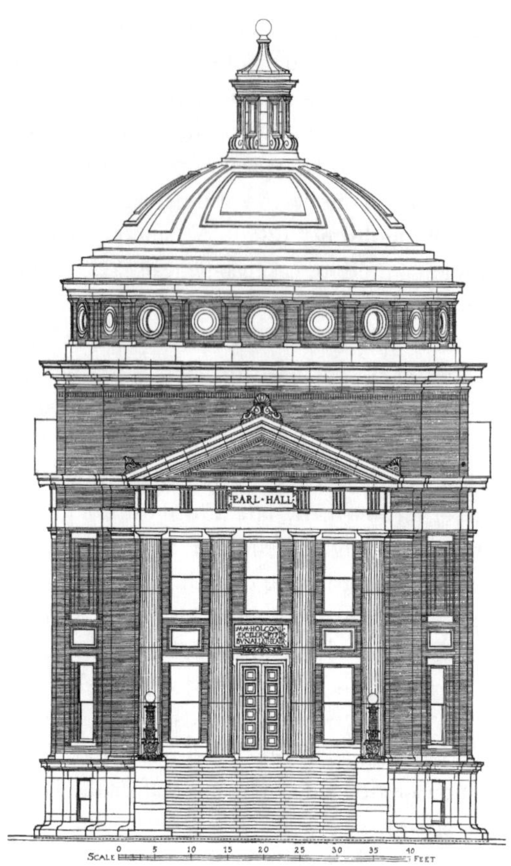

Classical Revival style
Earl Hall, ca. 1902
Columbia University, New York City

classicism The postmedieval practice of **classical** design principles and/or the study of classical literature. See also **classical orders, classical style.**

Classified Federal Heritage Building A building of the highest heritage significance that is listed in the Canadian **Register of Federal Heritage Buildings.**

clavel **1.** (pre-20c) A lintel or mantel. **2.** Same as **clevis.**

clay-and-hair A mixture composed of wet, raw clay and animal hair; used from colonial period to early 19c for **mortar** and **chinking;** the origin of the modern term **mud** for mortar.

cleanout, clean out 1. A plumbing drain pipe fitting with a cover for access to clear stopped lines; the cover may be bolted or a **trap screw.** 2. Same as **ashpit door.** 3. Any access panel for cleaning purposes, such as in a ventilating duct.

cleanout door Same as **ashpit door.**

clear, (pre-19c) **cleare, cleere, clere** 1. Without defects, especially a grade of wood without knots. Also known as **clear stuff.** See also **clear of sap, merchantable stuff, neat.** 2. Glass or plastic sheet that is transparent. 3. Without obstruction. See also **clear height, clear span, in the clear.**

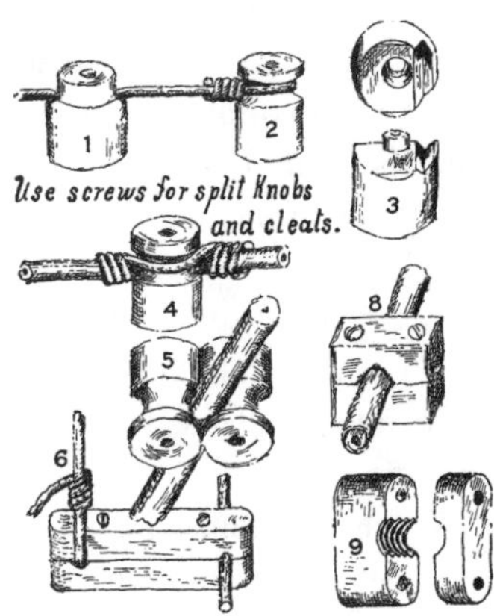

cleat

clearcole (19c) Sizing composed of ground white lead, water, and glue; used to prevent oil-base paint from seeping into a surface.

clear height The unobstructed vertical height in a space.

clear of sap (pre-19c) Same as **heartwood.**

clear span Any type of structural element without intermediate supports, such as a clear span roof; may **span** between exterior walls, columns, or piers.

clear stuff (pre-WWI) Wood that is **clear.** Also known as **free stuff.** See also **merchantable stuff.**

clearstory Same as **clerestory.**

cleat 1. A hardware device with two raised arms used for fastening a line on a pier or winding up an awning cord or similar item. 2. A short strip of wood used to fasten boards together edge to edge. See also **batten.** 3. A small insulating device used to support electric wires; typically porcelain with a bottom and top piece screwed to the surface; used with an electric wiring system with exposed wires on the surface of walls and ceilings; typically used only in commercial, industrial, or agricultural buildings because of its unsightly appearance; common from the 1880s; extremely dangerous due to fire hazard. See also **electric wiring, knob-and-tube, wooden cleat.** 4. Same as **ledger.** See also **shelf cleat.**

cleave board (pre-19c) A rived board; types include **clapboard, shake.**

cleaved Same as **cleft.**

cleft Split along a natural structural line by a wedge or hammer, such as a **cleave board** or a slate. Also known as **cleaved.**

clerestory, clearstory, (pre-18c) **cleerstory** The portion of a building raised above an adjoining roof and having windows in the wall to light, and sometimes ventilate, an interior space; common in churches where the nave is higher than the side aisles. Also known as **overstory.**

clerestory window A window in a wall of a **clerestory.**

clerk of the works A representative of the building owner who is continuously on site during construction to ensure that the work is performed according to the contract; typically accounts for the materials used and, sometimes, the workmen's time and prepares **as-built drawings.**

Cleveland Park granite A silver-gray to yellowish, fine-grained, mica schist granite formerly quarried in the Cleveland Park neighborhood of Washington, D.C., near the site of the National Zoo.

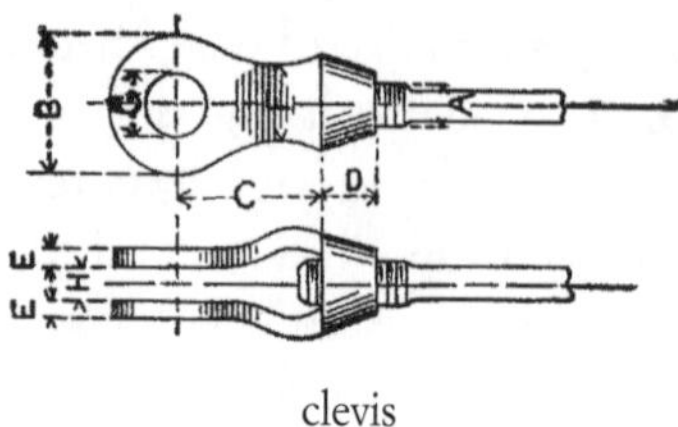

clevis

clevis A U-shaped metal device that has a hole through both ends for a pin or bolt; used in bridges and trusses to attach rods to other members.

clevis bolt Same as a **Lewis bolt.**

CLG **Certified Local Government**

cliff dwelling Dwellings built by native peoples in the southwestern U.S. and northern Mexico under cliff overhangs and on cliff tops; typically constructed of natural stone slabs with mud mortar; roofs were earthen-covered poles or the underside of the ledge above; galleting common in the mortar joints.

clinch **1.** To fasten a board by hammering over the protruding point of a nail. **2.** The grip of **plaster** on its backing. See also **key.**

clincher Same as **clinch nail.**

clinch joint A wood **lap joint** fastened with **clinch nails.**

clinch nail A broad-headed **wrought nail** or **wire nail** that is malleable enough to be clinched without breaking. See also **clinch.**

clinker block Same as **cinder block.**

clinker brick A vitrified, overburned **brick** that clinks when struck; generally darker in color than other bricks from the same clay and misshapen; often used as headers in Flemish bond. Also known as **glazed brick.**

clip A device for holding or clasping building or structural elements together, including (1) a metal device for attaching a tee or angle iron to steel beams without welding or bolting; (2) a device for preventing roof slates or tiles from slipping. See also **clip angle.**

clip angle A short length of metal angle used to attach two structural members together, typically with bolts. See also **clip.**

clip bond A brick wall bond formed by cutting off the inside corners of the stretchers on one side of the wall and laying diagonal headers behind them with stretchers on the other face of the wall; the clipped stretchers alternate from side to side of the wall and the bond produces a wall pattern entirely composed of stretchers. See also **plumb bond.**

clipped gable Same as **jerkinhead.**

cloaca (pre-20c) A latrine or sink.

cloacina temple (pre-20c) A latrine building; named after the main sewer of Rome.

cloak rail A horizontal board with projecting pegs attached to a wall; used for hanging coats or other items.

cloakroom **1.** Same as **coatroom.** **2.** A room for storing coats and other outerwear adjacent to a building entrance; may contain a toilet room; often a place to meet in a public building.

clock-spring balance (20c) Same as **tape-balance.**

clock tower An ornamental tower with a large clock in one or more of its faces; used on public buildings.

clock turret A small tower rising out of the main roof of a building with a clock in one or more of its faces.

cloistered arch Same as **cloistered vault.**

cloistered vault, cloister vault A **quadripartite vault** with a square base and sides that curve upward toward the center; also known as a **coved vault** because of the cove shape of its four sides. See also **vault.**

close Same as **closed newel.**

close coupled Same as **coupled.**

closed cornice Same as **box cornice.**

closed mortise A **mortise** joint in which the tenon is entirely surrounded by wood. Also known as **blind mortise, stub mortise.** See also **open mortise, through mortise.**

closed newel **1.** The inside of a winding stair that is a solid shaft or a continuous wall. See also **hollow newel, open newel. 2.** (19c) Same as **close string.**

closed string, close string A stair **string** that entirely covers the ends of the treads and risers; typically an inclined board or plate with parallel top and bottom edges; may be built against a wall or with both sides exposed. Also known as **curb string.** See also **housed string.**

closed-string stair **1.** A **stair** with closed strings on both sides of the treads and risers; may be built between and abutting two parallel walls. Also known as **box stair.** See also **closed newel, open string stair. 2.** Same as **close-string stair.**

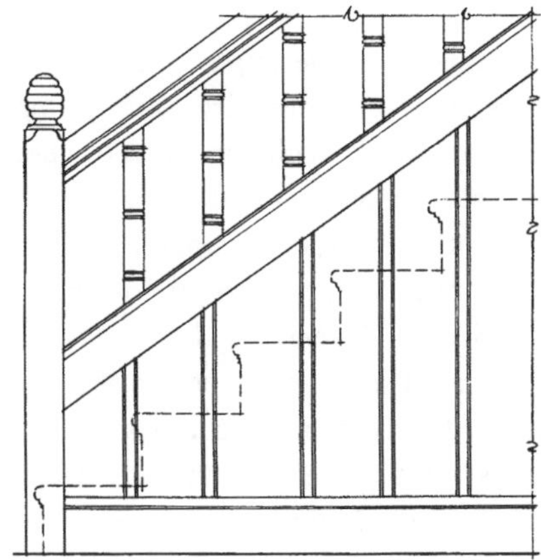

closed-string stair (sense 1)

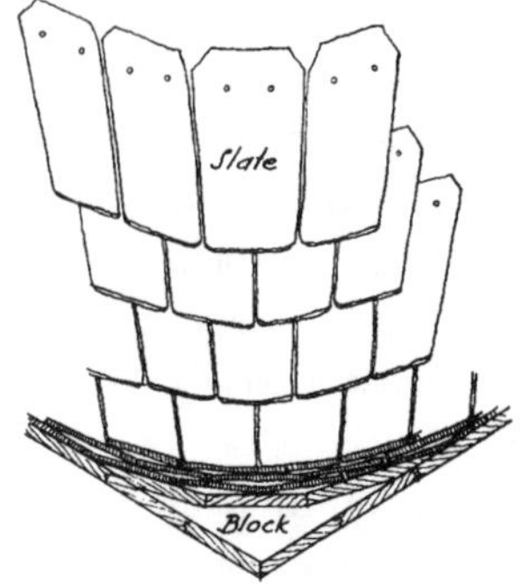

closed valley

closed valley A roof valley in which the slates or shingles on both slopes meet in the middle, hiding the valley flashing.

close-grained Wood with narrow, often faint, annual rings that produce an indistinct **grain** pattern when cut. Also known as **fine-grained** See also **coarse-grained.**

close pile A foundation **pile** located so that it touches the adjacent pile.

closer **1.** The last stretcher **brick** that completes a course of brickwork; may be of any length; types include **king closer, quarter closer, queen closer. 2.** A hardware device that returns a door to the closed position after it has been opened.

close stool A raised seat with a hole in a latrine building.

close-string stair **1.** A **closed newel** dogleg stair without a well. **2.** Same as **closed-string stair.**

closet **1.** (18c–present) A small room used for storage; types include **catery closet, cupboard, hot closet, walk-in closet, wardrobe.** See also **pantry, water closet. 2.** (to mid-18c) A small, secluded room. **3.** (Chesapeake Bay region) A small space enclosing the top of a stair.

closure **1.** A short masonry unit used adjacent to a jamb or corner to maintain the bond pattern. **2.** (19c) A short wall between, but not attached to, two columns.

clout nail A **wrought nail** with a fat midsection and a nearly flat head; typically used for fastening iron hardware to wood; named for its use in attaching clout plates to axletrees.

cloverleaf molding A molding with a cross section in the shape of a semicircle above a pair of quarter rounds; typically used as a wood screen molding.

clubhouse, (pre-WWII) **club-house,** (pre-19c) **club house** A building used as a private club.

clubroom, (pre-19c) **club room** A room used for activities of a private club; sometimes synonymous with **clubhouse.**

club stable The horse **stable** of a private club; typically luxuriously appointed, with a covered courtyard for washing the horses.

clump A compact group of trees or shrubs surrounded by open ground.

clustered column A vertical support with the appearance of several abutting columns; less massive than a **clustered pier.**

clustered pier A massive, vertical, masonry support surrounded with engaged columns; common in Gothic Revival and Romanesque Revival style church interiors; may be part of a **vaulting shaft.** See also **clustered column.**

clustered window A window with glass lights, or tracery openings, that are clustered together.

CMHC **Canada Mortgage and Housing Corporation**

CMU **Concrete masonry unit**

coach house Same as **carriage house.**

coach screw Same as **lag bolt.**

coach steps A set of one or more steps at the edge of a drive or road used for getting into a carriage; typically stone.

Coade stone, Coade's stone A trademark for a molded and fired clay **cast stone** invented by Eleanor Coade and manufactured in London by the Coade Company and its successor Coade & Sealy, from the 1770s to mid-19c; used for mantelpieces, capitals, urns, and similar interior and exterior elements, often with bas-relief decoration.

coal bin A walled storage area for coal; commonly with a low wood wall on one or more sides; often located in a basement or cellar and supplied by a **coal chute.**

coal chute A shaft or conduit that leads downward to a **coal bin** or other storage area.

coal gas Lighting gas manufactured by distilling coal and scrubbing the product to remove odors and particles; the most common gas lighting fuel 1817–ca. 1890. See also **water gas.**

coal hole cover A round, cast-iron cover over a **coal chute** opening in a sidewalk that connects to a basement **coal bin;** typically the name of the coal company is cast in **sunk relief** on the top. See also **coal scuttle.**

coal scuttle An access hatch in a basement wall or sidewalk for loading coal into a **coal bin** or **coal chute.** See also **coal hole cover.**

coal tar **Tar** produced as a by-product of making coal gas or coke. Also known as **gas tar.** See also **aniline color.**

coal tar color Same as **aniline color.**

coal tar indigo A deep blue-black **aniline color** paint pigment. See also **indigo.**

coaming The raised lip around a roof scuttle, or similar opening, to keep out water.

coarse-grained **1.** Descriptive of wood with widely spaced, distinctive annual rings that produce wide **grain** markings when cut. See also **close-grained, open-grained. 2.** Descriptive of stone composed of large, distinct particles that are visible on the cut surface. See also **fine-grained.**

coarse stuff The material for the base coat of a **plaster** finish; typically consists of lime paste with sand and well-beaten hair; other fibers used include Manila, sisal, jute, wood, and asbestos. See also **scratch coat, fiber plaster.**

coarse textured Same as **open-grained.**

coast redwood Same as **redwood.**

coat A single layer of a liquid or paste material, such as paint, varnish, or plaster, that forms a solid film on a surface.

coatroom A room used by the public to temporarily store coats, baggage, and packages. See also **cloakroom.**

cob An earth and straw mixture used as **nogging.**

cobalt blue **1.** A deep blue glass color. **2.** A pure blue paint **pigment** composed of cobalt oxide and alumina; often used with zinc oxide for azure tints; expensive and, therefore, somewhat rare for building paints.

cobalt glass A deep blue glass manufactured with cobalt oxide. Also known as **metz glass, blue glass.**

cobalt green A green oil-paint pigment composed of a mixture of zinc oxide and cobalt oxide.

cobble **1.** A stone that is 3–12 inches in diameter; smaller than a **boulder,** larger than some **gravel.** See also **riprap. 2.** Same as **cobblestone.**

cobblestone **1.** A naturally occurring round stone approximately 3–4 inches in diameter, smoothed by water; used for paving late 18c–early 19c and sometimes for stone walls. Also known as **cobble. 2.** (20c) Roughly cut small stone blocks used for paving. See also **Belgian block.**

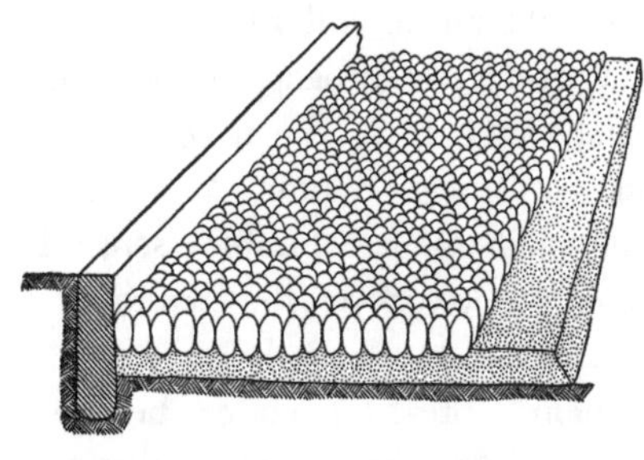

cobblestone (sense 1)

cobblestone face A molded finish on the face of a **concrete block** that resembles a cobblestone wall.

cobweb rubble **Random rubble** with stones of approximately the same size; common in pre-WWII suburban and country house foundations. Also known as **web wall.**

cock **1.** A mechanical device for adjusting the flow of gas or liquid in a pipe; types include **ball cock, bibb cock, urinal cock, stop cock.** See also **faucet. 2.** Same as **weathercock.**

cock bead, cocked bead A **bead molding** that projects beyond adjacent surfaces; called **return-cocked** if the bead meets the adjacent surface directly, and **quirked** if it has a groove adjoining the bead; types include **rail bead, return bead.**

cock brass Same as **cock metal.**

cockel stair Same as **winding stair.**

Cockeysville dolomite A white **marble** with light brown, wavy veins and floral markings quarried in the vicinity of Cockeysville, Maryland; polishes medium well.

cocking Same as **caulking.**

cocking piece Same as **sprocket.**

cockle stair (pre-20c) Same as **spiral stair;** in reference to the shape of a cockleshell.

cockloft An unfinished, low-height space between the ceiling joists and the roof rafters.

cock metal (19c) A **brass** alloy of copper and lead, of various proportions; used for plumbing fixtures. Also known as **cock brass.**

cockpit A pit or ring used for cockfights.

cock tenon, (pre-19c) **cock tenant, cock tennant** Same as **dovetail.**

code See **building code, housing code, zoning code.**

code compliance The process of ensuring that a site meets the requirements of a **building code;** typically involves review of a proposed design by a design professional, such as an **architect,** and a **building official.**

code enforcement The active enforcement of **building code, housing code,** and **zoning code** regulations in existing buildings; typically includes on-site inspections by a **building official** and administrative or legal sanctions against the owner of a property that is not in compliance.

coelanaglyphic relief Same as **sunk relief.**

coenotaph (18c) Same as **cenotaph.**

coffeehouse A place where coffee drinks and other refreshments are sold; sometimes included lodging in the 17c and 18c.

coffer One of multiple deeply recessed ceiling or soffit panels; originally part of stone vaulting, may be any material including wood or plaster; typically rectangular or octagonal with edge moldings; may have decoration, such as a rosette in the center. Also known as **caisson.**

coffer
National City Bank
New York City, ca. 1909

coffin nail (19c) A **nail** used to fasten sheathing. Also known as **doubling nail.**

C of O Abbreviation for **certificate of occupancy.**

cog **1.** A projecting tenon on the end of a joist, especially one formed by notching the bottom corner. **2.** A square-sided notch at the top of a **summer beam** or other girder that receives an unnotched joist.

cogging Same as **caulking.**

coigne, coin **1.** A wedge-shaped stone block resting on an inclined surface to provide a level bed for the blocks above. **2.** Same as **quoin.**

coil **1.** A helix-shaped pipe, especially in a water heater. **2.** A continuous, bent pipe, such as in an air conditioner or boiler, used for heat exchange.

coke breeze Cinders formed by the burning of coke coal; used as aggregate in **breeze concrete.**

colarin **1.** (18c) Same as **collar** (sense 2), especially a cincture of a Tuscan or Doric column between the astragal and the annulets. Also known as **collarino.** **2.** Same as **orlet.**

cold cement (18c) A gluelike substance used to bind bricks together before carving them into capitals or similar shapes, composed of a mixture of Cheshire cheese, milk, egg whites, and quicklime. See also **cement, hot cement.**

cold grapery A greenhouse without artificial heat used for growing grapevines.

cold room A refrigerated room cooled by blocks of melting ice.

cold-short iron A brittle **wrought iron;** easy to forge at low temperatures. See also **red-short iron.**

Cold Spring granite One of several medium- to coarse-grained granites quarried in the vicinity of Odessa, Minnesota; varieties include Agate, Carnelian, Diamond Pink, Pearl Pink, Pearl White, Rainbow, and Red and are generally pinkish or reddish in color.

colier (18c) Same as **collar** (sense 2).

collar **1.** A decorated band around a column or similar element. **2.** The necking of a Doric, Ionic, or Tuscan column. **3.** Same as **collar beam.** **4.** Same as **thimble** (sense 1). **5.** A timber framework at the mouth of a mine shaft.

collar beam, (pre-19c) **coller beame, collor beame** A horizontal member that connects a pair of rafters above their base to form an A-shape; typically used to prevent sagging caused by the weight of the roof without diagonal truss members, thereby providing headroom in an attic space, or sometimes to resist spreading when there is no tie beam at the wall plate level, such as with a **camp ceiling.** Also known as **collar, collar tie.**

collar bolt A **bolt** with a collar or shoulder at the head.

collar brace One of a pair of curved timbers that support a collar beam in a heavy timber roof truss; the top is notched into the collar beam near its center and curves downward toward the outer wall, where it is notched into a vertical post.

collar joint A continuous vertical mortar joint between the inner and outer wythes of a masonry wall.

collar roof A gable roof with rafters attached by collar beams.

collar screw A **machine screw** with a disk at the base of the head that increases the surface area of the head. See also **shoulder screw.**

collar tie Same as **collar beam.**

collection The entire group of cultural artifacts possessed by a museum.

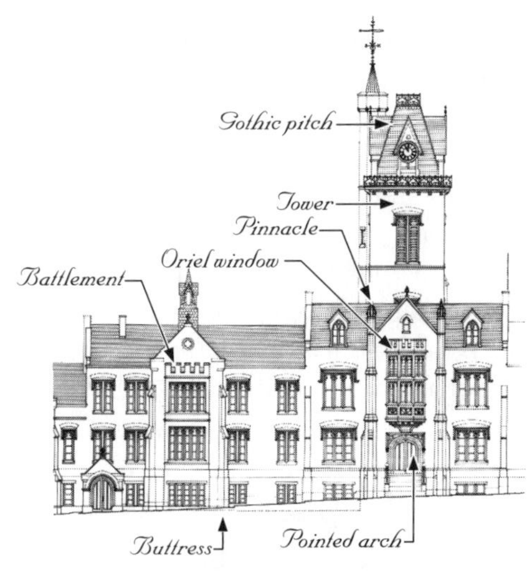

Collegiate Gothic style
Bethany College
Bethany, West Virginia, ca. 1858–71

Collegiate Gothic style Architecture in the style of the late-Gothic universities of England, especially Oxford and Cambridge; common for North American campuses beginning in the late 19c. See also **Gothic Revival.**

coller (pre-19c) **1.** Same as **cincture. 2.** Same as **collar.**

collerino (pre-19c) The **necking** of a column capital.

colliery A coal mine and all of its buildings and structures; may include a **coal breaker.**

collonado (pre-20c) Same as **colonnade.**

collum (pre-19c) Same as **column.**

colonial architecture **1.** Buildings constructed by European settlers, sometimes with African or native labor, during the various North American Colonial periods; types include **Dutch Colonial, French Colonial, French Regime, Georgian, Garrison Colonial, New England colonial, Norse American architecture, postmedieval architecture, Southern colonial, Spanish Colonial,** with building types that include **Cape Cod, saltbox. 2.** Buildings constructed after the Colonial period and designed in the Colonial style; types include **Colonial Revival style, Dutch Colonial, Georgian Revival.**

colonial buff The color of **barium yellow.**

colonial columns (post-WWI) Any of various classical-inspired columns; typically not accurate revivals.

colonial panel door A wood door with stiles and rails with rectangular cross sections and flat, recessed panels; common in the early North American colonies.

Colonial Revival style Architectural styles beginning in late 19c inspired by the study of colonial buildings, especially English and Dutch styles; variations include **Cape Cod, Four Square, Dutch Colonial, Garrison Colonial,** and **Georgian.**

colonial siding (20c) **Weatherboarding** with wide boards having a rectangular cross section, rather than tapered; until mid-19c, typically beaded on the face adjacent to the lower edge.

colonial sticking A door panel **sticking** with a cross section in the shape of a cyma molding.

colonnade A series of columns supporting an entablature; may include a roofed walkway beside the columns; types include **peripteral, portico.**

colonnette, colonette A miniature column.

colophony (pre-20c) Same as **rosin.**

color See **chroma, chromachronology, Munsell system, Ostwald system, pigment.**

Colorado travertine A cream to rose **marble** quarried in Colorado; trade names include Colorcreme, Colorosa.

Colorado Yule A white **marble** with veins of creamy yellow quarried on Yule Creek in the vicinity of Marble, Colorado.

colorant A general term referring to any material used as a dye or pigment.

colored glass **Glass** having a color throughout the material. Also known as **pot metal glass.** See also **stained glass.**

Color Rendering Index (CRI) A measure of the ability of a **lamp** to produce the same color appearance when reflected from an object as a reference source; in units of 1–100.

color temperature The temperature at which a theoretical blackbody would emit the same color radiation as a light source; used to specify electric lamp colors.

colossal order A classical order more than one story in height, such as a colonnade that extends the full height of a multistory building. See also **classical orders, cornicione.**

Columbia One of various shades of blue-gray **marble** quarried in Tuolumne County, California.

Columbian A white, clouded **marble** quarried in the vicinity of Proctor, Vermont; polishes medium well.

columella Same as **colonette.**

column, (pre-19c) **collum** A slender, vertical element that supports part of a building or structure; types by shape include **channeled column, classical orders, engaged column, H-column, knotted column, wreathed column.** See also **colonnette, pier, columniation, coupled, intercolumniation, mortuary column.**

column head Same as **capital.**

columniation A system of describing **classical style** buildings based on the arrangement of the exterior columns; the number of columns at the front facade is designated as diastyle (2 columns), tetrastyle (4), pentastyle (5), hexastyle (6), heptastyle (7), octastyle (8), enneastyle (9), decastyle (10), and dodecastyle (12); the number and position of portico columns on a building are designated **amphiprostyle, apteral, prostyle, pseudoprostyle, peripteral, pseudoperipteral;** the number of rows of columns is defined as **astylar, monopteral, dipteral;** shapes of rows include **cyclostylar, cyrtostyle, orthostyle.** See also **hypostyle, intercolumniation.**

Colusa sandstone A blue-gray, very even-grained **sandstone** quarried in Colusa County, California.

comb **1.** The projection of the top row of shingles or slates over a roof ridge or hip to cover the ridge joint; may extend uniformly on one side or alternately project from each side. Also

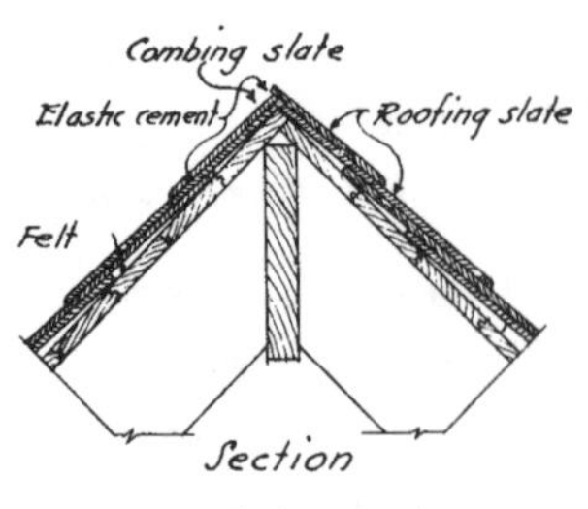

comb (sense 1)

known as **roof comb. 2.** A roof ridge ornament with regular vertical projections; usually of metal.

comb grain Same as **vertical grain.**

combination arch A terra-cotta **end-construction arch** with keystones made of **side-construction tiles.**

combination frame A pre-WWII wood framing system that combines elements of the **timber frame** and **balloon frame** systems; the sills, corner posts, and girts are mortise and tenoned timbers, while the studs, joists, rafters, and top plate are nailed 2× lumber. Also known as **braced frame.**

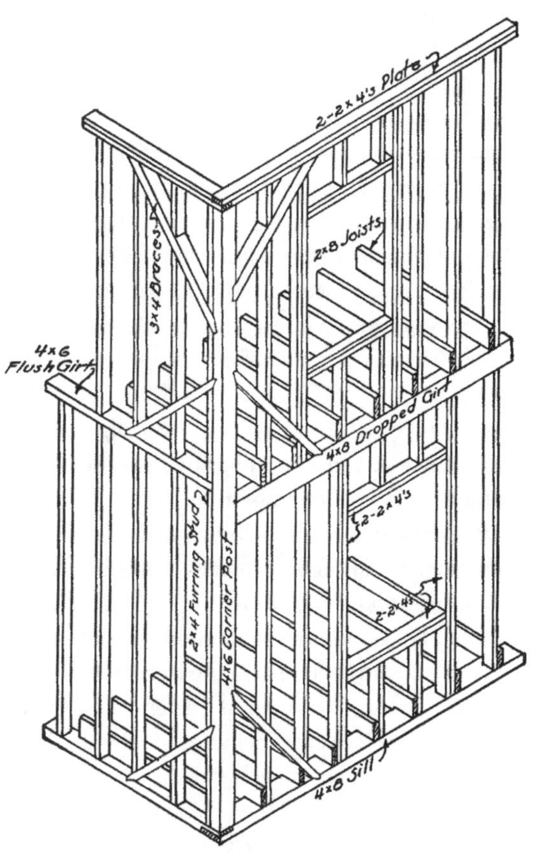

combination frame

combination stair A staircase with a secondary set of steps to the first landing; typically to provide access to service areas.

combination wall (20c) A foundation with a concrete footing and wall to grade level and masonry above.

combined furring and lathing An expanded-metal lath product with raised V-shaped ribs that act as the furring.

commercial archaeology The study of artifacts, structures, signs, and symbols of the American commercial process; includes both mass-produced and vernacular forms of the machine age: transportation facilities, such as highways and bus stations; roadside development, such as diners, strip retail, and neon signs; business district buildings, such as movie theaters and department stores; and recreation facilities, such as amusement parks.

commode A covered washstand with a basin, sometimes plumbed with a drainpipe.

commode step One of two or more spiral-shaped steps with curved risers; projects beyond the side of the stringer at the bottom of a stair, with the newel typically starting on the uppermost commode step. See also **bull-nosed step, curtail.**

common ashlar A **quarry cut** stone block.

common beam One of several floor joists, as opposed to a **beam** (sense 1) or **girder.**

common bond A brick wall bond with a course of headers or a course of Flemish bond after every five or six courses of **running bond** stretchers. Also known as **American bond.**

common brass A ductile **brass** alloy composed of copper and approximately 36 percent zinc.

common brick 1. A standard size and shape brick; typical dimensions are 3½–3⅝ × 8 × 2¼ inches (90 mm × 200 mm × 57 mm). Also known as **building brick, standard brick, stock brick. 2.** (19c) The average brick of a particular kiln run. **3.** (19c) Same as **salmon brick.**

common iron (19c) The cheapest grade of iron.

common nail A nail with a large head, typically used for framing; sizes include **fourpenny nail, sixpenny nail, eightpenny nail, tenpenny nail, twentypenny nail, sixtypenny nail.**

common pitch **1.** A gable roof pitch in which the length of the rafters equals three-quarters of the length of the span. See also **pitch.** **2.** A slope of 45 degrees.

common purlin One of several purlins spanning between two principal rafters of a **timber frame** roof; used to support vertically oriented sheathing boards and connect the principal rafters. Also known as **rib.** See also **principal purlin.**

common rafter One of a series of sloped roof beams that span from the top of the exterior wall to the ridge; in a **timber frame** building are smaller than, and between, the **principal rafters.** Also known as **spar.** See also **rafter.**

common varnish (18c) A varnish composed of oil of turpentine dissolved in turpentine.

common wall Same as **party wall.**

community plan An official land use and physical development plan, typically including **heritage conservation** objectives and an inventory of **heritage sites,** prepared by a Canadian local government under section 709-713 of the **Municipal Act.**

community planning See **planning.**

compact limestone A fine-grained **limestone** composed of calcium carbonate, sometimes with small particles of clay or sand.

company town A residential community built and owned by a private company to house its workers.

compartment One of a series of subdivided interior spaces; typically separated by partitions. See also **room.**

compartment ceiling A ceiling divided into panels by raised moldings, especially when the panels are of different shapes or sizes.

compass brick **1.** A brick having a rounded face, used for building a curved wall. **2.** Same as **arch brick** (sense 1).

compass head, compast head A curved top on an architectural element; typically a semicircle.

compass-headed roof A roof in the shape of a semicylinder or smaller portion of a cylinder; typically with curved-top rafters.

compass roof, (pre-19c) **compast roof** **1.** Same as **compass-headed roof.** **2.** A roof with a truss in which the lower edge of the rafters, collar beam, and braces is approximately in the shape of a semicircle. See also **collar brace.** **3.** (pre-19c) Same as **compass head,** such as an arched door or window.

compass timber A curved or crooked timber.

compass window (pre-19c) **1.** Same as **bow window.** **2.** A window with a **compass head.**

compatible use (Canadian) An **adaptive use** that maintains or restores the historical exterior appearance of a building and does not require irreversible alteration of architecturally or historically significant interior building elements.

compliance alternative A formally adopted **equivalent** to a building code requirement.

compo Abbr. of **composition.**

compo board Abbr. of **composition board.**

Composite order A heavier form of the **Corinthian** order with a capital that combines the top of an Ionic order and the bottom of a Corinthian order. From top to bottom, the typical Composite order is shown in the figure. The order typically includes a pedestal; the corners of the abacus are cut off at a 45-degree angle, the sides of the capital bow inward and the center of each face is decorated with a fleuron; the dentils are large blocks like a bracket;

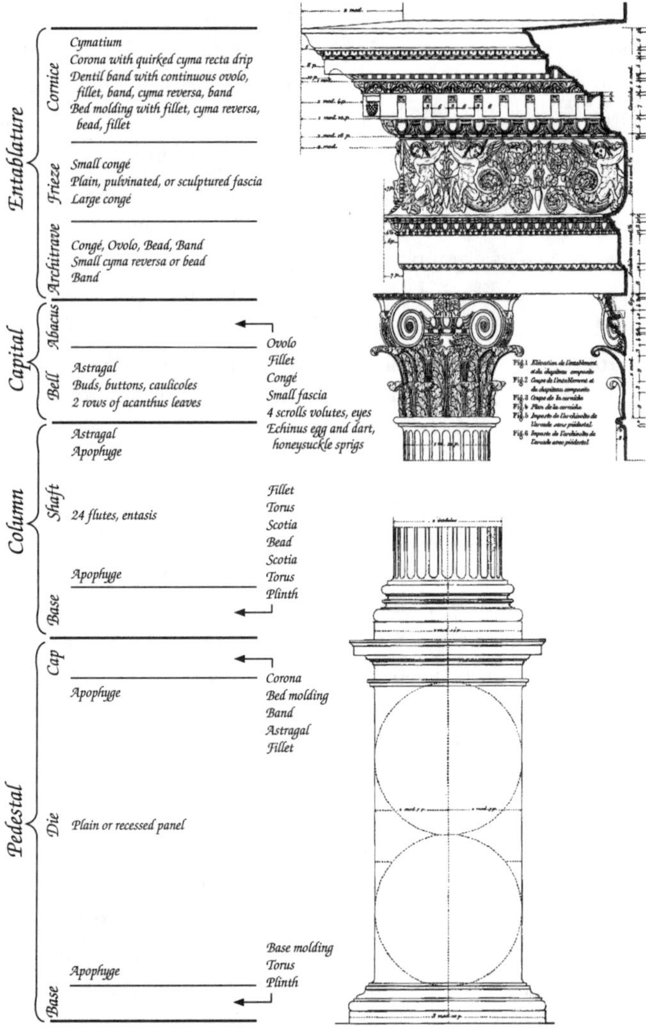

Composite order

the soffit of the corona between the dentils is plain; the Composite orders typically support an attic wall above the entablature. Also known as **Italic, Roman order.** See also **bud, button, caisson, caulicole, Classical orders, dentil, fleuron, Greek Revival style, lip of the bell.**

composite arch Same as **mixed arch.** See also **arch.**

composite wire fence A fence system composed of light-gauge, galvanized-steel wire mesh, with steel-pipe posts and top rails, cast **malleable iron** decoration, and **soft steel** scrollwork; manufactured in the U.S. from the mid-1880s to WWII; typically featured fleur-de-lis cresting until 1916. See also **wire fence.**

composition (late 18c–present) Any of several pastes that harden upon exposure to the air; used for cast or sculpted bas-relief ornament; types include mixtures of linseed or fish oil with whiting and animal-hide glue, or wood fibers and glue, or papier-maché, or plaster; used since the 17c and very common beginning in the 1890s. Also known as **compo.**

composition board A type of **wallboard** composed of compressed fibers; types include **Asbestos Air Cell Board, fiberboard, hardboard, Homosote, particle board, Sackett Board.**

composition shingle Any of various types of shingles made from a mixture of binder materials with fibers; types include **asbestos shingle, asphalt shingle;** first produced in the late 19c.

Compostone A trade name for **concrete block** manufactured in Jacksonville, Florida.

compound arch **1.** Same as a **built arch.** **2.** Same as a **mixed arch.** **3.** An arch with a multilayered archivolt that recedes from the face of the wall.

compound beam A **built beam** composed of two members stacked or side-by-side and fastened together so that they act as a single structural unit. Also known as **built-up** beam. See also **Clark's design, keyed beam.**

compound column A central column surrounded by other smaller columns; typically attached by a **shaft ring.**

compound order Same as **Composite.**

compound pier Same as a **clustered pier.**

compound vault A **vault** formed by the intersection of multiple vaults; types by number of intersecting vaults include **polygonal vault, tripartite vault, quadripartite vault, quinquepartite vault, sexpartite vault, septempartite vault, octopartite vault, decapartite, dodecapartite;** types include **cloister vault, cross vault, domical vault, groin vault, oblique vault, panel vault, segmental vault, stilted vault, star vault, Welsh vault.**

comprehensive plan A **master plan** for a local government area that includes various elements of **planning,** such as **land use,** transportation, and capital improvements; implemented by various methods, such as **zoning** and **historic districts.**

compressed glass (19c) **Sheet glass** tempered by pressing hot glass in cold molds. See also **tempered glass.**

compression shrinkage, compression set Permanent loss of volume of wood caused by crushing of the cells; often caused by swelling of the wood due to high moisture content, pressing against another element, and later shrinkage due to lower moisture content.

compressor **1.** (19c–present) A machine that pressurizes air or other gases. **2.** (pre-20c) A machine that compresses fibrous material such as hay or cotton. See also **cotton press.**

compting house (to early 19c) Same as **countinghouse.**

compting room (to early 19c) Same as **counting room.**

concamerate To arch over with a vault, especially one with coffers.

concave joint A **mortar joint** approximately shaped as an arc of a circle tangent to the corners of adjacent masonry units. Also known as **rodded joint.**

concave mansard roof A **mansard roof** with a concave lower slope. Also known as **French roof.**

concealed sprinkler A type of **sprinkler head** with its entire body concealed behind a cover plate on the ceiling or wall surface. See also **flush sprinkler.**

conch A concave construction in the form of a quarter sphere or less, as in the head of a semicircular niche.

concha 1. A sculptured, concave door head in the stylized form of the inside of a scallop shell; common in the massive walls of Spanish Colonial style buildings. **2.** A half dome above an apse. **3.** Same as **conch. 4.** The smooth, curved interior face of a **pendentive. 5.** (18c) Same as **expanding vault.**

conclave (pre-20c) A closet or inner room.

Concord granite A light gray **granite** quarried in the vicinity of Concord, New Hampshire; used for building stone, including the late 19c Library of Congress in Washington, D.C. See also **Swenson Buff Antique.**

concrete A structural building material formed by mixing water, **cement, sand,** and **aggregate** (such as crushed stone); typically placed in forms with steel reinforcing bars and allowed to harden; commonly used for foundations, structural framing, floor slabs, and pavement; types include **cast stone, cinder concrete, gypsum concrete, precast, reinforced concrete, stone concrete.** See also **asphalt concrete, portland cement.**

concrete block A molded concrete masonry unit with vertical hollow core holes; made with water, cement, aggregate, and, sometimes, coloring; first patented as **Foster Block** in 1855, common in the U.S. by the late 1860s and in Canada after ca. 1900; standard-weight block aggregates include gravel, sand, and crushed stone; lightweight block aggregates include shale, clay, slate, blast-furnace slag, sintered fly ash, coal cinders, pumice, and scoria; finishes include **chiseled, cobblestone face, cross tooth, duck-bill tooling, granite face, panel face, plain face, rock face, split face, tooled face,** and various bas-relief patterns; types include **Boyd block, Casberg block, cinderblock, Compostone, Frear stone, Hydrostone, Miami stone, pattern block, screen block, Straublox, Textile Block, Unit Block;** also known as **artificial stone, cement block, concrete tile.** See also **concrete masonry unit, block veneer.**

concrete masonry unit One of various cast concrete building blocks which can range in size from a **brick** to a **concrete block** measuring 8 × 12 × 16 inches; abbreviated CMU. See also **concrete block.**

concrete pipe (20c) Cylindrical pipe manufactured from portland cement concrete; typically of large diameter with interlocking ends; used for **sewer pipe** and water mains.

concrete plaster Same as **bond plaster.**

concrete tile (late 19c) Same as **concrete block.**

condemnation 1. (U.S.) The taking of real estate by a government agency for a public purpose, such as constructing a highway, with just compensation paid to the owner. See also **eminent domain, inverse condemnation. 2.** The declaration by a government agency that a building is unfit for human habitation and is to be vacated and repaired or demolished.

condenser 1. (20c) A machine used to condense a gas into a liquid as part of an air-conditioning or refrigeration system. **2.** (19c–present) A device used with a steam engine to condense steam exhaust and increase power by decreasing back pressure. **3.** The worm of a still in which vapors are condensed as liquor. **4.** (18c) Same as **compressor.**

condition assessment Inspection and analysis of an existing structure to identify symptoms and causes of problems; may include testing and monitoring in addition to visual inspection.

condition report Same as **historic structure report.**

condominium (mid-20c–present) **1.** One of several individually owned apartments or commercial spaces within a building. **2.** A building containing individually owned units. See also **cooperative.**

conductor A rain **leader** or **downspout.** Also known as **conductor pipe, rainwater conductor.** See also **conductor head, lightning conductor.**

conductor head An open-topped box that receives stormwater from a scupper or gutter and funnels it into a downspout; types include **hopper head.**

conductor pipe Same as **conductor.**

conduit **1.** (19c–present) A hollow pipe used for installing electric wiring, telephone cable, or similar wiring. **2.** (19c–present) A passageway or covered trench containing utilities such as water and gas lines and wiring. **3.** A pipe or channel for conveying fluids. See also **drain, sewer.**

cone joint A plumbing **joint** made by connecting tapered-end pipes with a sleeve that has inverted conical ends.

cone tile, cone hip tile A roof tile in the form of a truncated cone; used along a roof hip.

conge (18c) A ring or ferrule used at the ends of wood pillars to keep them from splitting; later imitated in stonework. See also **spudd and ring.**

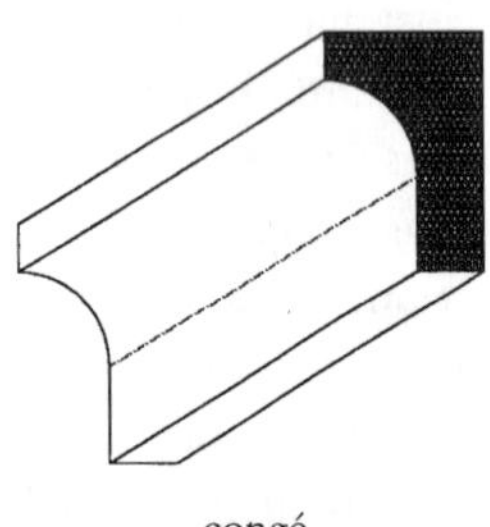

congé

congé, (pre-20c) **congee** **1.** A concave molding with one side of the quarter round concave curve tangent to a plane surface and the other side intersecting a fillet that is parallel to the plane surface; commonly used in the **classical orders.** **2.** (19c) Same as **apophyge.**

conglomerate Stone composed of rock fragments cemented together; types include **breccia, puddingstone.**

conical roof A roof with a circular plan that tapers upward to a point; used for round towers in the **Romanesque Revival style.**

conical vault, conic vault An **expanding vault** in the shape of a truncated semicone; most often used in a pendentive transition between an octagonal space above to a square space below or over a trapezoidal-shaped space. See also **conoidal vault.**

conjectural restoration The replacement of missing elements or the removal or repair of existing work based on speculation or theory due to insufficient physical evidence or incomplete historical documentation.

Connecticut brownstone A warm brown, fine-grained arkosoic sandstone quarried in Connecticut. See also **brownstone.**

Connecticut marble A coarsely crystalline, white, dolomite **marble** quarried in Canaan, East Canaan, Falls Village, and Milford, Connecticut, into the 19c.

Connecticut serpentine A **serpentine** marble quarried in the vicinity of Milford and New Haven, Connecticut, in the early 19c.

conoidal vault An **expanding vault** with the cross section at the small end in the shape of a semicircle and at the large end in the shape of a semiellipse with its long axis vertical; the ridge line is a sloped straight line.

conservation (20c) **1.** The skilled repair and maintenance of cultural artifacts, including buildings and historic or artistic materials, with the aim of extending their longevity and aesthetic qualities. See also **architectural conservation, preservation, restoration.** **2.** The protection of environmental quality.

conservation archaeology **Archaeology** that is limited to the minimum amount of excavation required to achieve research objectives; preserves unexcavated portions of the site for future, more sophisticated study.

Conservation Assessment Program A U.S. federal program administered by the **National Institute for the Conservation of Cultural Property** that provides independent, professional short-term surveys of the collections, sites, and environmental conditions of museums and, where appropriate, historic structures.

conservator (20c) An individual who practices **conservation,** especially in regard to an individual building or museum artifacts; types include **architectural conservator, fine arts conservator.** See also **curator.**

conservatory A greenhouse attached to a house and used as part of the living area. Also known as **orangerie.**

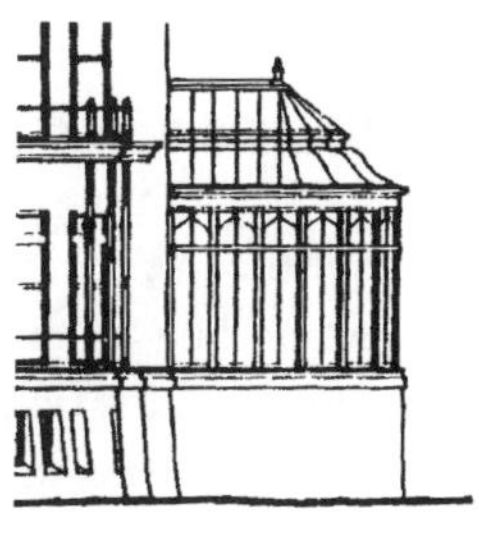

conservatory

console **1.** A thick, ornamental bracket with parallel, plane sides, especially when in the form of reverse scrolls; typically carved with elaborate decoration and sculpture. **2.** A projecting carved ornament on the keystone of an arch that supports a decorative cornice, bust, figure, or vase.

consolidation **1.** The stabilization of a deteriorated material by infusing it with another material, such as injecting epoxy resin into rotten wood or chemicals into stone. **2.** The combining of multiple real estate holdings, especially land, into a single parcel; typically part of a **development** process.

construction **1.** The act or business of building a structure. **2.** The building or detail which has been put together, such as a house of **wood frame construction.** See also **new construction.**

constructional (19c) Of a type or grade used in **construction,** such as constructional cast iron or constructional timber.

construction documents (20c) The data that set forth the detailed requirements for a restoration, renovation, or new construction project; typically include **working drawings** and **specifications.** See also **articles of agreement.**

construction joint Any **joint** that is a result of the normal sequence of construction, such as the joint between subsequent pours of concrete. See also **control joint, expansion joint.**

construction loan Short-term financing of a development project during the initial construction period; typically finances both hard and soft costs, and is replaced by a **permanent loan.**

construction observation On-site visit by the design architect or engineer to determine whether the construction materials and techniques are generally in conformance with the **construction documents;** includes analysis of building conditions discovered during construction and review of testing and inspection reports. Also known as **site observation.** See also **inspection, supervision, testing.**

Construction Specifications Institute (CSI) A national U.S. organization devoted to assisting professional specification writers; publishes model specification sections and a standardized format and numbering system.

constructive use The indirect harm or proximity impact of a U.S. federally funded transportation project on a historic site, park, wildlife refuge, or recreational area that is so severe that the value of the site is substantially impaired; negative impacts may result from noise, air pollution, and general unsightliness. See also **Section 4(f), Section 106.**

consultation process A process of preservation conflict resolution, especially the method required of U.S. federal agencies by **Section 106** in order to seek ways to reduce or avoid harm to historic properties, which might otherwise result from a federally assisted **undertaking;** involves the agency, a state historic preservation officer, and the Advisory Council on Historic Preservation; typically, the outcome is a binding **Memorandum of Agreement.**

contact period The time period during which Europeans first interacted with North American native peoples in a particular locality. See also **postcontact, precontact.**

containment (Canada) The construction of physical barriers to prevent unauthorized access to a site or building. See also **stabilization.**

contemporary Living or existing in the same time period; an ambiguous term that may mean of the same historical time, or of the present time, as in **modern.**

contingency The portion of a **development budget** allocated to costs that are likely to be incurred but are unknown at the start of a project; may be used for **hard costs,** such as a **change order,** or for **soft costs;** often established as 10 percent of the hard costs for a restoration project.

continuous coil spiral A decorative motif in the form of interlocked scrolls.

continuous hip A shingled roof hip that has been curved with **erectors** so that the courses run smoothly around a corner.

continuous impost **1.** The uninterrupted flow of a vaulting rib from the ceiling to the base of a column; found in the Gothic Revival style. **2.** Arch moldings that continue down the face of a supporting wall or pillar without a visually defined **impost.**

contract administration Architectural services provided during the construction phase of a project; typically includes construction observation, reviewing shop drawings and samples, processing change orders, and approving certificates of payment from the contractor. See also **architectural design.**

contraction joint Same as **control joint.**

contractor (late 18c–present) An individual or organization that contracts to perform construction work for a fee; types include **general contractor, subcontractor.** Also known as **undertaker.** See also **builder, supplier.**

contracture The narrowing of a column in a straight line toward one end. See also **entasis.**

contrasted arch An ogee or other arch with a reverse curve. See also **arch.**

contre-imbrication A decorative pattern in the form of overlapping rows of arches. See also **imbrication.**

contributing resource A building, site, structure, or object adding to the historic significance of a property or district.

control date The exact date to which a historic resource is restored or interpreted. See also **control period.**

control joint A groove or small embedded strip in the surface of a monolithic material, such as concrete, that is intended to limit shrinkage cracking to that location. Also known as **contraction joint.**

controlled photography Photography designed to produce relatively distortion free, scaled photographs to document a subject; usually with **large-format photography;** may be used to record a building or structure as a substitute for **measured drawings;** typically corrects for parallax by using **rectified photography** or **orthophotography** and, as far as possible, eliminates distortions and variations from varying light levels and color balance. See also **field photography, photogrammetry.**

control period The time period to which a historic resource is restored or interpreted; the beginning and ending dates are known as **terminus a quo** and **terminus adquem,** respectively. See also **control date, period of significance.**

Convention Concerning the Protection of the World Cultural and Natural Heritage A set of principles regarding preservation of historic and natural sites throughout the world adopted by the member states of UNESCO in 1972; includes a list of important cultural and natural properties nominated by member countries. Also known as **World Heritage Convention.** See also **World Heritage Committee.**

conversation room A sitting room in a private clubhouse.

conversion Change of use of a property, such as from apartments to condominiums or from a house to offices.

convex-conoidal vault A **conoidal vault** with a straight spring line and upwardly curved ridge line connecting the large and small ends; typically part of a **compound vault.** See also **expanding vault.**

cookhouse, (pre-19c) **cook house,** (18c) **kuch house, kuck house** A building for a kitchen that is separate from the main house.

cookroom (18c–19c Delaware) Same as **kitchen.**

cooling tower A device used to cool water by evaporation by trickling it over a series of vanes; used in conjunction with a building **air-conditioning** system.

coop An enclosure or cage for small animals, especially one with woven sides used for poultry.

co-op Same as **cooperative.**

cooperative, co-operative, co-op (20c) An apartment building that is jointly owned by the residents. See also **condominium.**

copal The gummy resin of various tropical trees; color ranges from colorless to yellowish to brown-black; used in varnishes, lacquers, and linoleum.

copal varnish Any varnish made with copal gum dissolved in a solvent. See also **hard oil, varnish.**

cope-and-stick A door or window sash with solid stick moldings on the rails and stiles, with the rails coped at the ends where they abut the molding on the stiles.

coped **1.** Cut to conform to the irregular outline of an abutting piece, such as where the end of one piece of molding overlaps another at an inside corner. See also **scribed. 2.** Having a **coping.**

copies (pre-19c) Same as **coppice.**

coping **1.** A water-resistant covering of the top of a wall; typically overhangs the sides of the wall to provide a drip for rain; common materials include stone, terra-cotta, and metal; types include **featheredge coping, parallel coping, saddle-back coping.** Also known as **tabling.** See also **footstone. 2.** The process of breaking marble to size in the plant.

coping course The row of roofing tiles at the edge of a roof that form the coping of the wall below. See also **field course.**

coping stone A stone block used to form a coping. See also **coping, footstone, parallel coping.**

copper A ductile, corrosion-resistant, metal element; reddish yellow in its pure state, bluish green when oxidized by exposure to the weather; used for sheet metal and electric wire, and as an alloy component. See also **bronze.**

copper colored **1.** The warm reddish yellow color of polished **copper. 2.** The light bluish green color of oxidized copper.

copper green A light bluish green oil-paint pigment composed of copper salts.

copper napthenate solution An aqueous solution of copper napthenate; used as a **wood preservative.**

copper pipe A pipe of solid, drawn copper; typically of small diameter and connected with soldered fittings; used for water supply.

copper-red brass A ductile alloy of copper and approximately 0.08 percent iron.

coppice, copse, (pre-19c) **copies** A dense thicket of small trees, especially a group of saplings sprouting from the stumps of trees that are periodically cut back.

copse Same as **coppice.**

coquillage Carved decoration in the form of stylized seashells.

coquina A slightly consolidated limestone, largely composed of seashells, formerly quarried on Anastasia Island, Florida, beginning in the late 17c, and on some Caribbean islands; used to construct various Spanish Colonial buildings, including houses and fortifications.

cora A draped female figure used architecturally. See also **caryatid.**

coral A white or pink building stone cut from former coral reefs in Florida and the West Indies; the many internal air pockets make it an excellent insulator.

coral marble Any **marble** containing coral fossils.

coral rock Limestone largely composed of coral.

corbeil A sculptured ornament in the form of a basket of fruit and flowers.

corbel **1.** A stepped portion of a masonry wall; the steps may be on top, as in a **crowstep** parapet, or below, as at the edge of an opening or supporting a belt course. See also **pannier.** **2.** A stepped arch impost that projects from a wall. See also **raked brick.**

corbel arch The bridge over an opening formed by laying successive horizontal courses closer to the middle. Also known as **Maya arch.** See also **corbel vault.**

corbel course A horizontal masonry band with continuous or intermittent corbels. See also **corbel table.**

corbel piece Same as **bolster** or **lookout.**

corbel step Same as **crowstep.**

corbel table Projecting masonry supported by a series of individual corbels, often with small arches between the corbels.

corbel vault A continuous **corbel arch** over a space; used by the ancient Mayas of the Yucatan. Also known as **Maya arch.**

corbil (18c) Same as **corbel.**

cord See **sash cord.**

cordon Same as **stringcourse.**

Cordova Pink A deep pink, coarse-grained **granite** mottled with black and quarried in Llano County, Texas.

core **1.** Rough masonry that is finished with plaster or ashlar. **2.** A cylindrical sample drilled out of the earth, masonry, wood, or concrete to inspect or test hidden materials. **3.** The interior part of a wood veneered element, such as a door. **4.** (20c) A vertical stack of service elements grouped together in a high-rise building; typically includes elevators, stairs, toilet rooms, and mechanical rooms and shafts. **5.** A center hollow space in a brick or concrete block.

core sample Same as **core** (sense 2.).

Corinthian order The most ornate and recent of the Greek **classical orders,** used in most Roman buildings. From top to bottom, the typical Corinthian order is shown in the figure. The **Roman Corinthian** order adds a pedestal; the corners of the abacus are cut off at a 45-degree angle, the sides bow inward, and the center of each face is decorated with a **fleuron;** the modillions are in the form of a double scroll supported by an acanthus leaf and are crowned with a small cyma reversa; the **caissons** between the modillions have a large

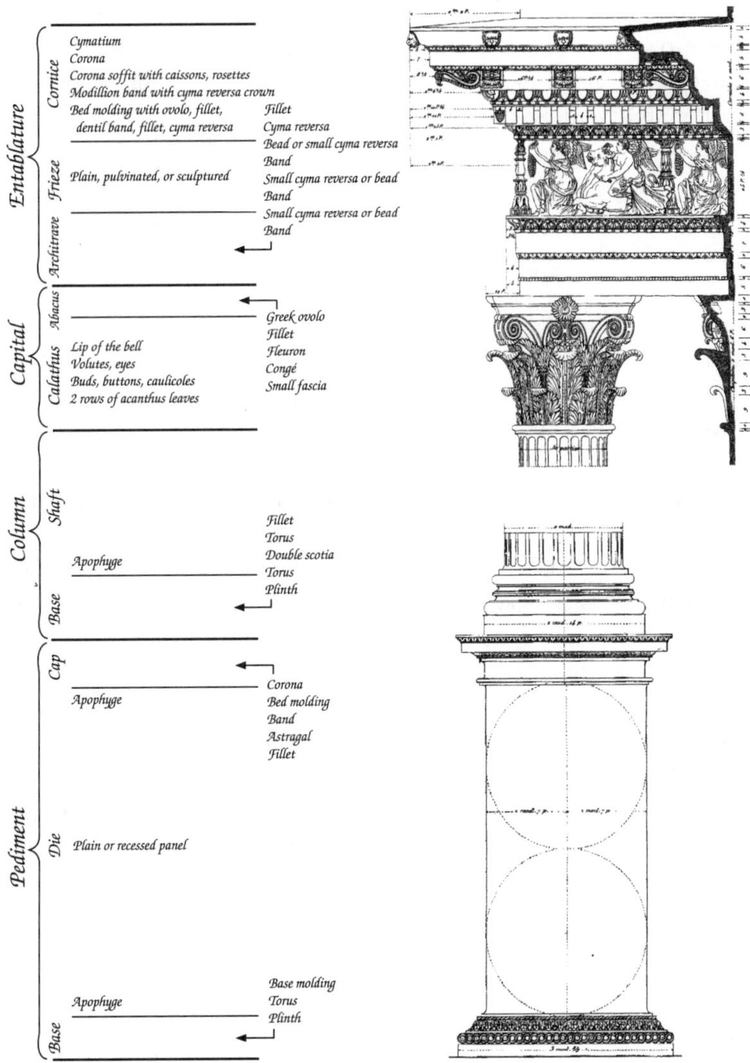

Corinthian order

rosette in their centers; the Corinthian orders typically support an attic wall above the entablature. See also **French order, Greek Revival style, lip of the bell.**

cork The lightweight, elastic bark of the cork oak tree; used for insulation, floor tile, and composite materials; *Quercus suber.*

corkboard (19c) A thick, lightweight sheet manufactured from ground cork particles and paper pulp; used for sound and heat insulation.

cork fossil (19c) Same as **asbestos.**

corkscrew stair Same as **spiral stair.**

Corktown cottage (Michigan) A one-story, gable front, clapboard house with a side entry hall;

the entry hall opens on one side to a front parlor and on the rear to a rear parlor, and a dining room is located at the rear of the building; both the rear parlor and the dining room are also connected to small side bedrooms; typically a kitchen was added behind the dining room; built 1820s–1850s; named for Detroit's oldest neighborhood built by Irish from County Cork.

corkwood The lightweight, porous wood of several Caribbean island trees, including *Anona palustris* and *Ochroma lagopus.*

corncrib, (pre-20c) **corn crib** A roofed structure for holding harvested ears of corn; typically raised above the ground and with side openings for air circulation; pre-WWII farm outbuildings commonly constructed of wood with slat sides sloping outward, now mostly metal; some midwestern Canadian and U.S. examples are large and have a central drive aisle. See also **cornhouse, corn loft.**

corner bead **1.** A metal ground for forming a sharp corner with plaster or drywall; covered by the finish coat. **2.** Same as **angle bead.**

corner block A square block used to trim casing at the upper corners of door and window surrounds; typically decorated with a milled bull's-eye. See also **head block.**

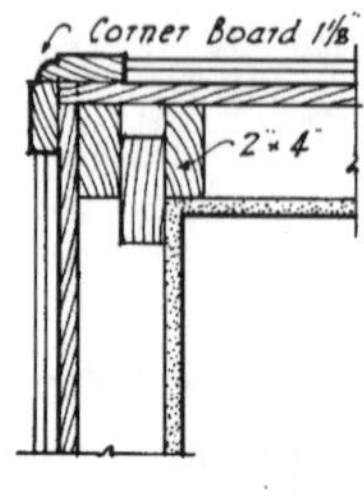

corner board

corner board One of a pair of boards installed with an L-shaped plan at an outside corner of a building with wood siding; clapboard or shingle siding usually abuts the sides.

corner capital Same as **angle capital.**

corner chimney A fireplace and chimney located in the corner of a room; typically the stack is shared with another fireplace in an adjoining room. Also known as **angle chimney.**

corner post The vertical member at an outside corner of a **wood frame** structure; may be a single timber, as in a **principal post,** or built-up of several studs, as in **stick built** construction.

corner stone (18c) A single, fire-resistant stone forming a chimney jamb; extends from the hearth to the bottom of the mantel. See also **cornerstone.**

cornerstone, (19c) **corner-stone,** (pre-19c) **corner stone** **1.** A decorative ceremonial stone block placed at or near a corner of a building to commemorate the start of construction; may be inscribed or contain a time capsule. **2.** Any stone block that forms part of the corner of a wall. See also **corner stone.** **3.** A stone **boundary marker** located at a turn in the property line.

corner tile (pre-19c) Same as **hip tile.**

cornhouse, (pre-19c) **corn house** **1.** (pre-19c) A building in which shelled corn or corn ears are stored. See also **corncrib, corn loft, fodder house.** **2.** (pre-18c) Same as **granary.**

cornice, (pre-19c) **cornish** **1.** The projecting moldings forming the top band of an **entablature,** wall, or other element; types include **barge cornice, box cornice, double cornice, Gothic cornice, modillion cornice, raked**

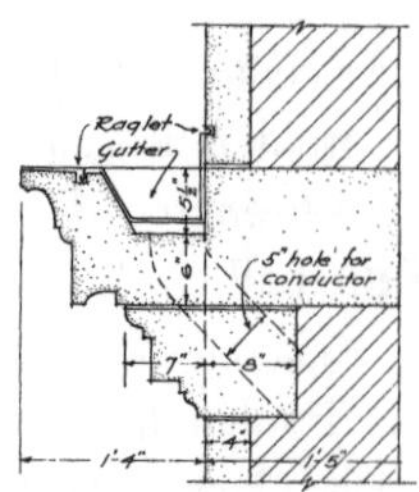

cornice (sense 1)

cornice, roof cornice, single cornice, wall cornice. See also **classical orders, corona, crown molding. 2.** The projecting molding at the top of a door or window casing. See also **architrave, chambranle. 3.** (19c) Same as **picture molding.**

cornice hook An S-shaped hook used to hang artwork from a cornice or picture molding.

cornice return The extension of a cornice in a new direction, especially where the **raked cornice** of a gable end returns horizontally a short distance.

corniche (18c) Same as **cornice.**

cornicione A large cornice proportioned to the entire height of a building, rather than to one story; common in **classical** style buildings. See also **colossal order.**

corn loft, (17c) **corne loafte** A building **loft** where corn is stored. See also **corn crib, cornhouse.**

corona 1. The vertical face of the principal projecting member of a **cornice.** See also **fascia board. 2.** On a cornice, the entire large projecting element with a rectangular cross section; the bottom surface is known as a **soffit;** typically has a **drip** and a **cymatium** molding above and a **bed molding** below. Also known as **larmier.**

coronet Any relief decoration above a door or window; for example, a pediment. See also **architrave, crown molding, overdoor.**

corporation cock, corporation stop The shutoff valve connecting a water or gas main to the pipe that leads into a building. See also **stop cock.**

corps de logis The main portion of a large house, as distinct from the wings. See also **avant de corps.**

corpse house (pre-19c) A building in which dead bodies were placed in the winter until the ground thawed enough to allow burial; typically next to a church; often a cellar.

corredor In the **Spanish Colonial** style, an arcade along one or more sides of an interior courtyard.

corridor 1. A relatively long, narrow passage or hall connecting multiple suites or apartments, such as in a hotel or office building. **2.** (pre-20c) A wide passage or gallery in a building or surrounding a quadrangle, usually connected to multiple rooms or suites. **3.** A covered passageway around the perimeter of a **fortification. 4.** (southern U.S.) A covered carriageway.

corrosion The chemical reaction of metal with other elements to form various compounds; may produce a stable patina (e.g., bronze) or rapid decay (e.g., rusting iron); water and oxygen are common activating agents; **galvanic corrosion** can affect all metals; types affecting copper and its alloys include **atacamite, azurite, brochantite, bronze disease, verdigris;** types affecting iron include **rust;** types affecting silver include **argenite.** See also **oxidation, rust jacking.**

corrugated glass A glass sheet with a cross section in the form of a regular sine wave, with parallel ridges and valleys; manufactured by pressing hot glass in a mold.

corrugated iron **Corrugated metal** sheets composed of iron or steel.

corrugated metal Sheets of metal stiffened by bending or rolling to produce parallel ridges and valleys; the cross section may be in various forms, including a curved, regular sine wave or straight lines with sharp bends; used for roofing and siding, and as floor and roof decking; types include **corrugated iron, corrugated plate, corrugated sheet, steel decking.**

corrugated plate (19c) A bent iron plate with a cross section in the form of an upward curving circle segment with horizontal flanges; typically 8¾ or 12³⁄₁₆ inches wide; multiple pieces used to span between bridge stringers to support the concrete paving or floor beams. See also **buckled plate, zore.**

corrugated sheet (19c–present) **Corrugated metal** manufactured from sheet metal.

cortina Corbeled stonework below a projecting windowsill or balcony on **Spanish Colonial** buildings; typically in the form of a stylized hanging banner with tassels and often layered in appearance; from the Spanish for **curtain.**

cottage **1.** A small, informal house of any style, often with a steeply pitched roof. **2.** (19c–early 20c) A country or resort house used as a summer residence; may be a small dwelling (such as those found at church campgrounds) or a mansion (such as those at Newport, Rhode Island). **3.** (19c–mid-20c) A suburban house.

cotton gin See **ginhouse.**

cotton house (southern U.S.) A **warehouse** used for storing cotton on a plantation.

cotton press A mechanical device that compresses processed cotton fibers into a bale; beginning in the 1840s, a tall wood frame with a large-diameter vertical screw rotated by a pair of sweeps pulled by mules and often protected by a pyramidal roof supported on four cornerposts; by the late 19c, beater, geared, hydraulic, toggle, rolling pressure, and windlass forms were developed; typically located adjacent to a **ginhouse.** Also known as **compressor.**

couch (18c) One coat of paint or varnish on a surface.

Council on Environmental Quality (CEQ) An independent U.S. federal agency created by the **National Environmental Policy Act of 1969.**

counter **1.** A horizontal work, display, or serving surface, such as in a store or restaurant. **2.** (20c) A work surface in a residential kitchen, especially one on top of cabinets. See also **countertop.**

counter arch An arch that resists the thrust of another arch.

counterbrace, (19c) **counter-brace, counter brace** **1.** A truss tie designed to resist variable live loads that would change the shape of the truss, and to dampen vibration; typically a diagonal member between panel-points. **2.** A subordinate brace crossing a main brace of a truss, used to resist forces in both directions.

counter ceiling, counter sealing (19c) A second ceiling installed above a main ceiling for sound and/or fire insulation; typically **sound boarding** with **pugging** above.

counter cock Same as **pantry cock.**

counterfeit architecture A **trompe l'oeil** that has the appearance of three-dimensional architectural elements.

counterflashing, counter flashing Sheet metal, or other waterproof material, on the face of a wall that overlaps and seals the top of vertical **flashing** below; typically in the form of an inverted L-shape with the upper end laid in a mortar joint or inserted in a reglet.

counterfloor, counter floor **1.** The lower-level boards of a wood **double floor;** furring and sound insulation are laid on top and support the finish floor. **2.** (pre-20c) Same as **subfloor.**

counterfort A buttress or reinforcing wall perpendicular to a foundation or retaining wall;

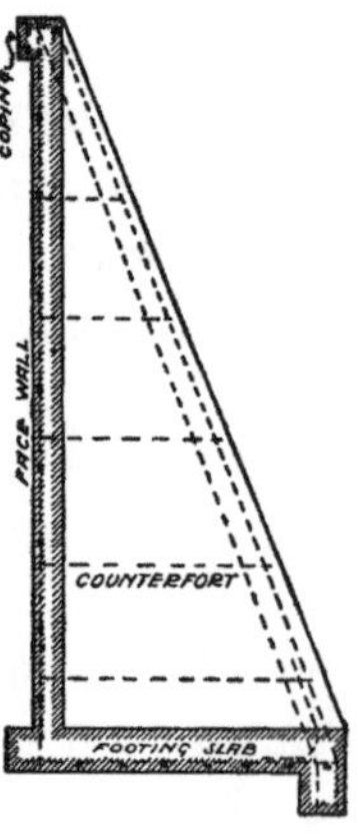

counterfort

may be on the side opposite the earth or on the earth side of the wall.

counterlath **1.** A batten spanning across the ceiling joists and to which the plaster lath is fastened perpendicularly; used to level the ceiling. **2.** Lath placed on a wall after the opposite face of the framing is plastered. **3.** Lath strips nailed parallel to the framing to level the surface and raise the lath to provide a plaster key. **4.** A roof tile lath strip installed perpendicular to two **gauge lath** to determine the spacing between them.

counterlight A window placed directly opposite another window on a facing wall. See also **cross light.**

countermure, (19c) **counter-mure** **1.** A low wall built next to another wall to fortify it or to prevent adjacent construction from damaging it. **2.** (19c) The veneer on a masonry wall.

counterpoise A heavy weight on an element, such as a corbel, that prevents movement due to other forces.

counter-retable The rear face of a **retable** that is in the form of a screen.

counterscarp wall The outer sloped wall or bank of a ditch that is part of a fortification. See also **fosse, scarp.**

countersink **1.** To make a recess to receive a piece of hardware, such as a screw or hinge, so that when installed the top will be flush with or below the surface. **2.** To drive a nail below the surface of the wood. See also **blind nailed, screwed and plugged.**

countersink nail A nail with a head that is beveled on the bottom so that it will sink into the surface. See also **nail.**

countersunk slab A horizontal stone slab with the middle cut down so that a raised rim is left on the edges; used on plumbing fixtures.

counter terrace (pre-19c) An earthen terrace constructed on top of another terrace, such as for a **parterre.**

countertop, counter top The cover slab of a **counter;** may be of various materials, including wood, stone, and plastic laminate on a substrate.

countervault Same as **inverted arch.**

counter-vent (pre-WWI) Same as **back vent.**

counter wall **1.** A building wall with its face on a property line that abuts an existing wall of another building. See also **party wall. 2.** Same as **countermure.**

counterweight A heavy component used to counterbalance the weight of a movable element; may be connected with a cable over a pulley, such as with an **elevator,** or be at one end of a lever on a pivot, such a leaf of a **bascule bridge.**

countinghouse, (19c) **counting-house,** (pre-20c) **counting house,** (to early 19c) **compting house** The building or room in which the accounting and other administrative functions of a business are performed.

counting room, (to early 19c) **compting room** A room in which the accounting and other administrative functions of a business are performed. Also known as **countinghouse.**

country seat A rural residence, especially an imposing home of a gentleman.

Countryside Institute A not-for-profit organization headquartered in Washington, D.C., that assists small communities to achieve a sustainable local economy while enhancing the quality of life; administers the International Countryside Stewardship Exchange.

county A political and geographic subdivision of a state in the U.S. See also **parish.**

couple (19c) A pair of rafters and a tie beam that form a simple triangular truss. See also **main couple.**

couple bolt (19c) A bolt with a square or hexagonal head at one end and threads to receive a nut at the other; the most common form of bolt.

couple close Same as **coupled.**

coupled Two elements tied or paired together, including (1) a pair of columns or pilasters located so that they nearly touch; typically used in multiples with wider spacing between the pairs; common in various Classical Revival styles; see also **intercolumniation;** (2) a **couple** of rafters; (3) **coupled windows.**

coupled windows A pair of windows that abut.

coupling See **pipe coupling.**

coupon A small piece of iron or steel cut from a structural member for testing for mechanical and chemical properties.

course **1.** A horizontal row of repetitive elements, especially masonry, tile, or roofing units; types include **blocking course, coping course, stringcourse, tumbling course.** Also known as **layer.** See also **bond, coursed. 2.** A layer of repetitive elements with joints radiating from a common center, as in a **rowlock arch.**

coursed **Stonework** or other masonry installed with courses of equal height units; all courses are not necessarily the same height; types include **brickwork, coursed ashlar, coursed rubble, range ashlar.** See also **uncoursed.**

coursed ashlar **Stonework** installed with courses composed of equal height **ashlar** blocks; all courses are not necessarily the same height; vertical joints may be of various patterns, such as **running bond.**

coursed rubble **Rubble masonry** with interrupted coursing and stones of irregular size and shape.

coursing joint **1.** A continuous horizontal **joint** between two masonry courses. **2.** A sloped joint between two voussoirs.

court **1.** Same as **courtyard. 2.** A level space for playing a game, such as tennis or basketball; may be exterior or interior.

courthouse, (18c–19c) **court-house,** (pre-19c) **court house** (mid-17c–present) A building designed to house one or more **courtrooms** and related facilities, such as judge's chambers and jury room; sometimes includes government administrative offices.

courtroom An interior space that houses a judicial court; typically with a judge's **bench, jury box, witness stand,** and **seating;** may be located in a **courthouse.**

courtyard An exterior space surrounded on three or four sides by buildings and/or walls.

coussinet **1.** The first stone of a curved arch that rests on the impost; the bottom bed is horizontal and the top is sloped. **2.** The scroll at the top of an Ionic capital, including the two volutes.

cove Any concave surface in the form of a portion of a cylinder, such as a vault. See also various phrases beginning with **cove** and **coved.**

cove and bead A solid sticking mold with a quarter round cove, fillet, and quarter round bead; the bead is at the outer edge of the mold. See also **bead and cove.**

cove bracketing The curved framework that supports plaster lath for a coved ceiling.

coved arch, coved vault Same as **cloistered vault.**

coved base A quarter hollow base molding; typically ceramic tile.

coved ceiling A cove-shaped transition between a ceiling and wall.

cove molding A molding in the shape of a cove.

covered passage Same as **covered way.**

covered way **1.** A roofed and open-sided passage connecting buildings or parts of a building; sides may be partially enclosed. Also known as **arcade, breezeway, covered passage. 2.** A passage in a fortification protected from enemy fire, especially a banquette or corridor on top of the counterscarp behind the embankment of the glacis. Also known as **covert way. 3.** (19c) A beam pocket left in a wall to accommodate roof rafters. **4.** Same as **cellar door.**

covering tile Same as **imbrex.**

cover plate A removable metal cover. See also **hinge plate.**

covert way (pre-20c) Same as **covered way.**

coving (pre-20c) The overhang of the upper stories of a building, especially with a plastered cove over the sidewalk.

coving jambs A curved or concave jamb; common on the inside edge of a mantelpiece.

cow barn A **barn** in which cows are kept; typically the cow stalls are at a lower story, with a hayloft above. See also **bank barn, cow stable.**

cowhouse A building where cows are kept. See also **cow stable.**

cowl A sheet-metal device that covers the top of a chimney, duct, or pipe to keep out rain; often designed to rotate with the wind; types include **ventilator, wind cowl.**

cow shed A **shed** in which cows are sheltered. See also **cow stable.**

cow stable Any building where cows are kept in stalls, especially for milking. See also **cow barn, cowhouse, cow shed, dairy, stable.**

CPM Abbr. for **critical path method.**

CPM diagram The graphic display of a **critical path method** analysis of a series of activities; typically has a series of parallel horizontal lines representing each activity with the length corresponding to the time to complete the activity, and arrows connecting the lines in the proper sequence; the critical path is graphically identified as a line moving through the diagram. See also **master plan.**

CPVC Abbr. for **chlorinated polyvinyl chloride.**

Crab Orchard stone A variegated, buff and gray quartzite quarried in Cumberland County, Tennessee; easily split in layers.

crack See **check, shake, split.**

crackle glass A type of **obscure glass** with a fine network of cracks on the surface. Also known as **ice glass.**

cradle vault Same as **barrel vault.**

craftsman sticking A door panel **sticking** with a rectangular cross section flush with the face of the rail or stile.

Craftsman style A small house and furniture style popular in the U.S. in the early 20c, popularized by Gustav Stickley's magazine **The Craftsman;** an outgrowth of the **Arts and Crafts movement,** which concentrated more on interiors than exteriors, especially in the illustrations of architect Harvey Ellis; exteriors could be any style, with typical features including irregular massing, low-slope gable roofs with wide eaves and exposed rafters, projecting beam ends or knee braces supporting bargeboards, porches with square-tapered columns or piers, and pergolas; common interior features included connected spaces separated by low-height walls, little or no applied ornament, straight lines, varnished wood (especially white oak), built-in benches and cabinets, box beams on the ceilings, and painted or **prairie plaster** walls; often used in conjunction with **bungalow** construction.

Craig pink A reddish pink **marble** with few veins quarried in the vicinity of Knoxville, Tennessee; polishes well.

crammed Packed tightly with material, especially clay **chinking** between the logs of a wall or an **earthen floor.**

cramp A metal strap used to fasten adjoining masonry stones together, especially when used to attach face stone to the backing; shaped in the form of a large staple or a double dovetail and inserted in recesses cut in the top of the stones; often seated in lead. Also known as **clamp, crampon, crampoon, dog, wall clamp.**

crampon Same as **cramp.**

crampoon (18c) Same as **cramp.**

crandalled The hand-cut surface texture of soft stone blocks with approximately ⅛-inch-deep grooves made with a crandall chisel; may be roughly parallel furrows or random; See also **furrows, stonework, tooth-chisel.**

crane An iron bracket that swivels into a fireplace; used to hang cooking pots; typically has a horizontal bar with a U-shaped end and a diagonal brace; may support a **trammel.** See also **randle bar.**

crapaudine door A door that rotates on pivots centered at the top and bottom. See also **door.**

crawl space A low-height space between the bottom of the floor of the lowest building story and the grade; may have an earthen or paved floor.

crazing A network of hairline cracks on a surface; found in various materials including concrete, ceramic glazes, and paint. See also **alligatoring.**

crazy (pre-20c) Full of cracks or dilapidated. See also **crazing.**

cream antique A slightly mottled, creamy white **marble** quarried pre-1920 in the vicinity of Brandon, Vermont. Also known as **Middlebury Cream.**

creamery The part of a dairy barn used to process raw milk; often a separate structure connected to a barn by a covered passage.

cream Lauville A cream white **marble** with numerous indistinct grayish, bluish, or yellowish veins quarried in the vicinity of Clarendon, Vermont; polishes medium well.

cream Pavonazzo A cream colored **marble** with variously colored veins quarried before ca. 1920 in Brandon, Vermont.

cream statuary A light cream colored **marble** with very pale brown waves; polishes medium well.

creeper A brick abutting the extrados of an arch and cut to follow the curve.

cremone bolt A locking device for french doors that includes two vertical rods that run the entire height of the door and are attached in the middle with a turning mechanism; when in the locked position, the rods act as bolts, sliding into the head and sill of the doorframe.

crenel, crenelle One of a series of open spaces between the merlons of a **battlement.** Also known as **embrasure.**

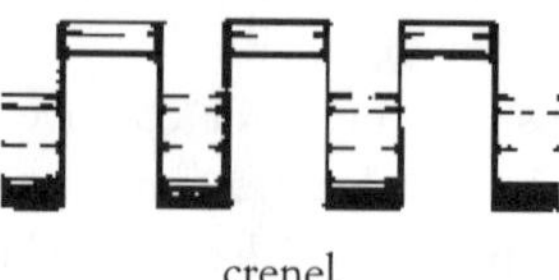

crenel

crenelet A small **crenel.**

crenellated, crenelated Having a parapet wall in the form of a **battlement** (sense 1).

crenellated molding, crenelated molding A molding band with a continuous bead that forms the outline of a **battlement** by a series of right-angle turns.

crenelle Same as **crenel.**

Creole Several varieties of bluish black and white mottled **marble,** some with heavy black clouding, quarried in Pickens County, Georgia. Also known as **Georgia creole.** See also **Georgia marble.**

Creole cottage A side-gabled, timber frame, one-story house built by Acadian immigrants to Louisiana 18c–early 20c; typically raised on piers with a front porch covered by a steeply pitched roof, clapboard sheathing, and a brick chimney adjacent to a gable end.

creosote An oil distilled from coal tar; used as a wood preservative and a base for shingle stains. Also known as **heavy oil.**

crescent A shape similar to the visible part of the moon in its first or last quarter, such as (1) (18c–19c) a row of town house fronts constructed in the approximate shape of a circular or elliptical arc; (2) a scrollwork cutout in a crescent shape.

cresting **1.** Same as **battlement** (sense 2). **2.** Decoration in the form of a series of ornate,

cresting (sense 2)

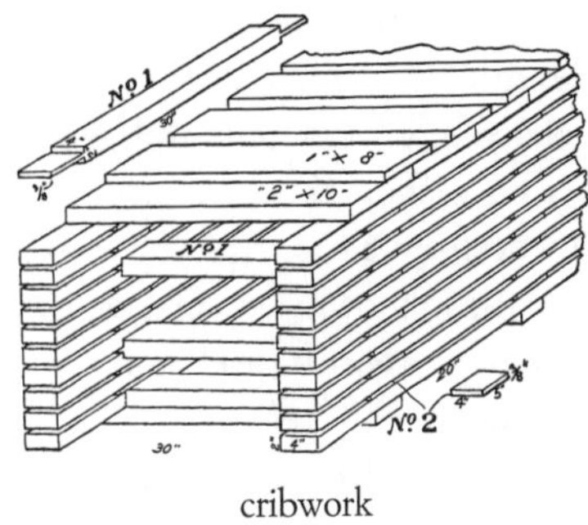

cribwork

pointed shapes located at the top of a parapet or roof ridge. Also known as **roof crest.**

crest table A saddleback stone coping with a raised astragal molding along its ridge; common in battlements.

crest tile Tile that covers a roof ridge and has projecting ornamentation across the top.

CRHP Canadian Register of Heritage Properties

CRI Color Rendering Index

crib, (18c) **cribb** **1.** (early 18c to present) Any small, wooden building constructed with open spaces between the boards or logs that form the walls; typically used for storage of crops; types include **corncrib.** **2.** A **foundation** constructed of a series of parallel timbers laid at right angles on alternate layers and connected with drift bolts; may be permanent or be used as the base for **shoring.** **3.** Same as **pen.** **4.** A timber shaft lining in a mine. **5.** Same as **cribwork.** **6.** A **retaining wall, wharf,** or similar structure constructed of **cribwork.** **7.** Same as **manger.** **8.** (20c) The space between two adjacent **cross ties** of a railroad track.

cribbled A random pattern of small depressions dotting the surface of stone, wood, or metal to produce a background pattern.

cribwork A framework constructed of a series of parallel timbers, laid at right angles on alternate layers, connected with drift bolts, notches, or chains, and filled with stone; used for retaining walls, wharves, and similar structures.

cricket A small element placed to create a slope away from a low point where a sloped roof abuts a vertical element, such as at the upper side of a roof surrounding a chimney; typically with two slopes in the shape of a miniature gable roof covered with flashing or shingles.

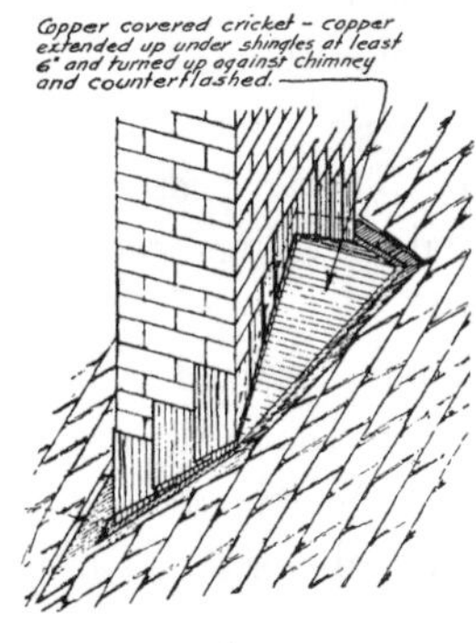

cricket

crimson A red paint pigment with a tinge of blue, composed of **mercuric sulfide.**

criosphinx A **sphinx** with the head of a ram and the body of a lion.

cripple **1.** Same as **jack** in reference to various framing members; types include **bottom cripple, cripple jack, top cripple.** See also **rafter, stud.** **2.** A short framing beam that spans between two joists or rafters. See also **header.**

cripple jack A cripple rafter that spans between a valley rafter and a hip rafter.

crisis archaeology Limited **archaeology,** performed in a short time, before development activity destroys a site; typically involves **excavation.** Also known as **emergency salvage archaeology, rescue archaeology, salvage archaeology.**

criteria The general standards by which the significance of a historic property is judged. See also **National Register criteria.**

critical path method (CPM) A construction scheduling device that diagrams the interrelationships between activities and identifies the critical path that optimizes the sequence of operations to minimize the construction period.

crocket **1.** One of a series of ornamental stone carvings that rise above a gable end coping or similar sloped surface in Gothic style buildings; typically in the form of stylized foliage rising on a thick stem. **2.** An ornamental end piece that rises above a roof ridge; common with terra-cotta ridge caps.

crocket capital A column capital decorated with crockets.

crook **1.** A curve or bend in any element, especially the sideways **warp** of a board with the broad face remaining flat. **2.** A stair rail cap that bends right or left. See also **easement, ramp.**

crooked tile (pre-19c) Same as **pan tile.**

crop, (pre-19c) crope **1.** A finial or other carved ornament, especially in stone. **2.** The process of cutting off or trimming an element.

croset Same as **crossette.**

cross A plumbing pipe fitting with a straight section with two side branches entering at right angles. See also **sanitary cross.**

cross above bible Same as **cross and bible.**

cross and bible (colonial New England) A six-panel door with a center stile and upper rail forming a cross shape. Also known as **Christian door, cross above bible.** See also **colonial panel door.**

crossbar **1.** Same as **bar** (sense 1c). **2.** A horizontal iron bar blocking a window or other opening; may be part of a **grate.**

crossbeam, (pre-20c) cross beam **1.** A large beam spanning from one outside wall to another and tying them together; typically perpendicular to the main axis of the space; may be the bottom chord of a truss. Also known as **tie beam** beginning in the 19c. **2.** A bridge beam that spans between the trusses and supports the stringers or deck. Also known as **spanner.** **3.** (17c) Same as **collar beam.**

crossbeam (sense 2)
St. Joseph Bridge, Missouri
by the Detroit Bridge and Iron Co.

cross bearing A series of **bearers** that support the top or bottom of an interior load-bearing partition that is parallel to, and between, a pair of joists; may rest on a **bearing cleat;** typically 2 × 6s.

crossbolt lock A key-operated lock that actuates two bolts in opposite directions; most common on bookcase doors. See also **lock.**

cross bond 1. A brick wall bond with courses of Flemish bond alternating with courses of stretchers and the joints of every other row of stretchers centered on a vertical line of headers. 2. Same as **English cross bond.**

cross bracing Diagonally crossed struts or ties in an X-shape between floor joists, bridge posts, or other structural members; each strut or tie connects the top of one member to the bottom of the adjoining member. Also known as **cross bridging.**

cross bridging **Bridging** in the form of continuous **cross bracing** between joists or similar members; types include **strap bridging, wire tension bridging.** See also **single bridging.**

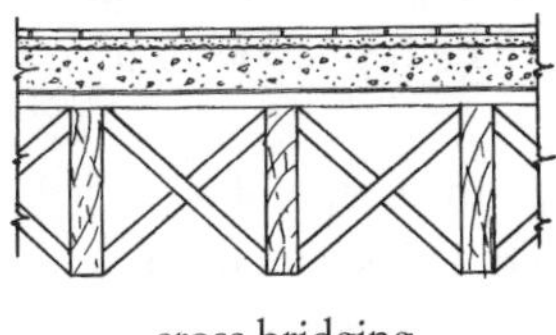

cross bridging

cross-church A **cruciform** church plan.

crosscut Wood or other material that has been sawn across the grain. See also **ripped.**

crosset 1. Same as **crossette.** 2. Same as **orillon.**

crossette, crosset, croset 1. The sideways extension of the moldings forming an architrave at a wall opening, generally between the top of the architrave and the top of the opening. Also known as **dog-ear.** See also **shouldered architrave.** 2. The notched side of a voussoir in a joggled arch; supports the adjoining voussoir. 3. The projection of an impost block past the face of an arch. 4. The horizontal extension of the top of a voussoir in a flat arch that rests upon the stone block below.

cross-furring Furring strips installed across ceiling joists to level the ceiling. See also **shredding.**

cross gable Two gable roofs that intersect at right angles.

cross-garnet A T-shaped **hinge** of various decorative forms; typically surface mounted like a **strap hinge,** rather than with a mortised butt like a **T-hinge.** Also known as **butt and strap, cross-tail hinge, garnet hinge.**

cross grain A wood **grain** pattern with markings that are not parallel to the sides of the board; types include **diagonal grain, spiral grain.**

crossing 1. The square space of a cruciform church, or similar structure, created by the intersection of the nave and chancel with the transept. Also known as **intersection.** 2. Intersection of two elements in the form of a cross, such as the ridges of a cross gable.

cross joint Same as **head joint.**

crosslight, (pre-20c) **cross light** 1. The light from windows in walls at right angles to one another. 2. Same as **counterlight** when referring to lighting from the rear and sides of class rooms or lecture halls.

cross panel A door **lying panel** in the shape of a horizontal rectangle.

cross quarters Same as **quatrefoil.**

cross rib Same as **arch rib.**

cross section The real, or imaginary, view of an object cut at a right angle to its length or primary plane, such as a molding or beam.

cross-sill A **sill** of a **timber frame** structure that runs in the direction of the short dimension of the plan; may rest on the foundation walls at the ends or span between walls at one of the interior bents. See also **main sill.**

cross springer A cross **rib** in a **groin vault.**

cross-tail hinge, cross-tailed hinge (19c) Same as **cross-garnet** or **T-hinge.**

cross tie One of a series of sleepers that connect and support the rails of a **railroad track;** most often made of a hardwood timber, sometimes composed of reinforced concrete beginning in late 20c. Also known as **railroad tie, tie.**

cross tongue One of a pair of hardwood tongues inserted into the shoulder of a timber frame tenon and into corresponding slots in the mortised timber; used to stiffen a joint.

cross tooth-chiseled A **tooth-chiseled** stone finish with overlapping grooves in two directions, or a similar finish on a pre-WWII molded concrete block; typically the grooves are at a 45-degree angle to the horizontal.

cross vault **1.** A vault formed by the intersection of two or more simple vaults; varieties include **groined vault, Welsh vault. 2.** The square plan shape formed by the intersection of two perpendicular barrel vaults.

crowfoot A dark zigzag marking in stone.

crown **1.** The head or top part of an arch; the extent of the crown is not exactly defined. **2.** The top projecting portion of a cornice.

crown backer A wood molding used as the bottom or top of a combination crown molding.

crowned table A **table** (sense 1) with a cornice above; most often used with bas-relief sculpture or an inscription.

crown glass Sheet glass cut from a hand-blown circular table of glass, with a raised center known as the crown; typically each table is 42–44 inches in diameter with a light sky-blue or green color; imported to North America late 17c–early 19c and manufactured regionally in the early 19c; individual panes have a surface pattern of concentric circles. See also **bull's-eye, window glass.**

crowning **1.** Any decorative feature at the top of a building; may include an **acroterion, cornice,** or **pediment. 2.** Installing a floor or roadway so that the top surface rises toward the center; used to counteract compressive stresses or produce proper drainage. See also **camber.**

crown land (Canada) Land that is owned by the federal or provincial government.

crown molding **1.** The horizontal molding at the top of any feature, especially an interior wall or piece of furniture; angles away from the vertical surface. See also **spring mold. 2.** (19c) Same as **cyma recta.**

crown plate Same as **bolster.**

crown post A vertical post in a timber frame roof truss, especially the single post in a **king truss.** Also known as **kingpost.**

crown tile **1.** Same as **plain tile. 2.** Same as **ridge tile.**

crow step One of a series of corbeled notches at the top of a wall; common on gable ends in **Dutch Colonial** buildings.

crowstone, crow stone **1.** The capstone of a gable end coping that supports a finial or cross. **2.** The top stone of a crow step gable wall.

cruciform In the shape of a Christian cross with two straight line segments intersecting at right angles, such as a **cross-church.**

crusher run Crushed stone as it comes from a crusher machine, with a mix of sizes ranging from powder to gravel; used for foundation and paving bases.

cryolite glass Same as **milk glass.**

crypt A cellar space below the nave or choir of a large church, especially of the Gothic Revival style; often used for burials.

cryptoflorescence Same as **subflorescence.**

crystal chandelier A glass **chandelier,** typically hung with prisms to refract the light from the fixture into different colors. See also **flint glass.**

crystal glass Same as **flint glass.**

crystalline limestone See **marble.**

crystalline verdigris Same as **distilled verdigris.**

crystal palace (19c) Any large exhibition hall with an iron frame and glass walls and roof; so-called from the original built in Hyde Park, London, in 1851.

C-scroll Scrollwork in the shape of the letter C; common on the ends of wrought-iron work.

C-shape lamp An **incandescent lamp** with a candle-flame shape with curved tip. See also **B-shape lamp, flame-shape lamp.**

CSI **Construction Specifications Institute**

CSI format Same as **uniform construction index.**

Cube style (Canada) Same as **foursquare.**

cubic Three-dimensional measurement expressed as a standard volume equal to a cube with sides of a fixed length, such as a cubic yard or cubic meter.

cubicle **1.** (pre-20c) A **bedroom** or other private room. **2.** (20c) A partitioned sleeping area in a **dormitory. 3.** (20c) A work or study area partitioned off within a larger space; may include fixed furniture, such as a desktop and shelves.

cubicular Of, or pertaining to, a **bedroom.**

cubiform capital Same as **cushion capital.**

cuddy A small closet or pantry.

Cudell trap A 19c **nonsyphoning trap** with a floating interior rubber ball that prevents backflow.

cuezcomate Circular Mexican granaries with thatched roofs and stuccoed wattle walls.

cul-de-four A semidome; used over a semicircular space or at the end of a barrel vault. See also **conch.**

cul-de-lampe A decorative corbel that supports a column, oriel, statue, or other projecting feature; typically in the form of an inverted cone.

cul-de-sac **1.** A passage open only at one end, such as a **blind alley. 2.** (20c) A dead-end street with a circular turnaround at the end.

cull **1.** The process of sorting superior or inferior material from the rest. **2.** Any poor-quality or rejected material that has been sorted out from the rest, such as **cull lumber.**

cullet Broken pieces of window glass, especially when intended to be remelted. See also **plate glass.**

cull lumber The poorest grade of lumber, of insufficient quality to be labeled as one of the standard grades.

cultural affiliation The archaeological or ethnographic culture to which a collection of sites, resources, or artifacts belong.

cultural artifact Any physical manifestation of human activity, including **archaeological artifact, building, cultural landscape, object, structure.**

cultural landscape The portion of the exterior environment that has been modified, influenced, or given special cultural meaning by people; includes large parks, a group of farms, countryside, and streetscapes; for **National Register** purposes, typically with **historic significance** and **integrity.** See also **built environment, sense of place, townscape.**

cultural property Same as **cultural resource.**

cultural resource **1.** An object, document, or any part of the built environment that has significance in archaeology, architecture, art, or history. **2.** A building, site, structure, object, or district evaluated by the National Register process as having significance in prehistory or history.

culture A group of people linked together by shared values, beliefs, and historical associations, together with the group's social institutions and physical objects necessary to the operation of the institution.

culture sequence The sequence of cultural traits or traditions in a local area over time as determined by **archaeology.**

culver hole (19c) A recess in a masonry wall for a beam end; from the similarity to openings in a **culver house.**

culver house A masonry **dovecote** with exterior wall openings for pigeons to enter.

culvert A covered water channel, constructed to allow flow under a road or other construction; types include **arch culvert, box culvert,** and **pipe culvert.** (*See illustration p. 132*)

culvert

culver tail, culvertail Same as **dovetail.**

Cumberland house A one-story, side-gable house with two front doors and windows and a front porch; built 1880–1940 in eastern and central Tennessee; named for the Cumberland Plateau region.

cup Wood that is warped across the face of the board; common in floorboards, where either the edges or the center are raised.

cupboard A shallow **closet** with shelves for dishes and similar objects.

cupola (sense 2)

cupola, (pre-20c) **cupolo,** (pre-19c) **cupalo, cupilo** **1.** A hemispherical-shaped roof or ceiling, such as the dome of the U.S. Capitol. **2.** A small structure projecting above a roof that provides ventilation or is used as a lookout, especially with a hemispherical roof on a circular or polygonal drum. See also **belvedere, monitor.**

cupolated A building with one or more cupolas.

cup shake **1.** A roofing **shake** with a curved cross section formed by splitting along an annual growth ring. Also known as **ring shake.** **2.** A naturally occurring internal crack in a tree that is parallel to an annual growth ring. Also known as **shell shake.**

curator One who manages a museum, library, or similar institution, or a particular collection within such an institution; may supervise a **conservator.**

curb, (pre-20c) **kerb, kirb** **1.** A low wall restraining the base of a dome. **2.** A framing member that supports the bottom of the upper set of rafters of a **curb roof.** **3.** A continuous raised edging that directs the flow of water, such as the masonry or concrete along a paved drive or roadway, or the lip of a shower stall. See also **curbstone.** **4.** (pre-20c) A **retaining wall** for an earth bank. **5.** Same as **well curb;** the primary meaning of the term before the 19c. **6.** Same as **curb plate.** **7.** Same as **roof curb.**

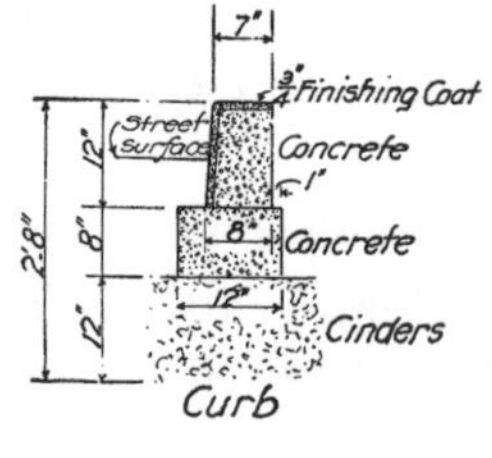

curb (sense 3)

curb plate **1.** The **wall plate** of a **curb roof** or dome. **2.** Same as **well curb.** **3.** The plate of a **roof curb.**

curb roof A roof with a low-sloping upper section adjoining a steeper-sloped section below; types include **gambrel roof, mansard roof.**

curbstone A linear stone block used to form a **curb** (sense 3).

curb string (pre-20c) Same as **closed string.**

curf (19c) Same as **kerf.**

curley gray Tennessee A medium pink **marble** with wavy veins of darker pink, quarried in the vicinity of Knoxville, Tennessee; polishes well.

curling stuff (18c) Same as **cross grain.**

curly grain A wood **grain** pattern formed by curved fibers, may be several inches in diameter. See also **swirl.**

current function For National Register purposes, the category for the current or anticipated use of a property or portion of a property. See also **use.**

curstable A stringcourse formed of stones with carved moldings.

curtail A scroll-shaped end of an architectural element.

curtail step A bottom step of a stair with a projecting, rounded end or ends; typically with a scroll-shaped handrail above. See also **bullnosed step, commode step.**

curtain An outer masonry wall of a fortification rampart with a parapet between two towers or bastions. See also **fortification.**

curtain wall **1.** (19c–present) A non-load-bearing exterior wall supported by the skeleton frame of a building; typically used in mid-rise and high-rise buildings; may be of any material, including masonry or glass. **2.** (19c) The flat wall between two protruding masses of a building; may be any type of wall, such as load bearing or without a roof. **3.** A thin masonry or concrete wall section supported by a series of piers; used for garden walls and foundations. See also **panel wall.** **4.** (late 19c) A self supporting exterior masonry wall used in **cage construction.**

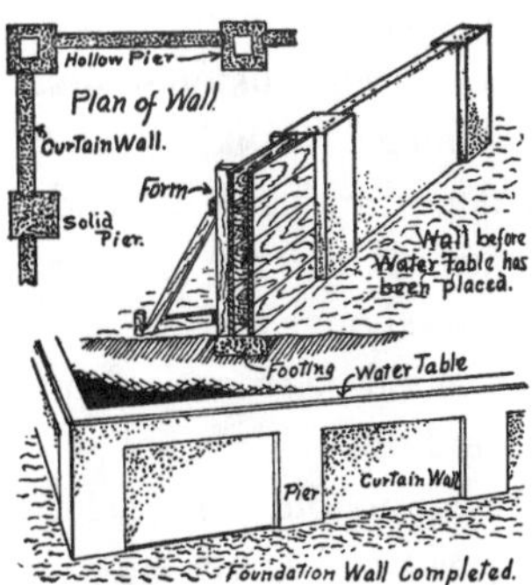

curtain wall (sense 3)

curticone (18c) A truncated cone.

curtilage A fenced yard of a residence, including the house and outbuildings.

curvilinear tracery Same as **flowing tracery.**

cushion A convex bow of any building element not commonly in that form. See also **cushion capital, cushion rafter, cushion edge, pulvinated.**

cushion board A cloth-covered shelf in a pulpit; used to support a bible.

cushion capital **1.** A column capital with a shape that appears to be pushed outward by the weight above. **2.** A capital that is bowl-shaped on the bottom and rises to a cubical top with a molded abacus; common in **Romanesque Revival** architecture.

cushioned edge A rounded or chamfered edge, such as that used at the edge of a tiled wall area, or along the corner of a concrete column or beam. See also **bullnosed.**

cushion rafter A relieving rafter partially supporting a principal rafter.

cusp A point formed by two intersecting curves; may have decorative foliation; common in arches and tracery of the Gothic Revival style.

cusped arch An arch with cusps or foliations at the intrados, such as a trefoil arch.

cuspidal, cuspidate Ornamented with cusps.

customhouse, (19c) **custom-house,** (pre-19c) **custom house** A building or office in which import duties are collected and vessels officially entered into the country; may have attached warehouse areas.

cut An excavation below the existing grade. See also **cut and fill.**

cut and fill, cut to fill The excavation of soil from one part of a construction site combined with its deposition on another part of the site. See also **cut, fill.**

cut and mitered string A cut string of a stair with the risers mitered into the vertical portion of the notches.

cut bracket A scroll-cut board used as a bracket or decoration; common on the face of stair stringers as the apparent support of the tread. See also **bracketed string.**

cut in Same as **let in.**

cut nail A **nail** with a shaft that is machine cut from sheet steel; wedge-shaped and sometimes case hardened; first produced in the 1790s and common by 1805; machine-formed heads were introduced circa 1815.

cutout, cut-out A device for interrupting an electrical circuit, such as a **fuse** or **circuit breaker.** See also **ceiling cutout.**

cut roof Same as **truncated roof.**

cut stone, cutstone Finished stone blocks, usually with rectangular faces, which have been shaped by cutting.

cut splay Brickwork in which the bricks are cut to fit an angled meeting of two surfaces, as in a splayed opening or a sloped sill.

cut string, cut stringer A notched stair stringer.

cut string stair A stair with the ends of the treads and risers resting on a cut stringer on one or both sides. See also **closed string stair, stair.**

cut terrace A terrace excavated out of a sloped hillside.

cut under Wood lath with beveled edges installed on solid timber so that there is a wider key space for plaster behind the face of the laths.

cyanotype See **blueprint.**

cyclical maintenance The periodic, recurring repairs, replacement of deteriorated elements, and conservation of a property based on a maintenance schedule.

cyclone cellar Same as **storm cellar.**

cyclostylar A structure with a circular colonnade; typically without an enclosed space in the center. See also **columniation.**

cylinder **1.** A geometric shape in the form of a circular tube. **2.** The center portion of modern locks, inserted directly into a round hole in a door or into a mortised latchset.

cylinder glass **Window glass** manufactured by hand blowing glass into a cylindrical mold, then cutting the cylinder to make a flat sheet; used late 19c–early 20c; types include **patent plate glass, picture glass.** Also known as **broad glass, spread glass, sheet glass.**

cylinder lock A lock with a central cylinder that rotates when a key lifts the internal tumblers; used in combination with a **dead-bolt lock, latch lock,** or **mortise lock.** See also **tumbler lock.**

cylinder system A pre-WWII water-heating system with a cylindrical, pressurized, hot water reservoir located below the level of the faucets; typically heated by a **waterback.** Also known as **pressure-cylinder system.** See also **tank system.**

cylinder-tank system A pre-WWII water heating system with both a **cylinder system** and a **tank system.**

cylindrical vault Same as **semicircular vault.**

cyma, cima, scima Same as **ogee.**

cyma recta A classical style molding with a projecting ogee curve, typically one concave and one convex quarter round, bounded by vertical fillets; when the molding is set so that its top is projecting, the bottom curve is convex and the top curve is concave. See also **cyma reversa.**

cyma reversa A classical style molding with an ogee curve, typically one concave and one convex quarter round bounded by vertical fillets; when the molding is set so that its top is projecting, the bottom curve is concave and the top curve is convex. See also **cyma recta.**

cymatium **1.** A small cyma molding **2.** The molding at the top of a classical style cornice; often a large **cyma recta.** See also **talon.** **3.** A small crown molding of any shape.

cypress, (pre-20c) **cipress, cipresse, sipres, cypresse** Any of the softwood trees of the genus *Cupressus;* types include **bald cypress, Monterey cypress, pecky cypress, pond cypress.** See also **American cypress.**

cyrtostyle A semicircular, or similarly shaped, portico with columns. See also **columniation.**

D

d Abbr. for **penny** in sizing nails; from the abbreviation for **denarius,** a Roman coin and, later, an English silver penny of equivalent value.

dabbed **1.** A rough stone finish made by a heavy pick or hammer; used for hidden work such as foundation stones; typically used on granite or other hard stones. Also known as **pick dressing.** **2.** Same as **daubed.**

dado **1.** A plain, flat surface between a base and a surbase molding, such as the die of a pedestal or the wall surface below a chair rail; wall dados often have paper or low-relief decoration. See also **wainscot.** **2.** A recessed rectangular groove, as in molding or to form a joint in millwork; forms include **blind dado, stop dado, through dado.** See also **pocketed, trench.**

dado panel One of the panels decorating a dado.

dado rail The molding at the top of a wall dado.

dagger The elongated, symmetrical, pointed shape of an opening in Gothic style **tracery,** with two cusps that divide it into equal portions that approximate the shape of a dagger. See also **mouchette.**

dairy, (pre-19c) **dary** **1.** (early 18c) A room or building in which milk is kept cool until the cream rises and is made into butter or cheese. Also known as **milk house.** **2.** A farm that produces cow's milk, butter, and cheese. **3.** (19c–present) A store or restaurant that specializes in milk products.

dallage [French] Paving or a floor of stone or tiles.

dam A structure used to impound water, such as for a reservoir or millpond; typically constructed across a stream or riverbed; may be of earth, wood, masonry, or concrete; components may include **gatehouse, spillway, waste gate, waste weir.**

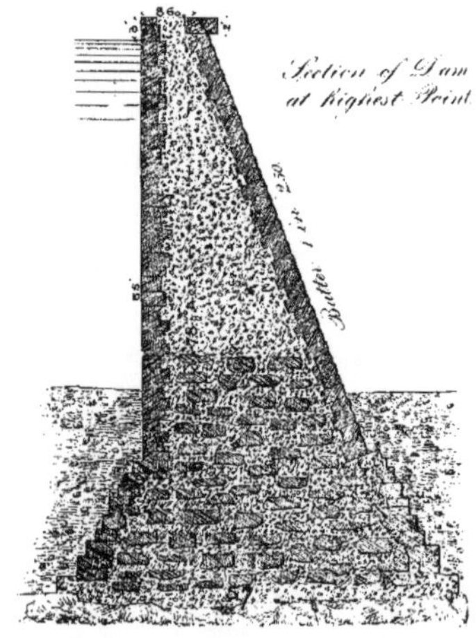

dam

dammar The gum of the dammar pine tree, *Dammara orientalis,* or similar species found in Australia, New Zealand, and the East Indies; used in varnishes.

dammar varnish Colorless **varnish** made with **dammar** resin dissolved in a solvent.

damp course Same as **dampproof course.**

damper An adjustable plate in a flue or duct; prevents downdrafts in a fireplace flue or adjusts the flow of air in a duct; may be a metal diaphragm or a cast-iron or soapstone device.

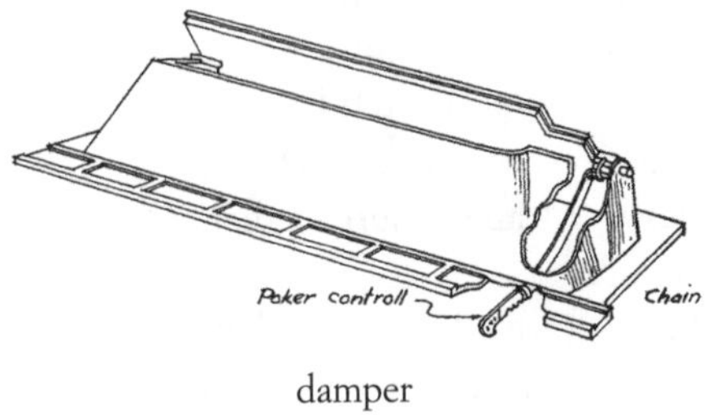

damper

dampproof barrier A horizontal moisture barrier in a masonry wall that prevents the capillary movement of water; typically formed by injecting chemical solutions containing silicone or aluminum stearates.

dampproof course A continuous horizontal membrane in a masonry wall that is impervious to water.

dampproofing A surface-applied coating used to seal out water. See also **waterproofing.**

Danby A light cream tinted, slightly translucent **marble** with yellow, greenish gray, irregular mottling or streaks, quarried in the vicinity of Danby, Vermont; polishes medium well. Also known as **Mountain White.**

dance pavilion A shelter with a wood floor suitable for dancing; typically open-sided and located in a park or garden.

dancette Same as **batons rompus.**

dancing step, dancing winder Same as a **balanced step.**

Danish arch (Virgin Islands) Same as a **semi-elliptical arch.**

dap **1.** A notch or **gain** cut in one wood member to receive another member. **2.** A notch at the end of a wood joist cut in the profile of the side of a steel beam; used so that the joist can be inserted between the flanges and supported by the beam.

Dark Blue Columbia A color variety of **Columbia.**

Dark Blue Rutland A dark bluish gray **marble** with white mottling quarried in the vicinity of West Rutland, Vermont; polishes well.

Dark Cedar Dark pink to dark chocolate **marble** quarried in the vicinity of Kizer and Knoxville, Tennessee; polishes well.

Dark Chocolate A dark brown **marble** quarried in the vicinity of Knoxville, Tennessee; polishes well.

Dark Columbia A color variety of **Columbia.**

Dark ivory green A light gray to ivory white **marble** with veins of yellowish to olive green quarried in the vicinity of West Rutland, Vermont; polishes fairly well.

Dark Lepanto A **marble** with red, pink, and dark gray fossil fragments in a gray background quarried at Bluff Point in the vicinity of Plattsburg, New York; polishes well. Also known as **French Gray.**

Dark Republic A dark chocolate **marble** with small white markings quarried in the vicinity of Knoxville, Tennessee; polishes highly.

Dark Tennessee See **Chocolate, Dark Cedar, Dark Chocolate, Dark Republic, Tennessee marble.**

Dark Vein True Blue A dark bluish gray **marble** with dark, winding veins and large and small white spots quarried in the vicinity of West Rutland, Vermont; polishes medium well.

dart The vertical element in the shape of a stylized arrow between the ova in an **egg and dart** molding.

dating The process of establishing the age or period of construction of a **cultural artifact,** including a building or structure; may include documentary research and stylistic or physical analysis, such as **radiocarbon dating** or **den-**

drochronology. See also **datum, historic structure report.**

datum **1.** A **bench mark,** or horizontal line or plane from which heights and depths are measured; used in civil engineering design and surveying. Also known as **datum line, datum plane, datum point.** **2.** A reference point of known age or period at an **archaeological site;** may be one of several used as reference points in **dating** the cultural artifacts.

datum line See **datum** (sense 1).

datum plane See **datum** (sense 1).

datum point See **datum** (sense 1).

daub, (pre-18c) **dawb** The rough mortar, clay, or plaster smeared on a surface; used for **chinking** in a log cabin or **wattle and daub.**

dawb (pre-18c) Same as **daub.**

day The space between two window mullions.

daylight An open space or clear distance between jambs of a window.

de-accessioning The process of disposing of unwanted **cultural artifacts** in a **collection;** may include selling or exchanging items such as art objects or buildings.

dead **1.** A door or window that cannot be opened or that provides no light. **2.** Impervious to sound. **3.** Same as **flat.**

dead bolt A lock without a spring that latches it automatically when the door closes.

dead coloring A first coat of paint with a matte finish that is covered with a glossy finish.

deadening **1.** Same as **deafening.** See also **double deadening.** **2.** (early 20c) Thermal insulating materials placed in the interstices of a structure. **3.** A wash or coating on a surface that dulls the brilliancy of its color or roughens its polish. See also **dead gold.**

dead floor (19c) A floor with **deafening** (sense 1) inside.

dead gold Unburnished gold leaf. See also **deadening** (sense 3).

dead house A building that contains the remains of the dead; for example, the large oval structures built by the Natchez tribe of Native Americans to house bones, fetishes, and a perpetual fire, or the tiny houses built by Native Americans on the Northwest coast to house remains. See also **mortuary, totem pole.**

deadlatch (19c) A **latch bolt** that can be locked in an open or closed position.

dead level A line or surface that is perfectly horizontal.

deadlight, (pre-19c) **dead light** **1.** Same as **fixed light.** **2.** An opaque material used in place of window glass.

dead load The portion of the weight supported by a structure that is due to the weight of the structure itself, as opposed to the **live load.**

deadlock, dead lock (19c–present) A lock with a **dead bolt.**

deadman A buried element that resists the push of earth against a retaining wall or anchors a fence post; attached with wire cable or wood guys.

dead shore, (pre-20c) **dead shoar** **1.** Any vertical **shore.** **2.** A vertical prop used as a temporary support and left in the structure; typically a wood timber surrounded by masonry.

dead wall **1.** (pre-20c) Same as **blank wall.** **2.** (19c) A wall with **deafening** (sense 1) inside.

dead well (19c) Same as **dry well.**

deafening (19c–mid-20c) **1.** Sound insulating materials placed in the interstices of a structure to reduce sound transmission; examples include **backplaster, felt, mineral wool, pugging,** and sawdust. Also known as **deadening, sound insulation.** See also **counterceiling, dead floor, dead wall, double deadening.** **2.** Incombustible materials placed in the interstices of a building to increase fire resistance, especially when located between joists.

deal **1.** (pre-20c U.S.) A thin board, less than one inch thick; used for paneling or finish flooring.

2. (Canada) A square-sawn softwood board of varying dimensions according to period.

deambulatory A choir aisle that continues around the apse of a church.

decapartite vault A **rib vault** formed by the intersection of ten curved vault surfaces; used to cover a square space with eight cells of triangular plan; has two diagonal ribs, one rib bisecting the square, and two ribs that pass through the apex and divide the triangles formed by the diagonal ribs into thirds.

decastyle See **columniation.**

decay The decomposition of organic material; may be caused by **fungi** or **weathering.**

decay tunnel Linear decay of the interior of a large timber while the exterior wood remains intact; caused by fungi progressively digesting wood cells along the fibers starting at moist end grain. See also **boxed heart rot.**

deciduous cypress Same as **bald cypress.**

deck A floor that is exposed to the elements, such as a porch or roof deck. See also **decking.**

deck beam A beam that supports a structural deck, especially a **bulb tee.**

deck bridge A **bridge** that carries a roadway or railway on the upper chords of the trusses. See also **through-truss bridge.**

decking The structural floor material that spans between beams of a skeleton frame; types include **corrugated metal, reinforced concrete, wood decking.**

deck plate A purlin at the break in a two-slope roof, with a flat deck on top, that supports the top of the lower rafters and the foot of the upper rafters.

Decorated style Architecture in the style of the English Gothic during the period 1280–1380; typical elements include pointed arches with head molds, large windows divided by mullions, elaborate cusped window tracery with geometric patterns or flowing lines, and a profusion of surface decoration and moldings. See also **geometrical tracery, Gothic Revival style.**

decoration Treatment applied to the surface of a building or structure to enhance its beauty; types include **gilding, glazing, graining, lincrusta Walton, paint, stenciling, wallpaper.** See also **interior decoration, ornamentation, polychromy.**

decorative art Decoration and ornamentation applied to such useful things as buildings and furniture; first use of the term is attributed to English architect A. W. N. Pugin in *Gothic Ornaments,* an 1831 study of Gothic church art and furniture.

decorator **1.** A person who is primarily engaged in producing **decorative art. 2.** (20c) A person engaged in **interior design,** especially **interior decoration** of houses.

decorum (18c) Building ornamentation relative to the economic standing of its occupants.

Dedham granite A pink, epidotic **granite** quarried in the vicinity of Dedham, Massachusetts; used for building stone (e.g., Trinity Church, Boston).

dedication **1.** The process of donating land to the public, such as for a road; often part of the development of a tract of land. **2.** A ceremony officially initiating the use of a building, such as a church or city hall, by the public.

deed A written document that transfers ownership of **real estate;** may be recorded by a government agency such as a Recorder of Deeds or Land Title Office. See also **title search.**

deep yellow brass A ductile alloy of copper and approximately 15.3 percent zinc.

Deer Isle **1.** A pinkish lavender tinted, medium gray, coarse-grained **granite** quarried in the vicinity of Deer Isle, Maine. **2.** A dark green, nearly black **marble** quarried on Deer Isle, Maine, before ca. 1870.

deferred maintenance Property **maintenance** that has been left undone over an extended period. See also **demolition by neglect.**

deformed bar A **reinforcing bar** with a surface pattern created by deforming a **plain bar;** used in **reinforced concrete** to increase the bond with the surrounding concrete; of many shapes including cup bars and **twisted bars.**

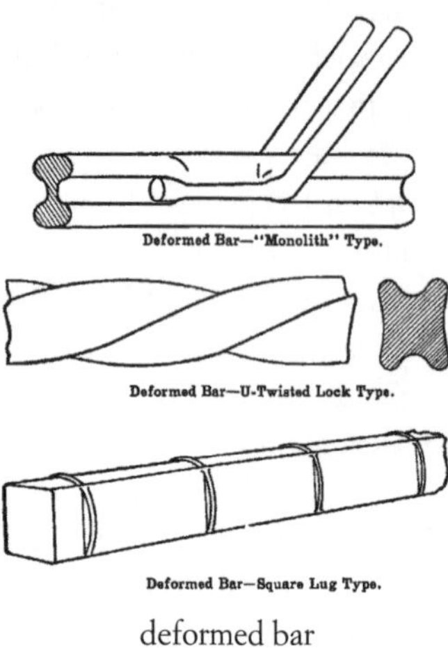

deformed bar

degradation The loss of the original condition of a **cultural artifact** over time owing to natural elements or human activity; mostly used in reference to **conservation** of objects, rather than buildings. See also **deterioration, patina, weathering.**

degree The number of degrees of angle of a circle used by a segmental arch (e.g., an 80-degree arch); arches with the same number of degrees are called **similar arches,** and similar arches with the same radii are known as **equal arches.**

dehumidifier A mechanical device that reduces the amount of moisture in the air of a building; typically cools the air and then reheats it. See also **desiccator.**

delamination Separation of the layers of a laminated material, such as plywood.

delay of demolition A temporary halt in demolition of a building or structure, usually ordered by a court or local government agency; may be based on legal grounds, such as failure to obtain a **demolition permit,** or be a legislated waiting period to allow preservationists time to attempt to save the building or structure.

deluge system A **sprinkler system** with open heads; fire detectors activate a valve that allows water to flow to all sprinkler heads simultaneously; used in areas where flammable materials are stored and water damage is of little importance.

demi-bass (18c) Same as **demi-rilievo.**

demicolumn An engaged column in which only one-half of the column projects from the wall.

demimetope A partial **metope** in a Doric frieze, as at an inside corner.

demi-rilievo, demi-relievo A sculpted surface that is engaged with the background, with portions of some figures completely undercut.

demolition The intentional destruction of all or part of a building or structure; in **restoration** or renovation projects, may include removal of structural elements, partitions, mechanical equipment, and electrical wiring and fixtures. Also known as **razing, wrecking.** See also **dismantling, exploratory demolition.**

demolition by neglect The destruction of a structure caused by failure to perform maintenance over a long time period; some localities (e.g., New Orleans) have ordinances prohibiting demolition by neglect. See also **deferred maintenance, demolition.**

demolition permit Written authorization by the appropriate government authority to raze all or part of a building or structure. See also **delay of demolition.**

demonstration project A project designed to demonstrate the feasibility of a particular method or course of action so that others will undertake similar efforts in the future; typically funded by a government agency or private foundation.

den 1. (late 18c–present) A room in a dwelling reserved for the solitary work or leisure of a resident. 2. (20c) An intimate room used for the casual entertainment of the residents of a dwelling.

dendrochronology A process used to date historic structures and living trees by comparing the sequence of annual rings of a sample of wood with a known standard piece from the same geographic area.

Dennett's An early 20c flooring system consisting of concrete placed between rolled iron beams; the concrete is flush with the top and bottom of the parallel beams; typically finished with plaster below and a wood floor above.

density A planning or **zoning** measure of the ratio of a quantity (such as the number of residents, buildings, or **gross floor area**) per a given area (such as acres or hectares).

density transfer See **transfer of development rights.**

denticle (18c) Same as **dentil.**

denticulated Doric A Doric order in which the mutule band has a dentil band and shallow mutules that are not seen in elevation; from bottom to top, the frieze is composed of cyma reversa, dentil band, soffit of the corona with mutules and caissons, corona, and cymatium; the mutules have 18 guttae.

denticulus The molding that supports dentils.

dentil In classical cornices and entablatures, one of a series of small, decorative blocks that alternate with a blank space; typically rectangular with moldings above and below. See also **interdentil, Venetian dentil.**

dentil band 1. A molding that has the profile of a **dentil** without the adjoining interdentils cut away; used in a classical **bed mold.** 2. A narrow, projecting band with the height of a dentil, as if the dentils had been removed from a typical classical bed mold. 3. A horizontal molding composed of alternating dentils and interdentils.

Department of Transportation Act of 1966 U.S. federal legislation that declares a policy of preserving natural and historic sites along highways.

dependency A subsidiary building adjoining the principal building, often one of a symmetrical pair.

deposition The process of accumulation of **cultural artifacts** and natural materials at an archaeological site over a period of time partly as a result of human activity; also used to refer to the material itself.

depot 1. A warehouse for storage, transfer, and, sometimes, sale of merchandise, such as a furniture depot or grain depot. 2. (U.S.) A transportation system station or terminal, such as for a railroad or stagecoach line; may be for freight, passengers, or both.

depreciable property **Real estate** that is **income property** or is used in trade or business; typically has **depreciation** each year because of its theoretical loss in value over time; may be eligible for an **investment tax credit.** See also **investment property.**

depreciation An economic calculation of the decreased monetary value of a building or structure because of physical deterioration over time; based on government regulations or generally accepted accounting practices rather than on actual market value.

depressed arch Same as **drop arch.**

depreter Stucco with tooled imitation ashlar joints and small, dry stones pressed into the surface. See also **pebble-dash.**

depth A measurement of the distance downward or backward from a surface, such as the distance between the intrados and the extrados of an arch, top to bottom of a beam, or front to back of a building or lot.

derelict Deserted or abandoned, especially a building that has not been maintained. See **demolition by neglect.**

desalinization Removal of salt from masonry, typically by applying clay poultices or by electrolysis.

desiccant A drying agent, especially a chemical that absorbs moisture from the air.

desiccator A device that removes moisture from the air or an object, typically by heat or use of a **desiccant.** See also **dehumidifier.**

design **1.** A planned arrangement of forms, shapes, lines, and/or colors; may be intended to serve a useful purpose or be decorative or artistic. **2.** The quality of **integrity** applying to the elements that create the physical form, plan, space, structure, and style of a property. **3.** A preliminary illustration, such as a sketch or drawing, as opposed to the executed work, such as a statue or building.

designated building (Canada) Same as **Federal Heritage Building.**

designated historic site Same as **historic site** (sense 2). See also **protected site.**

design controls Regulations governing alterations to buildings and structures in historic towns or districts; typically legislated by a local government and usually restricted to the exterior appearance and materials. See also **design guidelines.**

design guidelines Recommendations for control of new construction, as well as alterations and additions to existing buildings and structures, in historic towns or districts; typically adopted and published by the local regulating agency. See also **design controls.**

destructive testing **Testing** the quality of a material by a method that alters or destroys the sample or element; includes crushing concrete samples to determine compression strength, loading structures to failure, analyzing mortar samples, and removing core samples from timber beams. See also **inspection, nondestructive investigation, nondestructive testing.**

detached A freestanding building, as opposed to one with a **party wall.**

detail **1.** A minor or subordinate part of a building or structure, such as a column capital, molding, porch, or structural connection. **2.** A drawing of a **detail** (sense 1).

deterioration The loss of the original condition of a **cultural artifact** over time due to natural elements or human activity; used more often in reference to buildings and structures than to objects. See also **degradation, weathering.**

determination of eligibility (DOE) A decision by the U.S. Department of the Interior that a district, site, building, structure, or object meets the National Register criteria for evaluation, although the property is not actually listed in the National Register; nominating authorities and federal agency officials commonly request determinations of eligibility for federal planning purposes and in cases where a majority of private owners has objected to National Register listing; does not make the property eligible for such benefits as grants, loans, or tax incentives that require listing on the National Register as a prerequisite.

developer A person or organization that manages the process of developing **real estate,** especially involving the construction of buildings or other facilities for lease or sale; typically has an ownership interest in the project, arranges for purchase of the property and financing, hires the **architect** and **contractor,** obtains **zoning** approvals and a **building permit,** and leases or sells the completed project.

development **1.** A completed real estate improvement project, especially the buildings and public improvements, such as roads and sewers; often used to refer to a suburban single-family housing project. **2.** The process of producing real estate improvements. See also **developer, property management, redevelopment.**

development potential The difference between the current use of a property and another, more intensive possible **use;** often a comparison of the existing development to higher-density new construction. See also **highest and best use.**

device A sculptured emblem; often includes a motto.

devitrified glass A crystalline, opaque glass manufactured by exposing sheet glass to extremely high temperatures.

DeWint green An olive green oil-paint pigment composed of a mixture of artificial green and orange pigments.

diabase The same as what is now known as **diorite;** named in 1807.

diaglyph Relief sculpture that is sunk below the surface.

diagonal bond A brick wall bond with diagonally laid parallel headers.

diagonal bracing A series of diagonal structural members that stiffen a frame; types include cross bracing, K-bracing, and knee bracing.

diagonal buttress A buttress that bisects the 270-degree angle at the outside corner of a building.

diagonal grain A wood **cross grain** pattern in which the markings are at an angle to the edge of the cut board; caused by sawing at an angle with the outer edge of the log.

diagonal rib A projecting rib that crosses a **rib vault** with a square or rectangular plan from corner to corner. Also known as **angle rib, ogive.**

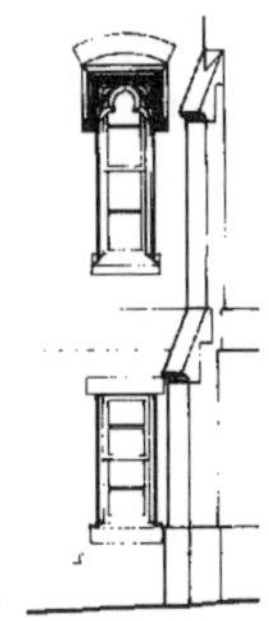

diagonal buttress

diagonal sheathing Sheathing boards installed at a 45-degree angle on the exterior of balloon frame or platform frame building to provide wind bracing.

diagonal tie A diagonal truss member used to prevent the bent from racking.

dial **1.** (pre-19c) A **sundial** on the wall of a building; typically consists of a horizontal projecting metal rod at the apex of radiating lines cut into or painted on a wall or metal disk. **2.** The face of a clock.

diamond A grid pattern created by rows of shingles, **slate,** or **weather tiling** with V-shaped bottoms.

diamond fret **1.** A fret or meander with straight lines forming diamond-shaped patterns with acute and obtuse angles. **2.** A fret or meander with the line forming right angles set at 45-degrees to the edge.

diamond glass Same as **quarrel.**

Diamond Gray A gray, coarse-grained granite with brown and black markings, quarried at Isle, Minnesota.

diamond lath Same as **diamond mesh.**

diamond mesh A type of **expanded-metal lath** with diamond-shaped holes. Also known as **diamond lath.**

diamond nail A **nail** having a rhomboidal-shaped head.

diamond notch In log construction, an interlocking **notching** system used at the corners; the diamond-shaped end of the log is held by V-shaped notches.

diamond work A masonry wall in which the units are set at a diagonal to form a grid; may be **tapestry brick** or other materials.

diaper, diaper-work A pattern formed by interconnected, repetitive elements covering a flat surface; often with decorative elements within the shapes of a bas-relief grid; may be brick, plaster, wood, or other materials. See also **semé, tapestry brick.**

diastyle See **intercolumniation.**

dichromatic brickwork Brick masonry constructed with two contrasting colors of brick to form decorative patterns; the trim color may be used to imitate the outline of classical revival details, such as quoins and hoodmolds, or patterns based on the brick bond, such as diamonds and zigzags; common late 19c–WWI, especially in Ontario, Canada, where the most frequent color combination is buff trim on a red background.

die The middle portion of a pedestal between the base and cap; typically a cube with flat, plain faces.

die square Smoothly finished faces accurately cut at right angles, especially when referring to timbers dressed and exposed as the finished surface.

differential settlement The downward movement of various parts of a building or structure at different rates caused by varying amounts of soil compaction below the foundation; typically causes cracking and sometimes results in structural problems. See also **settlement.**

diffuser A device for directing and dispersing air flow from a duct into a room, especially from a ceiling. See also **register.**

diglyph A decorative element on the frieze of a **Doric** entablature, composed of a rectangular block with two vertical, equally spaced, V-shaped grooves, or **glyphs;** alternates with the metopes; typically centered on the axis of the column below; used in place of the more common **triglyph** in some post-Renaissance classical buildings. See also **hemiglyph, hemitriglyph.**

dimension lumber Sawn wood with a rectangular cross section of a specified size, especially with standard nominal dimensions larger than 4 × 5 inches. Also known as **dimension timber.** See also **lumber, scantling.**

dimension shingle (19c–present) A shingle cut to a standard width.

dimension stone, dimensioned stone Stone blocks precut to specific sizes and shapes. See also **ashlar, rubble.**

dimension timber Same as **dimension lumber.**

dimension work Masonry built with **dimension stone.**

diminished arch (19c) An arch, of any shape, having less rise than a semicircle.

diminished bar A sash bar that is narrow on its inside edge.

diminished column A column with straight sides that taper inward toward the top, in the form of a truncated cone. See also **entasis.**

diminished stile A door **stile** that is narrower at the top to provide for a glass light that is wider than the paneling at the bottom of the door. See also **diminished stile.**

diminishing courses Slate courses that gradually get smaller from the eaves to the ridge of a roof.

diminution The decrease in size of a classical column shaft toward the top; typically the top is five-sixths of the size of the bottom; the sides may be straight or curved. See also **entasis, diminished column, swelling.**

diner **1.** (20c) A railroad dining car. **2.** (ca. 1924–present) A restaurant constructed from, or that resembles, a railroad dining car; by the 1960s, indicates a prefabricated restaurant building of any shape or style; the interior features a long counter with fixed stools in front of the food preparation area, where primarily grilled foods and home-style cooking are served; may also have seating at booths and/or tables and chairs.

dinette (20c) A dining alcove in an apartment. See also **breakfast nook, dining room.**

dingle The enclosed porch of a house, originally for use in inclement weather.

dining hall A large room used for group dining, especially at a school or college. See also **mess.**

dining room, (17c) **dininge roome** (late 18c–present) A room used for eating food while seated at a table; types include **dining hall, mess.** Also known as **eating room.** See also **breakfast nook, breakfast room, dinette.**

Diocletian window Same as **Palladian window.** See also **thermal window.**

diorama (19c–present) **1.** A large mural intended to realistically re-create one or more historical scenes; often on a wall with a circular or semicircular plan in a darkened room with special lighting and/or slide projectors to create an optical illusion of depth and change. **2.** A building containing a diorama mural for public viewing. **3.** A museum exhibit with human and/or animal models and a painted background that creates a realistic scene.

diorite A dark, granular, crystalline, igneous rock; typically composed of acid plagioclase and hornblende, with pyroxene or biotite; color ranges from greenish gray to black; often found with inclusions of other crystalline minerals; used as a **building stone** and gravel. Also known as **green stone, trap rock.**

dipteral Having two rows of columns on the outside face of the building, especially when they surround the perimeter. See also **columniation.**

diptere, dipteron A dipteral building.

dirt and stick chimney (southern U.S., 18c–19c) Same as **stick chimney.**

discharging arch Same as **relieving arch.**

discharging piece A structural element that supports a portion of the load on another element. See also **relieving arch.**

discontiguous district A historic or archaeological district containing two or more geographically separate areas.

dismantling The process of temporarily taking apart a structure (or some portion of it) so that it can be reused or reassembled. See also **demolition.**

displacement The movement of residents and businesses out of a neighborhood owing to rent increases and/or **redevelopment;** may be related to **gentrification.**

disposal field Same as **leaching field.**

disposition (19c) The arrangement of parts of a building in relation to one another, such as the rooms in plan or the major exterior masses.

distemper Water-base paint that has pigments mixed with size and an emulsion of egg yolk or egg white; used for interior murals or decorative painting. Also known as **tempera.**

distemper ground A wall surface prepared for application of distemper paint.

distilled verdigris Dark green crystalline copper acetate, $Cu(C_2H_3O_2)_2 \cdot H_2O$, manufactured by dissolving **verdigris** in distilled vinegar and slowly evaporating the liquid; used as a paint pigment. Also known as **crystalline verdigris.**

distillery A place where grain is distilled to produce alcohol or alcoholic beverages by use of stills and other equipment. See also **brewery.**

distribution (18c) The orderly arrangement of the parts of a plan or elevation.

district A geographically definable area, urban or rural, possessing a significant concentration, linkage, or continuity of sites, buildings, structures, or objects united historically or aesthetically by plan or physical development; may also comprise individual elements separated geographically but linked by association or history. See also **discontinguous district, historic district.**

disturbed An **archaeological site** at which the **deposition** has been physically altered so that analysis of **cultural artifacts** is difficult or impossible; may be the result of natural processes (e.g., erosion or plant growth) or of human activity (e.g., plowing or development).

distyle A **classical style** building with two exterior columns at the front facade. See also **columniation, distyle in antis.**

distyle in antis A **classical style** building having a front facade with two columns between the antae at each end. See also **columniation, in antis.**

ditch A long, narrow trench or channel dug in the earth; used for drainage or defense; types include **foss, wormditch.** See also **canal, drain.**

ditriglyph The spacing related to a Doric style entablature, with the following meanings: (1) The distance from the center of one metope to the center of a third metope, spanning two half triglyphs and one whole triglyph; (2) An **intercolumniation** of two triglyphs centered between adjoining columns, rather than the usual **monotriglyph;** (3) A single metope and its adjoining two triglyphs; (4) (18c) The space between two triglyphs.

divan (19c) A smoking room, typically furnished with Turkish-style cushioned benches around the perimeter.

divided light A window or door in which the glass is divided into several small panes. See also **muntin.**

division (18c) A fence or building wall that subdivides a larger area.

dobie Slang for **adobe.**

document **1.** An original written record, such as a deed. **2.** An original product, such as a lockset, of known provenance and used as the basis for modern reproduction.

documentation **1.** Any evidence that supplies factual information about a subject. **2.** The data that record the existing and prior condition of an existing building, structure, or site; typically includes measured drawings, earlier as-built and original working drawings, historic and contemporary photographs, historic references to the appearance and materials, and, sometimes, archaeological research. **3.** The process of tracing the history and establishing the authenticity of a **cultural artifact.** See also **historical research.** **4.** The National Register information that describes, locates, and explains the significance of a historic property.

documentation standards The requirements for describing, locating, and stating the significance of a property for listing in the National Register.

dodecapartite vault A **rib vault** formed by the intersection of twenty curved vault surfaces; used to cover a pentagonal, semicircular, or trapezoidal space; typically has an open circle at the apex, rather than a boss.

dodecastyle A **classical style** building with twelve exterior columns at the front facade. See also **columniation.**

DOE Abbr. for **determination of eligibility.**

dog **1.** A metal clamping device, such as used to secure architectural terra-cotta to a structure. See also **shutter dog, timber dog.** **2.** Same as **cramp.**

dog-ear (18c) Same as **crossette.**

dog iron Same as **timber dog.**

dogleg **1.** Any bent shape similar to that of the rear leg of a dog. See also **chevron. 2.** A **parquet floor** pattern of rows of elongated hexagons.

dogleg stair, doglegged stair A stair with two parallel, straight flights with an intermediate landing; one side of the lower flight is in the same vertical plane as one side of the upper flight.

dog nail **1.** A large **wrought nail** with either a projecting bill on one side of its head or a conical head; used to fasten hinges and locks to doors. **2.** (20c) A nail with a head designed to be countersunk.

dog's-tooth bond Any brick wall bond in which headers from opposite faces of the wall overlap each other without passing entirely through the wall. See also **dog's-tooth course.**

dog's-tooth course, dogtooth course A decorative masonry band formed by a row of bricks laid at a 45-degree angle to the face of the wall so that the corners form a zigzag pattern. See also **dog's-tooth bond.**

dogtooth, dog tooth **1.** One of a series of square-based pyramidal, projecting carved ornaments resembling a row of teeth; typically in the form of the points of four stylized leaves radiating from the apex of a pyramid; used in **Gothic Revival** architecture, especially of the **Early English** style. **2.** One of the bricks used to form a **dog's-tooth course.**

dogtrot house A one-story log house composed of two pens separated by a passageway and a single gable roof covering all three areas; the passageway was frequently enclosed later as a center hall; built primarily in southern U.S. in the 18c and 19c.

dolerite Same as **diorite.**

dolomite A compact **building stone** composed of crystalline calcium magnesium carbonate; colors range from white to grayish-white; frequently referred to as **marble.** Also known as **bitter spar.** See also **snowflake marble.**

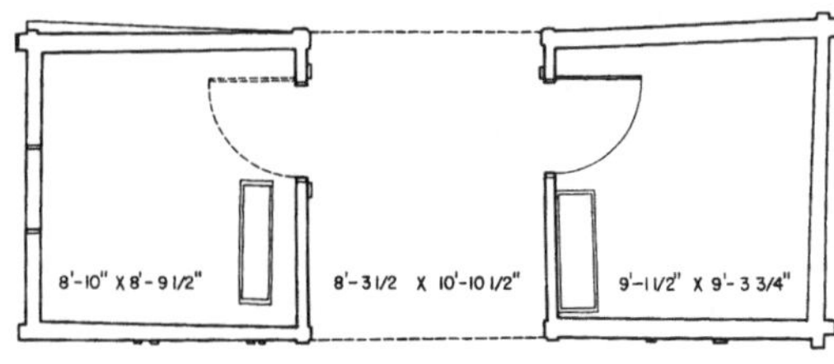

dogtrot house
Long-Hutchison Farm, Tenant Barn
Abbeville County, South Carolina

dome A large, curved shape with a circular base covering a portion of a building; most often a hemisphere but may be any arched shape, especially a segment of a circle, ellipse, or parabola; may be structural, as in masonry or cast-iron construction, or supported by other structural elements; forms include **double dome, elliptical dome, imperial dome, saucer dome, semidome, Turkish dome.** Also known as **hemispherical vault.** See also **cloistered vault, cupola, domical vault, eye of the dome, interdome, sail vault, vault.**

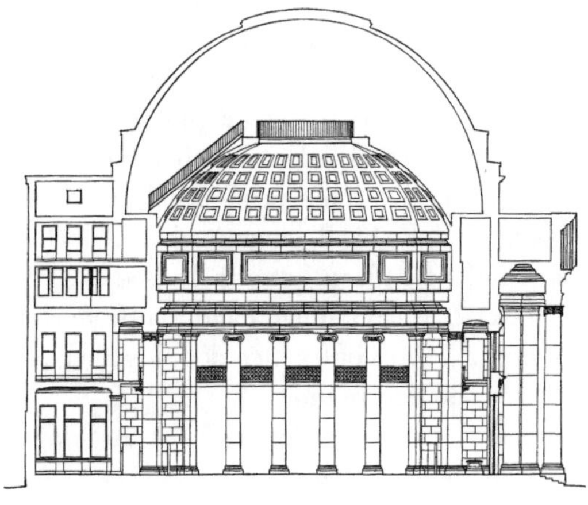

dome
Girard Trust Co.
Philadelphia, Pennsylvania, ca. 1908

dome light **1.** Any window or opening in a dome. See also **eye of the dome. 2.** (19c) A curved ceiling with a skylight above a stairway.

domestic architecture All of the various building types used as residences.

domestic hot water Heated water used for laundry, washing, and bathing.

domestic water The water used within a building.

domical vault A **rib vault** in which each rib, except the ridge rib, has the same radius, radiates from the apex, and is continuous from one side of the vault to the other; most commonly a groined vault formed by the intersection of four expanding vaults that slope up toward the center of the vault; when covering a square space, forms a **cloistered vault.**

dook A wood **nailer** block installed in a masonry wall. See also **wood brick.**

door A swinging or sliding panel that closes an opening in a wall and provides passage through it; types include **access door, accordion door, batten door, bifold door, blank door, blind door, crapaudine door, double-acting door, double door, double-framed door, double-margin door, dutch door, falling door, flap door, fire door, folding door, french door, half door, hollow-core door, jib door, ledged door, overhead door, overhung door, revolving door, sash door, solid-core door, swing door, trapdoor, Venetian door, weather door, wicket door;** common components include **panel, rail, stile.** See also **hand, hinge, jamb, leaf, lock.**

door band **1.** A large **bar** or **bolt** used as a door **lock. 2.** A large **hinge band** that fastens the vertical boards of a batten door together. Also known as **doorbrand.**

doorbell, (pre-20c) **door-bell** **1.** A ringing device to announce the arrival of visitors; until the early 19c, a bell hung on a spring attached to a wire and pull knob, then usually a gong struck by a lever activated by a wire; replaced by electric bells starting in the late 19c. See also **bell hanging. 2.** A bell that hangs on a door and rings when the door is opened.

doorbrand, door brand Same as **door band.**

door buck Same as **buck.**

doorcase, door-case **1.** The trimmed opening surrounding a **swinging door.** See also **cased opening. 2.** The recess into which a **sliding door** rests when it is open.

door check Same as **door closer.**

door closer A mechanical device that automatically closes an opened door and prevents it from slamming; typically operated by a pneumatic piston.

doorframe, (19c) **door-frame** **1.** The structure and trim surrounding and supporting the top and sides of a door; includes the jambs, head, and casing. See also **doorcase, doorpost. 2.** The components of a paneled door that hold the panels in place, including the rails, stiles, and muntins.

door girt A horizontal member that spans between the end posts of the center bents of a **timber frame** barn above the upper level doors.

door hanger A device used to suspend a sliding door from a track.

door head The top, horizontal members of a doorframe.

doorjamb One of the two facing jambs of a door.

doorknob The rotating handle of a **lockset.**

doornail **1.** A large nail that is struck by a door knocker. **2.** A large-headed nail clinched to fasten the parts of a batten door together.

doorplate A metal plate inscribed with the occupant's name; typically with a brass or silver-plated finish; common on houses during the 19c; sometimes incorporated into the escutcheon plate surrounding a bellpull.

doorpost, door post The jamb of a door, especially when a timber frame post without casing; may be a **hanging post.**

door pull Hardware used to open or close a door; does not include a latching device.

door roller A wheeled device used to support the bottom or top of a rolling door. See also **door track.**

doorsill A **sill** (sense 2) at the bottom of a door.

doorstead (pre-20c) All of the parts of a door, doorway, and enframement.

doorstep **1.** The sill of a door when raised above the outside level. **2.** The landing and two or three steps outside of a door. See also **stoop.**

door stone A doorsill formed by a single stone.

doorstop **1.** The portion of the cased opening against which a door rests when closed; may be rabbeted into the jamb or be a separate stop bead. **2.** A bumper that stops the swing of a door when opening; may be wood or metal and fastened to the floor or wall.

door strap Same as **door hanger.**

door strip A weatherstrip used on a door.

door track A metal floor strip or top rail on which a sliding door rolls.

door transom See **transom, transom bar.**

door tree Same as **doorpost.**

doorway The opening and surrounding trim of a passage between rooms or an entrance to a building. See also **notched doorway.**

doorway plane (19c) The splayed jamb and intrados of an arched doorway.

dooryard The open area outside an exterior door, especially the front door of a building.

d'or [French] Golden colored.

dorado, dorada [Spanish] Gilded or golden colored.

Dorchester stone An olive gray, fine-textured, carboniferous sandstone quarried in the vicinity of Shepody Mountain, New Brunswick; used as building stone in eastern Canada and U.S.

dore Having **gilding** on the surface.

Doric order, (18c) **Dorick order** The earliest type of classical Greek architecture. From top to bottom, the typical Greek Doric order is shown in the figure. The Greek Doric column does not have a base; the Roman Doric order has different proportions than the Greek and adds a column base (with a plinth, torus, bead, and fillet) and a pedestal; many variations of the typical order are found; the caissons between the mutules are recessed with raised moldings at the edges and form a rhombus with corners at the center of each edge; the Greek Doric orders typically support a gable roof with a pediment end and a triangular tympanum surrounded by cornices. See also **classical orders, denticulated Doric, Greek Revival style.** (*See illustration p. 150.*)

dormant, dormant window (pre-20c) Same as **dormer window.**

dormant-tree (18c) A large **summer beam** that spans across a house.

dormer **1.** (pre-19c) A sleeping room. **2.** Same as **dormer window.**

dormered Constructed with dormer windows.

dormer window **1.** A small structure that projects from a sloping roof, with a window in the downslope end; used to light an attic space and to provide headroom; may have a gabled, shed, or other shaped roof. Also known as **dormant, dorment, dormont.** **2.** A window in the end of a **dormer** (sense 1). See also **wall dormer.** (*See illustration p. 151.*)

dormitory A room or a building where many people sleep, especially students at a school or college; may also include dining facilities and study areas; from the term for a large sleeping room for monks. See also **barracks.**

Dorset Italian A white **marble** with scattered, grayish green and dark green crystals quarried in Dorset, Vermont; polishes fairly well.

Dorset Mountain A bluish-white tinted **marble** mottled with light gray quarried in the vicinity of East Dorset, Vermont, starting in 1825; polishes medium well.

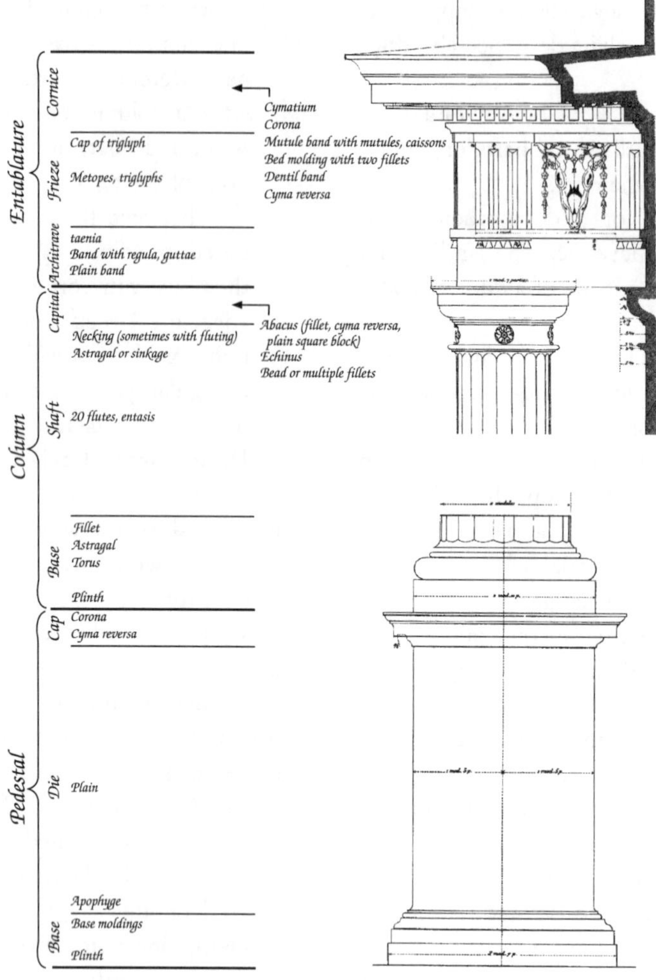

Doric order

Dorset stone A light cream to very light greenish **marble** clouded with light gray quarried in the vicinity of South Dorset, Vermont; polishes fair to medium well.

Dorset White See **Dorset stone.**

dosseret A column capital with a large raised element above a standard capital; may be decorated or plain.

dot A small tile at the intersection of four larger tiles; may be marble or ceramic; typically a square placed at a 45-degree angle to the grid of the larger tiles.

double-acting door A **door** that swings in both directions from a closed position; typically has a **double-acting hinge.**

double-acting hinge A **hinge** that allows a door to swing in both directions from the closed position; typically a spring-mounted double butt hinge.

double architrave, (18c) **double-faced architrave** An **architrave** (sense 2) with a bead

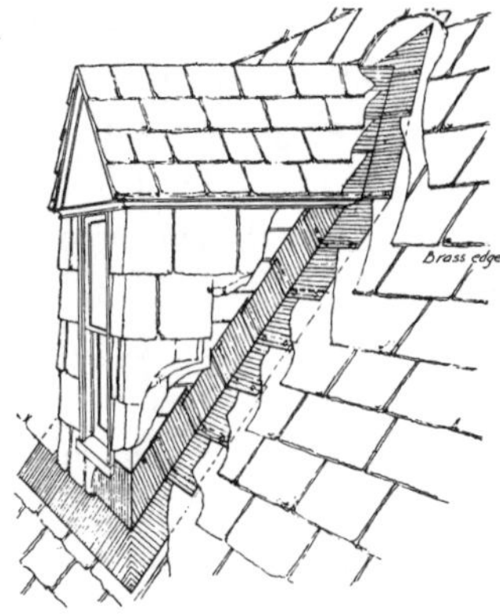

dormer window (sense 1)

molding at the edge of the opening, a flat band, a cyma or ovolo molding, a second flat band, and a raised molding adjacent to a fillet at the outer edge; the second flat band is stepped out from the first band; generally used in more elaborate spaces than a **single architrave.**

double baluster A baluster in the shape of two small balusters set base to base with a torus between them.

double bead A pair of adjoining **bead** moldings; commonly used on the edge of shelves.

double boiler A large water heater composed of two water boilers; typically one boiler is inside the other boiler; the two boilers may also abut onc another. See also **water boiler.**

double capital Same as **dosseret.**

double cone One of a series of ornaments in the form of truncated cones alternately joined at their bases and apexes.

double cornice (18c) A **cornice** that includes a cymatium on top and corona and bed molding below. See also **single cornice.**

double deadening (early 20c) A wood frame floor with both a **counterceiling** and a finish floor laid on sleepers above a subfloor.

double decker A two-unit house in which each of two stories is an individual apartment; common in New England.

double dome An outer dome built over an inner dome, with a space between them; used to provide a different shape or decorative finish on the inner vault.

double door **1.** A pair of swinging doors that close an opening by meeting in the middle. Also known as **folding door. 2.** (pre-20c) Same as **bifold door. 3.** (pre-20c) A door of double thickness. **4.** A pair of swinging doors with hinges on the same jamb; used for security, such as in a prison.

double faced **Ornamental cast iron** with full relief moldings on both front and back.

double-faced architrave (18c) Same as **double architrave.**

double floor **1.** A floor constructed with separate floor and ceiling joists. Also known as **double-framed floor.** See also **binding beam. 2.** A floor with joists supported by a **girder.** See also **single floor.**

double-framed door A **door** with stiles, rails, and panels set within a frame of stiles and rails.

double-framed floor Same as **double floor** (sense 1).

double gable roof A roof composed of two parallel gable roofs that form the shape of the letter *M* on the end wall. Also known as **M roof.**

double glazing **Insulating glass** with an inner and outer pane, usually with a sealed air space between them.

double house Same as **semidetached.**

double hung (early 19c–present) A **window** with two sashes that slide past each other vertically; either both sashes are hung with cord, pulley, and counterweight on each side, or (19c) the bottom sash has cords and counterweights on each side; typically the lower sash is inside the upper sash; types by number of panes range from **one over one** to **twelve over twelve.** See also **single hung.**

double lock A **lift-lock** with two parallel lift chambers that allow boats to pass upstream and downstream simultaneously.

double-margin door A single **door** with the appearance of a double door; the center stile is double wide with a vertical bead or similar device at the center, producing a double margin.

double pen A type of **log house** with two interior spaces separated by a log wall; typically with a doorway in the wall. See also **dogtrot, saddlebag.**

double-pile A building floor plan that is two rooms deep. See also **double pen, single-pile.**

double quadrangular truss A **Whipple truss** with diagonal counterbraces that overlap two panels; used for long-span bridges.

double quarter See **quarter.**

double-quirked bead An **angle bead** with quirks at both sides. See also **quirk bead.**

double skylight A skylight with glazing at the ceiling level and above the roof; the inner glazing typically is **obscure glass** or **colored glass.**

double spruce Same as **black spruce.** See also **spruce.**

double-strength glass **Window glass** that is ⅛ inch thick.

double studded A wood frame wall having closely spaced **studs,** or twice the usual number of studs; used to provide security or to add additional strength.

double sunk A panel (or similar element) that recedes from the main surface in two steps. See also **sunk panel.**

double triangular truss Same as **lattice truss.**

double vault An outer vault built over an inner vault, with a space between them; used to provide a different shape or decorative finish on the inner vault.

double water glass See **water glass.**

double worked A building element, such as a door, that has moldings or decoration on both sides. See also **single worked.**

double-worked siding A clapboard that has been milled to give the appearance of two narrow clapboards on each piece.

doubling A course of slates, tiles, or shingles that is two layers thick at the eaves.

doubling nail (19c) Same as **coffin nail.**

douche bath (19c) A plumbing fixture that sprays water over the body. See also **bath, bidet, Scotch bath.**

doucine (18c) Same as **cymatium.**

Douglas fir A large softwood tree with light yellowish to reddish, strong, straight-grained, pitchy wood, sometimes with dense knots; found in western North America from northern Mexico to British Columbia and lumbered mostly in northern California, Oregon, and Washington; typically used for sheathing, framing lumber, and millwork; *Pseudotsuga taxifolia;* also known as **Oregon pine, red fir, red pine.** See also **white fir.**

Douglas pine A very large softwood tree with a reddish, coarse-grained, strong, heavy wood; found on the U.S. Pacific coast; *Pseudotsuga douglasii.* See also **Douglas fir, pine, spruce.**

Douglas spruce Same as **Douglas pine.** See also **spruce.**

Dove Blue A general designation for dark bluish gray marbles, including **Columbia, Dark Blue Rutland, Dark Vein True Blue, Dove Blue Rutland.**

Dove Blue Rutland A uniformly blue-gray **marble** quarried in the vicinity of West Rutland, Vermont; polishes medium well.

dovecote, dovecot (18c–present) A structure that houses tame pigeons; has multiple openings in an exterior wall leading to nesting boxes; typically mounted on a post or a building wall. Also known as **dove house, pigeon house.**

dove house (19c) Same as **dovecote.**

dovetail, (pre-19c) **dufftail, duftail,** (pre-18c) **dove tayle** A tenon, especially of wood, cut in a flared shape similar to a bird's tail; typically used to make a **dovetail joint** or to connect the end of one timber frame element to another element.

dovetailed Interlocked by a single **dovetail** or a **dovetail joint.**

dovetail fret A fret or meander that forms dovetail-shaped patterns.

dovetail hinge A **hinge** with surface-mounted, wedge-shaped straps with the narrow ends at the joint; used for casement windows and cabinet doors. Also known as **butterfly hinge.**

dovetail joint **1.** A series of interlocking dovetails and mortises used to join two pieces together; types include **lap dovetail, secret dovetail;** used in wood casework to make strong corners and in **timber frame** construction to make locked joints. Also known as **fantail joint.** **2.** Same as **dovetail notch.**

dovetail molding A molding decorated with a series of equilateral triangles, with the apexes alternately at the top and bottom.

dovetail notch An interlocking **notching** system used for a **log house** in which the end of the log is wider at the outside of the dovetail-shaped notch.

dovetail tenon Same as **dovetail.**

dowel **1.** A **pin** used to attach elements together; typically a short cylindrical wood rod; used in millwork and log structures. See also **treenail.** **2.** A dovetail masonry cramp. **3.** A piece of wood driven into a wall as a nailer. **4.** A short reinforcing bar used as a splice between adjoining sections of concrete or masonry.

doweled door A wood door with rails and stiles fastened with dowels rather than tenons.

doweled window A wood window with rails and stiles fastened with dowels rather than tenons.

dowel pin Same as **dowel** (sense 1).

dowel screw A double-pointed screw used for hidden fastening of wood. Also known as **stair rail screw.** See also **wood screw.**

downspout A rainwater **leader** that is surface mounted on the exterior of a building; typically fabricated of sheet metal, including copper, galvanized iron or lead, and, beginning in the mid-20c, aluminum. Also known as **conductor, rainwater conductor.** See also **boot, conductor head.**

down zoning The process of making the **zoning** for an area or site more restrictive; may include lowering the permitted **density** and/or height or changing the **use;** sometimes used to decrease development pressures in historic districts.

drab **1.** Any yellowish to greenish brown color, such as khaki or olive green. **2.** Dull, faded, or monotonous in appearance.

draft, (Canada, pre-20c) **draught** **1.** The relatively narrow, tooled border on the face of a stone block, parallel to the face of the wall and finished with a different texture than the central portion. Also known as **margin.** See also **sunk draft.** **2.** A flow or current of air; types include **forced draft, natural draft.** **3.** (pre-20c) A latrine, sewer, sink, or similar element. See also **draft house.** **4.** A beveled face on the side of a casting that allows it to be withdrawn from the mold. **5.** A preliminary drawing or plan; in the 17c, same as **plan** or **plat.**

draft house (pre-20c) An **outhouse** used as a latrine.

draft stop **1.** A hanging wall around the edge of an opening in a ceiling, such as a stairwell, that restrains smoke from passing upward during a fire. See also **bulkhead.** **2.** A vertical fire-resistant partition that divides an attic into separate areas.

draft stopping Same as **fire stopping.**

draft tube A watertight tube that connects a water **turbine** to the **tail race;** used to increase the effective head of water.

dragged A stone finish produced by pulling a steel drag with a serrated edge across the face of a block.

dragging beam, dragging piece Same as **dragon beam.**

dragon beam **1.** A horizontal, diagonal tie beam that supports the end of a hip rafter and bisects the inside corner of a wall; the outer end is supported by the wall plates and the inner end by an angle brace or ceiling girder. **2.** (18c) One of two braces under a breastsummer, meeting at an angle on the shoulder of the kingpiece. **3.** A diagonal girder that projects past a corner post of a **timber frame** building to support the **overhang.**

dragon piece, dragon tie A wood tie between the intersection of a vertical and a horizontal timber and the middle of an angle brace between them.

dragon's blood A deep reddish brown pigment composed of one of various plant resins; sources include the fruit of the trees *Dracaena draco* and *Pterocarpus draco* and the rattan palms *Calamus rotang* and *Calamus draco.*

dragon summer A large **dragon beam.**

drain **1.** Any pipe or channel that carries stormwater or sewage; may be open or covered and above or below grade; types include **barrel drain, box drain, french drain, gunbarrel drain, rubble drain.** See also **drain gate, drainpipe, sewer.** **2.** The outflow plumbing fitting for any container or receiver of liquid, such as a sink, tank, or flat roof; types include **catch basin, roof drain, trap.**

drain gate (19c) An inflow opening to a sewer that is covered with a grate.

draining tile (pre-20c) Same as **drain tile.**

drainpipe Any **pipe** used to convey drainage liquids; types by use include **soil pipe, waste pipe;** types by orientation include **branch, stack;** types by material include **asbestos cement pipe, bituminized fiber pipe, cast-iron pipe, concrete pipe.** See also **sewer pipe.**

drain tile Terra-cotta pipe; typically with a circular or hexagonal cross section and used for underground installations to drain groundwater; (19c) also composed of a flat tile covered with a semicircular tile. Also known as **draining tile.**

drain trap Same as **trap.**

drain well (19c) Same as **dry well.**

drapery The sculptured representation of clothing, curtains, and other fabric.

draught (Canada, pre-20c) Same as **draft.**

drawbolt lock (19c) A **dead bolt** that may be shut with a knob or locked with a key.

drawbore, drawbore pin A tapered wooden peg used to fasten a **mortise and tenon** joint; typically the holes in the mortised timber are slightly offset from the hole in the tenon, so that hammering in the draw pin pulls both parts snugly together.

drawbridge A **bridge** that opens vertically or horizontally to allow passage of ships; types include **bascule bridge, swing bridge.** See also **vertical-lift bridge.**

drawing room, drawing-room **1.** (19c) A large, formal room used for receiving guests or retiring to after dinner. See also **parlor, saloon.** **2.** (late 18c) The room to which the ladies withdraw from the men after dinner; an abbreviated form of the original **withdrawing room.** See also **morning room, sitting room.**

drawings See **working drawings.**

drawn Wood, especially rived boards, that has been finished by hand shaving the surface, often with a draw knife. See also **dressed, dubbed.**

draw pin Same as **drawbore.**

dressed Finished by cutting or smoothing, as in **dressed stone** or **dressed lumber.** See also **drawn, dubbed.**

dressed-and-matched boards Same as **tongue-and-groove** boards.

dressed faced A smooth exposed face on a block of ashlar.

dresser (pre-WWII) In a kitchen or pantry, a cupboard or sideboard with shelves used for storing dishes or preparing food; may have solid or glass doors.

dressing (19c) **1.** The projecting moldings on the walls and ceilings of a room. **2.** The enframements of openings on the outside of a building.

dressing room (mid-18c–present) A room used for changing clothes; may adjoin a bedroom or be part of a theater or store. See also **green room.**

drier A component of paint that speeds the drying of the oil base; typically composed of metals such as lead, manganese, cobalt, calcium, iron, or zinc in a chemical compound solution.

drift (19c) The outward thrust of an arch.

drift bolt An iron or steel rod driven into a hole in heavy timbers.

drip **1.** A groove or projection on the bottom of an overhanging element that prevents rainwater from running down the wall below the overhang. **2.** (18c) Same as **corona.** See also **water nose.**

drip joint A metal flashing or roofing joint formed with a projecting lip that sheds rainwater.

drip ledge On a coping or similar element, a slightly angled piece that forms a shallow valley and directs water away from a building.

drip loop (19c) A hanging loop in an electrical service wire where it enters the building; used to prevent water seepage.

drip molding Any projecting molding that forms a drip.

dripping eaves Sloped eaves, without a gutter, that project beyond the face of the wall.

dripstone **1.** A hoodmold on the outside of a wall, especially in Gothic Revival architecture. **2.** A splash block cut from stone; used in Shaker communities in the 19c and early 20c.

driveway floor The upper level of a hay barn, accessible to a wagon or motorized equipment. See also **bank barn.**

drop **1.** Any hanging or pendant ornament. **2.** One of a series of **guttae.**

drop arch **1.** A **two-centered arch** in which the centers are below the spring line; the centers are often on the level of the top of the imposts of a stilted arch. **2.** A **multicentered arch** in which some of the centers are below the spring line.

drop black A black paint **pigment** manufactured from organic charcoal, especially burnt animal bones; typically composed of calcium phosphate [$Ca_3(PO_4)_2$] plus a small amount of carbon; may have a brownish tinge if made from soft bones; common in pre-19c house paints; originally sold in small lumps or drops. Also known as **bone black.** See also **ivory-black, lampblack, sugarhouse black.**

drop bolt A vertical **slide bolt** that engages a hole in the paving below a gate or large door; varieties include **cane bolt.**

drop feed Water distributed downward from a rooftop. See also **house tank.**

drop panel A thickened portion of a concrete slab that extends downward around a column to resist shear forces.

dropped girt Same as **sunk girt.**

drop siding Horizontal board siding with either a top front rabbet and a bottom rear rabbet that laps the board below or tongue-and-groove edges; installed flat against the wall; types include **German siding, log cabin siding, O-G novelty.** Also known as **matched siding, novelty siding.** See also **clapboard, siding.**

drop tracery The hanging tracery that borders the soffit of a Gothic Revival arch.

drove **1.** A chiseled stone finish with fine parallel grooves cut with a drove chisel. **2.** Same as **tooled.** See also **dragged.**

drum **1.** One of the cylindrical blocks that form a column. **2.** The exterior vertical wall, with a circular or regular polygonal plan, that supports a cupola or dome. **3.** The bell of a capital.

Drummond light A bright light produced by heating lime to incandescence in an oxyhydrogen flame. Also known as a **calcium light.**

dry arch An arched opening in a foundation to raise a portion above grade and keep it dry.

dry area A sunken **areaway** adjacent to a foundation wall; its purpose is to keep the wall dry.

dry deposition The deposition of dry pollutants on a surface; includes particles and gases. See also **acid rain, wet deposition.**

drying room, drying closet, drying loft A room for drying clothes, especially when equipped with mechanical heating and ventilation.

dry-laid Masonry construction built without the use of mortar, including **dry-stone.**

dry line Same as **occult line.**

dry-pack A mortar mixture with just enough water added to form a stiff putty; used to pack narrow spaces with minimal movement after installation; used under **bearing plates** and in **underpinning.** See also **grout.**

dry-pipe system A **sprinkler system** with pipes containing air or nitrogen under pressure; during a fire, a dry-pipe valve fills the pipes with water; often used in historic building interiors, especially when there may be danger of freezing. See also **preaction system, wet-pipe system.**

dry-press brick (20c) Bricks produced by forming relatively dry clay in molds under pressure.

dry rot Lumber decay caused by fungi, especially by *Merulius lacrimans* and *Coniophora cerebella;* named for the ability of the fungus to grow in relatively dry wood because it can transport water along its tendrils.

dry seam A fissure or fracture in a building stone that makes it unfit because of potential structural failure.

dry-stone **Dry-laid** stone masonry.

dry wall A **dry-laid** masonry wall.

drywall (20c) A wall and ceiling finish material composed of sheets of **gypsum board** nailed or screwed to the backing, with the joints covered with tape and drywall compound; named for the relatively dry application methods in comparison to **plaster.**

dry well, drywell A subterranean pit to which stormwater or liquid waste is directed so that it can seep into the ground; typically formed of dry-laid masonry or a gravel-filled hole. Also known as **dead well, drain well.** See also **cesspool.**

D-trap A plumbing drain trap that is approximately in the shape of the letter *D* turned sideways; may have a single semicircular bend or a similarly shaped box below the sink outflow pipe; not used after the 19c.

dubbed, (17c) **dubd** Trimmed and smoothed with an adze; used for timber and boards. See also **drawn.**

dubbing out The filling of depressions in a masonry wall before applying stucco.

Duchess County, Duchess **Marble** quarried in the vicinity of South Dover, Duchess County, New York.

duck-bill tooling A chiseled stone finish in the form of staggered rows of small, scalloped projections, or a similar finish on a pre-WWII molded concrete block; named for the similarity of the shape of the projections to a duck's bill.

duckboard (20c) A low platform composed of wood slats fastened to battens; used as walkways on rooftops and muddy ground; term originated with trench warfare during WWI.

ducking stool, (18c) **ducking stoole,** (17c) **duckinge stoole** A device for immersing someone in water as a punishment; of various forms, including a chair on a pole or a seat on a frame with large wooden wheels; required by law in every county of Virginia and some other states through the early 19c.

duct **1.** Same as **air duct.** **2.** An enclosure with a rectangular cross section for electric cables. See also **bus duct.**

dufftail, dufttail (pre-19c) Same as **dovetail.**

dugout An earth structure constructed by excavation; may be partially or completely below grade; typically the roof is formed of earth-covered poles; often used on the treeless plains, especially during construction of the Union Pacific Railroad and by Native Americans.

dull-glaze Any matte-glazed ceramic finish, such as that used on **architectural terra-cotta.**

dumbbell tenement A **tenement house** with two or more flats per floor and with indented light shafts at the middle of both sides, giving the plan of each floor a dumbbell shape.

dumbwaiter A small elevator used for moving food from a lower-level kitchen to the dining room; common during the 19c; originally a small cupboard on wheels used for serving diners.

dummy breast A false fireplace and chimney breast.

dungeon (pre-20c) A secure cell in a jail or prison.

Dunville stone A buff colored, fine-grained freestone quarried in the vicinity of Dunville, Wisconsin; does not polish.

duplex **1.** An apartment with rooms on two levels. **2.** A house with two dwelling units; may be divided vertically or horizontally.

Duprene A synthetic rubber compound used for electric wire insulation; developed in the 1930s. See also **rubber insulation.**

dustbin An enclosure for trash receptacles.

dust flue, dust shaft A trash chute.

Dutch arch Same as **French arch.**

Dutch bond Same as **English cross bond.**

Dutch brick A narrow, hard, yellow brick used for pavers and fireplace interiors; imported from England pre-19c. Also known as **Dutch clinker.**

Dutch colonial Buildings built by Dutch settlers and their descendants from early 17c to early 19c in various styles adapted from those in Holland; found primarily along the Hudson River and Delaware River valleys and on Long Island, New York; urban buildings are similar to those in 17c Holland, typically with steeply pitched gable roofs and the entrance in the parapeted gable end facing the street (not commonly built after ca. 1730); common urban elements include dagger-shaped wall anchors, **crow step** parapets, and paired end chimneys; rural houses typically are one story with stone walls and a side-gable roof or, sometimes (after mid-18c), a **gambrel roof;** rural house roofs have little or no overhang at the gable end and often, after mid-18c in the southern Hudson River valley, flared eaves; houses often have a battened or paneled **Dutch door.**

Dutch Colonial style An architectural style loosely based on **Dutch colonial** buildings; started ca. 1890 and continues to the present; nearly always with a **gambrel roof** and multi-paned double-hung windows; often with dormer windows and/or front-facing gambrel end, neither of which were found in the original.

Dutch corner A brick wall **bond** formed at a corner by ending one course with a two-thirds stretcher and the courses above and below with a full stretcher or a header; used in English bond and Flemish bond. See also **English corner.**

Dutch door A door divided horizontally so that the top and bottom parts can be opened separately; introduced in North America by Dutch settlers; used to provide ventilation by opening the top half while preventing passage of animals and children. See also **half door.**

Dutch foil Foil made from **Dutch metal.**

Dutch gable A gable wall with reverse-curve sides capped with a pediment.

Dutch gold Same as **Dutch metal.**

Dutch leaf Same as **Dutch foil.**

Dutchman **1.** A repair made with a piece of the same material inserted in a sharp-edged mortise. **2.** A shim.

Dutch metal An extremely malleable alloy of copper and zinc; typically manufactured as an imitation gold leaf, or to make **Dutch metal powder** or **Dutch foil.** Also known as **Dutch gold, Dutch, Dutch mineral, tombac.**

Dutch metal powder A fine, gold-colored powder composed of **Dutch metal;** used for bronzing.

Dutch mineral Same as **Dutch metal.**

Dutch pink A transparent yellow paint **pigment** composed of an extract of oak bark or quercitron precipitated by alum on a base of carbonate of lime; favored in the late 19c because it retained its hue in gaslight; used for yellow, green, and olive tints. See also **lake color.**

Dutch roof Same as **gambrel roof.**

Dutch shutter Interior window shutters with upper and lower sections that can be opened and closed independently.

Dutch tile A glazed terra-cotta wall tile made in the Netherlands; typically with a dark blue pattern on a white background and often with an illustration in a central panel. See also **chimney tile.**

dwarf door **1.** A short door. **2.** The lower half of a **Dutch door.**

dwarf wall **1.** A wall or partition that does not extend completely to the ceiling. **2.** Same as **knee wall.** **3.** An exterior wall less than a full story in height.

dwelling house A **house** (sense 1); in law, sometimes includes its various outbuildings, such as a carriage house or smokehouse.

dwelling plantation (Maryland) Same as **home plantation.**

dwelling unit A room or group of rooms that are the residence of one or more people; may be an **apartment, dormitory,** or **house.** See also **barracks, hotel.**

D-window A semicircular or semielliptical window; from its resemblance to the shape of the letter *D* on its back; common beginning in the late 18c. Also known as **lunette.** See also **fanlight.**

Dyer breccia A **marble** with a brick red ground mass with fragments of pinkish white to cream, bluish gray, or deep red, quarried before ca. 1920 in the vicinity of Manchester, Vermont. Also known as **equinox marble.**

dynamo (19c–present) A dynamo-electric generator or motor; changes rotational power into electricity or vice versa.

dyostyle Same as **distyle.**

dyptere (18c) Same as **diptere.**

E

ear **1.** Any small projecting element at the sides of a member. **2.** Same as **crossette** (sense 1).

Early English style Architecture in the style of English Gothic buildings constructed in the period 1189–1272; typical elements include pointed arches, shaft rings, circular cusped tracery, lancet windows, boldly projecting buttresses and pinnacles, and steeply pitched roofs. See also **Gothic pitch, Gothic Revival style.**

Early Romanesque Revival Same as **Romanesque Revival** (sense 1).

earlywood Same as **springwood.**

earth Relatively soft, natural, underground soil material, including clay, sand, silt, and decayed organic material, as opposed to gravel, boulders, or stone. See also **earthwork.**

earth cellar An underground storage structure with earthen walls and, usually, an earth-covered roof; used for keeping perishables cool. See also **root cellar.**

earth closet A commode or latrine in which dry earth is used as a deodorizer. See also **water closet.**

earth color One of the paint colors originally made from an **earth pigment;** popular in the mid-19c and in International Style interiors of the 1950s.

earthen floor A hard-packed clay floor; common in buildings 17c–early 19c, and later in outbuildings and poorer rural dwellings.

earthen pipe A large-diameter **socket sewer pipe** composed of terra-cotta.

earthfast (20c) A wood frame building supported directly on the earth, as opposed to having a masonry foundation; types include **poteau-en-terre, posts in the ground.** See also **mud sill.**

earth lodge Any of several types of earth shelters built by Native Americans. See also **dugout, hogan.**

earth pigment Paint pigment made from naturally occurring mineral deposits; prevalent pre-1800; types include **French ocher, yellow ocher, burnt sienna, raw sienna, burnt umber, raw umber.**

earth pit (pre-20c) A trench or pit covered with a glazed sash to protect plants in cold weather.

earthquake washer A round cast-iron plate attached to a **tie rod** or **bolt;** often used to reinforce masonry buildings in cities such as Charleston, South Carolina, and San Francisco, California, after earthquake damage or for **seismic retrofit** to prevent earthquake damage.

earth table An exposed, continuous masonry plinth course at ground level that projects forward of the wall above; located immediately above the **foundation** and below the **ledgement table** or **water table.** Also known as **grass table, ground table.**

earthwork **1.** A constructed mound or rampart of earth, including a part of a **fortification** or a

Native American **mound.** **2.** Any construction that involves moving, forming, and/or compacting earth, especially **cut and fill.** See also **catchwork, sitework.**

eased A building element, such as a stair nosing, with a slightly rounded corner.

easement, (pre-20c) **esement** **1.** A deed restriction on a property giving someone besides the owner rights to use or enjoy the property, and may also restrict its **use** or **development;** types include **facade easement, open space easement, right of way, preservation easement.** See also **restrictive covenant, title search.** **2.** A curved portion of an architectural element, such as a handrail or molding, that makes a smooth transition between two straight portions. See also **ramp.**

east end The chancel end of a Christian church; from the medieval practice of locating a church with its main axis oriented east and west, with the altar and related areas at the east end. See also **east window, westwork.**

eastern hemlock **1.** A **hemlock** tree with light buff colored, moderately strong, lightweight, flexible, coarse-grained wood; found in mountain valleys from northern Alabama to New England, and northern Wisconsin and Michigan to Canada; commonly used for lumber and sheathing until early 20c; *Tsuga canadensis.* Also known as **American hemlock, Canadian hemlock.** **2.** (19c) *Tsuga mertensiana.*

eastern red cedar A small softwood tree with aromatic, reddish brown to purplish brown heartwood and whitish sapwood of medium strength and low stiffness; found in eastern North America; used for posts, framing, trim, and to line storage closets; lumbered locally in small quantities; *Juniperus virginiana.* Also known in southern U.S. as **juniper, Virginian juniper.** See also **cedar, western red cedar.**

eastern spruce Same as **black spruce.**

eastern tamarack A deciduous softwood tree of the larch family with light brown, hard, strong, flexible, resinous, coarse-grained heartwood and whitish sapwood; found from northern West Virginia to Labrador and west to the Yukon Valley; durable in contact with soil; used for lumber and millwork; *Larix laricina.* See also **larch, tamarack.**

eastern white pine A common softwood tree with creamy white to reddish brown, soft, straight-grained wood; found in northern U.S., Appalachia, and Canada; used for all types of wood construction; the most common pre-20c timber tree, used mainly for interior millwork by the end of the 19c; *Pinus strobus.* Also known as **white pine.**

Eastlake style (late 19c–present) An architectural style characterized by rich, geometric ornamentation and heavy brackets, especially scrollwork, in the form of stylized plants; most often seen as a variation of the **Stick Style** or **Queen Anne style;** after Charles Lock Eastlake, a 19c English furniture designer and architect.

Eastman Blue A medium bluish gray **marble** quarried in the vicinity of West Rutland, Vermont; polishes medium well. Also known as **Oxford Fleuri.**

Easton marble Any of various green marbles quarried in the vicinity of Easton, Pennsylvania; variety includes **frozen green.** also known as **Pennsylvania green.**

east window A large window at the chancel end of a Christian church, especially a rose window in a square-ended building; typically faced east in Medieval churches. See also **east end.**

eat house (18c) Same as **restaurant.**

eating shed (19c southern U.S.) A **mess hall** for plantation slaves.

eat room (18c) Same as **dining room.**

eave cornice, eve cornice (18c) Same as **roof cornice.**

eaves, eave, (pre-20c) **eves** The projection of a roof beyond the wall below; most often used to refer to the edge or underside of a roof; types include **sprocked eaves.** See also **cornice.**

eaves board A beveled sheathing board at the edge of the eaves, with its upper edge the same thickness as the other sheathing boards and the lower edge thicker; used to give the last course of tile or slate the same slope as those above. See also **eaves lath.**

eaves catch Same as **eaves board.**

eaves channel A small gutter cut in the top of a masonry wall to direct rainwater from an eaves to a downspout, especially when in the top course of a cornice.

eaves lath A strip of wood used to raise the bottom course of roof tile or slate so that it has the same slope as the other courses. See also **eaves board.**

eaves trough A gutter hung from an eaves.

ebonite Same as **vulcanite.**

ebonizing An artificial finish applied to various woods to give them the black, lustrous appearance of ebony wood; popular during the Victorian era for both interior millwork and furniture. See also **black shellac.**

echinus A convex molding of a classical style capital immediately below the abacus; of various profiles; often with carved egg and dart ornament.

echinus and astragal An egg and dart molding above a bead and reel astragal.

echo (pre-20c) An elliptical or parabolic vault that produces a reverberating reflection of sound back to its origin. See also **centrum phonicum, centrum phonicampticum, whispering gallery.**

Eclecticism (late 19c–present) Architecture that freely uses earlier European styles; may use elements of a particular style in ways not found in the original or combine features of several styles in a single building; partially a reaction to those architects who believed in a single universal style such as **Greek Revival** or **Gothic Revival;** common for large public buildings mid-19c–late-19c.

École des Beaux-Arts The "School of Fine Arts" founded in 1648 in Paris to teach painting and sculpture; courses in architecture (begun in 1819) emphasize study of **classical** Greek and Roman buildings, axial symmetry, and composition; students are grouped in ateliers supervised by a master; strongly influenced North American architects in the late 19c and early 20c, beginning with Richard Morris Hunt, the first American to study at the school (1846–1852). See also **beaux arts, vista.**

eco-museum An economic enterprise within a **historic site** that also is interpreted for visitors as a museum exhibit.

economic life The period of time during which it is economically viable to keep a building, equipment, or a building component in use; determined in part by the **life expectancy** and maintenance costs of the component; can be extended by **restoration, rehabilitation,** or replacement, including **new construction.** See also **depreciation.**

economic viability The extent to which a property is economically self-sustaining with or without subsidies. See also **feasibility study.**

economy brick Oversized **brick** with a nominal size of 4 × 4 × 8 inches.

ecphora (19c) The projection of any architectural member beyond the one immediately below it.

edge butt hinge Same as **butt hinge.**

edge grain Same as **vertical grain.**

edge laid Flooring or paving installed **edge to edge.**

edgelong (pre-20c) Same as **edgewise.**

edge molding Any of various moldings with two convex curves connected by a fillet or concave curve; typically a quarter round on top meets a horizontal fillet that connects to a quarter round with a smaller radius.

edge roll **1.** Same as **bowtell.** **2.** A raised rim around the edge, such as on a lavatory sink.

edgeshot (pre-20c) A board that has been planed on the edges.

edge to edge Installed with the long edges butted against one another, especially boards.

edge veneer Wood veneer used to cover the edge of a door stile or similar element; often thick enough to be planed.

edgeways (18c) Same as **edgewise.**

edgewise Installed so that the long, narrow edge is exposed to view; often used to refer to bricks used for paving. Also known as **edgelong, edgeways.**

edging **1.** A border formed of a different material, such as bricks or shrubs around a planting bed. **2.** A molding profile cut at a corner of a wood member. **3.** Process of cutting the edge of wood members, such as rafters, to a particular level.

edifice A dignified and important building or structure. See also **pile.**

efflorescence Water-soluble salts leached out of masonry or concrete by capillary action and deposited on a surface by evaporation; typically white; usually crystalline sulfates of sodium, potassium, magnesium, calcium, and iron. Also known as **saltpetering.** See also **exfoliation, scaling, spalling, subflorescence.**

egg and anchor A convex molding with a series of bas-relief ovoids alternating with anchors with two flukes; typically each **ovum** is surrounded with a raised lip and the **anchors** point downward. See also **echinus, egg and dart, egg and tongue.**

egg and dart A convex molding with a series of bas-relief ovoids alternating with stylized barbed arrow heads; typically each **ovum** is surrounded with a raised lip and the **darts** point downward. See also **echinus, egg and anchor, egg and tongue.**

egg and tongue A convex molding with a series of bas relief ovoids alternating with stylized pointed tongues; each **ovum** is surrounded with a raised lip and typically the **tongues** point downward. See also **echinus, egg and anchor, egg and dart.**

eggshell A **glossy** paint finish with a fine, crinkled surface, similar to that of an egg.

egress requirement **Building code** regulations related to the minimum number, length, width, and type of exit corridors, doors, and stairways; alternative methods of egress are often necessary to satisfy these requirements in an existing or historic building or structure.

Egyptian Revival style An architectural style using Egyptian motifs, such as massive papyrus or lotus columns, bas-relief symbols (e.g., a **feroher**), and, sometimes, statuary (e.g., a **sphinx**); typically has battered walls; primarily used in public buildings and monuments during the 19c.

eightpenny nail (8d nail) A **nail** approximately 2.5 inches long; 85 iron common nails weigh one pound. See also **eightpenny spike, penny.**

eightpenny spike (8d spike) A **spike** approximately 6 inches long; 10 steel-wire spikes weigh one pound. See also **eightpenny nail, penny.**

EIS **Environmental Impact Statement**

elastic bitumen Same as **elaterite.**

elastic mineral pitch Same as **elaterite.**

elastomeric (20c) A flexible, elastic material that is in a plastic state during forming or application; used as a **sealant** or **backer rod.**

elaterite A dark brown, subtranslucent, elastic, resinous mineral hydrocarbon, found in soft masses; used through early 20c for caulking and roofing. Also known as **elastic mineral pitch, elastic bitumen, mineral caoutchouc.**

elbow Any construction that approximates the shape of a bent human elbow, including (1) a plumbing **pipe fitting** that changes the direction of the pipe; typically available in angles of 11.5, 22, 45, and 90 degrees; also known as **ell, L;** see also **bend;** (2) a return of a wall or parapet; (3) the facing sides of a window recess, especially when finished with paneling.

elbowboard (19c) An interior windowsill that can be used as an armrest.

elbow rail (19c) A chair rail or other wall molding placed at a height that makes it convenient to use as an armrest.

electrical Related to the furnishing of electric power and light for a building or site; typically includes main power **service cable, electric wiring,** outlets, light fixtures, and control devices. See also **electrical system, engineering.**

electrical code A **building code** that governs the safe and healthy design of electrical systems for a structure.

electrical conductor (18c) Same as **lightning conductor.**

electrical metallic tubing (EMT) Metal conduit with a circular cross section used for electric wiring. See also **electrical nonmetallic tubing.**

electrical nonmetallic tubing (ENT) Electrical **conduit** with a circular cross section and made of plastic or other nonmetallic material. See also **electrical metallic tubing.**

electrical rod (18c–19c) Same as **lightning rod.**

electrical system The entire apparatus for supplying and distributing electricity; typically includes dynamos, transformers, meters, cables, circuit breakers, wires, switches, light fixtures, lightbulbs, and outlets.

electric arc welding Same as **arc welding.**

electric box (late 19c–present) A box with a cover on one open side used for splicing **electric wiring** and sometimes making a connection to a **light, outlet, switch,** or other device; typically of stamped steel with round openings for conduit and wires, sometimes made of plastic beginning in late 20c; types include **junction box, outlet box, pull box, switch box.**

electric burner (19c) A **gas burner** with a mechanism for ignition by an electric spark.

electric candle (19c) A type of **arc light** with parallel carbon rods separated by insulating material. Also known as **Jablochkoff candle.**

electric elevator Any type of **elevator** operated by electric power. See also **geared traction elevator.**

electric fire extinguisher (19c) A thermostatically controlled **sprinkler system** or carbon dioxide extinguisher that operates when the temperature exceeds a certain level.

electric lamp (19c–present) A device that generates artificial light when electricity is passed through it; types include **arc lamp, fluorescent lamp, incandescent lamp.** Also known as **lamp, lightbulb.**

electric lock (19c–present) A lock that can be opened from a remote location by an electric currect passing through a magnetic coil around the bolt.

electric main (19c–present) A **main** that supplies electricity; typically consists of one or more insulated copper cables in an underground iron or concrete conduit.

electric railway (19c–present) A **railroad** with electric power supplied to the locomotives.

electric service See **service cable, service conduit.**

electric tower **1.** (19c) A tower that supports an **arc light.** **2.** (20c) A tower that supports electric transmission wires.

electric wiring (19c–present) Thin, continuous metal with a circular cross section and various insulation and protection systems used to carry electric current; typically copper and (after mid-20c) sometimes aluminum; system types include **armored cable, BX cable, flexible metal conduit, knob-and-tube, nonmetallic cable, office wire, porcelain cleats, rigid metal conduit, wooden cleats, wooden molding.** See also **insulated wire.**

electrolier (19c–WWII) An **electric light fixture,** especially one that is hung like a chandelier.

electroplate bronze A decorative **electroplated** bronze coating on another metal, especially iron; often used on 19c lighting fixtures.

electroplated Covered with a thin layer of metal deposited by electrolysis.

elegant (mid-18c–present) Refined and tasteful, especially when a symmetrical design; used to refer to interiors, landscapes, and buildings.

elemi, gum elemi A resin obtained from various tropical trees, such as *Icica icicariba;* used in pre-WWI varnishes. See also **spirit of wine varnish.**

elevation **1.** One of the faces of a building. **2.** A drawing of a face of a building or an interior wall, with all of the features shown as if in a single vertical plane. **3.** The height above a bench mark or sea level. **4.** The height of a facade of a building.

elevator **1.** A mechanical device for lifting people and objects on a platform; the platform may be open or enclosed with a cage or cab; types include **belt-driven elevator, geared traction elevator, hydraulic elevator, screw elevator.** **2.** A mechanical device with a continuous belt and a series of buckets used for lifting granular materials. **3.** A storage building equipped with an elevator (sense 2), such as a **grain elevator.**

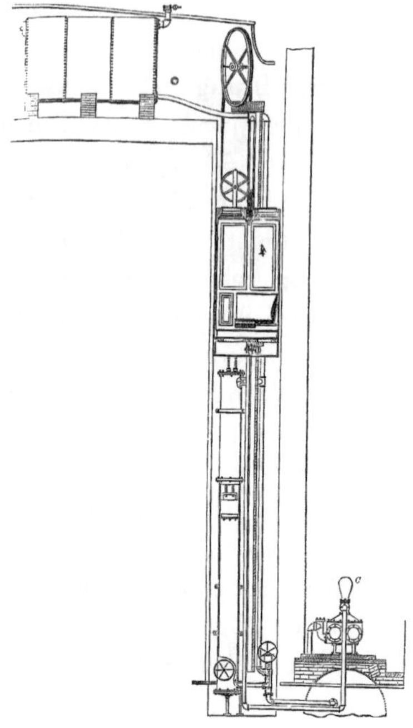

elevator (sense 1)

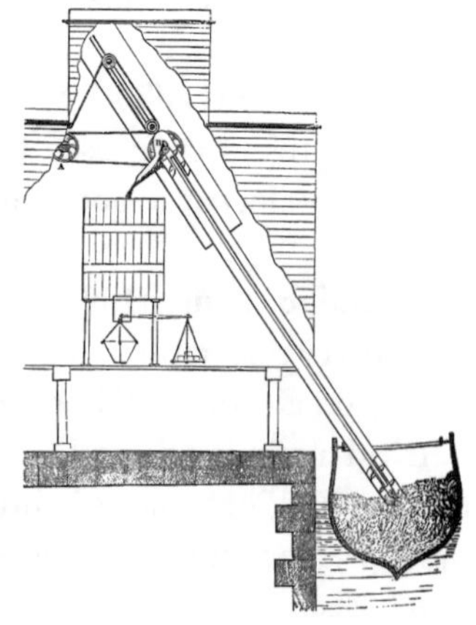

elevator (sense 2)

elevator lobby A waiting area for passengers in front of elevator doors.

eligibility The ability of a property to meet National Register criteria.

Elizabethan pitch A steep gable roof **pitch** in which the length of the rafters is greater than the span.

Elizabethan Revival See **Tudor Revival.**

ell, el, L **1.** (19c–present) An addition to a building that creates an L-shaped floor plan; usually added at the rear of the original structure. **2.** Same as **elbow.**

elliptical arch, elliptic arch **1.** An **arch** that has an intrados in the shape of a true semiellipse, with centers on the spring line; difficult for a mason to lay out and therefore rare. **2.** A technically incorrect term for a three-centered or five-centered arch that approximates a semiellipse. Also known as **basket-handle arch.**

elliptical dome, elliptic dome A **dome** with a cross section in the shape of an arc of an ellipse; may have a circular base or, more often, be an ellipsoid with an elliptical-shaped base.

elliptical stair A winding stair in which the plan of its inside edge is in the shape of an ellipse.

elliptical torus A ring molding with a cross section in the shape of a partial ellipse; a variety of **thumb molding.**

elm See **American elm.**

Elwood sandstone A light to dark buff colored sandstone quarried in western Pennsylvania.

embankment A continuous engineered **bank** of earth; typically a **fill;** uses include seawalls, levees, and highways and railroads crossing sunken areas.

embattlement Same as **battlement.**

embossed **1.** (19c–present) Decorated with bosses or relief figures, especially when produced by mechanically pressing material into a die. See also **repoussé.** **2.** (pre-19c) Same as **relief.**

embossed molding A molding manufactured by **wood embossing;** the width is typically less than 3 inches.

embrasure **1.** A wall opening enlarged on the interior side by splaying the jambs. **2.** Same as **crenel,** especially when designed for a gun emplacement in a **fortification.**

emergency generator (20c) An electric generator that operates when the main power source fails; typically uses diesel or gasoline fuel. Also known as **standby generator.**

emergency salvage archaeology Same as **crisis archaeology.**

eminent domain The right of a government to take private property for its own use, typically through a process of **condemnation.** See also **expropriation.**

eminently hydraulic lime A hydraulic lime that sets under water in three to four days and is very hard within a month.

empire cloth Same as **varnished cloth.**

Empire style The architectural style common in France during Napoleon's First Empire (1804–15); characterized by elaborate neoclassical bas-relief decoration. See also **Adam style, Second Empire style.**

EMT Abbr. for **electrical metallic tubing.**

enabling legislation Laws that confer legal power on a governing body, such as an architectural review board or local government, to regulate private activities; regulations created by such a body may include historic districts or zoning.

enamel **1.** A high-gloss paint; manufactured before WWII by adding varnish or natural resins to the paint. **2.** A smooth, hard, vitreous, shiny coating manufactured by firing a glazed material at high temperature; used on metals and ceramics, such as **porcelain enamel.**

en axe [French] On axis; used by practitioners of beaux-arts design.

encarpus A relief sculpture in the form of a garland or festoon of flowers and fruit.

encaustic tile A vitrified floor or wall tile with a decorative pattern of variously colored clays; manufactured by filling a recess cut into the clay tile base before firing; popular in late 19c.

encorbelment The projection of each course of masonry beyond the face of the course below. See also **corbel.**

encrinal marble Cut marble with surface markings of shells or fossils embedded in the stone, especially fossil encrinites.

end bedded Same as **face bedded.**

end board A board that closes the end of a cornice; cut so that the edge follows the profile of the cornice.

end-construction arch A **floor arch** constructed with **end-construction tiles.**

end-construction tile A structural clay tile unit installed in an **end-construction arch** with the axes of the air cells and webs vertical and perpendicular to the beams.

end girt A wood **girt** member that spans between the middle of the center post and the corner posts of the end bent of a **timber frame** building. See also **side girt.**

end grain The **grain** of the face of a piece of wood cut perpendicular to the vertical axis of a tree.

end scarf joint A scarf joint in which the ends of two wood members are interlocked end to end by means of a mortise and tenon joint with a cross-shaped cross section.

end scroll Same as **volute.**

end splice A wood frame butt joint in which the two members are joined by a board or **strap anchor** nailed across the joint; used for beams or joists above a support.

energy audit The analysis of the **energy efficiency** of an existing building or mechanical system; usually performed to determine ways to reduce energy costs.

energy efficiency The relative efficiency of energy use of any construction or product; may refer to the energy consumed by operating the heating and cooling systems of an entire building, the insulating value of an element such as a wall or window, or the amount of electricity used by an appliance or light fixture. See also **energy audit, infiltration.**

enfilade The arrangement of a series of doors opposite one another to give a continuous view.

enframement Projecting moldings surrounding a wall opening such as a window or fireplace.

engaged column A column attached to the wall behind it. Also known as **attached column.** See also **demicolumn, pilaster.**

Engelmann spruce, Engelmann's spruce A large **spruce** tree with a yellowish white to reddish brown, lightweight, soft, fine-grained wood; found in upper elevations of the Rocky Mountains from New Mexico and Arizona to the Yukon Territory; used regionally for lumber and millwork; *Picea engelmannii.*

engineer A licensed professional who practices **engineering.** See also **architect.**

engineer brick, engineered brick Oversized **brick** with three brick heights plus three joints equaling 9 inches, rather than the more common 8 inches; standard sizes include **engineer modular, engineer standard, engineer Norman.**

engineering The design of the civil, structural, mechanical, and electrical portions of a construction project. See also **architectural design, electrical, mechanical, structural.**

engineer modular A standard sized **engineer brick** with dimensions of $3\frac{1}{2}$–$3\frac{5}{8}$ × $7\frac{1}{2}$–$7\frac{5}{8}$ × $2\frac{3}{4}$–$2\frac{13}{16}$ inches.

engineer norman A standard sized **engineer brick** with dimensions of $3\frac{1}{2}$–$3\frac{5}{8} \times 11\frac{1}{2}$–$11\frac{5}{8} \times 2\frac{3}{4}$–$2\frac{13}{16}$ inches.

engineer standard A standard sized **engineer brick** with dimensions of $3\frac{1}{2}$–$3\frac{5}{8} \times 8 \times 2\frac{3}{4}$–$2\frac{13}{16}$ inches.

engine house **1.** (late 18c–present) A building used for storing a fire engine and related equipment; often contains a dormitory for firemen and, until the 1920s, a stable for horses. **2.** A storage building for railroad engines. **3.** (19c–present) A separate building used as an **engine room.**

engine room A room containing equipment used to generate power, heat, and/or electricity. Also known as **machinery space.**

English basement A **basement house** with the entry at or near grade; found in North America after 1840; in the 19c the basement level typically contained a reception room and dining room and the cellar contained a kitchen and storage rooms.

English bond A brick wall **bond** with a surface pattern of alternate courses of stretchers and headers, with each course having stretchers on one face of the wall and headers on the other face; varieties include **English cross bond;** common through the 18c. Also known as **block bond.** See also **English corner.**

English brass A ductile **brass** alloy of copper and approximately 29.26 percent zinc, 0.7 percent tin, and 0.28 percent lead.

English Colonial Construction by English settlers in the period 1607–1775 in various architectural styles, including **Adam style, Georgian style, postmedieval architecture.**

English corner A brick wall **bond** at a corner formed by ending one course with a header and a bat, and the courses above and below with a full stretcher; typically the length of the header and bat equals two-thirds of a stretcher; used in **English bond** and **Flemish bond.**

English cross bond An **English bond** with the stretcher course joints alternately centered on a header or the next stretcher course. Also known as **St. Andrews cross bond.**

English flooring A **parquet floor** pattern formed by elongated rectangular strips with the joints aligned in alternate rows, as in a running bond.

English frame (17c–early 18c Chesapeake region) **Timber frame** construction in which sawn timbers are connected with mortise and tenon joints and supported on a foundation, as opposed to other less difficult earthfast wood frame building systems.

English garden (mid-18c–19c) A large, informal landscape with open grassy areas and clumps of plantings that define scenic vistas, in imitation of the English country estates landscaped by Capability Brown and others; often include irregular lakes and follies.

English Gothic See **Gothic.**

English house **1.** (17c) A house built with English construction techniques, as opposed to those of Native Americans. **2.** (17c–18c Chesapeake region) An **English frame** building.

English ochre Same as **ocher.**

English style See **English garden.**

en grisaille Flat ornamentation without color, such as windows with rough, uncolored crown glass set in lead sash; from the French for gray monochrome paintings in imitation of bas-relief. See also **grisaille glass.**

enneastyle See **columniation.**

enriched (18c–19c) Having **enrichment.**

enrichment (18c–19c) Decoration added to the surface, especially sculpted relief ornament.

en suite A suite of rooms with the doors on axis with one another.

entablature In classical architecture, the entire band of horizontal elements above the column capitals; from bottom to top, the entablature is composed of the **architrave, frieze,** and **cornice.** See also **trabeated.**

entablement **1.** (18c) Same as **entablature.** **2.** (19c) A series of platforms at the cap of a pedestal supporting a statue.

entasis The convex curve of the shaft of a classical style column; typically the shaft is vertical at the bottom third and curves inward toward the top; commonly used in North America 19c–present. See also **diminished, diminution, swelling.**

enterclose (pre-20c) **1.** An interior passageway between rooms or between a hall and a door. **2.** Same as **partition.**

entering angle An angle formed by the outside of a fortified wall that points toward the interior of a **fortification.** See also **salient angle.**

entresole, entresol (18c–19c) In a house, a **mezzanine** between the ground floor and the main first floor.

entry **1.** A door, gate, or passage used to enter a building. **2.** (19c–present) The first space entered in a building from the outside, when not a living space; may include a vestibule, stair hall, or reception hall.

envelope See **building envelope.**

environment The sum of all the physical features at a particular location, including the **natural environment** and the **built environment.**

environmental conditions The elements that act upon the physical nature of anything; in reference to **cultural artifacts,** typically includes heat, light, temperature, and air quality and humidity. See also **actinic light, degradation, humidistat.**

environmental impact All of the identifiable social and physical effects of a development or a government policy. See also **Environmental Impact Statement.**

Environmental Impact Statement Under the National Environmental Policy Act of 1969 (NEPA), all major U.S. federal actions significantly affecting the quality of the human environment must be preceded by an Environmental Impact Statement (EIS). An EIS is a detailed statement assessing (1) the environmental impact of the proposed action; (2) any adverse environmental effects that cannot be avoided should the proposal be implemented; (3) alternatives to the proposed action, (4) the relationship between local short-term uses of the environment and the maintenance and enhancement of long-term productivity; and (5) any irreversible and irretrievable commitments of resources that would be involved in the proposed action. See also **avoidance, mitigation.**

Environmental Protection Agency (EPA) An independent U.S. federal agency that regulates environmental pollution, including air, water, and noise from sources such as automobiles, pesticides, solid waste, and manufacturing activity.

E.O. (U.S.) Abbr. for Executive Order.

EPA **Environmental Protection Agency**

EPDM (late 20c) Abbr. for **ethylene propylene diene monomer,** used for membranes for roofing and waterproofing.

épi A decorative finial extending upward at the apex of the intersection of hip rafters or a similar location; commonly made of sheet metal or terra-cotta.

epistyle Same as **architrave.**

epoxy, epoxy resin (late 20c) A plastic material formed by the polymerization of an epoxide; typically flexible and thermal setting; often used as an adhesive, coating, or filler, or in a plastic repair that replaces missing building elements; may be mixed with filler such as microballoons.

epoxy paint A hard, durable paint that has an epoxy **vehicle;** typically two or more components are mixed immediately before using.

EPS Abbr. for **expanded polystyrene.**

equal arches See **degree.**

equilateral arch, equilateral pointed arch A pointed **two-centered arch** in which the apex and centers form the corners of an imaginary equilateral triangle; the centers are located on the spring line at the base of each intrados, and the radius equals the span. Also known as **arch of the third point, lancet arch, tierce point arch.**

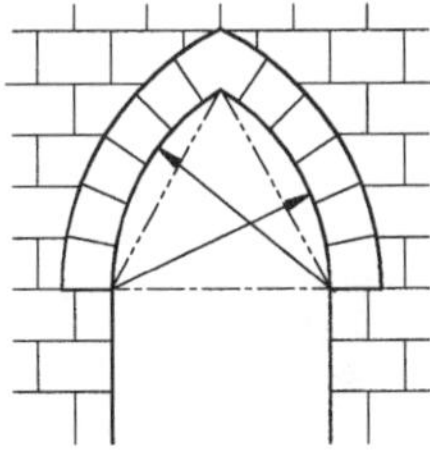

equilateral arch

equilateral pitch A roof **pitch** that forms a 60-degree angle with the horizontal. Also known as **true pitch.**

equilateral roof A roof with a cross section in the form of an equilateral triangle.

equinox marble Same as **Dyer breccia.**

equity The residual cash value of **real estate** after it has been sold at market value and all liens against it, including any mortgages, have been paid.

equivalency The use of alternative life safety systems to meet the requirements of a **building code,** such as providing sprinklers in an open stairway. See also **compliance alternative, life safety, timed exit analysis.**

erector A curved wood filler used to raise and curve the roof sheathing to form the base of a **continuous hip.**

erosion Wearing away of the surface of a material; typically used in geology and construction to refer to **weathering** and in metallurgy to refer to **corrosion.**

escalator (ca. 1902–present) A moving stair with a continuous metal belt of combined tread and riser sections; originally a copyrighted term.

escape Same as **aphophyge.**

escarp Same as **scarp.**

escarpment Any steeply sloped bank or wall of a fortification. See also **scarp.**

escoinson Same as **scoinson.**

escutcheon A decorative metal plate that surrounds the opening for a keyhole, doorknob, heating pipe, or similar element.

esonarthex **1.** An arcaded porch in front of a **narthex,** such as those found in **Romanesque Revival style** churches. **2.** The inner portion of a Greek Orthodox church, as opposed to the **exonarthex.**

espagnolette A locking device for french doors composed of a vertical rod with hooked ends that engage catches in the head and sill when the rod is rotated by turning a handle or key; may be surface mounted or inside the meeting stile. See also **cremone.**

Esperanza A dark bluish gray **marble** with lines of a darker shade quarried in the vicinity of West Rutland, Vermont; polishes medium well.

estufa (pre-20c) Same as **kiva.**

Etowah A light reddish pink **marble** with a few clouds of darker shade quarried in the vicinity of Tate, Georgia; polishes highly. also known as **Georgia Etowah.** See also **Etowah Pink.**

Etowah Pink A light pink to dark red, large-grain variety of **Georgia marble** with greenish gray and greenish black veining quarried in the vicinity of Tate, Georgia; polishes highly. Also known as **Georgia Pink.** See also **Etowah.**

Euclid Blue Stone A deep blue-gray building stone quarried in Cuyahoga County, Ohio. See also **bluestone.**

eustyle See **intercolumniation.**

evaluation The process by which the significance and integrity of a historic property are judged and eligibility for National Register listing is determined.

evaluative testing A preliminary excavation and analysis of an **archaeological site** to determine its significance. See also **shovel testing, subsurface investigation, excavation.**

excavation **1.** The process of digging a hole in the earth for a building or structure **foundation,** or the hole itself. **2.** The controlled removal of underground material at an **archaeological site;** types include **shovel testing, subsurface investigation.** See also **evaluative testing.**

excessing The process by which federal agencies dispose of unwanted real estate; includes offering the property to other federal, state, or local government agencies, **Section 106** review, and sometimes a public auction.

excess property Property, especially **real estate,** that is not needed by the owner; may be disposed of by **excessing.**

exchange A space or building in which specialized commodity or financial transactions take place, such as a cotton exchange or stock exchange.

Executive Order 11593 A presidential directive to federal agencies to preserve, restore, and maintain their cultural properties.

exedra **1.** A classical style stonework bench with a curved plan. **2.** (pre-20c) An apse, niche, or similar recess. **3.** (pre-20c) A small, private room.

exfoliation The flaking off of successive surface layers of stone; may be due to **salt decay** or to **freeze-thaw action** within the stone. See also **efflorescence, scaling, subflorescence.**

exonarthex The outer portion of a **narthex** vestibule of a Greek Orthodox church.

Exotic Revival style Any of the 19c–early 20c imitations of nonclassical foreign architecture, including **Arabesque style, Byzantine Revival style, Egyptian Revival style, Oriental style, Swiss Chalet style.** See also **alhambraic, Moorish.**

expanded-metal lath **Sheet-metal lath** manufactured by slitting and pulling apart sheet metal; various hole patterns include **Bostwick lath, diamond mesh, herringbone lath, hy-rib lath, oblong mesh, Truss-Loop lath, Trussit;** used as plaster lath and concrete reinforcing; patented in England in 1840 and first manufactured in the U.S. ca. 1896.

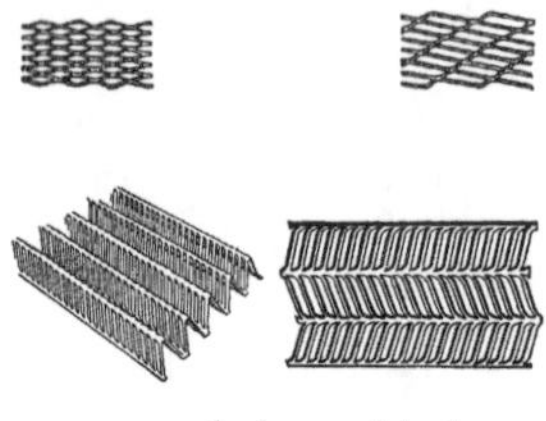

expanded-metal lath

expanded polystyrene (EPS) A 20c rigid foam plastic material composed of polystyrene encapsulating gas cells; commonly used for rigid insulation.

expanded slag A lightweight material produced by injecting steam into molten slag; used for aggregate and built-up roof gravel.

expanding vault A vault with a cross section that is larger at one end than the other; types include **conical vault, conoidal vault, convex-conoidal vault.** See also **domical vault.**

expansion anchor A **bolt** with an expandable device at the end; inserted into a hole drilled into masonry or other material. Also known as an **anchor bolt, expansion bolt.**

expansion bolt Same as **expansion anchor.**

expansion joint **1.** A continuous slot used to divide large building elements, such as walls and floor plates, into smaller panels; accommodates expansion and contraction caused by temperature change and movement caused by wind effects; closed with elastic sealant or a metal cover. **2.** A pipe joint that permits lengthwise expansion and contraction; typically composed of four right-angle bends forming a U-shape.

expansion tank In a hot water heating system, a metal **tank** that holds air to allow expansion of the volume of the water as the temperature increases.

expert witness A person who provides expert opinions during a court case or public hearing; typically qualified by experience and credentials.

exploratory demolition Limited removal of existing building fabric to determine the composition and condition of hidden features.

exposed aggregate A textured stucco or concrete finish formed by mixing stone aggregate with the finish coat or concrete and exposing it by brushing, water blasting, or other methods before final hardening. See also **pebble-dash, stucco.**

expropriation Same as **eminent domain.** See also **condemnation.**

extant Still existing or remaining, rather than destroyed or extinct.

extant drawings Same as **measured drawings.**

extended use An increase in the functional life of an existing building through intervention, such as **adaptive use** or **rehabilitation.**

extender A material (such as clay or chalk) added to paint to make it flow better and reduce its cost. Also known as **filler.**

extension **1.** Same as **addition.** **2.** (19c) A projecting portion of a main building; may be built at the same time. **3.** A portion of an element, such as a pipe or beam, that is added onto the existing portion.

extension bolt lock Same as **crossbolt lock.**

exterior slope The outside slope of a fortification embankment that is immediately below the **superior slope.** Also known as **talus.** See also **interior slope.**

external orthography See **orthography.**

Extra Dark Albertson A medium bluish gray **marble** with black and white veins quarried in the vicinity of West Rutland, Vermont.

Extra Dark Blue Same as **Dark Blue Rutland.**

Extra Dark True Blue A dark blue **marble** quarried in the vicinity of West Rutland, Vermont.

extrados **1.** The outer boundary of the **voussoirs** of an **arch.** **2.** The exposed face of voussoirs.

extradosed An **arch** in which the extrados is expressed by cutting the outer edge of the **voussoirs** parallel to the **intrados** and which has a well-defined **archivolt.**

Extra White Rutland A white **marble** with a few dark markings, quarried at West Rutland, Vermont.

extruded joint A convex **mortar joint** projecting past the face of adjoining masonry units.

extrusion (20c) An element formed by pushing a malleable material, such as clay, metal or plastic, through a die hole.

eye **1.** Same as **oculus.** **2.** The flat, circular disk at the center of a volute. **3.** One of the small openings between the bars of Gothic tracery; often triangular. **4.** An opening in the side of a sewer pipe that receives another pipe. **5.** A small metal loop that engages the end of a hook.

eyebar, (19c) **eye bar** A metal **truss** tension member having an enlarged end with an eye used to make a pinned connection to the structure; types include **upset-bar.** See also **American system.**

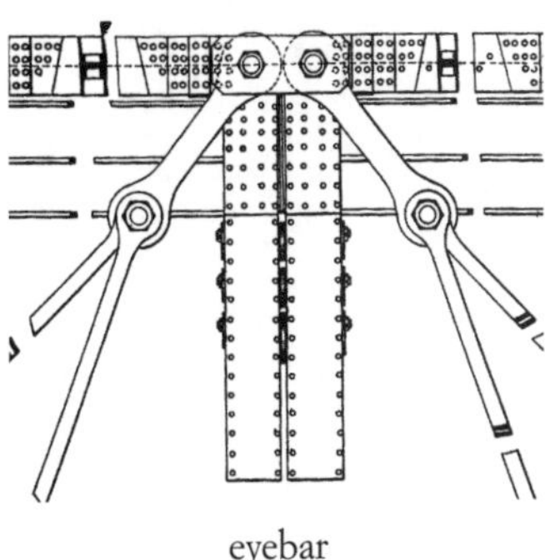

eyebar

eyebolt, (19c) **eye bolt** A **bolt** with a threaded end and a head formed by bending the shaft into a closed loop. See also **screw eye.**

eyebrow **1.** A low, curve-headed dormer without side walls; typically used on shingle or slate roofs, with the courses continuous over the top of the dormer. **2.** (18c) Same as **listel.**

eyebrow window Same as **frieze-band window.**

eyecatcher (18c–19c) A building or folly that serves as a focal point or the termination of a vista in a garden.

eye of the dome The aperture or skylight at the top of a dome. Also known as **oculus.** See also **dome light** (sense 1).

F

fabric, (pre-19c) **fabrick** **1.** The physical material of a building, structure, or object in its completed form. See also **original fabric.** **2.** (pre-19c) Same as **building.**

facade **1.** (19c–present) Any of the exterior faces of a building. **2.** (pre-20c) The front wall of a building, or the wall in which the principal building entrance is located, especially when highly ornamented.

facade easement A **preservation easement** that restricts future changes to the exterior appearance of a building; may apply to an entire building or a designated portion.

facadism (late 20c) Preserving the facade of a building while demolishing or drastically altering the rest of the building.

faccia **Marble** with a clear face.

face **1.** The front or exposed surface of a building element, including (a) same as **facade;** (b) (18c–present) the exposed side of a masonry unit, such as a stone block or brick, in a wall; see also **face bedded, face brick, face joint, face measure, face plan, face stone, faced;** (c) (18c–19c) same as **fascia;** (d) the vertical front of an arch showing the voussoir faces; (e) the side of a door or window jamb toward a room; see also **faced, face string, facing, casing.** **2.** The process of making the surface of a stone block smooth.

face bedded Stone installed with the bedding plane parallel to the wall surface.

face brick A high-quality brick used on the exterior face of a building wall. Also known as **stock brick.**

faced **1.** Veneered with another material, such as a brick wall faced with stone. See also **face, faced block, faced wall, facework.** **2.** Covered with molding or trim. See also **facing.**

faced block A **concrete block** with a face layer of .5 to 1 inch of fine concrete molded onto a coarser concrete base block; used to make highly detailed blocks popular ca. 1902–WWII; typically with a **sand finish.**

faced wall A masonry wall in which the facing units and the backup units are bonded together so they both support the loads.

face joint The exposed surface of a **mortar joint** between arch voussoirs.

face jointing The exposed pattern of masonry mortar joints. See also **ashlar, bond, rubble.**

face measure The dimension across the face of any wood element, exclusive of rabbets or solid molds.

face nailing Nailing from the finish face toward the rear of the wood.

face plan (19c) An **elevation** drawing of the front of a building.

face stone One of the stone blocks used to finish the face of a masonry wall.

face string Same as **finish stringer.** See also **open string stair.**

facet A flat, projecting fillet between column flutes.

facette (18c) A column groove with a rectangular cross section.

facework (19c) The **facing** of a masonry wall, especially when on the main facade and of superior quality to that used on the other facades.

facing **1.** Any type of nonstructural **veneer** or **trim** that covers a surface for decoration or protection. See also **face.** **2.** (19c) Wood trim on the exterior of a building. **3.** (19c) The joining of two timbers by means of a rabbet. **4.** (18c) Same as **face** (sense le).

facing tile A structural clay tile unit used in interior or exterior walls and left with an exposed face.

factory A building or group of buildings used for the manufacture of goods; typically includes machinery.

factory construction (19c–WWII) A construction system characterized by brick walls and open wood joists; used for small manufacturing plants.

factory sash (20c) A window sash with small, rectangular lights.

fading A loss of color intensity caused by exposure to light or **weathering.**

FAIA **Fellow of the American Institute of Architects**

faience Glazed earthenware ceramics; originally referred to a particular style of 16c–18c French pottery but, beginning in the late 19c, also used for ceramic tile and architectural terra-cotta, especially in the Arts and Crafts style.

failure Collapse, rupture, or fracture of a structural element such as a beam or column.

Fair Housing Act of 1988 U.S. federal legislation that includes **accessibility** requirements for residential multifamily properties.

fair market value Same as **market value.**

fall (18c–19c) One of the stepped terraces of a **falling garden.**

fall garden (18c–19c) See **falling garden.**

falling door Same as **flap door** (sense 1).

falling garden (18c–19c) An area landscaped with a series of stepped, sodded terraces with sloped embankments at the sides. See also **fall, flat.**

falling wainscot (18c) A wood partition hinged at the top so that it can be lifted up to create a larger space.

false **1.** A nonfunctional architectural element, such as **false arch, false attic, false front, false window.** **2.** (18c) A building element added for reinforcing the structure or improving the functional use.

false arch An opening having the form of an **arch** but which does not provide structural support.

false attic A completely enclosed space between a roof and the ceiling below, and without rooms or windows.

false body A paint or varnish consistency that is thicker than normal.

false front A building facade that extends above the roof or beyond the side walls in order to give the impression of a larger structure.

false pile A **pile,** or other construction, installed on top of a driven pile to extend it upward to the foundation.

false plate (17c–18c Chesapeake Bay region) A timber **plate** that supports the foot of the rafters and is supported by overhanging ceiling joists or tie beams; often 4 × 5 inches in cross section. Also known as **raising plate.** See also **top plate, wall plate.**

false ridgepole A board installed above a ridgepole to support the cresting or scroll cut to form a cresting.

false roof (19c) A ceiling below the roof, following the shape and slope of the actual roof structure.

false thatched roof A wood shingle **thatched roof.**

false window A glazed window frame in a wall with no opening behind it; used to preserve the symmetry of a facade or room. See also **blank window.**

falsework Temporary scaffolding that supports a structure during construction or demolition.

fan **1.** Same as **fanlight.** **2.** A mechanical device with rotating blades for circulating air. See also **plenum fan, vacuum fan.**

fan Fink truss A **Fink truss** with radial reticulation at the triangular panels that adjoin the diagonal upper chords.

fanlight, fan light A window in the arched opening over an entry door; through the 19c, restricted to a window with radial muntins, but now refers to any curved window over a door; common in **Georgian** buildings. Also known as **fan, fan-sash, fan window, sunburst light.** See also **overdoor.**

fan-sash (19c) Same as **fanlight.**

fantail joint Same as **dovetail joint.**

fan tracery Gothic style fan vaulting **tracery** with slender, branching ribs that divide as they ascend to form a fan-shaped pattern.

fan vaulting A Gothic vaulting system composed of vaults formed by a convex line rotated in a semicircle around a vertical axis, with the bottom of the line tangent to the face of the supporting clustered shafts and the top of the line intersecting a flat ceiling; always decorated with **fan tracery.**

fan window **1.** Same as **fanlight.** **2.** Any arch-headed window with a horizontal base.

F. A. Pink A light pink **marble** with fine specks quarried in Blount County, Tennessee; polishes highly.

FAR Abbr. for floor area ratio.

farmer's paint Same as **casein paint.**

farmhouse (19c–present) A dwelling **house** located on a farm.

farm stable Any kind of structure, often a barn, in which cattle or horses are kept in stalls. See also **stable.**

farrowing house A shelter for sows and their litters; includes a pen with an open-bottomed fence, so that the piglets are not crushed when their mother rolls over.

fascia, (18c) **fatio, facia** **1.** A flat, wide, horizontal band on a wall surface, especially the bands of an **architrave.** See also **fillet.** **2.** (18c) A projecting, horizontal molding above a window; typically with a cyma reversa base, two plain courses of brick, an astragal, and a boultin at the top. **3.** (19c) A projecting brick course in an exterior wall anywhere below the top story. See also **stringcourse.**

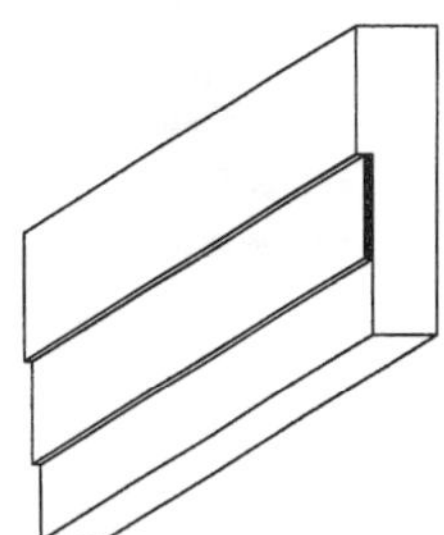

fascia (sense 1)

fascia board The board that forms a horizontal band at the edge of an eave.

fasciated Having multiple fascia bands; may be formed by projecting moldings or decorative colors.

fashionable (18c) In a **classical** style, as opposed to more ordinary vernacular work; used to refer to architectural elements.

FASLA **Fellow of the American Society of Landscape Architects**

fast (19c) A hardware device used for fastening a door or window in the closed position.

fastigium The pediment of a classical style portico.

fast joint hinge A **hinge** that has a permanently fixed pin attached to both leaves.

fatigue The weakening of metal due to repeated stress, such as bending; may lead to failure by fracture.

faubourg (Louisiana, French-speaking Canada) Same as **suburb;** used in New Orleans to refer to the pre-20c subdivisions developed outside of the Vieux Carré, such as faubourg Marigny.

faucet A plumbing device that regulates the flow of water at the end of a pipe; types include **bath-cock, hose bibb, pantry cock, urinal cock.** Also known as **bibb, petcock, tap.** See also **gate valve.**

faucet

faucet joint Same as **spigot and faucet joint.**

faux bois Same as **graining;** from the French for "false wood."

favo **Marble** or stone honeycombed with voids.

favus A marble paving tile with a hexagonal shape used to make a honeycomb pattern; sometimes used to refer to tiles of other materials such as flagstone or terra-cotta.

fc Abbr. for **footcandle.**

feasibility study An analysis of the alternative economic development possibilities for a historic property; the analysis typically considers alternative uses, as well as building code, zoning, financial, environmental, design, and historic significance factors. See also **economic viability.**

feasible and prudent alternative An alternative that avoids or minimizes harm to historic sites and other protected areas under **Section 4(f)** or **Section 106** and is **feasible** because the alternative could be built as a matter of sound engineering, and is **prudent** because it would not result in unique problems, truly unusual factors, or cost and community disruption of extraordinary magnitudes; must be adopted by the federal agency unless it can be shown to be not feasible and prudent.

feather **1.** Same as a tongue on a tongue-and-groove board. **2.** Same as **loose tongue.**

feather-cone fir Same as **noble fir.**

feathered Having a thin, sloped edge or transition, such as drywall compound over a joint.

featheredge brick Same as **arch brick** (sense 1).

featheredge coping A wall **coping** sloped so that the coping stone is thicker on one side of the wall than the other. Also known as **wedge coping.**

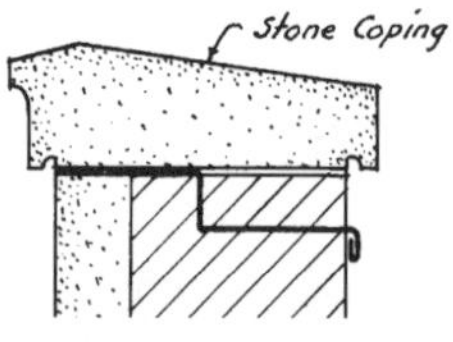

featheredge coping

featheredged, feather-edged, (pre-19c) **feather edged** A building element with a tapered cross section.

feather joint A joint formed by inserting the feather edge of one element into a V-shaped mortise in the end of another element.

feather-tongue spline A **spline** (sense 1) with a beveled edge.

feature A fixed result of human activity at an **archaeological site;** examples include **midden heap, mound, petroglyph,** or the remains of a fire pit.

Federal Heritage Building Any federally owned building that has been designated by the Minister of Canadian Heritage under the Federal Heritage Buildings Policy; types include **Recognized Federal Heritage Building, Classified Federal Heritage Building.** See also **Federal Heritage Building Review Office.**

Federal Heritage Building Review Office (FHBRO) An office of the National Historic Sites Directorate of Parks Canada that assists federal government departments in evaluating their buildings, provides advice on interventions to **Federal Heritage Buildings,** and maintains the **Register of Federal Heritage Buildings.**

Federal Preservation Officer (FPO) The official designated by the head of each U.S. federal agency to be responsible for coordinating the agency's activities under the National Historic Preservation Act of 1966, as amended, and Executive Order 11593, including nominating properties under that agency's ownership or control to the National Register.

Federal style Architecture style strongly influenced by the **Adam style** and a postcolonial successor to **Georgian style;** found throughout the eastern U.S., especially in New England seaports, ca. 1776–early 19c; typically symmetrical in elevation and plan, often with relatively simple brick or clapboard exterior walls and ornamentation at the entrance, such as a paneled door with fanlight and sidelights; interiors often have oval, circular, or octagonal rooms, elaborate door, window, and fireplace enframements, and delicate classical motifs including pedimented architraves supported on pilasters decorated with urns, festoons, rosettes, and oval patera. See also **Greek Revival style.**

feedway The aisle between stalls in a barn.

feeling The quality of **integrity** through which a historic property evokes the aesthetic or historic sense of past time and place.

Fellow of the American Institute of Architects (FAIA) An honorary title bestowed on members of the AIA.

Fellow of the American Society of Landscape Architects (FASLA) An honorary title bestowed on members of the ASLA.

felt **1.** A fabric composed of matted, compressed organic fibers; may be impregnated with asphalt or other water-resistant binders; types include **boiler felt, roofing felt. 2.** A thick fabric manufactured by weaving asbestos fibers. Also known as **asbestos felt.**

felt-and-gravel Same as **built-up roof.**

felt grain Same as **bastard grain.** See also **felting, quarter grain, silver grain.**

felting (pre-20c) The process of splitting or sawing wood along the **felt grain,** with each cut or split along a plane through the original center of the log.

felt insulation A felted **insulation** material, such as asbestos or hair, manufactured in sheets; typically .25–1 inch thick, 16.5–48 inches wide, and up to 10 feet long; common before WWII; sometimes attached to metal lath panels .5 × 24 × 42 inches. See also **flexible insulation.**

femerell, femeral, fumerell A roof lantern or cupola that ventilates the interior; typically with louvers on the sides.

femme-fleur An electric light fixture in the form of a female nude intertwined with flowers; manufactured in the late 19c and early 20c.

femur Same as **shank.**

fence, fencing A vertical wall or railing enclosing an outside area; types include **ha-ha, paling, palisade, picket fence, post-and-plank fence, rail fence, wire fence, worm fence.** See also **ditch.**

fender A low brass or iron hearth railing to catch burning coals from a fireplace; common 18c–19c. See also **fireguard.**

fendre A crack in a piece of **marble** or other stone.

fenestral **1.** A window opening or sash covered with translucent paper or cloth, rather than glass. **2.** (19c) A small window.

fenestration The arrangement of windows in a building facade.

feroher An Egyptian symbolic decoration in the form of a disk with a pair of long, horizontal wings; used in **Egyptian Revival style** architecture. Also known as **winged disk.**

ferrament, (pl.) **ferramenta** (pre-20c) Same as **ironwork.**

ferrocement (20c) A thin **reinforced concrete** shell made with alternating layers of cement mortar and steel mesh; term first used by the Italian engineer Pier Luigi Nervi.

ferroconcrete (20c) Same as **reinforced concrete.**

ferrocyanide blue Same as **Prussian blue.**

ferrosilicon Same as **silicon iron.**

ferrule **1.** A metal cap or ring on the end of a wood post to protect and strengthen it. **2.** A short pipe connector. **3.** A flanged section that connects a stovepipe to a masonry flue or breach stack. See also **thimble.** **4.** A type of connection between a water main and a building service line.

festoon A decoration in the form of a garland or drapery hanging from two end points, with the two ends hanging vertically; typically composed of leaves, fruits, flowers, and similar objects; found almost exclusively on Classical Revival buildings. Also known as **swag.** See also **encarpus.**

FHBRO **Federal Heritage Building Review Office**

fiberboard A type of **composition board** composed of compressed wood fibers; typically somewhat flexible and in sheets measuring 4 × 8 feet; most often .5 inch thick.

Fiberglas Trade name for **fiberglass.**

fiberglass A 20c material composed of spun glass fibers; various uses include **batt insulation, rigid insulation,** fire-resistant fabrics, and reinforcing a synthetic resin composite that is formed in a mold and used to replicate complex shapes.

fiber optics (20c) Bundles of continuous, tiny, glass rods that transmit light; used for lighting with a remote source, especially incandescent and metal halide lamps.

fiber plaster, (pre-20c) **fibre plaster** **Plaster** mixed with chopped fibers, such as hair or wood, for reinforcing. See also **coarse stuff.**

fibrous slab (19c) Plaster mixed with wood fibers; introduced in 1851 as an interior finish.

fibrous wrapped insulation Electric wire surrounded by organic fiber-based insulation; types include **circular loom, insulating paper, insulating thread, rubber insulation, varnished cloth;** forms include felted material, paper, thread, woven fabric, or yarn; treated with gums, oils, varnishes, or impregnating compounds to increase moisture, heat, and shrinkage resistance; first used in 1879.

field **1.** A repetitive decorative pattern on a surface, often surrounded by a border. **2.** The relatively large expanse of flat wall between openings in a masonry wall; typically composed of stretchers. **3.** Same as **on site;** typically used in the phrase "in the field."

field courses The rows of roofing tiles that make up the main body of a roof. See also **coping course.**

fielded panel A **raised panel** with a smooth, flat center.

field photography **Documentation** photographs taken of a site, building, structure, or object, usually with 35mm film; compare **large-format photography.**

field quarter, field quarters A **quarter** (sense 3) on a plantation used by the field hands and their families.

field records **Documentation** of a site, building, structure, or object recorded on site; typically include sketches, notes of measurements taken, and **field photography.**

fieldstone Naturally occurring **stone** of a size usable for construction; also known as **rubble.** See also **stonework.**

fier place (17c) Same as **fireplace.**

fiftypenny nail (50d nail) A **nail** approximately 5.5 inches long; 11 iron common nails weigh one pound. See also **penny.**

figure **1.** A sculptural representation of a person or animal. **2.** A pattern produced on the surface of wood, usually across the grain, by natural deviations from the normal **grain;** types include **burl, silver grain, swirl.**

figured glass Same as **obscure glass.**

figured novelty (19c–present) A type of **novelty siding** board with multiple grooves creating false joints to give the appearance of narrow-width boards.

filigree Intricate ornamental openwork.

fill **1.** Earth used to raise the existing grade level; may be natural soil or crushed stone. See also **backfill, cut and fill.** **2.** A nonstructural topping placed on top of a structural floor, such as cinder concrete on top of a brick floor arch.

filled (17c–18c) Packed with clay, stone, or other material, especially the space between studs, exterior weatherboards, and interior lathing. See also **nogging.**

filler **1.** Any of various colored paste compounds used to fill the pores and imperfections of a finish material, such as wood or marble, before finishing. See also **badigeon.** **2.** Same as a paint **extender.**

filler pile A pile driven between **gauge piles.**

fillet **1.** A narrow, flat molding; typically used to separate other moldings; variations include **back fillet, sunk fillet.** Also known as **listel.** See also **annulet, band, cincture.** **2.** A small molding with a rectangular cross section; may be used as a decorative molding, doorstop bead, or shelf ledger. **3.** The flat surface between adjoining column flutes. Also known as **flat arris, ridge crest, stria.**

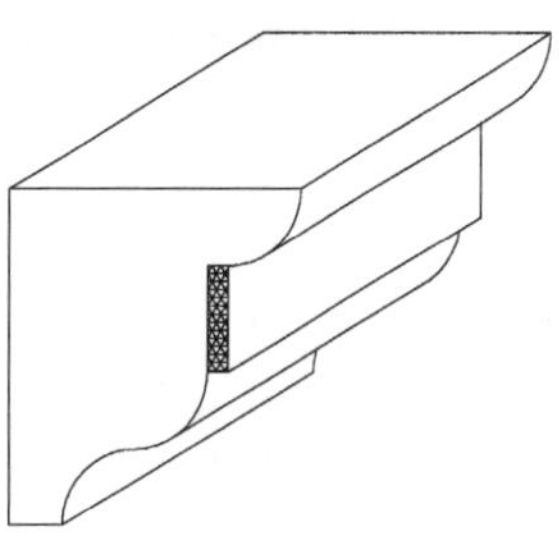

fillet (sense 1)

filleted round Same as **roll molding.**

fillet gutter A narrow gutter on the slope of a roof formed by turning sheet-metal flashing over a wood strip; used on the slope above a chimney and in other similar situations.

filleting Mortar used as **flashing** at the juncture of a sloped slate roof with a parapet wall; the mortar forms a trough that extends up the wall and over the bottom courses of slates, and is lapped by one course of slates.

fillet weld A **weld** bead with a triangular cross section; often used to connect two pieces of metal that butt at right angles.

filling **1.** Rough masonry used for the interior of a masonry wall or the spandrel of an arch. See also **nogging.** **2.** (pre-WWII) Same as **backfill.**

filling-in brick Same as **salmon brick.**

filling-in stuff Same as **filler.**

fillister A rabbet, especially one cut around the inner edge of a window sash to receive glass;

typically on the outside face of the sash and sealed with putty or wood trim.

final grade Same as **finish grade.**

fine arts conservator A **conservator** of fine art objects, which may be portable or part of a building or structure.

fine-grained **1.** Same as **close-grained.** **2.** Stone composed of small, distinct particles visible on the cut surface. See also **coarse-grained.**

fine stuff Lime paste used for a plaster **finish coat;** types include **plasterer's putty.**

finger joint A series of feather joints resembling interlaced fingers.

finial A pointed ornament; always symmetrical and frequently circular in cross section; typically used at the peak of a roof, especially in the Gothic Revival style. See also **hip knob, pyramid.**

finish **1.** The surface coating, treatment, or texture of any material; types include **cabinet finish, inside finish, paint, polished, varnish.** See also **stonework.** **2.** The material on an exposed surface of a building, especially the interior; types include **ceramic tile, drywall, flooring, paneling, paving, plaster, plastic laminate, stone.**

finish board (ca. 1925–50) Same as **drywall;** available only ⅜ × 47¾ inches by lengths of 5–10 feet before WWII.

finish carpentry Interior wood trim cut on site and installed over plaster or another finish; finish elements include **baseboard, casing, picture molding.** See also **millwork, rough carpentry.**

finish coat **1.** The hard, dense, top layer of a **plaster** finish, composed of **fine stuff.** Also known as **hard finish, setting coat.** See also **sand finish, skim coat, white coat.** **2.** The top layer of a painted surface applied over an **undercoat.** Also known as **setting coat.**

finished size The dimension of any wood element, including rabbets and solid molds, after final milling and sanding.

finish flooring The top surface finish material of a floor; types include carpet, **encaustic tile, floorboards, floor tile, linoleum, parquet,** and marble. Also known as **upper floor.** See also **folded floor, pavement, straight joint floor.**

finish grade The final ground level of earthwork or sitework when grading is complete.

finish hardware The exposed metal fittings used for fabricating and installing doors, windows, and cabinets; includes **hinge, knob, lock, sash lift, tieback.**

finishing (18c) Same as **crowning** (sense 1).

finish nail, finishing nail A thin nail with a small head, typically used for face nailing trim.

finish stringer, finish string The inclined trim on the exposed side of a rough face stringer; may be purely decorative or may support treads and balusters. Also known as **face string, string board.** See also **rough stringer.**

Fink truss A triangular **truss,** usually with a central equilateral triangle flanked by a pair of reticulated end triangles, each in the form of a king truss; the standard type has a horizontal bottom chord; variations include **cambered Fink truss, fan Fink truss, suspension truss;** invented by Albert Fink.

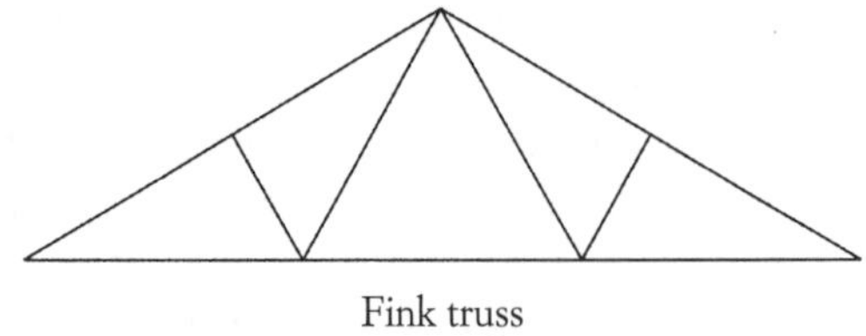

Fink truss

fir **1.** One of various softwood trees of the genus *Abies;* includes **balsam fir, white fir.** **2.** One of various similar trees of the genus *Tsuga* or

Pseudotsuga; includes **hemlock fir, Douglas fir.** See also **hemlock, pine.**

fir balsam Same as **balsam fir.**

fire See **accidental fire, arson.**

fire alarm A device that signals the presence of fire; may be manually controlled (e.g, a pull station) or automatic (e.g., a **fire detector**); may be a local bell, gong, or flashing light; or may send a signal to a central or remote station.

fireback, fire back **1.** A cast-iron lining of a fireplace firebox; typically with bas-relief decoration; movable firebacks that covered the chimney back were common in 17c and 18c; 19c firebacks typically are three-sided to cover the entire interior of the firebox. Also known as **chimney back, iron back.** See also **firebox, scotchback.** **2.** The rear wall of a **firebox.** Also known as **chimney back.**

fire bar (pre-20c) Same as **fire grate.**

fire bell A bell used for a **fire alarm;** typically refers to a large bell with a clapper, as opposed to an electric gong.

fire blocking **Blocking** across a void in a building to prevent the spread of fire; in wood frame construction, typically is a solid piece of lumber that fills the space between studs or joists. See also **fire stop.**

fireboard A decorative panel that closes a fireplace opening when not in use and prevents drafts; may be composed of wood, cast metal, or sheet metal. Also known as **chimney board.**

firebox **1.** The space enclosed by the jambs and back of a **fireplace.** **2.** The part of a boiler or furnace where the fuel burns.

fire brick A heat-resistant **brick** made with refractory clay; commonly used to line fireplaces and flues.

fire bridge A brick partition across the throat of a masonry furnace.

fire chamber The part of a furnace in which the fuel is burned.

fire cut A sloped end of a wood joist that rests in a pocket in a masonry wall; slopes down toward the end of the joist so that the bottom extends to the back of the pocket and the top is at the inside face of the wall; allows the joist to fall out of the pocket without pulling down the wall if the joist collapses during a fire.

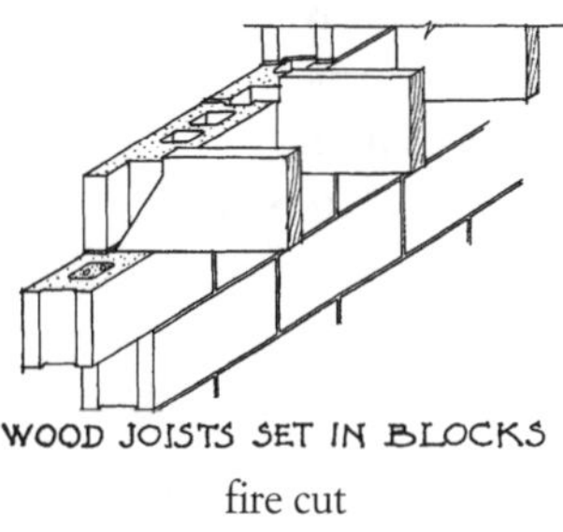

fire cut

fire damper A vane or louver in an **air duct** that closes automatically in the presence of smoke or high temperatures to prevent the passage of fire.

fire detector An automatic sensing device that detects the combustion products or heat of a fire; types include **flame detector, heat detector, smoke detector, wireless detector.** See also **automatic fire detection system, fire suppression system.**

fire door **1.** (20c) A sheet-metal-clad door that automatically closes in the event of a fire; typically designed to slide across a doorway when a fusible link melts. **2.** (20c) Any **fire-rated** door. **3.** The access door to a **fire chamber.**

fire escape **1.** A system of metal ladders and platforms on the exterior of a building used for egress during a fire; common late 19c–late 20c, especially to retrofit existing buildings; typically no longer permitted by building codes. **2.** A chute or other device for emergency egress during a fire.

fire gilding Same as **amalgam gilding.**

fire gilt Same as **amalgam gilding.**

fire grate A **grate** used to support the fire in a **fireplace** or **fire chamber.** Also known as **fire bar.**

fireguard, (pre-20c) **fire guard** **1.** Same as **fender.** **2.** A wire-mesh device that covers a fireplace opening and prevents sparks from escaping.

fire hole **1.** Same as **fire pit.** **2.** (pre-20c) A hole cut in ice through which to draw water to fight a fire in winter.

firehouse, (pre-20c) **fire house** **1.** A **building** used for sheltering fire-fighting equipment, sometimes with quarters for firefighters; type includes **truck house.** **2.** (pre-20c) A **house** with a fireplace, as opposed to an unheated outbuilding.

fire hydrant A **hydrant** designed for use by firefighters; typically with large-diameter male threaded spouts for attaching fire hoses. Also known as **fireplug.**

fire kiln See **kiln.**

fire loss risk reduction Construction methods and/or use of a **fire suppression system** that reduces the likelihood of fire damage to a building or structure and its contents; not necessarily intended to improve **life safety.** See also **fire resistant, fire stop, fire wall.**

fire main A **water main** used for fighting fires.

fire marshal The state, provincial, or local government official responsible for enforcing building code provisions related to fire prevention.

fire pit A hole in the ground that contains an open fire; also known as **fire hole.**

fireplace, (18c) **fire place,** (17c) **fier place, fyer place** A structure that partially encloses an open wood or coal fire; typically constructed of masonry; components may include **cheeks, chimney, chimney breast, damper, enframement, fireback, fireplace surround, flue, hearth, hearthstone, mantel, mantelpiece, smoke chamber, smoke shelf, throat.** Also known as **chimney, hearth.** See also **stove, furnace.**

fireplace surround The incombustible material bordering a fireplace opening; commonly brick, tile, or stone. See also **enframement, hearth, mantelpiece.**

fireplug Same as **fire hydrant.**

fireproof An element or assembly that can resist fire; typically used to refer to construction that is more fire resistant than the standard type. See also **fire rated.**

fireproof construction **1.** (late 19c–mid-20c) Building construction that uses noncombustible materials, especially a steel frame protected with a fire-resistant covering. **2.** (early 19c) Building construction in which exterior masonry walls enclose a wood frame.

fireproof floor (19c) A fire-resistant floor supported by iron or steel beams; construction includes **tile arch,** segmental brick vaults, and reinforced concrete slabs. See also **fireproof, fire resistant, mill construction, semimill construction.**

fireproofing Any material designed to increase the fire resistance of construction components (e.g., **structural steel**); material types include **brick, concrete, drywall, plaster, sprayed asbestos, terra-cotta.**

fireproofing tile A **structural clay tile** unit used for fireproofing.

fire protection system All of the devices that warn of and suppress fires at a site; elements may include **fire detector, fire alarm, fire suppression system.** See also **electric fire extinguisher.**

fire pump A **water pump** that increases the pressure from the water supply to the various standpipes, sprinklers, and hoses of a fire suppression system.

fire rated A building material or construction assembly that has been scientifically tested to determine its fire resistance over a particular period of time (e.g., a one-hour wall assembly); used in building codes. See also **fire-proof.**

fire-resistant A material that resists the spread of flames and heat during a fire; may be incombustible or of low combustibility; often used to protect other materials (e.g., terra-cotta wrapped around a steel column or beam).

fire-resistive See **fire-resistant.**

fire-retardant chemical (FRC) Any of various chemicals used in a **fire-retardant treatment;** types include phosphates, sulfates, and polymers.

fire-retardant treatment Application of a fire-retardant substance to a material to increase its fire rating, such as applying a **fire-retardant chemical** to fabric or coating wood with **intumescent paint.**

fireroom (pre-19c) A room with a fireplace.

fire silvering **1.** Same as **amalgam silvering.** **2.** Silver plating by applying powdered silver to metal and then heating.

fire spot The remains of a **fire pit.**

firestone, (pre-19c) **fire-stone** A fire-resistant type of stone, especially sandstone; often a light brown, Western sandstone in 19c U.S.; used as a **hearthstone, chimney back,** and **chimney jamb.**

fire stop, fire-stop, fire stopping **1.** Construction that blocks the passage of fire in concealed hollow spaces; types include **fire blocking.** See also **fire wall.** **2.** (pre-20c) Same as **fire bridge.**

fire suppression system Any of various mechanical systems that automatically extinguish a fire; types include **foam extinguishing system, sprinkler system.**

fire telegraph (19c–early 20c) A telegraphic **fire alarm.**

fire tower **1.** A **watch tower** used to look for forest or building fires. **2.** A continuous stair within a fire-resistant enclosure in a high-rise building. **3.** A **beacon tower** with a burning fire, used as a **lighthouse.**

firetrap, (pre-20c) **fire trap** A building likely to trap the occupants in case of fire, either because the building is extremely flammable or it does not have sufficient emergency egress.

fire treated Treated with a fire-retardant substance; see **fire-retardant treatment.**

fire tube One of a series of tubes in a boiler through which combustion gases pass to heat water.

fire wall Any fire-resistive wall constructed to separate buildings from one another or to subdivide a large building into smaller spaces; typically continuous from the foundation through the roof; may be constructed of masonry, drywall, or plaster materials.

fire zone A **building code** designation of the relative fire risk of various areas of a local jurisdiction based on density and use.

fir pine Same as **balsam fir.**

first-class construction (19c–WWII) A building code classification for a building with fire-resistant construction, with floors constructed of iron, steel, or reinforced concrete beams filled in between with terra-cotta or other masonry arches, or concrete or reinforced concrete slabs. See also **second-class construction, third-class construction.**

first floor **1.** (U.S.) Same as **ground floor.** **2.** (British Commonwealth) The building story immediately above the ground floor. Also known as **piano nobile.**

first-person interpretation The **interpretation** of a historic site by interpreters who dress, speak, and live in the mode of the historical period.

fish A metal plate used in a **fish joint;** typically one of a pair. Also known as **fish piece, fish-plate.** See also **fish strap, flitch plate.**

fish beam (19c) A beam that bellies out in the middle, especially on the underside.

fish bladder Same as **mouchette.**

fish joint Wood timbers or steel rails connected end to end by overlapping **fish** bolted through the timbers or rails.

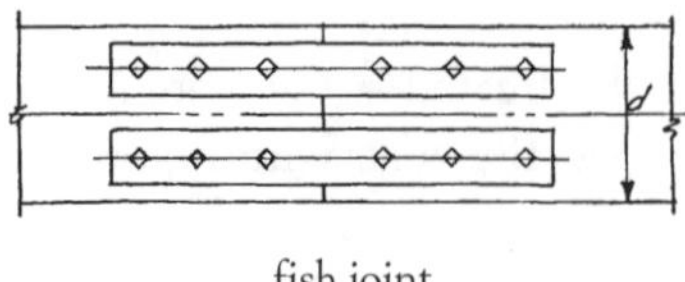

fish joint

fish piece Same as **fish.**

fishplate, (19c) **fish plate** **1.** Same as **fish.** **2.** An **anchor plate** made of a small iron or steel plate with a hole in the center.

fish-scale A pattern created by rows of shingles or slates with curved bottoms. See also **shingle, slate.**

fish strap A narrow, thin metal bar with a rectangular cross section used as a **fish** to connect the butted ends of two wood beams.

fishtail burner A **gaslight burner** that creates a flat flame with a fishtail shape; invented in England ca. 1820.

fitting See **pipe fitting.**

fittings The equipment and apparatus attached to a mechanical system, such as gas fittings or steam fittings. See also **fixture.**

five-centered arch An **arch** with five centers for the radii of the intrados; types include **basket-handle, cinquefoil, five-point arch.**

five orders See **Classical order.**

fivepenny nail (5d nail) A **nail** approximately 1.75 inches long; 200 iron common nails weigh one pound. See also **penny.**

fivepenny spike (5d spike) A **spike** approximately 4.5 inches long; 17 steel-wire spikes weigh one pound. See also **penny.**

five-point arch The shape of an elliptical arch approximated with five segments of a circle, a five-centered arch. See also **haunches, scheme, three-point arch.**

fixed glass Window glass held in a frame that does not open.

fixed glazing Any type of **glazing** held in a frame or sash that does not open; types include **fixed glass, fixed light, fixed sash.** See also **storefront.**

fixed light **Fixed glazing** with a single pane.

fixed sash **Fixed glazing** held in an immovable window sash.

fixture Operating equipment connected to a plumbing, gas, or electrical system; types include lights, bathtubs, sinks, and water closets.

flabelliform Fan shaped, as in the palmette decoration on an **anthemion.**

flag, (pre-19c) **flagg** A thin stone used as paving.

flagging (Canada) The process of putting a tag or notation on record of a particular property to notify a **building inspector** of a **heritage designation** or other restriction. See also **mandatory referral.**

flagstone, (18c) **flagg stone, flag stone,** (17c) **fflagg stone** **1.** A stone that can be split into flags; includes some sandstones and mica schists. **2.** Same as **flag.**

flake white A pure, flaky form of **white lead.**

flambé An iridescent ceramic glaze.

flambeau A lighting fixture in the form of a flaming torch.

flame detector An automatic device that detects the radiant energy of a fire, including flames and glowing embers; typically a line-of-sight device; the least common type of **fire detector.**

flameproofing See **fire-retardant treatment.**

flame-shape lamp An **incandescent lamp** in the shape of a candle flame with a wavy surface. See also **B-shape lamp, C-shape lamp.**

flange **1.** A projecting lip of a metal member, such as the horizontal parts at the top and bottom of a steel beam or the bottom edge of a sheet-metal vent. **2.** The collar at the end of a cast-iron pipe.

flanged T, flanged tee Rolled steel or iron in the form of a T-shape with flanges projecting downward from the top corners.

flange joint (19c) A bolted or riveted connection of the projecting flanges of two elements, especially the ends of two wrought-iron pipes.

flange tile Same as **soffit block.**

flanker A timber side piece.

flanket (pre-19c) An iron band used to connect the abutting ends of lead or iron pipes; screwed over a band of leather or hemp with oil, tar, or tallow caulking.

flanks (19c) Same as **haunches.**

flank window (pre-19c) Same as **sidelight.**

flap (19c) **1.** One of the folding sections of a folding door or shutter. **2.** One of the pair of leaves of a hinge.

flap door **1.** A small **door** or **shutter** hinged at the bottom. **2.** Same as **cellar door.**

flap hinge **1.** Same as a **strap hinge.** **2.** A hinge in which one of the leaves is attached to the face, rather than the edge, of the door or shutter. See also **butt hinge.**

flare header A **brick** burned on one end so that the end is darker than the rest of the brick.

flash glass, flashed glass Clear sheet glass with a thin coating of colored glass; typically the colored layer is **ruby glass;** often **brilliant cut.** Also known as **cased glass, covered glass, coated glass, doubled glass.**

flashing **1.** Sheet metal or other flexible material formed to prevent water from entering a building or structure at joints or intersections, such as where a roof intersects a wall or chimney. See also **counterflashing.** **2.** Irregular gloss or color of a painted or varnished surface; typically caused by insufficient sealing of the substrate.

flash patching The process of smoothing and leveling an irregular floor surface with a thin coating.

flat **1.** (19c–present) A rental dwelling unit that occupies all or part of a single floor of a building; in the late 19c, usually signified a unit that was lower-priced than an **apartment** but more expensive than a **tenement.** **2.** Having a dull, nonglossy finish. **3.** Abbr. for **flat bar.** **4.** (pre-20c) A level field, such as a terrace in a **falling garden.** **5.** (pre-20c) Same as **floor** (sense 2).

flat arch **1.** An arch with a horizontal, or nearly horizontal, intrados; types include **camber arch, jack arch, joggled arch.** **2.** A **tile arch** with a horizontal top and bottom.

flat arris On a column, the edge where the flat face of a **fillet** adjoins the concave curve of a **flute.** See also **arris, sharp arris.**

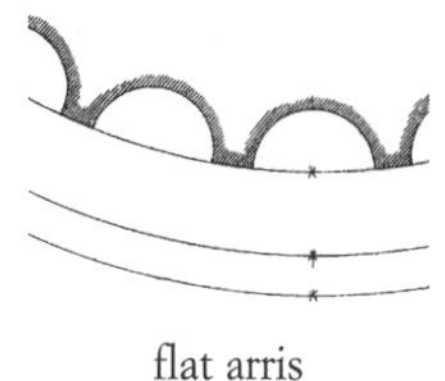

flat arris

flat astragal A **flush molding** used as a door **astragal.**

flat bar (19c–present) A solid metal **rolled section** with a rectangular cross section. Also known as **flat.**

flat-cut Wood cut lengthwise from a log with the cut face tangent to the growth rings; prone to excessive cupping and wear. Also known as **flat-sawn, tangent sawn.** See also **bastard cut, flat grain, flitch, quartersawn.**

flat grain The surface **grain** pattern of wood that has been **flat-cut;** typically has a flame-shaped pattern with alternating wide **springwood** and **summerwood** bands.

flat house, flat-house (19c) Same as **apartment house.**

flatjack A pressurized jacking device in the form of a thin steel envelope that applies uniform pressure on the surface of top and bottom plates; can be inserted into a cut-out mortar joint to test compressive strength and compressive deformity in situ.

flat joint (pre-WWI) Same as **flush joint.**

flat panel A wood **panel** that is the same thickness throughout. See also **sunk panel.**

flat plate slab A **reinforced concrete** floor slab of uniform thickness and with no dropped beams.

flat point A **nail** with a straight or cupped end that is driven into the wood; used on some types of wrought or cut nails to reduce splitting of the wood.

flat Pratt A **Pratt truss** with horizontal top and bottom chords and rectangular panels with a single diagonal chord; the diagonals slope downward from the top outer corners toward the middle of the truss.

flat rail **1.** A flat metal bar spiked along a line of wood stringers to form a railway **rail;** used ca. 1830–40. Also known as **strap rail.** **2.** A flat-headed railway **rail.**

flat roof A roof with a pitch sufficiently low that it can be walked upon easily; may be a true horizontal plane or have a low **pitch** (typically not more than 1 in 20) for rainwater drainage; may be surrounded by a **parapet** or have only a **gravel stop** at the perimeter. See also **terrace roof.**

flat-sawn Same as **flat-cut.**

flat slab See **flat plate slab.**

flat sliced Same as **plain sliced.**

flatting coat (19c) A coat of flat paint.

flat Warren A **truss** with horizontal top and bottom chords, vertical end posts, and zigzag diagonal chords.

flèche **1.** Same as **spire,** especially a small wood one over the intersection of the nave and transept of a Gothic style church. **2.** A redoubt in a **fortification,** typically composed of two walls with a V-shaped plan. **3.** Same as **broach.**

Flemish bond A brick wall bond with courses of alternating headers and stretchers; the headers are often **clinker brick;** types include **Flemish cross bond, Flemish diagonal bond, Flemish spiral bond;** used in the Chesapeake region beginning in early 17c and common in U.S. until mid-19c. Also known as **block bond.** See also **Flemish double stretcher, rowlock wall.**

Flemish cross bond A brick wall **Flemish bond** with courses of headers alternating with courses of stretchers, with the headers centered on the stretchers of the course above and below.

Flemish diagonal bond A brick wall **Flemish bond** formed with alternating Flemish bond and stretcher courses, with joints arranged to create continuous diagonals of stretchers.

Flemish double stretcher A brick wall bond formed by alternating courses of one header with two stretchers, with the headers centered over the joint between the two stretchers.

Flemish spiral bond A brick wall **Flemish bond** in which the joint between the stretcher and header is centered on the header below, with each offset in the same direction.

Flemish tile (pre-19c) **1.** Same as **pantile.** **2.** Same as **Dutch tile.**

fleur-de-lis An ornament in the shape of a stylized flower with three pointed petals projecting above and below a horizontal bar; the center petal is vertical, and the two side petals are C-shaped.

fleuron **1.** A carved flower located at the center of the abacus of a Corinthian capital; appears to grow from the center leaf below. **2.** A stylized plant form used as a crowning decoration.

flew (pre-19c) Same as **flue.**

flexible insulation An insulating material composed of a mat of loosely felted fiber covered on one or both sides with paper or fabric, .25–1 inch thick and 17–36 inches wide; used within voids of wood frame construction. Also known as **blanket insulation, quilt insulation.** See also **batt insulation, felt insulation.**

flexible metal conduit A spiral-wrapped steel tube used to provide an **electric wiring** conduit through existing buildings; the wires are threaded through the conduit after it is fished through concealed spaces; developed before 1900 and, by the 1930s, one of the most common retrofit wiring systems for commercial buildings. See also **armored cable, Greenfield conduit, rigid metal conduit.**

flier, (18c) **flyer** One of a series of steps with parallel risers in a stair. See also **winder.**

flight A continuous run of steps between landings of a stair.

flint **1.** A dark colored, nearly opaque, impure form of quartz, similar to **chalcedony;** typically occurs in small nodules in limestone or chalk. Also known as **flintstone.** **2.** Quartz pieces in any kind of stone; term used by quarrymen and stoneworkers.

flint brick A dense, hard fire brick manufactured from ground flint.

flint glass A highly refractive, decorative clear glass composed of white sand, red lead, and small amounts of potash and niter; often used for prisms on chandeliers.

flintstone Same as **flint** (sense 1).

flint wall A masonry wall constructed of flints set with a large amount of mortar.

flitch **1.** (20c) All of the thin, longitudinal slices of wood cut from a single log for veneer; sometimes used to refer to one of the individual pieces of veneer. **2.** (pre-20c) A plank attached to the side of another member to form a compound beam. **3.** (19c) One of several sawn planks connected by a **stub-shot** at the end of the log.

flitch beam, flitched beam **1.** A wood **built beam** reinforced with a continuous metal section; may be a pair of plates or channels on the outside of the wood or a plate sandwiched between two wood members; the former type is often used to reinforce existing beams. **2.** (pre-20c) A plank used as a beam, especially one split from its **stub-shot.**

flitch plate An iron or steel plate used in a **flitch beam.**

floated coat Same as **brown coat.**

float glass (mid-20c–present) A type of **window glass** made by floating molten glass on a bed of molten metal; used in place of plate glass by late 20c.

floating elevator (19c) Same as **hydraulic elevator.**

floating foundation Same as **mat foundation.**

floating house (18c) A houseboat or a similar flat-bottomed boat used for commercial purposes.

floating screed A **screed** formed with a strip of plaster or mortar.

floor, (pre-18c) **floore, flor, flower** **1.** The construction system that supports the horizontal plane at the base of a room or other enclosed space; construction types include **balloon frame, earthen floor, pavement, platform frame, reinforced concrete, slab-on-grade, timber frame.** See also **binder beam, buckled plate, carcass floor, double floor, double-framed floor, fireproof floor, floor joist, subfloor.** **2.** The interior surface on which one walks. See also **apparatus floor, finish flooring, floorboard, floor level, floor covering, paving.** Also known as **flat.** **3.** Same as **story** (sense 1); types include **first floor, ground floor, upper floor.**

floor arch **1.** A **tile arch** or low-rise, brick **segmental vault** that spans between two iron or steel beams and supports the floor above. **2.** A masonry vault that supports a floor above;

supported on bearing walls, massive columns, or piers.

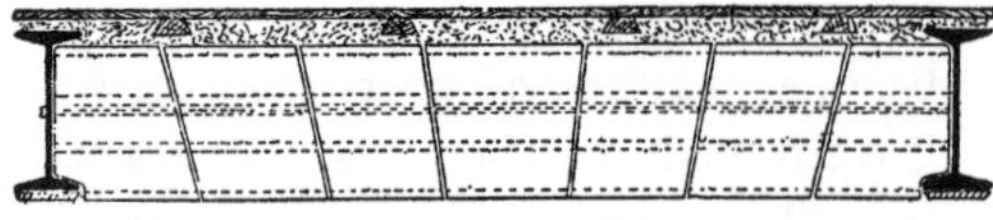

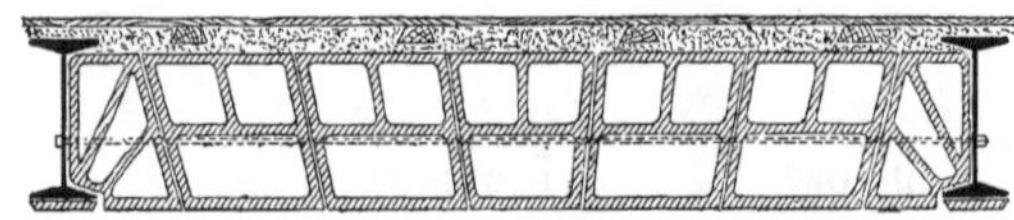

floor arch

floor area ratio (FAR) A multiple of the lot area used in **zoning** regulations to determine the gross square footage (gsf) that can be devoted to a particular use; the formula is: lot area × FAR = gsf.

floor beam Same as **cross beam.**

floorboard, (before late 20c) **floor board** One of the wood boards that compose a floor; may be rough sawn for a subfloor or planed and sanded for a finish floor; joint types include **butt joint, dowel, lap joint, spline, tongue-and-groove;** fastening types include **blind nailing, face nailing, pegged.**

floor drain A **drain** with a grate on top and a **trap** below, mounted flush with a floor.

floor finish A protective film and/or coloring on flooring. Finishes for wood floors include wax, **polyurethane, oil varnishes, shellac,** oils, **Swedish finishes, stains,** and **paint.**

floor hinge Same as **floor spring hinge.**

flooring Same as **finish flooring.**

flooring brads (18c) Large finish nails used for attaching wood flooring.

flooring nail A **nail** used for tongue-and-groove flooring; typically has a square-ended point so that the nail does not split the wood.

floor joist A joist used to support a floor.

floor level **1.** The height of the top of a floor above an established bench mark. **2.** The location of the floor of a **story** within a building, such as **basement, ground floor, first floor.**

floor load The weight supported by a floor in a building; often expressed as pounds per square foot; used in structural calculations. See also **live load, dead load.**

floor mold Same as **shoe mold.**

floor oil A late 19c–early 20c finish for wood floors; composed of a drying oil (such as linseed oil or crude petroleum), a wax (such as beeswax or paraffin wax), and spirits (such as turpentine or kerosene); applied over varnished floors or used as an inexpensive **varnish** substitute.

floor plan A scale drawing showing the arrangement of one level of a building projected onto a horizontal plane; typically indicates walls, door, windows, and dimensions; may also be overlaid with other information, such as a plumbing or electrical system; types include **gas plot, ground plan.** See also **as-built drawing, measured drawing.**

floor plate One of various bent plates used to support bridge decks; types include **buckle plate, corrugated plate, zore.**

floor sink A **sink** recessed into a floor; may have a cover grate.

floor spring hinge A self-closing door **hinge** mechanism that is mounted on the floor and has an internal spring. See also **checking hinge.**

floor tile, flooring tile **1.** (mid-19c–present) A structural clay tile unit used as a structural floor or roof support; types include **booked**

tile, foot tile. See also **tile arch.** **2.** A ceramic tile that can be used as a floor finish; types include **encaustic tile, glazed tile, quarry tile.** Also known as **paving tile.** **3. Resilient flooring** cut in geometric shapes, usually 8–12 inches square; types include **asphalt tile, cork, linoleum, vinyl asbestos tile, vinyl tile.**

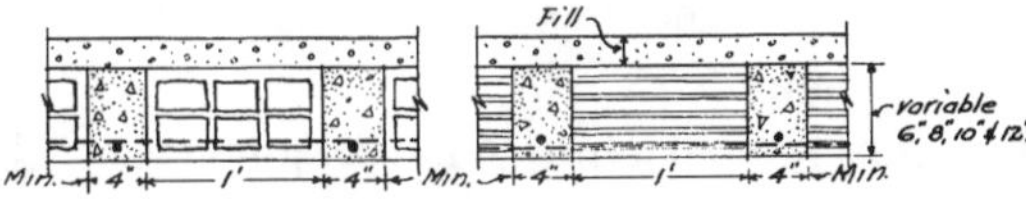

floor tile (sense 1)

floor timber (19c) One of the main beams supporting a floor.

Florence A light bluish gray **marble** with dark streaks or mottlings quarried in the vicinity of Florence Station, Pittsford Township, Vermont; polishes medium well.

Florentine arch An arch in which the voussoirs are larger at the crown than at the impost.

Florentine Blue A light or dark dove blue **marble** with dark blue veins and white spots quarried in the vicinity of Pittsford Township, Vermont.

flounder house A house built with a blank side to allow for future expansion; so-called because a flounder fish has both eyes on the same side of its head; in Alexandria, Virginia, a small, shed-roofed, one-room-deep house built to satisfy regulations requiring construction of a house within six months of purchasing the property.

flourished (18c) Decorated with foliage or festoons.

flower de Lys (18c) Same as **fleur-de-lis.**

flower garden The area in a **garden** where flowers are planted; usually arranged to give a pleasing appearance.

flowing tracery Gothic style **tracery** with continuously curving, interlaced stone mullions with a cusp at the edge of each opening. Also known as **curvilinear tracery, undulating tracery.**

flue, (pre-19c) **flew** A **vent** passage for **chimney** gases; may be masonry, terra-cotta, or metal; types include **stovepipe.**

flume An inclined, open-topped conduit for conveying water; used in manufacturing (e.g., for an ore-washer), in power generation (e.g., for a mill wheel or turbine), and in agriculture and transportation. See also **aqueduct.**

fluorescent lamp (20c) The bulb of a **fluorescent light;** typically a long, cylindrical tube with electrodes at both ends; the tube is filled with a gas, such as mercury vapor, that glows when current passes through it.

fluorescent light (20c) A lighting fixture with a **fluorescent lamp.** See also **incandescent lamp, neon.**

flush bead A recessed bead whose top is flush with the adjoining surfaces; types include **center bead.** Also known as **plowed bead.**

flushboard A plank placed on top of a dam to raise the water level, such as with a millpond.

flush box Same as **flushing box.**

flush box sill A pre-WWII box sill in which the wall plate and the sole plate are let into the ends of the joints, so that the top of the sole plate and the bottom of the wall plate are flush with the top and bottom of the joists. See also **box sill.**

flush door A door with a single, plain surface on its face; types include **hollow-core door, solid-core door.**

flush girder A wood frame girder whose top is flush with the top of the joists. (*See illustration p. 190.*)

flush gutter A built-in gutter on the surface of a shingle roof composed of sheet metal flashing and a board projecting from the sheathing; the flashing extends under the shingles above and over the board; may be of two forms: (a) an

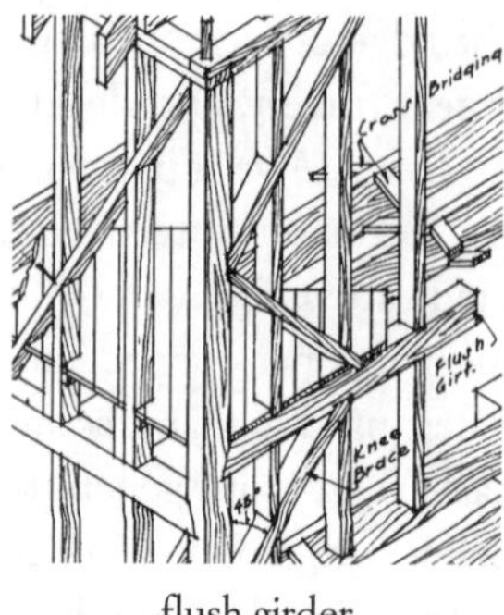

flush girder

inclined plank perpendicular to the roof sheathing and supported with brackets; (b) a vertical board parallel to the eaves, sometimes with moldings, with a sloped, tapered board forming the bottom of the gutter. Also known as **gutter strip, Philadelphia gutter.**

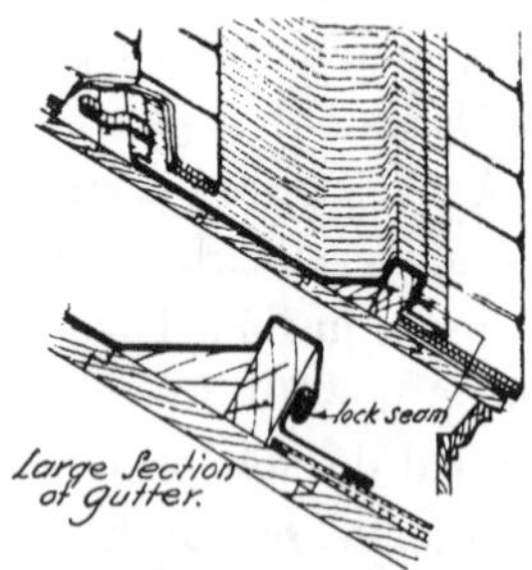

flush gutter (sense 1)

flushing box A metal lined, wood **flush tank;** typically mounted on a wall and connected with a pipe to the rear of the water closet; operated with a pull chain. Also known as **flush box.**

flush joint **1.** A **mortar joint** in which the mortar is cut even with the face of the masonry units; types include **high joint.** Also known as **hick joint, rough cut joint.** **2.** Any joint in which the exposed surfaces of adjoining members are in the same plane, especially in millwork; may have a strengthening plate behind; type includes **sypher joint.**

flush mold An applied door or window molding that is flush with, or below, the surface of the rails and stiles.

flush panel A wood panel whose surface is in the same plane as the adjoining surfaces of the surrounding rails and stiles; typically the edges of the rails and stiles have a bead mold to hide the joint.

flush plus rodded joint A **mortar joint** even with the face of the masonry unit and with a concave line at the center. See also **concave joint.**

flush sprinkler A type of **sprinkler head** that has most of its body behind the ceiling or wall surface on which it is mounted. See also **concealed sprinkler.**

flush tank A box or vessel for holding water used to flush a water closet bowl; typically an oak **flushing box** in the 19c, porcelain in the 20c.

flute One of a series of parallel linear grooves with a curved profile, especially when sepa-

flush tank

rated only by a **flat arris** or **sharp arris;** typically semielliptical on column shafts of Greek orders, such as the **Doric order,** and semicircular on Roman orders, such as the **Corinthian order.** Also known as **striga.** See also **cabled flute, canal, cannelated, channel.**

fluted glass Sheet glass with parallel abutting grooves; manufactured by pressing hot glass in a mold.

fluted torus A molding with a semicircular cross section with parallel grooves.

flying bond Same as **garden wall bond.**

flying buttress An exterior wall buttress composed of one or more **half arch** openings; used in Gothic churches to resist the outward thrust of the vaults and arches at the exterior wall of the clerestory; typically with no wall above the arch, and with a massive pier as the abutment of the half arch.

fly lattice (18c) Same as **screening.**

fly loft The space above a theater stage where the scenery backgrounds are raised and stored.

fly wire (18c) Same as **screening.**

foam extinguishing system A **fire suppression system** that uses bubbles containing a gas that displaces the normal amount of oxygen in the air and reduces the ability of combustion to continue; types include **carbon dioxide system, halon gas system.**

fodder house A building used to store fodder, especially corn stalks, for cattle or horses. See also **corn house.**

foil **1.** A leaf-shaped opening in carved **tracery.** See also **dagger, mouchette.** **2.** One of a series of round openings tangent to the intrados of an arch; forms include **trefoil, quatrefoil, cinquefoil, multifoil.** **2.** Thin, flexible sheets of metal; types include **aluminum foil, gold leaf, paillette, silver leaf.**

foiled arch Any **arch** with foils, such as a **two-cusped arch** or **trefoil arch.**

folded floor (19c) Wood flooring in which the joints at the ends of the boards are aligned to form a continuous line across the floor.

folding door **1.** (19c–present) Any door with multiple hinged leaves that open to one side; types include **accordion door, bifold door, folding partition.** **2.** (pre-20c) Same as **double door** (senses 1 and 2).

folding partition A floor-to-ceiling height folding door used to subdivide a room into smaller spaces.

foliage Sculptural decoration in the form of a cluster of stylized leaves, especially when used on capitals, friezes, and pediments.

foliated **1.** Decorated with foils, especially Gothic style tracery. **2.** Carved ornamentation in the form of stylized leaves.

foliated joint A flush carpentry joint formed by two overlapping rabbeted edges.

folk architecture Any building constructed by local people using traditional practices and customs for design and construction; may follow a regional pattern adapted to local materials and climate, especially during prerailroad eras before the mid-19c; building shapes and construction techniques often brought by immigrants from other regions or countries; types include **Cape Cod house, Carpenter Gothic, dugout, foursquare, I-house, log cabin, pueblo, sod house, timber frame, wigwam.** See also **high style, vernacular building.**

follower pile A second **pile** driven on top of an initial pile that has not reached the required level underground, or the required resistance. See also **false pile.**

folly **1.** (19c–present) A picturesque building built as a landmark in the landscape; often constructed to resemble a Gothic **ruin.** **2.** A building left incomplete because the owner's dreams outstripped his or her resources.

font **1.** A basin containing water used in baptisms; often a stone vessel supported on a short column. **2.** (19c–present) A reservoir for fuel for an **oil lamp.**

fontstone A stone fashioned into a **font.**

foot **1.** The bottom part of a rafter that rests on the wall plate. Also known as **toe.** **2.** A unit of length measure that equals 12 inches or one-third yard or 30.480 cm; in pre-19c North America varied between 11 and 14 English inches, depending on the country or city-state of origin of the inhabitants; originally based on the length of the human foot. See also **front foot, linear foot, square foot.**

foot base A molding used above a plinth.

footcandle (abbr. **fc**) (19c–present) A measure of brightness equal to the light that falls on a surface 1 foot away from a standard candle; sunlight is approximately 125 fc, and a single batswing gas burner is approximately 16 fc 12 inches away; typically, historic fabrics should receive less than 5 fc of light to avoid damage. See also **actinic light.**

footer Same as **footing.**

footing **1.** The bottom portion of a **foundation** that distributes the load of a wall or column onto the earth; typically wider than the element it supports. Also known as **footer.** See also **spread footing.** **2.** The lower outer slope of a **seawall.**

footing beam (19c) A roof tie beam.

footing stone (19c) A wide, flat stone used as a footing. Also known as **bottom stone.**

footpace, foot-pace **1.** (pre-20c) A landing in a continuous straight run of steps. **2.** (pre-20c) Same as **pace** (sense 1).

foot rail The bottom rail of a railing or balustrade.

footstall **1.** The decorative treatment at the base of a pillar or pier. **2.** The pedestal that supports a pillar or statue.

footstone **1.** The lowest coping stone on a sloped gable end, with a horizontal bed and a sloped top. Also known as **skew.** See also **foot table, fractable, kneeler, skew corbel, springer.** **2.** A grave marker placed at the feet of the deceased. See also **headstone.**

foot table A stone at the bottom of a gable end coping with a horizontal top and bottom. See also **footstone, fractable.**

foot tile (pre-20c) A **floor tile** that is 12 inches square.

footwalk (pre-20c) Same as **sidewalk.**

footway (pre-20c) A footpath or **sidewalk.**

forced air heating A **heating** system that uses **forced ventilation** to circulate hot air from a furnace to the spaces within a building.

forced draft **1.** Same as **forced ventilation.** **2.** A **draft** of air induced in a chimney or furnace by mechanical means. See also **natural draft.**

forced ventilation The circulation of air within a building by use of a fan, air ducts, and registers; introduced by Desaguliers in the British House of Parliament in 1736; not common in public and commercial buildings until ca. 1860. See also **ventilation.**

forcing house A **greenhouse** used to stimulate plant growth before its normal season.

fore-and-aft (19c) In the direction of front-to-rear; used to describe partitions, or similar elements, in town houses.

forecourt A courtyard at the main entrance to a building; typically enclosed by the wings of the building and/or a wall or fence.

forest marble Any **marble** that resembles a forest landscape when cut into slabs. Also known as **landscape marble.**

forge **1.** An open hearth or fireplace where iron is heated to make it malleable for shaping or making wrought iron. **2.** A building containing one or more forges (sense 1); may be a small smithy or a large building containing milling equipment. **3.** (19c–present) A building containing a furnace in which wrought iron is made directly from iron ore.

forge-pig Same as **white iron.**

formal garden (20c) A **garden** laid out in a geometric pattern or systematic design.

formeret Same as **wall rib.**

Formica (mid-20c–present) A trademark name for a **plastic laminate** phenolic resin material originally developed as an electrical insulator; commonly used for facing countertops and kitchen cabinets.

formstone A cast concrete synthetic stone typically applied to the surface of existing houses.

fornication **1.** A vaulted or arched space. See also **fornix.** **2.** The process of constructing a vault.

fornix (pre-20c) **1.** An **arch** or **vault,** especially a barrel vault below the main level of a building; from the Roman term for a brothel. **2.** A triumphal arch. **3.** A sally port in a wall.

fort, (17c) **forte** **1.** An independent **fortification** that can be garrisoned to defend against attackers; typically includes a ditch, rampart, and parapet or palisades around the perimeter. See also **fortification, fortress.** **2.** (19c–early 20c) An Indian trading post.

Fort Dodge Alabaster, Fort Dodge Gypsum A white or white-clouded **alabaster** quarried in the vicinity of Fort Dodge, Iowa.

fortification **1.** The science or process of fortifying a place. **2.** A complex of military structures designed to make it difficult to approach

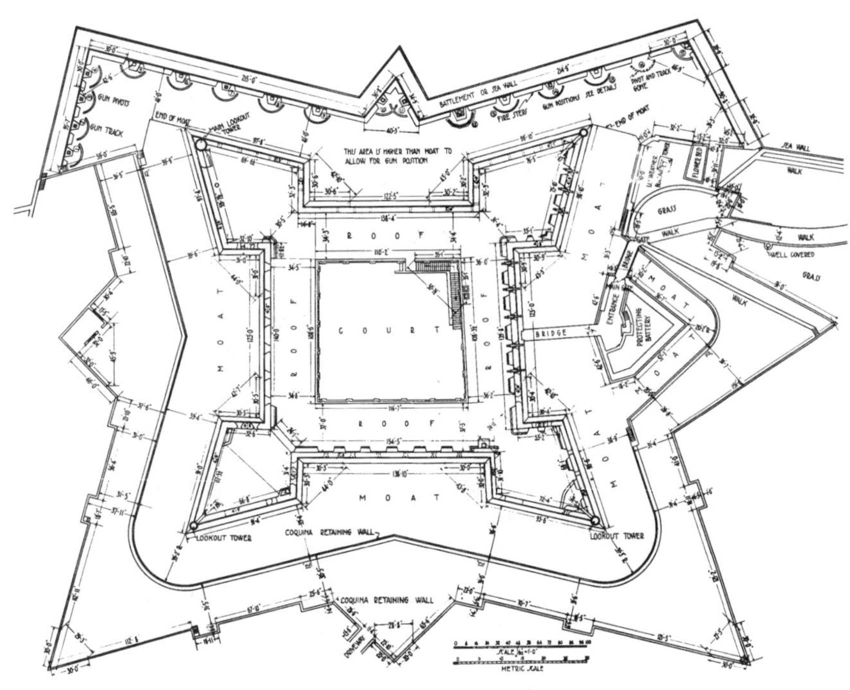

fortification (sense 2)
Fort Marion
St. Augustine, Florida

the structures and possible to defend them; elements may include **barracks, bastion, battery, battlement, blockhouse, breastwork, caponier, casemate, cavalier, cheval-de-frise, corridor, counterfort, counterscarp, curtain, ditch, embrasure, exterior slope, flèche, foss, glacis, gorge, lunette, orillon, palisade, parapet, rampart, ravelin, redan, redoubt, sally port, scarp, sconce, spur, tenail, terreplein, throat, tread, trench, turret, vantmure.** See also **fort, fortress.**

fortress A military structure designed to be defended against attackers; See also **blockhouse, fort, fortification.**

fortypenny nail (40d nail) A **nail** approximately 5 inches long; 200 iron common nails weigh one pound. See also **penny.**

foss, fosse A ditch or moat of a fortification.

fossil Geologically preserved remains of a natural phenomena, such as a mineralized plant or animal, or the shape of ripples on the bottom of a body of water embedded in sedimentary rock.

fossil cork (19c) Same as **asbestos.**

Foster block A **concrete block** made of sand and lime and patented by Ambrose Foster of Wisconsin in 1855; manufactured in the midwest and eastern U.S. in the late 1850s.

foundation The base of a building that rests directly on the earth and carries the load of the superstructure above; typically wider than the wall or column above it so that the weight is spread over a larger area to prevent settling of the building; components may include **crib, footing, foundation wall, pile, sand foundation, timber post foundation.** See also **slab-on-grade.**

foundation stone (19c) **1.** Same as **cornerstone. 2.** Any of the stones used in a foundation.

foundation wall The structural perimeter wall between the **footing** and the **ground floor** of a building, partially or completely below grade; typically constructed of masonry or concrete.

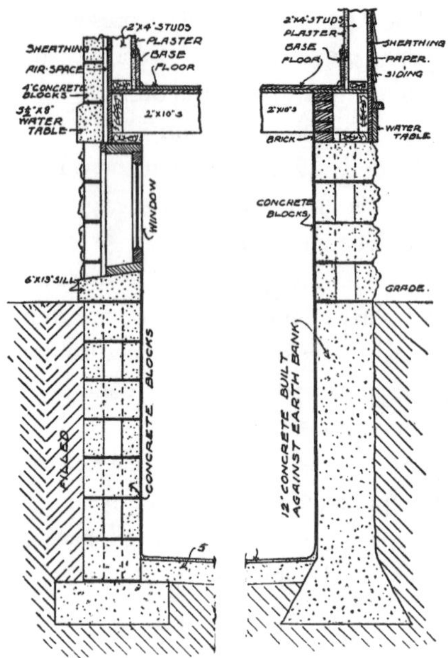

foundation wall

foundry, (pre-19c) **foundery** A place or building in which metal is cast in molds to manufacture finished products. See also **ironworks.**

foundry brick Same as **salmon brick.**

foundry iron Same as **gray iron.**

found space Space within an existing building envelope that is added to the usable floor area during rehabilitation; examples include converting attic or basement areas to habitable space and inserting mezzanine levels.

fountain **1.** A basin that receives flowing water, especially a jet that sprays into it; may be for drinking or purely decorative. **2.** A jet or spray of water. Also known as **jet d'eau.**

fountainmoreau's bronze A metal alloy that imitates bronze; composed of 90 percent zinc, 8 percent copper, 1 percent cast iron, and 1 percent lead.

four-centered arch An **arch** with four centers for the radii of the intrados; types include **two-cusped arch, ogee arch, Tudor arch.**

fountain (sense 1)

four-leaved flower A high-relief carved stone ornament with four radial petals and a raised ball, or round hollow, at the center; used in **Gothic** style architecture, especially the **Decorated style.**

four over four, 4 over 4 A double-hung window with four panes in both the upper and lower sashes; each sash is divided into quarters by vertical and horizontal center mullions. See also **twelve over twelve.**

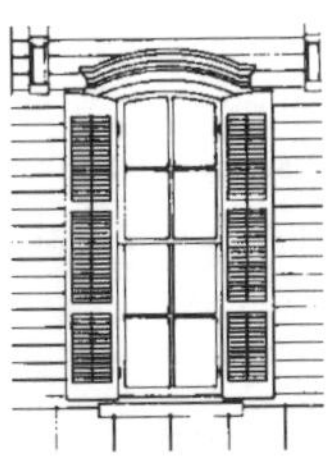
four over four

four over six, 4 over 6 A double-hung window with four panes in the upper sash and six panes in the lower sash; the upper sash is divided into quarters by vertical and horizontal center mullions, and the lower sash has three rows of two panes. See also **twelve over twelve.**

fourpenny nail (4d nail) A **nail** approximately 1.5 inches long; 300 iron common nails weigh one pound. See also **penny.**

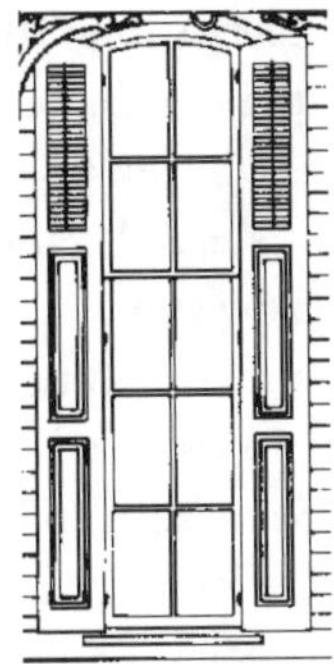
four over six

fourpenny spike (4d spike) A **spike** approximately 4 inches long; 23 steel-wire spikes weigh one pound. See also **penny.**

four ply Having four overlapping layers, especially the layers of felt in a **built-up roof.**

foursquare A 20c house form characterized by one-and-a-half to two-and-a-half stories, a square plan with a room in each corner and a center stair, and a hipped roof. Also known as **Cube style.**

fowlery (19c) A **fowl house** or poultry yard.

fowl house (Georgia and South Carolina) A **henhouse** or similar building for sheltering such fowl as ducks, geese, guinea fowl, or turkeys.

fox bolt A bolt secured by a **foxtail wedge** driven into its split end.

foxtail pine A softwood tree with reddish, hard, tough, close-grained wood that is extremely durable; found in California; *Pinus balforiana.* Also known as **hickory pine.**

foxtail wedge A hard metal or wood wedge used in a dovetail-shaped mortise to secure a tenon; when the tenon is driven onto the wedge inside the mortise, the tenon splits and forms a dovetail joint.

foyer **1.** A large entrance hall. **2.** The space outside an auditorium where the audience gathers during intermission. **3.** (19c) A gathering room, especially in a theater for actors or dancers.

FPO Federal Preservation Officer

fractable, fract table A gable end coping that rises to the peak in multiple steps or curves. Also known as **shaped gable.** See also **foot table, boltel, crow step.**

frame **1.** A structural support system in which all of the vertical loads are carried by columns and/or studs. See also **framing, wood frame.** **2.** One of a series of wall panels formed of surface molding or stencils; intended to unify a room by creating panels between doors and windows and over doors; common 1920–WWII in Colonial Revival, Mediterranean, bungalow, and Craftsman houses.

frame building A **building** built with a **wood frame,** especially when the exterior wall is wood, rather than masonry; types include **balloon frame, half-timbered, platform frame, timber frame.**

framed floor (19c) A floor construction system in which the binding beams are carried by larger girders.

framed square A wood **panel** held by rails and stiles with square, rather than molded, edges.

framing The structural system of beams, columns, and studs that supports a building; types include **reinforced concrete, steel frame, wood frame.**

frank To join a rail and stile by mitering the molded edge and cutting off one member square, and mortising a notch in the other member; typically used in window sash.

Franklin (late 18c–early 19c) Same as **lightning rod;** named for Benjamin Franklin.

Franklin stove **1.** An open front, wood burning, cast-iron stove with a hearth that projects into the room; smoke and room air are exhausted through a series of baffles at the rear to increase heat efficiency; originally portable with andirons, later versions had coal grates and could be closed by doors at the front; invented by Benjamin Franklin. **2.** (mid-19c to present) Any open front, cast-iron stove. See also **Rittenhouse stove.**

frass The fine wood powder left by wood-boring insects such as powder-post beetles and carpenter bees.

FRC Abbr. for **fire-retardant chemical.**

Frear stone A **concrete block** produced by the process of casting in a mold under pressure; patented by George Frear in 1868.

Frederick County marble Same as **calico marble.**

Freedley White An extremely light bluish gray **marble** quarried in the vicinity of Freedley, Vermont, starting in 1909. Also known as **White Freedley.**

free of sap Lumber that has only **heartwood.**

freestone Any stone without pronounced bedding planes, so that it can be worked equally well in any direction; usually a **sandstone** or **limestone.**

free stuff Same as **clear stuff.**

freeze **1.** (18c) Same as **frieze.** **2.** (Canada) A temporary halt to alteration or demolition of a **heritage site** by resolution of a municipal council.

freeze-thaw action The deterioration of a building, paving, or structural element owing to the internal pressure of freezing water in small cavities; may cause spalling or displacement of masonry.

freight station A structure for loading and unloading cargo from a railroad car or truck; typically includes a raised platform or loading dock and a building with offices and a storage area. See also **railroad station.**

French arch A horizontal support formed over a wall opening by laying bricks at approximately a 45-degree angle from both sides of the top of an opening to meet a wedge-shaped brick in the center; technically not a true **arch.** Also known as a **Dutch arch.**

French basement A **basement house** with raised steps to the main entry one story above grade, with the entry level containing a reception room and dining room, a basement level at or near grade containing the kitchen and storage rooms, and a cellar below the basement containing storage areas; found after ca. 1864.

French blue Same as **ultramarine blue.**

french casement A pair of **casement** windows that swing inward and are fastened by an espagnolette. Also known as **french window.** See also **french door.**

French Colonial (U.S.) Buildings of various styles constructed during the French settlement of the lower Mississippi valley during the period from 1700 to the Louisiana Purchase in 1803; these traditional forms continued in use in New Orleans until at least the 1860s, and into the 20c in rural areas; typical house elements included a single story with steeply pitched side gable or hipped roof, timber frame with nogging, French doors, and casement windows with board shutters; the stuccoed urban cottages of New Orleans were built immediately adjacent to and slightly above the sidewalks; rural houses typically are raised on a brick basement and have a porch covered by the main roof. See also **Creole cottage, French Regime.**

French Creek granite A dark-colored, fine-grained, hard granite quarried in the vicinity of French Creek, Pennsylvania; nearly black when polished.

french door A **french casement** that extends to the floor so that it can be used as a door; most common for access to balconies.

french drain A line of terra-cotta drain tiles installed with open joints outside the base of a foundation wall to remove groundwater and prevent basement walls from leaking; typically covered with muslin or other fabric and surrounded by small stones to keep out dirt.

French Eclectic style An architectural style for U.S. houses loosely based on the various styles of farmhouses and manor houses of Brittany and Normandy in France; may be symmetrical with Renaissance detailing, asymmetrical with informal, medieval details, or a towered **Norman cottage;** typical elements include a steeply pitched hipped roof that curves toward the horizontal at the eaves, dormers, masonry or stucco walls, and decorative half-timbering.

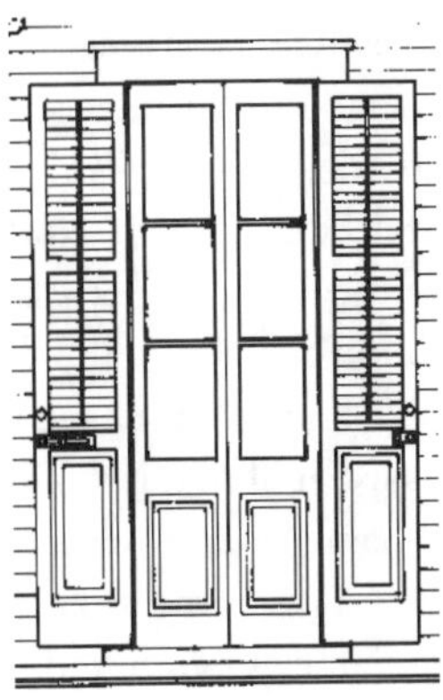

french door

french flyer (pre-19c) A staircase that ascends with a straight flight to a quarter-turn landing, then up one step to a second quarter-turn landing, then a straight flight parallel to the first flight. See also **flier.**

French gray Same as **dark Lepanto.**

French ocher A clear, bright yellow **ocher** paint pigment manufactured from earth deposits in France; the highest quality yellow ocher available; lighter in color than **yellow ocher.**

French order A variation of the **Corinthian** order, adapted with native French symbols, such as the fleur-de-lis and cock's head.

french polish A glossy wood finish obtained by rubbing with a mixture composed of shellac, sometimes with varnish gum, dissolved in alcohol.

French Regime (Canada) Dwellings and churches of various styles constructed by French settlers ca. 1601–1759. See also **French Colonial, Quebec style.**

French Renaissance Classical architecture in the style of the French Renaissance beginning in the mid-16c; influenced the **Renaissance Revival style** common in North America in the late 19c–early 20c. See also **beaux arts, Second Empire.**

French roof **1.** Same as **concave mansard roof.** **2.** A **mansard roof** that is nearly flat on top.

French sash Same as **casement.**

french section (19c) Same as **zore.**

French truss Same as **cambered Fink truss.**

French window Same as **french casement.**

fresco Decorative **wall painting** done with water-soluble pigments on fresh plaster or stucco; the pigments bond permanently with the lime mortar or plaster.

fresco secco Decorative painting with water-soluble pigments on dry plaster.

fret, (18c) **frette** **1.** Same as a **meander.** **2.** Perforated or relief ornamental work of wood or stone. See also **diamond fret, dovetail fret, fretwork.**

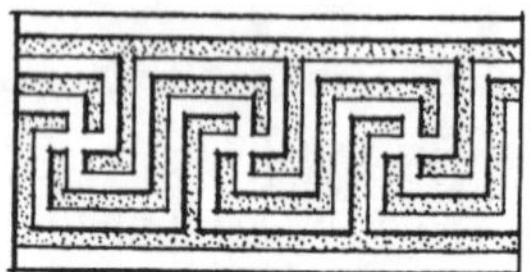

fret (sense 2)

fretwork **1.** A screen or lattice composed of intricate, interlaced openwork. **2.** A relief **fret** pattern, especially a rectilinear **meander.**

friable asbestos Loose asbestos fibers that can be crumbled or powdered by hand pressure; pose the greatest risk of causing cancer. See also **asbestos abatement.**

friction strip The thin wood strip on the edge of a **banded door.**

Friendsville Pink A lightly variegated pink **marble** quarried in the vicinity of Friendsville, Tennessee; polishes highly.

frieze, (18c) **freese, freeze, frize** **1.** The flat, middle portion of an entablature; may be **pulvinated** or decorated (e.g., a **historical frieze, marine frieze, symbolic frieze,** or **zoophorus**). **2.** Any long, narrow horizontal band on a building.

frieze-band window A rectangular window with a bottom hinged, inward opening sash located in the frieze of a Greek Revival house facade. Also known as an eyebrow window. See also **Greek Revival style.**

frieze panel **1.** Same as **metope.** **2.** One of the top panels of a door that has at least three rows of panels.

frieze rail A rail below a **frieze panel,** such as found on a paneled door.

frigeratory (18c) A cool place to make or store items in the summer.

frise A curly figure in **marble.**

frog A depression in the largest face of a **brick.** Also known as **panel.**

frontal (19c) A small pediment, or other decoration, above a minor door or window.

front brick A high-quality **face brick** used on the front of a building; in the 19c **pressed brick** was often used on the main facade and lesser quality brick on the sides of a building. See also **brick.**

front foot A linear foot measured along the side of a lot that faces the main street; usually used in reference to value (e.g., $100 per **front foot**).

front-gabled Same as **gable-front.**

frontispiece **1.** (18c–early 19c) A subsidiary element of the principal facade, such as a door enframement or window pediment, with ornate decoration that makes it visually prominent. **2.** The principal facade, especially when more ornate than the other facades.

fronton (pre-20c) A pediment over a window or door.

front window A double-hung window in which the height of the meeting rails is above the center of the opening.

front yard (19c–present) A open area in front of the main entrance to a house; may be fenced or landscaped. See also **yard.**

frosted bulb An **incandescent lamp** with an acid-etched interior surface; typically used with a tungsten filament starting in the 1920s.

frosted glass Various fine, crystalline patterns etched into clear glass to provide privacy.

frosted work Any surface pattern similar to that of frost on a windowpane.

frost line The maximum depth to which the ground freezes in winter; varies by locality.

frowy, (pre-20c) **frowey** Wood that is soft and easily worked without splintering.

frozen green A variegated, green **marble** quarried in the vicinity of Easton, Pennsylvania; polishes highly.

fruit garden (pre-19c) Same as **orchard.**

frustum **1.** A solid stone drum of a column. **2.** (19c) A broken shaft of a column.

fuchsite A brilliant, dark emerald-green, chrome mica **schist** with lighter veins and spots quarried in the vicinity of Shrewsbury, Vermont; used as a **marble;** named for the German chemist von Fuchs.

fugitive color A paint **pigment** or **colorant** that fades when exposed to sunlight.

full bound A window sash in which all the rails and stiles are of equal size. Also known as **same rail all around.**

full cape A **Cape Cod house** with two windows on each side of the front door.

full-centered arch (19c) Same as **round arch.**

full frame Same as **timber frame.**

full-glaze A thick, lustrous, smooth **architectural terra-cotta** glazed finish.

full hydraulic lime A **hydraulic lime** that sets under water in six to eight days and continues to harden for months.

fulling mill A building in which woolen cloth is compacted by heat, moisture, and pressure or beating.

full pitch Same as **whole pitch.** See also **pitch.**

full tail A **rafter tail** that is the same size as the main portion of a rafter, as opposed to a **reduced tail.**

fumed oak Oak with a silvery, weathered appearance made by exposing the filled and sanded wood to ammonia fumes; used for millwork and furniture, especially in the **Mission style.** Also known as **weathered oak.**

fumerell Same as **femerell.**

function The purpose for which a building, site, structure, object, or district is used. See also **current function, historic function, use.**

functionalism **1.** (19c) The visual expression of use and structure in the design of buildings after ca. 1860; common for railroad stations, exposition buildings, factories, and office buildings. **2.** (20c) An architectural design principle which holds that the form, structure, and materials of a building should be based on the most functional solution to the **program,** rather than on an academic or personal style, and that the various elements should be visually expressed separately; often expressed by the dictum "form follows function." See also **modern architecture.**

fungus, (pl. **fungi**) One of a group of simple organisms including molds, mildew, and mushrooms; many varieties consume wood by exuding digestive enzymes; need moisture, warmth, oxygen, and food for growth.

funnel **1.** (18c–19c) The **chimney throat** and **flue** of a chimney. **2.** (18c–early 19c) The outlet of a toilet hole; typically made of wood and often lined with metal. Also known as **pissduit.**

furbishing The process of polishing or finishing a metal surface. See also **refurbishing.**

furnace **1.** A device for producing hot air to heat a building; the heated air is moved through the building by ducts, vents, and/or fans; most

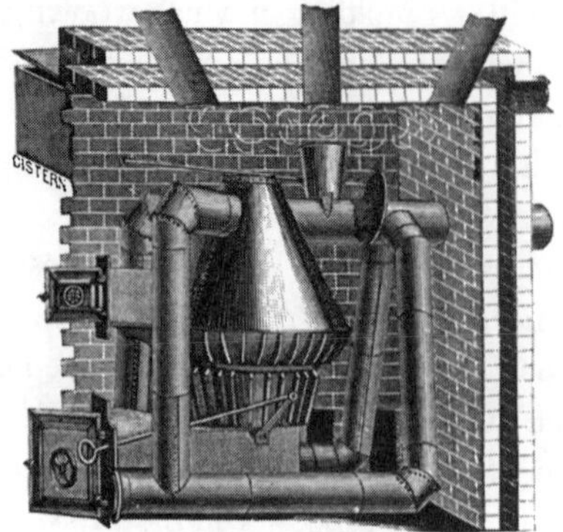

furnace (sense 1)

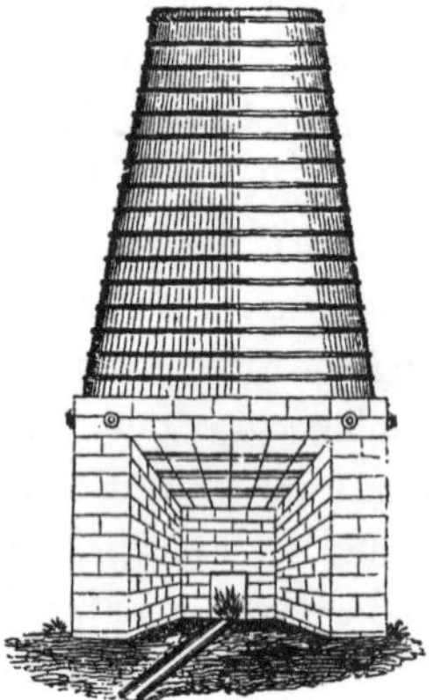
furnace (sense 3)

often coal-fired ca. 1880–mid-20c; also fired by natural gas, wood, or oil. See also **boiler, duct, stove.** **2.** The firebox of a steam boiler. **3.** A masonry structure used for smelting metal ores. See also **foundry.**

furnace coil A coil in a furnace; used for heating water.

furring **1.** A series of parallel wood or metal strips used to support and level plaster lathing, drywall, or sheathing, and to form an air space; used on walls, beams, columns, and ceilings. **2.** Any material used as a raised base for plaster, such as **furring tile.** See also **combined furring and lathing, cross furring, furring brick, furring strip.** **3.** (18c–19c) Wood members that extend the rafters at the base to form the eaves or to support a cornice. **4.** (18c) A wood strip that fills the sag on top of a rafter to make a straight nailing surface.

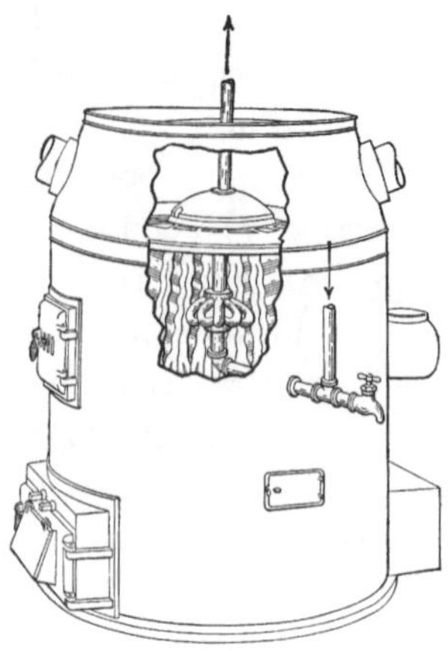
furnace coil

furring brick A hollow brick that is grooved on one face for furring the inside face of a wall.

furring channel A small metal channel used for furring.

furring strip A thin piece of wood with a rectangular cross section; typically a 1 × 2 or 1 × 3; used to level a surface, such as for lath or drywall; types include **strapping.**

furring tile A nonbearing structural clay tile unit installed on the inside face of masonry walls as a base for plaster.

furrow Same as **bat** (sense 2).

Furst-Kerber travertine A buff-colored **limestone** with many small pores.

fusarole, (pre-20c) **fusarol** Same as **astragal.**

fuse An electrical device with a metal strip that melts during a sustained current overload on the circuit; used to refer to both the portion that contains the fusible metal and the entire apparatus. See also **circuit breaker.**

fusible cutout (19c) Same as **fuse.**

fusible link A mechanism that releases when heated to excessive levels; used to shut a **fire door** automatically and open a **smoke vent.**

fust (pre-20c) The **shaft** of a column. See also **frustum.**

fyer place (17c) Same as **fireplace.**

G

gabbro A family of granular, igneous **stone** composed of basic plagioclase combined with a ferromagnesian mineral; used as a building stone; varieties include **Minnesota Black, Opalescent;** commercially known as **granite.**

gabion A woven container filled with earth or gravel and used in the building of an engineering work, such as a **revetment** or **retaining wall;** pre-20c containers were typically bottomless wicker baskets 2 feet in diameter by 3 feet tall, then most often cylindrical iron strapwork, and by late 20c woven wire in various shapes.

gable A wall that encloses the end of a **gable roof;** a triangular **gable end** below a roof overhang, or various shapes when parapeted, including **boltel, Dutch gable, shaped gable.**

gableboard Same as **bargeboard.**

gabled tower A tower crowned by a **gable roof** or a **cross-gable,** rather than a spire.

gable end **1.** The exterior wall of a building at the peaked end of a **gable roof,** from ground level to the top. **2.** The triangular portion of the end wall of a building at the peaked end of a gable roof, between the height of the eaves and the ridge.

gable end stud A stud between the horizontal top plate of a gable end wall and the pair of rafters above.

gable front A building with a **gable roof** and the main entrance in one of the gable ends. Also known as **front-gabled.** See also **side-gable.**

gable-front-and-wing A house with a gable end facing the street and an **ell-**shaped wing at the rear.

gable log One of the horizontal logs that fill the **gable end** of a log cabin.

gable pole A wood pole or bar that holds thatch in place at a **gable.**

gable post A vertical wood member below the ridge of an overhanging **gable roof** that supports the top of the bargeboards.

gable roof A pitched **roof** with two inclined planes having equal angles that meet at a peak in the center and terminate at a vertical **gable;** variations include **cross gable, square gable;** in the 19c sometimes also meant having exposed rafters in the interior. Also known as **V-roof.** See also **pitch.**

gable shoulder Corbeled masonry that supports a **gable springer.**

gable springer The stone at the base of a gable coping; types include **foot table, footstone.**

gablet A small gable or gable-shaped canopy, such as at the top of a buttress or over an entrance. See also **dormer.**

gable wall Same as **gable end.**

gable window **1.** A window in a **gable end.** **2.** A window with a gable top.

gadroon, godroon **1.** An ornamental motif composed of a line of overlapping, or parallel, convex petal shapes; typically made by notching a molding with a rounded cross section. **2.** An olive- or ruffle-shaped architectural ornament with fluted or reeded decoration; from the French jewelers' term for repetitive, linked bracelet medallions.

gage (Canada, pre-20c U.S.) Same as **gauge.**

gain **1.** Same as **tusk.** **2.** A groove across the width of a board or plank, especially when used for a millwork **dado** joint. **3.** A beveled cut at the end of a joist where it rests on a girder or trimmer. See also **gained in.**

gaine A pedestal or pilaster that supports a sculptured head or bust; has a rectangular cross section and tapers downward in approximation of a human figure.

galbe The rounded contour of a decorative object, such as a baluster or console.

galería In a Spanish Colonial style building, a porch with an arcade or columned front, typically wide enough to accommodate furniture. See also **gallery.**

galerie **1.** (Southern Mississippi valley) Same as **veranda.** **2.** [French] Same as **gallery.**

galleria **1.** A skylighted interior passageway for pedestrians, lined with retail shops. Also known as **arcade.** **2.** A building containing such a passage.

gallery **1.** A large, relatively narrow room, especially one connected to other similar rooms; found in large 17c–18c houses. See also **galleria.** **2.** A room, or building, used for the display of collections of art or other objects. See also **art gallery, museum.** **3.** A raised seating area that overlooks the main level, as in an auditorium or church. **4.** A raised passageway partially open on one side; typically supported by columns or corbels. See also **balcony.** **5.** An underground passageway, especially in a **fortification.** **6.** The upper story over the aisle of a church; located below the clerestory and triforium. **7.** (southern U.S., West Indies) Same as **veranda.** **8.** (early 19c–present) A roofed seating area from which to view outdoor events. **9.** (southern U.S.) Same as **galerie.**

gallery of mirrors Same as **hall of mirrors.**

gallet A small chip off a stone block.

galleting Stone chips used to fill the joints of rubblework; inserted into wet mortar. Also known as **garreting, packing.**

galley kitchen (20c) A narrow kitchen with cabinets along one wall; from the nautical term for the cooking area on a ship.

gallows **1.** A wooden framework used to hang criminals; of various forms, including **gibbet.** **2.** A rectangular frame composed of two vertical posts and a horizontal beam used for hoisting.

galvanic corrosion A type of **corrosion** caused by an electric current generated by two different metals touching in the presence of water, with the less **noble** metal being corroded.

galvanized, (19c) **galvanised** **1.** Protected with a zinc coating; used to protect iron and steel from rust; originally referred only to electroplated tin covered with molten zinc but now includes hot-dipped zinc alloy coatings. **2.** Same as **electroplated.**

galvanized pipe **Black iron pipe** with a **galvanized** coating.

gambrel roof (19c–present) A **roof** shape characterized by a pair of shallow pitch slopes above a steeply pitched slope on each side of a center ridge. Also known as **Dutch roof.**

gang sawed, gang-sawed Rough lumber or stone cut by a gang saw with multiple vertical saw blades set as a gang in a single frame; produces a relatively smooth finish with some parallel markings and scratches. See also **chat sawed, shot sawed, stonework.**

gang shower A **shower room** with multiple shower heads in the same space.

gantry, (pre-20c) **gauntry** **1.** A freestanding truss or girder with end supports; types include (a) the support of a traveling crane or winch; (b) the frame spanning over railroad tracks to support signal lights. **2.** A frame that holds barrels in a horizontal position. **3.** An interior ramp for rolling barrels.

gaol, goal (17c–18c) Same as **prison;** used to confine both criminals and debtors. See also **jail.**

garage An enclosed space used for storage of automobiles; may be a detached structure or part of a larger building. See also **carport.**

Garauna A tropical hardwood tree with brownish, veined wood imported from South America; used for veneer wood. Also known as **Brazil wood.**

garçonnière (Louisiana) A dormitory for young men; typically attached to or nearby the great house of a plantation but with no interior connection.

garde-manger (20c) A storage room for meat.

garden Land used for growing vegetables, flowers, fruits, herbs, or other small plants, especially for pleasure or when adjacent to a residence; types include **botanical garden, English garden, flower garden, formal garden, fruit garden, kitchen garden, pleasance, pleasure ground, parterre, public garden, wall garden, wilderness.** See also **pall-mall, trompe l'oeil.**

garden apartment (20c) A **walk-up apartment building** located in a parklike setting; typically with two or three stories above grade.

garden city A satellite community built outside of an established major city by followers of Sir Ebenezer Howard's design principles, late 19c–early 20c.

garden house **1.** An open-sided or enclosed **summerhouse** in a garden or park; often octagonal in plan. **2.** (southern U.S.) Same as **outhouse** (sense 2). **3.** A small shed used for storing garden implements.

garden wall bond A brick wall bond in which courses of headers alternate with three or more stretchers; commonly used for two-wythe boundary walls.

gargoyle A projecting stone waterspout; typically carved in the form of a monster or other grotesque; common on **Gothic** style buildings.

garite (pre-19c) Same as **garret.**

garner Same as **granary.**

garnet hinge Same as **cross-garnet.**

garret, (pre-19c) **garratt, garrett, garette, garite, garrit, garrot** **1.** A finished attic room with a sloping ceiling. **2.** (pre-20c) An unfinished space below the sloping roof in an attic story. **3.** (regional St. Louis) Same as **porch.**

garreting (pre-20c) Same as **galleting.**

Garrison Colonial A side-gable, two-story house with an overhanging second story at the front; based on the postmedieval houses of Massachusetts and Connecticut; typically with clap-

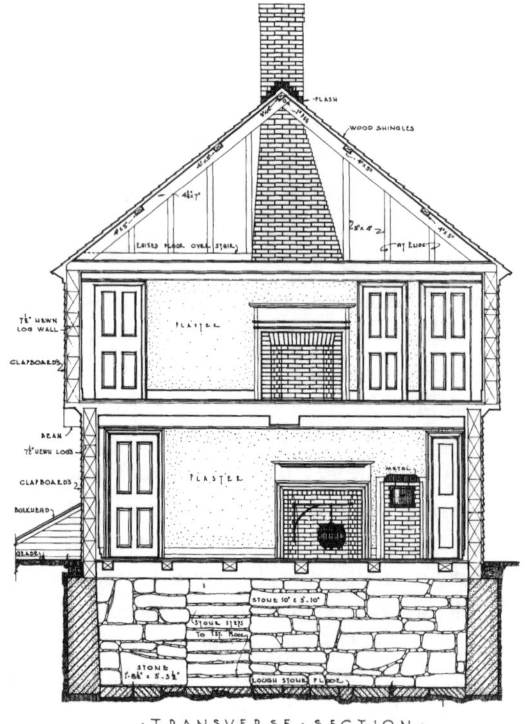

garrison house
McIntire Garrison House
York County, Maine

board siding, multipaned double-hung windows, and pendants at the overhang; first floor may be masonry veneer; common 17c–early 18c and in 20c revivals.

garrison house A fortified house, often of squared timbers with loopholes and an overhanging second story; common in parts of northeastern U.S. in the 17c and 18c.

gas A flammable, gaseous mixture used for lighting and heating; initially a manufactured product such as **coal gas** or **wood gas,** and later **water gas,** then supplanted by natural gas. See also **gas lighting, gasworks.**

gas boiler A **water boiler** heated by a gas flame.

gas bracket A wall bracket that supports a **gas fixture.**

gas bracket

gas burner The tip of a **gas fixture** that shapes the flame; types include **Argand, batswing, fishtail, ratstail, Welsbach.**

gas fitting The process, or trade, of providing gas piping, fixtures, and appliances within a building.

gas fixture An interior gas lighting device; types include **gas bracket, combination fixture, gasolier.** See also **gas burner.**

gas heater A gas-fired **water heater;** typically small with a copper or cast iron coil; through WWI, used to heat a separate storage boiler; combined tank and heater units were first manufactured ca. 1905.

gas holder (pre-WWI) Same as **gasometer.**

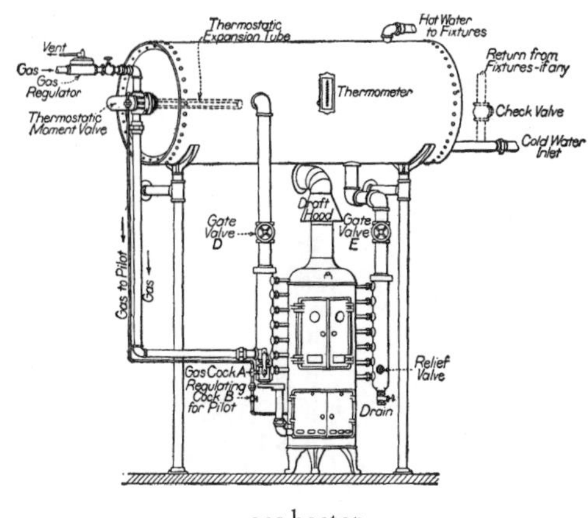

gas heater

gas house An industrial building that encloses a **gasometer;** typically cylindrical or with faceted sides.

gas jet Same as **gas burner.**

gas lighting Illumination by means of a **gas fixture;** first streetlights in U.S. installed in Baltimore in 1817; manufactured at a **gasworks** by heating coal and storing the gas in a **gasometer;** common in buildings in some urban areas beginning ca. 1830 and widespread by the end of the 19c; typically transfused through wall brackets in principal rooms, pendents or lanterns in passageways and stairways, and a newel post light at the base of the main stair. See also **gas.**

gas log A radiant heating device with a ceramic core in the stylized form of logs; used in a fireplace and heated with an open gas flame.

gas main See **main.**

gasolier, (19c) **gasalier** (19c–present) A hanging **gas fixture** similar to a chandelier; typically has three or more burners. (*See illustration p. 206.*)

gasolier-electrolier (late 19c) Same as **combination fixture.**

gasometer (19c–present) A tank for storing lighting gas; typically a large, cylindrical, iron tank with an open bottom that rests in a water tank; the iron tank rises as gas is pumped

gasolier

into it. Also known as **gasholder.** See also **gashouse.**

gas pipe Any of the distribution pipes that supply lighting or heating gas; typically of **black iron** with threaded fittings.

gas plant Same as **gasworks.**

gas plot (pre-WWI) A diagram of the layout of gas pipes and fixtures in a theater. See also **gas table.**

gas port An opening that provides access to an underground gas valve.

gas service See **service pipe.**

gas table (pre-WWI) A control panel for the gaslights in a theater. See also **gas plot.**

gas tank (pre-WWI) Same as **gasometer.**

gas tar Same as **coal tar.**

gas trap Same as **trap.**

gas welding **Welding** produced by simultaneously melting the metal on both sides of a joint and a rod of filler metal with a gas flame, usually with an oxyacetylene torch.

gasworks, (19c) **gas works** A manufacturing plant for lighting and heating **gas.** Also known as **gas plant.** See also **gas lighting, gasometer.**

gate **1.** A movable barrier across an opening in a dam, fence, railing, or similar enclosure; often refers to an openwork panel swinging on

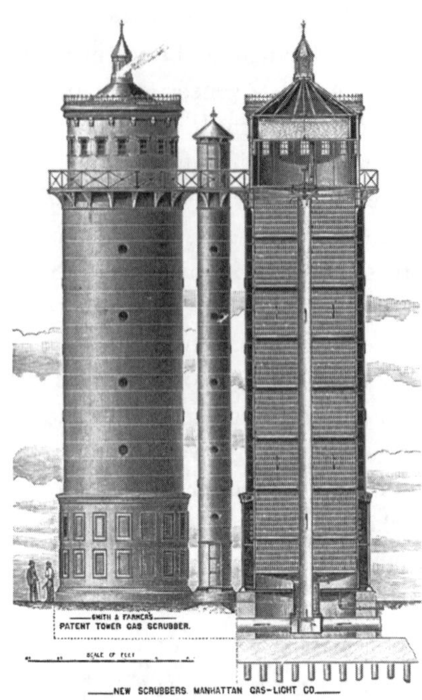

gasworks
Manhattan Gas-Light Co., ca. 1876

hinges; types include **balance gate, swing bar, tail gate, water gate.** See also **door, gatepost.** **2.** Same as **gateway,** especially when an imposing, ceremonial entrance. **3.** A device or structure for controlling water flow; types include **gate valve, sluice gate, water gate.**

gate chamber The recess that a gate swings into when open.

gate hinge A **strap hinge** in which the knuckle on one leaf interlocks with a lug projecting from the other leaf; the leaf with the lug may be mounted on the gatepost pointing up or on the gate pointing down. See also **hinge.**

gatehouse **1.** A house beside or over a **gate;** used as the station or residence of a gatekeeper. **2.** At a reservoir, the building containing the **water gates** and/or their controls. See also **waste gate, waste weir.**

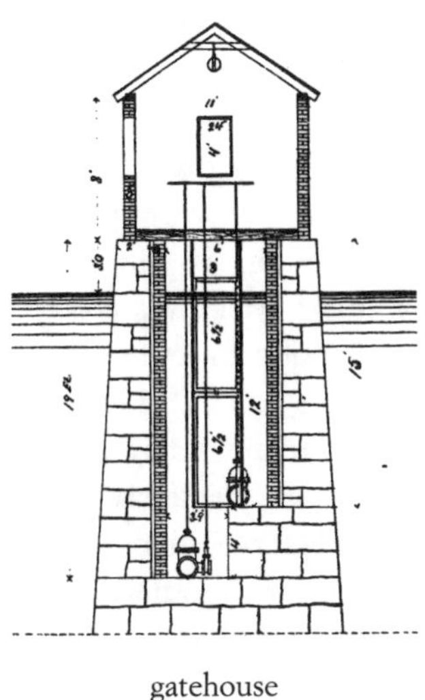

gatehouse

gatepost One of the two posts on each side of a gate; may be a **hanging post** or **shutting post.**

gate valve A valve for gas or liquids that is closed by a sliding plate; commonly used where the main utility service enters a building. See also **waste gate.**

gathering in The space where a fireplace narrows to the chimney throat.

gauge, gage **1.** A standard dimension, quantity, or amount, such as (a) the width between the rails of a railroad track; types include **narrow gauge, standard gauge, broad gauge;** (b) the diameter of wire; (c) the thickness of sheet metal; (d) the distance between centers of rows of bolts or rivets; or (e) a mixture of ingredients, such as **gauge mortar, gauged stuff.** See also **gauged, gauge pile.** **2.** The exposed portion of an installed slate, tile, or similar element. **3.** An indicator of a physical condition, such as a steam pressure gauge or a **gauge glass.**

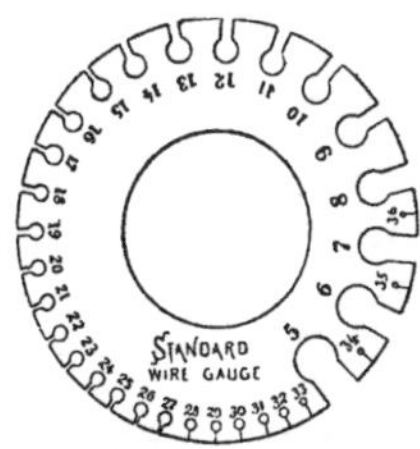

gauge (sense 1b)

gauged, gaged **1.** (19c) Properly proportioned or sized, as in **gauged stuff** or **straight gauged.** **2.** (pre-19c) A floorboard that has been undercut where it crosses a beam or joist so that the top surface is level with adjoining boards.

gauged arch An arch constructed of **gauged brick.**

gauged brick, gaged brick **1.** A brick shaped to conform to a curve, as in an arch brick. **2.** Bricks that have been sorted or formed to a particular dimension.

gauged joint (19c) A **mortar joint** finished by **tuck pointing.**

gauged stuff, gaged stuff A quick-setting plaster finish coat material; typically composed of approximately three-quarters fine stuff or plasterers' putty and one-quarter plaster of paris or Keene's cement. Also known as **gauging plaster.** See also **gauge mortar.**

gauged work Plastering done with **gauged stuff,** such as for repairs or applying decorative moldings.

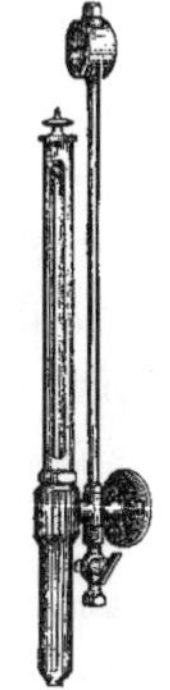

gauge glass

gauge glass A vertical glass tube that shows the water level in a boiler.

gauge lath One of a series of wood **lath** strips installed in horizontal, parallel rows on rafters to support slates or tiles; typically located directly under the nail holes. See also **counter-lath.**

gauge mortar Any rapid-setting mortar; typically with plaster of paris as an ingredient.

gauge pile, gauged pile One of a series of **piles** installed at accurately measured locations, typically at regular intervals; often connected by a pair of horizontal runners that guide the filler piles.

gauge work Rubbing or shaping bricks for use in an arch. See also **gauged arch, gauged work.**

gauging plaster, gaging plaster Same as **gauged stuff.**

gavel (18c) Same as **gable.**

gazebo, (19c) **gazabo,** (19c) **gazeebo** An open-sided, decorative shelter in a garden or park. See also **belvedere.**

gazebo porch Same as **pavilion porch.**

geared traction elevator An **elevator** with a platform supported by cables over a pulley and a counterweight; operated by a worm gear driven directly by steam or electric power.

geison The projection at the bottom of a tympanum formed by the top of the cornice; may be deeper than the depth of the architrave molding to create a recess for sculpture within the pediment.

gemeled (pre-20c) Coupled (e.g., a pair of columns), or a **gemel window.**

gemel hinge Same as **hook-and-eye hinge.**

gemel window A pair of adjoining windows; often divided by a mullion.

general contractor The building **contractor** who has legal responsibility for the entire construction project and who coordinates the work of all of the subcontractors.

generator A machine that produces electricity. See also **dynamo.**

Genessee Valley bluestone A dark bluish-grey sandstone quarried in the Genessee Valley of New York; used as a flagstone.

genteel (18c) Refined, stylish, and fashionable; used to describe architectural design. See also **fashionable.**

gentrification The process of higher-income people moving into a **transitional area** and restoring or renovating much of the existing housing stock; typically accompanied by the displacement of many of the existing residents and businesses because of higher rents or purchase of the buildings they occupy.

geocode A 14-digit identification code used by **Parks Canada** for location of historic buildings and structures. See also **Borden system, UTM.**

geodaesia (18c) The science of surveying.

geographical area An area of land containing historic or archaeological resources that can be identified on a map and delineated by boundaries.

geometrical decorated See **Decorated style.**

geometrical stair A winder stair in which the outside of the winders is supported by walls forming three sides of a rectangle, and the inside is unsupported and without newels, typically with a curved edge. See also **wreathed stair.**

geometrical tracery Window **tracery** with geometric shapes formed by the mullions, especially circles and cusped circles. See also **Decorated style.**

George Washington slept here A phrase that mocks the frequent association of historic buildings with George Washington or some other notable historical figure; the fact that General Washington was billeted at many locations during the Revolutionary War was justification for many early local preservation actions.

Georgia Cherokee A light gray **marble** that is slightly clouded and veined quarried in the vicinity of Tate, Georgia; polishes highly. See also **Cherokee.**

Georgia Creole Same as **Creole.**

Georgia Etowah Same as **Etowah.**

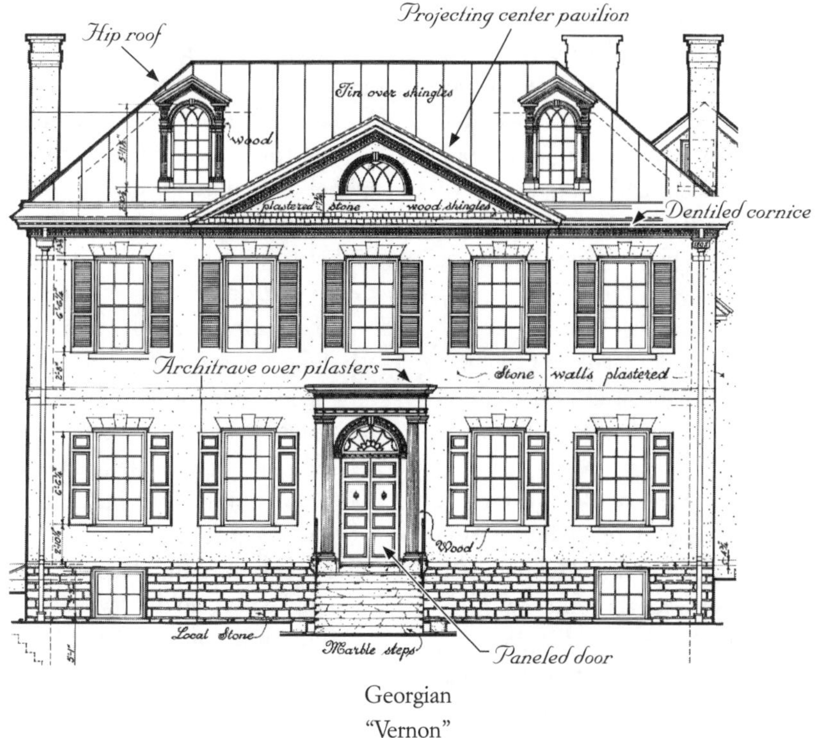

Georgian
"Vernon"
Philadelphia, Pennsylvania, ca. 1741

Georgia Green A dark yellowish green **marble** with small white specks quarried in the vicinity of Tate, Georgia; polishes highly. Also known as **Georgia serpentine, Georgia Verde Antique.**

Georgia Kenesaw A white **marble** quarried in the vicinity of Tate, Georgia; polishes highly.

Georgia marble Any of the coarse-grained varieties of **marble** quarried in Georgia; most often white, white clouded, pink, or light grey, with a sparkling crystalline structure; varieties include **Creole, Etowah, Etowah Pink, Georgia Green, Georgia Kenesaw, Georgia Silver Gray, Georgia White, Mezzotint;** used for building stone and, occasionally, for carved work.

Georgian **Classical** architecture built by British settlers along the U.S. Atlantic coast ca. 1700–76, although scholars in the 19c and early 20c extend the period to the end of the reign of George IV in 1830; now generally agreed that the use of the style largely ended at the beginning of the Revolutionary War; characterized by symmetrical elevations and plans, with axial entrances, heavily influenced by the **Palladian style;** typical elements include a rectangular plan with a projecting center pavilion, two main stories, hipped roof, paneled front door (often enframed with pedimented architrave and pilasters), wood single-hung multipaned windows with thick muntins; dentiled cornice; in northern U.S., buildings typically are frame with clapboard siding, while usually brick in the south. See also **Adam Style, colonial architecture, Georgian Revival, Federal style.**

Georgian Revival The studied use of **Georgian** elements in the architecture of later periods, especially the late 19c and early 20c; traditional Georgian details are often exaggerated in scale or repeated to accommodate larger buildings, and are often mixed with such noncolonial elements as bay windows, elaborate porches and dormers, and irregular floor plans. See also **Colonial Revival.**

Georgia pine, Georgia pitch pine Same as **longleaf pine.**

Georgia Pink Same as **Etowah Pink.**

Georgia serpentine Same as **Georgia Green.**

Georgia Silver Gray A light silver gray **Georgia marble** quarried in the vicinity of Tate, Georgia; polishes highly.

Georgia Verde Antique Same as **Georgia Green.**

Georgia White A nearly pure white **marble** quarried in the vicinity of Tate, Georgia; polishes highly. See also **Georgia Kenesaw.**

German glass (19c) Same as **cylinder glass.**

German siding A flat-faced type of **drop siding,** with a concave top that forms a tongue overlapped by the notched bottom of the board above. Also known as **simple drop siding.**

German silver A white alloy composed of nickel, zinc, and copper; first manufactured in Hildburghausen, Germany. Also known as **white copper.**

Germantown lampblack A variety of **lampblack.**

ghost mark A pattern or outline indicating that earlier construction has been removed; includes outlines created by different paint colors, missing plaster, and patched holes; may be small (e.g., a filled nail hole) or large (e.g., the outline of a building that has been demolished on a remaining structure).

giant order Same as **colossal order.**

giant sequoia A gigantic softwood tree with soft, straight-grained, reddish purple-brown, brittle, decay-resistant heartwood; found only in California at high elevations; used for lumber, millwork, and exterior trim before WWII; *Sequoia gigantea.* Also known as **sequoia.** See also **redwood.**

gib A wedge-shaped piece of metal driven through a rectangular eye to hold other pieces together; used in metal trusses.

gibbet A **gallows** composed of a post with a projecting horizontal beam.

gibbet-tree Same as **gibbet.**

Gibbs surround A heavy masonry door or window enframement with alternating courses of long and short stone blocks similar to quoins, or intermittent large blocks, and a projecting multiple-block keystone; named after the Scottish architect James Gibbs, (1682–1754), who published the influential **Book of Architecture** in 1728.

gilding **1.** A thin, decorative coating of gold; applied as gold powder or **gold leaf.** Also known as **gilt.** **2.** Silver leaf or **paillette** colored gold with yellow-tinted varnish. See also **bronzing.**

gilt Same as **gilding.**

gilt varnish (18c) A clear varnish composed of sandarac gum, aloes, gutta percha, and litharge; used to protect gilding.

gimlet screw (pre-WWI) A pointed **wood screw.**

gimp A braided fiber trim used to cover edges or seams of wall-hung fabric.

gimp nail A tack with a rounded or faceted head; used in upholstery. See also **rosehead, nail.**

gingerbread The ornate scrollwork on the exterior of houses, especially of the **Carpenter Gothic** style.

ginhouse, (18c–19c) **gin-house, gin house, ginning house** A building in which cotton is ginned to separate the seeds from the fibers; the cotton gin, invented by Eli Whitney in 1793, originally was powered by a foot pedal; beginning in the 1830s larger gin stands powered by mule or steam engine were housed in a room raised on columns eight feet above the ground;

processed fibers were tossed into a ground-level **lint room.** Also known as **ginnery.** See also **cotton house, cotton press.**

gin mill (U.S.) A bar where hard liquor is served.

girandole **1.** (pre-1830) A branched candleholder, especially one attached to a circular, convex, wall-hung mirror. **2.** (ca. 1840–70) A freestanding metal candleholder with a marble base and hung with prisms, especially when cast with relief sculpture of historical figures or scenes; often in sets of three for decorating a mantel or sideboard. **3.** (late 19c–present) A branching chandelier or bracket light.

girder A large beam that supports other beams or joists; types include **angle girder, binding beam, bowstring girder, half-lattice girder, lattice girder, plate girder, principal joist, riveted beam girder, summer, truss girder, trussed girder, tubular girder.** See also **girt.**

girder beam (18c) Same as **girder.**

girder bridge A bridge supported by girders that span directly between abutments and support crossbeams.

girt **1.** A horizontal member that encircles a wood frame building at upper floor levels and supports the joists, posts, and studs; used in **balloon frame** and **timber frame** buildings; types include **breast girt, end girt, overhanging girt, purlin girt, side girt.** Also known as **intertie.** See also **ribband.** **2.** In a steel frame industrial building, a horizontal member connecting the exterior columns or bents and supporting the siding.

girt roof (18c Virginia) Same as **principal roof.**

glacis The sloped ground below a fortified wall, open to give a clear field of fire. See also **fortification, scarp.**

glass, (pre-18c) **glasse** An amorphous, light-transmitting material composed of melted silica, usually quartz sand, and two or more metallic oxides; various manufacturing methods produce **compressed glass, crown glass, cylinder glass, float glass, heat-strengthened glass, patent plate glass, plate glass, rolled glass, tempered glass;** varieties include **adventurine, art glass, carrara glass, cased glass, devitrified glass, flint glass, kelp glass, laminated glass, lime glass, marbleized glass, mosaic glass, obscure glass, potash glass, slag glass, soda glass, tinted glass, water glass, window glass, wire glass;** the color depends on the amount of impurities in the silica as well as the amount and type of metallic oxides; types of **colored glass** include **alabaster glass, canary glass, cobalt glass, iridescent glass, grissaille glass, milk glass, onyx glass, opal glass, ruby glass;** the shape of the glass surface depends on the method of manufacture; shapes include **beveled glass, corrugated glass, fluted glass, jealous glass, kinkled glass, ondoyant glass, prismatic glass, ribbed glass;** finishes include **cameo glass, flash glass, granulated glass, ground glass, half-clear glass, picture glass, painted glass, stained glass.** See also **glazing, insulating glass.**

glass block A hollow, nonstructural glass masonry unit installed with mortar joints; typically used in exterior walls to transmit light while ensuring visual privacy; first manufactured in 1932.

glass flooring A floor composed of glass tiles held by a metal frame.

glass house **1.** (19c) Same as **greenhouse.** **2.** A building in which glass is manufactured. **3.** (19c) A building with a large glass skylight, such as a photographer's studio.

glass seam Coarsely crystalline calcite in veins of **limestone;** has a glasslike appearance compared with the rest of the stone.

glass tile **1.** A cast glass shape used for a light-transmitting floor; may be clear or colored;

typically has a ground glass finish. **2.** Glass in the size and shape of a ceramic tile. **3.** A roofing tile composed of glass and in the same shape as a terra-cotta tile; used for skylights.

glass wool Spun glass fibers; used for insulation. See also **fiber glass.**

glassworks A site where glass is manufactured.

glaze See **glazing.**

glazed brick **1.** A **brick** with a glossy fired enamel finish on the exposed faces; may be of various colors. **2.** Same as **clinker brick.**

glazed tile Ceramic tile with a glossy fired finish.

glazer's point Same as **glazier's point.**

glazier's point, glazer's point A small piece of cut sheet metal used to hold a pane of glass in a wood-framed window; always pointed on the bottom; top may be pointed or of various bent shapes, including a **tin tack.** Also known as **sprig.**

glazing **1.** The clear or translucent material through which light passes into a building; most often **glass** but includes other materials such as **acrylic** or **polystyrene.** See also **double glazed, isothermal glazing.** **2.** A translucent or transparent decorative coating used to protect the finish below and to give a uniform, glossy surface; in painting, typically a mixture containing linseed oil and, sometimes, **pigment;** in ceramics, a hard, glassy coating fused onto the surface, such as **faience.**

glazing bar Same as **muntin.**

glazing compound Any type of **sealant,** such as **putty,** used at the edges of a pane of glass to prevent leakage of air or water.

glazing panel (19c) A section of **stained glass** or **leaded glass** set in cames to be installed in a window sash or other frame.

glebe, gleeb (17c–18c) Farmland set aside for the use of an Anglican minister or for income for the church; often the location of the **parsonage.**

glebe house, gleeb house (17c–18c) Same as **parsonage.**

globe A spherical ornament, especially a relatively large one, such as on top of a steeple. Also known as **ball.**

globe valve **1.** A **valve** with a spherical chamber inside. **2.** A **valve** with a ball that shuts off the flow.

globular-shape lamp An **incandescent lamp** with a spherically shaped end.

glory A graphic representation of a halo surrounding a holy person.

gloss The reflective quality of a finish; varieties of paint gloss include **glossy, semigloss, satin, eggshell, flat.**

glossy A highly reflective finish, as opposed to a **matte** finish. See also **eggshell, flat, gloss, semigloss.**

glow light (late 19c) Same as **incandescent light.**

glue A viscid cement or adhesive; types include **casein glue, hide glue, isinglass glue, marine glue.**

glyph **1.** (pre-20c) A groove or channel, especially when vertical. See also **triglyph.** **2.** A recessed pictograph.

glyphtoteca, glyphtotek (19c) A building in which to exhibit sculpture; after a ca. 1848 building commissioned by Ludwig I of Bavaria for the sculptures from the Temple of Aegina.

gneiss A dense, dark, metamorphic building stone composed of quartz and orthoclase feldspar, with mica, hornblende, and other minerals; of various textures, colors, and compositions; typically has two cleavage planes; some varieties commercially marketed as **granite.**

gold A heavy, ductile, elemental metal; often used for **gold leaf;** imitations include **Dutch metal, similor.** Also known as **Royal metal.**

gold bronze **Bronze powder** with a gold color.

golden fir Same as **red fir.**

golden section A rectangular shape in the proportion of the length of the side of a square to the length of the square's diagonal.

gold leaf Gold beaten into extremely thin sheets; typically between 1/200,000 to 1/250,000 inch thick; used primarily for **gilding.**

gold size See **size.**

gooseneck A reverse curve bend, such as a flexible plumbing pipe fitting composed of two attached elbows.

gorge Any of various elements with a shape resembling a human throat, including: **1.** (18c–19c) Same as **cyma recta. 2.** (18c) An inverted cavetto. **3.** Same as **gorgerin. 4.** A concave molding wider than a scotia but not as deep; typically used for door or window surrounds. See also **gula. 5.** A **fortification** curtain wall between two bastions. **6.** An entrance into a bastion, or similar element, of a **fortification. 7.** A drip groove under a coping. See also **chimney gorge.**

gorgerin, (18c) **gorgerine** **1.** A narrow slot at the top of the shaft of a Doric column. **2.** On a Doric capital, the narrow area between the echinus and the shaft. **3.** A fillet or other band that divides a capital from the shaft of a column. Also known as **hypotrachelium, necking.**

gorgon, gorgoneion A sculptured stone representation of the mythical monster, with a huge mouth and teeth, serpentine hair, and glaring eyes.

Gothic See **Gothick, Gothic Revival.**

Gothic arch A **pointed arch** in which each side is formed by a segment of a circle with its center on the spring line; may be an **equilateral arch** or an **acute-pointed arch.** See also **arch.**

Gothic cornice A Gothic style cornice, typically with a sculptured band at the bottom, a deep projecting drip molding, and steeply sloped weathering that continues up to the gutter or parapet at the top.

Gothick A spelling of **Gothic** favored by 18c designers in the style; typically they borrowed the ornamental motifs of medieval Gothic architecture but not the construction techniques.

Gothic order An order of a column of one of the various Gothic styles. See also **Gothic Revival.**

Gothic pitch A steeply pitched roof used in the Gothic Revival style, often as great as **whole pitch.** See also **Gothic roof, pitch.**

Gothic Revival Imitation of various medieval Gothic architectural styles starting at the beginning of the 19c and widespread ca. 1840–70; known by the Romantic movement's proponents of Christian medieval architecture as the "only proper style"; common style for churches, colleges, and rural houses, and used for isolated examples of all types of buildings; styles copied include **Decorated style, Early English style,** and **Perpendicular style,** while looser adaptations were found in the **Carpenter Gothic, Collegiate Gothic,** and **High Victorian Gothic;** typical house elements include symmetrical facades, gable dormers, steeply pitched roofs with cross gables, scrollwork bargeboards, and hood molds over

Gothic Revival
Holy Trinity Episcopal Church
Nashville, Tennessee, ca. 1852

square-headed or pointed-arched windows. Also known as **neo-Gothic.** See also **Gothic roof, Gothic survival, Gothick, tracery.**

Gothic roof A roof with a **Gothic pitch;** used on Gothic Revival style buildings.

Gothic sash (18c) A multipaned window **sash** with curved muntins at the top forming pointed arch shapes.

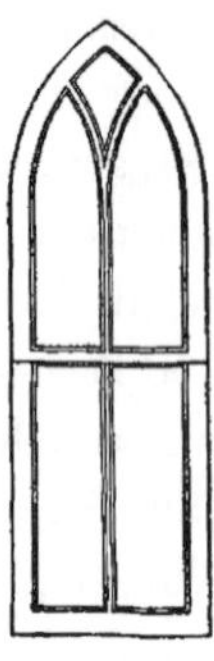

Gothic sash

Gothic survival Buildings constructed with medieval Gothic construction methods and style after the medieval period; use by European settlers in North America is relatively rare.

gouache A water-base paint composed of pigment, whiting, gum arabic, and water; typically used for decorative interior painting.

gouge work Woodwork with chiseled patterns, such as found on Dutch colonial mantels and the trim of houses in New Jersey and Pennsylvania.

government anchor (20c) A round steel rod bent to form a V-shaped saddle and inserted in a hole in the end of a steel beam as a masonry **anchor;** typically of .75-inch diameter and 18 inches long after bending.

Government Architect (19c) The supervising architect of the U.S. Treasury Department; oversaw construction of most U.S. government buildings during the 19c.

grade The height of the surface of the ground, especially in relation to a building; an element that is **at grade** is on the same level as the ground. See also **finish grade.**

grade beam A reinforced concrete beam at or below **grade** that spans between piles, piers, or isolated footings; may support the perimeter of a building or the edges of a suspended slab. Also known as **ground beam.**

gradine, gradin A raised step or ledge at the back of an altar.

gradino A decorative scene on a **gradin.**

graduated panel door A door with a series of cross panels that vary from wide at the bottom to narrow at the top.

graffiti The plural form of **graffito,** generally used in the 20c to indicate the result of people scratching or spray painting words or symbols on a building, structure, or object.

graffito (pl. **graffiti**) **1.** A decorative pattern produced by scratching the top layer of a two-color stucco finish. Also known as **sgraffito, black and white work. 2.** A decorative or symbolic pictograph scratched onto a hard surface. See also **graffiti, rock art.**

grain 1. The three-dimensional arrangement of the fibers and pores of wood; types include **bastard grain, close-grained, coarse-grained, open-grained, silver grain. 2.** The pattern of fibers and pores on the cut surface of wood; patterns include **burl, cross grain, curly grain, flat grain, quarter grain, silver grain, swirl, uneven grain, vertical grain, wavy grain.** See also **figure, graining, raised grain. 3.** The surface texture of a material composed of small particles, especially stone.

grain elevator An **elevator** (sense 3) used for grain; usually a large structure in which threshed grains, such as corn or wheat, are lifted from wagons or trucks into an elevated storage bin and later placed in railroad cars or

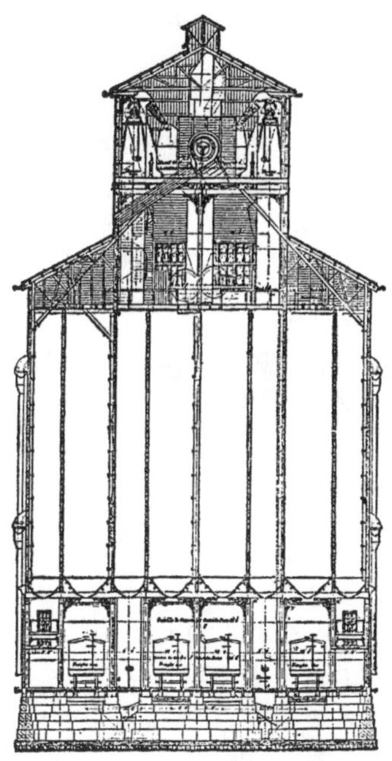

grain elevator

freighters for shipping to market. See also **granary.**

graining Painting that imitates the grain of finish wood; often used on wood to produce the appearance of a more expensive wood; popular in the U.S. from the 18c through mid-19c. Also known as **faux bois.** See also **cissing, marbleized.**

grain tin The best quality of commercial tin.

granary Any building used to store threshed or husked grain, such as wheat or corn. Also known as **cornhouse, garner.** See also **grain elevator.**

Grand Central Station decision A 1978 ruling by the U.S. Supreme Court in *Penn Central* vs. *City of New York,* which stated that a local government has the right to designate a property as historic and that a development restriction is not a taking that requires compensation to the owner.

grandstand, (19c) grand stand The principal viewing platform or seats at a racecourse, parade, or similar event; often covered with a roof.

Grange hall The meeting place of a local lodge of the Order of Patrons of Husbandry, an organization of farmers founded in 1867; named for the ancient term for a farm or barn.

granite 1. A hard, strong, igneous stone composed primarily of quartz and orthoclase feldspar, with mica, hornblende, and other minerals; great variety of color depending on the mix of minerals; quarried in Maine and New Hampshire since the late 18c, with increasing use in buildings in the early 19c with the advent of water-power driven saws; varieties include **Cold Spring granite, Concord granite, Cordova Pink, Dedham granite, Deer Isle granite, Grindstone Islands granite, Hallowell granite, Jonesboro granite, Leetes Island granite, Lithonia granite, Little Rock granite, Lyme granite, Magnet Cove granite, Missouri Red granite, Mount Airy granite, Mount Waldo granite, Oglesby Blue granite, Oriental, Palmer granite, Quincy granite, Red Beach granite, Richmond granite, Rocklin granite, Rockport granite, Rockville granite, St. George granite, Stone Mountain granite, Stony Creek granite, Swenson Buff granite, Swenson Pink granite, Texas Pink granite, Varitone Mahogany, Vinalhaven granite, Weymouth seam face granite, Westerly granite. 2.** Similar igneous building stones, such as **gabbro, gneiss.**

granite block A type of **concrete block** with exposed granite aggregate. Also known as **Boyd Block.**

granite faced block Same as **granite block.**

granulated glass **Obscure glass** with a roughened surface finish.

grapery A greenhouse used for cultivation of grapes.

grapevine joint A tooled **mortar joint** that is flush with adjacent masonry units at the edges and has a projecting bead at the center; may have two colors of mortar as in **tuck pointing.**

grapevine ornament, grapevine pattern Same as **vignette** (sense 1) or **vineyard.**

graphite A black mineral with a metallic sheen composed of carbon; used as **graphite paint** pigment and as a lubricant.

graphite paint A black paint with **graphite** pigment used on metal surfaces; typically mixed with silica and linseed oil.

grass house A dome-shaped dwelling of the Native American Wichitas and Caddoans; constructed of bent poles supported by a cubical log frame and thatched with grass attached to horizontal rods; banked with earth at the bottom.

grass table Same as **earth table.**

grate **1.** (18c–19c) A **cast-iron** container used to burn coal in a fireplace; often had urn-shaped sides in the 18c; hung from fireplace walls or supported on feet. **2.** A horizontal metal grid that supports burning coal or wood in a furnace or stove; typically **cast iron.** Also known as **grating.** See also **gridiron.** **3.** Same as **grating** (sense 1).

graticulated (18c) Divided into squares; the modern term is **reticulated.**

grating **1.** A series of bars set close together in order to prevent passage; may be vertical, such as across a door or window opening, or horizontal, such as a drain cover; may be wood or metal. **2.** Same as **grate** (sense 2). **3.** (19c) Same as **crib** (sense 2).

gravel Small pieces of stone that are larger than **sand** (2.0 mm) and of varying sizes including **pebble gravel, cobble, riprap.**

gravel roof A **built-up roof** with a protective layer of **pebble gravel** on top; used on flat roofs. Also known as **tar-gravel roof.** See also **slag roof.**

gravel stop A continuous band of bent sheet metal with a vertical or sloped projection that prevents gravel on a built-up roof from rolling off the edge.

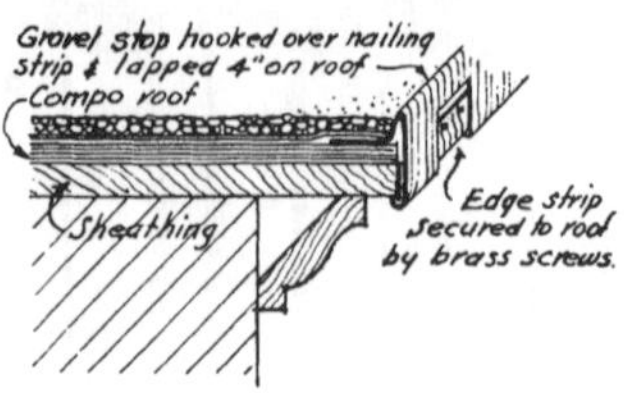

gravel stop

gravestone A stone marker at a grave; typically inscribed with the name and dates of birth and death of the deceased; types include **footstone, headstone, table.** See also **cenotaph, monument, tombstone.**

graveyard Land used for burying the dead; often enclosed with a fence or wall. Also known as **burial ground, cemetery, churchyard.**

gravity hinge A **hinge** that allows a gate or door to close itself due to its weight; such as a **rising hinge.**

gravity supply tank A **house tank,** or hot water tank, used in a **tank system.**

gravity system A hot-water heating system in which the hotter supply water from the boiler is circulated upward through pipes and radiators due to displacement by the heavier cooler water in the return pipes, as opposed to being circulated by a pump.

gravity ventilator A **ventilator** (sense 2) that operates by the normal rise of hot air in a building.

Gray Canyon sandstone A light blue-gray, fine-grained **sandstone** quarried in Ohio; fire resistant and even-textured. See also **Blue Amherst.**

gray iron, grey iron A soft, crystalline metal composed of iron and carbon; has a dull gray color when broken; flows easily when melted; used for **cast iron.**

graywacke slate (pre-20c) A dark gray, fine-grained slate or shale containing mica and sand.

gre, gree (pl. **grece, greese**) (pre-19c) A step or stair.

grease trap A large plumbing drain **trap** with internal baffles that collect kitchen grease; used in commercial and institutional kitchens; may be attached directly under a sink or in the drain line inside or outside the building.

grease trap

great house (southern U.S., West Indies) The main house occupied by the owners of a plantation, as opposed to the other residential buildings, such as the **overseer's house** or **quarters.** Also known as **big house.**

great prickly-coned pine Same as **Sabine's pine.**

great room (pre-19c) The largest or most important room of a building.

grecque Same as a **meander,** especially a simple, single-line form.

Greek key Same as **meander.**

Greek masonry A dry-masonry wall composed of large stone blocks set without mortar.

Greek ovolo A convex molding with a cross section in the form of a half hyperbola joining a fillet; used on a Corinthian style abacus.

Greek pitch (19c) A low-rise gable roof **pitch** with a vertical rise of one-ninth to one-seventh of the span, or 12.5–16 degrees from the horizontal; the norm for premedieval Greek building roof pitches was a rise of one-eighth of the span or 14 degrees. See also **Roman pitch.**

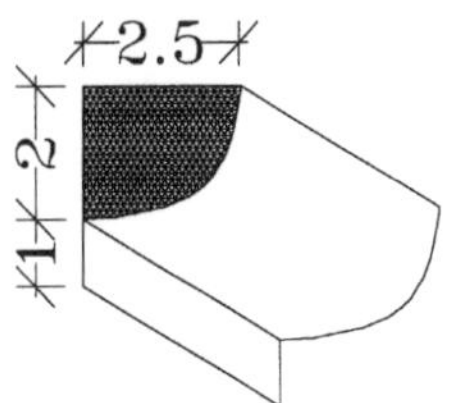

Greek ovolo

Greek Revival style A style of architecture based on Classic Greek temples; used for both public buildings and houses; typical elements include low-pitch gable or hipped roofs, pedimented gable ends, simple architrave bands at the eaves, entry porches with Doric style columns and entablature, front door with narrow sidelights and rectangular fanlight, multipaned double-hung or triple-hung windows; common in the U.S. ca. 1820–60. Also known as the **National style** in the mid-19c. See also **Corinthian, Doric, frieze-band window, Ionic, neoclassical.** *(See illustration p. 218.)*

green **1.** Not yet seasoned or cured; for example, newly cut timber or recently placed concrete or plaster. See also **seasoned wood. 2.** An open, sodded area, including: (a) public land in or adjacent to a town or village; and (b) (18c–early 19c) a lawn adjacent to a private dwelling. See also **greensward.**

green brass A ductile alloy of copper with approximately 15.0 percent zinc and 0.3 percent iron.

Green County sandstone A light gray, even-grained, soft **sandstone** quarried in Green County, Pennsylvania; easily worked when first quarried.

Greenfield conduit A trademarked **flexible metal conduit;** still in use.

greenhouse, (18c) **green-house, green house** A building, or portion of a building, with glazed roof and walls used for growing plants; typically

Greek Revival style
Dr. John Mathews House
Painsville, Ohio, 1829

has artificial heat; specialized varieties include **conservatory, hothouse, orangery, palm house, rose house, winter garden.** Also known as **glass house.** See also **Rendle system.**

greenroom **1.** In a theater, a backstage room where performers wait to go on stage; originally decorated in green. **2.** A space where green materials, such as unfired pottery or uncut cloth, are kept. **3.** (pre-20c) An examination room in a medical school.

greenstone Any green volcanic rock, such as **diorite.**

greensward (pre-20c) A grassy area, such as a **lawn.**

green verdigris See **verdigris.**

gridiron A frame with iron bars used to support cooking pots above a fire; usually has a rectangular pattern of parallel bars. See also **grate.**

gridiron plan A town or city street layout based on a rectangular or square grid.

griffe A claw, or other carved shape, projecting from the round base of a column toward each corner of a square plinth block; used in the Gothic Revival style. Also known as **spur.**

Griffith's zinc white Same as **lithopone.**

grillage A foundation composed of a layer of adjacent parallel beams supported by one or more similar perpendicular layers; used to distribute the vertical load from a column over a large area; may use timbers or rolled iron beams; iron grillage is typically embedded in concrete.

grille **1.** (19c) An elaborate wrought-metal gate or similar device that acts as a barrier to entry. **2.** Lacy metalwork that covers an opening, such as a cast-iron cover over a ventilating duct or ironwork outside a window. See also **grate.**

Grindstone Islands granite A red and pink **granite** quarried on the Grindstone Islands in New York; used for building stone, including two large columns in the New York State Capitol.

grisaille See **en grisaille.**

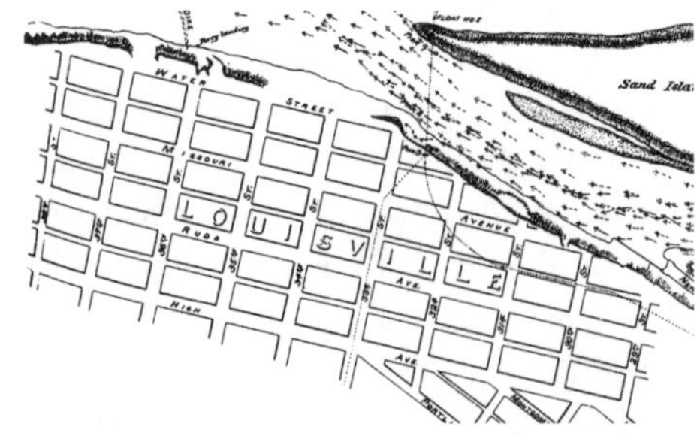

gridiron plan

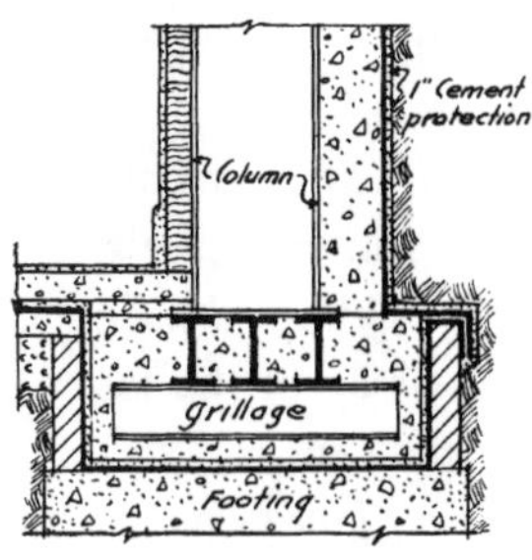

grillage

grisaille glass A decorative stained-glass window in which the pattern or illustration is done entirely **en grisaille** in tones of gray and black.

gristmill, (19c) **grist-mill,** (pre-20c) **grist mill** A **mill** for grinding grain.

groin **1.** The line formed by the intersection of two vaults. **2.** A wall or berm constructed perpendicular to a shoreline to reduce beach erosion; often a **riprap wall.**

groin arch **1.** Same as **groined vault. 2.** Same as **groin rib;** forms an arched shape.

groined vault Construction in the form of intersecting vaults that have a **groin** or **groin rib;** most often with two semicircular barrel vaults with their axes crossing at right angles, a 90-degree groin angle at the springing, and covering a square space; may also be other combinations of shapes, such as a semicircular vault intersecting a semielliptical vault to cover a rectangular space, or a **Welsh groin.** Also known as **groin vault.**

groining A structural system of groin vaults.

groin point (19c) A **groin** without a rib.

groin rib A projecting stone rib along a groin of a **groin vault.** Also known as **springer.**

groin vault Same as **groined vault.**

groove, (18c) **grove** A continuous recess cut in a member; typically rectangular in cross section. See also **flute, tongue and groove.**

gross floor area The total area of all the levels of a building, especially as defined in the **zoning** for a locality.

grotesque A sculptural decoration in the form of a fantastic beast or human, often surrounded by foliage and flowers; types include **gorgon, gargoyle,** half-human and half-animal figures, and a man or beast emerging from a flower. See also **sphinx.**

grotto, (18c) **grotta** A simulated cave in a garden, usually with a fountain; may be constructed of stone or artificial materials.

ground beam **1.** (19c) Same as **sleeper. 2.** (19c) Same as **groundsill. 3.** Same as **grade beam.**

ground floor The floor or story of a building located at, or slightly above, the adjoining **grade;** implies all of the construction up to the floor above, excluding the **basement** or **cellar.** Also known as **first floor, ground story.** See also **upper floor.**

ground frame (pre-19c) Same as **groundsill.**

ground glass Glass with a finely roughened, translucent surface produced by grinding, acid etching, or sand blasting; varieties include **half-clear glass.**

ground joist (19c) A joist supporting a basement floor.

ground lease A contract for use of land, usually for an extended period of time, such as 99 years; typically ownership of improvements, such as a **building,** reverts to the landowner at the end of the lease.

ground niche (19c) A niche, or similar recess, in which the floor is level with the surrounding grade or ground floor.

ground plan A **floor plan** of the ground floor of a building. Also known as **ground plot.**

ground plate Same as **groundsill.**

ground plot **1.** Same as **ground plan. 2.** Same as **lot.**

ground rent Rent paid for use of land, rather than a building, especially under a **ground lease.**

grounds **1.** Strips of wood used with a plaster finish as trim nailers and guides in plastering;

typically ¾–⅞ × 2 inches. **2.** Blocks of wood placed in a masonry wall for attachment of trim, furring, or jambs.

groundsill, ground-sill, ground sill, (19c) **groundsel,** (pre-19c) **groundsell** The lowest horizontal timber in a wood frame building into which the wall members are framed; typically rests on top of the foundation wall; **timber frame** types include **cross sill, main sill.** Also known as **ground frame, ground plate, sill.** See also **mudsill, sole.**

ground story The story of a building at **ground floor** level.

ground table Same as **earth table.**

groundwork **1.** Excavation and/or fill prior to laying a **foundation.** **2.** (pre-20c) Same as **foundation.** **3.** (pre-19c) Same as **groundsill.**

grouped Individual buildings placed close together.

grouped columns, group of columns A center pier closely surrounded by multiple smaller shafts, or three or more columns on the same pedestal. See also **coupled.**

grouping (19c) The architectural form of the major exterior elements of a building; for example, a main pavilion plus its wings or the base, shaft, and capital division of the facade of a tall building.

grout **1.** A mortar mix with sufficient water added so that the mortar flows without the ingredients separating; often used to fill narrow openings in a masonry wall and below a **bearing plate;** types include **nonshrink grout.** See also **dry-pack.** **2.** A cementitious material used to fill the exposed joints between ceramic tiles.

grove **1.** A group of trees, especially when closely spaced and without underbrush. **2.** (18c) Same as **groove.**

growth ring Same as **annual ring.**

grozed, grosed (pre-20c) Cut or smoothed with a grozing iron; composed of a cut pane of glass and a smoothed lead pipe joint or smoothed lead **came.**

guard bar **1.** (19c) A horizontal safety rail across a window opening; typically a single bar. **2.** On a pair of sliding glass doors, a bar placed between the stile of the inner door and the jamb to prevent entry.

guardhouse, (19c) **guard-house,** (pre-19c) **guard house** **1.** A building in which sentries are stationed; typically a small structure. **2.** A military **jail.**

guard lock A dike or dam that separates two bodies of water; used to dam and raise the level of a stream or to reduce tidal level changes; may be used in combination with a **lift-lock.**

guardrail, (19c) **guard-rail** **1.** A **railing** used to prevent falls or entry to a dangerous area; may be a single horizontal bar or a more elaborate design. **2.** A rail on the inside of the main rail of a railroad track that keeps the wheels from slipping off the track; used at tight curves and switches.

guard timber A timber placed along the edge of a bridge roadway to keep vehicles from hitting the side.

Guastavino tile, Guastavino vaulting (late 19c–early 20c) Ceramic tile set in quick-setting portland cement mortar to form fire-resistant, lightweight, vaulted ceilings similar to those of Catalonia; popularized by architect/builder Rafael Guastavinos y Moreno (1842–1908) in projects such as C. W. Vanderbilt's Biltmore estate in Asheville, North Carolina, and the main building at Ellis Island, New York.

gudgeon A pintle-shaped portion of a wrought-iron hinge, fixed to a jamb and supporting a strap with an eye.

guele (18c) Same as **gula.**

guest chamber (pre-19c) Same as **spare room.**

guesthouse, (19c) **guest-house,** (pre-19c) **guest house** **1.** A secondary dwelling used for the temporary housing of guests. **2.** (pre-20c) A building used for housing and entertaining travelers; for example, an **inn.**

guglia A building, or portion of a building, shaped like a pyramid.

guildhall **1.** (17c) A hall or building in which a trade group or guild meets. **2.** Same as a town or city hall.

guilloche A bas-relief decorative band with continuous, interlocking, curved patterns, such as a ribbon that creates linked circles. See also **fret, meander.**

guilloche

gula, (pre-20c) **gola,** (18c) **gule,** (18c) **guele** **1.** (18c–19c) Same as **ogee,** especially a **cyma reversa;** of Italian origin. **2.** (18c) Same as **cavetto.** **3.** (19c) Any molding or group of moldings having a large concave profile. Also known as **gorge.**

gum elastic (19c) Same as natural rubber. Also known as **caoutchouc.** See also **gutta percha.**

gun-barrel drain A small-diameter drain with a cylindrical cross section.

gunstock stile A **diminished stile** on a door, with a sloped reduction in width; typically the sloped portion is across the width of the lock rail.

Gunter's chain An iron chain with 7.92-inch-long links used to measure land through the 19c; 100 links equal 66 feet, and 100,000 square links equal an **acre.** See also **survey.**

gusset, gusset plate **1.** A triangular metal plate that connects and/or stiffens the ends of truss members or other framework. **2.** An angle iron or bracket that stiffens a connection or joint.

gut (18c) Same as **gutter.**

gut job Same as **gut rehab.**

gut rehab Rehabilitation of a building that includes removal, or gutting, of most of the nonstructural interior construction; may include removal of partitions, architectural finishes, and mechanical, plumbing, and electrical systems.

gutta (pl. **guttae**) **1.** One of six small, dovetail-shaped drops located on a **Doric** architrave below the **taenia** and centered on the **triglyph** above. See also **regula.** **2.** One of 18 or 36 short cylindrical drops exposed at the bottom of a **mutule** on a Doric cornice. Also known as **campana, drop, tree nail.** **3.** Abbr. for **gutta percha** or other similar gums.

gutta percha A brownish red natural gum similar to rubber, made from the sap of the evergreen Malaysian trees *Isonandra gutta* and *Dichopsis gutta;* insoluble in water; used as a **rubber insulation** substitute for electric **insulated wire** ca. 1900 through the 1920s.

guttae Plural of **gutta.**

gutter A horizontal or slightly sloped trough that collects rainwater; may be located at the bottom edge of a roof slope or be a channel cut in the ground; types include **arris gutter, canale, fillet gutter, flush gutter, parallel gutter, parapet gutter, pole gutter, vertical gutter.**

gutter board **1.** One of the boards that supports a lead gutter. **2.** A board that bridges over a gutter between the road surface and the top of the curb; used to permit vehicle access. Also known as **gutter plank.** **3.** (18c) A board placed in a roof valley to provide a flat surface on which to lay tiles or lead.

guttered Notched, especially the interior corner of a timber frame post; used so that the larger members do not project through the plaster finish.

gutter hook A cast-iron hook that supports a hung gutter.

gutter member The decorated face of a gutter that forms part of a cornice or other architectural ornament.

gutter plank Same as **gutter board** (sense 2).

gutter spout **1.** Same as **downspout.** **2.** Same as **gargoyle.**

gutter strip Same as **flush gutter.**

gutter tile A concave terra-cotta roof tile; may be a **tegula,** semicircular, or other curved shape; used in **normal tiling** or to form a roof valley. See also **undertile.**

guy wire A tensioned wire or cable that stiffens a structure; usually sloped and one of several.

gymnasium **1.** A room or building used for exercise and sometimes for sporting events; from the Greek for "training naked." **2.** (pre-20c) A Latin or classical school, as opposed to a technical school; usually of lower-level instruction than a college or university.

gymnosperm See **softwood.**

gypsum A white, crystalline mineral composed of hydrated calcium sulfate, $CaSO_4 \cdot 2H_2O$; used in **plaster** and **drywall.** Also known as **plaster stone.** See also **alabaster, gypsum crust, gypsum plaster, plaster of Paris.**

gypsum board A type of **wallboard** composed of a relatively thin sheet of gypsum plaster with a paper facing and backing; used in a **drywall** system; varieties include **Sheetrock.** Also known as **gypsum wallboard.** See also **plasterboard.**

gypsum concrete A type of **concrete** composed of a mixture of gypsum, aggregate, and water.

gypsum crust A surface deposit on marble and limestone formed by the reaction of calcite in the stone with airborne sulfur dioxide (SO_2); typically more friable than the stone substrate; usually contains dark soot particles that turn the stone black in sheltered areas not washed by rainwater.

gypsum lath **Plasterboard** composed of a gypsum core with paper facing; may be perforated to form a **key.**

gypsum plaster A hard, fire-resistant, quick-setting **plaster** with ground and calcined gypsum mixed with a retarder as the main ingredient; base coats are gypsum mixed with sand and hair; finish coat is neat gypsum plaster.

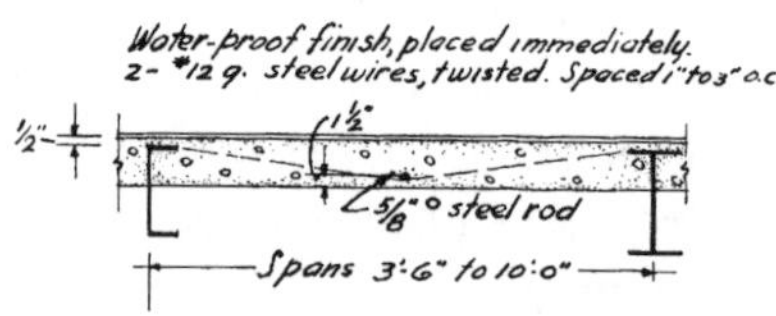

gypsum roof deck

gypsum roof deck A structural roof deck composed of gypsum concrete with a reinforcing mesh and supported by gypsum formboards.

ha-ha, (pre-20c) **haw-haw** A retaining wall, fence, or hedge hidden from view in a ditch; often used to improve the view from a house or main building while keeping out livestock. Also known as **aha, ha-ha wall, ha-ha fence, scarped ditch, sunk fence.**

ha-ha fence A fence hidden from view in a ditch. Also known as **sunk fence.**

ha-ha wall Same as **ha-ha.**

habitacle, habitacule (pre-20c) **1.** A dwelling. **2.** A niche or recess.

habitation site An **archaeological site** where people lived or worked over a period of time.

HABS **Historic American Buildings Survey**

HABS/HAER Standards The U.S. Secretary of the Interior's Standards for Architectural and Engineering Documentation as published in the *Federal Register* on September 29, 1983; defines the products acceptable for inclusion in the Building Survey and Engineering Record collections in the Library of Congress, including **measured drawings, large-format photography,** and written data. See also **documentation.**

hacienda (Mexico, southwestern U.S.) The main house on a large ranch.

hack A yard, shed, or frame used for air-drying green bricks.

hacking **1. Ashlar** in which the bond pattern is interrupted with two short-height courses instead of one standard course. **2.** Laying bricks so that the bottom edge is set in from the plane surface of the wall. See also **random-coursed ashlar.**

HAER **Historic American Engineering Record**

Hague Convention Short for the International Convention for the Protection of Cultural Property in the Event of Armed Conflict, a 1954 United Nations–sponsored treaty that includes measures for the protection of historic sites during war or natural disaster; U.S. and Canada, especially.

hairpin filament bulb Same as **carbon filament bulb.**

half-and-half solder A metal **solder** composed of equal parts lead and tin; no longer used in plumbing.

half arch One-half of a full **arch;** typically used with a quarter round window or in the lower part of a buttress. See also **flying buttress, straining arch.**

half bath (20c) A small room with a **lavatory** and **water closet.** See also **bathroom.**

half Cape See **half house.**

half-clear glass Sheet glass with a partially ground finish. See also **ground glass.**

half door A short **door** installed in the frame with space left above and below the door. See also **Dutch door.**

half-dovetail lap A **lap joint** in which a trapezoidal notch in one wood member is overlapped by a corresponding projection on the end of another member; often used to connect a collar beam to a rafter.

half-dovetail notch An interlocking **notching** system used at the corners in log construction; the shape of the ends of each log is a trapezoid.

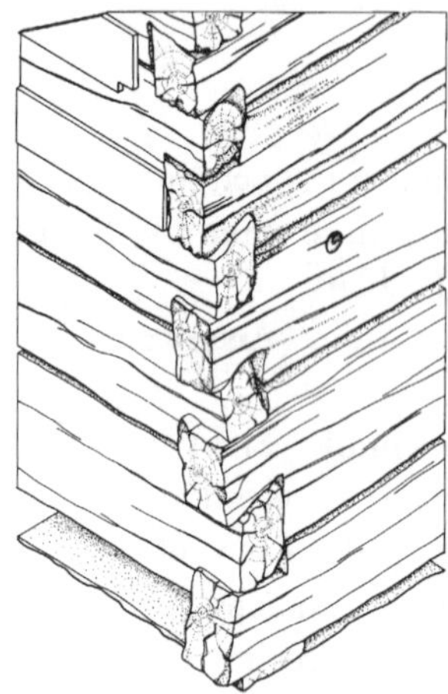

half-dovetail notch

half frame Same as **combination frame.**

half-hipped roof Same as **gambrel roof.**

half house A **Cape Cod** or **saltbox** house that has two windows on one side of the front door and none on the other side; also known as **half Cape.** See also **side hall house.**

half lap A **lap joint** in which a rectangular notch in the end of one wood member overlaps a corresponding notch in the end of another member.

half-lattice girder (19c) A metal girder with upper and lower flanges connected by diagonal struts that form triangular openings. See also **lattice beam.**

half moon Same as **ravelin.** See also **lunette.**

halfpace, (18c) **half-pace, half pace,** (17c) **halfe pace** A stair landing that connects parallel flights traveling in opposite directions; typically with a rectangular plan. See also **half quarterpace, pace.**

half pitch, ½ pitch A gable roof in which the slope of the rise is equal to half of the span, or 45 degrees above the horizontal. Also known as **true pitch.**

half quarterpace A stair **landing** in the shape of a 45-degree triangle; where a stair makes a right-angle turn, with the balance of the **quarterpace** occupied by winders.

half rail A projecting molding at handrail height on the wall enclosing a staircase; often above a **wainscot.** Also known as **surbase.**

half relief, half-relief A **relief** sculpture or form that is intermediate between **bas-relief** and **high relief;** projecting forms are less than half of the natural circumference; not an exact term. Also known as **medium relief, mezzo-relievo.**

half round A semicircular **molding.**

half S-trap (pre-WWI) Same as **P-trap.**

half-timbered **1.** A building constructed with a timber frame infilled with plastered nogging so that the timbers form a geometric pattern on the exterior; rare in North America; New England examples are usually sheathed with **weatherboard.** See also **post and pane. 2.**

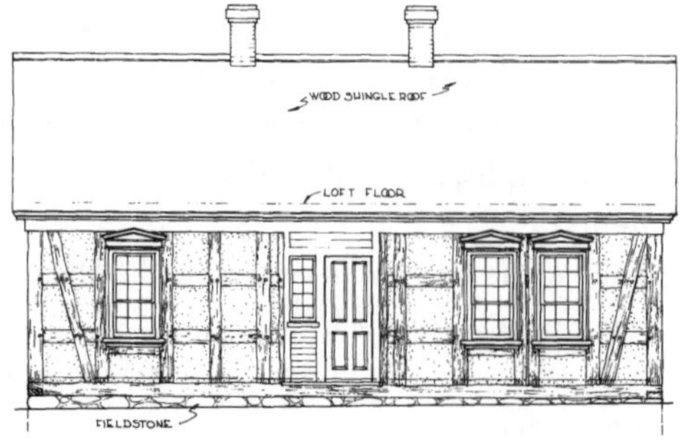

half-timbered (sense 1)
Rusch Cottage
Washington County, Wisconsin, ca. 1845

Having the exterior appearance described in sense 1 but constructed with various other framing systems and finish materials; common in the **Queen Anne style** and **Tudor Revival style.**

half-tuck pointing Same as **beaded joint.**

half-turn stair A **stair** with three flights at right angles and a U-shaped plan; may have winders or a quarter-pace landing at the turns.

half Y-branch A drainpipe fitting similar to a **Y-branch,** with the branch pipe entering at a 60-degree angle.

hall **1.** A large room for public assembly, such as the **hall** of the House of Representatives; types include **dining hall, lecture hall.** **2.** A building devoted to public or fraternal use, such as **city hall** or Faneuil **Hall** in Boston. See also **praise hall.** **3.** (19c–present) A passageway that connects multiple rooms on a floor, especially within a dwelling. See also **corridor, hall chamber, living hall, stair hall.** **4.** (pre-19c) A large private residence, especially on a plantation, such as Gunston **Hall** in Virginia. **5.** (17c–18c) A large ground-floor space in a dwelling, with direct access from the exterior; the principal entertaining space, as well as a place for cooking, eating, and sleeping. See also **servant's hall.**

hall-and-parlor (17c) A common type of small, one-story, side-gabled house with two rooms; the larger hall room was entered directly from the outside and served as both living space and kitchen; the smaller parlor room was entered from the hall and typically was used as a bedroom; variations include porches, rear additions, and center or end fireplaces; found mainly in southeastern U.S.

hall back chamber A room located behind a hall. See also **chamber.**

hall chamber A room located above a hall. See also **chamber.**

hall of mirrors A large room in which the walls are covered with framed mirrors, especially in 18c French style; origin is Hall of Mirrors at Versailles. Also known as **gallery of mirrors.**

Hallowell granite A light gray, fine-textured **granite** quarried in the vicinity of Hallowell, Maine; used for building stone (e.g., in the New York State Capitol).

halon gas system A **foam extinguishing system** that uses halogen gases to extinguish fires; used primarily for historic interiors and museum collections that would be damaged by water from a **sprinkler system;** commonly installed in the period ca. 1970–90; new systems are now outlawed in the U.S. because of environmental concerns regarding halon gas.

halving joint A **joint** formed by two boards with equal shaped rabbeted grooves along their edges; the boards are lapped so that the grooves interlock.

hammer beam A short wood beam spanning from a bearing wall to the end of a wall bracket and carrying a vertical member that helps support a principal rafter.

hammer beam truss A timber frame roof **truss** with one or two pairs of hammer beams; common in Gothic style architecture.

hammer-dressed Stone blocks roughly smoothed with only a hammer. See also **bush hammered, nigged, stonework.**

hammered work Metalwork made by hammering, such as **wrought iron** or **repoussé.**

hanch (18c) Same as **haunch.**

hand The direction in which a door opens; if one stands with one's back to the hinged jamb, a door that swings to the left side is **left hand,** and a door that swings to the right side is **right hand.**

hand arch An arch constructed without centering support, typically by using a template as a guide.

hand-hewn Wood roughly squared with hand tools such as a broad axe.

handicap accessibility See **accessibility.**

hand-planed Smoothed with a hand-held planing tool; may be a flat surface or molded.

hand plate A thin protective sheet attached to a door where it is handled in opening and closing; typically metal or glass with various finishes, including porcelain-glazed metal. See also **push plate.**

handrail A **rail** or **railing** with the top at hand height; used to prevent falls (e.g., along the edge of a floor opening) and to provide a hand grip (e.g., at the side of a stair); elements may include **ramp, swan neck, twist.** See also **baluster, guardrail, half rail.**

hand-sawn Manually sawn wood, as opposed to **hand-hewn** or **mill sawn;** typically refers to **lumber.**

hand-split rail See **split rail.**

hand-tooled, hand tooling The hand-chiseled surface texture of stone blocks; markings may be parallel or random. See also **stonework.**

hangar 1. (20c) A storage building for airplanes; from the French term. 2. [French] An open shed or lean-to.

hanger See **beam hanger, door hanger.**

hanger board The insulating board that supports an **arc lamp;** has a hand switch and hooks that complete the electrical connection when the board is hung in place.

hanging buttress A buttress-like projection from a masonry wall supported by a corbel; used to visually complete a series of buttresses or to resist the thrust of an arch.

hanging pew (18c) An elevated, enclosed pew; may be hung from roof trusses or raised on posts; built in Anglican churches in Virginia by the local gentry.

hanging post **1.** A vertical roof truss element, such as a **kingpost** or **queenpost. 2.** The portion of a doorframe on which the door hinges are mounted. **3.** The gatepost to which a gate is hinged. Also known as **hinge post, swinging post.** See also **shutting post.**

hanging rail The rail to which the hinges are attached on the top or bottom of a door, shutter, or sash. See also **hanging stile.**

hanging stair A stone **stair** supported by individual hanging steps projecting horizontally from a wall on one side, sometimes with corbels or brackets.

hanging step One of the individual stone steps of a **hanging stair.**

hanging stile **1.** The stile of a door or casement window to which the hinges are attached. **2.** Same as **blind stop.**

hanse arch Same as **haunched arch.**

hapse (18c) Same as **hasp.**

hardboard A dense, smooth-surfaced **composition board** composed of highly compressed fibers; varieties include **Masonite.**

hard-burned Clay masonry units, such as bricks, fired at high temperatures and partly vitrified, resulting in high compressive strength and low absorption. See also **clinker brick.**

hard costs The portion of a development budget directly related to construction costs; includes monies paid to construction contractors and testing agencies. Also known as **bricks and mortar.** See also **land costs, soft costs.**

hardened glass (19c) Same as **tempered glass.**

harder steel (19c) Same as **hard steel.**

hard finish Same as a plaster **finish coat.**

hard kiln run brick A hard-burned **brick** suitable for exterior use. Also known as **face brick.**

hard maple The wood of the **sugar maple** tree and related species.

hard oil (mid-20c) An inexpensive varnish composed of a drying oil, made by heating rosin or copal, and turpentine or a substitute; used only in interiors.

hard pan Earth composed of a dense, compacted mixture of clay, gravel, and/or sand.

hard solder **1.** A **brass** alloy composed of copper and zinc and used in **brazing** to join two pieces of metal; melts above 800 degrees Fahrenheit. **2.** Any **solder** that melts at high temperature, as opposed to a **soft solder.**

hard soldering Same as **brazing.**

hard steel A very hard, brittle, high-carbon **steel** with more than 0.60 percent carbon content; used for springs and rails. Also known as **high steel, ingot steel.** See also **high test iron.**

hardware See **builder's hardware.**

hardware cloth A square **mesh** formed of woven steel wire; typically galvanized; most commonly 2 or 2.5 meshes to the inch. Also known as **wire cloth, wire lath.**

hardwood **Wood** cut from a broadleaf tree that produces fruits and flowers, typically deciduous; often denser and harder than wood from evergreen trees; used for fine millwork and flooring, and, before ca. 1865, for framing and siding; types include **alder, ash, birch, black cherry, brazil wood, butternut, mahogany, maple, oak, poplar, satin wood, tulip tree, walnut.** See also **softwood.**

hasp, (18c) **hapse, haspe** A hardware device used for locking a gate or rustic door; may consist of a hinged plate that engages a large **staple** and is locked with a padlock, or simply a staple and hook. See also **lock.**

hatch **1.** (19c to present) An opening in a floor or roof with a removable cover. See also **scuttle, trapdoor.** **2.** A half door or gate with an opening above.

hatched molding Same as **notched molding.**

haunch, (18c) **hanch** One of the pair of outer ends of the intrados of an **arch** between the crown and the abutments; the extent of the haunches is not exactly defined. Also known as **hanse, reins.**

haunched arch, haunch arch An **arch** in which the haunches have a different curve than the crown, especially when distinguished by the design of the archivolt.

haunched beam A beam that is narrower at the middle than at the ends.

hayloft The open, upper level of a barn used to store hay. See also **loft, haymow, hay room.**

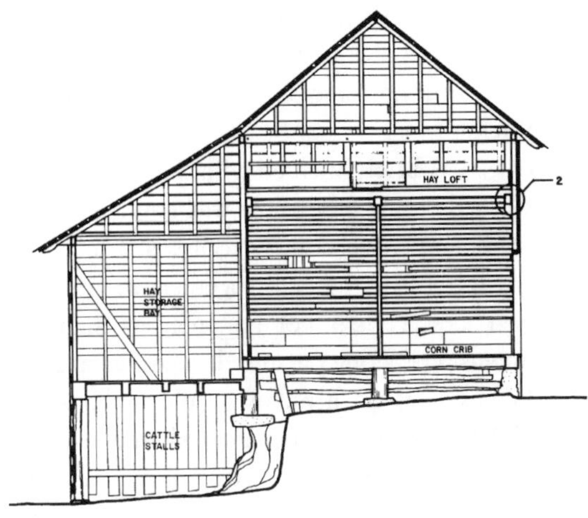

hayloft
Harper-Featherstone Farm
Abbeville County, South Carolina

haymow A large space within a barn used for storing a mow of hay. See also **hayloft, hay room.**

hay room, hay-room (18c) A space within a stable used for storing hay. See also **hayloft, haymow.**

hazardous material Any material that can directly or indirectly cause bodily harm to the occupants of a building; types include **asbestos, PCB.**

H-beam An **H-section** used as a beam.

HCF **Heritage Canada Foundation**

H-column An **H-section** used as a column. Also known as **Bethlehem column.**

HCRS **Heritage Conservation and Recreation Service**

head **1.** The covered portion of a tile, slate, or shingle, as opposed to the **tail.** See also **back.** **2.** Same as **head tile.** **3.** The top of an architectural element, especially a door or window opening. **4.** The enlarged upper end of a **nail.**

head block A rectangular wood block used at the upper corners of window and door casings; installed with the longer dimension vertical; sometimes decorated with a milled bull's-eye and horizontal moldings. See also **corner block.**

header **1.** A **brick** oriented with the smaller end exposed on the face of the wall and the smallest dimension vertical; typically used to bond two wythes of the wall together. **2.** A brick used as a voussoir of an arch; its shortest dimension is along the intrados, and its middle dimension is on a radius of the arch. **3.** In **stick frame** construction, a wood lintel over an opening that supports the structure above; may be a single 2× or be built-up of two or more pieces. Also known as **header beam.** **4.** A short joist or rafter that runs perpendicular to the length of the others and supports the end of one or more joists or rafters; used to frame around openings and projections such as a stairwell or chimney breast. See also **trimmer, tailpiece.** **5.** The top rail of a window sash.

header beam Same as a **header** (sense 3).

header bond A brick bond composed entirely of **header courses;** common in pre-19c Annapolis and the eastern shore of Maryland. Also known as **heading bond.**

header course A brick **bond course** composed of continuous headers. Also known as **heading course.**

header joist Same as **header** (sense 4).

header tile A structural clay tile unit with a recess for brick headers; used as backup.

head gate **1.** The upper **gate** of a **lift-lock.** See also **tail gate.** **2.** A gate that controls the flow of water into a flume, sluice, or similar conduit.

headhouse A building enclosing the headframe and machinery at the top of a mine shaft.

heading bond Same as **header bond.**

heading course A course of brick composed entirely of headers.

head joint, (19c) **header joint,** (19c) **heading joint** **1.** The vertical **masonry joint** between two adjacent masonry units, or the sloped joint between adjacent voussoirs. Also known as **cross joint.** **2.** Any joint across the end or top of an element, such as the end of a floorboard. **3.** Same as **butt joint** (sense 3). **4.** The horizontal millwork at the top of a door opening.

headless brad A **brad** (sense 2) with no projection at the head.

head lining The horizontal wood member between the interior face of a **window head** and the trim; typically with a tongue projecting into the window head. See also **jamb lining.**

head molding Same as **hood mold.**

headpost A post at the closed end of a horse or cattle stall that supports the side wall rails or boards.

headrail (19c) The horizontal **rail** at the top of a doorframe.

headroom The clear vertical distance between a floor or stair tread and the ceiling or other overhead obstruction.

headstone **1.** A stone marker placed at the head of a grave; typically inscribed and sometimes decorated with carving. **2.** (pre-20c) The principal stone of a building, such as a cornerstone or keystone.

head tile A half-length tile used at the eaves. Also known as **head.**

head tree Same as **bolster.**

heart **1.** The portion of a **came** that connects the two flanges; typically a rectangular bar shape. **2.** Same as **heartwood.**

heart-and-dart Same as **leaf-and-dart.**

heart bond A brick **bond** in which two headers butt in the center of the wall and the joint is covered by headers above and below.

hearth, (pre-19c) **harth** **1.** The level portion of a **fireplace** that supports the fire or grate. **2.** (18c–present) The floor in front of a fireplace that is covered with a fire-resistant material. See also **hearthstone.** **3.** (to early 18c) Same as **fireplace.**

hearthstone A stone slab used for a **hearth.** See also **firestone.**

hearth trimmer One of a pair of trimmer beams that supports the sides of a hearth, especially in conjunction with a **trimmer arch.**

hearting (19c) The interior portion of a masonry wall or element, rather than the face.

heart pine Heartwood lumber cut from original growth **pine** forests; has dense, thin growth rings that produce an exceptionally strong wood with a straight grain. See also **southern yellow pine.**

heart shake An internal crack or **shake** across the center of a tree. See also **star shake.**

heartwood The center portion of a tree trunk that is no longer growing or carrying the sap; often harder, denser, and of a different color than the **sapwood.** Also known as **clear of sap.**

heat aspiration The circulation of fresh air by heating the room air and thereby inducing an upward draft; typically accomplished by building vertical masonry chases adjacent to a chimney flue; apparently first used by Desaguliers to ventilate the British House of Parliament in 1723. See also **ventilation.**

heat detector An automatic device for detecting the combustion products of a fire; originally developed in the 1860s; an alarm sounds when a fixed temperature is reached or the rate of temperature rise exceeds a predetermined rate; types include **line detector, spot detector.** See also **electric fire extinguisher, fire detector, fire protection system.**

heating Artificially raising the temperature of an interior space through use of heating devices such as a **fireplace, furnace, heat pump, radiator, or stove** and heating systems such as **forced-air heating, hot-water heating, steam heating.**

heating, ventilating, and air conditioning (HVAC) The mechanical systems that control the temperature, fresh-air flow, and, sometimes, the humidity and airborne dust level inside a building. See also **air conditioning, heating, ventilation.**

heat pump An electrically powered forced ventilation **air-conditioning** and **heating** device employing a heat exchanger; the most common type operates as a standard air conditioner for cooling and reverses the cycle for heating.

heat-strengthened glass (20c) **Glass** that is reheated and cooled after initial manufacture to increase its break resistance. Also known as **annealed glass.** See also **tempered glass.**

heave-off hinge Same as **loose-joint hinge.**

heavy oil Same as **creosote.**

heavy spar Same as **barite.**

heavy timber construction A building code designation indicating a building frame is fire resistant due in part to the large size of the wood framing members; the structural beams and columns are a minimum of 6 inches in any dimension. See also **slow-burning mill construction, timber frame.**

heavy-wooded pine Same as **ponderosa pine.**

heel **1.** The lower end of a **stud** or **rafter.** See also **bird's-mouth, seat cut.** **2.** (19c) Same as **cyma reversa.**

heel cut Same as **seat cut.**

heel joint The **joint** at the end of a **truss** where a diagonal top chord intersects the bottom chord; for a timber truss, may be a cast-iron shoe, wood bolster, or gusset plate.

heel post **1.** Same as **pintle.** **2.** A post at the open end of a horse or cattle stall that supports the side rails or boards. **3.** A **hanging post** on which the hinges of a gate are fastened.

helix **1.** Anything with a spiral shape, especially the three-dimensional geometric form of a line wrapped around a cylinder at an incline. **2.** The spiral pattern of a **volute,** especially with a progressively projecting center, such as on a Corinthian capital; represents a spirally rolled acanthus stalk. Also known as **caulicole.**

helix stair An open **stair** with a circular plan; the outer ends of the treads trace a **helix** shape; more commonly known as a **spiral stair.**

helm roof A spire formed by four steeply inclined planes, each having a gable at its base.

hem The raised border of the **volute** of an **Ionic** capital.

hemiglyph One-half of a V-shaped **glyph,** especially a 45-degree chamfer on the outside vertical edges of a **triglyph.** Also known as **semiglyph.**

hemispherical vault A masonry dome with a semicircular cross section.

hemitryglyph A half **triglyph,** as at an interior corner.

hemlock One of various softwood trees of the genus *Tsuga;* species include **eastern hemlock, mountain hemlock, western hemlock;** *tsuga* is the Japanese word for hemlock.

hemlock-fir Same as **eastern hemlock.**

hemlock pitch A pitch made in North America by boiling down the sap of the hemlock tree. Also known as **Canada pitch.**

hemlock-spruce Same as **eastern hemlock.**

hemp house (20c) A theater in which scenery and equipment are lifted into the fly by hand-operated stage rigging made of hemp rope rather than by electric winches.

henhouse, (19c) **hen-house,** (pre-19c) **hen house** A building used for sheltering chickens or other fowl; typically with elevated nesting boxes. Also known as **chicken house, fowl house, poultry house.** See also **chicken coop.**

heptastyle Having a row of seven columns across a facade or portico. See also **columniation.**

herbarium A room, building, or institution that houses a collection of dried plant specimens for scientific study.

heritage **1.** Property that is inherited. **2.** Something other than property, such as tradition or culture, that is passed on from preceding generations. **3.** Anything from the past that has meaning or value for the present and the future; includes physical **cultural artifacts** and the natural environment, as well as intangible cultural values; the term is more commonly used in Canada and by international organizations than in the U.S. See also **World Heritage Committee.**

heritage area (Canada) **1.** A synonym for a designated historic district or conservation area that denotes a neighborhood unified by similar use, architectural style, and/or historical development. **2.** A generic term used to signify those geographical areas included in the Environment Canada-Parks Service Program; types include National Parks, National Marine Conservation Areas, National Historic Sites, and Historic Canals. See also **historic district, heritage corridor.**

heritage building (Canada) Same as **historic building.**

Heritage Canada Foundation A national, non-profit, membership-based organization established in Canada in 1973 to encourage Canadians to identify, protect, and enhance their cultural, built, and natural environments.

heritage conservation (Canada) **Historic preservation** and the **conservation** and presentation of **heritage** (sense 3) by various means.

Heritage Conservation District (Canada) A **heritage area** designated under the Provincial Heritage Act.

heritage covenant (Canada) A **restrictive covenant** placed on a heritage property by the current owner to ensure its future preservation. See also **heritage easement.**

heritage designation (Canada) Designation of a site, building, structure, or object as a provincial or municipal **heritage site** or **heritage object;** the government may decline permits to alter or demolish a property with a provincial heritage designation or **freeze** a designated municipal property.

heritage easement A **preservation easement** on a **heritage building** that is given or sold by the owner to another party. See also **heritage covenant.**

Heritage Regions (Canada) Introduced by Heritage Canada in 1988; conservation of heritage resources as a catalyst for rural and regional development.

heritage resource (Canada) A site, building, structure, or environment that may have architectural, historical, contextual, archaeological, cultural, and/or natural interest and that may warrant national designation for historic significance.

heritage river (Canada) **1.** A river or section of a river that has been determined by the Canadian Heritage Rivers Board to have outstanding Canadian natural heritage, human heritage, and/or recreational value. See also **Historic Canal.**

heritage significance See **significance.**

heritage site (Canada) A place or area, including buildings, structures, plants, landforms, and objects, that has heritage **significance.**

heritage village (Canada) A collection of historic buildings that has been moved to a site for use as an **outdoor museum.**

herm A column in the form of a three-quarter-length human figure on a pedestal. See also **atlas, caryatid, term.**

hermitage (pre-20c) A bower or hut in a garden, theoretically suitable for a hermit.

herringbone blocking Solid blocking between joists or studs with alternate blocks offset to allow for end nailing.

herringbone bond **1.** A brick wall bond with concealed diagonal headers laid at right angles to each other in a herringbone pattern. **2.** A brick floor pattern composed of stretchers in an interlocking herringbone pattern.

herringbone bridging Same as **single bridging.**

herringbone lath A type of **expanded-metal lath** with thin ribs separated by diagonal slots in a herringbone pattern. See also **Trussit.**

herringbone matched **Book-matched** wood or stone veneer panels with a diagonal grain that alternates directions.

hewed stuff (18c) **Hewn** lumber.

hewn, hewed, (pre-18c) **hewen** Material roughly cut or shaped with hand tools from basic materials, such as logs or rocks. See also **hand-hewn.**

hexapartite vault Same as **sexpartite vault.**

hexastyle Having a row of six columns across a facade or portico. See also **columniation.**

H-hinge A **hinge** shaped like the letter H; has T-shaped leaves, with the portion next to the knuckle narrower than the ends; typically a surface-mounted **strap hinge,** sometimes mounted as an **offset hinge** or with one leaf on the face of the swinging element and one leg against the jamb. Also known as **parliament hinge, side hinge.**

hick joint Same as **flush joint.**

hickory pine Same as **foxtail pine.**

hide glue A glue composed of gelatin manufactured by boiling animal hides, horns, and hoofs in water; the most common type of glue for joining wood.

hide paint A **paint** made with a hide glue and gelatin **vehicle.**

hieracosphinx A **sphinx** with the head of a hawk and the body of a lion.

highest and best use The use of **real estate** that provides the greatest economic return; used to determine **appraised value** and in a **feasibility study;** may involve **development** or **redevelopment** with (or without) consideration of **zoning** and historic designation restrictions.

high joint A masonry **flush joint** with narrow grooves adjacent to the edges of the masonry units; may also be decorated with a center groove.

high relief A sculptured feature carved or molded so that some portions are free of the background, or **à jour.** Also known as **alto-relievo.** See also **relief.**

high-rise An inexact term for a relatively tall building, as opposed to a **low-rise** building; often defined in building codes as more than 75 feet tall.

high roof A steeply pitched **roof** with a slope greater than 60 degrees with the horizon.

high steel Same as **hard steel.** See also **high test iron.**

high-stoop house (19c) A town house with an exterior stair 6–12 risers high to the main-floor entrance, where the drawing rooms and dining room were located; the kitchen was located either in the basement (e.g., in New York and Washington) or in a separate building (e.g., in Philadelphia, New Orleans, and Baltimore).

high style The more ornately detailed version of an architectural style; used in contrast to simpler examples, both from different periods or of the same period. See also **vernacular.**

high test iron (19c) A high-strength **wrought iron;** typically with a minimum ultimate strength of 50,000 pounds per square inch and a minimum elongation of 18 percent in 8 inches. Also known as **tension iron.**

High Victorian The more ornate architecture and interior design work of the post–Civil War Victorian period, which combines a variety of stylistic sources with great freedom; types include **High Victorian Eclectic, High Victorian Gothic, High Victorian Italianate.**

High Victorian Eclectic The late 19c practice of **eclecticism.** See also **High Victorian.**

High Victorian Gothic A late 19c form of the **Gothic Revival style,** which freely mixed French and Italian Gothic styles with the various English Gothic styles; influenced by the writings of the English medievalist John Ruskin (1819–1900), who advocated emulating Venetian Gothic buildings in the *Stones of Venice* (1851–53); characterized by complex, polychrome masonry exteriors, often with bays, towers, and turrets; typically with contrasting colors and/or textures of brick or stone, especially as horizontal bands and arch voussoirs in alternating colors; used most commonly for churches and public buildings. Also known as **Victorian Gothic, terminus.** See also **Collegiate Gothic, Ruskinian.**

High Victorian Italianate An inexact stylistic classification intended to separate more ornate, late 19c **Italianate** buildings from simpler, earlier examples.

hinge, (pre-20c) **henge** Hardware that supports a door or window and allows it to open and close; types include **anchor and collar, back flap hinge, blind door hinge, blind hinge,**

butt hinge, checking hinge, cross-garnet hinge, double-acting hinge, dovetail hinge, fast joint hinge, flap hinge, floor spring hinge, gate hinge, gravity hinge, H-hinge, HL-hinge, hook-and-band hinge, hook-and-eye hinge, lift-off hinge, locking hinge, loose pin hinge, offset hinge, pew hinge, pintle hinge, pivot hinge, reinforced hinge, rising hinge, setback hinge, side hinge, single-action hinge, spring hinge, spring-butt hinge, strap hinge, T-hinge, turnover hinge, water-joint hinge; components may include **acorn, hinge band, hinge pin, hinge plate, leaf, knuckle, pintle.**

hinge band A strap that is one of the pair of leaves of a **hinge.**

hinge nail A nail with a wide midsection and a rounded head; used with hinges because of its resistance to working loose.

hinge pin The cylindrical rod that connects the knuckles of a **hinge.** See also **pintle.**

hinge plate A thin, decorative plate that covers an exposed leaf and screws of a **butt hinge;** attached with small machine screws; typically with incised patterns.

hinge post The timber or post that supports the hinges of a door or gate. Also known as **hinging post.** See also **hinge.**

hinging post Same as **hinge post.**

hip **1.** An inclined line formed where two sloping roof surfaces turn an outside corner of a building; joint types include **Boston hip, square hip, woven hip.** See also components beginning with **hip.** **2.** Same as **hip rafter.**

hip-and-valley roof A **hip roof** on a building with an irregular plan, with valleys at the inside corners.

hip bevel **1.** The double angle cut at the head of a hip rafter where it abuts other roof framing members. **2.** The double bevel on the back of a hip rafter that allows the sheathing to lie flat. **3.** The angle between two slopes of a roof separated by a hip.

hip board A **ridgepole** used at a hip.

hip jack A **jack rafter** with its upper end supported by a **hip rafter** and its lower end supported by a wall plate.

hip knob A projecting ornament on the apex of a hip; may be a vertical wood post used to join the hip rafters or, more typically, a sheet-metal or terra-cotta decoration. See also **finial.**

hip mold, hip molding **1.** A molding that covers the joint at a **hip.** **2.** The back of a hip rafter. See also **hip bevel.**

hipped gable Same as **jerkinhead.**

hip rafter A rafter along a roof **hip;** supports the top ends of the **hip jack** rafters on two different roof slopes. Also known as **hip.**

hip roll Same as **hip mold** (sense 1); typically with a circular cross section.

hip roof, hipped roof A roof that slopes inward from all exterior walls; forms a **pyramid roof** above a square plan; has a ridge shorter than the length of the building above a rectangular plan. Also known as **Italian roof, umbrella roof.** See also **hip-and-valley roof.**

hip tile A **roof tile** formed to cover a roof hip; typically with the shape of a hollow, truncated cone sliced along its axis, and installed so that each piece overlaps the one below it. Also known as **corner tile.**

historic **1.** Mentioned, celebrated, or having influence in history. See also **historic building, historic context, historic district, historic landscape, historic structure, heritage.** **2.** Same as **historical.** **3.** (20c) Related to past human cultural activity, including prehistoric.

historical **1.** Belonging or relating to history or historians; a generally more inclusive term than **historic.** See also **historical significance.** **2.** Containing the representation or representation of facts. **3.** True to history, as opposed to fictional.

historical archaeology **Archaeology** that studies the physical remains of literate cultures; typically performed in conjunction with **historical research;** may include excavation, recovery, restoration, and evaluation of artifacts, and study of existing buildings for determination of **historical significance.** See also **crisis archaeology.**

historical architect A licensed architect who specializes in the preservation of historic buildings and structures; typically has special expertise about early building techniques and materials; prepares **historic structure reports,** coordinates the work of other specialists involved in a project, such as an **architectural historian, archaeologist, engineer, historic interiors specialist,** and **landscape architect,** and produces the **construction documents** for the **architectural conservation, restoration,** or **rehabilitation** work.

historical frieze, (18c) **historical freeze** A **frieze** decorated with bas-relief scenes illustrating a historical event.

historical function **1.** The original use of a building, structure, site, or object. **2.** The use of a building, structure, site, or object at the **control date** or during the **control period.** See also **historical significance.**

historical marker **1.** A permanent, descriptive sign or plaque affixed or adjacent to a historic building or other historic site. **2.** A commemorative monument. See also **site marker.**

historical monument (19c) A building or site having architectural or historical significance; municipal, state, or national significance.

historical research The study of **documents,** photographs, publications, and other data concerning a historic site, building, structure, or object; typically includes research on the architecture, construction, and users of the property. See also **documentation, historical archaeology, historic structure report, primary research.** **2.** The study of any subject in history.

historical significance The importance of an element, building, or site owing to its involvement with a significant event, person, or time period, or as an example of a past architectural style. See also **significance.**

historical society An organization that promotes the study of history, typically for a defined geographic area; may also maintain an **archive, museum,** or **historic site** and sponsor public education programs.

Historic American Buildings Survey (HABS) A division of the U.S. National Park Service that documents the appearance of historic buildings; the documentation, which includes photographs, measured drawings, and written historical information, is archived in a permanent collection at the Library of Congress; began as a New Deal project for architects in 1933 and was rejuvenated in 1966; primarily continued by student teams during the summers and by federal agencies altering National Register buildings. See also **Historic American Engineering Record.**

Historic American Engineering Record (HAER) A program of the U.S. National Park Service that documents the appearance and construction of exemplary engineering works, such as bridges and mills; documentation includes photographs, measured drawings, and written historical information and is archived at the Library of Congress; the program was begun in 1969; documentation is primarily prepared by teams of students during summer months. See also **Historic American Buildings Survey.**

historic building **1.** A building famous because of its association with a historic event or with the history of a locality. **2.** (20c) Any building recognized by a competent authority as being historically significant or contributing to the historical significance of a **historic district** or **heritage area,** especially those listed (or eligible to be listed) in a national, state, provincial, territorial, or local government register or inventory of historic places. Also known in Canada as **heritage building.** See also **Historic American Buildings Survey, historic structure, National Register of Historic Places.**

Historic Canal (Canada) An administrative term for those canals operated by the Department of Canadian Heritage for purposes of navigation as well as for protection, enjoyment, and interpretation of their cultural and natural heritage values.

historic context An organizing structure for interpreting history that groups information about historic properties that share a common theme, common geographical location, and common time period; used as a foundation for decisions about the planning, identification, evaluation, registration, and treatment of historic properties, based upon comparative significance.

historic district A definable **geographical area** that contains a number of related historic sites, buildings, structures, features, or objects united by past events or aesthetically by plan or physical development, and that has been designated on a local, state, or national register of historic places; may encompass a neighborhood or all of a small town; some districts may comprise individual elements separated geographically but linked by association or history; the oldest in the U.S. is located in Charleston, South Carolina. Also known in Canada as **heritage area** or **Heritage Conservation District.** See also **architectural review board.**

historic district survey The cataloging of each of the buildings and landscapes within an existing or proposed historic district; typically, each site is evaluated and rated for its level of contribution to the district; may be used to determine district boundaries.

historic function The use of a district, site, building, structure, or object at the time it attained historic **significance.**

historic interiors specialist An architect or other professional specially trained and experienced in the documentation, investigation, research, and analysis of the finishes, furnishings, fixtures, and decorative arts of historic building interiors; may be an expert in a subfield, such as historic lighting or paint analysis.

historic landscape **1.** A landscape that is famous because of its association with a historic event or with the history of a locality. See also **cultural landscape.** **2.** Any landscape listed (or eligible to be listed) in a national, state, provincial, or local register or inventory of historic places, or that contributes to the historical significance of a historic district. See also **National Register of Historic Places.**

historic marker A commemorative **monument, plaque,** or sign located on or near a historic site, building, structure, or object; may be placed by a government agency or a private organization, such as a historical society. See also **site marker.**

historic preservation Encompasses a broad range of activities related to **preservation** and **conservation** of the **built environment** by physical and intellectual methods; by the late 20c, its principles also contributed to protection of prehistoric archaeological and paleontological sites; early North American activities include the founding of the American Antiquarian Society in 1812 and the purchase of

Independence Hall by the city of Philadelphia in 1816 to prevent its demolition.

historic property Same as **historic resource.**

historic resource Any district, site, building, structure, or object determined to be historically significant.

historic significance See **historic function, historical significance.**

historic site **1.** (U.S.) The place where historically significant events or cultural activities have occurred. See also **Historic Sites Act.** **2.** (Canada) Any place formally recognized by a competent authority—usually a federal, provincial/territorial, regional, or municipal government—as being historically significant. See also **heritage site, Historic Sites and Monuments Act, National Historic Site.**

Historic Sites Act U.S. federal legislation enacted in 1935 that provides for the preservation of historic American sites, buildings, objects, and antiquities of national significance, including the designation of national historic landmarks and historic units of the National Parks System. See also **Antiquities Act.**

Historic Sites and Monuments Act Canadian federal legislation enacted in 1952–53 that enables the minister of Parks Canada to designate historic sites of national importance and creates the Historic Sites and Monuments Board.

historic structure **1.** A **structure** that is famous because of its association with a historic event or the history of a locality. **2.** Any structure listed (or eligible to be listed) in a national, state, provincial/territorial, or local register or inventory of historic places, or that contributes to the **historical significance** of a **historic district.** Also known in Canada as **heritage structure.** See also **historic building, Historic American Engineering Survey, National Register of Historic Places.**

historic structure report (HSR) A written summary of a detailed analysis of a historic **building** or **structure** and its site; typically includes **historical research,** data from nondestructive testing, descriptions of the property and its physical condition, drawings, photographs, analysis of which components are original or later additions, and recommendations for appropriate preservation treatment; begun by the National Park Service in the 1930s.

history See **architectural history, historic, oral history.**

hit-and-miss window A window with a fixed, glazed sash over a wood grate; the openings of the grate can be closed by sliding a second interior wood grate into place; used in stables to provide light and ventilation.

HL-hinge A wrought-iron **H-hinge** in which the bottom of one leaf extends horizontally to form an L-shape.

hob A shelf that projects from the side of a fireplace and is used to heat containers or to support a grate. See also **bath stove.**

Hodgkinson beam A cast-iron beam with a large bottom flange; typically the cross-sectional area of the bottom flange was six times the area of the top flange to compensate for the low tensile strength, irregularity, and brittleness of 19c cast iron; based on experiments by Englishmen Eaton Hodgkinson and William Fairbairn in the 1830s and 1840s.

hog A masonry wall with a different number of courses at each end; constructed with tapered mortar joints and/or special sized units; typically used to correct a leveling error.

hogan, (pre-20c) **hogun** A Navaho dwelling; typically constructed with log walls and an earth-covered roof.

hog-backed Cambered, as in a roof ridge; may be used to resist sagging or to prevent structural failure.

hog court (17c) Same as **sty.**

hog house, (17c) **hogg howse** (pre-19c) A building that shelters hogs; may be a long, open shed or be completely enclosed.

hoist **1.** (pre-19c) A beam with a block and tackle used for lifting objects. **2.** (19c–present) A machine for lifting objects; beginning in late 19c, includes an **elevator.**

hoist (sense 2)

hoistaway (19c) Same as **hoist** (sense 2).

hoistway A vertical shaft within a building for a **hoist,** such as an **elevator.**

holdfast A projecting element, such as a long, flat-headed nail or a large staple, that holds another element or to which something is fastened.

holiday A spot that has been missed during painting.

hollow A recessed **bead,** especially a **quarter hollow.**

hollow block **1.** A brick or other terra-cotta with openings for ventilation. **2.** Same as a **concrete block.**

hollow brick A brick with vertical interior perforations; used to build lightweight fire-resistant partitions.

hollow chamfer A chamfer with a concave surface.

hollow-core door (20c) A wood **flush door** with internal voids between the flat sheets on the faces, as opposed to a **solid-core door.**

hollow masonry unit (20c) A brick or block that is less than 75 percent solid in the bedding plane. See also **concrete block, solid masonry unit.**

hollow-metal door (20c) A metal door with internal voids between the sheet metal on the faces; most often a steel **flush door.**

hollow mold Any concave molding.

hollow newel The inside edge of a winding stair that is in the shape of a hollow cylinder, with no newel posts. Also known as **open newel.** See also **closed newel.**

hollow pile A **pile** in the form of a hollow metal cylinder.

hollow pottery (19c) Building elements composed of **terra-cotta** formed with interior voids, such as **architectural terra-cotta** or **structural terra-cotta.**

hollow quoin A vertical notch in the masonry of a canal lock that receives the gatepost.

hollow tile A **structural clay tile** unit with vertical hollow cells; used to build interior masonry partitions and as backup block for brick veneer; may be fabricated with plaster keys.

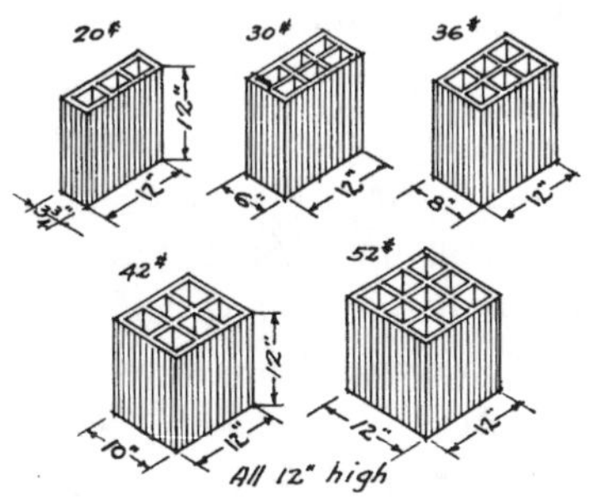

hollow tile

hollow wall A masonry wall in which the facing and backing are bonded by masonry units and are separated by a vertical internal air space. See also **cavity wall.**

holly See **American holly.**

holophane shade (early 20c–present) **1.** A translucent glass electric-light shade with a bas-relief pattern that is revealed when the light is turned on; introduced after the bright tungsten filament bulbs were developed ca. 1907. **2.** A clear glass electric light with vertical prismatic grooves that diffuse the light.

home farm (Delaware) Same as **home plantation.**

home house (southern U.S.) The part of a farm or plantation that includes the owner's dwelling and related outbuildings. Also known as **home house quarter.** See also **home plantation.**

home house quarter Same as **home house.** See also **quarter.**

home lot The legal land area on which a **home house** is located.

home plantation (southern U.S.) The farm land adjacent to, or including, the owner's house, especially when one of several tracts of land owned by the same individual. Also known as **dwelling plantation, home farm, homestead, manor farm, mansion farm, mansion plantation.** See also **home house, master seat.**

homestead **1.** A house and its adjacent land. **2.** A farm occupied by the owner and family. See also **home plantation.** **3.** The permanent residence of a family. **4.** In the U.S. and Canada, a **quarter section** of public land purchased from the federal government and used for a family farm; the U.S. Congress passed the **Homestead Act** in 1862, and the Canadian **Dominion Lands Policy** in 1872.

Homestead Act U.S. federal legislation, enacted in 1862, permitting settlers to occupy a **homestead** on designated public land in the western states and own it after five years. See also **section, township.**

homesteading **1.** The process of acquiring land by occupying and using it; may be done through a government program, such as the **Homestead Act,** or without official sanction. See also **preemption.** **2.** (late 20c) The process of acquiring a house for little or no money from a government in exchange for renovating or restoring and occupying the property.

Homosote (20c) The trade name for a **composition board** material composed of chopped wood fibers; used for sheathing and finish work; typically 4 × 8 feet; in late 20c, some types made from recycled newspapers.

honed The very smooth surface texture of soft stone blocks; produced by rubbing. See also **rubbed, stone work.**

honeycomb work Same as **stalactite work.**

honeysuckle ornament, (19c) **honey-suckle ornament** A bas-relief **honeysuckle pattern;** often used on anthemions or other Greek Revival style architectural elements.

honeysuckle pattern, (19c) **honey-suckle pattern** A decorative motif in the stylized form of a honeysuckle plant; used on **honeysuckle ornament** or as a repetitive element in Greek Revival style interiors.

hood **1.** A projecting sheet-metal construction at the top of a fireplace opening or over a cooking stove to contain and vent smoke and odors. **2.** A projecting shelflike element over an exterior wall opening. See also **hoodmold.**

hoodmold, hood molding A projecting molding over a wall opening; used to divert rainwater away from the wall opening. Also known as **head molding.** See also **label.**

hook **1.** A hardware device with a bent or curved end; used temporarily to hold another element in position. **2.** An L-shaped device that is driven into a jamb to support various types of **hook hinges;** its vertical leg is a round bar, and its horizontal leg is tapered and pointed. Also known as **pintle.** **3.** (pre-19c) Same as **shutter dog.**

hook-and-band hinge A **hook-and-eye hinge** in which the eye is formed by a surface-mounted strap. Also known as **band-and-hook hinge, strap hinge.** See also **hinge.**

hook and butt Same as **hooked scarf joint.**

hook and eye A hardware fastener composed of a screw eye with a hook that engages another screw eye; used to latch doors and casement windows. See also **hook and staple, spring hook.**

hook-and-eye hinge A **hinge** with an **eye** on the swinging element supported by a L-shaped **hook** mounted on the jamb; may be a **hook-and-band hinge** or the eye may be the end of a flat spike driven into the hanging stile. Also known as a **hook and hinge, gemel hinge.** See also **hook and staple.**

hook and hinge (pre-19c) Same as **hook-and-eye hinge.**

hook and staple A hardware device with a hook on one element that engages a staple attached to another element; typically used to fasten a swinging element, such as a gate or door, in a open or closed position. See also **hook and eye.**

hooked scarf joint A **scarf joint** with a step cut into both members so that they interlock and cannot slide apart. Also known as **stepped scarf joint.**

hook hinge See **hook-and-band hinge, hook-and-eye hinge.**

hook strip A horizontal wood band used to mount metal coat hooks.

hoop-iron bond A **chain bond** composed of strap- or hoop-iron material.

hopper closet A **water closet** with a funnel-shaped receiver; may also have a **trap** below the hopper.

hopper head A hopper-shaped **conductor head.**

hopper window, hopper casement A triangular, bottom-hinged window sash that tilts inward and rests at an angle when opened; air enters the room at the top of the sash.

horizontal cornice The cornice at the base of a pediment. See also **raked cornice.**

horizontal plank-frame A 19c wood frame construction system with walls composed of layers of planks stacked solid; typically with 1 × 6 inch planks staggered to form a plaster key; found mainly in houses and industrial structures in the eastern half of the U.S. and in Ontario. See also **board wall, plank-frame.**

hopper closet

horn The extension of the stiles of the top sash of a double-hung window beyond the bottom of the meeting rail; typically with an ogee scroll cut. Also known as **lug.** See also **witch's tit.**

hornwork A projecting portion of a fortification composed of a curtain between two half-bastions connected by parallel walls to the main structure.

horse block A stone block or wood platform set near a driveway or street to assist in mounting a horse or carriage. Also known as carriage block or **upping block.**

horsed string (pre-WWI) Same as **cut string.**

horseshoe arch An **arch** in which the curve of the intrados continues below the spring line, so that the size of the opening at the bottom is less than at the spring line; may be a **round horseshoe arch** or the bottom of the intrados

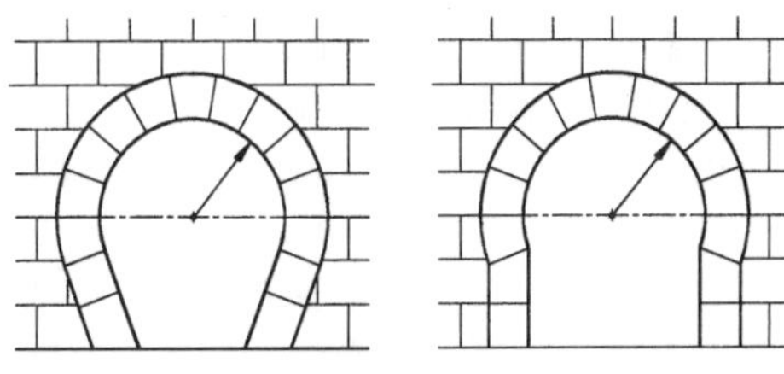

horseshoe arch

may be straight lines, either vertical or inclined.

hose bib, hose bibb A wall-mounted faucet with a male threaded end for attaching a hose. See also **hydrant.**

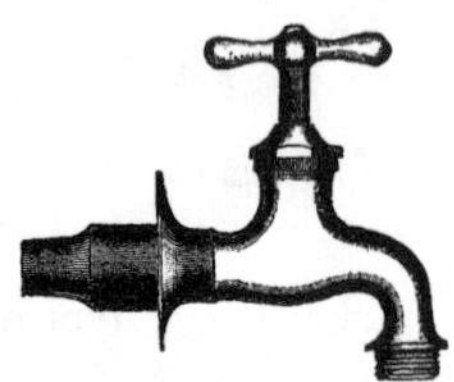

hose bib

hospital **1.** A building used for the reception, care, and medical treatment of the sick or wounded; typically refers to a facility with beds for overnight stays; specialized facilities, such as a **lying-in hospital,** were provided beginning in the 19c. See also **infirmary, lazaretto, sanatorium, sick house.** **2.** (pre-20c) A building or group of buildings used to shelter those in need, such as the poor, orphans, or the elderly. **3.** (18c–present) A building used for the shelter and care of the insane.

hot-cast porcelain Same as **opalin.**

hot cement (18c) A gluelike substance used to bind bricks together before carving them into capitals or similar shapes; composed of beeswax, brick dust, and powdered chalk; the mixture and the bricks are heated before application. See also **cement, cold cement.**

hot closet A closet next to a fireplace or oven that is used for drying things.

hotel (18c–present) A building with suites or rooms for rent by the day; typically includes public facilities for dining and entertainment; larger and of better quality than an **inn** or **tavern.**

hothouse, (19c) **hot-house,** (18c) **hot house** An artificially heated **greenhouse;** type includes **pinery.** Also known as **stove house.**

hot-tar roof A **built-up roof** that uses melted bituminous asphalt.

house, (pre-19c) **howse** **1.** A **building** used as a dwelling, especially for a single family; types include **apartment house, boardinghouse, bungalow, bunkhouse, dwelling house, gatehouse, great house, farmhouse, lock house, lodging house, manor house, mansion, overseer's house, Pueblo, quarter, ranch house, shooting box, stinash, tenement house, town house, villa;** forms include **basement house, catslide, clapboard house, Corktown cottage, cottage, detached house, duplex, floating house, foursquare, half house, hall-and-parlor, high-stoop house, log house, longhouse, Norman cottage, octagon house, piano-box house, raftered house, row house, saltbox, semidetached house, sod house, stone ender, Virginia cabin, Virginia house.** Also known as **casa.** See also **barracks, hotel, single-family dwelling.** **2.** A building name for the human activity that it shelters; types include **alehouse, almshouse, ash house, backhouse, bakehouse, balehouse, bank-house, bark house, bathhouse, beam house, bee house, brandy house, brewhouse, bunkhouse, carriage house, chaff house, chair house, chaise house, clubhouse, coach house, coal house, coffeehouse, cookhouse, cornhouse, corpse house, countinghouse, courthouse, cowhouse, custom house, eating house, farrowing house, firehouse, fodder house, garden house, gatehouse, ginhouse, glass house, glebe house, greenhouse, guardhouse, guesthouse, head house, hemp house, henhouse, hog house, hothouse, jury house, market house, meal house, meeting house,**

milk house, outhouse, playhouse, poorhouse, potato house, pot house, powder house, powerhouse, rolling house, roundhouse, scale house, shafthouse, slaughter house, slave house, smokehouse, spinning house, springhouse, stage house, statehouse, steam house, still house, storehouse, stormhouse, stovehouse, tobacco house, tollhouse, tomb house, transfer house, warehouse, washhouse, watch house, weaving house, woodhouse, workhouse.

house agent (19c) A **real estate agent** who sells or rents houses.

house apiary (19c) A building constructed to contain multiple colonies of bees. Also known as **bee house, bee shed.**

house bell One of a series of bells connected to copper wires so that the bells can be rung from remote locations; typically installed in or near the kitchen and used to signal the servants; wires may be exposed or hidden in hollow wood molding or **secret tubing.**

house drain Same as **house sewer.**

housed string, housed stringer A wood stair **string** rabbeted out in the shape of the ends of the treads and risers; the treads and risers are recessed in the rabbet and held in place with wedges.

house factor (19c) Same as **house agent.**

househead (pre-20c) Same as **housetop.**

housekeeping The regular removal of dirt and grime from the surface of building elements and **cultural artifacts.** See also **conservation, restoration.**

house museum A house that is furnished and maintained as an example of the setting of the life of a historical figure, such as the home of George Washington at Mount Vernon, or of a historic event, such as the Petersen House where President Lincoln died; used generically to refer to any type of building that is furnished and interpreted as a **museum;** first U.S. example is George Washington's headquarters in Newburgh, purchased by New York State in 1850.

house of correction Same as prison, **workhouse.**

house of ease (pre-19c) A **latrine** building.

house of God Same as **church.**

house of industry (19c) Same as factory, **workhouse.**

house of office (pre-19c) A **latrine** building.

house of prayer Same as **church.**

house of rendezvous Same as **brothel.**

house raiser Same as **house raising** (sense 2).

house raising **1.** The **raising** (sense 2) of a house frame, or the gathering of neighbors to construct a house frame. Also known as **house raiser, raising bee.** See also **barn raising.**

house sewer The main underground sanitary plumbing pipe within the perimeter of a building. Also known as **house drain.** See also **sanitary sewer.**

house tank A rooftop water tank that supplies domestic water under pressure to a building; the water is pumped into the tank and distributed by a **drop feed;,** 19c types include wood staves in a cylindrical shape, tinned-copper-lined rectangular wood boxes, and riveted wrought-iron tanks. See also **gravity supply tank.**

housetop The roof or top portion of the exterior a house; an inexact term. Also known as **househead.**

housing **1.** A recess cut in a piece of wood or other material to receive the end of another piece, such as the rabbeted recess in a string board that receives the ends of risers and treads. **2.** (19c) A niche for a statue. **3.** (18c) The hollow of a warped brick or tile. **4.** A casing or grille enclosing moving machinery, such as a fan or turbine. **5.** Dwellings in general.

housing code Government regulations that define the livability of a housing unit; typically includes minimum physical requirements for light, ventilation, security, room size, winter temperature, and interior painting. See also **building code.**

hovel **1.** A small, dilapidated dwelling. **2.** An open-sided shed for cattle.

hoveling **1.** A **chimney cap** formed by extension of two sides of a chimney top to support an arched or flat cover; typically the windward and lee sides are extended. **2.** An opening on one side of a chimney near the top.

Howe truss A bridge **truss** with repetitive rectangular panels with diagonal struts that all slope downward, or upward, toward the center of the truss; variations include triangular end panels and inclined top chords that form trapezoidal panels, or an overall triangular shape; varieties include **cambered Howe truss.**

H-pile (20c) A **pile** composed of an **H-section** driven into the ground.

H-section A rolled-steel shape with an H-shaped cross section with flanges with parallel faces; typically square in its outer dimensions; primarily used for structural columns and piles. Also known as **H beam, H column, H-pile.** See also **Bethlehem column, I-beam, WF section.**

HSR Abbr. for **historic structure report.**

hub The enlarged end of a plumbing pipe; may be threaded or smooth, such as a **bell pipe** or **socket sewer pipe.**

hubless joint (late 20c) A **drainpipe** joint connecting straight end pipes with a flexible gasket held in place by stainless steel hose clamps; most often used for cast-iron pipe.

Hudson River bluestone A dark, bluish grey sandstone quarried in the foothills of the Catskill Mountains near the Hudson River Valley of New York; split into flags for 19c New York City sidewalks and carved for the basin of Bethesda Fountain in Central Park. See also **bluestone.**

hull (pre-19c) The sheathed frame of a building. See also **carcase.**

human scale An inexact term implying that the **scale** of a building has an appropriate relationship to the size and proportions of the human body.

humidifier A mechanical device that adds moisture to the air in a building. See also **dehumidifier, humidistat.**

humidistat A device that measures and regulates the relative humidity of the air inside a building. See also **dehumidifier, humidifier.**

Hummelstown brownstone A reddish to purplish brown, dense **sandstone** quarried in Dauphin County, Pennsylvania.

Hungarian mosaic A **parquet floor** pattern of rows of chevrons.

hung lintel A steel angle or other shape suspended from the main building structure to support a wall; usually located at each floor level at the building perimeter to support a curtain wall.

hunting box Same as **hunting lodge.**

hunting lodge A residence used by hunters during hunting season. Also known as **hunting box.**

hunting miter A curved joint between straight and curved sections of a flush molding; used to avoid having to change the cross section of the molding for a wall panel or similar frame.

hut, (17c) **hutt** A small dwelling of inferior-quality construction. Also known as **cabin, cottage, hovel, shanty, shed.**

hut circle, hut ring (19c) A circular, raised mound, 15–50 feet in diameter, found in the Mississippi Valley; thought to be the base of Native American dwellings.

HVAC Abbr. for **heating, ventilating, and air conditioning.**

Hyatt light A type of **pavement light** invented by American Thaddeus Hyatt; produced in New York beginning in 1873.

hydrant A discharge pipe and valve connected to a water main; typically consists of a hollow vertical shaft with multiple male threaded spouts and a center rod connected to a valve at the bottom; types include **fire hydrant.** Also known as **fire plug, water plug.**

hydrant cesspool A plumbing floor-drain fitting in the form of a depressed hopper with a grille across the top: used as a drain directly below a yard hydrant or hose bib.

hydrated lime Calcium hydroxide, $Ca(OH)_2$, manufactured by machine-slaking **lime** (CaO) with enough water to convert the oxides to hydroxides; has mostly replaced **quicklime** in the 20c. See also **slaked lime.**

hydraulic cement A **calcareous cement** that can set under water; typically composed of calcined limestone that contains carbonate of magnesia; types include **portland cement, Roman cement, Rosendale cement, slate cement.** Also known as **water cement.**

hydraulic elevator (19c–present) An **elevator** with a platform supported on a piston that is raised and lowered by the pressure of hydraulic fluid in the cylinder; typically the cylinder casing is underground; limited to five or six stories of travel.

hydraulic lime A type of **lime** that hardens under water; typically manufactured from limestone containing 30–50 percent clay composed of silica and alumina; types include **full hydraulic lime, semihydraulic lime.** Also known as **water lime.**

hydraulic mortar A type of **mortar** that will harden under water; typically composed of **hydraulic cement, lime,** and **sand.**

hydraulic pile A **hollow pile** installed by excavating the earth with a jet of water.

hydraulic ram A **water pump** activated by water pressure. Also known as **water ram.**

Hydrostone A trade name for a T-shaped **concrete block** manufactured in Halifax, Nova Scotia; used for many houses in Halifax after an explosion in 1917.

hygrometer A device for measuring relative humidity.

hygroscopic Material that absorbs moisture from the atmosphere.

hypaethral, hypethral Roofless, such as a building, or portion of a building.

hyperthyrum, hyperthyrion, hyperthyron A **cornice** and **frieze** above a door or a window **architrave.**

hyphen A relatively narrow connecting link between the main building mass and a smaller wing; typically in the same style as the rest of the building. See also **link.**

hypophyge An aphophyge at the top of a column shaft.

hypostyle **1.** Any structure having a ceiling supported by columns. **2.** Having large and numerous columns. See also **columniation.**

hypotrachelium The neck at the top of the shaft of a Doric or Ionic capital, immediately below the **trachelium.** Also known as **gorgerin.**

hy-rib lath A trade name for a self-furring type of **expanded-metal lath.**

I

I-bar A small **I-beam.** Also known as **I-iron.**

I-beam An iron or steel beam with a symmetrical I-shaped cross section; typically the web is of uniform thickness and the flanges taper toward the outside; the rolled form was patented in the U.S. in 1844, and small sizes were available by the 1850s; usually an **American Standard beam** after 1890. Also known as **I-bar.** See also **skeleton construction, WF-section.**

ICCROM International Centre for the Study of the Preservation and the Restoration of Cultural Property

icebox (ca. 1880–present) A refrigerator that is cooled by blocks of ice and is used for keeping food fresh; may be movable or built-in; exterior is typically oak or ash lined with painted or galvanized sheet metal and insulated with sawdust, charcoal, or cork; also known as **ice chest.**

ice-breaker The V-shaped projection on the upriver side of a bridge pier; used to protect against ice floes and floating trees.

ice chest Same as **icebox.**

ice glass Same as **crackle glass.**

icehouse, (pre-20c) **ice-house, ice house** A building used for storing blocks of ice cut from lakes, ponds, and streams in winter; typically built mostly underground with masonry or timber walls lined with wood and with the hollow space filled with sawdust insulation; ice was shipped to southern U.S. from New England by sea pre-1799, then via the Mississippi River from Illinois and Wisconsin beginning in 1799.

ichnograph, ichnographia (pre-20c) A **plan** of a ground floor, especially a building plan drawn on a plat of the property. See also **ichography.**

ichnography **1.** (pre-WWI) The process of representing a building, or geometric figures, with line drawings; prepared using a straight edge and a compass as the primary tools. **2.** (pre-19c) A set of plans for a building that includes the **ichnograph** plan, a perspective view showing the front and one side, and an exterior elevation of the front. See also **scenography, sciography, orthography.**

ICOMOS International Council on Monuments and Sites

identification The process of gathering information about historic properties. See also **information potential.**

idglu Same as **igloo.**

IEEE Institute of Electrical and Electronics Engineers

igloo, iglu, (19c) **idglu** An Eskimo hut; made of wood and animal skins or snow blocks. Also known as **iglugeak.**

I-house A two-story **center passage, single-pile** house with a single room on each side of a center stair or passage that is aligned with the entrance in the middle of the long facade.

I-iron Same as **I-bar.**

ile (pre-19c) Same as **aisle.**

illuminance (late 20c) A measure of the quantity of light at a particular location; typically measured in footcandles (lumens/square foot) or lux (lumens/square meter).

illuminated tile (mid-19c) Cast-iron floor plates with inset glass prisms that provide light for a lower floor level.

imbrex **1.** A curved tile; typically a half-cylinder shape; used to cover the joint between **tegula** tiles; used in **Italian tiling.** Also known as **covering tile, roll roofing tile.** **2.** A semicircular shape used in **imbrication.**

imbrex (sense 1)

imbrication **1.** Tiles or shingles with a **fish-scale** pattern. **2.** Relief carving in the stylized form of overlapping fish scales; the scales may be an arc of a circle or similar shape. See also **contre-imbrication.**

impact The physical and socioeconomic effects of an undertaking or a new development on a site, building, or structure; includes direct effects, such as **demolition,** and indirect effects, such as noise pollution. See also **Environmental Impact Statement.**

impage Same as a door **rail.**

impastation (18c) Ornamental work made of **stuc.**

imperfect arch Same as **diminished arch.**

imperial dome A round roof form in the shape of an onion with a flared skirt at the base; common in Greek Orthodox churches. Also known as **onion dome.**

Imperial Mahogany A pinkish, medium-grained granite with black and gray markings quarried in the vicinity of Minneapolis, Minnesota.

imperial roof A pointed dome or ridge roof with an ogee profile.

imperial waste and overflow A bathtub plumbing fitting in the form of a narrow metal cylinder with a knobbed top; used to open and close the drain at the bottom of the tub and provide an overflow outlet near the top.

impost The stone block that receives the thrust of an arch, especially when it is a column or pier capital; types include **arched impost, continuous impost, dosseret, mutilated impost.** Also known as **chaptrel.** **2.** (18c) Same as a **skewback.**

impost block **1.** Same as **impost** (sense 1) **2.** Same as **dosseret.**

IMS **Institute of Museum Services**

inactive leaf The leaf of a **double door** that generally stays in the closed position.

in-and-out bond A masonry wall bond with headers and stretchers alternating vertically, especially at a corner. See also **quoin.**

in antis Having columns between antae, especially a classical style portico. See also **anta.**

in a wind, in wind (20c) An incorrectly installed jamb. See also **out of wind.**

inbond The bond of a masonry unit laid perpendicular to the face of the wall and that projects into the wythes behind the face, such as a **header.** See also **outbond.**

incandescent lamp (ca. 1880–present) An **electric lamp** with a metal base and a glass bulb containing a filament that glows when electricity passes through it; the bulb is typically filled with inert gases or encloses a partial vacuum; used in an **incandescent light;** first commercially manufactured successfully by Thomas A. Edison in 1879, with a hairpin loop carbon fiber enclosed in clear glass; **tungsten filament lamp** introduced ca. 1907 and the frosted bulb ca. 1925; base types include **bayonet base, screw base;** shapes include **B-shape lamp, C-shape lamp, flame-shape lamp, globular-shape lamp, T-type lamp.** Also known as **glow light, light-**

bulb. See also **fluorescent lamp, luminaire, neon.**

incandescent light A **light fixture** lit by an **incandescent lamp.**

incertum (pre-20c) Masonry composed of small, rough, or irregularly shaped stones embedded in mortar.

inch stuff (pre-WWI) Boards that are one inch thick.

incised work A decorative pattern cut into the surface of a finish material. See also **inlay, relief.**

inclined molding (19c) Same as **beveled molding.**

income property **Real estate** that produces income from rentals; may be residential (e.g., an **apartment house**) or commercial (e.g., an **office building** or **shopping center**). See also **depreciable property, investment property.**

incrustation The covering of a surface with another finish material, such as marble on brick or lacquer on wood.

indentation A pattern formed by a series of decorative depressions or pointed notches.

indented (19c) Toothed together.

indented molding A molding in the form of a series of pyramidal or toothlike projections.

Indian pipestone Same as **catlinite.**

Indian red A deep, rich, red paint **pigment** with a brownish-purple tinge, composed of iron oxide (Fe_2O_3); originally manufactured from earth rich in iron oxide found near the Persian Gulf (of the Indian Ocean), and by the 18c made from industrial waste acid containing iron scale. See also **roofer's red, Venetian red.**

Indian shutter An interior shutter with solid panels; often a **box shutter.**

Indiana limestone Same as **Bedford limestone.**

indigo A deep, blue-black paint **pigment** manufactured from the indigo plant; superseded as a house paint pigment in the 18c by **Prussian blue** and in the late 19c by the aniline color known as **coal tar indigo.**

industrial archaeology The scientific study and historical analysis of the remains of industrial facilities and artifacts, such as bridges, canals, railroads, steel plants, and water mills, including operating and redundant sites as well as ruins. See also **archaeology, Historic American Engineering Record.**

infill **1.** The **development** of real estate on land between or adjacent to existing buildings. **2.** Undifferentiated material used for fill between other materials, such as random rubble in a stone wall.

infiltration The passage of air into a room or building through cracks, joints, and other small openings; typically not desired for **energy efficiency.**

infirmary **1.** An office or small hospital used for the free treatment of the sick; may be part of an institution, such as a school. **2.** (pre-19c) A room or suite within a public institution, such as a prison or workhouse, used for treatment of the sick.

inflected arch **1.** Same as **ogee arch.** **2.** Same as **inverted arch.**

information potential The information that can be learned about history or prehistory through the composition and physical remains of a building, especially through **archaeology.**

infrared reflectography Analysis of paint by photographing reflected infrared light; used to determine hidden elements of decorative painting.

infrared thermography The use of photography or video that senses wavelengths in the infrared band to detect varying levels of heat output; uses include detection of heat loss from a building and determination of relative levels of moisture within building elements.

infrastructure Off-site utilities, services, and structures that serve a real estate development; may include water, gas, and electric service, water and sanitary sewer systems, roads, railroads, and schools; sometimes also used to refer to facilities within a site or building.

inglenook, ingle nook A sitting area with built-in benches in front of a fireplace; from the Scottish word **ingle** for fireplace. See also **chimney corner.**

ingot iron (19c) Same as **soft steel.**

ingot steel (19c) Same as **hard steel.**

inlaid work Same as **inlay.**

inlay A decorative pattern formed by placing finish material in shallow pockets cut into the main material; primarily refers to hard materials such as wood or stone. See also **mosaic, veneer.**

inn A building used for lodging, feeding, and entertaining travelers. Also known as **ordinary, tavern.** See also **hotel.**

inn yard An open area next to an inn used for saddling horses and similar activities. See also **yard.**

inner chamber (pre-20c) A room accessed through a hall or other room; typically a bedroom. See also **outer chamber.**

inner hearth Same as **back hearth.**

inside chimney A **chimney** stack that projects into the interior of a building. See also **breast, corner chimney, outside chimney.**

inside finish **1.** (19c) The interior wood trim and wall linings of tile, wood, or marble. **2.** (20c) All of the exposed interior surfaces, including flooring, plaster, tile, and paint. Also known as **interior finish.** See also **finish, cabinet finish.**

inside wall brick Same as **salmon brick.**

in situ In its original or proper site or position; from the Latin for "in position"; the term was originally used by geologists in the 19c.

inspection **1.** An on-site examination of construction to determine whether it is being performed according to the drawings, specifications, and building codes; may include examination of concrete reinforcement, repointing, steel connections, and waterproofing installations; the inspector may be a **building official;** typically, the inspector reports deficiencies to the architect, owner, and contractor. See also **construction observation, testing.** **2.** The examination of an existing building or structure to determine existing deficiencies; may also involve **testing** and **nondestructive investigation.**

inspection house, inspecting house (Maryland and Virginia) A warehouse used for government inspection of the quality of tobacco.

Institute of Museum Services A U.S. federally funded program that supports all types of museums, including historic houses and sites.

insulated column (18c) A freestanding column. Also known as **isolee.**

insulated glass, insulating glass Glazing formed of two or more sheets of glass separated by an airspace and sealed around the edge to provide increased thermal resistance; varieties include **double glazing, triple glazing.**

insulated wire Electric wire wrapped with a nonconducting material. See **insulation** for types.

insulating fabric Same as **varnished cloth.**

insulating glass Same as **insulated glass.**

insulating joint A pipe fitting in which electric insulation is used to attach a combination fixture to the gas pipe.

insulating paper A **fibrous wrapped insulation** for **insulated wire** composed of paper; Japanese mulberry paper is most common type; typically treated with moisture-resistant materials such as linseed oil before 1920; lacquered cellophane used in the 1930s.

insulating thread, insulating yarn A **fibrous wrapped insulation** for **insulated wire** composed of braided thread or yarn in layers; cotton impregnated with asphalt was the most common type; other types include felted asbestos and spun cotton or silk impregnated with paraffin or varnish.

insulating tube See **knob and tube.**

insulation **1.** A material used to reduce transmission of sound or heat; common pre-WWII materials include aluminum foil, **asbestos,** cork, corn stalks, cotton, **gypsum,** hair, jute, **limestone,** moss, paper pulp, wheat straw, wood; types include **batt insulation, fill insulation, felt insulation, flexible insulation, insulated glass, insulator quilt, loose fill insulation, metal foil insulation, rigid insulation.** **2.** A material used to prevent conduction or leakage of electricity, such as for **insulated wire** or an **insulator;** types include **Bakelite, fibrous wrapped insulation, glass, gutta percha, insulating paper, insulating thread, porcelain, rubber insulation, varnished cloth,** and thermoplastic insulation.

insulator A nonconducting electric wire support; typically glass or porcelain. See also **cleat, knob and tube.**

insulator quilt (late 19c–early 20c) A thick hair cloth used for sound insulation.

intarsia Wood **inlay.** Also known as **tarsia.**

integral lath A type of sheet-metal lath that is self-supporting without studs; cut and bent so that it has a cross section of continuous rows of 45-degree parallelograms, with alternate rows angled at opposite directions.

integrity A measure of the authenticity of a property's historic identity, evidenced by the survival of physical characteristics that existed during the property's historic or prehistoric period in comparison with its unaltered state; for example, a **historic building** of high integrity has few alterations or ones that can be easily reversed, and an **archaeological site** with high integrity is one that is relatively undisturbed; criteria evaluated include **association, design, feeling,** location, and **materials.**

intercolumniation The spacing between columns in classical style buildings based on multiples of the column diameter; typical spacings include **coupled, pycnostyle** (1 or 1½ diameters), **systyle** (2 diameters), **eustyle** (2¼ or 2⅓ diameters), **diastyle** (3 diameters), **araeostyle** (4 or more diameters), **araeosystyle** (alternately araeostyle and systyle); the diameter and spacing are measured just above the base of the columns; these multiples were not necessarily followed in practice; also measured in relation to entablature elements, such as **ditriglyph, monotriglyph.** See also **Classical orders, Tuscan intercolumniation.**

interdentil The space between two **dentils;** often less than the width of the dentils. See also **metoche.**

interdome The space between the inner and outer shells of a domed cupola.

interduce (pre-19c) Same as **intertie.**

interfenestration **1.** The space between windows. **2.** The art of arranging windows and other openings on a facade.

interfilling The material between the spaces of a timber frame or similar structure. See also **half-timbered, nogging.**

interglyph The space between two grooves, especially of a triglyph.

interior decoration The surface treatments and furnishings of the inside of a building; typically refers to those elements applied after construction is complete. See also **decoration.**

interior decorator Same as **interior designer;** usually refers to those who work primarily with residential properties.

interior designer (20c) One who designs the decoration, finishes, and furnishings of the interior spaces of a building; may contract for the supply and installation of finishes and furnishings in addition to designing them; may also design spaces with nonstructural partitions, especially in office buildings. Also known as **interior decorator.**

interior finish Same as **inside finish.**

interior slope The slope from the crest of an embankment to the building wall.

interjoist (19c) The space between two joists.

interlaced Connected with strapping in a crisscross pattern, such as a **lattice beam.**

interlaced arcade An arcade formed by a series of columns supporting arches with overlapping archivolts.

interlaced arch One of a series of overlapped archivolts; used in an **interlaced arcade** and common in Gothic **tracery.** See also **arch, Gothic Revival.**

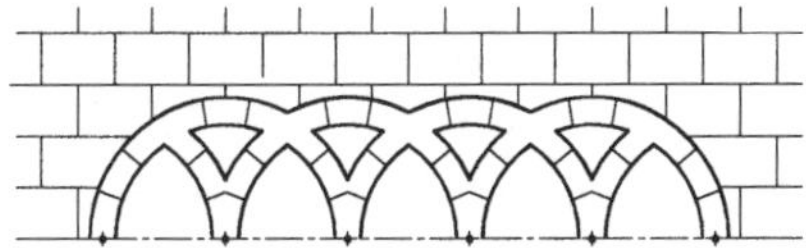

interlaced arch

intermediate rib A subordinate vault rib between primary ribs, especially between a **groin rib** and a **transverse rib** or **wall rib.**

Intermodal Surface Transportation Efficiency Act (ISTEA) U.S. federal legislation enacted in December 1991 that provides funding ($3 billion) to enhance the environmental, historic, and scenic features of intermodal transportation projects.

intermodillion The space between two modillions.

intermutule The space between two mutules, especially on an architrave.

internal dormer A vertical window set in a recess below a roof, with its head below the main roof surface.

internal orthography See **orthography.**

International Centre for the Study of the Preservation and the Restoration of Cultural Property (ICCROM) A school for the study of **conservation** and **preservation** of buildings and cultural artifacts established by UNESCO in 1959; located in Rome, Italy. Also known as the **Rome Center.**

International Council on Monuments and Sites (ICOMOS) An international, nongovernmental, professional organization composed of 65 national committees and 14 international specialized committees for the study and conservation of historic buildings, districts, and sites; founded in 1965; maintains a secretariat in Paris. See also **United States Committee of ICOMOS.**

International style Architectural style that originated in Europe after WWI and aimed to be without reference to historical design styles; incorporated the tenets of **functionalism;** isolated examples found throughout North America from ca. 1926 to the present, especially in California and northeastern U.S.; characteristics include defining volume rather than mass, ordering elements by regularity rather than axial symmetry, and avoidance of applied decoration; typical elements include non-load-bearing walls, projecting asymmetrical geometric forms, flat walls and roofs, and horizontal bands of windows set flush with the exterior wall surface; common materials

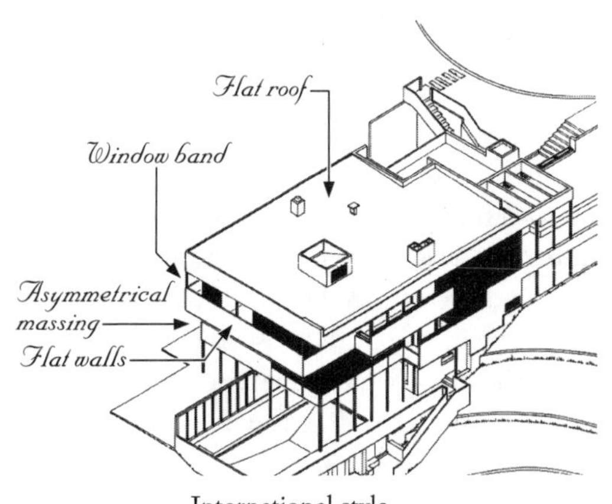

International style
Lovell (Health) House
Los Angeles, California

include concrete, steel, and glass; used for all types of buildings; the term originated with the 1932 Museum of Modern Art exhibition titled "Modern Architecture: International Exhibition" and the related book *The International Style: Architecture Since 1922,* both prepared by Philip Johnson and Henry-Russell Hitchcock. See also **Miesian, modern architecture.**

interpenetrate A decorative feature, such as a molding, that appears to enter another feature, such as a column, and reappears on the other side; common in the Gothic Revival style.

interpretation **1.** The presentation of information to the public regarding a **cultural artifact** at the location of the site, building, structure, or object; methods include guided tours, films, living history enactment, site markers, and museum exhibits. See also **first-person interpretation.** **2.** The analysis of historical research or an investigation of an **archaeological site.**

interrupted arch A segmental pediment with an ornament or gap at the center of the upper cornice. See also **broken pediment.**

intersecting arcade Same as **interlaced arcade.**

intersecting tracery **Tracery** formed by window mullions within a pointed arch; each vertical mullion splits at the spring line of the arch to form two mullions that follow the curve of the arch. See also **interlaced arch, net tracery.**

intersection Same as **crossing.**

intertie A horizontal timber frame member that binds posts together, such as a **girt,** or a tie beam in a roof truss. Also known as **interduce.**

intertriglyph Same as **metope.**

in the clear (pre-19c) The overall inside dimension of a space, such as between columns or exterior walls, or between floor and ceiling.

intrados **1.** The lower boundary or soffit of the voussoirs of an arch. **2.** The line formed by the intersection of the soffit and the face of the arch.

intumescent paint An interior fire-resistant paint that bubbles up in intense heat; used to increase the fire rating of wood trim and other flammable surfaces.

inventory A list of historic resources at a site or within a geographic area. See also **historic district survey.**

inverse condemnation The taking of a property by some action of a government agency that deprives the owner of any economic benefit from the property; used as a cause of legal action to recover damages or compensation. See also **condemnation.**

invert **1.** The elevation of the bottom of the inside of a sewer, especially where it enters a manhole or larger sewer. **2.** An inverted arch or vault, especially one that forms the bottom of a sewer; originally an abbreviation of **inverted arch.**

inverted arch An arch constructed upside down on the earth to support a building foundation; the spring line is above the intrados and the extrados below.

investment property **Real estate** used to produce both rental income and appreciation in **market value** for the owner. See also **income property, speculation.**

investment tax credit (ITC) A U.S. federal tax credit for a **Certified Rehabilitation Project** as defined in the Economic Recovery Tax Act of 1981 and the Tax Reform Act of 1986; available for **substantial rehabilitation** of a building listed in the **National Register of Historic Places;** administered by the National Park Service; equals the amount of the **qualified rehabilitation expenditures** up to a maximum of 20 percent of the **adjusted basis** of a **depreciable property.** See also **Certification of Significance.**

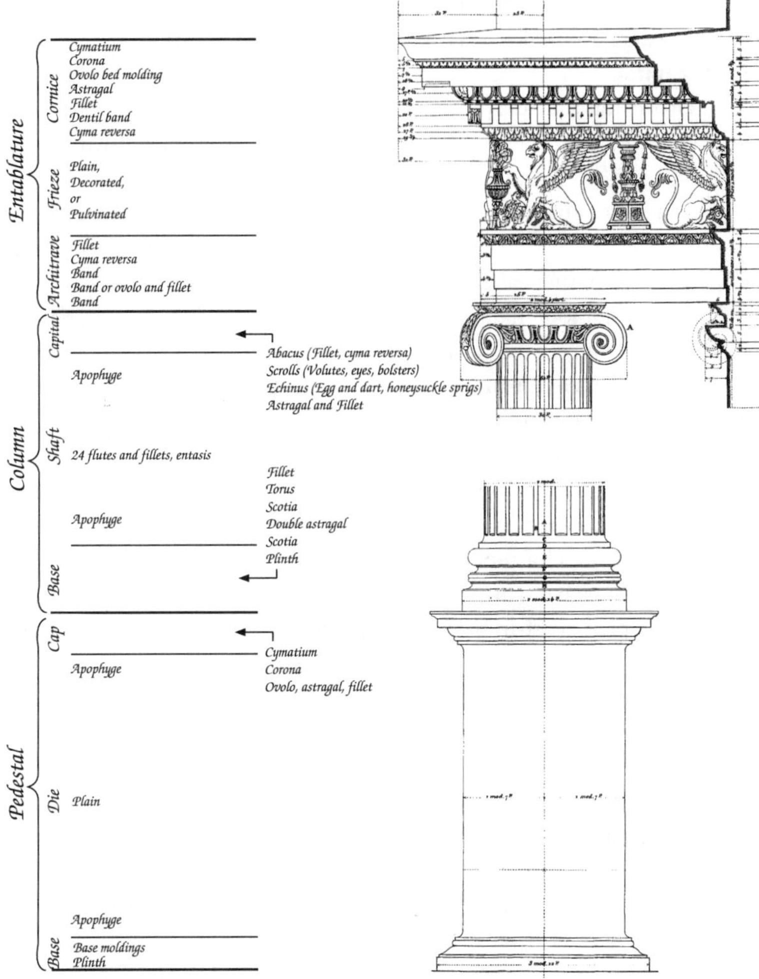

Ionic order

invisible hinge A hinge that cannot be seen when the door is closed.

inwrought Wrought metalwork with one or more additional metals worked into the base metal.

Ionic order, (pre-19c) **Ionick order** An order of the Greek classical styles. From top to bottom the Greek Ionic order is shown in the figure. The capital has a horizontal echinus scroll curving downward to form two volutes on both parallel faces with bolsters at each end; entablature with an architrave with (in order of appearance) a band, fillet, ovolo, band, cyma reversa, and fillet, a plain frieze or a zoophorus, and a cornice with a bed mold with cyma reversa, fillet, dentil band, fillet and ovolo, a corona, and cymatium; the Roman Ionic order often adds a lower torus or scotia to the base and a pedestal; many variations of these elements are found; the Ionic orders typically support a gable roof with a pediment end composed of a triangular tympanum surrounded by cornices. See also **attic base, channel, classical orders, Greek Revival style, Roman Ionic capital.**

I-rail (19c) An iron railroad rail that is approximately I-shaped in cross section.

iridescent glass Translucent glass manufactured with a diffractive sheen in imitation of antique glass.

iron, (pre-20c) **iren, irne** **1.** A malleable, elemental metal. **2.** The common name for many iron and carbon compounds such as **bar iron, Berlin iron, black iron, cast iron, common iron, iron steel, gray iron, mild steel, pig iron, white iron,** and **wrought iron;** although iron based, **steel** is sometimes considered a separate material; types by shape include **angle iron, cavity iron, channel iron, corrugated iron.** See also **passive iron.**

iron back (pre-19c) A one-piece cast-iron **fireback.**

ironbound Strapped together or wrapped with iron.

iron foundry A place where iron castings are made. See also **cast iron, ironworks.**

iron oxide Any of various compounds of oxygen and iron, including FeO, Fe_2O_3, and Fe_4O_5; often formed in the presence of water; as much as fifty times the volume of pure iron; used as a **pigment,** with various hues depending on the chemical composition, ranging from yellow to orange, red, and dark brown. Also known as **rust.** See also **Indian red, iron stain, rust jacking.**

iron pig An individual ingot of **pig iron.**

iron rust See **iron oxide.**

iron stain An **iron oxide** stain caused by rusting iron or steel. Also known as **iron mold.**

iron steel Steel-coated iron, or iron sandwiched between steel plates.

iron-wire fence A type of **wire fence** composed of woven wire in framed panels 7–10 feet wide, supported with cast-iron posts; manufactured from the late 1840s to ca. 1880 of ⅛–⅜ inch iron wire; **cast-ons** added in the 1850s; used for fencing, balcony railings, and window grilles.

ironwork, iron-work, iron work Ornamental or structural construction that uses **iron** or **steel;** types include **ornamental iron, structural steel.** Also known as **ferrament.** See also **cast iron, skeleton construction, wrought iron.**

ironworks, (19c) **iron works** A site where iron or steel is smelted or heavy **ironwork** is manufactured; may be an individual building or a site with multiple facilities. See also **iron foundry.**

irregular column (18c) A column not designed in the proportions of one of the five classical orders, especially one with unusual ornamentation.

irregular coursed A roughly coursed stone wall bond.

isinglass, isinglass-stone A transparent form of **mica.**

isinglass glue (19c) A strong, clear glue made from fish bladders and used in tempera paint.

isolated footing A **spread footing** that is separate from other footings, such as one of a series of column footings within a building.

isolee (18c) Same as **insulated column.**

isothermal glazing Two layers of glazing with a ventilated airspace between them; reduces heat buildup and protects existing stained-glass windows. See also **double glazed.**

ISTEA **Intermodal Surface Transportation Efficiency Act;** pronounced "iced tea."

Italianate An architectural style loosely based on that of rural Renaissance farmhouses in northern Italy; varies from picturesque villas with ornate detailing and asymmetrical massing to restrained and rigidly symmetrical town houses and commercial buildings; typical elements include multiple stories, bracketed cornices, low-pitched pyramidal roof, and

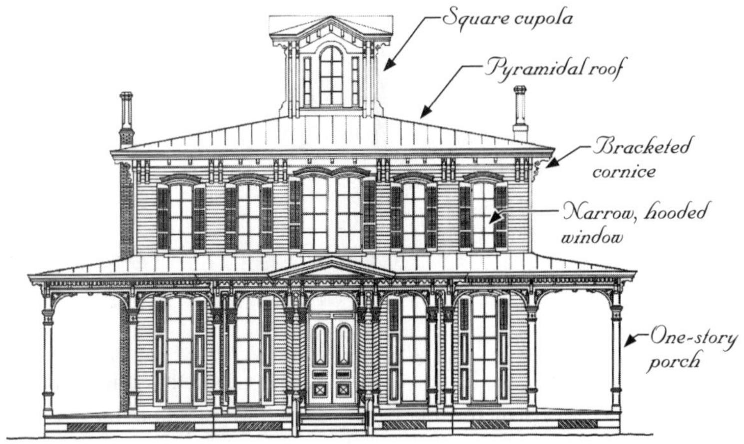

Italianate
Jackson's Clubhouse
Cape May, New Jersey

narrow, hooded, framed, or bracketed windows; often with a one-story front porch and occasionally with a square tower, bays, balustraded balconies, and a square cupola; some commercial buildings constructed with cast-iron fronts; found throughout the U.S. and Canada beginning in the late 1830s, rising to great popularity in mid-19c, and declining in use with the economic crash of 1873. Also known as **American style, Bracketed style, Lombard style, Round style, Tuscan style.**

Italian Renaissance Classical architecture in the style of the northern Italian Renaissance beginning in the 15c; influenced the **Renaissance Revival style** common in North America in the late 19c–early 20c. Also known as **Northern Italian Renaissance.**

Italian roof (pre-19c) Same as **hip roof.**

Italian tiling A terra-cotta roof covering composed of courses of two interlocked shapes: flat **tegula** tiles with turned-up edges and joints covered with curved **imbrex** tiles; used by the Romans and also known as **Roman tile.**

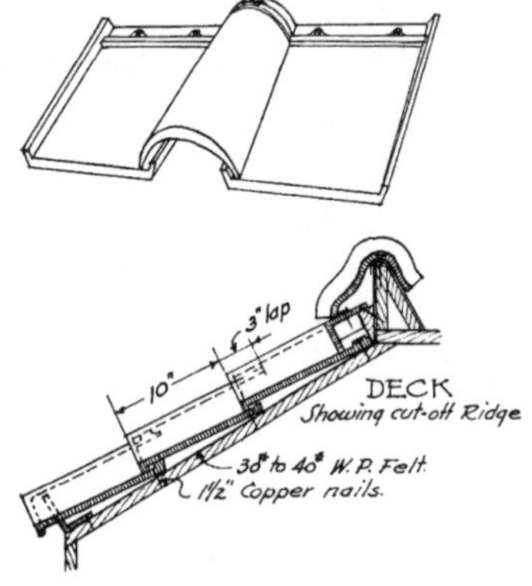

Italian tiling

Italian villa A house in the form of a rural, northern Italian Renaissance **villa;** popular in the mid-19c.

Italic order (pre-20c) Same as **composite order.**

ITC Abbr. for **investment tax credit.**

ivory-black A jet-black paint **pigment** manufactured using charcoal made from ivory chips left over from making ivory combs during the 18c and later also from animal bones; used for mixing pearl grays, warm olives, and bronze greens. See also **drop black, lampblack.**

J

Jablochkoff candle Same as **electric candle.**

jacal A Native American shelter constructed of upright poles infilled with thin wattle and daub walls made with wicker and adobe; found in northern Mexico and southwestern U.S.; some examples in Arizona have parallel walls of wicker filled with rammed earth.

jack **1.** Any building element shorter than others of the same type, such as a **jack rafter** or **jack rib. 2.** (18c) A machine with gears and chains that turn a kitchen spit.

jack arch, (pre-19c) **jak arch** An **arch** in which the intrados and extrados are level; used above square-headed openings. Also known as **straight arch.**

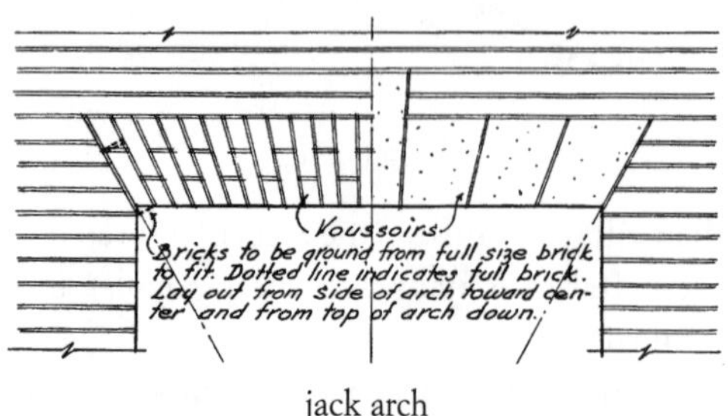

jack arch

jack architrave The lower fascia of an architrave that is divided into multiple fascias.

jackknife switch (late 19c–present) An electric **switch** with a copper blade with a handle on one end and a pivot on the other; when the blade is in the closed position, it is held by spring clips that complete the circuit; typically used for main circuits.

jackknife switch

jack post A steel column with a screw jack attached to one end.

jack rafter A rafter that is shorter than a common rafter, such as between a wall plate and hip rafter; type includes **valley rafter.** Also known as **cripple.**

jack rib A short **rib** in a vault or dome.

jack roof A single-slope roof section that does not extend to the ridge of the main roof.

jack stud A stud that is shorter than the height of the full wall, as at the side of a door. Also known as **cripple.**

Jacobean Revival style, Jacobethan Revival style Late 19c–early 20c architecture based on the style of late 17c English architecture, which combined elements of the **Pointed style** with **Palladian** influences of the Renaissance; most common for architect-designed buildings, especially in northeastern U.S.; typical elements include masonry walls with Gothic style detailing, steeply pitched gable roofs with parapeted gable ends, sometimes with flat-roofed towers and bays with castellated parapets; often with ornately formed ganged multiple chimney shafts and/or chimney pots. See also **Tudor Revival style.**

jacquard fabric A tapestry weave cloth manufactured beginning in the 1870s; typically used as a wall covering.

jail (late 18c–present) A building, or part of a building, used to confine accused or convicted criminals; typically refers to a place used for temporary imprisonment, such as for those convicted of petty crimes or those awaiting trial, as opposed to a **prison.**

jalousie **1.** Used to describe a porch or balcony enclosed with fixed louvered panels with adjustable slats. **2.** (19c) A venetian blind with wood slats. **3.** (20c) A window composed of narrow glass slats that can be adjusted.

jamb, (pre-20c) **jam, jaum, jaumb** The facing sides of a wall opening, such as a **door** or **window.** See also **cheek, chimney jamb, splay.**

jamb lining The vertical wood member between the interior face of a **window stile** and the trim; typically with a tongue projecting into the stile. See also **head lining.**

jamb post Same as **door post** or **window post.**

jamb shaft A small column, with base and capital, that forms part of the side of a door or window; found in Gothic style architecture. See also **angle shaft.**

jambstone A single vertical stone that forms a door or window jamb.

Janus-faced lock A rim lock with a case designed so that it can be used for both right-handed and left-handed doors.

japan Same as **japan drier.**

japan Same as **japan varnish.** See also **black japan.**

japan black Same as **black japan.**

japan drier A component of a paint mixture that speeds drying of the oil base; usually contains solutions of lead and manganese salts mixed in neutral linseed oil, resin, or gum and thinned with turpentine or mineral spirits; typically dark brown, but lighter colors are made using **sugar of lead** or **litharge.** Also known as **japan.**

Japanese lacquer A transparent varnish made by dissolving the plant resin urushiol in spirits; naturally dark brown, it is often colored with pigment; used in multiple layers for a smooth, shiny, thick finish on wood. Also known as **japan varnish.**

japanned Covered with a smooth, hard, glossy lacquer finish made by applying coats of **japan varnish** or a similar material; popular in the late 19c for wood, metal, and leather finishes.

japan varnish **1.** A hard, black varnish manufactured in Japan from the *Stagmaria verniciflua* plant. **2.** A varnish that imitates the Japanese product, such as a varnish of the 18c composed of amber and rosin dissolved in turpentine with ivory-black pigment. Also known as **japan.** See also **Japanese lacquer.**

jaspé Veined or clouded colors that imitate jasper; used in some linoleums.

J-bolt An **anchor bolt** with a J-shaped hook on the bottom.

jealous glass (18c–19c) A cast sheet glass with a surface of various oblong circular figures that are convex one side and concave on the other side; used in lower window sash to transmit light while maintaining privacy. See also **obscure glass.**

Jeffersonian, Jeffersonian Classicism Late 18c–early 19c **neo-classical** architecture based on that of Roman public buildings, such as the campus of the University of Virginia in Charlottesville designed by Thomas Jefferson; heavier and more monumental than the **Federal style** architecture of the period. Also known as **Early Classical Revival, Roman Republican, Roman Revival.**

jerkinhead, (19c) **jerkin-head,** (pre-19c) **jerkin head, jirkin head** A gable end that slopes back at the top to form a small hipped roof end. Also known as **hipped gable.**

jerkinhead

jerkinhead roof A roof with one or more **jerkin-heads.**

jerry-built, (pre-20c) **jerry built** Hastily and/or poorly constructed, usually with insufficient or insubstantial materials.

jesting beam A nonstructural beam used for decoration.

jet **1.** The opening at the end of a gas lighting fixture; type includes **batwing jet.** **2.** (pre-20c) A projection or overhang of an architectural element. Also known as **overjet.**

jet d'eau **1.** A spray of water in a fountain. **2.** (pre-19c) A water fountain with one or more spouts.

jett (pre-19c) **1.** To construct a **jetty** (sense 2). **2.** Same as **jet** (sense 2).

jetty **1.** A narrow, massive structure that projects into a body of water; used as a breakwater or landing place for ships. **2.** (pre-20c) An overhanging story of a building. Also known as **overhang, overjet, overset.**

jewel A faceted piece of glass in a colored glass window.

Jew's pitch (pre-20c) Same as **bitumen.**

jib door **1.** A **door** installed flush with the face of the wall without a casing trim, so that the door does not disturb the symmetry of the room; typically painted or papered to match the wall. See also **blank door.** **2.** (19c–present) Same as **jib window.**

jib lot (New England) A triangular-shaped piece of land.

jib window A **window** in which the sill is level with the floor; when the window is open, it can be used as a door. Also known as **jib door.**

jog An offset or change in direction of a line or surface.

joggle **1.** A locked stone or wood joint with an irregular outline (e.g., a **scarf joint**). **2.** A shoulder on a vertical element, such as a truss post, that receives the thrust of a strut. **3.** A tenon or dowel connecting two stone or timber elements. **4.** (19c) Same as **rabbet.**

joggle beam A wooden beam in which the components are connected with joggles.

joggled arch A **flat arch** with stepped voussoirs; each voussoir hangs on the adjacent one, rather than acts as a true **arch.** See also **crossette.**

joggle post A truss post with joggle shoulders supporting diagonal struts.

joiner's brad (18c) A finish nail 1–2.25 inches long used for hardwood wainscoting.

joinery, (pre-19c) **joynery** Fine wood architectural elements and furniture made by connecting their parts with shaped joints; includes **cabinetry, casework, millwork.**

joint The place where two or more separate elements come together; types include those used in carpentry such as **beaking joint, bridle joint, butt joint, dovetail joint, feather joint, fantail joint, finger joint, flush joint, foliated joint, halving joint, head joint, joggle, match joint, miter, mortise and tenon, quirk joint, scarf joint, shiplap, splay joint, sypher joint, tongue-and-groove,** metalwork such as **drip joint, flange joint, lap joint, pin joint, plumb joint, roll joint, saddle joint, sweated joint,** various kinds of **masonry joints** and **pipe**

joints, and **construction joint, control joint, expansion joint, bracket joint, heel joint, rust joint.** See also **normal cut.**

joint box A cast-iron fitting that connects the top of a truss post with the horizontal and diagonal members. See also **shoe.**

joint hinge Same as **strap hinge.**

joist, (pre-19c) **joyce, joyst, joyste, joys** **1.** One of a series of closely spaced, parallel **beams** that supports a floor or ceiling; typically 2× in wood frame construction by the late 19c. See also **binding joist, header, interjoist, sleeper, trimmer.** **2.** (pre-20c) A 3 × 4 inch **stud.** See also **split joist.** **3.** A **sleeper** on top of a structural deck.

joist anchor A metal device that attaches the end of a joist to a masonry or concrete wall; types include **side joist anchor.**

joist hanger A **beam hanger** that attaches the end of an individual joist to a beam or other structure; the light-gauge steel type commonly used today was in use by 1890.

joistile A **structural clay tile** unit used as part of a concrete flooring system; has a rectangular core with projecting lugs in the form of a flattened T-shape; used mainly in midwestern and southwestern U.S.

Jonesboro granite A red and pinkish gray, medium coarse-grained **granite** quarried in the vicinity of Jonesboro, Maine.

journeyman A skilled building mechanic who has completed his or her apprenticeship; may work under the direction of a **master.**

jubé Same as **rood screen.**

juffers (18c) Wood that is 4 or 5 inches square.

jump A stepped change in the level of masonry work, such as at the top or bottom of a foundation wall.

junction box (19c–present) An **electric box** used for splicing **electric wiring.**

juniper (southern U.S.) Same as **eastern red cedar** or **white cedar.**

jury box (mid-19c–present) A **box** that surrounds the jury's seats in a courtroom.

jury house A building adjacent to a courthouse and used for jury deliberations; common late 17c–early 18c northern Virginia.

jut-by A **Beverly jog** on a gambrel-roofed house.

K

kagge, kaggi A domed building built of snow and used by Eskimos for meetings; approximately 15 feet high and 20 feet in diameter.

kalsomine Same as **calcimine.**

karmang, garmang A permanent Eskimo dwelling built of seal skins stretched over whale ribs or poles and supported by a stone wall surrounding an excavation into the side of a slope.

K-bracing Diagonal bracing of a truss or skeleton construction bay that forms the shape of the letter *K* (e.g., members that connect the top and bottom of a column with the center of the column on the opposite side of the bay).

keel arch Same as **ogee arch.**

keel molding A projecting molding in the shape of a pointed ship's hull; may have a small fillet at the point; typically in the shape of two reverse curves in cross section.

Keene's cement A hard **plaster** material made by recalcining **plaster of paris** saturated with a solution of alum; invented ca. 1840.

keeper The socket into which the bolt of a lock slides. Also known as **catch.**

Keeper of the National Register The individual who has been delegated the authority within the National Park Service to determine the eligibility of historic sites for nomination to the **National Register of Historic Places;** first appointed in 1967.

keeping room (19c New England) A family living room or sitting room, as opposed to a formal parlor used for entertaining guests.

keg house (late 19c) A saloon that served liquor from small varnished kegs rather than from bottles; found mostly in the Plains states.

kelp glass Glass manufactured with kelp for the metallic oxides.

kennel **1.** A building used for housing dogs; may include a fenced enclosure. **2.** (pre-20c) Same as **canal** (sense 2).

Kentucky bluestone A light bluish gray, hard, durable sandstone quarried in Kentucky.

keramic (19c) Same as **ceramic.**

kerf One of a series of saw cuts made partially through an element; used on the back of a wood molding to assist in bending it or in any wood element to assist in chiseling a mortise. See also **back kerf.**

Kerite Trademark for an electric wire insulation composed of vulcanized rubber and oxidized linseed oil mixed with other vegetable oils; before 1920, used as a rubber substitute in **rubber insulation.**

kerosene A fuel oil initially distilled from bituminous coal and oil shale starting in the 1840s and later from petroleum; may be used in a **kerosene lamp** or various kinds of furnaces and heaters; patented by Abraham Gesner of Nova Scotia in 1854.

kerosene lamp An oil lamp fueled by **kerosene;** typically has an adjustable flat woven wick; most early types of oil lamps were converted to kerosene after the fuel came into common use in 1859; used in rural areas without electricity into the 1930s; may be portable, hung on a frame from the ceiling, or supported on a wall bracket. See also **oil lamp.**

kexen See **totem pole.**

key **1.** A tapered or wedge-shaped piece used to lock parts of a timber frame or other construction together. **2.** The portion of a plaster base coat that extends between and behind the lath and holds it in place. **3.** Same as **gib. 4.** (18c) A masonry bracket that supports an entablature, such as a **console. 5.** A roughened surface or recessed grooves that bond to stucco or some other coating. **6.** A device inserted in a hardware **lock** to open or close it.

key banding See **meander.**

key block Same as **keystone.**

key console A keystone with a projecting console.

keyed beam A **compound beam** in which two stacked wood members have a series of keys mortised into the abutting faces to provide shear resistance; typically each **key** is a pair of oak wedges but may also be pipe or solid wood or cast iron with a rectangular cross section.

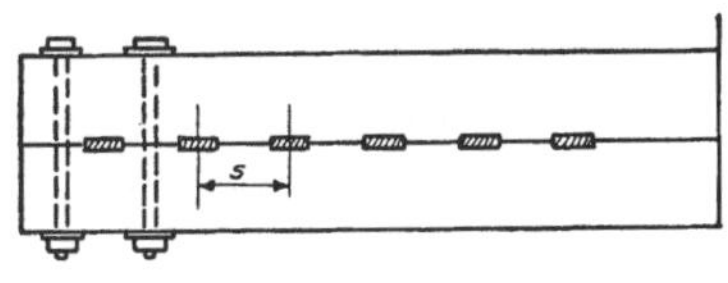

keyed beam

key pattern See **meander.**

keystone, (18c) **key-stone** The center voussoir of an **arch,** often larger or more ornate than the other voussoirs. Also known as **sagitta.**

key tenant Same as **anchor tenant.**

kickplate A metal or brass plate applied to the bottom rail of a door for protection.

kiln An oven, furnace, or other structure, usually constructed of brick, used to fire bricks, terracotta, and other ceramics, to calcine limestone, and to dry wood. Also known as **fire kiln.** See also **kiln dried.**

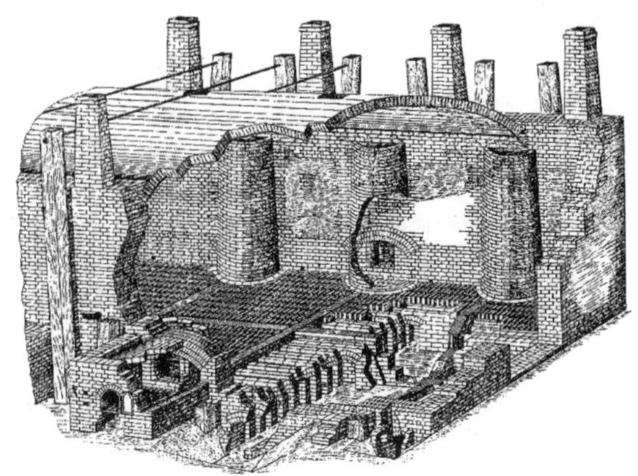
kiln

kiln dried **Seasoned wood** that has been dried mechanically in a kiln, as opposed to **air dried.**

kiln run An unsorted batch of bricks or terracotta from a particular kiln firing.

kingbolt, king bolt A vertical metal rod that connects the apex of a triangular roof truss to the middle of the tie beam; replaces a **kingpost.** Also known as **kingpin, king rod.**

king closer **1.** A stretcher brick cut to more than one-half of its length and used to complete a course that does not have an even number of stretchers. **2.** A stretcher brick cut diagonally so that one end is full width and the other end is one-half width. See also **brick, queen closer.**

King of Prussia marble A marble quarried in King of Prussia, Pennsylvania; colors range from white with gray veins to medium gray.

kingpiece, king's piece Same as **kingpost.**

kingpin Same as **kingbolt.**

kingpost, king-post The single vertical **hanging post** of a **king truss.** Also known as **crown post, broach post, kingpiece, king's piece, middle post, tree post.** See also **kingbolt.**

king-post truss Same as **king truss.**

king rod **1.** Same as **kingbolt. 2.** (19c) A metal rod used to support or brace a **kingpost.**

king's yellow (18c) Same as **orpiment.**

king-table In Gothic style architecture, a decorated masonry course under a parapet, typically with ballflowers.

king truss A triangular **truss** with a single vertical **king post** or **kingbolt** that connects the apex of the triangle with the middle of the horizontal tie beam; originally a timber-framed roof truss with two principal rafters, also used in iron and steel bridges; may have braces at the sides of the king post. Also known as **king-post truss.**

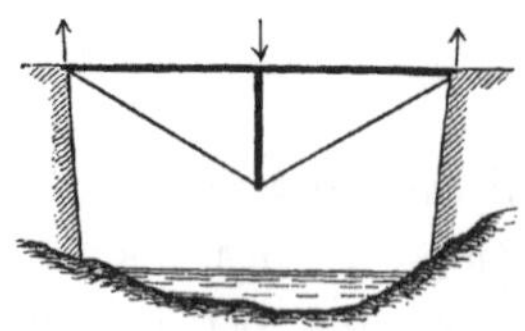

king truss

Kingwood stone Trade name for an antique yellow to purplish buff, medium- to coarse-grained quartzite quarried in West Virginia; composed of white quartz colored with spots of brown oxidized iron; used for building stone.

kinkled glass Glass in which the surface is covered with small, round bumps; synonym for **obscure glass.**

kiosk (19c–present) **1.** A small, ornamental pavilion or summerhouse used in parks and gardens; derived from similar structures in Iran and Turkey. See also **gazebo. 2.** A small structure used to display information or products; typically located in a public place.

kirb (pre-20c) Same as **curb.**

kitchen, (pre-19c) **kitchin,** (pre-18c) **kitchinge** A **room** used to prepare food; types include **galley kitchen, kitchenette.** Also known as **cookroom.** See also **cookhouse, kitchen cabinet, pantry.**

kitchen cabinet A cabinet used for storage in a **kitchen;** often with drawers and shelves; typically not permanently fastened to the wall of the building until the 20c. See also **countertop, cupboard, wall cabinet.**

kitchenette A small room or alcove with kitchen facilities.

kitchen garden A vegetable **garden.**

kitchen midden Same as **midden heap.**

kiva An underground room used for religious ceremonies by the Pueblo peoples of southwestern U.S. and northern Mexico; typically cylindrical in shape with adobe or stone walls, pole roof beams, and an earth-covered roof; the only opening is the hole in the roof for the ladder. See also **cliff dwelling, Pueblo.**

knee **1.** A bent or curved element used to stiffen a joint where two members meet at an angle, such as a **timber frame** column and beam; may be cut from a natural bend of a tree (e.g., where a branch joins the trunk). **2.** The convex part of a handrail between a sloped ramp and a horizontal portion at a landing. See also **swan neck.**

knee brace **1.** A **knee** or **bracket** formed by a short diagonal brace, such as between a beam and its supporting column; may be straight or curved. See also **knee timber, K-bracing. 2.** A relatively small diagonal brace used in **wood frame** construction. See also **stud brace.**

kneed architrave **1.** An **architrave** surrounding a wall opening with a sideways extension of the outer moldings at the bottom corners. **2.** Same as **shouldered architrave.**

knee iron (19c) A metal **knee** used to strengthen a joint.

kneeler One of a series of coping stones with a sloped top and a horizontal bed that projects into a gable wall. See also **footstone.**

kneeling rafter Same as **knee rafter.**

knee piece (18c) Same as **knee timber** or **knee rafter.**

knee rafter **1.** A **knee brace** between a principal rafter and a tie beam. **2.** A bent rafter, the lower end of which rests vertically on the wall plate or tie beam. Also known as **bent principal.**

knee roof Same as **curb roof.**

kneestone Same as **kneeler.**

knee timber A wood knee (sense 1), often cut from the naturally crooked part of a tree (e.g., where a branch joins the trunk) or from a branch of a **naval oak** artificially bent during growth.

knee wall A low-height wall between a floor and a sloped ceiling, such as in an attic; sometimes incorrectly used to mean a **dwarf wall.** See also **ashlaring.**

knob **1.** A rounded, projecting hand pull; may be fixed or rotate, such as a **doorknob.** **2.** Same as **boss** (sense 1).

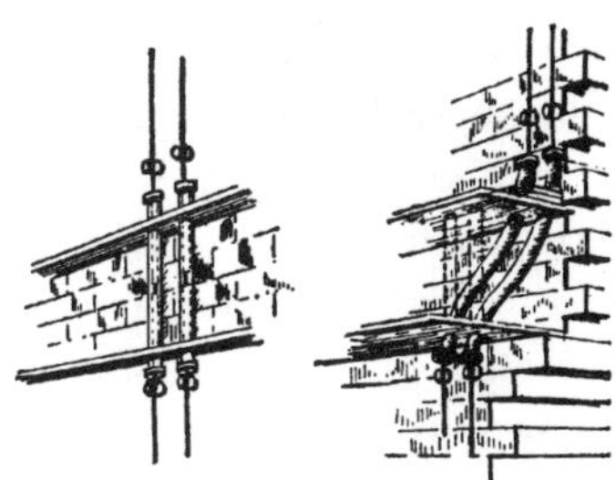

knob-and-tube

knob-and-tube An electric wiring system used in concealed spaces; wires are threaded through insulated tubes at joists and studs and are held along the surface of members by insulating knobs; typically made of porcelain, but also included glass and pottery. See also **electric wiring, porcelain cleats.**

knob lock A dead bolt lock operated with a knob on the interior face of the lock, rather than with a key.

Kno-fur lath A self-furring expanded-metal lath manufactured from steel sheet metal containing some copper and coated with carbon paint; used ca. 1925–50 in southern or coastal construction where corrosion is a problem.

knot **1.** See **knotwork.** **2.** A circular pattern of wood fibers caused by later growth of a tree around a branch; often denser than the surrounding wood. **3.** A geometric pattern in a flower bed that forms an interlaced design when viewed from above.

knot hole The void left in cut lumber by a **knot** that has separated from the surrounding wood and dropped out.

knotted column A **column** with a shaft carved to resemble a knot or two intertwined ropes.

knotted pillar Same as **knotted column.**

knotwork A bas-relief sculptural representation of interlaced cords. See also **knotted column.**

knuckle One of the hollow, cylindrical projections on the edge of a hinge leaf that holds the hinge pin; when the hinge leaves are at a 90-degree angle the shape resembles the knuckles on a human hand; may be cast or rolled metal.

knulling (19c) Same as **knurling.**

knurling A bead and reel or similar molding, especially one with elaborate divisions or decoration. Also known as **knulling.**

kraft paper (20c) A heavy, moisture-resistant, wood fiber paper.

K-truss A bridge truss with repetitive panels in the shape of the letter *K.* See also **truss.**

kyanized Wood impregnated with mercuric chloride; used to prevent decay.

L

L **1.** A bar or fitting for a pipe that makes a right-angle turn. **2.** Same as **ell.**

label Same as **hood mold,** especially when square headed.

label

labeled door A **fire-rated** door labeled according to the rating given it by a certified testing laboratory (e.g., a **B-label door**). See also **underwriters door.**

label stop A corbel or boss, or sideways projection, of the molding at the base of a hood-mold.

lac A resinous substance secreted by the East Indian lac insect; used for red dyes and for making **lacquer, shellac.**

lac dye A scarlet pigment refined from lac.

laced beam Same as **lattice beam.**

lacing The zigzag diagonal metal webbing connecting two structural sections to form a beam, column, or similar member. See also **lattice bar.**

lacing

lacing course A bonding course of brick or tile in a rubble stone wall; typically used at regular vertical intervals.

lac-luster (mid-20c) A flat varnish finish similar to that produced by shellac; may be inherent in the varnish or be developed by rubbing.

lacquer, (19c) **lacker** **1.** A transparent spirit varnish composed of a plant resin dissolved in alcohol; most often referred to as **shellac** and, after 1852, **Japanese lacquer;** often colored with pigments; used as a decorative wood finish and as a clear protective coating on brass and other polished metals. **2.** (1920s–present) A transparent coating composed of nitrocellulose in a fast-drying solvent; highly resistant to weathering.

lacuna (pl. **lacunae**) **1.** One of the recessed panels in a coffered ceiling or soffit. **2.** A space where something is missing or lost, such as a part of a building that has been removed or lost through deterioration.

lacunar **1.** Having sunken panels, such as a coffered ceiling or soffit. Also known as **lequear.** **2.** An arched roof or ceiling, especially the planking or flooring above a portico or piazza.

lac varnish Any **varnish** made with lac resin dissolved in a solvent; types include **shellac, water varnish.**

lady chapel In a large church, a **chapel** dedicated to the Virgin Mary; typically located east of the altar.

lag bolt A large-diameter bolt with a square or hexagonal head on one end and tapered threads on the other; used for attaching timbers to one another.

lagging Planks used as horizontal **sheeting** for an excavation; often installed between **soldier piles.**

lag screw A **lag bolt** with fine threads. See also **skein screw.**

laid on A wood framing member attached to the surface of the studs or other elements with nails, as opposed to being **let in.**

laja Flagstones used for flooring in adobe buildings.

lake color Any of various red paint **pigments** composed of organic compounds combined with metallic bases; the organic portions from wood and insect dyes were replaced by aniline colors in the late 19c; typically have **fugitive color;** bases include alumina, tin, lead, and chromium; colors include **Dutch pink, rose lake, rose pink, and Vienna lake.**

Lally column (20c) Trade name for a concrete-filled steel **pipe column** with end plates manufactured by Lally Column Company; used in house construction and repairs.

lamb's tongue **1.** An ovolo or quarter round molding with a fillet on the edge of a board, muntin, or sash. **2.** A 45-degree chamfer stop with a cyma profile; tapers from the full width of the chamfer to a point.

Lamella roof A reticulated barrel vault roof structure composed of a network of short wood members covered with sheathing; patented in 1925 and used for long roof spans.

laminated Any material built up in thin layers, such as plywood.

laminated arch, laminated rib A structural arch composed of multiple layers of material.

laminated beam **1.** Same as **flitch beam.** **2.** (20c) A wood beam composed of many overlapping pieces glued together.

laminated floor A structural floor constructed of a continuous series of 2× or 3× lumbers set on edge and nailed together; used for relatively long spans, such as in **slow-burning mill construction.**

laminated glass Two layers of **glass** sandwiching a layer of flexible plastic; when the glass is broken, the plastic holds the glass shards in place.

laminated mill construction A type of **slow-burning mill construction** with a **laminated floor.**

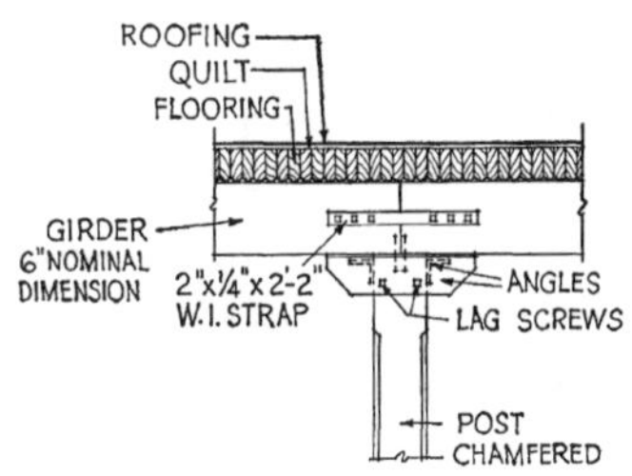

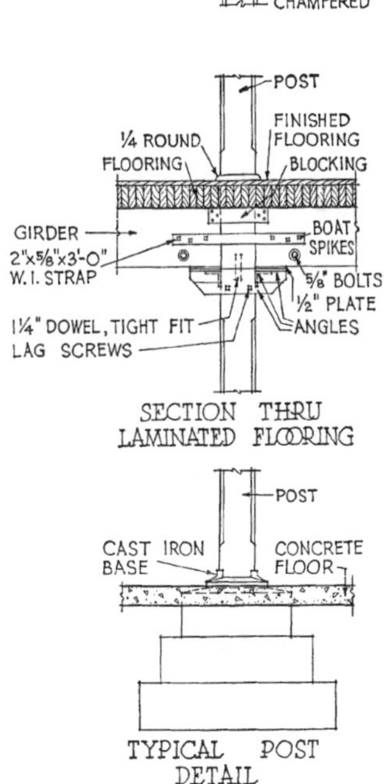

laminated mill construction

laminated plastic See **plastic laminate.**

laminated rib See **laminated arch.**

lamp **1.** A device that produces artificial light by a flame; may be portable or fixed; types include alcohol lamp, **Argand lamp, gas lighting, kerosene lamp, pentane lamp, oil lamp.** **2.** The bulb enclosing incandescent gas or a glowing filament in an electric light fixture; typically removable; types include **arc lamp, fluorescent lamp, incandescent lamp.** See also **light fixture.**

lamp bell A bell-shaped device that hangs over an **oil lamp** or **candle** to collect soot.

lampblack, (before mid-20c) **lamp black** A jet black pigment composed of amorphous carbon in the form of soot; manufactured by burning rosin, tallow, or coal tar distillates; often blue-gray when mixed with white lead, as in 18c paints. Also known as **smoke black, soot black.** See also **drop black, ivory-black, sugarhouse black.**

lamp globe A generally spherical glass cover for a **lamp.**

lamp head (19c) An electric light bulb.

lamp stove An oil-burning **stove.**

lanai Hawaiian name for a ground-level **terrace.**

lancet **1.** A light, or pane, shaped like a lancet window in a larger traceried window. **2.** Same as **lancet window.**

lancet arch Same as **equilateral arch** or **acute-pointed arch.**

lancet headed Having an acute-pointed arch at the top, such as a window or arch; may be an **equilateral arch** or narrower.

lancet window A narrow window with a **pointed arch** head; common in the Gothic Revival style. See also **lancet headed.**

Land Act U.S. legislation passed in 1796 that provided for the sale of lands in the Northwest Territory north of the Ohio River, with a minimum purchase of a 640-acre **section** for $2.00 per acre; established the federal system for surveying and selling public lands.

land costs The portion of a development budget allocated for acquiring **real estate;** typically includes the purchase price of the land and building, settlement costs, and transfer taxes. See also **pro forma.**

land description Same as **legal description.**

landing **1.** The floor area immediately adjacent to the top or bottom of a flight of stairs; may be an intermediate stair platform between floors or an area of a floor enclosed within the stairway; types include **halfpace, half quarterpace, quarterpace.** Also known as **footpace, pace.** **2.** A wharf, pier, or other place where boats dock to load and unload. **3.** A platform at a railroad station.

landmark **1.** A familiar or prominent building, structure, or landscape feature serving as a guide to a particular locality; often used to describe any historic property on a federal, state, or local **register.** See also **National Historic Landmark.** **2.** A fixed object that defines the boundary of a property; may be a **boundary marker, monument,** or a distinctive landscape feature.

landmarks register See **register.**

land records map One of a series of maps used by a government agency, such as a tax assessor or recorder of deeds, to record property size, boundaries, location, and ownership.

landscape, (18c) **landskip, landscipp** **1.** (19c) A rural view or prospect, especially a picturesque one. **2.** An exterior view. **3.** The whole of the exterior environment of a site, district, or region, including landforms, trees and plants, rivers and lakes, and the **built environment.** See also **cultural landscape, landscape architecture, landscaping, scenic, vernacular landscape, vista.** **4.** (18c) A painting of a rural scene; typically used as part of an overmantel.

landscape architect (19c–present) A professional with training in the design of **land-**

scape architecture; may have specialized training in historic plant materials and landscape construction techniques; a licensed profession in some jurisdictions. See also **architect.**

landscape architecture (late 18c–present) Designed, or sculptured, outdoor spaces, including **gardens** and **parks;** based on design principles; elements include plants, landforms, paving, furniture, minor related structures, and fencing; has largely replaced the earlier term **landscape gardening.** Also known as **landscaping.**

landscape gardening The process of producing **landscape architecture.**

landscape marble Same as **forest marble.**

landscape panel (18c) A panel in the middle of an overmantel suitable for installing a landscape painting; typically with the long axis of the rectangle oriented horizontally.

landscaping **1.** The process of designing and constructing **landscape architecture;** sometimes incorrectly used to mean gardening. **2.** Same as **landscape architecture.** **3.** The **vernacular landscape** setting for a building or complex.

land surveying See **surveying.**

land tie A **tie rod** that attaches a retaining wall, exterior stair, or similar structure to a **deadman.**

land use The way in which a particular property, district, or **study area** is used or is permitted or projected to be used in the future; categories of usage typically include residential, commercial, industrial, and farming; used in **planning** analysis and in **zoning.** See also **use.**

land use regulation Any type of government restriction on **development;** common methods of regulation include **zoning** and review by an **architectural review board;** such regulations typically are decided by a local government based on **planning** and public participation.

lane A narrow roadway between fences, hedges, or other confining structures; typically rural as opposed to an **alley.**

lantern, (pre-20c) **lanthorn** **1.** A structure with side windows that rises above adjacent roofs and lights the space below. See also **cupola, belvedere, skylight.** **2.** A transparent or translucent lighting fixture that encloses an open flame, especially when mounted on a lamppost or the exterior wall of a building. **3.** A glass-enclosed room that houses the light at the top of a lighthouse.

lantern light **1.** A small **lantern** (sense 1). See also **skylight.** **2.** (19c) A lamp or light in a lantern (sense 1).

lantern of the dead Same as **cemetery beacon.**

lantern stairs (19c) Winding stairs similar to those found in a lighthouse.

lantern tower **1.** A tall **lantern** (sense 1). **2.** A tower that supports a **lantern** (sense 2).

lap The length covered by a **lap joint;** typically measured from the upper edge of the bottom piece to the lower edge of the top piece; occasionally measured from nails in the bottom piece to the lower edge of the top piece.

lap dovetail A form of **secret dovetail** joint in which the ends of the boards are rabbeted, and the dovetail and the corresponding recess are cut into the thin ends of the boards.

lapis lazuli A rich blue mineral compound used to produce the paint pigment **ultramarine.**

lap joint **1.** A joint formed by overlapping two or more elements and mechanically fastening them, without rabbets, notches, or folds. Also known as **overlap joint.** **2.** A connection of two wood members created by cutting a notch in the bottom of one member and overlapping a corresponding notch in the top of the other member; types include **bevel lap, half dovetail lap, half lap.**

lapped work, (18c) **lapt work** (pre-19c) Carpentry that primarily consists of pegged lap joints rather than mortise-and-tenon joints.

lap siding Various horizontal lapped wood exterior siding arrangements. See also **clapboard, drop siding, weatherboarding.**

lap splice A splice in which the ends or edges of two pieces are overlapped and fastened together; commonly used in joists above a bearing partition.

lap weld A weld at the offset formed by overlapping metal plates.

larch **1.** One of various softwood trees of the genus *Larix;* includes **eastern tamarack, western larch. 2.** Same as **noble fir.**

larch fir Same as **western larch.**

large-format photography **Documentation** photography of a site, building, structure, or object taken with a large-format camera capable of producing negatives that are 4 × 5 inches or larger and uses **controlled photography** techniques.

Larimer column A patented steel column with a cross-shaped cross section; manufactured by bending two I-beams at right angles and riveting them together at the center with a small I-shaped filler between the webs.

larmier Same as **corona;** from the French *larme,* or "tear," because it is used to direct water away from the wall below.

latch Any of various wood or hardware devices that hold a door or shutter in a closed or open position and are operated without a key; types include **blind fast, latch lock, lift latch, rimmed latch, shutter bar,** and a pivoted bar on the stile that drops into a keeper on the jamb. See also **bolt, lock.**

latch bolt A latch lock bolt with a beveled end that automatically engages the strike plate when the door is closed.

latch lock A lock with a spring-actuated **latch bolt** that engages the strike plate when the door is closed; typically the bolt is momentarily opened by turning the doorknob. Also known as **spring latch, spring lock.**

Late Gothic Revival See **Collegiate Gothic, Gothic Revival.**

late medieval See **postmedieval.**

latewood Same as **summerwood.**

latex **1.** The thick, milky resin of the rubber tree, *Ficus elastica,* and similar plants that becomes elastic when dried. **2.** Synthetic rubber or vinyl.

latex paint A type of water-based paint; manufactured after 1940 with rubber- or vinyl-based binders and, after the mid-1960s, with acrylic binders. Also known as **synthetic rubber paint.**

lath, lathing **1.** A base material with small openings to support **plaster;** types include **split lath, wood lath, expanded-metal lath, sheathing lath, sheet metal lath, wire lath,** and various composition boards, including **Bishopric board, plasterboard; 2.** A wood strip used to support roofing shingles, tiles, or slates. See also **counterlath, gauge lath.**

lath and plaster A wall or ceiling finish of **plaster** supported on wood **lath.**

lathed and filled (18c) Finished with lath and plaster.

lath-laid and set A two-coat **plaster** finish supported on lath; after the first coat is laid on the lath, the surface is roughened and the second coat is laid over the first.

lath nail A small **cut nail** used for installing wood lath.

latia One of a series of peeled poles that span between the vigas of a flat-roofed adobe or stone building in the southwestern U.S. or northern Mexico; typically laid on a diagonal and left exposed, creating a herringbone-patterned ceiling.

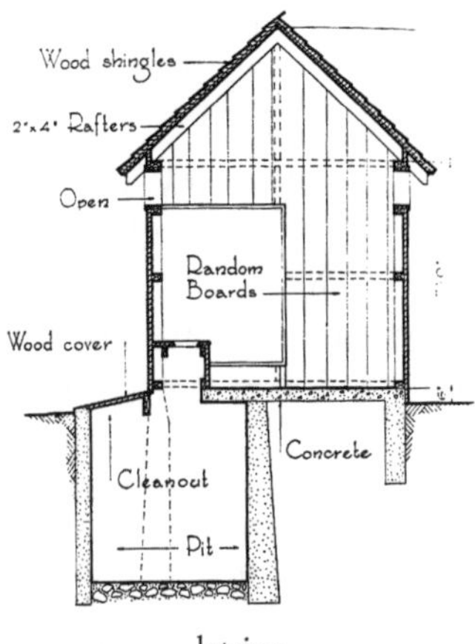

latrine

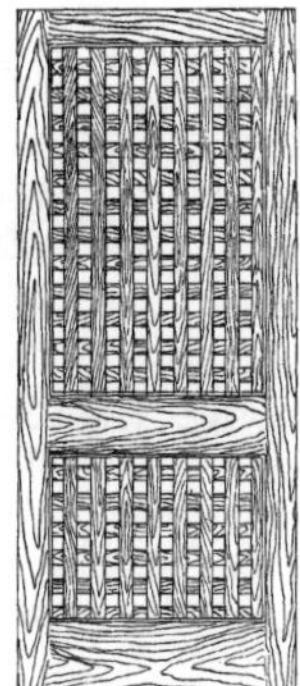

lattice door

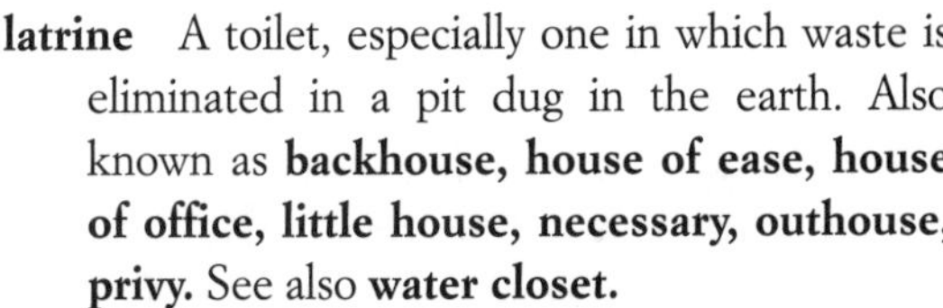

latrine A toilet, especially one in which waste is eliminated in a pit dug in the earth. Also known as **backhouse, house of ease, house of office, little house, necessary, outhouse, privy.** See also **water closet.**

Latrobe A stove set in a fireplace or against a chimney breast, which heats a room by radiation and the space above it by hot air; invented by Benjamin Henry Latrobe in the early 19c. Also known as **Baltimore heater.**

lattice Open screening formed by overlapping or interlaced grids of wood lath or metal bars.

lattice bar One of a series of short metal bars used in **lacing** two structural members, such as in a **lattice beam.**

lattice beam (19c–present) A metal beam with upper and lower flanges connected to overlapping, diagonal **lattice bar** struts. See also **half-lattice girder, lacing.**

lattice blind A window **shutter** with a wood lattice held by a frame of rails and stiles.

lattice door A door with a square-grid wood **lattice** above and below the lock rail.

lattice girder A large **lattice beam** that supports other beams.

lattice truss A **truss** consisting of overlapping inclined posts that form a pattern of squares and triangles. Also known as **double triangular truss.**

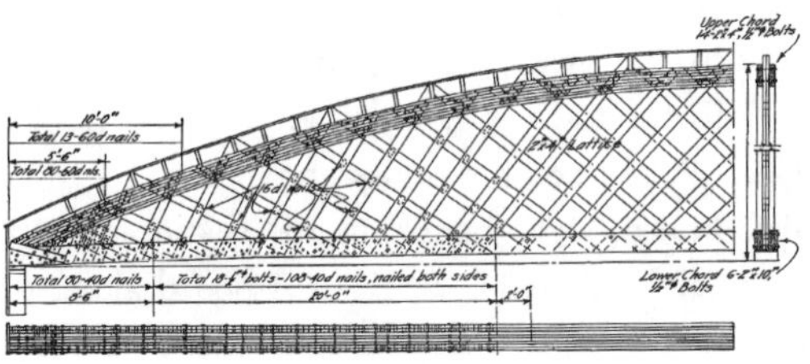

lattice truss

lattice window A **casement window** in which the sash is divided by the muntins or cames set in a diagonal grid. Also known as **trellis window.**

latticing A series of overlapping diagonal struts, especially in bridge trusses. See also **lattice beam, lattice truss.**

laundry A building or room used for cleaning and ironing clothes. Also known as **wash house.**

laundry tray Same as **laundry tub.**

laundry tub A deep sink used for washing laundry; often made of soapstone slabs. Also known as **laundry tray, washtub, wash tray.** (*See illustration p. 268.*)

laundry yard A open area where washed linens and clothes are hung to dry. See also **yard.**

laurel oak Same as **shingle oak.**

lavatory **1.** A room containing a sink for washing hands and, typically, a toilet. Also known as

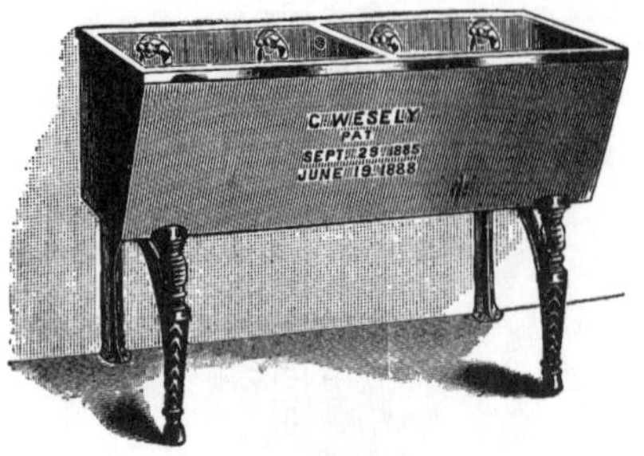

laundry tub

half bath. **2.** (pre-20c) A fixed or portable basin used for washing the hands and face. Also known as **washbasin, washbowl.** **3.** A plumbed basin, typically smaller than a sink. Also known as **washstand.**

lay To put down (e.g., to lay a floor or lay bricks).

layer A **course** of masonry units.

layer board, layer boarding **1.** Same as **gutter board** (sense 1). **2.** (19c) A board along the lower edge of a sloping roof next to a gutter. Also known as a **lear board.**

laylight A glazed ceiling opening to provide light to the space below; the light source may be natural or artificial; frequently used below a **skylight.**

lay stall (19c) A public place to deposit trash and garbage temporarily.

lazaretto (pre-20c) A quarantine building, or hospital ward, for people with infectious diseases; named for Santa Maria de Nazaret, a Church in Venice that maintained a prominent hospital. Also known as **pesthouse.**

LC **Library of Congress**

leaching cesspool A **cesspool** with unmortared joints that allow liquid to leach into the soil. Also known as **waste well.** See also **tight cesspool.**

leaching field A system of underground pipes that distributes the discharge of a **septic tank** through percolation into the soil; typically consists of a **tail drain** that connects **drain tile** in gravel-filled trenches arranged in a fork-shaped plan. Also known as **disposal field,** leach field, **septic field.**

lead **1.** A soft, malleable, heavy, elemental metal; shiny when cut but quickly oxidizes to a dull gray; used for roofing, flashing, plumbing, and stained-glass window cames; forms include **cast lead, lead pipe, milled lead, red lead, turned lead, white lead.** **2.** A lead **came.** **3.** Same as window lead (sense 2).

lead and tack (L&T) A permanent survey marker made by drilling a hole in paving, natural rock, or a similar material, filling it with lead, and hammering in a tack.

leaded glass Glass held in a sash by lead cames; types include **art glass, stained glass.** See also **lattice window, saddle bar.**

leaded zinc oxide White lead or lead sulfate added to zinc white and used as a white oil-base paint pigment in manufactured paints ca. 1896–ca. 1920.

leader A vertical pipe that carries a fluid, such as water or air, especially a **rain leader.** See also **downspout.**

leader head Same as **conductor head.**

leading Any kind of installed leadwork, such as **leaded glass** or a lead roof.

lead paint **Oil-base paint** that uses **red lead, white lead,** or other lead-based compounds for the pigment. See also **lead poisoning.**

lead pipe A pipe made of solid lead; typically 2 inches or less in diameter and with soldered joints; types include **cast pipe, soldered pipe;** used for water supply, short-branch drains, vents, and suction pipes from cisterns and wells; largely replaced by other types of materials by mid-20c; may be connected by a **blown joint** or **wiped joint.**

lead pipe coupling A device that makes a transition from a lead pipe to a different kind of metal pipe.

lead poisoning A nerve and brain disorder caused by ingesting, touching, or breathing the fumes of lead or lead compounds, including **lead paint** and water contaminated by **lead pipes.** See also **abatement.**

lead sash A window sash with **leaded glass** glazing.

lead sulfate See **sublimed white lead.**

lead tracery The decorative pattern of lead cames in a window.

lead white Same as **white lead.**

leadwork Elements made from **lead,** such as **lead pipe** plumbing or **cast lead** roofing.

leaf **1.** One of the two plates that form a **butt hinge. 2.** (19c–present) One of the folds of a folding door or shutter. **3.** Very thin metal foil, such as **gold leaf, silver leaf.**

leaf-and-dart A decorative band, often carved on a **cyma reversa,** of continuous alternating stylized darts and heart-shaped leaves. Also known as **heart-and-dart.**

lean-to **1.** (New England) A **shed roof** that abuts a larger structure and appears to lean against it. **2.** A small shelter with a single-slope roof with rafters that span from the ground to a horizontal beam, especially a rustic structure made with poles.

lean-to house Same as **saltbox.**

lear board Same as **layer board.**

leatherette (late 19c–WWI) Deeply embossed pressed cardboard sheets prefinished to resemble leather; used as a wall covering, especially for a dado.

ledge **1.** A small, horizontal, projecting element, such as a fillet or stop bead. **2.** The top surface of a projecting horizontal element, such as a **belt course. 3.** A horizontal board used as a cleat to fasten other boards together. See also **ledged door, ledger. 4.** A projecting shelf, especially when supported by brackets.

ledge batten Same as **ledge** (sense 3). See also **batten door.**

ledged door Same as **batten door.** See also **ledge.**

ledged partition A wall constructed of vertical boards fastened with horizontal cleats. See also **ledge.**

ledgement, ledgment (19c) Same as **ledge** (senses 1 and 2).

ledger **1.** A horizontal board attached to a wall or beam; used to support joist or rafter ends, shelves, and similar elements; types include **ribband, toe piece.** Also known as **cleat.**

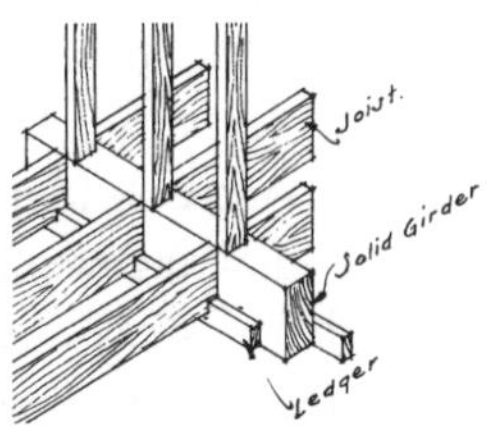

ledger

ledger stone A large stone mounted horizontally, especially one covering a tomb.

ledgment table **1.** The lowest horizontal molding on the exterior of a building, except for the **earth table.** See also **stringcourse. 2.** The prominent part of a plinth.

Lee marble A white, granular, dolomite **marble** quarried in the vicinity of Lee, Massachusetts; used for building stone.

Leetes Island granite A red and pink **granite** quarried in the vicinity of Leetes Island, Connecticut.

left-hand door See **hand.**

Legacy Resource Management Program A program for identifying and managing significant biological, geophysical, cultural, and historical resources existing on or involving all U.S. Department of Defense lands, facilities, and property.

legal description A written description of a **real estate** property, such as a plot of land or a condominium; typically includes the location, area, and **metes and bounds;** may be part of a **deed** or **survey.** Also known as **land description.**

length of board (17c) A unit of linear measure equal to one clapboard; typically equal to 4 or 5 feet.

lenticular truss A bridge **truss** shaped like a convex lens, with bowed top and bottom chords that meet at the ends.

lequear (pre-19c) Same as **lacunar.**

Lesbian cyma Same as **cyma reversa;** from the architecture of the island of Lesbos.

Lesbian leaf A **water leaf** divided by a projecting center rib. See also **water leaf and dart.**

let in, let-in A wood framing member, such as a **brace** or **ribband,** that is recessed in a notch or hole in another member, such as a **stud.** See also **laid on, mortise and tenon.**

levee A continuous raised embankment along a river to control floodwaters; from the French word *levé,* "raised"; common in the Mississippi valley.

leveler A small stone block used to fill the gap between larger stone blocks with broken coursing.

level of significance (U.S.) The geographical/political level at which a historic property has been evaluated and found to be significant; includes **local significance, state significance, national significance.**

leverage **1.** In real estate finance, the relationship between the constant rate of mortgage debt (say, 10 percent annually) and the average rate of net operating income on commercial property (say, 16 percent annually). **2.** The commitment of a large amount of private investment through a smaller expenditure of public funds or incentives.

lever board One of a series of adjustable slats in a shutter or jalousie; typically connected with a vertical bar so that all of the slats have the same angle. See also **louver board.**

lewis A wedge-shaped device inserted in a **Lewis hole** in the top of a stone block to aid in lifting during construction.

lewis anchor Same as **lewis bolt.**

lewis bolt A bolt having a flared end that is inserted in a **lewis hole** and secured with lead caulking or molten lead; used to hang soffit stones. Also known as **lewis anchor.**

lewis hole **1.** A dovetail slot in the top of a stone block that receives a **lewis.** **2.** In stone quarries, a method of cutting stone by drilling several holes close together and cutting away the material between them.

library (late 18c–present) A building or room used to display a collection of books for reading and study. See also **study.**

Library of Congress (LC) A national library administered by the U.S. Congress; the repository for HABS and HAER **documentation.**

lien A legal restriction on the deed of a property as security for an unpaid debt; a lien must be satisfied before **real estate** can be sold; types include **mechanic's lien.** See also **title search.**

lierne, lierne rib One of the subordinate cross, or branch, ribs in Gothic style vaulting; often purely decorative.

lierne vaulting A vaulted ceiling with lierne ribs.

life-cycle costing The analysis of the total cost of a building or structure over an extended period of time, including initial **hard cost** and **soft cost,** maintenance costs, and replacement costs based on the **life expectancy** of its components; typically compares alternative components and systems; may be used in conjunction with a **pro forma** to determine alternative economic returns.

life expectancy The predicted useful life of construction, fixtures, furnishings, or equipment before requiring major restoration, rehabilitation, or replacement. Also known as **useful life.** See also **life-cycle costing.**

life safety Protection of people against injury or loss of life, especially by fire. See also **equivalency, fire loss risk reduction, fire suppression system, timed exit analysis.**

life safety code **1.** A **building code** that deals only with **life safety** issues, such as the National Fire Protection Code. **2.** The part of a general building code concerned with life safety.

lift See **transom lift.**

lift latch A locking device that fastens a door by means of a hinged arm lowered into a hook on the doorjamb. See also **barrel bolt.**

lift-lock A structure that allows boats to be raised and lowered to pass between two bodies of water with different levels; typically includes two parallel walls with the ends enclosed by gates; components may include **head gate, flume, lock chamber, tail bay, tail gate;** types include **canal lock, double lock, guard lock, tide lock.**

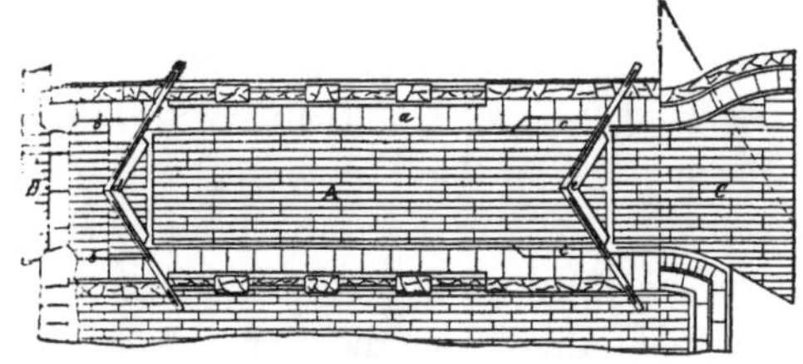

lift-lock

lift-off hinge Same as **loose-joint hinge.**

lift waterwheel A vertical **waterwheel** that can be raised or lowered to adjust to the water level.

light **1.** (18c–present) An individual **pane** of glass within a sash, or the multiple pieces of glass of an art glass window. **2.** An opening that lets light into a building; types include **angel light, bull's-eye light, skylight, spire light, vault light, window.** **3.** A source of artificial light, especially a **light fixture.** **4.** Visible electromagnetic energy.

light brick Same as **salmon brick.**

lightbulb Same as **electric lamp,** especially one with a globular shape; types include **fluorescent lamp, incandescent lamp.**

light fixture A fixed device that supports and, typically, encloses an electric lamp or gaslight; may include a lens, shade, and/or reflector; types by location include **ceiling light, wall light;** individual types include **arc light, Argand lamp, Bude light, Drummond light, combination fixture, fluorescent light, gasolier, lucigen, vapor lamp.**

light framing **1.** A general term indicating **stick frame construction using** lumber 2–4 inches thick or **light-gauge steel;** usually with 2 × 4 studs and 2× joists and rafters. **2.** (20c) **Lumber** with nominal dimensions of 2–4 inches thick and 2–4 inches wide. See also **structural joists and planks.**

light-gauge framing **Light framing** with **light-gauge steel** members.

light-gauge steel Structural members manufactured from cold-formed sheet metal, including joists, studs, and steel decking. See also **rolled section.**

lighthouse, (pre-19c) **light house** A tower or other structure supporting one or more lights to guide sailors at night; typically located at the entrance to a port or on a dangerous shoal; open fires were replaced by candles and oil lamps by the middle of the 18c and by Argand lamps and electric lights by the end of the 19c; quarters for the lighthouse keeper may be within or adjacent to the structure. Also known as **beacon house.** See also **light room.** (*See illustration p. 272.*)

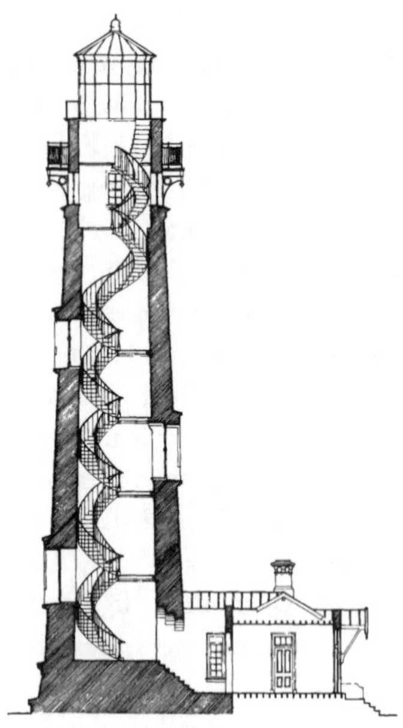

lighthouse
Pigeon Point Lighthouse
San Mateo County, California, ca. 1872

lighting See **color rendering, illuminance, lamp, light, luminance.**

lightning conductor A metal device that leads an electrical charge from lightning safely to the ground; typically a braided copper wire connected to a **lightning rod** on the roof and grounded to a water pipe or other underground metal element. Also known as **electrical conductor.**

lightning rod A projecting metal rod at the top of a structure that attracts lightning; attached to a **lightning conductor.** Also known as **electrical rod, Franklin.**

lightroom The room in a **lighthouse** that contains the illuminating equipment.

lightweight concrete Concrete made with aggregate that is lighter than stone; types include **breeze concrete, cinder concrete.**

lightwood A rot-resistant pine wood made hard and resinous by girdling the tree to kill it; used for foundations and fence posts.

Ligomur A variety of **Lincrusta-Walton.**

lime Powdered calcium oxide (CaO), manufactured by calcining a mineral calcium carbonate, such as limestone, marble, or sea shells; used in **mortar, plaster, whitewash;** types include **hydrated lime, hydraulic lime, poor lime, quicklime, rich lime, slaked lime, white lime.** See also **calcine.**

lime floor A floor composed of lime mortar.

lime flour (20c) Same as **lime.**

lime glass Glass manufactured with lime as an ingredient.

lime light Same as **Drummond light.**

lime plaster Plaster made with lime as the main ingredient; base coats are lime mixed with sand, hair, and plaster of paris; finish coat is lime, plaster of Paris, and, sometimes, marble dust.

lime powder (19c) Air-slaked **lime.**

lime proof green A green **aniline color** paint pigment used to tint calcimine and cement paints; originally manufactured from green earth called **terre verte;** alkali tolerant and very nonfading.

lime putty Same as **slaked lime.**

lime-sand mortar A masonry **mortar** composed of one portion of slaked lime mixed with 3–10 portions of sand; was the predominant mortar used for brickwork and stonework until the invention of **portland cement.**

limestone, (18c) **lime-stone** A sedimentary, freestone rock composed of calcium carbonate and formed from the shells and skeletons of marine organisms; used for **building stone, ornamental stone,** and **sculpture** and for producing **lime;** first quarried in North America in the 1790s; types include **compact limestone, coquina, coral rock, magnesian limestone, oolitic limestone, shelly limestone;** varieties include **Bedford limestone, Minnesota Makato, Missouri marble, Shadow Vein, Tyndall limestone.** See also **glass seam.**

lime stucco A stucco composed of lime, sand, and aggregates; may also contain pigments and waterproofing materials.

limewash Same as **whitewash.**

Lincrusta-Walton, lincrusta Walton A flexible, waterproof, embossed composition sheet composed of fiber, such as **cork,** oxidized **linseed oil,** and, sometimes, a backer such as canvas or thick paper; typically used as a wainscot and often finished with glazes to resemble tooled leather before mid-20c; later patterns included neoclassical motifs such as swags; first manufactured in 1875, patented in 1877, and in common use until the 1920s.

lineal foot Same as **linear foot.**

linear foot A unit of quantity equal to a **foot** measured along the length of an element; commonly used to measure building materials.

line detector A **head detector** composed of a length of heat-sensitive cable or small bore metal tube. See also **fire detector.**

linenfold Bas-relief wood carving in the stylized form of a cloth with symmetrical vertical folds; used in various styles based on medieval or postmedieval work, especially in the late 19c and early 20c. Also known as **linen pattern, linen scroll, napkin pattern, towel pattern.**

linen panel A wood panel decorated with a **linenfold** design.

linen pattern Same as **linenfold.**

linen scroll Same as **linenfold.**

lining An interior covering, especially boards on walls and ceilings, as opposed to **sheathing.**

lining paper Wallpaper that serves as a base coat for decorative wallpaper.

link **1.** Same as **eyebar.** **2.** (20c) The part of a building addition that connects to an existing building; typically recessed from the facade and often constructed of different materials from either the new or old structures; common when the style of the addition is dissimilar from that of the existing building.

linoleum A type of **sheet goods** flooring made with oxidized linseed oil and ground cork on a canvas backing; decorative patterns are printed on the top; typically 3/32-inch thick.

linseed oil An oil made from ground flaxseed; types include bleached, raw, refined, and **pale boiled oil;** used in **Lincrusta Walton, linoleum, oil-base paint, varnish,** and other building materials; typically produces a hard, glossy finish.

lintel A structural beam spanning over a door or window opening, or a facing, such as architectural terra cotta, that appears to be a structural beam. See also **back lintel, relieving arch, safety lintel.**

lintel construction Having a structural system composed of horizontal beams resting on vertical supports, in contrast to arched or vaulted construction.

lintel course A masonry course at the level of a door or window head that forms a visually distinctive band around the building.

lint room A room in which ginned cotton fibers are stored before they are taken to the **cotton press;** typically a ground-level shed attached to a **ginhouse.**

lip molding A molding with a profile in the shape of a pouting lower lip; common in **Perpendicular Style** elements designed to shed water, such as **ledgements.**

lip of the bell A **lip molding** that terminates the top of the bell of a Corinthian capital. Also known as **beak molding.**

lipped skew A terra-cotta **skewback block** with a groove that fits around the bottom flange of a steel beam; supports the end of a **tile arch** and provides fireproofing of the bottom of the beam.

liquid glass Same as **water glass.**

L-iron Same as **angle iron.**

list **1.** The top rail of a railing. **2.** Same as **listel.** **3.** A narrow strip of plank. **4.** The rough edge of a sawn board at the bark. **5.** A preliminary coat of **tinplate,** or extra tin that has accumulated on the edge of a surface. **6.** The tilt of an object, such as a boat, from the vertical. See also **out of plumb.**

listed size The standard size of a manufactured item, such as lumber, that may also be a **stock item.**

listel **1.** A small, square molding, such as a **fillet.** Also known as **list.** **2.** (18c) A decorative flat band. **3.** (19c) Same as **reglet.**

listing The process of placing a site, building, structure, or object on a historic register, such as the **National Register.** See also **nomination.**

litharge A light yellow pigment composed of lead monoxide (PbO) extracted from silver-bearing lead ore or made by oxidation of molten lead; used to manufacture **red lead, japan, gilt varnish.** Also known as **plumbic ocher.** See also **massicot.**

litharge of gold (18c) Same as **litharge.**

Lithonia granite A blue-gray, fine-grained **granite** quarried in Georgia.

lithopone A white, opaque, paint **pigment** composed of a mixture of zinc sulfide and barium sulfate; used as an oil-base paint pigment for flat paints after ca. 1901. Also known as **Griffith's zinc white.** See also **titanated lithopone.**

little house (18c) A latrine building.

Little Rock granite A syenitic **granite,** containing little quartz, quarried in the vicinity of Little Rock, Arkansas; used for building stone.

live load **1.** A floor load created by the addition of people and furniture to a building. See also **dead load, seismic load, wind load.** **2.** The term used to define the limit on the number of visitors to a historic site or a park at any particular time. See also **carrying capacity.**

live oak A spreading **oak** tree with yellow to light brown, hard, strong, close-grained wood with whitish sapwood; found along the Gulf and Atlantic coasts from northern Mexico to southeastern Virginia; limited use for knees, paneling, and parquet flooring; *Quercus virginiana.*

livery stable A commercial horse **stable** for boarding or renting horses and, sometimes, carriages; typically with minimal accommodations for humans.

living hall A large central circulation space in a house that includes a stair, fireplace, and sitting area; common in **Queen Anne style** houses.

living history enactment Role playing by costumed actors in a historical setting.

living room (U.S.) A sitting room in a dwelling for family or social gatherings.

load See **dead load, live load, wind load.**

load-bearing tile A **structural clay tile** unit that can support loading as part of a masonry wall.

loading dock A raised platform used for loading and unloading cargo, especially from a truck or railroad car; may be inside a building or be an exterior covered or uncovered platform.

loam An earthen mixture of sand, clay, and organic matter; mixed with lime and water for use as mortar or foundry molds.

lobby **1.** A **corridor, hall,** or **vestibule** serving as an **anteroom** to a room or suite of rooms. **2.** A furnished waiting area adjacent to a vestibule, such as in a hotel. **3.** (20c) A **vestibule** of a building used by the public. See also **elevator lobby.**

lobe A projection or division of a rounded architectural feature; used in reference to Gothic style tracery to describe both a **cusp** decorated with rounded forms and a **foil** of an opening.

lobed arch An arch with multiple foils at the intrados. See also **lobe, multifoil arch.**

loblolly pine A **pine** tree with a tall, round trunk and reddish-brown, coarse-grained, resinous, strong heartwood and creamy pink or yellow sapwood; found in wetlands and near streams from eastern Texas to southern Delaware; used for framing, sheathing, and millwork; lumbered primarily from 1870 to 1915; *Pinus taeda.* Also known as **southern pine, yellow pine.**

local historic district A locally designated **historic district;** may have related **design controls, design guidelines, zoning.**

local significance The importance of a property or district to the history of its community, such as a town or county. See also **level of significance.**

local vent A plumbing drain-pipe vent attached directly to the **trap** or fixture.

lock **1.** A hardware device that controls the opening of a door or window by means of a movable bolt; components may include **box, case, cylinder, hasp, keyhole, latch, strike plate;** types include **case lock, crossbolt lock, cylinder lock, dead bolt lock, door band, drawbolt lock, Janus-faced lock, latch lock, lift latch, mortise lock, rim lock, spring lock, stock lock, tumbler lock.** **2.** Same as **lift-lock.** See also **guard lock.** **3.** Same as a plaster **key** (sense 2). **4.** (19c) To provide the locks and other builder's hardware for a building; such language as "*to lock* a house" was often used in contracts.

lockband, lock bond A course of bondstones in a masonry wall.

lock chamber The space enclosed by the walls and gates of a **lift-lock.** See also **lock gate.**

lock gate One of the gates of a **lift-lock;** located at each end of the **lock chamber;** types include **head gate, tail gate.** See also **lock hatch.**

lock hatch A sliding board that opens and closes a **lock gate** or **sluice gate.** See also **lock paddle.**

lockhole Same as **keyhole.**

lockhouse The **lockkeeper**'s residence near a canal lock.

locking hinge (19c–present) A **hinge** with the pintle formed so that the hinge locks in the open or closed position; used for exterior window shutters.

lockkeeper **1.** A small, recessed box behind a door strike that surrounds the bolt when it is in the locked position. **2.** The person who operates a **lift-lock.** See also **lockhouse.**

lock paddle A small panel or board connected to a rod that opens and closes a lock gate. See also **lock hatch.**

lock rail **1.** The middle rail of a paneled door; typically where the door lock is mounted. **2.** The horizontal member that separates the top of a door from the transom sash above.

locomotive cinder concrete A lightweight, nailable concrete made with cinders from railroad engine coal; used in the early 20c.

locust A hardwood tree with tough, decay-resistant, coarse-grained, yellow to dark brown wood; originally native to the Appalachian Mountains and parts of Arkansas and Oklahoma, has been planted throughout U.S.; used for fence posts, poles, mine timbers, and occasionally for trim and millwork exposed to the weather; *Robinia pseudacacia.* Also known as **black locust, yellow locust.**

lodge **1.** Any of several types of portable or rustic dwellings used by Native Americans; types include **cavate lodge, earth lodge,** tepee, **wigwam.** **2.** A secondary dwelling on a large estate, such as a gatekeeper's lodge. See also **hunting lodge.** **3.** A permanent local meeting place of certain secret societies, such as the Freemasons.

lodge gate An entrance gate with an adjoining gatekeeper's lodge.

lodgepole pine A tall, slender **pine** tree with light brown, hard, stiff, brittle, straight-grained heartwood with thick, whitish sapwood; found in western North America from southern California to the Yukon River; used for lumber and log cabins; *Pinus murrayana.* Also known as **bird's-eye pine, screwpine.**

lodging chamber (pre-19c) Same as **bedroom.**

lodging room **1.** (pre-19c) Same as **bedroom.** **2.** (19c–present) A room rented as a residence; typically without a kitchen or bathroom.

lodging house A building with multiple rooms that are rented to travelers or longer-term residents. See also **boardinghouse, tavern.**

loft, (17c) **loaft** **1.** An upper-floor area below the rafters or main ceiling that overlooks a lower level; types include **choir loft, fly loft, organ gallery.** **2.** An upper floor used for storage, especially an unfinished space below the rafters; types include **corn loft, hayloft.**

lofted (pre-19c) Having a **loft.**

log-butt construction See **stovewood house.**

log cabin A small house with walls constructed of horizontal logs laid on top of one another and held in place with notched corners; typical construction elements include **cabin roof, chinking, gable log, notching, plate, sleeper;** built throughout forested regions of North America by settlers of northern European descent; often used interchangeably with **log house;** forms include **single pen, double pen, dogtrot, saddlebag.** See also **pen, round log construction, stovewood house.**

log cabin siding A type of **drop siding** with a curved profile that resembles horizontal logs when installed; typically approximately 1.5 inch thick.

loge **1.** A theater **box.** **2.** (20c) The front rows of a theater **mezzanine.**

loggia An open-sided, roofed space contained within the interior or exterior of a building, such as an upper-level colonnade. See also **balcony, porch, veranda.**

log house, (17c) **logg house, loged hows** A house with walls constructed of horizontal logs or squared timbers laid on top of one another and held in place with notched corners; typical construction elements include **chinking, gable log, notching, plate, sleeper;** types include **block house, log cabin.** See also **pen, round log construction, stovewood house, vertical log house.**

log pipe A large-diameter pipe bored out of a tree trunk, usually from an oak or alder; used until mid-19c for underground water supply mains.

Lombard style (19c) Same as **Italianate.**

London Farm decision A ruling by the Supreme Court of British Columbia that the court does not have jurisdiction to overturn a municipal heritage designation; the plaintiff argued that the property had insignificant heritage significance. Also known as *Murray v. Richmond.*

long bend **1.** A drainpipe **elbow** with a long, straight leg on the outflow end. **2.** Same as **sanitary bend.**

longhouse **1.** A Native American dwelling constructed of poles set in the ground and lashed together to form an arched or triangular-shaped frame connected with horizontal poles covered with birch bark; approximately 16 feet wide and 50–100 feet long, and divided into compartments 6–8 feet wide opening onto a continuous aisle; used by the Iroquois and other eastern tribes. **2.** (20c) A building with a common entrance used for both a dwelling and a barn.

longitudinal rib A rib at the edge of a vault oriented along the long axis of a building; may be a **wall rib.**

longleaf pine, (19c) **long leaved pine** A tall, softwood tree with very hard, strong, stiff, pitchy wood with yellowish orange to reddish brown heartwood and creamy pink or yellow sapwood; named for its very long needles; found in southeastern U.S. from eastern Texas to North Carolina; used for heavy girders, light framing, sheathing, and millwork; lumbered primarily 1870–1915; *Pinus palustris.* Also known as **Georgia pine, hard pine, southern pine, southern yellow pine, virginian pine, yellow pine.**

Longmeadow sandstone A dark reddish to orangy brown, fine and even-grained **sandstone** quarried in the vicinity of East Longmeadow, Massachusetts.

long room (pre-20c) A large room used for public entertainment.

long valley A diagonal rafter that runs from the wall plate to the ridge and forms one of the valleys of a dormer. See also **blind valley, short valley.**

looking glass (18c–19c) A large mirror, typically mounted in a frame (e.g., over a mantel).

lookout **1.** A short, cantilevered beam that supports an eave or cornice at the top of an exterior wall; typically concealed by the soffit or cornice. Also known as a **lookout rafter, tail, tailpiece.** **2.** An elevated place in a building to view the approach.

lookout rafter A **rafter** that acts as a **lookout** (sense 1).

loop Same as **crenel.**

loophole A narrow, vertical opening in a fortress wall through which small arms may be fired; typically with splayed sides that are larger on the interior. Also known as **oilet.**

loophole frame (19c) A wood frame surrounding a door with a transom window above, or surrounding two or more windows above one another; commonly used in stables.

loophole window A glazed opening in the shape of a loophole.

loose box Same as **loose stall.**

loose-fill insulation A type of **insulation** composed of individual loose pieces or fibers that create insulating air pockets when blown, poured, or pumped into place; types include **pouring wool insulation.**

loose-joint hinge (After mid-19c) A **butt hinge** that can be separated by lifting the single upper knuckle off a fixed pin on the lower knuckle; allows the door to be removed without removing the pin or the hinge; types include **olive-knuckle hinge.** Also known as **heave-off hinge, lift-off hinge.** See also **fast joint hinge, loose-pin hinge.**

loose-pin hinge A **hinge** with a removable pin; typically a **butt hinge.** See also **fast joint hinge.**

loose stall An enclosure within a stable large enough to allow an animal to move about inside. Also known as **box stall, loose box.**

loose tongue A thin wood **spline** used to join the grooved edges of two boards (or similar members) by slipping the spline into both pieces as the edges are brought together.

lot A surveyed parcel of land, especially of a size to accommodate a single building.

lot occupancy The portion of a piece of land taken up by a building footprint; typically regulated by **zoning** and expressed as a percentage of the lot area.

lounge, lounging room (19c–present) A place for relaxed conversation, especially in a hotel or club.

louver **1.** A covering for an opening with a series of angled, fixed slats with spaces between them to admit air; typically the slats slope downward and outward to protect

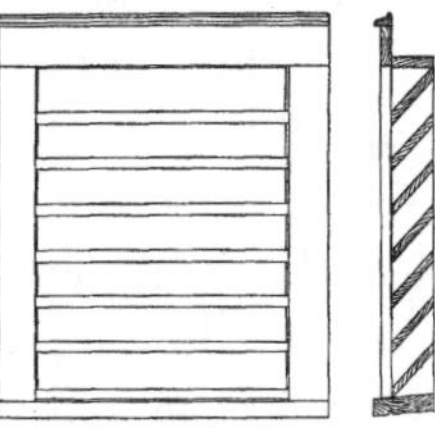

louver

against rain. Also known as **luffer.** See also **abat-vent, grille. 2.** (pre-WWI) Same as **louver window.**

louver board One of the individual wood slats in a louver or louver window. Also known as **luffer board.**

louvered Having louvers (sense 1).

louver shutter A **shutter** with fixed louver slats. See also **rolling slats.**

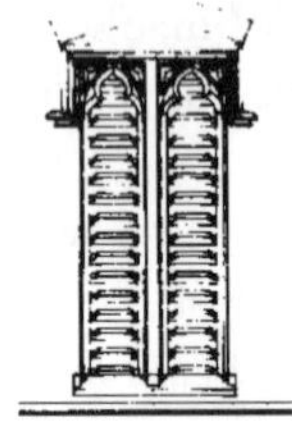

louver window

louver window (pre-WWI) An opening enclosed with louvers to permit the passage of sound and/or air, such as a belfry or in a gable end.

louver work Construction having slatted openings. See also **louver.**

louvre (pre-20c) Same as **louver.**

low-rise (20c) A relatively short multistory building as opposed to a **high-rise;** often defined in building codes as not more than 75 feet tall.

low steel Same as **soft steel.**

lozenge molding A molding band with raised lines forming hollow diamonds connected end to end; used in the Gothic Revival style.

L-plan An L-shaped floor plan.

L-sill A built-up sill in which the band beam is flush with the outside of the wall plate, forming an L-shaped cross section; the studs, or a sole plate, are nailed on top of the subfloor; used in **platform frame** construction. See also **T-sill, box sill.**

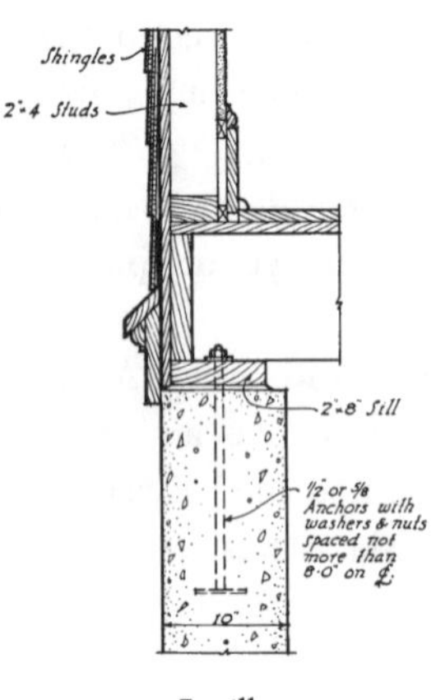

L-sill

L&T Abbr. for **lead and tack.**

lucarne (pl. **lucarna**) **1.** Same as **dormer,** especially when the window is directly above the cornice of an exterior wall. **2.** A small window in a spire; typically with a gablet and finial.

lucigen A 19c lighting fixture that burns sprayed oil; consists of a wall tank supported on brackets and connected to a jet with a gravity-fed pipe; the jet is connected to a compressed-air line; produces a larger, brighter flame than an ordinary **oil lamp.**

Lucite Trade name for **acrylic** plastic manufactured by DuPont Co.

luffer board Same as **louver board.**

luffer boarding Clapboard siding, especially with untapered weatherboards.

lug **1.** A vertical bead on the back of a window jamb that projects into the adjoining masonry. **2.** A horizontal top face at the ends of a

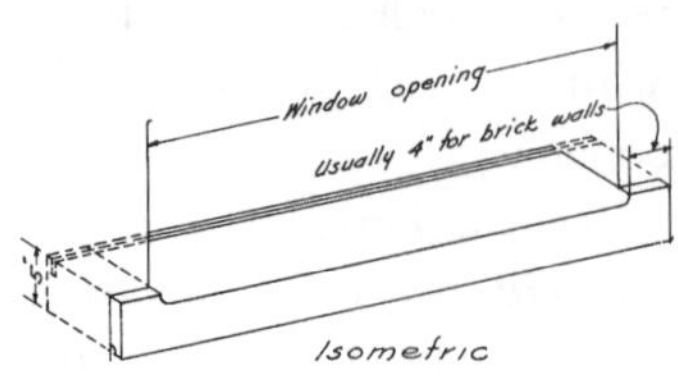

lug (sense 2)

sloped stone window or doorsill; supports the masonry jamb above; may be cut with the same profile as the moldings of the jamb. **3.** (pre-WWI) Same as **jamb,** especially a fireplace jamb. **4.** Same as **horn. 5.** The projecting end of a door or window stile; may be cut off during installation.

lumber **1. Wood** sawn or rived, and sometimes planed, for market, especially with a rectangular cross section with both dimensions nominally 1 inch or larger; types include **board, dimension lumber, light framing, plank, scantling, timber.** See also **structural lumber. 2.** (pre-20c) Old household items.

lumber house (pre-20c) A storage building for miscellaneous items and sometimes for wood lumber.

lumber measure Same as **board measure.**

lumber mill roof Same as **sawtooth roof.**

lumber room (pre-20c) A storage room for miscellaneous items.

lumberyard An open area in which wood lumber is stored, as well as the buildings in which a lumber building materials business is located. Also known as **timberyard.** See also **yard.**

luminaire (20c) An electric **light fixture.**

luminance **1.** (late 20c) A measure of the amount of light transmitted or reflected by a surface; typically measured in footlamberts (candelas per square foot). See also **illuminance, luminance ratio. 2.** The property of giving light.

luminance ratio The ratio of the **luminance** at different points on a surface or between different surfaces.

lumper A slang term for a social scientist, such as an **archaeologist,** ethnologist, or linguist, who tends to emphasize the criteria that place artifacts, languages, and other cultural groupings in a single category, such as when classifying a multitype **archaeological site** or an inventory or grouping of artifacts, as opposed to a **splitter.**

lunatic hospital A **hospital** (sense 1) used for confining those with mental disorders.

lunatic house A house used for confining a person with a mental disorder, especially a single individual.

lune (18c) Same as **lunette** (senses 1, 2, and 5).

lunette **1.** The approximately half-moon-shaped window or wall surface between the intrados and spring line of the edge of a vault; often decorated with mural painting. Also known as **lune, lunula. 2.** An arched opening in the side of a long vault formed by the intersection with a smaller vault, such as for a window. **3.** A small curved or circular opening in a coved or vaulted ceiling or in a roof. **4.** A fortification with a V-shaped front face, two parallel flanks, and an open gorge. See also **ravelin. 5.** A semicircular window. Also known as **D-window.** See also **fanlight.**

lunula (pl. **lunulae**) (18c) Same as **lunette** (senses 1, 2, and 5).

lustre A small, woven cotton bag saturated with rare earth oxides used in a **Welsbach burner** or similar gaslight; when the flame is lit, the cotton burns away and leaves a glowing network of ash.

Luxfer prism Trade name for a type of **prism light** manufactured beginning ca. 1896 by the Luxfer Prism Company. See also **Luxfer prism glass.**

Luxfer prism glass Trade name for a type of **prismatic glass** with sawtooth-shaped ribs on the interior face; used in windows to refract sunlight into an interior space; typically manufactured in 4 × 4 or 5 × 5 inch squares of variously angled ribs that were assembled into larger panels; the invention of Henry Crew and Olin Basquin was first exhibited at the Chicago World's Fair in 1893 and commercially produced ca. 1896–ca. 1933. See also **Luxfer prism.**

lyceum (19c) A building or hall used by a literary association for popular instruction.

lying-in hospital (19c–early 20c) A maternity **hospital.**

lying panel **1.** A rectangular panel with its longest dimension horizontal. Also known as **cross panel.** **2.** A wood panel with the grain running horizontally.

Lyme granite A deep red, coarse-grained **granite** quarried in the vicinity of Lyme, Connecticut; used for building stone (e.g., for Chaney Memorial Church, Newport, Rhode Island).

lysis A step or plinth above the cornice of a **podium** (senses 1 and 2).

M

M Abbr. for 1,000 units of building material, such as bricks or board feet of lumber; used in **board measure;** from the Roman symbol for 1,000. See also **board foot.**

macadam An exterior paving made of bitumen cement mixed with crushed stone; named for the Scottish engineer John L. Macadam (1756–1836).

machine finish, machined The smooth, machine-planed or -ground surface texture of soft stone blocks or metal. See also **stone work.**

machinery space (19c) Same as **engine room.**

machine screw A cylindrical metal rod with screw threads on one end and various shaped heads on the other end; used for fastening metal machine parts; used with a female threaded hole which may part of the machine or a separate nut; treads may be V-shaped or, more commonly, flat-topped with sloped or curved sides; types include **bolt, cap screw, carriage bolt, collar screw, set screw, shoulder screw, thumbscrew.** See also **wood screw.**

machine-tooled The machine-cut surface texture of stone blocks with continuous parallel furrows; may be 2–10 bats per inch; typically used on ashlar rather than trim. See also **bat, stone work, tooth-chisel.**

Madeira wood Same as **mahogany** (sense 1).

magazine A building or compartment for storage of explosives or projectiles. See also **powder house.**

magnesian limestone A fine grained **limestone** composed of calcium carbonate and magnesia, typically with small amounts of iron, silica, and alumina.

Magnet Cove granite A syenitic **granite,** with little quartz, quarried in the vicinity of Magnet Cove, Arkansas; used for building stone.

magnetic north The direction that a compass needle points; typically varies somewhat from true north by an amount that varies over time.

Maher v. City of New Orleans A 1976 decision of the U.S. 5th Circuit Court that the ordinance requiring maintenance of properties within the Vieux Carré historic district in the French Quarter of New Orleans was a permissible exercise of police power and not a taking of property.

mahogany **1.** A large, tropical, American hardwood tree with yellowish brown to reddish brown, fine-grained wood; used in fine millwork and trim; *Swietenia mahogoni.* Also known as **Madeira wood.** **2.** Various tropical trees with wood similar to *Swietenia mahogoni,* such as Philippine mahogany.

mail-order house A **ready-cut house** assembled from a package of pre-cut components ordered and, sometimes, delivered by mail; common in the late 19c and early 20c. Also known as **catalog house.**

main The primary utility supply pipe located in the public right-of-way; the service lines to individual buildings are fed from the main; types include **water main** and **gas main.** See also **corporation cock.**

main beam The beam that spans from the side of the main posts to the top of the center post of a **bent** of a **timber frame** building; typically supports the loft at the end bents.

main couple A pair of principal rafters that support other secondary rafters.

main disconnect See **service switch.**

main plate The top plate of the long side of a timber frame structure that supports the ends of the rafters. See also **purlin plate, timber frame.**

main post One of a pair of end posts at each bent of a **timber frame** building; runs from the **main sill** to the **main plate.**

main sill The **ground sill** of a **timber frame** structure that runs along the top of the foundation walls of the long sides of the building. See also **cross-sill.**

Main Street Canada A **Heritage Canada** program established in 1979 to encourage the economic revitalization of central business districts in small- to medium-sized communities through preservation; operates since 1993 as a series of services under community Heritage Development initiatives.

Main Street Program A program of the **National Trust for Historic Preservation,** with state and local goverment support, that encourages the economic revitalization of central business districts in small- to medium-sized communities through preservation; the four-point program includes design, organization, promotion, and economic restructuring.

maintenance The process of conserving a site, building, structure, or object over time to prevent deterioration, as opposed to **restoration** or **rehabilitation;** may include **inspection** and planning, as well as **housekeeping,** minor repairs, painting, mowing, and gardening. See also **capital improvement, deferred maintenance, preventive maintenance.**

making a baby Replacing a damaged slate by removing it, nailing a copper strap in place, inserting a new slate in the old slot, and bending up the end of the strap to hold the new slate in place.

mall **1.** A level, formal lawn or walk lined with straight rows of trees; originally from the pre-19c English game Pall Mall, where balls were struck with mallets along a turf alley; later a walkway in St. James Park, London. **2.** (20c) A wide pedestrian way between facing rows of buildings or stores. **3.** (mid-1950s–present) Same as **shopping mall.**

malleable cast iron Same as **malleable iron** (sense 1).

malleable iron **1.** A tough, malleable, low-carbon iron manufactured by heating cast iron surrounded by a decarbonizing powder red hot and cooling it slowly. Also known as **malleable cast iron.** **2.** Same as **wrought iron.**

Malone sandstone A light pink to reddish brown, strong, dense, hard quartzite quarried in the vicinity of Potsdam, New York; composed entirely of quartz grains cemented with silica. Also known as **Adirondack sandstone, Potsdam sandstone.**

mandatory referral A policy or legislation requiring that an application to one government agency be referred to another agency for review, such as an application to a building department for a building permit or demolition permit that is referred to an **architectural review board.** See also **flagging.**

manganese dioxide A black paint pigment compound; used to color mortar.

manger, (pre-19c) **mainger** A feeding trough or box that holds fodder for cattle or horses, typically in a stable or barn. Also known as **crib.**

manhole An underground pit or shaft for access to utilities, such as a sewer line or telephone cables; typically constructed of masonry covered with a stone slab before WWI, and supplanted by concrete construction with a cast-iron or steel cover by late 20c.

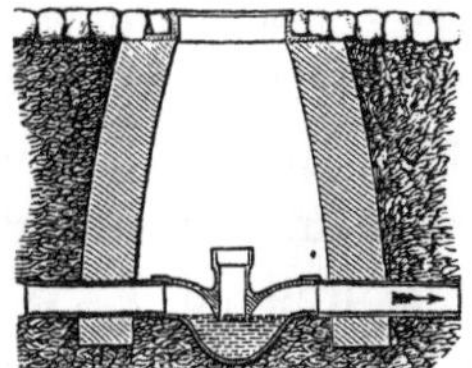

manhole

manhole cover A metal plate that provides access to a manhole; typically a cast-iron disk in a frame, with cast names and/or decoration.

manifesto A proclamation of policy or principles, especially when not widely accepted by a group or organization. See also **charter.**

man-made environment Same as **built environment.**

Mannheim gold A type of **brass** with the appearance of **gold;** developed in Mannheim, Germany. Also known as **tombac.**

manor **1.** (pre-revolution New York) A semifeudal estate leased in perpetuity to a patroon and subleased to tenant farmers in perpetuity or for the term of their lives. **2.** (southern U.S.) A large estate with tenant farms. See also **manor plantation.**

manor farm Same as **manor plantation.**

manor house The main house of a **manor** or **manor plantation,** especially when occupied by the patroon or owner; may be of any size or form.

manor plantation The principal farm of a **manor;** typically where the **manor house** is located. See also **home plantation.**

mansard, mansarde, mansart **1.** Same as **mansard roof.** See also **gambrel roof.** **2.** An attic room behind a mansard roof. See also **mansarde.**

mansarde **1.** A roof with dormer windows. **2.** Same as **mansard.** See also **mansard roof.**

mansard roof **1.** A two-pitched roof with a steep lower slope that rises from all of the formal facades of a building; hipped when used on a detached building; the nearly flat upper slope may not be visible from ground level; the lower slope typically starts from the cornice line of the floor below, and has multiple pedimented dormer windows; named from its frequent use by French architect Francois Mansart (1598–1666) and several contemporaries with the surname of **mansarde** or **mansart;** common in **Beaux-Arts** design and the **Second Empire** style; types include **bell cast roof, concave mansard roof.** Also known as **curb roof.** See also **gambrel roof.** **2.** (20c) A steeply pitched false roof in front of a parapet wall.

mansard style Same as **Second Empire style.**

mansart Same as **mansard.**

mansion **1.** (19c–present) A large and impressive house. **2.** Same as **mansion house.**

mansion farm (late 18c–early 19c Delaware) Same as **home plantation.**

mansion house **1.** (pre-19c) The principal dwelling house of a landowner; of any size or form. **2.** Same as **parsonage.** **3.** Same as **manor house.**

mansion plantation (late 18c–early 19c Delaware) Same as **home plantation.**

mantel, (18c) **mantle** **1.** (18c–present) Same as **mantelpiece** or **mantelshelf.** **2.** (pre-20c) The portion of a chimney above the fireplace opening that collects the smoke, especially when sloped like a hood.

mantel-board, mantelboard (19c) A wood **mantelshelf.**

mantelpiece, mantel-piece A mantelshelf and its pilaster-shaped supports. Also known as **mantel, parrel.** See also **overmantel.**

mantelpiece

mantel-tree, (18c) **mantle tree** **1.** A wood lintel above a fireplace opening. **2.** (19c–present) A stone lintel or an arch over a fireplace opening.

mantelshelf A shelf above a fireplace opening; may be part of a **mantelpiece.** Also known as **mantel.** See also **overmantel.**

mantle (pre-20c) Same as **mantel.**

manufacturer's drawing Same as **shop drawing.**

map A plan of a geographic area; types include **base map, ground plat, land status map, plat, subdivision, survey, topographic map, USGS map.**

maple Any of the many varieties of hardwood tree of the genus *Acer,* including **red maple, sugar maple.**

marble **1.** A metamorphic, partially crystalline **limestone** composed of calcium carbonate that may also contain magnesium carbonate; typically fine-grained and able to be highly polished; has a wide range of colors and patterns; used for statuary and fine masonry; often imported from Italy, first quarried in North America in the 1770s in Pennsylvania and Vermont; types include **encrinal marble, statuary marble;** varieties include **breccia marble, calico marble, Calway River marble, Carrara marble, Champion Pink, Cherokee, Cipollino, Clarendon, Cockeysville dolomite, Colorado travertine, Colorado Yule, Columbia, coral marble, Craig Pink, Cream Antique, Cream Lauville, Cream Statuary, Danby, Dark Blue Columbia, Dark Blue Rutland, Dark Ivory Green, Dark Lepanto, Dark Vein True Blue, Dorset stone, Dorset Italian, Dorset Mountain, Dove Blue Rutland, Dyer breccia, Eastman Blue, Esperanza, Extra Dark Albertson, Extra Dark True Blue, Extra White Rutland, F. A. Pink, Florentine Blue, forest marble, Freedley White, Frozen Green, Georgia marble, Missouri marble, onyx marble, snowflake marble, Tennessee marble, travertine, Vermont marble, Winooski marble.** See also **breccia, dolomite, dove blue, faccia, favo, frise.** **2.** One of various minerals that can be cut into slabs and take a high polish, especially **serpentine** and, in colonial times, **limestone;** varieties include **Connecticut serpentine.** See also **alabaster, dolomite, fuchsite, onyx marble.**

marbled Having a veined, clouded, or variegated appearance like marble.

marbleized Painted in imitation of the surface color and pattern of stone, especially veined marble; base materials may include slate, plain marble, cast iron, and plaster. See also **faux bois, ragging, scagliola.**

marbleized glass **1.** Multicolored glass with partially mixed colors resembling veined marble. **2.** (19c) Clear sheet glass with irregular veins; manufactured by shattering hot glass by plunging it into cold water, then remelting it.

marbleizing Painting a surface to imitate marble.

margin Same as **draft.**

marine archaeology, marine archeology Archaeological study of underwater sites, especially shipwrecks. Also known as **nautical**

archaeology, underwater archaeology.** See also **archaeology, wet work.**

marine frieze, (pre-19c) **marine freeze** A **frieze** decorated with symbols related to the sea, such as seahorses, tritons, and shells.

marine glue A waterproof glue made from shellac or rubber cement mixed with naptha or oil of turpentine.

marker See **historic marker, site marker.**

market **1.** A place where goods are sold from stalls; may be an exterior area or a large space within a building, or a combination of the two. See also **market house.** **2.** (19c–present) A food store, including specialized stores such as a **meat market.** **3.** (Regional U.S.) A unit of lumber measure equal to a barked log 19 inches in diameter at the small end and 13 feet long; approximately 200 board feet.

market analysis **1.** An economic study of the potential market for a proposed use for a site or building; may include demographic analysis of potential users and study of current rents or sale prices. **2.** Determination of the potential **visitor profile** of a historic site or museum.

market garden A garden where vegetables are raised for sale.

market house (pre-20c) A building used for a **market** (sense 1).

market place A square or other exterior area used for a **market** (sense 1).

market value The expected or actual sales price of **real estate** sold in an arm's length transaction after being advertised on the open market.

market wire (19c–WWI) **Soft steel** wire.

marouflage Attachment of a canvas to a wall surface with glue as a base for mural painting.

marquee Same as **marquise.**

marquetry A decorative pattern made of thin, inlaid wood veneers of different colors. See also **parquetry.**

marquise, marquee **1.** A projecting exterior sunshade or shelter at the approach to a door; may be of large size in front of a public building, such as a theater. **2.** An outdoor, tentlike shelter.

Maryland Verde Antique A mottled, light to dark grass green **serpentine** with veins of lighter green; quarried in Maryland.

mascarón (pl. **mascarónes**) [Spanish] A decorative element in the form of grotesque human heads; common on Mexican Spanish Colonial door knockers, and Renaissance Revival keystones.

Masonite Trade name for a wood fiber **composition board** with a hard, dense surface manufactured by the Masonite Corp.

masonry Stone, brick, or similar elements installed so that the weight of a unit bears on the one below, typically with mortar in the joints between the units; pre-20c often meant **stonework** as opposed to **brickwork;** types include **adobe, block veneer, brickwork, concrete block, Greek masonry, stonework.** See also **architectural terra cotta, bond, masonry joint, toothed.**

masonry bond See **bond.**

masonry construction A building with a **masonry** exterior; includes both those buildings with true masonry bearing walls and masonry veneer buildings. See also **frame construction.**

masonry joint The place where two masonry units meet; typically a **mortar joint;** types include **bed joint, coursing joint, expansion joint, head joint, pien joint, saddle joint, slip joint, rustic joint;** finishes include **tooled joint, struck joint.** See also **bond, dry laid, slip joint.**

massicot A light yellow pigment composed of lead monoxide (PbO) made by gently roasting **white lead.** See also **litharge.**

massing The overall composition of the exterior of the major volumes of a building, especially when the structure has major and minor elements; descriptive terms include **avant-corps, hyphen, link, pavilion.**

master-beam Same as **summertree.**

master plan **1.** A planning document designed to guide the future development of an entity; both a physical and administrative plan; may be for a building (indicating phased changes of use, alterations, and/or additions), for a site (indicating planned building, landscape, and access development), for a political jurisdiction (indicating proposed land uses and public improvements), or for an organization; implemented through more specific means such as **restoration** or **zoning.** See also **comprehensive plan. 2.** The overall graphic display resulting from the **critical path method.** See also **CPM diagram.**

master seat The principal farm of a large estate where the owner resided, such as the Mansion House farm which was one of five farms at George Washington's Mount Vernon. See also **home plantation.**

master vault (18c) A **vault** that covers one of the principal spaces of a building, as opposed to a **subordinate vault.**

mastic **1.** A natural gum resin obtained from the mastic tree, *Pistacia lentiscus;* used in lacquers and varnishes. **2.** (19c) A quick-drying cement made of a mixture of litharge, linseed oil, sand, and lime; used as a paste filler. **3.** A pasty cement made of tar boiled with powdered brick, lime, or similar materials. See also **asphalt mastic. 4.** (20c) Any compound that remains elastic after installation.

mastic varnish Any **varnish** made with **mastic** (sense 1) dissolved in a solvent.

mat **1.** A flat-painted or -glazed surface finish; the opposite of polished or glossy. Also spelled *matte.* **2.** A grid of steel reinforcing bars used in a concrete foundation. See also **grillage.**

match board (19c–early 20c) One of a series of **tongue and groove** boards of equal thickness, and, typically, equal width; typically used for subflooring or sheathing. Also known as **match lumber.**

match joint, matched joint, matching joint A joint formed by **matched boards** or **matched veneer.**

matched boards See **match board.**

matched veneer Wood or stone veneer pieces installed with the grain of adjoining pieces aligned at the edges; types include **book matched, herringbone matched.**

matching joint Same as **match joint.**

match lumber Same as **match board.**

Material Safety Data Sheet (MSDS) A summary of information related to health and safety hazards that may be experienced by a worker using a product; required by the U.S. **Occupational Safety Health and Safety Administration** (OSHA).

material, (pre-20c) **materiall** (19c–present) The substance of which something is composed or constructed; used as both singular, such as the stone material of a wall, and plural, such as the **building material** of a house. See also **fabric.**

materials **1.** A plural form of **material. 2.** The physical elements that were combined or deposited in a particular pattern or configuration to form a historic property. See also **fabric.**

mat foundation A continuous concrete slab foundation used support a building on soils of low bearing capacity; typically with **mat** reinforcing. Also known as **floating foundation.**

mat-glazed A thick, enamel, glazed finish with a mat surface on architectural terra-cotta. See also **architectural terra-cotta.**

mathematical tile (19c) A ceramic tile with geometric patterns on the exposed face.

matte Same as **mat.**

mausoleum A large **tomb** in the form of a building.

Maya arch Same as **corbel arch** or **corbel vault.**

Maya cement A **calcareous cement** made of lime and zaccab.

meal house A building used to store ground grain. See also **granary.**

meal room A room used to store ground grain.

meander A classical Greek style border decoration composed of various repetitive patterns of winding lines that form a continuous band; most commonly the turns are at right angles; typically expressed with bas-relief fillets. Also known as **aligreek, Greek key.**

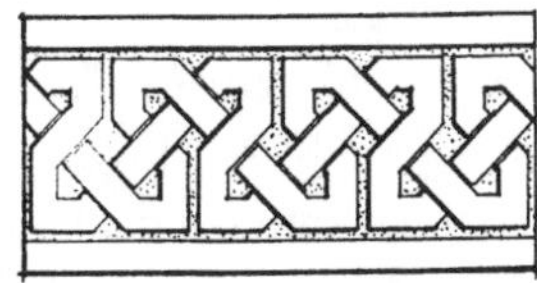

meander

measure See **board measure, foot, market, metric system, mil, minute, module, penny, perch, pH.**

measured drawings A set of drawings that accurately record an existing site, building, structure, or object, based on field measurements; typically includes plans, elevations, sections, and details; HABS/HAER Standards require ink lines on an archivally stable material, such as mylar. Also known as **as-found drawings.** See also **as-built drawings, controlled photography, select existing drawings.**

meat house **1.** (pre-20c) Same as **smokehouse.** **2.** A building where meat is stored.

mechanical Construction related to furnishing **heating, ventilating, and air conditioning, plumbing,** and a **fire suppression system;** restoration and renovation projects may include air conditioning and ducts, boilers, gas piping, water piping and drains, plumbing fixtures, fire sprinklers, and storm drains.

mechanical code A **building code** that governs the safe and healthy design of **heating, ventilating, and air conditioning** systems for a structure; sometimes also incorporates a **plumbing code.**

mechanical room A **room** devoted to mechanical equipment and controls, such as **boiler, furnace, ductwork, plumbing, water heater,** and so on. See also **electrical room.**

mechanic's lien A **lien** filed by a contractor or worker who claims to be unpaid for work performed on a construction project; may be satisfied by mutual agreement of the parties, or dismissed or upheld by court action.

medallion A bas-relief decorative panel set on a surface, especially when round or oval, and on an entablature. See also **ceiling medallion.**

medallion carpet A carpet with a central design feature in the form of a **medallion.**

medicine cabinet, medicine case A small, recessed storage cabinet with a mirrored door; typically located over the bathroom sink.

medium steel A medium-carbon **steel** with 0.25–0.60 percent carbon content; first used for structural shapes in the late 19c. Also known as **normal steel.**

meeting bar Same as **meeting rail.**

meetinghouse, (pre-19c) **meeting house,** (pre-18c) **meetinghowse** A Protestant place of worship; the term used by many denominations and sects before the 19c; largely replaced by **church,** except by Quakers.

meeting rail The bottom rail of the upper **sash,** or the top rail of the lower sash, of a double hung window; typically beveled so that the joint closes completely when the window is shut. Also known as **meeting bar.**

meeting stile One of the two stiles of a pair of doors or casement windows that abuts the adjoining stile when closed; may be in the form of an **astragal joint.**

melamine A colorless, wear-resistant, thermosetting plastic resin.

member **1.** One of the individual shapes that make up a **molding,** such as a water table that has three members. **2.** Any of the individual elements of a building, such as a framing member.

membrane roof A roofing surface covered with a thin, continuous, waterproof layer; most often used on a **flat roof;** types include **built-up roof, ready roofing, single ply membrane.**

Memorandum of Agreement (MOA) A written agreement between a U.S. federal agency, the State Historic Preservation Officer, and the Advisory Council on Historic Preservation defining how the agency will take into account and mitigate the effects of a project on affected historic properties under the **Section 106** review process. See also **consultation process, Programmatic Agreement.**

memorial arch Same as **triumphal arch.**

memorial slab An inscribed stone slab set in a wall as a memorial to the deceased.

memorial window A colored glass window installed as a memorial to a deceased person, or other cause; typically inscribed and bearing appropriate symbols.

mensa **1.** The top surface of an altar. **2.** The stone slab forming the top of an altar.

merchantable stuff (pre-WWI) Wood of a lower grade than **clear stuff.**

merchant bar A smoothly finished iron bar, ready for use, as opposed to a **mill bar.** Also known as **merchant iron.**

merchant iron Same as **merchant bar.**

merchant mill A large **mill** used for grinding grain; typically buys grain and sells flour and meal.

mercuric sulfide See **crimson.**

merlon One of a series of raised parapets of short length composing part of a **battlement.**

merlon

Merulius lacrimans A type of fungus that causes **dry rot.**

mesa dwelling A pueblo built on top of a mesa or cliff.

mesh **1.** A grid or network, especially made of wire; types include **hardware cloth, triangle mesh, welded wire mesh.** **2.** One of the open spaces of a grid.

meso-American architecture The architecture of the pre-Columbian native American cultures located in central and southern Mexico, Nicaragua, and Honduras, including the Aztecs, Mayans, and Toltecs. See also **pyramid.**

mess, mess hall A room used for group dining, especially at a military institution. See also **dining hall, eating shed.**

metal A class of ductile, opaque, conductive elements, such as **aluminum, chromium, copper, iron, nickel, tin, zinc,** and their alloys **brass, bronze, steel, monel.** See also **alloy, miscellaneous metal, noble.**

metal decking See **steel decking.**

metal fabric Same as **hardware cloth.**

metal flake paint Any paint containing metal powder; used to produce a gilded, bronzed, or silvered appearance, such as **aluminum paint.** See also **bronze liquid, Dutch metal powder.**

metal foil insulation Aluminum **foil** used to reflect radiant heat energy; in the second quarter of the 20c used in wood frame walls and roofs as sheets behind sheathing or plasterboard, crumpled up within stud spaces, and as backing for wire lath; after WWII most often used in combination with other insulating materials, such as **rigid insulation** or **batt insulation,** as both an insulator and vapor barrier.

metal lath, metallic lath Any of several types of plaster **lath** manufactured from metal; types include **expanded-metal lath, sheet-metal lath, wire lath.**

metal lumber (mid-20c) Rolled sheet metal used for framing members such as studs and joists; types include **Berlay metal lumber, Truscon steel joist.**

metal molding A surface-mounted electric wiring system with two to four insulated wires placed within a hollow rectangular or oval galvanized sheet-metal conduit; typically formed with separate backing and cap sections; developed by 1910 and common after WWI. Also known as **metal surface raceway.** See also **electric wiring, wire mold, wooden molding.**

metal roofing Any of various sheet-metal roof coverings; types include **Ag-panels, batten roof, standing seam roof, metal shingle, tin roof.**

metal shingle, metallic shingle A roof or wall **shingle** stamped from sheet metal; most commonly a **tin shingle,** may also be made of aluminum, bronze, copper, galvanized steel, zinc.

metal siding A type of **siding** made of stamped sheet-metal panels; typically imitate other materials such as ashlar stone, brick or clapboard.

metal stud Same as **steel stud.**

metal surface raceway Same as **metal molding.**

metalwork Any kind of building component manufactured of metal; may be cast, forged, repoussé, rolled, or wrought.

meter, metre A unit of length in the **metric system;** originally intended to be one ten-millionth of the circumference of the earth around a polar meridian; in the U.S. equals 39.37 inches.

metes and bounds The legal description of the borders of a piece of land; typically a series of compass headings and distances that form a closed shape when drawn or surveyed, and a description of one or more benchmarks or monuments; used to prepare a **survey.**

metoche The distance between dentils in the Ionic order.

metope The space on a **Doric** frieze between two triglyphs; may be a plain, flat surface or have elaborate relief carving. Also known as **intertriglyph.**

metope medallion A sculpted rosette located in the center of a metope on a doric frieze.

metric system A system of weights and measures based on the **meter;** developed in France at the time of the French Revolution. See also **centimeter, millimeter.**

metz glass Same as **cobalt glass;** named for the town of Metz, Germany.

mews **1.** (19c) A rear courtyard used for access to the stables in an urban area; name from the Royal stables of Buckingham Palace, built on the site of a former hawk mews in London. **2.** The carriage houses, especially with servant's quarters, surrounding a rear courtyard.

Mexican baroque Same as **barroco-mudéjar.**

Mexican onyx A variety of travertine **onyx marble** quarried in Mexico.

mezzanine **1.** A partial intermediate floor between two main floor levels, especially directly above the ground floor; often has a lower ceiling height than the other levels. Also known as **entresole.** **2.** (pre-20c) A window with a greater width than height, especially when used to provide light to an intermediate floor.

mezzo-rilievo, (pre-20c) **mezzo-relievo, mezzo rilievo** Same as **half relief.**

Mezzotint A variety of **Georgia marble** with heavy black clouding.

mica A transparent to translucent, colorless to jet black, layered mineral composed of silicates of aluminum or other metals, and an alkali, such as potassium or sodium; used in thin sheets for small windows and electrical insulation, and in powdered form for decorative painting; varieties include **isinglass, Muscovy glass.**

microballoons Small glass or phenolic spheres made by blowing gas through the molten material; an inert material used for various purposes, such as a filler in epoxy repairs and an abrasive in blast cleaning.

microclimate The exterior climate of a particular site.

microscopy The process of detailed examination of a small object or a surface with a microscope. See also **photograph microscopy.**

midden Same as **midden heap.**

midden heap A garbage dump, especially one associated with a prehistoric dwelling place; in coastal cultures, often largely composed of oyster or mussel shells. Also known as **kitchen midden, midden.** See also **archaeological site, mound.**

Middlebury Cream Same as **cream antique.**

middle post Same as **kingpost.**

midwall column Same as **midwall shaft.**

midwall shaft A relatively short column in an above-ground level wall opening; used in the Romanesque Revival style. Also known as **midwall column.**

Miesian In the style of Mies Van der Rohe, a German-born architect with many International Style works in North America; typical elements include total lack of applied decoration, exposed structural supports, visually free floating partitions, and reveals at joints between materials and surfaces.

mil A unit of thickness measurement equal to 0.001 inch; used to specify or measure coating and film thicknesses.

mild steel Same as **soft steel.**

mile post, milepost A marker along a roadway or railway placed at one mile intervals; often marked with the distance to a particular destination.

Milford pink granite A pink, medium- to coarse-grained **granite,** mottled with black mica spottings; quarried in the vicinity of Milford, Massachusetts.

milk glass A milky white glass colored with cryolite. Also known as **cryolite glass.** See also **opal glass.**

milk house, (17c) **milke howse** A **dairy** building used for storing milk, cheese, and butter.

milk paint Same as **casein paint.**

mill **1.** A structure containing an apparatus with **millstones** or rollers for grinding grain; typically a **windmill** or **watermill** before the introduction of the steam engine in the 19c; types include **gristmill, merchant mill. 2.** Any large building containing elaborate machinery for processing raw materials or manufacturing, especially with wood or steel skeleton construction with roof trusses; types include **fulling mill, rice mill, sawmill, spinning mill, sugar mill.** See also **factory, ginhouse, slow-burning mill construction.**

mill bar A roughly finished iron bar, as opposed to a **merchant bar.**

mill construction See **slow-burning mill construction.**

mill-dressed (19c) Same as **milled.**

milled Wood, or another material, finished by a planing mill. Also known as **mill-dressed.**

milled lead **Lead** rolled into sheets; a 19c substitute for cast lead; delaminates over time. See also **cast lead.**

mill floor See **mill construction.**

millimeter (mm) A unit of length or thickness that is 0.001 **meter;** in the U.S. equals 0.03937 inch.

mill-planed Same as **milled.**

mill pond A **reservoir** used to provide water to power a **water mill.** See also **mill race.**

mill race The canal or channel that carries water past a **millwheel.** See also **race tail, sluice.**

mill rind Iron hardware in the form of a Greek cross that holds the upper millstone in place.

mill run The standard quality material produced by a mill, such as **mill run steel.**

mill-sawn Sawn by a machine in a saw mill, as opposed to **hand-sawn** or **hand-hewn.**

mill scale The thin, rough layer of ferric oxide produced on iron or steel during hot rolling.

Millstone A pink, buff, and blue **granite** quarried in Connecticut.

millstone A large, quarried stone used to grind grain in a mill; often one of a pair of disk-shaped stones.

mill tail Same as **tail race.**

millwheel A **water wheel** used to power a mill.

millwork, (19c) **mill-work** **1.** (20c) Various wood items, such as doors, built-in cabinetry, or paneling, manufactured by use of a planing mill. See also **cabinetwork, odd work.** **2.** The manufacturing machinery of a **mill.** **3.** The planning and construction of the machinery of a manufacturing mill.

Milwaukee brick (19c) A cream colored **brick** manufactured in the vicinity of Milwaukee, Wisconsin.

minaret A slender tower adjoining a mosque; typically with balconies; traditionally used by the muezzin to issue the call to prayer.

mine An excavation for extracting minerals, coal, and similar substances, especially with underground shafts and/or tunnels; may include related facilities such as a **head house** and components such as **chamber, gallery.**

mineral caoutchouc Same as **elaterite.**

mineral cotton Same as **mineral wool.**

mineral spirits A volatile oil-paint or varnish **thinner** distilled from petroleum. Also known as **white spirits.**

mineral tar A type of **tar** produced by distilling bituminous minerals, such as shale, peat, and coal.

mineral wool A fibrous insulation made of spun mineral fibers manufactured by blowing air through molten slag; used as a sound and heat insulator by the late 19c. Also known as **mineral cotton, rock wool, slag wool.**

minium See **red lead.**

Minnesota Black A black, medium-grained **gabbro** quarried in the vicinity of Ely, Minnesota.

Minnesota Mankato A variously colored, semicrystalline, coarse-grained dolomitic **limestone** quarried in Minnesota; colors include cream to buff, yellow, gray, pink, and pink-buff.

minute **1.** A small unit of measure used in Classical revival modular systems; typically one-sixtieth of a column diameter. See also **module.** **2.** One-sixtieth of an angular degree.

mirador **1.** A rooftop belvedere in a Spanish Colonial style building. **2.** An oriel or bay window with a commanding view.

mirror A smooth, reflective surface; typically a sheet of glass with a **silvered** back, or polished metal.

mirror plate A high quality **plate glass** used for manufacturing mirrors.

miscellaneous metal The various small metal parts used in a building taken collectively, such as angles for lintels and metal railings; as opposed to **structural steel,** metal windows, **reinforcing bar,** or other major components.

mision [Spanish] **Mission.**

mission, mision **1.** Any type of building housing a group working for moral, political, or religious purposes in a foreign place, especially a permanent foreign embassy or legation. **2.**

One of the Spanish Colonial religious outposts located in Mexico, southwest U.S., and California and composed of a building or group of buildings; both the dwelling and work place of the Franciscans and other orders attempting to convert the native American population to the Catholic faith; typical elements include a series of connected buildings with a fortified appearance surrounding a central courtyard, massive plain stuccoed **adobe** or stone walls, fractable parapeted gables, bell tower of low height (often paired), red **mission tile** roofs, arched cloisters, exposed wood rafters with bricks spanning between them and cyma-shaped ends, **conchas, postigo.** See also **Barroco-mujédar style, Mission style.**

mission (sense 2)
Mission San Juan Capistrano
Orange County, California

Mission style An architectural style imitating some of the features of Spanish Colonial missions; originated in California in the late 19c, and most common for U.S. suburban houses in the early 20c; equally likely to have symmetrical facades with a hip roof, or asymmetrical facades with hip or gable roofs; typical elements include fractable parapets and dormers; mission tile roofing, overhanging eaves; smooth stucco walls and porches with large square piers; interior details often similar to the **Craftsman style.** See also **Spanish Colonial, Spanish Colonial Revival.**

mission tile A terra-cotta **roof tile** in the form of half of a truncated cone; laid alternately up and down, overlapping; typically 14–18 inches long.

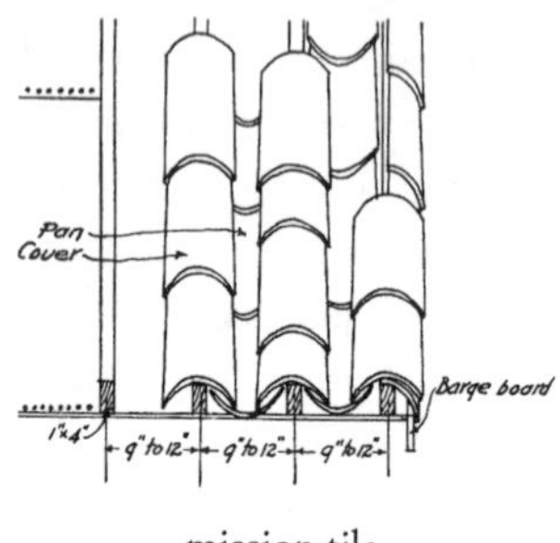

mission tile

Missouri marble A gray with bluish tint, crystalline **limestone** composed of shells and grains of calcite held in a mass of calcite; quarried in the vicinity of Carthage, Phoenix, and Marlo, Missouri.

Missouri Red granite A red, medium- to coarse-grain **granite** quarried in Missouri.

miter, (pre-20c) **mitre, myter, mytre** A **joint** between two elements meeting at equal angles; most commonly a right angle with the end of each piece beveled at 45 degrees. Also known as **miter joint.** See also **bevel joint.**

miter arch A structural support over an opening in a masonry wall formed by two stones that meet the abutments at a 45-degree angle, and form a right-angle **miter** in the center; technically not a true arch.

miter dovetail A **secret dovetail** corner joint with miter-cut projecting or recessed dovetails on the end of each board.

mitigation Any action taken to reduce **environmental impact;** methods include **avoidance, documentation** (including **crisis archaeology**), or moving the affected building or structure.

mitigative documentation program **Documentation** to **HABS/HAER Standards** of sites, buildings, structures, or objects that are threatened with demolition or substantial alteration by projects with U.S. federal involvement; required by the National Historic Preservation Act and administered by the regional offices of the National Park Service; typically performed by private contractors.

mitre joint, mitring joint (pre-20c) Same as **miter.**

mixed arch An **arch** with several centers, especially one of unusual form. Also known as a **composite arch.**

mixed use (20c) Having more than one **use** within a single building or zoning district; often used to distinguish from the single-use districts prevalent in the mid-20c.

mm Abbr. for **millimeter.**

MOA Abbr. for **Memorandum Of Agreement.**

modern architecture **1.** Building design in the currently fashionable **architectural style,** such as the various classical revival styles beginning in the 17c, and the **International Style** in the 20c. **2.** The term used beginning in the early 20c to describe a movement that combines **functionalism** with aesthetic ideals that include rejection of historical design precepts and styles; variations include **Art Deco, Art Moderne, International Style, organic architecture, Prairie style,** and many other offshoots in North America and other parts of the world.

Moderne See **Art Moderne.**

modernization The **renovation** or **alteration** of a building, typically with an attempt to make it look new or fashionable, as opposed to **restoration** or **rehabilitation.**

modern wainscot (late 18c) A dado made of flush boards.

modillion, (pre-19c) **modilion, mundillion** One of a series of scroll-shaped brackets supporting the corona of a cornice; common in **Corinthian** and **Composite** orders. See also **block modillion, console.**

modillion band A series of modillions alternating with open spaces.

modillion cornice A **cornice** with a **modillion band;** type includes **block cornice.**

modular brick A standard size **brick** with dimensions of 3½–3⅝ × 7½–7⅝ × 2¼ inches.

module One of various standard units of measure used to determine the proportions of a building and its elements; modular rules are common in various Classical revival styles starting in the Renaissance; typical modules include whole or partial column diameters or heights. See also **minute.**

moellon A mixture of rubble stones and mortar used to fill the interior of a masonry wall.

mogote A type of stone burial mound found in southern Mexico.

moisture meter A testing device that measures the amount of water in a material such as wood or brick.

mold, (pre-20c) **mould** Same as **molding.**

molded brick Same as **pressed brick.**

molded coping A stone coping with a **molding** cut into the lower front face of the coping stones.

molding, (pre-20c) **moulding** Linear decorative trim in various geometric profiles; term includes both the individual profile shapes and a composite of several shapes; plane forms include **fascia, band, beveled molding, chamfer, fillet, listel, panel strip, tringle;** convex forms include **astragal, bead, echinus, Greek ovolo, ovolo, quirk bead, reed, roll molding, torus, thumb molding, three-**

quarter round, and **zig-zag;** concave forms include **apophyge, cavetto, channel, congé, cove molding, ox-eyed molding, quirk moulding, roll molding, spring mold,** and **scotia;** double curved forms include **beak molding, bed molding, brace molding, chin-beak molding, cyma recta, cyma reversa, cymatium, keel, lamb' tongue, lip, ogee, treacle mold,** and **wave molding;** complex decorated forms include **anthemion band, bâtons rompus, bay leaf garland, billet molding, cable molding, chain molding, chevron molding, gadroon, lozenge molding, nailhead molding, nebulé, notch molding, paternoster, pellet molding, quirk bead, reeding, rose molding, star molding, tablet flower banding, torsade, trellis molding, twining stem molding, Venetian dentil, Vitruvian scroll;** types by use include **annulet, apron, back band, back molding, baseboard, base molding, bed molding, bolection, cant molding, cap trim, casing, chair rail, crown molding, dentil, drip, edge molding, hip mold, hood molding, picture molding, plate rail, raked molding, raking molding, rim molding, shoe mold, spring mold, stool, stop, surbase, wall molding, weather molding.** See also **corner block, flute, fret, head block, panel, plinth block, pampre, quirk, rabbet, rover, sticking, trim. 2.** Surface-mounted electrical conduit that is designed to be left exposed to view; types include **metal molding, wooden molding.**

mole **1.** A jetty, pier, or breakwater that protects a harbor or anchorage. **2.** (19c) An inexact term for any massive structure.

Monel, monel, Monel metal A 20c trade name for a silver colored, corrosion resistant **metal** alloy made of 67–70 percent nickel, 25–29 percent copper, plus small amounts of other metals including iron and manganese; invented by Robert Crooks Stanley and named for Ambrose Monell, president of the International Nickel Co.; used for manufactured products 1907–1950s.

monial (pre-20c) Same as **mullion.**

monitor, monitor top A linear, raised section of roof with vertical windows; used to light interior spaces. See also **cupola.**

monitoring The continual inspection or recording of the condition of a property; may be done automatically, such as with a **humidistat,** or visually, such as by crack width.

monitor roof A roof with a **monitor.**

monochromy A decorative pattern in different hues of the same color. See also **grisaille.**

monolith A vertically oriented architectural element, such as an **obelisk** or **pillar,** cut from a single stone block.

monolithic **1.** Having a uniform, continuous structure, such as a building with **reinforced concrete** walls, columns, and floor, or cut from a single piece of material, such as a **monolith. 2.** Concrete placed at one time without construction joints.

monopteral A circular classical style building with a single row of exterior columns. See also **columniation.**

monostyle **1.** Having a column with a single shaft, as opposed to a **compound column. 2.** Composed of a single column, such as a monument. See also **columniation.**

monotriglyph, monotriglyphic An **intercolumniation** interval of one triglyph, flanked by two metopes, centered between adjoining columns, plus a triglyph centered above each column; used in the **Doric** style. See also **ditriglyph.**

montant **1.** The part of a door, window, or panel stile that abuts the end of a rail. **2.** (19c) Any slender, vertical member. **3.** (18c) A panel stile.

Monterey pine A large, rapidly growing **pine** tree; found in southern California; *Pinus insignis.*

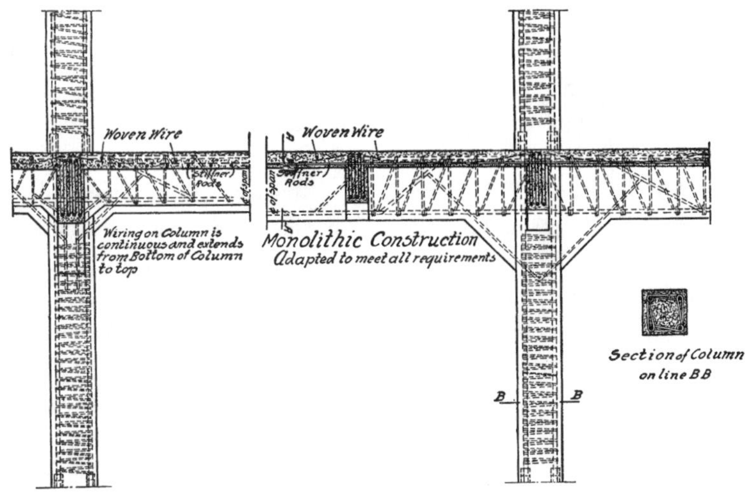

monolithic (sense 1)

Monterey Style An **architectural style** found in southwest U.S., especially California, after ca. 1830 that combines **Spanish Colonial** and **Greek Revival** style features; typical elements include adobe or stuccoed stone walls, pitched roofs with shingles or clay tiles, double hung windows, Greek Revival style wood trim at windows and doors, and cantilevered second-story porches. See also **Territorial Style.**

monument **1.** A commemorative building or structure that memorializes a person, place, or historic event, especially one of grand proportions and durable materials, such as the Washington Monument. See also **cenotaph, monolith, tomb, triumphal arch. 2.** An object constructed and placed as a permanent **boundary marker;** most often a stone pillar. **3.** An elaborate **gravestone,** especially when

Monterey Style
Casa Amesti
Monterey, California

sculptured. **4.** Any site, building, or structure with **significance;** for example, Mt. Vernon is known as a national monument. **5.** A formal designation of some units of the National Park Service.

Moorish In the style of the medieval Saracen architecture in Spain. See also **moresque, arabesque.**

Moorish arch A horseshoe arch, especially where the voussoirs alternate in color or decoration.

mopboard, mop board Same as **baseboard.**

moresque **1.** Moorish design, especially surface decoration of interlaced geometrical patterns in bas-relief and brilliant color. **2.** Same as **arabesque.**

moresque (sense 1)
Isaac M. Wise Temple
Cincinnati, Ohio, ca. 1865

mortar The material used to fill the joints of masonry; plastic when first mixed; various mixtures are used, including **adobe, brick dust mortar, cement mortar, clay-and-hair, gauge mortar, hydraulic mortar, lime-sand mortar;** the main function of the mortar is to evenly transfer the loads downward through the masonry units. See also **loam.**

mortar analysis Scientific determination of the components of a mortar sample by use of a microscope and chemical analysis.

mortar bond Same as **bond** (sense 2).

mortar joint A **masonry joint** between masonry units, such as brick or stone, filled with mortar to transfer the load, provide a bond between the units, and keep out the weather; types include **beaded joint, butter joint, concave joint, extruded joint, face joint, flush joint, flush plus rodded joint, gauged joint, grapevine joint, high joint, raked joint, ribbon joint, rope joint, ruler joint, rustic joint, struck joint, V-joint, weather joint;** construction types include **shove joint, slushed joint.** See also **bond, face jointing.**

mortess (pre-20c) Same as **mortise.**

mortgage button A round ivory decoration placed on the center of the top of the bottom newel of the main staircase; traditionally installed at the time the house mortgage was fully paid.

mortice (pre-20c) Same as **mortise.**

mortise, (pre-20c) **mortess, mortice** A recessed pocket cut into an element to receive hardware or the projecting end of another piece, especially with wood; types include **closed mortise, open mortise, through mortise.** See also **mortise and tenon.**

mortise and tenon A wood framing joint where a tongue or **tenon** cut into the end of one member is inserted in a rectangular **mortise** in another member; typically secured with a **treenail.** Also known as **mortised and pegged.** See also **drawbore.**

mortise bolt A bolt with its head recessed below the surface in a **mortise.**

mortised and pegged Same as **mortise and tenon.**

mortise lock A lock that is mortised into the edge of the stile of the door, so that the body of the lock is concealed from view when the door is closed.

mortuary **1.** A building for the temporary reception of the deceased. **2.** A **monument** or other memorial commemorating a deceased person. **3.** A **graveyard** or **cemetery.**

mortuary column One or two carved wood columns supporting a box containing the ashes or body of the deceased; built by the native peoples of the Northwest Coast.

mosaic, (19c) **mosaick** **1.** A surface finish made of small, inlaid stone, glass, or ceramic pieces forming a decorative pattern; used for flooring, walls, and counters; traditionally, cubes set in a mortar bed with small joints between the pieces; varieties include **opus Alexandrinum, opus lithostratum, opus sectile, opus tesselatum, vermiculated mosaic.** See also **tesserae, mosaic glass.** **2.** Any of various intricate parquet flooring patterns formed by multicolored woods. See also **parquet.**

mosaic glass Small pieces of colored glass used to form a pattern; most often cut from large sheets, may also be cast individually.

mosaic gold **1.** A yellowish compound composed of stannic sulfide; used in **gilding.** **2.** Same as **ormolu** (sense 2).

mosaick (19c) Same as **mosaic.**

mosaic rubble Same as **random rubble.**

mosquito bar (pre-WWI) Netting or screening installed over a door or window opening, or a bed, to keep out flying insects. See also **window screen.**

motif The theme or predominant feature of the design or decoration.

mouchette **1.** The curved, elongated, double-pointed shape of an opening in Gothic style **tracery,** with two cusps that divide it into two unequal portions. See also **dagger.** **2.** (18c) A pendant element of a **corona** soffit.

mould, moulding (pre-20c) Same as **molding.**

mound **1.** Earth heaped up by pre-Columbian Native Americans to form a huge geometric or stylized natural form in plan; found primarily in the eastern portion of the Mississippi valley. See also **midden heap, pyramid.** **2.** Same as **mount.**

mount An earthwork mound with a flat top; used as the base of a structure such as a fortification or summerhouse, as a feature or viewpoint in a landscape, or over a grave. Also known as **mound.**

mountain hemlock A **hemlock** tree with pale brown to red colored, strong, straight-grained, fine-textured heartwood; found in coastal areas from California to southern Alaska; used regionally for log cabins; *Tsuga mertensia.* Also known as **black hemlock.**

mountain pine A **pine** tree found at high altitudes from Arizona to Montana; *Pinus flexilis.* Also known as **white pine.**

Mountain White Same as **Danby.**

mountain white oak Same as **blue oak.**

Mount Airy granite A light gray to nearly white, medium-grained, biotite **granite** quarried in the vicinity of Mount Airy, North Carolina.

Mount Waldo A light to medium gray **granite** quarried in the vicinity of Mount Waldo, Maine.

mouth (18c) Same as **cavetto.**

mow floor The floor of a haymow in a barn; typically the main level.

M-roof A roof composed of two parallel gable roofs that form a center valley and are approximately M-shaped in cross section; common late 17c–early 18c. Also known as **trough roof, double-gable roof.**

MSDS **Material Safety Data Sheet**

mud A slang term for wet mixtures such as **concrete, mortar** or **plaster.** See also **clay-and-hair.**

mud brick Same as **adobe** (sense 1).

mud building See **adobe, pisé.**

Mudéjar-Gothic style An 18c Spanish Colonial adaptation of the earlier Moorish style from Spain; typical elements include raised geometric wall decoration, complex ogee arches, Tuscan style columns with zapatas, and floor brick spanning between wood joists. See also **Churrigueresque, Barroco-mudéjar style.**

mud house, (pre-19c) **mudd house** (pre-19c) A building with earthen walls or earthen nogging; typically of mud mixed with a binder such as straw or twigs. See also **adobe, pisé.**

mud jacking The process of using **pressure grouting** to lift a slab-on-grade to correct settlement.

mud mortar A **mortar** made of stiff mud. See also **adobe, cliff dwelling.**

mud set Tile laid in a wet **mortar** setting bed.

mudsill, mud sill **1.** A wood **sill** of a building or other structure that rests directly on the earth; used for sheds and other outbuildings, bridges, and dams. Also known as **bed sill.** **2.** A wood sill set into a concrete foundation or slab.

mugarnas, muqarnas Same as **stalactite work.**

mulberry A hardwood tree with rot-resistant wood; used for fence posts and occasionally for window and door sills and frames; the native variety is the red mulberry, *Morus rubra.*

mullion (12c–present) **1.** A vertical element between two window or door frames; typically not a structural support for the building. See also **muntin, window.** Also known as **munnion, monial.** **2.** A vertical framing member in the middle of a paneled door that runs between two rails. See also **paneled door.** **3.** A division between bays or panels of wainscoting.

multifoil Any arch, or tracery opening, with more than one **foil;** types include **trefoil, quatrefoil, cinquefoil.** Also known as **polyfoil.**

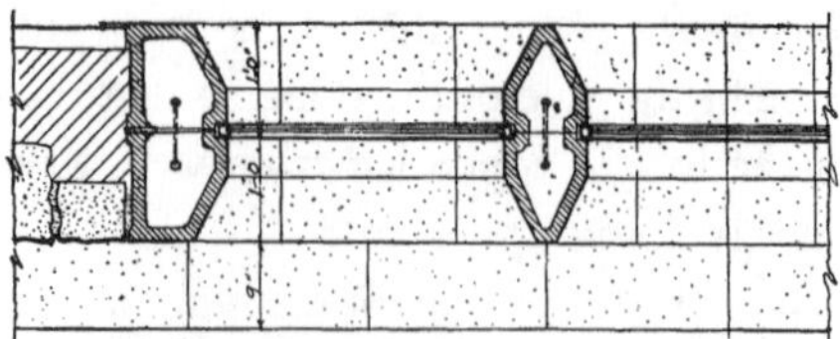

mullion (sense 1)

multifoil arch An **arch** that has an intrados with more than five cusps; common in **Arabesque style** architecture. Also known as **polyfoil arch.** See also **trefoil, quatrefoil, cinquefoil arch.**

multiple property listing A group of historic properties related by common theme, general geographical area, and period of time for the purpose of National Register documentation and listing.

municipality An incorporated local government jurisdiction, such as a town, township, or city, as opposed to a county, state, or province.

municipal planning See **planning.**

muniment room (pre-20c) A storage room in a house for important documents (especially deeds of title), silverware, and other treasures.

munnion (pre-20c) Same as **mullion.**

Munsell system A system of color indexing by hue, color saturation, and value; used in identifying and specifying finish colors; developed by the American Albert F. Munsell and first published as the *Atlas of the Munsell Color System* in 1915; all three attributes were combined into the Munsell color fan in 1947, and were developed into the Munsell Soil Color Chart by Nickersen in 1950.

muntin, muntin bar **1.** The small molding or bar that separates the individual panes of a multipaned window **sash.** Also known as **sash bar.** **2.** (pre-20c) Same as **mullion.**

Muntz metal, Muntz's metal A **brass** alloy made of copper and approximately 40 percent zinc that is malleable when heated; used in place of copper for roof sheathing; invented by G. F. Muntz of Birmingham, England. Also known as **yellow metal.**

muqarnas Same as **mugarnas.**

mural tower A tower that forms part of a fortification wall without projecting outside of the wall.

Murphy truss Same as **Whipple truss.**

Murray v. Richmond See **London Farm decision.**

musaick (19c) Same as **mosaic.**

Muscovy glass A transparent form of potassium-based **mica.**

museum A building or site used for housing, preserving, and interpreting a collection of **cultural artifacts,** some of which are on display; types include **art gallery, heritage village, house museum, outdoor museum;** from the term for a place devoted to the Muses of antiquity, such as the library and observatory established in Alexandria by Ptolemy (3c B.C.); first in the U.S. was the Charleston Museum, founded in 1773.

museum village See **heritage village, outdoor museum.**

mutilated impost An **impost** with moldings that do not project past the face of the pier below.

mutilated roof (18c) A roof that appears to be cut off, such as a mansard roof. See also **truncated roof.**

mutulary Doric A standard **Doric** order with a **mutule band.**

mutule One of a series of broad, low, rectangular blocks supporting the corona of a classical style cornice; often with parallel rows of guttae and a perimeter drip mold on the bottom face, and crowned with a fillet and cyma reversa. See also **Doric, gutta.**

mutule band The area immediately below the top half of a Doric style cornice; composed of mutules and caissons and has a continuous fillet and cyma reversa crown.

myter (pre-20c) Same as **miter.**

mytre (pre-20c) Same as **miter.**

N

nail, (17c) **naile** A metal fastener or pin hammered into materials to connect them together, usually tapered or pointed and having a thickened head; types by use include **back nail, clamp nail, clasp nail, clout nail, coffin nail, common nail, dog nail, finish nail, flooring nail, gimp nail, lath nail, picture nail, roofing nail, sheathing nail, trunk nail;** types by manufacture include **cut nail, wire nail, wrought nail;** types by shape include **brad, countersunk nail, diamond nail, flat point, rose nail, round-head nail, spike, sprig, square nail, tack;** types by size include **twopenny nail, threepenny nail, fourpenny nail, fivepenny nail, sixpenny nail, sevenpenny nail, eightpenny nail, ninepenny nail, tenpenny nail, twelvepenny nail, sixteenpenny nail, twentypenny nail, thirtypenny nail, fortypenny nail, fiftypenny nail, sixtypenny nail.** See also **penny, treenail.**

nail chronology Identification of the types of nails and dates used in a building or structure as a guide to the approximate period of construction of the original building and later alterations.

nailed in the edge (18c Philadelphia) Same as **blind nailing.**

nailer A block of wood, or other nailable substance, installed to provide attachment for furring, trim, or other elements; types include **blocking, dook, wood brick.**

nailhead A small, projecting, decorative feature that resembles the head of a nail; typically a flattened four-sided pyramid.

nailhead molding A molding with a series of sculpted projections in the form of a **nailhead.** See also **nailhead, tooth ornament.**

naked (pre-WWI) **1.** The main plane surface of a wall or floor from which molding and other elements project. **2.** Unsheathed or uncovered. See also **carcase, naked floor.**

naked floor, naked flooring (19c) Same as **carcase floor,** before applying the floor boards. See also **boarding joist.**

napkin pattern Same as **linenfold.**

Naples yellow **1.** A orangish yellow pigment composed of basic lead antimonate; used in house paints in the early 19c. **2.** (mid-19c–present) Other pigment compounds with a hue similar to sense 1.

narrow gauge, narrow gage A railroad track that is less in width between the rails than **standard gauge;** typically 48–56½ inches, measured perpendicularly at a point ⅝ inch below the top of the rail.

narthex The vestibule of a church or other religious building. See also **esonarthex.**

natatorium A building enclosing a swimming pool.

National Building Code A Canadian **building code** promulgated by the **National Research Council.**

National Center for Preservation Technology and Training An office of the U.S. National Park Service located in Natchitoches, Louisiana, that provides research, training, and information management regarding the art and sciences of historic preservation in the diciplines of architecture, archaeology, landscape architecture, conservation, and interpretation.

National Conference of the State Historic Preservation Officers A U.S. association of State Historic Preservation Offices headquartered in Washington, D.C.; lobbies Congress on behalf of the SHPO.

National Council for Historic Sites and Buildings A U.S. national private preservation organization formed in 1947; merged with the **National Trust for Historic Preservation** in 1954.

National Endowment for the Humanities (NEH) A U.S. federal agency that supports work to advance and disseminate knowledge in all disciplines of the humanities; programs include the Office of Preservation National Heritage Preservation Program, which funds housing and storage of museum objects, improved climate control, and the installation of security, lighting, and fire-prevention systems.

National Environmental Policy Act of 1969 (NEPA) U.S. legislation that requires preparation of an **Environmental Impact Statement** for all "major federal actions significantly affecting the quality of the human environment"; review must include disclosure and consideration of impacts on "urban quality, historic and cultural resources, and the design of the built environment"; applicable to all federally sponsored, funded, or licensed projects; regulations are issued by the **Council on Environmental Quality** (CEQ), an independent federal agency created under NEPA. See also **adverse effect.**

National Historic Landmark (NHL) A designation reserved for a **district, site, building, structure,** or **object** of exceptional significance to the U.S. as a whole, rather than just to a particular state or locality; NHL designation is conferred by the Secretary of the Interior; as of 1992, there were approximately 2,000 NHLs across the nation; since 1935 all NHLs are listed in the **National Register of Historic Places.**

National Historic Landmarks Program The National Park Service program that administers the process of designating a **National Historic Landmark.**

National Historic Preservation Act of 1966, as amended (NHPA) U.S. Federal legislation establishing the **Advisory Council on Historic Preservation,** expanding the **National Register of Historic Places,** and extending the **National Historic Preservation Programs** to properties of **State significance** and **local significance.** See also **Section 106.**

National Historic Preservation Programs The legislated U.S. Federal historic preservation programs administered by the **National Park Service;** includes the **Preservation Assistance Division, Historic American Building Survey, Historic American Engineering Record, National Historic Landmarks Program,** and the **National Register of Historic Places.**

National Historic Site Any place declared to be of national historic significance by the Minister responsible for Parks Canada.

National Institute for the Conservation of Cultural Properties (NIC) An organization that promotes the conservation and preservation of U.S. heritage, including works of art, anthropological artifacts, documents, historic objects, architecture, and natural science specimens; administers the **Conservation Assessment Program** and **Save Outdoor Sculpture!**

National Institute of Structural Technologies (NIST) A U.S. Federal agency that performs scientific research on building materials and systems.

National Landmark See **National Historic Landmark.**

National Park Land owned by a nation for use by all citizens; may be of historical and/or scenic significance; the world's first National Park was established at Yellowstone, Wyoming in 1872.

National Park Service (NPS) A bureau of the U.S. Department of the Interior whose purview includes the historic and cultural resources in the National Parks system, such as the Statue of Liberty, Independence Hall, and Mesa Verde, and the **National Historic Preservation Programs;** created in 1916.

National Register See **National Register of Historic Places.**

National Register Information System A computerized database of information on properties included in the **National Register of Historic Places.**

National Register nomination See **National Register of Historic Places, nomination.**

National Register of Historic Places A list of U.S. places of **significance** in American history, architecture, archeology, engineering, and culture on a national, state, or local level; places may be a **district, site, building, structure,** or **object;** established in 1935 by Act of Congress and the **tripartite agreement,** partially rejuvenated in 1960, and expanded by the **National Historic Preservation Act of 1966, as amended;** maintained by the **National Park Service.** Also known as the **National Register.** See also **determination of eligibility, Federal Preservation Officer, Keeper of the National Register, National Historic Landmark, nomination, State Historic Preservation Officer, State Historic Preservation Program, State Review Board, Thematic Group Format.**

National Research Council A Canadian Federal agency that produces the **National Building Code.**

national significance The importance of a property to the history of a nation; for National Register purposes, the importance to U.S. history.

National Style (mid-19c U.S.) Same as **Greek Revival style.**

National Trust for Historic Preservation (NTHP) A U.S. not-for-profit organization chartered by Congress in 1949 to further the cause of historic preservation; owns a limited number of historic properties and administers various preservation programs, such as the **Main Street Program, Office of Maritime Preservation,** and **Rural Heritage Initiative.** Also known as the **Trust.** See also **National Council for Historic Sites and Buildings.**

nattes Raised surface decoration in a woven pattern, such as **basket weave bond.**

natural bed Same as **bed** (sense 4).

natural cement Any type of **calcareous cement** made from a naturally occurring mixture of limestone and clay; types include **Roman cement, Rosendale cement.**

natural draft A current of air created by natural, rather than mechanical, phenomena, such as the wind or the temperature differential within a chimney flue.

natural environment The exterior **environment** that is substantially unaltered by human activity; includes land forms, trees and plants, rivers and lakes, and excludes the **built environment;** sometimes extended to include landscaped areas that appear natural or disturbed areas that have reverted to nature.

nautical archaeology Same as **marine archaeology.**

naval oak A **live oak** tree grown for use in ship building; plantations of trees were grown in southern U.S. under contract with the Navy.

naval stores Natural resin products used on wood boats; types include **rosin, tar, turpentine.**

nave The large central space of a **church** or other similar building; in a cross-shaped church, does not include the transepts or choir.

NCSHPO **National Conference of the State Historic Preservation Officers**

neat Undiluted, as in **neat plaster.**

neat plaster **Plaster** without sand.

nebulé, nebuly A projecting band with a bottom molding edged in the form of a continuous undulating curve with a series of symmetrical inward and outward bulbous shapes; from the heraldic term for a line of this shape; used in **Romanesque Revival style** architecture.

necessary, necessary convenience, necessary office, necessary place (Southern U.S.) A small **latrine** building.

neck **1.** Same as **necking** (sense 1). **2.** The narrow part of an **embrasure,** between the mouth and the sole.

necking The top of a column or pilaster shaft immediately below the capital, including any moldings; in the Doric and Tuscan orders, a cylindrical band between the fillet at the bottom of the capital and the astragal on the shaft. Also known as **gorgerin, neck.**

neck molding, neck moulding Same as **necking** (sense 2).

needle Same as **needle beam.**

needle bath A plumbing fixture for bathing that sprays water horizontally over the body with rows of fine jets.

needle beam **1.** A beam inserted through a hole knocked in an existing wall; used to support the wall above during repairs, underpinning, moving the building or structure, or demolition of part of the wall below; steel needle beams were used for the first time in 1890 during underpinning of the Chicago Chamber of Commerce Building. Also known as **needle.** **2.** Same as **cross beam.** **3.** A cross piece in a **queen-post truss** that supports a floor.

needle latch Same as **needle lock.**

needle lock A lock with steel pins, hung on pivots, that are moved by a key. Also known as **needle latch.** See also **cylinder lock.**

needle spire A thin spire that rises from a flat roof inside the parapet of a tower; commonly used with a decorative **battlement** parapet.

negro house (pre-20c southern U.S.) A dwelling used by African-American slaves. See also **negro hut, negro kitchen, negro quarter, slave cabin.**

negro hut (pre-20c lower southern U.S.) A house of inferior construction used as a dwelling by African-American slaves; most often a single-pen log cabin. See also **negro house, slave cabin.**

negro kitchen (pre-20c southern U.S.) An outbuilding used as both a kitchen and dwelling by African-American slaves.

negro quarter (pre-20c southern U.S.) A **quarter** (sense 3) used for African-American slaves. Also known as **negro house.**

neoantique (19c) **1.** Same as **neoclassical.** **2.** Architecture based on direct study of classical Greek and Roman architecture without reference to later examples, such as those of the Renaissance. See also **neoclassical.**

neoclassical, (19c) **Neoclassical** A return to architecture and art based on **classical** principles begun in Europe in the Italian Renaissance of the 15c, and again in North America in the late 18c; generally not a simple imitation of classical buildings; initially use of simple Roman orders with distinct massing of the elements was most common; succeeded by the **Greek Revival style,** and later in the 19c by the more ornate Roman Imperial style; after the Columbian Exposition in Chicago in 1893, popularity of the Renaissance styles was revived until the 1920s; watered-down versions continue to the present. See also **classical orders, classical style, classicism, Classical Revival style, Greek Revival style, Jeffersonian, neoantique, Vitruvian.**

Neoclassicism The revival of **classicism** in the 19c.

Neo-Gothic (19c) Same as **Gothic Revival style.**

Neo-Grec (19c) Same as **Greek Revival style.**

Neo-Greek (19c) Same as **Greek Revival style.**

neon **1.** An inert gas. **2.** Artificial lighting produced by passing a high-voltage electric current through a glass tube filled with neon or a similar gas. See also **fluorescent light, incandescent lamp.**

neoprene (20c) A synthetic rubber material.

NEPA **National Environmental Policy Act**

nerve (18c) One section of an ogive **rib** of a vault.

net tracery Gothic style window **tracery** with a series of openings of approximately the same size and shape that form a grid pattern. Also known as **reticulated tracery.** See also **interlaced arcade.**

neutron activation analysis Determination of the elemental components of a material by irradiating samples with a nuclear reactor; used to determine the composition of building fabric. See also **neutron probe.**

neutron moisture meter A portable device that indirectly measures hydrogen content by neutron thermalization; used to determine the water content of relatively thin materials. See also **neutron probe.**

neutron probe A device for elemental analysis using the prompt gamma neutron activation method; primary components are a small portable neutron source and a gamma ray detector; used to determine the amount of materials, such as water or salt, at a particular location. See also **neutron activation analysis, neutron moisture meter.**

New Art See **Art Nouveau Style.**

new construction The process, or completed product, of building a new structure or building, or an **addition** or **alteration** to an existing one, as opposed to **restoration, repair** or **rehabilitation.**

newel **1.** The vertical post that terminates a run of a stair railing; may be only at the bottom, or may be at each point where the rail turns; supports the railing, and sometimes the stringer; types include **closed newel, open newel, starting newel.** Also known as **newel post. 2.** The central column of a stone winding stair. **3.** A vertical post at the end of a bridge wing wall.

newel post Same as **newel** (senses 1 and 3).

newel stair, newelled stair A stair with newel posts supporting the railing at the turns.

New England Colonial **Colonial architecture** constructed in the New England region beginning in the early 17c; style includes **Georgian.** See also **Garrison Colonial, log house, postmedieval architecture, saltbox, stone ender.**

newgrounds (pre-20c) Land recently cleared of virgin forest.

New Orleans Charter The New Orleans Charter for the Joint Preservation of Historic Structures and Artifacts; principles governing the preservation of historic structures and the artifacts housed in them; finalized at a symposium in New Orleans in 1991, and adopted by **AIC, APTI,** and **NCSHPO.**

newsroom, (19c) **news-room 1.** A reading room for newspapers and other periodicals; typically associated with a hotel or similar establishment. **2.** (20c) A place where newspapers and magazines are sold. **3.** (20c) The room where copy for a newspaper is written and edited.

NGO Abbr. for **nongovernmental organization.**

NHL National Historic Landmark

NHPA National Historic Preservation Act of 1966

NIC National Institute for Cultural Conservation

NICCP National Institute for the Conservation of Cultural Property

niche A recessed space in a wall; typically semicircular in plan, with a conch at the top; most commonly used for placement of statuary; types include **angle niche, round niche, square niche.** See also **tabernacle.**

MEMORIAL ENTRANCE TO ARLINGTON NATIONAL CEMETERY

niche

nickel A hard, silver-gray, ductile, magnetic **metal** element. See also **nickel plated, stainless steel.**

nickel plated A thin layer of **nickel** electroplated, or deposited from a heated solution, on another metal to provide corrosion resistance; common late 19c–early 20c. See also **chrome plated.**

Nicolson pavement Paving composed of wood blocks set with the grain running vertically, the interstices filled with gravel and coal tar.

nigged A **stone work** surface dressed with a sharp pointed pick, rather than a chisel.

nigrosene black A bluish black **aniline color** paint pigment.

ninepenny nail (9d nail) A **nail** approximately 2¾ inches long; 75 iron common nails weigh a pound. See also **ninepenny spike, penny.**

ninepenny spike (9d spike) A **spike** approximately 6.5 inches long; 7.5 steel-wire spikes weigh a pound. See also **ninepenny nail, penny.**

ninepin alley (19c) A bowling alley.

NIST National Institute of Structural Technologies

NMC National Museums of Canada

noble A **metal** that is more resistant to corrosion than another metal; when two metals are in contact in the presence of water, the less-noble metal corrodes.

noble fir A large **fir** tree with light brown, reddish streaked, hard, strong, close-grained wood; found in the mountains of Washington and Oregon; used for millwork and flooring; *Abies procera.* Also known regionally as **feathercone red fir, bracted red fir, larch, Tuck-Tuck.**

nog One of a series of vertical wood members placed between the heavy framing posts of a timber framed structure. See also **nogging.**

nogging The material used to fill the wall spaces between the main vertical framing posts of a **timber frame** building; "used to control fire and vermine," as noted by General Skyler to Alexander Hamilton in the early 19c; material may include mud mixed with straw or twigs, **nog, brick nogging, cob, plaster, wattle and daub.**

noise pollution Unwelcome noises or noise levels from human activity. Also known as **sound pollution.**

nominal dimension A named, rather than actual, size, including: **1.** The size of a masonry unit plus one mortar joint, as in a 2⅔ × 4 × 8 inch brick; the actual dimension is smaller. **2.** (before mid-20c) The rough-sawn dimension of lumber, as in a 2 × 4 inch stud; the planed dimension is smaller by ⅛–⅜ inches. **3.** (mid-20c–present) A standardized cross sectional size of lumber that is **S4S;** actual dimensions are up to ½ inch smaller.

nominating authority The federal or state official authorized to nominate properties to the National Register of Historic Places.

nomination An official proposal to list a **historic resource** on a historic register, such as the **National Register of Historic Places;** states the significance and integrity of a historic resource or district; may include documentation on **associated historic contexts, associated property types, associative value.**

nonbearing Not part of the supporting structure of a building. See also **bearing wall, non-load-bearing tile.**

nonconforming building A building that does not meet the current requirements of a government regulations, such as the exit requirements of a **building code** or the size restrictions of a **zoning code;** may be **grandfathered.**

nonconforming use A **use** of a property that does not comply with the current **zoning** regulations; may be **grandfathered.**

noncontributing building See **noncontributing resource.**

noncontributing resource A building, site, structure, or object that does not add to the historic significance of a property or district.

nondestructive investigation Analysis of the condition and physical characteristics of a structure by methods that do not alter its condition; methods include use of **archaeology, boroscope,** document research, **mortar analysis, photograph microscopy, nail chronology, nondestructive testing, paint stratigraphy, salt meter,** and spraying water on masonry to check for leaks. See also **destructive testing.**

nondestructive testing **Testing** the quality of a material without damaging the sample or element; includes use of **CAT scan, infrared reflectography, hammer sounding, infrared thermography, moisture meter, neutron probe, ultrasonic testing, x-ray photography.** See also **destructive testing, inspection, nondestructive investigation.**

nongovernmental organization (NGO) A not-for-profit group, such as a preservation organization, involved in affecting and/or implementing public policy; typically used to refer to groups operating at the national or international level.

non-load-bearing tile A structural clay tile unit for masonry walls without vertical loading.

nonmetallic cable Insulated electric wires wrapped with a protective sheath; in use by early 1930s, now the most common type of cable; originally rubber-insulated wires sheathed with paper and cotton braid impregnated with moisture and fire resistant compounds; sheathing replaced by thermoplastics after WWII. See also **electric wiring, Romex.**

nonshrink grout A type of **grout** with additives that compensate for the normal shrinkage of calcareous cement as it dries; used in underpinning and other work where movement is a problem.

nonsyphoning trap Any plumbing drain **trap** designed so that the water seal is always maintained; types include **Bower trap, Cudell trap.**

nook A small recessed area connected to a main space. See also **breakfast nook, chimney corner.**

nook shaft A freestanding column or colonette set in a square recess at a jamb or an outside corner of a building; found in Gothic and Romanesque style architecture.

normal cut The portion of a saw cut at the end of a wood member that is perpendicular to its grain; used in wood truss joints. See also **seat cut.**

normal steel Same as **medium steel.**

normal tiling Any system of **roof tile** that has alternating and overlapping convex and concave shapes; types include **Italian tiling, pan-and-roll tile;** shapes include **gutter tile, imbrex, mission tile, Spanish roof tile, tegula.** See also **pantile.**

Norman brick A long **brick** with nominal dimensions of 2⅔ × 4 × 12 inches, and actual dimensions of 2³⁄₁₆–2¼ × 3½–3⅝ × 11½–11⅝ inches.

Norman cottage A large, asymmetrical house in the style of the farmhouses of Normandy; isolated examples built in the U.S. primarily in the 1930s; typical elements include a round tower with a tall, conical roof (often used as the entrance), two stories with one-story wings, steeply pitched roof with dormers, mixed brick, stone, and stucco walls, multi-paned casement windows, and sometimes decorative half-timbering. See also **French Eclectic style.**

Norman roof A steeply pitched, medieval style roof supported with wood king-post trusses, with the top of the principal rafters butting against projecting joggles at the top of the kingpost, and diagonal braces from the middle of the principal rafters to the base of the king-post. See also **postmedieval architecture.**

Norse American architecture The buildings of Scandinavian settlers in Labrador.

North Carolina pine Same as **shortleaf pine** (sense 2).

northern red oak A large **oak** tree with light reddish brown, close-grained, hard, extremely strong wood; found in the northeast U.S. and Canada, and as far south as northern Louisiana and west to eastern Kansas; used for lumber, flooring, and interior trim; *Quercus borealis,* and the larger *Quercus borealis maximus.* Also known as **red oak.**

northern white cedar A moderate sized softwood tree with pale yellowish brown, soft, aromatic, brittle, coarse-grained wood; found in wetlands in the Appalachian Mountains from northern Georgia to Nova Scotia, the Great Lakes states, and southern Ontario and Quebec; durable in contact with soil; splits easily; used for shingles, poles, and tanks; lumbered out in the Great Lakes states by WWII; *Thuja occidentalis.* See also **cedar.**

North River bluestone A dark bluish grey, fine-grained **bluestone** quarried in the vicinity of the North River, New York; used for flag pavers, curbstones, and trim.

Norway pine Same as **red pine.**

nosing A projecting molding or overhang, especially the portion of the front edge of a stair tread that overhangs the face of the riser below.

nosing bead A half round edge on a stair tread or similar projecting horizontal board. See also **bead.**

nosing return A piece of molding of the same shape as the **nosing** of a stair tread and covering the exposed end of the tread; typically has a mitered joint where it meets the nosing.

notched doorway An opening in an wall that is wider at the top than the bottom, with dwarf walls projecting into the opening from both sides; used in Native American pueblos and cliff dwellings in the Southwest U.S.

notched molding A band or fillet decorated with **notch ornament.**

notching The system used to connect the overlapping ends of logs at the corners of a **log cabin** or **log house;** types include **diamond notch, dovetail notch, half-dovetail notch, round notch, saddle notch, square notch.**

notch ornament A decorative pattern formed by a continuous series of notches on the edge of another element; commonly in the form of a V-shaped cut on a projecting right-angle corner.

notification The process of notifying property owners, public officials, and the general public of nominations to, listings in, and determinations of eligibility for the National Register.

novelty siding (19c) Same as **drop siding.**

NPS National Park Service

NRC National Research Council

NTHP National Trust for Historic Preservation

nubbly Having a surface texture composed of small, randomly spaced lumps or knobs.

nursery **1.** A room or suite used for the shelter and care of infants; typically part of a large house. **2.** A place where plants are grown for sale as transplants, especially trees and shrubs.

nut A piece of metal with a threaded circular hole through the center; usually square or hexagonal; used as a fastener on the end of a **bolt.**

O

OAHP **Office of Archeology and Historic Preservation**

oak, (pre-18c) **oake** One of many hardwood trees of the genus *Quercus;* varieties used for lumber include **black oak, blue oak, live oak, northern red oak, pin oak, scarlet oak, shingle oak, southern red oak, swamp white oak, western oak, white oak, willow oak.**

oak bark A rough-textured **architectural terra-cotta** finish resembling the bark of an oak tree.

oake (pre-18c) Same as **oak.**

oaker (pre-20c) Same as **ocher.**

oakum Coarse hemp fibers used for caulking; may be used alone, or as the backing for poured lead or asphalt. Also known as **white oakum.**

obelisk A freestanding, four-sided shaft that tapers inward toward the top, and is crowned by a pyramid shape; used as a commemorative monument, such as the Washington Monument in Washington, D.C., or a decorative element in **Classical Revival style** architecture.

object A material thing of functional, aesthetic, cultural, historical, or scientific value; typically primarily artistic in nature or relatively small in scale and simply constructed; may be, by nature or design, movable yet related to a specific setting or environment; may be listed in the **National Register** or be a **National Historic Landmark;** types include **boundary marker,** boat, **fountain, headstone, mile post, monument, sculpture, statuary.**

oblique arch **1.** Same as **skew arch.** See also **arch. 2.** Same as **rampant arch** (technically incorrect).

oblique vault Two vaults that intersect at an angle other than 90 degrees.

oblong mesh A type of **expanded-metal lath** with oblong shaped holes.

obscure glass, obscured glass Window glass with various surface patterns that transmit light while giving visual privacy; types include **crackle glass, ground glass, half-clear glass, granulated glass, jealous glass, kinkled glass, ondoyant glass.** Also known as **figured glass, pattern glass.**

obtuse angle arch Same as **blunt-pointed arch.**

o.c. Abbr. for **on center.**

occult line (pre-20c) A light line drawn with a lead or graphite pencil as a guide to the finished heavier pencil or ink lines of a drawing; typically erased upon completion of the drawing.

occupancy See **building occupancy.**

occupancy permit Same as **certificate of occupancy.**

Occupational Health Safety Administration (OSHA) A U.S. federal agency that issues worker safety regulations, including construction site safety regulations and requirements for manufacturers to produce a **Material Safety Data Sheet.**

ocher, ochre, (pre-20c) **oaker** A light yellow to brown earth (especially the mineral goethite) containing a compound of hydrated iron oxide (Fe_2OOH) and other minerals such as clay or quartz; used as a paint **pigment;** varieties include **French ocher, yellow ocher.** Also known as **English ochre.** See also **plumbic ocher, red ocher, Vandyke brown.**

octagon **1.** (18c) Same as **octangle.** **2.** A regular polygon with eight equal faces. **3.** (19c) A fortification with eight bastions.

octagon house A rare **house** type with the plan of the exterior walls in the form of a regular octagon; scattered early examples exist, such as Searight's Tollhouse on the National Road in Pennsylvania; popularized in the mid-19c by Orson S. Fowler; often two stories, with porches and an octagonal cupola; may be any architectural style, including **Greek Revival Style, Gothic Revival Style, Italianate Style.**

octagon rafter Any of the rafters that extend from an octagon-shaped wall plate to the pointed peak.

octagon roof A roof with an octagonal plan.

octahedrite Same as **anatase.**

octangle (pre-20c) Any plane shape with eight angles or faces, not necessarily equal in size.

octastyle, octostyle Having eight columns in a row on the front facade. See also **columniation.**

octopartite vault A **rib vault** formed by the intersection of eight curved vault surfaces; used to cover octagonal or irregular spaces, and for square spaces enclosed by walls, such as the base of a tower; has eight cells of triangular plan with both diagonal ribs and a pair of ribs that bisect the square.

oculus **1.** A round window, especially the opening at the top of a dome. Also known as **bull's-eye, eye of the dome.** See also **oeil de boeuf.** **2.** Any circular or oval architectural element, such as a wall panel or louver. **3.** The hooded surround of a round or oval window.

odd work **Millwork** that is not of a standard size or form.

odeion Same as **odeon.**

odeon, odeion, odeum A Classical Greek or Roman theater; often used as part of the name of North American theaters before WWII.

odeum Same as **odeon.**

oeil de boeuf A small, round or oval window, especially when incorporated in the design of a frieze or cornice. Also known as **bull's-eye, oculus.** See also **oxeye.**

office **1.** (17c–present) An interior space used for clerical activities. **2.** (19c–present) An interior space used for managerial and professional activities. **3.** (18c) The interior space used for activities that support a large residence, such as kitchens, storage rooms, and bakeries.

office building A building primarily devoted to clerical, executive, and professional use; typically a converted residence until mid-19c, then low-rise walkup buildings until 1860s, then up to 10-story elevator buildings with masonry bearing walls by 1870s, then steel skeleton buildings of increasing height, exceeding 100 stories by late 20c; reinforced concrete skeletons were used for relatively low height office buildings starting in the 20c. See also **Chicago School, skyscraper.**

Office of Maritime Preservation A department of the **National Trust for Historic Preservation** that fosters maritime preservation; provides information and services to maritime organizations and government agencies.

office wire (late 19c–WWI) Insulated copper wire used for interior wiring of telegraphs and, later, telephones; named for its use in telegraph offices. See also **electric wiring, telegraph wire.**

offset A short, perpendicular change in direction of the main line or surface, such as where a wall jogs for a few feet and returns to its original direction. See also **retreat, return, set-off.**

offset hinge Any door **hinge** with a knuckle and pin that projects past the casing on the jamb so that the door can open a full 180 degrees; sometimes used to provide doorway clearance as required by AAG.

offset pipe A curved plumbing-pipe fitting that connects two parallel pipes.

off site Located outside the boundaries of a construction site, as opposed to **on site;** used to refer to the location of stored materials or construction work, such as a sewer line or road.

O.G. Same as **ogee.**

O.G. door (pre-WWI) Any U.S. manufacturer's stock door made with ogee shaped moldings.

O-G novelty (20c) A type of **drop siding** board with a cross section profile of the finished face in the form of two double curves; has the appearance of thin, curved clapboard when installed.

ogee, O.G. **1.** Any of various moldings with an S-shaped cross section; types include **cyma recta, cyma reversa.** Also known as **cyma, ogive. 2.** Any decorative S-shape.

ogee arch A pointed **arch** formed by a pair of S-shaped curves, with the convex portions meeting at the top; most commonly a **four-centered arch** with two centers on the spring line and two centers above the spring line. Also known as **inflected arch, keel arch.**

ogee arch

ogee roof A double curved, pyramidal roof, with the concave portion rising to a point at the top. See also **bell roof.**

ogival The adjective form of **ogive.**

ogive **1.** Same as **diagonal rib. 2.** (ca. 1830–present) A two-centered **pointed arch. 3.** (18c) Same as **ogee.**

Oglesby Blue granite An azure blue, fine-grain, biotite **granite** quarried in Georgia; can be highly polished.

oil-base paint Any type of **paint** that has an organic or petroleum-based oil **base** or **binder;** typically **linseed oil** before 1940, then **alkyd;** mixtures by color include **drab, chocolate color, pearl color, stone color, straw color, turkey red, wainscot color.** Also known as **oil paint.** See also **oil stain, tung oil.**

oil burner A mechanical device that burns a spray of heavy petroleum fuel to heat a boiler or furnace; introduced in the 20c, and often retrofitted to coal-fired boilers.

oiled brick A **soft mud brick** manufactured by coating the inside of the mold with oil to make separation easier. See also **sand-struck brick, water-struck brick.**

oilet, oillet, oillette, oylet (pre-20c) **1.** A small **loophole. 2.** An eye hole, such as in a door.

oil-fired Heated with an **oil burner.**

oil lamp Any of various oil-burning light fixtures; types include **Argand lamp** (late 18c–mid-19c), **solar lamp** (ca. 1840–1859), **burning fluid lamp** (ca. 1825–1859), **kerosene lamp** (mid-19c–present).

oil of turpentine (pre-WWI) Same as **turpentine** (sense 1).

oil paint Same as **oil-base paint.**

oil stain A type of translucent **oil-base paint** without white or hiding pigments; used to color wood while revealing the grain.

oil varnish A clear, protective film made of hard resins in a drying oil, such as **linseed oil;** hardens by oxidation; developed in the second half of the 19c.

okote pine Same as **candlewood pine.**

olive One of a series of domed, ellipsoid decorations on a molding, such as **pearls and olives.** Also known as **bead.** See also **bead and reel.**

olive butt Same as **olive-knuckle hinge.**

olive hinge Same as **olive-knuckle hinge.**

olive-knuckle hinge A **loose-joint hinge** with the knuckles in the form of a small olive-shaped ellipsoid.

on center, o.c. The dimension between the center axis of a series of elements, such as wall studs that are 16 inches on center (16″ o.c.).

ondoyant glass (19c–20c) A type of **obscure glass** with a wavy surface to provide visual privacy; typically in different colors.

one-centered arch Any **arch** with a single center for the radius of the intrados; types include **horseshoe arch, semicircular arch, segmental arch, pointed arch, Syrian arch.**

one over one, 1 over 1 A **double hung** window with a single pane in both the upper and lower sashes. See also **twelve over twelve.**

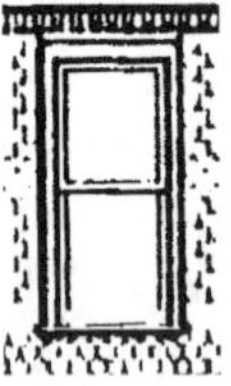

one over one

one-third running bond A brick **bond** having continuous courses of stretchers with the joints off-set one-third of the length of the stretcher above and below. See also **running bond.**

one-turn stair A **stair** with five flights at right angles, so that the top flight is directly over the bottom flight; may have winders, or a quarter-pace landing, at the turn.

onion dome See **imperial dome, Turkish dome.**

on site Located within the boundaries of a construction site, as opposed to **off site.** Also known as **field.**

Ontario poplar Same as **balsam poplar.**

onyx A translucent variety of **chalcedony** with banded colors; commonly white with brown, black, or red banding; used for interior decoration. See also **onyx marble.**

onyx glass Multicolored glass that resembles **onyx marble.**

onyx marble A translucent, compact form of travertine **marble;** typically clouded and banded in various colors, and resembling **onyx;** varieties include **Mexican onyx;** used for interior trim.

oölite Same as **oölitic limestone.**

oölitic freestone Same as **oölitic limestone.**

oölitic limestone A coarse-grained **limestone** composed of egg-shaped grains of calcium carbonate cemented together with the same material or mixed with clay and sand; quarried in Lawrence, Monroe, and Owen Counties, Indiana, and Alabama; varieties include **Bedford limestone, Shadow Vein.** Also known as **granular limestone, oölite, oölitic freestone.**

Opalescent A dark greenish gray, coarse-grained **gabbro,** with black and brown spotting, quarried in the vicinity of Cold Spring, Minnesota.

opalescent Any material, such as stone or glass, having the shimmering, cloudy appearance of pearl.

opalescent glass (1880–present) A milky, iridescent glass with multiple colors; manufactured by a process patented by Louis C. Tiffany in 1880.

opal glass A milk white, opaque glass, colored by 20 percent bone-ash calcium phosphate. Also known as **bone glass.** See also **milk glass.**

opalin, opaline (19c) **1.** A translucent, milky variety of glass. See also **milk glass. 2.** Fusible porcelain. Also known as **hot cast porcelain.**

open-air museum Same as **outdoor museum.**

open-air room Same as **sleeping porch.**

open cornice (20c) An overhanging eave having exposed rafter tails with a fascia board and spring mold across the ends and continued up the verge; the tails are often scroll-cut in one of various ornamental shapes; typically the roof sheathing is exposed to view from below.

open-grained Wood **grain** with large pores; typically needs to have a **filler** applied before painting. Also known as **coarse textured.** See also **coarse-grained.**

open mortise A **mortise and tenon** joint in which one or more sides of the tenon are exposed on the side; often used at the corner of timber frame sills. See also **closed mortise, through mortise.**

open newel A continuous winding stair without a newel post; types include **hollow newel.** See also **closed newel.**

open pediment Same as **broken pediment.**

open riser A stair **riser** defined by the surrounding treads and stringers, rather than being made of solid material.

open riser stair A **stair** with a series of **open risers.**

open sewer Any type of **sewer** that is unenclosed on top.

open slating Roof slates laid with space between adjoining slates in a course; used for economy, especially on farm buildings.

open space The area within a community or **planning** area that is unoccupied by buildings, structures or transportation networks; may be a **plaza, park,** farmland or part of the **natural environment.**

open space easement An **easement** requiring that property remain undeveloped; sometimes used to preserve historic cultural landscape.

open stair See **open-string stair.**

open-string stair **1.** A stair that has uncovered riser and tread ends. **2.** A stair with one or both sides not enclosed by a wall. Also known as **open stair.** See also **closed-string stair, cut string, stair.**

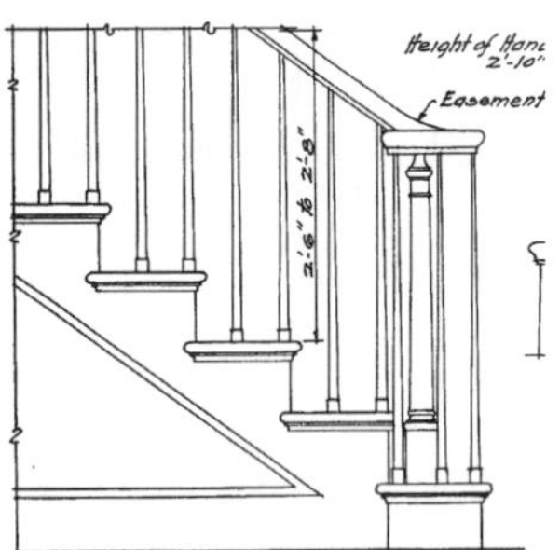

open-string stair (sense 1)

open-timbered A **timber frame** structure with exposed framing and sheathing, especially decorative roof trusses and rafters not covered by a ceiling.

open-timbered roof See **open-timbered.**

open valley A roof **valley** with the flashing visible between the shingles or slates on both sides. See also **swept valley.**

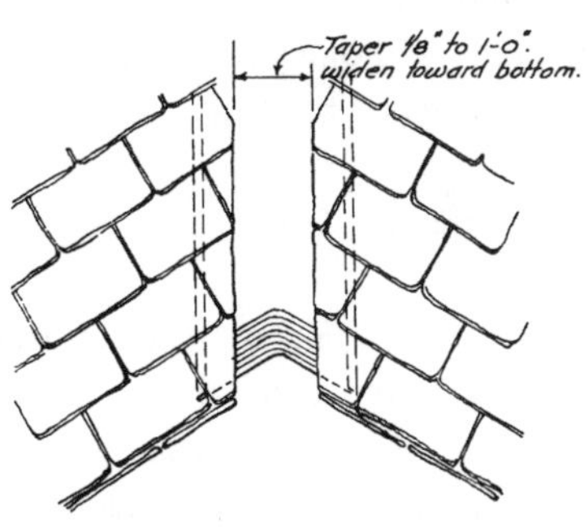

open valley

open web beam A truss with parallel top and bottom chords used as a beam, especially with a web of diagonal struts composed of a bent steel bars between chords formed of pairs of steel angles.

open web joist One of a series of **open web beams** used to support a floor; type includes **bar joist.**

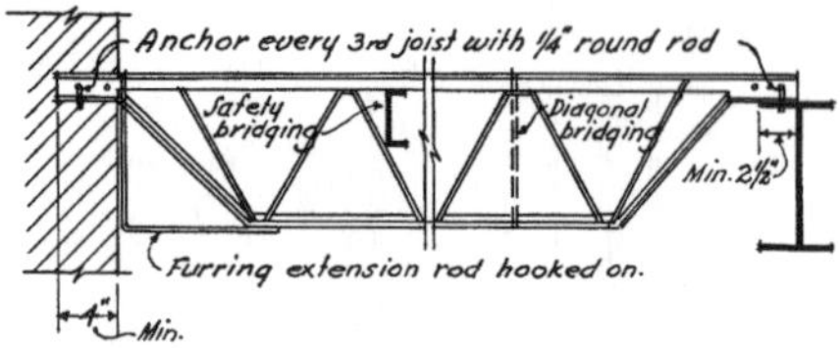

open web joist

openwork Decorative elements with a pattern formed by multiple holes; types include **pounced work, scrollwork.**

optical correction A change in the line of an element to improve its appearance, such as cambering the bottom of a beam so that it does not appear to sag, or providing **entasis** on a column shaft.

optick chamber (pre-19c) Same as **camera obscura.**

opus [Latin] Work or composition; used in architectural descriptions referring to masonry, mosaics, and paving.

opus Alexandrinum A type of stone **mosaic** work composed of a limited number of colors, such as white and black, and regular geometric pieces, usually cubes.

opus Graecanicum Greek style stone paving or inlay work.

opus lithostratum Any type of **mosaic** work composed of stone, including large pavers.

opus sectile Any type of **mosaic** work, or ornamental paving, composed of regular geometric pieces.

opus spicatum Masonry with a herringbone, or similar, pattern.

opus tesselatum A type of **mosaic** work composed of square pieces set in a square grid pattern.

opus vermiculatum Same as **vermiculated mosaic.**

oral history The recorded verbal recollections of a living person based on personal experience.

orange brass A ductile **brass** alloy of copper and approximately 0.73 percent zinc.

orange lead Same as **orange mineral.**

orange mineral (pre-20c) A brilliant orangish red paint pigment composed of lead tetroxide (Pb_3O_4); made by further heating of **red lead.** Also known as **orange lead.** See also **litharge.**

orange peel (20c) The textured surface of a film, such as **paint,** that resembles the skin of an orange.

orangerie, orangery **1.** (18c–19c) A **greenhouse** used for orange trees and other plants grown in tubs during the winter in northern climates; often unheated. **2.** (20c) Same as **conservatory.**

orangery Same as **orangerie.**

orange shellac A slightly orange, translucent **shellac** made from unbleached lac dissolved in alcohol.

oratory A small chapel, or room with an altar, for solitary prayer.

orb **1.** A plain, circular or spherical boss at the intersection of vault ribs. **2.** A sphere or globe.

orchard The ground or enclosure where trees are grown for their produce, especially fruit trees such as apples and pears. See also **grove, sugar-orchard.**

orchestra **1.** The portion of the main floor of a theater where the musicians sit, immediately in front of the stage. See also **orchestra pit.** **2.** The portion of the main floor of a theater between the orchestra pit or stage and the edge of the balcony above. Also known as **parquet.** See also **parterre. 3.** (18c) The gallery opposite the pulpit in a New England church.

orchestra pit A lowered area immediately in front of a theater stage where the musicians sit; allows a clear view for the patrons sitting in the front rows of seats.

order **1.** The sequence, shape, and dimensions of a column and the entablature above; may also include a pedestal supporting the column. **2.** A set of rules for determining the sequence, shape, and dimensions of a column and entablature; types include **attic order, Classical orders, Gothic order, rustic order.** See also **ordinance, suborder. 3.** A course of stone blocks, especially one of the stepped rings of an archivolt, shaped so that the soffit of the intrados is thinner than the wall at the extrados; common in the Romanesque Revival style.

order above order Same as **superposition.**

orders See **Classical orders.**

ordinance (pre-20c) A system of arrangement of architectural elements; may control details or the whole. See also **order.**

ordinary (17c–early 19c) Same as **inn.**

ordinary rubble Same as **rough rubble.**

ordnance iron A high tensile strength **cast iron;** used for cannons and bridge posts and top chords.

Oregon pine Same as **Douglas fir.**

organ gallery The raised floor within a church or theater that supports the organ and opens to the main space. Also known as **organ loft.**

organic architecture Building design based on natural forms that harmonize with the environment and give the impression of unity of a natural organism; theory was espoused by Louis Sullivan, Frank Lloyd Wright, and other architects beginning in the early 20c; examples are relatively rare.

organ loft Same as **organ gallery.**

organ screen A **screen** (sense 2) that blocks the view of an organ, especially in a church.

oriel A projection from the main wall of a building in the form of a **bay window** that starts above the ground level; may be supported on corbels, brackets, or an engaged column.

oriel

Oriental A pink with black and gray waves, medium-grained **granite** quarried in the vicinity of Morton, Minnesota.

Oriental style (19c–mid-20c) Any of various isolated adaptions of Middle Eastern or Far Eastern architecture built in North America late 18c–WWI; typically Italianate Style buildings with hipped roofs and multifoil arches; oriental features may include a Turkish dome, structural polychromy, and **moresque** decoration. See also **Exotic Revival style.**

orientation The relationship of a structure to the compass points or a site feature; may refer to the direction a facade faces, such as the south elevation, or the direction of a main axis, as in an east–west orientation. See also **siting.**

original **1.** A **cultural artifact** from which other copies are made. See also **document, reproduction. 2.** The first of its type or design.

original construction The portion of a building or structure that was present when it was first built; may remain intact, or have been subsequently altered or obscured by additions.

original fabric The **fabric** remaining from the **original construction,** especially with architectural or artistic value.

orillon A portion of a **fortification** composed of an earthen bank lined with a masonry wall, projecting at the shoulder of a bastion to protect the flank of the gunners. Also known as **crosset.**

Oriskany sandstone A Devonian **sandstone** quarried in the vicinity of Oriskany, New York.

orlet, orle **1.** A fillet molding immediately below a column capital, especially below an ovolo. Also known as **necking, orlo. 2.** (18c) The plinth of a column base.

orlo (18c) Same as **orlet.**

ormolu **1.** Bronze, or brass, gilded with powdered gold. **2.** A **brass** alloy composed of copper, zinc and tin, with the color of gold; often finished with lacquer or acid to give the appearance of gilded metal; used for lighting fixtures and decorative trim. Also known as **mosaic gold.**

ornament An object, or series of objects, added to the basic structure to enhance its visual appearance, especially sculptured forms; types include **anthemion, arabesque, boss, bucrane, buckler, diaper, foliage, gargoyle, garland, molding, orb, pendant, quernal, relief, rocaille, rose, scroll, swag, torsade, torsel, triglyph, trophy, window shield.** See also **decoration, molding, ornament in creux, ornament in rilievo.**

ornamental cast iron Decorative railings, brackets, spears and other architectural elements molded from cast iron; typically in the style of Louis XV, popular 1832–ca. 1900, especially in the lower Mississippi valley; types include **double faced, single faced, side backed out;** patterns include **bird of paradise, passion flower, Pontalba, rose, smooth oak, vineyard.**

ornamental iron Nonstructural **ironwork,** such as **ornamental cast iron** or **wrought iron,** as opposed to load-bearing construction, such as **structural steel.** See also **miscellaneous metals.**

ornamental plaster Decorative moldings and architectural features applied to plain plaster surfaces. See also **diaper, relief, run molding.**

ornamental stone Any type of stone used for interior finish work, as opposed to **building stone.** See also **stonework.**

Ornamented English Same as **Decorated Style.**

ornament in creux Decorative elements that are carved into the surface of a molding, such as **egg and dart** or **flute.**

ornament in rilievo, (pre-19c) **ornament in relievo** Decorative elements carved so that they are above the surface of a molding, such as scrolls or flowers and leaves.

ornate A building or element with elaborate decoration or ornamentation.

orpiment A pearly, lemon yellow paint pigment composed of arsenic trisulfide. Also known as **king's yellow.**

orthographic projection A graphic projection of an object onto a plane surface; typically at a reduced scale for buildings and other large structures.

orthography The art of drawing a correct vertical projection of a building, such as an elevation (external orthography) or section (internal orthography). See also **orthophotography, rectified photography.**

orthophotography A process of producing a photograph of a surface, such as a building facade, with computer correction of parallax distortions. See also **rectified photography.**

orthostyle (pre-20c) Aligned in a straight row, especially a classical style building with a straight row of columns on the facade. See also **columniation.**

OSHA Occupational Safety and Health Administration

Osmose A trade name for **sodium fluoride solution.**

ossature (pre-20c) The structural frame or skeleton of a building, or some portion of the building; from the French term for any kind of framework. See also **carcase.**

Ostwald system A system of color indexing used to identify and specify finish colors; developed by Wilhelm Ostwald of Germany. See also **Munsell system.**

oundy A wavy, curly, or scalloped element, such as a **molding** or stringcourse; sometimes used for **zigzag.** See also **nebulé.**

outbond The bond of a masonry unit laid parallel to the face of the wall, such as a **stretcher.** See also **inbond.**

outbuilding A **building** detached from, and appertaining to, the main house or structure; types include **carriage house, cookhouse, garage, privy, shed, smokehouse, stable, water cabin, wood shed.** Also known as **outhouse.**

outdoor museum A **museum** that displays cultural artifacts outside of a building, especially as a simulated historical scene; may be a historic site with existing buildings, a collection of historic buildings and/or objects moved from elsewhere, or a reconstruction; first U.S. example established by the Essex Institute in 1909 at Salem, Massachusetts. Also known as **heritage village, open-air museum.**

outer chamber, outward chamber (pre-20c) A hall used a living area in a dwelling. See also **inner chamber.**

outer hearth Same as **hearth** (sense 2).

outhouse **1.** Same as **outbuilding. 2.** A small latrine building. Also known as **backhouse, garden house, cloacina temple, necessary, privy.**

outlet (late 19c–present) An electrical device that contains one or more **sockets;** typically recessed in an **outlet box.** Also known as **receptacle.**

outlet box (late 19c–present) An **electric box** enclosing an **outlet;** typically recessed in a wall with concealed wiring or surface-mounted with exposed conduit.

out of plumb Not vertical; applied to building elements that should be vertical. See also **list.**

out of square Not at a right angle.

out of twist Same as **out of wind.**

out of wind, out of winding An unwarped, straight, plane surface, such as a board, especially when installed at right angles to another surface, as in a door jamb. Also known as **out of twist.** See also **wind.**

outporch An outer vestibule or an entrance porch; not an exact term.

outshot (pre-19c) Same as **addition.**

outside chimney A **chimney** with the stack outside the exterior walls of the building it serves. See also **inside chimney.**

outside casing The exterior wood trim at the top and sides of a window or door frame.

outside opening The overall dimension of the frame of a building element such as a window or door. See also **out to out, rough opening.**

outside sprinkler system A **sprinkler system** mounted on the outside of a building; creates a water curtain to protect the building from nearby fires; not common in North America.

outside to outside Same as **over-all dimension.**

out to out Same as **over-all dimension.** See also **outside opening.**

outwindow (pre–WWI) **1.** Same as **bay window. 2.** A projecting loggia, or similar element.

ova Plural of **ovum.**

oval, oval molding Same as **ovolo.**

ove Same as **ovum.**

over-all dimension The distance from one extreme of an element or structure to the other extreme, ignoring any projections, setbacks or recesses. Also known as **outside to outside, out to out.** See also **outside opening.**

overburden Same as **supercharge.**

overcoating Applying stucco over the exterior of an existing building.

overdoor **1.** A window above an exterior door, such as a **fanlight,** that is incorporated in the door enframement. **2.** A decorative element, such as an entablature or pediment, above a door.

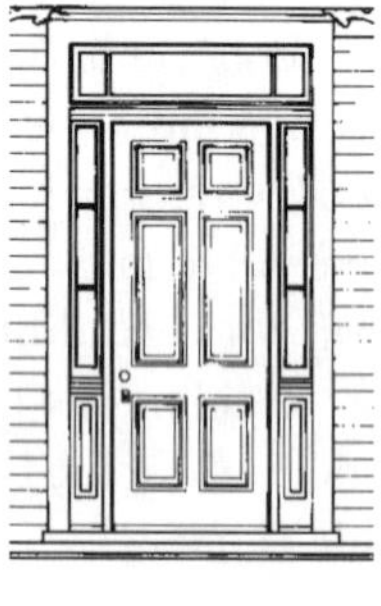

overdoor

overflow scupper A **scupper** opening through a parapet wall that allows rain water to drain off if the roof drains are clogged; may be above a **downspout.**

overglaze A second glaze applied to terra-cotta, or other ceramic, after the initial firing.

overhang The horizontal projection of a portion of a building past the element below; may be small, as in a molding, or large, as in an eave or story. Also known as **jet, jetty, overjet, overset.** See also **oversailing, overshoot.**

overhanging girt A horizontal **timber frame** member across the base of a building **overhang.**

overhead door A **door** composed of horizontal panels or slats hinged together, supported on a track at both sides, and opening upwards; may coil into a cylindrical shape, or be horizontal when in the open position; developed in the second half of the 19c. Also known as **overhung door, rolling door, rolling shutter.**

overhung **1.** Supported on rollers at the top, such as an interior sliding door or a barn door. See also **underhung.** **2.** Hinged at the top.

overhung door **1.** A **door** hinged at the top; typically held open with hook and eye. **2.** Same as **overhead door.** **3.** A door supported by overhead rollers.

overjet, over jet (pre-19c) Same as **overhang.** See also **jet, jetty.**

overlap joint, overlapping joint (pre-20c) Same as **lap joint.**

overlay A joist that spans between, and rests on, the cross-sills of a **timber frame** building; typically a log with flattened top and ends.

overmantel The decorative millwork above a fireplace mantel; may contain mirrors or inset stone panels; common in the 19c. See also **mantelpiece.**

over-restored A **restoration** that includes undocumented decorative or structural features not known to have been included during the **control period.**

overroof To install a new roof surface on top of an existing one.

oversailing Projecting beyond the face, especially corbeled brick. See also **overhang.**

overseer's house (southern U.S.) The dwelling of a plantation overseer; may be of any form or style, but typically relatively small and simple. See also **great house, quarter.**

overset Same as **overhang.**

overshoot **1.** A wide eave at a lower story, such as with a Dutch Colonial gambrel roof. **2.** The **overhang** along one side of a building, such as a **Pennsylvania barn.**

overshot wheel A **water wheel** mounted on a horizontal shaft and rotated by a stream of water that passes over the top and down one side. See also **breast wheel, undershot wheel.**

overstory Same as **clerestory.**

ovolo A convex molding, such as a quarter round, with the curved portion bounded by two fillets; varieties include **Greek ovolo, Roman ovolo.** Also known as **echinus, oval.**

ovum (pl. **ova**) The egg-shaped element of an **egg and dart** or **egg and anchor** molding.

owner Any individual or group of individuals, partnership, corporation, or public agency holding fee simple title to a property; does not include those holding other interests in a property, such as a leasehold. See also **developer.**

owner objection A notarized written statement from a property owner disapproving the nomination and listing of his or her property in the National Register, or a state, provincial or local register.

ownership Having the legal status of an **owner.**

oxeye An oval or round window, especially in a dormer or gable end. See also **oculus, oeil de boeuf.**

ox-eyed molding A concave **molding** that is less deep than a **scotia** and more deep than a **cavetto.**

Oxford Fleuri Same as **Eastman Blue.**

oxi (18c) A contraction of **oxygonium;** often used in reference to an **equilateral arch.**

oxidation, (pre-20c) **oxydation** The process of an element or compound chemically combining with oxygen; often a form of **corrosion.**

oxide jacking The displacement of building elements due to the expansion of iron and steel products as the metal rusts and becomes **iron oxide.** Also known as **rust jacking.**

oxycalcium light Same as **Drummond light.**

oxygonium (18c) An equilateral triangle. Also known as **oxi.**

oylet (pre-20c) Same as **oilet.**

P

pace **1.** An area raised one or more steps above the main floor level, such as around an altar or tomb or in front of a fireplace. **2.** (pre-WWI) Same as **landing.**

Pacific hemlock Same as **western hemlock.**

packing **1.** Same as **galleting. 2.** Material stuffed around a plumbing fixture valve stem to prevent leaks.

pad Leveled ground ready for construction of a building; may be raised, as in a terrace, or cut into a slope. Also known as **platform.**

paddock **1.** A fenced pasture enclosure for horses; typically adjoins a stable. **2.** A fenced, sodded area.

padstone A stone block inserted in a masonry wall to serve as a **bearing** support.

paillette, paillon A piece of metal **foil** used for gilding relief work; typically glazed or enameled.

paint Finely ground **pigment** and **binder** suspended or dissolved in a liquid **vehicle;** used to coat surfaces as a decorative and protective finish; may also include an **extender** or **drier;** use of factory-made products was widespread beginning in the last quarter of the 19c; types include **bituminous paint, calcimine, cement-water paint, distemper, epoxy paint, latex paint, metal flake paint, oil-base paint, stereochrome, vinyl paint, wax paint, whitewash.** See also **asbestine, finish coat, primer, stain, varnish.**

paint analysis The study of existing layers of paint to determine the sequence and approximate date of application; includes microscopic examination and microchemical analysis to determine colors, pigments, and media of any or all layers. See also **chromochronology, paint stratigraphy.**

painted canvas A water-resistant material used as flooring on porches and piazzas and occasionally on other surfaces.

painted glass Window glass having a surface colored or decorated by enamel paint (containing vitrifiable pigment) fused to the surface by intense heat. See also **colored glass, stained glass.**

painting The process of coating a surface with layers of **paint** to produce a finish. See also **bringing forward.**

paint remover Any of various compounds in liquid or paste form used to remove existing paint by chemical action; types include **caustic stripper, solvent stripper.** Also known as **stripper.**

paint stratigraphy The sequence of paint layers determined by **paint analysis.** See also **chromochronology.**

pair (pre-20c) A **stair** between floors; derived from the typical two flights with a landing.

palace (18c–19c) The official residence of an important government official, such as a governor's house.

pale **1.** (18c) A pointed wooden stake that is driven into the ground. **2.** A vertical wood fence element, especially with a round or semicircular cross section; typically with a flat or pointed top. See also **paling, picket. 3.** Same as **paling. 4.** The area enclosed by **paling. 5.** (18c) Same as **pile.**

pale boiled oil Boiled **linseed oil** that has been aerated at high temperature; used in glossy oil paints.

pale brick Same as **salmon brick.**

paleology The study of antiquity or antiquities, especially prehistoric antiquities; includes **archaeology.**

paleontological site A place containing **fossils** or other physical evidence of life from past geologic periods that can be investigated by **paleontology.**

paleontology The scientific study of **fossils** and other physical remains of life from past geologic periods. See also **archaeology.**

paling A fence constructed of a series of vertical **pales** abutting one another, or with small spaces between them, and fastened at the top and bottom to rails that are in turn supported by posts; typically, the pales are split or sawn saplings, with one round face. See also **picket fence.**

palisade, (18c) **pallisade, palisado,** (17c) **pallizade, pallizado** **1.** A defensive fence constructed of logs with pointed tops, set into the ground vertically and abutting one another. Also known as **stockade. 2.** (18c–19c) Same as **paling. 3.** (late 18c–early 19c) A fence with iron pickets.

Palladian Neoclassical architecture in the style of the Italian architect Andrea di Pietro della Gondola (1508–80), known as Palladio; popularized by his *Four Books of Architecture,* republished in England in the late 18c; typical elements include compact, symmetrical massing with a projecting, pedimented portico, flat

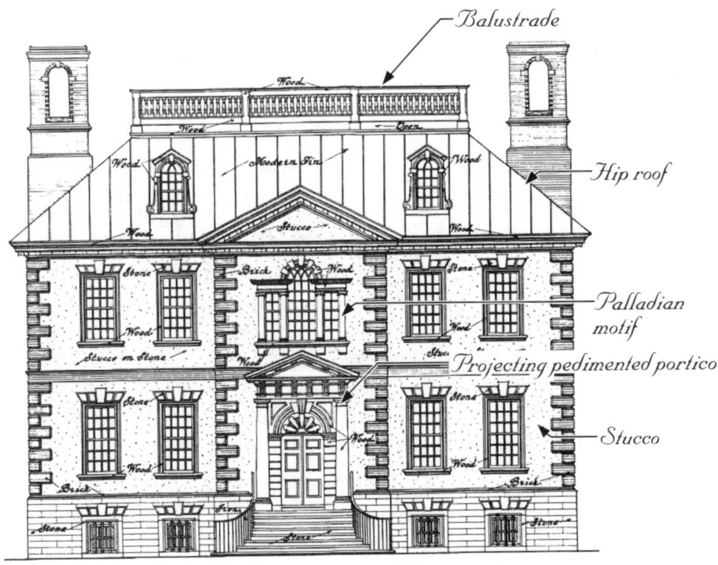

Palladian
Mt. Pleasant Mansion
Philadelphia, Pennsylvania, ca. 1761

or hipped roof with balustrade parapet, stuccoed brick, unframed window openings, and use of the **Palladian motif.**

Palladian base An **attic base** with beads and fillets at the edge of the scotia; used by Palladio.

Palladian motif A center round arch flanked by two rectangular openings extending from the base of the arched opening to the spring line of the arch. Also known as **serliana, Serlian motif, Venetian motif.** See also **Palladian window.**

Palladian window (20c) **1.** A Classical Revival style window in a **Palladian motif,** with a center fanlight, flanked by two rectangular windows. **2.** Any wall opening in the shape of a **Palladian motif.** Also known as **Diocletian window, serliana, Serlian window, thermal window, Venetian window.**

Palladian window

pallier, paillier (18c) A wide step or landing.

pallification (18c) The process of constructing a pile foundation.

pallisado **1.** Same as **palisade.** **2.** (18c) A decorative open fence.

palmate In the shape of fingerlike leaves or lobes radiating from a common center; decorative examples include **anthemion, honeysuckle, palmette.**

Palmer granite A pinkish, medium-textured biotite **granite** quarried in Maine.

palmette A classical style decoration in the stylized form of a palm leaf, such as an **anthemion;** carved or painted.

palm house A **greenhouse** in which to grow palms and other tropical plants in northern climates.

pampre A continuous carved decoration within a concave molding, especially a grapevine pattern.

pan **1.** The socket of a hinge. **2.** One of the spaces between posts in a timber framed building; typically filled with **nogging.** Also known as **pan piece.** **3.** A recessed portion of a metal stair that is filled with concrete.

panache The approximately triangular surface of a **pendentive** or the space between ribs of a **groin vault.**

pan-and-roll tile Terra-cotta **roof tile** with alternating flat and semicircular shapes; the semicircular tiles cover the joints between the rectangular tiles. Also known as **ridge and furrow.** See also **Italian tiling, pantile.**

pane, (17c) **paine** **1.** A piece of **window glass** set in an opening; typically refers to relatively small pieces. Also known as **light.** See also **beveled glass.** **2.** (pre-20c) A square or rectangular division, with a plane surface, of the elevation of a building. **3.** The flat side of a faceted element, such as one side of a spire or nut.

panel, (18c) **pannel** **1.** A small plane surface surrounded by moldings or depressed below or raised above the adjacent surface; typically rectangular but may be any geometric shape; may be ornamented; types include **flat panel, flush panel, linen panel, lying panel, raised panel, standing panel, sunk panel.** See also **paneled, paneling.** **2.** One of the openings in a truss, especially the division between two posts. **3.** The hewn face of a stone block. **4.** A section of fence between two posts. **5.** One of the sections of a **vault shell** between adjoining ribs. **6.** Same as **frog.** **7.** One of a series of rectangular shapes defined by wallpaper.

panel back, (19c) **pannelled back** A wood panel finish on a **window back** below a windowsill; typically the window casing continues to the floor. See also **back lining.**

panelboard The metal box that encloses the **electric wiring** connections between branch circuits and the feeder supply; typically has a hinged door and a series of **circuit breakers** and/or **fuses.** Also known as **panel box, power board.**

panel box Same as **panelboard.**

panel door A wooden **paneled door** with four or more panels held in a framework of stiles and rails; the most common type of door ca. 1700–mid-20c.

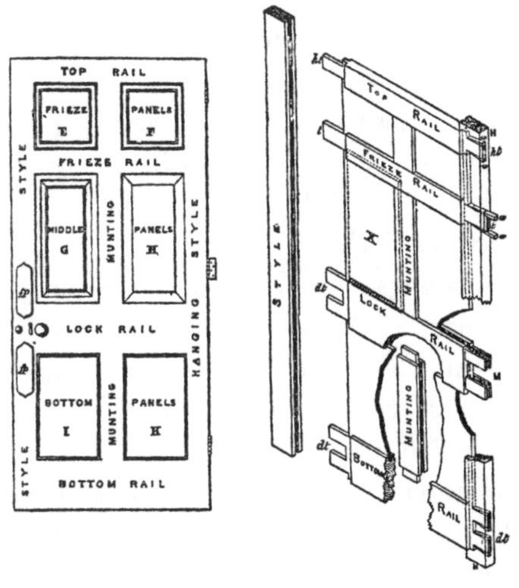

panel door

paneled **1.** Made with wood held in a frame, as in a paneled shutter; types include **bead and butt, framed square, raised panel.** See also **panel.** **2.** Divided by moldings into a geometric pattern, as in a paneled plaster ceiling. See also **frame.** **3.** Covered by **paneling.**

paneled door **1.** A wood door with flat or raised panels; components may include **cross panel, rail, mullion, standing panel, sticking, stile;** types include **Christian door, panel door.** See also **hinge, lock.** **2.** A door of metal or other material in the form of a **panel door.**

panel face A molded **concrete block** finish in the form of a projecting flat panel with beveled edges surrounded by a narrow flat margin; typically used for quoins on a **rock-faced** block wall.

paneling **1.** A finished surface composed of multiple, thin, wood panels held by rails and stiles and sometimes moldings; used for interior walls and ceilings and wainscoting. Also known as **panelwork.** See also **bolection molding, panel, sticking.** **2.** Any surface, such as stone or plaster, divided into panels. See also **paneled.**

panel mold One of various small moldings used as edging, especially when in the form of a **bolection molding.**

panel point The place where a strut and tie of a truss panel intersect.

panel strip **1.** A wide, thin, wood molding with a rectangular cross section; typically with dimensions of $\frac{1}{4} \times 2\frac{1}{4}$ inches; used for creating a surface-mounted wall **frame.** **2.** A narrow metal or wood batten that covers the joint between two sheathing boards or wood panels. **3.** A

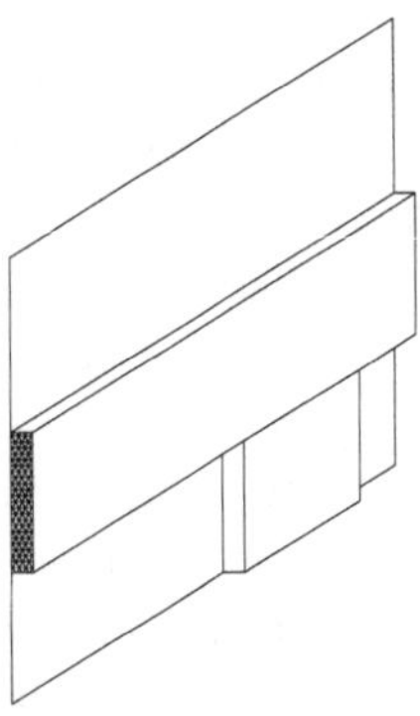

panel strip (sense 1)

molding between a panel and the surrounding stiles and rails, forming a secondary panel.

panel tracery Gothic style window **tracery** in sections within a large opening.

panel truss A structural truss having rectangular divisions with diagonal braces between opposite corners.

panel vault A **rib vault** having a central square panel connected with diagonal ribs to the corners of the larger square it covers.

panel wall **1.** In skeleton frame construction, a nonbearing masonry exterior wall supported at each floor and built between two columns. See also **curtain wall.** **2.** A brickwork garden wall composed of thin panels, typically one wythe thick, braced by a series of thicker piers.

panelwork Same as **paneling.**

panework The pattern formed by the division of a wall into panels, especially that of a Tudor style half-timbered house.

panic hardware A quick-release door lock that can be opened from the inside by pressing on a horizontal bar or other device; used on fire-exit doors beginning in the 19c.

pannel (18c) **1.** Same as **panel.** **2.** Same as a glass **pane.**

pannier (pre-20c) Same as **corbel,** especially one supporting a beam perpendicular to the face of a pilaster.

panopticon A building (usually a prison) designed with a system of radiating corridors such that all the corridors can be viewed from a central location.

pan piece Same as **pan** (sense 2).

pantheon (18c) A circular church or temple dedicated to all saints or gods; from the Roman temple of the same name built in 27 B.C.

pantile A terra-cotta **roof tile** with a flattened S-shape cross section, with the concave and convex curves of unequal sizes; installed so that the large curve overlaps the small curve of the adjacent tile. Also known as **Belgic tile.** See also **pan-and-roll tile, S-tile.** **2.** Sometimes incorrectly used to refer to **normal tiling.**

pantry A room or closet in which to store dry food and tableware; type includes **butler's pantry;** sometimes also used to refer to an outbuilding.

pantry case (pre-WWII) A built-in cabinet with doors and/or drawers; named for its use in a **butler's pantry.** See also **kitchen cabinet.**

pantry cock A faucet with a discharge pipe that rises vertically, then curves downward in a semicircle. Also known as **countercock.**

pantry radiator A cast-iron hot-water **radiator** formed with several horizontal sections on which plates of hot food can be set.

paper birch A hardwood tree with light brown, hard, tough heartwood; the sapwood is nearly white; found in northeastern U.S. and Canada from northern New Jersey to Labrador and west to Iowa and Manitoba; used for interior trim and millwork, especially where a light color is desired; *Betula papyrifera.* Also known as **white birch.**

paper hangings (pre-20c) Same as **wallpaper.**

papier-mâché A type of **composition** composed of a mixture of paper pulp and some form of glue, resin, oil, or size; used for molded ornament.

parabolic arch An **arch** in the shape of a parabola.

parade **1.** An area where military reviews are held, especially the level ground within a fortification. Also known as **parade ground.** **2.** (pre-19c) A public promenade or walk.

parade ground **1.** An outdoor place where parades are held. **2.** Same as **parade** (sense 1).

paradise (19c) Same as **parvis turret;** adapted by 19c antiquarians from the medieval word for *cloister.*

parallel coping A **coping** formed with flat stone pieces; typically used on sloped walls such as gable end walls.

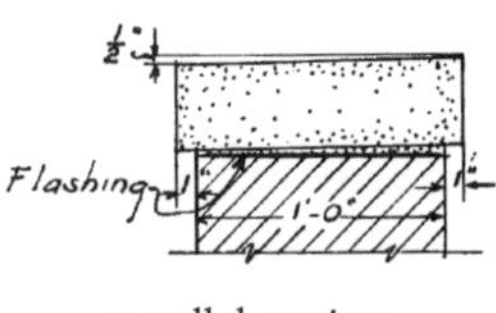

parallel coping

parallel gutter A built-in gutter at a roof eave, between two sloped roofs, or at the edge of a flat roof; typically with a deep, rectangular cross section; may also be a **pole gutter.**

parapet **1.** The part of a wall that projects above the adjacent roof; typically solid construction but may also be crenelated or pierced, such as a **balustrade.** **2.** A fortification wall or bank above a **rampart.** **3.** (pre-20c) Any low wall with a cap and base.

parapeted gable A gable end wall that projects above the roof; shapes include **boltel, fractable, square.**

parapet gutter A gutter concealed behind a parapet wall.

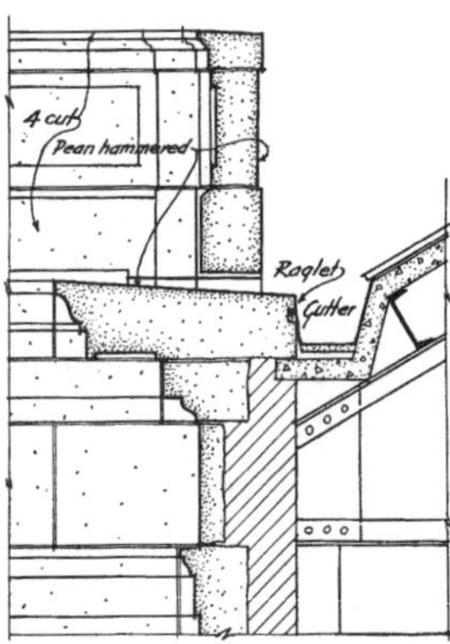

parapet gutter

parapet of the crenel The wall between the crenels and the banquette of a **battlement.**

para red Opaque red **aniline color** paint pigment.

parastas (pl. **parastades**), (pre-19c) **parastata** (pl. **parastatae**) (pre-20c) Same as **anta** or **pilaster;** especially when **in antis** and supporting an arch.

parcel A particular piece of land, especially a smaller part of a relatively large tract. See also **subdivision.**

parclose Same as **perclose.**

paretta **Pebble-dash** stucco with exposed pebbles; often the pebbles are colored for decoration.

parget **1.** The mortar used in **parging.** **2.** (pre-20c) Same as **gypsum,** especially from Montmartre or Derbyshire. **3.** (pre-20c) Same as **plaster,** especially a mixture of lime, sand, and hair.

pargeting, pargetting **1.** Any type of plaster, especially when stamped with low-relief decoration, such as a diaper pattern. **2.** (pre-WWI) Same as **parging.**

parging (19c–present) A rough coat of mortar on the surface of a masonry wall; used on the outside face of foundation walls and other below-grade surfaces or on the inside of facing or backup material; used for dampproofing. Also known as **pargeting.** See also **backplastering, stucco.**

Paris blue Same as **Prussian blue.**

parish A political and geographic subdivision of the state of Louisiana; equivalent to a **county** in other states.

Paris white **Whiting** imported from France.

park **1.** (19c–present) Public land used for outdoor recreation, ranging from a small urban plot, improved with landscaping, to vast natural areas, such as the Grand Canyon. See also **parking.** **2.** Picturesque woodland and pasture surrounding a country estate, often stocked with deer, sheep, or cattle. **3.** A large, open clearing or plateau in the Rocky Mountains.

parking **1.** Land resembling a **park** along or in a roadway, such as the strip of land between the street curb and private property or a median strip. **2.** (post-WWI) Land used for the temporary storage of automobiles.

parking lot An area on the ground surface used for parking vehicles; may be paved or unpaved.

Parks Canada The agency within the federal Department of Canadian Heritage that administers national parks, historic sites, and historic canals. Formerly known as **Canadian Parks Service.**

parliament hinge Same as **H-hinge.**

parlor, parlour, (pre-20c) **parler** **1.** (15c–mid-20c) A room for entertaining guests or callers; pre-19c also used for sleeping and eating; 19c residences often had a formal parlor for guests and an informal parlor for the family; typically located on the main floor of a house. See also **drawing room, hall, living room, sitting room.** **2.** (19c–WWI) A space for business furnished like a residential parlor, such as a dentist's parlor. **3.** (pre-18c) A principal ground-floor bedroom.

parquet **1.** Same as **parquetry.** See also **parquet floor.** **2.** Masonry with a **basketweave bond.** **3.** (pre-20c) The portion of the main floor of a theater nearest the stage; now known as the **orchestra.**

parquet floor A **parquetry** floor finish, where small individual pieces of wood of different colors make a decorative pattern; true parquet flooring is at least ⅞ inch thick; patterns include **assemblage, brixon plank, dogleg, English flooring, Hungarian, mosaic;** there are various imitations incorrectly known by the same name, such as **parquet veneer.**

parquetry, (pre-20c) **parqueterie** A mosaic composed of relatively thick wood pieces of different colors or grains; used for floors and furniture; types include **parquet floor, parquet veneer.** See also **marquetry.**

parquet veneer A thin **parquet floor,** often applied over an existing finish floor; types include **wood carpet.**

parrel (pre-20c) Same as **mantelpiece.**

parsonage, (pre-19c) **parsonage house** (19c–present) A residence of a minister; typically provided free by the church. Also known as **glebe house, parsonage house.**

parterre **1.** A flower garden with patterned beds separated by walks. **2.** A level terrace or open space surrounding a building. **3.** Theater seating located under the balconies.

particleboard (20c) A type of **composition board** composed of small wood chips and a resin binder.

parti-coated, party coated Having different tints or colors within the same finish coat. See also **parti-colored.**

parti-colored, party-colored, (pre-WWI) **party colored** Architecture with different tints or colors on different parts. See also **parti-coated, polychromy.**

parting bead A **parting strip** with a beaded edge, especially a wood one, ⅜–½ inch wide, used on a jamb to separate double hung window sashes.

parting lath Wood lath used as a **parting strip.**

parting slip A thin, vertical element between the sash weights of a box frame window; used to keep the weights from colliding.

parting strip Any thin element used to separate two adjoining members, such as a **parting bead.**

partition, (17c) **petition** A wall dividing the interior of a building, and one story or less in height; types include **folding partition, rolling partition, stud partition, partition wall, staggered stud partition, trussed partition.**

partition tile A structural clay tile unit for use in interior partitions; typically with integral furring ribs for plaster.

partition wall A masonry wall used to divide the interior of a building.

party coated Same as **parti-coated.**

party structure A structural element, such as a partition or floor, that separates real property owned by different people. See also **party wall.**

party wall A wall shared between two buildings that is partly on both properties; typically masonry; used to save space and expense in urban development. Also known as **common wall.** See also **counter wall, party structure.**

parvis, parvise **1.** A porch at the front of a church. **2.** A raised terrace at the front of a church. Also known as **paradise.**

parvis turret A small turret built over a church porch; often used as a library or study.

passage **1.** Any interior corridor connecting rooms in a building. Also known as **passageway.** **2.** (18c–19c) A relatively narrow space through the middle of a house, with exterior doors at front and back, a stair to upper levels, and doors to the principal ground-floor rooms. Also known as **hall.**

passage aisle A church aisle, adjoining the nave, with a narrow passageway from the front to back.

passageway **1.** Same as **passage** (sense 1). **2.** An exterior walkway or roadway between places, especially when between buildings or structures, such as a lane or pathway. Also known as **alley, passway.** **3.** Same as **covered way.**

passion flower An **ornamental cast-iron** pattern in the stylized form of intertwined vines with leaves and passion flowers.

passive iron Iron that has been heat- or acid-treated to be corrosion resistant.

passway (pre-20c) Same as **passageway** (sense 2).

pasticcio An architectural or artistic composition composed of a mixture of fragmentary parts of diverse styles or works within a single work. See also **pastiche.**

pastiche **1.** Architecture or art that copies the style of another designer or historical style. See also **postiche.** **2.** Same as **pasticcio.**

patent bronze A type of colored **bronze powder;** colors include blue, crimson, fire, lemon, and orange.

patent bush hammered The surface texture of stone blocks dressed with short, parallel scoring lines; used on all stones, especially granite; 4–8 cuts in ⅞ inch; originally cut with a **patent hammer** with a head holding a series of adjustable chisels; now largely machined. Also known as **scotching.** See also **bush hammered, stonework.**

patented wire Wire tempered by the process patented by James Horsfall of England.

patent light Same as **vault light.**

patent plate glass High quality, clear **cylinder glass.** See also **picture glass, plate glass.**

patera **1.** A dish-shaped bas-relief ornament, especially on a frieze; often with acanthus or rose petals. **2.** A circular ornament, such as a **rosette;** not technically correct.

paternoster, (18c) **pater-noster** An **astragal** or **baquette** molding with a continuous line of round or oval beadlike projections; named for the rosary beads used by members of the Catholic church. Also known as **bead molding, pearl molding.** See also **pearls and olives, pellet molding.**

patina **1.** The dark brown or green surface corrosion that bronze acquires over time, or the chemical imitation of this process. **2.** Any desirable surface quality acquired by a building element or work of art over time, especially when exposed to the elements.

patio **1.** An interior paved courtyard in the Spanish Colonial style, connected to the street by a passageway; typically contains a raised fountain or pool and perimeter plantings. See also **corredor, Spanish Colonial, zaguan.** **2.** (20c) A paved, ground level, sitting area adjacent to a residence. See also **lanai.**

patrol house (pre-WWI) Same as **firehouse.**

patten **1.** (pre-20c) The base course of a foundation wall. **2.** (pre-20c) The base ring of a column. **3.** (pre-19c) The sole plate of a timber frame. **4.** (pre-20c) The base of a weather vane.

pattern block A **concrete block** with a recessed decorative pattern on the front face. Also known as **shadow block.** See also **screen block.**

pattern bond The surface design created by installed masonry units; may or may not be related to the **structural bond.** See also **bond.**

pattern book A publication with drawings of buildings and decoration used as a design guide; sometimes copied exactly, most often approximated; imports common in North America beginning 18c; written by native architects, such as A. J. Downing, beginning 19c.

pattern glass Same as **obscure glass.**

pattern staining The discoloration of a surface due to uneven dirt deposition caused by different backing materials.

paumelle-knuckle hinge A loose-joint hinge with the knuckles in the shape of a small cylinder.

pavement A hard, finished road or walkway laid directly on the earth; the term is also applied to large interior floors; typically stone, brick or tile before the 19c, then other concrete materials were added; types include **ashlar pavement, asphalt concrete, Belgian pavement, cobblestone, concrete, macadam, mosaic, Nicolson pavement, pebble pavement, sets, terrazzo, Telford pavement, vulcanite pavement.** Also known as **paving.**

pavement light Same as **vault light.**

paver A thin block of stone, brick, tile, asphalt, or similar material used for **pavement;** typically, bricks and tiles are hard fired to make them stronger and impervious to water.

pavilion **1.** A summerhouse or outbuilding detached from a larger residence; from the original meaning of a tent or portable dwelling. **2.** A subsidiary portion of a monumental building, distinguished from the main mass by decoration or height. **3.** A structure not fully enclosed by walls, such as a **dance pavilion.**

pavilion porch A gazebolike structure projecting out of a verandah or porch.

pavilion roof A steeply pitched hip roof, with the smaller ends more steeply pitched than the long sides; common on early French Colonial houses.

paving **1.** The process of laying a **pavement.** **2.** Same as **pavement.**

paving stone A slab of stone used as a **paver;** typically rectangular.

paving tile A **flooring tile** or brick used as a **paver;** pre-19c typically square or rectangular and unglazed.

pavior (pre-19c) Material used for **pavement.**

PCB Abbr. for **polychlorinated biphenyl,** a potent carcinogen that is considered a **hazardous material;** existing 20c electrical and mechanical systems may contain PCBs that must be removed during rehabilitation. See also **abatement.**

Peach Bottom slate A deep blue-black **slate** quarried in Harford County, Maryland.

peak head window A narrow window with the top of the upper sash in the shape of a 45-degree triangle. See also **Gothic window.**

pearl colour (18c–19c) A greenish white paint **pigment** composed of **white lead** with small amounts of **Prussian blue** and **spruce yellow.**

pearl molding A **paternoster** molding with small, spherical beads.

pearls and olives An astragal molding with alternating small spherical and large ellipsoidal beads.

pearwood The light brown, fine-grained, delicately figured wood of the pear tree, *Pyrus communis,* or the white pear, *Pterocelastrus rostratus;*

used for **veneer,** often with **silver grain;** a native of Europe cultivated in North America.

pebble-dash, pebble dashing A nubbly textured **stucco** finish made by throwing or troweling pebble gravel onto the wet top coat; the pebbles remain exposed on the surface and may be applied clean or mixed in a cement slurry. Also known as **rock dash, rough cast,** and incorrectly as **slap dashing.**

pebble gravel A type of **gravel** with relatively small pieces ranging 4–64 mm in size.

pebble pavement A **pavement** with a surface of water-rounded pebbles closely set in clay or concrete; often different colors are used in a decorative pattern.

pecan One of several varieties of a large hickory tree having reddish brown heartwood with dark brown stripes and white to reddish sapwood; used for interior millwork; *Carya aquatica, Carya cordiformis, Carya illinoënsis, Carya myristicaeformis, Carya olivaeformis, Hicoria pecan.*

pecky cypress **Cypress** boards with a pattern of voids caused by fungal decay in the standing tree.

pedestal **1.** A low structure that supports a column or other element, or is part of a balustrade, most often with a square or rectangular plan; typically, a classical pedestal has a **base** with a **plinth** and **base molding,** a **die,** and a **cap** composed of a corona and bed mold. See also **classical orders, piedouche, podium, vagina.** **2.** (19c–early 20c) A casting on the abutment of a bridge that receives the strain of the main braces.

pedestal mouldings (18c) A **base molding** plus a **surbase;** used at the top and bottom of a wainscot.

pediment The triangular gable end of a classical building, or the same form used elsewhere; the pediment is composed of the **tympanum** with a horizontal cornice below and raked cornices at the sides; pediments over openings sometimes have curved tops; the classical pediment always had a low roof slope, such as **Greek pitch** or **Roman pitch.** Also known as **fastigum.** See also **broken pediment, fronton.**

pedimental Having the form of a **pediment.**

pediment arch Same as **miter arch.**

pedimented Having a pedimental or similar form, such as a gable end with a triangular wall enclosed by raked cornices and a horizontal cornice.

pediment pitch (18c) A low-slope gable roof used in classical buildings with pediments; types include **Greek pitch, Roman pitch.**

peeling **1.** (20c) The process of rotary cutting of veneer from a log. **2.** The detachment of a coating, such as paint, from the substrate because of lack of adherence; may be due to **weathering.**

peen hammered The surface texture of hard stone blocks produced by striking with a pointed tool, such as a peen hammer. See also **stonework.**

peg A wood pin used as a fastener or as a projecting element to hang clothes and other objects; in timber framing often a tapered piece with a square cross section driven into slightly misaligned round holes to draw the timbers tight.

pegboard A horizontal board with projecting pegs mounted on a wall; used to hang clothing and sometimes furniture.

pegged braced frame A **timber frame** with pegged mortise and tenon joints and diagonal corner braces. See also **braced frame.**

pegram truss A long-span bridge **bowstring truss** with triangular side panels formed by posts, tops that slope towards a center panel with X-bracing, and ties that slope down towards the middle.

pela Same as **Chinese wax.**

pellet molding A molding decorated with a row of hemispherical projections or flat discs. See also **paternoster.**

pellet ornamentation Having a surface decorated with hemispherical projections arranged in geometric patterns.

pen 1. A small enclosure for animals, with or without a roof. See also **coop, sty. 2.** (19c–20c) An individual, four-walled part of a log building; may be a **single pen,** or one of multiple pens combined to create a larger structure, such as **double pen, dogtrot, saddlebag;** sometimes used to refer to similarly shaped buildings constructed of other materials. Also known as **crib, rail pen.**

pencil cedar Same as **eastern red cedar** or **western red cedar.**

penciling Painting a thin line on the joints of a masonry wall, used to give the appearance of a narrow joint.

pendant, pendent 1. A hanging, ornamental architectural feature, especially when elaborately sculpted; typical examples include the bottom of a newel post that projects below the floor, a boss at the intersection of vaulting ribs, or the bottom of an arch keystone. **2.** (19c) Same as **chandelier.** See also **pendant light. 3.** (pre-19c) Same as **pendentive.**

pendant light A **light fixture** suspended from above; types include **chandelier, combination fixture, gasolier.**

pendant sprinkler The most common type of **sprinkler head;** projects below the finished ceiling; in use since ca. 1860; concealed types developed in the late 20c are often preferred for installations in historic buildings.

pendentive One of the four masonry transitions between a square base and a dome; the four tops form the circular base of the drum; two adjoining pendentives form an arch that rests on one wall of the base; typically a spherical triangle, the term is also used to refer to various other forms, such as a horizontal triangular stone block used as a lintel, corbeled courses, or arches. See also **panache, squinch.**

pendentive bracketing Multiple small arches that form a pendentive; one arch is at the bottom, two on the next level above, and so forth.

pendentive corbeling Corbeled masonry that forms a pendentive; often a series of concentric arches.

pendent post A short post that supports the wall end of a open wood truss and rests on a corbel or capital; supports the **tie beam** or **hammer beam** and diagonal **brace.** Also known as **wall-piece.**

penetrating oil A wood finish that soaks into the top of the floor boards.

penhouse Same as **penthouse.**

penitentiary (late 18c–present) A **prison,** especially where convicted criminals are to do hard labor and be reformed; typically a large building with individual cells. See also **jail, panopticon, reformatory.**

Penn Central case A 1978 landmark decision by the U.S. Supreme Court upholding the constitutional validity of local historic preservation ordinances; the Court rejected a claim by Penn Central Transportation Co. that the City's decision resulted in an unconstitutional "taking of property" without compensation and identified three factors to consider and balance in evaluating takings claims: (1) the character of the governmental action, (2) the economic impact on the property owner, and (3) the extent to which the action has interfered with distinct investment-backed expectations; confirmed the principle that as long as the owner has a reasonable economic use of the property, no taking has occurred. Also known as ***Penn Central Transportation Co. v. City of New York,*** **Grand Central Station decision.**

Penn Central v. City of New York See **Penn Central case.**

Pennsylvania barn A **bank barn** with an overshoot on the side opposite the bank; the livestock are housed in the masonry lower level and the timber frame haymow occupies the upper level.

Pennsylvania bluestone A blue-gray, gray-red, or gray-green, fine-grain, dense, hard sandstone quarried in Pennsylvania; used for pavers and trim. Also known as **Wyoming Valley stone.**

Pennsylvania green See **Easton marble.**

Pennsylvania truss A long span **Petit truss** with a curved top chord when used as a through truss or a curved bottom chord when used as a deck truss.

penny (d) A measure of nail size; attributed to a 100 nails originally equaling the weight of a certain number of English pennies, or, alternatively, costing a certain number of pennies; common nail sizes include **fourpenny nail, sixpenny nail, eightpenny nail, tenpenny nail, twentypenny nail, sixtypenny nail.** See also **d.**

penstock **1.** A large trough that carries water to a mill wheel; typically made of boards. **2.** A sluice or gate that controls the discharge of water from a pond or race. **3.** Same as **fire hydrant.**

pent Same as **penthouse** (senses 1 and 2); sometimes incorrectly used in late 20c to indicate any kind of roof projecting from a wall. Also known as **appentice.**

pentane lamp (19c–WWI) A lamp that burns pentane vapor; pentane is distilled from petroleum.

pentastyle **1.** Having a facade with a row of five columns. See also **columniation.** **2.** (18c) Having a facade with five rows of columns.

pentastylos (19c) A pentastyle building.

penthouse, (pre-19c) **pent house** **1.** A small, projecting roof or hood over an entrance or window that is cantilevered or supported by brackets. Also known as **appentice, pent.** **2.** A secondary structure with a shed roof, built against the main building; may have open or closed sides. Also known as **appentice, pent.** **3.** (20c) A secondary roof structure that covers the top of a stairway, water tower, or elevator shaft; originally referred only to a roof of a single slope, now any pitch, including flat. **4.** (20c) An apartment built on the main roof.

pentice Same as **appentice.**

pent roof, pent-roof **1.** Same as **shed roof.** **2.** A **penthouse** roof.

pepper box turret A turret with a circular plan and a conical roof; from its resemblance to a table top container for storing pepper.

perch A unit of measure of stone masonry; varies by locality, often a rod (16.5 feet) in length by one foot in height by the thickness of the wall; in some U.S. states, 25 cubic feet by law.

perclose, parclose A railing or screen enclosing a sacred place, such as a tomb or altar.

perfections A type of **western red cedar** shingle that is 18 inches long and $\frac{9}{16}$ inch thick at the butt edge.

perforated tracery Same as **plate tracery.**

pergola An open grid, supported by rows of columns, for growing vines; most often a series of wood beams supporting battens; may be attached to a building or covering a garden walkway; from the Italian *pergula,* meaning a projection from the roof.

peridromos The narrow walkway behind the exterior row of columns of a peripteral building.

perimeter drain A perforated pipe or terra-cotta drain tile with open joints, surrounded by gravel, used to drain ground water away from the base of a foundation wall.

period animation An interpretation of a historic site with people in **period costume** simulating work and recreation activities of the historical period at that location.

period architecture Architecture constructed during a particular historical period, such as Georgian or French Colonial. See also **period house.**

period costume A reproduction of clothing worn during a particular historical period; often designed to correspond with the control date at a historic site.

period exhibit An exhibit that reconstructs or simulates a historical scene; may be in a **museum** or **house museum.**

period house A house constructed in North America in one of several architectural revival styles of the first third of the 20c; based on study of **colonial architecture** or other earlier periods, especially farm or rural models; typically a large house constructed on a large suburban lot, with a front and back yard, that sometimes included a gate house, gardeners's cottage, guest house, stable, or similar structures; styles include **Dutch Colonial, Georgian Revival, Norman cottage, Spanish Colonial Revival.** See also **period architecture.**

period of significance The span of time when a property attained its significance that meets the National Register criteria. See also **control period.**

peripteral, (18c) **periptere** A classical building surrounded by a single row of columns supporting the roof and enclosing a covered walkway next to the exterior wall. Also known as **peristylar.** See also **columniation, peridromos.**

perispheric, perispherical Globe-shaped, especially a perfect sphere.

peristylar **1.** Same as **peripteral. 2.** Having a **peristyle.**

peristyle **1.** A row of columns with a covered walkway behind; may be **peripteral,** or enclosing an interior courtyard or room. **2.** An exterior space partly or wholly surrounded by a peripteral walk.

perling (19c) Same as **purlin.**

permanent loan The mortgage or other financing that replaces the **construction loan** of a development project and remains in place for a number of years. Also known as **take-out loan.**

Permastone A trade name for a cast stone veneer; has individual units in the approximate form of ashlar blocks, with mortared joints; typically applied to existing houses in cities such as Baltimore.

permit See **building permit, demolition permit, certificate of occupancy.**

perpend, perpender **1.** (pre-WWI) A stone bondstone with its ends exposed on both faces of a masonry wall, especially a squared ashlar stone. Also known as **through-binder, through-stone. 2.** (pre-20c) A vertical masonry joint, especially in brickwork with the joints aligned.

Perpendicular Style (19c–present) Architecture in the style of late English Gothic buildings constructed ca. 1377–1547; typical elements include pointed arches, large windows divided by vertical mullions from base to head, vertically paneled walls and ceilings, square headed hoods over small windows and doors, square and angular decoration, and boldly projecting flying buttresses and pinnacles. Also known as **Rectilinear.** See also **Gothic Revival style, label.**

perpend stone, perpent stone **1.** Same as **perpend** (sense 1). **2.** (pre-20c) A stone, pier, or buttress that projects from a masonry wall and supports a beam or roof.

perpend wall A stone wall composed entirely of perpends; typically a relatively thin wall.

perron A entrance landing with a parapet above a wide flight of steps; typically outside the main entrance, may also be in a large vestibule; often with elaborate architectural design.

Persian blind A exterior shutter with adjustable slats.

Persian order, (18c) **Persic order** An order of columns originally with the shaft in the form of a bound slave or captive; most common in North America in the form of figures representing virtues and vices, or Greek or Roman gods.

Persienne (19c) Same as **Persian blind.**

perspective A picture of a building or landscape constructed so that the view appears to be three dimensional; may be a small drawing or a large **trompe l'oeil,** such as one at the bottom of a garden that appears to continue an alley of plantings.

pesthouse, (19c) **pest-house,** (pre-19c) **pest house** A building used as a **lazaretto.**

petcock A small valve on a boiler or the end of a pipe for draining the water or testing the pressure.

Petit truss A long-span bridge **truss** with Y-shaped bracing within rectangular or trapezoidal panels; types include **Baltimore truss, Pennsylvania truss.** See also **Pratt truss.**

pew One division of fixed bench seating in a church; typically enclosed by a low paneled wall with a door until mid-19c, then most commonly a **slip.** See also **poppyhead.**

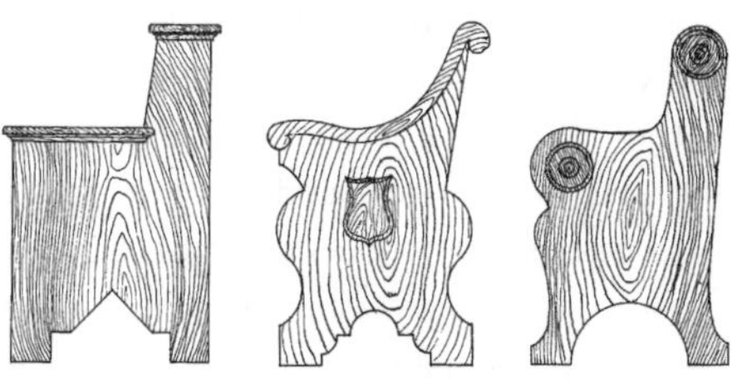

pew

pew chair A collapsible chair attached to the end of a pew for overflow seating in the aisle.

pew hinge A small **butt hinge** with a rising joint that projects from the face of the wall so that the door can open fully.

P.G. A sticking molding with a rectangular center groove and 45-degree beveled sides with a small horizontal fillet at the top and bottom; used to hold a wood **panel** in place.

pH A unit of measure of the acidity or alkalinity of a material; ranges from pH 0 (most acid) to pH 7 (neutral) to pH 14 (most basic).

Pharos, (18c) **phare** (pre-WWI) A lighthouse or beacon, especially a monumental one; named for the 3c B.C. lighthouse on the island of Pharos at the entrance to the port of Alexandria, one of the seven wonders of the ancient world.

Philadelphia gutter Same as **flush gutter,** especially a wood cant strip covered with lead flashing, placed on a shingle roof near the eaves to divert rain water to downspouts. See also **parallel gutter.**

Phillips head A type of screw with a cross-shaped recess in the head.

Phoenix column, Phoenix hollow column (late 19c) A round iron column that is composed of four quarter round segments with projecting flanges that are bolted or riveted together; also made with six or eight segments and in hexagonal and octagonal shapes; patented and first manufactured by the Phoenix Iron Company of Pennsylvania in 1862; used for bridge posts and building columns.

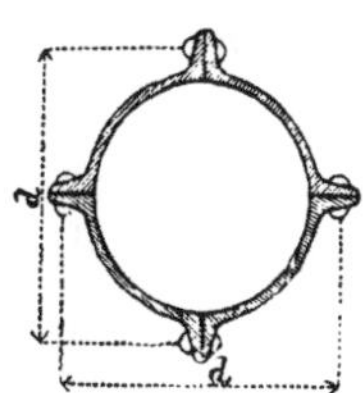

Phoenix column

phosphor bronze A **bronze** alloy composed of copper, tin, and a small amount of phosphorus; may be soft and ductile or hard and strong.

photocopy A **documentation** photograph taken using **large format photography** of a drawing or another photograph.

photogrammetry **1.** The process of producing drawings or maps by tracing outlines or contours while viewing stereo photographs with specialized plotters; used to accurately record an existing subject, including **measured drawings** of a building; developed to make topographic maps by aerial photography. See also **controlled photography.** **2.** The process of making precise measurements by the use of photography.

photograph microscopy **1.** The viewing of historic photographs with a microscope to detect evidence of the appearance of a historic structure at an earlier time. **2.** The process of recording a microscope image with photography.

photography The process of fixing a real image through the chemical action of light; often involves a two-step process of exposing film in a camera to create a negative through which light is projected to create a positive image; first used by the Frenchman Daguerre in 1839; types include **aerial photography, controlled photography, field photography, large format photography, orthophotography, photogrammetry, photograph microscopy, rectified photography, square-on photography, terrestrial photography.**

physical characteristics The visible and tangible attributes of a historic property or group of historic properties, including the architectural character and fabric.

piano A floor or story of a building, from the Italian.

piano-box house A vernacular style one-story, wood framed house type built in Tennessee during the late 19c; named for its fancied resemblance to a square grand piano; typical elements include an H-shaped plan, bargeboards, and a columned porch between the front wings.

piano nobile The principal floor of a building, especially of **Italian Renaissance** style architecture; typically one story above ground level, may also be above a mezzanine level.

piazza **1.** A covered walkway, such as a colonnade or portico, that adjoins a large public space. **2.** (18c–present) Same as **verandah;** most commonly used in southeast U.S. **3.** Same as **plaza.** **4.** (pre-20c, mid-Atlantic U.S.) A connecting link between buildings that also contains the main stair.

pick dressing Same as **dabbed.**

picked in Highlighted with a narrow line of contrasting color.

picket A pointed stick, bar, or post, most commonly wooden; types include: **1.** (mid-19c–present) One of a series of vertical elements set with space between to form a **picket fence;** of various wood or metal shapes, such as a 2 × 2 square with a pyramidal top, or a board with a scroll-cut top, or an iron rod with a spiked top; **2.** One of a series of double pointed stakes used in a **chevaux de frise;** **3.** One of series of large stakes driven into the ground to form a military stockade. See also **pale, palisade.**

picket casting One of various ornamental cast-iron or lead decorations that slide onto an iron picket or railing.

picket fence A fence composed of wood pickets, a top and bottom rail, and posts; typically the pickets are set 1–3 inches apart. See also **paling.**

picket hut A rustic dwelling with walls made by driving large stakes into the ground. See also **jacál.**

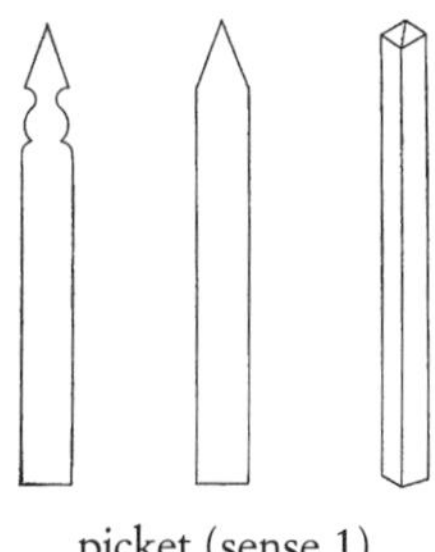
picket (sense 1)

picking **1.** A walkway paving composed of fine crushed shells. **2.** A hard-burned brick. See also **dabbed.**

pickled wood Wood with a bleached finish made by treating with acid, or a similar looking finish made by wiping off a white stain.

pictograph **1.** A stylized illustration used for communication. **2.** Symbols scratched or painted on in situ rock surfaces by prehistoric peoples.

pictou stone An olive gray, fine-grained, carboniferous sandstone quarried in the vicinity of Pictou Harbour, Nova Scotia.

picture gallery A room in a house or museum designed for the display of artwork, especially paintings. See also **gallery.**

picture glass Highly polished **cylinder glass.** See also **patent plate glass.**

picture molding A horizontal, projecting molding encircling the wall of a room a short distance below the ceiling or cornice; used to support hooks for hanging framed paintings and illustrations; typically with the back top corner rabbeted to receive the hooks, and 1.5–3 inches high. Also known as **picture slip.** See also **picture rail.**

picture mosaic A mosaic with a central decorative pattern surrounded by a border.

picture nail (pre-WWI) A **nail** with an ornamental head; typically the head is screwed on after the nail is driven into the wall; used to hang pictures on a wall.

picture rail A small metal rail supported on brackets and encircling the wall of a room a short distance below the ceiling or cornice; used to support hooks for hanging framed paintings and illustrations. Also known as **picture rod.** See also **picture molding.**

picture rod Same as **picture rail.**

picture slip (pre-19c) Same as **picture molding.**

picturesque Strikingly irregular and bold, such as a wild and unkempt landscape, or an asymmetrical building, especially one in ruins.

Picturesque movement A reaction to the dominant **Classical Revival style** architecture, beginning in the late 18c; popular motifs included landscapes with irregular planting beds, follys, and grottos, and asymmetrical buildings in the **Gothic Revival, Italianate,** and **Second Empire** styles; not well established in North America until the second quarter of the 19c.

piece mark A mark on a timber framing member that indicates where it is to be placed when assembled.

piedouche, (18c) **piedouch** A small pedestal or bracket for supporting an object such as a bust, vase, or candelabrum; smooth sided with cap and base moldings; typically square in plan.

piedroit An engaged rectangular pier without a distinct cap or base. See also **pilaster.**

pien, piend Same as **arris.** See also **pien check.**

pien check, (19c) **peen check** A rabbet at the bottom of the riser of a stone step that overlaps the top rear of the tread below.

pien joint, (19c) **peen joint** A joint between two stone steps formed by a **pien check.**

pier, (18c) **peer** **1.** A square or rectangular masonry or wood post projecting less than a story above the ground that carries the weight of a structure down to the foundation, especially when larger or squatter than a column;

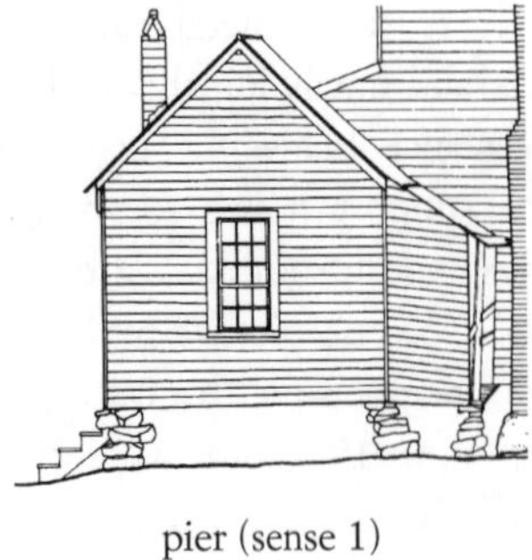

pier (sense 1)

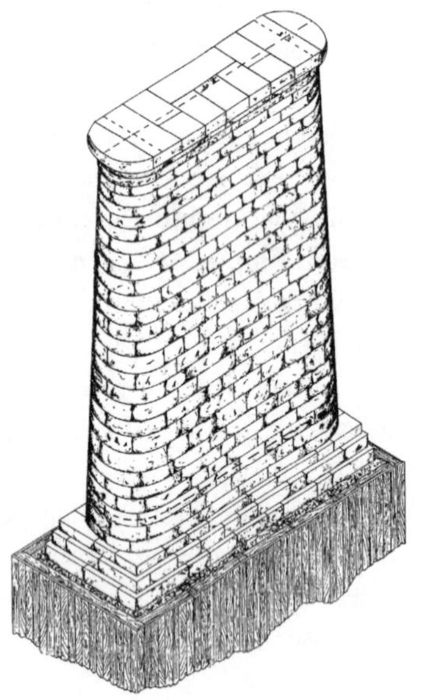

pier (sense 3)

may be below a wood frame or part of a wall between a series of openings. See also **clustered pier.** **2.** A wood post driven into the ground below water to support a structure, such as a dock or bridge. **3.** An isolated mass of masonry or concrete, or a cluster of piles, that supports a bridge or similar structure. See also **abutment, rocking pier.** **4.** A wooden walkway extending over the water, perpendicular to the shoreline. **5.** A post or portion of a wall that supports a gate or door. **6.** (20c) A masonry enclosure of a column to increase fire or water resistance.

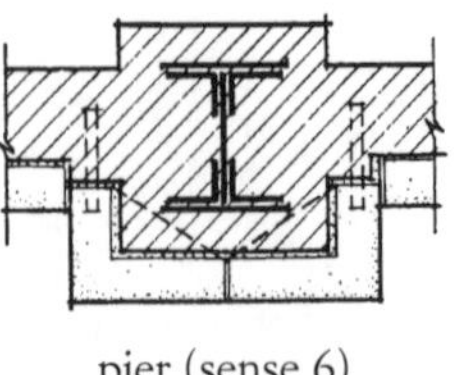

pier (sense 6)

pier abutment (19c) Same as **abutment** (sense 2).

pier arch (19c–present) An arch supported by piers, especially in a basilican church.

pierced work Any material having a decorative pattern formed by holes. See also **openwork.**

pier dam Same as **wing dam.**

pier glass A tall mirror that fills the wall space between two windows or doorways; often mounted above a pier table.

pig An individual ingot of **pig iron,** or other metal; from the fancied resemblance of a row of connected cast ingots to suckling piglets.

pigeon house A **dovecot,** especially a raised frame structure; often has a **pigeon roof.**

pigeon roof A **pyramid roof;** from the frequent use of the form on **pigeon houses.**

pig iron An oblong, cast ingot or **pig** composed of **iron** and carbon as it comes from the blast furnace, before it has been worked or cast at the foundry; types by composition include **all-mine pig, gray iron, Scotch pig, white iron.**

pigment The fine, colored particles in paint, stain, or similar materials; typically a crystalline compound; types used include **aniline color, lake color, ocher, verdigris;** specific colors include **American vermilion, barium white, barium yellow, barytes, blue verdigris, burnt sienna, burnt umber, chalk, chrome green, chrome yellow, cobalt blue, cobalt green, copper green, DeWint green, distilled verdi-**

gris, drab, drop black, graphite, green verdigris, Indian red, indigo, ivory black, leaded zinc oxide, lithopone, lime proof green, litharge, massicot, Naples yellow, Prussian blue, raw sienna, raw umber, red lead, red ocher, shell white, spruce yellow, sublimed white lead, titanated lithopone, titanium dioxide, turkey red, Tuscan red, ultramarine blue, ultramarine green, Vandyke brown, Venetian red, verdigris, violet oxide of iron, white lead, whitewash, whiting, yellow ocher, zinc chromate, zinc oxide white. See also **colorant, fugitive color.**

pig metal Any metal cast into the form of a **pig,** such as **pig iron.**

pilaster An **engaged column** of rectangular cross section, with base and capital; originally always part of a masonry structural pier, most North American examples are applied ornament; typically projects a distance that is one third or less of the width of the column. Also known as **parastas.** See also **anta, engaged column, piedroit, pilaster mass, pilaster strip.**

pilaster brick A brick which is notched half its width on one end and used to construct projecting piers or pilasters.

pilastered Constructed or ornamented with pilasters, especially when they are a prominent architectural feature.

pilaster mass **1.** A masonry pier structurally tied to the wall; typically without a base and capital. **2.** A structural masonry **pilaster** supporting a molded impost block that is the base of an arch; common in the **Gothic Revival** style.

pilaster strip A narrow, masonry pier with a low projection from the wall; typically without a base and capital; often used between windows or other openings to strengthen the wall.

pilastrata A series, or order, of pilasters. See also **colonnade.**

pile **1.** One of a series of foundation elements composed of a shaft driven into the ground; used to support buildings or structures on soft soil, or as part of a retaining wall; originally wood logs, steel has also been used since the late 19c, and concrete since the early 20c; types include **close pile, false pile, filler pile, follower pile, gauge pile, H-pile, hollow pile, hydraulic pile, pneumatic pile, pug pile, sand pile, screw pile, sheet pile, soldier pile;** related elements include **pile cap, pile hoop, pile plank, pile shoe, runner, sheeting, waler.** Also known as **pale.** **2.** A massive building or group of buildings, especially of masonry construction. **3.** (20c) The depth of a building from front to rear measured in number of rooms; most often **single-pile** or **double-pile.**

pile cap The construction on top of a number of piles that connects them together; may be a beam, plate, or block of concrete.

pile hoop A metal band placed around the top of a wood pile to keep it from splitting when driven.

pile pier A **pier** supported on piles.

pile plank A plank with a sharpened end used as a **sheet pile;** typically the end is cut at a 45-degree angle so that it is pushed against an existing adjoining pile as it is driven into the ground.

pile shoe A pointed metal fitting used on the end of a pile to assist in penetrating the earth.

piling A group of **piles** collectively.

pillage (18c) A square pillar with base and capital located behind a column and supporting an arch.

pillar **1.** An inexact term for a simple, massive, vertical structural support, especially one that is not a classical style **column,** with base and capital, nor a **pier;** common in Gothic Revival architecture. **2.** A large memorial column. **3.** (pre-19c) Same as **column, pier, pilaster** or **post.**

pillaret A small **pillar.**

pillory A punishment device having boards with holes that fasten the neck and wrists of a standing convicted offender; typically an ear or ears of the offender were nailed to the headboard; common in the 17c, used to mid-19c. See also **stocks.**

pillow work Same as **pulvinated.**

pilot door Same as **wicket door** (sense 1).

piloti (20c) One of a series of massive piers that support an open ground floor of a building; typically made of reinforced concrete; popularized by the French architect Le Corbusier starting in the 1920s.

pin **1.** A slender rod or peg used to connect two or more parts of a structure together; in **timber frame** construction typically wood with a circular or square cross section, and tapered; in a **pin connection** typically a cylindrical bar, sometimes with one or two heads. See also **hinge pin, pin joint, pintle, treenail.** **2.** A cylindrical metal bar used to connect the members of a truss at the joints. **3.** The bolt of a door. **4.** One of the small cylinders inside a lock that is moved by a key. **5.** Same as **pin knot.** **6.** Same as **pinnacle.**

pinacotheca (pre-WWI) An art gallery for paintings; from the name of the ancient lateral hall of Propylaea in Athens that displayed paintings.

pin connection A structural connection of a truss or bridge made by a **pin,** rather than by a rivet or turnbuckle. See also **pin joint.**

pine Any of the numerous softwood trees of the family *Pinus* and their wood; includes **candlewood pine, foxtail pine, Idaho pine, loblolly pine, lodgepole, longleaf pine, Monterey pine, ponderosa pine, red pine, Sabine's pine, scotch pine, shortleaf pine, slash pine, southern yellow pine, sugar pine, white pine, yellow pine.** See also **fir, spruce, sequoia, tamarack.**

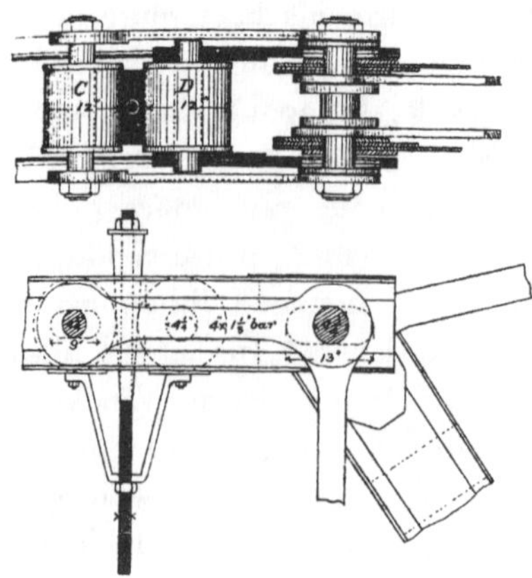

pin connection

pineapple (pre-19c) A pine cone; used as a symbol of hospitality, especially in various stylized forms as finials and bas-relief decoration.

pine fir Same as **balsam fir.**

pinery **1.** (18c–19c) A **hothouse** used for growing pineapple plants. **2.** (19c) A pine forest where lumber is harvested.

pin joint A **joint** made by connecting two members that have eyes at their ends with a **pin.** See also **pin connection.**

pin knot A wood knot smaller than 0.5 inch in diameter.

pin lock (19c) A door lock with a projecting cylindrical bolt.

pinnacle **1.** An ornamental, sculptured, vertical solid element; typically tapered to a point; used on top of buttresses, along roof balustrades, and surrounding the base of spires, especially on Gothic Revival style buildings. See also **finial.** **2.** A small turret with a pointed top.

pinning The process of attaching roof tiles with wood pins.

pinning in The process of filling the joints in a stone wall with chips or wedges of stone pushed into the mortar; typically used in the interior of the wall to avoid hollow spaces. See also **galleting.**

pinning under See **underpinning.**

pinning up The process of leveling lintels, beams, or piers by installing shims of slate, metal, or thin wedges of stone; also used to restore walls to the vertical.

pin oak A tall **oak** tree with light reddish brown, heavy, hard wood that checks badly in drying; found from North Carolina to Massachusetts and west to Kansas and Oklahoma; typically marketed as **red oak** for lumber and flooring; *Quercus palustris.*

pin plate A metal bearing plate with a pin on the bottom that fastens it to the masonry.

pin switch An electrical switch where the connection is made by a pin touching two plates.

pintle **1.** A hook-like, vertical pin that is the fixed pivot of a **pivot hinge** and receives the **pintle sleeve.** See also **hinge pin.** 2. A short metal post that supports the base of a wood column. See also **slow-burning mill construction.**

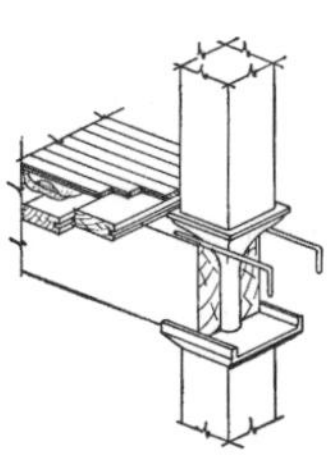

pintle (sense 2)

pintle hinge Same as **pivot hinge.**

pintle sleeve The half of a **pivot hinge** that slides over the **pintle.**

pioneer An inexact term for one of the first non-native peoples to explore a locality; especially one who prepares the way for others to follow, or is of the first generation of settlers.

pipe A long, narrow cylinder with a thin wall used to conduct a fluid or gas, such as water, steam, or natural gas; types by material or manufacture include **asbestos cement pipe, bituminized fiber pipe, black pipe, block-tin pipe, brass pipe, cast-iron pipe, cement pipe, copper pipe, earthen pipe, galvanized pipe, lead pipe, log pipe, PVC pipe, solid drawn, wrought-iron pipe;** types by use include **drain pipe, main, service pipe, sewer pipe, soil pipe, steam pipe, vent pipe, water pipe;** types by shape include **bell pipe.** See also **conduit, pipe fitting, pipe joint, solder.**

pipe collar An **ornamental cast-iron** railing or post decoration that slips over an iron or steel pipe; various turned and carved shapes are used.

pipe column (20c) A column composed of a steel pipe with base and top plates and sometimes a mechanism for adjusting its length, such as an integral screw jack; typically 3–6 inches in diameter; types include **Lally column.**

pipe coupling A straight **pipe fitting** for connecting two pipes. See also **bend, union.**

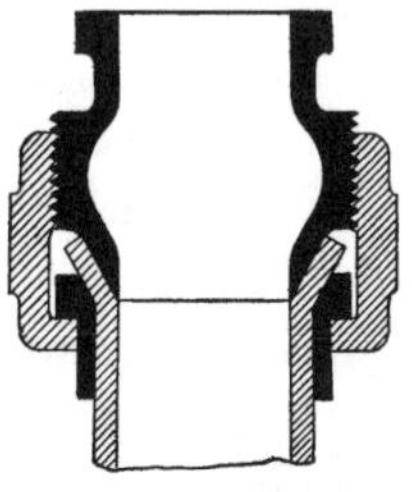

pipe coupling

pipe covering Thermal insulation wrapped around the outside of a pipe.

pipe culvert (19c–present) A **culvert** made with a large-diameter pipe of terra-cotta, cast iron, reinforced concrete, or galvanized sheet steel; may have a circular or elliptical cross section.

pipe fitting Any of various devices for connecting a **pipe** to another pipe or a plumbing fixture; types include **bend, cross, pipe coupling, pipe reducer, saddle, saddle hub, sweep tee, T-fitting, union, Y-branch.** See also **pipe joint.**

pipe joint Any **joint** that connects two pipes; types include **bell and spigot joint, blown joint, cone joint, expansion joint, hubless joint, inserted joint, lead pipe joint, putty joint, ring joint, rolled joint, sweated joint, threaded joint, water joint, wiped joint.** See also **bell pipe, pipe, pipe coupling, pipe fitting.**

pipe rail A handrail made from standard pipe and fittings; typically, threaded black pipe connected with various-shaped pipe fittings.

pipe reducer A **pipe fitting** for connecting pipes of different diameters.

pipework, piping A system of pipes, such as all of the plumbing pipes within a building.

piping Same as **pipework.**

pisé A construction system of rammed earth walls; earth is shoveled into a form and tamped; most often found in southwest U.S. or parts of Mexico, such as the prehistoric Native American Casa Grande ruin in Arizona, and in mid-19c U.S. Army outposts, such as Fort Laramie, Wyoming.

pissduit (17c) A funnel or channel that carries away urine and waste.

piston elevator (19c) Same as **hydraulic elevator.**

pit, (pre-19c) **pitt** **1.** (pre-20c) The orchestra seating in a theater immediately in front of the stage. See also **orchestra pit.** **2.** Any lowered area in a ground floor or an excavated hole in the ground. See also **sump.** **3.** (pre-19c) Same as **heartwood.** See also **pit wood.**

pitch **1.** (18c–present) The slope of a building element in relation to the horizontal, especially a roof; typically expressed as (a) a ratio of vertical inches to 12 horizontal inches, such as *3 in 12 pitch;* (b) a fraction computed by dividing the vertical rise by the entire span of a gable roof, such as **whole pitch, half pitch, quarter pitch;** (c) an angle of inclination above the horizontal, such as *30 degrees;* a steep pitch is one with a large angle between the horizontal and the roof surface; types include **common pitch, Elizabethan pitch, equilateral pitch, Gothic pitch, Greek pitch, pediment pitch, Roman pitch, true pitch.** **2.** The distance between rivet centers in iron or steel construction. **3.** The **rise** of an **arch.** **4.** A thick, dark brown to black, gummy substance produced from boiling down or distillation of tar or pine sap; used for caulking or sealing roofs; types include **Burgundy pitch, Canada pitch, Jew's pitch.** **5.** The angle of screw threads. **6.** (17c–mid-19c southern U.S.) The height of a wall between the sill and the wall plate. Also known as **between joints.** **7.** (18c South Carolina) Same as **gable roof.**

pitched Having a slope. See also **pitch** (sense 1).

pitch faced A rough, split, textured surface that projects forward from a tooled margin on the face of a stone block. See also **quarry face.**

pitch hole A depression below the main surface of a dressed stone block; typically found on one of the hidden faces.

pitching **1.** The process of applying **pitch** (sense 4), especially as caulking. **2.** (18c) Same as asphalt **paving.**

pitching piece Same as **apron piece.**

pitch mineral Same as **bitumen** or **asphalt.**

pitch pocket **1.** A cavity in softwood lumber filled with sap pitch. **2.** A box around a roof penetration, such as a steel shape supporting equipment, that is filled with asphalt to seal out water.

pitch roof Same as **gable roof.**

pitch tree Same as **Norway spruce;** named for the source of **Burgundy pitch.**

pit dwelling A residence that is excavated so that the living level is partly, or wholly, below grade; found in various Native American buildings in southwest U.S. and northern Mexico and some sod houses. See also **kiva.**

pit sawn Wood that has been sawn lengthwise by a two-person team, with the lower worker standing in a hole in the ground.

pit wood Heavy timbers used for pit frames in mines.

pivot Any type of pin that supports a rotating object, such as a door or window. See also **pintle, pivot hinge, pivot light.**

pivot bridge Same as **swing bridge.**

pivot hinge **1.** A two-piece **hinge** with one side having a vertical fixed pin or **pintle,** and the other side a **pintle sleeve** with a hole that fits over the pin; types include **rising hinge, gate hinge, hook-and-band hinge, hook-and-eye hinge, lift-off hinge, loose-joint hinge, pew hinge.** Also known as a **pintle hinge.** **2.** A double acting spring hinge supported on pivots, may be jamb mounted or the same as **floor spring hinge.**

pivot light A glazed sash that is opened and closed by turning on two pivots; may rotate vertically or horizontally; used for transom windows.

pivot span Same as **swing bridge.**

placard (pre-WWI) **1.** Same as **parging.** **2.** An interior door to a room decorated with a chambranle crowned with a frieze or gorge that is sometimes supported by consoles. **3.** The woodwork and frame of a door to a closet, or similar. **4.** A closet sunk in a wall so that only the door is seen. **5.** A shallow closet.

place brick (pre-19c) **1.** Same as **salmon brick.** **2.** A brick that is cut to shape on a flat, hard place before being air dried and fired in a kiln.

plafond, (18c) **platfond,** (18c) **platfound** (pre-WWI) **1.** A plain underside of a soffit, or similar architectural feature. See also **plancier.** **2.** An interior ceiling covering the bottom of a floor above. See also **plancher.**

plain An inexact term generally indicating an element or building that is smooth, flat and/or without ornamentation. See also various compound terms below.

plain bar An iron or steel bar with a round, square, or rectangular cross section and a smooth surface; may be used as a **reinforcing bar.**

plain face A flat, relatively smooth, finish on the face of a concrete block; not common until after WWI.

plain glass (18c) Window or mirror glass with a flat surface.

plain molding Any molding with a flat or continuous surface. Also known as **platband.**

plain rail A window meeting rail that is the same thickness as the rest of the sash. See also **check rail.**

plain sawn Wood cut longitudinally from a log with a series of parallel cuts entirely across the log; produces widest boards or flitches, with center pieces having **vertical grain** and outer pieces having **flat grain.** Also known as **bastard cut, bastard sawn, flat-cut, tangent sawn.** See also **pit sawn, quarter sawn, rift sawn.**

plain sliced Longitudinal **sliced veneer** flitches sliced from a log with a series of parallel knife cuts entirely across the log; produces widest flitches, most with **flat grain.** Also known as **bastard cut, flat sliced.** See also **quarter sliced, rift sliced.**

plain tile, (pre-20c) plane tile A thin, flat, rectangular roof tile; typically made of terra cotta. Also known as **crown tile, shingle tile, thack tile,** or simply **roof tile.** (*See illustration p. 342.*)

plaister (18c) Same as **plaster.**

P lam (late 20c) Abbr. for **plastic laminate.**

plan (18c–present) A drawing representing a horizontal view or cross section of a space, structure, system, or object; types include

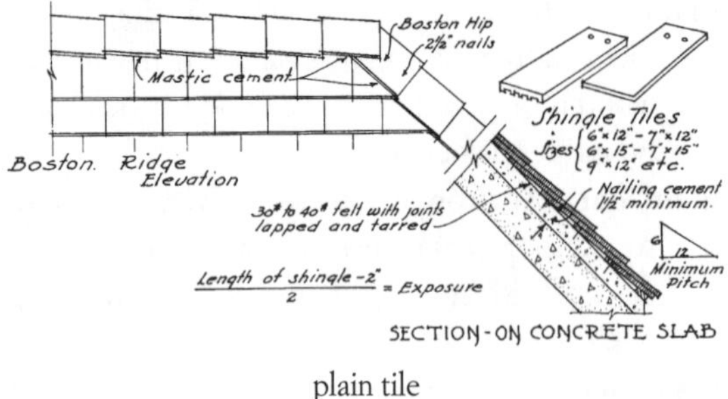

plain tile

detail, floor plan, ground plan, ichnograph, gas plot, raised plan. See also **working drawings, master plan, plans.**

planceer Same as **plancier.**

plancher (pre-WWII) **1.** A wood plank, especially used as a floor board. **2.** A wood ceiling board or **soffit board.** See also **plafond. 3.** Same as **plancier.**

planchette (pre-20c) A small plank.

planching (dialect) Wood flooring.

planching nail Same as **flooring nail.**

plancier, planceer, plancer (pre-WWI) **1.** The soffit or underside of any projecting element, such as a cornice. **2.** Same as **plancher.**

planed Wood smoothed with a tool with a sharpened wedge that cuts thin slices off the surface; done entirely by hand tools until ca. 1830, then gradually replaced by machine planers.

plane of a column An imaginary plane that intersects a column along its axis; in some classical Greek style buildings, the plane of the outer row of columns inclines slightly inward.

plane tile Same as **plain tile.**

plank A long, thin, wide piece of lumber with a rectangular cross section that is 1.5–4 inches thick and typically more than 4.5 inches wide; used as flooring, framing, or sheathing; when set horizontally on edge, known as a **beam** or **joist.** Also known as **plancher.** See also **board, timber.**

plank brace A diagonal 1× board installed as a brace at the corner of a wood frame building. See also **stud brace.**

plank-frame 1. Same as **horizontal plank-frame** or **vertical plank-frame.** Also known as **plank-wall.** See also **framing, plank house. 2.** (20c) A building framing system that uses lumber of 2 inch nominal dimension; for barns the lumber is double or tripled to achieve the required strength. **3.** A 2× used as a door or window frame; typically rabbeted on the inside edge.

plank house A building with exterior walls constructed of sawn planks set on edge with dovetail corners; used 17c–early 19c, especially for buildings requiring additional security, such as a jail or storehouse. See also **plank-frame.**

plank-on-plank 1. Same as **horizontal plank-frame. 2.** A type of **siding** or **fencing** composed of overlapping vertical planks, which alternate forward and back. See also **board-on-board.**

plank road A roadway constructed of transverse planks supported on timber sleepers.

plank-wall Same as **plank frame** (sense 1).

planned unit development (PUD) A **zoning** process that allows a developer relaxation from some regulations, such as restrictions on height or density, in exchange for creating public amenities, such as building roads or schools, or for providing a superior design; typically used for relatively large land parcels.

planning 1. (20c) The process of designing and guiding the future physical and economic **development** of any political jurisdiction; ranges from laying out the street network and open areas, such as in colonial Savannah, Georgia, to the use of such modern techniques as economic analysis and forecasting, historic districts, **preservation planning,** and **zoning;** variously referred to as **city planning, com-**

munity planning, municipal planning, town planning, urban planning. 2. The process of designing a complete building.

plant 1. The fixed mechanical systems needed to operate a building, including the heating, elevators, and lights. **2.** The buildings, structures, and equipment used for manufacturing at a particular site.

plantation 1. (pre-18c) A settlement of British colonists. **2.** (17c–19c) A farm. **3.** (18c–present) A large tract in the southern U.S. or West Indies where a cash crop such as tobacco, rice, indigo, or cotton was grown, typically using slave labor before it was outlawed in the 19c; mid-18c onward also implied a tasteful country seat of a gentleman and his family; building types may include **barn, great house, gin house, kitchen, overseer's house, outbuilding, quarters, stables, winnowing house.** See also **home plantation. 4.** (pre-20c) A grove of trees planted for harvesting lumber. **5.** (19c) A planted oyster bed. **6.** (New England) A small, unchartered district with a local government. **7.** (Newfoundland) A fish-processing plant.

planted An element, such as a molding, attached to the surface of another element; typically glued or nailed.

plaque A decorative or commemorative flat plate attached to a wall surface; typically metal, especially bronze, may also be terra-cotta, wood, or other materials. See also **site marker.**

plaster, (pre-19c) **plaister** A wall and ceiling finish material made of water and **quicklime** or **hydrated lime** or **plaster of Paris;** base coats are mixed with sand and, sometimes, hair or other fiber as a binder during application; typically applied as **three-coat work** with a **scratch coat, brown coat** and **finish coat** that are ½–1 inch thick; also used for cast ornaments and **run moldings;** components may include **coarse stuff, fine stuff, gauged stuff, Keene's cement, plaster of Paris;** types include **fiber plaster, gypsum plaster, lime plaster, prairie plaster, stucco, wood fiber plaster, zaccab, Zenitherm;** finish types include **hard finish, sand finish;** may be applied directly to masonry or over **lath.** See also **whitewash.**

plaster base Same as **plasterboard.** See also **base** (sense 5).

plasterboard, (19c) **plaster board** (late 19c–present) A composition panel used as a base for **plaster;** materials include alternating layers of gypsum plaster and felt, or fibrous felt, cork, asbestos, or wood fibers, or **gypsum lath;** typically 16 × 32 to 32 × 48 × .25–.5 inches. Also known as **plaster lath.** See also **drywall, lath.**

plaster bond A bituminous **dampproofing** applied to the inside of a masonry wall before application of a plaster finish.

plaster button A washer designed so that a screw can be inserted in the center and be attached through existing cracked plaster to the structure behind. Also known as **plaster washer.**

plasterer's putty Fine stuff that has been strained through a sieve to make an extremely smooth paste.

plaster lath Same as **gypsum lath.**

plaster of Paris, (pre-19c) **plaister of Paris** Partially dehydrated gypsum that forms a quick setting **plaster** when mixed with water; mostly a semihydrate of calcium sulphate, $CaSO_4 \cdot \frac{1}{2}H_2O$; used for **plasterwork,** especially cast ornaments and finish coats; first manufactured in a suburb of Paris. See also **composition, gypsum plaster, Keene's cement.**

plaster partition A thin partition composed of plaster on metal lath and small C-channel studs; typically two inches thick and used in offices late 19c–mid-20c.

plaster stone Same as **gypsum.**

plaster washer Same as **plaster button.**

plasterwork **1.** A finish constructed of **plaster,** especially an ornamental interior. See also **stuccowork.** **2.** Cast ornamental plaster, typically made with **plaster of Paris,** sometimes with reinforcing material.

plastic Any material that can be modeled, molded, or extruded; in the 20c the term is frequently used to refer to synthetic organic materials that are in a plastic state during manufacture, such as **acrylic, Bakelite, epoxy, polyethylene, polymethyl acrylate, polystyrene, polyurethane, polyvinyl chloride, vinyl.**

plastic art Sculpture or ornamental modeling done with materials that initially are soft and malleable, such as plaster or clay. Also known as **plastice.**

plastice (18c) Same as **plastic art.**

plastic laminate (P lam) (20c) Paper, cloth, or wood laminated with phenolic resin material; used for a washable finish, especially to face kitchen counter tops and cabinets; may have a wear resistant **melamine** overlay; types include **Formica.**

plastic pipe See **PVC pipe.**

plastic repair Modeling of a damaged or missing feature with a **plastic** material, such as **epoxy** or **plaster.** See also **plastic art.**

plat **1.** A surveyor's drawing of a measured piece of land. **2.** Same as **plot.** **3.** (pre-19c) Same as **ground plan.** **4.** (18c) A small lawn area adjacent to a house.

platband (pre-WWI) **1.** A slightly projecting molding with a rectangular cross section. Also known as **plain molding.** **2.** Same as **fascia.**

plate **1.** A continuous, horizontal member that distributes the vertical loads from a series of elements, such as studs or rafters; types include **deck plate, false plate, ground sill, pole plate, raising plate, sole, top plate, wall plate.** **2.** A thin piece of material, often steel or wood, used to reinforce a beam, column, or similar structural element. **3.** A horizontal piece used to distribute the concentrated loads from a structural element, such as the end of a beam or column, over a wider area; types include **bearing plate, pin plate, wall plate.** See also **bolster.** **4.** A thin layer of metal covering another metal, as in silverplate. **5.** Sheets of metal more than .25 inch thick; types include **tank iron.** See also **hand plate, push plate, sheet metal.** **6.** The top log of a log cabin wall that supports the ceiling joists.

plate beam A **built beam** made of iron or steel plates; typically connected with rolled shapes, such as **angle irons.** See also **angle girder.**

plate girder A **girder** built of steel or iron plates; type includes **angle girder.**

plate glass (ca. 1850–present) Large, thick sheets of polished, clear **glass;** manufactured by casting the glass on iron tables, rolling to the desired thickness, removing bubbles with pincers, and grinding and polishing; typically composed of white sand, sodium carbonate, lime, either alumina or manganese peroxide, and a large proportion of **cullet;** rare until after mid-19c; varieties include **mirror plate.** Also known as **polished plate.** See also **patent plate glass.**

plate iron (19c) Iron rolled into thin plates or sheet metal.

plate rail A narrow, grooved molding mounted on the upper part of an interior wall to hold decorative plates or other objects.

plate tracery Gothic style **tracery** formed by carving openings in a single stone rather than assembling several stones. Also known as **perforated tracery.**

platfond (18c) Same as **plafond.**

platform, (18c) **plat-form** **1.** A floor or similar level surface raised above the adjacent floor or

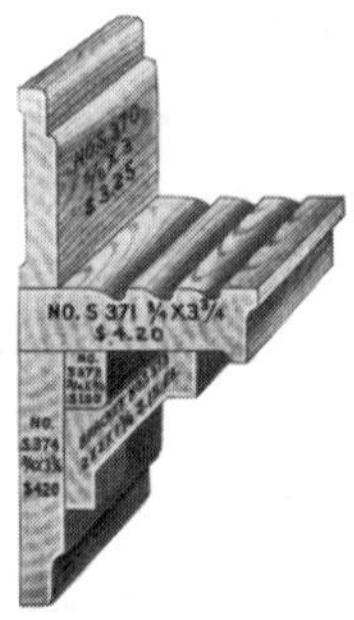

plate rail

ground level. **2.** Same as **pad. 3.** (18c) A series of horizontal beams that support a roof, or a flat roof itself, especially when used as a terrace. **4.** Same as **landing. 5.** (18c) Same as **plat** (sense 1).

platform frame A wood structural framing system for low-rise buildings in which a platform consisting of floor joists, a band beam, and the subfloor is constructed at each floor level; the stud walls run from the top of the subfloor to the bottom of the joists of the floor above; common for **wood frame** house construction by WWI and nearly universal after WWII. Also known as **western frame.** See also **balloon frame.** (*See illustration p. 346.*)

platform residence A group of houses built on a steep-sided, flat-topped mound by Native Americans in Florida; typically the mound is 20–50 feet high.

platform stair An **open string stair** with one or more landings between floors.

plating The process of lining one piece of colored glass with another piece to modify its color or intensity.

playhouse, (pre-19c) **play-house 1.** Same as **theater. 2.** (20c) A small shelter that children play in and that resembles a dwelling house.

plaza 1. An open public space or market in a city or town; often unpaved, especially in Spanish Colonial towns; beginning in the 19c often paved and landscaped with plantings and a fountain; typically a social center of Latin American towns. Also known as **piazza. 2.** A fortified town.

pleasance (pre-19c) A garden for pleasure.

pleasure ground (19c) A **park** or **garden,** especially a large landscaped area surrounding and belonging to a house or other building.

plenum chamber A space, often located between the finished ceiling and the floor structure above, that is pressurized to distribute conditioned air.

plenum fan A mechanical fan that pressurizes an interior space with outside air.

plenum system A building ventilation system that uses a **plenum** to distribute conditioned air; typically includes a **plenum fan.**

plexiform Having the appearance of a complex, interwoven network, such as **Romanesque Revival style** decoration.

Plexiglas A trade name for acrylic plastic sheeting, sometimes used for glazing.

plinth 1. The rectilinear block forming the lowest part of the base of a column or pedestal, often square in plan. See also **scamillus, socle, subplinth. 2.** Same as a **self-base** of a statue. **3.** The plain, continuous band between a base mold and the floor or ground level of any architectural feature, such as a **baseboard. 4.** A continuous, flat-faced, horizontal element projecting from a wall, such as a row of ashlars at the base of a rubble wall, several courses of brick forming a stringcourse, or the thick portion of a wall below the watertable.

plinth block A door or window surround **base block** that is adjacent to the floor.

plot 1. A measured piece of land; typically relatively small and often one of a series of similarly sized pieces, such as a cemetery or garden plot. **2.** Same as **plat.**

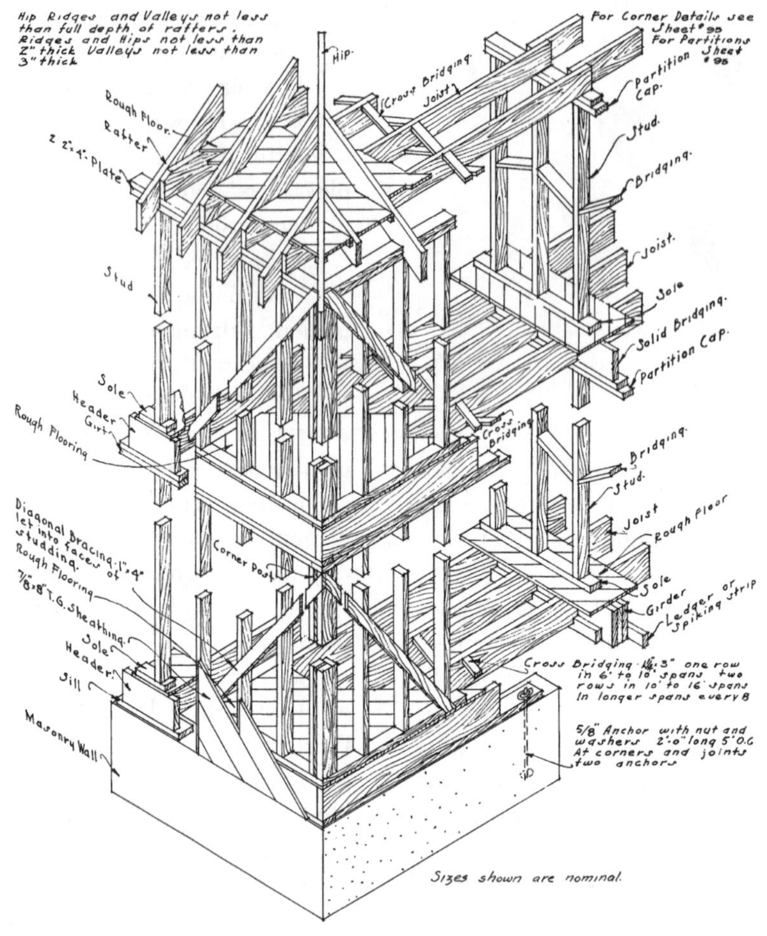

platform frame

plowed, ploughed Having a rabbeted groove; used to receive a tongue in a wood joint. See also **dado.**

plowed and tongued Same as **tongue and groove.**

plowed bead, ploughed bead Same as **flush bead.**

pluck A barbed nail or similar device hammered into masonry joints to attach woodwork.

plucked finish, plucker finish The rough planed surface texture of limestone blocks with small particles broken out; often used on the stone trim of buildings faced with a smooth finish. See also **stonework.**

plug 1. A small wedge of wood placed in a masonry joint as a **nailer. 2.** A water supply fitting with a male threaded end for attaching a hose, such as a fireplug.

plumb Vertical; perpendicular to a level surface. See also **out of plumb.**

plumbago (pre-20c) Same as **graphite.**

plumb bond A brick wall bond with a surface pattern composed entirely of stretchers in running bond, especially when created by a **clip bond.**

plumb cut A cut in framing lumber made on a vertical line, such as a cut on a rafter at the ridge. See also **seat cut.**

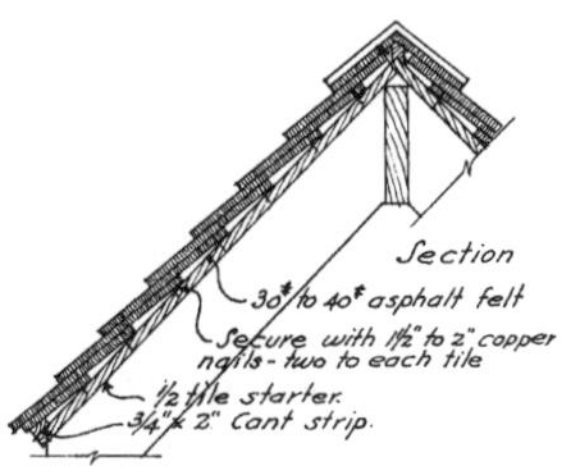

plumb cut

plumbery, plummery (pre-19c) The trade of manufacturing and installing **leadwork.** Also known as **plumbing.**

plumbic ocher Same as **litharge.**

plumbing **1.** A system of **pipes, pipe fittings, plumbing fixtures, tanks,** and **traps** that supplies water and/or gas and removes liquid wastes from a building; named for the trade of working in lead. **2.** The trade of installing plumbing (sense 1). **3.** (pre-20c) Same as **plumbery. 4.** Installing an element so that it is **plumb.**

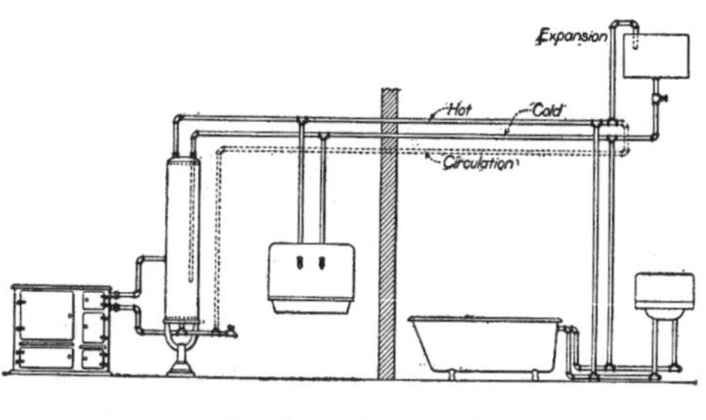

plumbing (sense 1)

plumbing code A **building code** that governs the safe and healthy design of plumbing systems for a structure; sometimes incorporated within a **mechanical code.**

plumbing fixture Any of various devices for supplying and holding bathing water and removing human waste; types include **basin, bathtub, grease trap, lavatory, laundry tub, sink, slop sink, urinal, water closet.**

plumb joint **1.** A lapped sheet-metal joint. **2.** A folded and soldered sheet-metal joint. See also **sweated joint.**

plummery Same as **plumbery.**

plunge bath (19c) Same as **plunge pool.**

plunge gauge A testing device with a movable rod that is used to measure movement across a crack.

plunge pool (19c–present) A small **swimming pool** that is deep enough to jump into.

ply One layer of a laminated material, such as two-ply or three-ply; used to refer to such materials as carpet backing, built-up roofing, and plywood.

plywood (20c) A fabricated panel of glued wood veneer layers; usually made with an odd number of plies and with the grain of adjoining plies laid at right angles to one another; sometimes made with a lumber core; patented in U.S. in 1865.

pneumatic elevator (19c) Same as **hydraulic elevator.**

pneumatic pile A hollow **pile** installed by creating a partial vacuum within it to excavate the earth from beneath it.

pocket **1.** Same as **sash pocket. 2.** The recess in a wall that receives a **pocket door. 3.** The recess at the side of a window that receives a folded interior shutter. **4.** The part of a flue below a stovepipe that catches soot.

pocket door A door that slides into a concealed recess in a wall; may be supported by a **door hanger** or by rollers on the floor.

pocketed An element, such as a stair tread, that has been inserted into a **dado** or similar recess.

pocket piece A access panel at the side of a window frame that opens the pocket for the counterweights; typically with a beveled joint at top and bottom.

Pocono sandstone A sandstone found in the northern Appalachian Mountains, especially Pennsylvania; named for Pocono Sandstone Knob in the vicinity of Huntington, Pennsylvania. Also known as **brownstone.**

podium **1.** A continuous pedestal forming a low wall that supports a row of columns. **2.** A platform with base, die, and cornice that supports a sculpture, monument, or classical building. See also **lysis. 3.** A raised platform used by a speaker addressing an audience; may be in the form of sense 2.

pointal (pre-WWI) Same as **poyntell.**

pointed arch A multicentered **arch** in which the upper curves of the intrados meet at an angle of less than 180 degrees; types include **acute-pointed arch, blunt arch, equilateral arch, lancet-pointed arch, ogee arch, ogive, Tudor arch, Venetian arch.** See also **pointed round arch.**

pointed arch

pointed architecture Architecture that employs the **pointed arch** of various Gothic styles. See also **Gothic Revival style.**

pointed finish The surface texture of stone blocks made with any pointed tool, such as a pick; may be coarse, medium, or fine; typically used on hard stone. See also **dabbed, peen hammered, rough pointed, stonework.**

pointed round arch An **arch** with a semicircular intrados and an extrados in the shape of a **pointed arch.**

pointed round arch

pointed tympanum A triangular **tympanum.**

pointed work **1.** Stone work with a rough, **pointed finish. 2.** Masonry with **pointing** or **repointing** work.

pointel (pre-WWI) Same as **poyntell.**

pointing The process of placing mortar (especially colored mortar) in a raked **masonry joint** after the units are laid; may be finished with a **tooled joint** or **tuck pointing;** sometimes used to mean **repointing.**

pole **1.** A long, slender, wood structural member with a circular cross section; typically a trimmed tree trunk; may be covered with bark. **2.** A surveying instrument with a length of one **rod.**

pole gutter A **parallel gutter** with a semicircular cross section.

pole plate A small **wall plate** that supports the foot of the common rafters and rests on the top of the tie beams.

pole structure A building or structure with a roof supported by unfinished, round, wood columns; commonly used for agricultural buildings.

police power The right of a government to restrict and enforce individual conduct and use of property to protect the public health, safety, and welfare; used as the basis for various property restrictions, including **building codes, zoning,** and preservation ordinances.

polished A glossy, very smooth surface texture on stonework and metals; common on marble, granite, gold, silver, and brass. See also **stonework.**

polished plate See **plate glass.**

poly Abbr. for **polyethylene.**

polychlorinated biphenyl Same as **PCB.**

polychromy, polychrome Having more than one color on the surface, especially buildings or statuary; may be painted on or be **structural polychrome.** See also **parti-colored.**

polyester (20c) A synthetic polymer resin compound; used for replicating cast ornaments and for making fiberglass-reinforced repairs.

polyethylene A synthetic resin manufactured from ethylene since ca. 1940; commonly used in 2–6 mm sheets as dampproofing under concrete slabs; destroyed by extended exposure to ultraviolet rays in sunlight unless **carbon-black-filled polyethylene** is used. Also known as **alkathene, poly, polythene.**

polyfoil Having multiple foils, especially more than five. Also known as **multifoil.**

polyfoil arch Same as **multifoil arch.**

polygonal rubble, polygonal masonry **Random rubble** formed of stones with polygonal-shaped faces. Also known as **polygonal masonry.**

polygonal vault A **vault** with more than four intersecting vault surfaces; typically octagonal in plan.

polymethyl acrylate A synthetic organic resin used to make **acrylic.**

polystyle Having many columns, especially a hall or interior court surrounded by columns.

polystyle colonnade A colonnade with many columns, such as one around a building.

polystyrene A synthetic polymer resin compound; used to make rigid **expanded polystyrene** insulation and **glazing.**

polythene Same as **polyethylene.**

polyurethane (post-WWII) A synthetic polymer resin compound; used to make flexible casting molds for replicating ornaments, used in **polyurethane varnish.**

polyurethane varnish A synthetic resin varnish developed after WWII; includes three types: moisture-cured, oil-modified, and water-based.

polyvinyl chloride (PVC) A synthetic vinyl resin in production since ca. 1930; commonly used in the late 20c for **PVC pipe.**

pommel, (19c) **pomel** A boss or knot, especially a ball-shaped top for a pyramidal or conical roof or pinnacle.

pond cypress A cypress tree similar to **bald cypress.**

ponderosa pine A tall, common **pine** tree with light red, lightweight, weak, fine-grained heartwood with whitish sapwood; found at upper elevations from northern Mexico to British Columbia; used for lumber, interior millwork, and flooring; referred to in some 19c references as a heavy wood, apparently in the mistaken belief that the Latin root *ponder sus* meant "heavy", rather than "ponderous"; *Pinus ponderosa.* Also known as **bull pine, heavy-wooded pine, pondosa pine, silver pine, western yellow pine, yellow pine.**

pondosa pine (20c) Same as **ponderosa pine.**

Pontalba An **ornamental cast-iron** pattern in the form of intertwined branching scrolls; originally manufactured in 1848 for the Pontalba building in New Orleans.

poop Same as **poppyhead.**

poorhouse, poor house (pre-20c) A public building or group of buildings used as a dwelling for paupers. See also **workhouse.**

poplar **1.** One of various hardwood trees of the genus *Populus* with greenish to tan, straight-grained, soft wood with no pronounced grain pattern; used primarily for painted millwork and the backing for veneer; includes **balsam poplar, California balsam poplar.** Also known as **white wood.** **2.** Wood similar to that of *Populus,* including **paper birch** and **tulip tree.** Also known as **poplar birch, tulip poplar, yellow poplar.**

poplar birch Same as **paper birch.**

poppyhead, poppy A carved finial on the end of a church pew; common in the **Perpendicular Style.** Also known as **poop.**

porcelain **1.** A fine, translucent, glazed ceramic made from kaolin clay and feldspar; first manufactured in Europe ca. 1470. **2.** A glazed, white ceramic plumbing or electric fixture, as opposed to one manufactured from metal. See also **opalin, porcelain enamel.**

porcelain cleat See **cleat.**

porcelain enamel A smooth, vitreous coating composed of sand and glass fired at approximately 1,000 degrees Fahrenheit; used as a finish on metal, such as the opaque white coating on cast-iron tubs, sheet-metal stoves, and similar fixtures, or the variously colored coatings on curtain wall spandrel panels. Also known as **vitreous enamel.** See also **porcelain.**

porch, (pre-20c) **porche** A covered and floored area of a building, especially a house, that is open at the front and, usually, the sides; typically partially enclosed with columns and railings; until mid-18c, used to describe a covered entrance to a building; the modern usage of the term was widespread in North America by the late 19c. Also known as **garret, piazza, veranda.** See also **portal, portico, wind porch.**

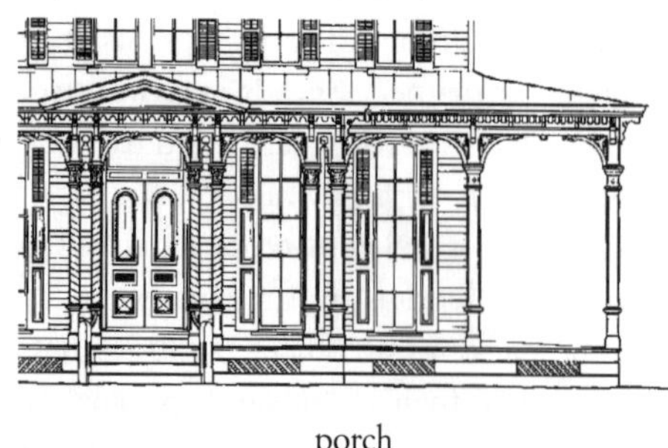

porch

porch chamber (pre-19c) **1.** An unheated room directly above a first-floor porch. **2.** A small room at one end of an upper-level porch or piazza; typically unheated and entered from the porch. Also known as **preacher room.**

porous earthenware **Terra-cotta** with numerous small voids created by mixing clay with sawdust and/or chopped straw, which is consumed during firing; used in the late 19c for fireproofing steel structures.

portal, (pre-WWI) **portail** **1.** A monumental gateway or entrance, especially one with a classical enframement. **2.** (19c) A vestibule formed of wainscoting that projects into a room. **3.** The entrance porch and related architectural features of a church or similar building. **4.** The smaller of two gates that are different sizes. See also **wicket. 5.** In the Spanish Colonial style, same as **arcade** or **porch.** See also **zaguan.**

portal brace One of a pair of concave quarter round braces that connect a vertical and horizontal member in ironwork; the form approximates an arched portal.

porte cochere **1.** A covered area over a driveway at a building entrance. Also known as **carriage porch.** See also **porch, portico. 2.** (pre-WWI) A doorway through which vehicles pass and that leads to a covered area for discharging passengers; from the French for a "gate for coaches".

portico A columned porch or ambulatory, especially at the main entrance to a Classical Revival style building; typically has a coffered ceiling. See also **in antis, prostyle.**

portiere A curtain across a doorway; used as decoration or in place of a door.

portland cement A hard, strong, **hydraulic cement** composed of calcium carbonate, calcium silicates, and calcium aluminates; first manufactured in England by Joseph Aspdin, who patented it in 1824 and named it for its resemblance to **Portland stone;** first, imported in the U.S. in 1865 and first manufactured in the U.S. in 1872.

Portland cement plaster A hard, fire-resistant **plaster** made of **portland cement,** sand, hydrated lime, and water. See also **Keene's cement.**

portland cement stucco A **stucco** composed of **portland cement,** sand, lime, and aggregates; may also contain pigments and waterproofing materials; finishes include **exposed aggregate, pebble-dash, sand-floated, sand-sprayed, smooth-troweled, spatter-dash, stippled.** See also **plaster.**

Portland stone **1.** A **brownstone** quarried in the vicinity of Portland, Connecticut, and used mainly for pavers. **2.** A light-colored, high-quality limestone quarried on the Isle of Portland, England; imported to North America in limited quantities in the 18c.

portón [Spanish] Same as **cancela.**

Port Orford cedar A large **cedar** tree with yellowish white, moderately soft, even-grained wood; found in a small area on the coasts of northern California and southern Oregon; used for venetian blind slats, millwork, plywood, and flooring; first lumbered after its discovery in 1854; *Chamaecyparis lawsoniana.*

post, (pre-18c) **poast** A slender column, generally round or square in section; usually wood but may also be metal or stone; timber frame types include **chimney post, center post, corner post, doorpost, jamb post, main post, prick post, purlin post, story post, window post;** truss types include **hanging post, king-post, pendent post, princess-post, queen-post;** other types include **gatepost, heel post, mile post, newel post, trellis post.** See also **strut.**

post-and-beam construction Any building **framing** system that primarily uses a series of vertical elements, such as columns, posts, or studs to support horizontal beams and rafters; types include **skeleton construction, wood frame.** Also known as **post-and-lintel construction, trabeated.** See also **arcuate, bearing wall, timber frame.**

post-and-girt framing Same as **timber frame.**

post-and-lintel construction Same as **post-and-beam construction.**

post and pane, post and petrail **Timber frame** construction in which vertical posts alternate with filled panes. See also **half-timbered, nogging, pane.**

post-and-plank fence A fence built of vertical posts with two or more horizontal sawn planks spanning between them. See also **post-and-rail fence, rail fence.**

post-and-rail fence A fence built of vertical posts with two or more horizontal rails spanning between them; may also support pickets or pales; typically the posts have horizontal holes into which the tapered ends of the rails are slipped. See also **post-and-plank fence, rail fence.**

post butt A block of stone or wood used as the base of a fence post.

postcontact The period after the first nonnative peoples entered a locality; the concept is important in **archaeology** (along with **precontact**) to distinguish between native and European cultural influences.

postern, postern door, postern gate **1.** A small door or gate beside a large one, especially in a fortification. **2.** A back gate or door.

post house, posting house, posting inn (pre-1930) A roadside inn where relays of horses and vehicles are kept for travelers.

postiche Architectural ornament added after the original work is completed, especially when inappropriate. See also **pastiche.**

postigo [Spanish] A **wicket** door set in a large door in a Spanish Colonial building. See also **postern.**

post in the ground (20c) An earth-fast wood framing system with posts set directly in the ground and tied together with a wall plate and weatherboards; used for all types of buildings during the 18c and into the early 19c, then used primarily for agricultural buildings. Also known as **pole structure.** See also **poteaux-en-terre, Virginia house.**

postmedieval architecture The architecture that continued the postmedieval construction techniques of English colonists during the 17c and early 18c, with many regional variations; typical original elements include a linear, one-room-deep plan; steeply pitched side-gabled roof without overhanging eaves; tall, massive chimneys of decorative form; weatherboard siding on the side walls; small casement windows with leaded diamond quarrels; batten door; typically timber frame with nogging, two stories and a central chimney north of New York, and one story brick or timber frame with two end chimneys south of New Jersey; often have later rear additions; supplanted by the **Georgian** style during the 18c. Also known as **postmedieval English.** See also **colonial architecture, Garrison Colonial, Norman roof, saltbox, stone ender.**

postmedieval English See **postmedieval architecture.**

post-mill A **windmill** in which the mechanism is elevated on a large central post that allows the vanes to rotate to face the wind. See also **smock mill.**

post-Renaissance architecture Classical revival architecture in Europe after the Renaissance.

post truss A rectangular, long-span bridge **truss** with inclined posts that slope toward a center triangular panel and diagonal ties from the top of each post to the bottom of the next post toward the center.

potash glass **Glass** manufactured with potash as an ingredient.

potato hole A cellar used to store potatoes; may be a separate structure or the lower part of a building.

potato house A building used to store potatoes; may be above grade or a **potato hole.**

pot chimney A chimney composed of multiple, stacked ceramic pots with no bottoms; used in Pueblo dwellings.

poteaux-en-terre [French] **Vertical log house** construction in which the posts are set in backfilled trenches dug in the earth. See also **post in the ground, poteaux-sur-sole.**

poteaux-sur-sole [French] **Vertical log house** construction in which the posts are supported on a horizontal timber sole that rests on a stone foundation. See also **poteaux-en-terre.**

pothouse, (18c) **pot house** **1.** (pre-19c) A building in which ceramic goods are made. **2.** Same as **ale house.**

pothunter A person who disturbs an **archaeological site** while looking for **cultural artifacts** without permission.

pothunting Collecting **cultural artifacts** from an **archaeological site** without permission.

pot metal **1.** An alloy of copper and lead; used for faucets and large containers. **2.** A type of **cast iron** used to make cooking pots.

pot-metal glass (pre-WWI) Same as **colored glass;** made by the addition of metal salts to the molten glass in a large pot.

Potomac breccia Same as **calico marble.**

Potsdam sandstone Same as **Malone sandstone.**

poultry house (18c–present, Maryland and lower South) Same as **henhouse.**

pounce, pounce powder A fine, colored powder; used to transfer decorative patterns by **pouncing.** Also known as **stamping powder.**

pounced work **Openwork** decorated with small, punched holes of various shapes or knife cuts. Also known as **punched work.**

pouncing Dusting a **stencil** with **pounce** to mark the outlines of a design on a surface to be painted.

pouring wool insulation **Loose-fill insulation** composed of chopped **rock wool.**

powder house A **building** used to store gunpowder or other explosives. See also **magazine.**

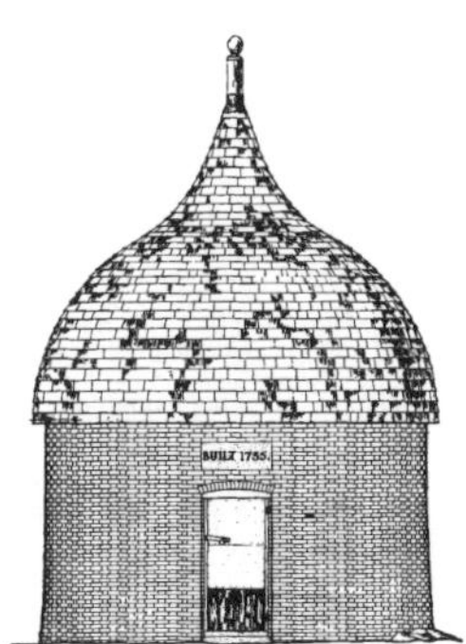

powder house
Marblehead, Massachusetts, ca. 1755

powdering, (18c) **poudering** **1.** A colored or metallic powder, such as bronzing, sprinkled on a surface for decoration. **2.** Decoration in the form of a small design repeated irregularly over a surface, such as stars scattered on a blue background.

powder magazine See **magazine.**

powder-post Wood riddled with powder-post borings or dry rot as evidenced by powdered wood fibers or frass.

powder-post boring A wormhole in wood made by the powder-post beetle; 1/16–1/8 inch in diameter; found in hardwoods along with powder frass.

powder room, powdering room **1.** (18c) A room in which to powder wigs or one's hair. **2.** (19c–present) A ladies lounge, especially adjacent to a toilet room.

powerhouse, (19c) **power house** A building containing machinery used to generate steam, water, or electrical power. See also **power plant.**

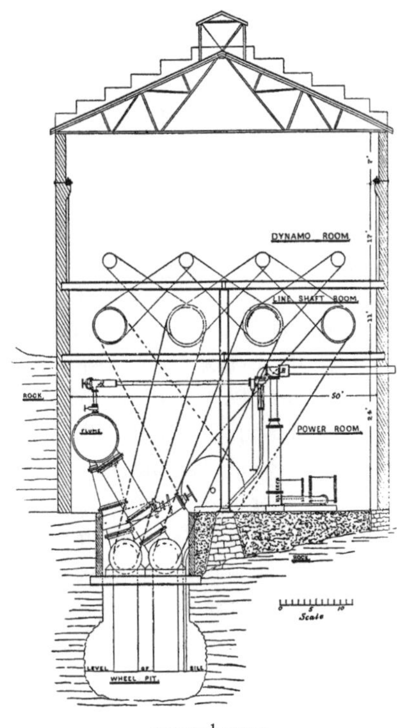

powerhouse

power panel Same as **panelboard.**

power plant (20c) A plant used to generate power, especially a central electrical plant; includes both the building and generating equipment.

power washing Same as **pressure washing.**

poy (pre-20c) A gallery or terrace with a railing that projects from a house.

poyntell, (pre-20c) **poyntill, pointal, pointel** (pre-WWI) A geometric pattern formed of small squares or lozenge-shaped pieces laid diagonally, usually tile or other paving.

prairie plaster A rough-finished, brown coat **plaster** used for **stucco** and interior plaster finish in Prairie Style houses; typically composed of portland cement and quartz sand, and sometimes contains small pebbles; often coated with glazes, stains, stippling, or scumbling of red, gold, and olive hues. See also **sand finish.**

Prairie School Same as **Prairie Style;** often used to refer to the work of Frank Lloyd Wright's contemporaries and followers, rather than Wright's work itself.

Prairie Style An architectural style centered in Chicago, ca. 1900–1920s; most notable practitioners were Frank Lloyd Wright and his followers; consciously rejected historical styles and based the overall form of houses on the rolling prairies of the Midwest; characterized by low-pitched hip roofs with wide eaves, casement ribbon windows, and spaces that flow into one another at right angles, typically without any curved forms; applied ornamentation is usually linear and never classical; isolated examples based on publications were designed by other architects throughout North America and Puerto Rico. Also known as **Prairie School.**

praise hall (19c Georgia) A small wood building built for prayer meetings held by plantation slaves.

Pratt truss A bridge **truss** with rectangular or trapezoidal panels formed by vertical posts, a top chord in compression, and a bottom chord in tension; diagonal ties slope downward toward the center; of various overall forms including triangular, rectangular with triangular end panels, **camelback truss,** and **flat Pratt.** Also known as **single quadrangular truss.**

preacher room (19c) Same as **porch chamber** (sense 2).

preaction system A **dry pipe system** that uses supplemental fire detectors installed near the sprinkler heads to start water flowing into the pipes; typically with pumps for quick delivery of water to the activated heads; used where the risk of water damage is greatest, such as irreplaceable historic interiors or computer rooms. See also **sprinkler system.**

precast (20c) A building material, especially **concrete,** that is molded before it is incorporated into a building; used for both structural and ornamental elements; products include **precast concrete, architectural precast concrete.**

precast concrete (20c) A structural or architectural element formed of **concrete** cast in a mold before it is incorporated into a building; typically composed of portland cement, sand, and dark-colored gravel reinforced with steel. See also **architectural precast concrete.**

precinct **1.** The area immediately surrounding a building; may be defined by a wall or fence or be inexactly defined. **2.** A local government geographic subdivision; typically smaller than a **ward** and often defined for voting or policing purposes.

pre-Columbian architecture The design of Native American structures constructed before Columbus's voyage to the Americas in 1492 and, more generally, before contact with European culture. See also **precontact.**

precontact The time before the first nonnative peoples entered a locality; the concept is important in **archaeology** (along with **postcontact**) to distinguish between native and European cultural influences. See also **pre-Columbian.**

precontract The period of a construction project between **bidding** and the signing of a construction contract; typically a time for analyzing bids and negotiating final terms.

precut house A **ready-cut house.**

predella **1.** Same as **gradino.** **2.** A step or platform below an altarpiece.

preemption The legal right of a settler on public land to purchase the property at a fixed price.

preengineered steel building (late 20c) A manufacturer's standardized package of steel rigid frame bents, girts, and purlins with corrugated metal roofing and siding; typically for industrial use and prefabricated. Also known as **prefabricated steel building, standard steel building.**

prefabricated A structure, or portion of a structure, that is manufactured with all of its parts cut to size and shipped ready to be assembled on site; typical products include curtain walls, movable partitions, and entire industrial buildings. See also **ready-cut house.**

prefabricated steel building Same as **preengineered steel building.**

prehistoric architecture The design of buildings and structures before written records were kept. See also **pre-Columbian architecture.**

prehistory The time before written records were kept in a locality or a society; may be the same as **precontact.** See also **protohistoric.**

premises A particular piece of **real estate,** including the land and all of the structures on it.

presbytery, presbyterium The space in a church between the altar and the apse or, in a large church, between the altar and the choir; typically raised to be visible from the nave.

preservation **1.** The protection of a material from physical deterioration or disintegration because of natural elements or human activity by various technical, scientific, and craft techniques; includes use of a **preservative,** as well as **maintenance, stabilization,** and **conservation.** **2.** (20c) The process of protection and enhancement of historic and heritage sites, structures, buildings, and objects through a broad range of physical and intellectual methods, including **conservation, interpretation, maintenance, reconstruction, restoration,** and **stabilization,** as well as legal, financial, political, and educational means. See also **heritage conservation, historic preservation.** **3.** (late 20c) "The act or process of applying measures to sustain the existing form, integrity, and material of a building or structure, and the existing form and vegetative cover of a site" (**Secretary of the Interior's Standards for Rehabilitation**).

Preservation Action (U.S.) A private national organization formed in 1974 to lobby for preservation.

preservation architect Same as **historical architect.**

Preservation Assistance Division An office of the U.S. National Park Service that provides technical services on preservation projects; oversees the investment tax credit program.

preservation commission An appointed local legislative body that administers preservation ordinances; typically adopts **design guidelines,** establishes historic districts, and places sites on a **register of historic places;** may also act as an **architectural review board.** Also known in Canada as **heritage commission.**

preservation easement A deed restriction on a property that limits future development in order to preserve all or a portion of its present appearance and/or use; may apply to any type of real estate, including a building, structure, garden, or landscape; typically given or sold by the owner of a property to a preservation organization. Also known in Canada as **heritage covenant.** See also **easement, facade easement.**

preservationist Anyone involved in promoting preservation (sense 2); may be a professional or layperson, a volunteer or someone employed in the field.

preservation planning A series of activities that develop goals, priorities, and strategies for identification, evaluation, registration, and protection of historic properties; often includes **planning** (sense 1).

preservative A coating or infusion used with a material to retard corrosion or rot; types include **paint, pressure treated, varnish.**

presidio A Spanish Colonial fort or outpost.

press See **cotton press, prize house.**

pressed brick A brick that has been hydraulically pressed while partially dry to create a dense, uniformly shaped unit; may have a smooth or ornamented face.

pressed glass Glass cast in a sharp-edged mold; used for pavement lights.

press-molded tile Ceramic tile manufactured by molding clay dust under pressure.

pressure grouting The process of pumping **grout** into voids below or within a structure; used to stabilize rubble masonry and concrete slabs-on-grade; variations include **mud jacking.**

pressure regulator A valve that automatically reduces the pressure of gas or water supplied to a building by a main.

pressure treated Wood injected with preservative chemicals (such as chromated copper arsenic) under high pressure; treatment retards rot. See also **wood preservative.**

pressure washing Cleaning a surface by spraying it with a pressurized stream of water; various cleaning agents may be added to the water. Also known as **power washing.** See also **blast cleaning.**

prestressed concrete **Reinforced concrete** with embedded high-strength steel cables in tension so that all of the concrete is in compression when loaded; used most often for beams and slabs.

preventive maintenance Regular, **cyclical maintenance** designed to prevent deterioration, as opposed to **repair** of perceived damage or loss.

pricked candlestick A candlestick with a **pricket.**

pricket A vertical, pointed spike that supports a candle. See also **pricked candlestick.**

pricking A process used to copy a drawing or design by pushing a needle through the original sheet to the surface below.

pricking up (pre-WWI) Same as **scratch coat.**

prickly spruce Same as **blue spruce.**

prick post **1.** (pre-WWI New England) A secondary or intermediate post, especially one between the corner posts of an end wall in a **timber frame** building. **2.** A side post of a roof truss, especially a **queenpost.**

primary research **Historical research** that relies on **primary source** documents such as personal letters, diaries, deeds, and the like, as opposed to research that relies on secondary sources such as published works. See also **oral history.**

primary source A **document,** photograph, or other material that dates from the historic period being investigated.

prime coat, primer coat The first coat of paint, used between old paint and new paint and to seal and bond the surface in preparation for the finish coats.

primer Any type of **paint** used for the **prime coat;** typically has more binder and less pigment than topcoat paint; types for metal include **red lead paint, red oxide paint, roofer's red, zinc chromate paint.**

princess A roofing slate that is 24 × 14 inches.

Princess Anne (regional) A less robust version of the **Queen Anne style** found in the vicinity of Louisville, Kentucky.

princess post A **post** in a triangular truss between a **queenpost** and the outside end; smaller than queenpost. See also **prick post.**

principal **1.** A term that designates one of the main members in a structural framework, as opposed to a subordinate member; types include **principal beam, principal brace, principal joist, principal post, principal rafter.** **2.** One of the ornaments that crown a canopy corner post.

principal beam A beam lying on top of a series of columns; sometimes the same as an **architrave.**

principal brace, principal sway brace A brace that stiffens a principal rafter, especially the diagonal strut between a vertical support and a tie beam.

principal building The main or most important building on a site, as opposed to an **accessory building** or **outbuilding.**

principal joist (pre-19c) A **girder** that supports a series of joists.

principal post A **corner post** of a **timber frame** building.

principal purlin A single large **purlin** spanning between two principal rafters of a **timber frame** roof and supporting several common rafters; typically located midway between the wall plate and the ridge. See also **common purlin**

principal rafter One of a pair of large rafters that extends from the wall plate to the ridge and supports one or more purlins; tenoned into the tie beam at the foot; often aligned with a supporting post or column. Also known as **blade.** See also **common rafter, main couple, principal roof.**

principal roof A roof frame with principal rafters, especially with a tie beam that forms a truss (e.g., a **king truss** or **queen truss**). Also known as **girt roof.**

prism **1.** A faceted piece of transparent material, such as glass or quartz, that refracts light into its component colors. **2.** A geometric solid with regular polygons for its ends and parallelogram sides connecting the ends. **3.** The straight portion of a civil engineering work, such as a canal or railroad cut, with a cross section in the form of a parallelepiped. See also **profile.**

prismatic glass Sheet glass with horizontal, triangular ribs that refract light; common in 19c–mid-20c industrial construction to direct light to interior spaces; also used for 19c residential skylights.

prism light **1.** A piece of glass cast in the shape of a pyramidal prism for use in a **pavement light;** types include **Hyatt light, Luxfer prism.** **2.** A window with **prismatic glass** glazing.

prison **1.** (late 17c–present) Any place used to confine or seclude persons involuntarily, including for punishment or reformation; types include **gaol, jail, penitentiary, reformatory, workhouse.** **2.** (20c) A public building used for confinement of convicted criminals; typically refers to a place used for long-term imprisonment, as opposed to a **jail.**

prison house (early 19c) Same as **prison** (sense 2).

prison rustic work Rusticated stone with a deeply pitted surface; used to give the appearance of rugged strength.

privy **1.** (18c–present) A **latrine** building. **2.** (pre-WWI) A private place (e.g., a **privy chamber**).

prize house (pre-20c U.S.) A building in which tobacco is compacted into hogsheads by use of a press known as a **prize;** this practice was generally abandoned by growers by 1860 because it was believed to be harmful to the leaves.

prize shed (19c U.S.) A small **prize house** attached to a tobacco warehouse.

processed shake A sawn wood shingle that has been textured on the exposed face to look like a split **shake;** typically of **western red cedar.**

profile **1.** The outline of a cross section of a building element, such as a molding. **2.** (pre-WWI) Same as **section.** **3.** A drawing of a cross section of the ground surface or a longitudinal section of a civil engineering work, such as a sewer line; typically with an exaggerated vertical scale. See also **prism.**

pro forma A summary of an economic analysis of the costs and value of a proposed real estate development; typically includes **land costs, hard costs, soft costs, equity,** and sales price or amount of the permanent financing. See also **life-cycle costing.**

program A written document that defines the intended functions and contemporary uses of a building, structure, or site; used to initiate an **architectural design** or **preservation** project.

Programmatic Agreement (PA) A method for fulfilling a U.S. federal agency's responsibilities under **Section 106** of the **NHPA,** using a single agreement establishing a compliance process for a large or complex project or for a series of similar undertakings that would otherwise require several individual requests for comments; most commonly used when: (1) effects on historic properties are similar and repetitive or are multistate or national in scope; (2) effects on historic properties cannot be fully determined in advance; (3) nonfederal parties, such as grantees or permit applicants, are delegated major decision-making responsibilities; (4) regional plans or land management plans are being developed; and (5) ongoing routine management activities at federal installations are required.

projecting angle Same as **salient angle.**

projecting table Same as **raised table.**

projection, (18c) **projecture** **1.** A drawing with a point-to-point correspondence with a three-dimensional form; **orthographic projection** is the most commonly used type in architecture. **2.** The extension of a molding or other architectural feature past the main surface of a wall or column.

promenade A place for strolling, such as a mall, sidewalk, terrace, or colonnade.

property **1.** Same as **real estate.** Also known as **real property.** **2.** An area of land containing a single historic resource or a group of resources; for purposes of the National Register, constitutes a single entry.

property management The process of managing **real estate,** including leasing and accounting and **maintenance** activities. See also **development.**

property type For purposes of a National Register **nomination,** a grouping of properties defined by common physical and associative attributes, such as buildings with the same architectural style or method of construction.

proportion The relationship of the size, shape, and location of one building element to all the other elements; each architectural style typically has its own rules of proportion. See also **classical orders, module.**

proposal A written offer from a contractor to perform work and/or supply materials; typically describes the extent of the work and its cost.

propylon A freestanding monumental gateway located in front of the main structure.

proscenium **1.** The portion of a theater stage between the drop curtain and the orchestra, typically including the **proscenium arch;** often projects forward into the orchestra pit; from the ancient Greek term for the stage in front of the wall that formed a background for the actors. See also **proscenium wall.** **2.** Abbr. for **proscenium box.**

proscenium arch **1.** The large opening in a **proscenium wall** that surrounds the stage and through which the audience views it; may be rectangular or shaped like an arch. **2.** An arch above such an opening; typically a relieving arch above an iron beam.

proscenium box A theater **box** near the proscenium arch. Also known as **side box, stage box.**

proscenium wall In a theater, a wall that separates backstage areas from the seating areas and surrounds the **proscenium arch;** typically constructed of a fire-resistant material such as masonry. See also **proscenium.**

prospect **1.** An extended view, especially from a high elevation. **2.** A picture of an exterior view, such as a perspective drawing or landscape. **3.** The facade of a building that faces a particular direction (e.g., the **west prospect**).

prostyle A **classical style** building with a projecting front portico having columns across its entire width (as opposed to **in antis**) but no columns at the side or rear. See also **amphiprostyle, columniation, pseudoprostyle.**

Protean stone A cast stone made from gypsum and resembling alabaster, popular in the 19c.

protected site A historic or prehistoric site that is protected by such physical means as fencing or by stabilization to prevent further deterioration.

prothesis A chapel in a Greek Orthodox church used for consecration of the Eucharist; usually adjacent to the nave, on the north side of the **bema.**

Protimeter A brand name for an electrical resistivity type moisture meter.

protohistorical The **postcontact** period in a locality before written records are kept.

protomai capital A column capital with carved animals or other figures projecting from each of four corners.

prototype Same as **original** (sense 1).

proud Projecting forward from the main surface.

provenance [French] The origin or source of a material or element, or the place where it is found. Also known as **provenience.**

provenience **1.** The exact location of a **cultural artifact** at an **archaeological site** as defined by a set of vertical and horizontal coordinates. **2.** (19c–present) Same as **provenance.**

prudent See **feasible and prudent.**

Prussian blue A transparent, deep blue paint **pigment** composed of any of several cyanogen compounds, especially ferric ferrocyanide [$Fe_4(Fe(CN)_6)_3$]; may have a purple, bronze, or green tinge; the earliest synthetic pigment, invented in Berlin, Germany, ca. 1704 by Diesbach and manufactured commercially by mid-18c; used for tinting interior paints or glazes. Also known as **Antwerp blue, Berlin blue, Chinese blue, ferrocyanide blue, Paris blue.**

pseudodipteral **1.** A **classical style** building with a double row of columns at the portico and a single row of columns at the sides; the rear may be a single or double row. **2.** A **classical style** building with the plan in the form of a dipteral building with the inner row of columns removed to provide a wide walkway between the columns and the wall of the building. See also **columniation.**

pseudoperipteral, pseudo-peripteral A **classical style** building surrounded with freestanding columns across the portico and engaged columns at the side walls. See also **columniation, peripteral.**

pseudoprostyle, pseudo-prostyle A **classical style** building in which the columns along the front portico are separated from the wall behind by less than a normal intercolumniation or are actually engaged in the wall. See also **columniation, prostyle.**

psychrometer An instrument used to measure relative humidity.

pteroma **1.** The space between the columns and the wall of a **classical style** building, especially along the sides of the building. **2.** A side wall of a **classical style** building.

pteron **1.** A side of a Greek **classical style** building; may be formed by a row of columns or a wall. **2.** Same as **portico.**

P-trap A plumbing drain trap that resembles the shape of the letter *P;* the vertical sink outflow pipe has a wide semicircular bend at the bottom that forms the trap and then a tight quarter bend to the horizontal outflow pipe; the most common form of trap in the 20c. Also known as **half S-trap.**

P-trap

public archaeology The **presentation** and **interpretation** of an **archaeological site** to the public while work is in progress.

Public Buildings Cooperative Use Act U.S. federal legislation passed in 1976 that allows and encourages nonfederal uses within federal buildings, and restoration and/or adaptive use of U.S.-owned historic buildings.

public garden (18c–19c) An urban **garden** for paying customers where refreshments are sold and amusements are held.

public house, (pre-20c) **publick house** Same as **tavern.**

public notice Notification via a local newspaper or by posting in a public place.

public participation The process whereby property owners, public officials, and the public have the opportunity to express their opinions before a decision is made, such as nominating or listing a property in the National Register; includes mailing notices to affected parties.

pudding stone A **conglomerate** stone composed of water-rounded rocks and pebbles cemented together. See also **breccia.**

puddle steel (pre-WWII) Steel made by stopping the **puddling** process in a furnace before oxidation produces **wrought iron.** Also known as **weld steel.**

puddling **1.** The process of making **wrought iron** from **pig iron** in a puddling furnace. **2.** The process of filling a cavity or lining a canal with clay to prevent water infiltration; sometimes mixed with sand; used behind retaining walls or sheet piling.

Puebla tile Polychromed wall tile with geometric patterns manufactured in the Puebla region of Mexico.

pueblo **1.** A communal dwelling of the Pueblo peoples of southwestern U.S. and northern Mexico; may be a cliff dwelling or a multistoried dwelling constructed of adobe or stone; characterized by a flat roof supported on vigas, a **kiva,** and originally, without openings on the lowest level. **2.** Any town or settlement of Native Americans or Spanish Americans in Latin America. **3.** The community of those who dwell in a **pueblo** (senses 1 and 2).

Pueblo Revival style A 20c architectural style loosely based on the **adobe** pueblos of the southwestern U.S.; used mostly for detached houses; typical elements include irregular massing with one or two stories, flat roofs, stucco walls with projecting vigas (real or imitation), and rounded parapets and corners; may be made of adobe or another masonry material. See also **Mission style, Spanish Colonial Revival.**

Pueblo sandstone A gray, soft, fine-grained sandstone with white and gray veining quarried in the vicinity of Turkey Creek, Colorado.

pugging Materials placed within wall or floor cavities to provide sound insulation and/or fireproofing; types of materials include coarse mortar, brown coat plaster, clay, and a mixture of sawdust and plaster; most commonly placed on boards spanning between floor joists.

pug pile A wood **sheet pile** with a dovetail-shaped tongue and groove joining adjacent piles.

pull See **door pull.**

pull box A large **electric box** with an access cover at the junction of two or more conduits; used to provide access for pulling and splicing electrical cables; typically made of heavy sheet metal.

pulley box, pulley case Same as **sash pocket.**

pulley mortise A mortise in a **pulley stile** for mounting a metal pulley; the mortise is in the form of an elongated hole through the stile, with shallow mortises at each end; the bottom mortise may be sloped to accommodate the pulley rope.

pulley stile, pulley style The board at the side of a double-hung window on which the pulleys for counterweights are mounted. See also **cased frame, pulley box.**

pulvinar The rounded side of an Ionic capital, formed by the ends of both scrolls.

pulvinated A building element that bows outward, especially the frieze of a **classical style** entablature. Also known as **pillow work.** See also **belly, bombé.**

pumping station A facility that pumps water, oil, or other fluid through a pipeline.

punch Abbr. of **puncheon.**

punched work Same as **pounced work.**

puncheon, (18c) **punchion, punchin,** (17c) **punchen** **1.** (pre-WWI) A short, vertical, framing timber, such as a squat queenpost or a short stud. See also **stanchion. 2.** (pre-20c) A vertical timber between two posts, added to help support the weight; typically shorter and thinner than the posts and fastened with iron hardware. **3.** (pre-20c) A wood post directly under a roof ridge. **4.** A split and hewn plank used as a floorboard in a log cabin; typically of 2-inch oak notched at the ends so that the planks lap the floor beams. **5.** (pre-19c) Same as **pale** (sense 1).

Purbeck stone A buff to gray, hard limestone with many fossils; imported to North America during the 18c from the Isle of Purbeck in England; used mainly for paving and hearthstones.

purfled Having elaborate edge decoration similar to lace, especially delicate wood or stone carving.

purlin, (19c) **perling** A horizontal beam in a roof structure that supports the **common rafters** or **subpurlins;** typically spans between **principal rafters** or parallel roof trusses. Also known as **side timber, side waver.** See also **common purlin, purlin plate.**

purlin brace In a timber framed structure, the diagonal strut extending from a roof truss to support and stiffen a purlin.

purlin girt One of the two horizontal members of an end bent of a **timber frame** building between the **purlin beam** and the **main beam.**

purlin plate A roof beam that supports the rafters between the ridge and the main plate of a **timber frame** building; supports the top of the lower set of rafters and the foot of the upper set in a curb roof. See also **deck plate, purlin post.**

purlin post **1.** A vertical element in a roof truss immediately below a purlin. **2.** One of a pair of posts that support a **purlin plate** at each bent of a **timber frame** building.

push button An electrical switch operated by pushing a button; may be a single button (e.g., for a bell) or a double button (for a light switch).

push plate A thin, protective sheet placed on a door where it is pushed in opening; typically metal or glass with various finishes, including porcelain-glazed metal. See also **hand plate.**

putlog hole, (18c) **putlock hole** An opening left in a masonry wall in order to support horizontal members in a scaffolding; after the scaffolding is removed, the holes usually are filled to match the wall.

putty **1.** A semisolid material used to caulk window panes; often composed of whiting and linseed oil, sometimes with white lead. Also known as **glazing compound.** **2.** Any of various mixtures used to fill holes in a surface before painting, including **plasterer's putty, Swedish putty.** See also **filler.**

putty joint A **pipe joint** sealed with putty, muslin cloth, and twine.

PVC Abbr. for **polyvinyl chloride.**

PVC pipe **Pipe** manufactured from **polyvinyl chloride;** typically .5–12 inches in diameter and connected by solvent in hub joints; commonly used for **drainpipe, vent pipe,** and **water pipe** beginning in the second half of the 20c.

pycnostyle Column spacing in a **classical style** building that is less than normal; typically 1 or 1.5 column diameters. See also **intercolumniation.**

pyramid **1.** A steep, stone-covered earth mound approximating a four-sided pyramid form built by pre-Columbian civilizations in Mexico and Central America; typically with steps leading to a small temple on top. See also **mound.** **2.** A four-sided pyramid form constructed of solid masonry, especially those built of stone in ancient Egypt. **3.** A three-dimensional geometric shape consisting of a polygonal base with faceted sides rising to a point; although usually with a square base, other architectural forms range from three to eight sides. See also **obelisk.**

pyramidion The pyramid-shaped apex of an obelisk or similar feature.

pyramid roof, pyramidal roof A hipped roof with four equal sides that meet in a point at the top. Also known as **pigeon roof.**

Pyrobar roof tile Trade name for reinforced gypsum roof decking product manufactured by U.S. Gypsum during the first half of the 20c; the short-span type has nominal dimensions of 3 × 12 × 30 or 4 × 12 × 30 inches, while the long-span type is 5 × 18 or 6 × 18 inches by up to 24 feet in length; the 3-inch type is solid, while the others have four horizontal core holes running the length of the block; the short-span types are sometimes used on edge for solid plastered partitions.

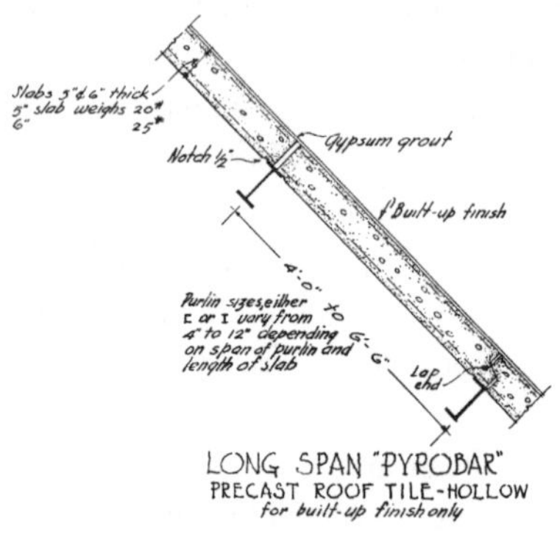

Pyrobar roof tile

qarmang Same as **karmang.**

quad Same as **quadrangle** (sense 1).

quadra **1.** A square border or frame enclosing a wall panel or painting, sometimes incorrectly used to refer to borders of other shapes. **2.** A square base or **plinth** at the bottom of a pedestal or podium. **3.** A decorative flat **band** or **fillet,** especially above and below the **scotia** of an **attic base.**

quadrangle **1.** A four-sided open space, most often square or rectangular in plan, formed by the enclosing walls of surrounding buildings, or sometimes the buildings themselves; typically refers to an institutional setting such as college or government buildings. Also known as **quad.** **2.** Any closed geometric figure with four straight sides and four angles; shapes include rectangle, square, trapezoid. **3.** A block of stone with quadrangular faces.

quadrangular truss (19c–present) A **truss** with multiple-braced four-sided panels; top and bottom chords may be inclined upward towards the center of the truss to form a shallow chevron shape; used for roofs and bridges; types include **single quadrangular truss, double quadrangular truss.**

quadratura (17c–18c) Trompe l'oeil perspective paintings on walls and ceilings of architectural scenes.

quadrel (pre-20c) A square brick, tile, or stone, especially an 18c whitish, air dried brick made of chalky earth.

quadrifrons A symmetrical classical style building with four identical faces.

quadripartite Composed of four sections, such as a **quadripartite vault.**

quadripartite vault A vault formed by four intersecting vault surfaces; typically used to cover square or rectangular spaces, types include **cloistered vault, groined vault, Welsh vault.**

quadro A four unit residential building in which each family occupies one corner of the structure.

quaint **1.** A romantically antique or old-fashioned style; a popular term during the Aesthetic Movement in the late 19c to refer to English style cottages and Queen Anne style houses. **2.** (pre-19c) Elaborately fashioned or ornamental.

Quaker shingle An unusually thick **shingle** used in Pennsylvania; typically .75 inch thick at the butt, 4 inches wide, and 26 inches long.

qualified rehabilitation expenditures Capital expenditures for the **substantial rehabilitation** of a building in an **investment tax credit** project; excludes acquisition costs, building enlargement costs, and routine maintenance costs.

quantity surveyor A professional who determines the amount of materials required for construction from drawings prepared by an architect; mostly found in British Commonwealth nations, such as Canada.

quarl pane Same as **quarrel.**

quarrel, (18c) **quarrey** A small, diamond-shaped element such as a window pane, mosaic tile or stone block, especially a diamond pane in a lattice window; may be square or lozenge-shaped; derived from the name for the four-sided head of a crossbow bolt. Also known as **quarl pane, quarry.**

quarry **1.** A pattern formed by a quadrilateral grid, or the individual four-sided elements of the grid, such as a tile. Also known as **quarrel.** **2.** A squared stone. Also known as **quarrel.** **3.** An open pit or shaft where stone is mined, usually by splitting the stone from its bed. **4.** Same as **quarrel.**

quarry bed Same as **bed** (sense 4).

quarry cut The roughly hewn finish of a stone block, indicating the block is cut to approximate size and shape, and has pick- or saw-marked faces. See also **dabbed, rough ashlar, rough pointed, squared stone, stonework.**

quarry faced **1.** A rough surface texture on the exposed face of a block of ashlar; typically with tooled margins. See also **pitch face.** **2.** The rough finish on the surface of stone as it has been split from its bed in the quarry. Also known as **rock face.** See also **quarry cut, split face.** **3.** **Stonework** masonry built of rough surfaced stones.

quarry sap The groundwater that is naturally present in stone at the time of quarrying. Also known as **quarry water.** See also **seasoned stone.**

quarry stone bond **Rubble masonry** composed of **quarry cut** stone blocks.

quarry tile A dense, unglazed, ceramic tile, commonly 6 × 6 × .5 inches, most often used for floors.

quarry water Same as **quarry sap.**

quarter **1.** (pre-20c) Same as **stud;** originally the standard size of a **single quarter** was 2 × 4 inches and a **double quarter** was 4 × 4 inches. See also **quarter partition.** **2.** A square panel, or tracery opening, divided by four cusps. See also **quatrefoil.** **3.** (pre-20c southern U.S.) The dwelling or group of dwellings where slaves and/or indentured servants and their families lived; most often a single-pen log cabin; may also refer to the area where these dwellings are located and/or the part of a plantation where these residents worked. Also known as **field quarter, negro house, negro quarter, quarters house, slave cabin, slave quarter.** See also **quartering house, quarters, servant's quarters.** **4.** (pre-19c Chesapeake region) One of several farms on a single tract of land, especially when subdivided from a large holding. **5.** One of the geographic divisions of a locality, such as the **French quarter** of New Orleans. **6.** Abbreviation of **quarter section.**

quarter bend A pipe **elbow** that makes a 90-degree turn. See also **sanitary bend.**

quarter cleft, quarter-cleft A log which has been split lengthwise into four equal pieces. See also **quarter sawn.**

quarter closer A stretcher **brick** cut to one fourth of its length and used to complete a course that does not have an even number of full stretchers. See also **king closer, queen closer.**

quarter cut Same as **quarter sawn.**

quartered Split or sawn into four equal parts. See also **quarter cleft, quarter sawn.**

quarterfoil Any architectural ornament or opening divided into four lobes or leaves. See also **quatrefoil.**

quarter grain **1.** A distinctive **grain** pattern found in some woods, especially oak, when they are quarter sawn; prominent medullary rays produce distinctive ripples across the **edge grain.** **2.** The radial grain of a tree. Also known as **bastard grain, silver grain.**

quarter head Same as **bill brad.**

quarter hollow A concave part of a molding in the shape of a quarter circle. Also known as **cavetto.**

quartering (pre-20c) The process of installing studs, or sometimes the wall itself.

quartering house (17c Chesapeake region) An outbuilding used as a dwelling by servants. See also **quarter.**

quarter line (Western U.S.) The original survey line defining a **quarter section** of government land.

quarter-notch The removed inside top quarter of a squared log that receives the floor beams of a log cabin.

quarterpace, quarter pace A square landing at a 90-degree turn between two flights of a stair. See also **quarterpace stair.**

quarterpace stair, quarter pace stair A stair with an L-shaped plan and a **quarterpace** landing at the turn. See also **quarter turn stair.**

quarter partition A **stud** wall. See also **quarter.**

quarter pitch A roof angle where the rise of a gable roof equals one quarter of the span, creating an angle of approximately 26.5 degrees.

quarter plate, ¼ plate A **ribband** that is notched into the studs one quarter of their width; typically a 1 × 5 let into a series of 2 × 4s.

quarter round, (20c) **quarter-round** A convex molding that is exactly, or approximately, a quarter circle in cross section. Also known as **ovolo, Roman ovolo, Vitruvius echinus.** See also **quarter hollow.**

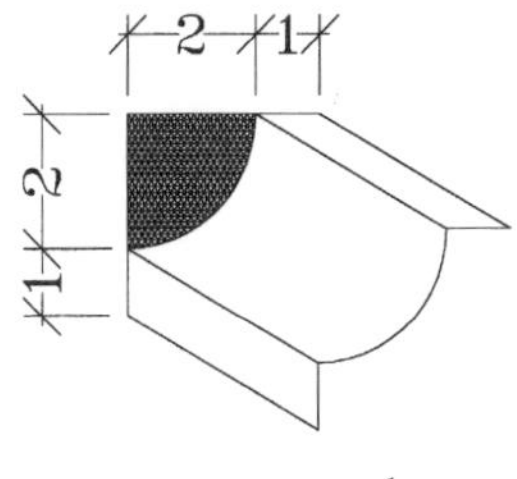

quarter round

quarter round window A window opening in the form of a quarter of a circle, with one of the straight sides horizontal; commonly found in Federal and Greek Revival style houses.

quarters **1.** The housing provided for soldiers or sailors, especially officers. **2.** Same as **quarter** (sense 3). See also **servants quarters.**

quarter sawn, quarter-sawn, quarter-sawed Boards produced by sawing a log lengthwise into four equal sections and then sawing each section into slices that are approximately radial to the original center of the log; produces boards with reduced likelihood of warping, and in some woods, such as oak, a distinctive grain pattern by exposing the medullary rays; there are several alternate ways of sawing the quarter sections into individual boards. Also known as **quarter cut.** See also **edge grain, plain sawn, quarter sliced, rift cut, silver grain, vertical grain.**

quarter section A tract of land that is .5 mile square and encloses 160 acres, one quarter of a full **section;** the standard size of a farmstead in portions of the western U.S. and Canada surveyed by the government. See also **Homestead Act.**

quarters house A dwelling in a **quarter** (sense 3).

quarter sliced veneer Wood **veneer** produced by slicing thin flitches diagonally across one quarter of a log. See also **quarter sawn.**

quarter stuff (pre-20c) Boards that are .25 inch thick.

quarter timber (pre-20c) Same as **stud.**

quarter turn stair, quarter-turn stair A **stair** with two flights and an L-shaped plan; may have **winders,** or a **quarterpace** landing, at the turn.

quarter winding A **stair** having continuous winders with a flattened S-shaped plan composed of two quarter circles.

quartz Silicon dioxide, the major ingredient of **sand** and many stones; colorless in its pure form, but frequently colored by trace impurities in nature.

quartzite A very hard, white quartz, nonporous arenite **sandstone,** with the sand grains completely cemented by silica; used as **building stone.**

quaternary ammonium compounds Chemical solutions, such as benzalkonium chloride, used to kill algae growths on buildings.

quatrefoil An architectural motif composed of four leaves in a radial pattern; typically refers to an opening for a window; in tracery, in the form of four intersecting circles; frequently found in **Gothic Revival style** architecture. Also known as **cross quarters.** See also **quarterfoil.**

quattro-cento In the style of the early Italian Renaissance during the 15c; from the Italian for "400," indicating the dates starting with the number 14, 1400 to 1499.

quay A solid structure for loading and unloading boats that is parallel to the shore line; most often of masonry construction, with a vertical or battered retaining wall and a paved top surface.

Quebec style A vernacular architectural style found largely in Quebec, eastern Ontario, and areas of the Maritime provinces; examples begin 17c and concentrate primarily late 18c–early 19c; typical elements include steeply pitched, tall, gable roofs over plain, thick masonry walls, widely spaced multipaned casement windows and dormers, with bell curve scrollwork at the base of the dormers; beginning late 18c facades tend to be classically symmetrical. Pre-1760 examples also known as **French Regime.**

Queen Anne arch An **arch** with a semicircular center flanked by flat wings; used in the **Palladian motif.**

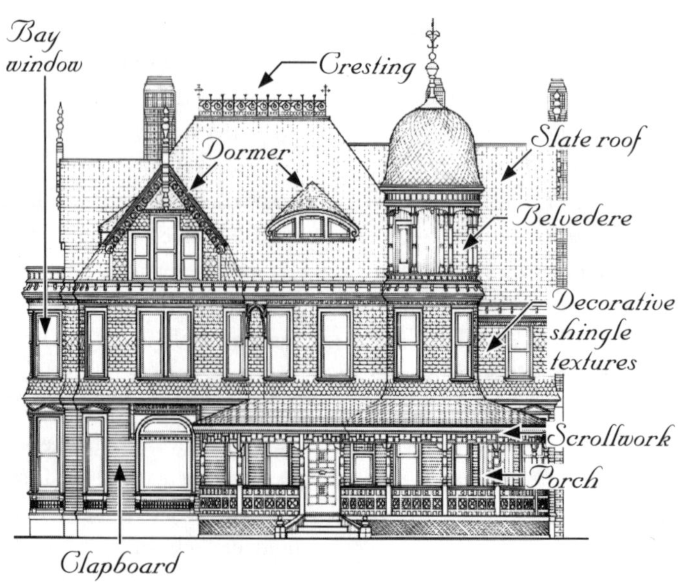

Queen Anne style
Long-Waterman House
San Diego, California, ca. 1889

Queen Anne style **1.** The architectural style prevalent in early 18c England during the reign of Queen Anne (1702–1714); typical elements include red brick exteriors with integral relief sculpture, stone parapets and sills, white painted trim, and asymmetrical massing. **2.** An architectural style prevalent in late 19c Britain and North America that featured a romantic reinterpretation of the earlier Queen Anne style; incorporates details and elements of many other styles, such as Flemish, Romanesque, Adam Style, and Second Empire; interiors have large doorways connecting public spaces and often feature a **living hall;** typical elements include robust, busy, asymmetrical exteriors, often with contrasting materials and/or textures between levels; gabled, hipped or mansard roofs, dormers, scrollwork brackets, and trim, porches, bay and oriel windows, turrets, and exuberant carving; British examples most often feature red brick exteriors with molded brick details, slate roofs, white, small paned windows, and sunflower motif decoration; U.S. and Canadian examples also include exuberant wood shingle, stone, stucco, and clapboard buildings with bold multicolor schemes. See also **Aesthetic movement, Eastlake style, Princess Anne.**

queen bolt A tension rod that replaces a **queenpost.**

queen closer **1.** A stretcher **brick** cut to less than one half length and used to complete a course which does not have an even number of full stretchers. See also **king closer, quarter closer.** **2.** A brick cut so as to have a nominal 2-inch horizontal face dimension.

queenpost One of the two vertical **hanging post** framing members in a **queen-post truss** framing system. See also **queen bolt.**

queen-post truss A triangular **truss** with two vertical **queenposts** forming both sides of a central rectangle; first used in wood roof framing, later in iron and steel bridges; components include **principal rafters, queenposts, straining beam, tie beam,** and sometimes **princess post, straining sill, struts.** Also known as **queen truss.**

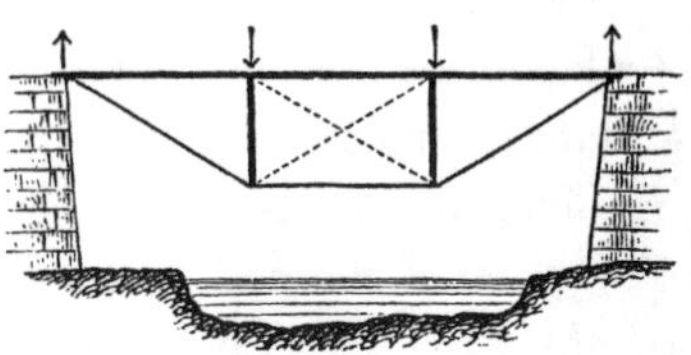
queen-post truss

queen rafter A **truss beam** rafter in the form of a shallow triangular truss composed of 2× lumber, with a short center post.

queen's metal An alloy similar to pewter composed of tin, antimony, zinc, and lead or copper; used for decorative work.

queen truss Same as **queen-post truss.**

quernal An ornamental figure formed of oak leaves.

quicklime Calcium oxide (CaO) or **lime,** produced by heating limestone or shells until they are reduced to powder. See also **hydrated lime, slaked lime.**

quicksilver **1.** The elemental metal mercury **2.** To coat glass with an alloy of mercury and tin to make a mirror. See also **quicksilver water.**

quicksilver water, quick water A mercury nitrate solution used for **gilding.**

quill (pre-20c) A small water pipe or faucet.

quilled Shaped like bundled quills, or fluted. See also **barley twist, reed mold.**

Quimby process A concrete forming and finishing system that uses boards equal in width to the height of each lift of concrete placed; each board has triangular strips of wood nailed to the edges to form a reveal between abutting boards; common in Philadelphia in the early 20c.

quincunx A geometric pattern of five objects, with one in each corner and one in the center of a square. See also **quincunxial arrangement.**

quincunxial arrangement A series of quincunxes located at the intersections of a diagonal grid; used for landscape plantings and mosaics.

Quincy granite A medium gray to dark bluish gray, medium- to coarse-textured hornblende pyroxene **granite** quarried in the vicinity of Quincy, Massachusetts; polishes to a high gloss; used for **building stone,** including King's Chapel and the U.S. Court and Custom House, Boston.

quinquepartite vault A **rib vault** formed by the intersection of five curved vault surfaces; typically used to cover a pentagonal, semicircular, or trapezoidal space.

quintefoil Same as **cinquefoil.**

quirk **1.** A V-shaped or rectangular groove that separates the other shapes of a molding. **2.** A piece removed from the complete geometric shape of a plot of ground or a room, especially a notch at a corner.

quirk bead A **molding** with a round cross section separated from adjoining surfaces by one or two quirk grooves; types include **angle bead, flush bead.** See also **double-quirked bead.**

quirk bead

quirk joint A stonework **masonry joint** with beveled edges on the adjoining stone blocks. See also **rustic joint.**

quirk molding, quirk moulding (19c) Any molding with one or more quirks; typically used to define the edges of other molding shapes.

quoin **1.** A large, rectangular block of stone used to physically and aesthetically fix an outside corner of a building; typically in a toothed form with alternate quoins projecting and receding from the corner; used extensively in Renaissance style architecture, and in later periods the form is often reproduced in brick, wood, stucco, and other materials. Also known as **angle stone.** See also **rustic quoin.** **2.** A masonry unit at an exterior corner, such as a **quoin header.** See also **hollow quoin.** **3.** The exterior corner of a building. **4.** A wedge-shaped **voussoir** stone in an arch. **5.** A stone block with a sloped bottom used to support a column on a incline.

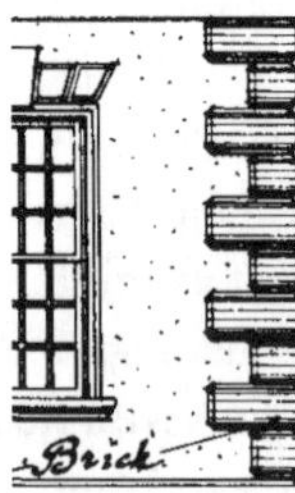

quoin (sense 1)

quoin header A masonry unit, such as a brick, located at a corner so that it is a header on one face and a stretcher on the other face.

Quonset hut A prefabricated structure in the form of a barrel vault with flat ends and composed of corrugated sheet steel reinforced with steel ribs and finished on the interior with fiberboard; developed in 1941 for the U.S. Defense Department as part of the build-up prior to World War II; the first Quonset huts were built at Fort Davis, Quonset, Rhode Island.

R

rabbet, (18c) **rabit** **1.** A continuous, rectangular notch, especially L-shaped and at, or near, the edge of a wood member; uses include the recess in a door jamb that forms the stop, jointing the edges of two boards, and the brick jamb recess that receives a window frame. **2.** A rectangular groove or slot cut in a piece of wood to receive another member, such as the slot in a door stile into which a panel is inserted. Also known as **rebate.** See also **dado, sticking.**

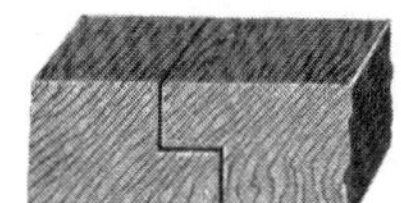

rabbet (sense 1)

rabbet bead A **bead molding** located at the inside corner of a rabbet. See also **flush bead, quirked bead.**

rabbet joint A carpentry **flush joint** with overlapped notched edges. See also **rabbet.**

rabit (18c) Same as **rabbet.**

raceway A rectangular enclosure for electric cables; typically made of heavy sheet metal. See also **conduit.**

rack An open framework that holds fodder, especially hay and straw, for cattle, horses, or sheep.

radial brick, radiating brick, radius brick Same as **arch brick** (sense 1).

radial sawn Same as **rift sawn.**

radiant heating A heating system that uses heat radiated from a finish surface, such as heating a concrete floor with below-grade pipes, or heating a ceiling panel by electric resistance.

radiator A hollow metal device that is supplied with hot water or steam by pipes to warm a space; typically cast iron or iron pipes through mid-20c; types include **pantry radiator.**

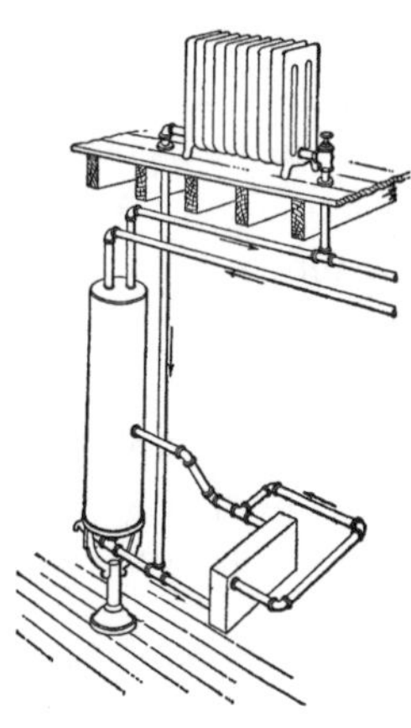

radiator

radiocarbon dating (20c) The scientific determination of the approximate age of a **cultural artifact** by analyzing the rate of decay of the radioactive element carbon 14; used to establish a range of possible origin dates of prehistoric organic materials.

radiograph An X-ray photograph; used to determine hidden construction.

radon A naturally occurring, invisible, odorless, radioactive gas formed by the decay of uranium in soil and rock; may be present in basements of existing buildings; decays rapidly but emits radioactive atomic particles (known as radon daughters) that can lodge in lung tissue. See also **alpha tracker.**

rafter **1.** One of a series of parallel, sloped, roof beams that support the sheathing or roof covering; types include **common rafter, hip rafter, jack rafter, principal rafter, valley rafter;** components may include **bird's mouth, foot, plumb cut, rafter tail, seat cut.** See also **purlin.** **2.** (19c) A regional term for a stud approximately 3 × 4 inches in cross section.

raftered house (17c Chesapeake region) A building without sidewalls so that the rafters rest directly on the ground; used for agricultural buildings.

rafter filling The continuation of a brick wall up between the rafter ends. Also known as **beam filling, wind filling.**

rafter tail The portion of a **rafter** that projects beyond the exterior wall to support the eaves; may also be a separate piece of lumber sistered to the actual rafter; types include **full tail, reduced tail.** Also known as **lookout.** See also **sally.**

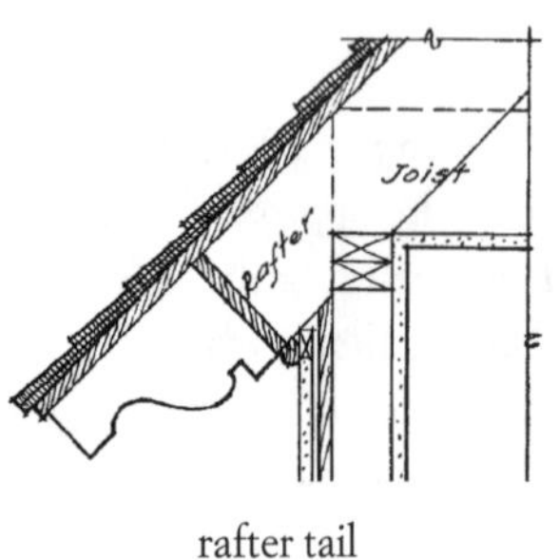

rafter tail

rag felt **Roofing felt** manufactured with cloth felt.

ragging **Marbleized** decorative painting with a surface glaze or paint that is partially removed with a roughly folded rag. See also **scumbling.**

raggle, raglet Same as **reglet.**

ragstone (pre-20c) Same as **flagstone.**

rag work Rough **stonework** masonry constructed with undressed flagstone or other flat stones.

rail **1.** A horizontal member of a **railing** or **fence;** may support vertical elements; may be wood or metal. See also **guard rail, rail post.** **2.** A **split rail** used as part of a **rail fence.** See also **rail cut.** **3.** A horizontal wood framing member of a door, sash, or wall paneling; types include **clamp rail, frieze rail, hanging rail, lock rail.** Also known as **impage.** See also **paneled door, stile.** **4.** One of a continuous pair of parallel iron or steel bars that form part of a **railroad track;** typically spiked to the cross ties; of various cross section shapes; types include **capped rail, flat rail.** **5.** The metal bar of a **railway** (sense 3).

rail bead A **cock bead** that projects from a flat surface and is not located at a reveal or corner.

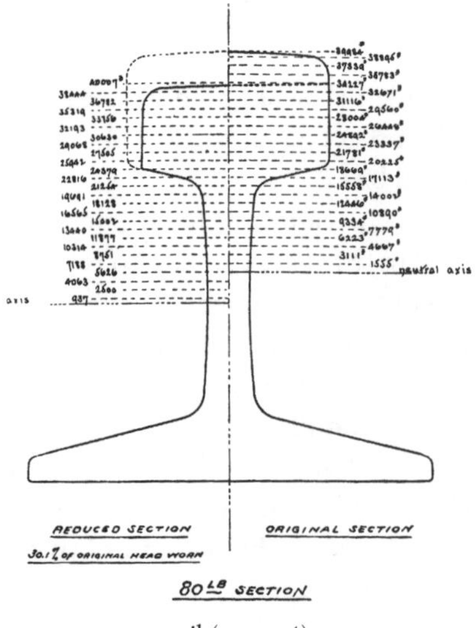

rail (sense 4)

rail fence A fence constructed of log rails; may have **split rails** or circular logs; types include **post-and-rail fence, worm fence.**

railing An openwork assembly at the edge of a balcony, stair or similar location to prevent someone from falling off it; typically constructed of a series of vertical posts supporting two or more horizontal rails; may also have vertical balusters between the rails; types include **guard rail, handrail.** See also **rail, balustrade.**

railing head A wrought-iron picket in the form of a square cross section split into four smaller squares and twisted into a spiral openwork decoration.

rail pen Same as **pen** (sense 2).

rail post, railing post **1.** Same as **baluster. 2.** Same as **newel post.**

railroad (19c–present) **1.** A system of transportation using vehicles rolling on **railroad track.** Also known as **railway. 2.** Same as **railroad track.**

railroad station (19c–present) The structure where a railroad train stops to load and unload passengers and/or freight; types range from a simple platform at grade to a large building with access to multiple, covered, raised platforms, including **depot, freight station, passenger station, terminal, train shed.**

railroad tie (19c–present) Same as **cross tie.**

railroad track (19c–present) A graded bed supporting two parallel rails connected to a series of cross ties, and forming a guide for the wheels of a railroad car or similar vehicle; includes the space between the rails plus at least 4 feet outside each rail; components include **ballast, cross tie, rail, spike.** Also known as **railway, track.** See also **crib, gauge.**

railway **1.** Same as **railroad. 2.** Same as **railroad track. 3.** Any metal track on which something rolls, such as a rolling crane in a manufacturing plant.

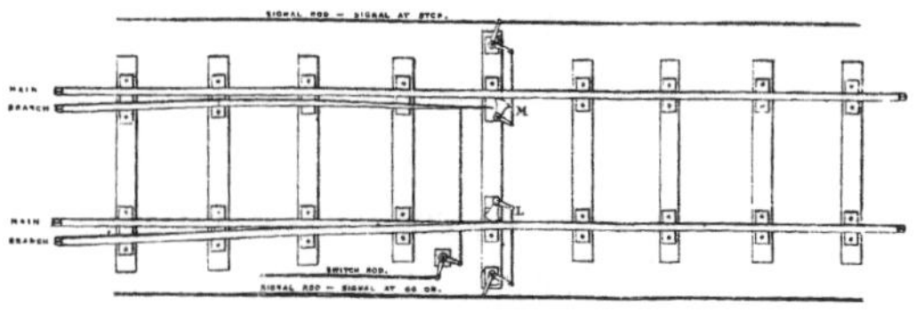
railroad track

rain bath (19c) An overhead **shower bath.**

rainbow roof A gabled roof with slightly convex, curved sides that approximate the semicircular shape of a rainbow.

rain leader A **leader** that carries stormwater away from a **conductor head, gutter,** or **roof drain,** especially when located in the interior of a building; typically of wrought or cast iron until the late 20c when PVC also became common. See also **downspout.**

rain water conductor (RWC) Same as **downspout.**

raised-field paneling Wood paneling with a series of **raised panels.**

raised girt A **timber frame** girt on an end wall with a top that is at the same level as the top of the floor beams. Also known as **flush girt.** See also **sunk girt.**

raised grain An uneven surface on cut wood with the harder summerwood above the softer springwood; caused by wetting and drying or erosion due to weathering.

raised mold, raised molding **1.** An applied door or paneling molding that overlaps the joint between the panel and the stiles and rails, and covers a portion of the stiles and rails. **2.** A mold that extends above the adjoining surface, such as a **bolection molding.**

raised panel A wood panel with beveled edges that fit into the sticking groove of the stiles and rails that surround it.

raised plan (19c) A building **section** or **elevation.**

raised skylight A skylight with the glazing frame supported on a curb above the roof surface.

raised table A **table** (sense 1) with a surface that is forward of the main wall surface; may have beveled edges adjacent to a raised molding frame. Also known as **projecting table.**

raiser (pre-WWI) Same as **riser.**

raising **1.** The process of lifting a timber frame bent, previously fabricated in a horizontal position, into the vertical position. **2.** The process of assembling the frame of a timber frame building by lifting and pushing the individual bents to an upright position and connecting them with girts and other timbers; typically requiring a large team of workers and consequently a social occasion as well; types include **barn raising, house raising.** Also known as **raising bee. 3.** The process of embossing sheet metal by hammering, stamping, or spinning. **4.** Same as **raising piece.**

raising bee Same as **raising** (sense 2).

raising hinge (18c) Same as **rising hinge.**

raising piece (pre-20c) A timber **top plate** that supports one or more beams or rafters on top of a brick or timber bearing wall. Also known as **raising.** See also **raising plate.**

raising plate (pre-WWI) **1.** Same as **raising piece. 2.** Same as **false plate.** See also **raising piece.**

raison (18c) Probably the same as **summer beam;** from the French for "reason."

raja One of a series of split pine logs that span between the vigas of an adobe building. See also **cedro, latia.**

rake The slope or **pitch** of a building element; especially a cornice, roof, or rafter.

rakeboard A sloped board or molding between an exterior wall and the roof soffit. Also known as **raking cornice, raked molding.**

raked A sloped or pitched surface, or a sloped element.

raked cornice, raking cornice **1.** The sloping cornice of a triangular pediment or gable end. Also known as **barge cornice.** See also **horizontal cornice. 2.** Same as **rakeboard.**

raked joint A recessed, tooled **mortar joint** with the flat face of the mortar parallel with the faces of the masonry units; made by scraping some of the mortar out of the joint after installing the bricks and mortar.

raked molding **1.** A molding with a sloped surface. **2.** Same as **raking molding. 3.** Same as **rakeboard.**

rake molding An angle-faced molding of various profiles with a flat back and top; often used as a **crown mold.** See also **raking molding, spring mold.**

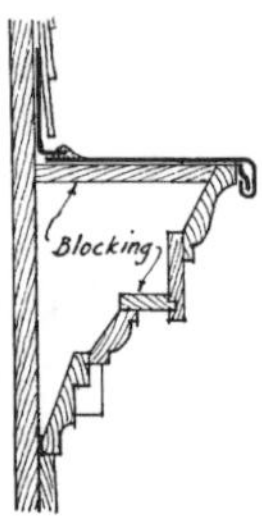

rake molding

raker A diagonal shoring brace. Also known as **raking shore.** See also **sheeting and shoring, wallpiece.**

raking arch Same as **rampant arch.**

raking bond A brick wall bond with the headers in a diagonal bond or herringbone bond pattern.

raking cornice Same as **raked cornice.**

raking molding Any molding installed on a slope, as opposed to being horizontal or vertical. See also **raked molding, rake molding.**

raking riser A slanted stair riser that slopes from the front of the tread above to the back of the tread below.

raking shore Same as **raker.**

raking table A **table** (sense 1) with a surface that is behind the plane of the main wall surface, with sloped edges; the edges are often molded. See also **projecting table.**

ram See **hydraulic ram.**

ramada An open-sided shelter with a thatched, pitched roof; often with palmetto thatching.

rammed earth See **earthen floor** or **pisé.**

ramp, (pre-20c) **rampe** **1.** A sloped surface that makes a transition between two different levels; includes a walking or driving surface. **2.** A sloped way on the interior of a fortification to the level immediately behind the parapet. See also **rampart.** **3.** A concave curve that makes a transition between a sloped and vertical portion of a handrail, such as a stair handrail that curves upward at the point where it joins the horizontal rail at an upper floor level or landing. Also known as **easement, easing.** See also **swan neck.**

ramp and twist A spiral, sloped, top surface used in a wide stone or wood handrail.

rampant arch An arch in which the impost at one side is higher than the other; used to support inclines, such as at a stair. Also incorrectly known as **oblique arch.**

rampant vault A barrel vault with a cross section in the form of a **rampant arch.**

rampart **1.** A continuous mound of earth piled up to form a barrier against attackers. **2.** The embankment of a **fortification** plus the parapet on top. Also known as **rampier, rampire.** See also **vantmure.**

rampart slope **1.** The interior slope of a rampart. **2.** Same as **ramp** (sense 2).

rampe (pre-20c) Same as **ramp.**

ramped Having a sloped surface. See also **ramp.**

rampier (pre-19c) Same as **rampart.**

rampire (pre-19c) Same as **rampart.**

ranch house **1.** (19c–present) The principal dwelling house of a western ranch. **2.** (20c) A single-family house form beginning in the 1930s and common after WWII; characterized by one story, an asymmetrical plan, and a low-pitch gable roof; often with an attached garage, rear patio or porch, front picture window in the living room, projecting cross-gabled wing at the front, and isolated exterior decorative details borrowed from earlier styles, such as window shutters or cast-iron porch supports.

randle bar An iron bar that projects from the jamb of an open fireplace to support cooking pots; may support a **trammel.** Also known as **back bar.** See also **chimney hook, crane.**

random ashlar **Stonework** composed of **ashlar** stone blocks of irregular height and length laid so that neither the vertical or horizontal joints are continuous. Also known as **broken ashlar, random rough bedded ashlar.** See also **random coursed ashlar.**

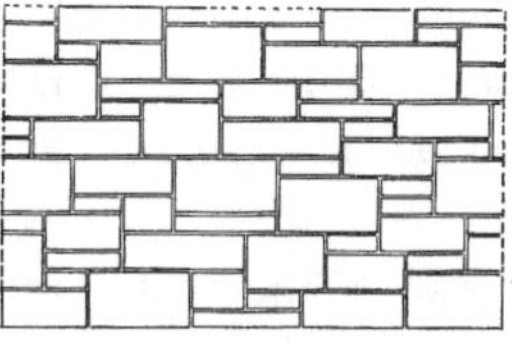

random ashlar

random broken coursed ashlar An **ashlar** masonry bond pattern with random sized stone blocks laid in short, discontinuous, interlocking horizontal courses, with varying sized stones within each course. Also known as **broken rangework.** See also **random ashlar, random coursed ashlar, stonework.**

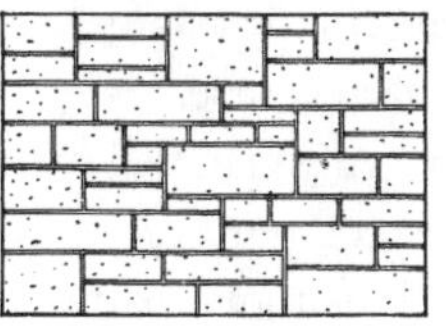

random broken coursed ashlar

random coursed ashlar An **ashlar** masonry bond pattern with random sized stone blocks laid in interlocking horizontal courses of different height, with varying sized stones within each course, some of which are **risers.** Also known as **random range ashlar, random rangework, random work.** See also **broken rangework, random ashlar, rangework, stonework.**

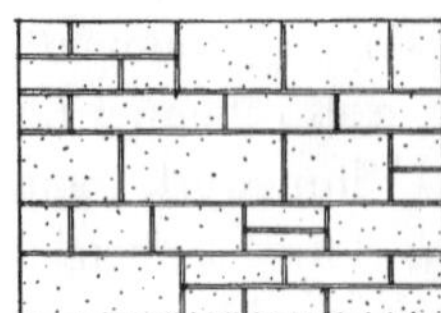

random coursed ashlar

random courses **Stonework** with horizontal courses of varying heights; may be **coursed rubble, random broken coursed ashlar** or **random coursed ashlar.** See also **riser** (sense 2).

random range ashlar Same as **random coursed ashlar.**

random rangework Same as **random coursed ashlar** or **random broken coursed ashlar.**

random rough bedded ashlar Same as **random ashlar.**

random rubble Uncoursed **rubble masonry** with stones of irregular size and shape with roughly flat faces; varieties include **cobweb rubble.** Also known as **mosaic rubble, polygonal rubble.**

random shingles Shingles of uniform length and **random width;** typically ranging 2.5–12 inches wide.

random slate **Rustic slate** laid with random lengths in each course.

random width Any material, such as floor boards or shingles, of varying width and installed without a regular joint pattern.

random work Same as **random coursed ashlar.**

range **1.** In **stonework,** a horizontal course of stone blocks; may be **ashlar** or **rubble.** See also **rangework. 2.** A permanently installed cooking stove, especially a large iron one built into a fireplace. **3.** A straight row of large objects, such as a range of columns. **4.** (18c) Architectural elements that are aligned or continue in a straight line, "thus the rails and panels of one side of wainscotting is said to run range." *The Builder's Dictionary,* 1734.

range (sense 2)

range boiler A water heater with a coil connected to a **water back** or **stove coil;** used in the first half of 20c.

rangework, range work **Ashlar** stone laid in continuous horizontal courses with even-height blocks within each course. See also **broken rangework, random rangework.**

ranging bond A brick wall chain bond with strips of wood laid in the joints as nailers.

rat-trap bond A brick cavity wall **bond** with a surface of rowlocks alternating with shiners, the rowlocks centered on the shiners in the

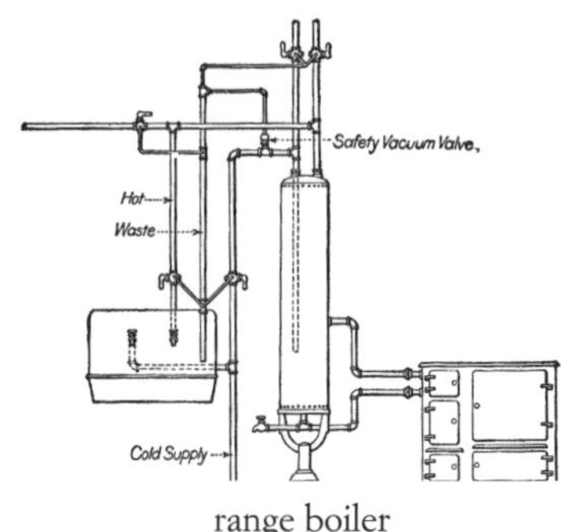

range boiler

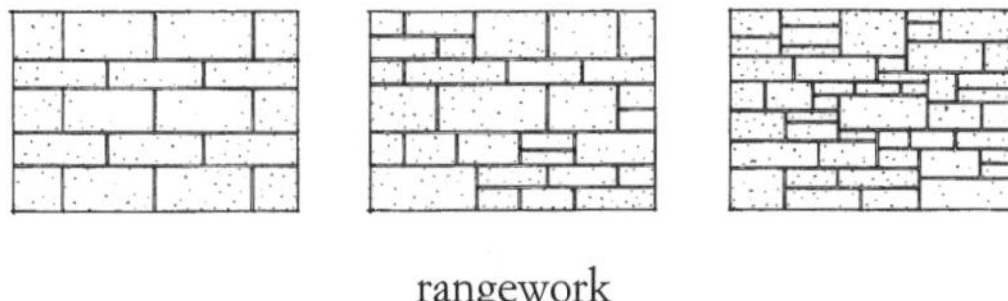
rangework

row below; the wall is one brick-length thick. Also known as **silver lock bond.**

ravelin A portion of a **fortification** in front of a curtain between two bastions, with two faces meeting in an acute angle pointed outward. Also known as **half moon.** See also **redan, lunette.**

Rawlplug A tradename for a wall plug fabricated of wood fiber surrounding a soft, hollow, metal cylinder.

raw Sienna A bright, clear, yellow paint **pigment** made from earth containing hydrated iron silicate. See also **burnt Sienna.**

raw umber A dark, greenish brown, or sometimes reddish brown, paint **pigment** made from earth containing hydrated iron oxide (FeOOH) and manganese oxide (MgO_2) mixed with clay or quartz; named for its original source in Umbria, Italy. Also known as **turkey umber.** See also **burnt umber.**

Raymond granite A light gray, medium-grained biotite-muscovite granite, with mica flecks and some black hornblende crystals, quarried in California.

razing The process of entirely destroying a building or structure without provision for reconstruction. Also known as **wrecking.** See also **dismantling, salvage.**

ready-cut house (pre-WWII) A house shipped to the builder with all the pieces precut to size. Also known as **catalog house, mail order house, precut house.** See also **prefabricated.**

ready roofing (19c–WWII) Same as **membrane roof;** types include **elaterite, Ruberoid, built-up roof.**

real estate Land and its permanent elements, such as buildings, driveways, fences, minerals, trees, and water. Also known as **property, real property.**

real estate agent A licensed agent who typically represents the **owner** or **developer** of **real estate** in selling or leasing the property; is, or works for, a **real estate broker.** See also **buyer's agent, house agent, Realtor.**

real estate broker A **real estate agent** licensed to manage a **real estate brokerage;** not necessarily a manager or head of the firm.

real estate brokerage A firm of real estate agents, always headed by a **real estate broker.**

real estate developer See **developer.**

real property Same as **real estate.**

Realtor (20c) A trademark for a **real estate agent** who is a member of the National Association of Realtors.

rear-vault A small vault between the inside face of a window and the molding surrounding the inside wall opening; used on thick Gothic style exterior walls.

reason-piece (18c) Same as **summer beam.**

rebar Abbr. for **reinforcing bar.**

rebate Same as **rabbet.**

rebate bead Same as **rabbet bead.**

receptacle Same as **outlet.**

reception room A room for the formal reception of guests; typically separate from a parlor or living room.

recessed dormer A **dormer** constructed so that all or part of the window is set below the main roof surface, creating a setback in the roof.

recessed dormer

recessed light fixture An electric light fixture with the lamp entirely above the ceiling.

recessed sprinkler A type of **sprinkler head** with most of its body within a recessed housing in the ceiling or wall surface. See also **flush sprinkler.**

Recognized Federal Heritage Building A building of the second highest heritage significance that is listed in the Canadian **Register of Federal Heritage Buildings.**

recondition (20c) The process of repair to a satisfactory functional state; typically used in reference to equipment and fixtures. See also **rehabilitation, restoration.**

reconstitution The reassembly of a dismantled or damaged building or structure, either **in situ** or at a new location; may be required by natural or humanmade disasters, such as earthquake or war, or by relocation as a preservation measure. See also **reconstruction.**

reconstruction The process of duplicating the original materials, form, and appearance of a vanished building or structure at a particular historical moment based on **historical research;** most often used at the original site; may be constructed using traditional and/or modern construction methods. See also **reconstitution, restoration.**

recording The process of preparing **documentation** of a site, building, structure, or object.

recreation pier (pre-WWI) A pier or wharf used for strolling and entertainment; may be multistoried and partially enclosed.

rectangled triangle (18c) A triangle with a right angle.

rectangular key A short bar with a rectangular cross section mortised into both the abutting faces of two wood members to provide shear resistance; typically cast iron, steel, or hardwood.

rectified photography A process of making photographic views of a building, or other subject, that are correctly proportioned in width and height to the original; includes mechanically correcting for distortions due to the fact that the camera lens is not directly in front of all parts being photographed; may be used to prepare **measured drawings** or reproduced and annotated as part of the **construction documents.** See also **orthophotography, photogrammetry.**

rectifier A device that converts electric power from alternating current to direct current.

Rectilinear Same as **Perpendicular Style.**

redan **1.** A projecting, V-shaped portion of a wall or parapet of a **fortification.** See also **lunette, ravelin.** **2.** A V-shaped buttress to a retaining wall.

red-barked fir Same as **red fir.**

Red Beach granite A red and pink **granite** quarried in the vicinity of Red Beach, Maine.

red cedar See **eastern red cedar, western red cedar.**

red deal The wood of a **scotch pine.**

redevelopment A **construction** or **rehabilitation** project at a site that has previously been developed; may involve demolition of existing buildings or adaptive use.

red fir **1.** A large softwood tree with reddish, soft, light, brittle, fine-grained wood with a straight grain; found at upper elevations in northern California and southern Oregon; used for framing lumber; *Abies magnifica.* Also known as **golden fir, red-barked fir, Shasta fir.** **2.** Same as **Douglas fir.**

red hill oak Same as **southern red oak.**

red lead A brilliant orangish red paint **pigment** composed of lead tetroxide (Pb_3O_4); made by heating **litharge** or **white lead,** or mined as the mineral **minium;** used in **red lead paint.** See also **orange mineral.**

red lead paint An **oil-base paint** with **red lead** pigment; used as a metal primer until the late 20c.

redlining The practice by a financial institution of refusing to lend money, or provide insurance, to residents or businesses located within a low-income or racially distinct neighborhood; from the image of drawing a red line around the area on a map.

red maple A moderate-sized **maple** tree with light brown, red tinged, hard, strong, stiff, fine-grained heartwood with wide, white sapwood; found in the eastern half of the U.S. and Canada, especially in the lower Mississippi valley; used for flooring and interior millwork; *Acer rubrum.* Also known as **swamp maple, water maple.**

red oak **1.** Same as **northern red oak.** **2.** The wood of several similar varieties of **oak,** including **black oak, northern red oak, pin oak, scarlet oak, southern red oak, willow oak.**

red ocher A red iron oxide paint **pigment** made by calcining **ocher;** sometimes also found in natural earth deposits.

redoubt An earthen or masonry wall, open at the sides and rear, used as part of a **fortification.**

red oxide Same as **Indian red.**

red oxide paint A reddish brown **paint** containing **zinc chromate** and **iron oxide;** used as a metal primer. See also **roofer's red.**

red pine **1.** A common, tall **pine** tree with pale red, hard, strong, fine-grained heartwood with yellow sapwood; found in northern U.S. as far west as Wisconsin and in Canada; wood is not durable in contact with soil; used for lumber, millwork, and flooring; peak production was ca. 1889; *Pinus resinosa.* Also known as **Norway pine.** **2.** Same as **Douglas fir.**

red-short iron A strong, tough wrought iron; difficult to forge except at high temperatures when the iron is glowing red. See also **cold-short iron.**

red spruce A variety of **black spruce;** found in the Appalachian mountains from North Carolina to New York, northern New England, Nova Scotia, and southern Quebec and New Brunswick; used primarily for pulpwood; *Picea rubra.* See also **spruce.**

reduced tail A **rafter tail** that has been cut to a smaller height than the main portion of the rafter. See also **full tail.**

reducer Same as **pipe reducer.**

reduct (pre-WWI) A quirk used to balance a shape, such as an angled wall added to a room to provide symmetry with a corner fireplace.

redwood An extremely large softwood tree with soft, straight-grained, reddish, decay resistant, moderately strong heartwood; color varies from a light cherry to dark mahogany with narrow, white sapwood; found in the Pacific Northwest and northern California; used for lumber, millwork, shingles, siding, silos, and exterior trim to the present; peak lumbering years were 1910–30; *Sequoia sempervirens.* Also known as **bastard cedar, coast redwood, sequoia, Washington cedar.** See also **giant sequoia.**

red-yellow brass A ductile alloy of copper and approximately 9.6 percent zinc.

reed One of the semicircular projections of a **reed molding** or a **cabled column.**

reed and bead A **bead molding** in the form of short lengths of reed molding alternating with two or three hemispherical beads. See also **reed molding.**

reed and tie A **reed molding** in the form of parallel cylindrical rods bound together by diagonal, overlapping ribbons; often with an overall semicircular cross section. See also **reeded torus.**

reeded torus A projecting molding having a semicircular cross section with parallel reeds on the surface; may be **reed and tie.**

reeding Reeds on a surface, such as on **reed molding.**

reed molding A surface in the form of parallel, linear, semicircular projections, resembling reeds bound together; variations include **reed and tie.** See also **barley twist, cable molding, reed and bead.**

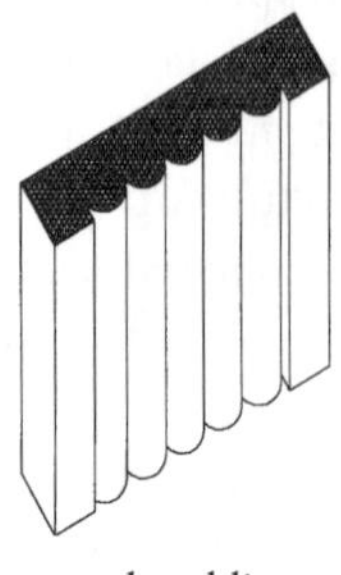

reed molding

reel One of a series molding decorations in the form of a pair of discuses on edge. See also **bead and reel.**

reel-and-bead, reel and bead Same as **bead and reel.**

re-entrant corner An inside corner.

refinish The application of a new finish, especially paint or varnish, to an existing surface; often includes removal of the remaining existing finish.

reformatory (late 19c–present) A **prison** for young offenders that includes programs for training and moral rehabilitation.

refractory mortar Mortar that can withstand high temperatures; typically a mixture of fireclay, ground ceramics, and sodium silicate.

refurbishing 1. The process of installing new equipment, fixtures, furnishings, and finishes in an existing building. See also **rehabilitation, remodeling. 2.** The process of **furbishing** an existing metal surface.

Regency Revival style A 1930s architectural style loosely based on the English Neoclassical style common during the Regency and reign of George IV (1811–30); typical elements include plain facade walls with quoins at corners and the main entrance, hipped roofs, a flat-roofed entry porch supported by cast-iron scrollwork, and a small octagonal window over the entrance.

register 1. A federal, state, provincial, territorial or local list of historic or culturally significant sites, buildings, structures, and objects. See also **Canadian Register of Heritage Properties, National Register of Historic Places, Register of Federal Heritage Buildings, registration. 2.** Any of various grilles with adjustable vanes for controlling air flow into a room, especially through a wall or ceiling. See also **diffuser.**

registered Licensed or certified by a provincial or state government to practice a design profession, such as architecture or engineering.

Register of Federal Heritage Buildings A register of Canadian federally owned buildings that have been designated a **Classified Federal Heritage Building** or a **Recognized Federal**

register (sense 2)

Heritage Building; maintained by the **Federal Heritage Buildings Review Office.**

registration The process that results in listing, or a determination of eligibility for listing, of historic or archaeological properties in a national, state, provincial, or local register or inventory of historic places, such as the **National Register of Historic Places.** See also **cataloging, nomination.**

registration requirements The attributes of **significance** and **integrity** qualifying a property for listing in a national, state, provincial, or local register or inventory of historic places, such as the **National Register of Historic Places.**

regle (pre-WWI) A groove or channel that guides a sliding element, such as a window sash or door.

reglet, (pre-20c) **riglet** **1.** (20c) A continuous slot in masonry or concrete that receives the end of counter flashing; sealed with lead wool or caulking. **2.** (pre-WWI) A narrow, flat molding used to form a design, such as a fret molding, or to cover a joint, such as a batten.

regrate (pre-WWI) To take off the top surface of old stone work to give it a fresh appearance.

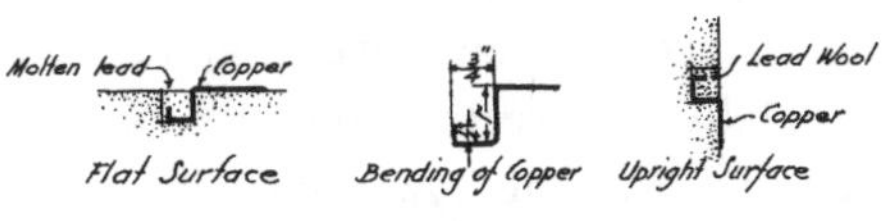

reglet (sense 1)

regula **1.** One of a series of small fillets above the guttae and below the taenia on a **Doric** architrave. **2.** (18c) Same as **orlet.**

rehab Abbr. for **rehabilitation.**

rehabilitation **1.** (post-WWII) To repair an existing building to good condition with minimal changes to the building fabric; may include **adaptive use, restoration.** Also known as **rehab.** **2.** (post-WWI) Same as **renovation.** See also **reconstruction, remodeling.** **3.** (late 20c) "The act or process of returning a property to a state of utility through repair or alteration which makes possible an efficient contemporary use while preserving those portions or features of the property which are significant to its historical, architectural, and cultural values." *(Secretary of the Interior's Standards for Rehabilitation)*

reinforced concrete (20c) A composite structural material made of concrete strengthened by iron or steel **reinforcing;** typically used to increase tensile strength; although experimental use in building began mid-19c, not in common use in North America until the 1890s. Also known as **steel concrete.** See also **steel lath and concrete.**

reinforced hinge, (19c) **reënforced hinge** (19c) A **strap hinge** with an additional layer of metal that covers the leaf and wraps around the knuckle.

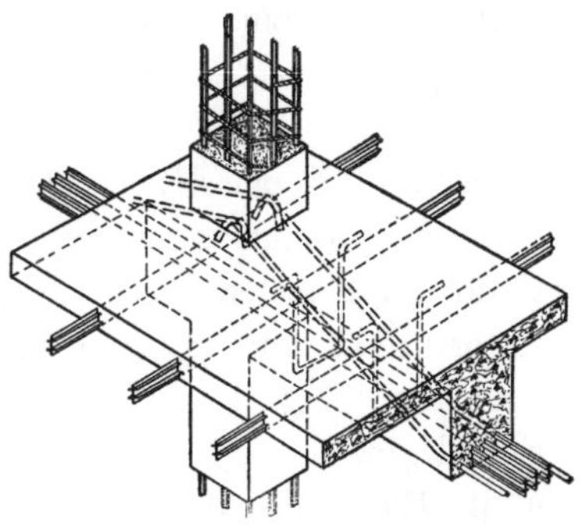
reinforced concrete

reinforcing **1.** Steel or iron used to increase the tensile strength of **reinforced concrete;** typically **reinforcing bars** and/or **mesh. 2.** Any element that adds structural strength to a building member.

reinforcing bar A metal rod or **bar** used as **reinforcing** in **reinforced concrete** construction; most often steel; types include **deformed bar, plain bar, trussed bar.** Also known as **rebar.**

reins (19c) A pair of arch haunches.

reinvestment A coordinated effort to invest public and private funds in an economically declining geographic area; most often used within a neighborhood that is physically deteriorated. See also **redlining.**

Reisner work Wood inlay with pieces of contrasting colors.

reja [Spanish] A wrought-iron grille in the **Spanish Colonial** style.

relevé [French; U.S., 19th c.] Same as **measured drawing,** especially one of an ancient building; from the drawings lifted from Classical buildings by students of the **École des Beaux-Arts.**

relief The raised surface of a sculpture that is engaged with its background, such as a frieze on a classical style pediment; the amount of forward projection ranges from **bas-relief** to **half relief** to **high relief,** or may be **sunk relief;** may be carved, cast or repoussé. Also known as **rilievo.** See also **à jour, anaglyph, coelanaglyphic, demi-relievo.**

relieving arch An arch built above a lintel or jack arch to support the weight of the wall above. See **arch, lintel.**

relieving joint A horizontal slot closed with elastic sealant that prevents the upper portion of an exterior finish material, such as brick or architectural terra-cotta, from resting on the material below.

relievo See **rilievo.**

relocation **1.** The process of moving a building or structure to a new location; typically placed on a new foundation. **2.** The process of moving businesses or residents to a new location; may be a result of **gentrification** or **redevelopment.**

remodeling (19c–present) The process of modifying an existing building, or space, for current use; used most often in connection with single-family houses; typically includes replacing some of the existing building fabric, such as kitchen cabinets, with new materials, and/or adding new components, such as a bathroom. See also **renovation, restoration, adaptive use.**

remuddle (ca. 1975–present) A humorous slang variation of **remodel;** used to refer to changes to historic buildings that destroy their original character and beauty; popularized by Clem Labine, founder of the **Old House Journal.**

Renaissance Revival style Architecture in the style of postmedieval, classical style European architecture, especially the **Italian Renaissance** style that began in the 15c and the **French Renaissance** style that began in the 16c. See also **Italianate, Palladian.**

rendered Covered with a coat of plaster, without lath. See also **rendering coat.**

rendering **1.** A finished architectural presentation drawing. **2.** Same as **rendering coat.**

rendering coat A **plaster** scratch coat applied on masonry. See also **scratch coat, stucco.**

Rendle System (19c–present) A metal greenhouse glazing support system with internal gutters for collecting the water that condenses on the inside of the glass.

renovation The process of repairing and changing an existing building for modern use, so that it is functionally equal to a new building; may include major changes; in Canada also refers to physical improvements in a neighborhood. See also **adaptive use, remodeling, rehabilitation, restoration.**

repair Fixing a deteriorated part of a building, structure, or object, including a mechanical or electrical system or equipment, so that it is functional; may involve replacement of minor parts. See also **conservation, maintenance, restoration.**

replica 1. An exact copy of an **original,** especially by the original artist or craftsman. **2.** (20c) Any copy or **reproduction,** including one produced by **reconstruction;** may involve a building element or an entire building.

repointing Repairing existing masonry joints by removing defective mortar and installing new mortar. See also **pointing.**

repoussé Decorative relief work composed of a thin, beaten sheet of metal; often beaten into a negative mold, such as the Statue of Liberty in New York Harbor.

reprise An inside corner formed by a single stone block.

reproduction A modern product that duplicates a **document;** may be an exact copy, or an **adaptation** with a different size, material, or production method. Also known as **replica.** See also **original, reconstruction, replica.**

reredos 1. (ca. 11c–present) A decorative screen or wall behind a church altar. Also known as **retable. 2.** Same as **fireback.**

rescue archaeology Same as **crisis archaeology.**

reservatory (18c) A water **reservoir.**

reservoir A storage structure for a gas or liquid, especially a basin for collecting and storing water for domestic use, irrigation, power, or transportation; types include **mill pond, side pond, standpipe.**

resilient flooring Various types of solid, flexible material used as finish flooring; types include **asphalt tile, linoleum, sheet goods, vinyl asbestos tile, vinyl tile.**

resin Any of various natural or synthetic organic polymeric semisolids; used in **epoxy, paint, plastic, varnish,** and other materials; types include **tar, turpentine, vinyl.**

resistance welding See **arc welding.**

resource 1. Any site, building, structure, or object that is part of, or constitutes, a historic property. **2.** Anything of cultural or economic value, including the **natural environment.**

resource development (20c) The extraction of raw materials from the environment through industrial activities, such as mining, logging, and harnessing water for power, domestic use, and irrigation.

resource type The general category of property that may be listed in a national, state, provincial, or local register or inventory of historic places, such as the **National Register of Historic Places;** types include site, building, structure, object.

respond A pilaster, or similar element, in the wall opposite each column of an arcade, or where the last arch of the arcade terminates.

ressaut The forward projection of an architectural element, especially a portion of a classical style entablature supported by one or two columns.

restaurant (19c–present) A commercial establishment where meals to order are served to the public; may be a separate building or within a hotel or other facility. Also known as **eating house.**

restoration (19c–present) The process or product of returning, as nearly as possible an existing site, building, structure, or object to its condition at a particular time in its history, using the same construction materials and methods as the original where possible; typically the period of greatest historical significance or aesthetic integrity is chosen; may include removing later additions, making hidden repairs, and replacing missing period work; often based on a **historic structure report;** first performed in the U.S. on the Touro Synagogue in Newport, Rhode Island, in 1828. See also **adaptive use, architectural**

conservation, conjectural restoration, control date, over-restored, rehabilitation, renovation, remodeling.

restoration architect An **architect** with special training and skills in **conservation, restoration,** and **reconstruction** of buildings and structures. See also **historical architect.**

restoration date Same as **control date.**

restoration period Same as **control period.**

restrictive covenant A deed restriction placed on a property by the current owner that affects the future use by all succeeding owners. Also known as **historic covenant** or **heritage covenant** when used to ensure future preservation. See also **easement.**

retable **1.** Same as **reredos.** **2.** A wall panel behind a church altar with an allegorical painting or bas-relief sculpture. See also **counter-retable, table.**

retaining bar (19c–present) A bent metal fabrication that covers the joint between two pieces of glass in a skylight and secures the panes to the frame.

retaining wall A wall that holds back the earth behind it; used for exterior changes of level, and in basements. See also **water wing.**

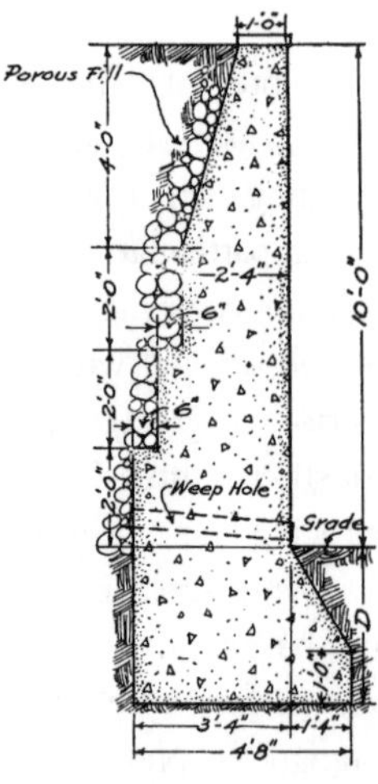

retaining wall

reticulated Divided into small geometric shapes by a grid; used to refer to Romanesque style decoration and various truss forms.

reticulated tracery Same as **net tracery.**

retiring room (19c–20c) A **bedroom** in a Shaker community; typically used as either a men's or women's dormitory.

retreat (pre-WWI) The receding of one surface, or element, behind another. See also **offset, return, reveal.**

retro-choir The portion of a large church beyond the altar; exclusive of a **lady chapel.** See also **antechoir, choir.**

retrofitting (late 20c) The process of installing new mechanical, fire protection, and/or electrical systems or equipment in an existing building; often required to meet current building code requirements.

return A surface that adjoins and recedes from the main face, such as the side of a molding that trims a window, or a small portion of a wall at right angles to the main facade. See also **offset, retreat, reveal.**

return bead **1.** A projecting three-quarter **bead molding** at an inside corner. **2.** A bead molding that is nearly a complete circle. See also **cock bead.**

return bend A U-shaped pipe fitting that changes direction 180 degrees.

return-cocked See **cock bead.**

returned archivolt An **archivolt** on the face of an arch with moldings continuing from its base horizontally along the wall.

returned molding A molding that changes direction, such as the right-angle turn at the base of the vertical portion of a hood mold.

return head The finish on two adjoining faces of a stone block, as at a corner.

return nosing A stair nosing that wraps around the side of an open string stair.

return piece One of the wings of a theater stage behind the proscenium wall.

return pipe A pipe that carries the condensed water in a steam heating system back to the boiler, as opposed to a **steam pipe.**

return trap A plumbing trap formed by a **return bend.**

return wall An interior masonry wall that abuts an exterior wall at an angle, usually 90 degrees, as opposed to a partition wall.

reveal **1.** A recessed edge, especially the exposed masonry surface between a window jamb and the main face of the wall. See also **offset, splay, return.** **2.** A continuous groove between adjoining plane surfaces. See also **dado.**

revenue property (Canada) Same as **income property.**

reversed photography The use of **photogrammetry** based on a historical photograph to establish the dimensions and shape of a missing feature.

reverse ogee Same as **cyma reversa.**

reversible **1.** Any restoration technique that can be undone in the future, by being reversed or removed, without damaging the original historic fabric. **2.** Hardware that can be used on either a right hand or left hand door.

revestiary (pre-20c) Same as **vestry.**

revestry (pre-20c) Same as **vestry.**

revetment **1.** A thin, finished facing on a masonry wall; may be of any material. **2.** A protective facing on an embankment, such as in a fortification, or on a river bank.

revitalization The planned economic and social improvement of a commercial or residential neighborhood or other geographic area through physical improvements and social and economic programs, such as a **main street program;** typically includes **rehabilitation** and **redevelopment** of private and public properties.

revival style Any style consciously imitating an earlier style; architectural types include **Byzantine Revival style, Chateauesque style, Classical Revival style, Colonial Revival style, Egyptian Revival style, Exotic Revival style, Georgian Revival, Gothic Revival style, Jacobean Revival style, Mission style, Pueblo Revival style, Regency Revival style, Renaissance Revival style, Romanesque Revival style, Spanish Colonial Revival style, Swiss Chalet style, Tudor Revival style.** See also **Eclecticism, period house.**

revolving door A pivoted **door** that is cross- or star-shaped in plan, and rotates within a cylindrical frame; typically used in commercial and public buildings so that the exchange of air when operating is minimized; invented in 1900.

revolving fund A source of loans or capital for development projects that relends or reinvests the money in new projects when it is paid back.

reweaving The repair of a damaged fabric by duplicating the original weaving with new threads.

rheostat An electrical device that regulates the flow of current by adjusting the resistance; often used as a dimmer switch for electric lights.

rib **1.** A molding on a ceiling, especially a vaulted one. **2.** One of the structural or decorative arches of a stone vault; types include **groin rib, intermediate rib, lierne rib, nerve, ridge rib, transverse rib, wall rib.** See also **rib vault.** **3.** (pre-19c) Same as **common purlin.**

RIBA Royal Institute of British Architects

riband Same as **ribband.**

rib band, ribband A thin strip of bent wood. See also **ribband.**

ribband, riband, ribbon A ledger board let into the inside face of studs to support the upper floor joists, or the outside face to support the ceiling joists; used in balloon frame construction; type includes **quarter plate.** Also known as **ribbon board, ribbon strip.** See also **girt, ledger.**

ribbed glass Window glass with small, raised, parallel Fresnel lens ribs; typically with 21 ribs to the inch and installed with the ribs oriented vertically to diffuse light throughout the space; used for factory skylights and windows late 19c–mid-20c.

ribbet (pre-WWI) Same as **rabbet.**

ribbing A system of decorative ceiling ribs, such as in the Gothic Revival style.

ribbon **1.** A narrow decorative band; may be painted or bas-relief. **2.** Same as **came.** **3.** Same as **ribband.** **4.** Same as **rib band.** **5.** Same as **ledger.**

ribbon board Same as **ribband.**

ribbon course A narrow course between large courses, such as slates or shingles laid with alternately large and small exposure to the weather.

ribbon grain Same as **roe.**

ribbon joint A mortar joint with grooves at the edges and a raised bead in the center.

ribbon window A horizontal band of adjoining window units without intervening wall section or columns; first used late 19c; common in various architectural styles including **Art Moderne, International Style, Prairie Style.** See also **curtain wall.**

rib vault, ribbed vault A vault that is structurally supported by arched ribs with thinner masonry panels bridging between them; the ribs typically lie in a vertical plane and are semicircular, semielliptical, pointed, three-centered or four-centered arches; used in Gothic style architecture; elements include **rib, vault shell, vaulting cell.** See also **compound vault, tracery vaulting, vaulting shaft.**

rice mill A building or group of buildings containing machinery used to thresh, winnow, clean, and polish rice grains; used various power sources in the 19c, including horses, tides, and steam engines. See also **winnowing house.**

rice stone glass (pre-20c) Same as **alabaster glass.**

Richardson courses (late 19c–early 20c) Stone or brick laid with alternately thick and thin courses.

Richardsonian In the style of Henry Hobson Richardson, especially **Richardsonian Romanesque.**

Richardsonian Romanesque Masonry buildings in the architectural style of Henry Hobson Richardson (1838–86) that are largely based on the Romanesque style of southeast France; typical elements include asymmetrical massing, round towers with conical roofs, massive walls with deep arched openings, hipped roofs with eyebrow dormers, pitch face rusticated stonework, and large double hung windows with a single pane in each sash. Also known as **Richardsonian.** See also **Richardson courses, Romanesque Revival style, Shingle Style, Syrian arch.**

rich lime A pure metallic calcium oxide **lime;** increases to at least twice its volume when slaked. See also **poor lime.**

Richmond granite A gray, fine-grained **granite** quarried in the vicinity of Richmond, Virginia; used for building stone, including in the Old Executive Office Building, Washington, D.C.

rider One of the heavy top rails of a **worm fence.**

ridge The line formed where two sloping roof surfaces meet at the top; may be horizontal or inclined. See also **valley.**

ridge and furrow **1.** Same as **pan-and-roll tile.** **2.** A roofing system with a series of small gable ridges alternating with gutter troughs; favored by Thomas Jefferson for low-slope roofs in the early 19c.

ridge beam Same as **ridge pole.**

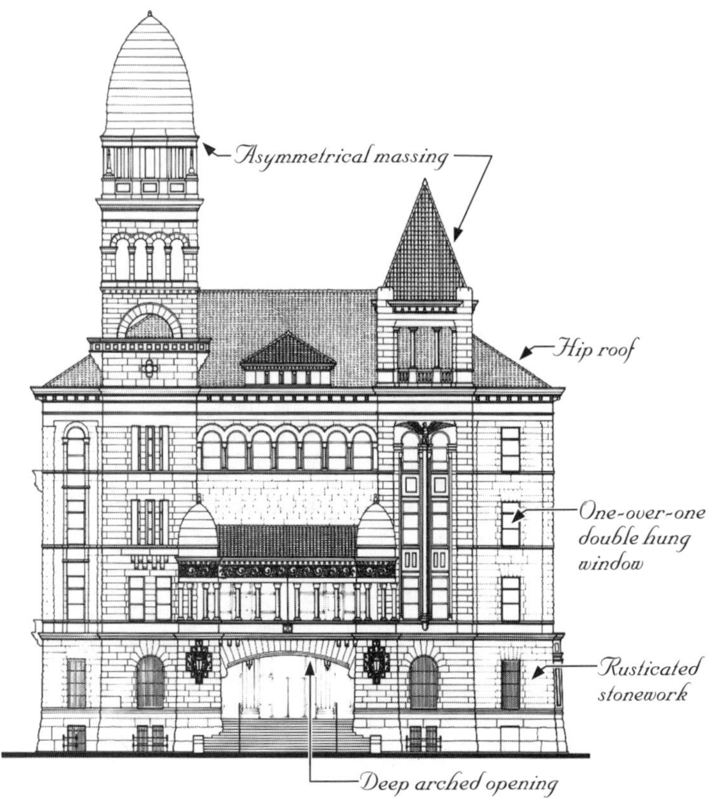

Richardsonian Romanesque
Bexar County Courthouse
San Antonio, Texas, ca. 1894

ridge board **1.** Same as **ridgepole.** **2.** A roof ridge cap formed by two boards nailed together in an inverted V-shape.

ridge course The top course of roofing slates, tiles, or shingles that ends at the ridge; typically cut to a shorter length.

ridge crest **Cresting** along a roof ridge. Also known as **fillet.**

ridge fillet A narrow, flat surface between column flutes.

ridge piece Same as **ridgepole.**

ridgeplate Same as **ridgepole.**

ridgepole, ridge pole The board between the tops of a series of rafters on both sides of a peaked roof; set with its length horizontal and the narrow edges at the top and bottom. Also known as **ridge beam, ridge board, ridge piece, ridgeplate, ridge tree.** See also **false ridgepole.**

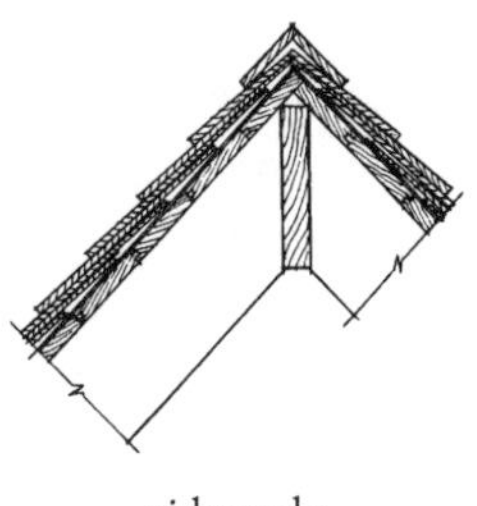

ridgepole

ridge rib A continuous, projecting rib connecting the apexes of the intermediate ribs of a **rib vault** with the center of the vault; may also continue to the wall rib or transverse **rib.** Also known as **lierne.**

ridge rod The portion of a lightning conductor that runs along a roof ridge.

ridge roll **1.** A batten with a curved top; used to support bent sheets of roofing metal at a roof ridge. **2.** A semicircular piece of sheet metal covering a roof ridge. Also known as **roll.**

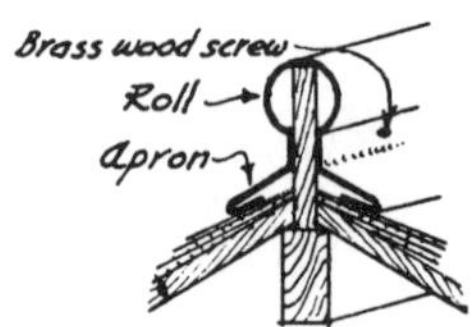

ridge roll (sense 2)

ridge roof Any type of roof having a **ridge.**

ridge spike A decorative **finial** at the end of a row of cresting on a roof ridge.

ridge tile A clay **roof tile** used to cover the top of a roof ridge; typically with a semicircular cross section, may also be V-shaped; may be plain or decorative. Also known as **crown tile.** See also **crest tile.**

ridge tree Same as **ridgepole.**

rift **1.** A principal plane of fracture in quarrying stone. **2.** A split in a material, such as a **rived** log.

rift board A board split, rather than cut, from a log.

rift-cut Same as **rift-sawed.**

rift sawn, rift-sawed, rift sawed **1.** Wood sawn radially through the center of a log; produces wedge-shaped boards used as **clapboard, shingle, veneer.** Also known as **radical sawn, rift-cut.** See also **quartersawn.** **2.** Wood with the grain across the width, rather than the more typical along the length; used for boards and veneer. See also **crosscut.**

right angle A 90-degree angle between two elements or lines.

right hand door See **hand.**

right of way **1.** The legal right to travel over or use land owned by someone else, including installation and maintenance of above or below ground utilities; may be recorded as an **easement.** **2.** The land used for a transportation corridor, such as a street or railroad.

right side The side of carpet or fabric intended to be exposed to view.

rigid insulation A stiff sheet material that incorporates numerous air cells; used on roofs, and as sheathing; types include wood or cane fiber, cork, and, after WWII, fiberglass and various plastic foamed materials, such as **expanded polystyrene;** fiber panels were used as an interior finish between WWI and WWII, both in 4 × 8 foot sheets and **beveled tiles.**

rigid metal conduit Metal pipe used to enclose an **electric wiring** system, with the wires threaded through the pipes and connectors; common in buildings constructed after 1880; originally fabricated using threaded iron gas pipe in .5–3-inch diameters; thinner-walled electrical metallic tubing used starting in the late 1920s. See also **flexible metal conduit.**

riglet (pre-20c) Same as **reglet.**

rilievo Same as **relief;** types include **bas-rilievo, demi-rilievo, mezzo-rilievo, alto-rilievo, cavo-rilievo.**

rim joist A joist along the edge of a floor or ceiling opening and parallel to other adjacent joists.

rim lock A surface-mounted **latch lock;** typically placed on the interior face of the stile; types include **Janus-faced lock.** See also **mortise lock, rimmed latch.**

rimmed latch (18c) A surface-mounted latch with a sliding bolt enclosed within a case. See also **rim lock.**

rinceau An ornamental running or scrolled ribbon of stylized vine with foliage, often with flowers and fruit; typically bas-relief; used on panels and friezes in the various classical and medieval architectural styles. See also **rocaille, scribbled ornament.**

ring **1.** Same as a column **cincture** or **annulet.** **2.** The stones composing an **archivolt.** See also **annual ring.**

ring bolt An eye bolt with an attached ring.

ring joint A connection of two circular flanges, such as a **pipe joint** at the abutting ends of two pipes. See also **flange joint, pipe fitting.**

ring shake Same as **cup shake.**

ring stone One of the exposed **voussoir** stones of an arch.

riparian right A legal right related to water flowing on the earth's surface, such as the right to divert water from a river.

ripped Wood that has been sawn lengthwise with the grain. See also **crosscut.**

ripping size The size of unmilled wood stock necessary to produce an element.

riprap, rip-rap, rip rap **1.** A type of **gravel** composed of large pieces of broken stone; used in rubble walls, and in landscaping and seawalls for erosion control. See also **cobble.** **2.** A foundation made of loose stones. See also **gabion.**

riprap wall A wall composed of a continuous pile of **riprap.** See also **gabion.**

rise **1.** The vertical distance from the center of the spring line to the bottom of an arch. Also known as **versed sine.** **2.** The vertical distance between two stair treads, or the total height from top to bottom of a stair. **3.** The vertical distance between the base of the rafters and the ridge of a roof. See also **rise and run.**

rise and run **1.** The ratio of vertical to horizontal distance of a slope, such as a roof slope of 3 in 12. **2.** The total vertical and horizontal distance of a flight of stairs, or an individual riser and tread.

riser **1.** The vertical portion of a stair step; type includes **open riser.** **2.** A pipe that distributes water, steam, or gas upward, or a main vertical electric power cable. **3.** A **stone** in a wall that is taller than one course.

rising arch Same as **rampant arch.**

rising-butt hinge Same as **rising hinge.**

rising damp The migration of underground water up a foundation wall or other below-ground structure by capillary action.

rising hinge A self-closing, **loose-joint hinge** with a spiral joint between the two knuckles; the door rises slightly as it is opened, allowing clearance over carpets. Also known as **raising hinge, rising-butt hinge, rising joint hinge.**

rising joint hinge **1.** Same as **rising hinge.** **2.** (pre-19c) An **offset hinge;** typically an H-hinge or HL-hinge.

rising line Same as **riser** (sense 2).

rising pipe Same as **riser** (sense 2).

risk assessment **1.** An environmental survey of an existing building to determine the extent of hazardous materials that may be present; for lead paint, may include atomic absorption spectroscopy, chemical spot tests, dust wipe tests, and x-ray fluorescence analysis; for asbestos, typically includes a visual survey, sampling, and laboratory analysis. See also **asbestos abatement, lead poisoning.** **2.** An inspection and analysis of the safety risks, such as tripping, inherent in the normal use of a facility. **3.** An insurance company analysis of the likelihood of a claim being filed.

Rittenhouse stove A cast-iron, open-front stove with splayed sides. Also incorrectly known as **Franklin stove.** See also **Rumford stove.**

rived, riven Split from a log, such as a **shake** or **rift board.** See also **quartered.**

riven Same as **rived.**

rivet, (pre-19c) **rivit** A metal device with a cylindrical shaft and two heads, used to connect two or more sheets or other elements; manufactured with a single head, and installed by inserting through a hole and peening or compressing the small end to create a second head; iron is typically installed hot so that the connection tightens as it shrinks while cooling; most commonly made with a domed head, may also have a flat, countersunk, or truncated conical head; used with cloth, leather, metal plate, and sheet metal. Also known as **bridge bolt.**

riveted beam girder (late 19c–WWII) A **girder** composed of a rolled I-beam with steel plates riveted to the top and bottom flanges.

riveted construction A structure, such as an iron bridge, fastened together by rivets.

RNC Abbr. for **rigid nonmetallic conduit.**

roasted iron oxide See **Venetian red.**

rocaille Ornamentation in the form of interlocked double scrolls covered with stylized foliage and shells; common in 18c rococo interiors, especially the French period of Louis XV; typically gilded. See also **rinceau, scroll.**

Rochester construction A type of **semimill construction** developed in Rochester, New York, with a separate steel girder that spans between the perimeter wall pilasters and supports the ends of intermediate floor beams.

rock art Artwork on natural rock; types include **petroglyph, pictograph.** See also **graffito.**

rock cork A light-colored variety of asbestos. Also known as **rock leather.**

rock dash Same as **pebble dash.**

rock face **1.** Same as **quarry face.** **2.** A molded finish on the face of a **concrete block** that resembles a pitched face stone block with a tooled margin; the most common type pre-WWII.

rocking pier A **pier** that supports a hinged shoe at the base of an iron bridge; used to allow thermal movement.

rock leather Same as **rock cork.**

Rocklin granite A light gray, medium-grained biotite-muscovite granite, with mica flecks and some black hornblende crystals, quarried in California.

rock maple The wood of the **sugar maple.**

Rockport granite A light gray, medium-grain **granite** quarried in the vicinity of Rockport, Massachusetts.

Rockville granite A pinkish gray, coarse-grained granite, with black mica flecks and large .5–.75 inch feldspar crystals, quarried in the vicinity of St. Cloud, Minnesota.

Rockwood limestone A light gray to buff, even-textured **oölitic limestone** quarried in the vicinity of Rockwood, Alabama.

Rock Wool A tradename for a type of **mineral wool.**

rod **1.** A thin, solid bar of metal with a diameter greater than 3⁄16 inch, especially when used as a tension member, such as a **tie rod.** See also **lightning rod.** **2.** A unit of length measure; equals 5.5 yards or approximately 5.029 meters; used in land surveying. See also **perch, square rod.**

rodded joint Same as **concave joint.**

roe A striped appearance in sawn wood, especially mahogany.

roll Same as **roll molding,** especially on a roof ridge. See also **ridge roll.**

roll and fillet A **molding** with a cross section in the form of a rolled piece of paper, with a radial, projecting fillet corresponding to the end of the sheet of paper; typically the curved upper half is slightly larger than the lower half; used in Gothic style architecture. Also known as **roll molding, scroll molding.**

roll billet molding A **billet molding** with short, cylindrical rods; typically with two or three staggered rows of billets. Also known as **round billet molding.**

rolled beam An iron or steel beam of solid section shaped by passing the raw metal billet through a series of rollers; first manufactured in the U.S. in 1854; rolled I-beams 4–15 inches high were available by 1875; types include **wide flange beam.**

roll-edged Same as **roll-rimmed.**

rolled glass **Sheet glass** manufactured by casting large sheets on an iron table and rolling to an even thickness. See also **plate glass.**

rolled iron Any iron bar or sheet formed by passing the hot, raw metal billet through a series of rollers.

rolled joint A **wiped joint** used to join the ends of two loose pipes by holding the wiping cloth stationary and rolling the pipes.

rolled section Any metal shape produced by shaping the billet by passing it through a series of rollers, especially a **rolled beam, rolled iron,** or **structural steel;** types include **angle, channel, H-column, I-beam, wide flange beam, T-beam, Z-beam.** See also **miscellaneous metal.**

roller coaster An amusement park ride with a train of small open cars that moves rapidly on an undulating elevated track; first used in Coney Island, New York, in 1884.

rolling door Same as **overhead door.** See also **overhung door.**

rolling house (pre-19c) A tobacco warehouse; named for the hogsheads of tobacco that were rolled along the road to the building. See also **tobacco house.**

rolling partition A floor to ceiling height folding door, supported on rollers, used to subdivide a room into smaller spaces.

rolling shutter Same as **overhead door,** or a similar device used on a window.

rolling slats Horizontal pivoted slats, on a shutter or blind, connected with a small wood bar so they can be opened and closed. See also **yoke pin.**

roll joint A sheet-metal joint formed by bending over the edges of two adjoining sheets twice; used in sheet-metal roofing. See also **rolled joint.**

roll molding **1.** Any molding of approximately cylindrical cross section. See also **angle bead, bead, boltel, edge roll, roll billet molding. 2.** Same as **roll and fillet.**

rollock Same as **rowlock.**

roll-rimmed A metal edge in the form of a semicircle, or fully round; used on cast-iron bathtubs, sinks and similar fixtures. Also known as **roll-edged.**

roll roofing A roofing material composed of heavy asphalt felt covered with a fine gravel topping; supplied in rolls.

roll roofing tile Same as **imbrex.** Also known as **covering tile.**

rolok Same as **rowlock.**

Roman arch Same as **round arch;** the only arch used by classical Romans; typically with wedge-shaped voussoirs.

Roman brick A thin, long **brick,** typically with nominal dimensions of 2 × 4 × 12 inches, and actual dimensions of 3½–3⅝ × 11½–11⅝ × 3½–3⅝ inches; sometimes manufactured in lengths of 16 inches or more; type includes **Tiffany brick.**

Roman cement A **hydraulic cement** made by heating and pulverizing naturally occurring chalky clay stone; invented and named by Joseph Parker in England ca. 1790.

Roman Corinthian See **Corinthian.**

Romanesque Revival style **1.** An architectural style based on the early medieval church buildings of various parts of Europe; common in the U.S. 1840–60; typical elements include relatively smooth-faced masonry walls, round arches supported by squat paired columns, steeply pitched slate roofs, and historically accurate carved stone moldings such as **batons rompus, billet molding;** the overall form and textures were similar to the Gothic style. **2.** Same as **Richardsonian Romanesque.**

Roman Ionic capital An **Ionic** capital with scrolls on all four faces, with the volutes projecting at 45-degree angles.

Roman mosaic Terrazzo with uniform pieces arranged in geometrical or figurative patterns.

Roman order **1.** Same as **arch order. 2.** Same as **composite.**

Roman ovolo Same as **quarter round.**

Roman pitch (19c) A gable roof **pitch** with a vertical rise of 2/5 of the span, or approximately 21.5 degrees from the horizontal; although some premedieval Roman building roofs were this steep (e.g., the pediment of the Pantheon at 23 degrees), most were of the lower **Greek pitch.**

Roman tiling Same as **Italian tiling.**

Roman travertine Same as **travertine.**

Rome Center, Rome Centre Abbr. for the **International Centre for the Study of the Preservation and the Restoration of Cultural Property (ICCROM).**

Romex A trademarked electrical **nonmetallic cable** with thermoplastic sheathing manufactured by Rome Cable Co.

rondelle A circular window light, especially a circular disk of colored glass used in a leaded window; often composed of **bull's-eye** glass. Also known as **roundel.**

rood screen A church **choir screen** separating the chancel from the nave, or the rear of the nave from the front of the nave; from the medieval English **rood** for a crucifix that is typically mounted on the screen.

rood spire A **spire** or **steeple** over the intersection of the nave and the transepts of a church.

roof The structure and finish that caps a building; forms include **barrel roof, cabin roof, compass roof, curb roof, dome, flat roof, French roof, gable roof, gambrel roof, Gothic roof, high roof, hip roof, hip-and-valley roof, imperial roof, jack roof, lean-to, jerkinhead, M-roof, mansard roof, Norman roof, octagon roof, ogee roof, pavilion roof, pent-roof, principal roof, pyramid roof, rainbow roof, ridge roof, rotunda, saddle roof, shed roof, single framed roof, spire, square roof, truncated roof, valley roof;** components may include **decking, purlin, rafter, roofing, sheathing, truss.** See also **pitch, roofage, roof deck.**

roofage (pre-20c) **1.** The materials forming a **roof. 2.** Same as **roofing.**

roof bearing A wood beam, or other support, built into an adobe or stone wall to support the **vigas.**

roof comb **1.** Same as **comb. 2.** Same as **cresting.**

roof cornice A cornice immediately below the eaves. Also known as **eave cornice.**

roof covering See **roofing.**

roof crest Same as **cresting.**

roof curb A continuous, raised lip that restricts the flow of water into a roof opening, such as below the edge of a skylight.

roof deck **1.** The structural **deck** of a roof. **2.** A level sitting area constructed above a roof. See also **terrace.**

roof drain A **drain** fitting used as the outflow for stormwater on a flat roof; typically circular with a sinklike depression and a domed strainer; connects to the **rain leader.**

roofer's red An oil-base paint for metal roofs, made with **Indian red** pigment.

roof garden A rooftop **terrace** with planters and potted plants, especially when on a tall building and used for serving food and drink; often with awnings for shelter from the sun or rain.

roof guard Any of various devices installed near the bottom of a sloped roof to prevent snow and ice from sliding off; types include **snow bird.**

roofing 1. The finish material that covers a roof; materials include **asphalt shingle, board, built-up roof, composition shingle, copper, corrugated metal, lead, membrane roof, painted canvas, roll roofing, roofing felt, sod, sheet metal, slate, thatch, roof tile, tin plate, tin shingle, wood shingle.** See also **sheathing.** 2. The process of installing roofing materials.

roofing felt A thick, coarse paper or felt impregnated with asphalt, tar, or a similar substance; used as temporary weather protection during construction, underlayment for roofing and siding, waterproofing, and layers of a **built-up roof;** typically manufactured in rolls 36 inches wide; types include **asphaltic felt, rag felt.** Also known as **tar paper.** See also **built-up roof, sheathing paper.**

roofing nail A **nail** with a wide, flat head and a short shank; used for fastening roofing felt, flashing, and shingles; often galvanized. Also known as **scupper nail.** See also **slate nail.**

roofing slate Any variety of slate that can be split into thin slabs suitable for making individual roof slates.

roofing tile See **roof tile.**

roof membrane See **membrane roof.**

roof pitch See **pitch.**

roof plate A **wall plate** that supports the bottom ends of the rafters.

roof tile Clay **tile** of various shapes used for **roofing** from mid-17c–present; forms include **Italian tiling, mission tile, pan-and-roll tile, pantile, plain tile, S-tile, Spanish roof tile;** may be pinned or nailed through preformed holes, or hung on battens by an integral hook shape on the bottom of the tile; special shapes include **crest tile, crocket, hip tile, ridge tile, strait, under-tile.**

rooftree, roof tree 1. (pre-20c) Same as **ridgepole.** 2. An entire roof or house.

roof truss A **truss** that supports the purlins of a roof; typically spans between the outer walls; always wood until the 19c.

room An interior space in a building separated by walls from other spaces; types include **assembly room, attic, auditorium, aviary, ballroom, banquet room, barroom, bathing room, bathroom, bedroom, box room, catery closet, choir, closet, corridor, counting room, dining room, dining hall, dormitory, drawing room, dressing room, eating room, electrical room, engine room, enterclose, fireroom, foyer, gallery, garret, gard manger, lodging room, kitchen, kitchenette, gallery, green room, gymnasium, half bath, hall, lavatory, laundry, library, light room, lint room, living room, long room, lyceum, magazine, mansard, meal room, mechanical room, mess, narthex, nave, newsroom, pantry, parlor, passage, picture gallery, porch chamber, preacher room, reception room, rotunda, sala, salon, saloon, showroom, sinkroom, sitting room, sleeping porch, smoking room, stackroom, steam room, summer room, sunroom, tambour, toilet room, traverse, tresaunce, vestibule, vestry, wardrobe, washroom, water closet.** Also known as **chamber.** See also **basement, breakfast nook, cellar, compartment, dinette, studio.**

root cellar An underground cellar used for the storage of potatoes and similar produce.

rope joint A protruding **mortar joint** in the form of a bead that is the full width of the space between adjoining bricks.

rope molding Same as **cable molding.**

rope torus Same as **cable molding.**

rope walk A long building or alley used for hand spinning rope yarn or laying rope; largely replaced by machinery by the end of the 19c.

rosace (pre-WWI) **1.** A center **ceiling medallion,** such as above a chandelier. **2.** Same as **rosette.**

rose **1.** An escutcheon plate, such as around a doorknob or encircling a gasolier pipe. **2.** A stylized carving of a wild rose; used in Gothic style decoration and on Corinthian capitals. **3.** A round ornament, such as a **rosace, rosette,** or **roundel.** See also **medallion, rose-en-soleil, Tudor rose.** **4.** Same as **rose pattern.**

rose banding Same as **rose molding.**

rose-en-soleil **1.** A stylized representation of a rose surrounded by petaled rays; the symbol of the British house of York. **2.** A stylized representation of a sun in the form of a circle with a face surrounded by petaled rays.

rosehead, rose head Same as **rose nail.**

rose house A **greenhouse** for growing roses.

rose lake A transparent, wine-colored, paint **pigment** composed of organic dye mixed with alum or tin; the original organic component of brazelein dye from brazilwood, sapanwood, or parnambue from South America was replaced by aniline color in the late 19c; a fugitive color used only on interior surfaces protected with varnish; slightly different shade than **rose pink.** Also known as **madder lake.** See also **lake color.**

rose madder Same as **rose lake** or **madder lake.**

rose molding A **molding** decorated with a line of sculpted stylized roses. Also known as **rose banding.**

rose nail **1.** A **wrought nail** with a round, faceted head; typically the head shape approximates a low, four-sided pyramid; used in rough carpenty, such as framing and sheathing. **2.** (late 19c–present) Any **nail** having a faceted head; the head may be nearly flat, domed, or conical. Also known as **rosehead.**

Rosendale cement A natural **hydraulic cement** produced from limestone containing calcium magnesia; found in the Hudson, James, Mohawk, and Potomac River valleys, and in Kentucky and Ohio; first manufactured ca. 1837 in Rosendale, New York.

rose pattern A 19c **ornamental cast-iron** pattern in the stylized form of intertwined scrolls, roses, and branches with leaves. See also **Tudor rose.**

rose pink **1.** A transparent, wine-colored, paint **pigment** composed of organic dye mixed with alum or tin; the original organic component of brazelein dye from brazilwood, sapanwood, or parnambue from South America was replaced by aniline color in the late 19c; a fugitive color used only on interior surfaces protected with varnish; slightly different shade than **rose lake.** See also **lake color.** **2.** Rose pink pigment mixed with whiting.

rosette **1.** A bas-relief sculpted, or painted, ornament in the form of a stylized flower with radial petals, or with a center flower surrounded by radial leaves. See also **mouchette.** **2.** A circular decoration cut into a surface; common on turned corner blocks. **3.** A circular porcelain block used to attach the wiring of a hanging electric fixture. See also **ceiling cutout.** **4.** A circle of gas jets.

rosette (sense 1)

rose window A large, round window filled with tracery and colored glass; common in Gothic and Romanesque style churches. See also **wheel window.**

rosin A hard, brittle, light yellow to black residue that remains after distilling **turpentine** from pine resin or pine wood. Also known as **colophony.** See also **naval stores.**

rosin paper A building paper manufactured by infusing heavy paper with **rosin;** used as a **slip sheet** below roofing and flooring.

rostrum An elevated platform or dais for addressing an audience.

rotary sliced Wood **sliced veneer** made by rotating a log and machine slicing it spirally; the most common method of cutting veneer after ca. 1935. See also **sawn veneer.**

rotunda **1.** A large, circular space covered with a dome, such as the central hall of the Capitol in Washington, D.C. **2.** A circular classical building, especially when domed.

rotunda roof A circular roof with a low slope and overhanging eaves.

rough arch An **arch** constructed with rectangular bricks and tapered mortar joints; typically used for relieving arches.

rough ashlar Masonry composed of unfinished **quarry cut** blocks of stone. See also **rubble ashlar, squared-stone masonry.**

rough carpentry The wood **framing** and **sheathing** of a building; elements may include **blocking, girder, joist, rafter, subfloor, stringer, stud.** See also **carcase, finish carpentry.**

roughcast, (18c–19c) **rough cast,** (17c) **ruffe cast** **1.** A coarse **stucco** finish made by throwing or troweling a mortar slurry on the wet base coats. See also **spatter-dash. 2.** Same as **pebble-dash.**

rough coat Same as a plaster **scratch coat.**

rough-cut joint Same as **flush joint.**

rough floor, rough flooring (20c) Same as **subfloor.**

rough hardware The metal connectors used in framing carpentry, such as nails, bolts, and hangers. See also **finish hardware.**

rough hewn Timber that has been cut to shape with a broad axe or similar tools without finish planing or sanding, leaving tool marks on the surface; sometimes a preliminary step to being **rough sawn.**

rough-in **1.** The stage of construction in which hidden work, such as portions of the mechanical, plumbing, and electrical systems, are completed. **2.** Any preliminary base work, such as installing the brown coat of plaster. See also **rough stuff, rough work.**

roughly squared Same as **squared stone.**

rough pointed Stone blocks roughly dressed with a pick so that projections of .5–1 inch are left on the face. See also **pointed finish, quarry cut, stonework.**

rough pointing An irregular, chipped stone finish; typically projects .5–1 inch forward of the **draft.** See also **smooth pointing, pitch faced.**

rough rubble **Rubble masonry** composed of uncoursed fieldstone, with rough faced stones of irregular size and shape projecting past the mortar joint. See also **random rubble.**

rough sawn Wood that has been sawn to shape without planing or sanding; typically with saw marks on the surface; may be a preliminary step to being **smooth four sides.** See also **nominal dimension, rough hewn.**

roughstring, rough stringer, rough string A stair **stringer** of lumber notched for the risers and treads; typically covered by the stair trim.

rough stucco A roughly finished **stucco** surface that is intended to be painted.

roughstuff, rough stuff (pre-WWI) A coarse paint applied between the **primer coat** and **finish coat;** used to fill in minor uneven areas. See also **coarse stuff.**

rough work (pre-WWI) The portion of a structure that is coarse and unsightly. See also **rough-in, rough stucco.**

roughwrought Metal **wrought** in a coarse way; may be the final finish or a preliminary stage in production.

round arch An **arch** with a semicircular shaped **intrados.** Also known as **full-centered arch, Roman arch, semicircular arch.**

round billet A **billet** in the form of a short cylindrical rod.

round billet molding Same as **roll billet molding.**

round church A church with a circular or polygonal plan, as opposed to the typical linear or cruciform plan; typically with a circular nave with lantern surrounded by a columned aisle.

roundel **1.** A deep, round niche with a free standing, or high relief, bust. **2.** A small, circular architectural element, such as a wall panel or window. **3.** Same as **rondelle.** **4.** An **astragal** or **bead molding.** **5.** (pre-20c) A semicircular bastion.

roundheaded Having a semicircular top, such a window head or a pediment.

round-head nail A **nail** with a hemispherical head. See also **rose nail.**

round horseshoe arch A **horseshoe arch** with an entirely circular intrados, as opposed to having straight legs at the bottom.

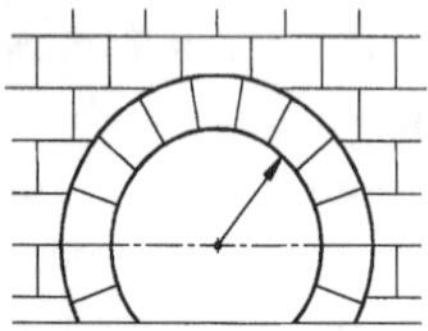

round horseshoe arch

roundhouse A railroad engine storage or repair building with an arced or circular plan; the engines are stored on segments of radial track served by a **turntable.**

round log construction The use of stacked horizontal round logs, rather than square hewn ones, to construct a building, such as a **log cabin** or **log house.** See also **round notch.**

round molding **1.** Same as **bowtell.** **2.** Same as **roll molding.**

round niche A **niche** with a circular plan; typically semicircular. See also **roundel** (sense 1).

round notch An interlocking **notching** system used for the corners of log cabins in which the bottom end of the upper log is cut in a rounded shape to match the overlapped lower log; the ends of the logs project past the face of the exterior walls.

round pediment A **pediment** with a curved top cornice; may be semicircular or segmental.

Round style (19c) Same as **Italianate.**

round window See **bull's-eye, oeil d'boeuf, rose window, roundel.**

routed A shape or depression that has been plowed with a plane or milled with a router machine.

rove (pre-20c) Same as **roof.**

rover An architectural element, such as a **molding,** that follows a curved line.

row A series of houses lining a street, especially row houses.

row house One of a series of three or more houses that abut one another, separated by party walls, with similar or identical floor plans; range from modest two-story dwellings to grand high-style houses. Also known as **terrace house.** See also **basement house, duplex, semidetached house, townhouse.**

rowlock, row-lock, (19c) **rollock, rolok** A **brick** oriented with the smallest face exposed on the face of the wall and the smallest dimension horizontal. Also known as **bull header.**

rowlock arch A segmental arch composed of full (unrubbed) rowlock bricks, especially when formed with concentric rows.

rowlock wall A **cavity wall** with a **Flemish bond** with rowlock headers and shiner stretchers.

royal door The center door leading from the narthex of a Greek Orthodox church into the nave.

royal metal Same as **gold.**

rubbed See **rubbed brick, rubbed work.**

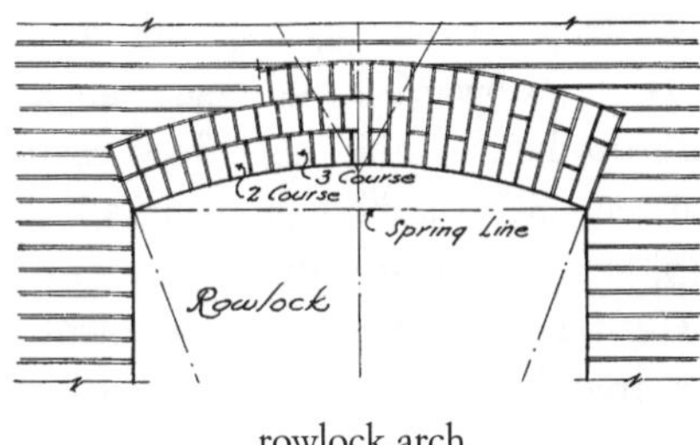

rowlock arch

rubbed brick Bricks that have been smoothed and/or shaped by rubbing them on a rough surface; typically have a lighter color than common brick; especially common with jack arch voussoirs and as decorative trim at the edge of 18c wall openings. See also **gauged brick, rubbed work.**

rubbed joint A glued wood joint fabricated by rubbing the adjoining boards together to expel air and excess glue.

rubbed work A smooth stone finish texture made by hand rubbing with powdered abrasive, including rottenstone, wet sand, or carborundum. See also **rubbed brick, stonework.**

rubber-base paint See **latex paint.**

rubber insulation An extruded or wrapped electric wire **insulation** composed of 20–40 percent rubber with fillers of chalk, lamp black, talc, white or red lead, or zinc oxide; the copper wire was tinned to protect it from the sulfur used in vulcanizing the rubber; used late 19c–1950s; types include **Duprene, gutta percha, Kerite.** See also **insulated wire.**

rubble Rough, irregular stones; may be natural or humanmade; size can range from gravel to large building stones. See also **rubble masonry.**

rubble ashlar Granite **squared-stone masonry.** See also **rubble masonry.**

rubble concrete (20c) Concrete containing large rubble stones.

rubble drain A drain constructed by filling a trench with rubble stones.

rubble masonry **Stonework** constructed with **rubble** stones of irregular size and shape; types include **coursed rubble, quarry stone bond, random rubble, rough rubble, snecked rubble.** Also known as **rubble work.**

rubble work Same as **rubble masonry.**

Ruberoid A tradename for a rubber-based type of **membrane roof.** Also known as **ready roofing.**

ruby glass A brilliant crimson glass; formerly manufactured by adding gold with tin oxide, copper oxide, or copper chloride; made with selenium in the 20c.

ruby glass

rudenture (pre-20c) Same as **cable molding,** especially in a **cabled flute.**

rugs Vertical scoring on the face of a stretcher brick produced by cutting or brushing the face with wire after forming.

ruin, ruins The partial remains of a building or structure that was once habitable. See also **folly.**

rule joint A hinged wood joint with a quarter round and fillet molding abutting a cove and fillet molding.

ruler joint A tooled **mortar joint** that is flush with the adjacent masonry units at the edges and has a narrow V-shaped groove at the center.

Rumford fireplace A shallow, masonry fireplace with splayed sides designed by American Benjamin Thompson (1753–1814), later Count Rumford, to maximize the amount of heat radiated into the room; design published by Thompson in 1796.

Rumford stove **1.** A cast-iron stove in the form of a **Rumford fireplace.** **2.** A brick cookstove invented by Count Rumford (rarely found in North America).

run The horizontal distance between the top and bottom risers of a flight of stairs. See also **rise.**

run molding A linear ornamental **plaster** molding that is formed in place. See also **running molding.**

runner One of a pair of horizontal timbers that connects two gauge piles, as a guide for locating the filler piles.

running bond A masonry **bond** with continuous courses of stretchers with each **head joint** centered in the stretcher above and below; variations include **one-third running bond, split bond.** See also **common bond.**

running dog Same as **Vitruvian scroll.**

running molding Any of several varieties of molding bands with surface decoration in the form of continuous interlocked patterns, such as **Vitruvian scroll** or **wave molding.** See also **run molding.**

running trap A U-shaped drain **pipe fitting** that forms a **trap;** typically used in a house sewer; variations include **running Y-trap.**

running trap

running Y-trap A **running trap** with the outflow leg bent downward at a 45-degree angle.

run with the land Indicates a **deed restriction** that remains regardless of changes in ownership, such as a **preservation easement.**

Rural Heritage Initiative A department of the **National Trust for Historic Preservation** that fosters rural preservation by creating a rural constituency, providing information and educational programs, and influencing public policy.

Ruskinian Following the design principles of John Ruskin (1814–1900), an English medievalist and architectural theorist. See also **High Victorian Gothic.**

rust **Iron oxide** produced by corrosion.

rust cement A compound composed of calcareous cement mixed with iron filings.

rusticated column A **column** having a shaft with projecting bands separated by rustic joints, or with a series of widely spaced projecting square blocks. See also **banded column, rustication.**

rusticated masonry Same as **rustication** (sense 1).

rusticated table A **table** (sense 1) that has a rough, rusticated surface.

rustication **1. Ashlar** masonry with stone blocks with chamfered, or rounded, edges that create deep grooves between the blocks that emphasize the horizontal joint pattern; the grooves may be all horizontal or both horizontal and vertical, as in a **running bond;** although the faces were originally rough-textured within the margins, may also be smooth in the Classical Revival style; common on the lower facade of Renaissance Revival style buildings. See also **banded rustication, chamfered rustication, rustic quoin, rusticated column, nigged, pitch face, vermiculation.** Also known as **rusticated masonry,**

rustic work. 2. A series of recessed, horizontal joints in imitation of true rustication, such as brick courses set behind the main face of the wall or chamfered wood.

rustic drab Same as **drab** (sense 1).

rustic frieze, (18c) **rustic freeze** (18c) A frieze composed of rusticated stone blocks.

rustic joint A **masonry joint** in the form of **rustication** (sense 1); types include **quirk joint.**

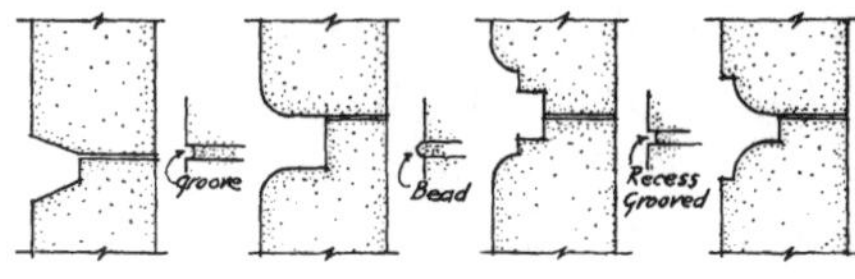

rustic joint

rustic order 1. Any of the classical styles with **nigged** or **pitch faced** stonework. See also **rustication, rustic work. 2.** (pre-19c) Same as **Tuscan order.**

rustic quoin A stone **quoin** with rough, split faces with chamfered edges; projects out from the main surface of the wall; used to give an appearance of rugged strength; often **pitch faced.**

rustic slate Slates of random width, length, and thickness; used to give a rough-textured appearance; typically laid in **diminishing courses,** may also be laid randomly.

rustic work 1. Construction intended to give the appearance of a rural building, especially with rubble stone and twisted branches for railings and brackets. See also **rustic order. 2. Pitch faced** masonry; may have grooved joints as in **rustication.**

rust jacking Same as **oxide jacking.**

rust joint (19c) A plumbing or sheet-metal joint formed by rapid chemical oxidation of iron filings between the pieces being joined; typically made by use of **rust cement,** or iron filings and sal ammoniac.

rutile A nonchalking type of **titanium dioxide;** used as a **pigment** in white paint; largely replaced the **anatase** type by mid-20c.

RWC Abbr. for **rain water conductor.**

S

S4S Abbr. for **surfaced four sides.**

Sabine's pine A large pine tree with a white, soft, resinous wood; found in California; *Pinus sabiniana.* Also known as **California nut pine, great prickly-coned pine, white pine.**

sacate de casa A Mexican grass used for thatching.

Sackett board (WWI–mid-20c) A trade name for a fire-resistant **composition board.**

sacristy Same as **vestry** (sense 2); typically with storage cabinets for vestments and sacred vessels; not common in North America until early 19c.

saddle **1.** A door **sill** with beveled edges on both long sides. **2.** Same as **bolster. 3.** A **pipe fitting** that straddles an existing pipe to make a connection.

saddleback coping A wall **coping** that is humped so that it is thicker in the middle than along the edges.

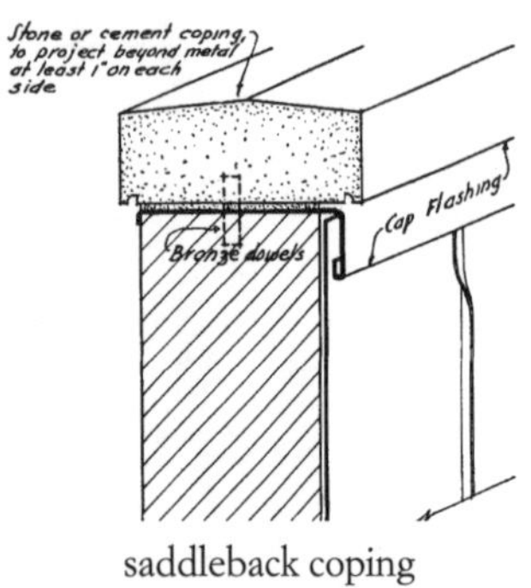

saddleback coping

saddleback roof Same as **saddle roof.**

saddlebag A type of **log house** with two back to back pens and a central chimney with fireplaces facing into both rooms.

saddle bar A small iron bar mounted across a **leaded glass** window sash to support the cames.

saddle board Same as **ridgeboard** (sense 2).

saddle flashing An inverted V-shaped flashing used under slates or tiles at a roof ridge, especially where it joins another portion of the roof. Also known as **saddle piece.**

saddle hub A cast-iron drain **pipe fitting** that overlaps a hole cut in the side of the main pipe; types include **T-saddle hub, Y-saddle hub.**

saddle joint **1.** A ridge at the ends of adjoining coping stones, or weathering stones, that form a raised joint to shed water. **2.** A sheet-metal **joint** with the edge of one sheet overlapping and straddling the turned-up edge of the adjoining sheet.

saddle-leaf tree Same as **tulip tree.**

saddle notch An interlocking notching system used for the corners of log cabins in which the top end of the lower log and the bottom end of the upper log are cut in an upside down V-shape.

saddle piece Same as **saddle flashing.**

saddle roof, saddleback roof A ridged roof with gable ends; may have a straight or curved ridge; typically the term is used for a relatively

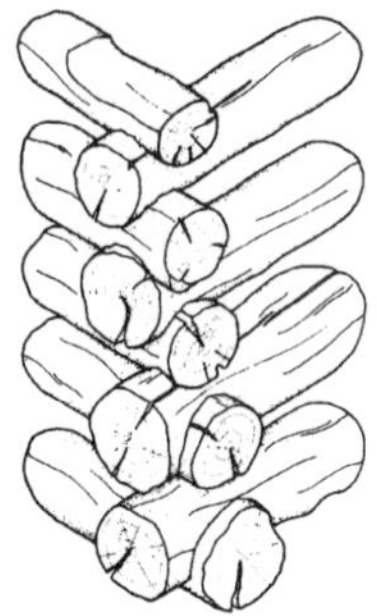

saddle notch

short gable roof in an unusual location, such as on top of a tower.

saddle stone The capstone of a gable end coping. Also known as **apex stone.**

safe lintel Same as **safety lintel.**

safety arch **1.** Same as a **relieving arch.** See also **safety lintel.** **2.** An arch under a bearing to distribute the load over a larger surface.

safety chain A small chain fabricated from interlocked pieces of sheet metal; each butterfly-wing-shaped piece has two triangular holes, and is threaded through its adjoining piece and bent in half; used for **sash cord.**

safety glass Any type of break-resistant window glass; types include **laminated glass, tempered glass, wire glass.**

safety lintel, safe lintel A wood lintel supporting the interior wythes of a masonry wall above an opening; typically below a relieving arch.

sagitta (pre-19c) An arch **keystone.**

SAH **Society of Architectural Historians**

sailing course Same as **stringcourse.**

sailor A **brick** oriented with the largest face exposed on the face of the wall and the longest dimension vertical.

sail over To project beyond the main face of a wall. See also **corbel.**

sail vault A dome in the form of a hemisphere with four sides cut away so that the base has a square plan; the shape resembles a square sail bellied out by the wind.

Saint Andrew's cross bond Same as **English cross bond.**

St. George granite A red and pink **granite** quarried in the vicinity of St. George, New Brunswick; used for building stone, including an 1897 addition to the Museum of Natural History, New York City, and for sculpture, such as the large granite vase located east of the U.S. Capitol.

sala **1.** The main living hall in an **adobe** or Spanish Colonial style house. **2.** [Spanish] Same as **room.**

sal ammoniac A salt composed of ammonium chloride; used as soldering flux and as an ingredient in **iron cement.**

sale stable A **stable** adjoining an auction house, with numerous small stalls.

salient angle An angle formed by the outside of a fortified wall that forms a projecting point. Also known as **projecting angle.** See also **entering angle.**

sally (pre-WWI) A projecting element, especially the foot of a rafter with a **seat cut.** See also **rafter tail.**

sally port A postern gate or underground passage to the outside of a **fortification;** used by sallying parties to counter attack; often a passage beneath the rampart to the glacis.

salmon brick A **soft-burned** brick named for its light, salmonlike color; typically used on the interior of a building due to its lack of weather resistance. Also known as **backing-up brick, chimney brick, common brick, filling-in brick, foundry brick, inside wall brick, light brick, pale brick, place brick, samel brick, sandel brick, soft brick.** See also **chuff brick, washed brick.**

salomonic column Same as **solomonic column.**

salomónica A column with a spiral twist; common in the Barroco-mudéjar style; from the Spanish for "Solomon," in reference to King

Solomon's Temple in Jerusalem. Also known as **solomonic column.**

salon 1. (19c–present) Same as **drawing room.** 2. (mid-18c–mid-19c) Same as **saloon** (sense 1). See also **parlor.** 3. (20c) Same as **saloon** (sense 4).

saloon 1. (mid-18c–19c) A large and elegant room for social receptions, displays of works of art, or public entertainment, especially a large public **parlor, drawing room,** or assembly room. Also known as **salon.** 2. A high hall with two tiers of windows; usually with a vaulted ceiling. 3. (19c) A place for selling and drinking liquor; typically larger and more elegant than a **barroom** (sense 2). 4. (19c) A public place for a specific activity, such as a hair **saloon** for dressing hair. Also known as **salon.**

saltbox A New England term for a two-story, steeply pitched side-gable roof house with a one-story lean-to addition that continues the back roof slope, or a similarly shaped house built in that form; common in the early 18c, and 20c revivals; named for its resemblance to the table-top container for granular salt; variations include **half house, three-quarter house.** See also **Cape Cod, catslide.**

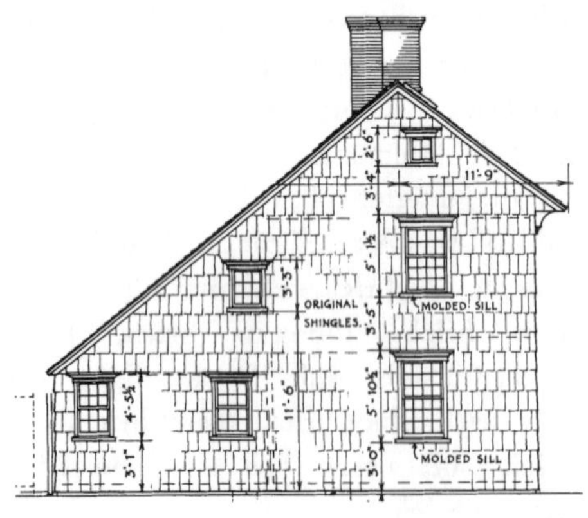

saltbox
John Howard Payne Memorial
Suffolk County, New York

salt decay Masonry damage caused by **subflorescence** of soluble salts; damage types include **exfoliation, scaling, spalling.** See also **efflorescence.**

salt glaze A glossy finish on clay masonry units formed by the thermochemical reaction of the silicates of the clay body with vapors of salt or other chemicals in the kiln; common on terracotta **sewer pipe.**

salt meter A device for testing the salt content of a building element.

saltpetering (pre-WWI) Same as **efflorescence.**

salvage Building components recovered during the process of partially or completely **razing** or **dismantling** an existing building, structure, or object.

salvageable A deteriorated building, structure, or object that is not beyond **repair, rehabilitation,** or **restoration.**

salvage archaeology Same as **crisis archaeology.**

samel brick (pre-19c) Same as **salmon brick;** originally meant a brick that was air dried before being heated in the kiln. Also known as **sandel brick.**

sample survey A limited **survey** of a **study area** or **archaeological site,** often based on a statistical sample of the entire area.

sanatorium A building, or institution, for treating a particular disease, especially by natural means; commonly used to refer to buildings with solariums and large amounts of natural ventilation used 19c–early 20c in the treatment of tuberculosis.

sanctuary The area surrounding the main altar of a church. See also **chancel, presbyterium.**

sand Small particles of rock, 0.06–2.0 mm in size; finer particles form **silt,** and larger pieces are known as **gravel;** typically composed of **quartz** grains.

sandarac, (18c) **sandarach** A gum exuded by the tropical sandarac tree; dissolved in alcohol or turpentine to make a white, hard, spirit varnish used pre-WWI for metal coatings.

sandblasting The process of **blast cleaning** with sand propelled by pressurized air or steam; process patented in 1870; not recommended for use with buildings or structures due to the permanent loss of surface finish, except for cleaning extremely abrasion resistant materials, such as cast-iron.

sand cushion Sand used as a sub-base below a concrete **slab-on-grade** or other pavement materials.

sanded **1.** A surface that has been smoothed by rubbing it with sandpaper or sand. See also **rubbed work, sand finish.** **2.** (18c) Having a **sand paint** finish.

sandel brick (pre-19c) Same as **samel brick.**

sand finish **1.** A colored, textured **plaster** surface similar in appearance to sandpaper; typically composed of a mixture of lime and sand, floated smooth. See also **prairie plaster, sand-floated.** **2.** A **faced block** finish composed of approximately 1 part Portland cement and 3 parts graded sand.

sand-floated A slightly textured stucco finish formed by sprinkling the partially hardened finish coat with sand and floating with a wooden float. See also **sand finish, sand-sprayed, stucco.**

sand foundation A level sand bed used as the base of a structure; most often a **sand cushion** used beneath a concrete **slab-on-grade,** may also be used beneath a **footing.**

sanding **1.** The process of producing a **sanded** finish. **2.** (18c) Having a **sand paint** finish.

sand-lime brick A **brick** manufactured by steaming a mixture of sand and lime. See also **chuff brick.**

sand mold brick, sand molded brick Same as **sand-struck brick.**

sand paint A granular, textured finish resembling ashlar stone made by throwing sand on wet paint; common on 19c exterior woodwork. Also known as **sanding.** See also **sand finish, sand-sprayed.**

sand pile A foundation support in the form of a compacted cylinder of sand in a deep hole; typically formed by driving a wood **pile** and withdrawing it, then ramming sand into the hole.

sand-sprayed A textured **stucco** finish formed by throwing a mixture of sand and Portland cement onto the wet finish coat; the sand remains exposed on the surface. See also **sand finish, sand-floated.**

sandstone Any stone composed of quartz sand grains cemented together with silica, iron oxide, or calcium carbonate; used as dimension stone, and sometimes as carved ornament, since colonial times; primarily quarried in North America in Appalachian regions; varieties include **Berea sandstone, bluestone, brownstone, Catskill sandstone, Colusa sandstone, Dorchester stone, Elwood sandstone, Gray Canyon sandstone, Green County sandstone, Longmeadow sandstone, Malone sandstone, Oriskany sandstone, Pocono sandstone, Portland stone, quartzite, Verte Island stone, Wakeman buff, Waller stone, Wilkerson sandstone.**

sand-struck brick A **soft mud brick** manufactured by coating the inside of the mold with sand to make separation easier; has sand particles embedded in the surface and, typically, slumped folds on the narrow faces. Also known as **sand mold brick.** See also **water-struck brick.**

sandwich beam A beam made with a flitch plate bolted between two wood members.

sanitarium Same as **sanatorium.**

sanitary base A flat **baseboard** with an integral quarter round top mold; may be used in conjunction with a **sanitary shoe;** named for the lack of intricate moldings that would collect dirt.

sanitary bend A drain pipe **elbow** with a large radius; used to prevent soil stoppage in the line; varieties include **sanitary cross, sanitary T-branch, sanitary Y-branch.** Also known as **soil pipe bend.**

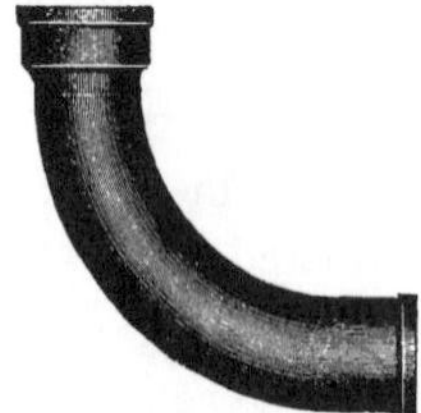

sanitary bend

sanitary casing A flat molding with quarter round edges.

sanitary cross A **cross** drain pipe fitting with the branches entering with downward curves. See also **sanitary bend.**

sanitary engineering A branch of civil engineering related to water supply, sewage, and waste disposal for cities and towns; pre-WWII also included water, sewage, and waste systems for building interiors. See also **sanitary sewer.**

sanitary sewer A sloping structure that carries fluid and solid sanitary waste, especially when underground; typically includes continuous sections of **sewer pipe** connected by various structures built of masonry or concrete. See also **house sewer, manhole, sanitary bend, sanitary engineering.**

sanitary shoe A flat **shoe mold** with a quarter round top. See also **sanitary base.**

sanitary T-branch A **sanitary bend** with the **T-branch** entering the main pipe with a downward curve.

sanitary Y-branch A **sanitary bend** with the **Y-branch** entering the main pipe with a tangent curve.

sap The fluid within a tree or plant. See also **quarry sap, sap stain, sapwood, seasoned wood.**

sapped (18c) Used to refer to wood that has had the **sapwood** removed. See also **barked, heartwood.**

sap stain An undesirable bluish gray or gray stain caused by mold in some sawn woods.

sapwood The relatively thin outer layer of a tree trunk that contains the growing cells and carries the **sap;** often lighter-colored than the **heartwood.**

sash The part of a **window frame** that holds the **glazing,** especially when movable; originally always wood, may also be metal, and in late-20c, plastic; types include **casement, fixed sash, leaded sash;** styles include **gothic sash;** components may include **meeting rail, meeting stile, muntin, rail, sash lift, stile.** See also **window.**

sash bar Same as **muntin.**

sash casing Same as **sash pocket.**

sash chain A thin chain **sash line** that attaches a hung window sash to a sash weight.

sash cord A small-diameter rope **sash line** that attaches a hung window sash to a sash weight; usually braided cotton.

sash door A **door** with a glass lite or lites in the upper half; typically the sash is fixed.

sash fast Same as **sash lock.**

sash fastener See **sash lock, window fastener.**

sash fillister Same as **fillister.**

sash frame Same as **sash.**

sash gate The movable portion of a **water gate** or valve that is raised and lowered like a double hung window sash to adjust the flow.

sash lift A hardware device that provides a grip for opening a double hung window; mounted on the bottom rail of the lower sash; may be a projecting hook or a recessed metal plate.

sash line (pre-WWI) Any line that is attached to a window **sash weight** and passes over the **sash pulley;** types include **sash cord, sash chain,** or **sash ribbon.**

sash lock Any of various hardware devices for locking a window sash, especially one that locks two sashes together; the most common is composed of a fixed piece, mounted on the bottom rail of the upper sash of a double hung window, that is engaged by a piece mounted on the top of the lower sash that rotates about a vertical axis. Also known as **sash fast, window lock.**

sash pocket The vertical space at the side of a hung window frame that encloses the hanging **sash weight** with a **pulley stile,** the inside and outside **casing,** and, usually, a **back lining;** may also include a **pocket piece.** Also known as **pocket, pulley box, pulley case, sash casing, window box.** See also **cased frame.**

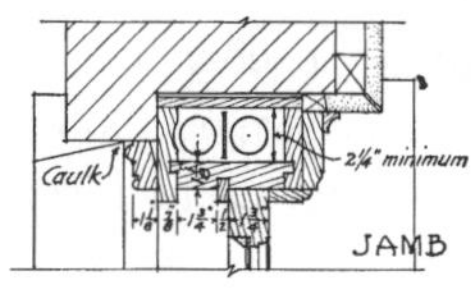

sash pocket

sash pulley A pulley that supports a **sash line** and is mounted in a hole at the top of a window **pulley stile.**

sash ribbon A thin, narrow strip of steel used as a **sash line** to attach a hung window sash to a **sash weight** or **tape-balance.**

sash sluice A **sluice** with the flow of water controlled by a **sash gate.**

sash weight The counterweight of a hung window sash that is supported by the **sash line;** typically a cast **window lead** until early 19c, then a long cast-iron cylinder.

sash window **1.** (pre-19c) A window with vertically sliding sash, as opposed to a casement

sash weight

window; types include **double hung, single hung, triple hung. 2.** (19c–present) Any type of **window** with the glazing in a movable **sash.** See also **fixed glass.**

satin A low-luster **gloss** paint surface.

satin varnish A late 20c type of **varnish** with a low-luster surface finish. See also **gloss.**

satin wood **1.** Any of several tropical hardwood trees with hard, brilliant yellow wood, with a satinlike appearance; used for fine veneer work; includes the Indian tree *Choroxylon swietenia.* **2.** A Florida hardwood tree with hard, orange wood with a satinlike appearance; used for veneer work; *Zanthoxylum flavum.*

saucer dome A **dome** with a low-rise segmental cross section and no supporting drum.

save To rescue a property or neighborhood from an immediate or long-term threat of **demolition** or other undesirable change or impact.

sawed The smooth surface texture of stone blocks with saw marks visible; used on all types of stone. See also **stonework.**

sawmill A place where logs are sawn into lumber by machinery; may include various buildings, yards, and equipment used for cutting and, sometimes, finishing and shaping the wood. See also **sawpit.**

sawn veneer Veneer wood sawn into thin, parallel flitches, as opposed to **sliced veneer;** the only method of making veneer until after WWI; types include **plain sawn, quarter sawn, rift sawn.**

saw pit, (pre-19c) **saw pitt** A deep trench used for hand sawing logs into lumber; typically has a framework on top for holding the timber in place during sawing by two workers; largely replaced by **sawmills** by the end of the 19c.

saw-tooth, saw-toothed **1.** Any serrated pattern with triangular notches similar to the teeth of a saw. **2.** A pattern created by rows of shingles with W-shaped butts. See also **shingle.**

saw-tooth roof, saw tooth roof A roof constructed of a number of adjoining parallel gable or shed roofs forming a serrated cross section similar to the shape of a saw blade; typically one side is of steeper slope or vertical and fitted with windows that are used to provide skylight to the interior of industrial buildings. See also **M-roof.**

saw-tooth truss An oblique-triangle-shaped roof **truss** with diagonal chords; used as part of a **saw-tooth roof.**

S-bracket A **bracket** with an S-shaped curve.

SCA **Society of Commercial Archeology**

scabbled, scappled A roughly dressed finish on a stone block, as opposed to a **tooled** finish or **rubbed work.** See also **stonework.**

scaffolding A temporary elevated platform used during construction to support the workers, especially masons, plasterers and painters. See also **putlog hole.**

scagliola (ca. 1600–present) An imitation marble composed of polished multicolored plaster and glue. See also **marbleized.**

scale **1.** The ratio of a drawing to the actual object; may be expressed as a ratio, such as 1:20 scale, or a unit that implies a ratio, such as ¼-inch scale (¼ inch measured on the drawing equals 12 inches on the building). **2.** The proportions of the elements of a building to one another and the whole, and sometimes to adjacent buildings; may be related to a **module.** See also **human scale.**

scale house A building containing, or adjacent to, a scale or scales used for weighing merchandise.

scaling **1.** The flaking off of a stone surface in thin pieces; often the result of **subflorescence** causing stress on the walls of the pores. See also **exfoliation, salt decay. spalling.** **2.** The deposition of minerals or corrosion on the interior of plumbing and equipment, such as pipes or boilers.

scallop The stylized shape of a scallop shell; includes an outline of a series of convex semicircles, and **scallop work.** See also **concha, wave molding.**

scalloped Having a **scallop** shape or outline.

scalloped capital A column **capital** with a square top and multiple convex semicone shapes tapering inward to a round shaft.

scallop tile A roof tile with the bottom edge cut in the shape of a semicircle, so that a row of tiles forms a **scalloped** pattern; may have a short straight edge on both sides of the semicircle.

scallop work Convex fluting in the form of a stylized scallop shell; common in Romanesque Revival moldings.

scalped, (18c) **scalpt** One or more sides of a log cut flat, as opposed to being left round; often used in reference to the exposed sides of log buildings and the surface of a corduroy road.

scamillus (pl. **scamilli**) **1.** A small bevel on the top or bottom edge of a Doric stone column drum, or bottom of a capital; used in the Greek Revival style to prevent chipping during installation. **2.** A plain stone block, without moldings, below a column **plinth** or a statue; used in **Classical Revival style** architecture based on Roman work.

Scamozzi capital (19c) Same as a **Roman Ionic capital,** named after an architect who frequently used it.

scantling (pre-WWI) **1.** The width and depth of framing **lumber** with a rectangular cross section; variously defined as having no dimension greater than 5 inches, or as having an area of 30 square inches or less, or as having one dimension less than 8 inches and the other 2–6 inches. **2.** Framing lumber of specified sizes. See also **bill of scantling. 3.** Same as **stud. 4.** The width, breadth, and length of a building element, such as a stone block.

scape **1.** The shaft of a column. **2.** The **apophyge** of a column shaft.

scape molding Same as **apophyge.**

scapple Same as **scabble.**

scapus (pre-19c) Same as **scape.**

scarcement A plain, flat ledge or setoff of a wall.

scarf joint A wood end joint formed by two members cut diagonally so that they overlap and, typically, interlock; pegs, glue, straps, or other devices are used to attach the members; types include **bridled scarf joint, bladed scarf joint, end scarf joint, hooked scarf joint.**

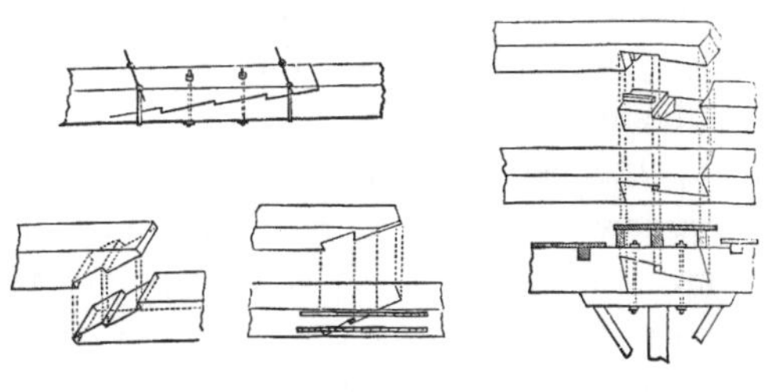

scarf joint

scarlet oak A moderately sized **oak** tree with pinkish to light reddish brown, hard, strong, coarse-grained wood; found from the southern central and eastern states to the northern southern states; used for interior millwork; often marketed as **red oak;** *Quercus coccinea.*

scarp The sloped bank or wall immediate below the rampart of a **fortification;** typically forms the inside of a ditch. Also known as **escarp.** See also **counterscarp, escarpment, fosse.**

scarped ditch A ditch with a **scarp** on one side; may be used as a **ha-ha.**

scenic Of or pertaining to a **landscape,** especially one that is beautiful or picturesque.

scenograph (pre-20c) A perspective drawing of a building or other object; typically shows both the front and one side. See also **ichnography.**

scheme, skeen, skene **1.** (pre-20c) A line drawing of an object or geometric shape, sometimes refers to a **plan. 2.** (pre-19c) Less than half a circle. **3.** (pre-19c) The crown of a **three-point arch** or **five-point arch,** formed of a relatively flat segment of a circle. See also **segmental arch.**

scheme arch (pre-19c) Same as **segmental arch.** See also **scheme.**

Schlitz glass A colored glass used in **Art Glass** windows.

school A place where instruction is given; may include a schoolroom within a larger building, or one or more buildings and related grounds.

schoolhouse A building used for a school, especially an elementary school.

scima (pre-19c) Same as **cyma.**

scintled brickwork, skintled brickwork **1.** A brick wall with the front faces of the bricks projecting irregularly. **2.** (19c) Brickwork with the brick set diagonally.

sciography (pre-19c) Same as **section** (sense 1).

scissor beam The two ties at the bottom of a **scissors truss** that cross in the shape of an open pair of scissors.

scissors truss, scissor beam truss A roof **truss** composed of two interlocking triangles with a common apex at the ridge. See also **scissor beam.**

scoinson The inside edge of a window jamb, especially with a large bead mold along an arch; used in the **Gothic Revival.** Also known as **escoinson.** See also **scoinson arch, sconcheon, scutcheon.**

scoinson arch An arch that is part of the depth of a wall and forms a shallow, flat niche, such as above a window.

sconce **1.** A wall-hung lighting fixture with an arm that supports the candle or lamp; often ornamental and may contain a reflector. **2.** (pre-WWI) Any small shelter such as a shed or covered stall. **3.** (pre-20c) Any detached **fortification,** such as a counterfort, or a work that defends a pass. **4.** (pre-19c) Same as **squinch.**

sconcheon, (pre-WWI) **scuncheon** The portion of a masonry wall jamb from the inside of the exterior reveal to the face of the interior wall; typically in the form of a rabbet that receives the door or window frame. See also **scutcheon.**

scotchback The space above and behind the throat of a fireplace. See also **fireback, firebox.**

Scotch bath A **douche bath** that alternately sprays hot and cold water.

scotching, (pre-20c) **scutching** **1.** A stone **pointed finish** made by a scutch hammer or similar tool. **2.** (20c) Same as **patent bush hammered.**

Scotch pig A very pure grade of **pig iron.**

scotch pine A large **pine** tree with pale reddish brown, tough, resinous heartwood; native of the British Isles and planted in North America; used for lumber, **red deal,** and sometimes millwork; *Pinus sylvestris.*

scotia **1.** A deeply concave, curved molding with both ends of the curve at right angles to the adjoining vertical faces, and one end of the curve projecting horizontally more than the other; most commonly with a small, hollow quarter round above a large hollow quarter round; used on the **attic base,** and other classical moldings. Also known as **casement, trochilus.** See also **quadra.** **2.** Any concave, curved molding. See also **cavetto.**

scrape A philosophy of a group of 19c English church restorers that favored removing church plaster hiding earlier decoration, as opposed to **antiscrape;** part of a general 19c restoration movement, intent on restoration to a Gothic ideal, that often ripped out substantial centuries-old, earlier additions, years old, and scraped and cleaned old work to make it look new.

scraper A small, vertical iron plate used for cleaning dirt off the bottom of one's shoes; typically located outside, adjacent to an entrance, and of various decorative forms.

scratch coat The first layer of a **plaster** finish, composed of coarse stuff; after application it is scratched with a comb to provide a grip for the **brown coat.** Also known as **rough coat.** See also **rendering coat.**

screed A guide for leveling plaster or concrete; typically placed along an edge of the work at the desired level; may be a wood or metal strip, or a **floating screed.**

screed clip A small sheet-metal strap with a hooked end used to attach a wood screed along the top of a steel joist; used with **steel lath and concrete.**

screen, (18c) **screene,** (17c) **scrime** **1.** Same as **window screen.** See also **screening.** **2.** A fine lattice work that shields one portion of a space from view; types include **choir screen, organ screen, rood screen.**

screen block A type of **concrete block** having a decorative pattern with openings entirely through the depth. See also **pattern block.**

screen door A door composed of a frame filled with stretched **screening;** used in warm weather to permit ventilation while preventing entry by insects; typically in addition to a standard type of door.

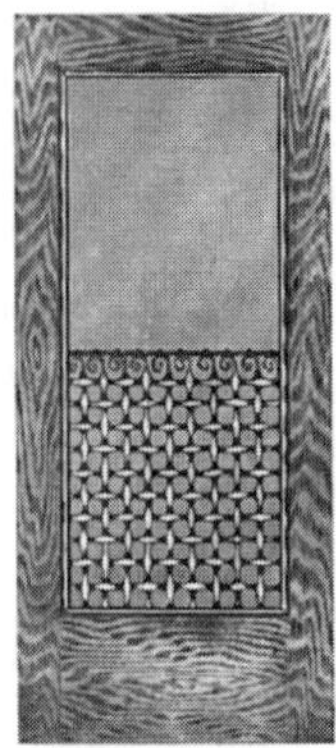
screen door

screening A woven wire cloth mesh with closely spaced, small diameter wires; used for **window screen, screen door,** and strainers. Also known as **fly lattice, fly wire.**

screw **1.** A cylinder encircled with a projecting helix; by the late 19c, standardized metal screw fasteners had a head, barrel, threads, and sometimes a point; types include **bolt, machine screw, wood screw.** **2.** Same as **wood screw.**

screw base An **incandescent lamp** with screw threads on the portion that is inserted in the socket.

screw bolt A **bolt** with a threaded end that connects to a **nut;** typically with a square head before the mid-20c, then most often hexagonal.

screwed and plugged Wood flooring fastened with countersunk screws covered with wood plugs.

screw elevator An **elevator** with a platform supported by a large screw; one of the earliest forms of elevator.

screw-end A threaded end on a metal bar.

screw eye A heavy wire bent into a loop with a projecting, pointed screw end; typically attached to wood as part of a **hook and eye.** See also **eye bolt.**

screw pile A **pile** in the form of a giant **screw;** installed by rotating into hard soil; in the 19c a wood pile with a metal screw tip, now a continuously threaded hollow metal cylinder.

screwpine Same as **lodgepole pine.**

screw rod A **tie rod** with threaded ends for nuts.

screw stair (pre-20c) Same as **spiral stair,** especially with a central post.

scribbled ornament Ornamental lines, curves, and scrolls randomly distributed over a surface. See also **rinceau, rocaille.**

scribed **1.** Marked with a pointed tool. **2.** An element that has been cut to fit an irregular form, such as a board with one edge cut to fit against a wall that is not flat; the board is first held against the wall and marked with a scribing compass, then sawn. See also **coped.**

scribed joint A overlapping joint between two pieces of molding, where one piece is **scribed** to the shape of the other piece; typically used at an inside corner.

scrime (17c) Same as **screen.**

scrole (pre-20c) Same as **scroll.**

scroll, (pre-20c) **scrowl,** (pre-19c) **scrole** **1.** Any spiral decoration; from the similarity to the end view of a rolled parchment scroll; types include **Vitruvian scroll, volute.** See also **rocaille, scroll molding, scrollwork.** **2.** A bas-relief sculptural representation of a partially unrolled parchment scroll; typically with an inscription. **3.** A spirally curved element, such as the end of a bannister rail. See also **twist.**

scroll molding, scroll moulding Same as **roll and fillet;** a recessed portion of the bottom curve is added in a few rare examples.

scrollwork, (pre-19c) **scroll work** Ornament with elaborate curved patterns that include **scroll** shapes; types include wood **openwork** ornament cut on a scrollsaw or bandsaw, and **wrought-iron** work. See also **Carpenter Gothic, Sorrento work.**

scrowl (pre-20c) Same as **scroll.**

scrub board Same as **baseboard.**

scuchon Same as **scutcheon.**

sculpture A three-dimensional artistic form produced by carving a solid material or modeling a plastic material; ranges from **bas-relief** to freestanding work, such as a statue.

scumbling **1.** An irregular, mottled glazing color produced by rolling a wadded piece of cloth or paper over the wet surface to expose the color below; leaves a random pattern of light and dark areas. See also **ragging. 2.** The process of blending nearly dry paint colors together by rubbing the surface lightly.

scuncheon (pre-WWI) Same as **sconcheon.**

scupper An opening that allows water to drain through a wall from a roof, terrace, or built-in gutter, or through a floor, such as in a warehouse; types include **overflow scupper.**

scupper nail (pre-20c) Same as **roofing nail.** See also **nail.**

scutched Dressed with a pointed or bladed tool; may include stone, brick, or wood materials. See also **scalped, scotching.**

scutcheon, scuchon, scutchin, scutchion **1.** (pre-WWI) Same as **escutcheon. 2.** (pre-19c) An angle of a building, especially an obtuse angle. See also **sconcheon.**

scutchin Same as **scutcheon.**

scutching Same as **scotching.**

scutchion Same as **scutcheon.**

scuttle **1.** An access hatch with a removable cover, especially in a roof. See also **bulkhead, coal scuttle, trap door. 2.** The cover of an access hatch.

seader (pre-19c) Same as **cedar.**

seal, (pre-18c) **seale** **1.** (pre-WWI) The process of enclosing the interior of wood framing with a finish material, especially wood boards, and, before early 18c, plaster. See also **ceil. 2.** (19c–present) The water in a plumbing trap that prevents sewer gases from entering the building. Also known as **water seal. 3.** To close a small hole or crack with a plastic material, such as **caulking, filler,** or **chinking.** See also **sealant, sealer. 4.** (pre-WWI) To attach an element, such as a block of wood, to a hole in a masonry wall by filling the remaining recess with a plastic material, such as plaster, mortar, cement, melted lead, or sulphur. **5.** The process of applying a **sealer.**

sealant (post-WWII) Any elastic material used to fill joints between elements, or cracks in a building, to prevent entry of water and air while allowing limited movement; types include **caulking, glazing compound, mastic.**

sealer Any liquid material used to close the surface pores of a finish material; typically transparent; used on concrete, plaster, and wood to keep dirt from accumulating, or to prevent stains or oils in the finish material from bleeding through paint.

sealing (pre-19c) Same as **ceiling,** especially when sealed with planks or boards.

seam **1.** A visible joint between two elements, such as the ridged overlap between pieces of sheet metal on a roof. **2.** The projecting ridge left by the mold on cast work, such as cast iron.

season check, seasoning check A small **check** or crack in **seasoned wood** that occurs during the drying process.

seasoned stone Stone that has hardened due to the drying of the **quarry sap.**

seasoned wood Wood that has had its natural moisture content reduced by drying to a stable level; typically 19–24 percent water by weight; may be **air dried** or **kiln dried.**

seasoning check Same as **season check.**

seat **1.** A built-in bench, or an individual fixed seat, such as in a theater. See also **seating, window seat. 2.** A surface that supports an architectural element, such as a beam or column. See also **bearing plate. 3.** The location of a residence, especially a **country seat** or **master seat.**

seat cut The horizontal bearing surface at the bottom of a sloped rafter; may extend entirely

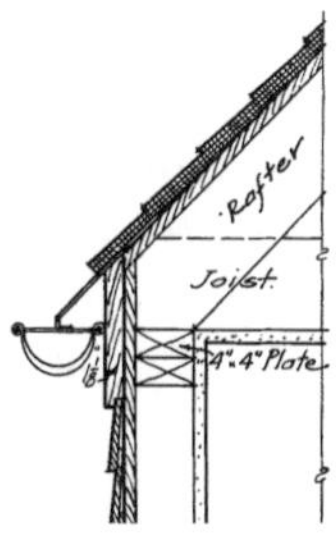

seat cut

across, or partially across, as with a **reduced tail** or **bird's mouth.** Also known as **bottom cut, heel cut.** See also **normal cut, plumb cut.**

seating Multiple seats for an audience, such as church pews or theater seats.

seawall, sea wall A revetment along a shore that resists erosion from wave action; typically covered with **storm pavement.** See also **bulkhead.**

secondary source A previously researched and published written account or report based on historical information; may be **primary research,** or be based on other secondary sources. See also **primary source.**

second-class construction (19c–mid-20c) A building code classification for wood frame construction with fire-resistant exterior walls, including those of brick, stone, iron, steel, concrete, reinforced concrete, and concrete block. See also **first-class construction, third-class construction.**

Second Empire style An eclectic architectural style loosely based on the French architecture common during the Second Empire of Napoleon (1852–70); common in northeastern and midwestern U.S. during the second half of the 19c; typical elements include a mansard roof with molded cornices above and below the lower slope, and patterned slates, bracketed eaves, cresting, projecting front tower or bay, dormers, and hooded or bracketed windows. Also known as **Mansard style.**

second-growth timber Wood cut from trees that have grown after the virgin forest was clear-cut; typically weaker and full of knots due to its relatively rapid growth.

Secretary's Standards Abbr. for *Secretary of the Interior's Standards for Rehabilitation.*

secret dovetail A **dovetail joint** where the dovetail does not show on the finished surface; types include **miter dovetail, lap dovetail.**

secret nailing (pre-20c) Same as **blind nailing.**

secret tubing Thin-walled zinc pipe used in concealed locations to carry wiring for **house bells.**

secret wedging See **foxtail wedge.**

section **1.** A drawing that illustrates the view seen if a structure were cut vertically, and the interior exposed. Also known as **sciography.** See also **rolled section.** **2.** A 1-mile-square division of U.S. public land that contains 640 acres; 36 sections comprise a **township.** See also **Homestead Act, Land Act, quarter section.**

Section 4(f) The part of the Department of Transportation Act of 1966 that prohibits U.S. federal approval of any transportation project that requires the use of historic sites, public parks, recreation areas, and wildlife refuges, unless (1) there is no **feasible and prudent alternative** to the use of the site, and (2) the project includes all possible planning to minimize harm to the site; applies to all federal transportation agencies, including the Coast Guard, Federal Aviation Administration, Federal Highway Administration, and Federal Transit Administration. See also **constructive use.**

Section 106 A portion of the **National Historic Preservation Act of 1966,** as amended; requires all U.S. federal agencies to take into account the effects of their undertakings on historic properties, and to afford the **Advisory Council on Historic Preservation** an opportunity to comment on any such undertakings.

See also **adverse effect, consultation process, undertaking.**

Section 110 A portion of **National Historic Preservation Act of 1966,** as amended; requires all U.S. federal agencies that own or control historic properties to preserve them by methods that include using them to the maximum extent possible, inventorying and nominating them to the National Register of Historic Places, and ensuring they are not "inadvertently transferred, sold, demolished, substantially altered, or allowed to deteriorate significantly."

sectional supply system A hot-water supply system that has multiple water heaters serving different portions of large buildings.

sectroid A curved **vault** surface between groins.

seadar (pre-19c) Same as **cedar.**

sedar (pre-19c) Same as **cedar.**

seeling (pre-20c) Same as **ceiling.**

seepage pit (post-WWII) A **leaching cesspool** that receives the discharge from a septic tank.

segment A portion of a circle, or other geometric shape; typically used to describe architectural members having an arc that is less than one half of a circle.

segmental arch A low-rise **one-centered arch** where the intrados is less than half of a circle; not common before 1850. Also known as **scheme arch.** See also **segment.**

segmental billet Same as **billet molding.**

segmental pointed arch A **two-centered arch** with the centers below the spring line; each half of the intrados is a circle **segment.**

segmental pointed arch

segmental vault A vault with a cross section in the form of a **segmental arch;** may be a **simple vault** or a **compound vault.**

segment top window A window with the top rail in the shape of a segment of a circle; both the upper and lower edges of the top rail of the upper sash may be curved, or the glass side may be curved and the head square.

segment top windows

seicento Design of 17c Italy; from the Italian for years that begin with the number 16.

seiling (pre-20c) Same as **ceiling.**

seismic code A **building code** that defines the minimum earthquake resistance of a structure; typically requires **seismic reinforcing** of existing buildings that are being altered.

seismic load The design load for potential seismic forces acting on a building during an earthquake; used in designing **seismic reinforcing.**

seismic reinforcing The structural strengthening of a building or structure to resist **seismic load;** may include introduction of shear walls, earthquake washers or partition trusses, and/or increasing the size of existing structural members.

seismic retrofit The **seismic reinforcing** or other alteration of an existing building or structure to improve earthquake resistance; may include **base isolation.**

select existing drawings For the purposes of the **HAS/HAER Standards,** drawings of historic buildings, sites, structures, or objects, whether of the original construction or later alterations, that portray or depict the historic value or significance.

self base The bottom support of a statue which is formed of the same piece of material.

sell (pre-20c) Same as **sill.**

sellar (pre-18c) Same as **cellar.**

seller (pre-18c) Same as **cellar.**

semé A pattern formed by rows of repetitive, unconnected designs covering a flat surface. See also **diaper.**

semiarch Same as **half arch.**

semicircular arch Same as **round arch.**

semicircular vault A **barrel vault** with a semicircular cross section. See also **simple vault.**

semicolumn, semi-column An **engaged column** that is a semicircle in plan. See also **demi-column.**

semidetached house One of a pair of houses that share a party wall between them. Also known as **double house.** See also **rowhouse.**

semidome A half dome, such as a **conch** or **cul de four.**

semigloss A **gloss** paint surface, midway between **flat** and **glossy.**

semihydraulic lime A **hydraulic lime** that sets under water in 15–20 days and is somewhat soft. See also **full hydraulic lime.**

semimill construction A more economical, less fire-resistant variation of **slow-burning mill construction** that has intermediate floor beams between columns and thinner plank floors; type includes **Rochester construction.**

seminary **1.** A school for special training, especially religious training. **2.** (pre-WWI) An academy grade school for men or women.

sense of place The total ambience of a **building, site,** or **cultural landscape;** includes both the visual impact of the built environment and human activities.

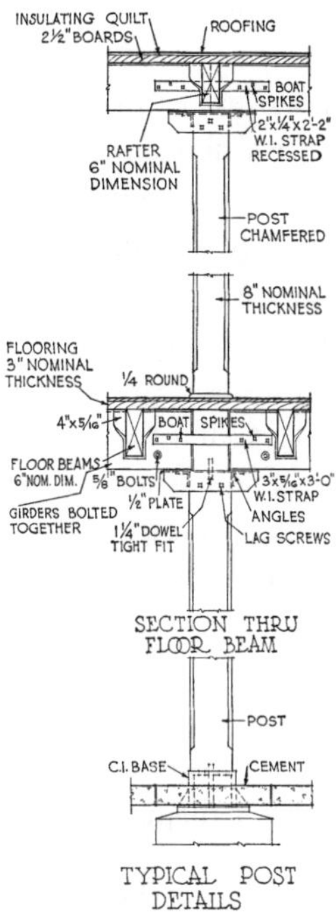

semimill construction

sentinel box (pre-19c) Same as **sentry box.**

sentinel house (pre-19c) Same as **sentry box.**

sentry box A small shelter for a sentry or watchman, especially with an open doorway; typically located next to an entrance or gate. Also known as **sentinel box, sentinel house.** See also **lookout, watchhouse.**

separation of occupancies A **building code** requirement to provide fire-resistant walls and/or ceilings between different uses within one structure; historic buildings may not have the fire-resistant separations required by current codes.

separator One of a series of cast-iron plates installed perpendicularly between the flanges of a pair of I-beams so that they are structurally connected; has a projecting lug in the center for a bolt that passes through both beam webs.

septempartite vault A compound **rib vault** formed by the intersection of seven curved vault surfaces; used to cover a square space and symmetrical about one horizontal axis and not the other; composed of half a quadripartite vault and half a sexpartite vault.

septic tank (post-WWII) A closed tank that processes sanitary sewage by anaerobic bacterial action; typically with multiple chambers and an automatic siphon that discharges the processed sewage to a **leaching field** or **seepage pit;** most often constructed of precast concrete, may also be cast-in-place concrete, masonry, or cast iron; used for individual house systems.

sequoia Either of two large softwood trees of the genus *Sequoia:* **redwood** or **giant sequoia.**

serliana Same as **Palladian motif.** See also **serlian motif.**

serlian motif Same as **Palladian motif;** first illustrated in *Architectura,* 1537, by Serlio.

serpentine **1.** A greenish stone composed of hydrous magnesium silicate with a mottled appearance resembling the skin of a snake; may also have a red or brown color due to iron oxide impurities; used for **building stone** and **marble;** some varieties are fibrous and are used as asbestos; varieties include **Deer Isle, Maryland Verde Antique, verdantique.** **2.** Having a sinuous curved shape, especially like a sine wave. **3.** (pre-19c) A spiral.

serpentine wall A brickwork garden wall one wythe thick with a plan in a wave shape of alternating arcs of a circle.

servants' hall A dining room for servants; most often located in a cellar of a large house, may also be an outbuilding.

servants' house A dwelling used by indentured servants or slaves; typically near the main house.

service cable The electric cable that connects a building to the utility company's main; may be strung overhead to the **service head,** or be in an underground **service conduit.** See also **service switch.**

service conduit The underground pipe containing the electric cable that connects a building to the main in the street; often encased in concrete.

service core The portion of a high-rise building where the service functions are grouped; typical elements include elevators, electrical rooms, janitor's closets, mechanical rooms, stairs, telephone rooms, toilet rooms.

service head A device that connects an overhead electric **service cable** to a building; often at the top of a vertical conduit that connects directly to the meter.

service pipe The pipe that connects a building to the gas, water, or steam utility main; types include **water service.**

service switch The main disconnect switch at the point where the electric **service cable** enters a building; typically adjacent to the meter.

set **1.** The finish plaster coat on a wall that is to be wallpapered. **2.** Same as **sett.**

setback **1.** A flat **setoff** of a wall. **2.** The construction of an upper story of a building a distance behind the outside wall of the floors below; often required by 20c zoning codes. See also **setback line.** **3.** (20c) The distance required between a building and the property line.

setback buttress A buttress located adjacent to, but not at, an outside corner of a building.

setback hinge A **rising hinge** with a notch that holds the door or shutter in the open position. See also **hinge.**

setback line The legal distance required between a property line and the face of a building; may be dictated by a deed restriction or local ordinance. See also **setback.**

setoff, set-off **1.** Same as **offset.** **2.** (pre-WWI) A ledge at the point were a wall decreases in width. **3.** A decorative contrast or setting.

setoff buttress A **buttress** that steps back toward the building as it rises, with sloped copings at each step.

sets A group of small, square stones used in **paving.**

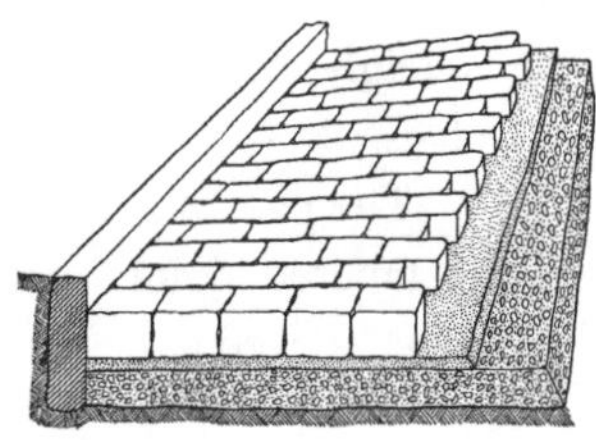

sets

set screw A small **machine screw** used to hold an adjustable part in a particular position; the head may be knurled, square, slotted, or recessed for a hexagonal allen wrench.

sett, set **1.** A supporting timber in a mine. **2.** The land controlled by the operators of a mine. **3.** A group of water pumps in a mine.

setting **1.** The physical environment encompassing a historic property; may include other on-site buildings and structures, natural and built landscape features, and the relationship to the street or nearby buildings. **2.** For purposes of the National Register, the quality of **integrity** applying to the physical environment of a historic property.

setting coat Same as **finish coat.**

settlement **1.** The downward movement of a building due to the compaction or movement of the earth below it. See also **differential settlement.** **2.** A group of dwellings constructed in a previously undeveloped area; sometimes defined as three or more houses built near each other.

sevenpenny nail (7d nail) A **nail** approximately 2.25 inches long; 120 iron common nails weigh a pound. See also **penny, sevenpenny spike.**

sevenpenny spike (7d spike) A **spike** approximately 5.5 inches long; 11 steel-wire spikes weigh a pound. See also **penny, sevenpenny nail.**

severey, severy A bay or division of a vaulted ceiling, especially in the Gothic Revival style.

sewer A sloped conduit for draining liquid waste, ranging from a 4-inch pipe to a large tunnel; types include **combined sewer, open sewer, sanitary sewer, storm sewer;** may include continuous sections of **sewer pipe** that terminate at a **manhole,** and other masonry or concrete structures. See also **French drain.**

sewer brick A dense, hard brick with low absorption used for building sewers, gutters, and similar engineered structures.

sewer pipe Any of various types of pipe suitable for underground use in a **sewer** line; types include **bituminized fiber pipe, cast-iron pipe, concrete pipe, drain tile, socket sewer pipe, vitrified sewer pipe.** See also **soil pipe.**

sexfoil A figure or element with six lobes. See also **foil.**

sexpartite, sextipartite Having six divisions. See also **sexpartite vault.**

sexpartite vault A compound **rib vault** formed by the intersection of six curved vault surfaces; used to cover a square, trapezoidal, or hexagonal space. Also known as **hexapartite vault.**

sextipartite Same as **sexpartite.**

sgrafito Same as **graffito.**

shack **1.** An inexact term for a roughly made one-room shelter; types include **storm house.** **2.** (Northwest U.S. and Canada) A **log cabin** with either upright or horizontal logs.

shade **1.** An interior window covering that screens out sunlight; typically adjustable vertically, and made of muslin fabric or paper. See also **blind.** **2.** (pre-20c) A glass case that covers valuable objects. **3.** A lamp shade. **4.** Same as **penthouse** (sense 1). **5.** Same as **shed** (sense 2).

shadow block Same as **pattern block.**

Shadow Vein A white, fine-grained **oölitic limestone** with delicate gray veining quarried in the vicinity of Russelville, Alabama, since 1827; virtually free of discoloration, cracks, and mud seams; used for **building stone.**

shaft **1.** The middle portion of a column or pier between the base and capital; typically two-thirds to nine-tenths of the overall column height. Also known as **fust, shank, tige, trunk, vivo.** See also **angle shaft, entasis, jamb shaft, midwall shaft.** **2.** A relatively plain middle portion of any vertical element, such as a tower or an entire building facade, especially when designed to resemble a column with base and capital. **3.** (20c) A vertical, enclosed space that connects multiple levels within a building, such as an elevator shaft. **4.** The portion of a chimney flue above the throat of the fireplace. **5.** A narrow, vertical excavation in a mine.

shafted impost Multiple engaged shafts in a wall or pier below an impost with horizontal moldings; arranged so that each shaft supports an impost projection that supports a corresponding archivolt; used in Gothic style architecture.

shafthouse A building that shelters the hoisting equipment at the top of a mine shaft.

shafting See **shafted impost.**

shaft ring A stone band of molding encircling a shaft of a clustered column, and attaching it to the center column; used in **Early English.**

shaft window A tall, narrow window, such as one of the lights in a Gothic Revival style window. See also **lancet window.**

shake **1.** (19c–present) A split, rather than sawn, wood **shingle;** typically 3–4 feet long, .5 inch thick, and of ash or cedar wood; common on log cabins and farm buildings. See also **processed shake.** **2.** A naturally occurring internal crack in a tree; typically caused by wind or frost; types include **cup shake, heart shake, star shake.** See also **check.**

shaken See **shaky.**

shaky Wood, or other material, that has cracks or shakes.

shambles (pre-20c) A slaughter house.

sham door Same as **blank door.** See also **door.**

shank **1.** One of the three vertical elements composing a **triglyph,** with a flat face and chamfered edges. **2.** (pre-19c) Same as a column **shaft.** **3.** The part of a nail between the head and the tapered point, or the straight part of a screw between the head and the threads.

shanty A small, roughly made hut or shed.

shaped gable Same as **fractable.**

shard A broken pottery fragment; used to date archeological sites where they are found.

shark's tooth (19c) Same as **dog tooth.**

sharp arris The edge between two column flutes, without an intervening **fillet.** See also **arris, flat arris.**

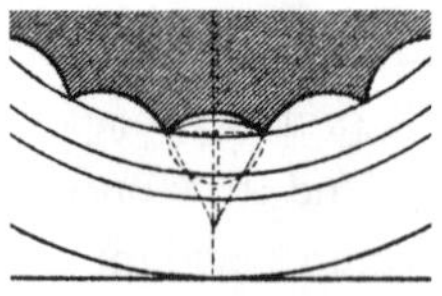

sharp arris

sharp sand A type of **sand** composed of grains with a broken, angular surface, as opposed to water-rounded grains.

Shasta fir Same as **red fir.**

shaved shingle A roughly rectangular wood **shingle** split from a log and shaved to a tapered cross section; typically approximately .5 × 4–6 × 18–24 inches.

shay house Same as **chaise house.**

shear steel A type of steel manufactured from **blister steel** sheared into short lengths that are stacked and drawn out.

sheathing, (pre-20c U.S.) **sheeting** Material used to enclose and strengthen the walls and/or roof of a wood-frame building; typically **sheathing board** or **plywood;** often the base for the exterior siding. See also **diagonal sheathing.**

sheathing board One of a series of wood boards used as **sheathing;** often with tongue and groove edges.

sheathing felt Same as **roofing felt,** when used to cover **sheathing.**

sheathing lath A combined exterior wood sheathing and stucco **lath** with beveled horizontal boards that form dovetailed keys for the plaster; types include **Byrkit lath.**

sheathing nail **1.** Any long **nail** used to fasten sheathing boards to the framing of a building. **2.** Cast bronze nails with a flat, countersunk head; used to fasten metal sheathing to the hull of a ship. See also **nail.**

sheathing paper A water-resistant coarse paper, such as **roofing felt,** attached to the exterior surface of sheathing for moisture protection; also used on top of a subfloor for sound insulation. See also **rosin paper.**

sheath pile (19c) Same as **sheet pile.**

shed, (17c) **shedd** **1.** A one-story shelter with a **shed roof;** typically open on one or more sides; types include **cowshed, toolshed, woodshed.** See also **outbuilding, penthouse, shack, shanty, train shed, weaving shed.** **2.** (17c–18c) A building wing or addition with a **shed roof** that abuts a higher wall. Also known as **lean-to, shade.**

shed dormer A dormer with a shed roof of flatter pitch than the main roof.

shed roof A roof with a single slope, with the rafters spanning from one outside wall to the opposite wall. Also known as **lean-to, pent roof.**

sheet brass **Brass** that has been rolled into **sheet metal.**

sheet glass **1.** Any **glass** manufactured in thin sheets directly from the furnace; types include **compressed glass, float glass, rolled glass.** See also **window glass.** **2.** (pre-20c) Same as **cylinder glass.**

sheet goods Any type of thin, composition floor finish that is manufactured in large rolls or sheets, for example **linoleum** or **sheet vinyl.**

sheeting **1.** One of a series of wood planks used in **sheeting and shoring;** typically installed vertically with a wood system, and as horizontal **lagging** between steel **soldier piles.** See also **sheet pile.** **2.** (pre-20c U.S.) Same as **sheathing.**

sheeting and shoring A temporary wall constructed during excavation to hold the side walls of the hole in place; originally vertical **sheeting** held in place by horizontal **walers,** vertical **shores** or **wallpieces,** and diagonal **rakers,** and sometimes **piles;** in large 20c excavations may have horizontal sheeting between vertical H-shaped steel piles, sometimes braced with steel sections, or may use **sheet piles.**

sheet iron (19c) Iron that has been rolled into **sheet metal.**

sheet lead See **milled lead.**

sheet metal Metal that has been rolled or cast into relatively thin sheets that can be formed by bending; technically 0.006–0.375 inch in thickness, the most common thicknesses range 0.01–0.10 inch (10–30 gauge); metal 0.006 inch thick, or less, is **foil,** and more than 0.25 inch thick is **plate;** types include **milled lead, sheet brass, sheet iron;** products include **Ag-panels, corrugated metal, expanded-metal lath, flashing, gold leaf, light-gauge steel, metal shingle, raising, tin roof;** used for various bent and/or repoussé fabrications, including **flashing, gutters, downspouts.**

sheet-metal lath A plaster **lath** formed from punched sheet metal; types include **expanded-metal lath, Sykes lath, Truss-Loop lath.**

sheet pile One of a series of broad, thin **piles** installed to form a temporary retaining wall during excavation; originally tongue and groove wood planks; replaced by interlocking steel piles in the 20c. Also known as **sheath pile.** See also **buckstay, pug pile, sheeting.**

Sheetrock (20c) A trade name for gypsum drywall products manufactured by U.S. Gypsum Co.; sometimes incorrectly used to mean **gypsum board.**

sheet vinyl A type of **sheet goods** flooring composed of polyvinyl chloride resin plus clay-based inert fillers and pigment; manufactured mid–late 20c with asbestos or felt backing; typically 1/16–1/4 inch thick. See also **vinyl tile.**

Shelburne marble Same as **Vermont marble.**

shelf angle A steel angle attached to the structure of a building so that one leg projects horizontally to support a brick, stone, or architectural terra-cotta veneer.

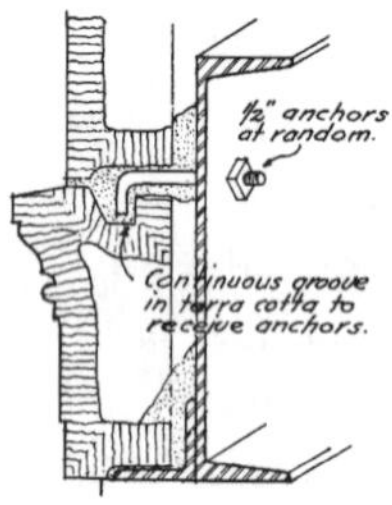

shelf angle

shelf cleat A wood **ledger** that supports the edges of a shelf, such as in a closet; may be rectangular in cross section or a notched molding.

shell **1.** The basic structure and enclosure of a building, exclusive of interior finishes and mechanical, plumbing, and electrical systems; often used to refer to a deteriorated building that has lost much of its original fabric. See also **carcase, concha, scallop, shell construction.** **2.** A cup-shaped piece of thin metal that covers the junction box above a ceiling-mounted electric fixture. **3.** The iron plates that form a boiler enclosure.

shellac A wood finish made from **lac** resin dissolved in alcohol; varieties include **button lac** and **orange shellac** made from natural lac, and **blonde** and **white shellac** made from bleached lac; used as a varnish and for sealing wood. See also **shell lac.**

shell construction (20c) A thin, curved, structural outer layer that distributes loads equally in all directions; most commonly used for roofs composed of concrete, may also be wood; first used for a concrete dome constructed in Germany by Bauersfeld and Dischinger in 1922. Also known as **thin shell concrete.** See also **reinforced concrete.**

shell heap Same as **shell mound.**

shell lac Thin sheets of melted purified lac resin; used to make **shellac.**

shell lime A type of **lime** that is made by heating oyster shells.

shell mound A **midden heap** largely composed of oyster or mussel shells. Also known as **shell heap.**

shell road A road, or driveway, paved with shells; common along the Gulf Coast, especially in pre-WWI suburbs.

shell shake A **cup shake** (sense 2) defect that is exposed upon sawing timber.

shell white A white paint **pigment** with a slightly yellowish tinge; made by pulverizing mollusk shells.

shelly limestone A coarse-grained **limestone** composed mainly of sea shells cemented together with calcium carbonate.

sherardized (20c) Iron that has been alloyed on the surface with zinc by coating with zinc dust and heating to 300–420 degrees; used to prevent rusting. See also **galvanized.**

shide (pre-19c) A wood **shingle.**

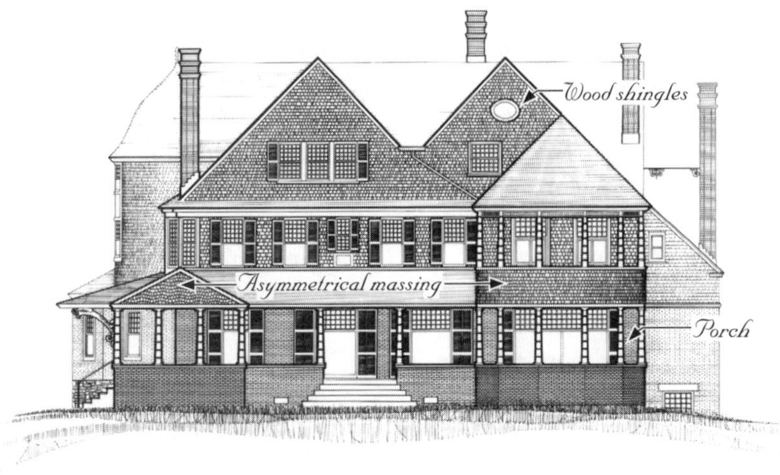

Shingle Style
Isaac Bell House
Newport, Rhode Island

shim A thin wedge used to fill the gap and/or adjust the spacing between building elements, such as between a window frame and the building structure, or between a steel column bearing plate and the concrete foundation.

shiner **1.** A **brick** oriented with the largest face exposed on the face of the wall and the longest dimension horizontal. Also known as **bull stretcher. 2.** A nail hammered through a board and showing on both sides.

shingle **1.** Thin overlapping elements for roofing or siding; installed so that the joint between adjoining shingles is covered by the shingle above, may also be installed **board fashion;** originally a wood **shake** or **shaved shingle** 18–36 inches in length with 4–11 inches exposed to the weather, by the middle of the 19c most shingles were sawn (often of **western cedar**), with the exposed **butt** ends often producing patterns such as **chisel, diamond, fishscale, sawtooth,** and **staggered;** substitute types by the end of the 19c include **metal shingle** and **composition shingle.** Also known as **shide.** See also **dimension shingle, Quaker shingle, roof tile. 2.** A small wooden sign.

shingle bolt A piece of log quartered and cut to length in preparation for splitting into shingles.

shingle nail (19c) A 1.5-inch **nail,** especially a cut nail.

shingle oak An **oak** tree found in the Mississippi River valley; commonly used for shingles; *Quercus imbricaria.* Also known as **laurel oak.**

Shingle Style An architectural style of the late 19c characterized by exterior walls covered with wood shingles, heavy asymmetrical massing, minimal exterior ornamentation, dormers, and open interior spaces; often has a random rubble stone foundation, porches, and an eyebrow dormer; partly a result of renewed interest in the shingled colonial houses of coastal New England, where the greatest concentration of examples are found; although best known for large, architect-designed houses and hotels, was also used for smaller suburban dwellings; most examples built 1880s; isolated work throughout North America continued into the early 20c; notable designers in the style included McKim, Mead, and White, and H. H. Richardson. See also **Queen Anne style.**

shingle tile Same as **plain tile.**

shingle timber Any wood suitable for cutting or splitting into shingles; types include **redwood, shingle oak, western red cedar.**

shiplap An overlapping, flush joint at the long edges of two boards; typically formed by a continuous, rectangular notch on opposite sides of both edges of each board; used to make a weathertight joint for siding.

shipping house (Carolinas) A warehouse on a plantation adjacent to a river; used to store rice until it was shipped to market.

ship spike Same as **boat spike.**

shoe **1.** Any stone, wood, or metal piece that encloses the bottom of a diagonal or vertical member, such as a wrought- or cast-iron truss post base, with connection points for the diagonal or horizontal members. See also **shutting shoe.** **2.** A plate that distributes the load at the bottom of a column to the foundation. **3.** The iron covering on the point of a driven pile.

shoe bolt A **bolt** with a countersunk head.

shoe mold Any type of **molding** that covers the joint between the bottom of a baseboard and the floor; types include **sanitary shoe.**

shoe tile A **structural clay tile** with a groove on the side that fits around the bottom flange of a steel beam to provide fire protection; usually used with a **tile arch.** See also **lipped skewback.**

shoot (pre-WWI) The thrust of an **arch.**

shooting box **1.** A small country house used as a dwelling by hunters. **2.** A very accurate carpentry tool for planing miters. See also **shot.**

shop **1.** A room or relatively small building where goods are manufactured. See also **mill, plant.** **2.** Same as **store** (sense 1).

shop drawing A detailed drawing produced by the fabricator or manufacturer of a particular building element; the shop drawing is typically approved by the architect during the construction period. Also known as **manufacturer's drawing.** See also **working drawings.**

shop front (pre-WWI) Same as **store front.**

shopping center (mid-20c–present) A site that contains one or more buildings with multiple retail stores, parking areas, and related facilities within a single development; typically one story with a linear plan. See also **shopping mall, shopping village.**

shopping mall (1950's–present) A **shopping center** with multiple retail stores facing each other across an interior pedestrian mall; originally uncovered, by late-20c the mall area is nearly always enclosed and climate controlled; first used for a shopping center in Harundale, Maryland developed by the Rouse Co. Also known as **mall.**

shopping village (early 20c) A **shopping center** with multiple buildings interspersed with parking areas; first built outside Kansas City in 1908.

shore A vertical or diagonal member used in **shoring** to support the structure; typically wood or steel; types include **dead shore, flying shore, raker.**

shoring A temporary system of support to a structure; used during restoration work to effect structural repairs, to move buildings, and during construction, especially for reinforced concrete and excavation work; elements include **raker, shore, waler.** See also **crib, needle beam, sheeting and shoring.**

shortleaf pine **1.** A **pine** tree with yellowish, moderately hard, strong, stiff, pitchy wood; found from eastern Oklahoma and Texas to southern Connecticut, but most common in the southeastern states; used for lumber, mill-

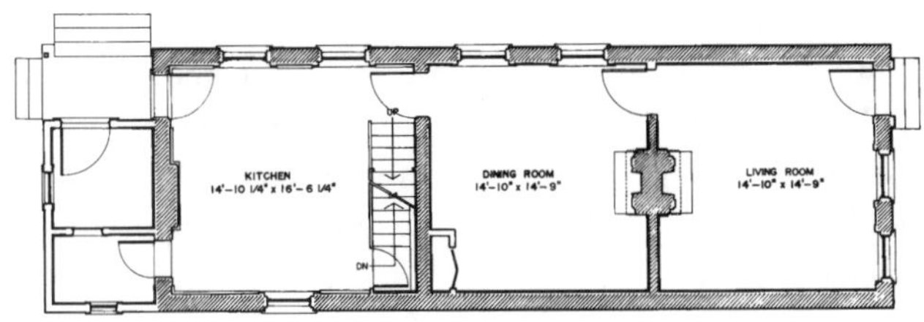

shotgun
Kuntz "Shotgun" House
Jefferson County, Kentucky

work, ceiling, and siding; *Pinus echinata.* Also known as **Southern pine, yellow pine. 2.** Any of the short-needled varieties of **Southern yellow pine,** including **loblolly pine** and **Pond pine.** Also known as **North Carolina pine.**

short valley A valley rafter that runs from the head of a dormer to the wall plate. See also **long valley.**

shot (pre-20c) Having a straight edge. See also **shooting box.**

shotgun A house form where the building is one room wide facing the street and each room connects directly to the next without hallways; typically the parlor was in the front and the kitchen in the rear; typical elements include a front porch, and a gable front or hipped roof; commonly built in Mississippi River valley cities from New Orleans, Louisiana, to Louisville, Kentucky, ca. 1880–ca. 1930.

shot sawed, shot sawn The rough, uneven surface texture of sawn stone **ashlar** blocks produced by using steel shot and chat sand during gang sawing; ranges from a pebbled surface to one ripped with irregular, roughly parallel grooves; used on soft stones. See also **chat sawed, stonework.**

shot tower A tall tower used to manufacture lead shot; molten lead is poured through a sieve at the top of the building, the pieces cool into solid balls as they fall, and drop into water at the bottom; used until late 19c.

shoulder **1.** An offset of any architectural element, typically at a right angle, where it increases in width, such as the area between a tenon and the outside face of a timber. See also **setoff. 2.** (20c) The graded area alongside a paved road or driveway; often graveled. See also **verge. 3.** The angle formed between the front face and the side flank of a fortification bastion.

shouldered arch A stone **lintel,** or **jack arch,** supported by two corbels; typically the corbels have a concave quarter round at the bottom, and rise vertically to the lintel; from the resemblance of the opening outline to a human neck and shoulders.

shouldered architrave An **architrave** surrounding a wall opening, with crossettes that extend outward at the top corners. Also known as **kneed architrave.** See also **crossette.**

shouldering **1.** The installation of mortar beneath the upper end of a slate or tile so that the bottom is parallel with the one below it and makes a tight joint. **2.** A rounded edge of an embankment.

shoulder piece A piece of material attached to a building element to form a **shoulder** (sense 1).

shoulder screw A **machine screw** with a barrel wider than the threads so that a shoulder is formed below the head.

shove joint, shoved joint A **mortar joint** between masonry units, such as bricks, formed by battering the end of the unit with mortar and shoving it against the adjoining unit so that some of the mortar is squeezed out of the joint; the preferred method of construction. See also **slush joint.**

shovel testing Limited hand **excavation** to determine the nature and extent of an **archaeological site.** See also **evaluative testing, subsurface investigation.**

show block (20c) A piece of wood **blocking** used as backing at the top edge of a wood framed gable end.

shower (20c) **1.** Abbreviation of **shower bath. 2.** A room or enclosure with one or more shower heads. See also **gang shower. 3.** Same as **shower head.**

shower bath **1.** (19c) A plumbing fixture for bathing that sprays particles or jets of water all over the body, typically from the side from tubes with a row of small holes, and positioned over a bathtub. **2.** (20c) A plumbing fixture for bathing that sprays jets of water down over the body from a wall-mounted fixture; may have a separate enclosure or be part of a bathtub. Also known as **douche bath, rain bath,** or simply **shower.**

shower bath (sense 1)

shower head A wall- or ceiling-mounted plumbing fixture with multiple small openings that create a water spray for a **shower bath.**

shower room Same as **shower** (sense 2).

show place **1.** (20c) An especially grand building, neighborhood, or city. **2.** (19c) A space for shows or exhibitions.

show room (19c) A room where a show is performed or an exhibition is displayed. See also **showroom.**

showroom **1.** A room where manufactured products are displayed for sale. **2.** (pre-20c) Same as **gymnasium.**

show window A large store window for display of retail goods; may be part of a **store front,** or a separate opening; typically backed by a partition that does not allow light into the interior.

showyard, (19c) **show yard** **1.** A fenced area for displaying cattle for sale. **2.** (19c) A fenced area for outdoor display of goods.

SHO Abbr. for **state historic preservation officer.**

shread head (pre-WWI) Same as **jerkinhead.**

shreading Same as **shredding.**

shredding, shreading Light furring attached to the underside of rafters to provide a nailer for lathing. See also **cross furring.**

shrine **1.** A place, building, or structure made sacred by association with a historic event. **2.** A place sacred to a holy personage, especially an altar, tomb, or chapel.

shrinkage crack A crack that occurs in building elements, such as concrete, masonry, and plaster, after installation due to tension caused by a decrease in volume as the components cure. See also **checking.**

shut-off valve A valve in a gas or water supply line that can completely seal off the flow to the building, a branch line, or a fixture; the main water shut-off typically is a **gate valve.** See also **stop cock.**

shute (re-20c) Same as **chute.**

shutter **1.** A hinged panel that closes a window or door opening in addition to the standard door or window; may be solid panels, or with cutouts or slats for ventilation, and located on the exterior or interior; typically one-half or one-quarter of the opening width, and made of a single board or multiple battens until mid-18c, then most often paneled or louvered; decorative, nonworking exterior shutters, not necessarily related to opening width, common after mid-20c; types include **box shutter, Indian shutter, lattice blind, louver shutter, Venetian shutter;** in some regions a solid panel is known as a **shutter** and a slatted panel as a **blind;** hardware includes **blind fast, H-hinge, shutter bar, shutter bolt, shutter dog, shutter eye, shutter hook, shutter lift, shutter worker.** See also **rolling slats, shutter box.** **2.** Any removable cover for a door, window or storefront. See also **rolling shutter.**

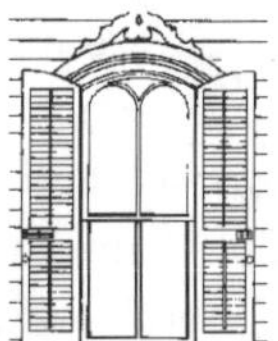

shutter (sense 1)

shutter bar A **lift latch** used on the inside stiles of a pair of shutters to fasten them in the closed position. See also **blind fast, shutter bolt, shutter hook.**

shutter bolt A hardware device for locking a pair of shutters, composed of a sliding bolt on one shutter that engages a hasp on the other. See also **blind fast, shutter bar, shutter hook.**

shutter box The cased recess that receives an interior **box shutter.** See also **sash pocket.**

shutter dog An iron piece of hardware that projects from an exterior wall and has a head that swivels to lock a **shutter** in the open position; typically composed of a square plate fixed to the wall, a short, horizontal, projecting rod, and a forged tongue that swivels on the end of the rod, with the bottom of the tongue larger so that gravity holds it in a vertical position; the tongue may be of various shapes, including S-shaped and dart-shaped. Also known as **turn, turn buckle.**

shutterette (late 20c) Bifold interior shutters.

shutter eye A metal eye attached to a jamb to support a **shutter.**

shutter hinge Same as **H-hinge.**

shutter hook A hook and eye that fastens a shutter in one position. See also **shutter bolt, shutter worker.**

shuttering All of the shutters on a building.

shutter lift **1.** A small **shutter bar** with a knob. **2.** A handle for raising a rolling shutter.

shutter worker A hardware device with a crank handle that opens and closes an exterior **shutter** from the inside; often includes a **blind adjuster** (sense 2).

shutting post The gatepost to which the gate is latched. See also **hanging post.**

shutting shoe An iron sleeve or stone with a hole that receives the end of the **drop bolt** that fastens a pair of gates in the closed, or open, position.

shutting stile The door or window **stile** that latches against the jamb. See also **hanging stile.**

siamese (19c–present) A plumbing fitting with a Y-shaped end with male threaded spouts; used on the face of a building for connecting a fire engine pumper hose to a standpipe; named after the Siamese twins Eng and Chang (1811–74).

sick house (pre-20c) A dwelling occupied by those too sick to work. See also **hospital.**

side backed out **Ornamental cast iron** with full relief moldings only on the front side, and a concave back. See also **single faced.**

sideboard **1.** A decorative dining room serving table, typically with drawers and cabinets below and shelves above, placed on a side wall; may be built-in or movable. **2.** (before mid-18c) A closet for storing tableware.

side box (pre-19c) Same as **proscenium box.**

side-construction arch A **floor arch** constructed with **side-construction tiles;** less common than an **end-construction arch.**

side-construction tile A structural clay tile unit installed in an **side-construction arch** with the axes of the air cells and webs vertical and parallel to the beams.

side-gabled, side-gable A gable-roofed building with the main entrance below the eaves of one of the sloping sides of the roof. See also **front-gabled.**

side girt A wood **girt** that spans between the end posts on the long side of a timber frame structure, at the same height as the end girts. See also **end girt, timber frame.**

side hall house A multistory house with a stair hall adjacent to an exterior wall; typically constructed with the intention of building a future addition that would make an **I-house.**

side hinge (pre-19c) A wrought-iron **H-hinge** or **HL-hinge.**

side joist anchor A metal strap connected perpendicularly across the top of several joists and anchored in an adjoining masonry wall.

side lap The amount of overlap between a slate or shingle edge and the joint of the course below.

side light, sidelight **1.** A narrow window adjacent to a door or wider window, and the same height as the door or window; most often one of a pair flanking an entrance door. **2.** (pre-20c) A window on the side of a building, as opposed to a skylight.

side light

side pond A water **reservoir** adjacent to a canal **lift-lock** to fill it when frequent passages have lowered the water level above the lock.

side post One of a pair of vertical truss posts equidistant from the center. See also **queen-post.**

side timber (pre-20c) Same as **purlin.**

sidewalk, (19c) **side walk** (19c–present) A walkway along the side of a road, especially when raised and improved with materials such as **ashlar pavement, asphalt concrete, brick, concrete, flagstone, gravel,** or **plank;** also used to describe similar types of walkways located elsewhere. Also known as **banquette, footway, sideway.**

sidewalk light Same as **vault light.**

side waver (pre-20c) Same as **purlin.**

sideway (pre-20c) A walkway beside a road; may be improved as a **sidewalk.**

side yard (19c–present) An open area at the side of a house. See also **yard.**

siding The nonstructural exterior wall covering of a wood frame building; types include **asbestos shingle, board and batten, clapboard, novelty siding, plank-on-plank, shingle, siding tile, weatherboard, weather slating,** and various substitute materials of metal, asbestos, asphalt, and vinyl.

siding tile (pre-WWI) One of a series of ceramic tiles that are nailed to wood frame buildings for **siding;** joints are filled with thin mortar. See also **tile veneer, weather tiling.**

Sienna See **burnt Sienna, raw Sienna.**

sign A fixed graphic display that conveys information.

signage All of the signs at a particular location.

significance **1.** (U.S.) The importance of a historic property as defined by the National Register criteria in one or more **areas of significance.** See also **historical significance.** **2.** (Canada) The aesthetic, cultural, educational, or scientific importance of an archaeological, architectural, paleontological, or scenic **heritage resource.** Also known as **heritage significance.**

silery (pre-19c) Same as **cilery.**

Silex A trade name for finely ground and sieved **silica;** used with oil or varnish as a wood pore filler.

silica A hard, brittle, transparent, crystalline compound composed of silicon dioxide (SiO_2); the basic component of quartz, sand, and flint; sometimes used in a very finely pulverized form to provide tooth to undercoat paints. See also **silicic acid.**

silicate paint Water-base paint containing pigments suspended in **water glass** (sodium silicate); used in making **stereochrome** paintings.

silicic acid A pure white, amorphous powder composed of precipitated **silica,** $SiO_2 \cdot nH_2O$; used as a paint filler and extender.

silicone (post-WWII) Any of several siloxane polymer resins with molecules composed of alternate silicon and oxygen atoms with attached organic radicals; chemically inert; used for caulking and sealing masonry walls.

silicon iron A type of **cast iron** containing 2–15 percent silicon. Also known as **ferrosilicon.**

sill, (pre-20c) **sell, cell, cill** **1.** The horizontal piece of lumber, or built-up section, that rests on the foundation and forms the base of a **wood frame** wall; types include **box sill, cross sill, L-sill, main sill, T-sill.** Also known as **ground sill.** See also **mudsill, sole.** **2.** The projecting horizontal base of a window or door; may be of any material; types include **sill stone, slip sill.** Also known as **doorsill, windowsill.**

sill catch A hardware device mounted on a window sill to engage a **blind fast** to lock an exterior shutter closed. See also **back catch.**

sillcock, sill cock Same as **bibb.**

sill course A masonry **stringcourse** that is continuous with the window sills, or immediately below them.

sill plate Same as **sole.**

sill stone A stone block in the form of a projecting exterior window or door **sill.**

silo An airtight structure or pit for storing cattle fodder; originally a pit or vat, in the 20c typically a cylindrical tower above a masonry or concrete pit, with an elevator to lift the fodder to the top.

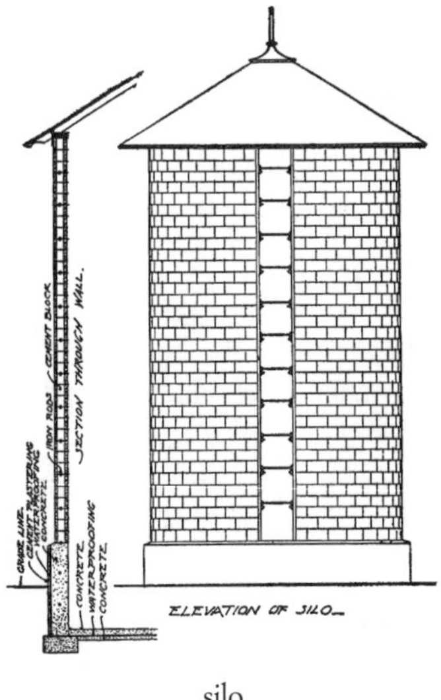

silo

silt Earth composed of extremely fine rock particles less than 0.06 mm in size; larger particles are **sand.**

silver bronze **Bronze powder** with a silver metal color. See also **silver powder.**

silvered Coated with a metal with the appearance of polished silver, especially the back of a **mirror** with an amalgam of tin or silver and mercury.

silver grain **1.** The distinctive silvery striped grain pattern of some radially sawn woods, especially oak, produced by exposed medullary rays. Also known as **bastard grain.** See also **quarter sawn.** **2.** The wood grain running circularly around a tree; exposed by a **bastard cut;** used for **bird's-eye maple.** **3.** The grain between the heartwood and sapwood of a tree.

silver leaf Extremely thin metal **foil** composed of silver.

silver lock bond Same as **rat-trap bond.**

silver pine Same as **ponderosa pine.**

silver powder A silver colored powder composed of bismuth, tin, and mercury; used for decorative finishes such as **japanning.** See also **silver bronze.**

silver spruce Same as **blue spruce.**

silver stain A transparent yellow **pigment** manufactured from silver and applied to the surface of **stained glass;** first manufactured 15c in Europe.

sima (pre-20c) Incorrect spelling of **cyma.**

similar arches See **degree.**

similor A ductile **brass** alloy composed of copper and zinc, the color of **gold.**

simple drop siding Same as **German siding.**

simple vault A **vault** with a single curved shape that does not intersect with other vaults; types include **annular vault, barrel vault, expanding vault, rampant vault, sail vault, segmental vault, semicircular vault, skew arch, spiral arch.** See also **compound vault.**

sine (18c) The **rise** of an **arch.**

single action hinge A spring-mounted self-closing **butt hinge** that opens in one direction.

single architrave, single-faced architrave An **architrave** (sense 2) with a bead molding at the edge of the opening, a flat band, and a raised molding adjacent to a fillet at the outer edge. See also **double architrave.**

single bridging **Bridging** with a single diagonal strut between a series of adjacent beams; the struts alternate direction at each space to form a herringbone pattern. Also known as **herringbone bridging.**

single cornice (18c) A **cornice** composed of a cymatium over a small fascia. See also **double cornice.**

single faced **Ornamental cast iron** with full relief moldings only on the front and a flat back. See also **double faced, side backed out.**

single-faced architrave (18c) Same as **single architrave.**

single-family dwelling A **house** designed to shelter one group of related individuals, typically with a single kitchen; often used to mean a **detached** house.

single floor A floor with only common joists spanning between bearing walls, without intermediate support. Also known as **single framed floor.**

single framed floor Same as **single floor.**

single framed roof A **roof** frame with only common rafters without intermediate supports or principal rafters; especially a gable roof with the attic floor joists acting as rafter ties, or with **truss beam** rafters with metal tie rods and a center post.

single house (Charleston, South Carolina) A multistory house with the narrow end facing the street and a center staircase with a single room on each side; typically the entrance, located on one long side of the house, is sheltered by a piazza that faces a garden.

single hung **1.** A **window** with one fixed sash and one vertically sliding sash; typically the sliding sash is at the bottom of the pair. **2.** A narrow window with a pair of **sash weights** on only one side of two vertically sliding sashes.

single pen, single-pen A **log house** or **log cabin** with one undivided room or **pen.**

single-pile A building floor plan that is one room deep, such as an **I-house.**

single-ply membrane (post-WWII) A roof covering composed of a single sheet of various rubberlike synthetic materials.

single quadrangular truss A **quadrangular truss** with diagonal tie braces within each panel; most often a **Pratt truss.** See also **single triangular truss.**

single quarter See **quarter.**

single sash A **window** with one sash in a cased opening; hinged at the top or bottom. See also **casement.**

single spruce Any of several **spruce** trees, including: (1) **white spruce,** (2) **Engelmann's spruce,** (3) **blue spruce.**

single triangular truss Same as **Warren truss.** See also **single quadrangular truss.**

single worked A building element, such as a door, that has moldings or decoration on one of two sides. See also **double worked.**

sink **1.** Any of various types of built-in watertight containers that receive cleaning wastewater; beginning in the 19c, typically rectangular with adjacent water faucets and connected at the bottom to a plumbing drain system, and without an overflow drain near the top; types include **laundry tray, slop sink.** See also **basin, lavatory.** **2.** (pre-20c) A hole or depression that receives refuse or human waste, including a **cesspool** and the hole below a **latrine.** See also **pit.** **3.** (pre-20c) A **drain** or **sewer** that receives wastewater. See also **area drain, sump.**

sink (sense 1)

sinkage **1.** (19c) A thin, rectangular groove in a classical style element. **2.** Any depressed area, such as for an entrance mat.

sink pipe The drain pipe of a **sink.**

sinkroom (pre-20c) A room with a sink; may be a scullery in a house with full plumbing, or the only room with running water in a country house.

sink trap A plumbing **trap** attached to the outflow pipe of a **sink.**

sinumbra An **annular lamp** with a reservoir with a wedge-shaped cross section; suspended from the ceiling, or set on a tall pedestal on the parlor table; patented in France in 1820, and popular in North America through the 1830s.

siphered (pre-19c) Same as **ciphered.**

siphon trap Any plumbing drain **trap** that forms a siphon, such as an **S-trap.**

siphon water closet A **water closet** that is flushed by water siphoned out of the bottom of the fixture; the **trap** at the base is refilled after flushing; usually with a **flush tank** above the bowl.

S-iron An iron tie rod with an S-shaped **anchor plate** at the end; used for attachment to a masonry wall.

sister A structural reinforcing member, such as a beam, attached to another similar member; commonly used to reinforce damaged, or undersized, existing wood beams.

site **1.** The land on which a building or other feature is located. **2.** For National Register purposes, the location of a significant event, a prehistoric or historic occupation or activity, or a building or structure, whether standing, ruined, or vanished, where the location itself maintains historical or archeological value regardless of the value of any existing structure; examples include a battlefield, a farm, an individual historic building, or the location of prehistoric rock art.

site coverage Same as **lot occupancy.**

site marker An interpretive **plaque** or sign located on or near a historic site, building, structure, object, or a scenic viewpoint; may be placed by a government agency or a private organization, such as a historical society. See also **historic marker.**

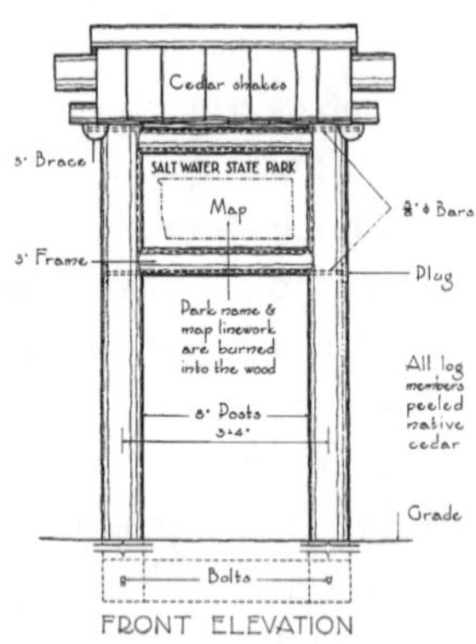

site marker

site observation Same as **construction observation.**

sitework The construction outside of a building, including earthwork, utilities, paving, and landscaping.

siting The placement of a building, structure, or object on a site in relation to natural features, boundaries, and other parts of the built environment. See also **orientation.**

Sitka spruce A large **spruce** tree of up to 150 feet in height with pale pinkish brown, soft, light, straight-grained wood; found on the Pacific coast from California to Alaska; used for millwork; *Picea sitchenis.* Also known as **tideland spruce.**

sitting room (late 18c–early 20c) A **room** in a dwelling for informal family socializing. See also **living room, parlor.**

sitz bath A tub shaped for bathing while sitting, especially with the legs and upper body not immersed in water. See also **bath, bidet.**

six over nine, 6 over 9 A double hung window with six panes in the upper sash and nine panes in the lower sash; the sashes are divided in rows of three panes.

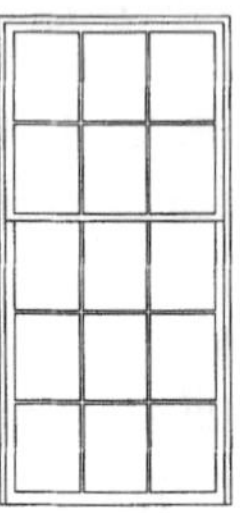
six over nine

six over six, 6 over 6 A double hung window with six panes in both the upper and lower sashes; each sash has two horizontal rows of three panes; common 1825–Civil War, and in Colonial Revival buildings.

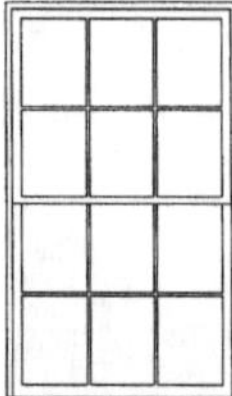
six over six

six part vault Same as **sexpartite vault.**

sixpenny nail (6d nail) A **nail** approximately 2 inches long; 150 iron common nails weigh a pound. See also **penny, sixpenny spike.**

sixpenny spike (6d spike) A **spike** approximately 5 inches long; 13 steel-wire spikes weigh a pound. See also **penny, sixpenny nail.**

sixteenpenny nail (16d nail) A **nail** approximately 3.5 inches long; 40 iron common nails weigh a pound. See also **penny, sixteenpenny spike.**

sixteenpenny spike (16d spike) A **spike** approximately 9 inches long; 4.5 steel-wire spikes weigh a pound. See also **penny, sixteenpenny nail.**

sixtypenny nail (60d nail) A **nail** approximately 6 inches long; 8 iron common nails weigh a pound. See also **penny.**

size, sizing A gelatinous solution composed of glue, resin, or starch used to smooth and seal a surface, such as wood or plaster, especially in preparation for applying gold leaf.

sized down A repetitive architectural feature, such as courses of slate, that gradually decreases in size.

sizing Same as **size.**

skeen (pre-19c) Same as **scheme.**

skeen arch (pre-19c) Same as **skene arch.**

skein screw Same as **lag bolt** with coarse threads. See also **lag screw.**

skeleton A timber or steel frame of a building before any other elements are placed on it. See also **skeleton construction.**

skeleton construction (late 19c–present) A building framing system composed of columns and girders forming a three-dimensional grid that supports the other elements, such as the floors and walls; initially cast or wrought iron during the last quarter of the 19c, then supplanted by steel by the 20c; typically the girders are a rolled **I-beam** or **wide flange beam,** and the columns are a **H-column, Z-column,** or a pair of latticed channels. Also known as **steel-cage construction.** See also **cage construction, curtain wall, monolithic, steel frame.**

skeleton paneling A wood molding grid pattern applied to a wall; the panels within the grid are the same material as the wall.

skeleton paneling

skene (pre-20c) Same as **scheme.**

skene arch, (pre-19c) **skeen arch** (pre-20c) Same as **segmental arch.** See also **scheme.**

sketch plan A **floor plan** produced as a free-hand sketch with the proper proportions and relationships of the elements; often done in the field as a basis for recording dimensions for measured drawings. See also **field records.**

skew **1.** Any architectural element with a sloped top, or not perpendicular. **2.** A coping with a sloped top, such as on a gable end wall. **3.** Same as **footstone.** See also **skew corbel.**

skew arch An arch that has the intrados at the two faces offset from each other so that the jambs below the arch are not perpendicular to the face of the wall. Also known as **oblique arch.** See also **angle of skew, skew vault.**

skewback, (19c) **skew back** **1.** A stone block with a sloped face that supports the end of a **segmental arch** or **flat arch.** **2.** A metal cap at the end of a wood truss that receives the pull of a **tie rod.** See also **anchor plate.**

skewback block (late 19c–present) A terra-cotta **structural clay tile** that rests on a steel beam and supports the end of a **tile arch;** may be located between the flanges of the beam or be a **lipped skewback.** Also known as **skewback tile.**

skew-back lintel (19c) A cast-iron lintel with end plates that form the skewbacks of an arch; typically has a T-shaped cross section; used as a tension rod to restrain the ends of the arch.

skewback tile Same as **skewback block.**

skew corbel A kneeler at the base of a gable coping that extends beyond the side wall; used to support the coping and, sometimes, to terminate the gutter or cornice on the side wall. Also known as **skew put, summer stone.** See also **skew table.**

skew fillet A fillet along a gable end wall that raises the sides of the abutting roof slates to divert water away from the wall.

skew hinge (19c) Same as **rising hinge.**

skew nailing (19c) Installing nails at less than a right angle to the surface. See also **blind nailing, toe nailing.**

skew put, skew putt (pre-20c) Same as **skew corbel.**

skew table **1.** A course of stones laid on a slope, such as below a gable coping. **2.** A single stone set at right angles to a gable coping at its base to prevent the coping stones from sliding down. See also **footstone, kneeler, skew corbel, table.**

skew vault A vault passage with an axis that is not perpendicular to the faces of the walls at the ends; typically a form of barrel vault with a spiral joint pattern; most often used for bridges. See also **angle of skew, skew arch.**

skim coat (19c–present) A smooth plaster **finish coat** composed of lime putty mixed with very fine white sand or plaster of Paris; typically about ⅛ inch thick.

skimming **1.** Same as **skim coat.** **2.** The process of applying a **skim coat.**

skinned Having had the bark (of a log) removed. See also **wane.**

skintled brickwork Same as **scintled brickwork.**

skintling Same as **scintled brickwork** (sense 2).

skirting, skirting board, skirt-board **1.** (18c–19c) Same as **baseboard.** **2.** The bottom rail of a wainscot, or wood paneled wall. **3.** (18c) An unnotched stringer board that covers and finishes the open side of stair risers and treads.

skirt-roof A false roof that encircles a building between two stories. See also **mansard roof.**

skylight, (pre-19c) **sky light** A glazed opening in the roof that lights a space directly below; may be of various forms, including gabled, pyramidal, sloped parallel to the roof, a structure raised above the roof with vertical windows, or (late 20c) a low rise plastic dome; types include **double skylight, lantern, raised skylight, slab skylight.**

sky line The upper outline of buildings or a landscape seen from a particular point of view.

skyscraper, (19c) **sky scraper** (ca. 1883–present) An exceptionally tall building; originally applied to early skeleton frame elevator buildings of 10–12 stories in New York and Chicago; the Woolworth Building in New York reached 792 feet by WWI, and the Empire State Building of 1930–32 was the world's tallest, at 1,250 feet, until late 20c; most often an **office building,** may also be other uses such as **apartment house, hotel.** See also **Chicago School, International Style, office building, tower, spire.**

slab **1.** A wide, relatively thin, plane piece of homogeneous material, such as stone. **2.** An outer plank cut from a log, with one curved and one straight side, or a rough, rived board. Also known as **clapboard.** See also **slab board, slab boarding.** **3.** (20c) Same as **slab-on-grade.** **4.** (20c) A reinforced concrete floor plate, especially when of uniform thickness.

slab board Same as **slab** (sense 2), especially a board with two flat sides and waney edges.

slab boarding Wood slabs used as siding.

slab dash A **slab plastering** stucco finish.

slab dashing (pre-WWI) Same as **slab plastering.**

slab house A Northwest coast Native American dwelling with roofing and siding constructed of split and smoothed planks supported on a pole frame lashed together.

slab-on-grade A concrete floor slab that is supported directly on the earth or fill. Also known as **slab.**

slab plastering A coarse-textured plaster used on exterior of English half-timbered houses, applied by dashing mortar on the wall and roughly troweling it; often imitated on houses of the **Tudor Revival style.** Also known as **slab dashing, slap-dash, slap plastering.** See also **spatter-dash.**

slab skylight A horizontal skylight composed of glass prisms attached with mortar or concrete to an iron frame; used for factory roofs and sidewalk vaults.

slabstone Any rock that easily splits into slabs.

slag The waste residue from the production of iron in a blast furnace, composed of silica, alumina, and lime; used in manufacturing **concrete block, mineral wool, slag brick, slag glass** and as gravel on a **built-up roof.**

slag brick A concrete **brick** manufactured from crushed **slag** and **lime.**

slag glass A type of **glass** manufactured from **slag.**

slag strip Same as **gravel stop.**

slag wool Same as **mineral wool.**

slaked lime **Quicklime** that has been steeped in water to prepare it for mixing with the other ingredients of **mortar;** may be in the form of wet **lime putty** or dry powdered **hydrated lime.** See also **whitewash.**

slap-dash, slap dashing (pre-WWI) Same as **pebble-dash** or **slab plastering.**

slap plastering Same as **slab plastering.**

slash pine A **pine** tree with orange to light brown, coarse-grained, brittle, resinous wood that is extremely heavy; not durable in contact with soil; found in coastal wetlands from eastern Louisiana to southern South Carolina; used for lumber and millwork; wood is often marketed as **longleaf pine;** *Pinus caribaea.* Also known as **southern yellow pine.**

slat **1.** Any thin, narrow piece of wood with an approximately rectangular cross section, especially when used in a louver or blind. See also **lath. 2.** (pre-20c) A slab of stone used for masonry veneer. **3.** (pre-20c) Same as a roofing **slate.**

slate **1.** Any kind of stone that splits easily into smooth, thin plates with even thickness, especially a fine-grained argillaceous rock composed primarily of sericite and quartz; imported from Britain (especially Wales) beginning in the 17c, and later quarried in Pennsylvania, Vermont, and Virginia; varieties include **graywacke, Peach Bottom slate, Welsh slate. 2.** A rectangular piece of slate stone, approximately ⅛–¼ inch thick, used to cover roofs or exterior walls in overlapping courses; typically punched with holes at the top for nailing. See also **open slating. 3.** An artificial material used as a substitute for slate.

slate-and-a-half A slate that is 1.5 times the width of the other slates; used to end a course at an edge or valley.

slate boarding (pre-20c) Same as **weather slating.**

slate cement **1.** A **hydraulic cement** made from argillaceous slate. **2.** Crushed slate mixed with a bituminous material.

slate hanging Same as **weather slating.**

slate nail A wide-headed **roofing nail** used for hanging slates; may be composed of aluminum alloy, brass, copper, or zinc. Also known as **slate peg.** See also **roofing nail.**

slate peg 1. (pre-20c) Same as **slate nail.** 2. A wooden peg used to attach the upper end of a roof **slate** to the **slating batten** below.

slating batten A **gauge lath** for a course of slates; used without sheathing.

slaughterhouse, slaughter house A building where animals are killed and butchered for market. Also known as **abattoir.**

slave cabin (southern U.S.) A small house for slaves; typically without cooking or bathing facilities. See also **quarters.**

slave quarter, slave quarters Same as **quarter** (sense 3).

sleeper 1. A horizontal timber that rests on, or just above, the ground; types include: (1) a nailer for flooring laid on the ground or structural deck; (2) One of the joist beams that rests on the first floor sills and supports the floor of a **log cabin** or **timber frame** building; (3) a **cross tie** used for spiking railroad rails; (4) (pre-18c) A timber frame building sill. 2. A diagonal board, on the rafters of a main roof, that supports the jack rafters of a dormer or cross gable. 3. (pre-19c) Same as **valley rafter.**

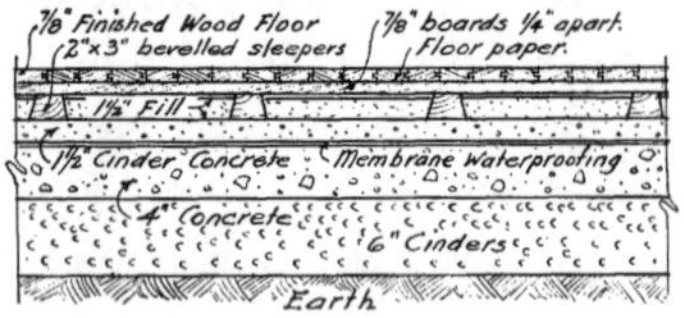

sleeper (sense 1)

sleeping porch A screened, unheated porch used for a sleeping place; commonly at an upper level of a house or on the first or second floor of a recreational building such as a lakeside cabin; used in late 19c to WWII to prevent tuberculosis and other diseases; often has interior casements, or hung sash that lowers into a pocket below the sill, for inclement weather. Also known as **open-air room.**

sleeping room Same as **bedroom.**

sleeve An open-ended fabrication, such as a tube or pipe, that forms the opening through a building element, such as a wall or floor, to allow the later insertion of another element such as a conduit, pipe, or piece of equipment.

sleeve nut A metal device with an internally threaded cylindrical hole and a hexagonal faceted exterior; the threads are opposite hand at each end; used to connect two halves of a tie rod and adjust its tension. See also **turnbuckle.**

sliced veneer (20c) Wood **veneer** that has been cut by a machine knife, as opposed to **sawn veneer;** types include **plain sliced, quarter sliced, rotary sliced.**

slick brick Same as **water-struck brick.**

slide bolt A door or gate locking device with a **bolt** that is manually slid into position; types include **drop bolt.**

sliding door A door that opens by rolling sideways, often into a pocket in the wall; typically one of a pair between parlors beginning in the early 19c; may be **overhung** or **underhung.** Also known as **pocket door.**

slip 1. (19c–present) One of the spaces created by a series of **pew** benches with integral backs and solid ends. Also known as **slip pew.** 2. A narrow space between two buildings. 3. A narrow berth for a ship, such as between two piers or rows of pilings.

slip joint A continuous slot between abutting masonry walls that allows for differential settlement. See also **construction joint, expansion joint.**

slip pew Same as **slip** (sense 1).

slip piece A projecting portion along the side of an element, that slides in a groove.

slip sheet Material, especially **rosin paper,** that allows movement between building elements, such as between a subfloor and finish floor.

slip sill A sill that is slipped between the jambs of an opening after they are in place, rather than supporting the base of the jambs.

slop brick Same as **water-struck brick.**

slope **1.** An inclined surface, especially of the ground. See also **exterior slope, interior slope, superior slope.** **2.** An angle measured against the horizon; may be calculated in angular degrees, or as a ratio of the horizontal distance to 1 foot of vertical distance, or a percentage equal to the vertical fall in 100 horizontal feet. See also **pitch.**

slope wall A masonry wall that is angled along the sloped face of an embankment.

slop sink A **sink** used for washing mops and similar activities; often mounted directly on the floor.

slot head A **screw** or **bolt** with a straight groove across its head.

slow-burning construction Same as **slow-burning mill construction.**

slow-burning mill construction A standardized type of factory building construction developed ca. 1835 by the Boston Manufacturers Mutual Fire Insurance Co.; has substantial exterior masonry walls with unpainted, heavy timber beams and columns, plank floors, and a minimum of concealed spaces and openings between floors; the beams span between columns without intermediate beams; elements may include cast-iron column bases, caps, pintles and beam boxes, segmental arches, corbeling under beam ends, saw-tooth roof, fish straps, timber dogs, scuppers at the perimeter of each floor, masonry-enclosed stair towers, fire shutters, wire glass, and laminated floors. Also known as **mill construction, slow-burning construction, standard mill construction.** See also **laminated mill construction, semimill construction.**

sluice **1.** An artificial channel for directing the flow of water, such as a flume leading to a mill wheel. See also **mill race.** **2.** A body of water controlled by a **sluice gate.** **3.** A long, sloping trough with a series of grooves or riffles along the bottom; used in mining to separate heavy gold from lighter materials carried in water along the trough.

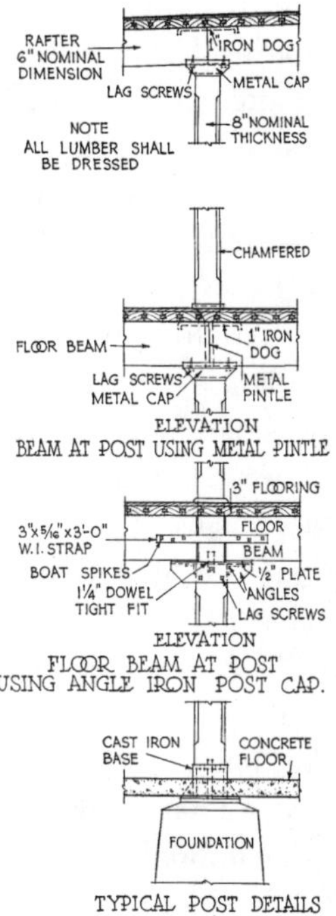

slow-burning mill construction

sluice gate A large gate valve, or similar mechanism, that controls the volume of water passing through to a **sluice** or **waste weir;** may have a **lock hatch.**

slum A pejorative term for a densely populated part of a city with decaying buildings inhabited by poor people with a high degree of social disfunction; often used with the added connotation of a place "where debauched and criminal persons live or resort" (*Funk & Wagnalls,* 1899).

slump block A type of **concrete block** with a rough face texture caused by sagging after removal from the mold; used to simulate **adobe.**

slushed joint, slushed-up joint A masonry joint, especially the head joints between bricks, filled with mortar after the bricks are laid by slushing in the mortar with a trowel; an inferior method of construction. See also **shoved joint.**

smalt **1.** Pulverized cobalt blue glass used for pigment in decorative painting and signs; typically applied dry to a surface with wet paint; common in house paints through the end of the 18c. **2.** (19c–20c) Pulverized clear glass applied to a wet paint surface; typically used to add sparkle to signs.

SMCRA **Surface Mining Control and Reclamation Act of 1977**

smith's shop A building used by a blacksmith to work iron. See also **forge.**

smith's work, smith work (pre-20c) Hand forged **builder's hardware.**

smock mill A **windmill** with a stationary base containing the mechanism and a cap that holds the vanes and is rotated to face the wind. See also **post mill.**

smoke bay A chimneylike structure on the interior of a one-story building formed by an attic partition sloping toward a gable end over an open fireplace at ground level; used primarily in 17c Chesapeake bay region houses. See also **smoke hole.**

smoke bell A metal bell or cone suspended over a gas light or oil lamp to collect the rising soot.

smoke black Same as **lamp-black.**

smoke board A board, or metal hood, that projects from the top of a fireplace opening to prevent smoke from entering the room.

smoke chamber The portion of a **fireplace** flue immediately above the throat and smoke shelf.

smoke consumer (19c) A device attached to a furnace to oxidize the partially burned combustion gases.

smoke detector A 20c automatic device for detecting the combustion products of a fire; may operate on the basis of a cloud chamber, ionization, or photoelectric detection. See also **fire detector.**

smoke extractor Any device that maintains or accelerates a chimney draft, such as a hood or ventilator at the top of the chimney.

smoke hatch Same as **smoke vent.**

smoke hole A hole in a roof to let smoke escape. See also **smoke bay.**

smokehouse, (pre-19c) **smoak house** (early 18c–present) An **outbuilding** used to smoke and store meat or fish; typically of small size (8–14 feet on a side), windowless and with an open fire in the center. Also known as **meat house.**

smokehouse

smoke panel A recessed area in the rear wall of a large fireplace; used pre-19c, probably to increase the draft.

smoke pipe Same as **smoke stack.**

smoke shelf A ledge above a fireplace firebox that prevents down drafts by inducing a rolling motion to the smoke.

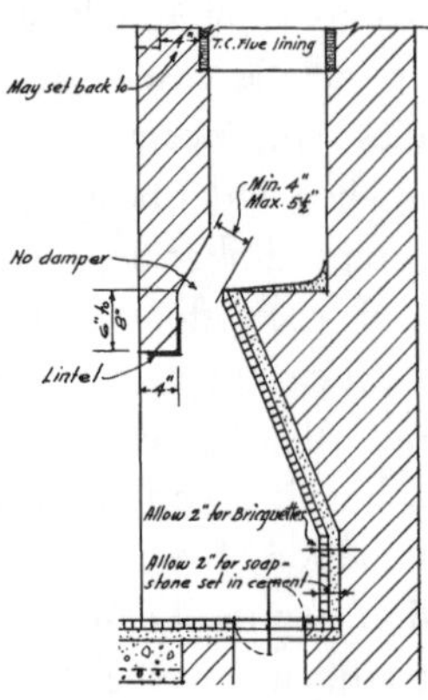

smoke shelf

smoke stack (19c–present) A chimney for a boiler, especially a cylindrical metal pipe of sheet or plate iron. Also known as **smoke pipe.** See also **chimney stack.**

smoke stop A smokeproof partition that separates portions of a building.

smoke tower (19c) Any tall architectural feature that encloses a chimney; used on some churches.

smoke vent **1.** Same as **smoke hole.** **2.** A roof hatch that automatically opens to let smoke from a fire inside a building escape. Also known as **smoke hatch.** See also **vent.**

smoke washer (19c) A device that precipitates smoke particles from exhaust by passing it through a water spray.

smoking room A room set aside for those who wish to smoke, such as in a hotel or clubhouse; common 19c–early 20c.

smooth finish **1.** An even, planed, sanded or ground surface texture of an exposed material, such as stone or wood. See also **machine finish, smooth-troweled.** **2.** The flat, even surface texture of brick formed with steel dies or pressed into molds.

smooth machine finish Same as **machine finish.**

smooth oak An **ornamental cast-iron** pattern in the stylized form of intertwined live oak branches with leaves and acorns; originated in New Orleans.

smooth pointing A fine, nearly flat, chipped stone finish; typically surrounded by a chiseled **draft.** See also **rough pointing, stonework.**

smooth-troweled A smooth stucco finish formed by floating the wet finish coat with a metal trowel. See also **stucco.**

SMSA Abbr. for **standard metropolitan statistical area.**

snake fence (19c–present) Same as **worm fence.**

snap switch (late 19c–present) An electric **switch** with a small handle that is rotated to turn the circuit on or off; internal springs keep the switch in either the open or closed position; typically wall-mounted flush for a small number of lights or wall outlets.

snap switch

snecked rubble **Rubble masonry** constructed of rubble stones laid to form a bond.

snow bird A small cast-metal device in the stylized form of an eagle, or a similar shape, used as a **snow guard;** typically one of a series on a slate or shingle roof.

snow board A continuous board attached to a sloped roof near the eave as a **snow guard.**

snowflake marble A coarse **dolomite** stone quarried in Westchester County, New York; not a true marble; used to construct St. Patrick's Cathedral and other buildings in New York City.

snow guard Any of various devices attached to a sloped roof near the eave to prevent large masses of snow from sliding off the roof; types include **snow bird, snow board,** and patented bent wire shapes installed in rows on slate or shingle roofs.

snow shed A structure covering a portion of a railroad to protect it from snow slides.

soap A stretcher brick whose back face has been cut off; typically used where the structure behind the brickwork does not permit a full-depth brick. Also known as **soap brick, split.**

soap brick Same as **soap.**

soapstone Steatite, a soft, foliated talc having a soapy-feeling surface; typically used in slabs for counters, hearths, fireplace surrounds, pavers, and sinks.

Society of Architectural Historians (SAH) A U.S. organization for members interested in **architectural history.**

Society of Commercial Archeology (SCA) A U.S. organization for members interested in the study of **commercial archaeology.**

socket **1.** Any cavity that receives the end of another member of the same shape, such as a beam, column, bolt, or pivot. **2.** The end of quarry shothole that remains after the explosion has split the stone. **3.** (20c) An electrical device that receives the prongs of a plug on a cord, such as from a light or appliance; typically part of an outlet.

socket bolt A door lock **bolt** that slides into a socket in the locked position.

socket pipe Same as **socket sewer pipe.**

socket sewer pipe (19c–present) A large diameter cast-iron or terra-cotta pipe with an enlarged opening at one end to form a hub that receives the end of the adjoining section of pipe; typically in 3 or 4 foot lengths. Also known as **earthen pipe, socket pipe, socket tile.** See also **bell pipe.**

socket tile (19c) A terra-cotta **socket sewer pipe.**

socket washer A cupped or countersunk washer, such as used on a bolt.

socle, zocle **1.** A plain, rectangular stone block that supports a statue or other object. Also known as **zocco, zoccolo.** See also **plinth.** **2.** A plain, projecting base supporting a wall or row of ornaments.

sod Intermingled grass plants, including the roots and topsoil held by the roots; sometimes mixed with other plants; includes an established lawn grown from seed, natural prairie, and cut pieces ready for transplanting or use in a **sod house.** Also known as **turf.**

soda glass A type of **glass** manufactured with soda (sodium carbonate) for the metallic oxide.

sodder (pre-19c) Same as **solder.**

sod house A type of prairie or plains house with bearing walls constructed of large bricks of cut sod; typically one story with a low-pitch, sod covered roof; most common mid-19c, constructed into the early 20c; the sod roof often replaced with more weathertight materials.

sodium fluoride solution An aqueous solution of approximately 7 percent sodium fluoride; used as a **wood preservative.** Also known as **Osmose.**

soffit, (pre-19c) **soffett, soffito** **1.** The bottom surface of an **arch,** especially when the arch has a square cross section. Also known as **archivolt.** **2.** The exposed underside of a relatively narrow surface, such as an architrave, beam, cornice, lintel, stairway, vault, or similar element. **3.** The flat underside of a roof eave or overhang. **4.** (pre-20c) Same as **ceiling.**

soffit board A horizontal board that covers an eave soffit. Also known as **plancer.**

soffit block A **structural clay tile** that covers the bottom of a steel beam to provide fireproofing; supported by the **skewback blocks** of a **tile arch.**

soffito (pre-19c) Same as **soffit.**

soft brick Same as **salmon brick.**

soft-burned Clay masonry units that have been fired at low temperatures; produces soft units with low compressive strengths and high absorption. See also **salmon brick.**

soft cast steel (19c) Same as **soft steel.**

soft costs The portion of a **development** budget for financing, fees, general overhead, and design costs; includes loan interest, permit fees, legal fees, architectural and engineering fees, geotechnical and environmental study fees, and developer fees. See also **hard costs, land costs, pro forma.**

soft mud brick A **brick** made by molding wet clay in a frame, especially by hand; types include **oiled brick, sand-struck brick, water-struck brick.** See also **stiff mud brick.**

soft solder Same as **solder** (sense 1).

soft steel A very malleable, low-carbon **steel** with less than 0.25 percent carbon content; commonly used as a substitute for wrought iron, and for rolled structural shapes, starting in the late 19c; the most common type used in construction. Also known as **carbon steel, ingot iron, low steel, low-carbon steel, mild steel, soft cast steel, structural steel.**

softwood Wood cut from a tree with needles that produces cones; typically evergreen; often softer and less likely to split than wood from hardwood trees; scientifically known as **gymnosperm;** types include **cedar, cypress, Douglas fir, hemlock, pine, spruce, tamarack.**

soil pipe **1.** A **drain pipe** that carries human waste between a water closet or urinal and a sewer; may also carry wastewater from bathtubs and sinks. See also **soil stack, waste pipe.** **2.** (19c) Cast-iron pipe used as a **house sewer.** **3.** Any type of **sewer pipe** used for a underground sanitary sewer line.

soil pipe bend Same as **sanitary bend.**

soil stack The vertical sanitary waste line in a building that is connected to the water closets and sinks. Also known as **waste stack.** See also **soil pipe.**

solar (pre-19c) Same as **solarium** (sense 2).

solarium **1.** A room with extensive glazing to let in sunlight, especially for medicinal purposes, such as in a hospital or sanatorium. **2.** (pre-19c) An upper-story room or an apartment on the roof, such as a loggia. Also known as **solar.** **3.** (pre-20c) Same as **sundial.**

solar lamp Any of various lamps developed in the 1840s to efficiently burn lard oil; the burner is surrounded by a glass reservoir so that the lard is melted by the heat produced; named by the manufacturers who claimed that the amount of light given off was equal to that of the sun; common ca. 1840–60, then displaced by the **burning fluid lamp** and the later **kerosene lamp.**

solder, (pre-19c) **sodder** A metal alloy that is solid at normal temperature but melts at relatively low heat and is used to attach metal pieces together; traditionally composed of lead and tin, lead in plumbing solder was outlawed in the U.S. in the late 20c; types include **aluminum solder, half-and-half, hard solder, soft solder.** See also **blown joint, brazing, soldered pipe, soldering, welding, wiped joint.**

soldered pipe A **lead pipe** fabricated by bending a flat sheet into a cylinder and soldering the joint. See also **cast pipe, blown joint, wiped joint.**

soldering The process of connecting two metal pieces by heating them and letting molten **solder** run into the joint; used to waterproof roofing and plumbing joints, and to connect window cames and electric wires.

soldier **1.** A **brick** placed vertically with its narrowest face exposed on the face of a wall. **2.** A vertical wood ground the size of a brick; used in a brick wall as a nailer for the baseboard.

soldier arch A jack arch composed of soldier bricks.

soldier course A horizontal row composed of **soldier** brick.

soldier pile One of a series of piles installed at intervals at the edge of an excavation to support the **lagging** in a **sheeting and shoring** system; in the 20c often a steel H-column.

sole **1.** The horizontal lumber which forms the base of a stud wall, typically the same dimension as the studs. Also known as **sill plate, sole plate.** See also **bed plate, sill.** **2.** A horizontal timber on the ground that supports shoring. Also known as **sole piece.** See also **sleeper.**

solenoid A mechanical switch activated by an electromagnet with a moving core; used in various devices such as remotely operated valves and door locks.

sole piece Same as **sole** (sense 2).

sole plate Same as **sole** (sense 1).

solid **1.** Cut or fabricated from a single piece of material. See also **worked out of the solid.** **2.** Without internal voids. See various phrases beginning with **solid** following.

solid blocking A rectangular piece of lumber fastened between two joists, or studs, that is the same depth as the framing; used as **solid bridging** and/or a **fire stop.**

solid bridging **Solid blocking** used as **bridging** between adjoining beams.

solid-core door (20c) A **flush door** that has a solid core between the flat sheets on the faces, as opposed to a **hollow-core door;** the core may be wood, such as a **stave door,** or a fire resistive material, such as gypsum.

solid door Same as **solid-core door.**

solid drawn (20c) A tube or **pipe** manufactured from a solid metal billet by drawing it over a cone-shaped mandrel.

solid floor (19c) A floor composed of continuous joists nailed side by side.

solid frame The rails and stiles of a paneled door that have **solid stuck.**

solid masonry unit (20c) A brick or block that is at least 75 percent solid in the bedding plane. See also **hollow masonry unit.**

solid mold A molding profile cut into the base material, as opposed to an **applied mold.** See also **solid stuck.**

solid stuck Any complex **solid mold** planed from a single piece of wood. See also **solid frame, sticking.**

solid vaulting A **vault** constructed with elements of uniform thickness, as opposed to rib vaulting.

solive (pre-20c) A secondary **beam,** such as a joist or rafter, especially when supporting a ceiling.

solomonic column, salomonic column A **twisted column** with a helical shaft and classical capital and base; often used in **baroque** architecture. Also known as **salomónica.** See also **cabled column, spiral fluted column, wreathed column.**

soluble glass Same as **water glass.**

solvent **1.** A liquid, such as water, alcohol, or acetone, that easily dissolves other materials; used in restoration cleaning. **2.** Same as **thinner.**

solvent stripper A **paint remover** with an organic compound as the active ingredient; solvents used include methylene chloride, methanol, or toluol; typically an additive, such as wax, is used to retard drying.

Somes Sound granite A light grayish buff, medium- to coarse-grained granite quarried in the vicinity of Somes Sound, Maine.

sommer (pre-19c) Same as **summer.**

son-et-lumière [French] "Sound and light"; a nighttime exterior dramatic interpretation of a historic site by the use of lighting and amplified voices and music.

soot black Same as **lampblack.**

sopraporta [Italian] "Above the door"; an illustrative painting above a doorway; typically framed by a continuation of the door moldings.

Sorrento work Fretwork cut with a jigsaw. See also **scrollwork.**

sound boarding A series of boards installed on ledgers between floor joists to support **deafening** in a **counter ceiling.**

sounding board **1.** A surface above a stage, or pulpit, that reflects the sound of a speaker, or music, towards the audience. Also known as **type.** **2.** One of a series of boards used for **sound boarding.**

sound insulation (late 20c) Materials used to decrease the transmission of sound from one part of a building to another, or from outside to inside. Also known as **deafening, deadening.**

sound pollution Same as **noise pollution.**

source See **document, primary source, secondary source.**

Southern Colonial **Colonial architecture** constructed south of Pennsylvania and Delaware beginning early 17c; styles include **Georgian.** See also **log house, postmedieval architecture.**

southern cypress Same as **bald cypress.**

Southern pine A 20c commercial wood group that includes **loblolly pine, longleaf pine, shortleaf pine, slash pine.** See also **Southern yellow pine.**

Southern red cedar Same as **eastern red cedar.**

southern red oak A medium sized **oak** tree with light red, heavy, coarse-grained wood that checks badly during drying; common in the Gulf and south Atlantic states, also ranges northward to southern New Jersey, Illinois and Indiana; used for lumber and millwork; *Quercus falcata,* (19c) *Quercus rubra.* Also regionally known as **red hill oak, Spanish oak, Spanish water oak, spotted oak, turkey oak.** See also **red oak.**

Southern yellow pine The several varieties of lumber quality pine tree found in southeastern US; includes **loblolly pine, longleaf pine, slash pine, shortleaf pine.** Also known as **Southern pine.** See also **yellow pine.**

spa A resort focused on the bathing in, or drinking of, natural mineral waters; common beginning late 18c.

space An enclosed, or visually defined, volume.

space heater An unducted hot-air furnace that is located within the space being warmed; may be attached to a permanent electric or gas supply, or have a self-contained propane or kerosene fuel source.

spackling, spackling compound A plasterlike material used to patch holes; typically composed of materials that do not shrink as they dry and, therefore, do not crack.

spall, (pre-20c) **spaul** A chip or flake removed from the surface of a masonry unit or concrete; may be a from a blow or a form of **spalling.**

spalled joint A masonry joint filled with chips of stone pushed into the mortar. See also **galleting.**

spalling The continuous formation of **spalls** on masonry units or concrete after installation; may have various causes including **freeze-thaw action, oxide jacking,** or **salt decay.** See also **exfoliation, scaling.**

span **1.** The clear opening distance between the abutments of an arch. **2.** For major arches, the horizontal distance between the skewbacks midway between the intrados and extrados. **3.** The distance between the bearings of a beam. See also **clear span.**

spandrel, (pre-20c) **spandril** **1.** The approximately triangular portion of wall between the extrados of two adjoining arches and the molding or arch above, or between an arched opening and a rectangular molding frame. **2.** (late 19c–present) In a **curtain wall** building, the panel between a window sill and the window head below. **3.** The triangular space beneath the string of a stair.

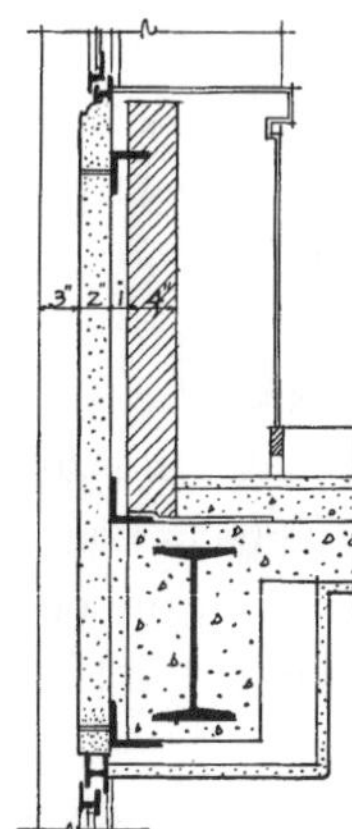

spandrel (sense 2)

spandrel beam A beam that spans between two exterior columns and supports the windows and wall above, especially in **skeleton construction.**

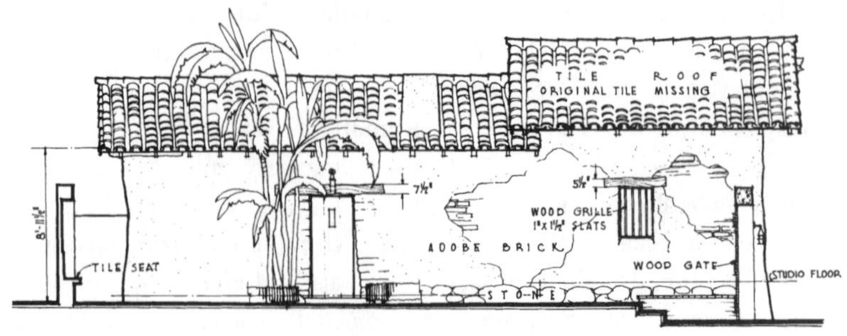

Spanish Colonial with Spanish roof tiles
El Cuartel
Santa Barbara, California

spandrel bracketing A pair of curved brackets that form an arch **spandrel** shape.

spandrel door A low-height door at the base of a **jib window.**

spandrel frame Any triangular wood frame, such as that formed by a stair stringer and the floor below.

spandrel glass (1955–present) A type of clear **glass** with an opaque colored coating on the back face; named for its use in curtain wall spandrels. See also **Vitrolite.**

spandrel step A solid stair step with a triangular cross section; used to make a flush soffit below the stair; typically a single piece of stone.

spandrel wall A wall supported on an arch **spandrel.**

spandril Same as **spandrel.**

Spanish brown **1.** A dark, dull reddish brown, earthen paint **pigment** containing iron oxide; commonly used 18c in oil-base paint as a primer or inexpensive finish coat. **2.** Same as **Indian red.**

Spanish Colonial The Spanish-influenced architecture built in Florida, Puerto Rico, southwestern U.S. and Mexico 16c–mid-18c; typically adapted Spanish baroque styles to local materials, such as **adobe** and **coquina;** most often used to refer to the **mission** complexes of the southwest U.S. and the **Mudéjar-Gothic** buildings of Mexico, also includes diverse examples such as the 1565 fortifications at St. Augustine, Florida; houses of the period often include massive plain stuccoed masonry walls, a central **patio,** pitched **mission tile** or thatched roof, or a flat roof with exposed wood rafters with bricks spanning between them and cyma-shaped ends, and features such as **cancela, concha, cortina, galería, mascarón, portal, postigo, reja, tejamaniles, zaguán** and **zapata.** See also **Barroco-mudéjar Style, Mission style, Monterey style, Territorial style.**

Spanish Colonial Revival style (1910–present) An architectural style beginning late 19c that is loosely based on stylistic elements of adobe **Spanish Colonial** and **Pueblo** buildings; most common in the period 1905–10; examples range from high style to vernacular; typical elements include smooth stucco walls imitating **adobe,** fractable parapet or parapeted dormer, irregular massing. See also **Monterey style, Mission style, Pueblo Revival style, Territorial Style.**

Spanish oak Same as **southern red oak.**

Spanish roof tile An interlocking terra-cotta **roof tile** with a convex, curved top that adjoins a narrow flat valley; typically about 9 × 13 inches. See also **mission tile.**

Spanish water oak Same as **southern red oak.**

Spanish whiting, Spanish white (18c) **Whiting** imported from Spain.

spanner A horizontal tie or cross brace, such as a roof **collar beam,** or a bridge **cross beam.**

span piece Same as **collar beam.**

span roof Same as **ridge roof.**

spar, (pre-19c) **sparr** **1.** (pre-20c) Any piece of **timber.** **2.** Same as **brotch.** **3.** A pole or timber used to fasten a door or gate. **4.** (pre-20c) Same as **common rafter.**

spare room A **bedroom** occasionally used for guests.

sparr (pre-19c) Same as **spar.**

spar varnish A glossy, transparent, exterior oil varnish originally developed for use on ship's spars; typically composed of linseed oil or tung oil mixed with resins.

spatter dash, spatter-dash, spatterdash A rough-textured **stucco** finish formed by throwing a stiff mixture of Portland cement and sand, or crushed stone, against the wet finish coat. Also known as **splatter-dash,** and incorrectly as **slab dash, slap-dash.** See also **pebble-dash, roughcast, slab plastering.**

spaul (pre-20c) Same as **spall.**

speaking tube A sheet-metal piping system connecting distant rooms that allows oral communication; used in large houses, offices, and between public lobbies and apartments mid-19c–early 20c.

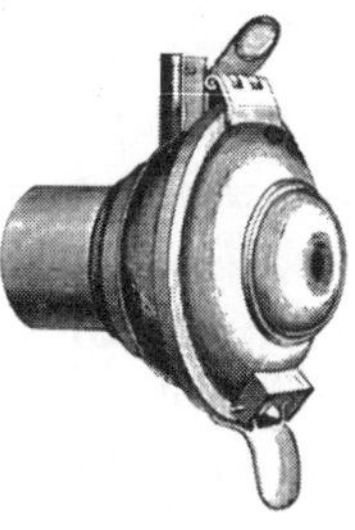

speaking tube

spear An **ornamental cast-iron** finial for a picket in the stylized form of a spear head.

special exception A zoning **variance,** often with specific criteria for approval spelled out in the **zoning code.**

specialties (20c) Miscellaneous minor building products, such as flagpoles or signage, that aren't part of a major **trade.**

specifications (late 18c–present) A written document that describes in detail the special contract conditions, and quality of materials and workmanship, of a construction project; part of the **construction documents** used for bidding and building a project; late 20c specifications are commonly organized in a standard CSI format that approximates the sequence of construction. See also **articles of agreement, plans.**

specs Abbr. for **specifications.**

spectatorium A diorama building in which the viewers are seated on a revolving platform.

speculation The purchase of an ownership interest in tangible property, such as **real estate,** based on its anticipated rise in **market value,** as opposed to its current value. See also **income property, investment property.**

spermaceti A brittle, fatty stearine found in the heads of whales, especially sperm whales; used in wax paints and as fuel in oil lamps. Also known as **cetaceum, white amber.**

sphinx **1.** Any one of several mythical Egyptian creatures with various combinations of heads on the body of a lion; types include **androsphinx, criosphinx, hieracosphinx;** used as ornamentation, or sculpture, on some Classical Revival buildings, especially those used by the Masonic Orders. **2.** A Greek mythical creature with the head, and sometimes breasts, of a woman, and the winged body of a lion or dog.

spigot **1.** A plug that stops the flow of liquid from a hole. **2.** The small end of a **bell pipe.** **3.** Same as **faucet.**

spigot and faucet joint (19c) Same as **bell and spigot joint.**

spigot joint Same as **bell and spigot joint.**

spike **1.** A large framing **nail** with a large, flat head; of larger cross section than a **common nail;** typically available in lengths of 3–9 inches; types include **wire spike;** types by size include **twopenny spike, threepenny spike, fourpenny spike, fivepenny spike, sixpenny spike, sevenpenny spike, eightpenny spike, ninepenny spike, tenpenny spike, twelvepenny spike, sixteenpenny spike.** **2.** One of a series of pointed metal bars, such as used on top of a wall to prevent someone from climbing over. **3.** A pointed iron bar with a square cross section and a slightly round flat head that projects on one side; typically 4.5–6 inches in length; used to attach rails to railroad ties and in construction of wood docks and wharfs; may be curved, serrated, or split to increase holding power. See also **split pin.**

spike nail Same as **spike** (sense 1).

spile (pre-20c) **1.** Same as **pile.** **2.** A wooden plug for a nail hole.

spillway The chute in front, or at the side, of a **dam** or **waste weir** that carries overflow water or water released from the gates; typically with a profile that is convex at the top and concave at the bottom to reduce erosion of the surface. Also known as **tumbling bay.** See also **waste weir.**

spindle A wood architectural element that has been turned on a lathe, including a **newel** or one of a series of thin, vertical, round elements of a railing or spindlework; from the resemblance to the wood rod, tapered at both ends, used in hand yarn spinning. See also **baluster.**

spindle work A decorative screen formed by a series of turned wood spindles.

spinning chamber (mid-18c–19c southern U.S.) A room used to make flax and/or cotton thread and yarn with a spinning wheel; also used as living quarters for servants.

spinning house (mid-18c–19c southern U.S.) A building used to make flax and/or cotton thread and yarn with spinning wheels; also used as living quarters for servants. See also **weaving house.**

spinning mill (19c–present) A building containing spinning machines for the manufacture of thread and yarn.

spinning room Same as **spinning chamber.**

spira The moldings at the base of a column or pilaster.

spiral fluted column A column with fluting that wraps around the shaft in a helical pattern. See also **solomonic column.**

spiral stair A stairway with a circular plan and wedge-shaped treads; the outer edge of the stair actually traces a helix, rather than a spiral. Also known as **cockle stair, corkscrew stair, helical stair, screw stair.** See also **newel, vise.**

spiral vault A barrel vault with a spiral, or helical, center axis; used to support a masonry **spiral stair.**

spire A steep, pointed roof approximately cone-shaped; common on church towers; types include **broach, needle spire.** See also **pyramid, steeple.**

spired Having a faceted roof that approximates a cone shape.

spirelet A small spire, such as a **pinnacle.**

spire-light, spire light A small window or dormer on the side, or at the base, of a spire.

spirit (pre-WWI) Same as **solvent** or **thinner,** especially alcohol or turpentine. See also **spirit varnish, spirits of turpentine.**

spirit of wine varnish (18c) A quick drying, translucent **spirit varnish** composed of **sandarac** gum, white amber, gum elemi, and mastic dissolved in alcohol from wine; used for varnishing gilt, leather, and picture frames.

spirits of turpentine (pre-WWI) Same as **turpentine** (sense 1).

spirit varnish Any quick drying, translucent **varnish** made of a resin or gum dissolved in a **spirit,** especially alcohol; types include **sandarach, shellac, spirit of wine varnish.**

splatter-dash Same as **spatterdash.**

splay A beveled or slanted surface, larger than a **chamfer,** that makes an oblique angle with another surface, especially an angled jamb.

splayed arch An arch with an intrados at one side of the wall larger than at the other side, creating a conical shaped soffit.

splayed coping Same as **feather edge coping.**

splay face molding Same as a **beveled molding.**

splay joint, splayed joint (19c) A joint between two beveled surfaces, especially between meeting rails of a double hung window.

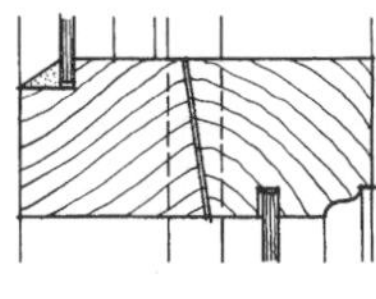

splay joint

splice The joining of any two elements lengthwise, such as two beams with a **scarf joint,** or two electric wires with their ends twisted together.

spline **1.** A thin, narrow element inserted into adjoining grooves in two pieces to attach them together; types include **loose tongue, feather tongue spline.** **2.** (pre-20c) A narrow board, such as those used for ceilings.

split **1.** A **crack** that passes entirely through a piece of wood, or other material, so that it is visible on two faces. See also **check, shake.** **2.** Divided into smaller pieces by striking or use of a wedge. See also **rived** and various phrases beginning with **split** following. **3.** Same as **soap.**

split bond A brick wall **blind bond** with the row of headers at every fifth or sixth course concealed behind stretchers which have been split lengthwise; the resulting surface pattern is **running bond.**

split face A rough, uneven, concave-convex surface finish produced by splitting stone or concrete blocks with a guillotine knife or other device. See also **stonework.**

split joist (pre-20c) One half of a **joist** (sense 2); nominally 2 × 3 inches in cross section.

split lath Thin wood lath strips made by riving wood; used before sawn wood lath became common in the 19c.

split pin A **spike** that is cleft at the point so that it spreads as it is hammered into the wood, making it less likely to come loose.

split rail A wood bar manufactured by splitting a cut log into smaller pieces by driving wedges into the ends. Also known as **rail.** See also **rail fence.**

split rail fence See **rail fence.**

split ring connector (20c) A wood truss connector in the form of a short metal cylinder with a gap; installed in a circular slot in each adjoining piece of wood, with a bolt through a hole drilled in the center of the ring.

split shake A **shake** (sense 1), as opposed to a **processed shake.**

split system An air-conditioning, or heat-pump, system with the fan coil inside the building and a remote condenser unit outside the building.

splitter A slang term for a social scientist, such as an **archaeologist,** ethnologist or linguist, who tends to emphasize the differences that make artifacts, languages, and other cultural groupings appear unrelated, such as when classifying a multitype **archaeological site,** or an inventory or grouping of artifacts; as opposed to a **lumper.**

splitwood, splittwood (18c) Rived wood materials such as **shakes** and **clapboards.**

spot detector A **heat detector** composed of an individual unit a few inches in diameter. See also **fire detector.**

spotted oak Same as **southern red oak.**

sprayed asbestos A fire-resistant coating composed of chopped **asbestos** fibers mixed with a cement and water, and sometimes mineral wool; sprayed on steel structure to form a coating .25–6 inches thick; used in the U.S. ca. 1900–86.

spray paint (20c) Any type of paint applied with a spray gun that atomizes the paint into a fine jet of mist by use of compressed air.

spread footing A **footing** that is wider than the wall or column it supports in order to spread the vertical load over a wider area; types include **isolated footing, strip footing.**

spread glass (19c) Same as **cylinder glass.**

sprig **1.** Same as **glazier's point.** **2.** A small, headless nail or brad.

sprig bolt Same as a **barb bolt.**

spring **1.** The resilience or bounce of a structure, such as a floor, roof, or stair. **2.** Same as **spring line.** See also **sprung.**

spring beam A large beam without intermediate support, such as a tie beam in a truss.

spring bolt A sliding lock bolt held in the closed position by a leaf spring; often used as synonymous with **spring lock.**

spring-butt hinge (19c–present) A self-closing **butt hinge** with an internal spring. See also **spring hinge.**

springer **1.** The first voussoir that curves upward from the spring line of an arch, immediately above the impost. Also known as **springing stone.** **2.** The place where the arch voussoirs meet the impost or other support. See also **spring-line.** **3.** The bottom stone of a gable coping; types include **footstone.** **4.** Same as **groin rib.**

spring head A natural spring that is the source of a stream of water.

spring hinge Any type of self-closing **hinge** with a steel spring; includes **floor spring hinge, spring-butt hinge.**

spring hook A hardware hook combined with a spring that closes the opening; used on a door to keep it latched. See also **hook and eye.**

springhouse, spring house A **structure** built over a natural spring; may be rustic or in an architectural style; used to protect the water and cool food and milk; sometimes large enough to sit inside.

springing course The horizontal masonry course that is in line with an arch **springer** (sense 2).

springing stone Same as **springer.**

springing line Same as **spring line.**

springing wall A buttress wall that resists the thrust of the end of an arch. Also known as **spring wall.** See also **flying buttress.**

spring latch Same as **latch lock.** See also **spring hook.**

spring line, springing line The imaginary line connecting the points where the intrados meets the abutments at each side of an arch; typically horizontal, may be sloped such as with a **rampant arch.** Also known as **spring.**

spring lock A hardware lock that fastens with a **spring bolt;** may be opened by sliding a handle or turning a knob; types include **latch lock.**

spring mold A wood **molding** planed from a board and installed with its back at an angle from the vertical in order to give the appearance of a large solid molding. Also known as **sprung molding.** See also **rake mold.**

spring wall (pre-20c) Same as **springing wall.**

springwood The less-dense springtime growth of an **annual ring;** typically lighter in color than the **summerwood.** Also known as **earlywood.**

sprinkler head A fire protection device activated by intense heat, or fire detectors, that sprays water from an overhead **sprinkler system;** typically has a metal plug that melts at 155 degrees; late 20c types may have a liquid-filled plastic plug that bursts at a particular temperature; types include **concealed sprinkler, flush sprinkler, pendent sprinkler, recessed sprinkler.**

sprinkler system An automatic fire protection system that delivers a water spray during a fire in a building; includes riser, main, and lateral pipes, sprinkler heads, valves, and often a fire pump and alarms; typically connected directly to the water main, and to a **siamese** and alarms; may be a **dry system** or **wet system;** types include **deluge system, outside sprinkler system, preaction system.** See also **fire suppression system, sprinkler head.**

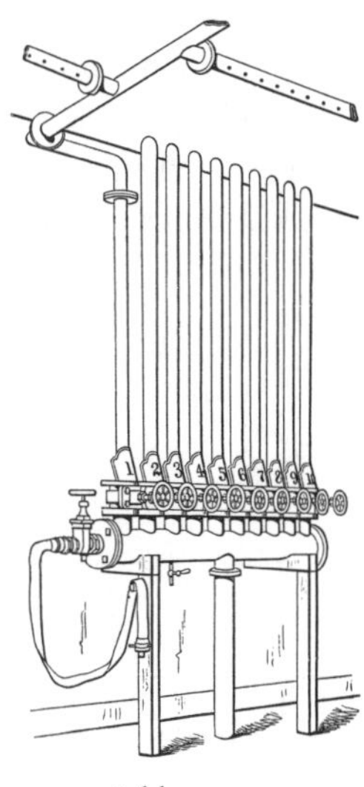

sprinkler system

sprocked eaves A roof **eave** formed by sprockets.

sprocket A small timber that slopes from the back of a rafter to the top of the masonry bearing wall to form an overhanging eave and a break in the roof slope. Also known as **cocking piece.** See also **sprocked eaves.**

spruce Any of the softwood trees of the genus *Picea,* with light, soft, moderately strong wood; types include **black spruce, blue spruce, Engelmann spruce, red spruce,**

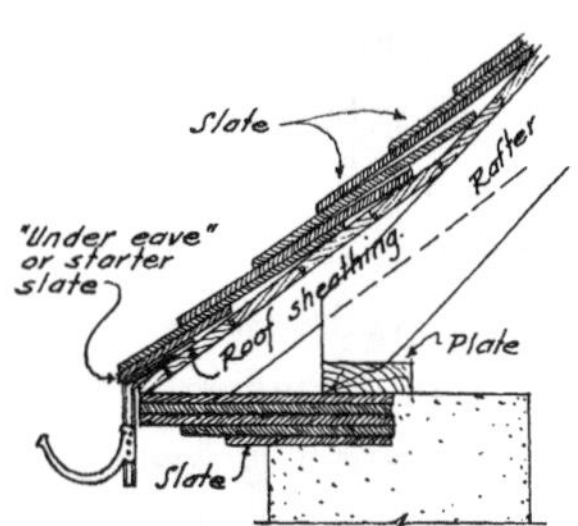

sprocked eaves

Sitka spruce, white spruce. See also **spruce-pine.**

spruce-pine **1.** Same as **yellow pine** (sense 1). **2.** Same as **black spruce.**

spruce yellow (pre-20c) An earthen paint **pigment** similar to, and slightly darker than, **ocher.**

sprung Having beveled joints between adjoining boards or planks so that the surface is flush.

sprung molding **1.** A molding bent in a curve. **2.** Same as **spring mold.**

spud (pre-20c) A dowel that projects from the bottom of a door post to attach it.

spudd and ring (pre-20c) A metal device for attaching a wood post to a stone base, composed of a ring, or ferrule, around the base of the post, with a projecting pin that is inserted into a hole in the stone. See also **thimble, spudd and ring.**

spur **1.** A diagonal wood brace, especially between a timber frame post and a tie beam or rafter. Also known as **spur brace.** **2.** A projecting portion of a wall, such as a **buttress.** **3.** A **fortification** wall that crosses part of a rampart and connects it to an interior part of the work. **4.** A projecting blockhouse or tower in front of a sally port in a **fortification.** **5.** Same as **griffe.** **6.** A **wing dam,** or similar projection into the water from the shoreline. **7.** (pre-19c) A piece of lumber such as a stud, joist, or door bar.

spur anchor A T-shaped **beam anchor** composed of a metal strap with one end wrapped around a metal rod; the strap is nailed to the wood beam and the rod is placed in the joint between masonry courses.

spur brace Same as **spur** (sense 1).

spur stone A projecting stone at the base of an outside angle of a building to prevent damage by vehicular traffic; typically with a round cross section, and often tapering up to a point against the angle.

square **1.** A measure equal to a sufficient amount of material to produce 100 square feet of finished surface; most often used for roofing and flooring. See also **squareage.** **2.** An urban public space, especially a park that is square in plan. **3.** A city block. **4.** A pane of glass. **5.** A molding with a square cross section. **6.** Any square-shaped object or outline. **7.** Forming a right angle, such as between vertical and horizontal element. See also **out of square.** **8.** A rectangular step of a **parapeted gable.** See also **fractable.** **9.** A square or rectangular planting **bed,** especially when part of a geometric garden design, such as a **parterre.**

squareage The amount measured in squares. See also **square** (sense 1).

square and flat A flat rectangular panel held by stiles and rails without edge moldings.

square and rabbet (pre-20c) Same as **annulet.**

square billet A cube-shaped projection used in a **billet molding.**

square droved A **stonework** finish of closely spaced, parallel, vertical grooves.

squared stone Roughly dressed stone blocks with rectangular faces. Also known as **roughly squared.** See also **quarry cut.**

squared-stone masonry Masonry with **random courses** composed of quarry cut, seam face, or split stones; intermediate between **rubble** and **ashlar.**

square edge and sound A grade of sawn timber, especially yellow pine timber, with flat faces without any **waney edges.**

square end A piece of lumber cut at a right angle across the end, as opposed to having a tenon, or other shape, at the end.

square flyers (pre-19c) A **staircase** with straight flights connected by quarter turn landings around a square well.

square foot (pl. **square feet**) A unit of measure equal to the area of a square with 1-foot-long sides; used in construction and surveying.

square-framed, (pre-20c) **square framed** An opening, such as a window or door, enclosed with square, rather than beveled or molded, edges.

square-headed, (pre-20c) **square headed** Having a flat top, especially a rectangular wall opening with a horizontal lintel and vertical jambs; also applies to the top of a bolt.

square hip A roof **hip** covered with rectangular shingles or slates parallel to the line of the hip. See also **Boston hip, woven hip.**

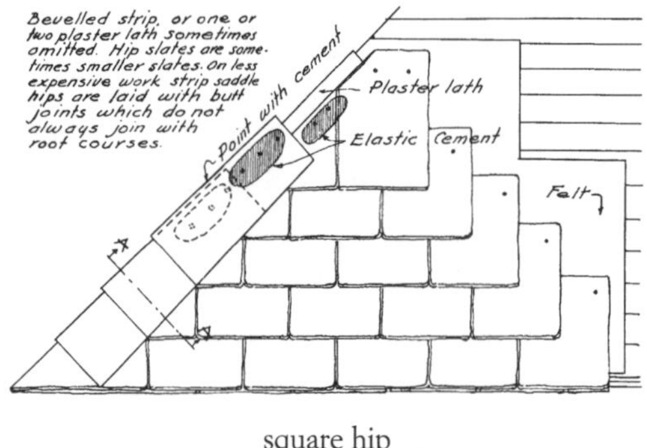

square hip

square inch A unit of measure equal to the area of a square with 1-inch-long sides; used in construction.

square measure A system of measuring areas in square units; units types include **square inch, square foot, square meter, square rod, square yard.** See also **square** (sense 1).

square meter A unit of measure equal to the area of a square with 1-meter-long sides; used in construction and surveying.

square nail (18c) A **nail** with a shank with a square cross section. See also **cut nail.**

square niche A **niche** with a square plan.

square notch A interlocking **notching** system used at the corners in log construction; shape of the end of the log is a square or rectangle; the least rigid type of notching.

square-on photography A type of **photography** where the plane of the camera film is parallel to the plane of the object being recorded to minimized size distortion between the elements; most often used in reference to the facades of a building. See also **rectified photography.**

square rod A unit of land measure equal to the area of a square with 1-**rod**-long sides; used in surveying; equals 1⁄160 acre, 30.25 square yards, or approximately 25.29 square meters.

square roof **1.** A gable roof with 45-degree slopes that form a right angle at the peak. See also **true pitch. 2.** A gable roof with a square plan.

square root angle (late 19c) A rolled metal **angle** with equal length legs with square ends, rather than the more common quarter round ends.

square sawn timber **Timber** sawn to a rectangular cross section; may have **wane.**

square staff A projecting wood **angle staff** molding, with a square cross section, at an outside corner of a plaster wall. See also **corner bead.**

square step A stone step with a rectangular cross section; installed so that the stair soffit below is stepped.

square turned A wood element, such as a newel, made with planed moldings on flat faces, rather than turned on a lathe to produce a circular cross section.

square yard A unit of measure equal to the area of a square with 1-**yard**-long sides; used in surveying.

squeeze A cast of an existing molding or ornament; made with a flexible material that can be peeled off after setting.

squinch One of a series of arches in the corner of a square base below a dome; each squinch is corbeled out from the one below to support a diagonal across the corner; may be part of a **pendentive.** Also known as **squinch arch.**

squinch arch Same as **squinch.**

stab To roughen a brick wall with a pick to provide a plaster key.

stability See **structural stability.**

stabilization The process of temporarily protecting a historic building or structure until **rehabilitation** or **restoration** efforts can begin; typically includes making the building weathertight, structurally stable, and secure against intruders on a one-time basis. See also **maintenance.**

stabilized adobe A type of **adobe** brick with a binder added to the mixture to increase weather resistance; binders may include asphalt, portland cement, or silicone.

stable A building where horses or cattle are cared for and kept; typically with food and tack storage areas, stalls, and, sometimes, living quarters for servants; types include **club stable, livery stable, breeder's stable, cow stable, farm stable, sale stable.** See also **carriage house.**

stable yard A open area for grooming and saddling horses next to a stable. See also **yard.**

stack **1.** Same as **chimney stack. 2.** A floor to ceiling built-in bookshelf, such as in a library. See also **stacks, stackroom. 3.** All of the vertical plumbing piping at one location; types include **soil stack, vent stack.**

stack bond, stackbond A masonry wall **bond** formed with the joints aligned both vertically and horizontally in a rectangular grid pattern.

stacked ashlar Stone blocks set with a **stack bond.**

stackroom A separate room in a library for the **stacks;** often with limited public access.

stacks The area with book shelves in a library.

stackstand (pre-WWII) A farm **structure** that stores hay off the ground; typically constructed with a low ring of posts supporting a raised platform and a tall central post.

stack yard A fenced **yard** for hay stacks.

staff **1.** Same as **staff bead.** **2.** A stiff plastic material composed of plaster of Paris mixed with water and a little glycerin and dextrin; first used for temporary buildings at the Exposition of 1878 in Paris, and later in Chicago for many buildings of the 1893 Columbian Exposition. **3.** Same as **cable** (sense 3).

staff bead **1.** An **angle bead** with decoration at the top and bottom; may be in the form of a capital and base. Also known as **angle staff, staff.** See also **Aaron's rod.** **2.** A **brickmold** with a round cross section.

stage **1.** A platform for performances, especially in a theater or auditorium; typically raised above the audience level. See also **proscenium.** **2.** A step, landing, floor or story. See also **staging.** **3.** A space or division between buttress setoffs. **4.** The horizontal division of a transomed window. **5.** A subdivision of geological strata.

stage box Same as **proscenium box.**

stage house An inn or other building where a stage coach regularly stops and/or the horses are kept.

staggered **1.** Two or more rows of objects that are offset from one another so that the objects form an imaginary zigzag line. **2.** A pattern created by rows of shingles where alternate shingles have greater and lesser areas exposed to the weather. See also **shingle.**

staggered stud partition A **partition** with two rows of studs that are less deep than the wall plates; the rows are offset so that each row is connected to only one wall finish; used for sound insulation.

staging Same as **scaffolding.**

stain **1.** A thinned form of paint that can be either semitransparent or opaque; semitransparent stains show wood grain and are typically oil-base; opaque stains may be oil-base or other clear resin, or after 1940, latex; typically semitransparent stains soak into the fibers of finish wood. See also **creosote.** **2.** A blemish from coloring that has penetrated the surface of a finish material; types include **sap stain.** **3.** A material that changes the color of glass by chemical action. See also **silver stain.**

stained glass **1.** Same as **colored glass** or **painted glass,** or a combination of the two, used to make a decorative window pattern. See also **mosaic glass.** **2.** Glass colored with a transparent stain, especially **silver stain,** that is applied to the surface and incorporated into it by heat.

stainless steel A highly corrosion resistant **steel** alloy developed in the 20c; typically contains 12–18 percent chromium and approximately 5 percent nickel; developed by Christian Dantsizen of Germany 1909–12 and used for architectural products beginning in the 1920s.

stair A series of steps for walking between different levels; types by plan include **quarter turn stair, half-turn stair, three-quarter turn stair, one-turn stair,** indicating 1–4 right-angle turns, **French flyers, geometrical stair, quarterpace stair, quarter winding, square flyers, straight stair, triangular flyers;** components may include **banister, baluster, carriage, curtail, half rail, handrail, newel, nosing, nosing return, riser, stringer, tongue and groove riser and tread, tread, waist, wreath;** types include **back stair, closed-string stair, close-string stair, cut string stair, dog-leg stair, hanging stair, newel stair, open riser stair,**

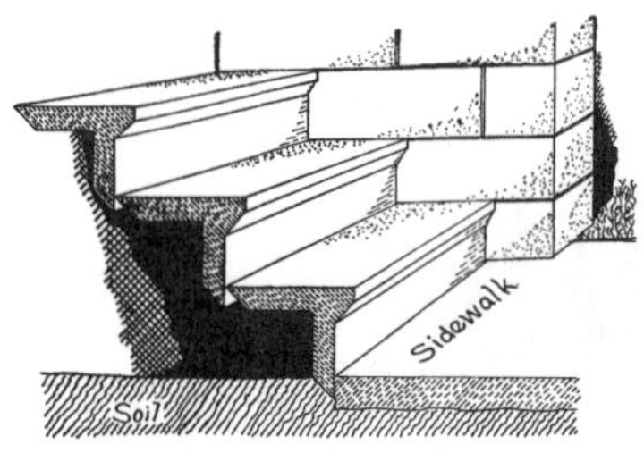

stair

open string stair, spiral stair, stile, trap stair, water stair, wedged stair. See also **below stairs, hollow newel, pair, staircase.**

stair carpet A carpet woven with a complete pattern the width of the stair; often installed with stair rods.

staircase, (pre-18c) **stair-case, staire case 1.** (18c–present) An entire **stair** with its railings, newels and other related components. Also known as **stairway. 2.** An entire stair plus its enclosing walls. See also **stair well, well staircase.**

stair dormer A dormer over the top of a stair that provides headroom for access to the attic level.

stair head The top of a **staircase.**

stair rail A handrail of a stair.

stair rail screw A **wood screw** with threads on both ends; used to connect sections of wooden handrail.

stair rod A small diameter metal rod with decorative ends installed across the back of each tread to hold a **stair carpet** in place. See also **stair wire.**

stair tower An enclosed staircase, especially a fire-resistant enclosure in a highrise building.

stair trimmer A **trimmer** beam that forms one of the sides of a stair well and supports one end of a header beam.

stair turret 1. A projecting tower that encloses a stair. **2.** A domed or conical roof over a stair that rises above the main roof surface.

stairway (19c–present) Same as **staircase.**

stair well A vertical space in a building that encloses a staircase. See also **staircase.**

stair wire A heavy wire used as a **stair rod.**

stake and rider fence Same as **worm fence.**

stalactite A pendent ornament on a vaulted ceiling.

stalactited Masonry that has icicle-shaped ornaments.

stalactite work Complex, decorative, Islamic vault corbeling that somewhat resembles natural stalactites; often has multiple arched corbel tables; may be masonry, plaster, or wood. Also known as **honeycomb work, muqarnas.**

stalk A stylized carved plant stem, such as a **caule** used on a Corinthian capital; may be fluted.

stall 1. A pen for an individual horse or cow in a barn or stable; typically 4–5 feet wide and 9 feet deep, with partitions on 3 or 4 sides; variations include **loose stall;** components may include **beaded board, stall post;** may include **manger, rack. 2.** (pre-19c) A theater seat separated from the others by arms or rails. **3.** A theater **box. 4.** A choir seat that is enclosed on the sides and back; sometimes used in Gothic Revival style churches. **5.** A booth in a **market house** for the display and sale of goods. (*See illustration on p. 448.*)

stall post The post at the end of a partition between stable stalls.

stamped metal Sheet metal that has been shaped by stamping or pressing with dies to form a raised or recessed decorative pattern on the surface.

stamping powder Same as **pounce.**

stanchion 1. A general term for a vertical post or bar that acts as a column to support a building element, such as a roof or awning. See also **puncheon. 2.** A metal post with one or more eyes that supports a rope or cable railing. **3.** A pair of metal rods that loosely hold a cow's head in a stall so that it can eat. **4.** (pre-19c)

stall (sense 1)

A vertical iron bar in the middle of a casement window frame.

stand **1.** A platform on which orators, viewers, or performers stand or sit. See also **rostrum, stage.** **2.** A counter or other fixture where merchandise is displayed. **3.** A place or building used for business, especially where one waits for customers, as in a hack stand or news stand. **4.** (pre-19c) A plantation or plot of land.

standard **1.** (pre-WWI) A column, pier, or post, especially in timber framing. **2.** (19c) The carved end of a church pew. See also **poppyhead.**

standard brick Same as **common brick** (sense 1).

standard finish A dull **architectural terra-cotta** finish; produced by spraying the block with clay slip before firing.

standard gauge, standard gage A standardized railway track width that allows rolling stock to travel between different railroads; in North America, 56½ inches, measured perpendicularly between the rails at a point ⅝ inch below the top of the rail. See also **broad gauge, narrow gauge.**

standard metropolitan statistical area (SMSA) A U.S. Census Bureau designation of a number of census tracts that make up a contiguous urban area; may include census tracts from more than one local government area; used to compile and report census data.

standard mill construction Same as **slow-burning mill construction.**

standard steel building (20c) Same as **preengineered steel building.**

standby generator (20c) Same as **emergency generator.**

standing The legal right of a person or group to participate in a court case or governmental hearing. See also **standing to sue.**

standing bolt (pre-20c) Same as **stud bolt.**

standing panel **1.** A rectangular **panel** with its longest dimension vertical. **2.** A wood panel with the grain running vertically.

standing seam roof A sheet-metal roof with vertical folded seams joining adjacent flat panels; the parallel seams run along the slope. See also **tin roof.**

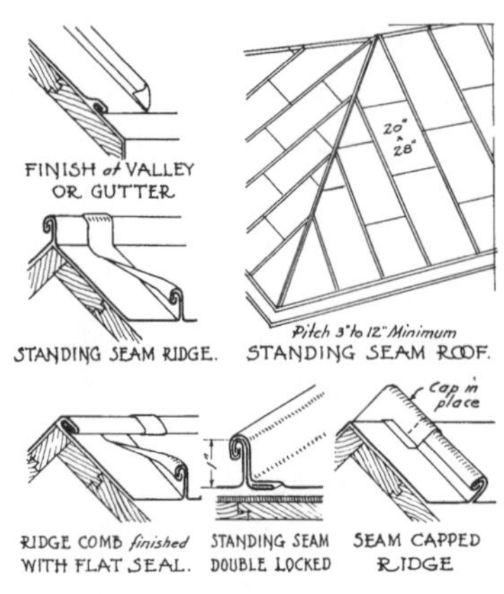

standing seam roof

standing to sue The legal right of a person or group to challenge in court the conduct of another, especially a governmental agency or official; generally plaintiffs must show (1) injury to a legally protected interest, (2) a causal connection between the injury and the governmental action, and (3) a likelihood that the injury would be redressed by a favorable decision; does not require an economic interest in a threatened historic building, or ownership of adjacent property, for example it is sufficient for an organization to demonstrate that its members appreciate, enjoy, visit, and use its architectural and aesthetic values.

standpipe **1.** (19c–present) A vertical pipe riser with multiple interior connections for fire hoses; always terminated at the building facade with a fitting for a fire engine hose; may also have a valved pipe connection to the water main; may be wet or dry. See also **siamese.** **2.** A tall, narrow, cylindrical tower that is filled with water to give it a head of pressure. **3.** A water tower that supplies water for fire fighting. **4.** A water-filled pipe tall enough that the water will flow into a boiler against the steam pressure. **5.** A vertical pipe that allows expansion of the water in a boiler or hot-water tank.

staple A U-shaped nail with two pointed ends; used as hardware to hold the end of a hook or the bolt of a lock, and in modern times as a fastener for various materials, including shingles, wire, and wire fencing. See also **hook and staple.**

star anchor A cast-iron **anchor plate** in the shape of a star. See also **earthquake washer.**

starling, (19c) **sterling** **1.** A series of abutting piles to protect a marine structure from waves. **2.** An individual pile in such a construction. Also known as **stockade.** See also **seawall.**

star molding, (pre-20c) **star moulding** A linear series of projecting star-shaped forms; used in Romanesque Revival architecture. See also **tooth ornament.**

star shake A radial internal crack in a tree, especially intersecting heart shakes. See also **shake.**

starting newel The **newel** that starts the railing at the foot of a stair.

star vault A **rib vault** with a star-shaped pattern of ribs and panels formed by the intersection of vault surfaces and decorative liernes; typically the stars are four- or six-pointed; used to cover square or rectangular spaces. Also known as **stellar vault.**

State Historic Preservation Program The program established by each U.S. state and approved by the Secretary of Interior for the purpose of carrying out the provisions of the National Historic Preservation Act of 1966, as amended, and related laws and regulations; typically nominates eligible properties to the National Register; headed by the **State Historic Preservation Officer.**

State Historic Preservation Office The U.S. state or territorial government agency that administers the preservation programs under the National Historic Preservation Act. See also **State Historic Preservation Officer.**

State Historic Preservation Officer (SHPO) The official in each U.S. state or territorial government designated by the governor to administer the **State Historic Preservation Program,** including assisting federal agencies and identifying and nominating eligible properties to the National Register; a key participant in the **Section 106** review process, also administers the federal Historic Preservation Funds; typically works with local governments on preservation planning issues and historic preservation ordinances.

statehouse (late 18c–present) The **capitol** building of a state government.

State preservation plan **1.** Same as **State Historic Preservation Program.** **2.** An administrative or strategic planning document designed to carry out preservation statewide.

State Review Board A board, council, commission, or other collegial body appointed by the SHPO that reviews and recommends National Register nominations processed through a **State Historic Preservation Program** prior to their submittal to the National Park Service; the members represent the professional fields of American history, architectural history, historic architecture, prehistoric and historic archeology, and other professional disciplines and may include citizen members.

state significance The importance of a property to the history of the U.S. state where it is located.

statuary Freestanding sculpture, as opposed to relief work.

statuary bronze A **bronze** alloy composed of 85 percent copper, 5 percent lead, 5 percent tin, and 5 percent zinc; highly resistant to weathering and corrosion.

statuary marble Any white, granular **marble** that is largely free of veins and is suitable for carving statues and other fine work; typically imported from Italy.

statue A sculpted three-dimensional representation of a person, animal, or mythological being; typically approximately life size. See also **caryatid, relief, statuette.**

statuette A small statue, especially one that is less than one half life size.

stave bent A curved wood element that has been shaped by wetting and/or steaming and bending it into the desired shape.

stave door A **solid-core door** with a core composed of vertical pieces of lumber glued together.

stay A general term for any support, prop, or anchor.

stay-bar (19c) A horizontal iron armature that reinforces the mullion tops of a tracery windows.

stay rod (19c) Same as **tie rod.**

steamboat Gothic Same as **Carpenter Gothic** style; found in the Mississippi River and Ohio River valleys during the second half of the 19c; from the resemblance to the decorative scrollwork on steamboats.

steam boiler A **boiler** that produces steam for heating or power.

steam boiler

steam chamber **1.** (pre-20c) Same as **steam room.** **2.** The part of a boiler where the steam is held.

steam chimney A vertical construction that leads exhaust steam from a boiler to the outside.

steam coil A **water heater** coil connected to a steam boiler. See also **steam injection heater.**

steam heating A system of heating a building by steam that condenses in radiators within the various rooms; may be a high-pressure or low-pressure central system; typically includes a boiler, steam pipes, return pipes, cast-iron radiators, and steam valves; types include **vapor heating.**

steam house A building where materials, such as wood, are steamed.

steam injection heater A large water heater that injects live steam directly into the water. See also **steam coil.**

steam pipe Any pipe that carries steam; in a heating system distinguished from the **return pipe** that carries condensed steam water; most commonly threaded iron pipe.

steam room A room where steam is released into the air for steaming materials or people. Also known as **steam chamber.**

steam turbine A **turbine** rotated by the force of pressurized steam.

steel A high-strength metal composed primarily of iron with 0.01–1.7 percent carbon; also has trace amounts of other elements such as chromium, copper, phosphorus, silicon, and sulphur; more malleable and stronger, and with less carbon content than **cast iron;** has less slag, and manufactured differently, than **wrought iron;** hardness increases as the carbon content increases, with strengths classified as **soft steel, medium steel, hard steel;** varieties include **alloy steel, blister steel, shear steel, stainless steel;** not commonly used for structural purposes until late 19c, entirely replaced iron for rolled sections manufactured by most companies by 1893. See also **light-gauge steel, structural steel.**

steel-cage construction Same as **steel frame.**

steel concrete Same as **reinforced concrete.**

steel decking Corrugated steel sheet metal used to span between floor or roof beams.

steel frame **Cage construction** or **skeleton construction** with a structural framework of steel columns and beams combined with various types of floor decks, including **reinforced concrete, floor arch, steel decking, steel lath and concrete,** and various exterior wall systems, including **architectural terra-cotta, curtain wall,** and **masonry;** may be fastened with rivets, bolts, or welds; common for large buildings by 1890.

steel lath and concrete A mid-20c floor construction system with steel lath laid perpendicular to the floor beams and covered with a concrete topping; the lath is both the formwork and the reinforcing; typically the concrete is 2 inches thick and the joists are spaced 12–24 inches on center. See also **reinforced concrete.**

steel stud A bent steel sheet-metal stud; typically with a rectangular C-shaped cross section with punched-out holes in the widest face; used in **light-gauge framing.** Also known as **metal stud.**

steelwork Any construction of steel.

steening The masonry lining of an underground well, vault, or cesspool; may be dry laid or mortared.

steeple **1.** The top of a tower that diminishes in stages with a small **spire,** or other shape, at the crown; most often on a **church,** occasionally used on other building types. **2.** An entire church tower. (*See illustration on p. 452.*)

stellar vault Same as **star vault.**

stem (19c) Same as **web.**

stenchtrap (pre-20c) Same as a plumbing **trap.**

stenciling Decorative painting with repetitive patterns applied by brushing paint onto the surface through openings cut in a stencil, or a series of stencils; common on interior walls during the first half of the 19c. See also **stippling, template.**

step **1.** Any horizontal offset of a vertical surface. **2.** A horizontal surface that is walked upon to change levels, especially when one of a series; types include **balance step, bullnose step, commode step, curtail step, hanging step, spandrel step, square step.** See also **stair.**

step joint A joint between the foot of a rafter and its supporting tie beam, with the tie beam notched to receive the rafter.

step log A log with staggered notches for use as a ladder or stair; used by pueblo inhabitants.

steeple (sense 1)
Philadelphia City Hall, Pennsylvania

stepped arch An **arch** with voussoirs shaped so that they have a horizontal top and vertical side that interlocks with a stepped joint pattern of the wall.

stepped flashing Individual pieces of flashing used where a sloped roof abuts a vertical masonry wall or chimney; the top portion of each piece is bent and inserted into a mortar joint; typically one piece of flashing is used for each slate, shingle, or tile.

stepped scarf joint Same as **hooked scarf joint.**

stepped voussoir One of the voussoirs of a **stepped arch.**

stereobate A masonry foundation above ground level, especially one that supports the peripteral columns of a classical style building. See also **stylobate.**

stereochrome A mural painting on plaster with pigments suspended in **water glass;** the pigments are fixed by chemical reactions among the lime, water glass, and fluosilicic acid. See also **silicate paint.**

stereotomy The art of dividing three-dimensional shapes into regular geometric sections; used in stone cutting to provide the proper sizes and shapes of stones for a building.

sterling (19c) Same as **starling.**

sterro metal A hard **brass** alloy composed of copper and approximately 40 percent zinc with small amounts of iron and tin.

stewardship The long-term care and protection of a historic property by an owner or the public, whether an individual, a private organization, or a public agency.

stiacciato Extremely flat **bas-relief** sculpture, from the Italian for "flattened out."

stick Any linear wood molding; from the word for shaping with a molding plane. See also **sticking.**

stick and clay chimney Same as **stick chimney.**

stick chimney A **wooden chimney** constructed of layers of parallel wood poles laid in alternate directions to form a hollow, rectangular shaft and covered with mud or mortar on the interior; common in exterior chimneys in **log cabins.** Also known as **cat and clay chimney, stick and clay chimney.**

stick chimney
El Capote Cabin
Guadalupe County, Texas, ca. 1840

stick frame Any **wood frame** construction system using primarily 2× lumber; types include **balloon frame, platform frame.**

sticking A planed molding, especially the projecting molding on the inside face of a door rail or stile, with a groove or rabbet that holds a panel or window pane in place; shapes include **colonial sticking, ogee, P.G.** See also **applied mold, bolection molding, paneled door, solid mold, solid stuck.**

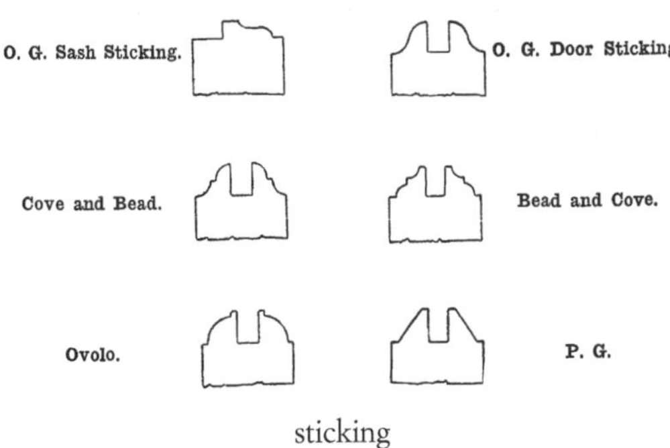

sticking

Stick Style An architectural style of wood framed houses that emphasized exterior wall patterns of varying textures divided by a rectangular grid of flat boards, sometimes with diagonals resembling half-timbering; common in the U.S. after ca. 1860; typical elements include asymmetrical massing, steeply pitched cross gable roofs, decorative trusses and brackets below overhanging eaves with exposed rafters; townhouse versions typically have flat roofs with only vertical banding surmounted by a large bracketed cornice; often based on pattern books of the 1860s and 1870s; largely supplanted by the more elaborate **Queen Anne Style** by the end of the 19c. See also **Carpenter Gothic, stickwork.**

stickwork Raised banding on an exterior wall, similar in appearance to **half timbered.** See also **Stick Style.**

stie (pre-19c) Same as **sty.**

stiffened wire lath **Wire lath** woven with round or V-shaped metal stiffeners approximately 8 inches on center.

stiffening girder Same as **stiffening truss.**

stiffening truss A truss designed to prevent oscillations in a suspension bridge or other structure by connecting upper and lower decks. Also known as **stiffening girder.**

stiff-leaf capital A **Gothic Revival** style column capital with stylized carved foliage.

stiff mud brick **Brick** manufactured by extruding clay through a die. See also **soft mud brick.**

S-tile A terra-cotta **roof tile** having a sideways S-shaped cross section with both curves of equal size; the convex side of one tile overlaps the concave side of the adjacent tile. See also **pantile.**

stile **1.** One of the main members of a millwork frame to which the others are attached, especially by mortise and tenon, such as the vertical framing members at the edge of a window **sash** or **paneled door;** may be horizontal in wall paneling; types include **diminished stile,**

gunstock stile, hanging stile, meeting stile, pulley stile, shutting stile. See also **rail, montant. 2.** Any plane surface forming a border. **3.** A fence post that supports rails. **4.** A stair with steep steps on both sides of a fence or wall.

still house (18c) A building containing a **distillery.**

stilted arch (late 19c–present) An **arch** that is raised higher than normal, especially with vertical jambs below the spring line that are supported on column capitals or a heavy molding; used to keep the top of arches of different widths at the same height.

stilted vault 1. A **vault** with the spring line of the wall ribs raised on a vertical pier above the imposts, or raised on a vertical wall above the surbase; used to raise the height of the clerestory windows. **2.** A vault with a rectangular plan formed by intersecting vaults of two different sizes, with the smaller vault raised so that the apexes of both vaults are at the same level; typically the vaults have a semicircular cross section; used first by the Romans, and later in French Romanesque architecture.

stinash A willow-framed lodge of the Modoc Native American peoples.

stippled 1. A textured plaster finish made by patting the wet surface with the end of a stiff brush. See also **stippling. 2.** A **brick** surface texture with multiple, small indentations.

stippling 1. A form of decorative painting with a gradual transition from one color to another; made by minute dots of color applied with a nearly dry brush. See also **stippled. 2.** The process of applying paint by tapping the surface with a nearly dry brush held vertically; used in **stenciling. 3.** The process of preventing drips and streaks by lightly pressing the tips of the bristles of a brush into a wet coating.

stirrup 1. An iron hardware device with a U-shaped seat that supports one end of a joist or beam; may be a **beam hanger** that supports a wood beam, or a cast-iron or welded steel device that supports an iron beam; used to attach one beam to another beam, or a beam to a wall. Also known as **bridle iron, stirrup iron.** See also **joist hanger. 2.** A **reinforcing bar** that wraps around the horizontal reinforcing bars of a concrete beam to connect them and increase shear resistance.

stirrup iron Same as **stirrup** (sense 1).

stitch bolt One of a series of bolts that connect two longitudinal structural members side by side, such as back to back steel channels.

stitch rivet See **stitch bolt.**

stockade 1. A defensible space enclosed by a palisade; often with loopholes. **2.** Same as **palisade. 3.** Same as **starling** (sense 1).

stockade fence Any fence formed by a series of vertical, round wood posts; the posts may be logs, as in a **palisade,** or saplings, as with **paling.**

stock brick A **common brick** suitable for exterior use. See also **face brick.**

stock goods Same as **stock item.**

stock item Any manufactured product regularly kept in warehouse stock by the distributor or manufacturer. Also known as **stock goods.** See also **stock size.**

stock lock A large, surface mounted, wrought-iron door lock with a wood block casing; typically pre-19c; type includes **Banbury lock.**

stocks A punishment device composed of a frame holding two planks with cutouts for holding the ankles and, sometimes, the hands of the offender.

stock size A product available from a manufacturer in standardized sizes; may stocked in a warehouse or made upon receipt of an order. See also **stock item.**

stockyard A fenced enclosure for keeping cattle and similar animals, especially prior to shipping or butchering.

stoker A mechanical device that automatically feeds coal to a furnace; from the worker who shovels coal into a furnace.

stone 1. A hard, naturally occurring material found in the earth; types by composition include **argillite, asbestos, brownstone, cobblestone, diorite, dolomite, gabbro, granite, gypsum, limestone, marble, onyx, quartzite, sandstone, serpentine, slabstone, slate, soapstone, trap rock;** types by size include **boulder, gravel.** See also **artificial stone, cast stone, crusher run, freestone.** 2. An individual piece of rock that has been separated from its natural bed; may be naturally occurring or quarried; categories include **ashlar, Belgian pavement, broad stone, cutstone, fieldstone, rubble stone, squared stone;** types by use include **apex stone, bond stone, coping stone, cornerstone, crow stone, curb stone, footing stone, footstone, quoin, spur stone, springing stone, summer stone.** See also **stonework.**

stone brick An extremely hard variety of **brick.**

stone color, stone colour A very light bluish gray **oil-base paint** with pigment composed of **white lead** with small amounts of **Prussian blue, spruce yellow** and **umber;** approximates the color of weathered limestone.

stone concrete **Concrete** made with crushed stone or gravel aggregate.

stone-ender A 17c type of timber frame house with stone gable end walls; almost exclusively found in Rhode Island; typical original elements include a steeply pitched side-gabled roof, a massive stone chimney incorporated into one gable end, clapboard siding on the side walls, small casement windows with diamond quarrels. See also **postmedieval architecture.**

stone lime **Lime** made by heating limestone or marble in a kiln.

Stone Mountain granite A uniform, light gray, medium-grain **granite** quarried in the vicinity of Stone Mountain, Georgia.

stone setting The process of installing dressed stone blocks, including both mortar joints and lead joints, such as between a column and its base. See also **stonework.**

stonework, stone work Masonry constructed with stone blocks or fieldstone; types include **ashlar, rubble masonry, squared-stone masonry, trimstone, veneer;** finishes include **dabbed, hammer dressed, honed, machine finish, pitch faced, plucked finish, polished, quarry cut, quarry faced, rough pointed, rubbed work, rugged, sawed, scabbled, shot sawed, split faced, striped, stunning, tooled.** See also **arch, bond, pitch hole, rangework, socket, stone, stone setting, vault.**

stoneworks A place where building stone is shaped.

Stonington Pink Gray granite A variety of **Deer Isle granite.**

Stony Creek granite A reddish, medium- to coarse-grained **granite** with bold veining quarried in the vicinity of Stony Creek, Connecticut.

stool The wood molding forming the shelflike cap of an interior window sill; typically milled with an angled rabbet on the bottom. Also known as **window stool.**

stoop, (pre-20c) **stoup** 1. An uncovered platform at the entrance to a house, typically with a set of steps with balustrade. 2. (New York region) The front steps leading up to the main floor of a house, including the landing. 3. (Northeastern U.S.) Any exterior set of steps with a level platform, such as a **porch** or **terrace.** See also **box stoop.** 4. (pre-20c Maryland to Connecticut) An uncovered platform with a pair of seats flanking a house entrance door; the seats are benches with backs perpendicular to the front wall; from the Dutch word **stoep.**

stop **1.** Any construction or device that arrests the swing of a door or casement window, or keeps a sliding member in place; types include **door stop, stop bead, window stop. 2.** A projecting stone that abuts the end of a molding, such as a **stringcourse** or **hood mold;** typically with carved ornament. See also **skew corbel.**

stop bead A small molding used as a door stop; typically rectangular in cross section, with an ogee shape on one edge. Also known as **stop.**

stop chamfer A corner **chamfer** that does not extend to the end of the timber or molding; typically terminated with a small, triangular plane surface. See also **stop molding.**

stop cock A shut-off valve in the middle of a line. See also **cock.**

stop cock

stop dado A **dado** groove that does not continue to the edge of the member.

stop molding A solid molding that terminates before the end of the member, or before it reaches an abutting member. See also **stop chamfer, stopped flute.**

stopped flute A column flute that stops approximately one-third of the shaft height above the base; the lower part of the shaft may be smooth, faceted, or have a shallow rectangular sinkage. See also **cabled flute.**

stopping Mortar that fills up a recessed masonry joint, such as in a **tuck.** See also **fire stop.**

store **1.** A place where retail merchandise is sold; may be a separate building or a portion of a building; may include a **counting room.** Also known as **shop.** See also **storehouse. 2.** Same as **storeroom.**

store front (19c–present) A ground-level facade of a shop with large sheets of plate glass in display windows with minimal sized mullions; typically with a recessed entrance. Also known as **shop front.**

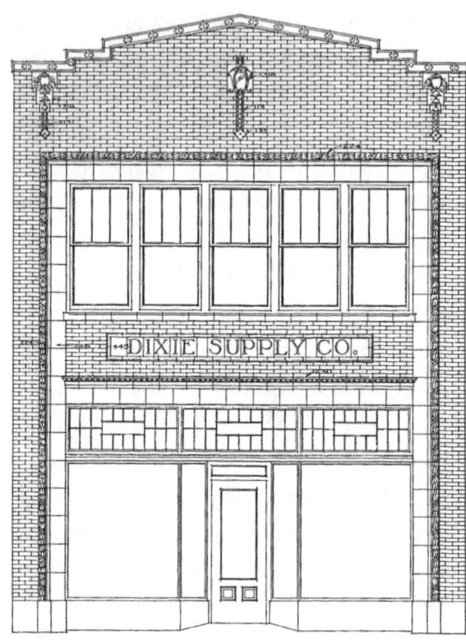

store front

storehouse A **building** where material goods are kept, especially food. See also **warehouse.**

storeroom, (pre-19c) **store room** A room used for storing goods. See also **lumber room, magazine, pantry.**

storey (pre-20c) Same as **story.**

storm cellar An underground **structure** used as shelter during tornadoes; common on the western plains. Also known as **cyclone cellar.**

storm door An additional exterior door, or projecting enclosure with a door, used to reduce the escape of heat in winter; typically lightweight and glazed; often removable during summer months. Also known as **weather door.**

storm house A **shack** used for shelter by workers or a guard, such as on a railroad.

storm pavement Flagstones, or other paving, covering a sloped **seawall.**

storm sash Same as **storm window.**

storm sewer A **sewer** that carries rainwater and the debris the water picks up on the surface.

storm window **1.** An additional window used to reduce the escape of heat in winter, and protect against severe weather; typically mounted on the exterior and removable during summer months; most commonly glass in a light wood sash, hung from the top of window frame, until after WWII, when aluminum frames came into use. **2.** (pre-WWI) A protected window in a roof, such as a **dormer window.**

story, (pre-20c) **storey** **1.** The space between two floors of a structure, or between a floor and roof; types include **attic, basement, cellar, ground story, mansard, piano nobile.** See also **floor.** **2.** The division on an exterior wall formed by two horizontal features that have the appearance of a floor, such as an entablature. **3.** (low country Carolinas and Georgia) The height of a wall from the sill to the wall plate.

story and a half A building with partial height second-floor walls below the gable eaves. See also **attic.**

story post **1.** A post that supports the beam below an exterior wall that starts at the second-floor level, such as with a recessed store front. **2.** A timber frame **main post** that is one story in height.

stoup **1.** A basin for holy water in the vestibule of a church; typically partly recessed in the wall. **2.** (pre-20c) Same as **stoop.**

stove **1.** A fixture that is used for heating a space or cooking; may burn fuel internally or, beginning in the 20c, use electric resistance heating; typically brick with cast-iron grates and stew holes until the 19c, then cast iron or, beginning in late 19c, sheet metal; types include **cast-iron stove, Franklin stove.** See also **furnace, water back.** **2.** Any room that is heated to above normal temperatures, especially for growing tropical plants or drying materials such as pottery. See also **stove house, stove room.**

stove (sense 1)

stove coil A continuous, brass or iron pipe in the firebox of a cast-iron stove; used to heat water. See also **range boiler, water back, water heater.**

stove glass Mica used for glazing in a cast-iron stove.

stove house Same as **hothouse.** See also **stove** (sense 2).

stovepipe A metal **flue** that connects a stove to a chimney or the exterior; typically fabricated from iron sheet metal.

stove plate **1.** A smooth-surfaced **cast iron** manufactured with a fluid, low-strength iron. **2.** A lid for a hole in a cast-iron stove.

stove room (pre-19c) A room heated by a stove, as opposed to a fireplace.

stovewood house A house with walls constructed of short logs laid in lime mortar perpendicular to the face of the wall, with square timber quoins; typically logs are white cedar with a length of 16–18 inches; found in northern Wisconsin.

straight arch, (18c) **streight arch** Same as **jack arch.**

straight course A row of slates or shingles with the butts in a straight line, as opposed to **staggered.**

straightening coat Same as **brown coat.**

straight gauged Installed in a straight line by use of a gauge, such as a row of slates.

straight grain Same as **vertical grain.**

straight joint floor **1.** A wood floor laid with the joints between the sides of adjoining boards continuous from one end of the room to the other, as opposed to a **broken joint floor.** **2.** A wood floor with boards with straight edges, as opposed to tongue and groove edges.

straight stair A **stair** with a single straight flight of steps between levels.

strainer **1.** An inverted wire basket inserted in the top of a downspout to catch debris. **2.** A pierced cup that is placed in a sink drain.

strainer arch Same as **straining arch.**

straining arch, strainer arch An **arch** used as a **raker** or **strut,** as in a flying buttress. See also **half arch.**

straining beam A horizontal **strut beam,** especially one that joins the top of two queenposts, or a similar member in other roof trusses. Also known as **straining piece.**

straining piece Same as **straining beam.**

straining sill A timber attached to the top of the tie beam of a **queen-post truss** between the queenposts, or between a **queenpost** and **princess post,** to prevent their movement due to loads from the diagonal struts. See also **strut beam.**

strait (pre-19c) A narrow **roof tile** used in alternate courses at the edge of a roof to maintain the joint pattern.

S-trap A plumbing drain trap in the form of a sideways S-shape; forms a siphon, and, therefore, not common after the 19c; variations include **half S-trap, three-quarter S-trap.** See also **P-trap.**

S-trap

strap **1.** An iron connector formed from a bent flat bar; of various forms, including a straight bar with holes for bolts or nails, and a **clamp, strap bolt, strap hanger,** or **strap loop.** **2.** Any element with a thin, rectangular cross section. See phrases beginning with **strap** following.

strap bolt (19c–present) **1.** A flat iron strap with one threaded end; sometimes nailed to the end of a joist to attach an anchor plate. **2.** A U-shaped bolt used as a clip.

strap bridging A mid-20c bridging system for steel joists composed of bent sheet-metal straps forming **cross bracing;** typically the straps are 18 gauge and 1⅛ inch wide for single strap bridging, and 20 gauge and 1 inch wide for continuous bridging; attached to the flanges with end hooks or nails.

strap hanger A **beam hanger** bent from an iron bar with a rectangular cross section. Also known as **stirrup.**

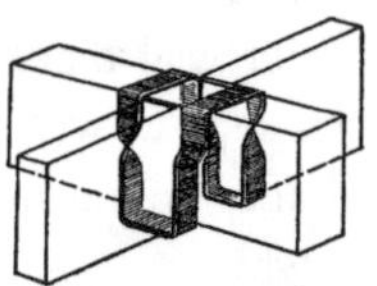

strap hanger

strap hinge A surface mounted **hinge** with rolled knuckles and wide leaves; commonly used on outbuildings for wide, heavy doors; types include **cross-garnet.** Also known as **joint hinge.** See also **gudgeon.**

strap loop A U-shaped iron strap; used as a clip.

strap ornament Same as **strap work.**

strapping A **furring strip** used to level a ceiling before applying lath or drywall.

strap rail Same as **flat rail.**

strap work Bas-relief decoration in the form of interlaced fillets, similar to fretwork; most commonly used on ceilings. Also known as **strap ornament.**

strata Plural of **stratum.**

stratification The deposition of archaeological artifacts and soils in identifiable layers or **strata** that represent different time periods at an **archaeological site.**

stratigraphy The process of interpreting **stratification.**

stratum (pl. **strata**) One of a series of layers of geological or archaeological material at a particular location.

Straublox **Cinderblock** patented by F. J. Straub in 1917 and first manufactured in Lancaster, Pennsylvania, in 1919.

straw color A pale yellow **oil-base paint** with pigment composed of **white lead** and **spruce yellow,** in the ratio of 10:1; named for the color of clean, ripe straw.

Streamline Moderne Same as **Art Moderne.**

street **1.** An urban roadway, especially when lined with buildings. See also **alley, passage.** **2.** The paved portion of a roadway between the sidewalks. **3.** (southern U.S.) A linear arrangement of slave cabins on a plantation; the cabins and the immediately surrounding land were collectively referred to as **the street.**

street architecture (19c) The architecture of building facades and public spaces.

street door A door of a building that faces a **street,** as opposed to a back door or side door.

street furniture The manufactured elements that are found in the public right-of-way, such as benches, streetlights, fire hydrants, mailboxes, and signs.

streetlight One of a series of lamps supported by a post along a street or similar public location; oil was used until the first gaslight installation in North America in Baltimore in 1817.

street railway, street railroad A urban railway at street level.

streetscape The **built environment** encompassing a street or road, including sidewalk and roadway paving, street furniture, buildings, landscaping, and signage. See also **townscape.**

streight arch (18c) Same as **jack arch.**

stretcher **1.** A full-size **brick,** or stone, with its longest dimension horizontal and its shortest dimension vertical at the face of a wall. See also **closer, soap, three-quarter brick.** **2.** A brick used as a voussoir of an arch, with its shortest dimension along the intrados and its longest dimension on a radius of the arch. See also **header.**

stretching course A masonry course composed entirely of stretchers.

stretching piece (pre-20c) Same as **strut.**

stria (pl. **striae**) Same as **fillet** (sense 3).

strié A decorative **paint** pattern of long, thin, vertical streaks made by brushing a thin paint over a base coat.

striga (pl. **strigae**), (pre-20c) **striges** A column **flute.**

striges (pre-20c) Same as **strigae;** from the Latin for the folds of women's dresses.

striker Same as **strike plate.**

strike plate A hardware device composed of a small metal plate with a hole that engages a beveled door latch as the door closes; mounted on a door jamb. Also known as **striker.**

string, stringer **1.** One of the inclined beams that support a stair; in wood construction typically

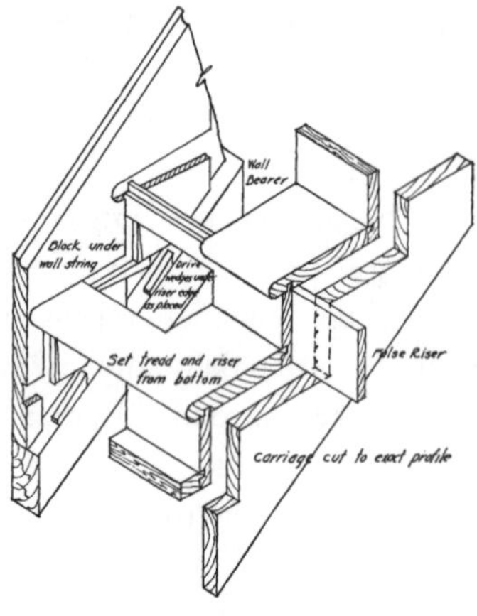

string (sense 1)

notched or rabbeted for the risers and treads; types include **bracketed string, closed string, cut string, cut and mitered string, face string, housed string, open string, rough string, wreathed string;** from the abbreviation for **stringpiece.** Also known as **bridge board, notch board. 2.** (19c) A horizontal beam that supports other framing members, especially a main lengthwise timber of a bridge. **3.** One of a series of longitudinal beams of a bridge that are supported by the **cross beams.** Also known as **bridge board. 4.** (19c) Same as **tie beam. 5.** (19c) Same as **stringcourse. 6.** The horizontal member at the bottom of a **bowstring truss.**

string board Same as **face string,** or a similar finish board covering the framing at the edge of a stair.

stringcourse, string course A projecting, horizontal molding separating parts of a wall surface, especially in masonry construction; types include **lintel course, sill course.** Also known as **belt course, sailing course, string.** See also **blocking course, curstable, water table.**

stringer Same as **string.**

stringpiece 1. Same as **string. 2.** (19c) A framing member at the edge of an opening; may be horizontal or inclined. **3.** Same as **string board.**

strip 1. An inexact term for a relatively narrow, thin piece of material, such as wood or metal. **2.** The process of removing a surface coating.

striped A **stonework** finish of deep, parallel grooves.

strip flooring Wood flooring composed of narrow-width finish floor boards; up to 4 inches wide.

strip footing A continuous **spread footing,** such as under a foundation wall. See also **isolated footing.**

stripper Same as **paint remover.**

stroked work (pre-20c) Stone finished with a fine, fluted surface, such as made with a drove chisel.

struck joint 1. A **mortar joint** that has been struck with a trowel so that it is flush with the bottom corner of the top masonry unit and slopes inward towards the bottom unit; creates a small ledge on the lower unit. **2.** Any mortar joint finished with the mason's trowel; shapes include **flush joint, V-joint, weathered joint;** often used incorrectly to mean **tooled joint.**

struck molding Same as **solid molding.** See also **stuck molding.**

Structolite (20c) A trade name for a dense, structural gypsum manufactured by U.S. Gypsum Co.

structural Pertaining to **structure** (senses 1 and 4). See also **structural stability.**

structural bond The interlocking or tying together of masonry units of a building element so that it acts as a single structural unit; methods include overlapping units, metal ties imbedded in the mortar joints, and the mortar or grout bond between adjacent wythes. See also **bond, pattern bond.**

structural clay tile Clay (including terra-cotta and fire clays) or shale that has been formed by extrusion with parallel air cells and fired for use as a masonry unit, especially in a **floor arch;** forms include **facing tile, fireproofing tile, floor tile, furring tile, header tile, hollow tile, load-bearing tile, non-load-bearing tile, partition tile.** Also known as **hollow pottery.** See also **concrete block, joistile, structural terra-cotta, tile arch.**

structural glass Glass panels used as a wall finish; types include **Carrara glass, Vitrolite;** common 1900–40; typically applied with asphalt mastic, sometimes with natural finish aluminum trim. See also **spandrel glass.**

structural investigation A systematic analysis of the **structural stability** of an existing building or structure. Also known as **structural examination.**

structural joists and planks (20c) **Lumber** that is nominally 2–3 inches thick and 5 or more inches wide.

structural lumber Lumber used for engineered framing that is 2 × 4 or larger; types include **structural joists and planks.**

structural polychromy Construction with materials of different integral colors for decorative effect, as distinct from applied coloring; types include **dichromatic brickwork.** See also **polychromy.**

structural shape See **structural steel.**

structural stability The relative structural soundness of an existing building or structure based on current and projected **dead load, live load, wind load,** and **seismic load** factors.

structural steel **1.** Any of various **steel** rolled sections, individually or collectively, used in the frame of a building or structure; typically designated by shape, depth of section in inches and weight in pounds per linear foot, such as H 16 × 57 before 1970, and 16 H 57 beginning in 1970; types include **angle, channel, H-column, I-beam, wide flange beam, Z-beam.** See also **miscellaneous metal.** **2.** Same as **soft steel.**

structural terra-cotta Terra-cotta clay that has been formed with parallel air cells and fired for use as a wall, partition, **tile arch,** or fireproof enclosure blocks; typically unglazed with mortared joints. Also known as **hollow pottery.** See also **architectural terra-cotta, structural clay.**

structure **1.** The components of a **building** or **structure,** individually or collectively, that support part of the weight of a building and its contents, or resist dynamic forces such as wind or earthquake; may include arches, domes, frame, skeleton, or walls. **2.** Any kind of human construction; often used to refer to an engineering work, as opposed to a building; types include **aqueduct, blast furnace, bridge, bulkhead, cistern, canal, corncrib, dam, distillery, fence, fortification, gazebo, glassworks, grain elevator, lighthouse, lift-lock, railroad, reservoir, roller coaster, root cellar, seawall, shot tower, silo, snow shed, springhouse, stack stand, starling, storm cellar, sty, tank, tetrapylon, tomb, tower, train shed, triumphal arch, viaduct, wellhead, well sweep, windmill.** See also **house** (sense 2). **3.** For purposes of the National Register, a functional construction made for purposes other than creating shelter. **4.** The internal and external form and arrangement of geological features, including the conjectured form before erosion.

strut A compression member of a **truss,** or similar frame; typically diagonal; types include **truss block.** Also known as **brace, stretching piece, strutting piece.** See also **post.**

strut beam **1.** (pre-20c) Same as **collar beam.** Also known as **strutting beam.** **2.** A horizontal member of a truss that braces other members. See also **straining arch, straining beam, straining sill.** **3.** A **trussed girder** member that is under compression; may be horizontal, such as the top member when trussed below, or diagonal when trussed above. See also **strut.**

strutting beam (pre-20c) Same as **collar beam.**

strutting piece (pre-20c) **1.** Same as **straining beam. 2.** Same as **strut.**

stub mortise A **closed mortise** used with a **stub tenon.**

stub-shot, stub-short (19c) **1.** The end of a log that connects a number of partially sawn planks; the planks are separated by splitting them apart. **2.** The end of a sawn plank that has been split from the log.

stub tenon A short tenon used in a **closed mortise** joint; usually used to prevent sideways movement of the end of a column or similar element without being pegged in place.

stuc (18c) Same as **stucco** (sense 2).

stucco **1. Plaster** applied on the exterior of a building; composed of lime and sand, and, starting in the 19c, sometimes various cements; types include **lime stucco, Portland cement stucco;** finishes include **bastard stucco, pebble-dash, roughcast, rough stucco, slab plastering, spatter-dash, tabby, troweled stucco.** See also **wash coat. 2.** A fine, white composition paste of various mixtures, including lime, white marble dust or limestone dust, and water; gypsum and glue water; and white marble dust, gypsum, fine sand, and water; used for statues and **stuccowork.** Also known as **stuck.**

stucco mesh A type of **wire cloth** used as lath for stucco; typically 17-gauge wire with hexagonal openings approximately 1.5 inches across. Also known as **stucco netting.**

stucco netting Same as **stucco mesh.**

stuccowork Fine interior decorative **plasterwork** made of **stucco** (sense 2), with bas-relief or cast ornaments on the surface.

stuck, (18c) **stuc** Same as **stucco** (sense 2).

stuck molding Same as **sticking.**

stud, (pre-19c) **studd** **1.** An individual vertical element in a wall of a **balloon frame** or **platform frame** building, typically one of a series of 2 × 4s spaced 16 inches apart, or one of the intermediate smaller verticals between the posts of a **timber frame** building; originally always wood, sometimes a **steel stud** beginning in mid-20c; types based on use include **king, queen, jack;** types by size include **double quarter, joist, single quarter, split joist.** Also known as **quarter.** See also **ashlar, double studded, stud brace, stud partition, two by four. 2.** A short projecting rod or bolt; types include **stud bolt, stud pin.** See also **stud screw.**

stud and mud (pre-20c) Same as **wattle and daub.**

stud bolt A bolt with screw threads on both ends; one end is permanently attached to the structure and the other receives a nut. Also known as **standing bolt.**

stud brace A diagonal 2× member at the corner of a wood frame building that is built in so that it interrupts the studs that fall between its ends; extends from the bottom of the wall plate downward to the top of the sole. See also **knee brace, plank brace.**

studd (pre-18c) Same as **stud.**

studio The working space of an artist, photographer, or craftsperson; may have special lighting provisions or equipment.

studio apartment (20c) An **apartment** with a single living space that includes a galley kitchen, plus an enclosed bathroom.

stud partition An interior partition with **stud** framing; may be covered with various materials, such as plaster and lath, or drywall.

stud pin A short **bolt** with a shoulder.

stud screw A **wood screw** with a large, round head.

study A room used for reading, writing, and contemplative thinking. See also **library.**

study area A defined geographic area for planning or survey purposes.

stuff Wood or plaster materials collectively; used in phrases such as **clear stuff, coarse stuff, inch stuff, merchantable stuff, thick stuff.**

stunning **1.** The deep scoring of a smooth sawn stone surface, especially marble; caused by sand particles. See also **stonework.** **2.** The process of loosening, or bruising, a stone surface by impact; may be done intentionally by direct hammer blows, or be accidental damage during cutting.

STURAA Surface Transportation and Uniform Relocation Assistance Act of 1987

sty, (pre-19c) **stie, stye** A pen for hogs with a small shelter. Also known as **hog court.** See also **farrowing house.**

style **1.** The overall appearance of the design of a building, structure, landscape, object, painting, or decorative design, including construction, form, space, scale, materials, and ornamentation; may be a unique individual expression or part of a broad cultural pattern. **2.** A category of similar things distinguished by characteristic construction, form, and ornament; may also be defined partly by the period of construction or manufacture. See also **architectural style.** **3.** (pre-20c) Same as **stile.**

Style 1900 Same as **Art Nouveau.**

style guide A publication that defines and illustrates architectural styles.

Style Moderne [French] Same as **Art Moderne.**

stylobate The raised, rectangular platform with continuous steps surrounding a Classical style building. See also **stereobate.**

styrene See **ABS, polystyrene.**

subarch One of multiple arches enclosed by a larger arch, common in **Gothic Revival** style window tracery, especially the **Perpendicular Style.**

subarcuated, (19c) **sub-arcuated** Having **subarches** beneath the main arches of a structure.

sub-base The earth or fill immediately below a paving base course, such as a layer of crushed stone below a layer of asphalt concrete.

subbase **1.** The lowest element of the bottom of an architectural feature, such as the bottom molding of a **base** or **baseboard.** See also **surbase.** **2.** (pre-20c) Same as **shoe mold.**

subbasement, sub-basement A story one or more levels below the **basement** level. See also **subcellar.**

subcellar A story below a **cellar,** as in a high-rise building with a deep foundation. See also **subbasement.**

subcontractor A specialized building **contractor** who typically works for the **general contractor** to perform work in a particular trade, such as masonry or millwork.

subdivision (20c) **1.** An individual building lot that is one of several parts of a piece of land. Also known as **parcel.** **2.** A group of lots divided from a single piece of land, or vice versa. **3.** A completed **development** of houses on subdivided lots, including site improvements such as roads and sewers.

subfloor The structural floor that supports the **finish flooring,** such as a concrete floor or the rough boards of a wood floor, not common before the 19c. Also known as **counterfloor, rough floor, underfloor.** See also **underlayment.**

subflorescence The migration, deposit, and recrystallization of soluble salts below the surface of masonry due to evaporation of internal moisture; may cause **salt decay.** Also known as **cryptoflorescence.** See also **efflorescence.**

sublimed white lead A white paint **pigment** composed of lead sulfate; made by heating white lead and sulfur to a gaseous state then condensing directly to a solid.

suborder A secondary, subordinate Classical **order** used on a building for decoration, in addition to the main order; types include **attic order.**

subordinate vault (18c) A **vault** that covers one of the minor spaces of a building, such as a passageway or archway, as opposed to a **master vault.**

subplinth, (19c) **sub-plinth** A horizontal band that projects outward below the principal **plinth.**

subpurlin, sub-purlin One of a series of relatively small roof beams that span from **purlin** to purlin.

subsidized housing Dwellings for lower-income residents whose construction, financing, or rental cost is partly paid by the government, or other organization.

subsill, sub-sill, sub sill **1.** A secondary supporting **sill** under a door sill, **window sill, mudsill,** or similar element. **2.** The horizontal wood framing member below a window or door sill.

substantial impairment Impacts of a U.S.-funded transportation project that are so severe that they substantially diminish or impair the protected activities, features, or attributes that qualify a resource for protection under **Section 4(f)** of the Department of Transportation Act of 1966, such as an increase of noise levels at a historic site with a traditionally quiet setting, or obstruction of the primary views of an architecturally significant building, or structural damage caused by vibration. See also **constructive use.**

substantial rehabilitation The extent of rehabilitation necessary to qualify for a **Certification of Significance** for an **Investment Tax Credit** project; the **rehabilitation expenditures** must exceed the amount of the **adjusted basis** and $5,000 within a 2-year period, or a 5-year period for a phased rehabilitation.

substruction (pre-20c) Same as **substructure.**

substructure A structure that supports another structure above, especially when below ground, such as a **foundation.** Also known as **substruction.** See also **superstructure.**

subsurface investigation Research to determine the existing condition underground; typically involves drilling and extracting core samples, or test pits; used to gather data for the design of buildings or structures, analysis of an existing building, or a preliminary survey of an **archeological site.** See also **excavation, shovel testing.**

suburb An outlying neighborhood or town near a city center, used primarily as a residential community; typically with single family homes; one of the earliest planned suburbs in North America was the 1857 Llwellyn Park outside New York City, with cottages designed by A. J. Davis; from the Latin *suburbium.* Also known as **faubourg, villa park.**

suburban Pertaining to, or located in, a suburb.

subway Any underground passage; used in some localities, such as New York City, to mean an underground railroad.

sucker The opening in the bottom of a water tank or reservoir.

sugar house (19c southern U.S.) Same as **sugar mill.**

sugarhouse black An inexpensive **drop black** paint **pigment** manufactured from bone charcoal that has been used to bleach sugar.

sugar maple A moderate sized **maple** tree with light reddish brown, hard, strong, stiff, fine-grained heartwood with wide, white sapwood; found in the eastern half of the U.S. and Canada; used for flooring and interior millwork; *Acer saccharum.* Also known as **hard maple, rock maple.**

sugar mill A building containing equipment used to produce raw sugar juice from sugar cane, typically with crushing rollers. See also **sugar refinery.**

sugar of lead Lead acetate; used to manufacture some types of **japan.**

sugar orchard The ground where sugar maples are grown for harvesting maple syrup.

sugar pine An extremely tall **pine** tree with light-colored, soft, straight-grained wood; found in Oregon and California; used for millwork, shingles, and lumber; commercially lumbered early 20c–present; *Pinus labertiana.*

sugar refinery (19c–present) A building containing equipment that refines raw or brown sugar juice by filtering, concentrating in evaporators, and crystallizing in molds; may contain various conveyor belts, boilers, and engines; typically a large building with one or more tall smoke stacks. See also **sugar mill.**

suite A series of connected rooms used for a single purpose. See also **en suite.**

sulfur, sulphur A brittle, pale yellow, nonmetallic, crystalline element. Also known as **brimstone.**

summer, (pre-19c) **sommer** **1.** (pre-19c) Same as **summer beam.** **2.** A stone lintel. **3.** A stone that caps a pier, or jamb, and supports the end of a beam or arch. Also known as **summer stone.** **4.** A beam that spans between the cross-sills of a timber framed building and supports the joists. **5.** (pre-19c) The condition where the sides of a wedge-shaped arch voussoir point to the center of the circle that forms the intrados of an arch.

summer beam **1.** A large **girder** or **binding beam** used in **timber frame** construction; typically spans the entire width or length of the building. Also known as **dormant tree, summer, summertree.** **2.** (pre-19c) A timber **girder** supported on the exterior wall of a building; may project past the ground-floor wall to support an overhanging story. Also known as **summer, summertree.** See also **breastsummer, chamber summer beam, dragon beam.**

summer cover A temporary decorative cover for a fireplace opening used during the summer months; may be cast iron or sheet metal. See also **fireback.**

summer house A residence used primarily in the summer. See also **summerhouse.**

summerhouse An open-sided pavilion in a park or garden for warm weather recreation. Also known as **summerroom.** See also **casino, gazebo, summer house.**

summer piece Same as **summer cover.**

summerroom (pre-20c) Same as **summerhouse.**

summer stone **1.** Same as **skew corbel.** **2.** Same as **summer** (sense 3).

summertree **1.** Same as **summer beam.** **2.** A timber beam acting as a lintel and supporting other beams. Also known as **master beam.** See also **breastsummer, summer.**

summerwood The denser wood that grows in summer and fall; often in an annual ring that is a darker color than **springwood.** Also known as **latewood.**

sump A pit or depression in a basement or cellar floor, or other paved area, that collects water; typically the water is removed by a **sump pump.**

sump pump A mechanical device for removing water from a **sump.**

sun (pre-WWI) Same as **sunburner.**

sunburner (late 19c–mid-20c) A lighting fixture with multiple lamps concentrated in front of a ceiling-mounted reflector covered with an inverted glass globe; typically electric, may also be gas. Also known as **sun, sunlight burner.**

sunburst light Same as **fanlight.**

sundial, (pre-20c) **sun dial** A device for measuring time by the shadow of a gnomon on a surface marked with radiating lines; may be on a horizontal or vertical surface, or a hollow spherical ornament. See also **dial.**

sunk draft A tooled **draft** on the perimeter of the face of a stone block that is below the main surface; often used with **pitch faced** blocks. See also **sunk face.**

sunk face A center portion of an exposed face of a stone block that is recessed below the surface of the perimeter **draft.** See also **sunk draft, sunk panel.**

sunk fence Same as **ha-ha fence.**

sunk fillet A recessed rectangular **dado** groove; used in moldings and to form a decorative pattern in a flat surface.

sunk girt A **timber frame** girt whose top surface supports the bottom of the ends of perpendicular floor beams. Also known as **dropped girt.** See also **raised girt.**

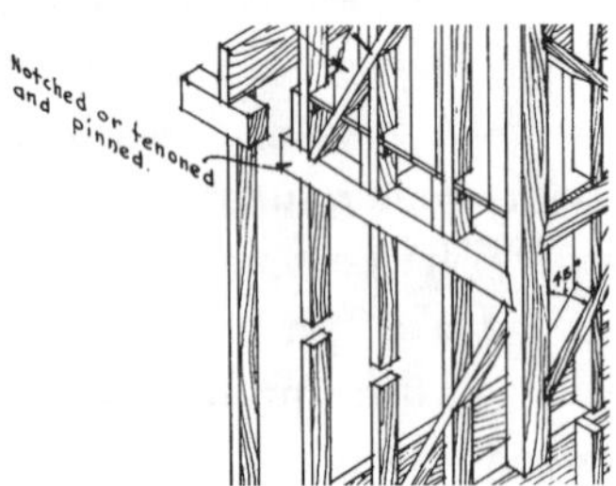

sunk girt

sunk panel A panel with its face below the adjacent surface. See also **double sunk, sunk face.**

sunk relief A **relief** sculpture, or letters, with a background that is lower than the main surface; made by cutting into a flat surface. Also known as **cavo-rilievo, coelanaglyphic relief.**

sun parlor (pre-20c) Same as **sun room.**

sunroom, (pre-20c) **sun room** Same as **solarium** (sense 1), especially in a house.

supercanopy An arch or gable above another arch or gable, or above a niche or recess.

supercapital An impost block above a column capital. See also **dosseret.**

supercharge To overload beyond bearing capacity; soil is sometimes supercharged to compact it before construction starts. Also known as **overburden.**

supercilium **1.** Same as **annulet;** forms the top member of a classical Roman style cornice; also refers to the fillets above and below a scotia on an attic base. **2.** Same as **corona.**

supercolumnar **1.** Erected above a row of columns. **2.** Having **supercolumniation.**

supercolumniation The placing one row of columns above another. See also **superposition.**

superficial contents (19c) Same as **superficial measure.**

superficial dimension (18c) Same as **superficial measure.**

superficial measure (pre-20c) The measured area of a surface, as opposed to a linear dimension or a volume; units may include **square,** square foot, and square yard. Also known as **superficial contents, superficial dimension.**

superimposition The support of one building layer by another; sometimes used to mean **superposition.**

superior slope The downward slope from the crest of a **fortification** embankment to the top of the **exterior slope.**

superposition The placing of one classical order above another; classical designers generally place the simple orders, such as Tuscan, at the base of a building and the increasingly more ornate orders in successive stories; typically followed the rule that the bottom of the column shaft above should be the same diameter as the top of the shaft below, giving a tapered appearance to the vertical line of columns; first used in the Theater of Marcellus in Rome (44–13 B.C.). Also known as **order above order.**

superstructure The structure of a building above the foundation. See also **substructure.**

supervision The direct management of labor at a construction site. See also **construction observation.**

supplier The company that provides materials for a construction project; the materials may be raw, such as sand or lumber, or manufactured, such as hardware or plumbing fixtures.

supply line The pipe that provides fresh water, steam, or gas to a fixture or piece of equipment. See also **return pipe, steam pipe.**

surbase, (pre-19c) **sur base, sir base** **1.** The molding or cornice at the top edge of a pedestal. **2.** A wall molding or decorative border above a base molding, dado or basement story. See also **subbase.**

surbased **1.** Flattened or depressed. **2.** Having a **surbase,** such as a surbased pedestal.

surbased arch A **drop arch** where the rise is less than half the span.

surbased vault A vault with a cross section in the form of a **drop arch** or **segmental arch.**

sure post (18c) A post used to reinforce an existing raised sill or beam.

surface arcade A series of arches engaged with a wall, with the surface appearance of an **arcade,** although purely ornamental. Also known as **blind arcade, wall arcade.**

surface board A **sheathing** board with a rectangular cross section. See also **match board.**

surface collection The gathering of **archaeological artifacts** from the surface of the ground without **excavation.**

surfaced four sides **Surfaced lumber** with a rectangular or square cross section that has been planed on all of the long sides; commonly abbreviated as **S4S.**

surfaced lumber **Rough sawn** lumber that has been planed on one or more of its exposed faces to remove saw marks; most North American lumber is **surfaced four sides** after mid-20c.

Surface Mining Control and Reclamation Act of 1977 (SMCRA) U.S. federal legislation that includes prohibition of coal mining that adversely affects any historic site listed in the National Register of Historic Places and requires that the Office of Surface Mining comply with **Section 106.**

Surface Transportation and Uniform Relocation Assistance Act of 1987 (STURAA) U.S. federal legislation requiring that historic bridges that are to be demolished during projects using federal funds be made available for donation to a "state, locality, or responsible private" entities who agree to maintain them, and that the Federal Highway Administration make funds available to preserve bridges that are no longer used to carry traffic.

surmounted arch A stilted **round arch,** with the spring line located above the imposts. See also **stilted arch.**

surmounted vault A **stilted vault** with a semicircular cross section above the springline.

surround Same as **enframement.**

survey **1.** A geometrically correct map of a piece of land; may show only the boundary lines, or other features such as buildings, driveways, trees, and topography. See also **metes and bounds.** **2.** The process of measuring and recording the features and boundaries of the land. See also **building survey, Gunter's chain.** **3.** The collection of data relative to a **study area;** typically includes both field investigation and research of documents; may be used to compile an **inventory;** types include **historic district survey, sample survey, windshield survey.** **4.** (British commonwealth) Evaluating the condition of an existing building.

suspended ceiling A finished **ceiling** attached to furring, or a **ceiling grid,** hung from the structure above; typically finished with **plaster, drywall,** or **acoustical tile.**

suspended light A **window pane** that does not abut the rails or stiles of a multipaned sash.

suspension bridge A **bridge** hung from cables that are strung between two towers or a tower and abutment. Also known as **wire bridge.**

suspension truss An inverted **Fink truss,** with all of the diagonals in tension.

sustaining wall (pre-20c) A structural wall, such as a **bearing wall** or **retaining wall.**

swag A **festoon,** especially one where the foliage, or drapery, is thick in the middle and thin at the supports.

swage bolt, swedge bolt (20c) An **anchor bolt** in the form of a round rod with one threaded end and a series of holes or depressions at right angles to one another along its length; typically .75–1.25 inches in diameter and 9–15 inches in length; used in concrete or masonry.

swamp cypress Same as **bald cypress.**

swamp maple Same as **red maple.**

swamp spruce Same as **black spruce.**

swamp white oak An **oak** tree with light-colored, heavy, strong wood; found in eastern and southeastern U.S.; *Quercus bicolor.* Also known as **white oak.**

swan neck **1.** A stair rail shape that curves upward from a sloped ramp until it is vertical, then turns horizontal, with a right-angle miter, for a short distance; often used to make a transition from the inclined portion to a vertical newel. **2.** The curved shape of each side of a pair of top cornices of a broken pediment; has a concave curve at the base that transitions to a convex curve ending in a scroll; sometimes used flanking a center finial with pineapple decoration.

sway bracing Bridge ties that resist vibration from variable live loads, such as wind or marching troops.

sweated joint A soldered metal **joint** formed by heating the assembled pieces so that the liquid **solder** runs into the gap between them; used for copper pipe and tin roofs.

sweat equity The interest in a property acquired by investing one's own labor or services in **rehabilitation** or **restoration;** sometimes used in low-income home purchase programs, such as **homesteading,** as the purchaser's equity.

sweating **1.** Condensation of water on a cool surface, such as a water pipe or window pane. **2.** Leakage of water from lead pipe joints. **3.** The process of making a **sweated joint.**

sweating room (19c–present) A room where people are sweated as a medicinal treatment, especially at a **spa.**

swedge bolt Same as **swage bolt.**

Swedish finish A synthetic ureaformaldehyde **varnish** developed after World War II.

Swedish putty **1.** A painter's **putty** used for filling large cracks or depressions; commonly contains oil-base paint, dry whiting or calcimine, glue dissolved in hot water, and dry color. **2.** A glazing putty composed of a white lead and oil paste.

sweep **1.** A long pole mounted on top of a post, with a bucket hanging from a rope above a well; used to draw water. **2.** (19c) A curve in a driveway leading to a building entrance.

sweep tee, sweep A plumbing **pipe fitting** with a curved side branch connected to a straight pipe section.

swelling **1.** The increase in diameter of a column toward the middle of its height; the middle is thicker than both the top and bottom. See also **entasis, diminution.** **2.** (18c) A projecting ogee molding, especially with a convex lower curve. See also **belly, pulvinated.**

swelling frieze (18c) A pulvinated frieze.

Swenson Buff Antique A light to medium grayish buff, fine- to medium-grained, muscovite-biotite **granite** quarried in the vicinity of Concord, New Hampshire. See also **Concord granite.**

Swenson Pink A light pink, medium- to coarse-grained, biotite **granite,** with black and pink stripes, quarried in the vicinity of North Berwick, Maine.

swept valley A roof **valley** covered with slates, tiles, or shingles that are in continuous courses with the adjoining roofs, as opposed to an **open valley.** Also known as **California valley.** See also **slate-and-a-half.**

swimming bath (pre-WWI) Same as **swimming pool.**

swimming pool (late 19c–present) A water reservoir constructed for recreational or therapeutic swimming; may be exterior or interior; type includes **plunge pool.** Also known as **swimming bath, swimming tank.** See also **bathhouse, natatorium.**

swimming tank Same as **swimming pool.**

swing bar **1.** A **gate** formed with a horizontal pivoting bar. **2.** An internal bar across a door or shutters supported by two sockets.

swing bridge A **drawbridge** that opens by turning horizontally on a **turntable** supported on a pier. Also known as **pivot bridge, pivot span, turning bridge.**

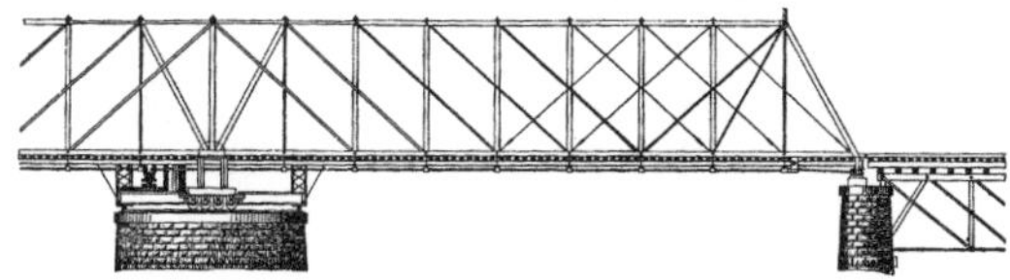

swing bridge

swing door, swinging door A **door** hinged so that it opens in both directions; may have a pivot hinge, double acting spring hinges, or other devices.

swinging post Same as **hanging post** (sense 3).

swirl **1.** The curling **grain** of cut wood around knots and crotches. **2.** A decorative pattern in coatings, such as paint and plaster, created by twisting the brush or trowel on the surface after the coating is applied.

Swiss Chalet style (19c) An architectural house style loosely based on the Swiss **chalet** prototype; first promoted in the U.S. by A. J. Downing in 1850, and in several pattern books through the end of the 19c; typical elements include two stories with front-gable, low-pitched roof, front balcony or porch with scroll work railings and decoration, and stickwork or board and batten siding.

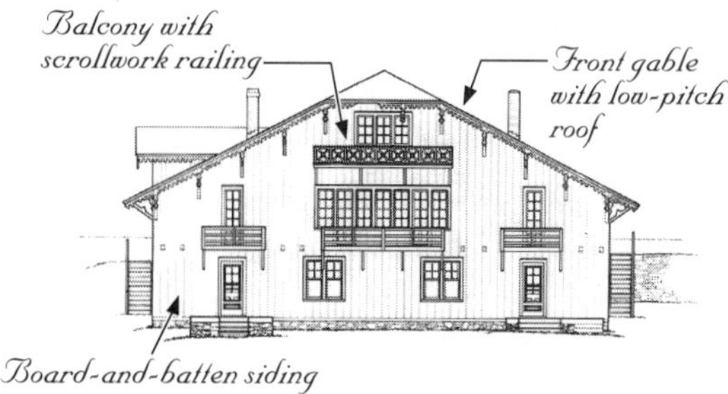

Swiss Chalet style
Montgomery Place, Swiss Cottage
by Alexander Jackson Davis, ca. 1867
Dutchess County, New York

switch **1.** A device for making and breaking an electric circuit; types include **jackknife switch, push button, service switch, snap switch.** **2.** A mechanical device that changes the route of a railroad train from one track to another.

switchboard An enclosure containing major electrical **switchgear;** typically self-supporting as opposed to a wall-mounted **panelboard.**

switchgear All of the major electrical disconnect switches and related devices in a large **switchboard;** most often used at the point where a heavy electric service line enters the building.

syenite An igneous rock similar to **granite,** except it contains little or no quartz.

Sykes lath A form of **sheet-metal lath** with rolled ridges approximately 2 inches apart and punched loops and holes. See also **lath.**

Sylvester process (early 20c) A waterproofing method for concrete consisting of alternating applications of hot solutions of castile soap and of alum.

symbolical freeze (18c) A **frieze** decorated with bas-relief religious symbols.

symmetry **1.** (19c–present) Having repetitive parts and proportions; in buildings most often refers to the bilateral form, with mirror images about an imaginary vertical line. **2.** (18c–19c) Having pleasing and harmonious proportions and form.

sympathetic An inexact adjective used to describe the character of new work, such as an **alteration** or **addition,** that is appropriate in relation to the existing historic architectural character and fabric.

synagogue A building or meeting used for Jewish religious worship and instruction; components may include **tebam.**

synthetic pigment An artificial paint **pigment** produced from chemicals, as opposed to an **earth pigment;** types include **American vermillion, aniline color, chrome yellow, chrome green, chrome oxide green,** and various shades of red.

synthetic resin Any of the various manufactured resins, as opposed to those derived from plants; types include **acrylic, epoxy;** used in paints, fillers, and molded ornaments.

synthetic rubber paint Same as **latex.**

sypher joint A carpentry **flush joint** made by overlapping the chamfered edges of two boards.

Syrian arch A **round arch** with the spring line almost at ground level; common in **Richardsonian Romanesque style** doorways.

systematic data recovery The scientific examination and recording of all of the material of a historic resource, especially at an **archaeological site;** involves partial or total disassembly.

systyle A spacing of a row of columns with two column diameters between column centers. See also **intercolumniation.**

T

tabby, (18c) **tappy,** (16c) **tapia** Concrete composed of oyster shell lime, water, sand, and whole oyster shells mixed in equal proportions; typically used to make walls with 10–12 inch-high courses; used by Spanish settlers in 16c Florida and in late 17c–mid-19c coastal Georgia and South Carolina.

tabernacle **1.** An ornamented recess or niche in a church that holds the vessels of the Holy Sacrament, an icon, or a relic; common in the Gothic Revival style. **2.** A freestanding ornamental canopy above an altar, tomb, or the items of sense 1. See also **tester.**

tabernacle frame A surround for an opening with columns or pilasters and a complete entablature; often with a corbeled pendant below windows and in the Gothic Revival style.

tabernacle work **1.** Ornate Gothic or Gothic Revival decorative work surrounding niches or stalls; typically with pinnacles and foiled openings. **2.** Architecture with multiple tabernacles.

table **1.** A rectangular panel on a stone wall or pedestal, often with an inscription, illustrative painting, or bas-relief sculpture; types include **crowned table, raised table, raking table, retable, rusticated table.** **2.** A horizontal molding or band that encircles the exterior of a building; types include **cornice, earth table, ledgement table, skew table, string course, water table.** See also **tablette.** **3.** A flat **tombstone** supported on piers. See also **table tomb.** **4.** A bas-relief front panel on a church altar. See also **retable.**

tablero A rectangular masonry panel, with a heavy, projecting, framed border, cantilevered over a battered **talud** that is part of a massive, stuccoed, rubble stone pyramid; hidden slabs of stone support the projecting frame; originated in Teotihuacán, near Mexico City, ca. 150, and later copied throughout central Mexico and as far south as Guatemala; from the Spanish for "panel."

tablet **1.** An inscribed slab of stone that is mounted on, or set into, a wall; often framed with moldings, scrolls, or a miniature order. See also **table.** **2.** Same as **tablette.**

tablet flower banding A molding composed of a row of flat, four-petaled flowers; used in **Decorated Gothic.**

table tomb A low tomb with a stone slab top. See also **altar tomb.**

tablette, tablet A coping stone with a thin, rectangular cross section.

tabling Same as **coping,** especially with tablettes.

tacamahac Same as **balsam poplar.**

tack A small, pointed **nail** with a flat head. See also **tin tack.**

tacky The sticky surface quality of some finish coatings after application; may continue for weeks with oil-base paints and varnishes.

taenia, (pre-20c) **tenia** A narrow, projecting fillet molding at the top of a classical architrave, with a flat face and top and a concave curved underside; located between the guttae and the triglyph in the Doric style.

tail **1.** The end of a member projecting into another element, such as the side of a stone window sill tailed into the masonry. **2.** The exposed portion of a shingle, tile, or slate, as opposed to the **head.** **3.** Same as **tailing.** **4.** Same as **rafter tail.** **5.** Same as **tail piece.**

tail bay **1.** The space enclosed by the walls of a canal lock between the **tail gate** and the lower water level. **2.** An end bay of a building, between a girder and a parallel exterior wall; one end of the perpendicular girders, and the joists or rafters, are supported by the wall. See also **case-bay, tail beam.**

tail beam Any beam that is tailed into a wall, such as a joist or girder supported by a pocket in a masonry wall. See also **tail joist, tail trimmer.**

tail drain The drain pipe that connects all the other drains of a **leaching field,** or similar system.

tail gate The lower gate of a **lift-lock** or **mill race.** Also known as **aft gate.** See also **tail bay.**

tailing The unexposed rear portion of a projecting cornice stone, or similar wall element, that acts as a counterweight.

tail joist **1.** Any joist that is tailed into a masonry wall. See also **tail, tail bay.** **2.** A joist used as a **tail piece.**

tailloir [French] Same as **abacus.**

tail piece **1.** Same as **lookout** (sense 1). Also known as **tail.** **2.** A short joist or rafter that is supported at one end by a **header.** Also known as **tail.** See also **trimmer, tail trimmer.**

tail race The portion of a **mill race** below, or after, the mill wheel. Also known as **mill tail.**

tail trimmer One of a pair of trimmer beams on each side of a chimney, or opening, that support a header that holds the ends of the tail piece joists or rafters; typically spans from one bearing wall to another bearing wall.

tail race

take into account The analysis by a U.S. federal agency of the effect of an **undertaking** on a historic property as defined by **Section 106;** typically done by use of an **Environmental Impact Statement** and the consultation process defined by the regulations of the **Advisory Council on Historic Preservation,** often resulting in a **memorandum of agreement.**

take-out loan Same as **permanent loan;** named for its replacement of the **construction loan.**

taking The acquisition of a property, in whole or part, by a government; owners have argued in court that the restrictions on development caused by preservation ordinances is a taking and must be compensated. See also **condemnation, expropriation.**

tall boy A tall, slender sheet-metal **chimney pot;** used to improve the draft of the chimney.

talon **1.** Same as **ogee.** **2.** (pre-19c) A cymatium with a fillet above, used as a crown molding for a door, pedestal, impost block, or similar location.

talud A pre-Columbian, battered, exterior wall surface; thought to have originated ca. 800 B.C. at the Olmec site located at La Venta, Tabasco, Mexico. See also **tablero.**

talus, talut **1.** A sloped architectural feature, especially a battered wall, or an inclined retaining wall against an embankment. **2.** Same as the **exterior slope** of a fortification.

talut Same as **talus.**

tamarack **1.** One of various trees of the larch family, especially **eastern tamarack.** **2.** Same as **lodgepole pine.**

tambac (pre-20c) Same as **tombac.**

tambaycke (pre-20c) Same as **tombac.**

tambour **1.** Same as **drum;** from the French term for the musical instrument. **2.** A lobby or vestibule, such as a church porch, designed to prevent drafts entering inside. **3.** A palisade that defends an entrance.

tangent sawn Same as **plain sawn.**

tan house A building used in tanning leather. See also **bark house, tannery.**

tank A fixed reservoir or vessel for holding a liquid or gas; typically constructed of wood or metal; types include **expansion tank, gasometer, water tank.** See also **boiler.**

tank iron Thick iron **plate** used for making large tanks.

tank system A pre-WWII water-heating system with a hot-water storage tank located above the level of the highest fixture; typically heated by a **waterback.** See also **cylinder system, cylinder tank system.**

tannery A place where leather is tanned; typically includes a **bark house, bark mill, tan house** and **tanyard.** Also known as **tanyard.**

tan pit Same as **tan vat.**

tan vat A lined pit for soaking leather in one of various solutions during the tanning process. Also known as **bark pit, tan pit.** See also **tanyard.**

tanyard **1.** The outside area of a **tannery;** typically includes several **tan vats** and lime pits. **2.** (pre-20c) Same as **tannery.**

tap **1.** To connect a utility service pipe to the main. **2.** Same as **faucet.**

tape-balance (20c) A support for the lower sash of a doublehung window in the form of a narrow steel tape wound around a spring mechanism. Also known as **clock-spring balance.**

tapestry A large woven illustration hung as a wall decoration.

tapestry brick Face brick laid in a decorative **bond** pattern with a combination of vertical, horizontal and/or diagonal elements, such as **basketweave.**

tapia **1.** A Latin American term for a mud or adobe wall. **2.** (16c) Same as **tabby.**

tappy (pre-19c) Same as **tabby.**

tar A sticky, water-resistant, black organic material manufactured by distilling minerals or resinous wood; types include **coal tar, mineral tar, wood tar;** used for built-up roofs, damp-proof courses, and manufacturing various construction products, such as roofing felt. See also **naval stores.**

tar-gravel roof Same as **gravel roof.**

tar paper Same as **roofing felt.**

tarrace (pre-20c) Same as **terrace.**

tarras (pre-19c) Same as **terrace** (senses 3 and 4).

tarrass (pre-19c) Same as **terrace** (senses 3 and 4).

tarrasse (pre-20c) Same as **terrace.**

tarris (pre-20c) Same as **terrace.**

tarsia Same as **intarsia.**

tassal Same as **torsel.**

tassel Same as **torsel.**

T-astragal A door **astragal** with an approximately T-shaped cross section.

tavern (mid-18c–present) A building used for the lodging, feeding, and entertainment of travelers. Also known as **inn, ordinary, public house.** See also **hotel.**

tax act certification See **Certification of Rehabilitation, Certification of Significance.**

tax credit project See **investment tax credit.**

tax incentive A reduction of taxes to be paid by an owner of a property in exchange for investing money and agreeing to meet certain requirements, such as preservation guidelines for **rehabilitation** or **restoration;** typically income taxes or property taxes are reduced or rebated. See also **investment tax credit.**

Tax Reform Act of 1976 (as amended) U.S. legislation that includes a provision for an **investment tax credit** against the federal income tax of an owner who invests in rehabilitating a **certified historic property** after obtaining a **certification of significance.**

tazza A shallow basin supported by a pillar, or foot, especially for a fountain; often one of several of increasing size from top to bottom; from the Italian term for a footed cup.

T-bar A small **T-beam.**

T-beam An iron or steel **rolled beam** with a T-shaped cross section; first manufactured in 1783. See also **I-beam, T-bar, T-bulb, tee beam.**

T-bolt A **bolt** with a T-shaped head.

T-branch A **pipe fitting** that is approximately T-shaped; the branching leg may be of equal or smaller size than the main pipe. See also **sanitary T-branch, T-fitting.**

T-bulb Same as **bulb-tee.**

T.C. **1.** Abbr. for **top chord.** **2.** Abbr. for **terra-cotta.**

TDD Abbr. for **telecommunication device for the deaf.**

TDR Abbr. for **transfer of development rights.**

teagle post A post supporting one end of a **tie beam,** such as below one end of a roof truss.

teasel tenon Same as **tease tenon.**

tease tenon, (pre-20c) **teaze tenon** A long tenon at the top of a **timber frame** post, with a two-step shoulder that fits into mortises in the bottom of two horizontal timbers that cross at right angles at the post; uses include attaching a girt and a tie beam to a post. Also known as **teasel tenon, teazle tenon.**

teaze tenon (pre-20c) Same as **tease tenon.**

teazle tenon (pre-20c) Same as **tease tenon.**

tebam A raised dais in a **synagogue** for the reader.

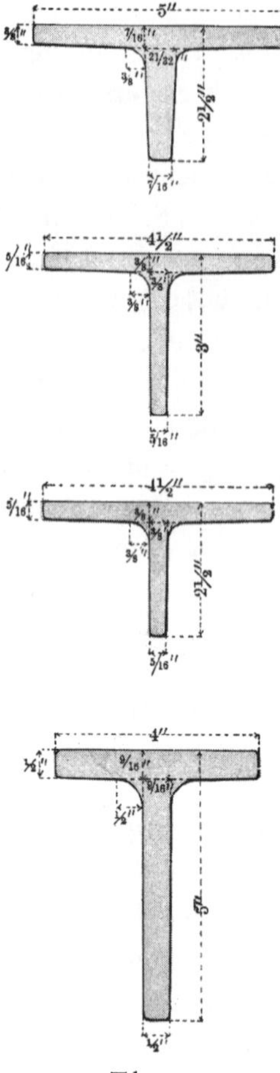

T-beam

tectonic Of, or relating to, architecture, building, or construction.

tee Any T-shaped element.

tee beam A reinforced concrete beam with a T-shaped cross section; the tension reinforcing in the bottom of the flange is often prestressed or posttensioned to increase strength.

tee-bulb See **bulb-tee.**

tee hinge Same as **T-hinge.**

teeth (pre-19c) A row of dentils.

tegula (pl. **tegulae**) A flat, terra-cotta roof tile with ridges at the vertical edges that are cov-

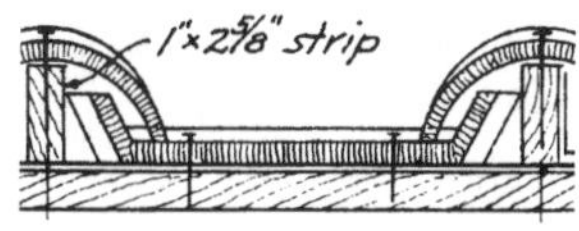

tegula

ered by an **imbrex;** used in **Italian tiling.** Also known as **gutter tile, under tile.**

tejamaniles Hand-split pine slats that span between rafters in the Morelia region of Mexico in **Spanish Colonial** style buildings.

telamon (pl. **telamones**) [Latin] Same as **atlas.**

telecommunication device for the deaf (TDD) A telephone that allows the sending and display of written messages for the hearing impaired.

telegraph wire (ca. 1885) An iron or low-grade steel **electric wire** strung between telegraph or telephone poles; sometimes **bimetallic wire.** See also **office wire.**

telephone wire (late 19c–present) Any type of wire used for telephone transmissions; typically an insulated, pure copper wire. See also **bimetallic wire, telegraph wire.**

Telford pavement A road paving with a base of large pieces of stone with the voids filled by small stones, covered with a layer of fine crushed stone, and rolled hard and smooth; developed by the Scottish road engineer Thomas Telford (1757–1834).

telltale Any of various devices for detecting building movement, such as a small, rectangular piece of window glass fastened on both sides of a building crack that breaks when there is movement; some late 20c telltales have two overlapping pieces with grid markings that are initially aligned.

telltale pipe An overflow pipe for a water tank that indicates when the level is too high.

tempera **1.** Same as **distemper** paint, or sometimes **calcimine,** especially when used in fine arts work. **2.** The process of painting with **distemper.**

tempered Moistened and mixed to the proper consistency; especially mortar, and clay for bricks.

tempered glass (19c–present) A high-strength glass manufactured by cooling the surface of the hot glass more quickly than the interior; both the open-hearth Siemen process and an oil bath were used for tempering in the 19c; breaks into small pieces when shattered. Also known in the 19c as **hardened glass, toughened glass.** See also **compressed glass, heat-strengthened glass.**

tempered steel Steel that has been hardened by repeatedly heating and quickly cooling it; during this process the color of the heated steel changes from light yellow to dark blue. Also known as **blue steel, case hardened.**

template **1.** A stiff sheet material with openings cut out to form a pattern guide, such as those used in **stenciling** or drafting. **2.** Same as **templet.**

temple **1.** Same as **synagogue.** **2.** A building in the form of a classical temple.

temple front A building facade with a classical colonnade, entablature, and pediment in the style of a Greek or Roman temple.

temple mound A **mound** that supported a Native American temple, such as the 90-foot-tall mound at Cahokia, Illinois, or those of Mexico.

templet, template (pre-20c) A bearing block of stone or wood; used to distribute the weight of a beam end in a masonry wall or over an opening, or to receive the thrust of the end of a truss.

temporary freeze (Canada) A halt to proposed alteration or demolition of a heritage site for 30 or 60 days by resolution of a municipal council.

temporary restraining order A court order that temporarily halts a proposed action, such as the **demolition** of a building.

tenail A wall between bastions of a **fortification;** joins the base of the angles between the flank and face of the bastions.

tender A construction bid or proposal; most often used in connection with public works, such as for bridge building.

tenement **1.** (pre-20c) Any residential rental property; may be a single-family house, or a room or apartment in a **tenement house.** **2.** (20c) An apartment building in poor condition and/or of substandard design.

tenement house A building with multiple dwelling units accessed by a single stair; typically two or more apartments share a common bathroom on each floor; types include **dumbbell tenement;** common in U.S. cities during the late 19c–WWI. See also **apartment house, tenement.**

tenia (pre-20c) Same as **taenia.**

Tennessee marble Any of the pink, gray, chocolate brown, black and white mottled varieties of **marble** quarried in the eastern part of Tennessee; used mainly in interiors; may have exposed shells or other remains of marine animals; varieties include **craig pink, curley gray Tennessee, dark cedar, dark Republic, F. A. Pink, Friendsville Pink.**

tennon (pre-19c) Same as **tenon.**

tenon, (pre-19c) **tennon** A tongue with a rectangular cross section projecting lengthwise from the end of a wood member, formed by cutting away a portion of the member; types include **tease tenon, stub tenon.** See also **dovetail, mortise and tenon, tusk.**

tenon bar A round bar used to provide a tension splice in a wood truss; may be one of a pair attached to angle irons on the outside of the butting ends of two members, or a single bar in a hole drilled lengthwise in the ends.

tenpenny nail (10d nail) A **nail** approximately 3 inches long; 60 iron common nails weigh a pound. See also **penny.**

tenpenny spike (10d spike) A **spike** approximately 7 inches long; 7 steel-wire spikes weigh a pound. See also **penny.**

tension bar A metal tension member in a truss or similar structure, in the shape of a bar or rod.

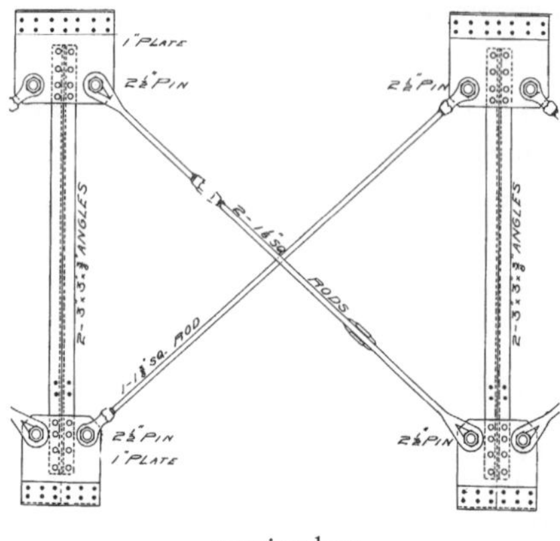

tension bar

tension iron Same as **high test iron.**

tension member A member in a truss, or similar structure, that is in tension; may be any shape, of wood or metal.

tension piece (pre-WWI) Same as **tension member.**

tent **1.** A portable shelter with an exterior surface of fabric or skin. **2.** (early 19c–present) A small house adjacent to a preaching **arbor;** used in place of the original fabric shelters.

term Same as **terminal figure.**

terminal **1.** A minor ornament at the end or top of an architectural element, such as the carved end of a church pew. See also **finial, poppyhead.** **2.** Same as **terminal figure,** especially when incorporated into an architectural element, such as a bracket. **3.** A station at one end of a transportation line, such as a bus, railroad, or truck line; those in cities are often large and ornate; may be used to include the adjacent railroad tracks as well as the building. Also known as **terminus.** **4.** Any station for an airline.

terminal figure A carving in the form of a pedestal that tapers outward at the top and merges into a animal, human or mythical figure; used for columns, statues, and consoles supporting entablatures; from those representing Terminus, the Roman god of boundaries; sometimes with two or four faces. Also known as **term, terminal, terminus, therme.** See also **atlas, caryatid, herm, vagina.**

terminal pedestal A tapered pedestal for a bust, with both objects forming a **terminal figure.**

termini See **terminus.**

terminus (pl. **termini**) **1.** Same as **terminal figure.** **2.** Same as **terminal** (sense 3).

terminus adquem The ending date of a **control period** or **period of significance.**

terminus a quo The beginning date of a **control period** or **period of significance.**

termite Any of numerous species of pale-colored, antlike social insects of the order *Isoptera;* typically consume dead wood; indigenous North American species have underground nests connected to their food source (such as the wood in a building) by shelter tubes made of mud; Formosan termites found in southern U.S. can nest above ground inside buildings. Also known as **white ant.** See also **carpenter ant.**

termite shield A projecting metal flashing on a foundation wall or pier that prevents termites from reaching the wood above.

terne, terne metal A corrosion resistant **alloy** of 67–90 percent lead and 10–33 percent tin.

terneplate, (pre-20c) **ternplate** Sheet steel coated with **terne** metal; used for sheet-metal roofs and flashings. See also **tinplate.**

ternplate (pre-20c) Same as **terneplate.**

terrace, (pre-20c) **tarrace, tarras, tarrasse, tarris,** (pre-19c) **terrass** **1.** An artificially leveled ground area; may have a retaining wall, or an embankment, at the edges; often one of a series used in landscape gardening to create, or overlook, a view; may be made by **cut** or **fill,** or a combination of the two; types include **built terrace, counter terrace, cut terrace.** See also **falling garden, parterre, patio, terreplein, xyst.** **2.** A paved sitting area adjacent to a building, without any enclosure; may be an extension of a partially enclosed veranda. **3.** A flat roof that is paved as a sitting area. See also **roof deck, roof garden.** **4.** (pre-20c) A balcony, or open gallery. **5.** (Canadian, pre-20c U.S.) A raised ground area supporting a row of houses, and by extension, the row houses themselves. **6.** Same as **terras.**

terrace of construction (pre-20c) Same as **built terrace.**

terrace roof A flat roof with a walking surface, such as pavers.

terra-cotta **1.** Fired ceramic clay, especially when used for architectural elements, such as **architectural terra-cotta, floor tile, hollow tile, roof tile, structural clay tile, tile arch, vitrified sewer pipe.** Also known as **hollow pottery.** See also **porous earthenware.** **2.** Sculptured, unglazed, reddish ceramic.

terra-cotta arch Same as **tile arch.**

terra-cotta lumber (19c) A soft, porous form of **architectural terra-cotta** that can be shaped and nailed; used in sheets for increasing fire resistance.

terras, terrace A defective area of a piece of marble that has been cut out and replaced with composition.

terrass (pre-19c) Same as **terrace.**

terrazzo A floor finish of stone chips laid in a mortar bed, then ground and polished smooth; typically composed of marble chips, less than 1.5 inch in diameter, laid in a nearly dry cement mortar, often with brass divider strips between sections of different colors;

type includes **Roman mosaic.** Also known as **terrazzo veneziano, trazzo, Venetian pavement.** See also **mosaic.**

terrazzo veneziano (pre-20c) Same as **terrazzo.**

terreplein, (pre-20c) **terre pleine** **1.** A level platform or terrace used in a **fortification,** such as the gun platform behind a rampart, or the field surrounding the outer wall. **2.** A large, level earthen civil engineering work, such the filled construction that carries a canal across a valley.

Territorial Style The architectural style of adobe buildings constructed by the military and settlers in the southwest U.S. during the late 19c, especially in New Mexico; typical components include brick copings on the parapets surrounding flat roofs, large windows with Greek Revival Style trim, relatively thin walls, and lime plaster stucco. See also **Monterey style, Spanish Colonial Revival style.**

terrones work [Spanish] From *terron,* "a clod of earth"; any kind of earthen construction, including **adobe, pisé.**

tessella (pl. **tessellae**) Same as **tessera.**

tessellated work A mosaic composed of small, square pieces. See also **Roman mosaic, tessera.**

tessellation **1.** Formerly, paving with large marble tiles. **2.** Finished with tesserae or mosaic tiles. **3.** Same as **Roman mosaic.**

tessera (pl. **tesserae**) A small mosaic tile; typically a cube of marble or glass, may also be brick, stone, or tile. Also known as **tessella.** See also **tessellation, trigonum.**

tester A flat canopy suspended over a tomb, pulpit, or bed; may be wood, fabric, or other materials. See also **tabernacle.**

testing **1.** Physical tests performed on building components during the construction phase of a restoration, renovation, or new construction project; may include concrete or mortar strength, and soil bearing capacity tests. See also **inspection.** **2.** Scientific tests of construction materials or assemblies under controlled laboratory conditions; may include tests for air infiltration, fire resistance, flame spread, pipe leaks, strength, color fading, safety, or moisture resistance. **3.** Field tests of existing building elements as part of an **inspection;** types include **destructive testing, nondestructive testing.**

testudo A **surbased vault** over a large space; from the Latin term.

tetrapylon A **structure** having four entrances, such as a **triumphal arch** with two intersecting vaults.

tetrastoon A courtyard enclosure with four porticos or arcades.

tetrastyle **1.** Having four columns across a facade. See also **columniation.** **2.** A building with a roof supported by four columns or pillars.

tewel (pre-20c) **1.** A louvered ventilation opening. **2.** A smoke flue.

Texas Pink granite A light pink, medium-grained **granite** quarried in the vicinity of Marble Falls, Texas.

Textile Block A trade name for **concrete block** with various bas-relief geometric patterns designed by Frank Lloyd Wright in the 1920s. See also **Unit Block.**

tezontle Rubble masonry of volcanic rock; found in Mexican Spanish Colonial construction.

T-fitting A T-shaped **pipe fitting** used to join three pipes. See also **T-branch.**

thack tile (pre-19c) Same as **plain tile.**

thatch A roof covering of straw, rushes, or similar plant materials; typically tied in bundles that are attached to horizontal rows of lath; used by early English colonists and in western expansion into the 19c. See also **false thatched roof.**

thatched roof (late 19c–mid-20c) A wood shingle roof with curved hips, valleys, verges, eaves, and sometimes rafters, that imitates the form of an English cottage roof covered with **thatch;** most common in the Tudor Revival style; in areas with tight curves the shingles are bent to follow the curve; the butts may be cut to form wavy courses. Also known as **false thatched roof.**

T-head A rod attached to a cross plate; used as an **anchor plate.** See also **T-plate.**

theater, theatre A **building** designed for live performances; elements may include **balcony, box, box lobby, box office, fly loft, foyer, green room, loge, mezzanine, orchestra, orchestra pit, parquet, parterre, proscenium arch, proscenium box, proscenium wall, stage, trap cellar, vestibule, wing.** Also known as **playhouse.** See also **hemp house, movie theater.**

thematic group format A format previously used for documenting and listing a group of historic properties related by a common **theme** for a National Register nomination; replaced by **multiple property submission.**

thematic nomination A National Register nomination with a **thematic group format.**

theme **1.** A trend or pattern in history or prehistory relating to a particular aspect of cultural development, such as dairy farming or silver mining. **2.** A category of historic activity; a site may be significant for and interpreted by several themes.

thermal window **1.** Same as **Palladian window;** from openings of this form found in the Roman thermae of Diocletian studied by Palladio in the 16c. Also known as **Diocletian window. 2.** (20c) A window with insulating glass.

therme (pre-19c) Same as **terminal figure.**

thermohygrograph A device for monitoring temperature and humidity.

Thermopane A 20c trade name for a hermetically sealed **insulating glass** manufactured by Libby-Owens Ford.

thermostat An automatic temperature regulating device that operates due to the expansion of a material or the differential expansion of two metals; may be connected to an electric circuit that operates a switch or solenoid, or mechanically control a fire alarm, steam valve, or similar apparatus.

therm window Same as **thermal window** (sense 1).

thicknessed (pre-WWI) Cut to a uniform thickness, such as a plank or board.

thick stuff (pre-WWI) Planks that are more than 4, but less than 12, inches thick.

thimble **1.** A metal or terra-cotta pipe set horizontally into a chimney to receive a stovepipe. Also known as **collar. 2.** A metal ferrule or cap that covers the end of a post, or similar member. See also **spud.**

T-hinge A **hinge** with one rectangular leaf that is mortised into the frame and a V-shaped leaf that is surface-mounted on the door, especially on a horizontal rail; common on heavy, wide, secondary doors and, when in a decorative form, on main entry doors. Also known as **butt and strap hinge.** See also **cross-garnet.**

thinner A volatile liquid used to thin paint binders or varnishes; evaporates during drying; types include alcohol, **mineral spirits, turpentine.** Also known as **solvent, spirit.**

thin shell concrete See **shell construction.**

third-class construction (19c–mid-20c) A building code classification for wood frame construction without fire-resistant protection; exterior may be wood, stucco, or brick veneer. See also **first-class construction, second-class construction.**

third point The vertex of an equilateral triangle. See also **arch of the third point.**

thirtypenny nail (30d nail) A **nail** approximately 4.5 inches long; 16 iron common nails weigh a pound. See also **penny.**

thole **1.** Same as **tholos.** **2.** A niche, or similar vaulted recess, for a votive offering. **3.** A knot or scutcheon at the apex of a timber vault.

tholobate The structural support immediately under a dome or cupola. See also **tholos.**

tholos, tholus **1.** A domed building with a circular plan, especially of the classical Greek style, such as the Jefferson Memorial. **2.** A dome or cupola, or a building having a dome as a predominant feature, such as the U.S. Capitol. See also **tholobate.** **3.** Same as **lantern** (sense 1).

tholus Same as **tholos.**

thorough bore (pre-20c) A hole drilled entirely through the material. See also **thorough-girt.**

thoroughfare An inexact term for a much traveled, unobstructed roadway.

thorough framing (pre-20c) All of the **carcase** framing of a **wood frame** building including window and door openings.

thorough-girt (pre-20c) Pierced entirely through the material. See also **thorough bore, through carved work.**

thorough light, through light (pre-19c) Having daylight from windows aligned on opposite sides of a room.

thrashing floor Same as **threshing floor.**

threaded joint A **pipe joint** where the **pipe fitting** and pipes have matching threads, as opposed to being soldered.

thready (18c) Veined, especially marble.

three-centered arch An **arch** with three centers for the radii of the intrados; types include **basket-handle arch, three-point arch, trefoil arch.**

three-coat work The standard **plaster** finish applied in three layers: **scratch coat, brown coat, finish coat.**

three-decker A single family house having three levels; from the term for a warship with three gun decks. See also **triple decker.**

three-hinged arch A structural support composed of two members curved in the form of an arch and attached at their apex and abutments with a hinge.

three-light fixture A chandelier, or sconce, with three electric lamps or gas jets.

threepenny nail (3d nail) A **nail** approximately 1.25 inches long; 400 iron common nails weigh a pound. See also **penny.**

threepenny spike (3d spike) A **spike** approximately 3.5 inches long; 30 steel-wire spikes weigh a pound. See also **penny.**

three-ply Having three layers, such as the layers of felt in a **built-up roof.**

three-point arch The shape of an elliptical arch approximated with three segments of a circle, a three-centered arch. See also **haunches, scheme, five-point arch.**

three-point gutter (18c) A tile roof valley lined with tiles so that a corner of the end tiles of the courses on each side of the valley meet a corner of the tile in the valley. See also **vertical gutter, swept valley.**

three-quarter brick A **stretcher** brick that has been cut to three-quarters of its normal length.

three-quarter Cape See **three-quarter house.**

three-quarter house A **Cape Cod house** or **saltbox** house with two windows on one side of the front door, and one window on the other side; also known as **three-quarter Cape.**

three-quarter molding A projecting **bead** molding at an outside corner, with a **three-quarter round** cross section.

three-quarter round A molding, or other element, having a cross section in the form of a three-quarter circle. See also **bead, three-quarter molding.**

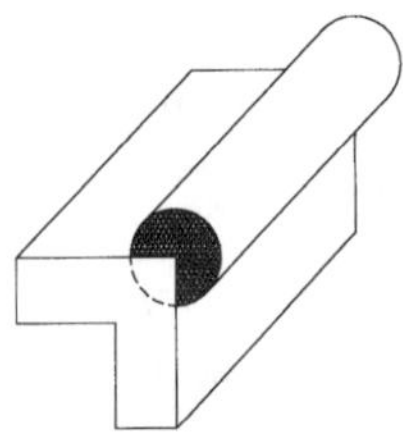

three-quarter round

three-quarter S-trap A siphoning plumbing **trap** composed of a pipe bent in a sideways S-shape with the outgoing side sloping downward at a 45-degree angle.

three-quarter S-trap

three-quarter turn stair A **stair** with four flights at right angles, and an open square or rectangular plan; may have winders, or a quarterpace landing, at the turns.

three-wire system An electric **service cable** with three wires.

threshing floor, thrashing floor A floor in a barn where grain is beaten to separate the grain from the chaff; typically a plank floor in the center bay of a timber frame structure.

threshold The **saddle** of an exterior door, or a similar element that separates the floor finishes on either side of an exterior door. See also **sill.**

throat **1.** Same as **chimney throat. 2.** The groove or recess cut into an overhanging stone element, such as a **drip.** Also known as **throating. 3.** In a **fortification,** the space between the flanks of a bastion, or between the rear ends of a redan. See also **gorge. 4.** The inside opening of an **embrasure. 5.** (pre-19c) An inverted cavetto. Also known as **gorge, gula.**

throating (pre-20c) Same as **throat** (sense 2).

through Same as **through stone.**

through arch An arched opening that passes entirely through a thick masonry wall. See also **vault.**

through-binder Same as **perpend** (sense 1).

through bolt A **bolt** that passes through all the layers of material and fastens them together with a nut.

through bond A masonry bond formed by a series of units, such as a stones or bricks, that passes perpendicularly entirely through a wall. See also **through-stone.**

through bridge A bridge where the roadway, or railway, passes between the arches, trusses, or other supports; types include **through girder bridge, through truss bridge.** See also **deck bridge.**

through bridge
Chester Park Bridge
by Cincinnati Bridge Co.
Hamilton County, Ohio

through-carved work, through carved work Sculpture or relief ornament with the spaces between elements entirely cut away or pierced through the piece. See also **à jour.**

through check A lumber **check** that extends between two faces of a timber or board. See also **through shake.**

through cut A roadway **cut** through a hillside with upward-sloping embankments on both sides.

through dado A **dado** groove cut across a member, such as a board, to both edges.

through girder bridge A **through bridge** that carries the roadway, or railway, on the lower chords of the girders.

through light (pre-19c) Same as **thorough light.**

through mortise A mortise hole that goes entirely through the element. See also **blind mortise.**

through shake A lumber **shake** that extends between two faces of a sawn timber or board. See also **through check.**

through-stone, through stone A building stone that is exposed on both sides of a masonry wall. Also known as **perpend, through.**

through truss bridge A **through bridge** that carries the roadway, or railway, on the lower chords of the trusses.

thumb latch A **lift latch** operated on one side of the door by pressing a thumb on a lever that passes through the door to the latch bar side.

thumb molding A projecting, convex molding that approximates the curve of the underside of the human thumb; typically a quarter ellipse cross section that is tangent to the horizontal at the top, and curves downward to less than a quarter ellipse on the bottom; types include **elliptical torus.**

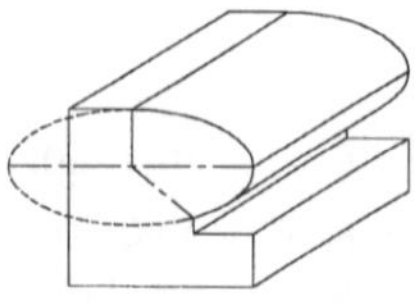

thumb molding

thumbscrew, (pre-20c) **thumb screw** A screw with a knurled or flattened head designed to be turned by hand without a wrench or screwdriver; typically a **machine screw.**

tideland spruce Same as **Sitka spruce.**

tide lock A **lift-lock** used in combination with a **guard lock** that controls tidal waters.

tide mill A **mill** powered by the flow of water due to tidal changes.

tidewater cypress Same as **bald cypress.**

tie **1.** A tension member of a truss, or other structure; often used for structural retrofit; types include **diagonal tie, land tie, tie chain, tie beam, tie rod.** See also **post, strut, X-brace.** **2.** A small-diameter **reinforcing bar** that wraps around and ties together the main bars. **3.** Same as **cross tie.**

tie back A **finish hardware** device located on a window casing to fasten curtains in their open position.

tie bar An iron bar shape used as a **tie rod.**

tie beam (19c–present) A beam which connects the bottom ends of two rafters together to prevent them from spreading apart, or a similar member at the bottom of a triangular truss. Also known as **cross beam, string.** See also **collar beam.**

tie bolt A long bolt used to connect timber frame members.

tie chain An iron tie across the spring line of an arch to resist the outward thrust; typically a rod with eyes at both ends that engage a hook set in the masonry.

tie iron Same as **tie rod.**

tie plate **1.** Same as **anchor plate.** **2.** An iron plate that attaches a railroad rail to a wooden crosstie.

tier **1.** A group of rows set one above another, especially seats in a theater or stadium, or tobacco hung in a warehouse. **2.** Same as **wythe.**

tierce point, tiers point (pre-20c) Same as **third point.**

tierce point arch Same as **equilateral arch.**

tierceron A secondary **vault** rib that springs from the intersection of two other ribs, or an intermediate rib springing from the base of a diagonal rib or arc doubleaux; used in Gothic style architecture.

tie rod, tierod **1.** Any rod in a structural frame, such as a truss, that is under tension; may replace a **tie beam,** or be a **tie bar, tie chain,** or **screw rod.** Also known as **tie iron.** **2.** A tension member that holds together parts of a building; most often a circular metal bar in combination with a **turnbuckle** and **anchor plate,** sometimes with an **upset screw end.** See also **tie bolt.**

tiers point Same as **third point.**

Tiffany brick A **Roman brick** with shades of yellow-brown spotted by dark iron pyrites; named after the brick used at the Louis Comfort Tiffany mansion in New York City.

Tiffany glazing An interior finish with blended glaze and accent colors on top of a different ground color; fashionable early 20c.

Tiffany shade **1.** A leaded glass electric light shade, with opalescent colored glass, manufactured by Tiffany Studios late 19c. **2.** Leaded glass shades inspired by those from the Tiffany Studios; commonly manufactured early or late 20c.

tige (pre-20c) The **shaft** of a column.

tight cesspool A watertight **cesspool** that is pumped out when full. See also **leaching cesspool.**

tignum Same as **building material;** used in civil law.

tile, (pre-18c) **tyle** **1.** Any one of a series of pieces of solid material used for **roofing;** most commonly a ceramic **roof tile,** may also be stone, **siding tile, weather tiling.** **2.** A small, geometric shape used for the finish surface of buildings, designed so that they butt or interlock to cover the entire surface; most commonly ceramic, may also be pieces of marble or other materials; types by use include **floor tile, siding tile, tile creasing, tile veneer, wall tile;** types by finish include **art tile, azulejo, Dutch tile, encaustic tile, mathematical tile, press-molded tile, quarry tile.** See also **glazing.** **3.** A building element composed of fired clay, including **book tile, drain tile, structural clay tile, vaulting tile.**

tile-and-a-half-tile A roof tile that is 1½ the width of a standard tile; used as a **verge tile.**

tile arch A floor system composed of **structural clay tiles** in the form of a **flat arch** or **segmental vault** spanning between parallel steel beams; provides both the structural support for the floor and the fireproofing of the beams; first used in the U.S. in 1873 as a replacement for heavier brick floor arches; the most common fire-resistant floor system during the second quarter of the 20c; the extension of the tiles under the beams for fireproofing was invented in 1883; typically 6–12 inches deep with lightweight concrete fill above; types include **end-construction arch, side-construction arch,** and **combination arch;** components include **end-construction tile, floor tile, lipped skew, shoe tile, side-construction tile, skewback block, soffit block.** Also known as **floor arch, terra-cotta arch.**

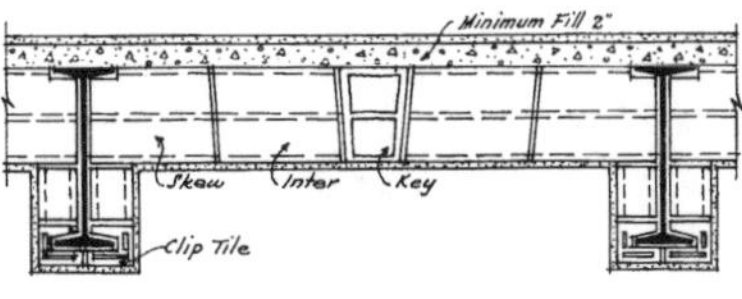

tile arch

tile batten A wood batten strip installed horizontally across the rafters to support **roof tile.**

tile creasing A double row of tiles used as a wall coping.

tilehanging, tile hanging Same as **weather tiling.**

tileing (pre-19c) Same as **tiling.**

tile pin A hardwood peg, or similar device, used to attach roof tiles; typically made of oak.

tilestone (pre-20c) A tile **paver.**

tile veneer Enameled or glazed ceramic tile attached to the exterior walls of a wood framed building; the tile is laid in a mortar bed and attached with metal ties; See also **architectural terra-cotta, siding tile.**

tiling, (pre-19c) **tileing** All of the **tiles** covering a surface plus any grout at the joints. See also **tilehanging.**

timber **Lumber** that is larger than 5 × 5 inches; types include **dimension lumber, second-growth timber, square sawn timber.**

timber bond A masonry wall **chain bond** formed by building a heavy **chain timber** into the wall.

timber brick Same as **wood brick.**

timber dog A metal strap with bent, pointed ends that is hammered into adjacent timber members to connect them; most often used on top of the butted ends of two beams, or for temporary fastening, such as for scaffolding. Also known as **dog.**

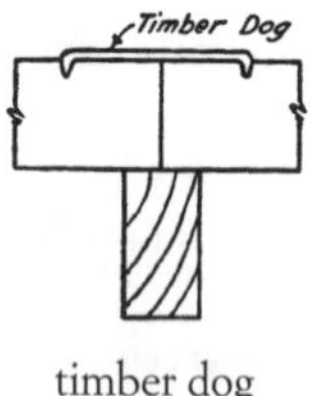

timber dog

timber frame A **wood frame** system with heavy corner posts, intermediate **posts, girts,** and **summers** supporting floor joists and rafters; the joists may be mortised to the girts or rest on top; the most common type of North American house framing ca. 1600–ca. 1800; typically used for barns and mills through the 19c, later in rural areas; other components may include **breast stud, dragon beam, ground sill, main beams, main plate, main sill, overlay, purlin beam, purlin plate, summer beam.** Also known as **English frame, post-and-girt, pegged braced frame.** See also **braced frame, clapboard house, dimension timber, half-timbered, guttered.**

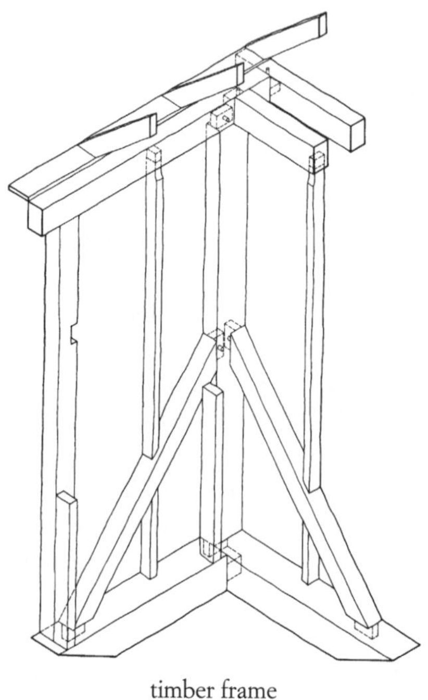
timber frame

timber post foundation A **foundation** composed of a series of posts placed in holes dug in the earth; typically the base of the posts is supported on a large rock, or is encased in concrete.

timberyard Same as **lumberyard.**

timed exit analysis A computer-generated analysis of the time required for the occupants of an existing building to leave in the event of a fire; used as part of an **equivalency** analysis.

tin **1.** A white, malleable, corrosion-resistant, elemental metal; used in alloys, such as **bronze,** and as a plating on other metals; types include **block tin, grain tin. 2.** Same as **tinplate.**

tin ceiling Embossed **tinplate** panels nailed to furring strips and painted as a finished ceiling, common 1850–1920 in homes and commercial buildings.

tinea Same as **annulet.**

tinned Coated with **tin,** such as **tinplate.**

tinplate, tin-plate Iron or steel sheets coated with tin, generally by dipping in a bath of molten tin; used as sheet-metal roofing and flashing beginning late 18c, and as tin shingles 19c; sometimes mistaken for **terneplate.** Also known as **bright tin, tin.**

tin roof **1. Tinplate** sheet roofing, bent or soldered together. **2.** The common name for any **sheet-metal** roof; types include **batten roof, standing seam roof.**

tin shingle A tin-coated steel **metallic shingle.**

tin tack, tinned tack **1.** A tin-coated iron or steel tack. **2.** A tinplate **glazier's point.**

tinted glass (20c) A colored **glass** produced by adding minerals to the ingredients; used to reduce light and heat transmission to the interior, especially on **curtain wall** buildings.

tip The fitting at the end of a gas lighting fixture that directs the flow of the gas.

T-iron **1.** An iron **T-head. 2.** An iron **T-bar.**

titanated lithopone A mixture of **lithopone** and **titanium dioxide;** used as a **pigment** for interior oil-base paint in the first half of the 20c.

titanium dioxide A naturally occurring mineral, TiO_2; used as a white paint **pigment** in manufactured paints ca. 1918–present as a substitute for **white lead;** also mixed with white lead until late-20c; the pigment manufacturing method was patented in 1911; two types available, **anatase** and **rutile.** Also known as **titanium oxide, titanium white.** See also **titanated lithopone.**

titanium oxide (early 20c) Same as **titanium dioxide.**

titanium white Same as **titanium dioxide.**

title search The examination of ownership documents for a particular property at a government agency such as a recorder of deeds or land title office; includes examination of **chain of title, deeds, easements,** and **liens.**

T-joint A **butt joint** with the end of one member attached to the side of another member.

tobacco barn (18c–present) A barn used for the curing and storing of tobacco leaves; forms vary by region. See also **tobacco house.**

tobacco house (mid-17c–19c southern U.S.) A building used for the curing and storing of tobacco leaves; typically wood with a series of tier poles across the width from which sticks carrying the tobacco are hung, and multiple doors for ventilation. See also **prize house, tobacco barn.**

tobacco house

toe Same as **foot** (sense 1).

toe joint The joint between the bottom of a vertical, or sloped, wood member and a horizontal member, such as at the base of a wall stud.

toe nailing Nailing the end of a stud, joist, or similar element at an oblique angle, so that the nail enters the side of the lumber and exits at the end of the piece. See also **skew nailing.**

toe piece A **ledger** that supports the bottom of a series of joist ends.

toilet (late 19c–present) Same as **water closet.**

toilet room (late 19c–present) A washroom with water closets and sinks, especially when designed to be used by more than one person at a time; often combined with a coatroom in the 19c. Also known as **washroom.** See also **bathroom, half bath.**

tolerance The variation in dimension allowed for a building surface or member, such as a concrete floor that has a tolerance of .25 inch in 10 feet.

tollhouse (pre-WWI) A gatekeeper's house located adjacent to the tollgate of a turnpike or bridge.

tomb **1.** A sealed cavity for permanent placement of the dead; may be carved from living rock or constructed of masonry. **2.** A **monument** that encloses the body of the dead, such as in a church or cemetery; types include **altar tomb, mausoleum, table tomb.** See also **cenotaph, monument, tombstone.**

tombac, (pre-20c) **tambac, tambaycke, tombaga, tombak** Several varieties of **brass** that imitate precious metals; types include **Dutch metal, Mannheim gold, white tombac;** may be in the form of foil; from the Malaysian word **tombaga.**

tombaga (pre-20c) Same as **tombac.**

tombak (pre-20c) Same as **tombac.**

tomb house **1.** A chapel or reception building for funeral services. **2.** Same as **mausoleum.**

tombstone A memorial stone marking a grave, especially when placed horizontally; typically inscribed with the name, birth and death dates, and sometimes a message and/or bas-relief sculpture; types include **table.** See also **gravestone.**

ton **1.** A unit of weight measurement; equals 2,000 pounds in U.S. and Canada, and 1,000 kilograms (2,204.6 pounds) in the metric system. See also **ton timber.** **2.** A unit of cooling measurement equal to 12,000 Btuh, or the approximate amount of heat necessary to melt 1 ton of ice in 1 hour.

tondino [Italian] A convex ring molding, such as a **torus** or **astragal.**

tondo A circular, sculptured medallion or painting.

tongue **1.** A projecting portion of a member, such as a **tenon,** or the continuous ridge on a **tongue-and-groove** board. See also **cross tongue, loose tongue.** **2.** A bas-relief ornament in the form of a stylized pointed tongue. See also **egg and tongue.**

tongue-and-groove A wood **joint** where the projecting tongue on the edge of one board fits into the recessed groove on the edge of the adjoining board. Also known as **plowed and tongued.**

tongue-and-groove riser and tread A **stair** constructed with tongues on the top of the risers and the back of the treads that interlock respectively with grooves on the bottom of the treads and the front of the risers.

ton timber (pre-19c) A unit of measure of the amount of timber that approximately equals 2,000 pounds—40 linear feet of round timber or 50 linear feet of hewn timber.

tooled **1.** A dressed stone surface finish with shallow chisel marks visible; forms include **boasted, bush hammered, carborundum finish, crandalled, duck-bill tooling, hand-tooled, machine-tooled, patent bush hammered, peen hammered, pointed finish, square droved, tooth-chiseled.** Also known as **tooled face.** See also **bat, stonework, tooled face.** **2.** An **architectural terra-cotta** finish imitating **tooth-chiseled** stone, with six or eight parallel lines to the inch.

tooled face Same as **tooth-chiseled.** See also **tooled.**

tooled joint Any **mortar joint** finished with a tool that compresses and shapes the mortar, other than a trowel; types include **beaded joint, concave joint, flush plus rodded joint, grapevine joint, raked joint, ruler joint.** See also **pointing, struck joint.**

toolshed A small shed used to store tools; typically in a garden.

tooth A slightly roughened finish surface; used to increase adherence of paint. See also **silica.**

tooth-chiseled The hand-cut surface texture of soft stone blocks with continuous parallel bats made by a tooth-chisel with 2–10 bats per inch; bats may be horizontal, vertical, or **cross tooth-chiseled;** used on soft stone, and imitated on molded **concrete block** and **architectural terra-cotta.** Also known as **tooled face, tooled.** See also **bat, stonework, machine-tooled, tooled.**

toothed Masonry that has been bonded together by temporarily leaving a series of projecting toothers on the end of the wall, and later filling in the gaps with the continuation of the wall.

toother A masonry unit, or several units, that project from one wall into another; used to connect masonry walls constructed at different times. See also **toothed.**

tooth ornament One of a series of pointed, carved ornaments, usually set in a concave molding band; typically a pyramid shape, often carved into a four-petaled flower; used in both the Romanesque Revival style and the Gothic Revival style; types include **dog tooth, nailhead molding, star molding.**

top beam Same as a **collar beam.**

top chord A **chord** along the upper perimeter of a **truss;** one of a pair with the **bottom chord.**

top coat Same as **finish coat.**

top cripple A short section of **cripple** stud framing above a header beam. See also **bottom cripple.**

topia, topiarium opus See **topiary art.**

topiarium opus Same as **topia.**

topiary art, topiary, topiary work (19c–present) The twisting and clipping of trees and shrubs into fantastic sculptured shapes in a formal garden; from the Latin word *topia* for a perspective mural fresco of a fanciful garden, such as those uncovered at Pompeii; boxwood and yew are the most commonly used plants; common in North America beginning 18c.

topographic map A map that indicates the shape of the surface of the ground, and other salient physical features such as buildings and roads; typically, 20c maps have a series of contour lines that indicate the elevation above sea level, building outlines, road edges, and identifying labels.

topography **1.** The physical features of a particular location, including the shape of the surface of the ground. **2.** The profession of drawing topographic maps.

topping out courses The uppermost courses of a masonry wall or chimney.

top plate A continuous, horizontal piece of lumber across the top of an exterior wall that supports the foot of the rafters, or other framework above it; laid flat on top of a masonry wall or wall studs. Also known as **plate, raising plate, wall plate.** See also **false plate.**

torch **1.** A sculptured representation of a torch formed by reeds bound together with ribbons; an erect torch symbolizes joy, from the Roman custom of marriage processions by torch light; an inverted torch symbolizes death; from the French word *torche.* **2.** To point slates with a mixture of lime and hair.

torch holder A wall bracket for holding a burning torch; types include **bracciale.**

torchère A tall metal torch used for artificial illumination; may be freestanding, or attached to a wall by brackets; typically with a gas or electric lamp.

tore (pre-20c) Same as **torus.**

tores A torus shape, especially at the base of a column.

torii The symbolic gateway to a Japanese Shinto shrine; composed of two columns with smooth shafts supporting a double cross beam with an upward curve, with a tie beam a short distance below the cross beam; both sets of beams project past the columns; used occasionally in North America.

torsade **1.** A twisted cord, such as used for curtains. **2.** An architectural **ornament,** or small **molding,** in the form of a twisted cord. See also **cable molding.**

torsal (pre-20c) Same as **torsel.**

torsel, torsal (pre-20c) **1.** A bearing block that supports a beam end in a masonry wall; may be stone, wood, or iron. Also known as **tassel, tossal.** See also **bearing plate. 2.** A twisted **ornament,** such as a scroll. See also **torso.**

torso **1.** (pre-20c) A column with a twisted shaft. See also **torsel. 2.** A statue in the form of the middle portion of the human body.

torus, (pre-20c) **tore** A large, projecting, semicircular molding, especially when used to ring the base of a column. See also **attic base, bead, thumb molding.**

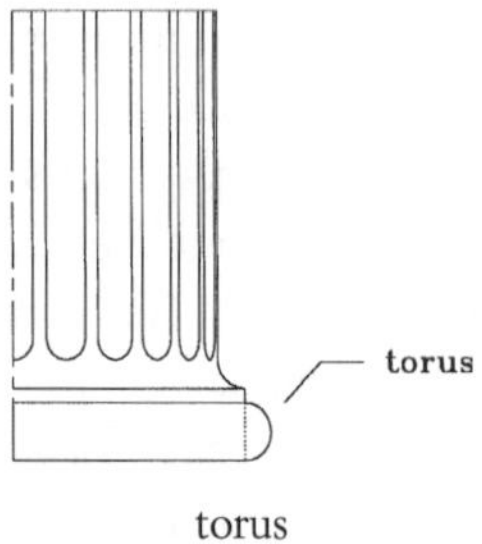

torus

tossal Same as **torsel.**

tossut The tunnel entrance to an Eskimo dwelling; typically approximately 10 feet long; used for protection from the elements in winter.

totem pole, totem post A carved wood column or post with a vertical series of stylized human and animal forms; created by the Haida native peoples located in the Pacific coast region of Canada and the U.S.; the house columns are known as **kexen** and the memorial posts are known as **xat.**

to the weather The portion of overlapping siding or shingles left exposed to the elements.

toughened glass (19c) Same as **tempered glass.**

tourelle A small projecting **turret** with a conical roof, especially one located at an outside corner of a building.

tow Hemp or flax fiber; used for caulking cast-iron pipe.

towel pattern Same as **linenfold.**

towel rail A device composed of heated pipes in the shape of a ladder; used for heating towels in a bathroom.

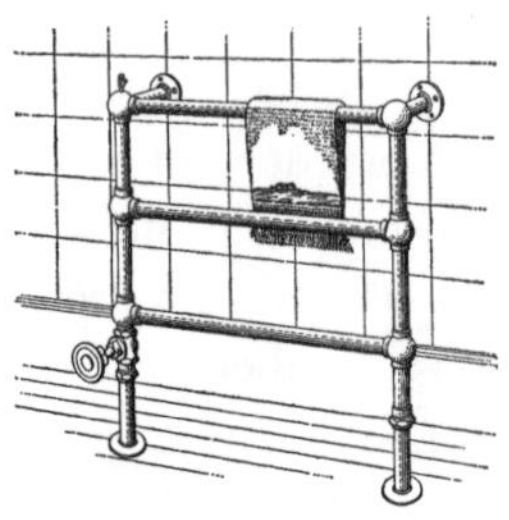
towel rail

tower A tall structure with a relatively small floor plan; may be an isolated structure, or part of a larger building; most commonly square or circular, with vertical sides; types include **bell tower, central tower, clock tower, gabled tower, mural tower, shot tower, water tower.** See also **steeple, toweret.**

tower clock A large clock used in a **clock tower;** typically with four dials.

toweret (pre-20c) A little **tower** or **turret.**

town **1.** A concentration of dwellings and related buildings surrounded by countryside; typically smaller than a **city** and larger than a **village.** **2.** Same as **township.**

town hall The building housing the administrative offices of a town; may also include related functions, such as a **jail.** See also **hall, market house.**

townhouse **1.** A city residence, as opposed to a country house. **2.** Same as **row house;** typically used to describe a relatively grand house, with more than two stories. **3.** (pre-20c) A town hall, or by extension: **4.** A public almshouse or workhouse, or a prison.

town planning See **planning.**

townscape **1.** The appearance and relationship of the exterior features of a town that determine its particular character. See also **cultural landscape, streetscape.** **2.** A concept developed in the 1940s that analyzes the urban exterior environment as a sequence of visual and spacial experiences for the moving spectator; influenced by the theories of 18c landscape architects.

township **1.** A political and geographic area within the boundaries of a municipal government, sometimes within and separate from a larger county; most common in northeastern U.S.; larger than a village and smaller than a city. Also known as **town.** **2.** A 6-mile-square subdivision of public lands in the western U.S.; designated by the **Homestead Act** in 1796, and laid out using a square grid with a north–south axis; the township is further subdivided into 36 **sections.**

towpath The walkway along the side of a **canal;** used by the mules that pull the barges.

T-plate A T-shaped connecting plate; used for wood construction, such as to attach a column and the beams it supports. See also **T-head.**

trabeated **1.** Having an **entablature.** **2.** Constructed with lintels or beams, as opposed to **arcuated.** See also **post and beam construction.**

tracery (17c–present) **1.** Decoration in the form of interlaced fillets or moldings, without foliage or other features of nature; may be pierced work or relief, such as **wall tracery.** See also **arabesque.** **2.** Interlaced Gothic style window mullions; types include **bar tracery, clustered tracery, fan tracery, flowing tracery, geometrical tracery, net tracery, panel tracery, pierced tracery, plate tracery, Y-tracery;** shapes may include **dagger, mouchette, quatrefoil, trefoil, triquetra;** the first recorded use of the term is by the architect Sir Christopher Wren (17c).

tracery (sense 2)

tracery vaulting A type of **solid vaulting** with decorative ribs forming patterns on the surface. See also **fan tracery, lierne vaulting, rib vaulting.**

trachelium The neck of a Doric or Ionic column immediately below the capital, and above the **hypotrachelium.**

tract A large, unbounded area of land; sometimes used with a place or name modifier to identify a particular parcel, such as **the Glover tract.**

trade One of the types of skilled construction work, including work traditionally associated with the main task; major categories include **sitework, concrete, masonry, ironwork, car-**

pentry, millwork, roofing, plaster, drywall, painting, specialties, elevator, plumbing, mechanical, sprinkler, and **electrical.** See also **CSI format.**

trading post The site of commercial exchanges between European traders and native peoples in sparsely settled areas; may have permanent buildings.

training stable Same as **breeder's stable.**

train shed A roofed enclosure for one or more train tracks with passenger platform that is open on one end for access by the trains.

train station Same as **railroad station.**

trammel A hook with rings that is attached to a fireplace **crane** or **randle bar** to hang a cooking pot.

transept The space that crosses at a right angle to the **nave** of a building, especially a church; may be larger in section than the nave, or of the same size, as in a **cruciform** building; typically referred to as **wings** in North America before 19c. See also **crossing.**

transfer house (pre-19c) A public tobacco warehouse where planters exchanged tobacco for bills of credit.

transfer of development rights (TDR) The process of allowing an owner of property whose development is restricted, such as through zoning or historic designation, to use the lost **development potential** at another site by increasing height, density, lot coverage, or similar features; first enacted in New York, New York in 1968. Also known as **Chicago plan, transfer of development potential.** See also **planned unit development.**

Transite A 20c trade name for **asbestos board** manufactured by Hohns Manville by pressure molding a mixture of Portland cement, water and asbestos; typically approximately ⅛ inch thick; used for fire- and rot-resistant wall, ceiling, and railing panels, and pipe.

transitional area A neighborhood or other geographic area that is changing from one type of use or resident to another. See also **gentrification.**

transitional style An architectural style characterized by elements of an older style blended with elements of a more modern style in the same building, such as the evolution of Romanesque into Gothic.

transom, (pre-19c) **transome** **1.** A fixed horizontal member that divides upper and lower portions of a window; may be made of stone, metal, or wood. **2.** (18c–present) A fixed horizontal member between the top of a door and a window above. **3.** (19c–present) A **transom window** (sense 1), especially one above an interior door.

transom adjuster A mechanical device that opens a **transom window** from below. Also known as **transom lift.**

transom bar A **transom** (senses 1 and 2) with a relatively slim cross section, especially one used between the top of a door and a fanlight or tympanum.

transom door (18c) A door with a glazed opening above.

transom lift Same as **transom adjuster.**

transom light Same as **transom window** (sense 1).

transom window **1.** A glazed opening above a door or window. See also **fanlight.** **2.** A window opening that is subdivided by a **transom** (sense 1). **3.** Same as **transom door.**

tranverse arch Same as **transverse rib.**

transverse rib An arched **rib** across the narrow dimension of a vaulted building, between and part of adjoining vaults, or supporting the roof structure; may be plain or molded. Also known as **transverse arch.**

trap **1.** A portion of a plumbing drain formed so that it holds water to prevent sewer gas from passing through; types include **bag trap, bell trap, D-trap, drum trap, grease trap, running trap, nonsyphoning trap, P-trap, S-trap.** Also known as **air trap, gas trap, stenchtrap, waste trap.** See also **trap screw. 2.** Same as **trap door. 3.** Same as **trap rock.**

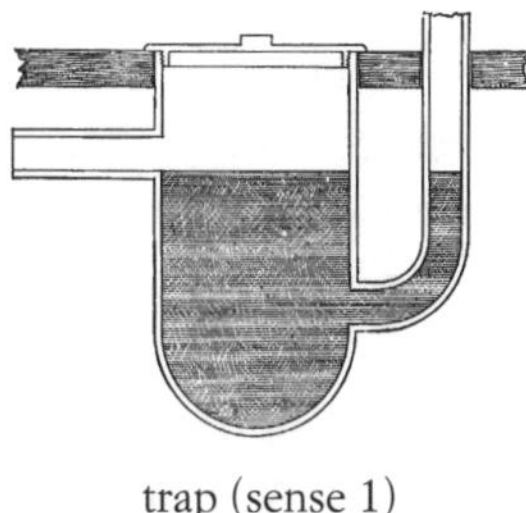

trap (sense 1)

trap cellar The space below a trap door in a theater stage.

trap door A **door** in a horizontal surface; may open up or down. See also **trap cellar, trap stair.**

trap rock Any dense, hard, dark, igneous rock, including **diorite,** basalt, and feldspar; named for its propensity to trap crystalline minerals in voids within the rock.

trap screw A round access plate with screw threads; used for a plumbing trap or pipe cleanout.

trap stair A narrow **stair** descending from a trap door.

traveler The moving part of a traveling crane, such the winch hung on rollers from an iron beam above a hay mow.

traverse 1. A screen that allows passage across a space without being seen; may be a curtain in a large room, a wood or metal lattice, or an elevated gallery or loft. **2.** Same as a **transom** (sense 1), or the horizontal member of a **chambranle. 3.** (pre-19c) Same as a panel **rail. 4.** (pre-19c) A groove planed across the grain of a board. See also **dado, trench.**

travertine A soft, creamy **marble** characterized by irregular surface pitting; the pits are elongated in one direction, and often interconnected; typically used in interior panels; varieties include **Furst-Kerber travertine.** Also known as **Roman travertine.**

tray ceiling A ceiling with a flat center and sloped sides; from its resemblance to an inverted tray. Also known as **camp ceiling.**

trazzo (pre-20c) Same as **terrazzo.**

treacle mold A molding with a cross section that curves downward from the horizontal approximately a quarter circle, then has a tight curve upward to a U-shaped drip groove; used as a drip or nosing.

tread 1. The top horizontal portion of an individual step of a stair; indicates both the top surface, and the slab or plank; the depth is measured from the front edge to the riser; types include **flier, winder.** See also **riser, run. 2.** A wearing surface, such as carpet or rubber, placed on top of a stair step. **3.** The horizontal surface behind a fortification banquet that one stands upon while firing weapons.

tread board A wood plank that forms a **tread;** may have a milled nosing and a rabbeted groove that receives the top of the riser below.

treated wood See **pressure treated.**

treble sash (pre-20c) Same as **triple hung window.**

trecento Design of 14c Italy; from the Italian for years that begin with the number 13.

treenail, trenail, trennel, trunnel 1. A hardwood pin used in mortise and tenon joints, especially **timber frame,** and to attach floorboards and planks. See also **dowel, tile pin. 2.** Same as **gutta** in classical style architecture, from the conjectured belief that the stone carving is a stylized representation of wood pins used to construct the original Greek temples.

tree post (pre-WWI) Same as **kingpost.**

trefoil A closed tracery shape with three foils divided by cusps or reverse curves, similar to a cloverleaf; may be pierced, or surround a panel with a decorated center.

trefoil arch A **three-centered arch** with an intrados in the form of a trefoil with a projecting cusp on each side; may be roundheaded or a **pointed trefoil arch.** Also known as **three-lobed arch, trilobated arch, trilobed arch.**

trefoil arch

treillage A frame used to fasten a tree or vine in making an espalier; often a large lattice grid attached to a wall. See also **trellis.**

trellis **1.** A lath lattice used as a screen. **2.** A framework or lattice that supports a climbing vine. See also **treillage.** **3.** (pre-20c) A summerhouse constructed mainly of lattice.

trellis molding An ornamental band composed of interlaced zigzag fillets that form a grid with diamond-shaped openings, similar in appearance to a lath **trellis;** typically bordered with other moldings a the top and bottom.

trellis post A column composed of lattice work connecting corner uprights; may be iron, such as part of a truss, or wood, as on a veranda.

trellis window Same as **lattice window.**

trenail Same as **treenail.**

trench **1.** A vertical-sided ditch cut into the earth, may be temporary, such as for laying pipes during construction, or relatively permanent, such as part of a **fortification.** **2.** A large groove cut across a wood member, such as in a **timber frame** stud that supports a bearer. See also **dado, traverse.**

trenching The process of cutting a narrow groove across areas of suspected ornament to determine the presence of decoration; the side of the cut is examined with a portable microscope.

trennel Same as **treenail.**

tresaunce (pre-20c) A passage in a building, or in a wall.

trestle **1.** A frame with a pair of uprights, sloped in toward the center, supporting a cross beam; may include additional uprights and cross bracing; most commonly timber, may also be iron or steel. **2.** Same as **trestle work.** **3.** A short intermediate stud or post in a wood frame. **4.** A carpenter's sawhorse.

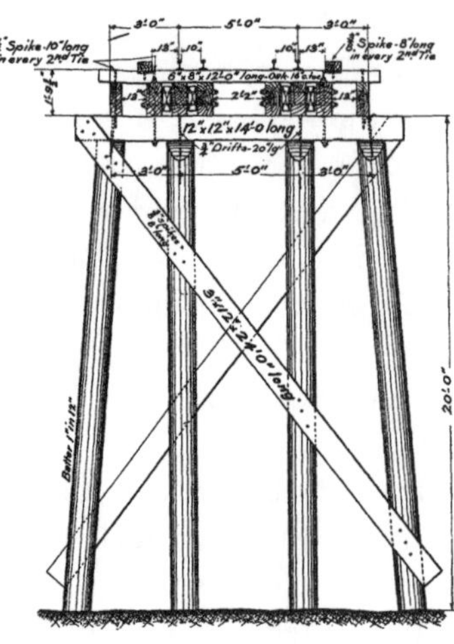

trestle (sense 1)

trestle bridge A bridge made up of a series of trestle frames, sometimes stacked in layers; common for pre-WWII railroad bridges.

trestle work A construction largely composed of trestles and their bracing, especially a **trestle bridge.**

triangle mesh A **mesh** of cold-drawn steel wire woven in a pattern of interlocking equilateral triangles; used as continuous **reinforcing** in concrete construction between WWI and WWII.

triangular arch **1.** A corbeled arch, or vault, such as used by the Mayans. **2.** An **arch** formed of two inclined stones.

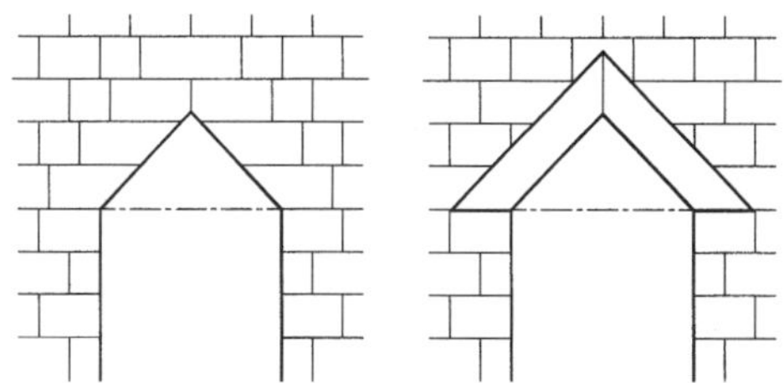

triangular arches (senses 1 and 2)

triangular flyers (pre-19c) A **staircase** with straight flights connected by 120-degree-turn landings around a well in the shape of an equilateral triangle.

triangular washer A metal washer with a triangular cross section; used as an **anchor plate** at the end of a tie rod that passes through a wall at an angle. Also known as **bevel washer.**

triangulation The design of a structure, such as a truss, that is entirely composed of straight members connected in triangles to provide rigidity. See also **reticulation.**

triapsidal A type of **church** with three apses; may be across the eastern end, terminating the two side aisles and the choir, or on three sides of the crossing.

triforium The space above the vaulting, and below the roof, of a side aisle of a church, with arched openings into the nave space; directly under the clerestory windows; typically with three arches in each bay forming an arcade, may also have one or two arches. See also **upper croft.**

triglyph A decorative element on the frieze of a **Doric** entablature, composed of three vertical shanks with chamfered edges that form two V-shaped **glyphs** and two **hemiglyphs;** alternates with the metopes; typically centered on the axis of the column below; thought to be a stylized representation of the ends of the ceiling beams used in the original Greek temples. See also **diglyph, hemitriglyph.**

trigonum **1.** A triangular **tessera.** **2.** A mosaic composed of triangular pieces.

trilobated arch Same as **trefoil arch.**

trilobed arch Same as **trefoil arch.**

trim, (pre-20c) **trimm, trimme** (19c–present) **Molding** surrounding windows and doors, copings, sills, and similar elements that contrast with the main wall surface; most often wood, may be of any material. Also known as **trimming, trimmings.** See also **casing.**

trimmed opening Same as **cased opening.**

trimmer **1.** One of a pair of joists or rafters that supports the ends of a header and forms the sides of a framed opening; typically a doubled joist or rafter, or wider than a common joist or rafter; types include **hearth trimmer, stair trimmer.** Also known as a **trimmer beam, trimmer joist, trimming beam.** See also **trimming joist.** **2.** Same as **trimmer arch.** **3.** (pre-20c) Same as **header** (sense 4).

trimmer arch A low-rise **half arch** supporting a fireplace hearth and spanning between a chimney breast and a **trimming joist** below the hearth; the low end is at the chimney breast. (*See illustration p. 494*)

trimmer beam **1.** Same as **trimmer** (sense 1). **2.** (19c) Same as **trimmer arch.**

trimmer joist Same as **trimmer** (sense 1).

trimming, trimmings (pre-20c) Same as **trim.**

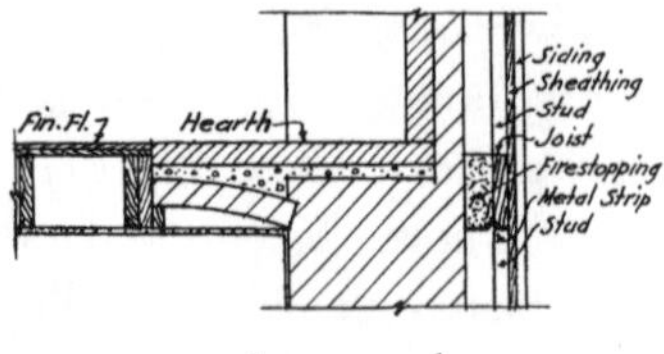

trimmer arch

trimming beam Same as **trimmer** (sense 1).

trimming joist (pre-20c) Same as a **header** that supports the trimmed joist ends at a chimney or stair well. See also **trimmer, trimmer arch.**

trimstone Decorative **stonework** used with masonry of a different material, such as brick; may include cornices, lintels, quoins, sills and surrounds.

tringle A narrow, straight **molding,** especially for the short section of the cap of the triglyph projecting above each triglyph on a Doric frieze; typically of rectangular cross section; from the term for a curtain rod on a canopy bed.

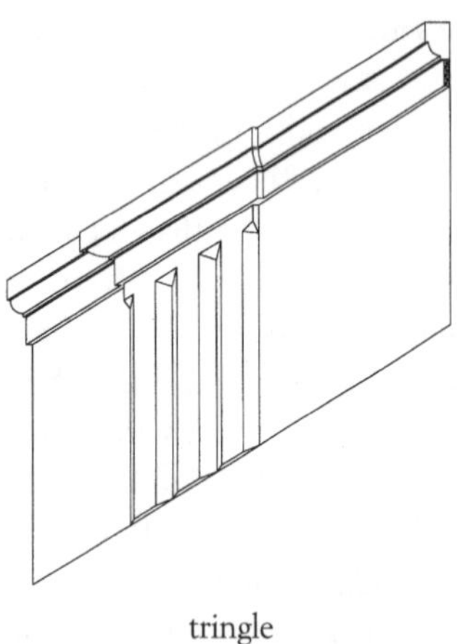
tringle

tripartite agreement An agreement among the American Institute of Architects, Library of Congress and National Park Service establishing the **Historic American Buildings Survey** and its administration.

tripartite vault A vault formed by three intersecting vault surfaces over a space with a triangular plan; typically used alternately with quadripartite vaults over the aisles of a polygonal apse, or similar space.

triple course A row of three layers of shingles at the bottom edge of an eave.

triple decker A three-unit house where each of three stories is an apartment, especially popular in the northeastern U.S. See also **double decker, three-decker, triplex.**

triple glazing **Insulating glass** having three layers of glass with air spaces between; often hermetically sealed.

triple hung window A window with three vertically sliding sashes that allow the window to open to two-thirds of its height; often used for access to porches or balconies. Also known as **treble sash.**

triple-riveted Fastened together with three rows of rivets.

triplet Any architectural feature composed of three elements.

triple window A window with two side casements and a single fixed sash in the middle.

triplex **1.** An apartment with three levels. **2.** A dwelling with three apartments. See also **triple decker.**

triquetra A triangle-shaped figure or ornament, especially three interlaced semicircles, or semiellipses, formed by tracery.

Triton A decorative feature in the form of the upper body of a man with a dolphin's tail holding a conch shell; may also have the forelegs of a horse; from the mythical son of Poseidon and Amphritrite.

triumphal arch A massive monument with a central archway as its main feature and decorated abutments; typically erected over a roadway to commemorate a significant historical event, especially victory in war; named for the

Roman victory pageant known as a **triumph.** Also known as **memorial arch.**

trochile (18c) Same as **trochilus.**

trochilus, (19c) **trochylis,** (18c) **trochile** Same as **scotia,** especially on an **attic base;** from the Greek *trochylos,* a pulley.

trochylus Same as **trochilus.**

trolley hanger A hardware device with wheels that runs on a grooved track and supports the top of a sliding or folding door.

trompe A curved partial vault that supports a projecting corner of a building, or similar member, as distinct from a **corbel** or **squinch.**

trompe l'oeil Two-dimensional decorative painting that appears to be a three-dimensional element of a building, such as a molding, coffer, or view into another space. See also **perspective.**

trophy An architectural **ornament** in the form a group of weapons, both offensive and defensive; often surrounding a tree trunk, or intermingled with foliage.

trough plate A steel **rolled section** with a flat center with sides that angle outward; multiple pieces are riveted together to form corrugated decking, typically with a 6-inch depth; used to support bridge and building floors late 19c–early 20c. Also known as **trough section.**

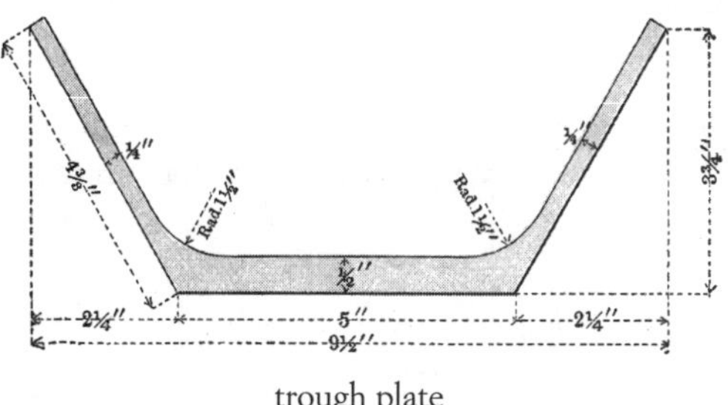

trough plate

trough roof Same as **M-roof.**

trough section Same as **trough plate.**

troweled stucco A smoothly finished exterior **stucco,** made by floating the surface with a metal trowel.

truck house A **firehouse** for a hook and ladder truck.

true A construction term indicating that the element is level or straight.

true pitch A steep roof **pitch** variously defined as: **1.** Same as **half pitch** (45 degrees above the horizontal). **2.** Having a rafter length equal to three-quarters of the span (approximately 47 degrees) **3.** (19c) Same as **equilateral pitch** (60 degrees).

true verdigris Same as **verdigris** (sense 1).

trumeau A pillar or pier between two adjacent openings, such as a double door, especially when supporting an arch **tympanum;** from the French.

truncated roof A **roof** with sloped sides and a flat top for a terrace; may have a balustrade around the flat center section. Also known as **cut roof.** See also **mansard.**

trunk (pre-19c) The **shaft** of a column or pilaster.

trunk dock (Carolinas) A wooden **sluice gate** that controls the flow of water from the trunk line canal to individual rice fields by raising or lowering boards held by grooves in the posts of a frame.

trunk duct A large, main **air duct** that connects to a series of smaller ducts.

trunk line The main line of a transportation system (such as a railroad or canal) or communications system (such as a telegraph) from which smaller branch lines diverge.

trunk nail A **nail** with an ornamental boss on its head; used for steamer trunks.

trunnel Same as **treenail.**

Truscon steel joist A mid-20c trade name for an **I-beam** joist built-up of two heavy sheet-metal channels.

truss **1.** A bridge or roof framing member composed of rigid diagonal, vertical, and horizontal members in the same plane, joined only at their ends and primarily either in compression or tension; composed of **chord** and **web** members that may be a **strut** or **tie;** forms include **Baltimore truss, Bollman truss, bowstring truss, couple, Fink truss, hammerbeam truss, Howe truss, K-truss, king-post truss, lattice truss, lenticular truss, panel truss, pegram truss, Pennsylvania truss, Petit truss, post truss, Pratt truss, quadrangular truss, queen-post truss, sawtooth truss, scissors truss, trussed arch, panel truss, Vierendeel truss, Warren truss, Whipple truss, W-truss.** See also **American system, batter brace, counter brace, double canceled, truss beam, truss bridge, truss girder.** **2.** A large ornamented bracket, modillion, or corbel; may be structural or purely decorative. See also **console.**

truss beam **1.** Any beam that is a component of a **truss.** **2.** A wood beam reinforced with components that form a low-height triangular truss; the reinforcing can be of various forms, including two wood sisters, or a tie rod passing over a short strut, or a **queen rafter.** Also known as **trussed beam.** See also **strut beam.**

truss block A **strut** that separates a compression member and a diagonal tie rod in a **truss,** especially in a **truss beam** or **trussed girder.** Also known as **distance block.**

truss bridge A **bridge** supported or stiffened by a **truss;** may be a **through bridge** or **deck bridge.** See also **beam truss bridge.**

trussed arch An arch-shaped truss with radial posts between parallel arched top and bottom chords.

trussed bar A **deformed bar** with diagonal extensions projecting upward at 45 degree angles; used in reinforced concrete beams in the early 20c.

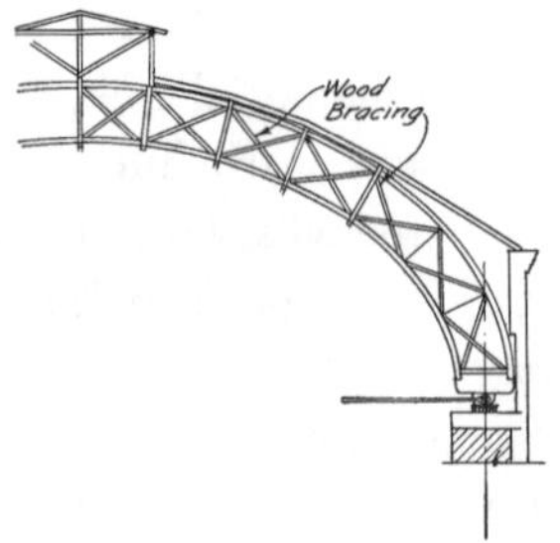

trussed arch

trussed beam Same as **truss beam** (sense 2).

trussed girder A **truss girder** in the form of a shallow **king-post truss** or **queen-post truss;** typical elements include **strut, strut beam,** and a **tie rod** with **turnbuckle.**

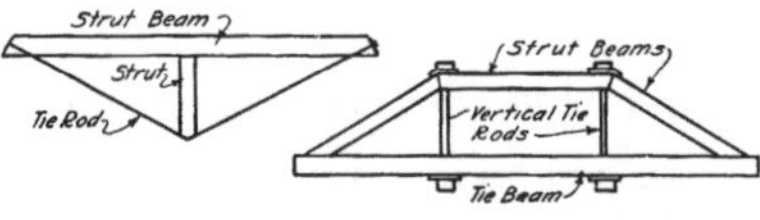

trussed girder

trussed partition A stud wall that incorporates a wood truss that spans over an opening below; the truss may be nearly the full height of the wall or a **braced header** between the head of a doorway and the ceiling; typically the two diagonal top chords of the truss are scarfed into a horizontal bottom beam.

trussed roof Any roof supported by trusses.

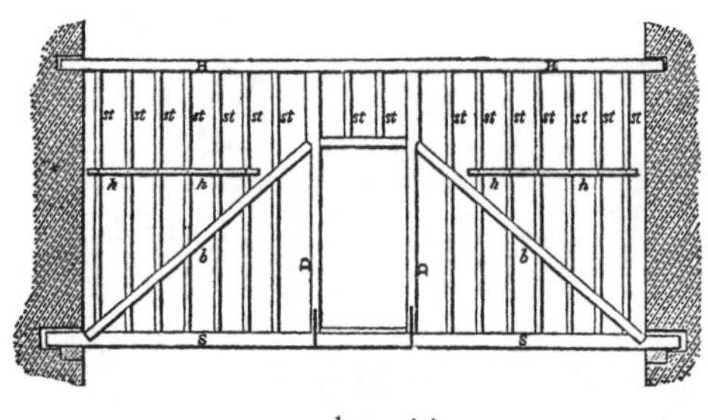
trussed partition

truss girder Any large beam in the form of a **truss;** type includes **trussed girder.** See also **truss beam.**

Trussit A trade name for a **herringbone lath** bent into a sawtooth profile and used to form plaster partitions 2–3.5 inches thick.

Truss-Loop lath A form of **expanded-metal lath** with truss-like loops. Also known as **Bostwick lath.** See also **lath.**

truss piece A **strut** in a **truss.**

truss rod A metal rod that connects the ends of a truss compression member and passes over a **truss block.**

Trust **1.** (U.S.) Abbr. for the **National Trust for Historic Preservation.** **2.** Abbr. for various state, provincial or local historic trust organizations.

trylon A tall, narrow, three-sided pyramid; term was invented to refer to the symbol of the 1939 New York World's Fair, the trylon and perisphere.

T-saddle hub A T-shaped **saddle hub** with the branch at right angles to the main pipe.

T-section Same as **T-beam.**

T-sill A built-up wood **sill** with the band beam inside the studs and the wall plate forming an inverted T-shape cross section; used with **balloon frame** construction. See also **L-sill.**

T-type lamp A tungsten filament **incandescent lamp** with a tip; manufactured 1909–20.

tube A long, hollow cylinder, or other hollow shape; typically refers to a flexible, or thin-walled, metal cylinder, as opposed to a **pipe.** See also **conduit, speaking tube.**

tube steel Rolled structural steel sections with a cross section in the shape of a hollow rectangle or square, with rounded corners.

tubular girder A large **box beam** used as a **girder.**

tuck **1.** To place mortar in narrow groove or joint. **2.** A narrow groove cut into the **stopping** in tuck pointing.

tuck-and-pat pointing Same as **tuck pointing.**

tuck and point Same as **tuck pointing.**

tuck joint A **mortar joint** made by **tuck pointing.**

tuck pointing **1.** The use of two mortar colors to simulate narrow masonry joints; the first color mortar **stopping** matches the brick or stone and is installed with a flush joint; the second color mortar is typically installed with a raised joint in a **tuck** groove cut into the first color mortar; technique developed 18c. **2.** (19c–present) Same as **repointing** of existing masonry joints; term most common in the midwestern U.S. **3.** Two-color false joints applied to brick-colored stucco. Also known as **tuck-and-pat, tuck-and-pat pointing, tuck and point.** See also **beaded joint, bricking.**

tuck-and-pat (18c) Same as **tuck pointing.**

Tuck-Tuck Same as **noble fir.**

Tudor arch A low-rise, pointed **arch;** typically **four-centered,** with the outside pair of centers on the spring line, and the middle pair below the spring line; in some examples, the middle pair of circle segments are replaced with straight lines; common in the **Tudor Revival style.**

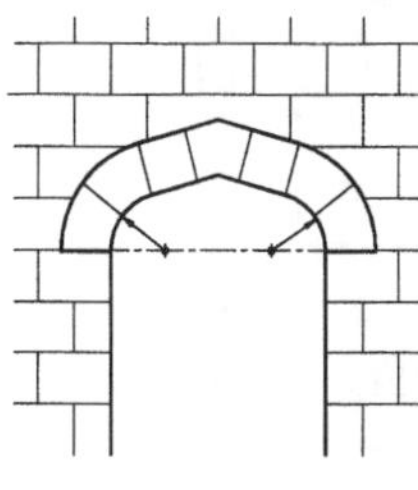

Tudor arch

Tudor flower A projecting ornament in the stylized form of a flat, three-petaled flower supported by a stem, with a diamond-shaped outline; used as cresting, alternating with a small trefoil or ball-flower; common in the **Perpendicular Style,** or projecting from a tracery cusp in the **Gothic Revival style.**

Tudor Revival style A house style ca. 1890–1940 loosely based on the domestic English architecture during the reign of monarchs of the House of Tudor, 1485–1558; typical elements include asymmetrical massing, steeply pitched, cross-gabled roof, decorative half-timbered patterns on upper exterior walls, tall, narrow, multipaned casement windows, massive chimney with chimney pots, **tudor arch;** used for small cottages to large mansions, and occasionally multistory commercial and apartment buildings, throughout suburban U.S. and Canada. See also **false thatched roof, Jacobean Revival, Perpendicular Style.**

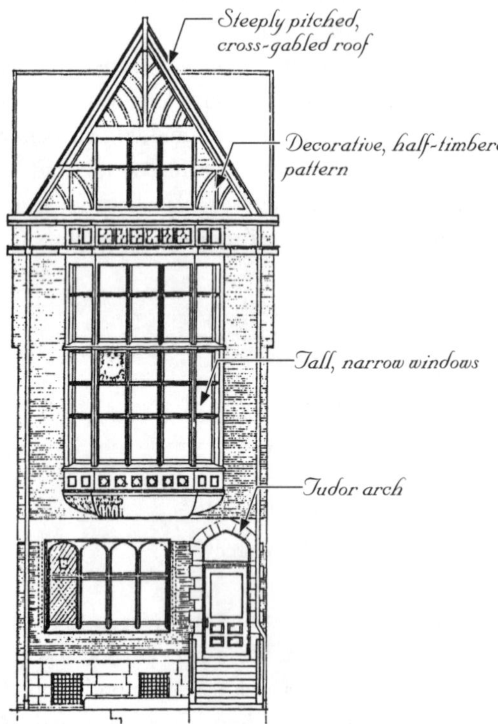

Tudor Revival style
Reginald De Koven Residence
Chicago, Illinois, ca. 1889

Tudor rose **1.** A stylized representation of two or three intertwined, or superimposed, wild roses; typically each flower is five-petaled; represents the union of the houses of Lancaster and York in 1486 to end the English War of the Roses. **2.** A rosette divided into quarters, with two of the quarters a different texture or color than the other two quarters.

tulip poplar Same as **tulip tree.**

tulip tree, tuliptree A large hardwood tree with light yellow to greenish brown, soft, lightweight, heartwood with creamy white sapwood; found from southern New York to northern Florida and west to the Mississippi valley; used pre-19c for framing, shingles, and weatherboards, later primarily for interior millwork; named for its tulip-shaped blossoms; *Liriodendron-tulipifera.* Also known as **poplar, saddle-leaf tree, tulip poplar, whitewood, yellow poplar.**

tumbler lock A **lock** with internal spring-loaded tumblers or rods that are moved by a key to release the bolt.

tumbling bay Same as **spillway.**

tumbling course A sloped row of bricks, such as a rowlock coping on top of a buttress.

tunck, yunk (Areas of U.S. with German settlers) Same as **whitewash;** from the German *tünchen.*

tung oil A drying oil made from ground tung tree nuts; used in **linoleum,** some types of **varnish,** and occasionally in **oil-base paint;** typically produces a flat finish.

tungsten A heavy, gray, powdery elemental metal; used to increase the strength of metal alloys and in **tungsten filament bulbs.**

tungsten filament bulb An incandescent electric lamp that uses a glowing tungsten wire, typically in a mixture of argon and nitrogen gas; first commercially available 1920s; typically with a **frosted bulb.** Also known as **tungsten lamp.**

tungsten lamp Same as **tungsten filament bulb.**

tunnel vault Same as **barrel vault.**

turbine A wheel with curved vanes around the perimeter enclosed in a casing and rotated by a fluid under pressure that passes through the casing; used for power; largely replaced the **water wheel** by end of 19c; types include **steam turbine, water turbine.** See also **water motor.**

turf Same as **sod.**

turkey oak Same as **southern red oak.**

turkey paint A bright red oil-base paint with **turkey red** pigment.

turkey red **1.** A brilliant red, nonfading paint pigment originally composed of sulfonated vegetable oil, especially castor oil treated with sulfuric acid; replaced by **alizarin red** late 19c. **2.** A bright red cloth dye made from madder root, or the cloth itself.

turkey umber (20c) Same as **raw umber;** named for earth mined on Cyprus and shipped through Constantinople.

Turkish dome An onion-shaped **dome** with a pointed top and a cylindrical base; named for its use in Byzantine architecture.

turn Same as **shutter dog.**

turn bridge Same as **swing bridge.**

turnbuckle **1.** A hardware device connecting two rods that are threaded with opposite hands; when rotated it either pulls the rods together or pushes them apart; used to adjust the tension of tie rods, or similar elements. See also **sleevenut.** **2.** Same as **shutter dog.**

turned Having a circular cross section that has been produced by turning on a lathe, or sometimes a similar molded or carved shape; may have **belly** and/or **waist.** See also **turning, square turned.**

turned lead (18c) A cast lead **came** with grooves for holding the glass formed by drawing the metal through a vice.

turnery Ornamental work that has been **turned;** term not common in construction.

turning An element, such as a column or baluster, that has been cut to shape by a tool while turning on a lathe. See also **turned.**

turning bridge Same as **swing bridge.**

turnkey job A construction project where the builder assumes the risks of cost overruns due to unforeseen circumstances, and upon completion turns the key in the door locks and gives them to the new owner; common for pre-19c church construction; in modern times often has the added connotation of the builder also selling the land for the project to the new owner upon completion of the building.

turnover hinge (19c) A **hinge** that allows a door or window to open flat against the wall; typically a butt hinge.

turntable A platform that rotates around a vertical axis; includes the device with a section of track on top used on railways to turn locomotives, and the mechanism with a center vertical pin that supports a **swing bridge.**

turpentine **1.** An oleoresin **solvent** distilled from pine resin; used in manufacturing oil paint and varnishes to thin the oil and make the coating easier to spread; varieties include **American turpentine, Canadian turpentine, Carolina turpentine.** Also known as **gum spirits, oil of turpentine, spirits of turpentine.** See also **naval stores, rosin, wood turpentine.** **2.** The thick, yellowish oleoresin exuded by pine trees.

turpentine varnish **1.** Any **varnish** made with resin dissolved in a **turpentine** solvent. **2.** Same as **common varnish.**

turret **1.** A small, projecting tower at the corner of a building, or above the roof a larger tower; types include **pepper box turret;** typically circular or octagonal in plan; roof shapes include **rotunda, dome, broach** and **spired.** See also

tourelle, toweret. 2. A short, rotating cylinder that contains a large gun in a **fortification;** constructed of iron plate. **3.** (pre-19c) Same as **cupola** or **belfry.**

Tuscan intercolumniation Widely spaced **Tuscan order** columns, as much as seven column diameters apart; the wide spacing originally made possible by wood architraves, rather than stone ones. See also **intercolumniation.**

Tuscan order The simplest order of the classical styles, developed by the Romans from the Doric. From top to bottom the typical Tuscan order is shown in the figure. A pedestal may be added below the base, and in neoclassical work rusticated bands may be added to the column shaft; typically the lowest of orders used with **superposition.** See also **Classical order.**

Tuscan red A bright red paint **pigment** composed of **iron oxide** mixed with **alizarin red.** See also **Indian red.**

Tuscan style (19c) Same as **Italianate.**

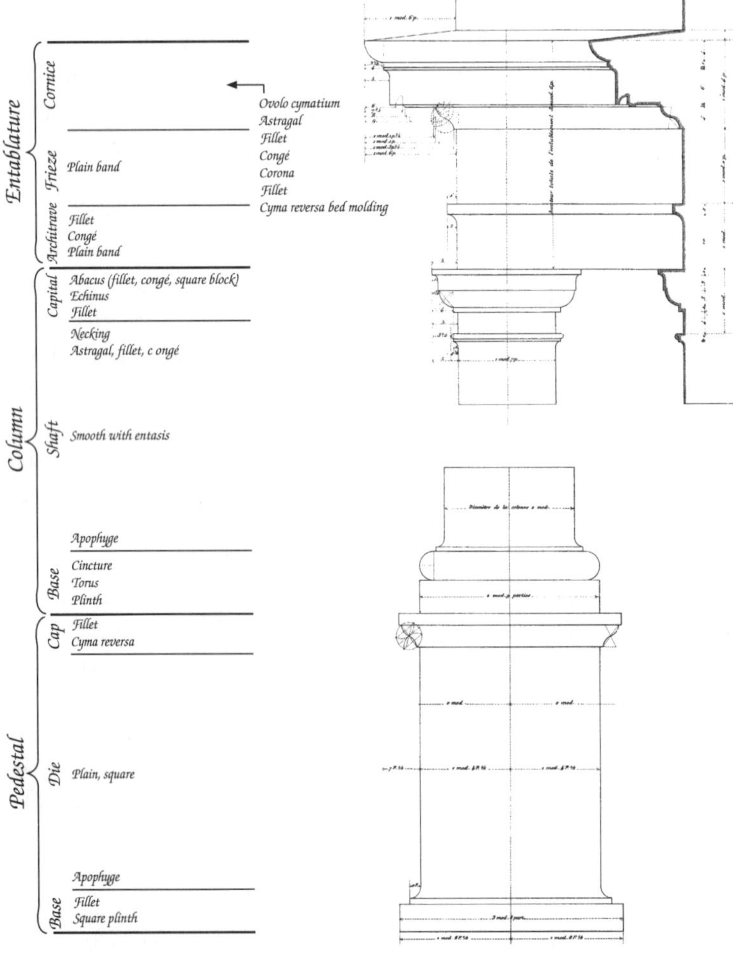

Tuscan order

tusk A beveled shoulder at the base of a **tenon,** such as that on a joist let into a girder; used to strengthen the tenon.

tusk tenon **1.** A **tenon** with a **tusk,** such as a **tease tenon.** **2.** A tenon that extends through a mortise and is fastened in place with a wood wedge through a hole in the projecting end.

twelve over twelve, 12 over 12 A double hung window with twelve panes in both the upper and lower sashes; typically in three horizontal rows of four panes; common until 1825, and in large Colonial Revival style windows; later windows typically had fewer panes as the **glass** making technology allowed larger pieces—**six over six, four over four, two over two,** and **one over one.**

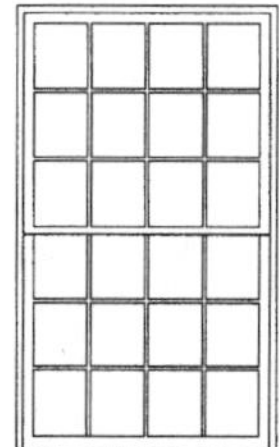

twelve over twelve

twelvepenny nail (12d nail) A **nail** approximately 3.25 inches long; 50 iron common nails weigh a pound. See also **penny.**

twelvepenny spike (12d spike) A **spike** approximately 8 inches long; 5 steel-wire spikes weigh a pound. See also **penny.**

twentypenny nail (20d nail) A **common nail** approximately 4 inches long; 20 iron common nails weigh a pound. See also **penny.**

twining stem molding A **molding** in the form of a stylized relief sculpture of a vine spiraling around a cylindrical stem.

twist **1.** An architectural element with a helical form, such as a continuous handrail at a turn. See also **scroll.** **2.** Same as **wind.**

twisted bar A **deformed bar** made by cold twisting a steel bar with a square cross section; used in reinforced concrete late 19c–early 20c.

twisted column **1.** Same as **solomonic column.** See also **wreathed column.** **2.** A column with a shaft in the form of two intertwined helixes. See also **cabled column, wreathed column.**

two by, 2× Sawn lumber with a **nominal dimension** of 2 inches on one of its faces, as in a two by four (2 × 4).

two-centered arch An **arch** with two centers for the radii of the intrados; types include **blunt pointed, equilateral pointed, acute pointed, segmental pointed.**

two-cusped arch A **four-centered arch** with two centers on or below the spring line and two centers above the spring line forming a pointed top; the intrados is said to be **cusped** or **foiled.** Also known as **foiled arch, pointed trefoil arch.**

two-cusped arch

two over two, 2 over 2 A double hung window with two panes in both the upper and lower sashes; each sash has a single vertical or horizontal center muntin. See also **twelve over twelve.** (*See illustration p. 502*)

twopenny nail (2d nail) A **nail** approximately 1 inch long; 800 iron common nails weigh a pound. See also **penny.**

twopenny spike (2d spike) A **spike** approximately 3 inches long; 41 steel-wire spikes weigh a pound. See also **penny.**

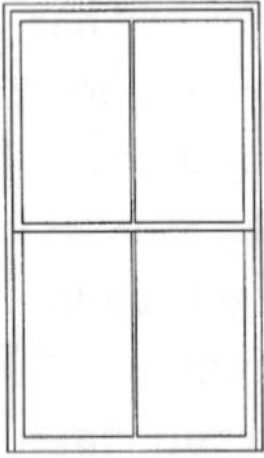

two over two

tyle (pre-18c) Same as **tile.**

tympan Same as **tympanum.**

tympanum **1.** The triangular, recessed wall of a Classical pediment, between the raking roof cornice above and the horizontal geison below; by extension, the wall enclosed by pediments of other shapes. **2.** A wall panel below an arch and above the transom of a square-headed door or window; often with relief sculpture, and supported by a **trumeau;** common in Gothic Revival style churches. **3.** The die or drum of a pedestal. **4.** (pre-20c) A door panel.

Tyndall limestone A buff, calcareous, Selkirk **limestone** mottled with dolomite and containing numerous coral fossils; quarried in the vicinity of Tyndall in southeastern Manitoba. Also known as **Tyndalstone.**

Tyndalstone Same as **Tyndall limestone.**

type (pre-19c) A wooden canopy above a pulpit; used as both a **sounding board** and a symbol of honor; elaborate examples had a polygonal plan with an ogee roof with a carved finial.

U

UBC **Uniform Building Code**

U-furring (20c) A bent sheet-metal shape that is approximately U-shaped in cross section; used to hold wire lath above a solid surface.

UL **Underwriters' Laboratory**

ultramarine blue An intense blue **pigment** composed of silica, alumina, sulfur, and soda; originally made in Europe from ground **lapis lazuli;** first synthesized in France in 1828, commercially available after 1830, common after 1850; often used to tint zinc oxide, glass, or mortar; nonfading, except when mixed with white lead; alkali resistant; name refers to the original source of lapis lazuli being across the sea, in Asia.

ultramarine green A green pigment used to tint mortar; a variety of **ultramarine blue.**

ultrasound meter A device that measures ultrasound waves; used to determine the passage of sound, and therefore air currents, through a wall or window, and to measure density or voids in materials.

ultraviolet light An invisible form of electromagnetic radiation with shorter wavelengths than visible light; may cause structural damage and fading in historic materials; a component of sunlight, fluorescent light, and, to a limited extent, incandescent light. See also **actinic light.**

umber See **burnt umber, raw umber.**

umbrage A deep recess in the building facade, typically forming a covered entrance at a doorway.

umbrella (18c) Same as **awning.**

umbrella roof **1.** (20c) Same as **hip roof.** **2.** A reinforced concrete or fabric roof in the approximate shape of an open umbrella.

unburnt Clay units that have not been fired in a kiln, such as **adobe.**

uncoursed Masonry laid without horizontal courses; the units may be rubble stone or squared, such as **ashlar.** See also **coursed, random ashlar, random rubble.**

uncut baluster A stone block with a rectangular cross section placed below the joint in the upper rail of a stone balustrade, as opposed to a **turned** baluster.

uncut dentil course A plain band occupying the normal position of a dentil band in a classical style entablature.

uncut modillion Same as **block modillion.**

undé, undée, undee, undy Having a wavy pattern, such as a **wave molding.**

undee Same as **undé.**

undée Same as **undé.**

underbuilt **1.** Construction that is of insufficient strength or quality. **2.** Construction that is below ground or beneath another structure. See also **underpinning.**

undercoat A layer of a finish material, such as plaster or paint, that is underneath the **finish coat;** not necessarily immediately below the finish coat.

under-conduct (pre-20c) An underground passage. See also **ventiduct.**

undercroft An underground chamber or passage, especially a vault below the main level of a church. See also **crypt, under-conduct.**

undercut **1.** A carved form or molding which overhangs itself. **2.** A floral or leafy ornament, or sculptural figure, that is nearly cut free of its backing surface.

underdrawn (pre-20c) A wood frame that has had a ceiling installed below the framing; by extension the installation of a ceiling, including its structure.

under floor **1.** (20c) Same as **subfloor.** **2.** (before mid-19c) A **ground floor,** as opposed to an **upper floor.**

underflooring (20c) Same as **subfloor.**

under frame (pre-19c) The framing supporting the first floor of a building, including the beams, joists, and sills.

underglaze The first coat of multiple glazed coats on **architectural terra-cotta.**

underhung A sliding door, or similar element, with rollers that ride a rail below, as opposed to **overhung.**

underlayment A layer of roofing felt, composition board, or other thin sheet material that covers the subfloor as a base for a finish floor; used to bridge gaps and irregularities.

underpinning, (pre-19c) **under pinning** **1.** The process of installing structural support under an existing wall or foundation; typically by placing short sections of concrete or masonry wall, or a series of piers, until the entire length of the wall or footing is supported; may also involve more elaborate construction; used to arrest settlement or lower the basement. Also known as **undersetting.** See also **shoring.** **2.** A foundation; including: (a) Footings, walls, and/or piers inserted as in sense 1; (b) (New England pre-20c) A masonry foundation, especially of a wood frame building; sometimes refers only to the portion above grade.

underpitch groin Same as **Welsh groin.**

underpitch vault See **Welsh groin.**

under sash (pre-19c) The lower sash of a **double hung** or **single hung** window.

undersetting (pre-20c) **1.** Same as **underpinning.** **2.** A pedestal or base.

undershot wheel A **water wheel** mounted on a horizontal axis and rotated by a stream of water that passes by the bottom portion of the wheel. See also **overshot wheel.**

undersiding (20c) Same as **sheathing.**

undertaking Any project, activity, or program under the direct or indirect jurisdiction of a U.S. federal agency, or licensed, permitted, or assisted by a federal agency, that can result in changes in the character or use of historic properties; **Section 106** requires the agency to **take into account** these effects.

underthroating The cove or **throat** of an exterior cornice that acts as a drip. See also **gorge.**

under-tile The bottom **roof tile** shape used with **Italian tiling,** or a similar system; varieties include **gutter tile, tegula.** See also **mission tile.**

underwater archaeology Same as **marine archaeology.**

underwriters' door (pre-WWI) A **fire rated** door assembly that has been approved by insurance company underwriters. See also **labeled door, Underwriters' Laboratory.**

underwriters' floor See **underwriters' door.**

Underwriters' Laboratory (UL) A private organization that conducts fire-resistance and safety testing on building material products and assemblies, and publishes standards and specifications; originally worked for insurance company underwriters.

undressed wood **Rough sawn** lumber.

undulated Having a wavy form, such as a **guilloche** molding. See also **undé.**

undulating tracery Same as **flowing tracery.**

undy Same as **undé.**

UNESCO **United Nations Educational, Scientific, and Cultural Organization**

uneven grain Wood **grain** with high contrast between the light and dark portions of the annual growth rings.

unframed door A **door** without stiles and rails at the edges, such as a **batten door.**

Uniform Building Code (UBC) A U.S. national **building code.**

uniform construction index (late 20c) A standardized outline of building trades and products agreed to by the **American Institute of Architects, Construction Specifications Institute,** and the Association of General Contractors; organized by **trade** and construction sequence, the 16 divisions are: (1) general conditions, (2) sitework, (3) concrete, (4) masonry, (5) metals, (6) wood and plastics, (7) thermal and moisture protection, (8) doors and windows, (9) finishes, (10) specialties, (11) equipment, (12) furnishings, (13) special construction, (14) conveying systems, (15) mechanical, (16) electrical; used for writing **specifications.**

Uniform Federal Accessibility Standards (UFAS) U.S. federal regulations that define **accessibility** design standards for all federal facilities.

union A threaded **pipe coupling** that can be unscrewed without twisting either of the two pipes connected.

Unit Block A trade name for a system of **concrete block** construction with units of trapezoidal and triangular plan shapes; developed by Alden Dow, a follower of Frank Lloyd Wright; used for houses in Midland, Michigan, 1930s.

United Nations Educational, Scientific, and Cultural Organization (UNESCO) A branch of the United Nations that includes administration of the **International Council on Monuments and Sites (ICOMOS)** and the **World Heritage Committee.**

United States Committee of ICOMOS (US/ICOMOS) One of the 65 ICOMOS national committees that facilitate worldwide information exchange on preservation concerns. See also **International Council on Monuments and Sites.**

unit of bond The smallest number of bricks needed for a complete sample of a repeating pattern; for example, a **Flemish cross bond** unit is 1.5 bricks long, while a **common bond** unit is 1 brick long.

universal transverse mercator (UTM) (20c) One of the internationally established coordinates used to produce a universal transmercator grid on maps and locate sites precisely. See also **geocode, UTM reference.**

upbrace An upward angled **brace.**

upholstered **1.** Having cushioned seating, such as fabric-covered padding for a window seat. **2.** (pre-20c) Provided with furnishings, such as curtains and furniture.

upper capital Same as **dosseret.**

upper croft (pre-19c) A triforium gallery above a side aisle of a church.

upper floor **1.** Same as **finish flooring** when on a subfloor. **2.** A floor level above the **ground floor.**

upping block (pre-19c) Same as **horse block.**

upset-bar A flat **eyebar** manufactured by pressing the end of the hot bar with a ram to form the eye.

upset screw end An enlarged-diameter threaded end of a round bar; used on a **tie rod** to provide attachment without reducing the cross sectional area.

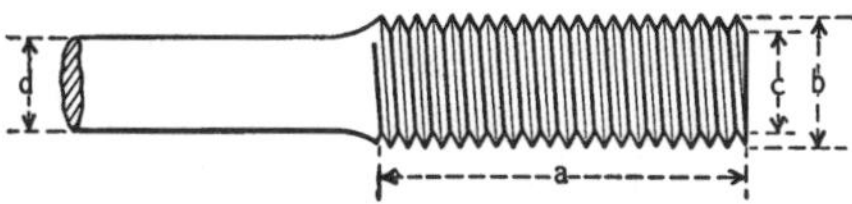

upset screw end

upstart (Regional) A building stone installed with the bedding plane not horizontal.

up to code Meeting **building code** compliance for an existing building.

urban design The design of public urban environments. See also **street furniture, townscape.**

urban planning See **planning.**

urban renewal A post-WWII effort to improve urban neighborhoods through massive **redevelopment;** typically resulted in wholesale demolition of most existing buildings in designated areas; U.S. urban renewal programs were federally funded and became obsolete by late 20c.

urinal **1.** A plumbing fixture used by males while standing; composed of a flushing device, a drain, and one of many varieties of bowl or trough. **2.** (19c) A compartment in a toilet room containing a urinal fixture.

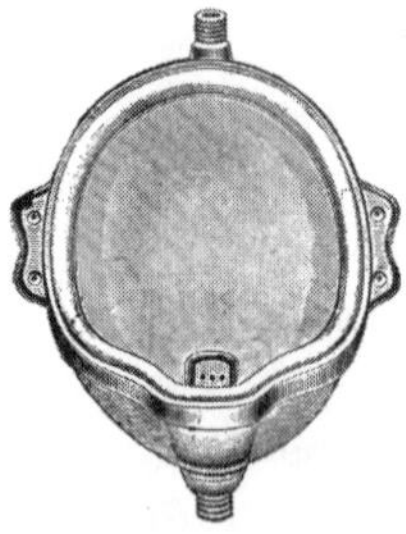

urinal (sense 1)

urinal cock A self-closing **faucet** for washing a urinal.

urn A large **vase** with a circular cross section, a footed base, and sometimes a cover; typically set on a pedestal; used as a decorative feature, such as in gardens and cemeteries and on balustrades.

use The activities permitted within a geographic area defined in a **zoning code;** typically divided into commercial, residential, industrial, and farming categories, often including various subcategories with gradations of permitted development intensity. See also **adaptive use, building occupancy, land use, zoning.**

useful life Same as **life expectancy.**

urn

USGS map A topographic map of a portion of the U.S. prepared by the United States Geological Survey. See also **universal transverse mercator.**

US/ICOMOS **United States Committee of ICOMOS**

Usonian Small, affordable houses designed by Frank Lloyd Wright, first half 20c, featuring flat roofs, carports, and open living spaces.

U-stud A bent sheet-metal stud with punched hooks for hanging metal lath; used to construct thin plaster partitions.

utility One of the services that supplies water, power, or communications to a structure; types include electricity, gas, steam, telephone, water.

utility brick An oversized **brick** with dimensions $3\frac{1}{2}$–$3\frac{5}{8} \times 11\frac{1}{2}$–$11\frac{5}{8} \times 3\frac{1}{2}$–$3\frac{5}{8}$ inches (90 × 290 × 90 mm).

utility room The space in a dwelling for service functions, such as laundry equipment, hot-water heater, furnace, and sometimes storage.

UTM Same as **universal tranverse mercator.**

UTM reference A set of **universal tranverse mercator** coordinates (easting and northing) that indicates a unique location on the grid on USGS maps; used to precisely locate historic sites for National Register nomination. See also **Borden system, geocode.**

V

vacuum fan A mechanical fan that draws air out of an interior space. See also **plenum fan.**

vagina The lower portion of a **terminus,** from its appearance of a sheath enveloping the lower portion of the figure.

valley The line, or angle, formed where two downward sloping roof surfaces meet at the bottom; may be horizontal or inclined; types include **swept valley, open valley.** See also **vertical gutter,** and various components beginning with **valley.**

valley board A wood board installed along the bottom of a roof valley to support the flashing, tiles, or slates. See also **vertical gutter.**

valley header A roof **header** between two valley rafters of a pair of gable dormers; used to support the lower ends of rafters without making a difficult end cut at the valley rafter.

valley jack A **jack rafter** with its lower end supported by a **valley rafter** and its upper end supported by a ridge.

valley rafter The long rafter along the bottom of a roof **valley;** supports the foot of the **valley jacks.**

valley roof A roof with two or more substantial valleys formed by the roof over a wing abutting the main roof.

valley shingle A wood shingle installed along a roof valley, with the grain parallel to the valley.

valley tile A large tile that forms the gutter in a roof valley.

value See **appraised value, assessed value, significance.**

valve **1.** A mechanical device that regulates the flow of liquid or gas through any type of conduit, pipe, or channel; types include **cock, faucet, gate valve.** **2.** (pre-20c) One of the leaves of a folding **door,** or one of a pair of double doors, such as a **French door.**

valve house A structure that encloses the large gate valves that control water flow from a reservoir.

vamure Same as **vantmure.**

Vandyke brown Any of various rich, deep reddish brown paint **pigment**s similar in color to that used by the Flemish portrait painter Van Dyck (1599–1641); may be made from decayed vegetable matter from lakes and bogs, or naturally occurring bituminous **ocher,** lignite, brown coal, or charred cork, or a mixture of **lampblack** and **Indian red;** used for glazing and staining.

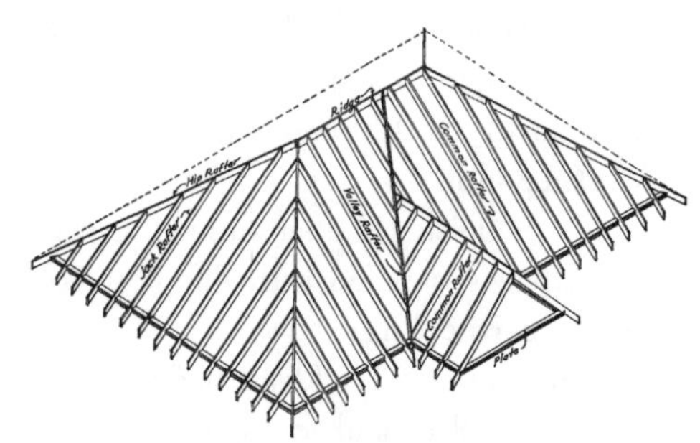

valley rafter

vane **1.** A thin piece of wood or metal that is rotated by the flow of water or gas, such as those on a **weather vane** or **windmill. 2.** (20c) A piece of sheet metal installed inside an air duct to direct the flow of air; used to reduce turbulence at bends and balance the amount of air flow.

vaneer (18c) Same as **veneer.**

vantmure, vamure The elevated walkway behind a **fortification** parapet. See also **terre-plein.**

vapor barrier (20c) A thin sheet material, or film, that is impervious to the passage of water vapor; used to prevent the movement of water vapor from one space to another, especially from a room to the inside of an exterior wall where it could condense in cold weather, or from the ground to a slab-on-grade.

vapor burner A device that vaporizes a volatile liquid, such as gasoline, so that it can be used for lighting or heating.

vapor heating A **steam heating** system where the pressure is near atmospheric; the condensate returns to the boiler by gravity.

vapor lamp A lighting device that includes a **vapor burner.**

vapor-tight globe (19c) The sealed glass bulb of an incandescent lamp.

varge board (pre-19c) Same as **bargeboard.**

variance The waiving of a **zoning** restriction, such as the width of a side yard, for a particular site; typically approved by a Board of Zoning Adjustment or similar body upon appeal by an owner for hardship reasons. See also **special exception.**

variegated A finish material surface, especially stone, that is dappled with different colors. See also **parti-colored.**

Varitone Mahogany A reddish, medium-grained **granite** with black and gray spottings quarried in the vicinity of Ortonville, Minnesota.

varnish, (pre-19c) **vernish** A resin, dissolved in a solvent, that forms a transparent, glossy, hard coating upon drying; most commonly used as a clear, or tinted, protective coating for wood; varieties include those named for the solvent, such as **oil varnish, spirit varnish, turpentine varnish, water varnish;** the resin, such as **amber varnish, copal varnish, dammar varnish, hard oil, lac varnish, mastic varnish, shellac, wax varnish, white varnish;** and other qualities, such as **gilt varnish, satin varnish, spar varnish, Swedish finish.** See also **floor oil, tung oil.**

varnished cambric Same as **varnished cloth.**

varnished cloth A **fibrous wrapped insulation** for electric wire composed of cotton or linen muslin treated with a mixture of benzine, boiled linseed oil, and resin. Also known as **varnished cambric, empire cloth, insulating fabric.**

vase **1.** A hollow vessel for household liquids; typically with a circular cross section; of various forms, including with a pair of projecting handles. **2.** Same as the **bell** of a Corinthian capital. **3.** The bas-relief representation of a **vase** (sense 1) as an architectural decoration; a common Renaissance Revival motif. See also **urn.**

vasistas A small grilled opening in a door, with a hinged panel, that can be opened to see who wants to come inside; a French corruption of the German phrase *"Was ist das?"* See also **wicket.**

vault **1.** An arched masonry ceiling or roof structure; forms include **simple vault, compound vault, panel vault, segmental vault, stilted vault, surbased vault, surmounted vault;** construction types include **double vault, rib vaulting, solid vaulting, tierceron;** components may include **boss, cell, cross springer, rib, panache, tracery vaulting, vaulting**

course, vault shell, voussoir. Also known as **voussure.** See also **cul-de-four, dome, master vault, pendentive. 2.** A wood or plaster ceiling in the form of a vault. **3.** An underground space, especially below a public sidewalk or street. **4.** A secure room for locking up valuables. **5.** A masonry burial compartment; often below a church or in a churchyard.

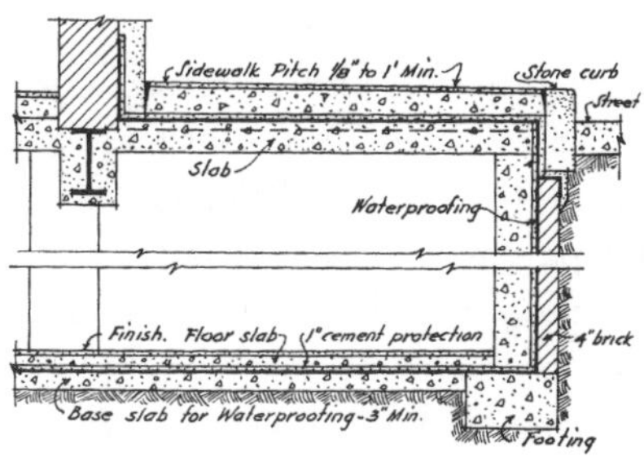

vault (sense 3)

vault bay One of a series of vaulted spaces separated by columns or piers, especially when between transverse arches. See also **bay.**

vaulted Constructed in the form of a **vault,** or covered by a vault, such as a vaulted aisle.

vaulting capital A pier capital that supports a rib, or ribs, of a vault. See also **vaulting shaft.**

vaulting cell A panel of a compound **rib vault** that can be built independently of the other parts of the vault. See also **cell, vault bay.**

vaulting course A horizontal course of wall springers that start a masonry vault above a wall; typically projecting or corbeled. See also **surbased vault.**

vaulting rib Same as **rib** (sense 2).

vaulting shaft (19c–present) A shaft that supports one of the ribs, or a group of ribs, of a **rib vault;** may have a simple cross section, or be a **clustered pier;** may start at the floor, a column capital, or corbel; used in Gothic style architecture. See also **wall shaft.**

vaulting tile A thin, lightweight clay tile used to form a **vault shell** between the vault ribs.

vault light A skylight in a sidewalk above a vault, composed of thick refractive glass pieces set in a frame. Also known as **patent light, pavement light, sidewalk light.**

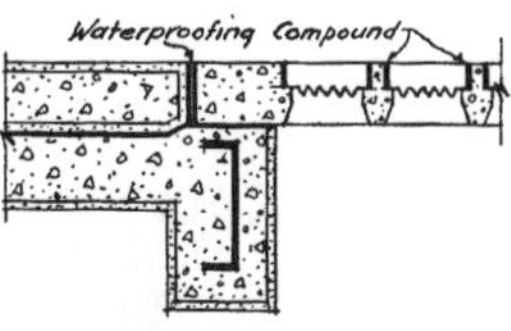

vault light

vault of the third point A vault with a cross section in the form of an **equilateral arch.**

vault shell The relatively thin masonry panels between the ribs of a **rib vault;** may be brick, stone, or **vaulting tile.** Also known as **vault skin.**

vault skin Same as **vault shell.**

vault stone (pre-19c) One of the voussoirs of a vault.

vegetable insect wax Same as **Chinese wax.**

vehicle The liquid base of a paint that includes all of the components that are initially liquid, including **binder** and **thinner,** without the solid components, such as **pigment;** some or all of the liquid evaporates after application; types include turpentine and oil for **oil-base paint,** water and acrylic resins for **acrylic paint,** water and vinyl for **latex paint,** melted hide glue and gelatin for **hide paint,** milk for **casein paint,** and epoxy for **epoxy paint.** See also **water-base paint.**

Veined Ebony A dark, medium-grained gabbro with black veins quarried in the vicinity of Mellen, Wisconsin.

vendue house (pre-19c) A building where auctions are held.

vendue office (pre-19c) A room where auctions are held.

veneer, (18c) **vaneer** **1.** A thin, decorative wood finish used for paneling or furniture; types include **marquetry, matched veneer, sawn veneer, sliced veneer.** See also **flitch.** **2.** Any relatively thin layer of material applied over a structural backing; types include **brick veneer, stonework, veneer plaster.**

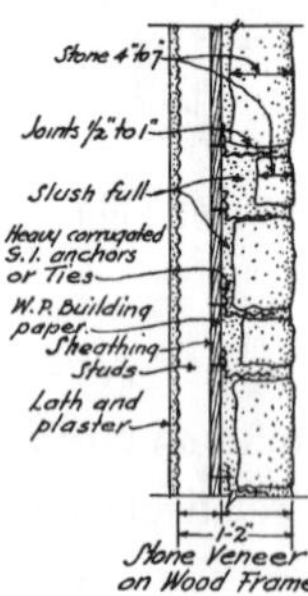

veneer (sense 2)

veneer plaster A thin layer of white plaster skimmed over drywall backing to give a plaster finish, developed second half 20c.

veneer tie One of a series of metal anchors used to attach masonry veneer to the **backup.**

Venetian Same as **Venetian mosaic.**

Venetian arch A form of pointed arch where the voussoirs are thicker at the crown than at the spring line.

Venetian blind **1.** (mid-18c–present) An interior window treatment of horizontal slats suspended by cloth tapes and arranged so that the angle of the slats can be adjusted by cords; popular in North America starting third quarter 18c. See also **blind.** **2.** (mid-18c–mid-19c) Same as **Venetian shutter.**

Venetian carpet A worsted carpet with a simple striped pattern; used in hallways and on stairs 19c.

Venetian dentil A projecting **molding** with rectangular dentils alternating with sloped interdentils; the direction of the slope may alternate from side to side.

Venetian door (pre-20c) A doorway with a central **door** opening flanked by two narrow windows; typically has an arch with glazing over the middle portion. See also **Palladian motif.**

Venetianed (19c) Having **Venetian blinds.**

Venetian molding Various moldings with repetitive individual projecting elements; types include **Venetian dentil.**

Venetian mosaic A form of **terrazzo** made with large marble chips. Also known as **Venetian.**

Venetian motif Same as **Palladian motif.**

Venetian pavement Same as **terrazzo.**

Venetian red A medium red paint **pigment** composed of iron oxide; manufactured in the 20c by roasting hydrated iron oxide mill scale from partially neutralized steel mill waste acid; lower grades used for painting barns; higher grades have very stable color. See also **Indian red.**

Venetian shutter **1.** (mid-18c–WWI) Any wood **shutter** with slats, such as a **louver shutter,** especially with adjustable slats. Also known as **Venetian blind.** **2.** (19c) An **overhead door** with horizontal slats attached to one another by a fabric strip.

Venetian varnish (18c) Same as **white varnish.**

Venetian window **1.** (pre-19c) Same as **Palladian window.** **2.** A semi-circular arched opening that is subdivided by a pair of round arches with a center mullion, and a circular light tangent to the intrados of the large arch and the extrados of the smaller arches.

Venetian window (sense 2)

Venice Charter The Decisions and Resolutions of the Second International Congress of Architects and Technicians of Historical Monuments held in Venice, Italy, in May, 1964; includes principles and guidelines for the rehabilitation and restoration of historic resources and infill construction in historic districts.

vent **1.** An opening, or conduit, for the escape of smoke, sewer gas, and similar noxious gases; types include **chimney flue, smoke hole, smoke vent, vent pipe.** **2.** A opening in an outside wall, or a roof, to provide ventilation to an interior space. **3.** (pre-20c) A wall opening, such as a **crenelle** or a **loophole.**

vent bonnet Same as **bonnet.**

vent brick A brick wall laid with gaps between adjoining units; often in Flemish bond with holes in place of headers.

vent-cap, ventilating cap The cover on the top of a plumbing **vent pipe.**

vent hole **1.** Same as **weep hole.** **2.** Same as **smoke hole.**

ventiduct (pre-20c) An underground passage, or large duct, used to convey and cool ventilating air. See also **air duct, under-conduct.**

ventilating brick **1.** A hollow **brick** used to form continuous air ducts within masonry. **2.** A brick wall with gaps left between adjoining bricks to allow air flow; commonly a brick stretcher alternates with a header-sized opening.

ventilation The process of supplying fresh air to interior spaces; first done in a systematic way through the use of **heat aspiration** in some 18c public buildings; mechanical ventilation with fans was not common until ca. 1860, and a constant supply of fresh air was not generally used until ca. 1880; may also involve **air conditioning,** or mixing with conditioned air. See also **forced ventilation; heating, ventilating, and air conditioning.**

ventilator **1.** Same as **vent register.** **2.** A louvered projection above a roof that provides air circulation to the interior space by exhausting warm air; of many forms, such as a **cupola,** or a sheet-metal hood over a vertical duct, such as an **acorn ventilator.** Also known as **gravity ventilator.**

vent pipe **1.** A plumbing pipe that allows sewer gases to escape to the atmosphere; typically extends above the roof. See also **branch, vent stack.** **2.** A pressure relief pipe; may be used for a steam boiler, hot-water tank, or compressed air system.

vent register A **register** that supplies, or exhausts, air to a space. Also known as **ventilator.** See also **ventilation.**

vent stack The vertical vent pipe that runs from the bottom to top of the plumbing system; typically used to indicate a **vent pipe** that connects several levels of drains.

veranda, verandah (second quarter 19c–present) An open-sided, raised sitting area with thin columns that support its roof; typically extends along an entire side wall, or wraps around a house or resort hotel. Also known as **galerie, piazza.** See also **apron, porch, portico.**

verbal boundary description A statement that gives the precise **boundary** of a property; may include a lot number, **metes and bounds,** or township and range; typically included on a survey or in a deed.

verdantique, verd antique **1.** Any of various types of veined **serpentine** with a marblelike appearance when polished; quarried in the vicinity of Marietta, Georgia; Milford, Connecticut; Westfield, Massachusetts; Roxbury and Cavendish, Vermont; Middle Gila River, New Mexico; San Bernardino, California; and in Harford County, Maryland; typically green, and may be mottled; used for interior decorative panels; originally named for its use in ancient buildings in Egypt, Greece and Italy. Also known as **verde antico. 2.** Same as **verdigris.**

verde antico Same as **verdantique.**

verdigris, (18c) **verdegrease 1.** The light bluish green surface corrosion or patina, composed largely of copper carbonate, that forms on copper-based metals such as bronze or sheet copper; similar compounds may also be brown or black due to pollution. Also known as **aerugo, true verdigris, verd antique. 2.** A green crystalline paint **pigment** composed of a mixture of several basic cupric acetates; originally manufactured by the action of acetic acid (vinegar) on copper sheets; varieties include **blue verdigris,** $Cu(C_2H_3O_2)_2 \cdot CuO$, and **green verdigris,** $2Cu(C_2H_3O_2)_2 \cdot CuO$. See also **distilled verdigris.**

verdigris green The color of **green verdigris,** common in late 18c–early 19c interiors. Also known as **copper colored.**

verge, (pre-20c) **virge 1.** The portion of a roof which extends past a gable end. See also **eaves. 2.** The shaft of a column, especially that of a colonnette; from the French term for "rod," and spoken with French intonation. **3.** The edge of the roof tiles that project over a gable. **4.** A grass edging, such as around a flower bed or along a roadway.

vergeboard, (pre-19c) **verge board** Same as **bargeboard.**

verge fillet A narrow board nailed to the ends of roof battens supported on top of a gable wall.

verge tile A **tile-and-a-half tile** used to complete a row at the **verge** (sense 3).

vermiculated mosaic A type of **mosaic** work composed of tesserae set in curvilinear lines named for their resemblance to the wiggling tracks of worms; used for shaded illustrations. Also known as **opus vermiculatum.** See also **vermiculation.**

vermiculated work Stone masonry with **vermiculation.**

vermiculation Decoration in the form of wide, wandering grooves carved in the surface of stone blocks, especially those used for **rustication;** named for a resemblance to the wiggling tracks of worms; found in Italianate style buildings imitating the palazzos of the northern Italian Renaissance. See also **vermiculated mosaic.**

vermiculatum opus See **vermiculated mosaic.**

vermiculite A pearly or bronzy colored, laminated micaceous mineral composed of hydrated magnesium-aluminum-iron silicate; typically heated to produce low-density, worm-like pieces; used as loose fill insulation, and lightweight aggregate in acoustical plaster or concrete.

vermilion (18c–present) A yellowish red paint pigment composed of mercuric sulfide (HgS); originally mined as **cinnabar;** beginning ca. 9c primarily manufactured from a mixture of mercury and sulfur; color varieties include Chinese vermilion, English vermilion, Dutch vermilion, and French vermilion. See also **American vermilion.**

Vermont marble Any variety of the white, blue-gray, or greenish gray **marble** quarried in Vermont. Also known as **Shelburne marble.** See also **Winooski marble.**

vernacular building A building built without being designed by an **architect** or someone with similar formal training; often based on traditional or regional forms.

vernacular landscape The portion of a **cultural landscape** created without design intent or designed by someone without formal training.

versed sine The **rise** of an arch, from the spring line to the highest point of the intrados.

Verte Island stone A red, hard **sandstone** quarried on Verte Island, Lake Superior.

vertical grain The wood **grain** pattern of distinct parallel light and dark lines running along the length of a board or panel; formed by wood cut so that the annual rings are oriented approximately perpendicular to the widest face; found in **quarter sawn** and **rift sawn** lumber and the center board from a log that is **plain sawn.** Also known as **comb grain, edge grain, straight grain.**

vertical gutter (pre-19c) A roof **valley** lined with lead or terra-cotta tiles. See also **gutter board, three-point gutter, valley board.**

vertical-lift bridge A **drawbridge** with a center section that opens by sliding upwards.

vertical log house A house with exterior walls constructed of a series of log posts installed with 2–6 inches between them and filled with chinking; some late 18c–early 19c examples of oak or cedar logs with **boussilage** chinking remain in the middle Mississippi valley between St. Louis and St. Genevieve, Missouri; types include **poteaux-sur-sole, poteaux-en-terre.**

vertical plank frame The exterior wall and structural support for the upper level and roof of a building constructed of vertical plank sheathing; the ends of upper floor joists are mortised directly into the planks; in areas such as Canada, New England, and Ohio, 2-inch-thick planks were rabbeted into a sill timber, and sometimes mortised and tenoned; later examples omit the heavy corner posts, and may be simply nailed together and/or omit the sill; primarily built pre-WWI, some one-story examples built as late as the 1930s. Also known as **board frame, box frame.** See also **boxing, plank frame.**

vertical sash A window sash that slides up and down; used in **double hung window, single hung window.**

vesica Same as **vesica piscis.**

vesica piscis A decorative, oval panel with pointed top and bottom, formed by the intersection of two segmental moldings; typically a glory surrounding an illustration of the members of the Christian Holy Trinity or the Blessed Virgin; from the Latin for "fish bladder," which it somewhat resembles; the term was first used by Albrecht Dürer (1471–1528). Also known as **vesica.**

vestiary (pre-19c) **1.** A changing room, or wardrobe. **2.** Same as **vestibule.**

vestible (18c) Same as **vestibule.**

vestibule, (18c) **vestible** **1.** (19c–present) A relatively small enclosed space between the outer and inner doors leading to a lobby or hall; used as an air lock to reduce drafts and loss of conditioned air. Also known as **vestiary.** See also **wind porch. 2.** (late 18c–present) An **antechamber** that is also an entrance lobby. **3.** (pre-19c) A narthex, porch, or other semienclosed space adjacent to a building entrance.

vestry **1.** A room in a church were the sacred vessels and vestments are kept; typically adjoins the choir. Also known as **sacristy. 2.** A changing room for the clergy; adjoins the chancel. See also **choir vestry, vestiary. 3.** (19c–present) A chapel or Sunday school room attached to a church, especially a nonliturgical church. **4.** (late 17c–present) A room used for the administrative meetings of the vestry of an Anglican or Episcopalian church; may be within the church or in a nearby **vestry house.**

vestry house (late 17c–present) A building used as a **vestry** (sense 4).

viability study See **economic viability, feasibility study.**

viaduct An elevated **structure,** supported on a series of arches, piers or trestles, that carries a roadway or railway over a valley or other depression. See also **terreplein, trestle.**

Victorian (late 19c–present) Any product or style used during the reign of Queen Victoria, 1837–1901; architectural styles of the period include **Eastlake style, Gothic Revival, High Victorian Gothic, Italianate, Queen Anne style, Renaissance Revival style, Richardsonian Romanesque.**

Victorian Gothic Same as **High Victorian Gothic.**

Victoria stone A type of **cast stone** first manufactured in 1868.

Vienna lake A transparent, wine colored paint colorant composed of organic dye mixed with alum or tin; organic component originally brazelein dye from South American brazilwood, sapanwood, or parnambue; replaced with **aniline color** late 19c; protected with varnish; a fugitive color used only on interiors. See also **lake color.**

Vierendeel truss A steel open web truss composed of rectangular panels with rigid joints between all the members and no diagonal members; invented 1896 by M. Vierendeel.

view **1.** What can be seen from a particular place or direction, especially a **landscape.** See also **prospect.** **2.** A graphic or photographic representation of what can be seen from a particular place. See also **landscape.**

viga A peeled log roof rafter in **adobe** construction, typically exposed to view from below, and often projecting outside the exterior wall; may support **cedros, latias,** or bricks. See also **canale, latia.**

vignette, vinette **1.** A running grapevine ornament, typically composed of a wavy stem with leaves, tendrils, and bunches of grapes. See also **vineyard.** **2.** Interlaced French style iron scrollwork; typically the bars have a square cross section and occasional right-angle offsets; common on balconets and entrance canopy supports of late 19c–early 20c classical work in the **beaux-arts** tradition.

villa **1.** (19c–WWII) A large country or suburban house; commonly includes formal gardens. **2.** (pre-19c) A country estate with a mansion with a formal garden, surrounded by farm land, out buildings, and countryside; from the Italian *villa rustica,* a term in use since Roman times.

village A small group of houses and related facilities surrounded by countryside; typically smaller than a **township, town,** or **city.**

villa park (19c) A **suburb** with large houses for the wealthy.

Vinalhaven granite A gray, even-textured, fine-grained **granite** quarried in the vicinity of Vinalhaven, Maine; used for building stone.

vinette Same as **vignette.**

vineyard An **ornamental cast-iron** pattern in the stylized form of intertwined vines with grapes and leaves; originated early 19c by artisans of Louis XV. See also **vignette.**

vinyl **1.** (19c–present) The chemical radical CH_2CH. **2.** (late 20c) Any of the plastics containing CH_2CH, such as vinyl chloride; typically tough, shiny, and flexible; used for a variety of building materials, including resilient flooring, siding, windows, and ornamental work.

vinyl asbestos tile A **resilient flooring** tile composed of vinyl resins reinforced with asbestos fibers, plus clay-based inert fillers and pigment; manufactured mid–late 20c; typically 9 × 9 or 12 × 12 inches square and 1/16 to 1/8 inch thick. See also **vinyl tile.**

vinyl paint (late 20c) Any of several types of **water-base paint** containing **vinyl.** See also **latex paint.**

vinyl tile A **resilient flooring** tile composed of polyvinyl chloride resin plus clay-based inert fillers and pigment; manufactured mid–late

20c; typically 9 × 9 or 12 × 12 inches square and 1/16 to 1/8 inch thick. See also **sheet vinyl, vinyl asbestos tile.**

violet brass A ductile **brass** alloy of copper and approximately 0.5 percent zinc.

violet oxide of iron A violet iron oxide **pigment** used to tint mortar.

virge (pre-20c) Same as **verge.**

Virginia cabin (pre-19c Chesapeake region) A crudely built, one-room **log cabin;** typically with round logs, no windows, a wood chimney, and a **cabin roof.**

Virginia house (late 17c–18c Chesapeake region) A **clapboard house;** may have a groundsill or **post in the ground** framing.

Virginia make fence Same as **worm fence.**

Virginian cypress (19c) Same as **bald cypress.**

Virginian juniper Same as **eastern red cedar.**

Virginian pine (18c) Same as **longleaf pine.**

Virginia rail fence Same as **worm fence.**

vise (pre-20c) A stone **spiral stair** with a solid newel.

visor roof (20c) A relatively small section of roof that projects on brackets from a flat wall surface; used in the **Mission style** below a parapet.

vista, (pre-19c) **visto** A distant view, especially when focused by parallel elements such as a formal garden, a lane bounded by trees, or the axial components of architecture; often further defined, or terminated, by a statue or fountain; commonly used in **Beaux-Arts** design. See also **eyecatcher.**

visto (pre-19c) Same as **vista.**

visual pollution A unpleasant view of a **cultural landscape;** often caused by advertising signs and/or buildings, structures, or activities that obscure a historic or scenic setting.

vitreous **1.** Having a glasslike quality. **2.** Same as **vitrified.**

vitreous enamel Same as **porcelain enamel.**

vitrified A clay material, such as brick or terracotta, fired to a glasslike consistency with the grains fused together and the pores closed. Also known as **vitreous.**

vitrified brick A type of brick that has been **vitrified** on all surfaces so that it is impervious to water; used for dampproof courses and paving.

vitrified sewer pipe Terra-cotta **sewer pipe** with a **salt glaze.** Also known as **vitrified soil pipe.**

vitrified soil pipe Same as **vitrified sewer pipe.**

vista

Vitrolite Panels formed of clear glass with colored glass laminated to one side; used as a wall veneer; common 1900–40. See also **Art Deco, Carrara glass, spandrel glass.**

Vitruvian In the style of architecture, or method of construction, recorded by Vitruvius, a 1c B.C. Roman architect and engineer who attempted to verbally define all of the components and rules of design in use at that time, in a series of 10 books, *De architectura;* beginning with 15c **Italian Renaissance** architect Alberti, translations of this treatise have been a reference for designers in classical styles.

Vitruvian opening A wall opening with jambs that slope inward toward the top; described by Vitruvius.

Vitruvian scroll A molding band pattern in the form of continuous, interlocked, S-shaped scrolls; typically used on classical style friezes of the composite order. Also known as **running dog.** See also **wave molding.**

Vitruvius echinus Same as **quarter round.** See also **Vitruvian.**

vivo (pre-19c) Same as **shaft** of a column.

V-joint **1.** A projecting, tooled **mortar joint** that is V-shaped, with the outside edges of the V touching the corners of the adjacent masonry units; may also have a flattened top in the shape of a fillet. **2.** A recessed V-shaped groove in a mortar joint formed by the end of a mason's trowel. **3.** A V-shaped groove formed by adjoining chamfered edges on tongue-and-groove boards.

V-notch Same as **saddle notch.**

voltaic light (19c) Same as an **arc light.**

volute A carved spiral relief form, especially one of the spiral scroll ends with a center **eye** on top of the side of an Ionic, Composite or Corinthian capital. See also **helix, hem.**

voussoir One of the individual masonry units of an **arch** or **vault,** usually wedge-shaped with the abutting faces aligned with a radius of the center; typically uniform in size, except in Gothic style arches. See also **arch brick, keystone.**

voussoir brick Same as **arch brick** (sense 1).

voussure (pre-20c) Same as a **vault.**

V-roof Same as **gable roof.**

vulcanite A dark, hard, vulcanized rubber; used late 19c for ornaments and electrical equipment. Also known as **ebonite.**

vulcanite pavement A type of **asphalt concrete** paving composed of a mixture of asphalt, coal tar, and gravel aggregate.

wagon headed (pre-20c) Having a **barrel vault** ceiling.

wagon roof (pre-20c) Same as **barrel roof.** See also **wagon headed.**

wagon vault (pre-20c) Same as **barrel vault.**

wainscot, wainscoting, (18c) **wainscott,** (17c) **wainscoate** **1.** A wood covering of an interior wall; most often **paneling;** may cover all or the lower portion of the wall; originally a high-quality oak imported into England from Scotland for paneling (wain scot-oak). See also **modern wainscot.** **2.** (19c–present) A covering that encircles the lower part of an interior wall; may be any material, including tile, marble, and Lincrusta-Walton. See also **dado.**

wainscot color (18c) An oil-base paint that resembles the color of new oak, with pigments composed of white lead and umber.

waist A portion of a member that is less thick than the adjoining portions, such as a narrow part of a turned baluster, or the thinnest part of a stair, between the bottom of a riser and the soffit below.

Wakeman buff A light buff, fine-grained **sandstone** quarried in the vicinity of Wakeman, Ohio; has faint spider web markings.

wale, waler A horizontal timber that connects vertical **shoring** members. See also **sheeting and shoring.**

walk-in closet A **closet** that must be entered to retrieve the stored objects, especially a clothes closet.

walk-up apartment building A low-rise **apartment house** without elevator service; typically four stories or less in height. See also **garden apartment.**

wall A solid vertical enclosure of rooms, buildings, or outdoor spaces; types include **bearing wall, blank wall, cavity wall, curtain wall, fire wall, partition, partition wall, party wall, retaining wall, springing wall, sustaining wall.** See also **fence, framing, surface arcade.**

wall arcade Same as **surface arcade.**

wall board An inclined framing member attached to a wall enclosing a stair, and supporting the **wall string.**

wallboard, wall board (1906–present) A type of interior wall or ceiling finish applied in large sheets that can span between studs; types include **composition board, drywall, plywood.**

wall box Same as **beam box.**

wall bracket Same as **bracket** (sense 2).

wall cabinet A **kitchen cabinet** mounted on a wall above the floor; typically approximately 12 inches deep and placed above a **base cabinet** and **counter.**

wall clamp **1.** Same as **clamp.** **2.** Same as **wall tie.**

wall column A **column** that is fully or partially enclosed within a wall.

wall cornice A **cornice** at the top of a masonry wall.

wall dormer A **dormer window** with its front wall flush with, and part of, the main building wall below.

Waller stone A buff or blue, medium fine-grained, even-bedded **sandstone** quarried in Scioto County, Ohio; easily worked and carved.

wall garden A dry laid stone wall with plants in the crevices.

wall hanger A **beam hanger** that is partly embedded in a masonry wall and supports the end of a wood beam. See also **beam box.**

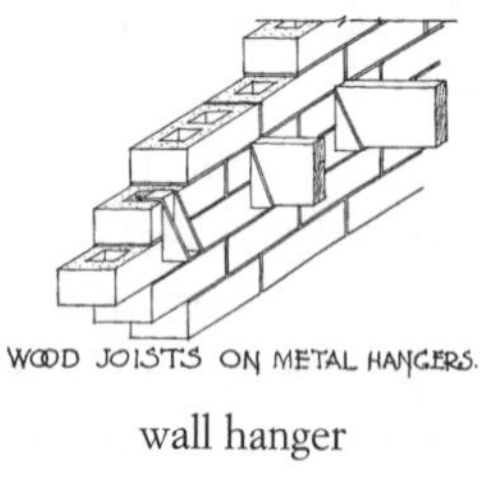

wall hanger

wall light A **light fixture** attached to a wall, or supported by a wall bracket; types include **bracket, sconce.**

wall molding (19c) A small **molding** installed in the angle between the edge of a casing trim, or other element perpendicular to a wall, and the wall, to hide the joint.

wall painting A decorative pattern or illustration painted directly on a plaster wall surface; types include **distemper, fresco, fresco secco.** See also **graffito.**

wallpaper (19c–present) A decorative wall and ceiling finish composed of printed sheets glued to the surface; wood pulp paper first used ca. 1850; may also be gilded, bronzed, or embossed. Also known as **paper hangings.** See also **anaglypta, Lincrusta-Walton.**

wall piece **1.** A decorative painting designed for a particular location. **2.** Same as **wallpiece.**

wallpiece, wall piece **1.** A vertical timber attached to a wall as the upper bearing of a **raker.** **2.** Same as **pendant post.** Also known as **wall plate.**

wall plate **1.** Same as **top plate;** originally referred only to lumber along the top of a masonry wall that supported the foot of the rafters or other framing; types include **pole plate.** See also **plate.** **2.** Same as **sole plate.** **3.** Same as **wallpiece.** See also **wall board.** **3.** Same as a **bearing plate** recessed in a masonry wall.

wall rib, wall-rib A projecting rib of a **rib vault** that abuts a perimeter wall and is parallel to the main axis of the vault. Also known as **formeret, longitudinal rib.**

wall seat (18c) A built-in bench against an exterior wall, such as along the sides of a church. See also **banquette, window seat.**

wall shaft An **engaged column** or **colonette** that is supported by a corbel or bracket, and appears to support a vault rib, or clustered ribs, above it. See also **vaulting shaft.**

wall space A flat, plain, interior wall surface available for hanging pictures or other decorations, or placing furniture.

wall stone Any type of stone suitable for building masonry bearing walls. See also **building stone.**

wall string, wall stringer A **string** that is attached to a wall enclosing a staircase. See also **wall board.**

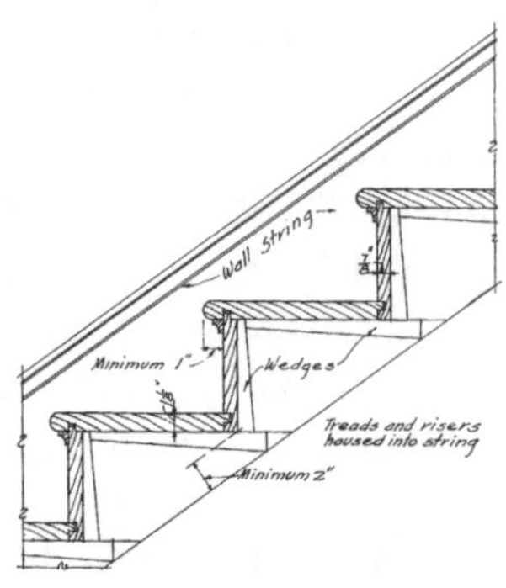

wall string

wall tie One of various metal devices for connecting the two parts of a cavity wall, or for attaching masonry **veneer** to its support, including **architectural terra-cotta, ashlar, brick veneer, ceramic veneer.** Also known as **wall clamp.** See also **cramp.**

wall tile Thin tile used as a wall finish; typically glazed ceramic tile, may also be terra-cotta, glass, plastic, or other material; may be square, rectangular, or other geometric shape; glued to the wall with mastic, or **mud set,** then the joints are grouted; types include **azulejo, Dutch tile.** See also **siding tile.**

wall tracery Relief **tracery** on an unpierced wall surface.

wall washer **1.** Same as **anchor plate. 2.** A recessed light fixture that bathes an adjacent wall with light.

walnut See **black walnut.**

wane A rounded edge on a sawn timber that was part of the original outside curve of the log. Also known as **bark edge, waney edge.**

waney edge Same as **wane.**

ward **1.** One of the divisions of patient rooms in a hospital; typically named for the type of treatment being administered, such as the **intensive care ward** or the **fever ward. 2.** A political and geographical subdivision of a local government; typically composed of multiple voting **precincts.**

wardrobe **1.** (pre-20c) A **walk-in closet** with shelves and hanging rods for storing clothes; originally the room where clothes were made and repaired. **2.** (pre-WWI) A cloakroom in a public building.

ward room (19c) A hall used for meetings with residents of a city ward.

wardroom (pre-19c) Same as **wardrobe** (sense 1).

warehouse A **building** for the storage of commercial products; often includes a **counting room;** during the colonial period, sometimes a room within a house; types include **inspection house, rolling house, tobacco house.** Also known as **bale house.** See also **store.**

warming See **heating.**

warming closet A compartment heated by pipes connected to a **water back** or **boiler;** used to keep food and plates warm.

warped Having an undesired twisted or bent surface, especially wood; types include **bow, crook, cup, wind;** warping of wood is caused by changes in its moisture content.

Warren girder Same as **Warren truss.**

Warren truss A truss with horizontal top and bottom chords, vertical ties, and diagonal struts and ties sloped alternately toward and away from the center. Also known as **single triangular truss, Warren girder, zigzag truss.**

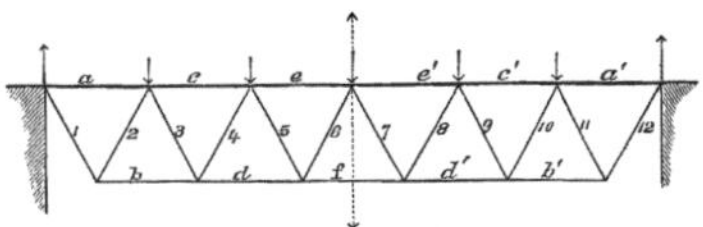

Warren truss

wash A sloped top surface of an exterior building element, such as a coping or window sill, designed to shed water.

washbasin Same as **basin** or **lavatory.**

washboard (pre-20c) Same as **baseboard.**

washbowl, wash bowl (pre-WWI) **1.** Same as **lavatory** (senses 2 and 3). **2.** Same as **laundry tray.**

wash coat A thin coat of plaster on masonry. See also **stucco.**

washed brick A poor-quality brick that was exposed to rain before firing. See also **salmon brick.**

washer **1.** A flat disk with a center hole used to increase the bearing area of bolts, tie rods, and similar devices; typically metal; types include cast iron, cast iron ribbed, cast iron beveled, square steel plate, circular pressed steel, malleable iron, **socket washer, triangular washer.** See also **anchor plate. 2.** A torus-shaped device with various cross sections, used to seal plumbing valves and other mechanical devices; may be rubber, leather, or other flexible substances. **3.** A plumbing outlet pipe for a water tank that is plugged when not in use.

wash gilding A bright gilt finish produced by heating metal coated with an amalgam of mercury and gold until the mercury is driven off, leaving a pure gold coating; used on fixtures and hardware. Also known as **water gilding.** See also **water silvering.**

washhouse, (19c) **wash-house,** (18c) **wash house** (18c–present) A building used for washing laundry, especially an outbuilding on a plantation, farm, ranch, or similar location. See also **laundry, water cabin.**

Washington cedar (19c) Same as **redwood.**

wash-out closet (pre-WWI) A **water closet** plumbing fixture with a single-piece bowl and trap.

wash-out closet

washroom **1.** (pre-19c) A room used for washing laundry. **2.** (19c–present) A place for washing the hands and face, especially in a public place or work place; typically combined with one or more water closet fixtures, and sometimes with a locker room and/or showers. Also known as **lavatory, toilet room.**

wash stand (19c) Same as **lavatory** (sense 3); originally a freestanding piece of furniture supporting a basin.

wash tray Same as **laundry tray, laundry tub.**

washtub Same as **laundry tub.**

waste gate A large valve that releases surplus water from a dam or reservoir. See also **waste weir, sash gate.**

waste pipe A **drain pipe** that carries the outflow of a sink, tub, or floor drain. See also **soil pipe.**

waste preventer (19c) A **ball cock** used in a water closet tank to prevent overflow.

waste stack Same as **soil stack.**

waste trap Same as **trap** (sense 1).

waste weir The channel or conduit that carries the outflow of surplus water stored behind a dam; typically the flow is regulated by a large gate valve; may be a **canal, spillway,** or entirely enclosed.

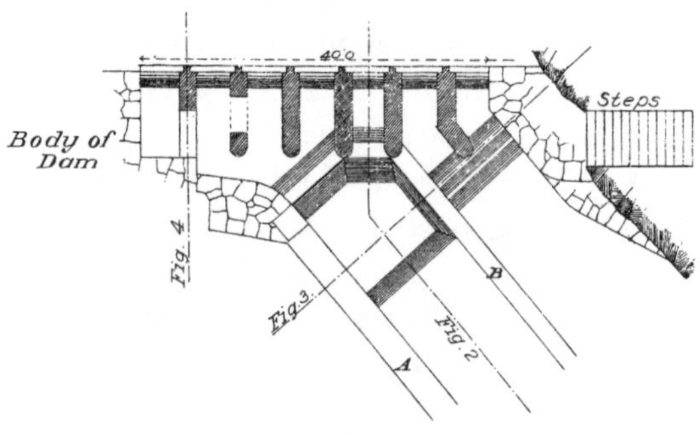

waste weir

waste well Same as **leaching cesspool.**

watch box Same as **sentry box.**

watchhouse, (pre-20c) **watch house** **1.** A shelter for a night watchman. See also **guardhouse. 2.** (pre-19c) A guardhouse with a lockup for prisoners.

watch tower An elevated structure of any type used by lookouts; may be a separate structure, or rise above the other portions of a building or wall.

water back A cast-iron water heater in the form of a box located at the back, and inside, the firebox of a wood or coal kitchen stove; used ca. 1830–mid-20c, typically in conjunction with a **range boiler.** See also **water front.**

water-base paint Any **paint** that uses water as a **thinner** or part of the **vehicle;** types include **acrylic paint, calcimine, casein paint, latex paint, tempera, whitewash.** See also **water color.**

water blasting A type of **blast cleaning** using a pressurized stream of water.

water board (18c) A **water table** (sense 1) with a distinct flat bevel.

water boiler A **boiler** that heats water directly, rather than boiling it; used for a hot-water heating system and/or producing domestic hot water.

water cabin (West Indies) A small **outbuilding** for washing dishes and bathing. See also **wash-house.**

water cement Same as **hydraulic cement.**

water closet **1.** (late 18c–present) A small room in which a flush toilet fixture is located. **2.** (late 19c–present) A toilet fixture for human waste that is flushed by running water; types include **hopper closet, siphon water closet, washdown closet, wash-out closet;** invented by Thomas Crapper, a London plumber. See also **earth closet.**

water color Paint that uses water as the **solvent;** types include **calcimine** and **distemper.** See also **water-base paint.**

water front **1.** A **water back** located in the front of a stove. **2.** The part of a city, or piece of property, that adjoins a body of water.

water gas A hydrogen-rich lighting gas manufactured by passing superheated steam through anthracite coal or petroleum; replaced most **coal gas** systems by 1890; superseded by natural gas.

water closet (sense 2)

water gate **1.** A device for controlling the flow of water, as at a dam, canal, or **water wheel,** or a **gate valve** on a water main. See also **lock paddle, sash gate, waste gate.** **2.** A gate in a fence or wall that controls access to a body of water. See also **water stairs.**

water gauge, water gage A clear, vertical glass tube connected to a boiler to show the water level inside.

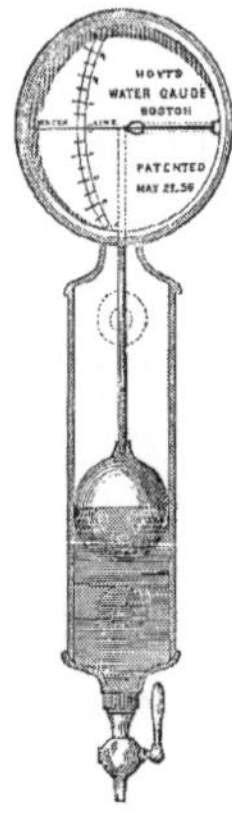

water gauge

water gilding Same as **wash gilding** or **water silvering.**

water glass, waterglass A glassy compound composed of sodium silicate or potassium silicate, or a mixture of both, known as **double water glass;** may be a solid mass, powdered, or dissolved in water to form a syrupy liquid; used as a fixative for **stereochrome** painting, hardening cast stone, and fireproofing fabrics. Also known as **liquid glass, soluble glass.**

water heater A device that produces hot water; typically includes an integral storage tank after WWI; types include **gas heater, range boiler, steam injection heater, water back, water boiler.** See also **boiler.**

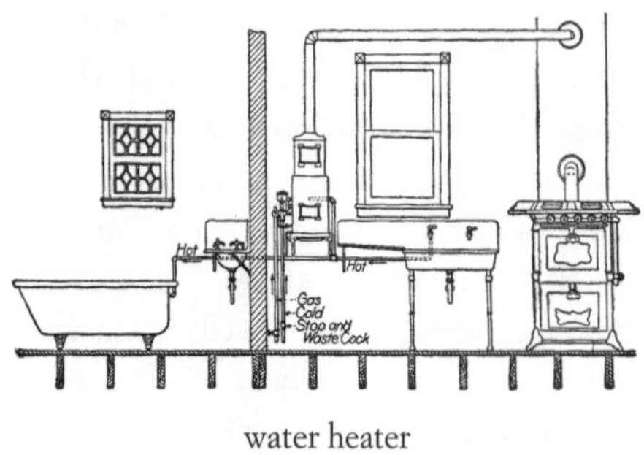

water heater

water joint A watertight joint, such as a **saddle joint.**

water joint hinge A **hinge** that is not affected by the action of rust; typically two connected eyes.

water leaf (18c–present) A Classical Greek ornament in the shape of a series of stylized lotus plants; used to decorate a projecting double curved molding; may have simple, smooth surfaces or be highly enriched; types include **lesbian leaf, water leaf and dart.** See also **water leaf capital.**

water leaf and dart A **water leaf** molding with a stylized dart between adjoining lotus plants.

water leaf capital A 12c Gothic style capital with **water leaf** ornamentation; a broad, smooth, double curved leaf covers each corner.

water lime Same as **hydraulic lime.**

water main A **main** supplying water; of various types of **water pipe,** including **log pipe, cast iron,** or **concrete pipe.**

water maple Same as **red maple.**

water mill Any type of **mill** with machinery operated by water power; typically rotary power is supplied by a **water wheel;** related structures may include **mill pond, mill race.**

water motor Any type of engine driven by water flowing through pipe, such as a **turbine,** or pressure on a piston head. See also **water pump.**

water nose (20c) The shape of the edge of a sill formed by cutting a quarter round **drip** groove in the bottom.

water pipe Any type of **pipe** used to supply water; types include **black pipe, block-tin pipe, brass pipe, cast-iron pipe, concrete pipe, copper pipe, lead pipe, log pipe, PVC pipe, wrought-iron pipe.** See also **drain pipe.**

water plug Same as **hydrant.**

waterproofing A coating or membrane applied to a surface, such as a foundation wall, to prevent the intrusion of water under pressure; materials used include **asphalt, asphaltic felt, tar,** and various synthetic membranes such as **EPDM.** See also **dampproofing, wearing coat.**

water pump Any type of pump for moving water; may be operated by electricity, gas, gasoline, hand, steam, or water; types include **booster pump, hydraulic ram, sump pump;** may be used to fill a reservoir or increase the pressure of water supplied by a main. See also **water motor.**

water ram Same as **hydraulic ram.**

water ramp A series of stepped ornamental pools with water flowing down them.

water repellent A surface treatment, especially of masonry or concrete, that resists water penetration.

water seal Same as **seal** (sense 2).

water service The **service pipe** that connects the water main to a particular building; heavy lead or galvanized wrought iron through the 19c, then gradually supplanted by copper; plastic pipe is occasionally used late 20c.

water shoot (pre-20c) An architectural feature that sheds water, such a **drip** or **water table.**

water silvering A bright silver finish produced by heating metal coated with an amalgam of mercury and silver until the mercury is driven off, leaving a pure, thin, silver coating; used on fixtures and hardware. Also known as **water gilding.** See also **wash gilding.**

water smoked **Brick** that have been heated slowly in a kiln to drive off the moisture before firing.

waterspout, (pre-20c) **water spout** An outflow pipe from a gutter; may be a short section that directs stormwater away from the building, or a **downspout** or **leader** that carries the flow to the ground, cistern, or sewer. See also **gargoyle.**

water stair, water stairs A flight of steps that leads down into the water for boarding boats.

water-struck brick **Soft mud brick** formed in molds slicked by water before the clay is inserted; common in New England before 1840. Also known as **slick brick, slop brick.** See also **sand-struck brick.**

water supply The entire system for providing **domestic water;** elements may include **reservoir, main, corporation cock, service pipe, pressure regulator, booster pump, riser, house tank, stop cock, drop feed, faucet.**

water table **1.** The projecting decorative molding of a masonry wall at the point where the wall thickens, often just below the first-floor joists. Also known as **water board, weather table.** See also **ledgement, earth table. 2.** The underground level at which the earth is saturated with water.

water tank A **tank** for storing water for drinking, bathing, or firefighting; types include **cistern, house tank.**

water tap **1.** Same as **faucet** (sense 2). **2.** The process of installing a **corporation cock.**

water tower A structure that supports an elevated water tank; used to create sufficient pressure to distribute the water through the mains and pipes of the system; originally in the form of a tower with bearing walls, may be any kind of structure.

water tube A horizontal, cylindrical, water-filled metal tube in a steam boiler that is heated by the combustion gases. Also known as **boiler tube.**

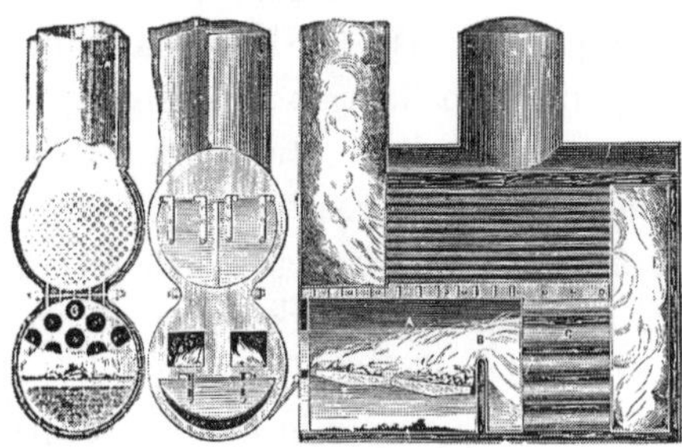

water tube

water turbine A **turbine** using water to rotate the wheel; typically in a horizontal position and held in a **penstock** supplied by a **flume.**

water valve A valve that controls the flow of water, especially in a pipe. See also **gate valve, waste valve.**

water varnish A **varnish** composed of gum dissolved in water, such as a type of **lac varnish.**

water well See **well.**

water wheel A large, cylindrical frame, with a series of vanes or buckets around the perimeter, that is rotated by flowing water; used to provide power, such as for a **water mill;** types include **breast wheel, overshot wheel, lift**

water wheel, millwheel, undershot wheel. See also **turbine, water motor.**

water wing A wall that projects along an embankment from a bridge pier.

waterwork Any structure built in water, or built to conduct or to protect from water; types include **aqueduct, canal, dam, dock, levee, lift-lock, mill race, pier, reservoir, seawall, tank.** See also **waterworks.**

waterworks, (pre-19c) **waterwork** **1.** A system to collect and distribute water to multiple buildings, especially in a city or town. See also **water supply, waterwork.** **2.** A water **pumping station** and/or treatment plant.

wattle and daub, wattle and dab Wall construction composed of **wattling** that is covered on both sides with a clay mud and straw daub; often plastered as a finish coat; used in some early colonial buildings as **nogging.**

wattling, (18c) **watling** Panels formed by vertical poles interwoven horizontally with thin branches, vines, or similar flexible plant material; similar to wickerwork; used for fences and **wattle and daub.**

wave A decorative motif in the form of parallel sine waves. See also **undé.**

wave molding **1.** A molding with an edge, or relief, of repetitive double curves in the form of breaking waves. Also known as **undé.** See also **scallop, Vitruvian scroll.** **2.** A linear molding composed of a convex molding between concave moldings; used in the Decorated Style.

wave scroll Same as **Vitruvian scroll.**

wavy grain A curly wave **grain** pattern on the surface of some sawn hardwoods, such as birch and mahogany.

wax paint A quick drying **paint** composed of wax dissolved in a solvent; typically **white wax** dissolved in turpentine resin and distilled turpentine; does not discolor like oil paint, but does collect dirt; used for illustrative painting on canvas, plaster, stone, or wood, such as the murals by LaFarge at the Boston Public Library and the Pennsylvania State Capitol.

wax varnish Any **varnish** composed of wax dissolved in a solvent.

wearing coat A layer of parging applied over waterproofing on the outside of a foundation wall.

weather The amount of exposed length on top of a shingle; measured along the slope. See also **lap.**

weather back A coating on the interior face of a wall with a material to resist water and/or wind penetration; materials used include **plaster, sheathing paper, tar.**

weatherbeaten A general descriptive term indicating deterioration of a structure due to exposure to the elements. See also **weathered, weather tint.**

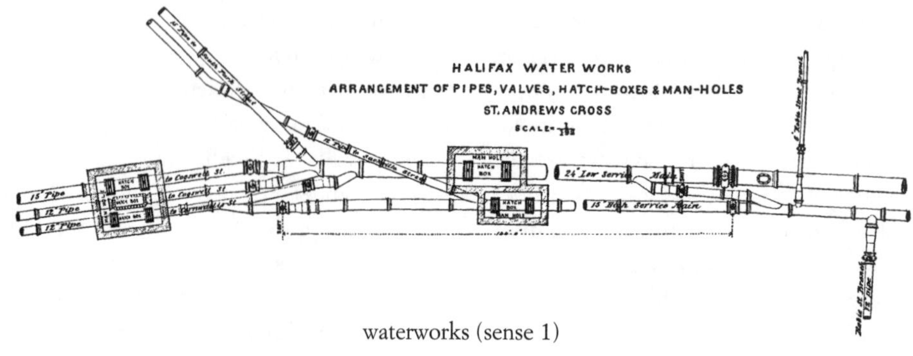

waterworks (sense 1)

weatherboard **1.** One of a series of horizontal boards used as an exterior wall covering. See also **weatherboarding.** **2.** A board at the top of an exterior wall that covers the joint at an overhanging eave or verge.

weatherboarding, (pre-19c) **weather boarding** A series of **weatherboards** used for exterior **siding,** and sometimes **roofing,** of a building; most often refers to **colonial siding,** may also be **clapboard, drop siding,** or flush **sheathing.**

weatherbreak (Southern U.S.) Same as **windbreak.**

weathercock, weather-cock, (pre-19c) **weather cock** Same as **weather vane;** from the common practice of having the Christian symbol of the crowing cock mounted on top.

weather contact A leakage of electricity due to wet weather. See also **weather cross.**

weather cross A short between electric wires due to wet weather or dampness. See also **weather contact.**

weather door (19c) Same as **storm door.**

weathered **1.** Deteriorated or aged due to exposure to the weather, for example shingles that have turned grey from exposure; agents include sun, rain, snow, humidity, wind, temperature changes, pollutants, moving water. See also **weatherbeaten, weather tint.** **2.** Having the top surface sloped to shed water. See also **drip, hood molding, water table.**

weathered joint Same as **weather joint.**

weathered oak Same as **fumed oak.**

weathering **1.** A projection from the face of a wall, with an inclined top to shed water and protect the wall below; types include **hood molding, water table, weathering stone.** **2.** The process of becoming **weathered** (sense 2).

weathering stone A projecting stone block with a sloped top designed to drip rain water away from a structure; typically placed between the top of the **cornice** and the bottom of the **balustrade,** or at the top of a **water table.**

weather joint A masonry **mortar joint** that slopes in toward the top and is tangent to the top corner of the bottom masonry unit; made with the mason's trowel, rather than a jointing tool. Also known as **weathered joint.**

weather molding Any **molding** with the top surface sloped to shed water, especially over a window or door.

weatherproof A general term indicating ability to withstand **weathering** (sense 2) without damage or loss of function.

weather slating Slates installed as **siding.** Also known as **slate boarding, slate hanging.**

weatherstrip, weatherstripping A narrow, compressible band used between the edge of a door or window and the jambs, sill, and head to seal against air and water infiltration; of various forms including felt, spring metal, plastic foam, and wood edged with rubber; types include interlocking and friction.

weather table Same as **water table** (sense 1).

weather tiling A series of thin terra-cotta tiles used in place of slates on a wall or roof; the butts are often shaped to create a decorative pattern, such as **fishscale** or **diamond.** Also known as **tile hanging.** See also **siding tile, tile veneer.**

weather tint Coloring caused by weathering, especially when considered to have a pleasing appearance.

weather vane A metal device mounted on a roof, with a vertical rod with a horizontal vane that is rotated by the wind; typically the vane is in the stylized form of an arrow that points towards the direction of the wind; may have crossarms below the vane indicating the cardinal compass points; often of decorative form;

types include **weathercock.** Also known as **vane.**

weave shed A large industrial **building** housing textile-weaving machines. See also **weaving house.**

weaving house (pre-19c) A building used for the making of textiles and for living quarters, especially on a rural plantation. See also **spinning house, weave shed.**

web **1.** The vertical center portion of an I-beam or similar structural shape. See also **flange.** **2.** The portion of a **truss** between the **top chord** and **bottom chord.**

web wall Same as **cobweb rubble.**

wedge See **foxtail wedge.**

wedge coping Same as **featheredge coping.**

wedged stair A **stair** with treads and risers fastened to a housed stringer, with slightly V-shaped rabbets, by wedges.

weeper A statue or relief sculpture in the form of a crying mourner; used on tombs.

weep hole An opening which allows moisture in the interior of construction to drain to the outside; used in masonry cavity walls, window frames, and curtain walls. Also known as **vent hole.**

weeping willow An ornamental **willow** tree with drooping branches; a symbol of mourning, especially in the 19c.

weight See **sash weight.**

weight-on roof Shingles held in place by the weight of a series of horizontal poles tied together on both sides of the ridge, or by stones.

weld A metal joint produced by **welding.**

welded wire mesh A steel **mesh** produced by cold-drawn steel wires laid in a rectangular grid at the overlaps; used as **reinforcing** in concrete construction second half 20c.

welding The process of connecting two pieces of metal by fusing the metal at the point of contact; typically done by hammering the heated, overlapping, tapered ends of metal sheets before the end of the 19c; generally replaced by **arc welding** and **gas welding** by mid-20c. See also **brazing.**

weld iron (late 19c–present) Same as **wrought iron;** due to its ability to be welded by hammering.

weld steel (late 19c–present) Same as **puddle steel;** named due to its ability to be welded by hammering.

well **1.** A pit or shaft excavated below the groundwater level as a source of fresh water; typically lined to keep the sides from collapsing; components may include **well casing, well curb, wellhead, well house.** See also **absorbing well, dry well.** **2.** A vertically oriented space within a building passing through two or more stories. Also known as **wellhole.** See also **stairwell.**

well brick A wedge-shaped brick used as **well casing.**

well casing A pipe, or other material, used to line a well. Also known as **well tube.** See also **well curb, well brick.**

well curb **1.** The low wall around the top of a well to prevent people or animals from falling into it; typically of wood in rural areas and stone in urban locations. See also **wellhead.** **2.** The wood, masonry, or concrete **well casing** inside a well hole to retain the earth.

wellhead A protective **structure** over the top of a well; typically includes a **well curb** and a roof, and often a water drawing mechanism, such as a **bucket and pulley,** is included. **2.** A naturally flowing spring. See also **well house.**

wellhole Same as **well** (sense 2).

well house An enclosed structure built over the top of a well, such as those used to cool dairy products on a farm; may contain a **water pump** and be multistoried to allow raising and lowering the well casing pipes. See also **well-head.**

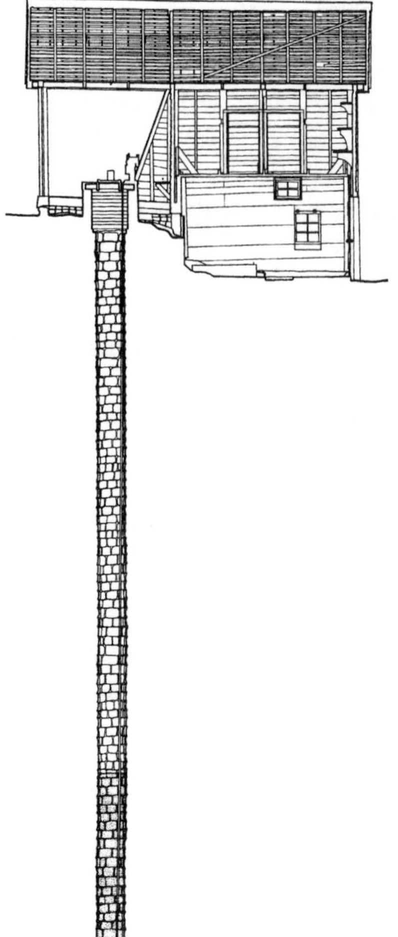

well house

well staircase **1.** A spiral stair with a hollow newel. **2.** A winding stair with an open well in the middle.

well trap A plumbing trap with a well, such as a **bell trap.**

well tube Same as **well casing.**

Welsbach burner A gaslight burner with a glowing **lustre;** invented ca. 1885, common from 1890 until replaced by electricity. See also **gas burner.**

Welsh arch A small, flat **arch** composed of a pair of corbeled skewbacks supporting a keystone; typically spans less than 12 inches; not a true arch form.

Welsh chimney A **stick chimney** supported above the ground on poles.

Welsh groin A **groined vault** where one of the intersecting barrel vaults is lower than the other vault; typically semicircular in cross section; first used in Romanesque architecture. Also known as **underpitch groin, underpitch vault.**

Welsh lay (19c) A paving slate with dimensions of 3 × 2 feet.

Welsh slate A dark gray, fine-grained slate imported from Wales through mid-19c.

west coast hemlock Same as **western hemlock.**

Westerly granite A red and pink, fine-grained **granite** quarried in the vicinity of Westerly, Rhode Island.

western cedar A small **cedar** tree found along the U.S. Pacific coast; *Juniperus occidentalis.* Also known as **yellow cedar.** See also **western red cedar.**

western frame Same as **platform frame.**

western hemlock A **hemlock** tree with pale yellowish brown, strong, straight-grained, fine-textured heartwood with a narrow band of white sapwood; found in coastal areas from California to Alaska; used for lumber, sheathing, and interior millwork to the present; lumbering peaked in 1927; *Tsuga heterophylla.* Also known as **Pacific hemlock, west coast hemlock.**

western larch A large, deciduous softwood tree with reddish brown, hard, strong, heavy, fine-grained wood that is extremely durable in contact with soil; found in high mountain valleys of the upper Columbia river basin and southeastern British Columbia; used for lumber and millwork; lumbered primarily 1910–30, with the high point ca. 1920; *Larix occidentalis.* Also known as **tamarack.**

western oak A large **oak** tree found along the Pacific coast of North America; *Quercus garyana.* Also known as **California white oak.**

western red cedar An enormous softwood tree with reddish brown, straight grained, very soft, medium- to coarse-grained wood that splits easily; found in the Pacific Northwest from northern California to southern Alaska; very decay and insect resistant; used primarily for shingles, and also for lumber, poles, and exterior trim; *Thuja plicata.* Also known as **British Columbia cedar, giant cedar, Pacific red cedar.**

western white pine A tall **pine** tree with pale brown to white, straight-grained wood; found in the far western U.S. and Canada; peak production 1930; used for lumber and millwork; *Pinus monticola.* Also known as **white pine.**

western yellow pine Same as **ponderosa pine.**

westwork The construction surrounding the entrance of a medieval style church; typically includes a pair of steepled towers flanking an arched entrance doorway; term is derived from the western-facing entrances of all medieval churches. See also **east end.**

wet deposition The deposition of waterborne pollution on an exterior surface; includes **acid rain** and particles. See also **dry deposition.**

wet site **1.** An **archaeological site** that has been continuously submerged below water since the deposition of the **archaeological artifacts** and has naturally preserved organic materials, such as wood and fabric, that normally deteriorate quickly; requires specialized excavation and preservation techniques for the fragile materials. **2.** A construction site for a **waterwork** that is normally partly or completely submerged.

wet system A **sprinkler system** with the pipes full of water at all times. See also **dry system.**

Weymouth seam-face granite A mottled brown and golden yellowish green, fine-grained **granite** quarried in the vicinity of Weymouth, Massachusetts; easily splits into plane sheets.

WF-section Same as **wide flange beam.**

WF-shape Same as **wide flange beam.**

wharf A structure for the loading and unloading of boats; types include **pier** and **quay.** See also **landing.**

wheel tracery **Tracery** in the approximate shape of a spoked wheel. See also **wheel window.**

wheel window A large **rose window** with radiating mullions or **wheel tracery** in the shape of a spoked wheel. Also known as **Catherine wheel.**

Whipple truss (19c–present) A **truss** with rectangular panels with more than two posts, diagonal ties, and X-shaped counter bracing at the center panel; end panels may be triangular or rectangular; named for the American engineer Squire Whipple (1804–88). Also known as **Murphy truss.** See also **quadrangular truss.**

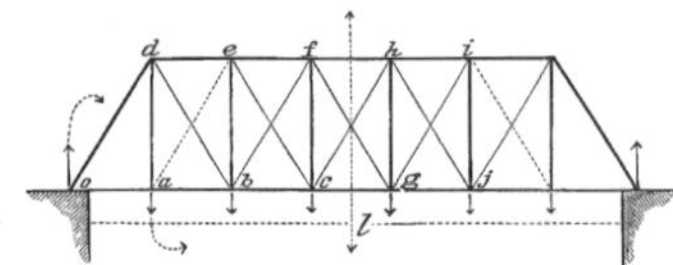

Whipple truss

whispering gallery A space covered with a vault or dome so that speech originating at one point of the space can easily be heard at another point; typically has an elliptical, or sometimes circular, cross section. See also **centrum phonicum, centrum phonicampticum, echo.**

white **1.** Having a surface that reflects the same color as the incident light. See also **pigment.** **2.** Without color, as in transparent or translucent materials, such as **white glass** or **white varnish.**

white amber Same as **spermaceti.**

white ant Same as **termite.**

white ash A hardwood tree with very light yellow, hard, close-grained wood that is tough, strong, and elastic; used for interior trim, sometimes as a substitute for oak; peak production in 1909; found throughout the eastern half of the U.S. and southeastern Canada; *Fraxinus americana.*

white birch Same as **paper birch.**

white brass A ductile **brass** alloy composed of copper and approximately 66 percent zinc.

white bronze A light-colored variety of **bronze** with a high tin content.

white cedar **1.** One of several large softwood trees with a fine-grained, straight, light-colored, soft wood; used for exterior siding, shingles, piers, interior trim; *Chamaecyparis lawsoniana* is found in the Pacific Northwest, *Chamaecyparis thyoides* is found in the eastern US and known as **juniper** in the southern U.S. **2.** Same as **American cypress.** See also **northern white cedar.**

white cement (20c) An iron-free Portland cement mixed with a white pigment; used to produce white mortar joints, and as a coating on brickwork.

white coat A polished **finish coat** composed of plaster made with lime putty, plaster of Paris, and marble dust or fine white sand. Also known as **white finish.**

white copper A white alloy of copper, especially **German silver.**

white finish Same as **white coat.**

white fir A softwood tree with white, moderately hard, moderately strong, straight-grained wood with knots; found on north slopes at moderate altitudes throughout western U.S.; not durable in contact with soil; used for house framing lumber, millwork, and sheathing; the small quantity lumbered peaked 1926; *Abies concolor.* See also **Douglas fir.**

White Freedley Same as **Freedley White.**

white glass **1.** A transparent glass that is nearly colorless. **2.** A translucent glass with a white tint. See also **obscure glass.**

white iron **1.** A hard, crystalline metal composed of iron and carbon; has a white or mottled color when fractured; used for manufacturing **wrought iron.** Also known as **forge-pig.** See also **gray iron.** **2.** Same as **tin-plate** iron. See also **black iron.**

white lead A highly opaque, white paint **pigment** composed of basic lead carbonate ($2PbCO_3Pb(OH)_2$); in pure form also known as **ceruse** or **flake white;** often mixed with hydrated lead oxide, typically in proportions of approximately 3:1; the most common oil-base paint pigment until ca. 1950, when it was outlawed in many jurisdictions due to the possibility of **lead poisoning.** Also known as **lead white.** See also **sublimed white lead, white lead and oil, white lead in oil.**

white lead and oil A white, linseed-oil-base paint composed of **white lead in oil** pigment and **linseed oil.**

white lead in oil A white pigment paste produced by grinding **white lead** in **linseed oil;** used to make **white lead and oil.**

white lime, (17c) **white lyme** **1.** Prepared lime for use in whitewashing. **2.** (pre-18c) Same as **whitewash.**

white limed (pre-18c) Whitewashed or plastered with lime.

white oak **1.** A large **oak** tree with light brown, hard, coarse-grained, extremely strong wood; attractively figured when quarter sawn; found throughout the eastern half of the U.S.; used for lumber, millwork, and flooring; lumbering production peaked 1920s; *Quercus alba.* **2.** Same as **swamp white oak.**

white oakum Same as **oakum.**

white pine 1. Same as **eastern white pine.** 2. Same as **western white pine.** 3. Same as **mountain pine.**

white shellac A clear, colorless **shellac** made from bleached lac dissolved in alcohol.

white spirit An oil paint thinner made from distilled petroleum; used as a substitute for **turpentine.**

white spruce 1. A **spruce** tree with pale yellowish white, soft, relatively weak, lightweight, stiff, straight-grained wood; found from northern New England and central states to Labrador, and west to Alaska; used for lumber, interior millwork, and pulpwood; *Picea glauca.* Also known as **blue spruce, spruce pine, eastern spruce, bog spruce, single spruce, swamp spruce.** 2. Same as **Engelmann spruce.** 3. (19c) A softwood tree; *Picea alba.*

white tombac A light-colored type of **brass** that includes arsenic. See also **Dutch metal, tombac.**

white turpentine Same as **American turpentine.**

white varnish (18c) A clear **amber varnish** composed of white amber (or mastic gum), oil of turpentine, and turpentine. Also known as **amber varnish, Venetian varnish.**

white walnut Same as **butternut.**

whitewash, whitewashing A surface coating applied as a creamy paste composed of **slaked lime** and water, and sometimes other ingredients such as salt, sugar, or whiting; most commonly used as an interior wall and ceiling finish before 19c, then commonly used on exterior wood, masonry, and concrete, or interior surfaces below grade; sometimes tinted with bluing, indigo, Indian red, lampblack, raw umber, or yellow ocher; varieties include **yeso.** Also known as **white lime.**

white wax 1. Same as **Chinese wax.** 2. Bleached beeswax. See also **spermaceti.**

whitewood, white wood, white-wood 1. Same as **poplar,** especially the wood of the **tulip tree.** 2. Any white or light-colored, fine-grained, easily worked wood similar to poplar.

whiting A finely ground, washed calcium carbonate powder made from chalk or limestone; used as a paint **pigment** extender, the base for **calcimine** paints, and a component of **composition** and **putty;** commonly imported into North America as **Paris white** or **Spanish whiting.**

whole pitch A gable roof **pitch** where the vertical **rise** equals the span, forming an angle with the horizontal of 63 degrees 30 minutes. See also **Gothic pitch.**

whorehouse Same as **brothel.**

wicket 1. A small door within a large **door** or gate. Also known as **pilot door.** 2. A small opening in a door for looking through, or passing food through. See also **vasistas.**

wide flange beam (20c) A steel **rolled beam** with an I-shaped cross section with wide, untapered flanges; used to increase the strength of a beam without increasing the depth. Also known as **WF-section, WF-shape.** See also **I-beam, H-column.**

wide gauge, wide gage Same as **broad gauge.**

widows walk A rooftop platform with an ornamental railing; from those on New England houses near the sea, used by captains' wives to look for returning ships; most often a deck on top of a mansard roof.

wigwam, wig-wam A Native American dwelling constructed of a wood framework covered with bark sheets or hides; most often dome-shaped in midwestern North America and oblong with an arched cross section in eastern North America.

wild black cherry Same as **black cherry.**

wilderness A portion of a formal garden that is designed and maintained to approximate, or symbolize, the natural condition; before 19c often with meandering paths through a dense grove of trees or a thicket.

Wilkerson sandstone A light gray, hard, medium-grained **sandstone** quarried in Pierce County, Washington; easily worked.

Williamsburg colors A set of pastel paint colors marketed since the 1920s as authentic Colonial era colors; later research indicates that the original paints generally had more intense color saturation.

willow Any tree or shrub of the genus *Salix;* types include **weeping willow, yellow willow.**

willow oak A moderately sized **oak** tree with reddish brown, heavy, strong, close-grained, knotty wood; found from eastern Texas to northern Florida, and along the Atlantic coast to Long Island; used for house framing lumber, millwork, and flooring; often marketed as **red oak;** *Quercus phellos.*

wind A **warped** twist in a wood member that was initially cut straight; rhymes with mind. Also known as **twist.** See also **out of wind.**

windbeam (pre-19c and Appalachian region) Same as a **collar beam.**

wind brace A diagonal brace between a principal rafter and a purlin in a **timber frame** roof; used to prevent movement of the frame due to wind loads.

windbreak, (19c) **wind-break** A fence, hedge, or similar device used to diminish the force of the wind; typically a line of evergreen trees planted adjoining a house or farm yard.

winder A **stair** step with a tread that is wider at one end; used for turning corners without a landing or for a **winding stair.**

wind filling Same as **beam filling.**

wind guard A **cowl** on top of a chimney.

winding stair Any **stair** composed entirely of winders; types include **geometrical stair, quarter winding, spiral stair.**

wind load The structural pressure on a building caused by the wind; may be a positive pressure caused by direct action, or a negative pressure caused by a pressure differential. Also known as **wind pressure.** See also **dead load, live load.**

windmill, (17c) **wyndemill** **1.** A **mill** powered by vanes turned by the wind; typically used for grinding grain; commonly in use until mid-19c, such as sugar cane mills in the West Indies; types include **post mill, smock mill. 2.** (19c–present) A tower structure with wind-powered vanes connected by a rotating shaft to a pump or generator; common on ranches and farms for pumping water and, 20c, generating electricity.

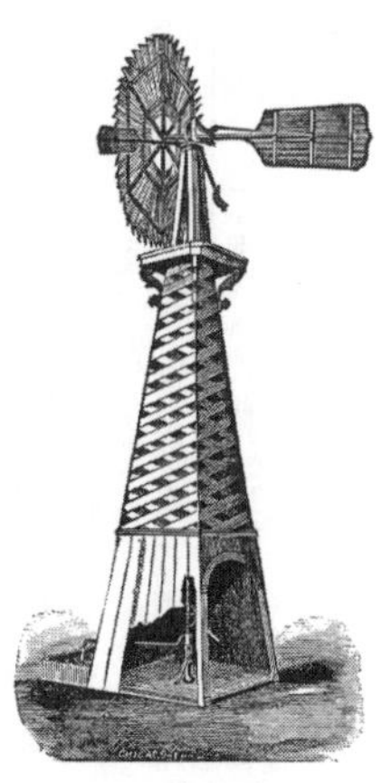

windmill (sense 2)

window An opening in an exterior wall to admit light and air, typically with glazing in a frame which can be opened; types include **awning window, blank window, casement window, clustered window, double hung, D-window, French casement, hit and miss window, hopper window, lancet window, lucarne, lunette, oculus, Palladian window, quarter round window, rose window, sash**

window, single sash, single hung, sliding window, store front, transom window, triple hung, wheel window; elements may include **back lining, came, elbow, fillister, glazing, head lining, jamb, jamb lining, meeting rail, mullion, muntin, pane, pulley stile, pulley box, rail, sash, sash lift, sash line, sash lock, sash pulley, sash weight, shutter, stile, stool, window back, window bars, window fastener, window frame, window screen, window sill, window glass, window lock, window pull, yoke;** from the Norse for "wind eye," a hole in the roof to let smoke escape; glazed windows were unknown before 5c. See also **clerestory, twelve over twelve.**

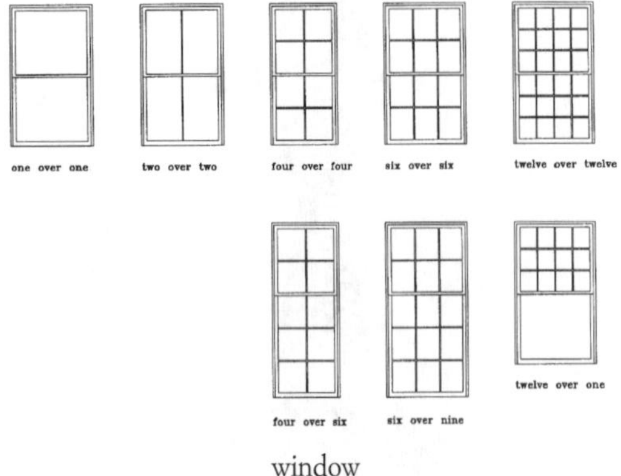

window

window back The interior finish on a wall breast below a window sill. See also **panelled back.**

window balance A spring that counterbalances the weight of a vertically sliding window. See also **sash weight.**

window bar **1.** Same as **muntin.** **2.** A movable wood or iron bar used to secure a shutter, or casement, in the closed position. **3.** (pre-WWI) An insect screen.

window bars A series of bars that keep one from entering, or leaving, through a window; vary from simple parallel vertical wood or metal bars to elaborate wrought-iron constructions. Also known as **window guard.** See also **grille.**

window board (pre-20c) Same as **stool.**

window box **1.** Same as **sash pocket.** **2.** A planting box outside a window.

window fastener Any type of hardware device used to hold a window sash in an open or closed position; types include **espagnolette, sash lock.**

window frame **1.** A wood or metal frame that holds the window **sash** in place and is set into a wall opening; members include **window head, window sill, window stile;** may be wood or metal; type includes **cased frame.** **2.** (before mid-19c) A wood framed wall opening to which the sash is directly attached; members include **window post.**

window glass Clear, smooth **glass** used for **glazing** ordinary windows; originally **crown glass,** then supplanted by **cylinder glass** ca. 1830, and then **float glass** 20c; typically ⅛ to 5/32 inch thick; varieties include **single-strength glass, double-strength glass.** Also known as **sheet glass.**

window guard (pre-20c) Same as **window bars.**

window head The horizontal cross piece that connects the stiles at the top of a **window frame.** Also known as **yoke.**

window hood See **hood mold.**

window lead **1.** A lead **came.** **2.** (pre-19c) A cast lead **sash weight.**

window-let, windo-let (19c) A small window.

window lift Same as **sash lift.**

window lock A hardware device that locks a window in a closed or partly open position; most often a **sash lock.**

window mirror A small mirror, or mirrors, fastened outside a window, so that a person inside can see a door or street below. Also known as **busybody.**

window pane An individual **pane** of glass in a window; types include **suspended light.**

window post One of a pair of vertical members in a **wood frame** building that form the sides of the opening for a **window frame;** may be a solid timber or double 2 × 4s.

window pull **1.** Same as **sash lift.** **2.** A plate with a recess mounted on a high window sash; used to open and close the window by a long pole with a metal hook on the end.

window sash Same as **sash.**

window screen **1.** A frame filled with **screening;** used to prevent insects from entering a building through the ventilation openings, such as windows and louvers. **2.** A latticework covering on a window that shields the interior from view.

window seat **1.** A bench built into a bay window, or similar recess. **2.** (pre-19c) A built-in bench that projects from the wall below a window. See also **banquette, wall seat.**

window shield The ornamental exterior wood trim at the top inside corners of a window; typically in the form of a quarter circle or triangle, often with fan-shaped fluting; common in **Queen Anne style** frame buildings.

window shutter See **shutter.**

window sill The horizontal **sill** at the base of a window; the term refers to both the interior and exterior portions, and to the base of a metal or wood **window frame,** as well as the projecting brick or stone on which the frame rests; often has a sloped top.

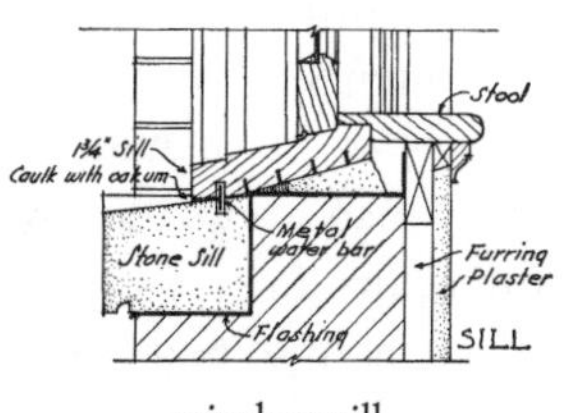

window sill

window soil (pre-19c) Same as **window sill.**

window stile One of the vertical sides of a **window frame.**

window stool **1.** Same as **stool.** **2.** A shelf forming the top of an interior window sill. See also **window seat.**

wind porch An enclosed vestibule that provides protection from drafts at the entrance to a building; often temporarily installed during the winter months.

wind pressure Same as **wind load.**

wind shake A **shake** (sense 2) that has been caused by the wind.

windshield survey A limited exterior **survey** of historic buildings and structures, sometimes conducted by driving through an area in a car; used to prepare a preliminary **inventory** of historic properties or other planning data.

wine cellar **1.** A below-grade storage room for wine. **2.** Any storage area for wine, especially with a temperature below normal room temperature.

wine vault Same as **wine cellar** (sense 1).

wing **1.** A relatively large side projection of a building, or other structure, that is smaller that the main mass, especially when one of a symmetrical pair. See also **ell.** **2.** (pre-20c) One of the sides of something that shuts, such as a double door **leaf.** **3.** Same as **wing dam.** **4.** Same as **wing wall.** **5.** The space at the sides of a theater stage that is hidden from public view; most often used in the plural.

wing dam, wingdam A pier or jetty that projects partway across a stream to divert the current; sometimes part of a pair used to raise the water level by starting diagonally from the shore then turning parallel to the flow, leaving a narrow channel in the middle. Also known as **pier dam, spur.** See also **wing wall.**

winged disk Same as **feroher.**

wing nut A threaded nut with a pair of flat extensions for hand tightening.

wings The fillets bordering a curved molding section.

wing wall The extension of one of the sides of a bridge abutment, or a dam, as a retaining wall; typically tapered downward. Also known as **wing.** See also **wing dam.**

winnowing house A building where grain is cleaned by blowing away the chaff and dirt with air currents; sometimes an elevated structure where the grain is dropped through a hole in the floor.

Winooski marble A reddish and brownish, variegated **marble** with white dolomite quarried in the vicinity of Mallets Bay, Vermont; used for interior finishes such as wainscoting and tile.

winter garden A large **greenhouse,** such as a courtyard with a glazed roof, for the permanent display of plants; often includes paved paths, fountains, and sculpture.

wiped joint A bulbous lead pipe joint formed by inserting the conical end of one pipe into another pipe and wiping with melted solder on a cloth; the completed joint is covered with a spherical mass of solder. See also **blown joint.**

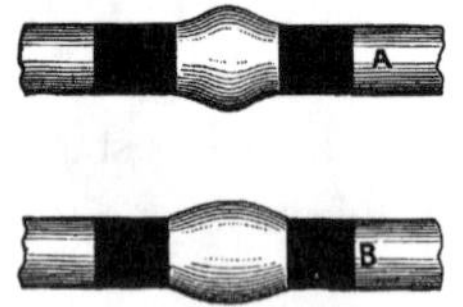

wiped joint

wire A slender strand of ductile metal less than 3/16 inch in diameter; typically with a circular cross section; originally made by hammering a billet; almost exclusively manufactured by drawing through dies of decreasing size by end 19c; used for communications, electric power, and attaching construction materials such as expanded-metal lath, rebars and ceiling grid; types include **market wire, office wire, patented wire, telegraph wire, telephone wire.** See also **electric wiring, rod.**

wire bridge (pre-20c) A **suspension bridge** hung on wire cables.

wire cloth Any type of mesh woven from wire; spacing and wire size ranges from the large **hardware cloth** to the fine **screening.** See also **chicken wire, stucco mesh.**

wire-cut brick **Brick** manufactured by extruding clay through a die and cutting off the individual bricks with a steel wire.

wire fence See **iron-wire fence, composite wire fence, chain-link fence, chicken wire.**

wire gauze (pre-WWII) Same as **screening.**

wire glass Sheet **glass** with an internal network of wires for reinforcement; typically .25 inch thick; used for break and fire resistance and security, such as in skylights and doors.

wire lath, wire lathing **Hardware cloth** used as plaster **lath;** in use by late 19c; types include **stiffened wire lath.**

wireless detector A battery powered automatic **fire detector,** motion detector, or similar device that signals a central station with radio waves; used to avoid installing wires that would damage historic plaster and other materials.

wire mold A trademarked two-piece metal molding system for **electric wiring,** first manufactured 1920s. See also **metal molding.**

wire nail A **nail** formed by cutting and forming wire, with a circular cross section and a sharp point; most often steel, may be of any metal, including copper or aluminum; of smaller cross section than a **cut nail, wire spike** or **wrought nail;** first imported from France late 19c; available in 2d to 60d sizes by 1893. See also **wire spike.**

wire spike A **spike** formed by cutting and forming steel wire, with circular cross section and a sharp point; of larger length and diameter than the equivalent **wire nail;** available in 2d to 16d sizes by 1893.

wire tension bridging A mid-20c bridging system for steel joists composed of continuous 14-gauge galvanized steel wire wrapped around the joists and woven between them to form **cross bridging.**

wiring The system of electrical wires for power and communication within a building.

witch's tit A turned, cylindrical wood lug that projects from the side of a double hung window sash.

withdrawing room (to early 19c) A room used for private conversation, such as a judge's chamber. See also **drawing room.**

withe Same as **wythe.**

wood The fibrous material of trees; common types of **lumber** wood used before WWII include **cedar, cypress, Douglas fir, hemlock, larch, locust, mulberry, oak, pine, redwood, spruce, tamarack;** common **trim** and **millwork** woods include **alder, ash, birch, black cherry, brazil wood, butternut, mahogany, oak, poplar, satin wood, walnut;** common **flooring** woods include **maple, oak;** variations within a log or piece include **heartwood** and **sapwood,** and **springwood** and **summerwood.** See also **artificial wood, lightwood, plywood, timber.**

wood block A solid timber element with vertical grain, 4–6 inches deep, used for paving, especially for mill floors and on bridge decks. See also **blocking, Nicolson pavement.**

wood brick A wood **nailer,** the size of a common brick, built into a masonry wall. Also known as **timber brick.** See also **dook.**

wood carpet An elaborate **parquet veneer** floor manufactured with the parquet pieces attached to a canvas backing.

wood carving A sculptured decoration made by cutting away parts of a piece of wood.

wood chimney Same as **wooden chimney.**

wood construction See **framing, truss, wood frame.**

wood decay See **boxed heart rot, carpenter ant, fungi, termite, testing, tunnel decay, wood pathologist, wood preservative.**

wood decking Thick tongue-and-groove planks used for a structural floor or roof deck.

wood embossing The process of making relief decoration on solid wood by subjecting it to heat and pressure by an embossing wheel or stamp, or burning in a mold. See also **embossed molding, wood fiber ornament.**

wooden chimney A chimney constructed of wood in any form, often with a protective interior coating of clay; types include **stick chimney.**

wooden cleats A pre-1900 **electric wiring** system with exposed, uninsulated wires held by wooden cleats; extremely dangerous due to fire hazard. See also **knob-and-tube.**

wooden hinge A hinge composed of a wood eye on the swinging element supported by a L-shaped wood pintle on the jamb; used for **log houses.**

wooden pavement (19c) **Pavement** composed of blocks of wood, such as **Nicolson pavement.**

wood fiber ornament A bas-relief ornament formed of wood fibers in suspension compressed with high pressure into a mold. See also **artificial wood, composition, wood embossing.**

wood fiber plaster Plaster mixed with finely chopped wood fibers; produces a lightweight, fire-resistant plaster finish. See also **fiber plaster.**

wood flour A fine sawdust; used in fillers.

wood frame Any **framing** system with structural members made of wood; types include **bal-**

loon frame, braced frame, platform frame, plank frame, pole structure, stick frame, timber frame.** See also **thorough framing, post and beam.**

wood gas An illuminating **gas** manufactured by the destructive distillation of wood during the 19c.

wood grain See **grain.**

woodhouse An outbuilding where wood is stored. See also **woodshed.**

wood lath Plaster **lath** composed of wood strips nailed in parallel rows with spaces between the strips to provide a **key;** originally **split lath,** then sawn wood strips, typically 1½ × ¼ × 48 or 1½ × ⅜ × 48 inches by late 19c; installed with staggered joints every 6–8 courses; displaced by **expanded-metal lath** beginning in 1896.

wood pathologist A scientist who studies the decay processes of wood.

wood preservative Any of various chemical compounds designed to kill fungi that consume wood; varieties include envelope types applied by brush or spray, including biocides such as **copper napthenate** or **zinc napthenate** and diffusion types applied as paste, pad, or rod, such as **borate** or **sodium fluoride solution.** See also **pressure treated.**

wood screw A **screw** with V-shaped screw threads on one end and a slotted head on the other end; the head may be flat or hemispherical; may have a straight barrel between the threads and head; almost exclusively with pointed ends after WWI; used for fastening pieces of wood together; types include **dowel screw, gimlet screw, lag bolt, Phillips head, slot head, stair rail screw, stud screw.** Also known simply as **screw.**

woodshed A small **shed** where firewood is stored. Also known as **woodhouse.**

wood spirits of turpentine Same as **wood turpentine.**

wood tar **Tar** produced by distilling pine or other resinous woods, chiefly as a byproduct of making alcohol and turpentine; the most common source of tar before WWI.

wood turpentine An oleoresin solvent distilled from pine wood; inferior in quality to **turpentine;** typically removed with steam from the waste wood of a pine tree, such as stumps and small branches; used in paints and varnishes. Also known as **wood spirits of turpentine,** and, incorrectly, as **oil of turpentine.**

woodwork **1.** Anything fabricated from wood. **2.** Interior trim or paneling.

work See **hammered work, metalwork, Reisner work, Sorrento work, stonework, woodwork.**

worked out of the solid (18c) An architectural element, such as a door jamb, cut from a single piece of wood, as opposed to being assembled from multiple pieces. Also known as **wrought out of the solid.**

workhouse **1.** (U.S.) A prison were minor criminals are confined and required to work. **2.** (pre-20c) A house or similar building used for manufacturing. **3.** (pre-20c) A **building** where able bodied vagrants or paupers are required to work. Also known as **bettering house, house of correction, house of industry.**

working drawings The architectural and engineering drawings that describe the appearance, location, type of materials, and quantity of the proposed construction work; typically include **plans, elevations, sections, details,** and related notes and schedules. Also known as **plans.** See also **architectural design, construction documents, engineering, shop drawings.**

workmanlike Having the high quality produced by a skilled worker.

workmanship **1.** The quality of execution of a craft or art. **2.** For National Register purposes, the quality of **integrity** applying to the physical evidence of the crafts of a particular culture, people, or artisan. **3.** (pre-20c) The amount of work produced by a craftsperson.

workmaster (pre-20c) A skilled or directing worker, especially one who designs, produces, or performs a work of importance.

workshop A room or building where goods are made or repaired by mechanics or artisans; typically refers to handicrafts as opposed to products manufactured in a factory.

World Heritage Committee The branch of **UNESCO** that administers the World Heritage Fund and selects sites for the **World Heritage List** and the List of World Heritage in Danger according to the **World Heritage Convention.**

World Heritage Convention Same as **Convention Concerning the Protection of the World Cultural and Natural Heritage.**

World Heritage List The list of the most significant historic and natural sites throughout the world; preservation of these sites is considered an international responsibility. See also **World Heritage Committee, World Heritage Site.**

World Heritage Site A **heritage site** that is listed on the **World Heritage List.**

wormditch (18c southern U.S.) A barrier formed by a **worm fence** next to a **ditch.**

worm fence A **rail fence** with a zigzag plan; the ends of the rails are laid across one another; the top rail may be supported on two split rails in an X-shape, or the ends of the rails may be held by a pair of posts. Also known as **snake fence, stake and rider fence, Virginia fence, Virginia make fence, Virginia rail fence.**

woven hip A roof hip covered with shingles with the butt end cut at an angle so that the bottom of the hip shingles continue the line of the adjacent courses.

wreath **1.** A decorative element in the form of a garland or band of foliage, often intertwined with flowers, fruits, and/or ribbons, especially in a circular pattern. **2.** A short, curved portion of a stair handrail, or string, at a turn; typically a portion of a circle in plan.

wreathed column **1.** Same as **solomonic column.** See also **cabled column. 2.** A column with a shaft spirally entwined by a raised molding. See also **twisted column.**

wreathed stair A **geometrical stair** with a curved well.

wreathed string A curved stair string in the form of a **wreath** (sense 2).

wreath piece Same as **wreath** (sense 1).

wrecking Same as **demolition.**

wrought Worked into shape, especially metal formed by hammering or forging; types include **hammered work, rough wrought.**

wrought iron **1.** Iron with a small amount of carbon, that has had its atoms aligned by beating and stretching the iron ingots; used for decorative hardware and ironwork, and in North America beginning early 19c, for structural components; types include **high test iron.** Also known as **weld iron.** See also **puddle steel. 2.** The common name for **mild steel** formed in the shape of decorative wrought iron.

wrought-iron pipe A pipe composed of **wrought iron;** typically of a diameter of 2 inches or less, and installed with threaded fittings; types include galvanized (for drains, vents, and water and gas supply), lead lined (for vents), enameled (for water supply), plain (for gas supply), asphalt lined (for gas and water mains), and cement lined (for gas and water supply lines); common in the 19c. See also **black iron pipe.**

wrought-iron work Products made by hammering or forging **wrought iron;** includes brackets, fences, grilles, hardware, railings, truss components, and window bars; also used to refer to **mild steel** products in the 20c. See also **wrought.**

wrought nail (late 18c–present) A nail that is hand-forged from iron or mild steel; although varying in shape, typically has a square cross section and a large head; gradually replaced by the **cut nail** beginning late 18c; common types include **brad, clasp nail, clout nail, dog nail, headless brad, rose nail, spike, sprig, tack.**

wrought out of the solid Same as **worked out of the solid.**

W-truss A triangular wood roof **truss** with diagonal struts in a W-shape.

Wyoming Valley stone Same as **Pennsylvania bluestone.**

wythe, wyth, withe **1.** (pre-20c) A brick wall separating chimney flues that is the width of a single stretcher brick. **2.** A single layer of wall thickness of masonry material; typically the depth of a brick stretcher; generally used to indicate the number of brick thicknesses of a solid wall, or one part of a cavity wall. Also known as **tier.**

X

xat See **totem pole.**

X-brace A truss **panel,** or similar structure, with a pair of diagonal braces from corner to corner that form an X-shape; may be **struts** in compression or **ties** in tension.

x-ray photograph A photograph of a portion of a building, such as a wall, using x-rays as a source; used to determine hidden construction details.

xyst (pre-20c) A garden **terrace** or walk; from the Latin for a tree-lined walk.

Y

Yankee gutter Same as **flush gutter.**

yard **1.** An outdoor area surrounded by buildings and fences where work is done or animals are kept, such as a **barnyard, churchyard, graveyard, inn yard, laundry yard, lumberyard, stable yard, stockyard, vineyard.** See also **courtyard, curtilage.** **2.** (19c–present) An open outdoor area adjacent to a house, such as a **front yard, back yard, side yard.** **3.** A unit of length measure equal to 3 feet or (U.S.) 0.9144018 meter, (Canada) 0.914399 meter.

Y-branch A drain **pipe fitting** with a branch pipe that enters the main pipe at a 45-degree angle. See also **half Y-branch.**

Y-branch

yellow birch A medium sized **birch** tree with reddish tinged, light brown, hard, strong heartwood with nearly white sapwood; found from the Appalachian Mountain region north to southeastern Canada and west to the Great Lakes region; used for flooring, veneer, and interior millwork; *Betula lutea.*

yellow cedar **1.** Same as **Alaska cedar.** **2.** Same as **western cedar.**

yellow cypress Same as **Alaska cedar.**

yellow metal Same as **Muntz metal.**

yellow ocher, yellow ochre Any of several solid yellow paint **pigments** made from **ocher;** darker than **French ocher,** may be clear or muddy in tone; used for mixing tans, creams, buffs, and olive green.

yellow pine **1.** The common yellow pine *Pinus mitis* with a yellowish, moderately hard, close-grained wood that is moderately pitchy; grows throughout North America east of the Rocky Mountains; used for lumber and millwork. Also known as **shortleaf pine, spruce-pine, bull pine.** **2.** Same as **Southern yellow pine.** **3.** Same as **ponderosa pine.**

yellow poplar Same as **tulip tree.**

yellow stain Same as **silver stain.**

yellow willow A North American variety of white **willow** with smooth, soft, tough wood; *Salix alba,* variety *vitellina.*

yeso A gypsum **whitewash** used in Mexico.

yoke **1.** A plumbing fitting that joins a branch line with the main line, typically at a 45-degree angle. **2.** Same as **window head.** **3.** (19c) A plumbing **pipe fitting** that connects hot and cold water faucets and mixes the water. **4.** A **tie beam, tie rod,** or similar connecting member.

yoke pin The metal staple that attaches one of a series of **rolling slats** to the vertical wood bar used to adjust the angle of the slats.

Y-saddle hub A Y-shaped **saddle hub** with the branch at an angle to the main pipe. See also **T-saddle hub, yoke.**

Y-tracery **Tracery** where the head of the mullions split in a Y-shape.

yunk Same as **tunck.**

Z

zaccab A **plaster** composed of lime, water, and a white earth found in the Yucatan peninsula; used by both ancient and modern Mayans.

zaguán A **porch, gateway,** or **passageway** connecting the interior patio with the street in an adobe or **Spanish Colonial** style house; typical elements include a clay tile roof and wood columns with zapatas. See also **patio.**

zapata A Spanish Colonial style bolster above a wood column; typically with flat sides and scroll-cut ends, often in the profile of a **console** or **cyma.**

Z-bar, zee bar A small iron or steel shape with a cross section approximately in the form of the letter *Z,* with a straight web with flanges projecting at 90 degrees on opposite sides.

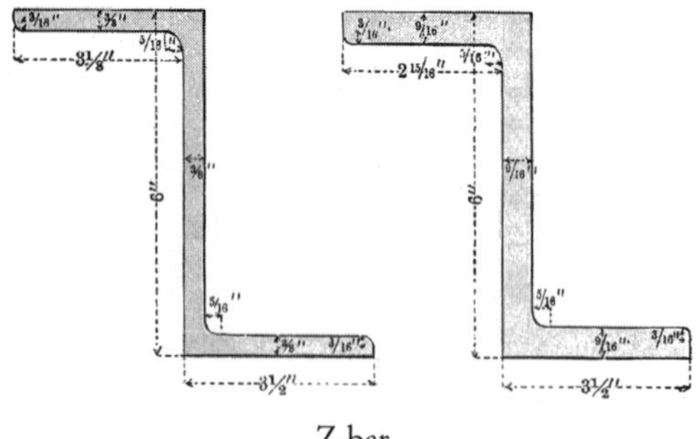

Z-bar

Z-bar column A column composed of four **Z-bars** riveted to a center connecting plate to form an H-shape with flanges extending from the corners; one to three cover plates sometimes added to increase strength; common late 19c.

Z-beam A iron or steel shape with a cross section approximately in the form of the letter *Z,* with a vertical web and horizontal flanges projecting on opposite sides of the web.

Z-column Same as **Z-bar column.**

zee bar Same as **Z-bar.**

Zenitherm A trade name for a 20c plaster product used to simulate stone.

Zenitherm

ziggurat A stepped pyramidal form in Art Deco style architecture; loosely based on the ziggurat temples of the Assyrians and Babylonians; sometimes the result of setbacks required by zoning.

zigzag A decorative line with short, straight, connected segments that turn abruptly; typically in architecture a continuous band of abutting V-shapes.

zigzag fence Same as **worm fence.**

zigzag moulding (19c) Same as **bâtons rompus.**

zigzag truss Same as **Warren truss.**

zinc A brittle, shiny, diamagnetic elemental metal with a fibrous structure; most often used for galvanizing and making alloys such as **brass;** also occasionally used beginning early 19c as sheet metal for roofing and decorative elements; melts at a relatively low 419 degrees C; exposed surfaces form a protective layer of **zinc carbonate.**

zinc carbonate See **zinc.**

zinc chromate A compound used as a bright greenish yellow paint **pigment;** the color is known as lemon yellow.

zinc chromate paint An **oil-base paint** with **zinc chromate** pigment; used as a **primer** for aluminum, iron, and steel.

zinc dust Powdered **zinc;** used in paint primers for galvanized iron.

zinc napthenate solution An aqueous solution of zinc napthenate; used as a **wood preservative.**

zinc oxide A white, opaque, oil-base paint **pigment** first used in house paints mid-19c; made by burning zinc in air to form zinc oxide (ZnO). See also **leaded zinc oxide.** Also known as **Chinese white, zinc oxide white, zinc white.**

zinc oxide white Same as **zinc oxide.**

zinc shingle A metal roofing shingle manufactured second quarter 20c; rectangular with interlocking edges, and held with a single nail.

zinc white Same as **zinc oxide.**

zocco, zoccolo Same as **socle.**

zocle Same as **socle.**

zoning (early 20c–present) The process of dividing a political jurisdiction into geographic zones with different mixtures of allowable **use,** size, siting, and form of real property, typically in conjunction with a **zoning code,** review of permit applications, and the administration of appeals, such as for a **special exception, planned unit development, transfer of development rights,** or **variance.** See also **planning.**

zoning code (20c) Government regulations that restrict the **use,** size, siting, and form of real property; typically includes restrictions on the **building envelope, floor area ratio, gross floor area, lot occupancy, use, setback.**

zoophorus, (pre-19c) **zoophoros** A sculptured **frieze,** especially with figures of people and animals; common in the Ionic order.

zore (19c) A bent iron plate having a cross section with a horizontal top with steep, downward diagonals on both sides, and horizontal flanges at the bottom; used to span between bridge stringers and support the concrete paving. Also known as **french section.** See also **corrugated plate.**

Z-section Same as **Z-beam.**

Illustration Credits

page

3 *acute-pointed arch* from Bucher.

3 *Adam style* from Historic American Buildings Survey.

10 *amphitheater* from McKim, Mead & White (Architectural Book Publishing, 1902), vol. II.

11 *anchor bolt* from AGS, 1st ed. (John Wiley, 1932).

12 *angle bead* from Southern Universal Catalog (Southern Sash, Door, & Millwork, 1923).

12 *angle buttress* from Historic American Buildings Survey.

13 *angle girder* from Boller (New York: John Wiley, 1890).

13 *angle iron* from Carnegie Steel Co., 1893.

15 *antepagment* from McKim, Mead & White (Architectural Book Publishing, 1902), vol. I.

16 *apophyge* from Bucher.

17 *apron* from AGS, 1st ed. (John Wiley, 1932).

17 *aqueduct* from Benjamin (D. Appleton & Co., 1880).

18 *arch* from Bucher.

23 *arch order* from Esquie (William Helburn, Inc.).

23 *arc lamp* from Horstmann (Frederick J. Drake, 1913).

25 *Art Deco* from Historic American Buildings Survey.

28 *astragal (senses 1 and 2)* from Bucher.

29 *astragal (sense 3)* from Southern Universal Catalog (Southern Sash, Door, & Millwork, 1923).

33 *balloon frame* from AGS, 1st ed. (John Wiley, 1932).

35 *baluster* from Southern Universal Catalog (Southern Sash, Door, & Millwork, 1923).

35 *band* from Bucher.

37 *bargeboard* from Historic American Buildings Survey.

37 *bargecourse* from AGS, 1st ed. (John Wiley, 1932).

40 *basket-handle arch (3-center)* from Bucher.

40 *basket-handle arch (5-center)* from Bucher.

41 *bath-cock* from Clow (Frederick J. Drake, 1906).

41 *bathtub* from Clow (Frederick J. Drake, 1906).

42 *bâtons rompus* from Bucher.

42 *batter* from Historic American Buildings Survey.

43 *battlement* from Historic American Buildings Survey.

44 *beam* from Boller (New York: John Wiley, 1890).

45 *beam hanger* from Voss (New York: John Wiley, 1926).

45 *beam truss bridge* from Boller (New York: John Wiley, 1890).

47 *bell (sense 1)* from Esquie (William Helburn, Inc.).

48 *bell trap* from Clow (Frederick J. Drake, 1906).
49 *belvedere* from Historic American Buildings Survey.
49 *bent sash* from Southern Universal Catalog (Southern Sash, Door, & Millwork, 1923).
50 *beveled molding* from Bucher.
53 *blast furnace* from Benjamin (D. Appleton & Co., 1880).
53 *blind door (sense 1)* from Southern Universal Catalog (Southern Sash, Door, & Millwork, 1923).
57 *bolt (sense 1)* from American Society of Civil Engineers (New York), vol. XI, 1882.
58 *Boston hip* from AGS, 1st ed. (John Wiley, 1932).
59 *bowl* from Clow (Frederick J. Drake, 1906).
60 *bowstring truss* from American Society of Civil Engineers (New York), vol. XXIII, 1890.
60 *box cornice* from AGS, 1st ed. (John Wiley, 1932).
62 *braced frame (sense 1)* from AGS, 1st ed. (John Wiley, 1932).
62 *braced header* from Voss (New York: John Wiley, 1926).
63 *bracketed cornice* from Historic American Buildings Survey.
64 *breakfast nook* from Southern Universal Catalog (Southern Sash, Door, & Millwork, 1923).
66 *bridge* from American Society of Civil Engineers (New York), vol. XX, 1894.
68 *buckled plate* from Carnegie Steel Co., 1893.
71 *built beam* from American Society of Civil Engineers (New York), vol. XVIII, 1888.
71 *bulb-tee* from Carnegie Steel Co., 1893.
72 *bull's-eye* from Southern Universal Catalog (Southern Sash, Door, & Millwork, 1923).
72 *bungalow* from Historic American Buildings Survey.
73 *bungalow door* from Southern Universal Catalog (Southern Sash, Door, & Millwork, 1923).
73 *bungalow window* from Southern Universal Catalog (Southern Sash, Door, & Millwork, 1923).
74 *butt hinge* from Historic American Buildings Survey.
76 *cabin* from Good (U.S. Department of the Interior, 1938).
78 *camelback* from Historic American Buildings Survey.
80 *cantilever* from American Society of Civil Engineers (New York), vol. XIV, 1885.
81 *capitol* from McKim, Mead & White (Architectural Book Publishing, 1902), vol. II.
83 *Carpenter Gothic* from Historic American Buildings Survey.
83 *cartouche (sense 2)* from Atlanta Terra Cotta, 1923.
86 *cavetto* from Bucher.
91 *chamfer (sense 1)* from Bucher.
91 *channel (sense 4)* from Carnegie Steel Co., 1893.
92 *Châteauesque style* from Historic American Buildings Survey.
93 *checkered plate* from Carnegie Steel Co., 1893.
97 *cinquefoil arch* from Bucher.
98 *cistern* from Radford Architectural Co., 1910.
99 *Clark's design* from Voss (New York: John Wiley, 1926).
100 *classical orders* from Esquie (William Helburn, Inc.).
100 *Classical Revival style* from McKim, Mead & White (Architectural Book Publishing, 1902), vol. I.
101 *cleat* from Horstmann (Frederick J. Drake, 1913).
102 *clevis* from Carnegie Steel Co., 1893.

103 *closed-string stair (sense 1)* from AGS, 1st ed. (John Wiley, 1932).
103 *closed valley* from AGS, 1st ed. (John Wiley, 1932).
105 *cobblestone* from Baker (New York: John Wiley, 1910).
106 *coffer* from McKim, Mead & White (Architectural Book Publishing, 1902), vol. I.
107 *Collegiate Gothic style* from Historic American Buildings Survey.
108 *comb (sense 1)* from AGS, 1st ed. (John Wiley, 1932).
109 *combination frame* from Voss (New York: John Wiley, 1926).
111 *Composite order* from Esquie (William Helburn, Inc.).
114 *congé* from Bucher.
115 *conservatory* from Historic American Buildings Survey.
119 *Corinthian order* from Esquie (William Helburn, Inc.).
120 *corner board* from AGS, 1st ed. (John Wiley, 1932).
120 *cornice (sense 1)* from AGS, 1st ed. (John Wiley, 1932).
122 *counterfort* from Radford Architectural Co., 1910.
126 *crenel* from Historic American Buildings Survey.
127 *cresting (sense 2)* from E. C. Hussey, 1876.
127 *cribwork* from American Society of Civil Engineers (New York), vol. XX, 1894.
127 *cricket* from AGS, 1st ed. (John Wiley, 1932).
128 *crossbeam (sense 2)* from Boller (New York: John Wiley, 1890).
129 *cross bridging* from Voss (New York: John Wiley, 1926).
132 *culvert* from American Society of Civil Engineers (New York), vol. X, 1881.
132 *cupola (sense 2)* from Historic American Buildings Survey.
132 *curb (sense 3)* from Radford Architectural Co., 1910.
133 *curtain wall (sense 3)* from Radford Architectural Co., 1910.
136 *dam* from American Society of Civil Engineers (New York), vol. III, 1875.
137 *damper* from AGS, 1st ed. (John Wiley, 1932).
140 *deformed bar* from Radford Architectural Co., 1910.
143 *diagonal buttress* from Historic American Buildings Survey.
147 *dogtrot house* from Historic American Buildings Survey.
147 *dome* from McKim, Mead & White (Architectural Book Publishing, 1902), vol. II.
150 *Doric order* from Esquie (William Helburn, Inc.).
151 *dormer window (sense 1)* from AGS, 1st ed. (John Wiley, 1932).
164 *elevator (sense 1)* from Benjamin (D. Appleton & Co., 1880).
164 *elevator (sense 2)* from Benjamin (D. Appleton & Co., 1880).
169 *equilateral arch* from Bucher.
170 *expanded-metal lath* from Radford Architectural Co., 1910.
171 *eyebar* from American Society of Civil Engineers (New York), vol. VII, 1878.
175 *fascia (sense 1)* from Bucher.
176 *faucet* from Clow (Frederick J. Drake, 1906).
176 *featheredge coping* from AGS, 1st ed. (John Wiley, 1932).
179 *fillet (sense 1)* from Bucher.
180 *Fink truss* from Bucher.
181 *fire cut* from AGS, 1st ed. (John Wiley, 1932).
184 *fish joint* from Voss (New York: John Wiley, 1926).
185 *flat arris* from Esquie (William Helburn, Inc.).
188 *floor arch* from Carnegie Steel Co., 1893.
189 *floor tile (sense 1)* from AGS, 1st ed. (John Wiley, 1932).

Illustration Credits

190 *flush girder* from AGS, 1st ed. (John Wiley, 1932).
190 *flush gutter (sense 1)* from AGS, 1st ed. (John Wiley, 1932).
190 *flush tank* from Clow (Frederick J. Drake, 1906).
193 *fortification (sense 2)* from Historic American Buildings Survey.
194 *foundation wall* from Radford Architectural Co., 1910.
195 *fountain (sense 1)* from Clow (Frederick J. Drake, 1906).
195 *four over four* from Historic American Buildings Survey.
195 *four over six* from Historic American Buildings Survey.
197 *french door* from Historic American Buildings Survey.
198 *fret (sense 2)* from Atlanta Terra Cotta, 1923.
200 *furnace (sense 1)* from E. C. Hussey, 1876.
200 *furnace (sense 3)* from Benjamin (D. Appleton & Co., 1880).
200 *furnace coil* from Hutton (David Williams Co., 1913).
204 *garrison house* from Historic American Buildings Survey.
205 *gas bracket* from Mitchell (Mineola, N.Y.: Dover reprint, 1876).
205 *gas heater* from Hutton (David Williams Co., 1913).
206 *gasolier* from Mitchell (Mineola, N.Y.: Dover reprint, 1876).
206 *gasworks* from American Society of Civil Engineers (New York), vol. VII, 1878.
207 *gatehouse* from American Society of Civil Engineers (New York), vol. XV, 1886.
207 *gauge (sense 1b)* from Benjamin (D. Appleton & Co., 1880).
207 *gauge glass* from Benjamin (D. Appleton & Co., 1880).
209 *Georgian* from Historic American Buildings Survey.
213 *Gothic Revival* from Historic American Buildings Survey.
214 *Gothic sash* from Southern Universal Catalog (Southern Sash, Door, & Millwork, 1923).
215 *grain elevator* from Benjamin (D. Appleton & Co., 1880).
216 *gravel stop* from AGS, 1st ed. (John Wiley, 1932).
217 *grease trap* from Clow (Frederick J. Drake, 1906).
217 *Greek ovolo* from Bucher.
218 *Greek Revival style* from Historic American Buildings Survey.
218 *gridiron plan* from American Society of Civil Engineers (New York), vol. XVII, 1887.
219 *grillage* from AGS, 1st ed. (John Wiley, 1932).
221 *guilloche* from Atlanta Terra Cotta, 1923.
222 *gypsum roof deck* from AGS, 1st ed. (John Wiley, 1932).
224 *half-dovetail notch* from Historic American Buildings Survey.
224 *half-timbered (sense 1)* from Historic American Buildings Survey.
227 *hayloft* from Historic American Buildings Survey.
237 *hoist (sense 2)* from Radford Architectural Co., 1910.
237 *hollow tile* from AGS, 1st ed. (John Wiley, 1932).
239 *hopper closet* from Clow (Frederick J. Drake, 1906).
239 *horseshoe arch* from Bucher.
240 *hose bib* from Clow (Frederick J. Drake, 1906).
245 *imbrex (sense 1)* from AGS, 1st ed. (John Wiley, 1932).
249 *interlaced arch* from Bucher.
249 *International style* from Historic American Buildings Survey.
251 *Ionic order* from Esquie (William Helburn, Inc.).

253 *Italianate* from Historic American Buildings Survey.
253 *Italian tiling* from AGS, 1st ed. (John Wiley, 1932).
254 *jack arch* from AGS, 1st ed. (John Wiley, 1932).
254 *jackknife switch* from Horstmann (Frederick J. Drake, 1913).
256 *jerkinhead* from Historic American Buildings Survey.
259 *keyed beam* from Voss (New York: John Wiley, 1926).
259 *kiln* from American Society of Civil Engineers (New York), vol. XXVI, 1892.
260 *king truss* from Boller (New York: John Wiley, 1890).
261 *knob-and-tube* from Horstmann (Frederick J. Drake, 1913).
262 *label* from Historic American Buildings Survey.
262 *lacing* from American Society of Civil Engineers (New York), vol. XX, 1889.
263 *laminated mill construction* from Voss (New York: John Wiley, 1926).
267 *latrine* from Good (U.S. Department of the Interior, 1938).
267 *lattice door* from Southern Universal Catalog (Southern Sash, Door, & Millwork, 1923).
267 *lattice truss* from Voss (New York: John Wiley, 1926).
268 *laundry tub* from Clow (Frederick J. Drake, 1906).
269 *ledger* from AGS, 1st ed. (John Wiley, 1932).
271 *lift-lock* from Benjamin (D. Appleton & Co., 1880).
272 *lighthouse* from Historic American Buildings Survey.
277 *louver* from Southern Universal Catalog (Southern Sash, Door, & Millwork, 1923).
278 *louver window* from Historic American Buildings Survey.
278 *L-sill* from AGS, 1st ed. (John Wiley, 1932).
278 *lug (sense 2)* from AGS, 1st ed. (John Wiley, 1932).
283 *manhole* from Benjamin (D. Appleton & Co., 1880).
284 *mantelpiece* from Southern Universal Catalog (Southern Sash, Door, & Millwork, 1923).
287 *meander* from Atlanta Terra Cotta, 1923.
288 *merlon* from Historic American Buildings Survey.
292 *mission (sense 2)* from Historic American Buildings Survey.
292 *mission tile* from AGS, 1st ed. (John Wiley, 1932).
295 *monolithic (sense 1)* from Radford Architectural Co., 1910.
295 *Monterey Style* from Historic American Buildings Survey.
296 *moresque (sense 1)* from Historic American Buildings Survey.
298 *mullion (sense 1)* from AGS, 1st ed. (John Wiley, 1932).
305 *niche* from Caemmerer (U.S. Government Printing Office, 1932).
311 *ogee arch* from Bucher.
312 *one over one* from Historic American Buildings Survey.
313 *open-string stair (sense 1)* from AGS, 1st ed. (John Wiley, 1932).
313 *open valley* from AGS, 1st ed. (John Wiley, 1932).
314 *open web joist* from AGS, 1st ed. (John Wiley, 1932).
315 *oriel* from Historic American Buildings Survey.
318 *overdoor* from Historic American Buildings Survey.
321 *Palladian* from Historic American Buildings Survey.
322 *Palladian window* from Historic American Buildings Survey.
323 *panel door* from Benjamin (D. Appleton & Co., 1880).

323 *panel strip (sense 1)* from Bucher.
325 *parallel coping* from AGS, 1st ed. (John Wiley, 1932).
325 *parapet gutter* from AGS, 1st ed. (John Wiley, 1932).
333 *pew* from Southern Universal Catalog (Southern Sash, Door, & Millwork, 1923).
333 *Phoenix column* from American Society of Civil Engineers (New York), vol. IX, 1880.
335 *picket (sense 1)* from Southern Universal Catalog (Southern Sash, Door, & Millwork, 1923).
336 *pier (sense 1)* from Historic American Buildings Survey.
336 *pier (sense 3)* from American Society of Civil Engineers (New York), vol. XX, 1889.
336 *pier (sense 6)* from AGS, 1st ed. (John Wiley, 1932).
338 *pin connection* from American Society of Civil Engineers (New York), vol. XVII, 1887.
339 *pintle (sense 2)* from Voss (New York: John Wiley, 1926).
339 *pipe coupling* from Clow (Frederick J. Drake, 1906).
342 *plain tile* from AGS, 1st ed. (John Wiley, 1932).
345 *plate rail* from Southern Universal Catalog (Southern Sash, Door, & Millwork, 1923).
346 *platform frame* from AGS, 1st ed. (John Wiley, 1932).
347 *plumb cut* from AGS, 1st ed. (John Wiley, 1932).
347 *plumbing (sense 1)* from Hutton (David Williams Co., 1913).
348 *pointed arch* from Historic American Buildings Survey.
348 *pointed round arch* from Bucher.
350 *porch* from Historic American Buildings Survey.
353 *powder house* from Historic American Buildings Survey.
353 *powerhouse* from American Society of Civil Engineers (New York), vol. XX, 1894.
360 *P-trap* from Clow (Frederick J. Drake, 1906).
362 *Pyrobar roof tile* from AGS, 1st ed. (John Wiley, 1932).
365 *quarter round* from Bucher.
366 *Queen Anne style* from Historic American Buildings Survey.
367 *queen-post truss* from Boller (New York: John Wiley, 1890).
368 *quirk bead* from Bucher.
368 *quoin (sense 1)* from Historic American Buildings Survey.
369 *rabbet (sense 1)* from Southern Universal Catalog (Southern Sash, Door, & Millwork, 1923).
369 *radiator* from Hutton (David Williams Co., 1913).
370 *rafter tail* from AGS, 1st ed. (John Wiley, 1932).
370 *rail (sense 4)* from American Society of Civil Engineers (New York), vol. XXIV, 1891.
371 *railroad track* from American Society of Civil Engineers (New York), vol. III, 1875.
372 *rake molding* from AGS, 1st ed. (John Wiley, 1932).
373 *random ashlar* from AGS, 1st ed. (John Wiley, 1932).
373 *random broken coursed ashlar* from AGS, 1st ed. (John Wiley, 1932).
374 *random coursed ashlar* from AGS, 1st ed. (John Wiley, 1932).
374 *range (sense 2)* from E. C. Hussey, 1876.
375 *range boiler* from Hutton (David Williams Co., 1913).
375 *rangework* from AGS, 1st ed. (John Wiley, 1932).
376 *recessed dormer* from AGS, 1st ed. (John Wiley, 1932).
378 *reed molding* from Bucher.

379 *register (sense 2)* from E. C. Hussey, 1876.
379 *reglet (sense 1)* from AGS, 1st ed. (John Wiley, 1932).
379 *reinforced concrete* from Radford Architectural Co., 1910.
382 *retaining wall* from AGS, 1st ed. (John Wiley, 1932).
385 *Richardsonian Romanesque* from Historic American Buildings Survey.
385 *ridgepole* from AGS, 1st ed. (John Wiley, 1932).
386 *ridge roll (sense 2)* from AGS, 1st ed. (John Wiley, 1932).
392 *rosette (sense 1)* from Atlanta Terra Cotta, 1923.
394 *round horseshoe arch* from Bucher.
395 *rowlock arch* from AGS, 1st ed. (John Wiley, 1932).
395 *ruby glass* from E. C. Hussey, 1876.
396 *running trap* from Clow (Frederick J. Drake, 1906).
397 *rustic joint* from AGS, 1st ed. (John Wiley, 1932).
398 *saddleback coping* from AGS, 1st ed. (John Wiley, 1932).
399 *saddle notch* from Historic American Buildings Survey.
400 *saltbox* from Historic American Buildings Survey.
402 *sanitary bend* from Clow (Frederick J. Drake, 1906).
403 *sash pocket* from AGS, 1st ed. (John Wiley, 1932).
403 *sash weight* from E. C. Hussey, 1876.
405 *scarf joint* from Benjamin (D. Appleton & Co., 1880).
407 *screen door* from Southern Universal Catalog (Southern Sash, Door, & Millwork, 1923).
409 *seat cut* from AGS, 1st ed. (John Wiley, 1932).
410 *segmental pointed arch* from Bucher.
410 *segment top windows* from Southern Universal Catalog (Southern Sash, Door, & Millwork, 1923).
411 *semimill construction* from Voss (New York: John Wiley, 1926).
413 *sets* from Baker (New York: John Wiley, 1910).
414 *sharp arris* from Esquie (William Helburn, Inc.).
416 *shelf angle* from AGS, 1st ed. (John Wiley, 1932).
417 *Shingle Style* from Historic American Buildings Survey.
419 *shotgun* from Historic American Buildings Survey.
420 *shower bath (sense 1)* from Clow (Frederick J. Drake, 1906).
421 *shutter (sense 1)* from Historic American Buildings Survey.
422 *side light* from Georgian, *American Architect & Building News,* 1899.
423 *silo* from Radford Architectural Co., 1910.
425 *sink (sense 1)* from Clow (Frederick J. Drake, 1906).
426 *site marker* from Good (U.S. Department of the Interior, 1938).
426 *six over nine* from Bucher.
426 *six over six* from Bucher.
427 *skeleton paneling* from Southern Universal Catalog (Southern Sash, Door, & Millwork, 1923).
430 *sleeper (sense 1)* from AGS, 1st ed. (John Wiley, 1932).
431 *slow-burning mill construction* from Voss (New York: John Wiley, 1926).
432 *smokehouse* from Historic American Buildings Survey.
432 *smoke shelf* from AGS, 1st ed. (John Wiley, 1932).
433 *snap switch* from Horstmann (Frederick J. Drake, 1913).

437 *spandrel (sense 2)* from AGS, 1st ed. (John Wiley, 1932).
438 *Spanish Colonial with Spanish roof tiles* from Historic American Buildings Survey.
439 *speaking tube* from E. C. Hussey, 1876.
441 *splay joint* from AGS, 1st ed. (John Wiley, 1932).
443 *sprinkler system* from Benjamin (D. Appleton & Co., 1880).
443 *sprocked eaves* from AGS, 1st ed. (John Wiley, 1932).
444 *square hip* from AGS, 1st ed. (John Wiley, 1932).
447 *stair* from Radford Architectural Co., 1910.
448 *stall (sense 1)* from E. C. Hussey, 1876.
448 *standing seam roof* from AGS, 1st ed. (John Wiley, 1932).
450 *steam boiler* from Benjamin (D. Appleton & Co., 1880).
452 *steeple (sense 1)* from American Society of Civil Engineers (New York), vol. XX, 1894.
453 *stick chimney* from Historic American Buildings Survey.
453 *sticking* from Southern Universal Catalog (Southern Sash, Door, & Millwork, 1923).
456 *stop cock* from Clow (Frederick J. Drake, 1906).
456 *store front* from Atlanta Terra Cotta, 1923.
457 *stove (sense 1)* from E. C. Hussey, 1876.
458 *S-trap* from Clow (Frederick J. Drake, 1906).
458 *strap hanger* from Voss (New York: John Wiley, 1926).
460 *string (sense 1)* from Voss (New York: John Wiley, 1926).
466 *sunk girt* from AGS, 1st ed. (John Wiley, 1932).
469 *swing bridge* from American Society of Civil Engineers (New York), vol. VII, 1878.
469 *Swiss Chalet style* from Historic American Buildings Survey.
472 *tail race* from American Society of Civil Engineers (New York), vol. XX, 1894.
474 *T-beam* from Georgian, *American Architect & Building News,* 1899.
475 *tegula* from AGS, 1st ed. (John Wiley, 1932).
476 *tension bar* from American Society of Civil Engineers (New York), vol. XXIII, 1890.
481 *three-quarter round* from Bucher.
481 *three-quarter S-trap* from Clow (Frederick J. Drake, 1906).
481 *through bridge* from Boller (New York: John Wiley, 1890).
482 *thumb molding* from Bucher.
483 *tile arch* from AGS, 1st ed. (John Wiley, 1932).
484 *timber dog* from Voss (New York: John Wiley, 1926).
484 *timber frame* from Historic American Buildings Survey.
485 *tobacco house* from Caemmerer (U.S. Government Printing Office, 1932).
488 *torus* from Bucher.
488 *towel rail* from Hutton (David Williams Co., 1913).
489 *tracery (sense 2)* from Historic American Buildings Survey.
491 *trap (sense 1)* from Clow (Frederick J. Drake, 1906).
492 *trefoil arch* from Bucher.
492 *trestle (sense 1)* from American Society of Civil Engineers (New York), vol. XXIII, 1890.
493 *triangular arches (senses 1 and 2)* from Bucher.
494 *trimmer arch* from AGS, 1st ed. (John Wiley, 1932).
494 *tringle* from Bucher.
495 *trough plate* from Carnegie Steel Co., 1893.
496 *trussed arch* from Voss (New York: John Wiley, 1926).
496 *trussed girder* from Voss (New York: John Wiley, 1926).

Bibliography

Aberdeen's Magazine of Masonry Construction. The Aberdeen Group, Addison, IL.

Adaptive Use: A Survey of Construction Costs. Advisory Council on Historic Preservation, Washington DC, 1976.

AIA Historic Resources Program. *A Guide to Historic Preservation.* American Institute of Architects, Washington DC, 1992.

Amburgey, Dr. Terry. "Wood pathology and wood timber deterioration." Lecture at APT *Structural Timber Framing and Trusses: Diagnostics* symposium, Philadelphia, PA, 1995.

APT/AIC New Orleans Charter for the Joint Preservation of Historic Structures and Artifacts. Association for Preservation Technology International and American Institute for the Conservation of Historic and Artistic Works, undated (adopted 1991).

APT Bulletin, Vol XI, No. 2, 1979.

Gillespie, Ann. "Early development of the *Artistic* concrete block: The case of the Boyd Brothers."

Ritchie, T. "Notes on dichromatic brickwork in Ontario."

Szabo, T., and J.K. Shields. "Simple remedial treatment of deteriorated wood in heritage homes."

Winkler, Erhard M. "The lightness (reflectance) of stone in the stone industry."

APT Bulletin, Vol XXIII, No. 3, 1991

Carden, Marie L. "Use of ultraviolet light as an aid to pigment identification."

Livingston, Richard A. and Thomas H., Jr. Taylor "Diagnosis of salt damage at a smokehouse in colonial Williamsburg."

Shellenbarger, Michael. "Tuck pointing history and confusion."

Architectural Woodwork Quality Standards, Guide Specifications and Quality Certification Program, Fourth Edition. Architectural Woodwork Institute. Arlington, VA, 1985.

Atlanta Terra Cotta Company. *Atlanta Terra Cotta Stock Designs.* Atlanta, Georgia. Privately printed, 1923.

Audels Carpenters and Builders Guide #1–4. Theo. Audel & Co., New York, 1939.

Audels Masons and Builders Guide #4. Theo. Audel & Co., New York, 1945.

Auer, Michael J., Charles E. Fisher III, Thomas C. Jester, and Marilyn E. Kaplan, R.A. (Eds.) *The Interiors Handbook for Historic Buildings, Volume II.* Historic Preservation Education Foundation, Washington, DC, 1993.

Badzinski, Stanley. *Carpentry in Residential Construction.* Prentice-Hall, Inc., Englewood Cliffs, NJ, 1972.

Banks, Elizabeth. *Creating Period Gardens.* Preservation Press, Washington DC, 1991.

Bates, Robert L. and Julia A. Jackson. (Eds.) *Glossary of Geology.* American Geological Institute, Falls Church, VA, 1980.

Benjamin, Park, Ph.D., LL.B., ed. *Appletons' Cyclopaedia of Applied Mechanics: A Dictionary of Mechanical Engineering and the*

Mechanical Arts, Vol 1. D. Appleton and Company, New York, 1880.

Bero, John F. "A designer's guide to invisible perils," In: *The Interiors Handbook for Historic Buildings,* Volume II. Historic Preservation Education Foundation, Washington DC, 1993.

Bettesworth, A. and C. Hitch. *The Builder's Dictionary: or, Gentleman and Architects's Companion.* London, 1734 (APT reprint, Washington, DC, 1981).

Birk, Sherry C. and John M. Bryan. *The Most Distinguished Private Place: Creating the Biltmore Estate* (Octagon Museum Exhibit Catalog). The American Architectual Foundation, Washington, DC, 1994.

Birkmire, William H. *Skeleton Construction in Buildings.* John Wiley & Sons, Inc., New York, 1907.

Boller, Alfred P. *Practical Treatise on the Construction of Iron Highway Bridges,* 4th Edition. John Wiley & Sons, Inc., New York, 1890 (1st Ed. 1876).

Brolin, Brent C. *Architecture in Context.* Van Nostrand Reinhold Company, New York, 1980.

Brooks, Hugh. *Illustrated Encyclopedic Dictionary of Building and Construction Terms.* Prentice-Hall, Inc., Englewood Cliffs, N.J., 1976.

Burkett, Randy. "Lighting renovations," *Building Renovation.* Cleveland, OH, Winter, 1994.

Caemmerer, H.P. *Washington: The National Capital.* U.S. Government Printing Office, Washington, DC, 1932.

Caravaty, Raymond D. and Harry C. Plummer. *Principles of Clay Masonry Construction.* Structural Clay Products Institute, Washington, DC, 1960.

Clow, George B. *Practical Up-to-Date Plumbing.* Frederick J. Drake & Company, Chicago, 1906.

Collingwood, G. H. *Knowing Your Trees.* The American Forestry Association, Washington, D.C., 1937.

Conservation Assistance Program, The. National Institute for the Conservation of Cultural Property, Washington DC, undated (ca. 1993).

Cooper, Gail. "Custom design, engineering guarantees, and unpatentable data: The air conditioning industry, 1902–1935." *Technology and Culture,* Vol. 35, No. 3. July, 1994.

Cummings, Abbott Lowell. *The Framed Houses of Massachusetts Bay, 1625–1725.* The Belknap Press of Harvard University Press, Cambridge, MA, 1979.

Dutton, Brian, L.P. Harvey, and Roger M. Walker. *Cassell's Concise Spanish-English English-Spanish Dictionary.* MacMillan Publishing Company, Inc., 1969.

Dwight, Pamela (General Ed.). *Landmark Yellow Pages.* Preservation Press, Washington DC, 1993.

Emery, H.G. and K.G. Brewster. *The New Century Dictionary of the English Language.* P.F. Collier & Son Corporation, New York, 1938.

Federal Assistance for Our Nation's Museums. Institute of Museum Services, Washington, DC, undated (ca. 1993).

Federal Register, Vol. 46, No. 220. November 16, 1981. Rules and Regulations, 36 CFR Part 60, National Register of Historic Places.

Ferro, Maximilian L., AIA and Melissa L. Cook. *Electric Wiring and Lighting in Historic American Buildings.* AFC/A Nortek Company, New Bedford MA, 1984.

Fischetti, David, P.E., "Early Truss Designers and Their Work." Lecture at APT *Structural Timber Framing and Trusses: Diagnostics* symposium, Philadelphia, PA, 1995.

Fleming, John, Hugh Honour, and Nikolaus Pevsner. *The Penguin Dictionary of Architecture.* Penguin Books, Bungay, England, 1972.

Fletcher, Bannister. *A History of Architecture on the Comparative Method,* 17th Edition. The

Royal Institute of British Architects and the University of London, London, 1967.

Frazier Associates. *Preserving Prince William: Building Codes and Historic Buildings.* Prince William County, VA, 1990.

Frazier Associates. *Preserving Prince William: Protecting Historic Properties from Arson and Accidental Fire.* Prince William County, VA, 1990.

Friedman, Donald. *Historical Building Construction.* W.W. Norton & Company, Inc., New York, 1995.

Funk, Isaac K. (Ed.). *A Standard Dictionary of the English Language.* Funk & Wagnalls, New York and London, 1899.

Gettens, Rutherford J. and George L. Stout. *Painting Materials, A Short Encyclopaedia.* Dover Publications, Inc., New York, 1966.

Girouard, Mark. *Sweetness and Light, The Queen Anne Movement 1860–1900.* Yale University Press, New Haven and London, 1977.

Harding, Louis Allen and Arthur Cutts Willard. *Mechanical Equipment of Buildings.* John Wiley & Sons, Inc., New York, 1917.

Harriman, Marc S. "Jeffersonian Invention." T&P Technology, *Architecture,* Volume 82, No. 4, April, 1993.

Harris, Cyril M. *Illustrated Dictionary of Historic Architecture.* Dover Publications, Inc., New York, 1977.

Haselberger, Lothar. "Deciphering a Roman Blueprint." *Scientific American,* New York, NY, June 1995.

Historic Preservation News. National Trust for Historic Preservation, Washington DC, February/March, 1994.

Holloway, Marguerite. "The Preservation of the Past." *Scientific American,* New York, NY, May 1995.

How to Apply the National Register Criteria for Evaluation. National Park Service, U.S. Department of the Interior, Washington, DC 1990.

Hryniuk, Margaret and Meta Perry. *Regina: A City of Beautiful Homes,* Centax Books, Regina, Saskatchewan, 1994.

Huot, William. *Huot's Handy Heritage Lexicon,* British Columbia Heritage Conservation Branch, 1985.

Hussey, E.C. *Home Building.* New York: Privately printed, 1876.

Hutton, William. *Hot Water Supply & Kitchen Boiler Connections,* David Williams Co., New York, 1913.

Indiana Limestone Handbook. Indiana Limestone Institute of American, Inc., Bedford, Indiana, 1977 (not copyrighted).

Inside the Beltway: A Dialogue With Decision Makers. Historic Resources Committee, The American Institute of Architects, Washington, D.C., November 3–6, 1994.

Kyriakos, Marianne. "Historic Wessynton: First in Peaceful." *Washington Post,* Washington DC, February 4, 1995.

Legislative Purposes of Legacy. CEHP, Inc., undated.

Lewandoski, Jan. "Field analysis of wood timber trusses." Lecture at APT *Structural Timber Framing and Trusses: Diagnostics* symposium, Philadelphia, PA, 1995.

Lief, Judith Siegel. "The American Diner: A Meeting Place of 20th-Century Building Materials." *Traditional Building,* Brooklyn, NY, January/February 1995.

Lounsbury, Carl R. *An Illustrated Glossary of Early Southern Architecture and Landscape,* Oxford University Press, New York/Oxford, 1994.

Lowndes, William S., Ph. B. *Plastering and Architectural Terra Cotta,* International Textbook Company, Scranton, PA, 1938.

Maitland, Leslie, Shannon Ricketts, and Jacqueline Hucker. *A Guide to Canadian Architec-*

tural Styles, Broadview Press, Peterborough, Ontario, 1992.

Mansion, J.E. *Harraps's Modern College French and English Dictionary.* Charles Scribners' Sons, New York, 1972.

Massey, James C., Nancy B. Schwartz, and Shirley Maxwell. *Historic American Buildings Survey/Historic American Engineering Record, An Annotated Bibliography.* HABS/HAER, National Park Service, U.S. Department of the Interior, 1992.

McAlester, Virginia and Lee, *A Field Guide to American Houses.* Alfred A. Knopf, New York, 1986

McBride, Dennis G. "Cast Stone, Precast Concrete & Architectural Precast Concrete." *Traditional Building,* Brooklyn, NY, January/February, 1995.

McClymont, J.J. "A List of the World's Marbles." *Through the Ages,* Volumes 43–45, Marble Institute of America, Farmington, MI.

Mitchell, Vance & Co. *Picture Book of Authentic Mid-Victorian Gas Lighting Fixtures.* Privately printed, 1876; reprint, with an Introduction by Denys Peter Myers, Dover Pictorial Archives Series. New York, Dover Publications, Inc., 1984.

Morris, Prof. Charles, (Ed.). *Universal Dictionary of the English Language.* Peter Fenelon Collier, New York, 1898

Morris, William, (Ed.). *The American Heritage Dictionary of the English Language.* American Heritage Publishing Co., Inc., Boston, 1973.

Moss, Roger. *Century of Color: Exterior Decoration for American Buildings, 1820–1920,* The American Life Foundation, Watkins Glen, New York, 1981.

Moss, Roger W. *Lighting for Historic Buildings.* The Preservation Press, Washington, DC, 1988.

Moss, Roger W. (Ed.), *Paint in America.* The Preservation Press, Washington, DC, 1994.

National Capital Planning Commission/Frederick Gutheim. *Worthy of the Nation.* Smithsonian Institution, 1977.

National Register Application Guidelines. Maryland Historical Trust, Annapolis, 1988

National Register Bulletin 15, How to Apply the National Register Criteria for Evaluation. National Park Service, U.S. Department of the Interior, 1991.

National Register Bulletin 16A, How to Complete the National Register Registration Form. National Park Service, U.S. Department of the Interior, 1989.

National Register Bulletin 18, How to Evaluate and Nominate Designed Historic Landscapes. National Park Service, U.S. Department of the Interior, 1989.

Neilson, William Allen, (Editor in Chief, *Webster's New International Dictionary of the English Language, Second Edition.* G. & C. Merriam Co., Springfield, MA, 1956.

Nelson, Lee H. *White House stone carving: builders and restorers.* U.S. Government Printing Office, Washington, D.C., 1992.

Old-House Journal, Volumes I–XXIII, Gloucester, MA.

Ortega, Richard I., P.E., R.A. "Monitoring wood timber framing." Lecture at APT *Structural Timber Framing and Trusses: Diagnostics* symposium, Philadelphia, PA, 1995.

Parker, John Henry. *ABC of Gothic Architecture.* James Parker and Company, London, 1900.

Parker, John Henry. *Classic Dictionary of Architecture.* James Parker and Company, London, 1875 (New Orchard Editions Ltd. reprint 1986).

Pehnt, Wolfgang. *Encyclopedia of Modern Architecture.* Harry N. Abrams, Inc., New York, 1964.

Pentz, Suzanne. "Case study: academy of music/wood pathology." Lecture at APT

Structural Timber Framing and Trusses: Diagnostics symposium, Philadelphia, PA, 1995.

Peterson, Charles E. (Introduction & Notes), *The Carpenters' Company of the City and County of Philadelphia 1786 Rule Book.* The Astragal Press, Mendham, New Jersey, 1992.

Pocket Companion for Engineers, Architects and Builders Containing Useful Information and Tables Appertaining to the Use of Steel, Twenty-Third Edition. Carnegie Steel Company, Pittsburgh, Pa., 1923.

Poppeliers, John C., S. Allen Jr. Chambers, and Nancy B. Schwartz. *What Style Is It?.* The Preservation Press, Washington DC, 1983.

"Preservation Standards." *BR Building Renovation.* Penton Publishing, Cleveland OH, Spring 1995.

Preservation Strategy, No. 3. Heritage Canada (ca. 1993).

Product Use Manual. Western Wood Products Association. Portland, Oregon, 1977.

Radford, William A. (Ed.). *Cement and How to Use It.* The Radford Architectural Company, Chicago, 1910.

Radford, William A. (Ed.). *Framing.* The Radford Architectural Company, Chicago, 1913 (Copyright 1909).

Ramsey, Charles George, and Harold Reeve Sleeper. *Architectural Graphic Standards.* John Wiley and Sons, New York, 1932 (reprint 1990).

Ramsey, Charles George, and Harold Reeve Sleeper. *Architectural Graphic Standards.* John Wiley and Sons, New York, 1970.

Ramsey, Charles George, and Harold Reeve Sleeper. *Architectural Graphic Standards.* Robert T. Packard (Ed.). John Wiley and Sons, New York, 1981.

Redwood Sales Manual. California Redwood Association. San Francisco, 1928.

Renfrew, Colin. "World Linguistic Diversity." *Scientific American,* New York, NY, January 1994.

Rybczynski, Witold. *Looking Around, A Journey Through Architecture.* Penguin Books, New York, 1992.

Rys, Michael. "Scarier and Scarier." *Parade,* August 14, 1994.

Saylor, Henry H. *Dictionary of Architecture.* John Wiley & Sons, New York, 1952.

Secretary of the Interior's Standard and Guidelines for Architectural and Engineering documentation: HABS/HAER Standards. (Originally published in the *Federal Register,* Vol. 48, No. 190, September 29, 1983), HABS/HAER Cultural Resources Program, National Park Service, Washington, D.C., 1990.

Scott, John S. *A Dictionary of Building.* Penguin, Baltimore, 1964.

Scott, John S. *A Dictionary of Building.* Viking Penguin, New York, 1984.

Sherwood, Susan I. and Frederick W. Lipfert (principal authors). *Acidic Deposition: State of Science and Technology,* Report 21, National Acid Precipitation Assessment Program, November 1990.

Shipway, Verna Cook, and Warren. *The Mexican House Old & New.* Architectural Book Publishing, New York, 1965.

Silman, Robert, P.E. "Inspection and analysis of wood timber framing & using fiber optics as an inspection tool." Lecture at APT *Structural Timber Framing and Trusses: Diagnostics* symposium, Philadelphia, PA, 1995.

Simpson, Pamela H. "Blocks Like Rocks." *BR Building Renovation,* Penton Publishing, Cleveland, OH, Spring 1995.

Slesin, Suzanne and Stafford Cliff. *Caribbean Style.* Clarkson N. Notter, New York, 1985.

Smith, T. Roger, F.R.I.B.A. *Greek Architecture.* The Chautauqua Century Press, Meadville, Pennsylvania, 1892.

Society for Commercial Archeology (membership pamphlet). Washington DC, undated.

Southern Universal Catalog. Southern Sash, Door and Millwork Manufacturer's Association, Atlanta, 1923.

Sprigg, June, and David Larkin. *Shaker Life, Work, and Art.* Stewaret, Tabori & Chang, New York, 1987.

Stevens, Edward F. *The American Hospital of the Twentieth Century.* New York: F.W. Dodge Corporation, 1928.

Storer, J.E. "Fossil Invertebrates in Building Stone at the PMAA." *Provincial Museum & Archives Notes No. 12,* Edmonton, Alberta, 1972.

Sturgis, Russell, et al. *A Dictionary of Architecture and Building: Biographical, Historical and Descriptive.* Macmillan, New York, 1901–02 (Dover reprint, 1989).

Sweet's Architectural Catalog. Sweet's Catalog Service, New York, 1927–1928.

"Trackdown." *Mileposts,* MTA Metro-North Railroad, New York, NY, February 1995.

Transactions, Vol. III. American Society of Civil Engineers, New York, 1875.

Transactions, Vol. VII. American Society of Civil Engineers, New York, 1878.

Transactions, Vol. XVI. American Society of Civil Engineers, New York, 1887.

Transactions, Vol XVII. American Society of Civil Engineers, New York, 1887.

Transactions, Vol. XVIII. American Society of Civil Engineers, New York, 1888.

Transactions, Vol. XX. American Society of Civil Engineers, New York, 1889.

Transactions, Vol. XXIV. American Society of Civil Engineers, New York, 1891.

Transactions, Vol. XXVI. American Society of Civil Engineers, New York, 1892.

Vanderwalker, F.N. *The Mixing of Colors and Paints.* Frederick J. Drake, Chicago, 1924.

Vlach, John Michael. *Back of the Big House.* The University of North Carolina Press, Chapel Hill and London, 1993.

Voss, Walter and Edward A. Varney. *Architectural Construction, Volume II, Book I, Wood Construction,* John Wiley and Sons, New York, 1926.

Voss, Walter and Edward A. Varney. *Wood Construction,* John Wiley & Sons, New York, 1926.

Ware, William R. *The American Vignola,* Third Edition. International Textbook Company, Scranton, Pennsylvania, 1937 (1st published 1904).

What is Glass Fibre-optics Lighting? Building Conservation International, Philadelphia, PA, 1994.

White, Anthony and Bruce Robertson. *Architecture & Ornament.* Design Press, New York, 1990.

Wigginton, Eliot (Ed.). *The Foxfire Book.* Anchor Press/Doubleday, Garden City, NY, 1972.

Wolf, Sara (Ed.). *The Conservation Assessment.* Getty Conservation Institute and National Institute for the Conservation of Cultural Property, 1990.